TABLE OF CONTENTS

THE DEEDS OF
AMHERST COUNTY, VIRGINIA, 1761–1807
AND
ALBEMARLE COUNTY, VIRGINIA, 1748–1763

by
The Rev. Bailey Fulton Davis

SOUTHERN HISTORICAL PRESS
% The Rev. S. Emmett Lucas, Jr.
P. O. Box 738
Easley, South Carolina   29640

ISBN 0-89308-147-7

DEDICATION

This work and Albemarle deed books in sequence will be dedicated to a
terrible tragedy. Counties, like people, have trees. Albemarle was
formed from Goochland, in the main, in 1744 and Amherst was cut from
Albemarle on May 1, 1761. In 1808 Amherst lost half of her area to newly
organized Nelson county.

Nelson County, Virginia, is a daughter of Amherst and a granddaughter of
Albemarle County. May 25th through May 27, 1771, Amherst suffered a
disaster when the James river was at flood stage. One hundred and fifty
persons were lost at that time. Nelson was then a part of Amherst.

On the night of August 19, 1969, and into the early morning hours of the
20th, Nelson experienced another horrible disaster. Amherst received a
great deal of property damage, but the loss of life centered in Nelson.
Rockbridge and other areas also were hard hit, but the blunt of the
attack was felt in Nelson.

I had worked at the polls all day on the 19th. A bad storm came up just
about closing time and someone brought me home in a car. We received
three inches of rain during the night, but little knew of what was taking
place in Nelson county.

My wife and I planned to go to Lynchburg on the morning of the 20th, but
I walked down first for the mail. Folk were talking of the fact that
Buffalo bridge was under water just North of the village of Amherst, but
had not yet realized the horror of Nelson. I did not walk across the
street to view a black man's body in an ambulance since I am not the
morbid type. We only knew that somewhere in southern Nelson a stream
had swept him to his death.

We went to Lynchburg, as planned, and saw that the James was raging out
of banks. We were working outside all day at our house at 1615 Langhorne
and commented on the fact that the air was filled with planes and "chop-
pers". We found one bridge closed as we left Lynchburg and the traffic
was terrible because of folk who had driven down to the river for a look.

The late afternoon and night news informed us of the tragedy, but the
full import of it all did not dawn for several days. We were able to
get into the Roseland section and to the railroad bridge which was washed
out over Tye. I was able to get up to Lovingston and about three miles
above to see the awful havoc in the Woods' Mill and Davis creek section,
but still did not get into the road back into Davis creek area.

About 150 people were lost and around 40 bodies have never been recovered.
The entire area was subjected to what can only be termed a meterological
freak.

The storm, Camille, crossed the Blue Ridge on the night of the 19th. It
had dumped rain on various areas enroute from its journey from the Gulf
Coast. Camille came over the Blue Ridge into Nelson and cold air from
the valley caused a terrible downpour to begin. Weather experts found a
barrel which was known to have been empty on the 19th and it contained
32 inches of rainwater. The rain began at about the State Fish Hatchery
and Tye River became a monster. Crab Tree Falls was not damaged, but the
bed was changed, rocks and trees were swept aside and bottom land was
ruined.

The little village of Massie's Mill was practically destroyed and many
perished in the area. Lawson Cox, recently retired Amherst rector, was
at his home up on the mountain and the next morning he and his wife found
chasms in the road and on their place that were over sixteen feet deep.
They were finally flown out in a "chopper".

The rain swept across the county and caused terrible loss of life in the
Davis Creek area. There is a road which leads off of Route 29 into the
region. I have been back in the section several times and still can not

comprehend the whole thing. Huge sections of the hills washed down upon houses and roads and over 50 people lost their lives. These great washes show only rock beneath where dirt and trees once abounded.

The Huffman family lost over twenty members. I went to the home of one of my members, Mrs. White, who was a Huffman. They had flown her mother and a brother out of the area. The clan lived in a cove on Davis creek. He told me that he was awakened by noise which he realized was a slide. He had 8 children and a wife. He managed to get 6 of them out and his wife was trying to bring out the baby and one more. He said that he looked back and, by lightning flashes, saw the house engulfed by the slide. His wife and the two children were lost.

I could go on and on with stories of horror and bravery, but all is being recorded by chosen writers who will leave a chronicle of the event. I attended their memorial service at Nelson County High School and the governor of Virginia was at the meeting. It was indeed a solemn affair.

To Albemarle's granddaughter I dedicate these works. The destruction of lovely stream beds and trees fade into nothing when we recall the awful loss of life.

BAILEY FULTON DAVIS

1970

FOREWORD

These records from Albemarle and Amherst counties, Virginia were abstracted over a number of years by the Reverend Bailey Fulton Davis,
former pastor of the Amherst Baptist Church of Amherst, Virginia, now
retired. The original works were mimeographed and each deed book published separately, and are now out of print.

It is because of the wide-spread interest in genealogy, and in early
Virginia records, that these deed books are being re-published with a
new full name index.

As it was necessary to re-type the material for publication, some
changes were made in the abstracts, mostly in the use of fewer abbrevia-
tions, to make the meaning of the abstracts clearer to the seasoned and
novice genealogist alike.

The Reverend Mr. Davis has compiled and published other books concerning this area of Virginia, which we hope to reprint in the future.
These are:

   AMHERST COUNTY VIRGINIA DEED BOOKS L-Z, 1807 - 1848

   AMHERST COUNTY VIRGINIA WILL ABSTRACTS 1761 - 1920

   AMHERST COUNTY VIRGINIA ORDER BOOK 1766 - 1769

   AMHERST COUNTY VIRGINIA IMPRESSED PROPERTY CLAIMS 1773 - 1784

   MARRIAGE BONDS OF AMHERST COUNTY VIRGINIA 1801 - 1854

   NELSON COUNTY VIRGINIA WILL BOOK A, 1807 - 1817

   NELSON COUNTY VIRGINIA DEED BOOK 1, 1807 - 1813

   NELSON COUNTY VIRGINIA MARRIAGES 1807 - 1837

As publisher of this volume, I want to express my deepest thanks
and gratitude to Morn Lindsay (Mrs. Herbert, Jr.) of Altamonte Springs,
Florida, formerly of Greenville, S.C. who so bravely undertook the
monumental job of retyping and editing the many different Deed Books
done by Mr. Davis over a period of years. Without her patience this
reprint would not have been possible.

INTERESTING ITEMS FROM ALBEMARLE COUNTY, VIRGINIA
ORDER BOOK 1744 - 1748 AS GATHERED BY COMPILER
BAILEY FULTON DAVIS

For some inexplicable reason there are no will or deed books in Albemarle
from formation date from Goochland in 1744 to 1748. It may be that
Tarlton's Raiders destroyed them, but there is no office statement to
answer the question of their being gone. We do know that Tarlton gets the
credit(?) for having destroyed the records of marriages back of about 1780.
A compilation has been made of extant marriages and also one has been made
in abstract of wills from 1748 to 1800.

I have not tried to jot down all items in this old order book, but have
confined myself to noting surveys, deeds, and other interesting items.
It is unfortunate that surveys and deeds do not give descriptions of areas,
but we are able to pick up many names. A study of later deeds will some-
times assist in this search for I have abstracted several deed books in
sequence.

My chief purpose is to give a survey up until May of 1761 for in that
period Amherst County was formed from Albemarle. I have abstracted deeds
of Amherst from 1761 through Deed Book Z. This brings searchers to a period near 1850.

One would have to search Goochland and Louisa for deed data prior to 1744.

SURVEY ITEMS

There are four reports which were made by JOSHUA FRY, Gentleman, Surveyor.
I have incorporated these by putting the page number to the left and acres
to the right. These pages and dates are as follows:

Page 21 - 1 January 1744 to 24 June 1745
Page 122 - 1 June 1745 to June 1746
Page 290 - 9 July 1747 to report - from June 1746 to June 1747
Page 364 - from June 1747 to June 1748

Page	Acres	Page	Acres
290 -	JAMES AGEE 400	21	JNO. BLACKBURN 395
290 -	MATT. AGEE 390, 400	364	" " 245
21 -	WM. ALLEN, Gent. 100, 400	364	NICHOLAS BODEN 50
122 -	" " " 288	290	COL. JNO. BOLLING 224
21 -	WM. HUNT ALLEN 394	122	JNO. BOSTICK 380, 400
364 -	GILES ALLIGRE (GEA) 248	364	" " 1270
122 -	THOS. ANDERSON 400	364	RICHARD BURKS 200, 200, 350
122	ADRIAN ANGLE 165	364	MANUS BURGER 222
364	ANGLE & H. HAMBLETON 370	290	HARDIN BURNLEY 400
290	CHRISTOPHER ANTHONY 388	364	" " 2216
290	JNO. ANTHONY 62	290	ZACHARIAH BURNLEY 394
290	EDMOND AYRES 400	290	GEO. BROOKE (BROKE) 100
290	MATTHIAS AYRES 400	122	PETER BROOKS 400, 545
364	" " 1600	290	CHAS. CARD 178
290	EDWARD BABER 325	364	LUKE CARROL 400
290	ROBERT BABER 200	364	HOWARD CASH 400, 400, 180
21	SAML. BAILEY 100	290	WM. CHAMBERS 190
364	JOSEPH & RICHARD BALLINGER 2000	21	JNO. CHILDERS 300
290	LEONARD BALLOW 400, 400, 150,	122	" " 215
	400, 400, 192	290	" " South River 212
290	LEONARD BALLOW, JR. 119	122	JOS. CHILDERS 200
290	CAPT. THOS. BALLOW	364	CHAS. CHRISTIAN 400, 68
290	THOS. BALLOW, JR. 145	364	JAS. CHRISTIAN 390, 323,
364	FRANCIS BARKER 230		400, 13, 400
364	ISAAC BATES 18	364	ROBT. CHRISTIAN 120,297,400
122	ANTHONY BENOIN(?) 636	364	COL. CHISWELL 2460
364	THOS. BIBB 308, 400	265	Apr 1747 MICAJAH CLARK 400
290	THOS. BIBE 95		on My Chunk Creek
364	JNO. BISWELL 400	364	JNO. COATS 200

Page	Acres
21	WM. NOLAND (NOWLAND) 400
290	" " 400
21	PATRICK OBRIAN (OBRYAN)400,400
122	" " 394,400
290	" " 280
364	ARTHUR OSBURN 400
122	GEO. PAIN 382
290	JNO. PAINE 320, 188
290	ALEXANDER PATTEN 71
290	DAVID PATTERSON 195, 198
364	" " 400
21	THOS. PATTERSON 370, 400
122	MARY PATTESON 200
290	CONSTANT PERKINS 100
21	WM. PERKINS 387, 400
290	" " 50
364	JNO. PETERSON(PATERSON?) 400
290	LEONARD PHILLIPS 123
290	THOS. PHILLIPS 9, 300
290	WM. PHILLIPS 180, 275
364	" " 200
290	JNO. PLEASANTS 1510
21	THOS. POTTER 400
364	RICH. POWEL 283
122	MOSES RAY 400
290	" " 400, 343,9
290	DANL. REYNOLDS 100
21	WM. RICKLEY 283
290	SAML. RIDGWAY 400
290	MILES RILE 251
290	ALEX. ROBERTS 225
290	JOHN ROBINSON 250
290	JOHN RODGERS 115
122	JOHN ROWLAND 100
122	PETER SALLE 400
122	SAML. SANDERS 396
122	STEPHEN SANDERS 400
122	THOS. SANDERS 400
122	DANL. SCOTT 380
122	SAML. SCOTT 400
364	WM. SCRUGGS 200, 400
290	SAML. SHANNON 150
290	JAMES SHASTED 150
290	JAMES SHEPARD 400
290	SAML. SHORT 394
290	ABRAHAM SMITH 200
364	JACOB SMITH 256
364	JAMES SMITH 400
122	JOHN SMITH 400
122	JOHN SNODDY 196
122	THOS. SOWELL 78
21	SAML. STEPHENS 200
122	" " 225
290	BENJ. STINNETT 400
290	JAS. STINNETT 227
122	ALEX. STINSON 385
290	" " 400
364	REV. MR. WM. STITH 276
364	JNO. STONE 365, 200
364	MARVEL STONE 390
364	THOS. STONE 230, 200
364	GEO. STOVALL 400, 340
364	GEO. TAYLOR 200
364	JAMES TAYLOR 337
290	THOMAS & DABBS 385, 350, 400, 380, 385
21	EDWARD THOMAS 140
290	HENRY THOMAS 172
290	JNO. THOMAS 100

Page	Acres
21	JOSEPH THOMAS 200
290	JOS. THOMPSON 345
364	ROBT. THOMPSON 200
364	PETER TOBLET 400
290	BISHOP TONEY 99, 150
290	HENRY TRENT 14, 175
290	WM. TROTTER 133
364	ARTHUR TULEY 400
122	THOS. TURPIN 222
290	JNO. WADE 128
122	JOEL WALKER 340, 400
290	" " not clear
290	JOSEPH WALTON not clear
290	THOMAS WALTON 9
364	WM. WALTON 400
122	JNO. WARD 300
364	JAMES WARREN 400
364	JNO. WARREN 276
290	DAVID WATKINS 295
122	JAMES WATKINS 400
364	THOMAS WATTS 335
290	JNO. WEBB 225, 392
290	JNO. WHEELER 374
21	SACKERVAL WHITEBREAD 400
122	" " 400
364	MATTHEW WHITTELL 400
364	DAVID WILLIS 125
21	EDWARD WOOD 350
364	ROBT. WOODING 390
290	BENJ. WOODSON 377, 400
122	OBADIAH WOODSON 285
122	JNO. WORLEY JR. 386
290	THOS. WRIGHT 200, 290
290	WM. WRIGHT 166
364	" " 2000
122	JNO. YOUNG 100
364	JNO. R. 195 name not clear

INDENTURED SERVANTS

SLAVE ITEMS

PEOPLE AND PLACES

Page

130 June 1746 JAS. MEREDITH, attorney.

 80 Nov. 1745 EDWD. MOLLOY & MARY BARNETT, adultery.

151 Aug 1746 ROBT. NAPIER, JR., & wife MARY - in a suit.

280 May 1747 Church wardens vs. PHEBE NOWLAND - debt; no inhabitant.

 41 July 1745 THOS. NUNN & wife CATON, swore that they were imported
            from Scotland 14 years ago; no rights received.

400 Aug 1748 JNO. & STEPHEN HEARD & PATRICK NOWLAND swore that left ear
            of DAVID REESE had "pies bit off" in fray with PATRICK
            NOWLAND.

276 May 1747 Church wardens vs. LORINDA SANDERS; debt; no inhabitant.

 65 Sept 1745 THOS. SOWELL; Lt.

130 June 1746 VINSENT SPROUCE & wife MARY - in suit.

101 Mar 1746 BENJ. WHEELER, ensign.

280 May 1747 Church wardens vs. JNO. WHEELER; debt; continued.

  5 Mar 1745 JNO. WOODY - road surveyor.

(I did not attempt to abstract all suits, but merely picked out a few
men and wives.)

CHILDREN

Many of these items pertain to children who were bound out. I use "BO"
to mean bound out.

169 Sept 1746 MARY ALLSUP B.O. to MARY LADD.

231 Feb 1747 MARY BARNETT's children B.O: CHAS.; LETTIE; NED; FRANCIS
            & WINEY(?). (Was she the same woman who was arraigned for
            adultery?)

 92 Jan 1746 JNO. BURKS' children B.O., not named.

215 Feb 1747 JNO. & FRANCIS CAMERON - children of JNO. & CATH. CAMERON -
            JAS. LEE to show why he detains them.

143 Aug 1746 SUSANNAH COLE - poor mulatto girl - B.O.

 11 Apr 1745 JNO. DANIEL, orphan about 15; B.O. to RICH. ELLIOTT, weaver.

  9 Mar 1745 GEO. DUNCOMB, orphan about 17; B.O. to THOS. MOODRICK(?),
            carpenter.

 92 Jan 1746 -------DUNKIN children B.O.

139 Jul 1746 STEPHEN & DAVID FIELDS B.O.

271 May 1747 CHAS. FIND, orphan B.O. motion of PHILLIP MATTHEWS.

345 Mar 1748 RHODY, ELIZ. & JNO. GORDON B.O. Sheriff to sell the
            estate of JNO. GORDON.

360 May 1748 ANN GREGGS alias SANDERS - to be B.O.; now in possession
            of JNO. HODNETT.

139 Jul 1746 JNO. HOWLAND(?) B.O.

 92 Jan 1746 ELIZ. MATTHEWS' children to be B.O.

6

281   May, 1747   PRUDENCE MAXBURY B.O.; poor child.

366   May 1748   ENGLISH MCCOY B.O. to LASARUS DAMERON, showmaker.

231   Feb 1747   B.O. children of CATHON NUNN: MARY & LUCRETIA. See people
                   and places for NUNN data.

       ANN SANDERS - see GREGG

214   Feb 1747   JAS. SANDERS, orphan, B.O.

 28   Jun 1745   MARY SEALES, orphan, B.O. to MANUS BURGER.

121   Jun 1746   SARAH & ANN SMITH B.O. - neglected by parents.

345   Mar 1748   JAMES SUBLETT - his guardian was RENE SHASTAIN, or RENEE
                   CHASTAIN.

219   Feb 1747   JNO. WARD B.O.

 62   Sep 1745   JOS. & HANNAH WELCH - mulattoes born to ELEANOR WELCH
                   B.O. to EDWIN HICKMAN - also GEO. WELCH, bastard, B.O.
                   to HICKMAN.

ESTATES AND HEIRS

I regret as much as anyone that these items, in various sections, are
fragmentary, but I have included all data.

361   May 1748   LEONARD BALLOW's will - SUSANNA BALLOW to administer and
                   heir, LEONARD BALLOW, to appear. Page 394, July 1748,
LEONARD, son of LEONARD, came with WM. BATTERSBY, attorney, and objected to
will of father. Claimed changes made without father's consent - vile
practices after his death. Susanna denied and appealed; p.400, Aug. 1748,
will approved.

  3   Feb 28, 1744 CHAS. BLANEY, dec'd...Sheriff, J. THOMSON, to summons
                     widow as to any estate.

 96   Jan 1746   JNO. BURKS, dec'd. THOS. McDANIEL, admr.

308   Aug 1747   WM. CANNON, dec'd. ISAAC BATES, former admr. JNO. CANNON,
                   heir, & THEODORICK WEBB to show cause. Page 312, JNO.
                   CANNON qualified.

       THOS. CHRISTIAN - see AMELIA CRAWLEY & admr., REBECCA CHRISTIAN.

  8   Mar 1745   WM. COLLINS, dec'd. MARGARET COLLINS, exrx.

 15   May 1745   AMELIA CRAWLEY - THOS. CHRISTIAN was her admr.; his exrx
                   is REBECCA CHRISTIAN.

314   Nov 1747   STEPHEN EDWARDS' will; JANE EDWARDS is to admr.

361   May 1748   MARTHA EVANS to show as to administration of her dec'd.
                   husband's estate - he is not named.

215   Feb 1747   JAS. FENLEY's will proved by ARCHIBALD BLACK. p.242, Mar
                   1747, JNO. FENLEY, an heir, MARGARET FENLEY to admr. p.
267, Apr 1747, she declined and DAVID BELL to admr.

121   Jun 1746   SAML. GLOVER's will: SARAH GLOVER to admr; THOS. JONES
                   "writ" it; reference to several legacies. Same page;
SAML. GLOVER in room of late father as road overseer.

344   Mar 1748   THOS. GOOLSBY's will - TABITHA & WM. GOOLSBY are to admr.
                   approved by heir, THOS. GOOLSBY.

Page
345 Mar 1748 Sheriff to sell estate of JNO. GORDON. RHODY, ELIZ. &
              JNO. GORDON to be B.O.

372 Jun 1748 Also in deeds: MICHL. HOLLAND's exrs.: HENRY MARTIN & wife
              POUNCEY, to GEO. PAYNE.

34   Jul 1745 STEPHEN JOHNSON's will: MARY JOHNSON to admr. p.82, Nov.
              1745 - same data.

79   Nov 1745 AMOS LADD's will; NOBLE LADD to admr.

79   Nov 1745 SAML. MAXBURY, dec'd. WM. CABELL, admr.

257 Mar 1746 WM. MAYO, dec'd. ANN MAYO to admr.

372   EDWD. McGEE, dec'd. JNO. GILMORE, admr.

299 Jul 1747 NICHOLAS MERIWETHER, dec'd. RO. LEWIS, admr.

186 Sep 1746 RICH. MOSBY, dec'd. BENJ. MOSBY, admr.

122 Jun 1746 THOS. PATTESON's will; MARY PATTERSON to admr. p.145,
              Aug. 1746, same data, but PATTESON here.

255 Mar 1746 ROBT. RODGERS, dec'd. JER. WHITNEY & wife SUSANNA (she
              is exrx.) vs. JNO. BIBY.

     1746   JNO. REED's will; ANDREW REED, admr., JNO. REED, bdm.

20   May 1745 EDWD. SCOTT, dec'd. SAML. SCOTT proposes to build court-
              house on EDWARD's land. (Note: Scottsville is now site
              of first seat of government.)

372 Jun 1748 JNO. SHROSBURY, dec'd. WM. HAMMOCK, admr. JEREMIAH
              SHROSBURY, brother of JNO., to show cause.

36   Jul 1745 JNO. STEPHEN's estate: SIMON MILES, exr., and heirs want
              an acct. p.44, THOS. STEPHENS - his orphan - WM. CABELL,
gdn. p.149, Aug, 1746, gdn. and ward mentioned. p.406, Aug 1748, CABELL
states that there is no estate on hand.

327 Dec 1747 MICHAEL THOMAS' will; EDWARD THOMAS, heir, to be called.

12   Apr 1745 THOS. UPTON's will, p.32, approved; MARY UPTON to admr.

3   Feb. 28, 1744. WENTWORTH WEBB's widow, MARY, to admr. p.363, May
1748, MARY has married THEODORICK WEBB. bdm.: ISAAC BATES & JNO. CANNON.

DEED ITEMS: CROSS INDEX OF PARTIES

Page   Grantor   Grantee

372 June 1748 JOS. ADCOCK to ALEX. SPEIRS. ELIZ. wife of ADCOCK.
22   June 1745 JNO. ANTHONY to HENRY MARTIN
139 Jul 1746   "   "   to JOHN TURRENTINE GOOLSBY
403 Aug 1748   "   "   " WM. HAMNER
305 Aug 1747 JOSEPH ANTHONY to JNO. COATS
314 Nov 1747   "   "   to SIMON CLEMONS
308 Aug 1747 JNO. AUSTIN to JNO. SNELSON - deed of trust
359 Mar 1748 DOUGLAS BAKER & wife JANE to DANL. JOHNSONTON (sic)
45   Aug 1745 JNO. BARNETT to JNO. WITT
415 Aug 1748 HANNAH BATES to BOBLE LADD
305 Aug 1747 ANTHONY BENNETT(?) to HENRY CARY
120 Jun 1746 SAML. BRIDGWATER to ISAAC BATES
360 May 1748 BENJ. BROWN & wife SARAH to ROBT. HARRIS
78   Sep 1745 REBCEA BUNCH to ALEXANDER MACKEY
248 Mar 1747 CHAS. BURKS to JNO. PLEASANTS
314 Nov 1747 JNO. BURNS to WM. HAMNER
360 May 1748   "   " & wife DINAH to WM. HAMNER

Page	Date	Grantor	Grantee

```
274   May 1747   WM. CABELL to WM. BATTERSBY
314   Nov 1747    "      "    & wife ELIZ. to WM. MEGGINSON
119   Mar 1746   HENRY CARY to PATRICK CAMPBELL
203   Nov 1746    "     "    "      "       "
 45   Aug 1745   HENRY CHILES to JAS. WALKER
 11   Apr 1745   JNO. CHISWELL & wife ELIZ. to ALEX. MONTGOMERY; to JAS.
                 REED: to SAML. BELL
119   Mar & Jun 1746   JNO. CHISWELL & wife ELIZ. to JAS. ROBERTSON; to
                 EDWD. MAXWELL; to JNO. LACKEY, to JAS. BARNETT; to JAS.
                 BELL; to JOSEPH BARNETT, to SAML. HOLLINGS
264   Mar 1746   JNO. CHISWELL & wife ELIZ. to JAMES MARTIN
359   Mar 1748    "      "       "      "     "  FERGUS RAY
140   Jul 1746   JOSIAH CLAPHAM to WM. SYMSON; to ALEX. PATTEN
 11   Apr 1745   WM. COCKRAM to WM. DUIGUID - deed of trust
167   Sep 1746   CHAS. COFFREY to JNO. GRILLS
120   Jun 1746   WM. CREASY to THOS. GREGG YARBOROUGH
120   Jun 1746   EDWD. DANIEL to JNO. FLOYD
385   Jul 1748   NICHOLAS DAVIES to JOSHUA FRY
359   Mar 1748   JNO. DOBBINS to WM. PATTESON
271   May 1747   ARTHUR DONELLY to DENNIS DOYLE
325   Nov 1747    "       "      "  FRANCIS ETHRINGTON
313   Nov 1747   JNO. DOUGLAS & wife JUDITH to ANDREW McWILLIAMS
362   May 1748    "      "     "    "      "  DAVID DOUGLAS
 45   Aug 1745   DENNIS DOYLE to BENJ. BROWN, JR.
 80   Nov 1745    "      "    JNO. MULLINS; ELIZ, wife of DOYLE
315   Nov 1747   RICH. & WM. EPPES to RICH. RANDOLPH; also p. 320
373   Jun 1748    "     "    "     "   "  JOSHUA FRY; also p. 385
361   May 1748   FRANCIS ETHRINGTON to MICHAEL THOMAS.
344   Mar 1748   JNO. FEARN to RICH. SOUTHERN
386   Jul 1748   JOS. FITZPATRICK to DENNIS DOYLE
385   Jul 1748   THOS. FITZPATRICK & wife JANE to ELIZ. BUSTARD
344   Dec 1747   JNO. FLOYD to ISAAC BATES
 33   Jul 1745   GEO. HOLMES GIVIN to ROBT. KING
252   Mar 1746   JOHN. GLOVER to SAML. GLOVER
201   Nov 1746   PHINEAS GLOVER to SAML. GLOVER
251   Mar 1746   ROBT. GLOVER & wife MARY to JAS. McNEAL
253    "    "     "      "     "    "    "    "  SAML. GLOVER
250   Mar 1746   SAML. GLOVER to JNO. GLOVER
251   Mar 1746    "      "     "  ROBT. GLOVER, & wife JUDY to JNO. GLOVER
 34   Jul 1745   THOS. GOOLSBY to SAML. SHELTON
190   Sep 1746    "      "    & wife TABITHA to LEONARD BALLOW
305   Aug 1747    "      "      "    "      "  to THOS. GOOLSBY JR.
 79   Nov 1745   JAMES GOSS & wife MARY ANN to THOS. PARTOR(?)
201   Nov 1746   JNO. GRAVES to GILES ALLEGRE
214   Feb 1747    "      "      "      "      "
 88   Jan 1746   WM. GRAY to EDMUND GRAY
233   Feb 1747    "     "    "  JOS. DABBS
292   Jul 1747    "     "    "  EDMUND GRAY, 2 deeds, wit: JAMES GRAY
 61   Sep 1745   EDWARD GREESHAM to ALEX. TRENT
 61   Sep 1745   DAVID GRIFFITH & wife ELIZ. to JNO. HENSON
345   Mar 1748    "      "       "      "     "  BENJ. MIMS
 25   Jun 1745   JAS. & BETSY GULSBY el al to JNO. FARRAR
 13   May 1745   BERNARD GAINES, son of DANIEL, from RO. ROSE, clerk, & wife
                 ANN.  (For good discussion on GAINES family see RAILEY's
                 Woodford County, Kentucky volume.)
167   Sep 1746   THOS. HARBOUR to JNO. MARTIN
 61   Sep 1745   THOS. HARCOURT & wife SARAH to JNO. BIBY
102   Mar 1746   CASTLETON HARPER & wife REBECCA to WM. HITCHCOCK
359   Mar 1748   CHAS. & ISABEL HEARD to JNO. HEARD
127   Jun 1746   JNO. HEARD to WM. MORIAL
233   Mar 1747   JAMES & ELIZ. HENDRICK to THOS. SHENNON
 61   Sep 1745   WM. HILL to ALEX. TRENT
 33   Jul 1745   MICHAEL HOLLAND to CHAS. LEWIS
372   Jun 1748    "       "    , his exors, HENRY MARTIN & wife POUNCEY,
                 to GEO. PAYNE.
360   May 1748   SAML. HOLLINGSHEAD to SAML. DAVIS
 25   Jun 1745   ROWLAND HORSLEY to JOSIAH PAIN
142   Jul 1746   GUILIELMUS HUDSON to JOSHUA FRY
```

Page	Date	Grantor	Grantee

120 Jun 1746 DANL. JONES to PAT. NOWLING; to DENNIS DOYLE
25 Jun 1745 RICH. KEARBY & ELIZ. KEARBY et al to JNO. FARRAR (see KERBY)
102 Mar 1746 RO. KENT to THOS. KENT
362 May 1748 RICH. & ELIZ. KERBY to PATRICK NAPIER
22 Jun 1745 JNO. KEY to DANL. HOLLODAY
271 May 1747 MARTIN KING to JNO. WITT
121 Jun 1746 MARTIN KING Jr. to JNO. ANTHONY
320 Nov 1747 " " " " HENRY MARTIN
305 Aug 1747 JAS. LEE to ROBT. HAMNER
21 May 1745 CHAS. LEWIS to CHAS. LEWIS, JR.
81 Nov 1745 DAVID LEWIS to DAVID & JAMES KINKHEAD
266 Apr 1747 JNO. LEWIS & wife ELIZ. to THOS. GOOLSBY
292 Jul 1747 JNO. LIVINGSTON, JR. to BERNARD GAINES
102 Mar 1746 THOS. LOWELL to CASTLETON HARPER
140 Jul 1746 CHAS. LYNCH to JAS. MANLY
360 May 1748 " " " THOS. WRIGHT
78 Sep 1745 JNO. LYON to HUGH BOYLES
22 Jun 1745 HENRY MARTIN to JNO. ANTHONY
313 Nov 1747 JAS McBANE to JNO. REID et al; to JNO. McWERTER
399 Jul 1748 JAS McCAN to JAS. MANLY
88 Jan 1746 JNO. McDANIEL to GILES ALLEGRE
201 Nov 1746 " " " " "
       McWILLIAMS - see ANDREW WILLIAMS
298 Jul 1747 HUGH MOOR to david bell
344 Mar 1748 " " & wife ELIZ. to JNO. STEVENSON
360 May 1748 WM. MOOR to WM. MOOR JR.
61 Sep ,745 CHAS. MOORMAN to DANL. MAUPIN
399 Jul 1748 THOS. MOORMAN & wife RACHEL to JNO. ROADS
120 Jun 1746 LEWIS MORGAN to MATTHIAS AYRES
372 Jun 1748 WM. NOWLAND & wife JANE to WM. CHAMBERS
215 Feb 1747 PATRICK NOWLIN to DENNIS DOYLE
344 Mar 1748 ARTHUR OSBORN to JNO. ANTHONY
214 Feb 1747 BRISSIE(?) PARISH to JNO. LUCAS
167 Sep 1746 GIDEON PATTESON to NATHL. JEFFRIES
36 Jul 1745 THOS. & MARY PATTESON to WM. DUIGUID
313 Nov 1747 WM. PHELPS to EDMOND TONEY
214 Feb 1747 ANTHONY POUNCEY to JNO. GRAVES; to JAS. SPEARS
201 Nov 1746 JNO REYNOLDS to JNO. THURMAN
13f May 1745 ROBT. ROSE, clerk, & wife ANN, to DUNCAN GRAYHAM; to
       MARGARET MUSKET: to JNO. GRAYHAM; to BERNARD GAINES, son
       of DANIEL GAINES
79   ROBT. ROSE clerk, to JAS. BARNETT, a release
272 May 1747 " " " THOS. JONES
371 Jun 1748 " " " " AMBROSE JONES; to EDMOND MANNING
118 Mar 1746 PETER RUCKER to JNO. LIVINGSTON
190 Oct 1746 STEPHEN SANDERS and wife PRISCILLA to JOEL WALKER
22 Jun 1745 WM. SANDERS to JNO. ANTHONY
101 Jan 1746 JACOB SHEPARD to JNO. HOWARD
101 Jan 1746 JAS. SHEPHARD to CHAS. BOND
399 Jul 1748 GEO. SLAWTER to JOHN ADAM CORN
139f Jul 1746 JNO. SMITH & wife JANE to PETER JEFFERSON
166 Sep 1746 LARKIN SMITH & wife MARY to CHAS. LYNCH
102 Mar 1746 DAVIS STOCKTON to JOS. KINKHEAD
313 Nov 1747 THOS. STOCKTON & wife RACHEL to SAML. BLACK
305 Aug 1747 RICH. TAYLOR to ANTHONY BROWNE
371 Jun 1748 " " " RICH. BURKS; to CHAS. BURKS
264 Mar 1746 WM. TAYLOR to JNO. CHISWELL;also p.292, July 1747
400 Aug 1748 EDWD. THOMAS to HENRY THOMAS; to JNO. THOMAS
400 Aug 1748 JNO. THOMPSON to JOHN LEWIS; release
78 Sep 1745 JAS. TOOLEY, JR. & wife ANN to JNO. LEWIS
304 Aug 1747 THOS. TURPIN to HENRY CARY
61 Sep 1745 ABRAHAM VENABLE to THOS. MARTIN
121 Jun 1746 JNO. WADE & wife ELIZ. to ANDREW HERSTON
78 Sep 1745 JAS. WALKER to ARTHUR BREADING
78 Sep 1745 " " " BRISSEL(?) PARISH
120 Jun 1746 " " " JNO. BOSTICK
236 Mar 1747 JOS. WALTON to GEO. SLAUGHTER
306 Aug 1747 ROBT. WALTON to DRURY TUCKER

Page	Date	Grantor	Grantee
264	Mar 1746	JAS. WARREN & wife ELIZ. to THOS. CHAMBERS	
139	Jun 1746	JAS. WATKINS to THOS. TURPIN	
22	Jun 1745	JNO. WEAD to GEO. HEARD - power of attorney.	
313	Nov 1747	SACKERVAL WHITEBREAD to JOS. FUQUA	
121	Jun 1746	ANDREW M. WILLIAMS (or McWILLIAMS) to BENJ. BROWN.	
360	May 1748	JNO. WILLIAMSON & wife PRUDENCE to JNO. THOMPSON	
25	Jun 1745	ABRAHAM & FRANCIS (sic) WITWORTH to JNO. FARRAR	
124	Jun 1746	HENRY WOOD to VALENTINE WOOD; deed of gift	
344	Mar 1748	ARCHIBALD WOODS & wife ISABEL to JNO. LOCKHARD	
233	Mar 1747	JONATHAN WOODSON to WM. HOOPER	
360	May 1748	THOS. WRIGHT to ALEX. MURRAY	

ALBEMARLE COUNTY, VIRGINIA DEED BOOK 1

Deed Book 1 contains wills and deeds, but I have not abstracted wills
since this has been well done. The book begins in 1748. We do not know
what became of the first wills and deeds, for there is no explanation in
the clerk's office. - Bailey Fulton Davis, 1970.

Page 1   Oct 1748 WM. DUIGUID, planter, to THOS. McDANIEL for Ь150,
          156 acres S. side Fluvanna River adj. THOS. BALEW.

Page 3   10 Dec 1748 WM. MATTHEWS to WM. CABELL for Ь40, 150 acres N. side
          Tye, adj. CAPT. CABELL near mouth of Joe's creek. Wit: GILBERT
BOWMAN, KATH. HARPER, TERRENCE C. MACDONALD.

Page 4   12 Jan 1740 HUGH DOBBINS & wife ANNE to JNO. CAMBELL for Ь50,
          390 acres(?-page is torn) N. Garden adj. RO. LEWIS, grantor,
WM. TAYLOR. Wit: CHARLES LAMBERT, THOS. FITZPATRICK, DAVID REES.

Page 6   10 Dec 1748 JNO. HEARD to JNO. BISWELL for Ь28, 275 acres both
          sides of Hardway-S. fork. Adj. MILDRED MERIWETHER, Jumping
Branch. Wit: JNO. HUNTER, CASTLETON HARPER, WM. CABELL.

Page 7   9 Sep 1748 WM. ALLEN to WM. HUNT ALLEN for Ь100, 650 acres of
          1185 acres, patented to WM. ALLEN 13 Aug (year hard to read) in
then Goochland County, on Slate River, Hunt's Creek. Wit: G. MARR, JAS.
TAYLOR.

Page 9   9 Sep 1748 WM. ALLEN to JNO. ALLEN for Ь110, 394 acres both
          sides of Slate, patented to WM. ALLEN 10 Oct 1746; also a tract
on both sides of Glover's road and both sides of Horn Quarter road; headwaters of Randolph's, Hatcher, and Joshua Creeks - 400 acres, pat. to
WM. ALLEN 1745. Wit: G. MARR, WM. HUNT ALLEN, JAS. TAYLOR.

Page 10   8 Sep 1748 EDMOND WOOD &wife MARY to ROBT. THOMSON of Goochland
          for Ь40, two tracts of 595 acres, whole of 2 patents, 13 June
1743 - 243 acres pat. to WM. CANNON & 350 acres pat. to EDMOND WOOD 1 Oct
1747, adj. branches of Hatcher's creek and Willis River.

Page 11 10 Feb 1748 COL. JNO. CHISWELL of St. James Parish, Hanover, to
          EDWD. STEVENSON(summary gives name as STINSON), planter of
Albemarle, for Ь28, 280 acres on Lynch and Taylor creeks, forks of Rock-
fish branches; part of pat. of 26 Mar 1739. Adj. JAS. MARTIN, THOS.
MERIWETHER, JAS. ROBERTSON. Wit: JAS. BELL, WM. SIMSON, JNO. HEARD.

Page 13 14 Feb 1748 JNO. CHISWELL, St. Martin's parish, Hanover, to
          LAWRENCE SMALL for Ь110, 200 acres on branches of Corbin creek,
branch of Rockfish near Blue Mountains, adj. JAS. BARNETT, JNO. REID;
part of pat. of 11 and 140 acres of 26 Mar 1739. Wit: JOS. BARNETT,
FRANCIS WRIGHT, JAS. ROBERTSON.

Page 16 14 Feb 1748 JNO. CHISWELL, St. Martin's Parish, Hanover, to

JNO. WRIGHT, farmer, for ₤40, 800 acres adj. ALEX. MONTGOMERY, the river branch, and grantor. Part of a pat. of 11; 140 acres 26 Mar 1739. (I misread just before this, for this is part of pat. of 11, 140 acres.) Wit: FRANCIS WRIGHT, JOS. BARNETT, JAS. ARMOR.

Page 18   13 Feb 1748 JNO. CHISWELL, as above, to JNO. WRIGHT for 5 sh., 800 acres adj. same as above. Wit: same as above.

Page 20   14 Feb 1748 JNO. CHISWELL, as above, to FRANCIS WRIGHT, farmer, for ₤15, 300 acres on Davis Creek, S. side Rockfish. Part of pat. above. Wit: JOS. BARNETT, JAS. ARMOR, JNO. WRIGHT.

Page 22   13 Feb 1748 JNO. CHISWELL, as above, to FRANCIS WRIGHT, farmer, for 5 sh., 300 acres, adj. as above. Wit: as above.

Page 23   13 Feb 1748 JNO. CHISWELL, as above, to JAMES ARMOR for ₤27, 400 acres N. branch Rockfish - part of above pat. adj. grantor. Wit: JNO. WRIGHT, FRANCIS WRIGHT, JOS. BARNETT.

Page 25   23 Dec 1748 EDWIN HICKMAN to THOS. GRAVES, St. Geo. Parish, Spotsylvania, 2 JNO. & BENJ. CLERK, Drysdale Parish, King & Queen - JOSEPH SMITH, HICKMAN, THOS. GRAVES & JONATHAN CLERK, 25 May 1734, pat. 3277 acres in Goochland; SMITH & CLERK died with no legal heirs - CLERK's part by will is in hands of his sons, JNO. & BENJ.   10 sh. their father's part 809¾ acres N. side Rivanna, N. fork James adj. JOHN KEMP; near Linch ford. Wit: EDWIN HICKMAN, JR., HIRAM GAINES, BENJ. WILSON.

Page 28   22 Nov 1748 MICHAEL WOODS to ANDREW WALLACE for ₤20, 400 acres Ivy Creek, 200 acres of it as dowry "with his daughter". Pat. to Capt. CHAS. HUDSON 26 Jul 1735, and by HUDSON deeded to WOODS 10 June 1737. Wit: ARCHIBALD WOODS, WM. WOODS, ROBT. LOGAN.

Page 30   22 Nov 1748 MICHL. WOODS to RO. LOGAN for ₤30, part of above tract on Ivy Creek adj. ANDREW WALLACE. Wit: WOODS as above, ANDREW WALLACE.

Page 32   26 Dec 1748 ANN MAYO, exrx. of WM. MAYO, Goochland, to ROBT. BARNET for ₤30, on both sides Rockfish branches; part of 800 acres pat. to WM. MAYO 13 Mar 1743. Wit: JAS. & JANE BARTLEY, JOS. BARNET.

Page 33   8 Sep 1748 WM. NOLAND & wife JANE to THOS. BLAKEY of Goochland for ₤50, 200 acres Arthur's Creek of Slate River. Pat. to WM. NOLAND 20 Aug 1747, and where he dwelleth. Wit: ISAAC BATES, JNO. WATKINS, PATRICK NAPIER.

Page 36   16 Sep 1748 BENJ. WHEELER to GILES ALLEGRE for ₤60, 300 acres both sides Mychunk Creek adj. RO. ADAMS. Pat. to WHEELER 3 Oct 1734. Wit: SAML. GEHEE, JUDITH ALLEGRE.

Page 38   1748 JNO.   BURKS to SAML. SPENCER for ₤35, 400 acres Tye River adj. JNO. MACHONY. (Note: Those who have studied my Amherst works know that land on Tye and Rockfish became Nelson after 1808. I drove down Rockfish to the village by that name the other day and saw the horrible results of the storm.

Page 41   8 May 1749 WM. MORRISON to ANDREW REID for ₤27, 500 acres on Rockfish. Wit: WM. CABELL, ALEX. REID, JNO. CONFEY.

Page 43   8 May 1749 WM. MORRISON to ALEX. REID for ₤27, 700 acres on Rockfish branches. Wit: as above.

Page 45   3 May 1749 SAML. MURRELL to WM. MILLER for ₤3, 20 acres adj. a path, Rockfish, opposite a small island, ALEX. PATTEN, WM. MILLER, JR. Wit: WM. CABELL, JNO. REID, WM. MALER.

Page 47   10 May 1749 ALEX. PATTON to JNO. THOMSON for ₤9-10, 172 acres both sides Taylor Creek adj. ARCHIBALD WOODS, mt. spur, a branch. Wit: WM. SIMSON, WM. MALER (MATER?), JNO. MORRISON.

Page 50   2 Nov 1748 JNO. JEMMESON to JNO McCOLLOCH for ₤11, 77 acres both

sides Moreman's river. Part of pat. of 177 acres, 6 Jul 1741. Wit:
NATHAN WOODS, JAS. WHAREY, JAS. WEIR.

Page 53   24 Jan 1749 ROBT. BABER, JR. of Lunenberg Co. and Cumberland
           parish to JNO. TIRN for ₺20, 300 acres adj. WM. CANNON, WENT-
WORTH WEBB, Beargarding Creek, pat. 12 Jan 1746. Wit: ISAAC BATES, THEO-
DORIC WEBB, STEPHEN RENNO. (Note: all parties are of Albemarle unless
otherwise stated.)

Page 56   21 Nov 1748 GEO. HEARD & wife ELENOR of Chas. City County, to
           WM. & JNO. HEARD, for ₺50, 400 acres Rockfish adj. near Blue
Mts., JNO. CHISWELL. Pat. Feb 1748 to WM. HEARD & JNO HEARD, son, to
GEO. HEARD, dec'd. Wit: JNO. GILMORE, STEPHEN HEARD, JAS. HEARD, JANE
GILLMORE, JNO. WEAD.

Page 58   21 Nov 1748 GEO. HEARD & wife, as above, to JAS. HEARD for
           ₺9-10, 130 acres Rockfish branches near Blue Mts. adj. WM. HEARD-
"Layed" off in dide(sic) granted WM. HEARD 3 Nov 1748. Wit: JNO. GILLMORE,
WM. HEARD, STEPHEN HEARD, JANE GILLMORE.

Page 60   24 Sep 1748 JNO. MAXEY & wife SARAH, of Goochland, to WM. TAX,
           JR., of same place, for ₺26, 400 acres both sides Troublesome
Creek of Slate adj. SACKERVAL WHITEBREAD. Pat. 25 Sep 1746. Wit: JNO.
HUGHES, WALTER MAXEY, EDWD. MAXEY.

Page 63   17 Feb 1748 JNO. MAXEY to SAMPSON MAXEY - gives and bequeaths -
           200 acres adj. N. side Great Creek on N. side Slate; ABRAHAM
BIGINGS. Wit: MATTHIAS AYRES, EDMD. WOOD, JNO. MOSSHAM.

Page 65   11 May 1749 FERGUS RAY to ALEX. HENDERSON of Augusta Co. for
           ₺60, 237 acres both sides Rockfish; part of tract pat. to JNO.
CHISWELL, of Hanover, and sold by him to FERGUS RAY. (Note: This Rockfish
area is part of devastated flood area of present Nelson.)

Page 68   27 Feb 1748 ANNE CHILES of Amelia to PAUL CHILES, for ₺80, 265
           acres N. side Attomack and Holladay rivers. Surveyed for HENRY
CHILES 1 Mar 1740. Wit: SILVANUS MAXEY, THOS. BALLOW, RICH. LEE.

Page 71   10 Nov 1748 JNO. GLOVER to BRYAN DOLEN for ₺1400 tobacco, 400
           acres S. side James and both sides of creek called Glover's on
Slate Creek.

Page 73   2 Jun 1749 JAMES ARMOR (MOT) and wife JANNET of St. Martin's
           Parish, Louisa (error - this is for grantee), JNO. RODES - note
error for grantor-- for ₺80, 400 acres N. branch Rockfish adj. Col. CHIS-
WELL's old line. Wit: JO. BECKLEY, DAVID HAMILTON, DAVID MARTIN, JNO.
RODES, BENJ. BIBB, JNO. LONGAN.

Page 76   8 Jun 1749 CHAS. BURKS to FRANCIS BROTHERS for ₺35, 275 acres
           both sides Frisbey Creek adj. WM. JONES; grantor. Wit: WM.
CABELL, SAM. GLOVER, JAMES GOSS. SARAH, wife of BURKS.

Page 79   29 Aug 1748 THOS. EDWARDS to WM. KANNON of Goochland for ₺90,
           400 acres S. side James; upper end of Willis Creek; branch of
Barren Lick. Adj. JNO. PAYNE, JNO. DAIN(?). Pat. to EDWARDS 5 July 1746.
Wit: ARCH CARY, JAS. ALLEN, JNO. BETTERFORD, WICKSON TINSON.

Page 82   8 Aug 1748 JNO. WOODY, planter, to CHRISTOPHER SHEPARD of
           Louisa, planter, for ₺25, 200 acres Byrd Creek. Wit: FRANS.
BAKER, CHAS. LYNCH, JNO. ANTHONY.

Page 84   2 May 1748 JNO WARREN to JNO. CHISWELL of Hanover, merchant,
           for 5 sh. 276 acres pat. 20 Sep 1747. Wit: CHAS. LYNCH, J.
POWER, H-- BROOKE.

Page 85   3 May 1749 JNO WARREN & wife SUSANNAH, to JNO. CHISWELL, as
           above for ₺200, lease, 276 acres. Pat. as above. Wit: as above.

Page 90   Delivered to Capt. CHAS. LYNCH - if CHISWELL views veins and
           mines and approves - will pay ₺200 and WARREN gets one fifth of

"oar"; reverts, if not worked within 8 months. (Alfred Percy refers to CHISWELL and mine ventures in what was to become Amherst in his fine work on Amherst. BFD)

Page 92 8 Aug 1749 PHILIP THOMAS, of Amelia, to GIDEON THOMAS - consid-
         eratin, a tract in Amelia - part of - on S. side Appomattox -
tract on Troublesome of Slate River - 400 acres adj. ANTHONY BENOINE.

Page 93 9 Aug 1749 CHAS. LYNCH to MOSES EDGAR for Ŀ20, 400 acres pat.
         1747. Adj. WM. WHITESIDES, COL. CHISWELL, TERRILL.

Page 96 9 Aug 1749 THOS. WATTS & wife SARAH to PETER BAYS for Ŀ35, 400
         acres N. side Pedlar. Wit: EDMOND H. HARRISON, RICH. POWELL,
THOS. SMITH.

Page 98 8 May 1749 EDMUND GRAY to JNO. SAUNDERS for Ŀ28, 200 acres
         Willis Creek, part of tract bought from WM. GRAY adj. Grantee.
Wit: STEPHEN SANDERS, WM. ACRES, WM. BLACKBURN.

Page 100 22 Apr 1748 JNO. BLACKBURN to WM. BLACKBURN for Ŀ5, 395 acres
         S. side of James, N. branch of Willis Creek above JAMES SANDERS'
survey. Wit: STEPHEN & G(?) SANDERS, WM. ACRES.

Page 102 7 June 1749 ELIZ. BAKER of Amelia to SAML. GLOVER for 5 sh.,
         376 acres in fork of Slate; pat. to GLOVER 20 Aug 1747. Wit:
JNO. GLOVER, JNO. DABYHEHORN, JNO. HUNTER.

Page 103 7 June 1749 SAML. GLOVER to SAML. BAKER(BACKER) of Amelia, for
         5 sh., the tract above. Wit: RO. KING, THOS. DAVIS, JNO. DARBY-
SHORN; receipt of ELIZ. BACKER.

Page 104 4 Aug 1749 DENICE DOYLE to PATRICK KNOWLING for Ŀ22, 200 acres,
         part of 400 acres patent.

Page 106 9 Aug 1749 GEO. HOMES GIVENS & wife ELIZ. to RICH. GIVENS for
         Ŀ35, 350 acres Slate river. Wit: RO. KING, ANTHONY CHRISTIAN,
JNO. WATKINS.

Page 107 9 Aug 1749 RICH. GIVIN to GEO. HOMES GIVEN for Ŀ35, 400 acres
         on a branch of Willis and Great Buffalo adj. MAJOR JNO. BOWLING.
Wit: as above. MILDRED, wife of RICH.

Page 109 27 Nov 1747 JNO. CHISWELL, of Hanover, to FURGUS REA for Ŀ12-12,
         237 acres both sides Rockfish adj. JAS. MARTIN. Wit: DAVID
MARTIN, JAS. ARMOR, DANL. LATHAMOR.

Page 112 10 Aug 1749 DENNIS DOYLE to WM. BATTERSBY for Ŀ15, 150 acres
         patented 12 Jan 1746 to ARTHUR DONALLY and by him to DENNIS
DOYLE. Wit: JNO. HARVIE, JAS. MEREDITH, THOS. FITZPATRICK.

Page 113 2 Sep 1749 JNO. COATS of Hanover, carpenter, to CHAS. THOMSON
         of Louisa, carpenter, for Ŀ30, 400 acres on Moor Creek, Cow
branch; part of 800 acres bought from JOS. ANTHONY adj. SIMON CLEMENTS,
THOS. BIBB and grantor, late tract of DENNIS DOYLE - now WM. BATTERSBY,
attorney. Wit: ALEX. GLASBY, MOUNTFORD M. ROBINSON, JAS. BUNCH. ELIZ.,
wife of JNO. COATS.

Page 114 14 Nov 1749 JNO. SMITH of Goochland to JNO. SMITH JR. for Ŀ10,
         400 acres middle fork of Cunningham Creek adj. MARTIN DUNCAN.

Page 116 1 Aug 1749 ALEX. TRENT of Cumberland Co. to JNO. COCKE of
         Henrico, for Ŀ10, land on Great and Little Buffaloe of Willis
river, pat. 12 Jan 1746 adj. ANTHONY SHERRON, SUSANNA CAMER, WM. RICE,
GRISWELL COLEMAN, WM. HILL. Wit: MATTHIAS AYRES, HUGH MAGARRACH, JNO. T.
ROGERS, THOS. TURPIN.

Page 118 1 Aug 1749 ALEX. TRENT of Cumberland to JNO. COCKE of Henrico
         for Ŀ40, 150 acres on Willis river adj. ANTHONY SHERRON, Great
Buffaloe, JAS. TERRY - all of 400 acres in fork of Buffalo, pat. to WM.
STILL 10 July 1745, and by him to ALEX TRENT 6 Sep 1745. Wit: as above.

Page 120   19 July 1749   FRANCIS KELLY to SAML. GAY of Augusta, planter,
           for Ł60, 600 acres adj. THOS. FITZPATRICK on S. & N. of a mount-
ain, Col. JOSHUA FRY. Part of tract bought from SAML. MAXEY; lease until
1 Aug 1754. Wit: CHAS. LAMBERT, HUGH DAUGHERTY, PATRICK NOWLIN.

Page 122   14 Nov 1749   SAML. BURK, planter, and wife ELIZ. to WM. CABELL,
           planter, for Ł40, 200 acres S. side Fluvanna; pat. 30 Aug 1744.
Adj. Woods' island, grantee. Wit: GILBERT BOWMAN, FORGUS REE, DAVID REES.

Page 124   13 Nov 1749   SAML. BURK & wife ELIZ. to THOS. WRIGHT, planter,
           for Ł15, 50 acres N side Tye; part of 350 acre pat. 25 June
1747. Wit: as above.

Page 126   12 Aug 1749   DENNIS DOYLE to WM. BATTERSBY for Ł70, 3 tracts.
           1) 400 acres adj. PAT. NOWLAND, Bisket run; pat. to DANL. JONES
3 June 1745, and by him to DENNIS DOYLE. 2) 400 acres on N Garding; pat.
to JOS. FITZPATRICK adj. COL. ROBT. LEWIS, THOS. MATHER, Widow BUSTARD,
bought from JOS. FITZPATRICK.   3) 800 acres Totare(?) Creek adj. THOS.
MERIWETHER, JAS. TULEY. Wit: JNO. HARVIE, ALEX. ROSE, JNO. FLEMING JR.

Page 127   14 Nov 1749   WM. WEBB to JNO. SOUTHERN for Ł15, 325 acres on a
           branch of Barrly(?) Garden adj. WM. PHELPS, grantee (where he
lives); part of pat. of WENTWORTH WEBB, dec'd 1 Mar 1747. Other 400 of it
to ABRAHAM WEBB by WENTWORTH WEBB.

Page 129   20 Aug 1748   JNO. THRASHER, planter, to JAS. SMITH, planter, for
           Ł100, 400 acres both sides Buffaloe near Blur Mts., pat. 1 Feb.
1738; also 388 acres adj. grantor; the river, DAVIS' path, Buffalo River.
Pat 20 Sept 1745. Wit: WM. CABELL SR. & JR., LUKE CARNELL, JAS. SHASTED,
JNO. HARRIS.   (One of the streams in Amherst still bears the name of
this man. It is in western section. BFD)

Page 131   15 Nov 1749   HENRY MARTIN & POUNCEY ANDERSON, exors. of MICHL.
           HOLLAND, dec'd, to PATRICK NAPIER for Ł54 - 6, 400 acres S side
North fork James. Adj. Cunningham Creek. Pat. 28 Sept 1730.

Page 131   (two pages so numbered) 20 May 1749   FRANCIS BAKER & wife MARY
           to WM. SHELTON of St. David's Parish, King William, for 5 sh.
lease 366 acres adj. ABRAHAM VENABLE, EBENEZER ADAMS; pat. to JAS NOWLING
of Goochland 1 June 1736 - 1 year - 1 grain of corn on demand. Wit: DAVID
WADE, ABRAHAM CHILDERS, JNO. WRIGHT.

Page 132   21 May 1749   FRANCIS BAKER & wife MARY to WM. SHELTON, as above;
           reference to lease above for Ł45, tract above. Wit: as shown.

Page 134   15 Nov 1749   JNO. ANTHONY & wife ELIZ. to HENRY MARTIN for Ł300,
           300 acres both sides Hardware; pat. 12 Mar 1739 to CHAS. LYNCH,
and by him to JNO. ANTHONY; also 109 acres adj; pat. 20 Sept 1745 to JNO.
ANTHONY. Wit: JOSEPH THOMSON, POUNCEY ANDERSON, JNO. BIBY.

Page 135   25 May 1748   BRISSET (BRISSEL?) PARRIS of Goochland to JNO.
           LUCAS for Ł20, 200 acres N side James and Burd Creek; bought
from JAS. WALKER. Wit: DAVID TOMLINSON, JNO. WOODY.

Page 137   14 Nov 1749   GEO. DAMERON & wife ANNE GHONS(?) to JNO. PETER
           for Ł10, 147 acres pat. 1 Dec 1747; S side Fluvanna adj. MICHL.
GHOMAS; MAJOR ALLEN HOWARD.

Page 139   23 Oct 1749   THOS. MERIWETHER of Hanover to JNO. SORREL for
           Ł40, both sides br. Mychunk or Beaverdam fork adj. BENJ. WHEE-
LER. Pat. to THOS. MERIWETHER 10 June 1740 - 200 acres. Wit: THOS.
WALKER, JNO. LEWIS, WM. HILL.

Page 141   20 Aug 1748   JNO. HARRIS, Gent., of Goochland, to JNO. DANL.
           CARNER & WM. CARNER for Ł12 by each. To JNO. DANL. CARNER 100
acres lower half of 200 acres on Buffalo Creek of Willis; pat to JOHN
HARRIS; other 100 acres to WM. CARNER. Wit: JAS. MEREDITH, G. MARR, JNO.
HUNTER.

Page 143   15 Aug 1749   JNO. WOODSON JR. of Cumberland to WM. MILLER of

of Goochland, for ₤50, 400 acres both sides Great Creek of Slate. Pat.
20 July 1748. Wit: JAS. MEREDITH, J.P. SMITH, JR., G. MARR.

Page 145   No date at top, but 20 June 1749 at end: Order to JAS. HOLEMAN,
            JNO. PAINE & WM. MILLER as to deed of May 1748, by JOS. FITZ-
PATRICK & wife MARY PERRIN to DENNIS DOYLE. JNO. FLEMING, deputy of Albe.

Page 146   8 Aug 1749 WM. WEBB to ABRAHAM WEBB - love of WM. WEBB for his
            brother ABRAHAM WEBB, 400 acres both sides Glover's road adj.
Major GEO. CARRINGTON, JNO. FLOYD, HUGH MOOR. Part of 725 acres pat. to
WENTWORTH WEBB.

Page 147   June court, 1749 JNO. ADAMS CORN - report on tract - apple
            trees, dwelling house - by JNO. ROBARDS, JNO. LADD, HENRY TRENT.
No total.

Page 147   June court 1749 Report on ARCHIBALD WOODS' land - 1 house,
            cultivated ground, 17 sheep. ₤83. Done 20 Jan 1749. DAVID Q.(J)
ROOS, JNO. AUSTIN, JNO. HARRIS.

Page 148   June court 1749 JNO. GRILL's land - Long - Branch of Moore's
            Creek at the Raged (sic) Mts.; 1 cabbin (sic), trees, tools, 1
slave. ₤95. DAVID ROOS, WM. CARROLL LEWIS, JNO. HARRIS.

Page 149   13 Feb 1749 JNO. MOSELEY of Goochland Co. to BENJ. CARTER of
            Louisa, for ₤20, 225 acres both sides branch of Bird Creek
(Phill's Creek) adj. RO. KENT, EBENEZER ADAMS dec'd, ARTHUR HOPKINS, PHIL-
LIP THURMOND. Pat. 25 Sept 1746. Wit: THOS. POOR, JNO. MOSELEY JR.,
WM. JOHNSON.

Page 151   24 Apr 1749 JAS HENDERSON to JOEL TERRELL for ₤9, 122 acres on
            branches of Meadow Creek, S side of Rivanna adj. JAS FIDLER,
HOWARD CASH, the grantee, CHAS. LEWIS. JUDITH, wife of JAS. HENDERSON.
Wit: DAVID LEWIS, ABRAHAM MUSICK, CHAS. SNEED.

Page 153   22 Sept 1749 ANTHONY HOGGATT to JNO. BOSTICK of Southam Parish,
            Cumberland, for ₤74 - 6. 743 acres, part of tract where grantor
lives, adj. NATHL. HOGGATT, GRAY ____. Wit: MARVIL STONE, NATHL. CHASTAIN,
NATHL. HOGGATT, JOEL WALKER.

Page 155   7 Feb 1749 JAS. MATTHEWS to JNO. JENNINGS JR. for ₤20, 150 acres
            next to N side Appomattox River. Wit: THOS. SANDERS, PHILLIP
MATTHEWS, RICH. LEE.

Page 157   8 Sept 1748 WM. CHAMBERS to THOS. SANDERS of St. James Parish,
            Goochland, for ₤145, 465 acres Fishpond Creek, part of tract
bought from HENRY CHILES who took it up. Adj. CHILES. Wit: GIDEON MARR,
STEPHEN SANDERS, NATHL. HOGGATT.

Page 160   13 Jan 1749 CHAS. LYNCH to RO. ADAMS for ₤250, 400 acres S side
            Rivanna, adj. Major CAR. Pat. 20 June 1733; also 445 acres adj.
MAJOR CAR, WILLIAMSON. Pat. 20 Aug 1748. Wit: THOS. & JNO. SMITH, SIMON
RAMSEY, WM. LEE.

Page 163   13 Feb 1749 SAML. BAILEY to JNO. HUNTER for ₤8, 100 acres
            GLOVER's Creek of Slate. Pat. 1 Oct 1747.

Page 164   29 Nov 1749 GEO. BROCK SR. to wife, KATHERINE - love - to
            support her, all estate. Wit: PATRICK NAPIER, JNO. ROGERS, WM.
GRYMES.

Page 164   25 Mar 1748 JNO. WARREN to JAS WARREN; JAS. WARREN, the Younger,
            Lunenberg, BETTY WHITTLE, wife of MATT. WHITTLE; SARAH COFFREY
wife of CHAS. COFFREY; ELEANOR RUCKER, wife of JNO. RUCKER; GRACE WARREN.
Last four of Albemarle. For ₤100,000 to be paid in equal proportions - one
eighth to each; minerals that may be discovered on 276 of JNO. WARREN's on
N side Buffalo Ridge (this is now Amherst) ₤200 excepted as working costs -
1000 years. To pay on feast day of St. Michael from sums earned. Wit: JNO.
HARVIE, JOSHUA FRY, JNO. COFFREY.

Page 166   14 Feb 1749 THOS. OGLESBY to HUGH MORRIS, planter, for ₤20,

200 acres S side Hardway, pat. 12 Jan 1746. Adj. GEO. DANARILL; grantee. Wit: WM. CABELL JR., ADRIAN ANGLIN, JNO. BRYANT. MARY, wife of OGLESBY.

Page 168   15 Nov 1749 JNO. CRAWFORD, Craven Co., province of S.C., to NELSON ANDERSON of Henrico, for Ŀ70, 590 acres Plumtree branch, N side Rivanna, adj. CHAS. LEWIS; pat. 400 acres and 190 acres 3 Oct 1784. Wit: DAVID CRAWFORD, JR., WM. TERRELL LEWIS, DAVID MARTIN, DAVID CRAWFORD, JNO. MARTIN.

Page 170   14 Feb 1749 THOS. OLGESBY to HUGH MORRIS, planter, for Ŀ20, 200 acres N fork Toter Creek, pat. 12 Jan 1746, adj. ARTHUR DONALLY, AMBROSE JOSHUA SMITH. Wit: WM. CABELL JR., ADRIAN ANGLIN, JNO. BRYANT. MARY, wife of OGLESBY.

Page 172   16 Feb 1749 THOS. McDANIEL to JAMES TULEY for Ŀ20, 350 acres pat. 1 Dec 1748; both sides Ballinger's creek adj. EPPES. Wit: JNO. PETER, DANL. SCOTT, JNO. TULEY Jr.

Page 174   4 May 1750 DAVID LEWIS to WM. TERRELL LEWIS - love - 200 acres on branches of Moor's creek where WM. TERRELL LEWIS lives, adj. main road of county, JOEL TERRELL, the mt. ridge. Part of pat. of DAVID LEWIS. Wit: JNO., DAVID & JOEL LEWIS.

Page 175   4 May 1750 DAVID LEWIS to DAVID LEWIS - love - creek as above, 200 acres near BENJ. WHEELER's road; grantor; Round Top Mt., JOEL LEWIS; Part of patent. Wit: JNO, WM. TERRELL & JOEL LEWIS.

Page 176   4 May 1750 DAVID LEWIS to JNO. LEWIS - love - creek as above, 200 acres, part of patent. Wit: WM. TERRELL LEWIS, JOEL and DAVID LEWIS.

Page 178   4 May 1750 DAVID LEWIS to JOEL LEWIS - love - creek as above. 200 acres adj. WM. LEWIS, hill side nigh DAVID LEWIS' plantation, Piney Mt. spurs. Part of patent. Wit: JNO., DAVID & W.T. LEWIS.

Page 179   8 May 1750 JNO. LACKEY, weaver, to JAMES LACKEY, tanner, for Ŀ6, 74 acres both sides S branch of Corbin Creek; branch of Rockfish near Blue Mts. adj. Col. CHISWELL. Wit: JAS. BARNETT, JOS. BARNETT, JNO. REID.

Page 181   12 Mar 1749 WM. MORRISON to JAMES MORRISON for Ŀ20, 420 acres Rockfish branches, adj. ANDREW REID, ALEX. REID. Wit: WM. CABELL, JNO. ROBINSON, JNO. CONFREY.

Page 182   12 Mar 1749 WM. MORRISON to THOS. MORRISON JR. for Ŀ20, 420 acres branches of Rockfish adj. grantor. Wit: as above.

Page 184   8 May 1750 WM. SUDDARTH, planter, to JAS. SUDDARTH, carpenter, in consideration of 200 acres on Red Bar Hollow, 200 acres S. branch of Hardway, part of 300 acres bought by WM. SUDDARTH from ABRAHAM VENABLE; 100 acres is where house stands of WM. SUDDARTH and reserved for LAWRENCE SUDDARTH.

Page 185   8 May 1750 JAMES WOODS to ROBT. ANDERSON for Ŀ10, 200 acres both sides Stockton's branch of Mecham. Adj. WM. WHITESIDES, AMBROSE JOSHUA SMITH, pat. 1 Apr 1749. Wit: HUGH MAGARROH, JOS. MILLER, MICHL. MONTGOMERY.

Page 187   8 May 1750 JNO. ADAM CORN and wife MARY to WM. WILLIAMS, of Goochland, for Ŀ30, 400 acres both sides Little Bremer Creek adj. BENJ. WOODSON. Wit: FRANCIS BAKER, TUCKER WOODSON, WM. CHRISTIAN.

Page 188   8 May 1750 WM. HARRIS to STEPHEN ROE for Ŀ5, 100 acres Beaver Dam. Adj. grantor's new line, side of mountain, THOS. SORREL.

Page 189   8 May 1750 SAML. DAVIS to WM. HARRIS for Ŀ50, 296 acres Green Creek adj. LEONARD PHILLIPS. Wit: HENRY MARTIN, WM. CABELL, JNO. HUNTER.

Page 190   8 May 1750 SAML. DAVIS to WM. HARRIS for Ŀ15, 100 acres Bryery branch of Green Creek adj. grantee near mouth of creek. Wit: as above.

Page 192   13 Feb 1749 EDMD. GRAY to WM. GRAY, New Kent County, for Ŀ885,
            34 named slaves. Wit: JAS. GRAY, JNO. SANDERS, CHAS. LEE, JOSHUA
CHAFFIN, JAS. LEE.

Page 193   25 Oct 1749 EDMD. GRAY to WM. GRAY of New Kent Co., for Ŀ400,
            5800 acres where EDMD. GRAY lives; head branches of Willis
River; pat. 29 June 1739 to WM. GRAY and sold to EDMD GRAY 4 Feb 1746.
Wit: As above.

Page 194   8 May 1750 EDMD. GRAY to WM. GRAY of New Kent Co., for Ŀ153,
            stock on several plantations in Lunenberg & Albemarle Co.
Wit: As above.

Page 195   8 May 1750 JNO. BISWELL to HENRY MARTIN for 5 sh., 275 acres
            both sides Hardaway, S. fork adj. MILDRED MERIWETHER, Jumping
Branch, the Falls. Pat. to JNO. HEARD & sold to JNO. BISWELL; also stock.
Deed of trust. Wit: JOHN ANTHONY, MITCHELL BAUGHAN, JNO. WOODY, JNO. BIBY.

Page 196   20 Apr 1750 GEO. KLEINHOFF of Chesterfield to ARCHIBALD CARY of
            Chesterfield, for Ŀ25, 400 acres N. branches of Willis; pat. 10
July 1745. Wit: JNO. HUNTER, JNO. FLEMING JR., DAVID BELL, JAS. MEREDITH.

Page 198   9 Apr 1750 ROBT. ROSE, clerk and wife ANNA to JNO. WILCOX of
            Urbanna, Middlesex Co., mariner, for 5 sh., 1020 acres, part of
23,700 to ROBT. ROSE 13 Aug 1744 adj. N. side Tye, AMBROSE JONES, CHAS.
LEWIS, a good spring. Wit: WM. HARRIS, JNO. PETER, HENRY TRENT, MICHL.
THOMAS, RICH. GIVIN. Lease for 1 year.

Page 199   10 Apr 1750 RO. ROSE as above to JNO. WILCOX, as above for Ŀ60,
            1020 acres above. Wit: as above.

Page 202   2 May 1750 ALEX. SPEIRS to THOS. JONES, Slate river; receipt
            for 2 bonds to PETER RANDOLPH & SPEIRS - charge of 2 law suits.
Wit: ANDREW BUCHANAN, CHAS. TRUMBULL, JR.

Page 202   5 Mar 1749 CASTLETON HARPER, planter, to CHAS. LYNCH & JNO.
            ANTHONY, Gents., for 5 sh., on bond to JOS. THOMPSON, Gent. and
Sheriff for HARPER as undersheriff, 50 acres where HARPER lives and 84
acres, furniture. Wit: JOSHUA FEY, JOS. THOMPSON, WM. HOOPER.

Page 204   3 Mar 1749 DRURY TUCKER to ABRAHAM CHILDERS for Ŀ000(?) tobacco,
            200 acres Rockfish, adj. EZEKIAH DAVIDSON; grantee. Part of
tract bought from ROBT. WALTON and pat. to WALTON. Wit: MATT. TUCKER,
LUCRETIA TUCKER, EZEKIAH DAWSON.

Page 205   3 Mar 1749 DRURY TUCKER to EZEKIAH DAWSON for Ŀ2000 tobacco,
            200 acres adj. THOS. TINDALL, part of tract bought from RO.
WALTON. Wit: MATT. & LUCRETIA TUCKER, ABRAHAM CHILDERS, JNO. NICHOLAS,Clk.

Page 206   19 Feb 1749 JAS. STINNETT to CHAS. PARKS for Ŀ17, 227(?) acres
            Huff Creek adj. JNO. WHEELER, JNO. GRAVES, BENJ. STINNETT. Wit:
WM. CABELL SR. & JR., JOS. CABELL.

Page 207   1 May 1750 ROBT. THOMPSON to FRANCIS MARSHALL of Cumberland
            Co., for Ŀ30, 570 acres; part of pat. of 20 July 1748; N. side
of road crossing land - Troublesome Creek; branch of Slate.

Page 208   14 Aug 1750 WM. HOOPER & wife MARTHA to HARDIN BURNLEY of St.
            Paul's Parish, Hanover Co., for Ŀ20, 280 acres N. side JAMES;
E. branches Hardware adj. Capt. HUDSON's former line. Wit: WM. CABELL JR.,
JER. WHITE, ALLEN ADDISON.

Page 210   14 Aug 1750 ANTHONY SHAWROON JR. to EDWD. GIBSON for Ŀ21 - 10,
            100 acres, part of Pat. 26 Mar 1739.

Page 212   8 Aug 1750 RICH. TAYLOR to PETER BONDURANT for Ŀ10, 200 acres
            both sides of Green creek of Slate. Wit: SHADRACK TURNER, JNO.
& MARY SPENCER.

Page 214   14 Aug 1750 WM. RICE to JOS. ADCOCK for Ł60, 440 acres pat.
            5 Sept 1749 adj. SUSAN CARNER, GRIZEL COLEMAN, GEO. HOLMES,
BENJ. STRANGE, RICHARD GIVIN. Wit: FRANCES CHILDERS, GOADRIDGE HUGHES.

Page 214   24 Feb 1749 JOS. THOMAS to JNO. MARTIN SR. for 5 sh., 200 acres
            pat. 20 Aug 1747; head branches Rock Island Creek. Wit: EDWD.
THOMAS, JNO. PETER, WM. THOMAS.

Page 216   25 June 1750 MARGARET FENDLEY, widow of JAS. FENDLEY - by will
            has 350 acres S. side Fluvanna - where she lives - life estate -
reverts to her son, JAMES FENDLEY - love - 150 acres to son, JAMES FENDLEY,
lower end; adj. Dug landing. Wit: WM. CABELL SR. & JR., SAML. BURKS JR.

Page 217   24 Jan 1749 BENJ. MIMS to WM. CABELL for Ł28, 200 acres S. side
            Fluvanna adj. grantee; cliff by river. JUDITH, wife of BENJ.
MIMS. Wit: SUSANNA MANASCHO, ELIZ. & JAS. SHARSTED.

Page 217   29 June 1750 JAS. FENDLEY to SAML. BURKS JR. for Ł85, 150 acres
            S side Fluvanna. See page above - p.216 when his mother gave it
to him. He gives pat. date to JAS. FENDLEY dec'd. as 22 Sept 1739. His wife
MARY, joins in deed. Wit: WM. CABELL SR. & JR., JOHN WRIGHT.

Page 219   14 Aug 1750 WM. FLOYD - signed also by WM. MATTHEWS at end - to
            SAML. BURKS Jr., for Ł100, 400 acres upper side of Pedlar. Wit:
WM. CABELL, MATT. JORDAN. (This is doubtless the famous FLOYD family of
Amherst. It will be recalled by researchers that Pedlar River became part
of area of Amherst. BFD)

Page 220   14 Aug 1750 JAMES IRELAND to TERISHA TURNER for Ł13-7-6, 147
            acres N. fork Green River adj. CHRISTOPHER ANTHONY. Pat. 20
Aug 1748.

Page 221   14 Aug 1750 DANL. REYNOLDS of Lunenburg Co. to JNO. PETER, for
            Ł6-10, 100 acres pat. 1 Dec 1748, S. side Fluvanna, adj. MICHL.
THOMAS. Wit: JNO. THOMAS, JAS. HILTON, WM. BALEY.

Page 222   14 Aug 1750 JNO. ANTHONY to HENRY MARTIN for Ł150, 400 acres
            pat. to ARTHUR OSBURN 10 June 1740, and by him deeded to JNO.
ANTHONY. On Rivanna River adj. JOSEPH KING, dec'd., Rockfish, ROBT. ADAMS.
Also 200 acres transferred by MARTIN KING Jr. to ANTHONY, S. side North
River adj. MARTIN KING.

Page 224   15 Aug 1750 THOS. TURPIN of Cumberland Co. to ARTHUR MOSELEY
            of Cumberland Co. for Ł25, 222 acres both sides Slate adj.
PATRICK OBRIAN, THOS. JONES.

Page 225   10 Apr 1750 RO. ROSE, Clerk, to JNO. PARKS, planter; rents and
            covenants - 100 acres, part of 3,700 acres pat. to ROSE- during
lives of WM. PARKS & JOHN PARKS, Jr. - to pay on 26 Dec each year 436 pds.
tobacco. Wit: MATTHEW DAVIS, GILBERT HAY, THOS. JOPLING, PHILLIP DAVIS.

Page 227   17 May 1750 JAMES COCKE, Gent., of Henrico to BENJ. WOODSON,
            for Ł40, 400 acres NE side Hardware adj. RICH. DAMAREL. Wit:
BOUTH WOODSON, BOUTH NAPIER JR., JO. FITZPATRICK, BOUTH NAPIER, BENJ.
WOODSON, JR.

Page 229   13 Nov 1750 THOS. FITZPATRICK to JACOB MOON for Ł110, 400 acres
            South Garden among mountains, Hardware branches. Pat. to RO.
DAVIS 10 Jan 1735, and by him to FITZPATRICK 10 Nov 1748. Wit: JNO. WEBB,
SAML. JORDAN, JNO. WARE. JANE, wife of FITZPATRICK.

Page 230   6 Oct 1750 THOS. JARRAL (JERRELD) to JNO. HOY for Ł24, 400
            acres S side James, N. branch, adj. SAML. STEPHENS. Wit: WM.
PERKINS, ARTHUR McDANIEL, THOS. GIBSON. MARY, wife of JARRAL.

Page 231   27 Aug 1750 NOBLE LADD to PETER JEFFERSON of St. James Parish,
            Goochland Co., for Ł105, 100 acres S. side James adj. JNO. LADD,
JNO. BOLING. Wit: JNO. STAPLES, THOS. TURPIN JR., JNO. SCOTT, JNO. LEAD,
WM. ROACH.

Page 233   27 Aug 1750   NOBLE LADD to PETER JEFFERSON, as above - bond to
            convey to JEFFERSON - where LADD lately lived - if wife will
release - Ŀ120 bond. Wit: JNO. STAPLES, THOS. TURPIN JR.

Page 233   13 Oct 1750   JNO. WHEELER to JNO. DAMERON for Ŀ7, 374 acres Huff
            Creek. (Note: this creek is still so called and is just west of
the village of Amherst Courthouse. BFD.) Wit: HENRY TRENT, THOS. LAWHORNE,
GEO. DAMERON.

Page 235   15 Oct 1750   ARTHUR BEARDING of Alb. to JNO. PERKINS for Ŀ20,
            200 acres on Great Byrd, where BEARDING lives, adj. JNO. LUCAS.
Wit: BENJ.-----; JNO. BYBEE, JOS. CABELL, JOS. THOMPSON JR., JNO. JOHNSON.
MARTHA, wife of ARTHUR BEARDING.

Page 236   13 Nov 1750   JAMES IRELAND, planter, to WM. HENDERSON of Louisa,
            planter, for Ŀ25, 296 acres N fork Green. Pat. 20 Aug 1748. Wit:
CHAS. THOMPSON, JNO. FORTUNE, MITCHELL BAUGHAN. JANE, wife of IRELAND.

Page 237   9 Aug 1750   JNO. GOODWIN & wife MARY to RICH. THOMPSON & ROBT.
            THOMPSON of Caroline for Ŀ50, 400 acres S side James, N branches
Slate. Adj. WM. NOWLIN. Wit: ROBT. & RICH. GEORGE, WM. HOLMAN, WM. TURNER.

Page 239   14 Nov 1750   ARTHUR HOPKINS of Goochland to WM. MEGGINSON for
            Ŀ5, 180 acres S side Fluvanna about 4 miles above Tye.

Page 239   13 Nov 1750   RICH. HALL to JNO. HALL for Ŀ10, 400 acres N side
            Fluvanna. Pat. 5 Nov 1743; adj. THOS. TINDALL, S side Hardware,
WM. CHAMBERLAIN, HUGH MORRIS. Wit: JAS. NEVIL JR., WM. OGLESBY, JNO. PETER.

Page 241   13 Nov 1750   JEDIAH BRISTOW of St. Peter's Parish, New Kent Co.,
            planter, to WM. WOODSON, planter, for Ŀ30, 400 acres S branches
Fluvanna adj. WM. CANNON. Wit: JAS. NEVIL JR., JNO. CANNON, JNO. LADD,
CHAS. BALLOW.

Page 242   14 Nov 1750   WM. BATTERSBY of Cumberland Co. to JNO. WALKER for
            Ŀ65, 50 acres S side Fluvanna, pat. to WM. CABELL 25 Sept 1746.
Adj. JNO. LADD. Wit: BOUTH NAPIER, THOS. PHELPS.

Page 243   15 Nov 1750   STEPHEN HUGHES & BOUTH NAPIER to JAMES MEREDITH of
            Cumberland Co. for Ŀ52-10, 400 acres N. side Pedlar, Horsley Ck.
Pat. to both, 20 Sept 1748.

Page 245   15 Nov 1750   BENNETT BALLOW to MATT. JORDAN for Ŀ20, 500 acres
            S side Fluvanna adj. LEONARD BALLOW. Wit: DAVID PATTESON, RICH.
BIRK, HUGH MAGARROCK.

Page 246   15 Nov 1750   CHAS. BALLOW to MATT JORDAN for Ŀ30, 150 acres S
            side Fluvanna adj. LEONARD BALLOW, Ballow Creek. Wit: as above.

Page 248   18 Aug 1750   ISAAC BATES to THOS. MARTIN of New Kent Co. for
            Ŀ53-15, 400 acres on Ned's Creek of Fluvanna, pat. to EDWD.
DANIEL 30 June 1743. Wit: RALPH FLIPPIN, ABRAHAM CHILDRES, GEO. MARTIN,
JNO. CANNON.

Page 249   10 Jan 1750   DANL. HOLLODAY & wife AGNES to CHAS GILLUM for
            Ŀ65, 300 acres N side Rivanna pat. 6 Apr 1734, adj. THOS. CARR.
Wit: W. LEWIS, JNO. RAGLAND, HENRY HARPER.

Page 251   12 Feb 1750   SAML. GLOVER to JAS. SPENCER for Ŀ18, 300 acres N.
            branches of S branches of Slate.

Page 252   12 Feb 1750   THOS. McDANIEL, carpenter, to JNO. LADD, planter,
            for Ŀ150, 156 acres S side Fluvanna adj. THOS. BALLOW, old
bounds of 6 acres. Wit: SAML. JORDAN, JNO. NICHOLAS, THOS. PLEASANTS.

Page 253   12 Feb 1750   CHAS. LEWIS SR. & wife MARY of Goochland to ALEX-
            ANDER BLANE for Ŀ60, 2000 acres pat. 12 Mar 1739. Part of tract.
Adj. GEORGE DOUGLAS, PETER LYONS. Sells 600 acres of said patent.

Page 255   12 Feb 1750   CHAS. LEWIS as above to PETER LYON for Ŀ40, 400 acres of above tract adj. ALEX. BLANE, JNO. BURNS.

Page 257   9 Feb 1750   ROBT. DAVIS to JNO. PARTREE BURKS for Ł50, 400 acres
            S side of Pedlar adj. WM. FLOYD. Wit: WM. CABELL SR. & JR.,
JOS. CABELL.

Page 258   12 Feb 1750   JAS. NEVIL & wife LUCY to JNO. COBBS of Goochland
            for Ł400, 500 acres S side Fluvanna adj. mouth of Watkins'
Creek, JAS. DANIEL, the county line, MAYO.

Page 259   28 Sept 1750   JOS. BENNING & wife SARAH to WM. SALLE for Ł30,
            400 acres both sides Crooked Creek of Slate. Wit: ADRAIN ANGLIN,
ABRAHAM SOBLET, WM. SALLE, ELLET LACY.

Page 261   12 Feb 1751   WM. RICKLES, Tinker, to MEREDITH MANNING for Ł40,
285 acres both sides Slate adj. JAS. GOSS, JNO. HUNTER. Wit: WM. SALLE,
RENNIE CHASTAIN and ?. MARY KATHERINE, wife of RICKLES.

Page 262   13 Feb 1750   HENRY BEARD to JNO. HARDMAN for Ł15, 250 acres,
            part of tract sold to BEARD, pat. by ABRAHAM CHILDERS 25 July
1746, both sides branch of Willis Creek. Wit: RENE CHASTAIN, EDWD. GIBSON,
JNO. CHILDERS.

Page 263   7 Feb 1751   JNO. PETER to son RICH. PETER for Ł10, 100 acres,
            pat. to DANL. REYNOLDS 1 Dec 1748, adj. MICHL. THOMAS - 50 acres
is part of 147 acres pat. to GEO. DAMERON 1 Dec 1748, adj. HENRY THOMAS,
MAJOR ALLEN HOWARDS. Wit: JOS., HENRY, & JAS. THOMAS.

Page 264   13 Feb 1750   JAS FENDLEY & wife MARY to WM. MEGGINSON for Ł106,
            200 acres S side Fluvanna adj. SAML. BURKS & grantor. Part of
300 acres pat. to JAS. FENDLEY, dec'd. 22 Sept 1749 - reversion by will.
MARGARET, mother of JAS., was to have made title.

Page 265   Apr 1751   JAS. NEVIL to JNO. WARE for Ł200, 100 acres adj.
            NOBLE LADD, DRURY TUCKER. Wit: JNO. TULEY, MICHL. THOMAS, DANL.
SCOTT.

Page 267   14 May 1750   CAPT. CHAS. LEWIS, Goochland Co., to JNO. LYON for
            Ł40, 400 acres Rich Cove adj. PETER LYON, JNO. BURNS.

Page 268   14 May 1751   CHAS. LEWIS SR. & wife MARY of Goochland to BAZELL
            MAXWELL - pat. of 400 acres 25 July 1741 - Rich Cove.

Page 270   13 May 1751   JNO. WOODY to JNO. HOWARD of Hanover for Ł33, 375
            acres Byrd Creek adj. JAS. JOHNSON; grantor. Pat. 16 Sept 1740.
Wit: ARTHUR & JOHN HOPKINS

Page 272   15 Dec 1750   ROLAND HORSLEY of Hanover to JOSIAS PAYNE of
            Goochland, for Ł120, 200 acres N side Rivanna. Part of 400 acres
pat. to ROBT. HORSLEY 17 Sept 1731. Wit: JNO. PAYNE, CHAS BOND, JNO. MIMS,
JOSIAS PAYNE JR.

Page 273   13 Nov 1750   JNO. MARTIN to JNO. BYBEE for Ł13, 100 acres on
            Barrenger's Creek adj. his own.

Page 274   2 Feb 1750   PAUL CHILES to JNO. WARD for Ł45, 265 acres both
            sides Holloday River. Wit: ANN, HENRY, & JNO. CHILES, RO. WATHEN.

Page 276   9 Apr 1751   WM. CHAMBERS of Granville Co, Province of North
            Carolina, to THOS. SANDERS for Ł50, 300 acres Holloday River &
Fish Pond Creek adj. his own; HENRY CHILES; grantor. Wit: STEPHEN SANDERS,
ANTHONY BENNIN, SAM. GLOVER.

Page 277   13 Feb 1750   JNO. SORRELL to BENJ. SNEED for Ł5, 200 acres Bea-
            ver Dam fork of Machunk Creek. Formerly that of THOS. MERIWETHER.
Wit: JNO. MORRIS, JAS. DEFOOR, WM. McGHEE.

Page 279   20 Dec 1750   JNO. SORRELL to JNO. HENDERSON for Ł33, 90 acres
            S side N Rivanna adj. Perry Creek. Wit: BENJ. SNEED, JNO. MORRIS,
WM. McGHEE, ROBT. HARDWICK.

Page 280   14 May 1751 THOS. SMITH to HIRAM GAINES for L40, 287 acres N.
            side Rivanna adj. where JNO. KEY lives. Wit: EDWIN HICKMAN,
DANL. HOLLODAY, JNO. GRAVES. MARTHA, wife of THOS. SMITH.

Page 281   24 Jan 1750 THOS. CHAMBERS of Louisa to DANL. MAUPIN for L50,
            100 acres N side Rivanna adj. county line, Ivy Creek mouth.
Wit: RO. HARRIS, CHS. SMITH, JAS. YOUNG, RICH. YANCEY.

Page 283   30 Apr 1751 MOSES HIGGINBOTHAM & wife FRANCES to JOS. HIGGIN-
            BOTHAM for 5 sh., 200 acres on Buffalo branches, part of 1340
acres bought from GEORGE BRAXTON, the Younger, of King and Queen 23 Apr
1745; adj. JAS. HIGGINBOTHAM. Wit: JAS. HIGGINBOTHAM, JNO. HIGGINBOTHAM,
THOS. JEFFERSON. (Note: My third son's wife, MARY GAYLE (nee PETTYJOHN)
is a descendant of this family through RUFUS ANDERSON HIGGINBOTHAM of Amherst County. This is somewhat later, but I have traced RUFUS ANDERSON
back into the family which has been pretty well written up by the late Mr.
and Mrs. WILLIAM SWEENEY, nee LENORA HIGGINBOTHAM. Mrs. SWEENEY used
to come here to work on her family. She said that her late husband has
spent big sums in research in the "old country", but at that time my son
had not married MARY GAYLE PETTYJOHN and I had not worked out her line via
ABSALOM HIGGINBOTHAM. Mrs. SWEENEY said that she was double-checking data
before she published it. On her last trip, prior to her last illness, she
pushed the announcement of the forthcoming book across the counter in the
clerk's office to me. She died before it was published and I have heard
unproved stories as to what she wanted done. If she left a will, it is not
of record here and I presume it is in state of New York. I received several indignant letters after her death wanting to know when I would get on
with the publication, but I assured each writer that I was in no way connected with the project. I wish that it would be released for posterity,
but can provide no official data as to prospects. BFD.)

Page 285   21 May 1751 MOSES HIGGINBOTHAM & wife FRANCES to JOSEPH HIGGIN-
            BOTHAM for 5 sh., 204 acres on Buffalo, bought from GEO. BRAXTON
as above. Adj. JAMES HIGGINBOTHAM. Wit: JNO., BENJ., & JAS. HIGGINBOTHAM.

Page 288   11 May 1751 MOSES HIGGINBOTHAM as above to JNO. HIGGINBOTHAM,
            for 5 sh., 200 acres Buffalo Branch, bought as above. Adj. WM.
MORRISON. Wit: JOS., BENJ. & JAMES HIGGINBOTHAM.

Page 290   11 May 1751 MOSES HIGGINBOTHAM as above to JNO. HIGGINBOTHAM,
            for 5 sh., 204 acres Buffalo branches bought as above, adj. JAS.
HIGGINBOTHAM. Wit: JOS., BENJ., and JAS. HIGGINBOTHAM.

Page 293   6 May 1751 MOSES HIGGINBOTHAM as above to JAMES HIGGINBOTHAM
            for 5 sh., 204 acres Buffalo Branches, bought as above, adj.
Mill creek; grantor. Wit: AARON HIGGINBOTHAM, WM. MORRISON, JNO. HIGGIN-
BOTHAM.

Page 295   6 May 1751 MOSES HIGGINBOTHAM as above to AARON HIGGINBOTHAM
            for 5 sh., 204 acres, bought as above, adj. JOSE. & JAS. HIGGIN-
BOTHAM, Mill Creek. Wit: JAS., JNO. HIGGINBOTHAM, WM. MORRISON.

Page 298   30 Apr 1751 MOSES HIGGINBOTHAM as above to JAMES HIGGINBOTHAM
            for 5 sh., 200 acres Buffalo branches adj. RUCKER. Wit: THOS.
JEFFERSON, JNO. & JOSEPH HIGGINBOTHAM.

Page 300   30 Apr 1751 MOSES HIGGINBOTHAM as above to BENJ. HIGGINBOTHAM
            for 5 sh., 204 acres Buffalo branches. Wit: THOS. JEFFERSON,
JNO. & JAS. HIGGINBOTHAM.

Page 303   6 May 1751 MOSES HIGGINBOTHAM as above to WM. MORRISON for 5 sh.
            204 acres Buffalo Branches adj. JAS. HIGGINBOTHAM; grantor; JNO.
HIGGINBOTHAM. Wit: JAMES, JNO. & AARON HIGGINBOTHAM.

Page 305   6 May 1751 MOSES HIGGINBOTHAM as above to WM. MORRISON for 5 sh.
            land on Buffalo branches. Adj. JOS. HIGGINBOTHAM. Wit: JAS, JNO.
& AARON HIGGINBOTHAM.

Page 308   1 Feb 1751 JNO. THOMSON to SAML. MAN for L23, 172 acres both
            sides Taylor Creek adj. ARCHIBALD WOODS, spur of a mountain.
Wit: JNO. REID, JAS. BARNET, THOS. MAN, JAS. ROBERTSON.

Page 310   12 July 1750 HOWARD CASH, planter, to JER. WADE, planter, for
            L20, 180 acres Thrasher's Creek adj. PEARCE WADE, JNO. BISWELL.
Pat. 12 July 1750. Wit: MICHL. SMITH, DAVID WADE, CHISLEY DANIEL. RUTH,
wife of HOWARD CASH.

Page 311   10 May 1751 HOWARD CASH & wife RUTH, to son STEPHEN CASH -love-
            Meadow Creek branches, 250 acres. Adj. ABRAHAM LEWIS, DAVID
LEWIS, JOEL TERRELL, part of a patent.

Page 312   6 Feb 1751 FRANCIS CALLOWAY & wife FRANCES to JNO. THOMSON,
            planter for L15, 200 acres Tomahawk Swamp branches, pat. 20
Sept 1745. Wit: JAS. FAIR, JAMES CALLAWAY, EDWD. BRIGHT, EDMOND FAIR,
RICH. WOODWARD.

Page 314   11 May 1751 JNO. BYBEE & wife JANE to DANL. KING of Hanover Co.
            for L70, 407 acres Ballinger Creek, part of where BYBEE lives
and pat. 14 May 1751.

Page 315   14 May 1750 SAML. SPENCER to STEPHEN TURNER for L10, 248 acres
            pat. 30 Mar 1743; N side Fluvanna adj. Capt. HOWARD. Wit: JNO.
PETER, EDWD. THOMAS, RICH. PETER.

Page 316   14 May 1751 NOBLE LADD to son, AMOS LADD; love - 300 acres N.
            side Fluvanna adj. New Breamer Creek, head of branch that "the
Indian shot JNO. LAWSON at". Wit: JNO. PETER, AMOS LADD, JNO. MOOR.

Page 317   14 May 1751 DANL. KING of Hanover to JNO. KING of Hanover for
            L25-15, 150 acres both sides Ballinger Creek adj. JNO. BYBEE,
JNO. MARTIN. Part of a tract.

Page 318   29 Mar 1751 NICHOLAS DAVIES (DAVIS), Gent., of Cumberland, to
            RICH. WOODWARD for L58-1-3, 800 acres Blackwater branches near
Fleming's mountain. Wit: JNO. ANTHONY, EDWD BRIGHT, JAS. CALLAWAY, JAS.
FAIR, EDMUND FAIR. Signed: DAVIES.

Page 320   29 Mar 1751 NICHOLAS DAVIES of Cumberland to JAMES CALLAWAY
            for L14-18-8, 200 acres Blackwater as above. Wit: as above save
subtract CALLAWAY and add RICH. WOODWARD.

Page 321   29 Mar 1751 NICHL. DAVIES as above to JAMES FAIR for L14, 200
            acres on above creek adj. grantor; JAS. CALLAWAY, EDMD. FAIR.
Wit: as above, but minus JAS. FAIR.

Page 322   29 Mar 1751 NICHL. DAVIES as above to EDMOND FAIR for L10, 155
            acres same creek adj. JAS. CALLAWAY. Wit: As above, but minus
EDMD. FAIR. In each deed DAVIES gave acreages as "according to his own
account".

Page 323   14 May 1751 RICH. WOODWARD to EDWD. BRIGHT for L15, 200 acres
            Blackwater Creek branches. (I am not conversant with creeks in
Albemarle area. I have been told that county once extended across James
into present Campbell county- and perhaps Bedford area - and there is a
Blackwater Creek in Lynchburg. Is this the same creek or another one? BFD)

Page 324   2 Mar 1750 JNO. DAVIS & wife REBECCA to JNO. DAUGATY for L30,
            122 acres adj. JOS. ANTHONY, HUGH DAUGHTY. Wit: HUGH DAUGHAURTY,
THOMAS BROWN, JNO. SMITH, JAS. DAVIS.

Page 325   14 May 1751 GEO. HANCOCKE of Chesterfield and DANL. PARISH to
            RICH. BURK for L17, 250 acres Wreck Island Creek. Wit: WM.
CABELL, JOSIAS PAYNE, JOS. CABELL.

Page 326   14 May 1751 ROBT. DAVIS to WM. FLOYD for L50, 200 acres both
            sides Pedlar adj. his own line. Wit: JNO. ANTHONY, MATT. JORDAN,
JNO. PETER.

Page 328   14 May 1751 ROBT. DAVIS to SAML. BURK Jr. for L100, 400 acres
            Pedlar branches adj. his own line, WM. FLOYD. Wit: WM. CABELL
Jr., JAS. & MOSES HIGGINBOTHAM.

Page 329   30 Jan 1750 WM. HILL to GILES ALLEGRE for Ł 8-11, Above HENRY WOODS'
            upper corner on Buck Isalnd Creek; survey about 13 years ago by
Major WM. MAYO. Pat; 345 acres. Wit: JNO. HOPKINS, MARTIN KING, JUDITH
ALLEGRE, GILES ALLEGRE JR.

Page 330   14 May 1751 CHAS. LYNCH to BOOKER SMITH of Cumberland Co. for
            Ł10, 600 acres Beaverdam Swamp adj. branch of Hardware. Wit: JOHN
SMITH JR., JNO. BYBEE, ABRAHAM EADES.

Page 331   25 May 1751 JNO. HENSON to JAS. SANDERS of Goochland for Ł130,
            400 acres both sides N branch Slate. Pat. to DAVID GRIFFITH 30
Mar 1748(?) and sold to JNO. HENSON.

Page 332   12 Aug 1751 SACKERVELL WHITEBREAD to WM. MARSHALL of Cumberland
            Co. for Ł21-10-6, S side James, Willis River fork, 400 acres
adj. Col. JNO. BOLING, JNO. CHILDERS. Wit: EDMD. WOOD, JOS. ADCOCK,
ANTHONY CHRISTIAN.

Page 333   15 July 1751 TYREE HARRIS, of Louisa, to JAS. BRADLEY for Ł30,
            315 acres on branches of Willis, pat. 15 Dec 1749. Adj. GIDEON
PATTERSON, EDMD. GRAY, WM. GRAY, JNO. COOK. Wit: CLATEN COOK, JNO. BROWN,
JNO. COOK.

Page 334   20 May 1751 JNO. AUSTIN to Col. JOHN CHISWELL for Ł30, 250
            acres both sides Moore's Creek adj. JNO. CARTER. Pat. to SAML.
DAVIS 29 June 1739. Wit: GILES ALLEGRE, WM. HOWARD, JUDITH ALLEGRE.

Page 336   9 Aug 1751 WM. ALLEN to JNO. ALLEN for Ł210, 140 acres both
            sides Fishing Creek, N side Fluvanna - includes two islands
called Elk Island. Pat. to WM. ALLEN 1746. Wit: HUGH MAGARROCK, WM. SALLE,
JNO. GOODWIN, ANTHONY CHRISTIAN.

Page 338   9 Aug 1751 JNO. ALLEN to WM. ALLEN for Ł110, 394 acres both
            sides Slate; Pat to WM. ALLEN 1 Oct 1747. Also tract on both
sides Glover's road and both sides Horn Quarter Road - heads of branches
of Randolph, Hatcher, and Joshua Creeks - 400 acres pat. to WM. ALLEN in
1747. Wit: as above.

Page 339   12 Feb 1751 ANTHONY BENNING to WM. SALLE for Ł60, pat. of 400
            acres adj. DUDLEY DIGGS; both sides Randolph Creek; N branch of
Willis. Wit: THOS. TURNER, DAVID BELL, HUGH MAGARROCK, JAS. GOSS.

Page 340   I Aug 1751 EDWD. MOODY to BENJ. MATLOCKS for Ł5, 50 acres
            Cunningham Creek adj. grantor; grantee; Capt. JOS. THOMPSON.
Wit: HENRY MARTIN, JNO. McGURK, WM. CRUTCHFIELD.

Page 341   26 Jun 1751 RICH. STOCKTON, weaver, and wife AGNES to Rev. Mr.
            SAML. BLACK for Ł150, 400 acres both sides Stockton Creek adj.
JOEL TERRELL. Wit: ANDREW WOODS, JAS. JOHNSTON, THOS. REID.

Page 344   18 Aug 1751 ANDREW WOODS to JAS. KINKHEAD for Ł20, 224 acres
            near the Great Mt. Wit: WM. WOODS, RICH. STOCKTON, AGNES
STOCKTON.

Page 345   12 Aug 1751 DAVID KINKHEAD to ANDREW WOODS for Ł20, 222 acres
            at foot of the Great Mt. adj. grantee. Pat. 5 Mar 1747. Wit:
RICH. & AGNES STOCKTON, JAS. KINKHEAD.

Page 347   13 Aug 1751 JNO. COBBS to RO. CARRILL for Ł16, 115 acres adj.
            BENJ. WOODSON; N side Cary Creek. Pat. 1 Dec 1748.

Page 348   2 Mar 1751 PAUL ABNEY, planter, to JNO. GRAVES, planter for
            Ł3, 100 acres adj. CHAS. LYNCH, WM. RANDOLPH. Wit: DAVIS
STOCKTON, ADAM GOUDYLOCK(?), RO. BRENTON, WM. WHITESIDE.

Page 350   4 Nov 1747 SAML. DAVIES to JNO. SHEELS for Ł00 (sic), 200 acres
            N branch Rockfish adj. COL. CHISWELL, Beavercreek, Woods' Swamp.

Page 352   13 Aug 1751 JAS. DANIEL - Sheriff - qualified. Bondsman, WM.
            CABELL, WILLIAM MEGGINSON.

Page 352   13 Aug 1751   JOSHUA FRY qualified as surveyor. Bondsman: JNO.
            HARVEY, JNO. ANTHONY.

Page 353   13 Aug 1751   WM. CABELL - asst. surveyor - Bondsman: JNO.
            HARVEY, BENJ. HARRIS.

Page 353   THOS. TURPIN on above date - asst. surveyor - Bondsman: JNO.
            HARVEY, BENJ. HARRIS.

Page 354   13 Aug 1751   THOS. JEFFERSON - asst. surveyor - bondsman: DAVID
            BELL, THOS. TURPIN.

Page 354   12 Nov 1751   LARKIN SMITH & wife MARY to PETER JEFFERSON, Gent.,
            of Goochland, for Ł15, 150 acres where LARKIN SMITH lives; part
of tract left him by father JOSEPH SMITH, on N side of N fork James, adj.
RICH. MERIWETHER, CHAS. LYNCH, PHILIP SMITH.

Page 356   11 Nov 1751   PETER RUCKER & wife ELIZA of Orange Co., planter,
            to DAVID ROSSE, planter.   Consideration - ROSSER to seat and
improve tract of 204 acres adj. BERNARD GAINES, dec'd; grantor; WM. GAINES.
Wit: JNO. RUCKER, AMBR. RUCKER, WM. MILLER, GEO. McDANIEL.

Page 357   11 Nov 1751   PETER RUCKER, son and heir of JNO. RUCKER dec'd,
            of Orange Co., planter, to AMBROSE RUCKER of Orange, planter;
by order of father's will - taken up by JNO. & pat. to PETER - 324 acres,
save 4 acres for DAVID ROSSER; adj. HARVIE, ROSSER. Wit: JNO. RUCKER, WM.
MILLER, GEO. McDANIEL.   ELIZ., wife of PETER RUCKER.

Page 358   10 Nov 1751   PETER RUCKER of Orange Co., planter, & wife ELIZA
            (someone has tampered with official record and put b by her
name) to JOHN RUCKER of Albemarle, planter, for 5 sh., 318 acres Harris
Creek, part of 5850 acres pat. to PETER RUCKER 12 Mar, 16th year of
George's Reign. Adj. JOHN HARRIS, JNO. LIVINGSTON. Wit: JNO. HARVIE,
JNO. GOUGH, WM. MILLER, AMBR. RUCKER. (This JOHN is ancestor of MARY
GAYLE PETTYJOHN who married my third son, THURMAN BLANTON DAVIS, and they
live on Harris Creek.

Page 361   11 Nov 1751   JAS. SHARSTED to WM. CABELL for Ł15, 150 acres
            Huff branches E side Tobacco Row Mts. - still our landmark -
adj. BENJ. STINNETT. Wit: JAS. FREELAND, JAS. CHRISTIAN, PHILIP DAVIS.

Page 362   1 July 1751   CHAS. BAILEY of Goochland to THOS. THOMERSON for
            Ł18, 180 acres both sides Bailey's Creek of Byrd, adj. THOS.
BAILEY. Wit: HUGH LEWIS VENABLE, THOS. & DAVID BAILEY.

Page 364   9 Nov 1751   PETER LYON SR. & wife MARGARET to ELISHAH LYON -
            400 acres pat. to CHAS. LEWIS Sr. 12 Feb 1750 and sold to
PETER LYON on Rich Cove; Ł24 and Ł24 for 100 acres. Wit: JNO. LYON;
BLANE; WM. TAINER(?).

Page 366   10 Oct 1751   JNO. GRAVES & wife LUCY to WM. GOUGE of Hanover,
            for Ł40, 350 acres in adj. tracts adj. N branch of James;
JNO. MORRIS, PAUL ABNEY, Mt. Falls Creek, WM. RANDOLPH - lease of 100 acres
of the tract adj. CHAS. LYNCH, WM. RANDOLPH. Wit: JNO. MORRIS, FRANCIS
GRAVES, MARY MORRISS, WM. GOOCH, JR.

Page 368   12 Nov 1751   WM. BARNET to RO. HARDEE for Ł15, 100 acres
            Ballinger's Creek adj. WM. MOOR. Wit: JAMES GEORGE, JNO.
HOPKINS, JOS. CABELL.

Page 370   11 Nov 1751   ABRAHAM CHILDERS to WM. BUGG for Ł33, 200 acres
            adj. Rockfish; EZEKIAH DAWSON, grantee. Bought from DRURY
TUCKER. Wit: WM. CABELL JR., WM. DEPRIEST, JNO. HUNTER.

Page 371   18 Oct 1751   JAMES FORD of Cumberland Co., King Wm. Parish,
            to MARY AGEE & husband JAMES AGEE - MARY is daughter of FORD -
love - 200 acres. Adj. MATT. AGEE, TURPIN, Hubard Creek. Wit: JNO.
BEAZLEY, DANL. FORD.   Mark of FORE (sic)

Page 372   8 Oct 1751   DANL. FORD, Cumberland Co., to ARTHUR MOSELEY of

Cumberland, for Ł35, tract on Joshua Creek of Slate adj. MATT. AYRES, WM. SALLEY. Pat. 3 Nov 1740. Wit: JNO. MAXEY, RO. MOSELEY, NATHL. MAXEY.

Page 374   4 Oct 1751   PETER BROOKS to HENRY PERKINS of Essex Co. for 5 sh, 2 tracts of 2,301 acres. 1) 945 acres adj. DABBS, OBADIAH WOODSON, JNO. HODNETT; grantor. 2) 1356 acres adj. grantor; JNO. WOODSON, ROGER WILLIAMS, GANNAWAY, TURPIN, WALKER, Capt. ANDERSON, CHAS. ANDERSON. Wit: JNO. GRIGGS, CALEB HINES, JNO. ELLATT.

Page 376   5 Oct 1751   PETER BROOKS & wife CATHERINE, to HENRY PERKINS of Essex for Ł110 - (seems to be repeat of deed above, but amount paid was Ł110. Perhaps PERKINS took an option on day before and then decided to buy. I have found several such items.)

Page 378   13 June 1751   THOS. HIGGINBOTHAM to ROBT. ROSE for Ł45, 3 pats. 1) 200 acres in Piney Woods - 1 June 1750. 2) 140 acres Piney River - 12 July 1750. 3) Pat. date as for 2 - 200 acres Piney Woods. Wit: JNO. WALKER, RO. GREEN, PATRICK MORRISON.

Page 379   12 Nov 1751   WM. CANNON, carpenter, to JNO. GOODWIN for Ł75, 400 acres N branch Willis, formerly that of THOS. EDWARDS by pat. 25 July 1746. Adj. JNO. PAIN, Barron Lick Creek. Wit: BENJ. HARRIS, JNO. CHILDERS, JOSEPH ADCOCK.

Page 381   13 July 1751   NICHL. DAVIES of Southam Parish, Cumberland Co. to WM. CABELL for Ł260, 240 acres; part of 400 acres bought from RICH. BURKS lower end. Also 75 acres S side Fluvanna - opposite 400 acres, pat. 20 Aug 1747. Wit: SAML. JORDAN, THOS. TURPIN JR., JNO.NICOLAS.

Page 383   10 Nov 1751   PETER RUCKER of Orange Co., St. Thomas Parish, & wife ELIZ. to JNO. GOUGH for 5 sh., 463 acres Harris Creek branches, known as PETER RUCKER's lot - save 10 acres adj. DAVID ROSSER; adj. ROSE's pat. by branch of Harris. Wit: WM. MILLER, DAVID ROSSER, JNO. RUCKER, GEO. McDANIEL.

Page 384   11 Nov 1751   PETER RUCKER & wife, as above, to JNO. GOUGH for Ł200, in possession of JNO. GOUGH for one year and reference to deed above - 463 acres, lines and wits. as above.

Page 386   3 Oct 1751   JNO. GIVODAN to RENE CHASTAIN for Ł150, several slaves. Wit: JOS. ADCOCK, HENRY RICE, JNO. ADCOCK.

Page 386   12 Nov 1751   GEO. HOLMES GIVIN & wife ELIZ. to EDWD. CASON of Spotsylvania for Ł20, 400 acres S side James, branch of Willis or Bolling Creek, adj. SACKERVAL WHITEBREAD, COL. JNO. BOLLING, THOS. POTTER.

Page 388   12 Nov 1751   GEO. HOLMES GIVIN & wife ELIZ. to JAMES PALMER for Ł23, 347 acres Wolf Trap branch of Mt. Creek adj. BOLLING, WOODS, STRANGE. Wit: HUGH MAGARROCK, JNO. HARDEMAN, SACKERVALL WHITEBREAD.

Page 390   12 Nov 1751   MOSES RAY &wife ELIZ. to JNO. GOODWIN for Ł10, 400 acres pat. 15 Dec 1749; S side Fluvanna near branch of Rock Island Creek. Wit: JNO. & RICH. PETER, JNO. GOODWIN JR.

Page 393   13 Nov 1751   HENRY MARTIN & wife JUDITH to HARDIN BURNLEY of Hanover Co., planter, for Ł500, 2 adj. tracts. 1) 350 acres pat. to CHAS. LYNCH 12 Mar 1739. 2) 109 acres pat. to JNO. ANTHONY 20 Sept 1745.   489 acres Hardware. Wit: JNO. SMITH JR., JNO. HOPKINS, JNO. HUDSON.

Page 395   13 Nov 1751   JNO. GRAVES of Caroline Co. to THOS. PARKS for 5 sh., 400 acres adj. BENJ. STINNETT - 1 yr. lease - rent of 1 ear of Lady corn on Lady Day.

Page 396   12 Nov 1751   JNO. GRAVES to THOS. SPARKS for Ł65, but probably PARKS since lease is mentioned.

Page 398   13 Nov 1751   JNO. CHILDERS, planter, to his son FRANCIS CHILD-ERS - love & 5 sh., 200 acres where son lives. Wit: BENJ. HARRIS, JNO. COBBS, JOS. ADCOCK.

Page 400   13 Nov 1751 ROBT. BABER & wife JANE of Lunenberg Co. to WM.
            BABER for Ҍ25, 300 acres both sides Wolf Pit Branch.

Page 401   14 Nov 1751 WM. HARRIS, Gent., to SAML. JORDAN & PATRICK
            NAPIER, Church wardens of St. Ann's Parish, for Ҍ135, 400 acres
for a glebe - both sides S fork Totier(?) Creek, pat. 25 July 1741. (I
think that this creek is Totier, but I am not sure. I recall getting lost
once while on sightseeing tour with my wife and we came into a road called
the Glebe Road somewhere near Scottsville.) Adj. MATT. HARRIS, Major
JOHN BOLLING, CHAS. LYNCH.

Page 403   14 Nov 1751 LUKE CARRELL (CARROLL) late of Albemarle, to JNO.
            MARR of St. Thomas Parish, Orange Co., for 5 sh., 400 acres
adj. branches of late Secretary CARTER's Mill Creek, CARTER, HOWARD CASH.
Wit: HENRY MARTIN, WM. CABELL JR., HUGH MAGGARROCH.

Page 405   15 Nov 1751 LUKE CARRELL, late of Alb., to JOHN MARR, as
            above, for Ҍ40, 400 acres in possession of MARR - reference to
grant, 1 June 1751. Wit: as above.

Page 406   13 July 1751 NICHL. DAVIES of Southam Parish, Cumberland Co.
            to RICH. BURK for Ҍ100, 160 acres; pat. of 400 acres bought
by NICHL. DAVIES from BURK; upper end. Wit: SAML. JORDAN, JNO. NICHOLAS,
THOS. TURPIN JR.

Page 407   10 Feb 1752 JNO. HEARD to CHAS. LAMBERT, Schoolmaster, for
            Ҍ40, 225 acres S. Garden or Thoroughfare, adj. MILDRED MERIWE-
THER, HOWARD CASH, his corner. Wit: DAVID LEWIS, HIRAM GRAVES, JNO.
GILMORE.

Page 410   11 Feb 1752 DAVID KINKHEAD to JOS. KINKHEAD for Ҍ20, 178
            acres N branches of Stockton, branch of Mecham River, adj.
ANDREW WOODS, the graveyard. Part of 400 acres pat. 5 Mar 1747.

Page 411   10 Feb 1752 DAVID KINKHEAD & wife WINNEFRED to JOS. KINKHEAD
            and BOROUGH KINKHEAD for 5 sh., 737 acres Rockfish branches,
pat. 12 Jan 1746, adj. Col. JNO. CHISWELL, end of a mt.

Page 413   11 Feb 1752 Same parties and same tract as above.

Page 416   11 Feb 1752 GEO. DAMERIL & wife ANN THANY, to THOS. TILMAN of
            Goochland Co. for Ҍ100, 400 acres both sides Hardware adj.
BENJ. WOODSON. Wit: MATT. JORDAN, ALEX. McCAUL, THOS. THORNELL.

Page 417   11 Feb 1752 JNO. RIPLEY to his son RICHARD RIPLEY for Ҍ40, 195
            acres both sides Walton's fork of Slate, pat. 12 July 1750.
Also 100 acres upper end of where JNO. RIPLEY lives, N side Walton's fork.
At Richard's death it goes to his daughter, JUDITH RIPLEY. Wit: JAS. GOSS,
SAML. JORDAN.

Page 419   8 Feb 1751 EDMUND MANNION to JAS. JONES for Ҍ55, 315 acres
            adj. ROES' pat.; the river.

Page 420   8 Feb 1752 Same parties and deed.

Page 422   11 Nov 1751 MEREDITH MANING to JAS. GOSS for Ҍ10, 35 acres N
            side Slate adj. WM. RICKLES, MOOR's Creek. Wit: SAML. JORDAN,
JNO. RIPOLEY, ABRAHAM CHILDERS. ELIZ, wife of MEREDITH MANING.

Page 423   Aug 13 1751 RICH. BURK to WM. HORSLEY for Ҍ100, 160 acres;
            part of 400 acres bought from NICHL. DAVIES - upper end. Wit:
JER. WHITNEY, JOS. CABELL, DAVID BARNET.

Page 424   18 Nov 1751 JNO. FENLEY to SAML. BURKS Jr., for Ҍ20, 200 acres
            devised by father, JAMES, dec'd, to my brother, CHAS. FENLEY,
and me by will. Pat. 20 Sept. 1745, both sides David's creek. Wit: CHAS.
FENLEY, WM. NICHOLLS, RO. KYLE, WM. MEGGINSON.

Page 425   11 Feb 1752 JNO. McWHORTER to ALEX. PATTON for Ҍ90, 120 acres
            bought from JAS. McCANNE 10 Sept 1747. Pat. 10 July 1745, save

1 acre sold to JNO. REID, JAS. ROBERTSON, & SAML. BELL for Presbyterian Church of Rockfish - school house and cemetery. Adj. EDWD. MALOY, EDWIN HICKMAN, JAS. HENDRICKS, JOSIAH CLAPPAM. (This old church and cemetery are still in existence.)

Page 427   10 Feb 1752 ALEX. MONTGOMERY to son, WM. MONTGOMERY; love and 5 sh., 255 acres Rockfish Settlement, part of tract bought from Col. JNO. CHISWELL of 640 acres. Wit: WM. CABELL, RO. DUNWOODY, THOS. BEGGS.

Page 428   11 Feb 1752 DAVID KINKHEAD, carpenter, to JOS. KINKHEAD and ANDREW WOODS for L300, slaves; deed of trust.

Page 429   14 May 1752 STEPHEN SANDERS to JER. PARKER REACH for L20, 100 acres. Wit: RICH. TAYLOR, JNO. SANDERS, WM. PASSLY.

Page 430   27 Apr 1752 SAML. RIDGWAY to DRURY MIMS of Cumberland Co., for several satisfactory services, 406 acres, N branches Willis, part of a tract adj. ANTHONY SHARRON. Wit: JNO. & SARAH RIDGWAY, W.STILL?

Page 432   25 Nov 1751 WM. GRAY of New Kent, St.Peter's Parish, to STEPHEN SANDERS, FOR L100, 405 acres. Wit: JNO. SANDERS, JER. REACH, CHAS. LEE, WM. PASLAY.

Page 433   16 Nov 1751 DRURY TUCKER & wife SUSANNA to ABRAHAM CHILDERS for L50, 400 acres adj. the river, WM. CANNON. Wit: THOS. TENDALL, WM. DEPRIEST, RICH. HALL.

Page 435   ---- 1752 BENJ. MIMS to JAS. SANDERS for L75, 100 acres Slate river adj. his own. Also 350 acres adj. THOS. GIBSON, WM. PERKINS, branch of Meredith's creek. Wit: JNO. SANDERS, WM. PASLEY, HENRY THOMSON, STEPHEN SANDERS, JOEL WALKER.

Page 436   15 Mar 1752 BENJ. MIMS to JAS. SANDERS for L70, 200 acres both sides GRIFFITH's; N branch Slate, adj. grantee. Wit: as above.

Page 437   9 June 1752 JNO. WADE & wife MARY to JNO. GREEN for L8, 128 acres, branches of Hat Creek near Blue Mts. Wit: DUNCAN CAMERON, JNO. & THOS. REID.

Page 439   12 May 1752 SAML. BURK Jr. & wife ELIZ. to JNO. FIDLEAR of Henrico, for L30, 300 acres S side Tye. Part of 350 acre pat. 25 June 1747. Wit: JAMES CLAIBORNE, JOS. CABELL, WM. CABELL Sr. & Jr.

Page 441   9 May 1752 SAML. BURK, JR. & wife ELIZ. to CHAS. FINLEY for L22-5, 200 acres; part of 400 acres left my brother, JNO. FENLEY, by father, JAMES FENLEY, and to SAML. BURK - N side Slate River Mt., branch of David Creek. Wit: LETISHA MARTIN, WM. MEGGINSON, JAS. SPEARS.

Page 442   8 May 1752 SAML. MURRIEL & wife LEIZ. to SAML. BELL for L12, 160 acres S. branches Rockfish. Part of 350 acre pat. 20 June 1747. Adj. grantor; Col. CHISWELL; grantee; EDWD. MALOY, JAS. WOODS. Wit: WM. CABELL, JR., JNO. SMALL, MOSES EDGAR.

Page 444   1 May 1752 CHAS. LYNCH to THOS. WRIGHT for L20, 400 acres branch of Joy creek adj. MICHL. HOLLAND, CHAS. HUDSON; pat. to CHAS. LYNCH. Wit: DAVID LEWIS, WM. TERRELL LEWIS, HENRY TILLY.

Page 446   12 Apr 1752 ANTHONY HOGGAT to JNO. FRANKLIN of Cumberland Co. for L50, 300 acres adj. JNO. BOSSHICKS(?), NATHL. HOGGATT. Wit: G. MARR, JNO. HUNTER, THOS. BARKER, DIANNA TANNER.

Page 448   11 June 1752 GEO. HILTON to WM. SPURLOCK of Goochland, for (blank sum), 200 acres both sides Raccoon Creek of Rivanna. Pat. 2 July 1750. HESTER, wife of GEO. HILTON.

Page 449   11 June 1752 THOS. WRIGHT to HENRY TILLY for L30, 200 acres Ivy Creek branches adj. MICHL. HOLLAND, ALEX. MURROW, CHAS.

HUDSON. Bought from CHAS. LYNCH. Wit: DAVID LEWIS, JNO. WOODS, WM. TERRELL LEWIS.

Page 450   20 Feb 1752   JNO. CHISWELL, of Hanover, to MICHL. MONTGOMERY
            for Ł50, 500 acres N. side Rockfish. Part of 11,140 acres pat.
1739. Adj. mouth of Davies creek, S. fork Rockfish, JOS. BARNETT, FRANCIS
WRIGHT. Wit: JNO. FALL, THOMAS JAMISON, MOSES EDGAR, WM. POLLARD.

Page 453   20 Feb 1752   JNO. CHISWELL of Hanover, to JNO. SMALL, for Ł40,
            400 acres N side Rockfish, part of pat. above, adj. grantor;
ALEX. MONTGOMERY. Wit: MOSES EDGAR, THOS. JAMISON, MICHL. MONTGOMERY, WM.
POLLARD. (Note: I am satisfied that the title used for Davis Creek -
where the terrible flood took such a toll - is really Davies creek and was
named for NICHOLAS DAVIES. I have found that many confuse Davis with
Davies and I have pointed out in Amherst that one of the worst offenders
was none other than A.B. DAVIES who was once Amherst clerk. My "D" Will
work of Amherst cites the errors.)

Page 455   11 Feb 1752   ALEX. MONTGOMERY to his son JOHN MONTGOMERY for
            20 sh. and love; 336 acres, part of 640 acres bought from Col.
JNO. CHISWELL and rest pat. 1747. On Buck creek, branch of Rockfish, adj.
grantor; CHISWELL. Wit: JNO. SMALL, JOS. MILLER, JOS. BARNETT.

Page 458   13 Mar 1752   ROBT. BARNET & wife MARY to DAVID CRAWFORD of
            Hanover, for Ł130, 200 acres; part of 400 acres pat. to WM.
MAYO 30 Mar 1743; also 211 acres adj. pat. 12 Jan 1746 to ROBT. BARNET;
adj. WM. MAYO, HICKMAN (now JNO. ROBINSON). Wit: JNO. REID, OWEN CRAWFORD,
JNO. DAVIS,JAS. BARNET.

Page 460   19 May 1752   ROBT. HOLT & wife ELIZ. to RANE CHASTAIN for Ł20,
            200 acres, part of a pat. adj. JOS. ADCOCK; COLEMAN; CARY. Wit:
THOS. TABB, JOHN HARRELSON, DRURY MIMS, BENJ. HARRISON.

Page 462   19 May 1752   RO. HOLT as above to ALEX. SPEIRS, Glasgow mer-
            chant, for Ł70, 215 acres Buffalo Creek branches, adj. RANE
CHASTAIN, JOS. ADCOCK; grantee (formerly HENRY CARY) part of 415 acres pat.
20 May 1749. Wit: THOS. TABB, JNO. HARRELSON, DRURY MIMS, RANE CHASTAIN.

Page 464   9 July 1752   JAMES DAVIS, planter, to PATRICK BISHOP for Ł30,
            312 acres Branham clearing, adj. E side of one of Ragged Mts.;
JOS. ANTHONY. Wit: CHAS. LAMBERT, DAVID LEWIS, JNO. SACKETT. MARY, wife
of JAMES DAVIS.

Page 466   25 May 1752   GEO. NICHOLAS, DINWIDDIE Co., to DANL. SCOTT of
            Cumberland Co. for 5 sh., 500 acres N side Fluvanna, part of
pat. of GEO. NICHOLAS, Gent., late of Williamsburg, dec'd, for 2600 acres,
Jan 1729. Adj. JNO. DOUGLAS' house. Wit: W. BATTERSBY, GIDEON MARR, JAS.
CLAIBORNE, SAML. JORDAN. Lease - 1 year.

Page 467   26 May 1752   SCOTT, above, pays Ł430 for the tract. Wit: as
            above.

Page 470   13 Aug 1752   JNO. MOORE & wife MARY to ARTHUR HOPKINS of
            Goochland, for Ł60, 800 acres N side James and branches of
Johns Creek, adj. Capt. CLARK, MICAJAH CLARK, JNO. HOPKINS. Wit: JNO.
SMITH JR., RICH. TAYLOR, OBADIAH WOODSON.

Page 472   30 July 1752   ALEX. HENDERSON of Augusta Co., planter, to JNO.
            McWHORTER for Ł70, 237 acres both sides Rockfish, N branch,
near Blue Mts., adj. Pounder branch, JAS. MARTIN. Wit: GEO. POWEL, WM.
SIMSON, ALEX. PATTON, SAML. MANN.

Page 474   6 July 1752   THOS. WRIGHT to ALEX MURRY for Ł18, 200 acres Ivy
            Creek branches, part of tract bought from CHAS. LYNCH. Wit:
JNO. McCORD, PETER HEARSTON, WM. TERRELL LEWIS.

Page 475   13 Aug 1752   WM. MILLS & wife MARY to MARTHA MASSIE of New
            Kent Co., for Ł200, 400 acres both sides Pedlar adj. Dancing
Creek.

Page 477   13 Aug 1752 SAML. STEPHENS to JNO. LEE for Ь105, 400 acres
            Slate branches adj. Mill Creek; pat. 12 Jan 1746. Also 225
acres with a line crossing the river, pat. 20 Aug 1748. Wit: JNO. HUNTER,
JAS. GOSS, JNO. McCORD.

Page 478   2 Apr 1752 JER. WADE to DAVID WADE for Ь35, 180 acres Thrasher
            Creek adj. PEARCE WADE, JNO. BRISWELL; N branch Thrasher. Pat.
to HOWARD CASH 12 July 1750. Wit: JAS. GEORGE, CHISLEY DANIEL, PEARCE WADE.

Page 480   13 Aug 1752 JNO. CLARK to BENJ. CLAR--JONATHAN CLARK, late of
            King and Queen Co., dec'd. - surveyed and took up with JOS.
SMITH, EDWIN HICKMAN & THOS. GRAVES, 3277 acres in then Goochland, N fork
James or Rivanna; pat. 25 May 1734. JONATHAN CLARK left will and pat. to
be equally divided between his two sons, JNO. & BENJ. CLARK. Will proved
in King and Queen, 9 Apr , in year above mentioned. Others divided to the
sons and conveyed 820 acres. Mutual division by sons - JNO. from BENJ.
5 sh., 410 acres adj. Lynch ford; between 2 mts.; MERIWETHER. BENJ. from
JNO. for 5 sh., 410 acres adj. MERIWETHER, JNO. KEYS, RO. DALTON's old
field, white oak marked MT.

Page 483   10 Aug 1752 SAML. JAMESON to JAMES WHAREY(?), for Ь40, Spring
            Creek branches, adj. CHAS. WILLIS (WILLS?); pat. 25 June 1747.
Wit: JNO. McCOLLOCH, JNO. JAMISON, ALEX. JAMESON. JEAN wife of SAML.

Page 484   27 Feb 1752 CHAS. LYNCH & wife SARAH to PETER JEFFERSON of
            Goochland, for Ь15, 100 acres N side Rivanna, adj. THOS. SMITH,
JNO. SMITH, Col. MERIWETHER; a ridge. Wit: JNO. SMITH JR., EDWD. CLARKE,
FRANCES MOLOY.

Page 486   13 Aug 1752 VALENTINE ALLEN to CHAS. PERROW for Ь250, 300 acres
            N side Fluvanna above Fishing Creek, pat. to WM. ALLEN, Gent.,
20 Sept 1745. Wit: ADRAIN ANGLING, JNO. SPEARS, JAS. BARNET.

Page 487   1 Mar 1752 JNO. BOSTICK of Cumberland Co. to WM. JOHNS of
            Chesterfield, for Ь100, 730 acres where JAS. STAPLES lives; 400
acres of it pat. to HENRY CHILES 1 Feb 1738; 330 acres adj. WM. GRAY,
NATHL. HOGGATT & adjs. 400 acres, pat. of 2000 acres, 1 June 1750. 730
acres adj. ANTHONY HOGGATT, WM. GRAY. Wit: WM. GRAY, JOSHUA DOSS(?), WM.
BALLARD, JAS. CLAIBORNE, GIDEON MARR, CHAS. LYNCH.

Page 489   10 Dec 1741 THOS. DOBBINS to RO. WEIR for Ь33, 166 acres Rock-
            fish branches adj. Col. CHISWELL. Wit: THOS. & JAMES BELL, MATT.
ROBERTSON.

Page 491   25 May 1752 WM. WOMACK to WM. JOHNS for Ь100, 400 acres both
            sides Willis Creek pat. 20 Sept 1751; adj. DANL. LOW, JOHN
SANDERS, JNO. COOCK (sic). Wit: BENJ. HARRIS, G. MARR, WM. TRIGG.

Page 493   14 Aug 1752 CHAS. LYNCH to MATT. JORDAN for Ь80, 250 acres
            adj. THOS. SOWEL. Wit: THOS. JEFFERSON, THOS. TURPIN JR.,
SAML. JORDAN.

Page 494   18 Mar 1752 RO. THOMPSON (TOMPSON), Cumberland Co., to WM.
            CHILDERS of Cumberland Co., 250 acres Glover's Creek and road
dividing tract of 500 acres between WM. CHIDERS and brother, MOSES CHILD-
ERS. Part of 1140 acres pat. to RO. THOMPSON 20 July 1748. Wit: JNO.
SCRUGGS, T. ATKISON, JOSIAH THOMSON.

Page 495   1 May 1752 ROBT. THOMPSON, as above, to son, ROBT. THOMPSON
            (THOMSON), 1045 acres S side James., adj. Little Buffaloe;
CANNON, both sides Hatcher's Creek; DANL. SCOTT, MARTHA AYRES.

Page 496   18 Mar 1752 RO. THOMPSON, as above, to MOSES CHILDERS, same
            county, 250 acres S side Glover's road. Part of 1140 acres
above. Wit: JOHN SCRUGGS, T. ATKINSON, JOSIAH THOMSON.

Page 497   1 May 1752 ROBT. THOMSON, as above, to son JOSIAH THOMSON,
            1045 acres S side James adj. Little Buffaloe, CANNON, both
sides Whispering Creek, Capt. JNO. BOLLING, HOLMES GIVIN.

Page 498   4 June 1752   Order by JNO. NICHOLAS, clerk, to JNO. HENRY, RO.
JENNINGS & JAS. LITTLEPAGE - ROWLAND HORSLEY & wife SUSANNA,
15 Dec 1750, to JOSIAH PAYNE, 200 acres N side Rivanna. Dower released
to HENRY & LITTLEPAGE on same day.

DEED BOOK 2 OF ALBEMARLE COUNTY, VA.

FOREWORD

I have made remarks about the terrible Nelson County, Va., flood. This
further data shows just a bit of the fine response made by my own Baptist
group to the needs. Federal and state funds are still being contributed
to rebuild roads and bridges which suffered enormous damage. I am not
able to give a complete report on assistance from other church groups, but
will mention splendid work done by a Methodist organization from the
Emmanuel Church of Amherst. Mrs. Roy Drummond and her workers went into
many homes and trailers (set up for those who lost homes) and learned
needs and raised funds to respond to the reports made on needs.

This is a report called Flood Relief Bulletin #2 from the Virginia Baptist
Evangelism and Missions Department. In part, this was written: "As of Nov.
8, 1969, thirty-five thousand dollars ($35,000) has been sent to the Va.
Baptist General Board for flood relief. In addition to this, over eight
thousand dollars ($8,000) has been sent directly to the Baptist Flood
Relief Committee of the Piedmont Baptist Association (this embraces part
of Amherst and Nelson counties and I have the Honor to be moderator of the
group), and an unreportable amount of money and supplies have been sent
directly to the churches and individuals in the stricken area. This is a
continuing need and churches may contact Rev. John Gordon, pastor of Cal-
vary Baptist Church, Lovingston, for names of families with such needs.
We are also aware that many Baptist groups and individuals have contributed through civic programs of relief.

"In addition to money, clothing, and other supplies that have been given,
many men have given generously of their time and talents to assist victims.
As an example, on one recent Saturday, 83 men gave over 650 man hours of
labor in repairing houses and churches.(This is not in the report, but
mention should be made of the splendid work done by the Mennonites who
came into the area and performed such tasks.) Mr. Gordon reports that 43
projects have been completed by these Baptist teams. Elwood Hurst, President of Baptist Men in Potomac Association, Al Pitts, President of the
Baptist Men of Fredericksburg Association, and Coy Hardee, Richmond, are
three examples of men who have given of themselves unselfishly in chan-
neling volunteer labor of a period of time into the area. Volunteer
labor continues to be the greatest need at this moment.

Flood Relief Committees of Piedmont and Rockbridge Baptists have made
these contributions: About $3600 has been put aside for pastors who need
salary aid. Several churches were so damaged that this aid was imperative.
$500 has been given to replace a pastor's library and for personal needs.
Right here I might put in a personal word as to the peculiar experience
of Rev. Eugene Campbell who moved from Elon Church in Amherst on the
morning before the flood of the horrible night to his new field in Rockbridge at Glasgow (near Natural Bridge) and suffered a great deal of damage. $1500 has been used to replace furniture; $200 has been donated for
food supplies. The Red Cross supplied most of the food.

$6,000 has been given to buy materials and supplies for repairing houses
and churches in Nelson and a footnote states that a request from Rockbridge for additional supplies will have been granted by the time that the
report reaches the pastors.

I realize that this is entirely inadequate to give a true picture of the
heroic work done by so many denominations, but I do not have their data
at hand.

It suffices to say that people of all faiths rose up with one accord to answer the Macedonian call. In my memory is still the sight of the refrigerated truck in Lovingston into which were placed bodies of unidentified dead. I am reminded of those days whenever I hear a "chopper" fly over my house. I also recall the statement made by Hugh Boyd, pastor of Jonesboro Baptist Church, when he spoke of the sadness experienced when he led a procession to inter seven bodies in one funeral service.

> Bailey Fulton Davis
> Amherst, Va., April 11, 1970.

ALBEMARLE COUNTY, VIRGINIA DEED BOOK 2

Page 1   8 Feb 1758 WM. HAMMACK to DANL. HAMMACK; no sum; 100 acres N
           side Little Mt. Wit: JNO. HENSLEE, DAVID WATTS, JNO. HAMMACK.
(It will be noted that there is a gap from 1752 to 1759 in these deed books 1 to 2. I suspect that the gap will have to be filled by inspection of Will Book 2, which may follow the pattern of Deed & Will Book 1, but I have not checked. If so, I shall try to go back and pick up the missing years after finishing Deed Book 3.)

Page 2   9 Feb 1758 JNO. KEY SR. to MARTIN KEY for Ł18, 150 acres; part
           of a pat. of 300 acres dated 10 Jan 1735; rest given to JOHN's daughter, MARY DAULTON - on Rivanna where JNO. KEY lives, N side, adj. BENJ. CLARK. Wit: JAS. NEVIL, GEO. KEY, JNO. GILLUM.

Page 3   11 July 1758 JNO. KEY SR. to GEO. KEY of Louisa, planter, for
           5 sh., 430 acres pat. 6 July 1741, adj. COL. MEREDITH, Key's Mills. Wit: BENJ. CLARK, NOELL JOHNSON, RO. ADAMS.

Page 5   9 Feb 1758 JNO. KEY SR. to son MARTIN KEY; love - 200 acres;
           part of 400 acres pat. 1732. Now divided to MARTIN and younger brother, JOHN KEY, adj. BENJ. CLARK, WM. TANDY. Where JNO. KEY lives. Wit: JAS. NEVIL, JOHN GILLUM, GEO. KEY.

Page 6   8 Mar 1758 JOS. KINKHEAD to ANDREW GREER for 5 sh., 178 acres
           on Stockton branch of Meechum. Wit: THOS. REID, HUGH ALEXANDER, JAS. KINKHEAD. Lease for yr.

Page 7   8 Mar 1758 JOS. KINKHEAD to ANDREW GREER for Ł40, 178 acres
           above, adj. ANDREW WOODS, pat. to DAVID KINKHEAD 5 Mar 1747, and by deed to ANDREW WOODS 12 Aug 1751, and by WOODS to JOS. KINKHEAD. Wit: THOS. REID, HUGH ALEXANDER, JAMES KINKHEAD.

Page 8   8 Mar 1758 JNO. BONDURANT SR. of Cumberland Co. to son JOHN JR.
           of Albemarle, for love, 200 acres, part of 400 acres pat. 12 Jan 1746, on Slate river branches of Flatt Creek; upper end where plantation now is. Wit: JAS. & ANN FORD.

Page 9   4 Mar 1758 JNO. JENNINGS to WM. JENNINGS for Ł15, 150 acres N
           side Appomattox River. Wit: JOEL WATKINS, GEO. NIX, JNO. MORROW.

Page 10   9 Mar 1758 HOWARD CASH to WM. BICKNELL - love - 100 acres Mill
           Creek, part of 400 acres laid off for WM. BICKNELL. Wit: THOS. POWEL, PHILIP SMITH, JACOB SMITH.

Page 11   1 Mar 1758 JNO. JENNINGS to GEO. NIX for Ł30, 200 acres N side
           Appomattox; upper part of 400 acres pat. 16 Aug 1756. Wit: JOEL WATKINS, JNO. MOREN(?), WM. JENNINGS.

Page 12   9 Mar 1758 JNO. COFFEY to JAMES COFFEY for Ł30, 124 acres on
           heads of branches of Hardware adj. grantor.

Page 13   9 Mar 1758 ALEX. BLANE to GEO. BLANE, planter, 200 acres pat.
           Mar 12 1739 to CHAS. LEWIS SR., Rich Cove. 600 acres of it bought by ALEX. BLANE. Adj. GEO. DOUGLAS.

Page 15   15 Feb 1758 THOS. BRUMIT, MARTHA & MARY REES to NATHL. HAGGARD
           for Ь30, 400 acres pat. to DAVID REES 25 Jun 1747 - to us by law;
DAVID is dec'd. On Moor Creek, branches, adj. E side Piney Mt., GEO.
BELL; Also signed by ANN BRUMIT(ET). Wit: BENEJAH GENTRY, ISHAM ROYALTY,
DAVID NOWLIN.

Page 17   9 Mar 1758 JAS. GATES to GIDEON TOMMAS for Ь18, 400 acres both
           sides Walton's fork; Arthur's Creek, adj. WM. NOWLIN, THOS.
PATTESON, WM. CHAMBERS. Pat. 10(?) Sep 1755. Wit: JAS. NEVIL, JAS. OWL,
STEPHEN GARROTT.

Page 18   9 Mar 1758 GIDEON TOMMAS to STEVEN GARRET for Ь10, 50 acres
           both sides Troublesome Creek adj. ANTHONY BENNING. PHILIP TOMMAS
got pat. 12 Jan 1746. Wit: JAS. NEVIL, ELIZ.(?) BLACKBURN, JNO. MASTERS.

Page 19   8 Dec 1757 JAS. SMITH, planter, to JACOB SMITH, planter, for
           Ь50, 344 acres both sides Buffaloe. Part of 788 acres bought
from JNO. THRASHER, adj. grantor. Wit; JAS. NEVIL, HENRY TRENT, WM.
CABELL, JR.

Page 20   29 Nov 1757 PHILIP SMITH, Chesterfield Co., to PETER RANDOLPH,
           THOS. TURPIN, JNO. NICHOLAS, THOS. WALKER, JNO. HARVIE, exors.
of PETER JEFFERSON's will - Ь25 paid by PETER JEFFERSON in lifetime and
5 sh. by exors., 200 acres N side Rivanna adj. THOS. SMITH, LARKIN SMITH,
MERIWETHER, HICKMAN. Devised to PHILIP SMITH by will of father, JOSEPH
SMITH. Until THOS. JEFFERSON is 21 - eldest son of PETER JEFFERSON - other
sons of PETER - choices to be made. Wit: THOS. SMITH, WM. HICKMAN, JNO.
DAWSON.

Page 23   8 Dec 1757 JAS. SMITH to PHILIP SMITH for Ь20, 244 acres both
           sides Buffaloe. Part of 388 acres bought from JNO. THRASHER,
adj. grantor, Puppie Creek (still known as such along with Thrasher's
Creek in western Amherst), JACOB SMITH. Wit: JAS. NEVIL, WM. CABELL JR.,
HENRY TRENT.

Page 24   2 Dec 1757 JNO. WALKER to RICH. HALL Jr. for 19000 tobacco, 50
           acres S side Fluvanna, pat. to WM. CABELL 5 Sep 1746, adj. JNO.
LAD. Wit: RICH. TAYLOR, EDWD. HUNTER.

Page 25   9 Mar 1758 JNO. GOODWIN SR. & wife MARY to WM. ANGLIN for Ь12,
           both sides Rock Island Creek of Fluvanna, 100 acres, part of 400
acres pat. to MOSES RAY 15 Dec 1749. Memo: this deed sent to STEPHEN FORD.

Page 26   9 Mar 1758 BOWKER SMITH of Goochland Co. to JNO. SMITH JR.,
           same parish of St. James, Northam, for Ь100, 600 acres Beaver
Dam Swamp, adj. branches of Hardware. Wit: MARTHA DAVIS, JNO. & GUY SMITH,
HENRY MARTIN.

Page 28   9 Mar 1758 PARTICK NOWLIN & wife SARAH to JNO. MOORE for Ь40,
           600 acres, 400 acres of it pat. to NOWLIN 15 Aug 1737 - both
sides Moor's Creek Bisket Run; 200 acres both sides Brisket Run and Cow
Branch; bought from THOS. HAYNES "Plumb Orchard". Wit: WM. HARRIS, JNO.
BRYANT, GEO. ROBINSON.

Page 29   9 Mar 1758 THOS. JOPLING to SAML. BAILEY for Ь10, 134 acres
           both sides Green Creek adj. grantor; RALPH JOPLING. Wit: JNO.
PETERS, NATHAN BOND, LEE HARRIS.

Page 31   24 Dec 1757 RALPH JOPLIN to JNO. COX for Ь50, 400 acres Green
           Creek, branches, adj. COL. EPES' Green Mt. tr. Wit: JNO.
GRIFFIN, RICH. & PERRIN FARRAR. KATHERINE, wife of RALPH JOPLIN.

Page 32   16 Jan 1758 SAMSON MAXEY & wife MARY to WM. BABER for Ь11-15,
           25 acres both sides Great Creek, branch of Slate, adj. ISAIAH
BURTON. Wit: ADRIAN ANGLIN, NATHL. & WM. BURTON.

Page 33   13 Apr 1758 JAS. IRELAND to GEO. EUBANK for Ь20, 300 acres adj.
           THOS. SOWELL, WM. HARRIS, JAS. HILL, mt. side, Beaver Dam fork
of Epes' Creek. Wit: JNO. MARTIN JR., LUCY & JNO. FORTUNE.

Page 34 5 Sep 1757 JNO. COOK of Cumberland Co., planter, to WM. VAUGHAN,
Bedford Co., planter, for ₺25, 400 acres Willis Creek adj. WM.
GAY, DANL. LOW, GIDEON PATTERSON. Pat. 17 Apr 1757. Wit: SOLOMON PASSLAY,
STEPHEN SANDERS, WM. LOW, TERRY BRADLEY.

Page 35 12 Apr 1758 WM. MEGGINSON & THOS. TURPIN, Cumberland Co., to
WM. CLARK of Cumberland Co, for ₺80, 1150 acres adj. PHILIP MAYS,
JAS. IRELAND; E. side Bent Creek. Wit: THOS. BEARD, ROBT. KYLE, JAS.
SPEARS.

Page 36 12 Apr 1758 JAS. MOBLEY to WM. MEGGINSON, Tillotson Parish -
consideration: 325 acres on Little Owens and 1 bay gelding worth
₺5, 75 acres on N side Fluvanna. Wit: THOS. BEARD, RO. KYLE, JAS. SPEARS.

Page 37 11 May 1757 LAMBETH BLACKBURN & wife MARY to THOS. ROBINSON for
₺30, 200 acres N branches Willis Creek.

Page 39 30 Mar 1758 THOS. CAWTHON & JOS. GOODE & wife ELIZ. to WM.BUGG,
for ₺28, land on N side Fluvanna & Bremer Creek. 1) 50 acres,
part of where GOODE lives above mouth of Calf Pasture Branch and joins
CAWTHON. 2) 350 acres pat. to CAWTHON and adjs. on N side Bremer Creek.
WALTON's surveys. Wit: SAML. JORDAN, ARCHELAUS MITCHELL, CHAS. CARD.
SUSANNAH, wife of CAWTHON.

Page 40 11 May 1758 STEPHEN HERD to ABRAHAM HERD, his son - love - 100
acres N side of 348 acres adj. JAS. DILLON, DAVID BARRET(?).

Page 41 2 May 1758 GEO. HUNT ALLEN to AMBROSE HUDGINS for ₺50, 400
acres Hatcher's Creek, head branches adj. THOS. TURPIN, GLOVER's
road; Horn Qtr. road. Wit: WM. SUBLET, GEO. RADFORD, JAS. MACK GLASSON.

Page 42 11 May 1758 WM. JOHNS to WM. LOW for ₺100, 400 acres both sides
Willis Creek adj. DANL. LOW, JNO. SANDERS, JNO. COOK.

Page 43 10 May 1758 ROBT. DONWOODY to DAVID CRAWFORD for ₺8, 74 acres
at foot of Blew(sic) mts. on head of 2 branches of Rockfish adj.
both.

Page 45 11 May 1758 RICH. PERKINS, Cumberland Co., to WM. BRADSHAW for
₺20, 200 acres both sides Cunningham Creek adj. PATRICK NAPIER.
Wit: WM. OGLESBY, HARDEN PERKINS, JNO. PETER. SUSANNAH, wife of PERKINS.

Page 46 3 Mar 1758 JNO. BYBE SR. to GEO. ROBINSON, merchant, for ₺5,
900 acres both sides Ballinger Creek where BYBE lives, adj. DANL.
KING, WM. BARNET, JNO. BARNET; also named slaves, stock, furniture and
about ₺50 of pewter. Deed of trust. Wit: HENRY MARTIN, GUY SMITH, WM.
COLEARD(?).

Page 47 11 May 1758 WM. PYRON (LYRON?, could by TRYON) and wife ANN of
Lunenberg to ARTHURNATIAS FEARS, for ₺40, 300 acres N side
Rivanna and both sides Ballinger Creek adj. NATHL. KING, JNO. LONG, JNO.
MARTIN, widow Hickman. Part of 400 acres pat. to THOS. HARBOUR 1 Aug 1734.

Page 48 11 May 1758 RICH. PETER to MATTHIAS AYRES for ₺8-15, 100 acres
pat. to DANL. REYNOLDS 1 Dec 1748, S side Fluvanna, adj. MICHL.
THOMAS.

Page 49 24 Feb 1758 ROBT. AYRES, planter, to DAVID CRAWFORD SR. for
₺20, 95 acres S branches Stoney Creek of Rockfish near Blue Mts.
pat. to AYRES-no date. Wit: BENJ. CLARK, NATHL. BARNET, SAML. DOCKE, DAV-
ID CRAWFORD JR., SUSANNAH & NATHAN CRAWFORD.

Page 51 25 Mar 1758 TARRY BRADLEY to ROBT. HASTIE of Pr. Edward Co.,
for ₺100, several slaves and a horse. 4 slaves. Wit: WM.
HOWARD, JNO. WIMBISH, ALLAN PARKER.

Page 51 19 May 1758 JOSEPH EADES (EDDES) to sons THOS. & JNO. EDDES -
love - 150 acres Toteer Creek adj. Rev. WM. STITH dec'd; equal
division. Wit: JNO. PETER, A. EDDES, HANNAH PETER.

Page 52   8 Jun 1758 BISHOP TONEY to JOS. CABELL for Ł45, 99 acres S side
          Fluvanna pat. 1 Apr 1754 adj. BENJ. MIMS, Grassey Patch Creek.

Page 53   3 Jun 1758 BISHOP TONEY to FRANCIS BAKER for 5 sh., 150 acres
          S side James. SARAH, wife of TONEY signed. Wit: DANL. JONES,
MARY F. JONES, ELIZ. RAY, NATHL. GILBERT (GILBATT?). 1 yr. lease

Page 54   4 Jun 1758 BISHOP TONEY & wife SARAH to FRANCIS BAKER - ref. to
          lease above - Ł40. Wit: As above.

Page 55   7 Aug 1758 JNO. REID to JNO. LOVING for Ł21-10, 100 acres
          Verdiman's Thoroughfare, adj. WM. WRIGHT, HARMER & King Co.
Wit: MATT. JORDAN, SAML. JORDAN, JNO. COBBS.

Page 56   7 Apr 1758 CHAS. LEWIS & wife MARY of Goochland Co., JAMES
          LEWIS & wife ELIZ. to FRANCIS JERDONE, Louisa merchant - CHAS.
owns 475 acres and intends to provide for his son, JAMES LEWIS - 20 sh.
paid by JERDONE with consent of JAMES LEWIS and L000 paid to JAMES. Tract
on Ivey Creek pat. to MICHL. HOLLAND, Hanover, 15 Mar 1744, and by him sold
to CHAS. LEWIS 24 Jul 1745. Adj. TERREL, LEWIS, THOS. MOORMAN, JAS.
FIDDLER. Wit: JNO. COBBS, JOS. HADEN, JNO. BRYANT.

Page 59   1 Jan 1757 JNO. SOUTHERN to second son, JAMES SOUTHERN (someone
          seems to have tampered with document and added "11" for whatever
that means) gift of 300 acres part of 325 acres bought from WM. WEBB.
Where WM. FALWELL formerly lived - 25 acres to be laid off at lower end of
where JOHN lives.

Page 60   1 Jan 1755 (perhaps the tamperer was trying to put 1755, but
          one above seems to be 1757 - others are 1755) JNO. SOUTHERN to
his third son, SAML. SOUTHERN; gift of 260 acres both sides Glover's road
adj. WM.WEBB, THOS. MARTIN, WM. WOODSON.

Page 60   1 Jan 1755 JNO. SOUTHERN to eldest son, WM. SOUTHERN, gift of
          100 acres, part of where JOHN lives - joins 45 acres bought from
JNO. FERN; tobacco warehouse.

Page 61   21 Jun 1758 WM. CABELL JR. to CALEB WORLEY, late of Pennsylvania
          for Ł50, 250 acres Beaver Creek, branches; E side and joining
Tobacco Row Mt...part of 2700 acres pat. adj. grantor, Smith Mt. Wit: JAS.
& JACOB SMITH, JNO. HIX.

Page 62   10 Aug 1758 GUY SMITH to WM. HOOPER for Ł20, 350 acres both
          sides S branches Hardware.

Page 63   14 Sep 1758 SAML. TALIAFERRO to ZACHARIAH TALIAFERRO of Caroline
          Co. for Ł22, 400 acres both sides Buck Island Creek of Rivanna
and both sides MARTIN KING's road, adj. MARK LIFELY. Wit: WM. CRUTCHFIELD,
CHAS. COBBS, WM. PEARCE.

Page 65   13 Sep 1758 ALEX. PARISH to WM. SPEARS for Ł60, 100 acres
          Cariot(?) Creek branches; N side Rivanna, adj. CHAS. LYNCH. Wit:
BENJ. SNEED, JOS. LAWRENCE, ROGER THOMPSON.

Page 66   4 Jan 1758 WM. SHELTON, planter, to AUGUSTINE SHEPHERD & wife
          SARAH, Hanover Co. - love of SHELTON for daughter, SARAH, and
his son-in-law, AUGUSTINE SHEPHERD. 100 acres Great Byrd branches adj.
ABRAHAM VENABLE. Wit: ELIZ. BAILEY, HUGH LEWIS VENABLE & MARY VENABLE.

Page 67   26 Aug 1758 ROBT. HARRIS, Fredericksville Parish, Albemarle, to
          son-in-law, JNO. RODES - love - several slaves. Wit: MATT. HARRIS,
JOEL TERRELL, JR., DAVID LEWIS, ANDREW WALLACE.

Page 67   23 Aug 1758 BRYANT DOLAIN to EDWD. GIBSON for Ł100, 450 acres -
          2 pats. S. side Slate River - Glover's Creek, adj. JNO. GLOVER,
SAML. GLOVER, then mention of 50 acres. Wit: JAS. HILL, HENRY SCRUGG,
WM. GIBSON. ELIZ., wife of DOLAIN.

Page 69   14 Aug 1758 ALEX. PARRISH & JOHN HENDERSON JR. to SAMUEL HEN-
          DERSON, Louisa, for Ł25, 200 acres N side N Rivanna and both

sides of Carrotte Creek. Wit: BENJ. SNEED, JNO. MORRIS JR.

Page 70   14 Sep 1758 MARY KING, widow of ROBT. KING of Halifax Co. to
          JNO. COCK, for Ł15, 290 acres - sold by husband to JNO. COCK in
lifetime - both sides Little Buffaloe - her dower, branch of Willis. Wit:
GIDEON MARR, J. MOORE(?), WM. HUDGINS.

Page 70   9 Nov 1758 JEA(?) ATKINS to HUGH MORRIS for Ł40, 400 acres,
          pat. 10 Sep 1755 - ROBT. DAVIS' Mill Creek, adj. NATHL. DAVIS,
N side Fluvanna. Wit: PETERFIELD TRENT, RICH. MURREY, JNO. TULER, JNO.
MURREY.

Page 70   8 Nov 1758 DAVID LEWIS & wife REBECCA to RICH. WOOD for Ł20,
          tract of Ivy Creek adj. SAML. ARNOLD, ROBT. DAVIS, WM. WOODS.

Page 73   8 Nov 1758 JNO. HODNETT to ISHAM RICHARDSON for Ł124, 408 acres
          S fork Willis, adj. RICH. RANDOLPH, JNO. GANNAWAY, ALEX. TRENT.

Page 74   9 Nov 1758 THOS. BOAZ SR. to THOS. BOAZ JR., Lunenberg - his
          son - love - 100 acres N side Appomattox adj. Mallery Creek.

Page 75   1 Nov 1758 EDWD DAY, Lunenberg, to WM. BUG for Ł20, 206 acres
          adj. JNO. DOUGLAS, part of pat. of ABRAHAM CHILDERS of 800 acres,
13 Sep 1753. Wit: SAML. JORDAN, JNO. HOWARD, ADRIAN ANGLIN, WM. CHAMBERS.

Page 76   9 Nov 1758 JNO. LEAK to RICH. RANDOLPH, Henrico, Ł15, 123 acres
          adj. CHRISTOPHER ARMSTRONG. Wit: MICHL. THOMAS, JNO. HANCOCK,
JACOB WEBB.

Page 78   10 Jan 175-- ALEX. PARRISH to PETER JOHNSON for Ł10, 250 acres N
          side Rivanna; both sides Spradling Spring Branch adj. ANTHONY
POUNCEY. Wit: BENJ. SNEED, JNO. DAWSON, SAML. HENDERSON.

Page 79   27 Dec 1758 WM. LEE, yeoman, & wife SARAH, to ROGER KILPATRICK,
          245 acres pat. 12 Jan 1746 on Hardway branches adj. MILDRED
MERIWETHER, THOS. FITZPATRICK. Wit: GEO. BLENE, THOS. MAXWELL, JNO.
MAXWELL, JAS. MAXWELL, JAS. DOUGLAS.

Page 81   27 Jan 1759 SAML. BELL of Orange N.C., to JNO. MILLER, Ł60, 260
          acres Rockfish near Blue Mts. adj. grantor; JNO. SMALL. Wit:
JNO. REID, ROBT. MILLER, THOS. MILLER, ALEX. REID.

Page 83   25 Aug 1758 WM. CABELL JR. to EDWD. WEIR for Ł50, 400 acres
          Puppy Creek branches, part of 2700 acres pat. 6 Dec 1753, adj.
Late Capt. RICH. TALIAFERRO, JNO. WATKINS, Tobacco Row Mt. Wit: DAVID
WOODROOF, HENRY KEY, and ?

Page 84   31 Oct 1758 ADAM GOUDILOCK to THOS. STOCKTON, York Co. Penn.,
          for Ł31, 400 acres Yellow Mts. br. adj. THOS. SHEELDS, Col. JNO.
CHISWELL. Wit: GEO. BERRY, CHAS. LAMBERT, JNO. BUSTER.

Page 86   27 Dec 1758 BEZALEEL MAXWELL to his son JNO. MAXWELL - love -
          100 acres W end of tract bought from CHAS. LEWIS, Goochland,
Senr. (sic) Adj. grantor; GEO. DOUGLAS, GEO. BLENE. Wit: ROGER KILPATRICK,
THOS. MAXWELL, JAS. MAXWELL, JAS. DOUGLAS.

Page 87   21 Sep 1758 JANE BALDWIN to daughter, DORETHET ATKINS, a slave
          Tony. Wit: THOS. TINDALL, BENJ. TINDALL.

Page 87   9 Nov 1758 WM. NOWLIN to JNO. NOWLIN - full satisfaction - 200
          acres lower side of my plantation; both sides Arthur's Creek.
Wit: W. CHAMBERS, THOS. BLAKEY, ISAIAH BURTON, JNO. GOODWIN.

Page 88   8 Nov 1758 THOS. LANKFORD from DAVIS STOCKTON - receipt for all
          debts due. Wit: ADAM GOUDILOCK, SAML. STOCKTON. Rec. 8 Mar 1759.

Page 88   8 Mar 1759 JOS. TATE, Roan Co. NC, to JNO. HADEN, Goochland,
          for Ł80, 400 acres, E of the Byrd, adj. JNO. CLARK, Elk Run fork,
RICH. ADAMS. Also 400 acres on Elk Run branches adj. RICH. ADAMS, EDMD.
LILLEY, ARTHUR HOPKINS. Wit: TANDY HOLMAN, ARCHELAUS MITCHELL, GIDEON MARR.
ALICE, wife of JOS. TATE.

Page 90   8 Mar 1759   GEO. DUNCAN & wife ANNE to RICH. PERKINS, Cumberland
Co., for L150, 200 acres both sides Hardware adj. JNO. STEVENS.
Pat. to HUGH MORRIS 13 Jun 1743. Wit: JACOB OGLESBY, WM. OGLESBY, JESSE
ATTKISSON.

Page 91   8 Feb 1759   JAS. SMITH, planter, to AARON HIGGINBOTHAM, blacksmith, for L100, 200 acres "where he lives", both sides Buffaloe
near Blue Mts. adj. JACOB SMITH, bought from JNO. THRASHER who had pat. 1
Feb 1738. Wit: JACOB & PHILIP SMITH, JNO. HICKS.

Page 93   4 Dec 1758   SAML. TALIAFERRO to JNO. BURRIS for L4, 225 acres
pat. 16 Aug 1756, adj. MARTIN DAWSON; Secretary's line. Wit:
JNO. HENDERSON JR., SUSANNAH HENDERSON, CHAS. MOREMAN.

Page 94   16 Dec 1758   DAVID LEWIS to JOEL TERRIL, son of JOEL TERRIL,
dec'd, Hanover.   Pat. of 2 tracts of 3000 acres, Moore's Creek,
branches, and Meador Creek - 2 pats. to LEWIS & JOEL TERRIL, dec'd. 1)
2300 acres 2) 700 acres.   DAVID LEWIS gave bond 4 Jun 1736 to JOEL TERRIL
to release 1600 acres.   TERRIL died before deed made, but left will and
gave to JOEL TERRIL Jr.   700 acres on Meador, 5 sh. Wit: HENRY CARTER,
ALEX. MACKEY JR., PRUDENCE LEWIS.

Page 95   10 May 1759   GEO. CARRINGTON, Cumberland Co., to DENNIS McCOR-
MICK, 5 sh., 55 acres adj. S by Bear Garden Creek; WALTER KING,
DAVID DOUGLAS, THOS. MOSS. Part of pat. of 2520 acres, 5 Sep 1749.

Page 96   12 Feb 1759   GEO. CARRINGTON, Cumberland Co., to CHAS. REYNOLDS,
for L22, 150 acres S side Randolph Creek adj. ISAAC BERRYMAN;
grantor; WALTER KING. Pat. as above. Wit: ISAAC BERRYMAN, SAML. HAMELTON,
NICHL. MORRIS, MAJOR BOLLING, TUCKER WOODSON, JNO. PALMORE.

Page 97   9 May 1759   GEO. CARRINGTON, Cumberland Co., to WM. MILLER, 5 sh,
227 acres Harris Creek branches, adj. GRAHAM. 1 yr. lease; 1
pepper corn on Lady Day next.

Page 98   10 May 1759   GEO. CARRINGTON, Cumb. Co., to WM. MILLER for L18,
tract above.

Page 100   7 May 1759   JOHN JOSLIN to JAS. EVINS(EVANS) consideration -
marriage contract - 195 acres Elk Island Creek branches, adj.
his own lines, pat. 22 Nov 1755. Wit: WM. CABELL JR., JAS. NEVIL, THOS.
WRIGHT.

Page 101   1 May 1759   JNO. BOSTICK SR. to VOLENTINE HATCHER for L30, 200
acres, part of where BOSTICK lives, adj. head of Little Willis
branch, WM. JOHNS, JOHN BOSTICK JR.

Page 102   23 Jan 1759   ABRAHAM VENABLE, Louisa, to daughter, ELIZ., wife
of JOSHIAH MORTON, Cumb. Parish, Lunenberg - love - both sides
Byrd Creek br., Great Creek or Tom's Creek, 510 acres adj. WM. MARTIN,
WM. BANKS. Wit: JNO. HARVIE, JNO. HENDERSON JR., HUGH LEWIS VENABLE, WM.
& JAS. VENABLE.

Page 103   23 Jan 1759   ABRAHAM VENABLE, Louisa Co., to daughter, ANN KING,
wife of PHILLIP KING, Cumb. Co., - love - Byrd Creek branches
adj. KENT, EBENEZER ADAMS dec'd.   460 acres adj. where HUGH LEWIS VENABLE
lives; Lewis Creek; his line. Wit: as above.

Page 105   24 Mar 1759   GEO. STOVALL SR., Bedford, to GEO. STOVALL JR., for
L20, 240 acres Stovall Creek, N side Fulvanna, adj. COL. MAYO,
COL. JNO. BOLLING. Wit: ELLIOT LACY, DAVID MATLOCK, MARY BECKHAM, JOS.
CREWS.

Page 107   23 Feb 1759   JNO. BURNS JR. to WM. ROSS for L36, 394 acres between Rockfish and Hicory Creek adj. JAS. LEWIS, JNO. BURNS, WM.
BURNS. Wit: NICHL. LYON, JACOB TYREE, JNO. LYON, JNO. COTTRELL.

Page 108   10 May 1759   WM. SALLE JR. to JAS. SUBLET for L26, 300 acres
Joshua Creek adj. where Turpin's road crosseth the creek, Lick
Branch. Wit: ADRAIN ANGLIN, WM. CHAMBERS, BRIANT REALY.

Page 109   11 May 1759   BRIANT REALY to PHILLIP HUCKER for Ł25, 50 acres
          Doble Trap; br. of Boaling Creek adj. JAS. PALMER, THOS.
CHRISTIAN, ADCOCK.   Wit: THOS. BLAKEY, WM. WALKER, ADRIAN ANGLIN.

Page 110   10 May 1759   HENRY THOMAS, Tillotson Parish, to THOS. ROBINSON
          for Ł20, 172 acres Rock Island Creek, S of Fluvanna, adj. EDWD.
THOMAS.   Wit: JNO. & WM. THOMAS, JNO. FROVEMEN.

Page 112   8 May 1759   DAVID WOODROOF SR., planter, to DAVID WOODROOF JR.
          love - 200 acres; part of 332 acres adj. grantor. Wit: DANL.
BURFORD, JAS. DANIEL, JNO. POWELL.

Page 113   1 May 1759   DANL. BURFORD to his son, JNO. - love - where JNO.
          lives - E side Harris Creek, 194 acres; part of 600 acres bought
from Col. GEO. CARRINGTON.

Page 114   10 Oct 1758   DAVID CHRISTIAN to JNO. COCKE for Ł30, 200 acres
          both sides Buffaloe, branch of Willis. Devised to me by father
in will. Adj. grantee; PAT. O'BRYAN. Wit: ALEX. TRENT, HENRY SCRUGGS,
PAT. O'BRYAN, BENJ. COLVARD, ISAAC CHRISTIAN.

Page 116   13 Apr 1759   JAMES SUDDETH to WM. SUDDETH for Ł20, 135 acres
          Hardware branches adj. CHAS. BLANY, ABRAHAM VENABLE. Pat. 10
Mar 1756.   PATIENCE, wife of JAMES SUDDETH.

Page 118   9 Feb 1759   THOS. FITZPATRICK to WM. HAMNER for Ł200, 497 acres
          Hardaway branches. Wit: WM. LEE, WM. LIFELY, GANALION BALEY,
HUGH DONATY.

Page 120   10 May 1759   JNO. CANNON to JOHN BATES, eldest son of ISAAC
          BATES 5 (sic) 250 acres S side Fluvanna adj. ABRAHAM CHILDERS,
JNO. PRIOR; grantor. Pat. of 1700 acres to WM. CANNON & 250 acres is part.
ELIZ. BATES, widow of ISAAC, has dower rights.

Page 121   12 Feb 1759   GEO. CARRINGTON, Cumb. Co. to NICHL. MORRIS for
          Ł15, 100 acres Randolph Creek branches, part of 2520 acres pat.
5 Sep 1749, adj. JEDIDIAH & JONATHAN PULLING; grantor;, ORLANDO HUGHES.
Wit: ISAAC BERRYMAN, TUCKER WOODSON, C. REYNOLDS, MAJOR BOLLING.

Page 123   11 May 1759   BOLIN CLARK, Bedford Co., to CHAS. MOORMAN, Louisa
          Co., for Ł125, 400 acres Totier Creek branches adj. MAJOR BOLLING,
CHAS. LYNCH.   Wit: PETER FIELD TRENT, JNO. HARDWICK.

Page 124   13 June 1759   WM. SHELTON & wife PATIENCE, planter, to PHILLIP
          KING, Cumberland Co., for Ł180, 349 acres Burd Creek branches
adj. ABRAHAM VENABLE, RICHARD ADAMS, EBENEZER ADAMS, dec'd. Wit: WM. WOOD,
HUGH LEWIS VENABLE, WM. VENABLE.

Page 126   12 June 1759   JAS. SANDERS to JAS. MEREDITH, for Ł37, 350 acres
          adj. THOS. GIBSON, WM. PERKINS, MEREDITH Creek.

Page 127   23 Feb 1759   WM. MOORE JR. to BENJ. MADDOX, Goochland, planter,
          for Ł40, 133 Acres Ballinger's Creek, adj. WITT. Wit: TARLTON
WOODS JR., BENJ. WEST, WM. MADDOX.

Page 128   14 Jun 1759   PETER BAYSE, Hallifax, to WM. GILLIAM for Ł70, 400
acres Pedlar Branches.   SARAH, wife of BAYSE.

Page 129   12 Jun 1759   Col. CHAS. LEWIS SR., Goochland, to GEO. DOUGLAS,
pat. of 400 acres Hickory Creek branches, for Ł30. Wit: JAS. DOUGLAS, WM.
MAXWELL, JOHN ADKINS, MICHL. SMITH.

Page 131   12 Jun 1759   CHAS. LEWIS SR., Goochland, to GEO. DOUGLAS for Ł4,
          400 acres pat. 6 Jul 1741. Rich Cove. adj. grantor. Wit: as above.

Page 134   10 Jun 1759   JNO. BURFORD, Planter, to THOS. GILLENWATERS, plant-
          er, for Ł13, 100 acres Harris Creek branches adj. GEO. McDANIEL.

Page 135   3 May 1759   JAS. MARTIN SR. to STEPHEN MARTIN for Ł22, 200 acres
          S side Meriwether branch - where STEPEHN lives. Wit: WM. MARTIN,

OBADIAH, JOHN & DAVID MARTIN; JAS. MARTIN JR., JNO. STAPLES.

Page 136   3 May 1759 JAS. MARTIN SR. to son JNO. MARTIN - love - 310 ac-
            res both sides Hughes' Creek. Wit: DAVID & WM. MARTIN, JAS.
MARTIN JR., JNO. STAPLES.

Page 137   3 May 1759 JAS. MARTIN SR. to son JAS. MARTIN JR. - love - 200
            acres S side Rockfish branches adj. MERIWETHER branch. Wit:
DAVID, WM., OBADIAH & JNO. MARTIN; JNO. STAPLES.

Page 138   3 May 1759 JAS. MARTIN SR. to son OBADIAH MARTIN - love - no
            acres mentioned, both sides Meriwether Branch. Wit: DAVID,
WM., JNO. MARTIN; JAS. MARTIN JR., JNO. STAPLES.

Page 140   3 May 1759 JAS. MARTIN SR. to son WM. MARTIN - love - 200 acres
            both sides Rockfish - where WM. lives. Wit: DAVID, OBADIAH &
JNO. MARTIN; JAMES MARTIN JR.; JNO. STAPLES.

Page 141   3 May 1759 JAS. MARTIN SR. to son DAVID MARTIN - love - 200
            acres S side Rockfish - where DAVID lives. Wit: WM., JNO.,
OBADIAH MARTIN; JAMES MARTIN JR., JNO. STAPLES.

Page 142   1759   THOS. STEVENS alias STEPHENS to WM. OGLESBY for
            Ⴑ300, deed of 27 June 1756, intended to convey 200 acres - mis-
take in deed made it more. Bond to describe it as 200 acres N side Hardware. Wit: ABRAHAM DANIEL, JNO. HOWARD.

Page 143   14 Jun 1759 DAVID GLASS, planter, to WM. SHELTON for Ⴑ37-10,
            275 acres N side Mt., Buck's Elbow, Moreman River; adj. RICH.
BLALOCK. Pat. 7 May 1759. Wit: DAN BURFORD, ARCH WOODS, JNO. McCORD,
ROBT. HARRIS.

Page 145   11 Dec 1758 THOS. STEPHENS to STEPHEN GOLDSBY & wife MARTHA -
            love - 50 acres N side Fluvanna; life estate. Adj. LEOND.
BALLOW; the road. Wit: JNO. PETER, JNO. THOMAS.

Page 147   9 Jun 1759 JNO. RIPLEY to his daughter, SARAH RIPLEY, for 5
            sh., 100 acres where he lives both sides Walton's fork, branch
of Slate. Adj. grantor. Pat. 12 July 1750, also stock and furniture.
Wit: RICH. TAYLOR, ANTHONY DIBRELL, JNO. PEARCY.

Page 148   28 Oct 1758 ELEANOR McWHORTER & JAS. McWHORTER to JOSEPH SMITH
            for Ⴑ20, 237 acres Rockfish. Part of pat. of 16,400 acres of
JNO. CHISWELL, 26 Mar 1739. Wit: JNO. MARTIN, WM. ROBERTSON, RO. McWHORT-
ER, DAVID MARTIN, CHAS. McANALLY.

Page 149   10 July 1759 JULIAS SANDERS & wife JEMIMA to WM. AMOS for Ⴑ40,
            250 acres adj. MW. BURTON, JNO. MORGAN, EDWD. LYON (or LYO?)
CHAMBERLYNE, JNO. ANTHONY, WM. SANDERS. Wit: TANDY HOLMAN, JNO. BRYANT,
JNO. MARTIN.

Page 151   12 Jul 1759 GEO. HILTON to WHITED RYAN (sic, but I have seen
            it as WHITEHEAD RYAN) for Ⴑ45, 400 acres both sides Racoon
Creek pat. 12 Mar 1739, and bought from JNO. BYBE.

Page 152   12 Jul 1759 MATT. JORDAN to JNO. EUBANKS, Orange Co., for Ⴑ100,
            150 acres adj. THOS. SOWEL.

Page 153   12 Jul 1759 THOS. STEPHENS & wife SUSANNAH to GEO. DUNCAN for
            Ⴑ100, 200 acres both sides Hardware adj. WM. OGLESBY. Part of
400 acres pat. to JNO. STEPHENS, father of THOS., 13 Dec 1738. Wit: JNO.
HOWARD, WM. MOON, WM. BIBB.

Page 154   10 Jul 1759 MARVEL STONE, Halifax Co., to JOEL WATKINS, Pr.
            Edward Co., for Ⴑ70, 392 acres Pedlar, adj. Davis' road, Cedar
Creek. Wit: NATHL. HOGGATT, JOEL WALKER, CH. GALLOWAY.

Page 155   1 Jul 1759 MARVIL STONE, Halifax, to WM. JOHNS for Ⴑ45, 400
            acres where STONE formerly lived. Deed of gift from JNO. BOS-
TICK, 8 Jun 1757. Adj. JNO. JENNINGS, Appomattox River. Wit: as above.
LUCY, wife of STONE.

Page 157   29 June 1759   ISHAM RICHARDSON & wife FRANCES to SARAH JOHNSON,
            Louisa Co., for ₺120, 200 acres both sides Little Willis adj.
GANNAWAY.   Part of 400 acres bought form JNO. HODNETT. Wit: JNO. GANNAWAY
JR., JNO. PARMER, RUBIN BOUGHMAN.

Page 158   3 Mar 1759   WM. PERKINS & wife LUCY to DAVID DAVISON for ₺50,
            400 acres adj. ARTHUR McDANIEL. Wit: CHAS. MAY, JNO. BENNING,
WM. WEBB.

Page 159   20 Jun 1759   JACOB EADES to JOHN RAMSEY, clerk, for ₺16-16, 300
            acres bought from WM. SUDARTH, both sides S fork Totier. Adj.
BOLLING CLARK, STITH. Wit: PETERFIELD TRENT, RICH. MURRY SR. & JR.

Page 161   9 Aug 1759   JNO. DUNCAN & wife JANE to RICH. MURREY for ₺35,
            200 acres both sides Hardway adj. THOS. TINDAL. Wit: EDWD.
HUNTER, A. MARTIN, FRANCIS MERIWETHER.

Page 162   26 May 1759   RO. LEWIS, Louisa Co., to CHAS. LEWIS the younger,
            for ₺120, 500 acres Hardway River, adj. tract bought by CHARLES
LEWIS from ROBERT LEWIS. Part of pat. 20 Jul 1738; North Garden. Wit:
SAML. HENDERSON, WM. CARRELL, SAML. TALIAFERRO.

Page 164   9 Aug 1759   WM. MARTIN(G) to PETER MARTING for ₺15, 162 acres
            Ballinger Creek. Signed MARTIN.

Page 165   4 Aug 1759   WM. CARROLL & wife MARY to SUSANNAH CARROLL for ₺15,
            180 acres N side Rivanna, adj. CHAS. LEWIS. Pat. 12 Jul 1750.
Wit: STEWARD CARRELL, JNO. BELL, GEO. TOMSON.

Page 166   9 Aug 1759   JNO. GOODWIN SR. to STEPHEN FORD for ₺25, 300 acres
            both sides Rock Island Creek, part of 400 acres pat. to MOSES
RAY 15 Dec 1749. MARY, wife of JOHN GOODWIN.

Page 168   11 May 1758   DAVID BELL & wife JUDITH, 1 - FRANCIS JERDON,
            Louisa, 2, merchant - JAS. LEWIS, 3 Bell owns 535 acres and owes
SAML. RICHARDS et al assignees of GEO. BUCKHANNON & WM. HAMILTON, London
merchants. Put lien of tract, 19 Sep 1752, to JERDONE & NINIAN BORG(?).
JERDONE agreed to convey to JAS. LEWIS 20 sh. and -- a sold by JAMES LEWIS
to FRANCIS JERDONE - sells 1535 acres in Albemarle & Cumberland both sides
Randolph Creek; bought from ISAAC BATES 16 Aug 1751, and rec. in Cumb.
Wit: JNO. FIELD, SR. & JR.; JNO. SPENCER. Page 170, 16 May 1759, order to
quiz JUDITH to SAML. JORDAN, JNO. COBBS, & JNO. CANNON. Done, 18th, by
JORDAN & CANNON.

Page 170   13 Sep 1759   SAML. HOPKINS to ARTHUR HOPKINS SR. for ₺200, 350
            acres adj. Dog(?) Pouit(?)

Page 172   12 Sep 1759   JNO. LOCKHART to DAVID LEWIS for ₺60, 250 acres
            Ivy Creek branches adj. DAVID LOCKHART, WM. WOODS. Wit: JNO.
STATHAM, CLAUDIUS BUSTER, JNO. BUSTER. MARGARET, wife of LOCKHART.

Page 173   4 Aug 1759   ALEX. MONTGOMERY, Orange Co. N.C. to RO. BARNET for
            ₺40, 260 acres Rockfish near Blue Mts. adj. JNO. WRIGHT, WM.
MONTGOMERY, JNO. SMALL. Pat. of 11,140 acres to JNO. CHISWELL and this
tract to ALEX MONTGOMERY 25 Apr 1745. Wit: JOS. BARNET, WM. & JOHN
MONTGOMERY.

Page 175   11 Apr 1759   PETER BONDURANT of Cumberland Co. to ANTHONY AGEE
            for ₺10, 200 acres Green Creek branches. Wit: CHAS.MAY, STEPHEN
FORD, MARTIN BINION.

Page 176   12 Sep 1759   JAS. LYLE, Chesterfield merchant and ALEX. McCAUL,
            Henrico merchant, to JAS. DILLARD - JAS. CHRISTIAN, dec'd.,
late of Albemarle, owned 200 acres N side Fulvanna and also Buffaloe
Island. Put in deed of trust 6 Aug 1756, to RICH. OSWALD & Co., London
merchants. Sold to LYLE & MCCAUL, ₺350 paid by DILLARD for said tract.
Page 178 - 13 Sep 1759, LYLE & McCAUL & JNO. HARVIE, Albemarle attorney,
and SAML. JORDAN bound to DILLARD for above deed.

Page 179   28 May 1759   JNO. BISWELL & wife ELIZ. to HENRY MARTIN for Ł150,
            275 acres both sides Hardware, S fork. adj. MILDRED MERIWETHER,
Jumping Branch, the Falls. Pat. to JNO. HEARD 1 Oct 1747, adn sold to
BISWELL 10 Dec 1748. Wit: GEO. FRANCISCO, JNO. FRANCISCO, THOS. GAY, JAS.
TAYLOR.

Page 181   13 Sep 1759   JAS. LYLE & ALEX. McCAUL - see p.176 - TO JAMES
            DILLARD to defend title - to JNO. HARVIE & SAML. JORDAN.

Page 182   13 Sep 1759   ISHAM DAVIS to CHAS. ELLIS for Ł10, 230 acres N
            side Pedlar adj. mouth of Cedar Creek. Wit: JNO. PETER, JOHN
DUNCAN, JNO. LOVING.

Page 183   8 Nov 1759   WM. CABELL SR. to THOS. DICKERSON for Ł45, 145 acres
            adj. JNO. HARRIS, Indian Creek, Piney River branches. Wit: CHAS.
MAY, ABRAHAM HEARD, ALEX. PATTON.

Page 185   9 Jun 1759   ABRAHAM CHILDERS JR. to ARCH. INGRAM, GEO. KIPPEN
            & Co., Glasgow merchants, for Ł34-117½, 300 acres S side Fulvan-
na. Deed of trust. Wit: SAML. JORDAN, RICH. MURREY, PETERFIELD TRENT.

Page 187   19 May 1759   JNO. SHARP & wife KATHERINE, to WARHAM EASLY for
            Ł175, 400 acres both sides Slate branches; Great Creek. Pat.
20 Aug 1745. Wit: ADRIAN ANGLIN, SAML. JORDAN, JNO. NICHOLAS.

Page 189   9 Aug 1759   DAVID COWAN & wife JANE, planter, to JNO. COWAN
            for Ł10, 268 acres Mitchum River adj. HENRY CARR, WM. WALLACE.
Wit: JOHN ANDERSON, JAS. COWAN, NICHL. WALLACE.

Page 191   8 Aug 1759   WM. WEBB to CHAS. TONEY for Ł20, 200 acres Randolph
            Creek branches and Bargain Creek. Adj. JAS. MOSS, GEO. CARRING-
TON, JNO. STEPHENSON. Part of pat. of WENTWORTH WEBB, dec'd., 12 Jan 1746.
Part belonging to ABRAHAM WEBB, dec'd. Wit: CHAS. MAY, WM. OGLESBY.

Page 192   1 Oct 1759   SARAH RIPLEY to JNO. BALLOW for Ł10-10, 150 acres
            adj. Ripley's Creek, N branch Walton's fork, except 100 acres
which "was gave to JUDITH RIPLEY(RIPPLY), daughter of RICH. RIPLEY - brother of SARAH RIPLEY. Lines of 100 acres, mouth of a branch into N side
Walton's fork, upper part of pat. to JNO. RIPLEY, father of SARAH, 20 May
1749, and by him "gave to daughter, JUDITH" Wit: JNO. THOMAS (2), JNO.
GOODWIN.

Page 194   14 Aug 1759   Order to quiz SARAH COCK, wife of JAS. COCK,
            Henrico, as to deed 15 May 1750, to BENJ. WOODSON - 400 acres.
WOODSON, 5 Apr 1759, sold to NOEL BURTON. Done, 22 Oct 1759, by WM. &
JOS. LEWIS.

Page 195   11 Oct 1755 JNO. DAUGHERTY, planter, to PATRICK NOWLIN, Planter,
            for Ł30, 122 acres S side Rivanna and small branch of Bisket
Run. Adj. JOS. ANTHONY, HUGH DAUGHERTY. Wit: CHAS. LAMBERT, JNO. GAY,
HUGH DAUGHERTY.

Page 197   22 Nov 1759   JNO. PAYNE, Goochland, to JNO. KIRBY for Ł25, 2
            tracts in fork of James. 1) Both sides Bremo Creek, 138 acres,
pat 20 Aug 1758. 2) Both sides Bremo, adj. NOBLE LADD, 320 acres pat.
20 Jun 1749. Wit: PHILIP WALKER, BARNET OWEN, HAWKINS KIRBY.

Page 199   13 Dec 1759 WM. BABER to WARHAM EASLEY - consideratin: EASLEY
     is to cancel and deliver a bond of Ł100 by WM. BABER to JNO. SHARP
who assigned it to EASLEY. Tract both sides Great Creek of Slate - 200
acres, pat. to WM. PHILPS, 16 Aug 1756, and by him devised to BABER, adj.
JNO. SHARP.

Page 201   13 Dec 1759   PATRICK NOWLIN, planter, to MICHL. DAUGHERTY for
            Ł40, 122 acres S side Rivanna and small branch of Bisket Run,
adj. JOS. ANTHONY, HUGH DAUGHERTY. Wit: MICHL. THOMAS, CHAS. LAMBERT,
LEONARD PHILLIPS.

Page 203   13 Dec 1759   ISHAM DAVIS & wife ELIZ. to ASHCRAFT ROACH for
            Ł20, 200 acres Wilderness Swamp adj. JNO. DAVIS. Wit: JAS.NEVIL.

Page 205   13 Dec 1759 THOS. SMITH & wife SARAH to JNO. TOOLEY for Ł10,
            350 acres pat. 20 Mar 1759, on Pedlar, adj. WM. MILLS, Maple
Creek, EDWD. WATTS Jr.

Page 206   28 May 1759 WM. HOOPER to ROBT. & JAS. DONALD & Co., 350 acres
            where HOOPER lives; deed of trust. Wit: MARY FRY, RO. SAUNDERS,
HENRY FRY.

Page 207   13 Dec 1759 HENRY BEARD, planter, to son EDWD BEARD - love -
            400 acres. adj. Col. BOLLING, (JNO.); ALEX. STINSON. Wit:
HARDIMAN & JNO. BEARD.

Page 208   8 Aug 1759 BENJ. SNEED to JNO. FORSIE, Louisa, for Ł55, 200
            acres Beaver Dam fork, branch of Meechum; per pat., adj. BENJ.
WHEELER. Wit: RICH. TIMBERLAKE, JNO. LOBBAN, WM. TIMBERLAKE.

Page 210   14 Feb 1760 WM. CABELL JR. to ROBT. WHITTEN for Ł120, 400 acres
            Beaver Dreek branches and E side Tobacco Row Mt. - Cabell's
Grove - part of pat. of 2700 acres 6 Dec 1753, adj. BENJ. STINNETT, HENRY
CHILDERS.

Page 211   14 Feb 1760 WM. CABELL JR. to JEREMIAH WHITTEN for Ł50, 400
            acres Beaver Creek branches; E side Tobacco Row Mts., part of
pat. above, adj. CALEB WOODEY, RO. WHITTEN.

Page 212   31 Jan 1760 JNO. THORNTON, Province of Georgia, Districk of
            Augusta, to JNO. BELL, Orange Co., for Ł170, 400 acres S side
Rockfish. Wit: WM.HARRIS, LEONARD PHILLIPS, JAS. BROWN, CHAS. MARTIN,
HENRY ROBERTS, ZACH. PHILLIPS.

Page 213   31 Oct 1757 JNO. LOW JR. to BENJ. ARNOLD for Ł135, 250 acres
            both sides Willis River. 40 acres of it bought from JNO. CHILD-
ERS; 200 acres bought from DANL. JOHNSON, where LOW lives; adj. JOHN CHILD-
ERS, NATHL. JEFFERIES, DANL. JOHNSON; grantor; JNO. COCK(COOCK). Wit: WM.
JOHNS, ALLEN PARKER, JOS. EVANS.

Page 215   6 Nov 1759 WM. JOHNS to ROBT. HASTIE, Pr. Edward Co., for Ł150,
            530 acres where JNO FISHER lives, adj. JNO. MOSSUM(?). Wit:
HEN DAWSON, I LE NEVE, JNO. FISHER.

Page 216   8 Apr 1760 WM. FOCKNER & wife PRISCILLA to WM. TERRELL LEWIS
            for Ł20, 132 acres pat 10 Sep 1754; branches of Moore's Creek.
Adj. JAS. WARREN JR., JOHN HARRISON, DAVID REESE.

Page 218   18 Dec 1759 WM. MEGGINSON to WM. PATTESON for Ł60, both sides
            David's Creek adj. JAS. FREELAND, JAMES FINLEY. Wit: THOS.
BEARD, JNO. PATTERSON, MACE FREELAND.

Page 219   10 Apr 1760 JOS. CABELL to JAS. MEREDITH for Ł100, 450 acres
            David Creek branches, part of pat. of 900 acres Sep 1759;adj.
grantor.

Page 220   10 Apr 1760 HENRY MARTIN to HARDIN BURNLEY, Hanover, planter,
            for Ł60, 290 acres, pat. to HENRY MARTIN, late of Albemarle,
10 Mar 1756. Adj. HUDSON, LYNCH, now BURNLEY.

Page 222   3 Apr 1760 JOS. CABELL to GREGORY MATTHEWS for Ł85, 1) 400 ac-
            res Davis Creek adj. LEE HARRIS, DAVID MONTGOMERY, COL. JNO.
CHISWELL. 2) 190 acres on Horseshew(sic) Mt. adj. JNO. HUNTER, WM. BURNS.
Wit: GEO. WILSON, JAMES MEDDICRAFT, ARTHUR HOPKINS, JNO. DAILEY.

Page 224   10 Apr 1760 MATT. TUCKER to JER. WADE for Ł35, 378 acres Hard-
            way branches adj. grantor; WM. MATLOCK, JAS. SHEPPARD, Court-
house road; CHAS. BOND. Pat., no date. Wit: CORNL. THOMAS, WM. GOLDSMITH,
PEARCE WADE.

Page 225   9 Dec 1759 JAS. DEFOE to WM. DANL. FITZ for Ł15, 146 acres;
            spur of the mt. near Hannah's Gap where DEFOE lives, adj.
MICAJAH CLARK. Wit: BENJ. SNEED, RO. & MICAJAH CLARK.

Page 226   13 Mar 1760 FRANCIS MERIWETHER to EDWD. MOSLEY for Ł13, 166 acres E branches of Taylor Creek of Rockfish adj. ARHCIBALD WOODS, FRANCIS ATHRINGTON.

Page 227　8 May 1760　DAVID LEWIS JR. to JNO. COFFEY JR. for Ł45, 90 acres head branches of Michum River and Ivy Creek adj. BENJ. TAYLOR, Grantor; JNO. LOCKHART. Part of pat. of JAS. WOODS and sold to THOS. LOCK-HART. REBECCA. wife of DAVID LEWIS.

Page 228　6 May 1760　DAVID LEWIS JR. & wife REBECCA to BENJ. TAYLOR for Ł20, 100 acres Ivy Creek branches adn Hardware, adj. Col. RO. LEWIS. Part of tract above.

Page 229　8 May 1760　HENRY WEAKFIELD SR., planter, to his son HENRY JR., love and Ł10, 91 acres, part of pat. of JNO. DOBBINS, adj. JAS. BELL, grantor, WM. WAKEFIELD. Wit: CHAS. LAMBERT, WM. STOCKTON, DAVIS STOCKTON. (I do not think that this is the same WAKEFIELD line of Kentucky with which I am acquainted. MARCUS WAKEFIELD, son of JAS. HEADY WAKEFIELD, married my mother's sister, IRENE BAILEY. I have five cousins by this union. I believe that this Wakefield family came into Kentucky from Pennsylvania.)

Page 231　8 May 1760　HENRY WEAKFIELD SR. to son WM. WEAKFIELD-love- Ł10, 76 acres, part of tract above, adj. HENRY JR., grantee. Wit: as above.

Page 232　8 May 1760　HENRY WEAKFIELD SR. to son JNO. WEAKFIELD, planter, love and Ł10, 94 acres pat. as above. Wit: as above.

Page 233　8 May 1760　WM. MOON & wife ELIZ. to JNO LEWIS for Ł35, 100 ac-res both sides Hardware. Part of 1000 acres bought from HARDIN BURNLEY, adj. grantor.

Page 234　8 May 1760　GEO. CARRINGTON, Cumberland Co., to PIERCE WADE, for Ł24-15, 413 acres Harris Creek branches, part of pat. 20 June 1753, of 6750 acres.

Page 235　28 Feb 1760　ELIZ. HIGGINS, New Kent, to son-in-law CHAS. BOLTEN JR., slave, Fanny. Wit: JNO. STRANGE, WM. APPLEBURY, WM. TUCKER.

Page 236　5 May 1760　WM. WEBB to WM. BOND for Ł60, 300 acres SE of tract of 400 acres pat. 30 July 1742, adj. JNO. FLEMING, JNO. SOUTH-ERN, grantor. Wit: WM. HOWARD, JNO. CANNON, BUCKLEY WALKER, JAS. BROWN. RACHEL, wife of WM. WEBB.

Page 237　29 Mar 1760　WM. BATTERSBY to RICH. MURRY for Ł150, 150 acres S side of Fluvanna adj. THOS. BALLOW, AMOS LADD. Also small tract of 6 acres. Wit: PETERFIELD TRENT, JNO. WATKINS, RICH. MURREY, JR. ELIZ., wife of WM. BATTERSBY.

Page 238　11 May 1759　DUNCAN SMITH & wife MARGARET to ROBT BABER of Bedford Co. Ł500 bond - SMITH & wife to release dower to tract on S side of Fluvanna, bought by ROBT. BABER dec'd. from JNO. PHELPS - heirs - where we live - on Dec 24th next. Wit: THOS. BABER, BUCKLEY WALKER, BETTY WALKER. Done, 14 Nov 1759. Wit: WM. WEBB, WM. WALKER.

Page 239　1 May 1760　JNO. BEAZLEY & wife BRIDGETT to SHELTON RAILEY for Ł46, 100 acres on Troublesome, branch of Slate. Part of pat. of SACKERVALL WHITEBREAD - now that of JOS. FUQUA. Adj. WM. LAX(TAX?), JNO. HUBBARD. Wit: CHAS. GARRETT, WM. FUQUA, THOS. GARRETT.

Page 240　22 Oct 1759　JNO. REA to HENRY MARTIN for Ł60, 200 acres S side Rivanna, adj. MARTIN KING's ford; grantee; ARTHUS OSBURN, dec'd, RO. ADDAMS. Wit: GUY SMITH, WM. CRUTCHFIELD, WM. PAYNE, JNO. SHEATS.

Page 242　28 Nov 1759　JNO. GRILLS to SOLLOMAN NELSON for Ł30, 200 acres Moore's creek, part of pat. adj. Dr.(?) ALLEGRE. Wit: JOEL TERRELL, HENRY CARTER, JNO. FRANCISCO.

Page 244　19 Dec 1759　DAVID LEWIS to JOEL TERRELL, son of JOEL, dec'd., Hanover - 3000 acres on Moore's Creek branches; Meador Creek.

2 pats. to DAVID LEWIS and JOEL TERRELL, dec'd. 1) 2300 acres 2) 700 acres.
LEWIS made bond 4 Jun 1736, to make deed to TERRELL, dec'd, to 1600 acres.
TERRELL died before deed was made and left will and devised 1100 acres to
sons JOEL & WM., 500 acres remainder. Adj. lines of JNO. DABNEY, FRANCIS
JOURDAN, road to Wood's Gap, TERRELL, WM. TERRELL LEWIS, grantee. 5 sh.
for 500 acres. Wit: WM. TERRELL LEWIS, JOEL LEWIS, HENRY CARTER.

Page 246   18 Oct 1759 THOS. PHELPS to THOS. TURPIN, Cumberland Co., for
            consideration of 200 acres - 75 acres head and both sides Brydle
Creek adj. grantor. Wit: DAVID & CHAS. PATTESON, THOS. SNELSON, RICH.
CHEATWOOD.

Page 247   8 May 1760 WM. CABELL JR. to HENRY CHILDERS for Ł27-12, 76
            acres Huff Creek branches and E side Tobacco Row Mts., part of
pat. of 2700 acres, 6 Dec 1753. Adj. BENJ. STINNETT.

Page 249   8 May 1760 HENRY MARTIN to JACOB MOON for Ł160, 275 acres both
            sides Hardway, S fork adj. MILDRED MERIWETHER, Jumping Branch.

Page 251   15 Dec 1759 JOS. THOMPSON to GEO. ROBINSON, merchant, for Ł147,
            5 slaves & stock. Wit: DAVID BYBEE, DAVID SHEPHERD, GILES
LETCHER.

Page 252   3 Nov 1759 JNO. GRILLS to JNO. SPENCER for Ł50, 390 acres
            Moore's Creek branches adj. JOEL TERRELL, DAVID LEWIS. Wit:
JOEL TERRELL, HENRY CARTER, JNO. FRANCISCO.

Page 254   12 Jun 1760 JNO. KING & wife HANNAH to JNO. STRANGE for Ł40,
150 acres both sides Ballenger's Creek adj. JNO. BYBEE, JNO. MARTIN. Part
of a pat. Wit: JNO. BRYANT, STEPHEN SEAY, THOS. DEVARD.

Page 256   12 June 1760 WM. CABELL JR. to RICH. PETER for Ł15, 150 acres,
            part of 450 acres pat. 23 May 1760; Harris creek branches be-
tween Bear and Cedar mts. adj. grantor, JNO. PETERS.

Page 257   12 Jun 1760 WM. CABELL JR. to WM. PETER for Ł15, 150 acres,
            part of tract above.

Page 259   12 Jun 1760 WM. CABELL JR. to JNO. PETER, JR. for Ł15, 150
            acres, part of above tract.

Page 261   7 Jun 1760 RO. MOSELEY, Cumberland, to DAVID LESEUR, King. Wm.
            County, for Ł68, 400 acres Joshua Creek, branches of Slate. Pat.
3 Nov 1750 to DANL. FORD, adj. MATTHIAS AYRES, WM. SALLEY. Wit: THOS.
SMITH, JNO. CHASTAIN JR., JANE CHASTAIN.

Page 263   20 Mar 1760 EDWD. HAMBLETON, Pr. Edwd. Co., to GIDEON MARTIN
            for 5 sh., 100 acres, where MARTIN lives; adj. MORRIS LANGHORN,
JOS. PRICE, JOBE MARTIN. Wit: ORSTON MARTIN, PHILIP BOND.

Page 265   8 Jul 1760 JNO. GRILLS to CHAS. WHITLOCK for Ł20, 319 acres
            Moore's Creek branches. Adj. JNO. BURRAS, DAVID LEWIS. Pat. to
GRILLS & sold to WHITLOCK. Wit: JOEL TERRELL, HENRY CARTER, JNO. FRANCISCO.

Page 267   8 Jun 1760 ROBT. SPOONER BAILEY to JNO. BAILEY for Ł25, 200
            acres head branches Rock Island Creek. Wit: THOS. BLAKEY,
ADRIAN ANGLIN, NATHL. BURTON.

Page 268   7 May 1760 JNO. HODNAT & wife LUCY to HIGGINSON BARKSDALE, of
            Cumberland Co., for Ł335, 820 acres Willis River adj. ALEX.
STINSON, JNO. SANDERS, ALEX. TRENT, HODNAT's spring branch. Wit: ALEX.
STINSON, BLIZARD MAGRUDER.

Page 270   12 Jun 1760 THEODORICK WEBB and wife MARY to HENRY SMITH for
            Ł50, 392 acres Bear Garden Creek. Wit: W. MEGGINSON, JOS.
CABELL, BUCKLEY WALKER.

Page 272   12 Jun 1760 WM. WALTON to CHAS. COBBS for 20 sh., 400 acres
            Slate river branches adj. Arthur's Creek.

Page 274   12 Jun 1760 WM. WALTON to ABSALOM JORDAN for 20 sh., 220 acres
            Slate River.

Page 275   2 Jun 1760 THOS. GRIGS YARBROUGH, Goochland, to GEO. THOMPSON,
            Louisa, son of JOS. THOMPSON dec'd., late of Albemarle, for Ŀ45,
400 acres N fork Cunningham Creek adj. MARTIN DUNCAN, Horse Penn branch.
Wit: PAT. NAPIER, JAS. THOMPSON, ASHFORD NAPIER, THOS. NAPIER, RENE & PAT.
WOODSON.

Page 278   8 May 1760 GIDEON THOMAS to CHAS. GATES for Ŀ25, 400 acres
            Walton's fork, Arthur's Creek, adj. WM. NOLAND, THOS. PATTESON,
WM. CHAMBERS. Wit: WM. GATES, HENRY RAKES, JOS. BENNING.

Page 280   8 Nov 1759 WM. NEW to JNO. KEY for Ŀ30, 400 acres both sides
            middle fork Spring Garden Creek, fork of James, adj. BENJ. &
RICH. COCKE. Wit: JNO. & RICH. FARRAR, GUY SMITH.

Page 282   14 Jan 1760 JAS. CHITWOOD to WM. DUIGUID & JNO. FEARN, church
            wardens, Tillotson Parish, Albemarle, for Ŀ40, 200 acres; tract
lateley recovered by county court chancery decree vs. THOS. MACKDANIEL,
infant, and eldest son of ARTHUS MACKDANIEL, dec'd. - THOS. BY JNO. NICHOLS,
guardian, on equal date made deed to CHITWOOD. Wit: GIDEON MARR, JNO.
NICHOLAS, JNO. CABELL, WARHAM EASLEY. See p.290 - McDANIEL here.

Page 283   7 Jun 1760 JNO. PLEASANTS, JR. Henrico, to JAS. BROWN for Ŀ14,
            150 acres Rockfish branches, pat. to PLEASANTS & ROBT. ABRAHAM
14 Feb 1756. Wit: THOS. MAXWELL, BESALEEL MAXWELL, JAS. MAXWELL.

Page 284   10 Jul 1769 RICH. WOODS & wife MARGARET, merchant, to WM.
            FORBES, schoolmaster, for Ŀ25, 175 acres head of Ivey Creek, adj.
SAML. ARNOLD, RO. DAY, WM. WOODS.

Page 287   26 May 1758 JNO. MONTGOMERY to ALEX. REID for Ŀ30, 100 acres
            Rockfish branches. Wit: DAVID & THOS. MONTGOMERY, WM. WRIGHT.

Page 289   10 July 1760 THOS. BAILEY to MOSES LOWREY for Ŀ8, 100 acres,
            part of pat. of 379 acres, 16 Aug 1756; Great Bird Creek adj.
THOS. THOMASON.

Page 290   14 Jan 1760 THOS. McDANIEL, infant, by JNO. NICHOLAS, guardian,
            to JAS. CHITWOOD - ARTHUR McDANIEL, father of THOS., in life
agreed to sell CHITWOOD 200 acres, part of 400 acres pat. both sides Ripley
Creek, branch of Slate. CHITWOOD sued and got judgment to say Ŀ12-7 -where
CHITWOOD lives; S side of 400 acres. Wit: JNO. CABELL, WARHAM EASLEY, G.
MARR.   Seems to EASLEY in first deed P.282.

Page 291   15 Jul 1760 JNO. HUBBARD, Orange Co, N.C., to WM. FUQUA for
            Ŀ35, 400 acres Turpin Creek adj. JOS. FUQUA, MATT. AGEE. Pat.
20 Aug 1757, adj. SACKERVALD WHITEBREAD. Wit: JNO. BEAZLEY, THOS. GARRETT,
JAS. TAYLOR.

Page 293   1 Aug 1760 RO. LEWIS SR., Louisa, to son RO. LEWIS Jr., Louisa,
            love - several slaves named and 1500 acres. Wit: NICHL. MERIWE-
THER, NICHL. LEWIS, EDMD. COBBS, DAVID MERIWETHER.

Page 294   14 Aug 1760 WM. McCORD to sister, AGNES McCORD - love and 5 sh.
            174 acres both sides Moorman River near Blue Ledge. Pat. to
JAS. McCORD, dec'd.

Page 296   9 Aug 1760 SAML. MAN, exr. of will of THOS. MAN, dec'd - appro-
            bation of ALEX. REID, exr. in trust and SARAH MAN, widow of
THOS., to JNO. REID for Ŀ43-5, 400 acres Rockfish branches adj. Col. JOHN
CHISWELL, JAS. WOODS. Pat. to THOS. MAN dec'd. 8 Aug 1746. Wit: DAVID
CRAWFORD, JAS. LACKEY, JAS. MORRISON, JOS. BARNETT.

Page 299   9 Aug 1760 JOS. BARNET to DAVID REID, Lancaster Co. Penn, for
            Ŀ32, 200 acres Rockfish. Wit: DAVID CRAWFORD, JNO. REID, JAS.
LACKEY, JAS. MORRISON.

Page 300   4 Aug 1760 JNO. HARRIS to THOS. WHITE, planter, for Ŀ500, bond

to make deed for 300 acres; part of 400 acres where HARRIS lives, adj.
GILBERT HAYES, Indian Creek, RO. ROSE. Wit: GILBERT HAY, JAS. MURREY, WM.
BICKNELL.

Page 301   24 Jun 1760 PAUL CHILES, Halivax Co. to ALEX. TRENT, Cumberland
            Co., for Ь100, Appomattox branches adj. THOS. SANDERS, grantor.
Pat. 10 Sep 1755. Wit: CHAS. MAY, BENJ. COLVARD, DANL. BATES, ARTHUR MOSE-
LEY, GEORGE ROBERTSON, RANE CHASTAIN.

Page 303   5 Sep 1759 DAVID LEWIS & wife MARY, WM. TERRELL & wife FRANCES,
            Louisa, planter; JOEL TERRELL to JNO. DABNEY, Hanover, planter,
for Ь100, 400 acres S side road to Woods' Gap; Ivey and Moore's Creek
branches, adj. WM. TERRELL LEWIS, DAVID LEWIS, FRANCIS JORDONE. Part of
2300 acres pat. 3 Oct 1734 to JOEL TERRELL & DAVID LEWIS, one of the
parties. Wit: WM. TERRELL LEWIS, JOEL LEWIS, HENRY CARTER.

Page 306   7 May 1760 Order to quiz FRANCES TERRELL, wife of WM. TERRELL,
            Louisa, as to above deed - directed to CHAS. BARRETT, THOS.
PAULETT & THOS. B. SMITH by JNO. NICHOLAS, Ablemarle Clerk. Done, 4 July
1760, by PAULETT & THOS. BALLARD SMITH.

Page 307   14 Aug 1760 SAML. SOUTHERN to TUCKER WOODSON - blank sum -
            260 acres both sides GLOVER's road, adj. NOEL BURTON, WM. WEBB,
JNO. CANNON, EDWD. DANIELS, WM. WOODSON, STEPHEN HUGHES - also signed by
JNO. SOUTHERN. Wit: JAS. & JOS. SOUTHERN.

Page 309   9 Jun 1760 JNO. LEAK to Col. RICH. RANDOLPH, Henrico, for Ь15,
            123 acres Green Creek adj. CHRISTOPHER ARMSTRONG, pat. 20 Aug
1748. Wit: JNO. HANCOCK, MICHL. THOMAS, SAML. HANCOCK.

Page 311   10 Aug 1760 BENJ. WOODSON to BENJ. WOODSON JR., Goochland, for
            Ь20, 200 acres, fork of James - known as Raccoon - pat. of 400
acres adj. WOODSON, Little Raccoon, WM. CREASY, GEO. HILTON. Wit: RENE,
PAT. & TRA WOODSON, RO. NAPIER, JAS. BAUGHAN.

Page 313   10 Sep 1760 BENJ. WOODSON to RENE WOODSON for Ь20, 400 acres,
            fork of James, Cary & Little Breamor Creeks. Wit: BENJ. WOODSON
JR., PAT. WOODSON, TRA WOODSON, RO. NAPIER, JAS. BAUGHON.

Page 314   3 Oct 1751 RENE CHASTAIN to JNO. GIVODAN for Ь160, several
            slaves. Wit: JOS. ADCOCK, HENRY RICE, JNO. ADCOCK.

Page 315   8 Sep 1760 THOS. LEE to PETER LEE for Ь30, 200 acres S side
            Fish Pond Creek of Appomattox, adj. HENRY CHILES. Wit: PETER
FORE, THOS. & ADDAM SANDERS.

Page 316   8 Apr 1760 WM. LAX, Halifax, to CHAS. GARRETT for Ь75, 400 ac-
            res both sides Troublesom Creek adj. SACKERVAL WHITEBREAD. Pat.
to JNO. MAXEY 25 Sep 1746, and bought by LAX. Wit: JNO. BENNING, GIDEON
THOMAS, JAS. BENNING.

Page 317   10 Nov 1760 CHAS. LEWIS, Goochland,to JNO. LEWIS, Goochland,
            for Ь600, 1850 acres both sides Tye, adj. Lewis Creek, Taylor
Creek. Wit: VAL. WOOD, ANDREW HARRISON, WM. HARRISON, THOS. GORDON.

Page 319   1 Sep 1760 JOS. CABELL to THOS. PATTESON, Planter, for Ь100,
            450 acres Head branches David's Creek near Slate river Mt...
Part of 900 acres pat. 20 Sep 1759, adj. grantor, Megginson's road, RO.
WALTON, JAS. MEREDITH.

Page 320   11 Sep 1760 JNO. HENDERSON to JOS. THOMPSON for Ь80, 400 acres
            N side Cunningham Creek. Wit: JNO. HENDERSON JR., WM. HARRISON,
JNO. WATKINS.

Page 322   25 Feb 1760 THOS. TURPIN SR., Cumberland, to JNO. BONDURANT SR.
            consideration of 125 acres - 400 acres both sides Turpin Creek,
Slate river - where BONDURANT lives. Wit: G. MARR, WM. H. ALLEN, PETERFIELD
TRENT, ALEX. TRENT. Order to quiz MARY, wife of TURPIN, to Cumberland
J.P.'s, done by GEO. CARRINGTON & THOS. PROSSER.

Page 324   11 Sep 1760   ORLANDO HUGHES, Cumb. Co., to GEO. WALTON, Cumb.Co.,
            for L60, 400 acres, part of 8 acres (sic) pat. 1757, adj. JNO.
PALMER, grantor, TONKHART PULLEN, ALEX. TRENT, DRURY SCRUGGS. Wit: BENJ.
WILSON, THOS. TABB, ROBT. BROWN, JACOB WINFREY JR.

Page 325   15 Oct 1760   THOS. HARBOUR, Halifax, to LEANDER HUGHES, Cumber-
            land, for L45, 400 acres N branches Horsley. Wit: MOORE LUMPKIN,
POWELL HUGHES, JNO. PIGG, SAML. VAWTER.

Page 326   15 Nov 1760   LANDER HUGHES, Cumb. Co., to DAVID CRAWFORD JR. for
L65, 400 acres N branches Horsley.

Page 327   13 Nov 1760   GEO. OLIVER to NICHL. COMAR for L7, 200 acres both
            sides middle fork of Slate, adj. SAML. STEPHENS.

Page 328   6 Nov 1760   WM. WALLACE to WM. WOODS & DAVID GASS, for L28, 300
            acres Micham Creek branches adj. DAVID MILLS, JNO. LAWSON. Pat.
16 Aug 1756. Wit: MICHL. WOODS, JAS. WALLACE, MICHL. WALLACE.

Page 330   13 Nov 1760   JNO. LEAK to OBADIAH MOORE for L17, 150 acres Hard-
            river, adj. THOS. FITZPATRICK, MILDRED MERIWETHER.   Ann, wife
of JNO. LEAK.

Page 332   13 Nov 1760   DAVID BARNETT to PETERFIELD TRENT for L12-10, 60
            acres where EDWD. COFFEY lives, Hardway branches adj. JACOB
CLEVELAND, NATHAN BARNETT. Wit: JNO. HENDERSON JR., MATT. JORDAN, ABRAHAM
CHILDERS.

Page 333   12 Jun 1760   JNO. GANNAWAY SR. to JR., love - 900 acres where
            SR. lives - all slaves - in my will. Wit: J LE NEVE, JNO.
SIMMONS, JNO. PEAK, GEO. PEAKE.

Page 335   13 Nov 1760   JNO. GANNAWAY JR. to SR., for L1000 - makes bond
            for SR. to use tract and slaves during lifetime. Wit: as above.

Page 335   12 Jun 1760   JNO. GANNAWAY ST. to JNO. PEAK SR. for L5, where
            PEAK lives, both sides Great Creek of Appomattox - 200 acres,
part of 400 acres pat. 10 Sep 1755. Wit: JNO. SIMMONS, GEO. PEAK, JNO.
GANNAWAY JR., JNO. PEAK JR.

Page 337   12 Nov 1760   JNO. GANNAWAY SR. to THEODORICK CARTER, son of JNO.
            CARTER, Henrico - love for THEODORICK CARTER, his grandson,
180 acres N fork Mayo Creek adj. JNO. PEAK, AUSTIN MARTIN, HENRY PERKINS.
MARY, wife of GANNAWAY. Wit: JNO. SIMMONS, GEO. & JNO. PEAK.

Page 338   13 Nov 1760   MATT. DAVIS to GILBERT HAY for L10, 140 acres,
            pat. 10 Sep 1755, S branch Piney.

Page 339   13 Nov 1760   JNO. DOUGLAS & wife MARY to JNO. LADD, planter, for
            L100, 400 acres both sides Rockfish, adj. WM. MATLOCK, RO.
WALTON, ABRAHAM CHILDERS.

Page 342   9 Oct 1760   PEARCE WADE to JNO. PARKS SR., for L110, 390 acres
            pat. 1 Jun 1760; Thrasher's Creek. MARY wife of WADE.

Page 343   27 Aug 1759   JNO. WINGFIELD & wife MARY; NICHL. JOHNSTON & wife
            ELIZ.; RO. WALTON & wife, REBECCA; RICH. HOLLAND & wife SARAH,
JOSEPH LEWIS & wife ANNE, and CHRISTOPHER HUDSON to JNO. HUDSON, 7 slaves
of estate of CHAS. HUDSON, dec'd, Hanover Co. - Assigned by CHAS. HUDSON
to be given to JNO. HUDSON, but by some oversight left out of will and
WM. HUDSON, eldest son, claimed them.   Lawsuit pending for sometime in
General court and finally WM. gave up his pretensions to JNO.   JNO. now
has them, but this deed to prevent any controversies - brotherly love for
JNO. - said slaves. Wit: JNO. GILLUM, PETER GILLUM, ORLANDER JONES. (WM.
seems to have felt that he did enought when he surrendered the slaves for
he does not sign.)

Page 344   12 Jul 1760   WM. STATON to WM. LEAK for L10, 122 acres, part of
            400 acres pat. to JNO. BALLOW 12 Jul 1750.   285 acres of pat.
to STATON from BALLOW. Adj. STATON, BENJ. HOWARD.

Page 346   27 Sep 1760   RICH. TILLIS, Bedford Co., to JNO. GOODWIN for Ł55,
           400 acres N side and adj. Fluvanna, adj. RICH. BURKS, MAJOR GEO.
CARRINGTON, REV. MR. STITH.   Pat. 23 May, last. Wit: HENRY THOMAS, JNO.
DANIEL, JAS. BRUMMIT.

Page 349   23 Oct 1760   JNO. WARREN to CHAS. CHRISTIAN, Goochland Co, for
           Ł16, 400 acres Rocky Creek of Buffalo adj. grantee, Col. BRAX-
TON. Wit: GEO. ROBERTSON, WM. LEAK, JAS. TAYLOR, THOS. BALLOW.

Page 349   23 Oct 1760   DAVID PATTESON to THOS. TURPIN, Cumb. Co. - consi-
           deration of 100 acres - 100 acres both sides branch of Elk
Creek where TURPIN's plantation is, adj. grantor. Wit: WM. DUIGUIS, JNO.
STAPLES, CHAS. PATTESON.

Page 351   12 Nov 1760   JNO. PEAK, SR. to JR., for Ł5, 100 acres N side
           Appomattox, adj. grantor. Wit: JNO. GANNAWAY JR., GEO. PEAK,
JNO. SIMMONS.

Page 352   23 Oct 1760   THOS. TURPIN, Cumb. Co., to DAVID PATTESON - con-
           sideration of 1-- acres - 100 acres Elk and Bridle Creeks adj.
grantee; near COLEMAN's road. Wit: WM. DUIGUID, CHAS. PATTESON, JNO.
STAPLES.

Page 353   12 Mar 1761   LEONARD PHILLIPS to GEO. BLANE for Ł30, 210 acres
           head of Green Creek adj. WM. HARRIS, side of a mt., top of a
mt. JOANNA, wife of PHILLIPS.

DEED BOOK 3 OF ALBEMARLE COUNTY, VA.

This abstract is dedicated to my third grandchild, Elizabeth Pettyjohn
Davis. She was born on September 2, 1970, at two in the afternoon at
Virginia Baptist Hospital in Lynchburg, Virginia, to grace the home of her
parents. Her father is my third son, Thurman Blanton Davis, and her
mother is Mary Gayle Pettyjohn. Elizabeth is my second granddaughter and
joins Margaret Ann and John Fulton Davis, my other grandchildren, who belong to John Fulton Davis and Joy Eddings.

Elizabeth is a descendant of several of the families which are found in
Albemarle before Amherst was to become a county in 1761. She has two
Watts lines, Higginbotham, Old, and Wheeler ancestors, so it seems fitting
that this should be dedicated to her.

Mary Gayle is the daughter of Thomas Watts Pettyjohn and Mary Hesson
Pettyjohn, Monroe, Virginia.

                              Bailey Fulton David
                              Amherst, Virginia
                              1971

Page 1   15 Dec 1760   THOS., JNO. & WM. JONES to JNO. HOY for Ł100, 340
           acres adj. FARSON(?). Wit: JNO. BOOKER HOY, ADDAM SANDERS, ASAPH
WALKER. (I am not using counties of these folk unless they lived in some
other county other than Albemarle. If no county is named, it is evident
that they were in Albemarle.)

Page 2   11 Feb 1761   BEZALEEL MAXWELL SR. & wife REBECCA to THOS. MAX-
           WELL for Ł10, -pat. 25 July 1741 to CHAS LEWIS and sold to
MAXWELL; 400 acres Rich Cove, Ł10, 60 acres, adj. grantee.

Page 3   10 Feb 1761   JNO. PERKINS, Goochland, to JOEL PERKINS for Ł50,
           200 acres Great Byrd Creek adj. WM. CREWS(?). Wit: DAVID &
STEPHEN NOWLIN, ABRAHAM PERKINS.

Page 4   12 Feb 1761   CHAS. BOND to son NATHAN BOND for Ł50, 100 acres N
           side Hardware adj. Shepherd Creek, RICH. DAMERON. Wit: JACOB
OGLESBY, SAML. RAY, HARDIN PERKINS, GEO. DUNCAN.

Page 5   13 Nov 1760 WM. GOUGE to BENJ. SNEED for Ŀ25, 350 acres-2 tracts
          near Rook's Ford; 250 acres adj. JNO. MORRIS, PAUL ABNEY, WM.
RANDOLPH, Mt. Falls Creek. 100 acres adj. CHAS. LYNN, WM. RANDOLPH. Wit:
WM. CARRALL, JNO. LOBBAN, SAMUEL HENDERSON.

Page 6   27 Dec 1760 CHAS. SMITH to RICH. LAWRANCE for Ŀ5, 200 acres N
          fork Hickory Creek adj. WM. MORRISON. Wit: THOS. HENDERSON, WM.
TILLER, JNO. LAWRENCE.

Page 7   8 Feb 1760 THOS. FITZPATRICK to DAVID COOK, for Ŀ62-8, 172 acres
          pat. in 1756, adj. his own line. Wit: JOS. FITZPATRICK, THOS.
BICKNELL, WM. FIELDER. (Note: many times this phrase, "his own" appears,
and I do not know which party is meant.)

Page 9   12 Mar 1761 LEONARD PHILLIPS to PETER FARRAR, for Ŀ25, 236 acres
          both sides Ivey Creek of Rockfish.

Page 10   12 Mar 1761 LEONARD PHILLIPS to WM. FARRAR for Ŀ25, 200 acres
          both sides Ivey Creek adj. grantor, ELIOT ROBERTS.

Page 11   13 Dec 1760 WM. GILLIUM to NICHL. DAVIS for Ŀ80, 400 acres
          Pedlar, pat. to THOS. WATTS 5 Apr 1748. Wit: MATT. WHITING,
BATHURST SHELTON, CHARLES BARKER, ALEX.. MULLIS(?), MARGARET BERNARD. MARY,
wife of GILLIUM. (Note: we often find NICHOLAS DAVIES named as DAVIS, but
we know that the first spelling is correct. I feel sure that Davis Creek
in present Nelson should really be Davies, for NICHL. owned much land in
area.)

Page 12   12 Mar 1761 CHAS. GARRETT(OTT) to THOS. GARRETT, for Ŀ11, 50
          acres on Troublesom Creek, pat. to Sackerval Whitebread; taken
from pat. to JNO. MAXEY. Wit: NANCY GANAY, SHELTON RILEY, JOS. GENEWAY.

Page 13   8 Dec 1760 WM. SPURLOCK, Goochland, to JNO. WEBB for Ŀ40, 200
          acres both sides Raccoon Creek of Rivanna. Wit: AMOS, GEO. HILTON,
ARTHUR COOPER.

Page 14   - Mar 1761 MATT. AGEE to his son JAMES AGEE, for Ŀ100, 400 acres
          Hubbard's branch, part of 1280 acres pat. 12 May 1759, adj. JNO.
HUBBARD, JAS. FORD. Wit: CHAS. GARRETT, SHELTON RAILE(?), JAS. FORD (2 such)

Page 15   28 Feb 1761 JAS. FORD to ANNE CHASTAIN, 100 acres Slate River
          branch, Pond branch, adj. WM. SOUTHERN, JNO. MAXEY. Wit: CHAS.MAY.

Page 16   11 Mar 1761 JNO. WEBB to NATHAN BARNETT for Ŀ10, 100 acres; half
          of tract bought from WM. SPURLOCK, Raccoon Creek; pat. 12 July
1760. Wit: WM. AMOS, ARTHUR COOPER, JAS. HILTON.

Page 17   12 Mar 1760 SAML. STOCKTON to WM. STOCKTON for Ŀ5, 204 acres S
          fork Meecham River, Stockton Mill Creek, where mill stands.

Page 18   27 Oct 1760 JNO. CHILDRES to his son, ABRAHAM CHILDRES - for
          many good services - 250 acres N branch Willis Creek, Beaver Pond,
adj. JNO. LOW, NATHL. JESSE(?), GIDEON MARR. Wit: JNO. HARRISTON, HENRY
ROLAND, WILLIS CHILDRES.

Page 19   11 Mar 1761 CASTLETON HARPER to ATHANASIUS FEAR for Ŀ35, 160
          acres Hardware Creek adj. THOS. SOWELL. Wit: JOS. DAVENPORT, CHAS.
WINGFIELD, HENRY CARTER.

Page 20   25 Oct 1760 WM. TRIGG, Bedford Co., to THOS. JEFFRIES for Ŀ50,
          400 acres both sides Tongue Quarter Creek, pat. to SACKERVIL
WHITEBREAD 20 Jul 1748. Wit: NATHL. JEFFRIES, AMBROSE HAMON, JULIUS (?)
DAVENPORT.

Page 22   - Jan 1761 JNO. BERNARD Sr., planter, to ABNER WITT for Ŀ75, 100
          acres North River adj. grantee-where BERNARD lives-bought from
JNO. WEBB - Goochland deed. MARY, wife of JNO. BERNARD. Wit: BENJ. MADDOX,
JNO. WITT SR. & JR.

Page 23   11 Feb 1761 ALEX HUNTER, Bedford, to RO. RUTLEDGE, Prince Edward
          Co., for Ŀ15, 275 acres David Creek adj. PHILIP MAYO, JNO.

PATTESON. ELIZ., wife of ALEX. HUNTER.

Page 24   28 Feb 1761 ALEX. HUNTER, Bedford, and wife ELIZ, to ALEX. DAVID-
          son, for Ł20, 344 acres Wolf Creek of Appomattox and both sides
Beard's Road, ajd. JOHN PATTESON. Wit: JAS. LAX, SEBREE(?) LAX, JAS. VEST.

Page 26   12 Mar 1761 ALEX. HUNTER as above and wife to JAS. VEST for Ł9,
          140 acres Bridle Creek adj. PHILIP MAYO; PHELPS(?).

Page 27   28 Feb 1761 ALEX. HUNTER & wife, as above, to NICHOLAS HAYS,
          Bedford, for Ł10, 200 acres on Wolf Creek adj. JOHN PATTESON,
PHILIP MATTHEWS. Wit: ALEX. JAMESON, JAMES VEST, JAMES LAX(TAX?).

Page 28   12 Mar 1761 AARON MACKENZEY, planter, to MARTIN KEY, planter,
          for Ł25, 200 acres adj. JNO. KEYS, HICKMAN & co.; Little Mt.
JEMIMA, wife of AARON MACKENZEY.

Page 30   12 Mar 1761 JAMES COFFEY to JAS. GARLAND for Ł85, 124 acres
          Middle Hardway in North Garden; part of tract bought by JNO.
COFFEY SR. from HUGH BOYLE and by JNO. to JAS. by deed. Wit: CHAS. LAMBERT,
WM. NORVALL, JNO. SMITH. ELIZ., wife of COFFEY.

Page 32   20 Aug 1760 JNO. WRIGHT, Orange, N.C., to THOS. JOPLING for Ł100,
          400 acres N side Rockfish; part of 800 acres bought from Col. JNO
CHISWELL, adj. ALEX. MONTGOMERY, CHISWELL.

Page 33   12 Mar 1761 THEODORICK WEBB to ANTHONY DIBRELL for Ł60, 400 acres
Walton Fork adj. WALTON, WM. WALTON.

Page 34   12 Nov 1760 DAVID WADE to WM. PARKS for Ł75, 180 acres, pat. to
          HOWARD CASH 12 Jul 1750; Thresher's Creek, adj. PEARCE WADE, JNO.
BISSWELL. ELIZ. wife of DAVID WADE. Wit: EDMD. POWELL, THOS. PARKS, JONA-
THAN STAMPER.

Page 36   24 Nov 1760 ROBT. BOWLING, Chesterfield, to SAML. RIDGWAY for
          Ł60, 200 acres mt. creek of Willis. Signed ROBERT BOWLING JR.
Wit: WM. ALLEN, BLIZZARD MAGRUDER, THOS. RIDGWAY.

Page 37   12 Aug 1760 WM. MEGGINSON to JNO. BROTHER for Ł40, 285 acres
          both sides of Bent Creek adj. JAS. FREELAND.

Page 38   11 Mar 1761 JAS. HARRIS & wife MARY to THOS. GRUBBS for Ł10, no
          acres, Moorman river. Wit: JNO. RODES, WM. SHELTON, JNO. McCORD.

Page 40   11 Mar 1761 RICH. BLALOCK, Cumberland Co., Province of Carolina,
          to JNO. RODES for Ł35, 200 acres Moormam River - Hercules Pillar.
Wit: JNO. McCORD SR. & JR., THOS. GRUBBS, WM. SHELTON.

Page 41   10 Mar 1761 RICH. BLALOCK as above to JNO. RODES for Ł35, 200
          acres S side Moorman and Middle Mt. Wit: as above.

Page 42   22 Oct 1760 SAML. TALIAFERRO to GEO. ROBINSON, Merchant, for Ł35,
          slaves named and ages; furniture. Wit: THOS. BALLARD, RO. CLARK,
DAVID SHEPHERD, GILES LETCHER.

Page 43   4 Mar 1761 JAMES CHRISTIAN to JEREMIAH WHITNEY for Ł67, 100 ac-
          res both sides Wreck Island Creek adj. grantor. Pat. 12 Jan 1746.
Wit: WM. DUIGUID, WM. KITCHEN, JNO. EVANS, DAVID ROGERS.

Page 45   4 Mar 1761 Same grantor and grantee as above for Ł67, 147 acres
          on same creek. Pat. 20 Sep 1745. Wit: as above.

Page 46   4 Sep 1760 SUSANNAH CHRISTIAN, widow of JAMES CHRISTIAN - her
          husband owned 200 acres on N side Fulvanna; suit in Henrico -
RICHARD OSWALD & Co., London merchants; JAS. LYLE & ALEX. McCAUL and they
sold to JAMES DILLARD who paid her Ł40 for her dower in 200 acres. Wit:
JNO. COLEMAN SR. & JR., WM. GILLIAM.

Page 47   7 Mar 1761 WM. MONTGOMERY, planter, to MATT. SMALL, weaver, for
          Ł6, 50 acres Rockfish, adj. JNO. SMALL, COL. CHISWELL. Wit: JNO.
REID, JAS. SMALL, JNO. LACKEY, THEOBALD MAIGHAN.

Page 49   27 Dec 1760 JAS. ROBERTSON to REBECCA ROBERTSON, widow of JAMES
          ROBERTSON, dec'd, for Ŀ38, 265 acres Taylor's Creek, branch of
Rockfish. Joins MATT. ROBERTSON. Part of pat. of JNO. CHISWELL, Hanover,
and by him deeded to JAS. ROBERTSON. JAS gave by will to son, JAMES. Wit:
JNO. RIED, JAS. BARNET, JAS. SMALL, THEOBALD MAGHAN.

Page 51   9 Apr 1761 JNO. WADE & wife ELIZ. to WM. TROTTER for Ŀ10, 200
          acres both sides Davis Creek.

Page 52   4 Apr 1761 THOS. JOPLING to DAVID ENICKS for Ŀ20, 400 acres,
          pat. 20 Aug 1760, on head branches Geady and Briery Creeks, adj.
his own line; MARY UPTON, JℕO. SNYDER. Wit: WM. COX, ROBT. JOHNSON, JNO.
PETER.

Page 54   11 Feb 1761 JNO. SCRUGGS to JNO. WEBB & THOS. SCRUGGS for Ŀ17-4
          furniture, etc. Wit: GEO. MILLER, JNO. NEVIL, ISHAM DAVIS.

Page 55   18 Mar 1761 GUY SMITH & ARTHUR HOPKINS to King George - SMITH
          has rec'd from WM. HARRIS & WM. CABELL JR. - co. levy. Wit: SAML.
JORDAN, JAS. NEVIL.

Page 55   18 Mar 1761 JNO. HUNTER to CHARLES MAY for Ŀ20, 200 acres; part
          of where JOHN HUNTER lives S side Slate and both sides Crooked
Creek, adj. WM. RICKLEAR, ridge path, Sheephill branch, HUGH GREE, WM.
BINION. Wit: JNO. FRY, PETER FIELD TRENT, EDWD HUNTER.

Page 57   20 Mar 1761 ARTHUR HOPKINS SR. to SAML. HOPKINS, Lunenberg, for
          Ŀ10, 2,950 acres adj. grantor, WOODY, CUNNINGHAM Creek, GEO.
HILTON, WM. CREASY, GEO. PAYNE, Burks Creek. Pat. - save 800 acres on river.
Wit: JNO. CABELL, ARTHUR HOPKINS JR., GUY SMITH.

Page 59   10 Jun 1761 JAS. WOODS, Amherst farmer, to SAML. WOODS, store-
          keeper, for Ŀ100, 350 acres N side N branch Meecham, adj. THOS.
REID, ROBT. ANDERSON, HENRY KERR, JNO. COWAN, WM. SETTLES. Wit: WM. FORBES,
JNO. DEPRIEST, SPENCER REFFIELD(?).

Page 61   11 Jun 1761 WM. WOOD to his son JNO. WOOD-love- 100 acres Ragged
          Mt. adj. TERRELL. Wit: CHAS. LAMBERT, JAS. GLEN, WM. BARNEY.

Page 62   11 Jun 1761 WM. WOOD, Planter, to RICH. DOLLINS, planter, for
          Ŀ16-13, 100 acres headwaters of Meecham, part of tract bought
from JNO. LEAK, adj. HENRY TERRELL, grantor, COL. JNO. CHISWELL, BENJ.
TAYLOR. Wit: as above.

Page 64   9 May 1761 ABRAHAM CHILDERS to WM. SORROW, Buckingham Co., for
          Ŀ17-10, 200 acres; part of pat. of 400 acres 10 Aug 1759; fork
of James and Spring Garden Creek adj. RICH. COCKE. Wit: DAVID ROSS, BEN
HOWARD.

Page 65   11 Jun 1761 MARTIN DAWSON to JNO. BUNRUS for Ŀ50, 300 acres S
          side branches of Buck Island Creek and Rivanna, adj. JNO. CARTER,
dec'd. Wit: JNO. WATKINS, JNO. COLEMAN, GEO. ANDERSON.

Page 67   11 Jun 1761 BENJ. MADDOX to WM. PEARCE for Ŀ36, 131 acres both
          sides of Cunningham Creek adj. EDWD. MOODY, PAT. NAPIER, JOS.
THOMSON, GILES LETCHER. 50 acres part of pat. of 250 acres of EDWD. MOODY.
Wit: JNO. KEY, JNO. WITT, ROBT. NAPIER. MARY, wife of MADDOX.

Page 68   2 May 1761 GUY SMITH, planter, to WM.BANKS, Goochland, planter,
          for Ŀ140, 375 acres adj. N side Rivanna; ROBT. HORSLEY, dec'd;
RO. ADAMS. Wit: SAML. EMMERSON, WM. WOODY, JNO. ROBERTSON.

Page 70   9 Jul 1761 WM. HARRIS to JNO. THURMOND for Ŀ30, 164 acres head
          of Bear Branch, of Rich Cove Creek. Wit: HENRY MARTIN, HENRY TRENT.

Page 71   8 Jul 1761 WM. BAYLEY to friend, ISAAC CREWS; love - slave boy
          named Dick, and girl, Diley. Wit: GEO. ANDERSON, JACOB WILLIAMSON,
FRANCES ANDERSON.

Page 72   2 Apr 1761 Col. JNO. CHISWELL, Williamsburg, to THOS. SMITH,
          planter, for Ŀ15, 150 acres; branches of Mitcham, adj. HUGH, JNO.

ALLEN, grantor, Little Mt. Wit: CORNELIUS NEVIL, JNO. SMITH, WM. PANNELL.

Page 74   2 Apr 1761 JNO. CHISWELL, as above, to BENJ. DOVE for Ŀ23, 230
           acres both sides fork of Meechem; part of a grant adj. THOS.
HUGHES, grantor, THOS. SMITH. Wit: as above.

Page 76   9 Jul 1761 RICH. MURRY to BENJ. TINDALL for Ŀ35, 200 acres adj.
           Hardaway River, THOS. TINDALL. Pat. 1 Jun 1750. Wit:JNO. WAT-
KINS, ARCHELAUS MITCHELL, JACOB MOON. SARAH, wife of MURRY.

Page 78   21 Dec 1760 Order by JNO. NICHOLAS to Cumberland J.P.'s: GEO.
           CARRINGTON, THOS.TABB, THOMAS PROSSER - as to ORLANDER HUGHES &
wife ELIZ., 11 Sep 1760, to GEO. WALTON for 400 acres. Wife released
rights 23 Feb 1761, to first two.

Page 79   1 May 1761 JNO. WEBB & wife MARTHA, to RICH. MELTON, planter,
           for Ŀ5, 400 acres. Wit: WM. AMOS, THOS. FITZPATRICK.

Page 80   14 Mar 1761 WM. BANKS & wife ELIZ, Goochland, to TURNER RICHARD-
           SON, Hanover, for Ŀ140, 666 acres in Alb. & Goochland, N side
James and branches of Byrd, adj. WM. MARTIN, JNO. KERBY, PETER MASSIE,
Rolling Path, PARRISH, EMMERSON, JNO. WALKER. 200 acres of it bought from
ABRAHAM VENABLE, Louisa, and rec. in Goochland. Rest pat to BANKS 26 Mar
1736, and 20 Aug 1747. Wit: JNO. WINSTON, JR., JNO. NORVELL, WM. NORVELL.

Page 83   4 May 1761 WM. BRYANT to JNO. WEBB for Ŀ20, 85 acres N side
           Fluvanna and E side Bremo Creek adj. Rich. Cove, FRANCES KERBY.
Wit: WM. AMOS, GEORGE HILTON, NATHAN BARNETT.

Page 85   9 Jul 1761 CHAS. TATE, Amherst planter, to JAS. SUDDARTH for Ŀ20,
           109 acres S Hardware, adj. SAML. JORDAN, WM. SUDDARTH.

Page 87   8 Aug 1761 JNO. SHELTON, Goochland Planter, to MOSES LOWRY,
           planter, for Ŀ20, 150 acres N side Byrd Creek adj. mouth of the
Great Creek, EBENEZER ADAMS, RO. RICHARDSON. Wit: JAS. & WM. GEORGE, RICH.
MELTON.

Page 88   13 Aug 1761 WM. WALTON to JAS. HILTON, Buckingham, for Ŀ260, 200
           acres, part of a tract adj. Hardway, Rockfish, James River. HILTON
gets all above Rockfish - 200 acres. Wit: RICH. PERKINS, JNO. MOORE. ELIZ,
wife of WALTON.

Page 91   4 Jul 1761 MARTIN KING to GEO. ROBINSON, merchant, for Ŀ7, stock,
           furniture. Wit: JNO. BYBE JR., DAVID SHEPHERD, GILES LETCHER -
9 months deed of trust.

Page 92   15 Jul 1761 ROWLAND HARSLEY to CHAS. GOODMAN who married my
           daughter, ELIZABETH - a slave, Roger. Wit: JER. BURNETT, MICAJAH
VIA, BOND BURNETT.

Page 93   10 Sep 1761 WM. FORBES, Schoolmaster, and wife MARY to JNO.
           SPENCER for Ŀ26, 175 acres head of Ivy Creek adj. SAML. ARNOLD,
RO. DAY, WM. WOOD. Wit: JOHN BELL, RICH. NALLEY, CHAS. LAMBERT.

Page 94   25 May 1761 JOS. FITZPATRICK, planter, and wife MARY PERIN, to
           JOHN GILLUM for Ŀ92-10, 180 acres and 10 adj. South Garden, adj.
WM. FITZPATRICK, RO. LEWIS, North Garden, HUGH MORRIS, THOS. FITZPATRICK,
JACOB MOON, WM. FITZPATRICK. Pat. to JOS., 1747. Wit: GEO. ANDERSON,
---WOODSON, WM. & JNO. FIELDER.

Page 97   10 Sep 1761 WM. BURTON to BENJAMIN HARRISON for Ŀ35, 400 acres
           fork of James and adj. N side Mt. Missery Creek, JNO. COBBS,
EDWD. PYE CHAMBERLEYNE, BENJ. & RICH. COCK. Wit: ARTHUR HOPKINS JR.,
AUGUSTINE SHEPHERD, MATT. TUCKER.

Page 99   19 May 1761 PATRICK NAPIER to JACOB WILLIAMSON for Ŀ50, 382 acres
           fork of James and N branches Cary Creek adj. BENJ. WOODSON, where
JACOB WILLIAMSON lives. Wit: THOS. NAPIER, ASHFORD NAPIER, RENE WOODSON.

Page 100   10 Apr 1761 RO. LEWIS, Louisa, Gent., to NICHOLAS LEWIS, love &
           5 sh., 11 named slaves. Wit: JNO. LEWIS JR., NICHL. MERIWETHER,

PEACHY R. GILMER.

Page 101   10 Sep 1761 WM. MOORE to NATHAN BARNETT for Ŀ6, 200 acres; part
            400 acres on branches of Cunningham & Raccoon creeks, upper end
on latter creek, adj. CHAS. HULSEY, WM. SPURLOCK.

Page 102   10 Sep 1761 WM. MOORE to WM. BRYANT for Ŀ6, 200 acres adj.
            NATHAN BARNETT; HANDCOCK; ARTHUR HOPKINS.

Page 103   8 Oct 1761 THOS. CAUTHORN to WM. BUGG for Ŀ28, 350 acres W
            branches Bremo Creek, fork of James, adj. JNO. PAYNE, JOS. WAL-
TON, JOS. GOOD, SAML. SHORT. SUSANNAH, wife of CAUTHORN.

Page 104   8 Oct 1761 HENRY MARTIN to WM. MOON for 20 sh., 270 acres both
            sides of S fork Hardware, adj. JACOB MOON, THOS. FITZPATRICK,
Jumping Branch, MILDRED MERIWETHER, JNO. BISWELL, PAUL MICHAUX.

Page 106   8 Oct 1761 STEPHEN HEARD, planter, to JNO. HUDSON for Ŀ5, 47
            acres adj. grantor, ABRAM VENABLE. MARY wife of HEARD.

Page 108   8 Oct 1761 STEPHEN & THOS. HEARD, heirs of ABRAHAM HEARD, to
            JNO. HUDSON for Ŀ255, 348 acres S fork Hardware, adj. VENABLE.
THOS. HEARD is set forth as son of STEPHEN HEARD.

Page 110   12 Oct 1761 JNO. CAMPBELL, Orange Co., N.C., to JAS. GLEN for
            Ŀ36, 150 acres Mitchum River branches, Rich Cove; pat to CAMP-
BELL, adj. HENRY TYREL, JAS. WARREN. Wit: WM. WOOD, JNO. WOOD, MICHL. ?__,
THOS. SMITH.

Page 112   16 Jan 1762 SAML. TALIAFERRO to THOS. GARTH for Ŀ20, 400 acres,
            pat. 16 Aug 1756, adj. THOS. CAUTHORN, HENRY WOODS, Indian Br.,
branch of Buck Island. ANNE, wife of TALIAFERRO.

Page 114   14 Jan 1762 SAML. TALIAFERRO to THOS. GARTH for Ŀ20, 50 acres
            adj. Buck Island, pat. 16 Aug 1756. ANNE, wife of TALIAFERRO.

Page 116   7 Dec 1761 JNO. BISWELL to PETERFIELD TRENT for Ŀ130, 190 acres
            N side Fluvanna; Hudson creek, adj. MICAJAH CLARK. Wit: BENJ.
COLWARD, JNO. BUTTERSWORTH COLWARD, JNO. SWANN.

Page 118   3 Dec 1761 THOS. EVENS to BENJ. DOD WHEELER for Ŀ60, 246 acres
            S branch Moor Creek adj. BEN WHEELER, grantor. MARGARET, wife
of EVENS. Wit: WM. CHEEK, MICAJAH WHEELER, JNO. LANGFORD, ABRAHAM MUSICK.

Page 120   11 Sep 1761 THOS. EVINS SR. to BENJ. DOD WHEELER for Ŀ60, 400
            acres pat. 6 Jul 1741, both sides S fork Moor Creek adj. JNO.
WARREN, BENJ. WHEELER. Wit: JNO. LANGFORD, MICAJAH WHEELER, CHAS. WHITLOCK.
MARGARET, wife of EVINS.

Page 122   11 Sep 1761 WM. BICKNELL, Amherst Co., & wife HANNAH, to JOHN
            LANGFORD SR. for Ŀ25, 204 acres More's Creek branches. Wit:
MICAHAH WHEELER, JAMES TAYLOR, BENJ. DOD WHEELER, SARAH TAYLOR.

Page 124   25 Nov 1761 ROBT. HARRIS to son-in-law WM. DALTON; 2 slaves.
            Wit: MILDRED & THOS. WALKER.

Page 124   12 Jan 1762 SAML. DALTON SR. & wife ANN to son, WILLIAM DALTON;
            love - tract formerly in Louisa, both sides N branch N fork James
above Little Mt., 404 acres adj. Wolf Trap Branch, Jacob's Run; also a
slave to their son, WM. Wit: GEO. MARTIN, ISAAC DAVIS, THOS. BURROWS, JNO.
HENSLEE.

Page 126   12 Nov 1761 JAS. TULER to MARTIN DAWSON for Ŀ4, 125 acres both
            sides of Ballinger's Creek adj. EPPS. Wit: SAML. HANCOCK,
TERISHA TURNER, EDMD. NEW.

Page 128   25 Jun 1761 ROBT. DUNCANSON, Fredericksburg mct. to WM. BROCK-
            MAN, Orange Co., planter, for Ŀ80, 400 acres; bought from RICH.
DURRETT & wife SARAH, Louisa Co. Deed, 22 July 1750; adj. WM. CRADDOCK.
Wit: DAVID WATTS, RO. MARTIN JR., RICH. WILSON, JNO. HAMMACK, THOS. STAPP,
THOS. EASTIN. (Note: this merchant was an ancestor of Catherine "Toddy"

BARRICKMAN who is wife of my brother-in-law, Clarence Ludlow Miller, and she has data on him. Just this morning, March 12, 1971, I went to Va. Baptist Hospital and had prayer with Mrs. Paul Brockman of my Amherst Church. She goes to surgery this afternoon and will be transferred to Lynchburg General. There is a good book written on the Brockman family, and those of Amherst stem from those of Orange, as I recall. I also note name of a David Watts as a witness. I am interested in the Watts line - that of my third son's wife Mary Gayle (N Pettyjohn) for she stems from THOS. WATTS who shows early in Alb. and owned land on Pedlar. His presumed son, CALEB, had wife SUSANNAH - and they had SAML. who married NANCY WILCOX. No luck to date on earlier WATTS & WILCOX - NANCY was dtr. of THOS. WILCOX & wife WINNIFRED---.)

Page 130   8 Dec 1761 JNO. BROCK to GEO. BROCK for L20, 95 acres both sides Great Bremo adj. JNO. PAINE, JOS. WALTON. Wit: CALEB STONE, GEO. BROCK, JEMMIMA LAWHORNE. JUDA, wife of JOHN BROCK. (The BROCK name is profuse in Kentucky.)

Page 131   24 Oct 1761 ALEX. CHISAM, Amherst Co., to GEO. BLANE for L40-10, 100 acres; 22 acres adj.; 122 acres; pat. of 12 May 1759, and deed of 13 Mar 1755. Rich Cove, adj. LEWIS, ALEX. BLANE. Wit: ALEX. BLANE, GEO. BLENE JR (sic), WM. ROSS.

Page 134   11 Mar 1762 proof, but dated ----1761. BENJ. WOODSON to grandson BENJ. FITZPATRICK - love, 200 acres on head of Cary Creek, part of 400 acres which I gave my son, BENJ. WOODSON, JR. JR. gets upper tract on Little Raccoon. Wit: THOS. & JOS. FITZPATRICK, THOS. GAY.

Page 135   19 Oct 1761 NELSON ANDERSON, Hanover Co., to RO. SHARP SR., for L120, 590 acres Plumb Tree branch adj. CHAS. LEWIS, BENJ. WHEELER. Pat. to JNO. CRAWFORD by 2 pats. of 3 Oct 1734(?), and by J.C. to N.A. by deed. Wit: WILLIAM STEPHENS, WM. SHARP JR., JAS. LEEK, CHAS. SNEED.

Page 137   11 Mar 1762, proof. THOS. HENDERSON & wife DORCAS, to WM. MAX-WELL, pat of 15 Jul 1760; 239 acres, head of Hickory Creek, for L40-10, adj. ALEX. PATTEN. Wit: JNO. & JAS. MAXWELL, JAS. DOUGLAS.

Page 139   Proved 11 Mar 1762. GEO. HILTON SR. to WM. AMOS for L30, 98 acres N side S fork Cunningham Creek. Wit: GEO. ANDERSON, RICH. MELTON, CALEB STONE.

Page 141   10 Mar 1762 WM. BURNS, N.C., to JOS. FITZPATRICK for L40, 180 acres head of Ivy Creek, pat. 12 Nov 1761. Wit: JNO. GILLUM, THOS. FITZPATRICK, JNO. GAY, BENJ. FITZPATRICK.

Page 142   11 Mar 1762 WM. BURNS, N.C., to THOS. FITZPATRICK for L5, 75 acres Kirby Creek - made to GEO. BURNS and on his order to WM. BURNS; pat. as above. Wit: as above.

Page 144   11 Mar 1762 WM. BURNS, N.C., to THOS. FITZPATRICK for L12-10, 193 acres, branch of Rich Cove, adj. JNO. BURNS, CHAS. LEWIS. Wit: as above.

Page 145   25 Sep 1761 RO. HARDIN to JAS. GEORGE, Goochland, for L26, 300 acres Bold Branch of Berrenger, N side Rivanna, adj. JNO. ROBIN-SON, JNO. BELLAMY. Part of pat. of 400 acres 12 Jan 1746. BETHSHEBA, wife of R.H. Wit: WM. GEORGE, WM. SOUTHERLAND, PHILLIP JONES, WM. GROOM.

Page 147   23 Nov 1761 NATHAN BOND & wife ELIZ. to GEO. PERRY JR., for L40, 100 acres N side Hardway, ajd. mouth of Shephard Creek, RICH. DAMERON, JAMES SHEPHARD. Wit: JACOB OGLESBY, JESSE MOORE, JNO. MOORE JR.

Page 148   11 Mar 1762 ALEX. FORTUNE, Caroline Co., to SILAS MELTON for L25, 175 acres S branches Hardware adj. JAS. HILL. Wit: WM. AMOS, RICH. MELTON, ALEX. BLAINE. (The MELTON line is of those of Mary Gayle Pettyjohn Davis, but I have done no research on it.)

Page 150   20 Oct 1761 JNO. CREASY to WM. CREASY for L10, 100 acres S fork Raccoon, bought from WM. Wit: PAT., THOS. & RICH. NAPIER.

Page 151   20 Oct 1761 THOS. CREASEY to WM. CREASEY for Ŀ10, 100 acres S
            fork Raccoon, bought from WM. Wit: THOS. & PAT. NAPIER, JNO.
CREASEY.

Page 152   11 Mar 1762 MATT. JORDAN & ABRAHAM CHILDERS, St. Ann Church
            wardens, to WM. BURTON - in division of Louisa and Albemarle -
glebe tract in their hands; Ŀ231-10, glebe tract. Wit: RICH. MURRY, JNO.
HARRELSON, JNO. COTTRELL.

Page 153   12 May 1762. Ref. to deed of 1 Aug 1759(?). RO. LEWIS to son
            RO. of Louisa; love - 10 slaves & 1500 acres. JR. sells to SR.
for 5 sh., slaves and 1500 acres.

Page 155   12 May 1762 RO. LEWIS SR. to JR.; ref. to deed above, 1500 acres
            adj. CAPT. CHAS. LEWIS, Hardware - also slaves - for love.

Page 157   3 May 1762 MARY WINGFIELD, Hanover, to son CHARLES WINGFIELD -
            love - 270 acres where he lives; part of tract given to MARY by
father, CHAS. HUDSON - 540 acres. Called Prospect. Wit: WM. COCK, THOS.
FORTUNE, WM. HITCHCOCK, JR.

Page 158   13 May 1762 CHRISTOPHER HARRIS to SAML. KARR, Augusta, for Ŀ65,
            331 acres both sides S fork Rockey Creek adj. HENRY BUNCH,
MORIAS JONES.

Page 160   19 Nov 1761 JAS. COLEMAN, Gent., Orange Co., to HENRY BARBOR &
            JNO. CARLTON, Orange Co, planters, for Ŀ40, 400 acres bought
from PHILIP WILSON, 14 Mar 1742, pat. to TIMOTHY DALTON, 1 Feb 1738; upper
side Chestnut Mt. adj. WM. CRADOCK - division to be made by grantees by
cited lines. Also line of DOWEL. Wit: JAS. MERIWETHER, AMBROSE COLEMAN,
DAVID FARGESON, JNO. VAUGN, JAS. COLEMAN JR., THOS. JONES.

Page 162   26 Apr 1762 JAS. COLEMAN, Orange, to SAML. SIMPSON, for 5 sh.,
            2 tracts - Fredericksville Parish. 1) 400 acres adj. McKILLIHITT,
W. HENRY, WM. CARR, MAJOR CARR. 2) 200 acres adj. HENRY, JAS. McKAMEY, WM.
CARR. Wit: AMBROSE COLEMAN, THOS. JONES, JAS. COLEMAN JR.

Page 163   26 Apr 1762 JAS. COLEMAN, Orange, to SAML. SIMPSON for Ŀ25, all
            possessions for 1 year in 2 tracts above.

Page 165   13 May 1762 HENRY CRUMPTON, alias MARTIN, to ANDREW HARRISON,
            Goochland, for Ŀ120, 180 acres N fork James, adj. Rivanna - part
of tract under will of JNO. MARTIN, late of New Kent, to wife of CRUMPTON,
and SILVANUS BRYANT - will of 16 Dec 1741, in New Kent.

Page 167   13 May 1762 JOEL TERRELL, JR. & wife ANN, to JNO. SUMTER SR.,
            for Ŀ100, 350 acres adj. JAS. FIDLER, HOWARD CASH, HUGH FRASER,
WILLIAMSON; THOS. MOREMAN.

Page 169   27 Feb 1762 JNO. SYMME, Gent. of Hanover, to THOS. WALKER,
            Louisa, Gent., for Ŀ400, a tract in Albemarle - formerly Hanover,
1650 acres where WALKER lives, adj. Turkey Run Mt. Formerly that of NICHO-
LAS MERIWETHER SR. and to JR. - his grandson, 5 Dec 1734. JR. died intestate and to his only daughter, MILDRED, wife of JNO. SYMME - MILDRED agreed
to deed but died before it was made. She left son, JNO. SYMME, infant, and
JOHN SR., has life estate - when MILDRED's eldest son is 21 - all of her
children - not named. Wit: RO. COBB, HENRY TYLER, JNO. HAWKINS, JNO.
WALKER, J. MOORE, ANDE JOHNSTON.

Page 171   13 May 1762 DAVID THOMPSON, Louisa, to HENRY HARPER for Ŀ40,
            400 acres Moor Creek, Cow Branch, part of 800 acres bought by
JNO. COLES(COTES?) from JOS. ANTHONY, adj. SIMON CLEMONS, THOS. BIBB, JNO.
COTES, DENNIS DOYLE, dec'd.- his Exr. is JAS. DAVIS.

Page 173   3 Apr 1762 RO. HARRIS, planter, to son RO. JR., love - on Blue
            Ridge, Doyle River, pat. of 521 acres 6 Dec 1753. Wit: JAS.
HARRIS, CHRISTOPHER HARRIS, WM. BROWN.

Page 174   3 Apr 1762 BENJ. BROWN, to dtr. LUCRETIA HARRIS; love; slave,
            Moll. Wit: JAS. HARRIS, CHRISTOPHER HARRIS, WM. BROWN.

Page 174   5 Jan 1760 Exrs. of PETER JEFFERSON - JNO. HARVIE, THOS. WALKER,
            JNO. NICHOLAS - at request of widow, JANE - have divided named
slaves by will of PETER. Wit: CHAS. LEWIS JR., J. MOORE, JNO.HENDERSON JR.

Page 175   3 Apr 1762 BENJ. BROWN, planter, to dtr., LUCRETIA HARRIS; love;
            Blue Ridge tract and Doyle's River - where she lives, adj. JNO.
STATHAM, BENJ. THURMAN - 400 acres. Wit: JAS. & CHRISTOPHER HARRIS, WM.
BROWN, BENJ. THURMAN. (Note that THURMAN is spelled as found in early
Louisa data. My mother-in-law was Emma Thurman, but it is said that old
PHILIP THURMAN SR. of Albemarle changed it to THURMOND and this is generally
spelling found hereabouts.

Page 176   13 Nov 1761 MICHL. JONES, Cumberland, to JNO. HARGIS for Ⱡ32,
            300 acres Long Branch of Moor Creek. Wit: WM. CHEECHE, ABRAHAM
MUSCIK, COTTEN BENGE.

Page 178   23 Nov 1761 BENJ. BROWN SR. to JR., Hanover, for Ⱡ71, 305 acres
            E side Doyle River, adj. SR. & JR., WM. RICE. Wit: RO. HARRIS,
WM. BROWN, JAMES HARRIS, JNO. MULLING.

Page 180   20 Mar 1762 DAVID GASS to WM. WOOD for Ⱡ100, 300 acres Meecham
            River, adj. DAVID MILLS, JNO. LAWSON. Wit: ARCHIBALD WOODS,
ANDREW WALLACE, MICHL. WOODS.

Page 182   19 Sep 1761 HARDEN BURNLEY, Hanover, Gent., to JAS. SANDDIGE,
            FOR Ⱡ45, 400 acres N fork Cunningham, adj. grantor. Wit: PETER
GILLUM, JNO. DURM(?), GREEN RICHESON, JNO. SMITH.

Page 183   30 Jun 1762 JNO. WEB & wife MARTHA, to THOS. TILMAN for Ⱡ20, 84
            acres N side Fluvanna and E side Bremo Creek, also a pat. to
JNO. CRAIM for a mill, adj. RICH. KOHE, FRANCIS KERBY. Pat. to WM. CRAIN,
28 Sep 1758. Wit: ABRAHAM CHILDERS & CREED CHILDERS.

Page 184   17 Jun 1762 ANDREW JOHNSTON, Augusta, to CHAS. DICK, Spotsyl-
            vania, for 5 sh., 200 acres adj. ROGER QUARRELS, JNO. MAJOR
DOWELL, WM. DYER - yr. lease - pepper corn on feast of Archangel Michl.
Wit: THOS. & JNO. WALKER, JAS. MAURY, JNO. MOORE.

Page 186   17 Jun 1762 - Same parties as above Ⱡ14, tract above sold out-
            right to DICK. Wit: As above.

Page 187   10 Jun 1762 BENJ. BROWN to granddaughter, LUCINDA PRICE, dtr.
            of my dec'd dtr. ELIZ, & son-in-law, JNO. PRICE - to longest
liver - 280 acres foot of Great Mts. adj. some in Louisa. Wit: RO. HARRIS,
RO. HARRIS JR., JAS. HARRIS.

Page 189   5 Jul 1762   BENJ. TAYLOR (signed TYLER) to RICH. WOODS for
            Ⱡ8-16, deed of trust on furniture etc. Wit: DAVID LEWIS, JR.,
WM. HIBIT, RO. ROZEN.

Page 190   8 Jul 1762 JNO. MITCHELL, Great Britain, and ANDREW SHEPHERD,
            Orange Co., factor, and merchant, to WM. DALTON for Ⱡ30, 277
acres adj. JNO. ENNISS.

Page 191   8 Jul 1762. Same parties as above to GABRIEL MAUPIN for Ⱡ15,
            204 acres N fork Rockey Creek adj. JOS. PHILLIPS.

Page 192   8 July 1762 Same parties as above to GABRIEL MAUPIN for Ⱡ15,
            318 acres Piney Run adj. TULLEY CHOICE, a mt.

Page 194   8 July 1762 Same as above to WM. KEATON JR. for Ⱡ25, 230 acres
            both sides N fork Rockey Run & Long Mt., adj. MITCHELL.

Page 195   --- 1760 JNO. MOORE to JNO. HENDERSON, The Younger, for Ⱡ40,
            600 acres; 400 acres of it pat. to PATRICK NOWLIN 15 Aug 1737;
both sides Moor's Creek or Bricke Run in pat.; 200 acres on both sides of
a branch of Bricket Run - now Cow Branch, bought by MM from MOWLIN and
known as Plum Orchard.

Page 197   8 Jul 1762 JNO. HENDERSON to son JNO. JR. for Ⱡ125, 490 acres
            200 of it pat. to HENRY RUNALLS 11 Apr 1732; N side Rivanna and

bought from RUNNALLS, 90 acres S side Rivanna and bought from JNO. SORRILL and joins where JH lives. 200 acres pat. to ARTHUR HOPKINS, 20 Apr 1732, on Lewis Creek near Red Bank falls - has manor where I live. Wit: GUY SMITH, CHRISTOPHER CLARK, JNO. COLEMAN.

Page 198   8 Jul 1762 JNO. HENDERSON SR. to son JR., love - slaves; 1 boy
            & 1 girl, Joe & Rachel. Wit: RICH. HARPER, JNO. COLEMAN.

Page 199   30 Jun 1762 DAVID LEWIS JR. & wife REBECCA to ALEX. BAINE,
            Henrico merchant, for ₤150, 200 acres where we live adj. WM.
WOODS, JNO. KINCAID, JNO. COFFEY, DAVID LOCKHARD(now KINCAID). Wit: JNO.
COFFEY, inner(sic); JNO. LEWIS, WM. GARLAND.

Page 201   30 Jun 1762 DAVID LEWIS JR. & wife REBECCA to ALEX. BAINE, as
            above, for ₤150, slaves: Beck, Affrican(sic) born, 25; Sam, Va.
born, about 9; Job ca. 7; suckling girl, Agy - last three are offsprings
of wench, Beck; cattle, beds. Wit: as above.

Page 202   9 July 1762 JNO. MOORE to son-in-law, JNO. HENDERSON, and my
            daughter, FRANCES HENDERSON - love - 3 slaves.

Page 202   3 Mar 1762 RICH. ADAMS, Henrico merchant, to RO. LEWIS, The
            Younger, Goochland, for ₤250, 800 acres Byrd Creek; pat. of 15
May 1755. Wit: THOS. ADAMS, PHIL WATSON, JNO. WOODSON, ALEX. McCAUL, JAS.
VAUGHAN, RO. LEWIS, M(sic); RO. SMITH, WM. WALTON, WM. HUDNELL, SIMON W.
WOOD.

Page 204   6 Mar 1762 RO. KENT, Hanover, planter, to ARMIGER LILLY, Gooch-
            land, planter, for ₤82-3-3, 297 acres both sides Great Byrd adj.
ADAMS, THURMON. Wit: WM. VENABLE, HUGH LEWIS VENABLE, THOS. & DAVID D.
BAILEY. LUCY, wife of KENT.

Page 206   12 Aug 1762 JACOB SNEAD to ALEX SNEAD for 5 sh., 200 acres pat.
            10 Sep 1755; both sides Ivy Creek adj. MICHL. HOLLAND, LEWIS.

Page 208   13 Aug 1762 DAVID THOMPSON & wife CATY to DAVID MILLS for ₤55,
            524 acres - 250 acres of it pat. 16 Aug 1756; 274 acres pat 10
Aug 1759, Lynch River branches. Wit: NICHL. MERIWETHER, JNO. LEIS JR.(LEWIS)

Page 211   20 Dec 1761 HENRY TILLEY JR. & wife JEAN(JANE) to PHILLIP THUR-
            MAN (This is the fellow who is said to have changed spelling to
THURMOND) for ₤30, 294 acres adj. Rich Meadow; CAPT. JOS. MARTIN, HENRY
BUNCH. Wit: DAVID THOMSON, CATY THOMSON, MARY NORTON.

Page 213   11 Aug 1762 WM. LEE to DAVID LEWIS JR. to secure ₤18-15-10;
            beds etc. Wit: WM. COFFEY, JNO. KINKHEAD.

Page 214   13 Aug 1762 JAS. TAYLOR to HENRY CARTER - yearly rents - where
            JT lately lived; lower clearing of the river; 4 slaves, from 25
Dec last, for 5 years at ₤60 per year.

Page 216   18 Feb 1762 SAML. HENDERSON & wife JEAN to JNO. FORD, Goochland,
            for ₤70, 200 acres N side N Rivanna adj. Carrole's Creek. Wit:
BENJ. SNEAD, BARTLETT FORD, WM. SPEARS - called SPENCER also later in
summery.

Page 218   23 Jul 1762 DAVID LEWIS to ALEX. BAINES, Henrico - power to
            collect money or tobacco from appended list - quite long. Wit:
CHAS. LAMBERT, THOS. MORROW, RO. BAINE. He listed them by counties and I
jotted down Amherst names: JOS. ALLEY, JAS. LECKEY, THOS. CARPENTER, WM.
FORBES, SPENCER RAYFEALD, JOS. MILSTREAD, JNO. MARTIN, CHAS. YANCEY - all
seem to have been small debts due.

Page 222   9 Sep 1762 JNO. LEEK & wife ANN, Amherst Co., to WM. WATSON,
            Hanover, for ₤56, 226 acres pat. to WALLER LEEK, 12 Jan 1746,
adj. THOS. FITZPATRICK, WM. FITZPATRICK. Wit: JOS. & THOS. FITZPATRICK,
JNO. HARRIS.

Page 224   9 Sep 1762 WM. FITZPATRICK & wife SARAH; JOS. FITZPATRICK &
            wife MARY, to WM. WATSON, Hanover, for ₤400, 390 acres pat. to
RO. DAVIS 10 Jan 1735. Wit: JNO. HARRIS, JNO. LEAK, THOS. FITZPATRICK.

Page 226   9 Sep 1762   JACOB CLEVELAND & wife MILDRED, planters, to ALEX.
             CLEVELAND, planter, for Ŀ18, 99 acres Hardware branches and N
Garden adj. JNO. LYONS, MILDRED MERIWETHER. Wit: JNO. FOSTER, JNO. HENLEE,
ELI CLEVELAND.

Page 228   7 Sep 1762   JOS. THOMAS, Buckingham Co., to JNO. MARTIN, JR. for
             Ŀ40, 628 acres. Wit: SAML. SHELTON, MICHL. THOMAS, JNO. COUCH.

Page 230   6 Sep 1762   HENRY CARTER to JACOB CLEVELAND for Ŀ11, 114 acres
             S fork Hardware. Wit: JNO. FOSTER, JNO. HENLEE, ELI CLEVELAND.

Page 231   6 Sep 1762   HENRY CARTER to JACOB CLEVELAND for Ŀ11, 70 acres S
             fork Hardware, adj. JNO. GILMORE, Mettle Branch. Wit: as above.

Page 233   9 Aug 1762   ARTHUNATIUS FEARS to CHAS. BOLTON for Ŀ35, 290 acres
             adj. JNO. STRANGE, JNO. LONG, Ballenger's Creek, HIGGINS.

Page 234   9 Sep 1762   VINCENT TULLOCK, Joyner, to JAS. KARR, Planter, for
             Ŀ34, stock, tools, etc., deed of trust. Wit: JACOB WATTS,
BARTHOLOMEW RANSEY.

Page 235   9 Sep 1762   DAVID MILLS & wife LUCY to JNO. SHIFFLETT for Ŀ16,
             100 acres adj. COURSEY, WM. DAVIS.

Page 236   4 Oct 1762   WM. COURSEY, SR., planter, to wife ANN - love - 245
             acres South Garden adj. JAS. BRAYDEN, JACOB CLEVELAND, bought
from CLEVELAND COFFEY; also 6 named slaves, stock. Wit: JNO. FOSTER, JNO.
RIPTO, MARY RIPTO.

Page 237   12 Oct 1762   JNO. DOLTON to PATRICK FISHER for Ŀ25, 100 acres S
             fork Wolf Trap branch adj. JNO. HENSLEE, WM. BROCKMAN, THOS. Mc-
COLLEY. Wit: JNO. HENSLEE, FULLELOVE BENNETT, WM. TERRELL LEWIS.

Page 239   14 Oct 1762   WM. COURSEY SR. & wife ANNE to JACOB WATTS for Ŀ25,
             400 acres adj. RIPPON, Co. line, spire of Piney Mt.

Page 242   24 Oct 1762   PETER HAIRSTONE to JOS. DAWSON, Amherst Co., for
             Ŀ48, 250 acres North Garden adj. RO. LEWIS. AGNES, wife of PH.

Page 244   o4 Oct 1762   JNO. DAVIS to SAML. MUNDAY for Ŀ10, 50 acres N side
             Turkey River. Wit: JNO. DOLTON, DAVID & RICH. HAMMOCK.

Page 245   12 Oct 1762   JNO. COWAN & wife MARGARET, to GEO. JOHNSTON for
             Ŀ18, 179 acres Meecham River branches adj. MICHL. WALLACE.
Part of 268 acres bought by JC on 9 Aug 1759.

Page 245   14 Oct 1762   BENJ. CLARK & wife ELIZ. to JNO. FRY for Ŀ310, 410
             acres N fork James. Part of 3,277 acres pat. to JOS. SMITH;
EDWIN HICKMAN & THOS. GRAVES, 25 May 1734. Also 1 moiety of 820 acres bought by BC and brother, JNO. CLARK, from SMITH et al, 13 Aug 1752.

Page 249   9 Sep 1762   PETERFIELD TRENT to BERNARD FRANKLIN, Orange Co.,
             for Ŀ24-3-4, 60 acres where EDWD. COFFEE lives on Hardware adj.
JACOB CLEVELAND; NATHAN BENNETT.

Page 251   30 Sep 1762   WM. COURSEY to son, JAMES COURSEY - WM. is feeble
             and very old - 9 named slaves, stock, furniture. If my wife
ANN outlives me JAS. to pay her Ŀ7 per year for support. Wit: JAS. TAYLOR,
DAVID VIA, LUKE HAMBLETON.

Page 252   9 Dec 1762   JNO. LOCKHARD to DAVID LEWIS JR. merchant, for Ŀ35,
             200 acres adj. both; DAVID LOCKHARD.

Page 253   11 Nov 1762   JACOB WATTS & wife ELIZ. to THOS. BOND for Ŀ30, 135
             acres Ivy Creek.

Page 255   10 Nov 1762   FRANCIS MERIWETHER, Spotsylvania, & wife MARY to
             ROBT. LEWIS, for Ŀ380, 144 acres adj. RO. LEWIS, DR. THOS. WALK-
ER, WM. SANDIDGE - part of pat. of NICHL. MERIWETHER, dec'd. Wit: GEO.
MARTIN, NICHL. MERIWETHER, MATT. ANDERSON, J. LEWIS.

Page 257   23 Mar 1762   THOS. MERIWETHER, merchant, to RO. LEWIS, merchant,
            for L400, 856 acres; part of pat. of Col. NICHOLAS MERIWETHER,
dec'd, and given by him to THOS., adj. Glebe, Mrs. ELIZ. MERIWETHER, where
her overseer, SAML. DOLTON, lives - JNO. MOORE. Wit: THOS. WALKER, THOS.
JOHNSON, WM. JOHNSON, GEO. MARTIN, J. LEWIS, MATT. ANDERSON.

Page 259   11 Nov 1762   MOURNING ADDAMS to son-in-law, CHAS. DOUGLAS, love
            and support - 2 slaves. Wit: HEZEKIAH HOLLAND, JAS. MOSELEY.

Page 260   11 Nov 1762   MOURNING ADDAMS to son-in-law, HENRY HARRIS as
            above - 1 slave. Wit: as above.

Page 261   11 Nov 1762   JOS. ANTHONY & wife ELIZ. to JAMES JONES for L150,
            800 acres, part of pat. of 2042 acres adj. PAT. NOWLIN.

Page 264   10 Nov 1762   WM. BROWN to mother-in-law, SARAH BROWN for L5,
            slaves given her by my father, BENJ. BROWN, dec'd. -- so written,
but she may have been his step-mother.

Page 264   10 Nov 1762   WM. BROWN to brother-in-law, RO. HARRIS JR., slave
            given by my father, BENJ. BROWN, dec'd, to HARRIS. Wit: RO. &
CHRISTOPHER HARRIS.

Page 265   10 Nov 1762   WM. BROWN to brother, BAZELEEL BROWN, for L2, all
            interest in slave given to BB by my father, BENJ. BROWN, dec'd.
Wit: as above.

Page 265   10 Nov 1762   WM. BROWN to brother, BRIGHTBERRY BROWN, L2, inter-
            est in a slave as above.

Page 266   12 Oct 1762   JOEL LEWIS to JNO. LEWIS for L100, 200 acres MOORE's
            Creek adj. WM., DAVID & WM. LEWIS, Piney Mt. spring, part of pat.

Page 267   12 Nov 1762   BENJ. BROWN, St. Martin's parish, Hanover, to JOHN
            PENIZ, same par. and co., for L28, 79 acres N side Doyle River
adj. grantor, WM. RICE, JNO. MULLINS.

Page 269   14 July 1762   GEO. ROBINSON to SAML. TALIAFERRO - receipt for
            full   payment on lien of 9 Oct 1760.

Page 269   8 Dec 1762   JNO. & DAVID LOCKHARD to JNO. KINKHEAD for L80, 356
            acres S branch of N fork Meecham River adj. MATT MILLS, JNO.
LOCKHARD, GEO. DAVIDSON.

Page 270   9 Dec 1762   Same parties as above - L80, for tract in hands of
            JNO. KINKHEAD for 1 year's lease.

Page 272   9 Dec 1762   DAVID LEWIS SR. & WM. TERRELL LEWIS to RICHARD BEN-
            NETT for L20, 100 acres, part of pat. to DL, SR. adj. WM. T.
LEWIS, ABRAHAM MUSICK, THOS. BENGES.

Page 274   26 Nov 1762   THOS. PLEASANTS, Goochland, to THOS. NAPIER for L70
            200 acres Rivanna River adj. PAT. NAPIER, ASHFORD NAPIER - for-
merly WM. CREASEY SR. Wit: DAVID POLLOCK, RICHARD MOORE, JNO. WOODALL,
STEPHEN, JNO. & RENE NAPIER.

Page 275   16 Nov 1762   JAS. REID, blacksmith, to RO. MILLER, planter, for
            L25, 311 acres Rockey Creek adj. CHRISTOPHER HARRIS, WM. KEATON,
PAT. WOODS, WILLIAM OWENS, county line. Wit: MOSIAS JONES, JNO. ABLE,
LEONARD DAVIS, JOSEPH WOODS, DAVID EPPERSON.

Page 276   17 Nov 1762   Exrs. of will of JAMES PATTON, Augusta - WM. THOMP-
            SON, JNO. BUCHANAN - to THOS. DOUGLAS for 5 sh, 200 acres bought
by JP from ROBT. ROSE & THOS. WALKER, 13 Apr 1745, in then Louisa Co. adj.
GOUGHT, HICKMAN, AMBR. JOSHUA SMITH, Prithes(?) Creek. Wit: JOEL TERRELL,
SAMUEL DOLTON, Jr., HEZ. RICE.

Page 277   8 Nov 1762   Same exors. as above to THOS. DOUGLAS for L22, 200
            acres bought as above and lines as above. Wit: as above.

Page 279   10 Mar 1763   WM. MAUPIN to GABL. MAUPIN for L25, 224 acres both

Yellow Run adj. grantor. Wit: THOS. MAUPIN, THOS. BALLARD.

Page 280   10 Mar 1763   MATT. MULLINS to WM. MAUPIN for Ł10, 190 acres S
            side Moorman River. Wit: as above.

Page 281   23 Sep 1762   WM. COURSEY, SR. to step-son, WM. COURSEY JR.,
            schoolmaster, and son of my wife ANNE COURSEY - love - 6 named
slaves, stock, furniture.

Page 282   10 Mar 1763   JOS. MARTIN & wife SARAH to THOS. KEYTON for Ł30,
            300 acres Rockey Creek adj. WM. KEYTON, RICH. VERNON, SUSANNA
MARTIN.

Page 283   5 Mar 1763   ABRAHAM CHILDRES to WM. VAUGHAN, Buckingham Co., Ł16,
            200 acres, part of pat. of 400 acres 10 Aug 1759, fork of James
and Spring Garden Branches, adj. BENJ. & RICH. COKE(COCKE). Wit: CREED
CHELDRES, WM. PAARCE.

Page 284   18 Jan 1763   JAS. WARREN SR., Amherst planter, to THOS. RAY for
            Ł25, 100 acres Mitcham River in Rich Cove. Wit: BARTHOLOMA
RAMSEY, EDWD. CARTER.

Page 287   9 Mar 1763   GEO. JOHNSON & wife ELIZ. to WM. WOODS for Ł50, 129
            acres Lickinghole Creek, branch of Rivanna, adj. MICHL. WALLACE.
Bought from JNO. COWAN, 9 Mar 1762. Wit: MICHL. WOODS, JAS. & WM. LITTLE.

Page 288   10 Mar 1763   STEPHEN CASH & wife JEMIMA, Amherst Co., to JOEL
            LEWIS for Ł35, 250 acres both sides Midon(?) Creek adj. ABRAM
LEWIS, DAVID LEWIS,JOEL TERRELL.

Page 290   2 Feb 1763   JNO. COWAN to WM. WOODS for Ł25, 68 acres Spring
            Creek of Micham River adj. DAVID MILLS, grantee. Pat. 25 Mar
1762. Wit: MICHL. WOODS, DAVID LEWIS, ARCHIBALD OWENS.

Page 291   14 Apr 1763   FRANCIS WHEELER to PAT. DAVIS for Ł100, 312 acres
            both sides Meecham River, pat 25 Mar 1762. MARTHA, wife of FW.

Page 293   8 Sep 1762   WM. GOOCH to JNO. PAYNE, Goochland, for Ł32, 400 ac-
            res on branches of Byrd Creek adj. ABRAHAM VENABLE, THOS. BAY-
LEY. Wit: JNO. PAYNE, JR., JNO. WOODSON, JNO. HOLLAND, JR., JNO. BAILEY.

Page 294   4 Jan 1763   DAVID MERIWETHER, of City of London, but now in Va.,
            Marrener (sic, but probably Mariner), to NICHL. MERIWETHER for
5 sh., 164 acres Taylor Creek, branch of Rockfish adj. ARCH. WOODS. Wit:
THOS. WALKER, ROBT. BAINE, THOS. JEFFERSON, THOS. GORDON, JNO. MOORE.

Page 295   5 Jan 1763   Same parties as above - Ł27-7-4½, property as
            above which was 1 year's lease. Wit: as above.

Page 297   15 Apr 1763   HENRY HAYS, Haberdasher, to ROBT. CLARK for Ł15,
            stock and watch in deed of trust. Wit: JNO. RICE, CHRISTOPHER
CLARK.

Page 298   12 May 1763   JOEL TERRILL & wife ANNE to JNO. DABNEY for Ł300,
            400 acres main road from the Blue Ridge to courthouse; Terrill's
Ordinary, adj. DAVID LEWIS, FRANCIS JORDAN, Moore's creek branches, WM.
TERRILL LEWIS, grantee, DAVIS LEWIS JR.

Page 299   12 May 1763   THOS. BOND & wife ELIZ to JAS. CARR for Ł30, 135
            acres. Wit: MOSIAS JONES, HENRY TURLEY.

Page 301   12 May 1763   HEZEKIAH RICE & wife MARY to JNO. MICHIE, Louisa,
            for Ł170, 100 acres, Horse Shoe or Penisula of Meecham. Pat to
JNO. HENRY and by him to MICHIE in Louisa and by MICHIE to RICE; also 120
acres adj.; pat. to JNO THOMSON Aug 1759, adn by him to RICE. Wit: MOSIAS
JONES, JOS. GRESHAM.

Page 302   6 Dec 1762   JNO. MORAN, Amherst Co., to NICHL. MORAN, planter,
            for Ł20, 141 acres both sides S bank of Stockson's Mill; one
half of pat. of 10 Aug1759. Wit: WM. WOOD, THOS. & EDMD. COFFEY, JNO.
CARTER, & another WM. WOOD.

Page 303   21 Feb 1763 HUGH FRAZIER to JOEL TERRILL for Ŀ30, 200 acres
             both sides Meadon Creek, branch of Rivanna adj. HOWARD CASH. Wit:
JNO. & ANNA DABNEY, JNO. PATTESON.

Page 305   11 Apr 1763 GEO. BRACKINRIDGE to DAVID LEWIS Jr. for Ŀ40, 200
             acres N side Stockton, branch of Meecham. Pat. to WM. LITTLE
1746, adj. JOHN WOODS.

Page 306   20 Dec 1762 ASHFORD NAPIER to ARCHIBALD INGRAM & GEORGE KIPPEN,
             Glasgow merchants, for Ŀ100-6-8, 200 acres, upper side Rivanna
where NAPIER lives, adn given to him by his father, RO. NAPIER, Dec'd.-
slave in hands of Col. JNO. COBBS, stock, deed of trust to be paid by 1764.
Wit: RO. NAPIER, JNO. ROBINSON, MARGARET SMITH, SAML. JORDAN.

Page 308   13 May 1762 JNO. RODES SR., Louisa, planter, to son DAVID RODES,
             for 5 sh. and love, 264 acres N fork Moorman and where DAVID
lives. Adj. grantor, mouth of Cabbin Creek branches. Wit: CLIFTON & JNO.
RODES, WM. WRIGHT, DAVID EPPERSON, THOS. GRUBBS.

Page 309   14 Jul 1763 RO. LEWIS to daughter, MARY COBBS, widow of SAML.
             COBBS, dec'd., and to granddaughter, JANE COBBS - 2 slaves.

Page 310   10 Dec 1762 JULIUS WEBB to JNO. PRICE for Ŀ9-5, 2 father(sic)
             beds, but sorry, at Ŀ3; 1 old fleast(sic) bitten horse, other
horses and stock. Wit: PAT. & JAS. HAWES.

Page 311   4 Jun 1763 JNO. MABE to CHAS. FARGERSON for Ŀ9-16-9½, 82 acres
             both sides Wolf Trap Branch, part of pat. to WM. MABE. Wit: JAS.
COLEMAN, JR., JOS. GRESHAM, REUBIN LINDSEY.

Page 321   17 Jan 1763 Dr. GILES ALLEGRE to WM. HOWARD, watchmaker and
             goldsmith - 5 sh., mineral rights - 3 Notched Road, S branchs
of Mechunk, where WH lives, adj. NAT. WINSTON, THOS. MERIWETHER. Wit: JNO.
MORRISON SR., GEO. MORRISON, JNO. & BARTELOT FORD.

Page 315   8 Jun 1763 NATHAN WOODS to son JOSEPH WOODS, love and 1 sh.,
             100 acres, N side Moorman, where JOS. lives, adj. old Louisa Co.
line. Part of pat. of 370 acres 25 Jun 1747. Wit: RO. HARRIS, RO. MILLER,
DAVID RODES, MATT. MULLINS, GABLE MAUPIN, WM. MAUPIN.

Page 317   11 Jun 1763 HARDEN BURNLEY, Hanover, to JOS. FITZPATRICK for
             Ŀ45, 427 acres both sides middle fork of Cunningham, where BENJ.
BRYANT formerly lived and where JF now lives. Wit: JNO. STAPLES, WM.
FITZPATRICK JR., BENJ. FITZPATRICK, REUBEN SHELTON BROWN.

Page 318   7 July 1763 FRANCIS JERDONE & wife SARAH, Louisa, to STEPHEN
             WILLS, Hanover, for Ŀ60, 424 acres adj. Ivy Creek, SNEED, CLARK,
FIDLER, above Mackie's Ford.

Page 320   7 July 1763 Same grantors above to THOS. BURCH & RICHINS BRAME,
             Caroline Co, for Ŀ60, 402 acres adj. as above.

Page 322   11 Aug 1763 DANL.MAUPIN, planter, to his son, THOS. MAUPIN,
             love, 490 acres adj. grantor, Grubb Creek.

Page 323   11 Aug 1763 DANL. MAUPIN to his son DANL. JR., planter, love,
             150 acres where he lives adj. the river, GABL. MAUPIN.

Page 324   11 Aug 1763 DANL. MAUPIN to his son, JNO. MAUPIN, love, where
             JNO. lives, 150 acres, adj. DANL. MAUPIN.

Page 325   11 Aug 1763 DANL. MAUPIN to son-in-law, ROBT. MILLER, planter,
             love, 137 acres where RM lives.

Page 326   7 Aug 1763 WM. QUARLES,Orange Co, to RICH. DURRETT for Ŀ45, 400
             acres both sides Prettis Creek above Little Mts. adj. HAYNES,
HICKMAN. Wit: MARY, RICH. & WM. WILSON.

Page 328   8 Sep 1763 THOS. WALKER to SAML. BOYD for Ŀ3-5-6, ½ acre lot
             in certain town called Charlottesville - lately laid off - #49
in plat.

Page 329   30 Dec 1762 WM. BURTON to chruchwardens, MATT. JORDAN & ABRAHAM
            CHILDRES, for Ł231-10, 400 acres for a glebe - both sides S fork
of Totear Creek pat. to WM. HARRIS 25 Jul 1741, adj. MATT. HARRIS, MAJOR
JNO. BOWLIN, CHAS. LYNCH. Wit: HENRY & CHAS. MARTIN, MICHL. THOMAS.

Page 332   3 Apr 1763 RICH. SURLS & wife ELIZ., to THOS. WALKER, for 5 sh.,
            400 acres Great Creek adj. NICHOLSON OLIVER, JAS. POWERS. Pat.
10 Aug 1759, 1 year lease. On p.333 is outright sale with no sum given.

Page 335   19 Feb 1763 JAS. HOPKINS from WM. PEARCE for Ł20, where "he
            lives", 150 acres Cunningham Creek. Wit: GUY WMITH, DICK HOLLAND,
WM. HORSLEY.

Page 336   9 May 1763 WM. CREASEY to BENJ. WOODSON JR., Goochland, for
            Ł6,400 acres or 40 acres in one place adj. Derick's branch, Rac-
coon Creek. Wit: ROGER THOMSON, RENE WOODSON, PAT. NAPIER, ---WOODSON, GEO.
ANDERSON, ASH NAPIER, RO. & JNO. NAPIER.

Page 338   8 Sep 1763 WM. TERRELL LEWIS to his daughter, ANNE McCONNELL,
            wife of JNO. McCONNALL, hatter - love - 250 acres adj. ABRAHAM
MUNCHKS, JAMES WARREN, JNO. HARRIS, JNO. GRILLS, JAS. DAVENPORT - for
their support.

Page 339   -- 1763 JNO. BURROWS to HENRY WOOD for Ł26, 110 acres Moore
            Creek branches and Ragged Mts., pat 10 Sep 1755 - The Grape Yard
Survey. Wit: SAML. BOYD, ALLEX. MACKEY, ISRAEL DAVIS.

Page 341   8 Sep 1763 THOS. WALKER to RICH. HARVIE for Ł3, lot in Char-
            lottesville - ½ acre - #14.

Page 342   8 Sep 1763 THOS. WALKER to ROBT. BAINE for Ł28-14; lots in town
            above - #'s 9, 10, 24, 33, 34, 59.

Page 343   8 Sep 1763 THOS. WALKER to SAML. WOODS for Ł9, lot in town
            above #'s 19 and 20.

Page 344   9 Sep 1763 THOS. WALKER to RICH. WOODS for Ł7-10 and Ł10-12,
            lots in town above - #'s 31 and 32.

Page 345   9 Sep 1763 THOS. WALKER to JNO. GRILLS for Ł15, lot in town
            above #18.

Page 346   9 Sep 1763 THOS. WALKER to GEO. ROBINSON for Ł5-1, lot in town
            above - #7.

Page 347   9 Sep 1763 RO. LEWIS to THOS. WALKER for Ł55, paid to JNO.
            LEWIS, Spotsylvania, who married ROBERT's daughter, ANN, also,
20 sh.; part of pat. to NICHL. MERIWETHER, dec'd., who conveyed to CHRISTO-
PHER CLARK who conveyed to RO. LEWIS - Hanover deeds - 435 acres adj. THO-
MAS MERIWETHER, oak in Orange Co. line, JNO. SUTTON.

Page 349   13 Oct 1763 JOSIAH MORTON & wife ELIZ., Lunenberg Co., to TURN-
            ER RICHARDSON SR., Hanover, for Ł120, 510 acres, branches of the
Byrd, adj. WM. MARTIN, grantee. Part of pat. of ABRAHAM VENABLE and given
by him to his daughter, ELIZ., wife of J. MORTON - ref. to Alb. deed of
gift. Wit: JAS. ADAMS. ABRAHAM CHILDRES, WM. VENABLE.

Page 351   11 Oct 1763 THOS. LAND & wife ANN, to WM. SUMPTER for Ł7-10,
            100 acres, part of 250 acres bought from WM. HENRY, Hanover, adj.
TRESSLE(?) DOLLINGS, JAMES ISBEL, grantor - very fine script and hard to
read.

Page 353   12 Oct 1763 THOS. HARDEN & wife MARY to RO. GRINNER - to pay
            debts and finding meat, drink, lodging, clothing and washing
suitable for poor persons - 100 acres N branch of N fork of Tamer, adj.
WM. HERRIN, JNO. DICKERSON, RICH. ALLIN; stock, furniture - long list. Wit:
JNO. DOWELL, WM. DOWELL, THOS. DICKERSON.

Page 355   13 Oct 1763 ABRAHAM ALLEN & wife MARY to JOS. EVE JR. for Ł17,
            200 acres both sides Land Spring Creek adj. THOS. LANDS, WM.
COURSEY, grantor.

Page 356   13 Oct 1763 THOS. RAY & wife MARTHA, to WM. FEIDLER for Ŀ15, 50
            acres, part of 100 acres bought from JAS. WARREN adj. HENRY
TERRELL, JAS. WARREN.

Page 358   12 Oct 1763 WM. HINES & wife MARY to WM. JOHNSON for Ŀ30, 200
            acres S branches James, adj. MAJOR THOS. CARR. Wit: JNO.
HENOLES(?), MICAJAH CLARK JR., RO. CLARK.

Page 359   10 Sep 1763 JACOB BOW adn wife JAMIMAH to THOS. RAY for Ŀ25, 83
            acres pat. 10 Nov 1757, adj. JNO. WARREN, HENRY TERRELL. Wit:
WM. FIELDER, MICHL. ISRAEL, JNO. MORAN, SOLOMON ISRAEL.

Page 361   14 Sep 1763 JNO. HARGIS to PETERFIELD TRENT for Ŀ35, 300 acres
            Long Branch of Moore; pat. to RO. EDGER, 13 Sep 1753, adn by
deed to MICHL. JONES and by him by deed to HARGIS. Wit: JNO. TILLER, JNO.
SMITH, JNO. SWANN.

Page 362   14 Oct 1763 CASTLETON HARPER to PETERFIELD TRENT for Ŀ7, 70
            acres adj. THOS. SOWEL, JAS. GARRET.

Page 363   21 Apr 1762 JNO. GEER & wife ELIZ, Johnston Co., N.C., to JNO.
            MILLER(AR), Augusta Co., for Ŀ70, 250 acres; in JM's hands by 1
year lease day before this, adj. Grannees Hill, WM. SHAW. Wit: GEO. ADAMS.
GEORGE PATTERSON, RO. MILLAR, JNO. ROARK, ANDREW MILLER, WM. LESSLEY.

Page 367   20 Apr 1762 JNO. GEER, Johnston Co., N.C. to JNO. MILLAR, Augus-
            ta., 5 sh., 1 yr. lease on above 250 acres.

Page 369   6 Dec 1763 ADAM GOUDLOCK, planter, to JOS. ANDERSON, planter,
            for Ŀ24, 182 acres Virgin Spring branch adj. MARTHA STOCKTON,
THOS. SHIELDS. Wit: JNO. & RO. STOCKTON, DAVIS WHITENDE. HANNAH, wife of AG.

Page 372   3 Nov 1763 JNO. FRY to HENRY FRY for 5 sh., 130 acres Brecry
            Creek; pat. to JOSHUA FRY, now dec'd. Wit: JNO. LOBBAN, JNO.
HARVIE (2 so signed). p.374 outright sale of tract to HENRY FRY, pat. as
above, 3 Nov 1752.

Page 377   8 Dec 1763 JNO. MILLAR, Augusta, to JAS. JOHNSTON, 5 sh., 250
            acres, 1 yr. lease, adj. Grannell Hill, WM. SHAW. P. 379,
outright sale of tract ot JOHNSON(sic), Ŀ60.

Page 382   4 Oct 1763 RICH. HAGGARD, Lunenbert Co., to THOS. WALKER for
            Ŀ20, 300 acres adj. MERIWETHER, BENJ. JOHNSON, MOOR. Wit: JNO.
COLEMAN, RICHARD WOODS, SOLOMON NELSON.

Page 384   25 July 1763 WM. SANDIDGE & wife BETTY, to JNO LEWIS for Ŀ130,
            200 acres adj. grantee, THOS. WALKER. Wit: JAS. MAURY, JNO.
MOORE, NICHL. MERIWETHER.

Page 387   9 Nov 1763 CHAS. ENGLISH & wife ANNE, to NICHL. CAIN, Louisa,
            for Ŀ30, 100 acres Key's Mill Creek adj. GIDEON CARR. Wit: DANL.
HAMMACK & WM. HAMMACK.

Page 389   12 Nov 1763 JNO. MULLENS, Goochland, to JAMES HARRIS for Ŀ40,
            200 acres adj. BENJ. BROWN. Wit: MOSIAS JONES, DAVID RODES, RO.
MILLER, JOS. WOODS, RO. MORRIS.

Page 392   27 Jun 1763 JNO. McCAULEY JR. to THOS. MERIWETHER & JNO. LEWIS
            for Ŀ15-1-6, 100 acres adj. JOS. GRAVES, WM. CRANSHAW, THOS.
McCAULEY, PAT. FISHER, JNO. CAVE, WM. GRANTHAM, JAS. COLEMAN. Bought from
DAVID WATTS who conveyed to JM. - seemingly COLEMAN bought tract. Wit:
NICHL. LEWIS, THOS. MADISON, NICHL. MERIWETHER.

Page 394   9 May 1763 JAS. MAURY to THOS. WALKER & JNO. LEWIS - MATTHEW
            MAURY, late of King William, Gent., by will to son, ABRAHAM
MAURY, to take sum and buy young slaves - mostly female - for two grand-
daughters, ANNE & MARY MAURY, daughters of JAMES, but if either died or was
married before 21, then to their brother, MATT. MAURY. ABRAHAM did not
execute trust and Louisa court appointed JAMES as guardian of his daughters
to receive from ABRAHAM Ŀ150. WALKER & LEWIS are trustees and sum paid -
5 sh., 4 slaves. Wit: NICHL. LEWIS, THOMAS MADDISON, THOS. WALKER.

Page 395 6 -- 1764 DAVID MILLS to JAS. MEREDITH for Ŀ16, 100 acres adj.
grantor. Wit: SAML. DOLTON, JAS. KEATON, BRADLEY MEREDITH.

Page 397 8 Mar 1764 JAS. HAMBLETON to MICHL WOODS for Ŀ80, 400 acres
Licking Hole Branch, adj. ANDREW McWILLIAMS. Pat of WM. LITTLE,
18 Nov 1756, and to JH from WL.

Page 399 8 Mar 1764 WM. WOODS to MICHL. WOODS for Ŀ100, 153 acres Licking
Hole, adj. grantee. Pat. 10 Jun 1737.

Page 401 8 Mar 1764 WM. WOODS to ADAM EDGER, Augusta Co., for Ŀ25, 178
acres Meecham River, pat. 23 Mar 1763.

Page 403 17 Jan 1764 JNO. ROBINSON, King and Queen Co., to JNO. RODES,
Louisa Co, for Ŀ107-10, 900 acres Meecham River. Part of pat. of
Col. JNO. CHISWELL and conveyed to JR. Adj. DAVID GLEN, BENJ. DOVE, grantor.
Wit: THOS. & JAS. WALKER, WM. CABELL, JR., JOS. CABELL, CORNL. THOMAS.

Page 404 17 Jan 1764 JNO. ROBINSON, as above, to WM. GRAYSON, for Ŀ57-10
521 acres Meecham River. Part of pat. above, adj. DAVID GLEN,
JAS. GLEN, WM. WILSON, JNO. ALLEN, THOS. SMITH, BENJ. DOVE, JNO. RODES.
Wit: As above.

Page 406 17 Jan 1764 JNO. ROBINSON, as above, to DANL. ONEALE for Ŀ31-12
304 acres Meecham River, pat. as above, adj. BENJ. DOVE, JNO.
RODES, grantor. Wit: as above.

Page 408 17 Jan 1764 JNO. ROBINSON, as above, to JAS. GLEN, for Ŀ44-15,
382 acres Meecham River, pat. as above, adj. DAVID GLEN, JNO.
RYAN, SHAROD MARTIN. Wit: as above.

Page 409 20 Jan 1764 GILES ALLEGRE to BENAGAH GENTRY for Ŀ30, 178 acres,
pat. of 1 Dec 1748. Bickett Run. Wit: ROBT. GENTRY, ABSALOM
McKINZIE, MOSES LISBA(?).

Page 411 7 Mar 1764 JNO. BYBIE, SR. & wife JEAN, to CHRISTOPHER MAC RAE
for Ŀ100, 353 acres both sides Ballinger's Creek adj. WM. BARNETT,
DANL. KING. Part of 1000 acres bought from THOS. HARBOUR. Wit: JNO., JOS.,
& WALTER MACKIE, PHILIP MacRAE.

Page 414 10 Aug 1763 WM. HARLOW, planter, to CHAS. DOUGLAS for Ŀ70,
slaves: Primus Tamer, Nane, & Will. Deed of Trust to be paid at
house of CD. Wit: THOS. DOUGLAS, WM. CUDING, JNO. LAND.

Page 415 18 Feb 1764 MARY DAVIS, St. Thomas Parish, Orange Co., to JNO.
OGG, same place, for Ŀ27, 100 acres adj. Kid Branch, RO. THOMPSON.
Given to her by her father, ROBT. THOMPSON.

Page 417 8 Mar 1764 THOS. WALKER to SAML. TALIAFERRO for 31 sh., lot #52
in Charlottesville.

Page 417 8 Mar 1763(sic) THOS. WALKER to JNO. McCONNELL for Ŀ5, lot # __
in Charlottesville. Certified in 1764.

Page 418 8 Mar 1763 RO. BAINE to RICH. WOODS, for 45 sh., Lot 59 in
above town.

Page 419 10 Feb 1764 WM. TAYLOR, Planter, to CLAUDIUS BUSTER for Ŀ30, 74
acres North Garden, adj. MILDRED MERIWETHER. Wit: JNO. BUSTER,
ELIZ. BUSTER, CHAS. LAMBERT.

Page 421 24 Jan 1764 WHITEHEAD RYON to WM. STONE, Henrico, for Ŀ15, 150
acres adj. both; Raccoon Creek, the roade(sic). ELIZ., wife of
W.R. Wit: CALEB STONE, ELIJAH STONE, ABRAHAM SEAY.

Page 422 11 Apr 1764 JAS. HILTON to JNO. WARE for Ŀ400, 200 acres adj.
James River and Hardware, Great Rockfish.

Page 424 12 Apr 1764 RO. SHARP to WM. BARTEM for Ŀ26, 100 acres Plumb
Tree Branch bought from NELSON ANDERSON by pat., 3 Oct 1734, adj.
Notched road, a run, MANUS BURGER.

Page 425 12 Apr 1764 THOS. WALKER to JNO. MOORE, planter, for Ł33, 33 acres adj. lines SE of Charlottesville, STEPHEN HUGHES, (now
CHILDRESS), NICHL. LEWIS, Prison spring - lot #10.

Page 426 12 Apr 1764 JNO. JAMESON to son-in-law, THOS. CREAGE, 100 acres
N side Moorman River and where TC lives, adj. grantor. Wit: RO.
MILLER, JAMES WHAREY, DANL. MAUPIN.

Page 427 12 Apr 1764 WM. COURSEY, JR. to BERNARD FRANKLYN, no sum, 245
acres South Garden and Hardaway branches - bought from CLEVELAND
COFFEY, also slave Deed of Trust. Wit: MARY CLEVELAND, BETTY CLEVELAND, JAS.
WILSON.

Page 428 12 Apr 1764 ARTHANASIUS FEARS to WM. GOOCH, JR., for Ł30, no
acres; adj. THOS. SOWELL, Hardware River. MARY, wife of AF.

Page 429 9 Feb 1764 HENRY HARPER to CHAS. LEWIS JR. for Ł40, 300 acres
adj. Col. RO. LEWIS, foot of the mt., pat. 30 Aug 1763 North
Garden. Wit: EDWD. CARTER, JNO. HENDERSON, CHAS. MARTIN, JNO. CLARKE.

Page 431 10 May 1764 BENJ. WHEELER, SR. to MICAJAH SPRADLING - love - 200
acres Moore Cr-ek branches. P.432 same parties and date - 2
slaves to MS for love.

Page 433 9 May 1764 ARMIGER LILLY, Goochland planter, to JNO. LOWRY, for
Ł25, 380 acres Byrd Creek branches, adj. JOS. TATE, EDMD. LILLY,
BENJ. JOHNSON. Wit: WM. LILLY, AARON LOWRY, JNO. CLARK.

Page 434 8 May 1764 WM. HOOPER to RICH. WOODS for Ł20, no acres, both
sides of Hardware. Part of where WH lives, adj. grantor.

Page 436 10 May 1764 DANL. MAUPIN, planter, to his son, WM. MAUPIN, planter, where WM liveth; Moorman River, adj. DM's old line, grantee,
DM., JR. 150 acres.

Page 437 8 May 1764 JAS. HAGGARD & wife SARAH to TANDY FORD for Ł16,
Little Mechunk Creek; N side Rivanna. Pat. 7 Aug 1761. Wit:GILES
ALLEGRE JR., BARTLET FORD, JNO. FORD, THOS. CATLET.

Page 439 9 May 1764 DAVID MERIWETHER, Amherst Co., to JNO. SCOTT, Cumberland, for 5 sh., pat. to THOS. MERIWETHER. 3 tracts. 1) 6 July
1741 - 400 acres. 2) 25 July 1741 - 400 acres. 3) 30 July 1742 - 950 acres.
Toter Creek Branches. Wit: JNO. HARVIE, JR., SAML. WOODS, WM. HIBBIT - 1
year lease.

Page 440 10 May 1764 Same parties as above, but here DM is of Alb., for
Ł550, tract above sold. Wit: as above.

Page 442 10 May 1764 THOS. WALKER to GEO. DUDLEY for Ł5, lot #47 in
Charlottesville.

Page 443 6 Jun 1764 Order to J.P.'s of Alb. to quiz MARY MERIWETHER, wife
of DAVID MERIWETHER, as to deed to JNO. SCOTT. Done on same day.
J.P.'s: RO. LEWIS, NICHL. MERIWETHER, NICHL. LEWIS.

Page 444 1 May 1764 FRANCIS JERDONE & wife SARAH, Louisa, to WM. GARRETT,
Louisa, consideration of 940 acres in Spotsylvania and Louisa to
FJ from WG and wife SARAH, 1 May 1764. 20 sh. N Garden, 1999 acres - 1200
of it bought from WM. TAYLOR, 30 Jun 1755; 790 acres pat. to FJ - 2 pats.
of 10 Nov 1757; 1 of 19 Aug 1758; 1 of 30 Aug 1763. Wit: J. LEWIS, RO.
FLEMING BIBB, JNO. CARR, JNO. HARVIE, RO. BAINE.

Page 446 12 Nov 1763 DAVID MILLS to WM. COLEMAN & wife BETTY - rents
paid - 100 acres- mineral rights excepted; adj. grantor, WM.
THOMPSON, N side Piney - 10 year lease, Ł1-5 per year for 4 years and Ł1
for rest of time - to care for 100 apple trees on tract. Wit: WM. MICHIE,
JAS. KEATON.

Page 448 31 Mar 1764 WM. HOWARD & wife JUDITH, to his father-in-law,
GILES ALLEGRE - dispute between them over slave woman given
JUDITH before marriage. They will receive a wench in their hands instead

of first woman - if G.A. will put it in his will, and then to JUDITH's eldest son. We have agreed with G.A. to receive tract where we live instead of Buck Island tract formerly given to JUDITH by father, then to our oldest living son. Wit: JNO. FORSIE JR., SUSANNA FORSIE.

Page 449 no date   JNO. GRILLS to GEO. KIPPEN & ARCH. INGRAM for Ƚ107-4-
               8½, Deed of Trust to these Glasgow merchants; 4 named slaves. Wit: ARCH BRYCES, RICH. HARVIE, ARCH B--seems to be BAYCRESS as in next deed below.

Page 450 19 Nov 1763 PHEBE BAILEY, exrx. and widow of WM. BAILEY, dec'd,
               to GEO. KIPPEN & Co. for Ƚ37, slaves. Wit: N. MITCHELL, ARCH. BAYCRESS.

Page 451 1 Oct 1762 JNO. CARR & wife BARBARA, of Louisa, to NATHL. POPE,
               Louisa, rents rec'd 150 acres adj. mouth of Powell's creek, THOS. CARR - 10 yrs. lease. Wit: RO. BAINE, JNO. HARVIE, J. LEWIS.

Page 453 1 Oct 1762 JNO. CARR, Louisa - St. Martin's parish, and wife, as
               above, to WM. TANDY, Louisa, and Trinity parish, rents received. 75 acres adj. grantee, the river - 10 yrs. lease. Wit: as above.

Page 455 13 Jun 1764 RENE WOODSON to ANTHONY MINTER, Cumberland Co., for
               Ƚ120, 400 acres James fork and Carey Creek, Little Bramer Creek. Pat. to BENJ. WOODSON, 24 Mar 1734, and sold to RW. Wit: JNO. STRANGE, WM. TUCKER, ROBT, THOS. & RENE NAPIER. FRANCES, wife of RW also a wit.

Page 458 11 May 1764 RICH. STOCKTON 7 wife AGNES to DAVID KINKHEAD for
               5 sh., 400(500?) acres both sides Stockton's Branch of Meecham, adj. DAVID STOCKTON, CHAS. LYNCH. Wit: THOS., MATT. & JOHN KINKHEAD - 1 yr. lease. On p.459 is outright sale to DK for Ƚ57, of tract. Wit: same.

Page 461 28 May 1764 DAVID KINKHEAD & wife WINNIFRED, to son JOHN KINK-
               HEAD for 5 sh., above tract. 1 yr. lease. Wit: THOS. & MATT. KINKHEAD, JAS. BLACK. P.463, next day, they sell to son for love and 1 sh. the tract leased and wits. were the same.

Page 465 28 May 1764 DAVID KINKHEAD & wife as above to JAMES BLACK for
               5 sh., 400 acres on Stockton. Wit: JNO., MATT. & THOS. KINKHEAD, SAML. CRAIG - 1 yr. lease. On p.467 they sell, on next day, the tract to BLACK for Ƚ16-10. Wit: the same.

Page 469 12 Dec 1763 JOS. CHILDRES & wife MARY, to ALEX. McCAUL, Henrico,
               for Ƚ120, 200 acres adj. ALLEN HOWARD; mouth of Rockhouse creek; main road. Wit: JNO. GRIFFIN, RALPH JOPLING.

Page 471 14 Jun 1764 THOS. MOREMAN & wife RACHEL, of Louisa and Trinity
               Parish, to RO. CLARK for Ƚ45; no acres; on Ivy Creek.

Page 472 21 Jan 1764 THOS. STOCKTON to ADAM GOUDYLOCK for Ƚ35-19-3, 400
               acres both sides Rockfish, adj. HENRY TERRELL, MOSES AYRES, MARTHA STOCKTON, DAVIS STOCKTON. Wit: SAML. & THOS. STOCKTON, JNO. ABNEY, RICHARD STOCKTON.

Page 474 14 Jun 1764 DAVID COOK to THOS. PEMBERTON, planter, for Ƚ30, 78
               acres North Garden, adj. HUGH MORRIS. Wit: JAS. & JNO. COFFEY, CHAS. MASSIE.

Page 476 14 Jun 1764 SOLOMON NELSON to JNO. MOORE for Ƚ80, 200 acres both
               sides Moore Creek adj. STEPHEN HUGHES; tract bought from Col. RANDOLPH; bought from JNO. GRILLS & grist mill thereon. Part of pat. of GRILLS. Wit: JNO. HENDERSON JR.

Page 478 11 Apr 1764 BENJ. COLVARD to JAS. & ROBT. DONALDS for Ƚ164-13-9½,
               deed of trust to these merchants; slave, furniture, books 7 accts. Wit: DANL. GAINES, JNO. SWANN, ELISHA COX(?).

Page 479 12 Jun 1764 WM. AMOS, carpenter, to company above to secure Ƚ17-
               -4-6½, slave, blue rug, tools, stock. Wit: BENJ. COLVARD, BENJ. DOD WHEELER, JNO. TOMPKINS.

Page 480 13 Jun 1764 SAML. STOCKTON & wife PRUDENCE; WM. STOCKTON & wife
        JANE (they appear in this order as wives in signatures so I assume
that I have them married to the right men) yeomen, to THOS. STOCKTON, wheel-
right, for Ł100, 100 acres both sides S fork Mitchum River. Pat. to both
6 July 1741.

Page 487 12 July 1764 WM. COX to DANL. McKINSY for Ł30, 594 acres adj.
        WALTON; Sect.'s rolling road; THOS. NAPIER, Rockfish Branch, JNO.
DOUGLAS. Wit: JOHN TOMPKINS, THOS. HICKMAN, THOS. TILMAN.

Page 483 12 Jul 1764 JNO. McCULLOCK & wife MARY to JOSIAS HUNSMAN for
        Ł40, 342 acres S branches of Moorman; Wit: THOS. MERIWETHER, WM.
WOODS, CHAS. MARTIN.

Page 485 9 Aug 1764 NOEL BURTON, Goochland, to JNO. MOOR for Ł125, 400
        acres N side Hardware, adj. RICH. DANIELS (DAMRIL?). Wit: GEO.
PERRY, JER. WADE, THOS. TILMAN.

Page 486 11 Apr 1764 ABRAHAM VENABLE, Louisa, to his son, WM. VENABLE;
        love - 500 acres both sides N branch Great Byrd, lines a little
above Horsepin branch, WM. MARTIN, HOLLARD, GRUBS. Wit: WM. LILLEY, PHILLIP
KING, JNO. LOWRY.

Page 488 14 Dec 1763 PAT. NAPIER & wife MARTHA, to DAVID STAPLES for Ł35,
        106 acres both sides Cunningham Creek adj. WM. PEACE. Wit: ASH-
FORD & THOS. NAPIER, WM. PEARCE.

Page 490 7 Aug 1764 ELIZ. HIGASON to JNO. STRANGE for Ł25, 100 acres
        Ballingers Creek, part of where she and THOS. BABER lived, adj.
Wakeley's branch; LAURENCE MARTIN'S branch, BOLTON. Wit: WM. PEARCE,
CHAS BOULTON, PETER ROY, THOS. BABER, DANL. KING.

Page 491 23 Mar 1764 CHAS. BOLTON to JNO. MARTIN, Goochland, for Ł45, 290
        acres both sides Ballinger's Creek, adj. JNO. LONG, widow DICKER-
SON, JNO. ALLEWAY. Wit: JNO. MOSELEY, JNO. BRITH, WM. PACE. ELIZ, wife of
CHAS. BOLTON.

Page 493 9 Aug 1764 COL. ARTHUR HOPKINS to JNO. HADEN, Goochland, for
        Ł400, 1150 acres both sides Rivanna, adj. BURKS; rock house;
grantor; SAML. HOPKINS; CAPT. JOS. THOMPSON - 350 acres of it known as Dog-
point and on N side and bought from Col. WM. RANDOLPH, dec'd. 800 acres
on upper side pat. to AH.

Page 494 9 Aug 1764 GEO. DAVIDSON & wife MARY, to JAS. WHAREY for 5 sh.,
        170 acres S side Blue Ridge, 1 yr. lease. On next page and same
day, outright sale to JW for Ł40.

Page 497 9 Aug 1764 DANL. ONEAL to THOS. McCOLLOCK for Ł60, 303 acres
        Meecham River; branches of; part of pat. of Col. JNO. CHISWELL
and by him sold to JOHN ROBINSON of King & Queen, and by lawful deed to
D.O. Adj. SAML. TRUSLER, BENJ. DOVES (formerly); JOHN RODES. Wit: JAS.
ADAMS, JNO. McCULLOCK, MICHL. WALLACE, JNO. WOODS.

Page 498 Page torn off - WM. BARNETT SR. to CHRISTOPHER MacRAE for Ł20,
        seven--page torn off - adj. COL. JEFFERSON, JNO. BARNETT. Wit:
JOHN WITT, JAS. HOPKINS, PHILLIP MacRAE.

Page 500 13 Dec 1763 JOS. GOODE to JAS. LYLE, Chesterfield, for Ł37, 180
        acres both sides Bremer Creek, pat. 16 Aug 1756. Wit: RICH.
MACKACSHAN, THOS. McCORMECK, SAML. JORDAN, JNO. TUGGLE, JOS. GOODE JR.,
SAML. JORDAN(2).

Page 501 21 Jan 1764 NATHAN BARNETT, Prince Edwd. Co., to JNO. WEBB, for
        Ł12, 100 acres; upper end and both sides of Raccoon Creek, for-
merly that of WEBB and sold to NB. Wit: PAT. & RO. NAPIER, JNO. BARNETT;
GEORGE THOMPSON, WM. PEARCE, RICH. & ASHFORD NAPIER.

Page 502 25 Jun 1764 GEO. BROCK to SAML. JORDAN, factor for ARCH.INGRAM
        and GEO. KIPPEN, Glasgow merchants; 5 sh., 100 acres Bremo Creek,
branch of Fluvanna, adj. WM. STONE, JNO. MELTON, JNO. MOORE. Wit: J. MOORE,
RICH. WOODS, RO. CLARK, JNO. HARVIE. Deed of trust.

Page 505   18 Jan 1764   PETER JOHNSON, Planter, to friend, CHRISTOPHER CLARK,
           Planter, - gift - where I live - 250 acres adj. ANTHONY POUNCIE.
Wit: JNO. CLARK, HENRY ROLAND, MICAJAH CLARK.

Page 506   30 Oct 1763   Order to J.P.'s - JNO. BISWELL & wife, ELIZ, to
           PETERFIELD TRENT, 7 Dec 1761 - 190 acres. Done by RO. LEWIS &
NICHL. MERIWETHER, 1 Nov 1763.

End of Deed Book 3

AMHERST COUNTY, VIRGINIA

COURTHOUSE MINIATURES

DEED BOOK A 1761 - 1765

This work is dedicated to the Blue Ridge Chapter of the National Society of Daughters of the American Revolution, Lynchburg, Virginia. My wife, Mildred Miller Davis, has recently transferred her membership to this Chapter after some years of pleasant association with the John Fitch Chapter in Bardstown, Kentucky.

FOREWORD

This work is sent out in preliminary commemoration of the two hundredth birthday of Amherst County, Virginia, in 1961. In the year 1761 Amherst was formed from Albemarle, which in turn was formed from Goochland. In 1807 Nelson County was cut off of Amherst County, so all deeds up to that date include land that is now in Nelson County.

The compiler is a Kentuckian and so is his wife, Mildred Miller Davis, but she is descended from George Gillespie and his son, William Gillespie. The latter married Ann Hudson, daughter of Joshua Hudson, and William was a Revolutionary soldier who went to Madison County, Kentucky. The names of George Gillespie and Jushua Hudson appear in the court orders here showing that they rendered assistance to the Continental Army.

He suggests that anyone wishing to locate any particular tract should acquire a Virginia Highway map. This will not give all creeks and branches, but will enable one to get a fairly accurate idea of the location of most of the land herein. Piney River divides Amherst County from her daughter, Nelson County, and any mention of sites on the south side of that river will indicate that the land is in present Amherst. Taylor Creek, Tye River, and Rockfish River references also indicate Nelson County land. This is not, by any means, an exhaustive list of Nelson County creeks and branches, for there are many more. It will be noted on modern maps that the James River divides Lynchburg from Amherst County, but the river is not so called in these early documents. The James River runs around a large portion of Amherst, but in the early days it was called the Fluvanna(h) River and you will so encounter it in many deeds. Buffalo or Buffaloe River is in Amherst and is north of the village of Amherst. It has its headwaters in the mountains to the northwest of Amherst. Little Piney and Piney are in this same area to the northwest of Amherst Courthouse. Huff's Creek is also west and northwest of Amherst. Rocky Creek is east of Amherst in the section known as Buffalo Ridge. This has never been regarded as very productive land. Stovall's Creek is in the southeast section. Partridge Creek is also in this area. Higginbotham and Rutledge are in the Sweet Briar neighborhood which is south of Amherst. Muddy, Miller, Salt, Harris, Lone Buck, Otter, Little Otter, Cedar, Dancing, Puppie(y), Maple, are some of the streams in the west and southwest. A great many of these are tributaries of the Pedlar River which is the stream which you will meet a great many times. Davis Creek is quite often mentioned and it is north of the county seat of Nelson, Lovingston. I had hoped to include a riparian map of these counties, but I am unable to locate anything that I deem suitable.

The same statement can be made as to a map for the mountains of the two counties. The name of Tobacco Row Mountains will appear again and again in these deeds. The map shows that this is a rather long section to the west and southwest of Amherst, but there is one particular peak that is to the southwest that is a landmark and is known as Tobacco Row. The village of Elon nestles at the foot of this peak and the mountain can be spotted for miles on clear days because of some white buildings that are atop it. The western boundaries of Amherst and Nelson are now in the George Washington National Forest. The famous Blue Ridge Parkway skirts the western borders of the two counties. The Big Priest and Little Priest are two of the many peaks in Nelson. Amherst folk love their "Sleeping Giant of Amherst" and it is a gorgeous sight to stand at the "Traffic Circle" in Amherst on a clear day and to gaze at this spectacle. Mount Pleasant, Long Mountain, Cold Mountain, Enchanted Mountain, Big Friar, Little Friar - one could go on for sometime just calling the names of the spots in western Amherst.

Beautiful drives are to be found in many of these areas. One of the favorite expeditions that my wife and I like to take is the drive up U.S. 29 north of Amherst for a few miles. One looks to the west and the Blue Ridge never presents the same appearance to the admirers. We turn west of U.S. 151 and go by the Winton estate at Clifford, where Patrick Henry's mother is buried, and go into Nelson as we cross Piney River. There is a breathtaking side trip that one can take on this drive. One can turn to the west on U.S. 56 and go to the beautiful Crab Tree Falls and then on to the Parkway. Nelson County is justly proud of the Falls and efforts are being made to save them from future commercialization. The main drive that we mentioned takes us up the scenic Rockfish Valley to Afton.

We leave the discussion of the historic homes to others who are better qualified, but there are many in the two counties. Winton, Kenmore, Tusculum, Edgehill, Red Hill, the Glebe (Miner Hall), Mt. San Angelo, and others, dot the terrain of Amherst County. Nelson nestles the Thomas Fortune estate and there are other ancient homes there, too. The spacious campus of Sweet Briar College is always shown to our visitors.

You will see references to New Glasgow and when you consult a map you will note that it is a station on the Southern Railroad. Do not be misled, however, for New Glasgow became the village of Clifford in 1883. Clifford is on U.S. 151 and the Winton estate, previously mentioned, is nearby.

This is an abstract and does not pretend to include the poles and degrees. One can easily obtain a copy of any deed by writing to the Circuit Clerk of the County. Pd. stands for pounds, sh. for shillings; AC for Amherst County. All counties otherwise mentioned are in Virginia, unless stipulated. "Lines" refers to names of adjoining property owners. Some deeds are disappointing in that there is seemingly no data in them to give approximate location, but it is included whenever given.

We wish to thank Miss Helen Edgemon and Miss Mildred Edgemon for their invaluable assistance. They are on the Sweet Briar College Library Staff and have typed the stencils and have run the mimeograph for me [for the original edition]. My wife has given me sympathetic audience as I have taken my discussion of the work to her. The staff at the courthouse, Mr. William Sandidge, Circuit Clerk; Mrs. Raymond Gregory, Deputy; and Mr. Lloyd Storey, Deputy; have been patient with me as I have visited the courthouse. We do not claim infallibility for our work and assume all responsibility for any errors that might accidentally creep into a compilation of this sort. However, we have tried to be as painstaking as possible and send this work forth with the hope that it will be a pleasure and profit to those who use it.

It joins a small group of works that have been done on the county of Amherst. The first one that we have encountered is that of Hardesty and Brock. I have indexed the names in the biographical sections of Amherst and Bedford and followed the pattern employed in my Kentucky index on the Sixth Edition of the book of Kentucky History by Perrin, Battle, and Kniffin. I have not attempted to print it, though, for so few libraries have original copies of this book by Hardesty and Brock. Mrs. Bess Willis Shrader issued a work in 1946 on Amherst and Nelson County citizens of recent years. The two modern contributions of great merit to genealogists are those of Mr. William Sweeny and his wife, Mrs. Leonora Higginbotham Sweeny. Mr. Sweeny compiled Amherst marriages from 1761 to 1801. Mrs. Sweeny published her excellent book, Amherst County in the Revolution with Excerpts from the Lost Order Book. She is the Grand Lady of Amherst Genealogy in my eyes and she comes here from her New York home to do research. It is always a pleasure to find her poring over the records when I enter the record room. She has been most encouraging in this project.

If I am spared to do so, I plan to issue additional works in this series.

Bailey Fulton Davis

Amherst Baptist Church
Pastor's Study
January 22, 1960

ABSTRACTS OF DEEDS AND ALL OTHER ITEMS
IN DEED BOOK A
OF AMHERST COUNTY, VIRGINIA

Page 1.   JOHN REID, JAMES NEVILL, JOHN ROSE, & JOSEPH CABELL, Amherst County Gentlemen, bound in the sum of one thousand pounds to our Sovereign Lord King, GEORGE the Third, June 1, 1761. JOHN REID has been appointed Sheriff by Governor under searl of Colony on May 2, 1761, and is
accountable for all sums of money and Tobacco by him received. Court held
at HENRY KEY's on June 1, 1761. GEORGE SEATON, Clerk.

Page 1f.   JOHN REID, JAMES NEVILL, & JOHN ROSE*, Amherst County Gentlemen,
bound to our Sovereign Lord King, GEORGE the Third, for five hundred pounds, June 1, 1761. JOHN REID was appointed Sheriff for Amherst Co.
by Governor of Colony under seal dated May 2, 1761. He is hereby bonded to
collect all fines, Quitrents, forfeitures, and Americaments and to pay them
to His Majesty's Revenues on or before the second Tuesday in June annually.
Court held at HENRY KEY's, June 1, 1761. *(For interesting information on
RUCKER, ROSE, FLOYD and several other Amherst familes, consult Alfred Percy's
Piedmont Apocalypse.)

Page 2.   JOHN REID, WILLIAM CABELL, & JAMES NEVIL, Gentlemen of Amherst Co.
bound to King George III for one thousand pounds. REID's appoint-
ment is set forth as in the two items above and he is bound to collect taxes.
Court held at HENRY KEY's, Sept. 7, 1761.

Page 3.   1 Jun 1761. JAMES CULL, Amherst County, to DAWSON WADE of Colony
of Virginia, for 10 sh., 60 acres on South branch of North fork
of Davis's Creek. Lines: JOHN WADE's corner. CULL will execute any other
acts or conveyances to assure and convey within the next twenty years.
Court held at HENRY KEY's on June 1, 1761. GEORGE SEATON, Clerk.

Page 4f.   6 July, in first year of the Reign of our Sovereign Lord George
the Third, by the grace of God of Great Britain, France, and Ireland, King, Defender of the Faith, etc..1761..WILLIAM FLOYD & ABBEGAL, wife,
of Amherst County and Parish, to RODERICK MACCULLOCK, of Amherst Co., 369
acres on Stone's Creek in cove of the Tobacco Row Mountain. Rent of one
pepper corn upon the feast day of St. Michael the Archangel. Signature of
WILLIAM FLOYD and mark of ABEGAIL. She had been privily examined. Court
held at HENRY KEY's, 6 Jul 1761.

Page 6.   6 Jul 1761. WILLIAM FLOYD & wife, ABIGAIL of Amherst, to RODERICK
MACCULLOCK...Reference to lease made and fifty pounds for 369
acres on Stone's Creek in the cove of the Tobacco Row Mountains. Signature
of FLOYD and mark of wife, ABIGAIL. Court held at HENRY KEY's, 6 Jul 1761.
GEORGE SEATON, Clerk.

Page 9.   3 Aug 1761. BENJAMIN STINNET, AC, to JAMES ISHAM, AC. STINNET in
consideration of a certain promise made by him to JAMES ISHAM at
time of his intermarrying with his daughter has bargained, sold, etc., to
ISHAM 100 acres near Tobacco Row Mountain on Huff's Creek. It is lower part
of 400 acres patented to BENJAMIN STINNET on June 1, 1750, and is now in
ISHAM's possession. Mark of STINNET. Court held at HENRY KEY's, 3 Aug 1761.

Page 10.   1 Aug 1761. WILLIAM MONTGOMERY & wife JANE to THOMAS SHANNON, AC,
for 40 pds, 208 acres on Rockfish River and part of 640 acres
bought of JOHN CHISWELL by ALEXANDER MONTGOMERY and conveyed by him to WILL-
IAM MONTGOMERY by deed of 10 Feb 1752. Lines: top of a mountain. Signature
of WILLIAM MOUNTGOMERY(sic) and mark of JANE. Wit: DAVID CRAWFORD, JACOB
BROWN, JOHN LOVING. Court held at HENRY KEY's, 3 Aug 1761.

Page 12f. 7 Dec 1761. WILLIAM CABELL, SR., AC, to DANIEL McKINSEY (MCKEN-
ZIE on margin) for 50 pds, 150 acres on both sides of Ivy Branch
of Tye River. Lines: SAMUEL MARKSBURY, dec'd. Wit: WILLIAM MANRAW & HENRY
FRANKLIN. Court held at HENRY KEY's, 7 Dec 1761.

Page 14. 7 Dec 1761. SAMUEL MILLER, AC, to JAMES MONTGOMERY, Blacksmith,
AC, for 24 pds, 200 acres which SAMUEL MILLER purchased of JOHN
BURNS by deed 10 Apr 1755. South side of and joining Cove Creek and part of
222 acres by patent to JOHN BURNS on 24 Apr 1753. 22 acres sold by JOHN

BURNS to ALEXANDER CHISM and to avoid mistakes this is included in descrip-
tions. Lines: JAMES LEWIS' corner; Cove Creek; Capt. CHARLES LEWIS; ALEXAN-
DER CHISM. Turf and twig parcel "in lieu of the whole". Court held at
HENRY KEY's 7 Dec 1761.

Page 15.   1 Dec 1761. THOMAS JOPLING, AC, to JOHN ROBERTS, AC, 25 pds.
            for 300 acres...North side of South Fork of Rockfish. Lines:
Widow UPTON, Widow JOHNSON. Mark of THOS. JOPLING. Wit: THOMAS FARRAR,
WILLIAM COX, JAMES JOPLING. Court held at HENRY KEY's 7 Dec 1761, and THOS.
FARRAR & JAMES JOPLING certified as to deed. At court held at the court-
house 1 Mar 1762, THOS. JOPLING ack. receipt of payment. This first court-
house was in what is now Nelson county.

Page 17.   1 Mar 1762. HUGH WILLOBY(sic), AC, to CHARLES TATE, AC, 10 pds.
            for 100 acres, branches of South fork of Rockfish and part of
371 acres pat. to HUGH WILLOBY 7 Aug 1761. Lines: CHARLES MCANALLEY. Proved
at court held at courthouse 1 Mar 1762. AGNES WILLOBY, wife of HUGH, privily
examined. HUGH made his mark.

Page 18f.   27 Feb 1762. SAMUEL MANN & wife MARGARET, AC to NATHANIEL MANN,
            AC, for 7 pds. for 31 acres on Taylor's Creek, branch of Rock-
fish and part of 172 acres granted to ALEXANDER PATTON by patent 12 Jan
1746, and now in possession of SAMUEL MANN. Lines: ARCHIBALD WOODS. SAMUEL
MANN signed and MARGARET made her mark. Wit: THOS. REID, ALEX. REID, ALEX.
REID, JR., JAMES MCALEXANDER JR., JOHN REID.

Page 20f.   2 May 1761. BENJAMIN HIGGINBOTHAM, AC to RICHARD DAVIS, AC, for
            60 pds, 204 acres on branch of Buffalo River. Tract of 204 acres
granted to BENJAMIN HIGGINBOTHAM by MOSES HIGGINBOTHAM, 14 May 1751, in Albemarle. Signed by BENJ. HIGGINBOTHAM & wife, ELIZABETH. Wit: MOSES, JOHN,
& JAMES HIGGINBOTHAM. Court held at HENRY KEY's, 7 Sep 1761.

Page 21.   5 Sep 1761. JAMES WOODS, AC, to MARY WOODS, wife of SAML. WOODS.
            JAMES WOODS for natural love and affection for his daughter,
MARY WOODS, and for the better maintainance and livelyhood of her, conveys
to her and lawfully begotten heirs of her body 200 acres in Amherst County
and negro boy named Adam. Lines: JOHN MORRISON, DAVID CRAWFORD, JR., JOHN
REID, side of a mountain. Part of 400 acres to JAMES WOODS by "patton" at
Williamsburg, 28 Aug 1746. Mark of WOODS. Wit: ALEXANDER REID, JOHN FARRER,
PETER FARRER, THOS. REID.

Page 23.   5 Oct 1761. GEORGE CARRINGTON, Parish of South Ann(?), Cumber-
            land Co., to JAMES CREWS, AC, for 16 pds. for 200 acres...next
to JAMES CREWS...N side of Harrises Creek and part of pat. to GEORGE CAR-
RINGTON 20 Jun 1753. Wit: JAMES NEVIL, HENRY KEY, NATHANIEL WATKINS, WM.
CABELL, JR., JOSEPH CABELL.

Page 25.   25 Sep 1761(?) and proven in court on 1 Mar 1762. JOHN SUTTEN-
            FIELD, AC, to HENRY KEY, AC, for 20 pds. 8 sh. 3 p., one dark
bay about seven and branded on near buttock and household goods. Wit: JOHN
PETER, DANIEL AARON(X).

Page 26.   16 Sep 1761. JOHN HICKS, AC, to HENRY KEY, for 7 pds. 14 sh. 2p.
            one black horse about four and branded on near buttock, five
head of cattle, one feather bed and furniture now in HICK's possession.
Mark of HICKS. Wit: JOHN GREGORY(X) & JOHN PETER.

Page 26.   26 Nov 1761. PATRICK MORRISON, AC, to HENRY KEY, 19pds, 17sh.
            1p...mare, colt, 3 cows & 2 calves & household goods. Wit: JOHN
PETER, ELIAS SMITH(X), JOHN MANNING(X).

Page 27.   13 Nov 1761. JOHN JONES, AC, to HENRY KEY, AC, for 28 pds. 7p,
            2 cows and calves and other stock and all my household goods.
Wit: JOHN PETER & SUSANNAH NEVIL(X).

Page 28.   1 Mar 1762. ANGUS FORBES & wife, CATHERINE FORBES (spelled
            FORBAS in deed) for 10 pds, 66 acres on Rockfish, to CHARLES
YANCEY, AC.

Page 30.   24 Oct 1761. WILLIAM ROSS to ALEXANDER CHISM, for 10 pds, 394

acres. Lines: JAMES LEWIS - near Hickory Creek; JOHN & WM. BURNS. Wit:
GEORGE BLENE & GEORGE BLENE, JR., ALEX. BLENE.

Page 31. 3 May 1762. BENJAMIN STINNET, AC, to BENJAMIN STINNET, JR., for
love and affection borne his son, BENJ. JR., 150 acres on Huff's
Creek and middle part of 200 acres patented to BENJ. Sr. Lines: JAMES ISHAM.

Page 32. 25 Mar 1762. ALEXANDER MONTGOMERY, JR. of St. Matthews Parish of
Orange Co, NC, to ROBERT BARNETT, AC, 15 pds. for 250 acres on
both sides of Buck(?) Creek and part of 450 acres pat. to ALEX. MONTGOMERY,
Sr., at Williamsburg, 25 Jun 1747, and sold by him to ALEX., JR., and now
in BARNETT'S possession. Wit: WILLIAM MONTGOMERY, JOHN BARNET, THEOBALD
WAIGHAN (or MAIGHAN).

Page 33. 9 Mar 1762. HUGH WILLOUGHBY & wife, AGNES, AC, to CHARLES McAN-
ALLY, AC, for 5 pds., 100 acres on branch of South Fork of Rock-
fish and part of 371 acres pat. at Williamsburg to WILLOUGHBY 7 Aug 1761.
Lines: JAMES NEVIL. Wit: JOHN REID, JAMES NEVIL, CHAS. TATE(X).

Page 34. 3 May 1762. WILLIAM BUTTER, AC, to THOMAS WEST, AC, 22 pds. for
95 acres...N branch of Davis's Creek. Lines: JAMES McALEXANDER.
BUTTER made his mark and FRANCIS BUTTER, his wife, also signed.

Page 36. 5 Jul 1762. JOSEPH BALLENGER & SARAH BALLENGER, wife, and RICH-
ARD BALLENGER, AC, to JOSEPH MAYS, AC, 60 pds. for 400 acres.
Lines: Ballenger's Mountain, EDWARD CARTER. Wit: GEORGE SEATON, WM. CHEEKE,
SAMUEL HINSLEE.

Page 38. 26 Mar 1762. ADAM LACKEY, AC, weaver, to JOHN LACKEY, JR., 53
pds. for 200 acres, part of tract pat. to CHARLES SMITH, now of
Augusta, of 400 acres on Hockory Creek. Wit: JOHN LACKEY, SR., DAVID CRAW-
FOR, JR., DAVID MARTIN, JOEL CRAWFORD, JAMES LACKEY, JAMES TROTTER or
TOTTER(X).

Page 40. 16 Mar 1762. ROBERT WILBUN, AC, to GABRIEL PENN & CO., Merchants
of AC...Deed of Trust for 100 pds...one negro man, Daniel, formerly belonging to JOYN WARREN SR.; furniture, horses, & "rest of my estate". To be paid by 10 Jun 1765.

Page 41. 8 May 1762. JOHN DAVIS, Albemarle Co., to JAMES TULLEY SR. of
Albemarle, 57 pds, 10 sh. for 400 acres. Lines: ROBERT DAVIS,JR.
Wit: GEORGE MILLER, ISHAM DAVIS, EDMUND NEW, MARTIN DAWSON(X).

Page 42. 27 Apr 1762. JOHN DEMPSEY to GEO. MILLER, Factor of ARCHIBALD
INGRAM & Co., Glasgow merchants, 11 pds, 2sh, 1p...Deed of trust,
cattle & horses. Wit: WM. JOHNSTONE, JNO. LOVING, GEO. SEATON.

Page 44. 6 Apr 1762. JOHN ROBINSON, Esq., King & Queen County, to LANGS-
DON DEPREIST, AC, 50 pds. for 400 acres...Lynches' Creek...N side
of Rockfish, part of tract granted to JOHN CHISWELL by patest and now property of ROBINSON. Lines: JOHN BILL(?), Lynches Creek. Wit: GEORGE CARRING-
TON, JOS. CABELL, CORN. THOMAS, WM. CABELL, JR.

Page 45. 6 Apr 1762. JOHN ROBINSON of King & Queen Co. to EDWARD STEPEHN-
SON, AC, 35 pds. for 224 acres on Lynches Creek; N side of Rock-
fish and part of a tract pat. to JOHN CHISWELL and now property of ROBIN-
SON. Lines: MARTHA ROBINSON, JAS. MARTIN, LANGSDON DEPRIEST. Wit: GEORGE
CARRINGTON, CORN. THOMAS, JOS. CABELL, WM. CABELL JR.

Page 46. 6 Apr 1762. JOHN ROBINSON, Esq., King & Queen Co., to JOHN
THOMPSON, AC, 31 pds. for 275 acres on both sides of Rockfish;
part of tract granted to Col. JOHN CHISWELL by patent and now property of
ROBINSON. Lines: JOHN SMALL, SAMUEL BELL, JOHN ROBINSON. Wit: GEORGE CAR-
RINGTON, CORNELIUS THOMAS, JOSEPH CABELL, WM. CABELL JR.

Page 47. 6 Apr 1762. JOHN ROBINSON, King & Queen Co., to JOSEPH MILLER,
AC, 11 pds. 14 sh. for 90 acres; S side of and joining Rockfish
and part of tract pat. to JOHN CHISWELL and now property of ROBINSON.
Lines: MICHAEL MONTGOMERY, JOSEPH BARNETT...now in MILLER's possession.
Wit: GEORGE CARRINGTON, CORNELIUS THOMAS, JOSEPH CABELL, WM. CABELL JR.

Page 49.   5 Jul 1762.   JOHN FIDLER (alias LOVING) and wife SARAH, AC, to
VALENTINE BALL, AC, 65pds. for 2 tracts of 590 acres on both
sides of Tye River. 350 acres and part of which was patented to SAMUEL
BURKS JR., 25 Jun 1746. Small Ivy Island mentioned.   240 acres granted to
JOHN FIDLER, alias LOVING, by patent on 2 Jun 1760. BURKS' line mentioned
and now in possession of BALL. X of SARAH.

Page 50.   5 Jul 1762.   ROBERT BARNETT, AC, to JOHN FARRAR, AC, 50 pds. for
260 acres on Rockfish near the "Blew Mountains". Lines: JOHN
WRIGHT on Rockfish, WILLIAM MONTGOMERY, JOHN SMALL. Part of 11,140 acres
pat. to JOHN CHISWELL 25 Mar 1739, and by him conveyed to ALEXANDER MONT-
GOMERY 25 Apr 1745, and conveyed by MONTGOMERY to ROBERT BARNETT 4 Aug 1759.
Wit: SAMUEL HENSLEE, MATTHEW HARRIS, THEOBALD MAIGHAN.

Page 52.   2 Jul 1762.   HENRY TENISON SR., AC, to JOHN SIMS TENISON for 5
sh., 100 acres. Lines: HENRY TENISON JR. & SR.

Page 53.   2 Jul 1762.   HENRY TENISON SR., AC, to HENRY TENISON JR., for 5
sh., 100 acres. Lines: JAMES CHRISTIAN on Porrage Creek.

Page 54.   3 Jul 1762.   SARAH LYNCH, Bedford Co., to GEORGE McDANIEL, AC,
70 pds. for 400 acres on headwaters of Bowling's and Stovall's
Creek. She is possessed of it by King's Letters Patent. Wit: DANIEL BURFORD,
HENRY TENISON, PATRICK MORRICE, WILLIAM CANDLER, HENRY GUTTRY.

Page 55.   3 Jul 1762.   SARAH LYNCH, Bedford Co., to GEORGE McDANIEL, AC,
10 pds. for 100 acres on Head branches of Stovall's creek. Wit:
DANIEL BURFORD, HENRY TENISON, PATRICK MORRICE, WILLIAM CANDLER, HENRY
GUTTRY.

Page 57.   6 Sep 1762.   AARON HIGGINBOTHAM & wife, CLARY, AC, to WILLIAM
CABELL, JR., & CORNELIUS THOMAS, Church Wardens of Amherst Parish; 120 pds. for 204 acres for glebe for parish. On branch of HIGGINBO-
THAM's old Mill creek and part of tract granted to Col. GEORGE BRAXTON,
late of King and Queen, and by him conveyed to MOSES HIGGINBOTHAM, and by
him to AARON HIGGINBOTHAM. Lines: BRAXTON. Mark of CLARY.

Page 58.   14 Aug 1762.   CARTER BRAXTON, King William Co., to WILLIAM CA-
BELL JR. & CORNELIUS THOMAS, Church Wardens for Amherst Parish
and successors - 5 pds. for glebe use - 50 acres on branch of HIGGINBOTHAMS
Old Mill Creek of Buffalo; part of larger tract of late Col. GEO. BRAXTON,
King and Queen Co., and by him devised to the said CARTER BRAXTON. Lines:
AARON HIGGINBOTHAM. Wit: AMBROSE LEE, AARON & SAMUEL HIGGINBOTHAM.

Page 59.   1 Mar 1762.   JOHN WOODS, Albemarle Co, & SUSANNAH, wife, to
CHARLES YANCEY, AC. 38 pds. for 232 acres, Rockfish River. Lines:
ARCHIBALD WOODS, COL. CHISWELL. Wit: THOMAS REID, MARGARET ANDERSON(X),
JOHN PRICE, JAMES DUNWOODY, JOEL CRAWFORD.

Page 61.   7 Jun 1761.   GEORGE CARRINGTON, Parish of So-Ham in Cumberland
Co. to ISAAC WRIGHT, AC. 27 pds, 19 sh. for 466 acres on Harris
Creek. Linds: DANIEL BURFORD, SHELTON's line. Wit: CORNELIUS THOMAS, JOHN
WOODROOF, JOHN LOVING,DANIEL BURFORD.

Page 63.   27 Jul 1762.   JOHN PARTREE BURKS, Bedford Co., to HUGH MORRIS,
Albemarle Co.; 10 pds. for 420 acres on Maple Creek, granted by
pat. to BURKS. Lines: MICAJAH CLARK. X of BURKS. Wit: CORNELIUS THOMAS,
GABRIEL PENN, AMBROSE LEE, ROBERT DAVIS.

Page 64.   6 Sep 1762.   DAVIS ROSER, Bedford Co, planter, to JOHN RUCKER,
AC, Planter, 40 pds. for 204 acres. Lines: BERNARD GAINES, AM-
BROSE RUCKER. Wit: JOHN GOFF(X), AMBROSE RUCKER.

Page 66.   22 May 1762.   JAMES HIRD, AC, to JOHN PRICE, AC, one red cow.
Wit: JOEL CRAWFORD. X of HIRD.

Page 66.   22 Jul 1762.   JOSEPH KING, AC, to JOHN PRICE, AC, 4 pds. 10 sh.;
one brindle cow & calf; one black cow. X of KING. Wit: JAMES
& RO. DUNWOODY.

Page 66. 9 Jun 1762. JOHN HOWARD, Goochland, to STEPHEN TURNER, AC, 100
      pds. for 178 acres on N side of Fluvanna River. Lines: WILLIAM
CABELL's corner. Part of 2380 acres granted by patent to ALLEN HOWARD 30
Jul 1742. Wit: MOSES SWEENY, JOSEPH UPTON, JOHN HAMPTON, SAMUEL PARKER.
(X's for UPTON, HAMPTON, & PARKER.)

Page 68. 1 Sep 1762. ELIAS DEHART, AC, to SIMON DEHART, SR., AC, 10 pds
      for 138 acres, part of a larger tract, both sides of Poridge
Creek. Lines: CHRISTIAN's corner; it being upper end of tract pat. to
ELIAS DEHART 20 Aug 1760. A note within body of deed says that this is
made for SIMON DEHART "Senere".

Page 70. 22 Aug 1762. ARCHIBALD WOODS & wife ISABEL, Albemarle, to
      MICHAEL WOODS, Albemarle, 198 pds. for 243 acres on Taylor's
Creek, branch of Rockfish. Part of 400 acres pat. to ARCHIBALD WOODS 30
Jan 1741. Wit: WILLIAM SHAW, JAMES LACKEY, JOHN COWAN, WILLIAM WOODS.

Page 72. 4 Oct 1762. ZACHARIAH PHILIPS, AC, to ANNE NEAL, AC; 6 pds.
      for 144 acres on N fork of Nassau Creek. Lines: LUNSFORD LOMAX.

Page 74. 1 Oct 1762. ROBERT BARNETT, AC, to WILLIAM MONTGOMERY, AC, 30
      pds. for 187 acres; S side of Hatt creek near the Nassau Moun-
tain. Lines: Late Col. WILLIAM RANDOLPH. Pat. to ROBERT BARNETT 10 Dec
1755.

Page 76. 26 Jan 1763. ELIAS DEHART, AC, to WILLIAM DUIGUID, Buckingham
      Co., 25 pds. for 112 acres, both sides of Porridge Creek. Lines:
DEHART, WILLIAM TACKET. Part of 300 acres tract pat. to ELIAS DEHART 20
Aug 1760. Wit: AARON DEHART (X), MATHEW WHITELL(?), JAMES BECKHAM, JAMES
WARREN JR.(X), JOHN WARREN JR.

Page 78. 9 Aug 1762. WILLIAM WARD, AC, 12 pds. to AMBROSE JONES, AC...
      household goods...Deed of trust. To be repaid by next 10 March.
Wit: JOHN WARD(X), EDMUND MANION, JOHN LOVING.

Page 79. [This bond is being inserted in its entire form because of its
      interest. Note very poor punctuation.]   This Indenture wit-
nesseth that JOHN WARD Late of Amherst County hath put himself and by
these presents doth voluntarily of his own free will and accord Put himself Apprentice to AMBROSE JONES of the said County to Serve him from the
Day of the date hereof for and during the Term of one year next Insuing
During all which term the said Apprentice his said Master faithfully
shall serve his Secrets keep his lawful commands gladly and everywhere
obey he shall do no Damage to his said Master nor see it done by others
without leting or giving notice thereof to his Said Master he shall not
waste his Master's goods nor Lend them unlawfully to any he shall not
commit fornication nor contract Matrimony within the said Term at Cards
or dice or any other unlawful games he shall not Play Whereby his said
Master may have Damage with his own Goods, nor the Goods of others he
shall not Abscond nor absent himself from his said Master's services day
nor night without his leave nor haunt Ale houses, Taverns or Playhouses
but in all things behave himself as a faithful Apprentice ought to do
During the said Term, and the said Master shall use the utmost of his
Indeavour to Procure and Provide for him Sufficient meat Drink apparel
Lodging and Washing Fiting for an Apprentice during the said Covenants
and agreements, Either of the said Parties bind themselves unto the other
by these Presents In Witness whereof the said Parties have Interchangea-
bly set their hands and Seals this Sixteenth day of February and in the
third year of our Sovereign Lork King George the third and in the year
our Lord Christ one thousand Seven hundred and Sixty three. X of WARD
and signature of JONES.   Memorandum that the within named AMBROSE
JONES agreed before signing the within Indenture that whenever the within
Bound JOHN WARD should Satisby Pay and Discharge a Debt of nine pounds
Seventeen shillings and six pence which he is Justly indebted to the said
JONES by Bond, that then the said JONES is to Discharge and free the said
Apprentice from any further Servitude. Witness this Sixteenth Day of
February 1763. AMBROSE JONES. Test: JOHN REID, GABRIEL PENN.   At a
Court held for Amherst County at the Courthouse the 7th Day of March,
1763, This Indenture was proved by the oaths of the witnesses and ordered
to be recorded. GEORGE SEATON, Clerk.

Page 80. 20 Jan 1763. CHARLES SMITH, AC, to JOHN LACKEY, 10 pds. for 75
acres. Lines: Trees marked by RICHARD LAWRENCE and ADAM LACKEY;
JAMES JOHNSON. Wit: ROBERT DUNWOODY, JAMES DUNWOODY, SAMUEL MORRAL, JR.,
JAMES DINWIDDIE, JR.

Page 81. 20 Jan 1763. CHARLES SMITH to RICHARD LAWRENCE, 10 pds. for 75
acres. Lines: Marked trees "maid" by RICHARD LAWRENCE and ADAM
LACKEY...Hickory Creek to the side of a mountain...JAMES JOHNSON. Wit:
SAMUEL MORRAL, JR., JOHN LACKEY, JOHN DAWSON, JOHN LAWRENCE(X).

Page 82. 28 Dec 1762. CALEB WORLEY, AC, to SAMUEL AYRES, Hanover Co.,
125 pds. for 250 acres...Branch of Beaver Creek on East and
joining Tobacco Row Mountain...part of a tract of 2700 acres pat. to
WILLIAM CABELL, JR. Lines: WILLIAM CABELL, JR., Smith's Mountain, JACOB
BROWN. [On page 83 it is stated that WORLEY's wife was examined as to
dower rights, but her name is not given.]

Page 84. 9 Nov 1762. JOHN BENGER of Spotsylvania, to PETER CASHWELL, AC,
49 pds 18 sh 4 p for 832 acres on branch of Higginbotham's Mill
Creek, branch of Camp Creek. Lines: MEREDITH, RICHARD DAVIS, HIGGINBOTHAM,
ROSE's line...part of a larger tract of 2163 acres pat. to ELLIOTT BENGER,
father of JOHN BENGER, at Williamsburg, 25 Nov 1743. Wit: GABRIEL PENN,
AMBROSE PORTER, JAMES HIGGINBOTHAM.

Page 85. 7 Mar 1763. WILLIAM WRIGHT & wife, ESTHER, AC to ROBERT WRIGHT,
AC...5 sh. and for natural love and affection borne ROBERT
WRIGHT as their son...166 acres on S branch of Davis Creek and pat. to
WILLIAM WRIGHT 1 Jun 1750. Mark of ESTER(sic) and turf and twig possess-
ion given.

Page 87. 1 Oct 1762. BARNARD GAINES & wife SARAH, St. Ann's Parish,
Essex Co., to JOHN THOMAS of same; 5 sh. for 450 acres which
GAINES bought from ROBERT ROSE, Clerk, and recorded in Albemarle. Land is
known as Aberfoil. Lines: Stake at line of tract of 1100 acres which is
part of tract of 9600 acres and which is known by name of Starksbury
Plain...patent line...to corner of 450 acres; part of tract and granted
by ROBERT ROSE, Clerk, by deeds of lease and release unto MARGARET MUS-
CHELT and along her lines to the beginning.

Page 88. 2 Oct 1762. BARNARD GAINES & wife SARAH, St. Ann's Parish,
Essex Co., to JOHN THOMAS of same parish and county. 35 pds.
for 450 acres and description is same as that of deed on page 87.

Page 90. Order to SIMON MILLER and PAUL MICOU, Justices of Essex Co., to
examine SARAH GAINES as to dower rights in deeds and apart from
her husband, BARNARD GAINES, October 1 and 2, 1762, to JOHN THOMAS. Order
sent by GEORGE SEATON, Clerk of AMHERST Co., 4 Oct 1762, and the justices
reported that they had performed their duty on 20 Nov 1762.

Page 91. 7 Mar 1763. DAVID CRAWFORD, JR., & wife ELIZABETH, planters,
to ABRAM WARWICK, Taylor, for 50 pds, 200 acres on both sides
Hickory Creek...then patented in Albermarle...and part of 400 acres taken
up and patented by JOHN BARNS and by BARNS transferred to DAVID CRAWFORD,
and transferred by JOHN CRAWFORD to DAVID CRAWFORD, JR. Pat. 3 Nov MDCCL
--or so it appears. Lines: Rockfish Road and Hickory Creek.

Page 93. 7 Feb 1763. JAMES BARNETT, AC, to WILLIAM BARNETT, AC, 1 pd.
5 sh. for 50 acres...S branch of Rockfish...JAMES BARNETT's
heirs...the said WILLIAM BARNETT, excepted. Wit: FRANCIS MERIWETHER, JOHN
PRICE, WILLIAM RAY.

Page 95. 25 Feb 1763. ABRAHAM WARWICK, AC, to WILLIAM TILLER, AC, 25
pds. for 100 acres and part of tract which ABRAHAM WARWICK
bought from DAVID CRAWFORD. Lines: ALEXANDER CHISHOLM, TERISHA TURNER,
JOHN LYON. X of WARWICK.

Page 96. 7 Mar 1763. HENRY ROBERTS, AC, to BENJAMIN MOOR, AC, 50 pds.
for 384 acres. This land formerly belonged to MORRICE ROBERTS,
deceased. Lines: JOHN LYON, JOHN SORREL, JOHN CRAWFORD. X of HENRY
ROBERTS.

76

Page 97.   19 Nov 1762.   JOHN ROBINSON, King and Queen Co., to JAMES
            MONTGOMERY, AC. 20 pds. for 207 acres, S side of Rockfish and
part of tract granted to JOHN CHISWELL, Gent., and now property of ROBIN-
SON. Lines: WILLIAM HARRIS, JOHN MONTGOMERY. Wit: GEORGE CARRINGTON,
CORNELIUS THOMAS, JOSEPH CABELL, WILLIAM CABELL, JR.

Page 99.   7 Mar 1763.   JOHN FREEMAN & wife, ABIGAIL, AC, to PARAN FARRAH,
            20 pds for 300 acres. Wit: MATTHEW TUCKER, CHARLES BOND, JR.,
JOSEPH BALLENGER.

Page 100.   7 Mar 1763.   JOHN FREEMAN, AC, to NATHAN BOND, AC, 84 pds. for
            300 acres...Stone House Creek. Said 300 acres being part of
two joining tracts granted to JOHN FREEMAN. Wit: MATTHEW TUCKER, CHARLES
BONDS, Jr., JOSEPH BALLENGER.

Page 102.   7 Mar 1763.   JOHN FREEMAN & wife, ABIGAIL, AC, to JONATHAN
            STAMPER, AC...40 pds for 200 acres. Lines: Stonehouse Creek.
Wit: MATTHEW TUCKER, CHARLES BOND, JR., JOSEPH BALLENGER.

Page 104.   21 Jan 1763. ELIAS DEHART, AC, to WILLIAM TACKETT, AC, 3 pds
            for 50 acres...part of larger tract on Porage Creek and on
both sides. Lines: CHRISTIAN; part of tract patented to ELIAS DEHART 20
Aug 1760. Wit: JOSEPH MAGANN, HENRY TENISON, SR., JOHN LAMASTER JR.(X)

Page 105.   7 Mar 1763.   AMBROSE JONES, Eldest son and heir at law of
            THOMAS JONES, and wife DOROTHY, late of St. Anne's Parish,
Albermarle, Deceased, and Administrator of all the goods, etc., of THOMAS
JONES at time of his death, and JAMES JONES, another of the sons of
THOMAS JONES, and DOROTHY,his wife, to GEORGE SEATON of AC...Lease made
between ROBERT ROSE, late of St. Anne's of Essex, Clerk, and THOMAS JONES,
on 8 April MDCCXLVI, and recorded in Albermarle of 14 May in year named...
200 acres on Tye River in Albermarle, now Amherst, and where THOMAS JONES
then lived...W side of the river by a small run near the Main Road...
leased for natural lives of THOMAS JONES & wife and ten years to survivor
of the two...THOMAS JONES died on...day in year MDCCLIX...now for 40 pds
from SEATON the heirs of THOMAS JONES sell him remainder of DOROTHY, widow of THOMAS JONES, in lease. Signed by AMBROSE & JAMES JONES & GEORGE
SEATON, Clerk of Amherst County.

Page 108.   27 Apr 1763. JAMES WOODS, AC, farmer, to RICHARD McCLAIN, AC,
            100 acres for 8 pds...Lines: SAMUEL MILLER, JANE WHITE, FRAN-
CIS MERIWETHER; X of JAMES WOODS. Wit: SAMUEL WOODS, WILLIAM McMULLAN,
JAMES BELL.

Page 109.   23 Apr 1763. WILLIAM CABELL & wife, MARGARET, AC, to WILLIAM
            CABELL, the Younger...for love and affection unto their loving
son, WILLIAM CABELL, JR. and in consideration of a certain promise made
to him (with reservations hereinafter mentioned:...1785 acres on N side
of and joining Fluvana River and known as CABELL's Great Low Grounds.
Lines: Elm on N side of Fluvana and some small distance above the Swift
Islands...crossing Fendley's and Stephens' Creeks and a branch of the
Pounding Mill creek...Joe's Creek...Tye River...and reserving to himself
terms of leases granted by him to JOHN JUDE & JOHN LEWIS...the plantation
whereon "his people now works". X of MARGARET. Wit: WILLIAM FANNING,
THOMAS WRIGHT, JOSEPH CABELL, WILLIAM WALTON.

Page 110.   30 Apr 1763. WILLIAM CABELL & wife, MARGARET, AC, to JOHN
            CABELL, Buckingham Co., for love and affection which they bear
their loving son, JOHN CABELL, and in consideration of certain promises
made (with reservations hereinafter mentioned) 790 acres, N side of and
adj. Fluvana River...40 acres part of which is an island in the Fluvana
and known as Woods' Island...200 acres one other part in the fork of Tye
River...400 acres one other part thereof beginning at mouth at Owen's
Creek...part of tract of 4800 acres pat. to WILLIAM CABELL on Sept 12,
1738...150 acres lying opposite land belonging to estate of WILLIAM MEG-
GISON, deceased, and granted to HUGH DENHAM by patent and by him sold to
WILLIAM ARRINGTON, deceased, and by him devised to his son, NEVES ARRING-
TON, and by him sold to WILLIAM HORSLEY, Deceased, and by said HORSLEY
sold to WILLIAM CABELL. Reserving leases granted to THOMAS HUGHES, JOHN
SMITH, GILBERT BOWMAN, HENRY GOTHERD, & ROBERT IRONS and use of plantation

"his hands now works"...liberty for his son, WILLIAM CABELL, JR. and his heirs forever to fish on any parts of Wood's Island. X of MARGARET. Wit: WILLIAM WALTON, WILLIAM CABELL, JR., JOHN DAWSON.

Page 112. 30 Apr 1763. WILLIAM CABELL, AC, to WILLIAM, ROBERT, & JOHN HORSLEY, infant sons of WILLIAM HORSLEY, AC, deceased. During WILLIAM HORSLEY's lifetime CABELL agreed to convey to him the fee simple estate in 200 acres in Albemarle in exchange for another tract in Gooch- land which HORSLEY then owned...did moreover promise the said WILLIAM HORSLEY that in consideration he had intermarried with MARY, the daughter of the said WILLIAM CABELL, he would convey to him the Fee tail estate of 160 acres of land lying and being in Albemarle being part of 400 acres pat. to RICHARD BURKS and by him conveyed to WILLIAM CABELL...for love borne by WILLIAM CABELL unto his grandsons, WILLIAM, ROBERT, & JOHN HORS- LEY and for their better support and maintenance grants to them 1575 acres in Amherst and Buckingham on both sides of the Fluvana and adjacent to Elk Islands and pat. to WILLIAM CABELL 20 Sep 1759 and which includes the above mentioned 200 acres. Also 160 acres which is upper part of tract of 500 acres pat. to RICHARD BURKS and by him conveyed to WILLIAM CABELL and adj. the 1575 acres on N side and adjacent to Fluvana near the Elk Islands on the Great Bank...Reservations: should any of the heirs fail to leave lawfully begotten heirs...then it descends to heirs of WILLIAM CABELL. To be divided as will of WILLIAM HORSELEY stipulates in County Court of Albemarle. Wit: WILLIAM WALTON, JOHN DAWSON, JOHN CABELL.

Page 114. 2 May 1763. WILLIAM ROBERTSON, AC, to ALEXANDER McMULLAN, AC, 20 pds. for 125 acres formerly in Albemarle and on Rockfish. Lines: ARCHIBALD WOODS, COL. CHISWELL, ROBERT WEIR. Wit: GEORGE STOVALL JR., ROGER CAZY, JOHN SMALL.

Page 116. 2 May 1763. JAMES TOOLEY of St. Anne's Parish, Albemarle, to ADAM REID, AC...15 pds. for 250 acres on Three forks of Pedlar and "pattented" to JAMES TOOLEY 25 Sep 1762.

Page 117. 2 May 1763. ROBERT DAVIS, AC, to CORNELIUS THOMAS, AC, 20 pds for 169 acres on branch of Maple Creek. Lines: MARVEL STONE, SAMUEL BURK JR., ARTHUR TOOLEY, MICAJAH CLARK.

Page 119. 2 May 1763. JOSEPH BARNETT, AC, to JOHN LYON & RACHEL MORRI- SON...25 pds. for 10 acres...both sides of Corbbins Creek... part of Tract granted to COL. JOHN CHISWELL by patent and by him conveyed to JOSEPH BARNETT 22 May 1746.

Page 120. 25 May 1763. JOHN ROBINSON, King and Queen, to THOMAS JOPLING, AC, 22 pds. for 258 acres, S side of Rockfish and part of larg- er tract pat. to JOHN CHISWELL and now property of ROBINSON. Lines: WILL- IAM HARRIS, on S side of Rockfish; JAMES MONTGOMERY, JOHN MONTGOMERY. Wit: WILLIAM CABELL, JR., CORNELIUS THOMAS, JOSEPH CABELL.

Page 122. 4 July 1763. CHARLES McANALLY, AC, to DAVID PROFITT, Tillot- son Parish in Buckingham, 30 pds. for 100 acres...a branch of S fork of Rockfish. Lines: Fendley's Mountain, JAMES NEVIL.

Page 123. 4 Jul 1763. THOMAS BALLOW, AC, to ALEXANDER CHISNELL, AC, 10 pds. for 150 acres...part of 400 acres pat. to THOMAS BALLOW at Williamsburg 12 May 1759, S side of Tye. Wife of BALLOW examined, but not named.

Page 125. 2 Jun 1763. JOHN GILMORE, AC, to GABRIEL PENN, AC...one grey mare; bay mare and colt; horse, other stock and many other items. Deed of trust for one month and to be paid by July 1 next. X of GILMER. Wit: LARKIN GATEWOOD & THOMAS LUMPKIN.

Page 127. 2 Jul 1763. JOHN WILLIAM SR., AC, to GABRIEL PENN, AC, 21 pds 12 sh 9 p and half penny...Deed of trust containing many items, for one month. Wit: THOMAS LUMPKIN, ABRAM SMITH.

Page 129. 5 Sep 1763. JOHN WADE, AC, to WILLIAM WHITSITT, AC, 40 pds for 200 acres on North fork of Davis' creek, branch of Rock- fish. Line of WILLIAM TROTTER. Half of tract bought from WILLIAM WRIGHT.

78

On page 130 ELIZABETH WADE, wife of JOHN WADE, is examined as to dower
wishes and rights. [I should like to point out that this WILLIAM WHIT-
SITT is the ancestor of the Dr. WILLIAM WHITSITT who bacame President of
the Soughern Baptist Theological Seminary in Louisville, Kentucky, and
who became involved with his fellow Baptists about interpretations concerning historical matters. BFD.]

Page 131.   4 Aug 1763.   JOSEPH CREWS & wife, AGNES, AC, to WILLIAM DILL-
            ARD, Hanover Co., 40 pds. for 195 acres...both sides of Rocky
Run, a branch of Buffalo River, and part of 400 acre tract where JAMES
WARREN now lives. Wit: JAMES DILLARD, THOMAS ROBBERTSON (sic), MARY ANN
TENISON (X).

Page 133.   14 Mar 1763.   JOHN PARTREE BURK, Bedford Co., to WILLIAM SHU-
            MAKER (SHOEMAKER in margin), AC, 5 sh. for 145 acres...branch
of Pedlar called Dancing Creek. X of BURK. Wit: CHARLES TULEY, CORNE-
LIUS THOMAS, WILLIAM FLOYD, JOHN ISONS(X).

Page 134.   5 Sep 1763.   HUGH WILLOUGHBY, AC, to HENRY KEY, AC, 40 pds.
            for 171 acres...part of 371 acres pat. to HUGH WILLOUGHBY at
Williamsburg on 7 Aug 1761...S branch of Rockfish. Lines: WALTER KING,
bounds for whole 371 acres; 100 acres already sold to CHARLES McANALLY;
100 acres sold to CHARLES TATE, and remaining 171 is land and plantation
whereon WILLOUGHBY now liveth. X of WILLOUGHBY.

Page 136.   1 Aug 1763.   RICHARD NALLY, AC, to PETER FIELD TRENT, Albe-
            marle Co., 10 pds. for 80 acres. Lines: MERIWETHER. Now in
possession of TRENT. Wit: GEORGE SEATON, HENRY TRENT, DAVID MONTGOMERY.

Page 137.   7 Apr 1763.   RICHARD NALLEY, Planter, AC, to JOEL TERRELL,
            Fredericksvill Parish, Albermarle, 54 pds. 8 sh...various
items of stock and furniture. Deed of trust. Wit: WILLIAM TERRELL,
LEWIS & SARAH LEWIS. Page 138 Endorsement by JOEL TERRELL to PETER
FIELD TRENT for use of JAMES & ROBERT DONALDS & CO. and acknowledged by
RICHARD NALLEY. Wit: JOHN SWANN. Dated 22 July 22, 1763.

Page 138.   8 Jul 1763.   HENRY TENNISON, AC, to ALEXANDER McCAUL, Henrico
            Co., 32 pds...tract where TENNISON now lives...200 acres on
both sides of Porridge Creek...Deed of trust until 1 Jun 1764. X of
TENNISON (sic) and NEILL CAMPBELL, attorney for ALEXANDER McCAUL. Wit:
MATTHEW JORDAN, JO. RAMSEY, GEORGE MILLER.

Page 140.   5 Sep 1763.   GEORGE TAYLOR, AC, to HENRY TAYLOR, AC, 10 pds.
            for 70 acres. Lines: Piney River at ROSE's line.

Page 142.   3 Oct 1763.   JAMES NEVIL, DAVID CRAWFORD, CORNELIUS THOMAS,
            THOMAS JOPLING, & HOWARD CASH, AC, bound to our Sovereign
Lord George the Third for one thousand pds...NEVIL appointed Sheriff of
Amherst County by the President of the colony under its seal, September,
last past...during Pleasure. Marks of JOPLING & CASH.

Page 143.   Same men as above bound to the King for 500 pds, 3 Oct 1763,
for NEVIL to collect all fines, etc.

Page 143.   Same men bonded as in two previous items to collect taxes.

Page 144.   1 Oct 1763.   RICHARD McCARY, AC, to JACOB TYRE, St. Ann's
            Parish, Albermarle, 32 pds. for 150 acres...both sides of
Nassau Creek. Lines: JOHN KARMER...now in TYRE's possession. Wit:
WILLIAM TILLER, CHARLES TEATET, JOHN CRAWFORD. Page 146, wife of McCARY
examined, but name is not given.

Page 146.   2 May 1763.   JOHN PETER, JR., AC, to JOEL FIELD, St. Ann's
            Parish, Albermarle, 35 pds. for 150 acres...part of tract
granted by patent to COL. WILLIAM CABELL at Williamsburg, 23 May 1760...
branch of Harris' Creek and between the Bear and Cedar Mountains. Lines:
CABELL. Page 147, wife of JOHN PETER, JR., examined, but not named.

Page 147.   2 Nov 1763.   JEREMIAH WADE, Albemarle, PEARCE WADE, JOSEPH
            BALLENGER, & RICHARD BALLENGER, AC, to GEORGE SEATON, AC, 5sh.

two tracts of 400 acres each...one beginning at MAY's line; CARTER's line.
Second tract - CARTER's line. 800 acres in all and part of tract of 2000
acres on S side of Buffalo under Tobacco Row Mountains and pat. to JOSEPH
& RICHARD BALLENGER and late in tenure and occupation of JEREMIAH &
PEARCE WADE...to be conveyed under decree in Albemarle County. One
pepper corn to be paid on Lady Day next, if demanded. Wit: PATRICK ROSE,
W. HANSBROUGH, ALEXANDER REID.

Page 149.   3 Nov 1763.   JEREMIAH WADE, Albemarle, PEARCE WADE, JOSEPH
            BALLENGER & RICHARD BALLENGER, AC, to GEORGE SEATON, AC; 160
pds. for sale of the land leased in previous document above...two tracts
of 400 acres each. Lines: MAYS, CARTER. Wit: PATRICK ROSE, W. HANSBROUGH,
ALEXANDER REID.

Page 152.   28 Mar 1763.   PEARCE WADE & JOSHUA FOWLER, AC, promise to pay
            DRURY TUCKER or heirs, etc., 50 pds. on or before 20 Oct ensu-
ing...bond of 110 pds. Wit: WM. CABELL, JR., ROBERT YANCEY, RICHARD
POWELL.

Page 153.   3 Oct 1763.   ANGIS FORBES, AC, to JOHN McGUIRE, AC...7 pds. 10
            sh. for 66 acres...S branch of Taylor's Creek. Lines: CHARLES
YANCEY. Wife of ANGIS FORBES, KATHERINE FORBES, signs the deed.

Page 155.   14 Oct 1763.   NICHOLAS MERIWETHER, Frederick Parish, Albemarle,
            to PETER FIELD TRENT, St. Ann's Parish, Albemarle...20 pds.
for 164 acres. Lines: ARCHIBALD WOODS. Wit: JOHN HARRIS, NEILL CAMPBELL,
LEONARD PHILLIPS.

Page 156.   7 Jul 1763.   JOHN HUNTER, Buckingham, to JOSIAH WOOD, 40 pds.
            for 400 acres on Nassau Creek and the Admiral Mountain. Lines:
WALTER KING. Wit: WILLIAM CABELL, MATTHEW TUCKER, JOSEPH CABELL.

Page 157.   7 Nov 1763.   RICHARD PETER, AC, to STEPHEN GOOLSBY, AC. 50 pds
            for 150 acres...part of 450 acre tract granted to WILLIAM CA-
BELL, JR. by Williamsburg patent, 23 May 1760. Branch of Harris' Creek
between the Bear and Cedar Mountain. Lines: RICHARD PETER & JOEL FIELDS.
Page 159, HANNAH PETERS, wife of RICHARD PETER(S) examined as to dower
wishes and rights. Nov. 7, 1763.

Page 159.   4 Mar 1764.   JOHN BENGER, Spotsylvania Co., to LAURANCE CAMP-
            BELL, Spotsylvania Co., 82 pds. 1 sh. for 547 acres...branch
of Naked Creek and Higginbotham Mill Creek. Lines: MOSES HIGGINBOTHAM,
RICHARD DAVIS, RICE MEREDITH, BRAXTON. Part of greater tract pat. to
GEORGE BRAXTON, 25 Nov 1743. Wit: GEORGE SEATON, JAMES & JOSEPH HIGGIN-
BOTHAM. Page 161, ELIZABETH, wife of JOHN BENGER, examined 5 Mar 1764
as to dower rights and wishes.

Page 161.   5 Mar 1764.   JOHN GREEN, AC, to JEANE (JANE) SHIELDS, AC, 12
            pds. for 115 acres on head of Hatt Creek. Part of 175 acres
pat. to JOHN GREEN 12 May 1759. Lines: Col. WILLIAM RANDOLPH, dec'd.
X of GREEN.

Page 162.   5 Mar 1764.   GREGORY MATHEWS, Buckingham, to JOHN MURREL, Al-
            bemarle, 25 pds. for 190 acres on Horse Shoe Mountain and
joining lands of JOHN HUNTER & WILLIAM BURNS. Pat. to JOSEPH CABELL, 20
Sep 1759. Wit: WILLIAM TILLER, JESSE MILLS, STEPHEN GEE.

Page 164.   5 Mar 1764.   DAVID PROPHET, AC, to JAMES MATHEWS, AC, 20 pds
            for 100 acres and part of 371 acres pat. to HUGH WILLOUGHBY
at Williamsburg, 7 Aug 1761. Branch of S fork of Rockfish. Lines: JAMES
NEVIL, HUGH WILLOUGHBY.

Page 165.   5 Aug 1763.   WILLIAM BRYANT, Bedford Co., to HENRY TRENT, AC,
            150 pds. for 400 acres...N side of and joining Fluvana River.
Lines: John's Creek, RICHARD TILLIS. X of BRYANT. Wit: GEORGE COX JR.,
MICAJAH COX, OBEDIAH HENRY TRENT. Wife of WILLIAM BRYANT examined as to
dower rights and wishes, but not named, 5 Sep 1763.

Page 167.   24 Aug 1763.   JOHN LEAK, AC, to ALEXANDER McCAUL, Henrico Co.
            87 pds. for 400 acres on both sides of the S fork of Rockfish.

Deed of Trust. Signed by LEAK & NEILL CAMPBELL as attorney for McCAUL. Wit: JACOB LINDSEY, CHARLES IRVING.

Page 169. 25 Jan 1764. SAMUEL MURREL, JR., Augusta County, to JOHN WEBB, Albemarle Co., 48 pds. for 200 acres...part of a tract JOHN SMALL had of JOHN CHIZELL...branch of Rockfish. Lines: CHIZELL's at foot of the mountain. Wit: NEILL CAMPBELL, THOMAS BALLEW, JAMES HALLY-BURTON, LEONARD BALLAWE(X).

Page 171. 10 Jun 1763. ARCHIBALD WOODS, Fredericksville Parish, Albemarle, 125 pds. for 157 acres on Taylor's Creek, branch of Rockfish...residue of 400 acres granted to WOODS by patent at Williamsburg, 30 Jan 1741. Lines: Col. CHISWELL. This 400 acres was conveyed by ARCHIBALD WOODS on 22 Aug 1762, to his son, MICHAEL WOODS...243 acres and MICHAEL WOODS conveys this to DAVID MERIWETHER. Wit: FRANCIS MERIWETHER, ROBERT McWHERTER, WILLIAM ROBERTSON. (Note: see next deed as to 243 acre transaction mentioned herein.)

Page 174. Order to NICHOLAS LEWIS & NICHOLAS MERIWETHER, Justices of Albemarle to examine ELIZABETH WOODS, wife of ARCHIBALD, as to dower rights, 20 Jul 1763. Done 1 Mar 1764. Marginal note says original was delivered to BENJ. TALIAFERO.

Page 175. 10 Jun 1763. MICHAEL WOODS, Parish of Fredericksville, Albemarle, to DAVID MERIWETHER, St. Anne's Parish, Albemarle, 125 pds. for 243 acres...Taylor Creek, branch of Rockfish...part of 400 acres pat. to ARCHIBALD WOODS 30 Jan 1741. This tract was conveyed by ARCHIBALD WOODS to MICHAEL WOODS 22 Aug 1762, and was recorded in Amherst 4 Oct 1762. Wit: FRANCIS MERIWETHER, ROBERT McWHIRTER, WILLIAM ROBERTSON. Marginal notation says original was delivered to BEN. TALIAFERRO.

Page 178. 20 Jul 1763. Order to NICHOLAS LEWIS & NICHOLAS MERIWETHER, Justices of Albemarle Co., to examine JANE WOODS, wife of MICHAEL, relative to dower rights and wishes in above conveyance. Done on 1 Mar 1764. Original delivered to BENJ. TALIAFERRO.

Page 179. 17 Jan 1764. JOHN ROBINSON, King and Queen, to SAMUEL SHELTON, Albemarle...135 pds. 4 sh. 4 p. for 800 acres...S side of Rockfish and on S branch of Davis' Creek...part of larger tract pat. to Col. JOHN CHISWELL and now property of ROBINSON. Wit: GEORGE CARRINGTON, CORNELIUS THOMAS, JOSEPH CABELL, WILLIAM CABELL, JR.

Page 181. 17 Jan 1764. JOHN ROBINSON, King & Queen, to JOSEPH BARNET, AC, 10 pds. for 120 acres on Corbin's Creek...part of larger tract pat. to Col. JOHN CHISWELL and now property of ROBINSON. Lines: MICHAEL MONTGOMERY, JOSEPH BARNET, JOHN SMALL, FRANCIS MERIWETHER, JOHN REID. Wit: GEORGE CARRINGTON, CORNELIUS THOMAS, WM. CABELL JR., JOSEPH CABELL.

Page 183. 17 Jan 1764. JOHN ROBINSON, King and Queen, Esquire...to GEORGE CAMPBELL, AC. 10 pds. 15 sh. for 110 acres; head branch of Rockfish...part of larger tract formerly granted to Col. JOHN CHISWELL. Lines: ROBINSON, ROBERT GARLAND, Wit: GEORGE CARRINGTON, CORNELIUS THOMAS, JOSEPH CABELL, WILLIAM CABELL, JR.

Page 185. 17 Jan 1764. JOHN ROBINSON, King and Queen, to JACOB WRIGHT, AC, 65 pds. 16 sh. for 990 acres...N side of and joining Rockfish...part of larger tract pat. to JOHN CHISWELL, 400 acres of which JOHN CHISWELL conveyed to JOHN WRIGHT and by JOHN WRIGHT conveyed to JACOB WRIGHT...590 acres residue vested in JOHN ROBINSON. Lines: THOMAS JOPLIN, JOHN ROBINSON. Wit: GEORGE CARRINGTON, CORNELIUS THOMAS, WM. CABELL, JR., JOSEPH CABELL.

Page 187. 17 Jan 1764. JOHN ROBINSON, King and Queen, to MICHAEL MONTGOMERY, AC...30 pds. for 200 acres...Short's branch, branch of Rockfish...part of a larger tract pat. to Col. JOHN CHISWELL and now property of ROBINSON. Lines: JOSEPH BARNET. Wit: GEORGE CARRINGTON, CORNELIUS THOMAS, JOSEPH CABELL, WM. CABELL, JR.

Page 189. 17 Jan 1764. JOHN ROBINSON, King and Queen, to THOMAS JOPLIN,
AC, 12 pds. 12 sh. for 530 acres...N side of and adj. Rockfish
and tract formerly conveyed by JOHN CHISWELL, Gent., to JOHN WRIGHT and
by WRIGHT to THOMAS JOPLIN...190 acres being residue and property of JOHN
ROBINSON. Lines of the whole: JOHN ROBINSON, JOHN FARRAR. Wit: GEORGE
CARRINGTON, CORNELIUS THOMAS, WM. CABELL, JR., JOSEPH CABELL.

Page 191. 7 May 1764. ROLAND HORSLEY BIRKS, Bedford Co., to MARY BRYANT,
Bedford Co, 40 pds. for 400 acres...both sides of Jon's Creek
of N side of Fluvannah River. Lines: NICHOLAS DAVIS, RICHARD & ROLAND
BIRKS. Page 192, SARAH, wife of ROWLAND HORSLEY BIRKS, examined as to
dower rights and wishes.

Page 193. 7 May 1764. ROWLAND HORSLEY BIRKS & wife SARAH, Bedford Co.,
to WILLIAM STATON, AC...20 pds. for 400 acres...both sides of
Harris Creek and joining N side of Fluvannah River. Lines: Captain
CHARLES LYNCH, Rev. WILLIAM STITH, GEORGE CARRINGTON.

Page 195. 7 May 1764. ROWLAND HORSLEY BURKS, Bedford, and wife SARAH,
to JOHN GOODWIN, AC...40 pds. for 400 acres...both sides of
John's creek and joining N side of Fluvanna. Lines: RICHARD BURKS,
NICHOLAS DAVIS. Signed: "BIRK".

Page 197. 7 May 1764. JOHN LYON, AC, to BENJAMIN MOORE, AC, 97 pds. for
41 acres. Lines: "top of a mountain".

Page 199. 7 May 1764. WILLIAM TILLER, AC, to JOHN LYONS, AC, 35 pds.
for 100 acres. Lines: ALEXANDER CHISUM, TERISHA TURNER,
ABRAHAM WARWICK.

Page 200. 7 May --   BENJAMIN MOORE, AC, to JOHN DAWSON, AC, 20 pds.
for 100 acres...Fork of Cove and Hickory Creek of Rockfish.
Lines: JOHN LYON, JOHN SORRELL, JOHN CRAWFORD.

Page 202. 7 May 1764. RICHARD POWELL, AC, to JACOB SMITH, AC. 20 pds.
for 200 acres. Lines: DAVID WATKINS on waters of Puppies
Creek; JAMES SMITH, RICHARD POWELL. Wife of POWELL examined, but name
not given.

Page 204. 28 Dec 1763. NATHANIEL MANN to WILLIAM ROBERTSON... 20 pds.
for 31 acres on Taylor's Creek...part of 172 acres pat. to
ALEXANDER PATTON, 12 Jan 1746. Lines: SAMUEL MANN, ARCHIBALD WOODS. Wit:
FRANCIS MERIWETHER, DAVID MERIWETHER, ROBERT WEIR, ALEXANDER McMULLAN,
EDWARD MOURLY.

Page 207. 29 Dec 1763. NATHANIEL MANN to WILLIAM ROBERTSON...20 pds.
for 143 acres..branch of Taylor's creek. Lines: SAMUEL MANN. Wit:
ROBERT WEIR, ALEXANDER McMULLAN, FRANCIS MERIWETHER, DAVID MERIWETHER,
EDWARD MOURLY.

Page 210. 6 May 1764. WILLIAM CABELL, AC, to ELIZABETH REE, AC, 29 pds
1 sh. 5 p. for 200 acres on Castle Creek, branch of Tye River.
Lines: JAMES DICK, JOHN ROSE, late Rev. ROBERT ROSE. Wit: ALEXANDER
McMULLAN, JAMES MENE, DRURY BOWMAN(X).

Page 211. 4 May 1764. WILLIAM CABELL, AC, to DRURY BOWMAN, AC. 60 pds.
for 400 acres...S side of Tye River on Camp Creek. Lines: JOHN
MACKENNY, JOHN PEARTRE BURKS; ROSE.

Page 213. 6 May 1764. DRURY BOWMAN, AC, to WILLIAM CABELL, AC, 60 pds.
for 400 acres S side of Tye River on Camp Creek. Lines: JOHN
MACKENNY, JOHN PARTREE BURKS, ROSE. Wit: ALEXANDER MCMULLAN, JAMES MENE,
HESAKIAH STUTTON(?) (X).

Page 214. 7 May 1764. JOHN LOVING, AC, 5 sh. for love of my son, WILL-
IAM LOVING, one negro girl named Fanny.

Page 215. 7 May 1764. JOHN LOVING, SR., to JOHN LOVING, JR. "for love
borne my son, JOHN LOVING JR." Both of AC...one negro girl,
Hannah. 5 shillings.

Page 216. 7 May 1764. MICHJAH MOORMAN & wife, SUSANNAH, AC, to RICHARD
POWELL, AC, 120 pds. for 244 acres, granted to EDWARD LYNCH
and including survey of 250 acres adj. same, the whole containing 494
acres...N side of Fluvana. Lines: Hollow next above the Ferry landing;
CHARLES LYNCH, deceased.

Page 218. 7 May 1764. MICAJAH MOORMAN & wife, SUSANNA, to EDWARD LYNCH,
all of Bedford [Note: Item before this on same date styles
MOORMAN & wife as being of Amherst. BFD.] 10 pds. for 150 acres, N side
of Fluvannah, part of 394 acres now granted to EDWARD POWELL. Lines:
mouth of a hollow next above the Ferry landing. Marginal notation that
the original was delivered to CHARLES H. LYNCH 21 Sep 1852.

Page 220. 20 Nov 1763. JAMES BONDS & wife, MARY, AC, to THOMAS WILLIAMS,
AC, 25 pds. for (?) acres (not given) on Stovall's Creek. Wit:
MICAJAH TERRILL, JOHN LEMASTER, HENRY TENISON, JOSEPH FROST, GEORGE STO-
VALL, JR.

Page 223. 4 Jun 1764. HENRY KEY, AC, to JOHN KEY -- JOHN is brother of
HENRY -- AC. 36 pds. for 71 acres, pat. to HENRY KEY at
Williamsburg 10 Sep 1760. Lackey's Thoroughfare and line of JAMES
LACKEY mentioned.

Page 225. -- Feb 1764. WILLIAM BLAIR & wife MARY, Albemarle, to EDWARD
BOWMAN, AC, 40 pds. for 150 acres, part of tract pat. to MI-
CHAEL THOMAS 10 Jul 1745, and by him conveyed to WILLIAM BLAIR by deed of
sale. S side of Rockfish. Wit: WILLIAM BOWMAN, DAVID BURKS, DRURY
BOWMAN(X).

Page 227. 2 Jul 1764. JACOB WRIGHT & wife, ELIZABETH, AC, to WILLIAM
HARRIS, Albemarle...70 pds. 15 sh. for 590 acres, N side of
and adj. Rockfish...part of 990 acres belonging to JACOB WRIGHT...Wit:
JAMES NEVIL, MATTHEW TUCKER, JOSEPH DAWSON. WRIGHTS signed with X's.

Page 229. 2 Jul 1764. JOHN WOODROOF, AC, to JOHN OWNSBY, AC, 10 pds. 10
sh. for 132 acres on Harris Creek. Lines: DAVID WOODROOF; and
part of a greater tract pat. to GEORGE CARRINGTON, Cumberland Co, 20 Jun
1753, and "acknowledge" to DAVID WOODROOF, Sr., in Albemerle, and falling
to the above JOHN WOODROOF by heirship.

Page 231. 2 Jul 1764. SUSANNAH COTTRELL & HOWARD CASH, Executors of
THOMAS COTTRELL, "Deceised", AC, to PHILLIP SMITH, AC, 50 pds
for 500 acres, part of 700 acres pat. to SUSANNAH COTTRELL & HOWARD CASH
30 Aug 1763. Lines: JOHN TALIAFERRO, JACOB SMITH, AARON HIGGINBOTHAM,
ZACHARIAH TALLIAFERRO. CASH & COTTRELL signed with X's.

Page 233. 2 Jul 1764. SAMUEL MARKSBURY, AC, to ZACHARIAH TALLIAFERRO,
AC, 100 pds. for 400 acres, granted to SAMUEL MARKSBURY by
deed 18 Sep 1739, from JAMES CHURCHILL, to SAMUEL MARKSBURY The Elder...
part of a tract of 1500 acres pat. to JAMES CHURCHILL 1 Feb 1738, and
which SAMUEL MARKSBURY held by Heirship "being the Eldest Son and heir
at law of SAMUEL MARKSBURY, Deceased." Lines: LITTLEPAGE, CHEWS, Tye
River. Wit: JACOB SMITH, JACOB BROWN.

Page 235. 6 Jun 1764. JOSEPH McGANN, AC, to ALEXANDER McCAUL, Merchant
in Henrico Co., 86 pds. 2 sh. 5 p. half penny...Deed of Trust.
All of his tract where he now lives between Porrige Creek and Harris
Creek...200 acres. Wit: RICHARD HOLLAND, WILLIAM COX, EDMUND COBBS.

Page 239. 26 Jan 1764. PATRICK NOWLIN, AC, to WILLIAM CHECKE, AC. 25
pds 18 sh. for 156 acres, branch of Routledge's Creek..."Run-
eth" into Mr. BRAXTON's line. 156 acres in all, but one tract of 48
acres mentioned. Wit: JOHN KNIGHT, ANNE KNIGHT(X), JOSEPH MAGANN.
NOWLIN signed with X.

Page 241. 31 Mar 1764. GEORGE HAYS, AC, to ZACHARIAH TALLIAFERRO...
Tobacco crop now lying in my tobacco houses, one of which
stands on the land and plantation of GEORGE MUNRO, and the other upon my
own plantation...stock. Wit: DAVID ROSS & WILLIAM LOVING.

Page 243. 2 Jul 1764. ALEXANDER REID, AC, to MARY REID, AC...20 pds.
for 250 acres, head branches of Corbin's Creek, pat. to JOHN
REID bearing date 1755 and since the death of the said JOHN REID descended to the aforesaid ALEXANDER REID as eldest son and heir at law of him
the said JOHN REID which the said ALEXANDER REID hath bargained and sold
to his sister, MARY REID.

Page 247. 2 Jul 1764. ALEXANDER REID, AC, to NATHAN REID, AC, 50 pds.
for 400 acres on a branch of Rockfish. Lines: COL. CHISWELL,
JAMES WOODS, side of a mountain, formerly granted and "conveyed" from
SAMUEL MANN, Executor(?) of THOMAS MANN to JOHN REID by deed of date,
25 Feb 1760, and since death of JOHN REID descended to ALEXANDER REID as
Eldest son and heir at law...hath bargained and sold unto his brother,
NATHAN REID.

Page 249. 6 Aug 1764. HAWARD CASH & SUSANNAH COTTRELL, Executors of
THOMAS COTTRELL, AC, to ROBERT CHILDERS, AC, for 20 pds. for
200 acres. Lines: JOHN TALLIAFERRO, HOWARD CASH, RICHARD POWELL, JAMES
SMITH. CASH & COTTRELL signed with X's. Wit: ZACHARIAH TALIAFERRO,
ROBERT JOHNSTON, S. MURPHY.

Page 251. 4 Aug 1764. JOHN GOODWIN, AC, to JOSEPH GOODWIN, AC. JOHN
for the paternal affection borne for (which I have and do
"bar") to my said son JOSEPH GOODWIN...all of that tract which is at this
Tim(sic) laid of (sic) for him"seituat" ...200 acres joining N side of
Fluvaner(sic) River. Lines: RICHARD BURKS, near mouth of John's Creek,
part of 400 acres JOHN GOODWIN bought from ROWLAND HORSLEY BURKS. Wit:
DANIEL BURFORD, AMBROSE RUCKER, JOHN BURFORD, ELIJAH BRYANT.

Page 253. 6 Aug 1764. PEARCE WADE & wife MARY, AC, to JOHN GOODWIN, AC,
25 pds. for 105 acres on W side of Harris Creek.

Page 255. 3 Sep 1764. ROBERT WHITTEN & wife, SARAH, AC to NICHOLAS
EASTIN, AC...85 pds. for 137 acres, E side of the Tobacco Row
Mountain and known as Cabell's Cove...part of 400 acres bought by ROBERT
WHITTEN from WILLIAM CABELL 14 Feb 1760. Lines: HENRY CHILDRESS, ROBERT
WHITTEN. X of WHITTEN. Wit: JAMES(?) CAGANN(?), GABRIEL PENN, ROBERT W.
GRIMES.

Page 256. 3 Sep 1764. JOHN LEAK, AC, for love and affection borne my
three daughters: MARY, JUDITH, & ELIZABETH LEAK...one negro
girl, Jane, and her increase to be equally divided among them in the year
of our Lord, 1776, and if any daughter dies the survivors are to have
that share. Also all of my substance that falls to me from my father's
estate...save and excepting land. Wit: GEORGE SEATON, NEILL CAMPBELL.

Page 257. 19 Jul 1764. JOHN LEAK & wife ANN, AC, to NEILL CAMPBELL,
Albemarle, 110 pds. for 410 acres. Lines: Bear Branch, S fork
of Rockfish. X of ANN LEAK. Wit: BEN HOWARD, JOSEPH CHILDERS, WILLIAM
HIX, CHARLES IRVING. Memorandum: 60 feet square excepted as a burying
place...when the said LEAK's wife is buried.

Page 260. 3 Sep 1764. ZACHARIAH TALLIAFERRO, AC, to SAMUEL MARKSBURRY,
AC, 100 pds. for 740 acres, pat. to ZACHARIAH TALLIAFERRO 10
Sep 1755. Lines: AARON HIGGINBOTHAM, JAMES SMITH, Late Capt. RICHARD
TALLIAFERRO, Horsley's Creek, Branches of Buffalo, JOSEPH HIGGINBOTHAM.
The wife of ZACHARIAH TALLIAFERRO appeared and relenquished dower rights,
but her name is not given.

Page 263. 1 Oct 1764. MICAJAH TERRELL & wife SARAH, AC, to ABRAHAM
NORTH, Cumberland Co, 150 pds. for 200 acres on Bowling Creek.

Page 265. 12 Mar 1764. DAVID RICHARDS, AC, Cooper, 3 pds. 10 sh. to
ABRAHAM SMITH, AC, Carperter...cow and calf. Deed of trust.
Wit: WILLIAM DIVER.

Page 266. 24 Oct 1764. JOHN BENGER, AC, heir of ELLIOTT BENGER, AC,
deceased, to BENJAMIN JOHNSTON, son of WILLIAM JOHNSTON, and
own brother to ELIZABETH, wife of JOHN BENGER of Spotsylvania and Parish
of St. George...50 pds...BENJAMIN JOHNSTON is surety unto ROGER DIXON,

for 425 pds. for BENGER...mention made of plan of land hereunto annexed, but not with this deed...part of larger tract granted to GEORGE BRAXTON and by him to THOMAS CHEW; also two tracts in Spotsylvania where BENGER lately lived and by CHEW to ELLIOTT BENGER, Esq., deceased...also 14 negroes, cattle, furniture, crops...also actual right in an estate left to me in England by will and wills. Deed of Trust. Payment to be made at dwelling house of BENJAMIN JOHNSTON by o Oct 1764. Wit: CHARLES Mc-PHERSON, ROBERT JOHNSTON, JAMES HIGGINBOTHAM, JOHN HIGGINBOTHAM. Memo as to lines: One red oak corner to Mr. GEORGE BRAXTON; a "popular" corner to Mr. ROSE, white oak to"HUKINGBOTHAM" ; RICE MEREDITH.

Page 270.   24 Oct 1764.   JOHN BENGER, AC, and son and heir of ELLIOTT BENGER, Spotsylvania county, to BENJAMIN JOHNSTON, son of WILLIAM JOHNSTON, and own brother to ELIZABETH, wife of JOHN BENGER... BENGER appoints him attorney-in-fact here and in England..."for all that part of his the said BENGER's estate that now is and lies in the Kingdom of England". JOHNSTON is of Spotsylvania...JOHNSTON is also appointed High Steward of BENGER and General Steward in Colony and England and is to make leases, etc. and transact all business for JOHN BENGER. This is done because of "my frailty". Many "underminded people have over-catched me craftily"...so as almost to deprive me of that Freedom which belongs to a free subject and JOHNSTON is to allow me enough to support my family for this is true intent and meaning of this present...so that these evilminded persons may not deprive me of my estate so unjustly..." advises him of a mortgage of large sum and it is legally done by BENGER. Wit: CHARLES McPHERSON, ROBERT JOHNSTON, JAMES & JOHN HIGGINBOTHAM.

Page 278.   20 Aug 1764.   EDWARD MANION, AC, 12 pds. 9 sh. 9 p. to JAMES JONES. Deed of Trust. Pocket knife, grey mare paces natural, two feather beds, four cows and 3 calves. Wit: WILLIAM LOVING, EDWARD EIDSON, GEORGE CAMPBELL(X).

Page 279.   3 Dec 1763.   DAVID PATTERSON, Gent., and wife MARY, Buckingham Co., Tillotson Parish, to JAMES LONDON, AC, 20 pds. for 400 acres N side of Fluvanna...tract granted to DAVID PATTERSON. Wit: JAMES DILLARD, JESSE EVANS, MOSES LONDON, CHARLES PERROW. Page 280 - order from GEORGE SEATON, Clerk of Amherst Co., to Justices of Buckingham: JOHN STAPLES, JEREMIAH WHITNEY, & CHARLES PATTERSON to examine MARY PATTERSON, wife of DAVID, as to dower rights. Return signed by WHITNEY & PATTERSON on 4 June "in the fifth year of the Reign of our Sovereign Lord, etc."

Page 282.   5 Nov 1764.   WILLIAM MARTIN & wife, FRANCES, AC, to DAVID MERIWETHER, AC, 165 pds. for 200 acres...all given to WILLIAM MARTIN by his father, JAMES MARTIN, by deed 3 May 1759, and recorded in Albemarle...both sides of Rockfish. Wit: SAMUEL WOODS, JAMES LEAKEY, JOHN JACOBS.

Page 285.   5 Nov 1/64.   JAMES HULSE, AC, to CHARLES YANCEY, AC...25 pds. for 64 acres on S side of Taylor's Creek. Lines: JOH (sic) WOODS.

Page 288.   27 Apr 1764.   CHARLES PARKS, Halifax Co., to JOHN OWNBEY JR., AC, 10 pds. for 359 acres, N branch of Buffalo and N side of Fluvanna. Lines: AMBROSE PORTER, BRAXTON & Co., the late Secretary's Line; JAMES WILLIAMSON. Wit: JONATHAN JOHNSON, JAMES OWNBEY, ELIZABETH WILLIAMSON.

Page 290.   27 Apr 1764.   CHARLES PARKS, Halifax Co., to JONATHAN JOHNSON, AC...40 pds. for 200 acres...N branch of Buffalo and N side of Fluvanna. Lines: BRAXTON & Co., JAMES WILLIAMSON. Wit: JOHN OWNBEY, JAMES OWNBEY, ELIZABETH WILLIAMSON.

Page 292.   5 Nov 1764.   ROBERT GRISSOM, AC, binds himself to THOMAS MERRITT, AC, to learn carpenter's trade.

Page 293.   5 Nov 1764.   JOHN KENNEDY, AC, to GEORGE CEPPIN & CO, Merchants in Glasgow, 22 pds. to KIPPEN (two spellings noted) & Co. Deed of Trust...stock, etc., and 80 acres on N side of Buffalo and joining CARTER BRAXTON & JONATHAN JOHNSON. Wit: NEILL CAMPBELL, EDMUND

COBBS, CHARLES IRVING.

Page 294.   4 Jul 1764.   RICHARD HOLLAND & wife, SARAH, to THOMAS PLEAS-
ANTS, Goochland Co.; WILLIAM CABELL, Sr., AC; GEORGE ROBINSON;
REILL CAMPBELL, PETER FIELD TRENT, Albemarle; FRANCIS SMITH, Han (sic)
County; JOHN CLARK, Henrico Co., WILLIAM PEARCE, Albemarle; JOSHUA FOWL-
ER, AC, & JAMES GEORGE, Goochland...446 pds. 12 sh...Deed of trust...
negroes, tobacco crop "made and now growing". Wit: JOHN DAWSON,
FRANCIS WEST.

Page 296.   28 Aug 1764.   LUNSFORD LOMAX, Gent., Caroline Co., to JOHN
LOVING, AC...Plantation let to JOHN LOVING...200 acres...adj.
and surrounding the courthouse...and known as the Nassau Tract...3 years
to begin on 25 Dec, next ensuing. 30 pds. annual rent, if rent not paid
then LOMAX and heirs can repossess it. LOVING will within three years
plant at least 200 peach trees and 100 apple trees and provide fence for
same...shall not work over four tithables and must not "committ waste"
and must remove only timber necessary for plantation uses. Wit: LUNS-
FORD LOMAX, JR., RALPH LOMAX, THOMAS LOMAX, HUGH ROSE. Memo: LOMAX has
the right to build thereon such store houses as he may deedm necessary
for the receiving of goods and merchandise. This was recorded at a
court held and continued at the courthouse, 6 Nov 1764.

Page 299.   4 Feb 1765.   JAMES NEVIL, THOMAS JOPLING, HENRY KEY, & GEORGE
SEATON bonded to King George III for 1000 pds. NEVIL was
appointed sheriff 27 Sep, last, and is hereby bonded to collect taxes.

Page 300.   12 Sep 1764.   HENRY KEY, AC, to ALEXANDER McCAUL, Henrico Co,
Factor for GEORGE KIPPEN & Co., Merchants in Glasgow, 5 sh.
to secure payment of bond of 1559 pds. 11 sh. 9 p...Deed of trust...298
acres pat. to KEY, 20 Sep 1759; 278 acres with same patent date; 258
acres with same patent date; 400 acres pat. 16 Jun 1756; 171 acres that
is part of 370 acres pat. to HUGH WILLOUGHBY 7 Aug 1761 and by him conveyed to KEY; also ten slaves. Wit: NEILL CAMPBELL, CHARLES IRVING,
ARCHIBALD BRYCE, JOHN OLD.

Page 302.   9 Oct 1764.   JOHN LOVING SR., AC, to ALEXANDER McCAUL, Henrico Co., Factor for GEORGE KIPPEN & Co., Merchants in Glasgow,
5 sh. to secure bond of 189 pds. 10...one tract in Spotsylvania of 400
acres and patented to JOHN LOVING 10 Mar 1756, and joining former tract
pat. to him 3 Sep 1762. Amherst tract of 400 acres pat. to LOVING 2 Jun
1760. Tract in Lunenberg, now Halifax, of 200 acres pat. to JOHN LOVING
10 Aug 1759. Also, four slaves. Note is to be paid to ALEXANDER McCAUL
at his store in Albemarle. Wit: NEILL CAMPBELL, W. HANSBROUGH, JOHN OLD.

Page 305.   15 Sep 1764.   RICHARD NALLEY & ABRAHAM NALLEY, AC, 27 pds. 5
sh. 8 p.3 farthings...to SAMUEL WOODS, Merchant in AC...Tobac-
do now grown on RICHARD NALLEY's plantation or places "where I now lives"
Wit: JOSEPH NALLEY, ABRAHAM HARGUS, JAMES C. WOODS(X), X of ABRAHAM
NALLEY.

Page 306.   28 Feb 1765.   SAMUEL MANN, Augusta Co., to ROGER KASEY, AC...
46 pds. 10 sh. for 141 acres...both sides of Taylor's creek.
Wit: FRANCIS MERIWETHER, CHARLES YANCEY, ALEXANDER McMULLAN, DAVID
MERIWETHER.

Page 308.   4 Mar 1765.   WILLIAM CABELL, JR., AC, to LEONARD TARRANCE JR.
AC, 100 pds. for 674 acres...both sides of Bever(sic) creek
of Buffalo...part of 2700 acres pat. to WILLIAM CABELL 6 Dec 1753.
Lines: JOSEPH BALLENGER, SAMUEL AIR, JEREMIAH WHITTEN, ROBERT WHITTEN,
BENJAMIN STINNETT, THOMAS PARKS, Top of BALLENGER's Mountain; DANIEL's
line; CABELL's line.

Page 310.   1 Mar 1765.   THOMAS TOMSON, St. Fredericksdale Parish of
Louisa Co., to JAMES GLEN, his son-in-law, AC...10 sh. for
love, respect, and good will for his son-in-law...119 acres on headwaters of Bever Creek and part of a larger tract pat. to TOMSON...also one
negro girl. Wit: MOSES CLARK(X), WILLIAM WOOD, THOMAS GLEN, JOHN FREE-
MAN. Memo: If JAMES GLEN sells this land he must "buy another for his
son, TOMSON, to same value".

Page 312. 1 Mar 1765. THOMAS TOMSON, Louisa Co., to MOSES CLARK, who is
his son-in-law, 5 sh. for 105 acres on headwaters of Bever
Creek and part of larger tract pat. to TOMSON. Lines: TOMSON's patent
line; JAMES GLEN; to MOSES CLARK, SR. & to MOSES CLARK, JR., grandson.
Wit: JOHN FREEMAN, JAMES GLEN, WILLIAM WOOD, THOMAS GLEN.

Page 315. 14 Feb 1765. JOHN RYAN, AC, to JOHN PATRICK, Augusta Co., 180
pds. for 425 acres in Albemarle and Amherst...Rockfish and
Muckham Rivers...part of tract pat. to JOHN CHISWELL and conveyed by him
to JOHN ROBINSON and by him to JOHN RYAN. Lines: Pointers in Albemarle
County.

Page 316. 24 Sep 1764. CLAIBORNE RICE, AC, to GEORGE KIPPEN & Co.,
Glasgow merchants...Deed of trust of slaves. Wit: NEILL
CAMPBELL, CHARLES IRVING, JOHN OLD.

Page 318. 11 Jul 1764. SAMUEL STAPLES, AC, to HENRY KEY...Deed of
trust...68 pds. 15 sh 2p., stock and furniture. X of STAPLES.
Wit: JOHN PETER, GEORGE HOPPER, ELIZABETH HOPPER(X).

Page 319. 7 Jan 1765. Deed of trust, by JOHN PETER, SR., AC, to HENRY
KEY...20 pds...household goods, etc.

Page 321. 4 Mar 1765. CHARLES TATE, AC, to HENRY KEY, AC...18 pds for
100 acres...South fork of Rockfish...part of 371 acres granted
to HUGH WILLOUGHBY by pat. at Williamsburg 7 Aug 1761. Lines: CHARLES
McANNALLY, WILLOUGHBY. Wit: NEILL CAMPBELL, JOHN PETER, JOHN SNYDER.

Page 323. 4 Mar 1765. JOHN ROSS & wife, ISABEL, AC, to ALEXANDER McCAUL
of Henrico Co., 35 pds. for 100 acres. Lines: ROSS, MAJOR
HENRY; RANDOLPH; Rackoon (sic) Creek. Wit: NEIL CAMPBELL, JOHN KIPPEN,
SAMUEL MURPHY.

Page 324. 1 Apr 1765. LARKIN GATEWOOD & wife, CATHRIN, AC, to JOHN
ROWSE, AC, 28 pds. 15 sh. for 115 acres...part of tract GATE-
WOOD bought of CARTER BRAXTON. Lines: Turkey Mountain ridge; GABRIEL
PENN. Signed to deed: CATHREEN GATEWOOD & CATHERINE in exam.

Page 326. 22 Oct 1764. LUNSFORD LOMAS, Caroline Co., to WILLIAM BIBB,
AC...62 pds. 10 sh. for 192 acres...pat. to LOMAX 3 Nov 1750.
Lines: HARMER KING, Rucker's Run. Wit: JOHN LOVING, RICHARD TANKERSLEY,
RALPH LOMAX, THOMAS LOMAX.

Page 328. 1 Apr 1765. ABRAHAM WARWICK, AC, to JOHN DAWSON, AC...35 pds
for 100 acres...Rich Cove near Rockfish...Lines: JOHN CRAW-
FORD, Cove Creek, ALEXANDER CHISAM, JOHN LYONS. Wit: AMBROSE PORTER,
RICHARD TANKERSLEY, HARRIS TONEY.

Page 330. 2 Aug 1764. SAMUEL SHENAN(sic), AC, to THOMAS SHANNON, AC,
10 pds. for 75 acres...branch of Rockfish near the Blue Mountains. Lines: SAMUEL SHANNON. Wit: ALEXANDER REID, ANDREW REID, JAMES
REID.

Page 333. 1 Oct 1764. DANIEL MACKINZIE & wife, SARAH, Albemarle, to
JAMES BROWN, AC...51 pds. 15 sh. for 150 acres...branch of
Tye...and pat. to DANIEL McKINZIE 4 Jul 1759, and of record in the Secretary's office. X's for DANIEL & SARAH McKINSEY. [Note: Several different spellings are employed herein.]

Page 335. 10 Apr 1765. JOSEPH BALLENGER, AC, to RICHARD BALLENGER, AC,
50 pds. for 232 acres...branch of Beavor (sic) Creek and part
of 2000 acres pat. to JOSEPH & RICHARD BALLENGER. Lines: Top of Ballen-
gers Mt., JOSEPH MAYS. Wit: HENRY FRANKLIN, DRURY TUCKER(X).

Page 337. 4 May 1765. WILLIAM CABELL, AC, to WILLIAM PHELPS, AC, 120
pds. for 170 acres, both sides of Raven Creek of Buffalo.
Wit: JOHN OWEN, JOHN DAWSON, JOHN SAVAGE(X).

Page 338. 10 Apr 1765. JOSEPH & RICHARD BALLENGER, AC, to HENRY FRANK-
LYN, AC, 42 pds. for 156 acres on branch of Beavour [Note:

the clerks seem to have a difficult time spelling this one. BFD.] and part of 2000 acres pat. to JOSEPH & RICHARD BALLENGER. Lines: GEORGE SEATON. Wit: DRURY TUCKER(X), HENRY FRANKLYN JR., JAMES FRANKLYN.

Page 340.   10 Apr 1765. RICHARD BALLENGER, AC, to JOSEPH BALLENGER, AC,
             50 pds. for 412 acres on branch of Beavour Creek and part of
2000 acres pat. to the said parties. Lines: GEORGE SEATON, "on end of
Tobacco Mountain".

Page 342ff. 4 Nov 1765. DANIEL BURFORD, JAMES NEVIL, CORNELIUS THOMAS,
             JAMES DILLARD, JOHN RUCKER, AMBROSE RUCKER, BENJAMIN RUCKER,
and GEORGE McDANIEL bonded for 100 pds. for DANIEL BURFORD who was appointed sheriff by governor of colony 19 Oct, last. He is herein bonded to
collect fees.

Page 343.   Same men are bonded for DANIEL BURFORD to collect taxes as
             sheriff under commission from the governor of the colony.

Page 344.   Same men bonded for DANIEL BURFORD to collect all fines as
             sheriff. These three bonds were acknowledged and recorded at
the courthouse on 4 Nov 1765.

End of Deed Book A

AN ABSTRACT OF ALL ITEMS IN DEED BOOK B

AMHERST COUNTY, VIRGINIA

Bicentennial Commemorative Issue

1761 - 1961

FOREWORD

I have furnished a rather elaborate foreword on the County in my abstract of the first deed book which I issued in 1960. It is only necessary to say here that this commemorated the Bicentennial of the County of Amherst, Virginia. There is a long item in Henning's Statutes concerning the founding of Amherst on May 1, 1961. On that date we were cut from Albemarle. Albemarle, in turn, was cut from Goochland and that county was cut from Henrico. One could write at length of many prominent men who were born in Amherst and what is now Nelson County, daughter of Amherst, but space forbids it. It is sufficient to mention but a few of them: JOHN FLOYD, PETER CARTWRIGHT, members of the CABELL and RIVES families; WILLIAM HARRIS CRAWFORD, Ambassador to France and presidential candidate in 1824; ANTHONY RUCKER, and others. I can but refer one to Hardesty and Brock, William and Lenora Higginbotham Sweeny and their works on Amherst, and the excellent little booklet on Nelson County by J.B. Coincon. My good friend, Alfred Percy, Jr., Elon Road, Madison Heights, Virginia, plans to issue a book this summer, treating historical aspects of the county to further commemorate the Bicentennial. It will also have illustrations to embellish it and I trust that those interested in procuring it will get in touch with him at his address. He has previously published Piedmont Apocalypse, and it has much Amherst data in it.

I wish to express my thanks to my son, Bailey Fulton Davis, Jr., who has cut out stencils and done the tedious mimeograph work for me [in the original issue]. I also wish to extend words of appreciation to members of the Amherst Board of Supervisors for financial aid in preparing this and other commemorative Bicentennial issues. These men are: Bernard H. Camden, Chairman; William E. Sandidge, Circuit Clerk and as such secretary to the Board; James Davis; Ben Wailes; W.M. "John" Fulcher, and E. O. Baldwin.

Bailey Fulton Davis
Director of Bicentennial

DEDICATION

This Bicentennial Issue is dedicated to the memory of my mother-in-law, Emma Thurman Miller, 1889 - 1957. No words of mine can adequately express the love and esteem which I held for her in life. She was an invalid for years and was noble throughout the experiences incident thereto. It is eminently fitting that I sould thus memorialize her in this work, for she was a descendant of early Amherst Countians.

One of her ancestors, WILLIAM GILLESPIE, married ANN HUDSON here in 1777. He was a Revolutionary soldier and migrated to Madison County, Kentucky. ANN HUDSON was the daughter of JOSHUA HUDSON who came to Amherst from Orange County, Virginia. WILLIAM GILLESPIE was a son of GEORGE GILLESPIE, but the mother is unknown since we only have the record of his second marriage in Louisa. The claims of JOSHUA HUDSON and GEORGE GILLESPIE were both allowed in Order Book items relative to assistance furnished the Continental Army.

Emma Thurman's line is herein given without any attempt to supply the dates in my possession:

1. Mary Gillespie, daughter of William and Ann Hudson Gillespie, married Henderson Thurman in Madison County, Kentucky.

2. James Thurman married Polly Harris in Madison County, Kentucky.
3. Perry Thurman married Mary Belle Thompson in Madison County, KY.
4. Emma Thurman married Pleasant Green Miller in Anderson County,KY.

DEED BOOK B

Page 1.   20 Apr 1765. SAML. SPENCER SR., Buckingham, to SAML. SPENCER,
           BUCKINGHAM, for love and affection borne by Sr. to Jr., 500
acres S side Berry's Mt., part of 2000 acres pat. to Sr. on 10 Sep 1755.
Lines: FRANCIS WESTBROOK SPENCER, THOS. LAYNE. Mark of Sr. Wit: CHAS.
LAYNE, WM. SPENCER, FRANCIS WESTBROOK SPENCER.

Page 2.   20 Apr 1765. SAML. SPENCER SR., Buckingham, to MARY PATTESON,
           wife of CHAS. PATTESON,AC, for love and affection borne his
daughter, MARY, and son-in-law, CHAS. PATTESON, 500 acres on S side
Berry's Mt. and S side Rucker's Run and joining same, part of 2000 acres
pat. to SAML. SPENCER SR. 10 Sep 1755. Wit: WM. SPENCER, FRANCIS WEST-
BROOK SPENCER, SAML. SPENCER JR.

Page 4.   6 May 1765. SAML. SPENCER SR., Parish of Tillotson, Bucking-
           ham, to STEPHEN TURNER, AC, for 10 pds., 400 acres pat. at
Williamsburg to SS, Sr. 12 Jan 1746. Lines: Swan's Creek, WM. MAYS (or
MAYO). Wit: SAML. SPENCER JR., FRANCIS SPENCER, CHAS. PATTESON.

Page 5.   3 Jun 1765. JAS. LONDON, AC, to JOS. WILSHER & ARTHER ROBERT-
           SON, AC. 30 pds for 400 acres. Lines: Both sides of Hooker's
Creek.

Page 6.   3 Jun 1765. GEO. CARRINGTON, Cumberland Co., to RICHARD SHEL-
           TON, AC,, for 6 pds. 12 sh., 132 acres Harris Creek. Lines:
WM. MILLER, GRAHAM. Part of 6750 acres pat. to CARRINGTON, 20 Jun 1753.

Page 7.   11 Jan 1765. ALEX. CHISEM, AC, to JOHN DAWSON, AC, 80 pds.
           for 394 acres, Rich Cove near Rockfish. Lines: JAS. LEWIS(?),
near Hickory Creek, JOHN BURNS, WM. BURNS. Wit: WM. TILLER, JAS. LYONS,
JOHN CHISAM(X), WM. CHISAM(X).

Page 9.   5 Jun 1765. ANN NAIL, AC, to WM. MARTIN, AC., for 20 pds.,
           144 acres N fork of Nassau Creek. Lines: LUNSFORD LOMAX.
Mark of ANN NAIL in one place and ANN NEIL in another.

Page 10.   1 Jun 1765. JOHN VALENTINE EATON, AC, to WM. MARTIN, AC, 40
           pds. for 82 acres S branch of Nassau. Lines: JOHN HARMON
(NARMON?). Wit: JOHN PETER, HENRY KEY, SUSANNA PETER(X). Wife examined,
but not named, of EATON.

Page 11.   6 May 1765. CHAS. LYNCH, Bedford Co., to MARTIN DAWSON, AC,
           for 4 pds, 206 acres in 2 tracts. 1) 156 acres on Nuton's(?)
Creek. Lines: HENRY GUTREY, JAS. FROST. 2) 50 acres on Newton's Creek.
Wit: JOHN DAWSON, LEONARD TARRENT, JOS. DAWSON.

Page 12.   3 Jun 1765. LEONARD TARRANT, JR., AC, to JOHN TARRANT, AC,
           for 40 pds, 241 acres both sides of Beavour Creek of Baffilo
(sic), part of 2700 acres pat. to WM. CABELL JR. 6 Dec 1753. Lines:
CALEB WORLEY, THOS. PARKS, ROBT. WHITTEN, JER. WHITTEN. Mary, wife of
LEONARD TARRANT JR., consents.

Page 14.   3 May 1765. CARTER BRAXTON, King Wm. Co., to GEO. LEE, son
           and heir of AMBROSE LEE, dec'd. Pursuant to will of AMBROSE
LEE, 40 pds. paid by late AMBROSE LEE, 200 acres N side of joining Buffalo; part of 1370 acres surveyed for AMBROSE LEE out of larger tract belonging to CARTER BRAXTON. Lines of GEO. PENN of Buffalo. Wit: JOHN
FRY, CORNELIUS THOMAS, JOS. CABELL, WM. CABELL JR.

Page 15.   3 May 1765.   CARTER BRAXTON, King Wm., to RICH. LEE, son of
            late AMBROSE LEE, AC, pursuant to AMBROSE LEE's will and for
40 pds. paid by late LEE, 200 acres on N side of Buffalo - part of 1370
acres bought by Lee from BRAXTON.   Lines: DUDLEY GATEWOOD, Glebe line,
JOS. HIGGINBOTHAM, AMBROSE LEE, dec'd., FRANCIS LEE.   Wit: JOHN FRY, JOS.
CABELL, CORNELIUS THOMAS, WM. CABELL JR.

Page 16.   3 May 1765.   CARTER BRAXTON, King. Wm., to GERRARD BANKS, Cul-
            peper, for 74 pds, 340 acres E side Buffalo of ---River and on
Turkey Mt., part of larger tract of Braxton.   Lines: JOHN ROWSEY, LARKIN
GATEWOOD.   Wit: JOHN FRY, JOS. CABELL, CORNELIUS THOMAS, WM. CABELL JR.

Page 17.   3 May 1765.   CARTER BRAXTON, King Wm., to FRANCIS LEE, son of
            late AMBROSE LEE, AC, pursuant to will of LEE and for 40 pds.
paid by LEE, 200 acres N side of Buffalo, part of 1370 acres bought by
LEE from BRAXTON.   Lines: AMBROSE LEE on Buffalo; GEO. LEE - reserving to
FRANCES LEE, widow of AMBROSE LEE - uses of land during lifetime or widowhood.   Wit: JOHN FRY, CORNELIUS THOMAS, JOS. CABELL, WM. CABELL JR.

Page 18.   3 May 1765.   CARTER BRAXTON, King. Wm., to DUDLEY GATEWOOD.
            Pursuant to last will of AMBROSE LEE - 74 pds. paid by late
LEE, 370 acres N side of Buffalo and part of tract sold to
late A. LEE.   Lines: GEO. PENN, GEO. LEE, Glebe line, A. LEE, dec'd. Wit:
JOHN FRY, CORNELIUS THOMAS, JOS. CABELL, WM. CABELL JR.

Page 19.   3 May 1765.   CARTER BRAXTON, King Wm., to GEO. PENN, AC, pur-
            suant to will of AMBROSE LEE, for 80 pds., 400 acres N side
Buffalo - part of 1370 acres surveyed for LEE, dec'd.   Out of larger
tract of BRAXTON's.   Lines: AMBROSE LEE, dec'd. Buffalo River.   Wit: same
as preceding deed.

Page 20.   7 May 1765.   JOHN ROBARDS, AC, to NEILL CAMPBELL, Alb. Co.,
            for 26 pds, 300 acres.   Lines: Widow UPTON, Widow JOHNSON,
Rockfish River.   Wit: GABL. PENN, LETTFIELD TRENT, JOHN DIGGS.

Page 22.   20 Jun 1765.   SAML. MORIAL, AC, to ROBT. MORIAL for 10 sh., 69
            acres branch of Rockfish near Blue Mts.   Lines: SAML. MORIAL,
JOHN CHISWELL.   Wit: DAVID CRAWFORD, SAML. WOODS, WM. DEPREIST.

Page 23.   1 Jul 1765.   HOWARD CASH, AC, to JOEL CASH, AC, for 5 pds, 300
            acres Br. of EDWARD CARTER - Mill Creek.   Lines: WM. BICKNEEL's
100 acres deeded to him by HOWARD CASH - part of 400 acres pat. to HOWARD
CASH 12 Jul 1750.   Wife of HOWARD CASH consents.

Page 24.   5 Apr 1765.   JOHN BURFORD, AC, to WM. PENDLETON, AC, for 30
            pds., 196 acres Harris Creek.   Lines: Capt. JOHN HARVEY, GEO.
McDANIEL.   Wit: AMBROSE RUCKER, GEO. McDANIEL, HENRY TRENT.

Page 25.   1 Jul 1765.   HOWARD CASH, AC, to STEPHEN CASH, AC, for 5 pds.,
            200 acres Stone House Creek, part of 440 acres pat. to HOWARD
CASH 3 Mar 1760; bound by a line already marked off in upper part of
tract for 200 acres.   Wife of HOWARD CASH consents.

Page 26.   1 Jul 1765.   PIERCE WADE, AC, to ALEX. McCAUL, Henrico, for 5
            sh., to secure bond to GEO. KIPPEN & CO., Glasgow Merchants,
of June 1, 1765, and one in McCAUL's possession of same date - tract where
WADE now lives - 308 acres.   Lines: JOHN GOODWON, JNO. WALES, WM. STAITON,
JAS. CREWS(W), EDWARD EIDSON.   Also slave, Tobey.   Wit: NEILL CAMPBELL,
RICH. HARVIE, JOHN KIPPEN.

Page 27.   1 Jul 1765.   MINOS WRIGHT, AC, to KILLIS WRIGHT, AC, 15 pds,
            100 acres N side and adj. Fluvanna - lower part of 390 acres
which MINOS WRIGHT lately recovered of JOHN FRY.   Lines: N side of Tye;
to mouth of the Great Branch, Back line.

Page 28.   4 Mar 1765.   SAML. STAPLES, AC, to HENRY KEY, AC, 70pds 3sh
            11p, 200 acres pat. to SAML. STAPLES at Williamsburg 2 Jun
1760.   Lines: LUNSFORD LOMAX, Nassau Creek; for 500 years - one pepper
corn due on feast of St. John Baptist if demanded.   Conditioned upon KEY
and heirs paying the debt with interest 24 Jun 1767.   Mark of STAPLES.

Wit: JOHN PETER, THOS. ALFORD, JAS. MATTHEWS(mark), GEO. HOPPER.

Page 30.   13 Apr 1765.   JOHN MOORE, Parish of Fredericksville, Alb. Co.,
            to JOHN COLEMAN of same, for 50 pds., 370 acres on Tobacco Row
Mt., branch of Huff's Creek. Lines in pat. of 15 Aug 1764. Wit: PETT-
FIELD TRENT, THOS. DEVER(R)IX(X), GEO. BOURN, JOHN HARVIE.

Page 31.   1 Jul 1765.   STEPHEN TURNER, AC, to CHAS. PATTERSON & wife,
            MARY, for love borne by TURNER for them - 37 acres N side of
Fluvanna and joining it. Part of land bought and recorded by STEPHEN
TURNER from JOHN HOWARD.

Page 32.   14 Mar 1765.   VALLENTINE BALL, AC, to GEO. KIPPEN & Co., Glas-
            gow merchants, 5 sh. to secure 55-1-8 half penny - land where
he now lives - 540 acres, slave Lucy - to be paid by 14 Mar 1766. Wit:
NEILL CAMPBELL, WM. ANGUS, THOS. REID, HUGH ROSE.

Page 34.   13 Dec 1764.   THOS. JEFFERSON, Gent., Albemarle Co, to JAS.
            COFFEY, Planter, Alb. Co, for 100 pds, 364 acres. Lines: Tye
River (chesnut tree near it). Wit: JOHN HARVIE, SAML. WOODS, WM. COFFEY,
JAS. GLEN. Proven in courthouse by the above witnesses 5 Aug 1765.

Page 36.   5 Aug 1765.   LEONARD GOFF, son and heir of JOHN GOFF, dec'd,
            and wife ANN, AC, to GEO. McDANIEL, AC, in consequence of
agreement between McDANIEL and late JOHN GOFF - 500 acres consideration -
Stovall Creek and conveyed by McDANIEL to LEONARD GOFF of equal date; they
convey to McDANIEL 153 acres on Harris Creek.

Page 37.   5 Aug 1765.   GEO. McDANIEL & wife, MARGRETT, AC, to BAYLOR
            WALKER, King and Queen, for 60 pds, 136 acres S branch of
Harris adj. the Tobacco Row Mts. Line: JOHN HARVIE.

Page 38.   5 Aug 1765.   GEO. McDANIEL & wife MARGRETT, AC, to LEONARD
            GOFF, JOS. GOFF, JOHN GOFF, AMBROSE GOFF, & ELIJAH MORAN, AC,
in consequence of agreement with the late JOHN GOFF and in consideration of
153 acres on Harris Creek conveyed to McDANIEL by LEONARD GOFF, son and
heir of JOHN GOFF, bearing equal date with these presents - 500 acres on
Stoval Creek, 400 of which was pat. to SARAH LYNCH 20 Sep 1759, the other
100 acres pat. on same date to SARAH LYNCH. Reservation to ANNE GOFF,
widow and relict of JOHN GOFF, the plantation whereon she now lives during her natural life or widowhood in lieu of her dower in the 153 acres,
and to be fivided between the above persons, agreeable to the will of
JOHN GOFF.

Page 39.   5 Aug 1765.   PATRICK MORRISON, AC, to HENRY KEY, AC, for 50
            pds., 228 acres pat. to MORRISON at Williamsburg 15 Aug 1764.
Lines: N side Piney, running down same, and crossing the river. Wife of
MORRISON consents.

Page 41.   22 Jul 1765.   THOS. WRIGHT, AC, to JOHN WELCH, AC, for 35 pds,
            200 acres N side Tye River. Lines: SAML. BURKS, JR. Wit:
JOHN PETER, GAB. PENN, HENRY KEY, ANDREW LACKEY. Wife of Wright consents.

Page 42.   5 Aug 1765.   WM. HARTGROVE, orphan and son of BENJ. HARTGROVE,
            apprentices himself to ROBT. MONTGOMERY, Wheelwright, for five
years. Wit: SAML. MURPHY, JOHN LOVING, JR.

Page 43.   12 Mar 1765.   JEREMIA WHITTEN, AC, to WM. CABELL, AC, for
            56-17-6, 400 acres; land where WHITTEN now lives on Tobacco
Row Mt. (X) of Whitten. Wit: JOHN DAWSON, THOS. MEGGINSON, JOHN SAVAGE(X)

Page 44.   31 Aug 1765.   JOHN DEPRIEST, AC, to JAMES HULSEY, AC, for 10
            pds., 89 acres both sides Pounder Branch. Lines: JAS. MARTIN.
Wit: FRANS. MERIWETHER, DAVID MARTIN, SAML. CALDWELL, DAVID MERIWETHER,
JOS. SMITH.

Page 45.   13 Jul 1765.   SAML. BELL, "Orringe" Co. NC, to FRANS. MERIWE-
            THER, AC, for 100 pds., 400 acres Rockfish river. Lines: JOHN
MILLER; MELOY; WOODS; MORREL; SAML. BELL. Wit: OLIVER ORR(X), THOS. BELL,
DAVID MERIWETHER.

Page 46.   2 Sep 1765.   RICH. POWELL, AC, to JOHN WOODROOF, AC, for 5 sh.
           242 acres on Fluvanna. Wife of POWELL consents.

Page 47.   2 Sep 1765.   JOHN WOODROOF, AC, to RICH. POWELL, AC, for 5 sh,
           217 acres on Harris Creek. Wife of WOODROOF consents.

Page 48.   2 Sep 1765.   DAVID MARTIN, AC, to SAML. CULLWELL (CALWELL), AC,
           for 150 pds, 200 acres on Rockfish. Lines: Chiswell's old line.

Page 49.   Order to DAVID CRAWFORD & FRANS. MERIWETHER, Gent., to examine
           MARY MARTIN, wife of DAVID, as to conveyance to SAML. CALWELL.
14 Sep 1765. Recorded 28 Sep 1765.

Page 50.   30 Aug 1765.   DAVID CRAWFORD, AC, to JOEL CRAWFORD, AC, for
           100 pds. 400 acres on branch of Rockfish and bounded as by
pat. to EDWIN HICKMAN at Williamsburg 9 Feb 1737, and conveyed to JOHN
MORRISON by EDWIN HICKMAN in 1741 and by MORRISON to JOHN ROBESON; conveyed by JOHN ROBESON to DAVID CRAWFORD - 25 acres cleared on W side of
the road and 10 acres of tendable wood land joining thereto to be enjoyed
by my son, JOEL CRAWFORD.

Page 51.   20 May 1765.   ROBERT HARRIS, Parish of Frederickville, Alb. Co,
           to his son-in-law, JOEL CRAWFORD; slaves: Lewis, a boy, and
Juliany, a gir. Wit: DAVID CRAWFORD, NATHAN CRAWFORD, JOHN JACOBS.

Page 52.   22 Apr 1765.   WM. BRUCE, AC, to JACOB EADS, AC, for 15 pds,
           150 acres S fork of Rockfish. Lines: HENRY KEYS. Wit: HENRY
KEY, WM. HARTGROVE, THOS. SARGENT(X), JOHN STRATTON(?)(X).

Page 53.   2 Sep 1765.   ZACH. TALIAFERRO, AC, to JACOB SMITH, AC, for 20
           pds, 400 acres Franklin & Moll's Creek. Lines: JAS. SMITH,
HOWARD CASH, PIERCE WADE, BENJ. TALIAFERRO. Wit: WM. HANSBROUGH, JOHN
LOVING, JOHN WRIGHT. Wife of TALIAFERRO consents.

Page 54.   24 Sep 1765.   JOHN LYON, AC, to TERISHA TURNER, Alb. Co., for
           36 pds, 100 acres. Lines: JOHN DAWSON, TERISHA TURNER, JOHN
LYONS. Wit: JOHN DAWSON, CHAS. TEDBET(?), MARTIN DAWSON.

Page 55.   1 Oct 1765.   DAWSON WADE, AC, to CHAS. TATE, AC, for 10 sh, 60
           acres S branch of N fork of Davis Creek. Lines: JOHN WADE.

Page 57.   1 Jun 1765.   THOS. HENDERSON, AC, to MATT. HARRIS, AC, for 15
           pds, 110 acres both sides Rockfish. Lines: S. side of Col.
JOHN CHISWELL's old line, crossing Buck Creek; fork of David Creek; WM.
HARRIS. Pat. to THOS. HENDERSON 20 Sep 1751.

Page 58.   7 Oct 1765.   SAML. MARKSBERRY, AC, to CHAS. TALIAFERRO, AC,
           for 11 pds, 162 acres joining CHAS. TALIAFERRO's old line.
Lines: AARON HIGGINBOTHAM, PHILLIP SMITH. Wit: ZACH. TALIAFERRO, JOHN
LOVING JR.(?), JOHN WRIGHT.

Page 60.   7 Oct 1765.   THOS. SHANNON, AC, to WM. CROW, AC, for 45 pds,
           300 acres branch of Rockfish near the Blew(sic) Mts. Lines:
WM. SIMSON, SAML. SHANNON, JOHN MORRISON. Wit: WM. PATTON, SAML. SHANNON,
THOS. PATTON.

Page 61.   7 Oct 1765.   THOS. SHANNON, AC, to SAML. SHANNLN, AC, 10 pds.,
           100 acres branch of Rockfish near the Blew(sic) Mts. Lines:
WM. SIMSON. Wit: WM. PATTON, THOS. PATTON, THOS. SHENNAN(sic).

Page 63.   1 Jul 1765.   RICH. LAWRENCE, AC, to JOS. MORRIS, AC, for 20
           pds, 75 acres Hicory Creek of Rockfish. Wife of LAWRENCE
consents.

Page 64.   5 Oct 1765.   GRIGORY (GREGORY) MATHIS (signed MATHEWS), AC, to
           ZACH. PHILLIPS, AC, for 45 pds, 400 acres on Davis Creek.
Lines: LEE HARRIS, DAVID MONTGOMERY, Col. JOHN CHISWELL - "continued"
from JOS. CABELL to GRIGORY MATHIS by deed of sail(sic). Wit: JOHN DAW-
SON, THOS. WEST, LEE HARRIS.

Page 66.   5 Oct 1765.   THOS. FITZPATRICK, Alb. Co., to WM. FITZPATRICK,
          son of the aforesaid THOS., for love and 5 sh., part of 340
acres pat. to THOS. in 1763, 170 acres and part of the 340 acres N fork
of Nassau - to be equally divided between my two sons, WM. & JOHN. WM.
to have uper (sic) end of tract. Wit: JOS. FITZPATRICK, ALEX. FITZPAT-
RICK, JOHN FITZPATRICK.

Page 67.   5 Oct 1765.   THOS. FITZPATRICK Alb. Co. to JOHN, son of THOS,
          for love and 5 sh, part of 340 acres pat. in 1763 to THOS. -
170 acres - description same as in above deed - John to have lore(sic)
end. Wit: WM. & ALEX. FITZPATRICK.

Page 68.   7 Oct 1765.   HENRY CHILDERS & wife, SUSANNA, AC, to JOHN CHIL-
          DERS, Alb. Co, for 35 pds., 138 acres br. of Huffis Creek,
part of 276 acres surveyed for HENRY CHILDERS and bought from WM. CABELL
JR. Lines: BENJ. STINNET, ROBT. WHITTEN. Marks of CHILDERS & wife.

Page 69.   7 Oct 1765.   SAML. MARKSBERRY, AC, to JOHN PARKS, JR., AC, for
          49 pds 1 sh, 223 and 1/8 acres, part of larger tract bought by
S.M. from ZACH. TALIAFERRO. Lines: E side of Piney Mt., TALIAFERRO's Mt.

Page 70.   2 Sep 1765.   WM. MARTIN, AC, to MW. TILLER, AC, for 24 pds,
          144 acres N fork of Nassau. Lines: LUNSFORD LOMAX - conveyed
to WM. MARTIN by ANN NEAL last June.

Page 71.   7 Oct 1765.   JOHN WEBB & wife USLEY, planters, to JAMES LYON,
          planter, for 60 pds, 200 acres Rockfish. Lines: CHISELL's at
foot of the Mt. JOHN WEBB bought it from SAML. MURRIL; rec. in AC.
Signed USSLEY WEBB.

Page 73.   7 Oct 1765.   WM. FLOYD & wife EBEDIAH, AC, to SAML. GIST of
          Hanover, formerly Goochland, 100 pds., 200 acres S side of the
river (Pedlar), pat. to ROBT. DAVIS 1 Apr 1749, and by him conveyed to WM.
FLOYD. Rec. in Alb. Co. (X) of wife.

Page 75.   16 Sep 1765.   JOHN DAWSON, AC, to TERISHA TURNER, Alb. Co.,
          for 3 pds, 100 acres Rich Cove and Cove Creek of Rockfish.

Page 76.   1 Aug 1765.   ELIAS SMITH, AC, to PATRICK MORRISON, AC, for 10
          pds, 50 acres pat. to JOHN MAYFIELD 1 Jun 1750, and conveyed
in Alb. by MAYFIELD to ELIAS SMITH. Lines: PHILIP DAVIS, ROSE. (X) of
SMITH. Wife of SMITH consents.

Page 77.   5 Oct 1765.   JOHN CARTER, AC, planter, to THOS. GORLEY, AC,
          planter, for 5 pds, crop of corn, foder(sic), hemp sead(sic).
Wit: SAML. WOODS, ROBT. JOHN KNIGHT, RICH. NALLEY.

Page 78.   30 Sep 1765.   JOS. NALLEY, AC, planter, to SAML. WOODS, AC,
          Merchant, for 5-6-11, hemp crop. Wit: RICH. NALLEY & WM. W.
NEALY or McNEALY.

Page 79.   4 Oct 1765.   HENRY MAGUFFY, AC, to CHAS. McPHERSON & NINIAN
          MINZIES, Henrico, for 36 pds, 200 acres head of Harris and on
Tobacco Row. Lines: Col. LOMAX. Wit: THOS. REID, THOS. POWELL, RODERICK
MACCULLOCK. (X) of MAGUFFY.

Page 80.   7 Oct 1765.   WM. CABELL, AC, to JULIAN NEAL, AC, for 22 pds,
          247 acres. Lines: JOHN SNYDER, CAPT. NEVIL - 188 acres and
435 in all.

Page 81.   27 Sep 1765.   RICH. NALLEY & ABRAHAM NALLEY, AC, to SAML.
          WOODS, AC, for 35 pds, hemp crop where wee (sic) now live this
year; corn, and flax. Wit: MICHAEL McNEELY, FRANS. MOORE. (X) of
ABRAHAM NALLEY.

Page 82.   7 Oct 1765.   NIEL CAMPBELL, Alb. Co.; VALENTINE BALL & wife
          SUSANNA, AC, to NATHANIEL WOODROOF, AC, for 40 pds, 270 acres
S side and next to Tye - upper part of tract property of CAMPBELL & BALL.

Page 83.   7 Oct 1765.   GEO. CARRINGTON, Cumberland Co, to THOS. WATTS,
            AC, for Ŀ19-4, 243 acres branch of Harris Creek. Lines: JAS.
CURSE, ISAAC WATTS, JAS. CREWS, part of greater tract of 6750 acres pat.
to GEO. CARRINGTON 20 Jun 1753.

Page 84.   7 Oct 1765.   JACOB BROWN, AC, to HENRY KEY, AC, for 20 pds,
            90 acres pat. to JACOB BROWN at Williamsburg 7 Jul 1763, on N
side of Tye on branch of Black Creek. Lines: Col. LOMAX, AMBROSE JONES,
WILCOX. Wife of BROWN not named, but consents.

Page 85.   2 Oct 1765.   JOHN CHRISTIAN & DRURY CHRISTIAN, AC, to DAVID
            PATTESON, Buckingham, pursuant to decree of Gen. Ct. 400 acres
N side and joining Fluvanna - just below Buffalo Island; upper part of
1000 acres pat. to ROBT. CHRISTIAN 30 Sep 1743 - DRURY & JOHN CHRISTIAN
hold indefeasible estate of inheritance in fee simple. Wit; JAS. DILL-
ARD, JOHN COLEMAN, JAS. CHRISTIAN, THOS. PATTESON, SAML. WEAVER(X).

Page 87.   21 Aug 1765.   MARY REID, AC, to THOS. CARPENTER, AC, for 37
            pds, 270 acres pat. to JOHN REID 25 Mar 1762, head branch of
Corben's Creek, branch of Rockfish. Lines: JAS. BARNET. Wit: SAML.
WOODS, JOHN REID, ALEX. REID JR.

Page 89.   7 Oct 1765.   ROBT. WHITTEN, AC, HECTOR McALESTER, for 100 pds,
            263 acres both sides of Beavour Creek. Lines: NICHOLAS EAST-
ING, JER. WHITTEN, WM. CABELL's order of Council tract; BENJ. STENNET.
(X) of WHITTEN. Wit: WM. HENRY, THOS. REID. Wife of WHITTEN consents.

Page 90.   7 Oct 1765.   GEO. CARRINGTON, Cumberland Co, to ROBT. WHITTEN
            AC, Ŀ13-10, 270 acres. Lines: PIERCE WADE, JAS. CREUSE.

Page 91.   12 Jul 1765.   HENRY ROSE, AC, to JOHN ROSE, AC. This is an
            exchange of land. Lines: CHAS. ROSE, JOHN LEWIS, JOHN ROSE -
S branch of Castle Creek - 10 sh - belongs to JOHN ROSE. Exchange: Land
of JOHN ROSE next to CHAS. ROSE, JOHN LEWIS, JOHN ROSE, part of 23,700
acres pat. to ROBT. ROSE, Clerk, 10 Aug MDCCXLIV (or so it appears, but
it has been erased and it is difficult to read) - 174 acres. Lines: JOHN
ROSE, CHAS. ROSE, LEWIS. This is JOHN ROSE from HENRY ROSE -10 sh. paid
by HENRY to JOHN - land pat. to JOHN ROSE XX day of Aug MDCCL. Lines:
JAS. DICKIE; plan drawn by WM. CABELL XXIV day of Nov MDCCL. Wit: H(?)
ROSE, J.R.; PAT. ROSE, FRANCES LANDRUM.

Page 93.   28 Oct 1765.   AMBROSE JONES, AC, to JOHN GIZZAGE FRASER, AC,
            120 pds, 135 acres N side of Tye - granted by order of Council
to ROBT. ROSE, Clerk, and THOS. CHEW, and sold by ROSE to AMBROSE JONES
and rec. in Alb. Co.; 264 acres adj. pat. to AMBROSE JONES 15 July MDCCLX.
Lines: LUNSFORD LOMAX, JAS. JONES. Wit: H.T.(?) ROSE, PAT. ROSE, RALPH
LOMAX. HUGH, CHAS, & JOHN ROSE.

Page 95.   23 May 1766.   JOHN WELCH, AC, to GEO. KIPPEN & Co, Glasgow
            merchants, for 5 sh, Deed of Trust for 25 pds. on 9 Jan 1765,
and 10 pds. on same date - 250 acres on Tie, land bought of THOS. WRIGHT,
dec'd., rec. in AC. Wit: NEILL CAMPBELL, WM. WALTON, WM. COX, GEO.
MUNROE(X).

Page 96.   2 Jun 1766.   BENJ. STINNET, JR., AC, to HENRY CHILDRESS, AC,
            for 65 pds, 150 acres branch of Huff middle part of 400 acres
granted to BENJ. STINNET SR. Lines: JAS. ISHAM, BENJ. STINNET. STINNET
& wife USLE signed with X.

Page 97.   9 Oct 1765.   GEO. SEATON, AC, to GEO. KIPPEN & Co., Glasgow
            merchants - 5 sh. to secure bond of 9 Oct 1765, of 479 -e-4.
400 acres joining HENRY FRANKLIN & JOS. BALLENGER and bought of JER. WADE
and also 400 acres bought of PIERCE WADE, rec. in AC. Also 400 acres in
Henrico left by Mr. WATSON to his daughter, ELIZ., wife of GEO. SEATON,
also 23 slaves, all named. D.of T. Wit: HENRY ROSE, JOHN FRASER, NEILL
CAMPBELL. Memo: 400 acres from PIERCE WADE is excepted.

Page 99.   1 Jul 1765.   JAMES CRUSE & wife, MILDRED, AC, to JOS. DAWSON,
            AC, for 100 pds, 344 acres. Lines: 200 acres formerly that of
WM. MILLER & joining same, JNO. BURFORD, 140 acres formerly belonging to

DANL. BURFORD.

Page 100. 7 Jul 1766. JONATHAN STAMPER & wife, RACHAEL, AC, to JNO.
ROWZEE, AC, for 18 pds, 124 acres heads of branches on N side
of Buffalo. Lines: Late Sect. CARTER, 124 acres pat. to STAMPER 16 Sep
1765. STAMPER & wife signed with (X).

Page 102. 7 Jul 1766. GEO. TAYLOR, AC, to NEILL CAMPBELL, Alb. Co., for
100 pds., 240 acres head of S fork of Buffaloe and where TAY-
LOR now lives. Lines: WM. CAMPBELL. Memo. GEO. TAYLOR is to "have his
life" in the said line.

Page 104. 7 Jul 1766. GEO. TAYLOR, AC, to SAML. MURPHY, AC, for 50 pds,
170 acres S. side and joining N branch of Piney - part of
tract pat. to GEO. TAYLOR 20 Sep 1751. Lines: 4th branch of Crawley's
Creek, HENRY TAYLOR's corner on the ridge, up river to beginning. In
possession of MURPHY. (X) of TAYLOR.

Page 105. 14 Jul 1766. CARTER BRAXTON, King Wm., to MATT. TUCKER, AC.
for 36 pds, 144 acres both sides of Buffaloe - part of tract
of BRAXTON's. Lines: GEO. SEATON, N side of Buffaloe, BRAXTON; in TUCK-
ER's possession. Wit: GEO. SEATON, EDMD. WILCOX, HUGH ROSE, WM. WALTON,
GABL. PENN.

Page 106. 4 Aug 1766. JNO. CRAWFORD, AC, to WM. CRAWFORD, AC, for 15
pds, 92 acres head of Maloy's Creek.

Page 107. 15 Jul 1766. THOS. HAMILTON, AC, to ABRAHAM NAIBOURS, Prince
Edward, Deed of Trust - great many items - poplar leaf as
stock mark. Wit: THOS. PAULET, ISAAC NAIBOURS, FRANCIS NAIBOURS. MARY
HAMILTON joins in and makes mark along with THOS.

Page 108. 15 Jul 1766. CARTER BRAXTON, King Wm., to GEO. SEATON,AC, for
865 pds, 2268 acres, part of tract of GEORGE BRAXTON, late of
King and Queen, pat. 25 Nov 1743, and given by GEO. BRAXTON to CARTER
BRAXTON in his last will and rec. in King and Queen, and now of record in
Sect's office of this Colony - land formerly in Goochland and now in AC.
Lines: AMBROSE LEE (now GEO. PENN's); on N side of Buffalo, glebe corner,
JOHN BENGER, GABL. PENN, up river, across the river, CARTER BRAXTON. AC.
Given as 2268 in the beginning and 2228 later. Wit: WM. CABELL, JR.,
EDMD. WILCOX, GABL. PENN.

Page 110. 1 Sep 1766. JNO. MCGUIRE, AC, farmer, to CHAS. YANCEY, AC,
farmer, for 7 pds. - no AC stated - S branch of Taylor's
Creek. Lines: CHAS. YANCEY. (X) of McGUIRE.

Page 112. 4 Aug 1766. NATHAN CRAWFORD, AC, to ANNE CRAWFORD, Sr., AC,
for yearly rents and covenants - 200 acres where she now lives,
rent 9 sh. 1 peny (sic) on or before May 1st, during her natural life or
widowhood. Signed by both parties. Wit: JNO. & WM. CRAWFORD, CHAS.
YANCEY.

Page 113. 1 Sep 1766. JARVIS JACKSON & MARY JACKSON, Bedford, to HENRY
TRENT, AC, for 30 pds, 400 acres "boath" sides John's Creek of
the N side of Fluvanna. Lines: NICHOLAS DAVIS, crossing John's Creek,
RICH. & ROWLAND BURKS, "with the priviledges of Hunting, Haucking, Fishing, and Fowling". (X) of MARY JACKSON.

Page 114. 11 Mar 1766. THOS. SHANNAN, "Juner" to THOS. SHANNON "Senor",
both of AC. for 1 sh., 75 acres that Jr. had of SAML. SHANNAN
on a branch of Rockfish near the Blew Mts. Lines: JAS. HENDRICKS. Wit:
SAML. SHENNAN, WM. CRAWFORD, (X) of ANN CROW.

Page 116. 1 Sep 1766. JACOB EADS to HUGH PATRICK, both of AC, for 15
pds, 150 acres branch of S fork of Rockfish. Lines: HENRY
KEYS. (X) of EADS.

Page 117. 1 Sep 1766. GEO. SEATON, AC, to CARTER BRAXTON, King Wm., for
₤739-12-3, 2268 acres both sides of Buffalo and formerly conveyed to SEATON by CARTER BRAXTON 15 Jul 1766. Also, four young negroes:

Sam, Agg, Cresy, & Peter, with future increase of females. One penknife and all houses and orchards. Deed of trust to be repaid by Oct. 15 next.

Page 119. 4 Aug 1766. DANL. McBEN, AC, to SAML. MURPHY, AC, for 12 pds, 81 acres S side and joining N branch of Piney. Lines: SAML. MURPHY. Wit: SAML. CRAWLEY, DUNCAN CAMERON, JOHN SALE.

Page 120. 1 Sep 1766. EDMUND WILCOX, AC, to RICH. CORBIN Esq., King and Queen, for 200 pds, 1120 acres N side Tye. Lines: AMBROSE JONES, by side of river, CHAS. LEWIS, a spring - according to a survey by ROBT. BROOKE on 3 Apr 1742 - and whereof EDMUND WILCOX is now seized as son and heir of JNO. WILCOX, dec'd. Deed of trust if repaid by 25 Oct 1767 with interest from Oct. 25 next ensuing.

Page 122. 30 Jul 1766. JAS. BUSH, AC, to McPHERSON & MINZIES, Henrico merchants, 5 sh. to secure debt of bond as of 30 Jul 1766, of Ƚ106-16-2 half penny and principal is Ƚ53-8-1 penny farthing - 75 acres joining THOS. PARKS & HENRY CHILDERS and piece of land that PETER FIELD TRENT bought of BENJ. STINNETT and same land JAS. BUSH obught of JNO. STINNETT; also 373 acres that JAS. BUSH bought from GLOVER DAVENPORT and where JOHN BERRY lives joining WM. CABELL JR. & THOS. PARKS; also one survey on Piney about 300 acres - bay mare, colt, 11 cattle, cow and calf, cow marked with JNO. STINNETT's mark and calf with his own mark. One cow with DRURY TUCKER's mark and calf with mine. Two red "Earlings" and other stock and household goods. Wit: THOS. REID, GABL. PENN, WM. PENN, (X) of BUSH.

Page 124. 8 Aug 1766. ROBT. WHITEN, AC, to McPHERSON & MINZIES, Henrico merchants, 5 sh. to secure debt Ƚ66-6-7 half penny and principal of Ƚ33-3-3-3 farthings. 270 acres on Harris Creek. Lines: PEIRCE WADE, JNO. GOODWIN, JOS. DAWSON, THOS. WATTS. Land ROBT. WHITEN bought of GEO. CARRINGTON SR. and rec. in AC - also stock and house hold goods. (X) of WHITEN. Wit: THOS. REID, GABL. PENN, JNO. BARRET, JOHNSON BIEN.

Page 126. 20 Jun 1766. JAS. WARREN, AC, to McPHERSON & MINZIES, Henrico merchants, 5 sh. to secure debt of Ƚ15-5-1 both sides of Stoney Creek, 205 acres. Lines: CHAS. CHRISTIAN, WM. DILLARD, and piece of land or Col. JOHN CHISWELL whereon JNO. WARREN lives and land whereon JAS. WARREN now lives. (X) of JW. Wit: THOS. REID, GABL. PENN, WM. PENN.

Page 127. 1 Sep 1766. JULIAN NAIL (NEAL) & wife MARY, AC, to JNO. SNYDOR, Abl., now AC, for 10 pds, 247 acres on branches of Rockfish. Lines: JNO. SNYDER, Capt. NEVIL. Signed: JULIAN NEAL.

Page 128. 1 Sep 1766. JESSE MILLS, AC, to NATHANIEL DAVIS, AC, for 40 pds, 350 acres branch of Buck Creek of Pedlar. Lines: Maple Creek, EDWARD WATTE, JR, THOS. MILLS. LUCY, wife of JESSE MILLS, consents.

Page 129. 6 Oct 1766. ELIZ. RAY, AC, to JAS. BROWN, AC, for 60 pds, 200 acres Castle Creek, branch of Tye. Lines: JAS. DICKIE, JOHN ROSE, Late "Reverent" ROBT. ROSE. (X) of E.R. Wit: THOS. SHENNAN, WM. RAY, JNO. JACOBS. Wit. to peacable possession: HUGH ROSE, CHAS. ROSE, RALPH LOMAX.

Page 131. 3 Sep 1766. GEO. SEATON, AC, to McPHERSON & MINZIES, Henrico merchants, Ƚ184-14-9 pence farthing, 400 acres both sides Beaver Creek, which SEATON bought of PEIRCE WADE. Lines: EDWARD CARTER, RICH. BALLENGER - 400 acres which SEATON bought of JER. WADE. Still head and worm and penknife - Deed of Trust to be repaid by Sept 28, 1767. Wit: THOS. REID, GABL. PENN, JNO. BARRET.

Page 134. 6 Oct 1766. JULIAN NEAL, AC, to JAS. BROWN, AC, for 20 pds, 188 acres in the Dutch Thoroughfare. Wit: RICH FARRAR.

Page 135. 6 Oct 1766. JACOB MICHAUX & wife SALLEY, Parish of Southam in Cumberland, to CORNELIUS THOMAS, AC, for 100 pds, 838 acres "Sout" branch of Rockfish. Lines: STEPHEN JOHNSON, Lick branch, "Seedar" branch - part of 3226 acres pat. to JAS. NEVIL, dec'd, 12 Jan 1746, and left by will of NEVIL to SALLEY, wife of JACOB MICHAUX.

Page 136. 8 Oct 1766. DUNCAN GRAHAM, Caroline Co., & wife MARY, to
          BATTALE HARRISON, AC, for 67 pds, 268 acres Harris Creek near
Tobacco Row Mts. and part of larger tract of GRAHAM. Wit: EDWARD TINSLEY,
DAVID TINSLEY, REUBEN HARRISON. Commission on p.137 for EDMUND PENDLETON,
JOHN TAYLOR, WALKER TALIAFERRO, Gents., to examine MARY GRAHAM. PENDLE-
TON & TAYLOR, Caroline justices, report on 1 mar 1770.

Page 139. 8 Oct 1766. DUNCAN GRAHAM & wife MARY, Caroline, to EDWARD
          TINSLEY, AC, for 185 pds, 740 acres on Harris Creek near To-
bacco Row Mts., and part of larger GRAHAM tract. Wit: BATTAILE HARRISON,
REUBEN HARRISON, DAVID TINSLEY.

Page 141. 31 Oct 1766. WM. TACKETT alias JNO. TENNISON, AC, his certain
          attorney, to JNO. LEMASTERS, AC, for 5 pds, 50 acres both
sides of Porage Creek; part of tract granted to ELIAS DEHART. Lines:
CHRISTIAN. Wit: JAS. LONDON, ELEAZAR LEMASTER, JNO. LEMASTER(X).

Page 143. 3 Nov 1766. HENRY TRENT, AC, to JOS. GOODWIN, AC, for ₤14-2-6,
          113 acres N side of Johns Creek, part of greater TRENT tract.
Wit: JAS. DILLARD, RICH. SHELTON, WM. HORSLEY, SAML. BAUGHEN.

Page 144. 11 Nov 1766. THOS. WHITE, AC, to GILBERT HAY, AC, for 90 pds,
          136 acres pat. to THOS. WHITE 15 Jul 1760 on Little Creek, S
branch of Indian Creek. Lines: HENRY ROSE, formerly JOHN HARRIS' corner;
another tract of 301 acres pat. to JOHN HARRIS and part of 400 acres, 10
Sep 1755. Wit: JOS. LIVELY(X), HENRY ROSE, THOS. PARKS, RACHEL WHITE(X).

Page 146. 21 Nov 1766. JOHN BURROWS, AC, to McPHERSON & MINZIES, Henri-
          co merchants, 5 sh. to secure debt for ₤11-2-4-3 farthings
and due on 22 Oct 1766 - bay mare, other stock, and household goods.
Wit: GAB. PENN, THOS. REID, JOHN BARRET.

Page 147. 3 Jun 1766. ARCHY BURDEN, AC, Deed of Trust to secure
          ₤21-18-2 half penny - horse, household goods - to McPHERSON
& MINZIES, Henrico merchants. Wit: GAB. PENN, WM. PENN, JOHN BARRET.

Page 148. 28 Jul 1766. THOS. SHANNON, AC, to ABRAHAM HARGIS, AC, for 55
          pds, 208 acres branch of Rockfish - part of tract "sould" to
ALEX. MOUNTGOMERY and containing 640 acres and bought of JOHN CHISWELL by
ALEX. MOUNTGOMERY and by him to WM. MONTGOMERY and by WM. MONTGOMERY to
THOS. SHANNON. Lines: Top of a mt. (X) of SHANNON. Wit: RICH. NALLEY,
JNO. MOUNTGOMERY, JNO. THOMSON.

Page 150. 24 Jan 1767. JOHN HEARD, Hallifax (sic), to JAS. REID, AC,
          for ₤45-10, 200 acres and part of 400 acres pat. to GEO. HEARD
1 Feb 1748. Lines: ANDREW REID & formerly to JOHN CHISWELL; NATHANIEL
BARNET, pat. line formerly belonging to WM. MEHO, Gent., JAS. HEARD. Wit:
SAML. SHENNAN, ALEX. MILLER, JOHN SHIELDS, ALEX. REID. Page 151, SUSANAH
HEARD, wife of JOHN HEARD, consents before ARCHIBALD GORDON & HUGH INNES,
J.P.'s of Halifax, 17 Jan 1767.

Page 152. 19 Aug 1766. GEO. BODINGHAM, AC, for love and affection borne
          to my loving son, DANL. CONNER, AC, all goods and chattels,
cattle, and hogs. Wit: DAVID & MATT. MOUNTGOMERY.

Page 152. 3 Nov 1766. NEILL CAMPBELL, Alb. Co., to GROVES HARDING, Hen-
          rico, for 30 pds, 300 acres. Lines: JOS. UPTON, Widow JOHNSON,
S branch of Rockfish.

Page 154. 3 Nov 1766. NEILL CAMPBELL, Alb. Co., to GROVES HARDING, 120
          pds, 410 acres.

Page 155. 24 Nov 1766. THOS. PANNELL, AC, to CHAS. RODES & SAML. COL-
          WELL, AC, for 21 pds, Deed of Trust - stock & household goods.

Page 156. 6 Oct 1766. CORNELIUS THOMAS, GEO. HILTON & wife, BETHEMA,
          HENRY HOPSON & wife, MARTHA, JOHN HUGHES & wife, JUDITH, JACOB
MICHAUX & wife Salley, to JAS. NEVIL, for ₤83-6-8, 799 acres. Lines: JNO.
HUGHES; lines running by the upper end of Augusta; Rich land; S fork, JAS.
NEVIL; pointers near Tye; part of greater tract of JAS. NEVIL, dec'd, and

given to above parties by his will. Wit: EDMUND WILCOX, HENRY KEY, WM.
HORSLEY, LEONARD PHILLIPS, JAS. BROWN, GEO. CARRINGTON. Page 158 -
wifes examined.

Page 158. 27 Oct 1766. JNO. HUGHES & wife, JUDITH, Cumberland, to COR-
           NELIUS THOMAS, AC, for 100 pds, 838 acres S side of Rockfish,
joining land according to line formerly laid off between JACOB MICHAUX &
HUGHES. Lines: N side of Ivery Creek, Barons (sic) known as lick branch;
deed of THOMAS from MICHAUX referred to for courses; MICHAUX's wife,
SALLY, joined in deed; Cedar branch all pat. land of estate of JAS. NEVIL
dec'd; JAS NEVIL. Wit: BENNETT HENDERSON, JOS. GOODWIN, WM. CABELL JR.,
SAML. JORDAN, JOS. CABELL.

Page 160. 24 Feb 1767. THOS. JEFFERSON, Alb., to GEO. CLASBY, AC, for
           95 pds, 300 acres. Lines: Red oak on N side of Piney; point-
ers on S side of Piney. Pat. to THOMAS JEFFERSON 27 Jun 1764. Wit:
DABNEY CARR, RICH. HARVIE, SAML. WOODS.

Page 161. 6 Jan 1767. LUNSFORD LOMAX, Gent., & wife JUDITH, Caroline,
           to JOHN LOVING JR., AC, for 44 pds, 112 acres. Lines: WM.
LOVING. Part of tract of 6134 acres conveyed to LOMAX by BENJ. WALLER,
attorney for WALTER KING, Merchant of Bristol, and THOS. MANN RANDOLPH
Dec 1, 1764; rec. in Gen. Ct. Wit: HENRY ROSE, LUNSFORD LOMAX, JR.,
RALPH & THOS. LOMAX.

Page 163. 6 Jan 1767. LUNSFORD LOMAX & wife JUDITH, Caroline, to WM.
           LOVING, AC, for 116 pds, 291 acres - 3/4 part of 6134 acres
described above. Same wit. as above.

Page 165. 2 Mar 1767. CHAS. LINCH (sic), Bedford Co., to MARTIN DAWSON,
           AC, for 4 pds, 337 acres on N side of Fluvannah on Nuton's ck.

Page 166. Rec. 2 Mar 1767, but no date on deed. JNO. & ROBT. MILLER,
           AC, to ALEX. PATTON,AC, for 70 pds, 181 acres branch of Rock-
fish. Lines: WHITE's corner, PATTON's corner, S side of S branch of
Rockfish, MORRISON's corner, S side of S branch of Rockfish, MORRISON's
corner. (X) of JOHN MILLER. ROBT. & HANNAH MILLER sign, and on p.168
she is shown to be wife of JNO. MILLER.

Page 168. 2 Mar 1767. CHAS. LYNCH, Bedford, to JOHN BAUGHAN, AC, for
           50 pds, 158 acres both sides of Bolling's Creek. Lines: JOHN
LYNCH, CHAS. LYNCH's old lines.

Page 170. 3 Mar 1767. JAMES RAY, AC, to GEO. BLAIN, AC. RAY apprenti-
           ces himself to BLAIN for 3 years from 9 Feb last past - to
learn sadler's trade, which trade BLAIN now follows.

Page 170. 3 Feb 1767. JAS. JONES & wife MARY, AC, to RICH. TANKERSLEY,
           AC, for 100 pds, 315 acres N side of Tye and opposite mouth of
Piney, part of larter tract granted by order of Council to ROBT. ROLES
(sic, but ROSE is meant), Clerk, and THOS. CHEN (CHEW) and sold by ROBT.
ROSE to EDWARD MANION & rec. in Alb. Wit: HENRY ROSE, LEONARD TARRNAT
JR., AMBRAS JONES.

Page 172. 3 Nov 1766(?). THOS. HENDERSON, AC, to ELIOT ROBERTS, AC, for
           100 pds, 3 "tracks" of 721 acres N side of Rockfish - one is
part of 400 acres pat. to THOS. HENDERSON 1751 and on both sides of Rockfish; sold to GREGORY MATTHEWS by THOS. HENDERSON and by G.M. sold to
MATT. HARRIS - namely that part which lyeth on S side of Rockfish and on
S side of Buck Creek. Other two tracts granted to THOS. HENDERSON - one
of 81 acres 10 July 1755. Lines: CHAS. LEWIS, Col. JOHN CHISWELL.
Other tract pat. to him on 10 Mar 1756. Lines: Capt. CHAS. LEWIS -
pointers on the river. Notation in margin that the original was delivered to WM. HARRIS for ROBERTS 7 Mar 1788.

Page 174. 4 May 1767. JOHN WAID & wife, ELIZ, AC, to WM. HORRALL, AC,
           for 3000 pds. tobacco - 114 acres and part of 214 acres "adj.
the track" where JOHN WADE now lives containing 300 acres on N branch of
Davis Creek. JOHN & ELIZ. signed with (X).

Page 176. 4 May 1767. JAS. CULL & wife, MARY, AC, to JOHN BRYAN, AC,
          for 16 pds, 46 acres branch of Davis Creek. Lines: WM.
WRIGHT, EDMUND WILCOX, Clerk.

Page 178. 4 May 1767. GEO. CARRINGTON, CUMBERLAND, to JAS. CREWS, AC,
          for 30 pds, 578 acres on branch of Harris Creek. Lines:
PIERCE WADE, MOSES HIGGINBOTHAM, CARRINGTON's line, DANL. BURFORD.

Page 179. 3 Nov 1766. JOS. UPTON, Alb, to THOS. JOPLING, AC, for 60 pds,
          400 acres. Lines: Bryary Branch. Wit: GEO. SEATON, EDMUND
WILCOX, NEILL CAMPBELL. (X) of UPTON.

Page 181. 10 Dec 1766. GEO. SEATON, AC, to THOS. CLAIBORNE, King Wm.
          Co., for 112 pds, 400 acres on Byffaloe (sic); Lines: JAS.
BALLENGER, AARON HIGGINBOTHAM, EDWARD CARTER. Also 24 Negroes named in
Deed of Trust. Wit: EDMUND WILCOX, GABL. PENN, WM. HORSLEY.

Page 182. 4 May 1767. GEO. SEATON, AC, to HENRY ROSE, AC, ROSE on bond
          for SEATON in trespass action brought against him by THO.
WHITEHEAD, insurance broker; SAML. SMITH; lines drapier; EDWARD GARLINC;
Sugar Baker of Bristol, surviving assignees of estate, debts, and effects
of THOS. KNOX & JAS. CLARK, late of the same place, merchants and partners Bankrupts in the Gen. Ct. vs. the same said GEO. SEATON - 60 pds.
sterling - to secure ROSE, SEATON sells 400 acres on Buffaloe. This land
was bought from JER. WADE and adj. lands of EDWARD CARTER, JOS. BALLENGER,
and AARON HIGGINBOTHAM and 24 slaves also named - which have been previously mtgd. to certain creditors.

Page 184. 4 May 1767. DANL. BURFORD, JAS. NEVIL, CORNELIUS THOMAS, Gent,
          EDWARD WARE, HOWARD CASH, & CHAS. TALIAFERRO bonded to King
Geo. for 1000 pds. for BURFORD to collect taxes for present year.

Page 184. Same day and men as above for BURFORD to collect levy laid
          and assessed on the Tithable persons and proportion of the
public levy now due from the said county as it is settled at the last
session of the Gen. Assembly.

Page 185. 6 Jul 1767. JOHN DEMPSIE, AC, planter, to JNO. ROSE, Executor
          or ROBT. ROSE, Clerk, dec'd, AC, - Ł8-4-5 horse and sheep Deed
of Trust upon demand. Wit: NEILL CAMPBELL, GILBERT HAY.

Page 186. 1 Jun 1767. GILBERT HAY, AC, to HENRY ROSE, AC, for 10 sh, 2
          acres on Little Piney. Lines: Corner tree between HENRY ROSE
& DUNCAN CAMERON - part of larger tract. Wit: JNO. BARRET, MARTIN DAW-
SON(X), WM. MARTIN.

Page 187. 1 Jun 1767. GILBERT HAY, AC, to GEO. KIPPEN & Co., Glasgow
          merchants - Ł91-10 for 538 acres both sides of Little Piney
and which HAY bought of HENRY BUNCH & MATT. DAVIS and where he now lives.
Deed of Trust - by June 1st next ensuing. Wit: HENRY ROSE, JOS. GOODWIN,
NEILL CAMPBELL.

Page 188. 17 Mar 1767. THOS. MANN RANDOLPH & wife, ANNE, Goochland, to
          JNO. DEPRIEST, AC, - consideration of 270 acres in AC - have
sold 265 acres pat. and lying in AC, on head of N fork of Nassau Creek
at a place called Indian Cove. Wit: CHAS. BALLOW, WM. KITCHEN, THOS.
HOOPER, SAM. JORDAN, JOS. CABELL, WM. CABELL JR. Page 90, Order to JOS.
WOODSON & JOHN WOODSON, Gent. J.P.'s of Goochland, to examine ANNE RAN-
DOLPH; done 11 Jul 1767.

Page 191. 2 Jun 1767. JNO. LOVING, AC, to JNO. LOVING JR., for 40 pds,
          100 acres. Lines: WM. WRIGHT, HARMER & KING Co. - land deeded
to JNO. LOVING from JNO. REID on 7 Aug 1758. Wit: NEILL CAMPBELL, EDMUND
WILCOX, WM. HORSLEY. Memo: above tract made over by mtg. to me for GEO.
KIPPEN & Co., and I have rec'd. the consideration and hereby in their
name relenquish all right or title to it. NEILL CAMPBELL, for KIPPEN.
Wit: EDMUND WILCOX and WM. HORSLEY.

Page 192. 2 May 1767. JNO. SANDIDGE & wife, KEZIAH, AC, to JNO. PENN,
          Spotsylvania, for 50 pds, 200 acres N side of Sandidge Spring

Branch. Lines: Buffaloe River at mouth of said spring - where SANDIDGE
now lives and which he bought from CARTER BRAXTON and surveyed by Col.
WM. CABELL, JR. 13 Sep 1764. (Orig. del. to JOHN PENN JR. 15 Aug 1808.)

Page 194. 13 Jan 1767. LUNSFORD LOMAX & wife JUDITH, to LUNSFORD LOMAX
JR., Caroline, 7851 acres in AC conveyed to LL, Sr., by WALTER
KING on Oct. 25, MDCCLI and formerly mtgd. by LL, Sr., to PHILIP GRYMES,
Dec'd. Also 6134 acres and containing 400 acres on Purgatory Swamp and
these two were conveyed to LL, Sr. by BENJ. WALLER, atty. for WALTER KING,
Bristol merchant, and THOS. MANN RANDOLPH, heir and devisee of WM. RAN-
DOLPH Dec'd, on Dec. 1, MDCCLXIV - ref. to deed, but not located - LL, Sr,
obtained pat. for 3553 acres on Horsley Creek, AC, and several pats. on
Harris Creek for 1150 acres and has undoubted right to convey any part or
whole except mtgd. tract - has come to agreement from sales to executors
of PHILIP GRYMES, dec'd, and to other creditors of LL, Sr. - 10 sh. for
all tracts. Wit: RALPH LOMAX, THOS. LOMAX, JAS. MICOU, MUNGO ROYE(?).

Page 196. 1767. LUNSFORD LOMAX, the Younger, Caroline, to SOLOMON CAR-
TER, AC, for 31 pds. 6 sh., Horsley Creek - 156½ acres. Lines:
LOMAX, part of 3553 acres granted by Council Order to LUNSFORD LOMAX, the
Elder, Caroline, and conveyed by him and wife, JUDITH, to LL, the Younger,
13 Jan 1767, and rec. in AC.

Page 197. 20 May 1767. HENRY TAYLOR, AC to HENRY KEY, AC, for 50 pds -
73 acres S side of N branch of Piney - part of 400 acres pat.
to GEO. TAYLOR at Williamsburg 20 Sep 1751. Lines: Mr. ROSE, where WM.
WALTON; Page has been torn and shows only S and T, but on next page appeared the name of SAML. TARRANT.

Page 198. 8 Apr 1767. MARY GRYMES, BENJ. GRYMES, & PEYTON RANDOLPH,
three of the executors of PHILIP GRYMES, dec'd, grant power of
attorney to WM. CABELL JR., AC, to sell 7881 acres and all slaves specified in a mtg. from LUNSFORD LOMAX, Gent., to PHILIP GRYMES, dec'd on Aug
27, 1756. Five percent commission. Wit: P. PELHAM JR., JNO. TAZEWELL
(PR), JOS. CABELL, CORNELIUS THOMAS.

Page 199. 7 Jun 1767. WM. CHECKE & wife ELIZ., AC, to THOS. WIATT, AC,
for 32 pds 10 sh, 108 acres on branch of Rutledges Creek.
Lines: JAS. MENCES - will defend all claims except that of SARAH NOWLIN,
wife of PATRICK NOWLIN, to her dower rights.

Page 201. 3 Aug 1767. COLBARD BLAIR, & wife SARAH, AC, to WLTR. POWERS,
Augusta Co, for 20 pds, 154 acres. Lines: JAS. COLBARD BLAIR.
Pat. to COLBARD BLAIR, 10 Jul 1766. (X's) of BLAIR & wife. *

Page 202. 3 Aug 1767. JOHN DENNEE & wife ELIZ, AC, to JNO DEPRIEST, AC,
for 35 pds, 200 acres branch of Rucker's Run. Lines: Col.
LOMAX. Signed by JOHN DENNY & (X) of wife.

Page 203. 7 Jul 1767. MARY GRYMES, widow; PEYTON RANDOLPH, Esq.; BENJ.
GRYMES; and JOHN ROBINSON, Gent., Executors of PHILLIP GRYMES,
dec'd; and LUNSFORD LOMAX, the Younger, Caroline Co., to JESSE MILLS, AC,
LUNSFORD LOMAX, the Elder, Caroline, mtgd. on 7 Aug 1756, and rec. 21 Oct
1756, in General Court - to secure loan to LOMAX by PHILLIP GRYMES, late
of Middlesex, 7881 acres - money not repaid - mutually agreed between
MARY GRYMES, widow, and executors that land be sold to discharge debt and
interest thereon - and they appointed WM. CABELL, the Younger, atty, in
AC Court - LUNSFORD LOMAX & wife, JUDITH, 13 Jan 1767, (Proved in AC) conveyed to LUNSFORD LOMAX, the Younger, 128 pds. 10 sh. by JESSE MILLS -
396 acres, part of said tract and formerly granted to HARMER, KING, RAN-
DOLPH, & LOMAX by order of Council - Tye River. Lines: ROSE. Wit: GEO.
SEATON, WM. WALTON, JNO. RYAN, EDMUND WILCOX, clerk.

Page 206. 6 Jul 1767. PETER TALIAFERRO, Spotsylvania, Joiner, and ANNE,
wife, to WM. HANSBROUGH, AC, for 30 pds, 400 acres, land devis-
ed by his father, RICHARD TALIAFERRO, to PETER. Head of Joe's Creek.
Lines: Col. JAS. NEVIL, Doctor WM. CABELL - S fork of Rockfish; Fenley's
Creek. Wit: FRANS. MERIWETHER, S. MURPHEY, HENRY KEY, WM. LOVING, ZACH.
TALIAFERRO, RICH. McCARY.

*Orig. del. to POWERS Oct 1779.

Page 207. 3 Aug 1767. LUNSFORD LOMAX, the Younger, Caroline, to CHAS.
          TALIAFERRO, AC, for 15 pds. 12 sh, 104 acres on Horsley Creek,
part of 3353 acres granted to LUNSFORD LOMAX, the Elder, and wife, JUDITH,
Caroline Co, Gent., and conveyed to LL, the Younger, 13 Jan 1767, and
proved in AC.

Page 209. 10 Apr 1767. JOHN THOMSON, AC, to JAS. WOODS, AC, planter,
          for 62 pds, 275 acres "boath" sides Rockfish - part of tract
granted to Col. JNO. CHISWELL and now property of THOMSON. Lines: JNO.
SMALL on N side Rockfish; JNO ROBERTSON; crossing river to SAML. BELL.
Wit: ALEX. REID, JR., JNO. BARNET, SAML. WOODS, MICHAEL McNEELY.

Page 210. 18 Aug 1767. JNO. BEAZLEY & wife, BRIDGETT, Buckingham, to
          NEILL CAMPBELL, Alb., for 150 pds, 400 acres on Long Mt. (X)
of BRIDGETT. Wit: BEN HOWARD, THOS. FITZPATRICK(X), CHAS. BEAZLEY(X),
LEONARD BALLOW, Sen.(X), WM. COX, MATT. JORDAN, JAS. HALEYBURTON. Page
212, Order to BENJ. HOWARD, JACOB LINSAY, & CHAS. MAY, J.P.'s of Buckingham to examine BRIDGETTE BEAZLEY, apart from husband, 9 Sep 1767. Done
on 27 Nov 1767, by LINSAY & MAY.

Page 214. 7 Apr 1767. SAML. SHANNON, AC, to JNO. MORRISON, AC, for 27
          pds 13 sh, 175 acres branch of Rockfish near Blew Mts. Lines:
THOS. SHANNON, WM. CROW, WM. SIMPSON. Wit: JAS. DUNWOODY, JOEL CRAWFORD,
ROBT. DUNWOODY.

Page 216. 16 Oct 1766. JAMES COLBERT BLAIR, AC, intends in a short time
          to move to province of South Carolina and gives power of attor-
ney to ALEX. BAGGS, Augusta, to sell 166 acres both sides of S branch of
Middle Fork of Pedlar, 30 pds. Wit: GEO. SEATON, EDMD. WILCOX, WM.
HORSLEY. (X) of BLAIR.

Page 217. 7 Sep 1767. JNO. DEPRIEST, AC, to ABRAHAM WARWICK, AC, for
          14 pds, 73 acres on S fork of Nassau Creek. Lines: LOMAX; in
WARWICK's possession.

Page 218. 7 Sep 1767. ABRAHAM WARWICK, AC, to JNO. WOOD, Alb., for 10
          pds, 70 acres on branches of Nassau Creek near the Rockey Mt.
Marginal notation: Delivered to JAS. HOPKINS 11 Aug 1783.

Page 219. 1 Aug 1767. CHAS. LYNCH, Bedford, to PETTIS THACKER, AC, for
          20 pds, 155 acres Newton's creek. Wit: JO. MAGANN, PETER
CARTER (X), BOYCE EIDSON(X).

Page 220. 13 May 1767. WM. FLOYD, AC, to JOB CARTER, AC, for 50 pds,
          400 acres N side of N branch of Horsley. Lines: NATHANIEL
DAVID, WM. CABELL, Col. LOMAX. Wit: DAN. BURFORD, JAS. SYMONS, SOLOMON
CARTER;(X) PETER CARTER; (X), ANTHONY ROGERS.

Page 222. 7 Sep 1767. JAS. MENEES, AC, to WM. WHITSETT, AC, for 30 pds,
          300 acres branch of Rutledge. Lines: JAS. MENEES, JR. Wit:
DAVID WOODROOF, ISAAC WRIGHT. Page 223, MARGARET, wife of JAS. MENEES,
Sr., consents.

Page 223. 7 Sep 1767. JAS. MENEES, SR., to JAS. MENEES, JR., AC, for 5
          sh, 300 acres. Wit: DAVID WOODROOF, ISAAC WRIGHT. Page 224,
MARGARET, wife of JAS. MENEES, SR., consents.

Page 224. 7 Sep 1767. JAS. MENEES, AC, to BENJ. MENEES, AC,, for 5 sh.,
          300 acres. Lines: WM. WHITSITT. Wit: same as above. Page
225, MARGARET, wife of JAS. MENEES, consents.

Page 226. 4 Sep 1767. JOHN ROBERTS, AC, & wife MARY ANN to JNO. SAND-
IDGE, AC, for 35 pds, 180 acres on Horsley. Lines: WM. CABELL. Wit:
POWELL HUGES, DUDLEY GATEWOOD.

Page 228. 7 Sep 1767. THOS. WILLIAMS, Bedford, to JOHN BALLOW, Bucking-
          ham, for 30 pds, 260 acres both sides Stovall's Creek. Lines:
GEO. STOVALL. Page 229, ESTHER, wife of THOS. WILLIAMS, consents.

Page 230. 4 Jul 1767. PERRIN GILES, AC, to WM. PARKS, 5 sh. to secure
          him on bond to McPHERSON & MINZIES as of due date of 1 Jul
1769 - Negro woman Sall, beds, cattle marked with a low fork in right
ear and smooth crop in left; mare. Deed of Trust. Wit: WM. PENN, THOS.
REID.

Page 231. 6 Sep 1767. JAS. SMITH & wife, MARY, AC, to PATRICK LOWRY,
          Augusta, for 110 pds, 200 acres N side and joining N fork of
Pedlar and on side of Long Mt. Pat. to JAS. SMITH 10 Jul 1766. Lines:
JOS. HIGGINBOTHAM. Page 232, RODERICK McCULLOCH & DAVID CRAWFORD privily
examine MARY SMITH, wife, 1767.

Page 233. 7 Sep 1767. JNO. PARKS, SR., AC, to THOS. LANDRUM, AC, for
          5 sh., 100 acres. Lines: Rock on S side of Pyna(sic) River;
leased 10 Apr 1750, to JNO PARKS by ROBT. ROSE, Clerk, dec'd., and rec.
in Alb. Co. Lease conveyed to LANDRUM.

Page 235. 27 Jul 1767. JAS. NOWLING, AC, to AMBROSE RUCKER, AC, for 6
          pds, 12 acres. Lines: JAS. MENEES. Wit: JOS. GOODWIN, DAVID
TINSLEY, GEO. McDANIEL, JNO. GILES(X).

Page 236. 7 Sep 1767. JAS. NOWLING, AC, to STEVEN HAM, AC, for 3 pence,
          106 acres. Lines: JAS. MENEES on branch of Rutledge; AMBROSE
RUCKER, JNO. HARVIE.

Page 238. 7 Sep 1767. JAS. MENEES, AC, to STEPHEN HAM, AC, for 5 sh.,
          23 acres. Lines: branch of Rutledge.

Page 239. 7 Sep 1767. STEVEN HAM, AC, to JAS. MENEES, AC, for 5 sh, 29
          acres. Lines: branch of Rutledge.

Page 249. 3 Aug 1767. JAS. MURRAY to NEILL CAMPBELL, Factor for GEO.
          KIPPEN & Co., Glasgow merchants - 5 sh. to secure Ł70-15,
horses and mares - one of them is a dark bay mare of English blood;
cattle, sheep, hogs, heads of tobacco, bed, etc. and one pen knife. Wit:
WM. LOVING, GEO. MUNROE(X). (X) of MURRAY; Deed of trust or bill of sale.

Page 241. 3 Aug 1767. STEPHEN GOOLSBY, AC, to NEILL CAMPBELL, Factor
          for KIPPEN & Co, Merchants in Alb., for Ł25-16-11, 150 acres
and where GOOLSBY lives. Wit: WM. LOVING, JOS. BALLENGER, JOS. CHILDERS
(X).

Page 242. 4 Sep 1767. JAS. WARREN, AC, to ICHABOD CAMP, AC, for Ł37-10,
          168 acres. Lines: N side Rockey Run; WM. DILLARD. Wit: THOS.
REID, GABL. PENN, WM. PENN, JNO. BARRET. Mark of WARREN.

Page 244. 8 Sep 1767. MARY GRYMES, etc. - see page 203 for estate
          details - Ł81 paid for 202 acres to GEO. BLAIN, branch of Tye.
Lines: WALTER KING.

Page 246. 1 Mar 1767. MATT. SMALL, AC, to JNO. SMALL, for 24 pds, 50
          acres formerly "lade" off from tract granted to WM. MONTGOMERY
and sold by him to JNO. SMALL and laid off for MATT. SMALL. Lines:
Branch of Rockfish; top of the Mt., JNO. SMALL, CHISWELL. Wit: FRANS.
MERIWETHER, JNO. THOMPSON, SAML. WOODS, JNO. WEBB.

Page 248. 5 Oct 1767. BAYLOR WALKER, King & Queen, to ABRAHAM PENN, AC,
          for 71 pds, 136 acres on S branch of Harris Creek and adj.
Tobacco Row Mts. Lines: JOHN HARVIE.

Page 249. 7 Sep 1767. BENJ. HIGGINBOTHAM, AC, to ALEX. BAGGS, Augusta,
          HIGGINBOTHAM under Power of Atty. from JAS. COLBERT BLAIR as
of 16 Oct 1766 - 30 pds - both sides of the S branch of Middle Fork of
Pedlar - pat. to BLAIR 10 Jul 1766. Wit: JNO. LOVING JR., JNO. LOVING,
WM. LOVING. (Note: no acreage stated here in in P of A, p.266, it is
set forth as 166 acres. BFD.)

Page 250. 12 Sep 1767. JOS. BLAIR, AC, to WM. BLAIR, AC, for 10 pds,
          stock, etc. (X) of BLAIR. Wit: JNO. OLD, HENRY ROSE, CLOUGH
SHELTON. Bill of Sale.

Page 251. 10 Jul 1767. GEO. TAYLOR, AC, to JAS. & ROBT. DONALDS & Co.,
        Glasgow merchants, for Ł39-9-3, 170 acres. Lines: Crawley's
Creek, SAML. MURPHEY, DUNCAN CAMERON, HENRY TAYLOR; part of 400 acres
pat. to GEO. TAYLOR - Deed of trust. Wit: EDMD. WILCOX, WM. MITCHELL,
LUNSFORD LOMAS JR., JOS. TURNER.

Page 252. 14 Sep 1767. JAS. STINNET, "Cenior", AC, to DANL. EDMONDS,AC,
        for 10 pds, 75 acres, part of 227 acres N fork of Huff Creek.
Lines: JNO. DAMERON, THOS. PARKS, JAS. ISON, Little Branch. ANN STINNET,
wife, makes X. Memo: EDMONDS is to have no part of rent due from THOS.
WITINGTON for the plantation for ensuing year. Wit: JNO. KENNEDY, JNO.
STINNETT.

Page 253. 21 Sep 1767. LARKIN GATEWOOD, AC, to WM. PENN, AC, for 65 pds,
        173 acres N branch of Buffalo. Lines: JNO. BENGER, top of
Turkey Mt., GABL. PENN. Wit: GABL. PENN, JOS. MAYS, JNO. BARRET. Page
254, CATH. GATEWOOD, wife of LARKIN, consents.

Page 254. 2 Nov 1767. MARY GRYMES, widow, etc - see page 203 for estate
        data to JOS. DILLARD, for Ł119-17, 513 acres Tye river and
branches. Lines: ROSE.

Page 257. 5 Oct 1767. LUNSFORD LOMAX, the Younger, Caroline, to EDWARD
        WARE, AC, for Ł64-8, 214 acres on branch of Horsley. Lines:
WAUGH, SOLOMON CARTER, LUCY CARTER; part of 355 acres pat. to LL, Sr. See
page 194. Wit: ZACH. TALIAFERRO, JNO. RYAN, JNO. TUGGLE, THOS. LANDRUM.

Page 258. 2 Nov 1767. GEO. CLASBY & wife MARY, AC, to LUCAS POWELL of
        Alb., for 100 pds, 300 acres both sides N fork of Piney and
granted to THOS. JEFFERSON by pat. 27 Jun 1764, and by T.J. to G.C. and
recorded in AC 24 Feb 1767. Wit: WM. MITCHELL, JNO. RYAN, WM. WALTON.
(X) of CLASBY.

Page 259. 2 Nov 1767. WM. MONTGOMERY & wife JANE, AC, to JNO. SHIELDS,
        AC, for 65 pds, 187 acres branch of Hatt. Lines: Col. THOS.
MANN RANDOLPH.

Page 261. 2 Nov 1767. GEO. STOVALL JR., JAS. DILLARD, WM. WALTON, GABL.
        PENN, ALEX. REID JR., ALEX. REID, JNO. RYAN, JACOB SMITH,
JESSE MILLS, AMBROSE PORTER, ABRAHAM PENN, WM. BIBB, JAS. CHRISTIAN, WM.
FLOYD, JOS. DILLARD, & WM. LOVING bonded to King Geo. III for 1000 pds.
for GEO. STOVALL JR. who was appointed sheriff by governor under Colony
seal on 17 Oct last past to perform duties of office.

Page 261. Same men and date as above for STOVALL to collect fees.

Page 262. Same men and date for STOVALL - 500 pds - to collect all Quit
        Rents.

Page 263. 7 Dec 1767. HENRY MORRIS & wife, ELIZ, Prince Edward Co., to
        MOSES SWINEY, AC, for 55 pds, 142 acres S side of Bear Mt.,
pat. to MORRIS 10 Jul 1767. Lines: Capt. JNO. HARVIE. (X) of ELIZABETH.

Page 264. 7 Dec 1767. PATRICK, AC, to JNO. WEBB, AC, for 25 pds, 150
        acres branch of S fork of Rockfish. Lines: HENRY KEYS.
SUSANNA PATRICK, wife of HUGH, consents.

Page 266. 4 Sep 1767. JNO. SANDIDGE, & wife KEZIAH, AC, to JAS. GATE-
        WOOD, AC, for 120 pds, 400 acres. Lines: S side Buffaloe,
crossing Tribulation Creek twice; Sandidge's Spring. Wit: THOS. REID,
W. PENN, DUDLEY GATEWOOD, THOS. LUMPKIN. (X) of KEZIAH.

Page 268. 14 Apr 1767. BENJ. DENNY, AC, to LAURENCE SUDDORTH, AC, for
        30 pds, 94 acres both sides main branch of Rucker's Run in
Cove of a Mt. Signed: DENEE.

Page 269. 4 Sep 1767. JOS. WILTSHIRE & ARTHUR ROBINSON, AC, to LARKIN
        GATEWOOD, AC, (BARBARY WILTSHIRE & MILDRED ROBINSON, wives,
named later in deed) for 50 pds, 400 acres on Hooker's Creek. Lines: JNO.
CHRISTIAN. Clerk has it ARTER ROBBERSON. Wives consented.

Page 272. 21 Sep 1767. THOS. PHILIPS, AC, to HENRY KEY, AC, for 30 pds,
           273 acres both sides Cubb Creek. Lines: JNO. MACLAKIN. SARAH
PHILLIPS, wife, consents. Wit: WM. WALTON, ELIAS SMITH(X), MOSES MOTT(X).
Grantors signed with (X).

Page 274. 7 Dec 1767. LUNSFORD LOMAX, the Younger, Caroline, to JACOB
           EADES, AC, for Ł11-5-6, 50 acres branch of Purgatory Swamp be-
low Fenley's Gap. Lines: JOHNSTON. Part of 400 acres conveyed by WALTER
KING, Bristol Merchant, and THOS. MANN RANDOLPH to LUNSFORD LOMAX, the
Elder, 1 Dec 1764, and proved in Gen. Court; conveyed by LL Sr. and wife
JUDITH, to LL Jr., 13 Jan 1767, recorded in AC.

Page 275. 11 Sep 1767. JNO. MAYFIELD, AC, to WM. CABELL, AC, for 20 pds,
           93 acres heads of branch of N fork of Piney. Wit: JAS. PAMP-
LIN, VALENTINE BALL, JAS. DILLARD.

Page 276. 7 Dec 1767. MARY GRYMES, widow, etc. See p.203 for estate
           data - to AUGUSTINE WRIGHT, AC, for Ł85-5, 341 acres on Tye.

Page 278. 7 Mar 1768. JNO. KEY, AC, to RICH. DERBY, Alb., for Ł6-10,
           96 acres Cov of a Mt. on a branch of Rockfish. Lines: JAS.
LACKEY, JNO. LACKEY. Wit: MATHEW CONELY, WM. HORALL. (Note: word "Jr."
has been marked through on JOHN KEY's signature.

Page 280. 7 Mar 1768. GEO. SEATON, AC, to CARTER BRAXTON, King Wm., for
           Ł473-15, 1295 acres both sides of Buffalo and part of tract
which SEATON bought lately from BRAXTON. Lines: Late AMBROSE LEE, late
JNO. BENGER, GABL. PENN.

Page 281. 6 Feb 1768. JOS. EATTEN, AC, to WM. MOORE, AC of Tye River,
           for Ł31-15, horses, cows, etc. Memo: before signing, EATTON
makes over his bed and bed "cloaths" and his wife's "wearing cloaths".
Wit: JNO. BARNET, NATHANIEL BARNET.

Page 282. 30 Jan 1768. DAVID CRAWFORD, JNO. CRAWFORD, JOEL CRAWFORD,
           CHAS. YANCEY, NATHANIEL BARNETT, & JNO. JACOBS, AC, to ROBT.
YANCEY; NATHAN CRAWFORD, AC, two negro children - Dick and Anakey, "which
were willed and bequeathed by the late DAVID CRAWFORD" to his son, WM.
CRAWFORD, now dec'd, and "we the above named persons" defend the title.
Wit: THOS. DANNALL, ANN CRAWFORD.

Page 282. 2 Mar 1768. ABRAHAM HARGIS, AC, to JOHN FARRAR, AC, for 70
           pds, 208 acres, part of 600 acres bought of "Coll" JOHN CHIS-
WELL by ALEX. MONTGOMERY and by him conveyed to WM. MONTGOMERY and by him
sold to ABRAHAM HARGIS. Liens: Top of a Mt. Wit: JNO. SAMLL, JAS. LYONS,
JNO. DIGGES. Page 204, JEAN HARGIS, wife of ABRAHAM, consents.

Page 284. 2 Mary 1767. HENRY CHILDRESS, AC, to JNO. WHITEHEAD, AC, for
           60 pds, 150 acres branch of Huff. Lines: JAS. ISHAM, BENJ.
STINNETT SR. (X) of HENRY CHILDRESS.

Page 285. 27 Feb 1768. SAML. BAUGHAN, AC, to JAS. & ROBT. DONALDS Co.,
           Glasgow merchants, for 5 sh., to secure debt - 158 acres Boll-
ing's Creek. Land pass. by MITCHELL BAUGHAN, AC, at his death. Lines:
JONATHAN JOHNSTON, JOS. GOFF. Stock, utensils. Wit: THOS. LUMPKIN, JOHN
WIATT, WM. MITCHELL.

Page 287. 7 Mar 1768. JNO. SMALL, AC, to JNO. LYON, AC, for 53 pds, 2
           tracts together, and part of tract of Col. CHISWELL and part
of which was granted to SMALL - 127 acres laid off for LYON by Capt. JAS.
HIGGINBOTHAM, Assistant Surveyor - 50 acres which formerly belonged to
MATT. SMALL and whereon WM. LYON now lives. 127 acres. Lines: JNO. SMALL,
old and new surveys - Lines of 50 acres, JNO. SMALL, JOHN CHISWELL, Top
of a Mt.

Page 288. 7 Mar 1768. ANGUS FORBUS, AC, to JNO. DAVIS, AC, 46 acres
           branch of a Mt. on N side of Rockfish. Lines: JNO. MONTGOMERY,
Col. CHISWELL. CATHERINE FORBES (sic), wife of ANGUS consents.

Page 289. 30 Sep 1767. JNO. CABELL to JNO. WEBB - lease - "my plantation above the mouth of Owen's Creek on N side of Fluvanna -
from Jan 1 next for 5 years - annual rent 2500 pds. of Tobacco - for
every tithable over 5 worked WEBB shall pay 500 pds. extra of Tobacco.
He shall build as soon as convenient a Tobacco house 40 ft. long and 20
ft. wide - 12 ft. pitch - framed and braced - white oak to be sawed. One
"Corne" house - 20 ft. long, 12 ft. wide, and 8 ft. pitch - sawed logs
and Dufftailed(sic) - both to be done in good workmanlike manner and he
is to plant an apple orchard on High land - 100 trees of grafted fruit
and fenced to prevent being barked and spoiled by creatures of any kind.
He shall trim them each year. All tended ground to be put in fence at
least ten good "loggs heigh" and staked and ridered - mauled stakes of an
equal length. (X) of WEBB. Wit: FRANCIS WEST, JACOB WEBB(X).

Page 291. 7 Mar 1768. JNO. CABELL to JNO. HARGROVE Sr. - lease - part
of my plantation where HARGROVE now lives - to be divided by
Straight Line of fence to be run from the hill to the river joining upper
end of a Tobacco House upon the "heigh" ground. Lower part next Tye is
his part from Jan 1 next for five years. 1900 pds. of Tobacco per yr. -
boat to be kept in good repair and to be delivered to CABELL at end of
lease well corked and tarred. "He shall set all the said JNO. CABELL's
faely (sic) over the said Ferry Free". He is to build Tobacco House -
for specifications see deed just prior to this one. Wit: THOS. WRIGHT,
JNO. HARPER (X), HEZEKIAH HARGROVE.

Page 293. 7 Mar 1768. GEO. LEE, orphan of AMBROSE LEE, to SAML. MURPHEY.
Apprentice bond to learn art of a house carpenter and joyner
(sic) until LEE is of 20 years of age.

Page 294. 22 Jan 1768. GEO. SEATON, AC, to NEILL CAMPBELL, St. Anne
Parish, Alb. Co., and ALEX. McCAUL, Henrico, for sum mentioned
in deed of mtg. made by SEATON to GEO. KIPPEN & Co. on 9 Oct 1765, and
rec. in AC - 5 sh. - also estate contained in a mtg. made by SEATON to
THOS. CLAIBORNE, King Wm,.as Trustee in Trust - to be sold after making
and finishing the 1768 crop -- CAMPBELL & McCAUL to be paid principal and
interest and then CLAIBORNE is to be paid. Wit: GEO. DONALD, JAS.
VAUGHAN, WM. WILSON.

Page 295. 6 Jan 1768. JNO. PARKS, Sr, AC, to Gen. KIPPEN & Co., Glasgow
merchants, 10 sh. to secure debt - note made 5 Jun 1764, and
acct. of 48 pds. by Book act at their store in Alb., 390 acres on THRESH-
ER's Creek. Land which PARKS bought from PEERCE WADE, rec. in Alb; also
2 slaves. Wit: JNO. HARVIE, NEILL CAMPBELL, JNO. OLD, CLOUGH SHELTON.

Page 297. 16 Dec 1767. GEO. BLANE, AC, to GEO. KIPPEN & Co, Glasgow
merchants, for Ł55-2-1½, 202½ acres. Lines: WALTER KING,
where BLANE lives. Deed of Trust. Wit: NEIL CAMPBELL, JNO. OLD, JAS.
HALEYBURTON.

Page 299. 7 Mar 1768. WM. CABELL, AC, to JOS. EATON, AC, for Ł31-15,
150 acres on Cuffy's or commonly called Rackoon. Lines: JOHN
HENRY, GEO. MONROE. Wit: ED. WILCOX, WM. HORSLEY. ALEX. REID.

Page 300. 1 Feb 1768. NATHANIEL WOODROOF, Senior, AC, to GEO. KIPPEN &
Co, Glasgow Merchants, for 30 pds - Tye River - land WOODROOF
bought from VALL BALL; rec. in AC - 270 acres. Deed of Trust. Wit:
VALENTINE BALL, HANNAH WOODRUFF, JNO. OLD, WM. SPENCER.

Page 301. 3 Aug 1767. JNO. DEPRIEST, AC, to ROBT. DONALDS & Co., 25 pds,
200 acres branch of Rucker's Run, part of larger tract pat. to
JNO. DENNEY and which DEPRIEST bought from DENNY. Lines: Col. LOMAX.
Deed of Trust. Wit: WM. MITCHELL, CHAS. ROSE, THOS. REID, HECTOR McALES-
TER. Note; Alb., 16 Sep 1767, JNO. DEPRIEST discounted Ł3-8-9 as part
payment, HECTOR McALESTER.

Page 302. 7 Mar 1768. GEO. STOVALL, JR., WM. WALTON, WM. CABELL, DANL.
GAINES, CORNL. THOMAS, WM. LOVING, & GABL. PENN - 500 pds.
bond to King Geo. III. STOVALL appointed Sheriff under seal of Colony
17 Oct. last past. Bond to collect levies.

Page 303. Same men and date as previous entry - 1000 pds -- for STOVALL
as Sheriff to receive all land and poll taxes.

Page 304. 7 Mar 1768. THOS. ALFORD & wife, ELIZ, AC, to WM. BICKNALL
Sr., AC, for 45 pds, 140 acres. Lines: DANL. AARON, JNO. HAR-
MER. Side of Mt. Wit: JNO. LOVING, LAWRENCE SUDDATH(X), WM. ALFORD.
(X) of ELIZ. ALFORD.

Page 306. 5 Oct 1767. LUNSFORD LOMAS, Jr., Caroline, to JNO. TUGGLE,
AC, for Ł22-7-6, 44 and 3/4 acres branch of Rucker's Run.
Lines: Top of a Mt., LOMAX. Part of 6134 acres. See page 194. Wit:
GABL. PENN, JAS. DILLARD, JNO. KEY, JR.

Page 307. 12 Apr 1768. JOS. GOFF, AC, to JNO. HARDWICK, AC, for 25 pds,
115 acres head of Boling Creek. Wit: SAML. BAUGHON(X), JNO.
GOFF, WM. GETTRY(X), ANTHONY ROGER(X), PETER CARTER(X).

Page 308. 2 May 1768. LANGSDON DEPRIEST, AC, to WM. DEPRIEST, AC, for
5 sh., 144 acres Lunch Creek on N side Rockfish; part of 400
acres conveyed to LANGSDON DEPRIEST on 6 Apr 1762, and rec. in AC. Lines:
The late JAS. BELL, LANGSDON DEPRIEST. In possession of W.M.

Page 309. 1 May 1768. STARK BROWN, AC, to JAS. GATEWOOD, AC, apprentice
bond of BROWN to GATEWOOD until BROWN is 21 to be taught "Art
and Mistory of a cooper and also to be taught how to read and write".
(X) of BROWN.

Page 310. 4 Apr 1768. LUNSFORD LOMAX, the Younger, Caroline, to PHILIP
PAYTON for 60 pds, 422 acres branch of Horsley. Lines: CHAS.
TALIAFERRO, Widow CARTER. Part of 3553 acres etc. See page 194. Wit:
EDMD. WILCOX, WM. HORSLEY, G. WALKER, Jr, JNO. HARVIE.

Page 311. 2 May 1768. JNO. WEBB, AC, to ABRAHAM EADES, Sr., St. Ann's
Parish, Alb., for 30 pds, 150 acres branch of S fork of Rockfish - formerly granted to W. BRUCE by pat. and by him to JACOB EADES and
he sold it to HUGH PATRICK and he granted it to JNO. WEBB. Lines: HENRY
KEY. USELEY, wife of JNO. WEBB, consented.

Page 312. 30 Apr 1768. HECTOR McALESTER, Alb. Co., to JNO. BARNES, City
of Bristol in Great Britain, merchant; for 100 pds, 263 acres
both sides of Bever Creek. Lines: NICHOLAS EASTIN, JEREMIAH WHITTEN, WM.
CABELL's Order of Council Tract, BENJ. STENNET - bought by McALESTER from
ROBT. WHITTEN and rec. in AC. Wit: WM. MITCHELL, JNO. BARNET, GEO.
SEATON, THOS. RICHARDS.

Page 313. 2 May 1768. SAML. CROUCHER, orphan, son of WM. CROUCHER, late
of Caroline, apprentices himself to SAML. MURPHEY, AC, to
learn art of a house carpenter for two years and 8 months. Wit: THOS.
REID.

Page 314. 12 Apr 1768. JNO. MURRELL & wife, RACHEL, AC, to THOS. EADES,
AC, for 5 pds, 35 acres on Davis Creek - part of where MURRELL
now lives. Wit: JNO. LOVING, Jr., ROBT. WRIGHT, ROBT. MONTGOMERY.

Page 316. 6 Jun 1768. JNO. LOVING, AC, & wife SARAH, to WM. LOVING, AC,
for 20 pds, 98 acres. Lines: JNO. LOVING JR, (formerly LUNS-
FORD LOMAS's); pat. to JNO. LOVING on 25 Sep 1762. Wit: GABL. PENN,
AMBROSE RUCKER, ROBT. MONTGOMERY. Memo: NEIL CAMPBELL ack. receipt of
consideration and that land is made over to him for GEO. KIPPEN & CO.

Page 317. 6 Jun 1768. JAS. COFFEY, AC, to WM. COFFEY, AC, for 36 pds,
120 acres. Lines: Coxes Creek, over the river, Elk Creek.

Page 318. 6 Jun 1768. HUGH ROSE, AC, to JNO. DEMSEY, AC, 75 acres lease.
Lines: Dempsey's Mt. on north; PRICE on south; the ridge on
upper end which divides Naked Creek from Tye on upper end of his plantation on the west - during term of his and wife, JANE's, lives. To com-
mence from date hereof - yearly rent to be paid on Oct. 6th - 30 sh. for
every tithe or Hireling employed for more than one month every year.
DEMPSEY will plant 150 apple trees and fence them so that number of trees

will be bearing fruit at expiration of lease. Timber is to be conserved.
Wit: JNO. HARVIE, HENRY ROSE, CHAS. ROSE. (X) of DEMPSEY.

Page 319. 6 Jun 1768. ROBT. JOHNSTON, AC, to WM. FLOYED(sic), AC, for
30 pds, 310 acres both sides Maple Creek, branch of Pedlar.
Lines: ARTHUR TULLY. In possession of FLOYD.

Page 320. 6 Jun 1768. REUBIN SEAYRS LOVING, AC, apprentices himself to
JNO. JOHNSTON, AC, for 4½ years to learn art of house carpen-
ter or joiner. Wit: WM. & JNO. LOVING. Rec. for REUBIN SEAYRS LOVING, an
Infant, etc, and JNO. JOHNSTON, Carpenter, 6 Jun 1768.

Page 321. 4 Jul 1768. GEO. SEATON, AC, to CARTER BRAXTON, King Wm., for
187 pds. 10 sh, 750 acres S side and adj. Buffalo and upper
part of tract of SEATON lately mtgd. to CARTER BRAXTON.

Page 37. 23 Mar 1768. THOS. MONTGOMERY & wife, BRIDGET, AC, for love
and affection for their dutiful and well beloved son, ROBT.
MONTGOMERY, 200 acres on Davis Creek - half of 400 acres which THOS.
MONTGOMERY bought of WM. WRIGHT. Lines: T. MONTGOMERY & WRIGHT.

Page 323. 4 Jul 1768. THOS. JOPLING, AC, to BENJ. CHILDERS, AC, for
love borne by JOPLING for his son-in-law, BENJ. CHILDERS - 200
acres S side Rockfish. Lines: Col. JNO. CHISWELL, MICHAEL MONTGOMERY,
JOSIAH JOPLING.

Page 324. 4 Jul 1768. THOS. JOPLING, AC, to his son, JOSIAH JOPLING,
530 acres N side and joining Rockfish - and to heirs and assignees right to henceforth lawfully hold, etc. Marginal note that the
original deed was delivered to JAS. JOPLING 14 Mar 1792.

Page 325. 4 Jul 1768. THOS. JOPLING, AC, to JNO. GRIFFIN, his son-in-
law, AC, 323 acres. Lines: WM. HARRIS, JAS. MOUNTGOMERY, JOHN
MOUNTGOMERY, CHISWELL, BENJ. CHILDERS, S side of Rockfish. Marginal
notation that the original was del. to (blurred) SHELTON, 7 Oct 1789.

Page 326. 24 Mar 1768. WM. WRIGHT & wife, ESTHER, AC, for love borne
their son, JNO. WRIGHT, 200 acres on Davis Creek - part of
tract whereon WM. WRIGHT now lives. Lines: WM. WRIGHT, JNO. WADE, Col.
CHISWELL.

Page 327. 23 Mar 1768. WM. WRIGHT & wife ESTHER, AC, for love borne
their son, JAS. WRIGHT, 180 acres on Davis Creek, part of
where WRIGHT now lives. Lines: WM. WIRGHT, top of a ridge betweeen WM.
HIBITS & JAS. WRIGHT. Marginal notation: Orig. del. to JAS. WRIGHT.

Page 329. 8 Jun 1768. CARTER BRAXTON, King Wm., to RICE MEREDITH, AC,
for 5 sh, 48 and 3/4 acres, Higginbotham's Mill Creek, part of
a tract of 25,000 acres pat. to GEO. BRAXTON JR., at Williamsburg, 25 Nov
1743. Wit: GABL. PENN, EDMD. WINSTON, THOS. LUMPKIN.

Page 330. 4 Jul 1768. SAML. MAXBURY, AC, to WM. CARRELL, AC, for 40 pds,
276 acres on Buffaloe. Lines: JNO. PARKS, JR., Horsley Creek.
In possession of CARRELL.

Page 331. 11 Jun 1768. JOS. BARNETT & wife, MARY, Augusta Co, to MATT.
NIGHTINGALE, AC, for 130 pds, 333 acres S side of Rockfish and
both sides of Corbins Creek. Lines: JNO. SMALL on Rockfish, DAVID REID,
Late Col. CHISWELL, MICHAEL MONTGOMERY, ALEX. REID, FRANCIS MERIWETHER.
Wit: ROB. BARNETT, JNO. BARNETT, JR., JNO. BARNETT.

Page 333. 4 Jun 1768. DANL. GAINES, AC, to JOS. MAGANN, AC, for 15 pds,
124 acres where MAGANN now lives and part of tract where GAINES now lives
and adj. tract known as MAGANN's Ordinary and on which BATTAILE HARRISON
now lives. For 30 yrs. next ensuing and MAGANN covenants not to remove
and house to his own land; will not leave land "uninclosed" nor carry the
"loggs" to his own land. At end of lease will deliver up the plantation
in tolerable good order.

Page 333.   25 Mar 1768.   JOS. MAGANN, AC, to DANL. GAINES, AC, for 130
            pds, 200 acres between Porridge and Harris Creek and joining
GAINES' land; also 2 slaves to ensure GAINES on bond to GEO. KIPPEN & Co.
Deed of Trust.   Wit: BENJ. RUCKER, ANTHONY RUCKER, ISAAC TINSLEY.

Page 335.   4 Jul 1768.   JNO. DEPRIEST, & wife, ELIZ, AC, to WM. MARTIN,
            AC, for Ł99-7-6, 200 acres at the head of N fork of Nassau
Creek at Indian Cove.   Wit: JNO. GRIFFIN, ZACHARIAH JONES.

Page 336.   15 Apr 1768.   LUNSFORD LOMAX Jr., Caroline, to HENRY BARNES,
            AC, for 68 pds,17 sh, 306 acres on Ruckers Run, part of 6134
acres - see page 194.   Wit: ZACH. TALIAFERRO, RICH. TANKERSLEY, ROBT.
TAYLOR, PATRICK ROSE.

Page 337.   3 Oct 1767.   DUNCAN GRAHAM, Caroline, to HUGH ROSE, Power of
            Attorney to sell 2000 acres in AC, on SE side and near Tobacco
Row Mts.   Wit: JNO. ROSE, RICH. HARVIE.

Page 337.   4 Jul 1768.   PATRICK ROSE to JNO. SALE - lease - 100 acres
            lower end of plantation whereon JNO. SALE lives.   Lines: PAT-
RICK & HENRY ROSE, also HIGGINBOTHAM's entry on N side; 7 years - rent
due each Dec. 1, 10 pds. 40 sh. for all tithable worked above five.   Wit:
JOHN BIBB, WM. PARKS, DAN. DAINES.

Page 338.   4 Apr 1768.   HUGH ROSE, AC, to PATRICK P. MORRISON; lease.
            200 acres.   Lines: WARD's old shop; to hold during term of his
own and wife, ELIZ, and son, PATRICK's lives - yearly rent on April 10
of Ł1-1-6 (except during first three years when it is to be rent free)
but MORRISON to pay all taxes due our Sovereign Lord the King.   He is to
plant 200 peach and 100 apple trees and fence them and shall yearly
manure and prune them.   5 pds. consideration.

Page 340.   8 Jun 1768.   JOHN GIZZAGE FRASER to AMBROSE JONES, AC, for
            Ł78-10, 135 acres N side Tye - part of larger Order of Council
tract to ROBT. ROSE, Clerk, and THOS. CHEW and sold by ROSE to JONES, rec.
in AC, and then by JONES to J.G. FRASER, 8 Oct 1768, rec. in AC.   Wit:
LUNSFORD LOMAX, JR., GEO. SEATON, EDMD. WILCOX, HENRY BARNES.

Page 340.   4 Jul 1768.   PATRICK ROSE, AC, to JAS. JACKSON, AC, for 40 sh.
            per year lease, 100 acres mouth of Jackson Creek to old Order
of Council line of ROBT. ROSE, dec'd - to JACKSON & wife, MARTHA, for
natural lives.   Wit: DANL. GAINES, WM. MITCHELL.

Page 341.   21 Dec 1767.   LUNSFORD LOMAX, Jr., Caroline, to THOS. POWELL,
            AC, for Ł49-12-6, branch of Horsley, 165 and 3/4 acres. Lines:
SOLOMON CARTER. Part of 3553 acres - see page 194.   Wit: ZACH TALIAFERRO,
THOS. WAUGH, CARABY VEALE, RICH. LAWLESS(X).

Page 342.   16 Jul 1768.   JOS. CRUIZE & wife AGNIS, AC, to WM. GATEWOOD
            Jr., AC, for 15 pds, 290 acres S side of Buffaloe and N side
Rocky Run.   Lines: Col. JOSHUA FRY, Dec'd.   Wit: SAML. MURPHEY, JNO.
PHILIPS, MARTIN DAWSON(X), THOS. REID.

Page 343.   5 Sep 1768.   ABRAHAM EADES & wife SUSANNA, Alb. Co, to THEO-
            DORIC WEBB, Buckingham, for 30 pds, 150 acres branch of S fork
of Rockfish; pat. to WM. BRUCE 25 Sep 1762. Lines: HENRY KEYS, Grantors
made their marks.

Page 344.   5 Sep 1768.   JOHN ROWZIE, AC, & wife MARY to RICH. GATEWOOD
            (This appears to be ROUZIE in deed), for 35 pds, 115 acres,
part of tract bought by J.R. for CARTER BRAXTON. Lines: Ridge of Turkey
Mt., GABL. PENN.   Possession of GATEWOOD.   Wit: LAWRENCE CAMPBELL, JNO.
STOAKES.   Grantors made (X).

Page 345.   19 Feb 1768.   SAML. BAUGHAN, AC, to JNO. HARDWICK, AC, for 25
            pds, no acres mentioned.   Lines: JONATHAN JOHNSTON, JOS. GOFF;
on N branch of Boleing Creek.   Deed of Trust.   Wit: JNO. BURFORD, FRANCIS
WALKER, DANL. BURFORD, JR.

Page 346.   5 Sep 1768.   JOS. KINKEAD, Augusta, to MICHAEL CRAFT, AC, for
          50 pds, 369 acres head of N fork of Rockfish - part of tract
pat. to DAVID KINKEAD.   Wit: JULIUS WEBB, JNO. BURGER, JNO. MARTIN.

Page 347.   5 Sep 1768.   DANL. BURFORD, AC, to DANL. BURFORD JR., AC, for
          love borne by son, DANL. JR., land laid off for him, both
sides Harris creek, escepting 2 acres whereon the Mill stands; 76 acres
S side of Harris Creek, ROSE' s line - part of 600 acres I bought of Col.
GEO. CARRINGTON.   Wit: JNO. BURFORD, JAS. CREWS, CATH. KIPURS(?)(X).*

Psge 348.   20 Aug 1768.   JER. WADE, Alb. Co., to JNO. PARKS, AC, for 40
          pds, 378 acres head of "Frankling" and Tharahers creeks, in
the coves of the Mts.   Wit: MATT. TUCKER, JOS. BALLENGER, DRURY TUCKER(X)
Wife of WADE consents.

Page 349.   5 Sep 1768.   GEO. CARRINGTON, Cumberland, to RICH. PETER, AC,
          for Ł14-6, 179 acres Harris Creek.   Lines: EDWARD EDSON,
PIERCE WADE.

Page 350.   5 Mar 1768.   MURTAUGH CONNELL (or MURLAUGH) to JAS. SMITH, AC,
          crop, household goods, and horse for six years or until debt
is paid that SMITH is surety for - 8 pds - in JOHN KEYS' hands.   Also
corn at JNO. EDMONDS, Sr.

Page 351.   14 Jul 1768.   WM. RODGERS, Alb. Co., to MANUS BURGER, AC, 137
          acres on top of the Blue Ridge Mts., adj. Rockfish Gap.   Wit:
RICH. HARVIE, JNO. BURGER, JNO. HARVIE.   Signed: ROGERS.

Page 352.   17 Jul 1768.   WM. RODGERS, Alb. Co., to MANUS BURGER, AC, for
          50 pds, 142 acres on Top of the Blue Ridge Mts. - a Naked
Ridge; head of a branch of Rockfish.   Wit: JNO. HARVIE, JNO. BURGER,
RICH. HARVIE.

Page 353.   20 Aug 1768.   JER. WADE, Alb. Co., and St. Ann's Parish, to
          JOS. BALLENGER, AC, for 10 pds, 114 acres Top of Smith's Mt.
and in cove on side of same.   Lines: WM. CABELL, JR., JOS. BALLENGER.
Wit: MATT. RUCKER, RICH. BALLENGER, DRURY TUCKER(X).   Wife of WADE consents.

Page 354.   JAS. MAYFIELD, AC, to JOS. HIGGINBOTHAM, AC, planter, for 26
          pds, stock, household goods, etc. Deed of trust.   Wit: JNO.
HIGGINBOTHAM, JAS. HIGGINBOTHAM.   (X) of MAYFIELD.

Page 355.   30 Mar 1768.   WM. CLARK & wife, MARTHA, Cumberland Co, (Sur-
          viving executor of last will and testament of JAMES MEREDITH
late of the same county, dec'd) to CHAS. ELLIS, AC, JAS. MEREDITH in
life time bargained and agreed with CHAS. ELLIS, the elder, now dec'd,
the father of said CHAS. ELLIS, aforesaid - 400 acres on N side of Pedlar in Alb., but died before conveying.   CHAS. ELLIS, the elder had paid
the consideration - WM. CLARKE and wife, MARTHA, FRANCIS, JAS., JNO.
FLEMING, & WM. MIGGINSON, Executors of JAS. MEREDITH, did exhibit their
bill in chancery for recovery of the consideration money then due - CHAS.
ELLIS died before determination of suit - and in his will, 8 Jun 1760,
devised the 400 acres to his son, CHAS. ELLIS, and appointed DANL. BUR-
FORD, CORNELIUS THOMAS & JOSIAH ELLIS, executors of his will - whereuopn
WM. CLARKE et al revived their suit vs. the executors - and it was ordered that the plaintiffs convey the said 400 acres on Pedlar in Alb. to
person "Intitled" to it under the will of CHAS. ELLIS the elder and that
executors of ELLIS pay to pltffs Ł58-17-6 and interest on 32 pds at 5%
per annum from Dec 20, 1753 and cost of 441 pds. of Tobacco and 50 sh. -
or 500 pds. of Tobacco.   400 acres in AC on Pedlar.   Lines: CHAS. ELLIS,
WM. HORSLEY estate, dec'd, unknown owner to East.   Wit: GEO. CARRINGTON,
WM. PRYOR, MILTON BURFORD.   Marginal notation that the original deed
was delivered to CHAS. ELLIS, 1784.

*Marginal notation for deed on page 347, that the original deed was
delivered to ELIAS WILES(?), Admr., 11 Jan 1811.

Page 357. 22 Jun 1768. MARY MAYO & GEO. CARRINGTON, executors of will
          of DANL. MAYO, Cumberland, to WM. CABELL, AC, - MAYO in will
of 8 Dec 1760, devised among other things - that land in Alb. should be
sold by executors, and WM. CABELL "pretending a right" to 400 acres; 200
acres; and 100 acres - part of land to be sold - commenced chancery suit
in county court of Cumberland vs. executors and WM. MAYO, infant, heir of
DANL. MAYO, and obtained a decree that title be vested in WM. CABELL.
They have also offered for sale 800 acres (remainder) and WM. CABELL has
agreed to buy that, too, for 600 pds N side and adj. Fluvanna - tracts
all adjoin - now in AC. Wit: MILTON BURFORD, WM. PRYOR, DAVID REYNOLDS.
Marginal notation that original was delivered to NICH. CABELL.

Page 358. 24 Aug 1768. JNO. SCOTT & wife, MARGARET, St. Ann's Parish,
          Alb. Co., to JAS. LONDON, JR., AC, for Ł46-2, 461 acres branch
of Porrage, part of larger tract granted to MARGARET FRY who has since
married the said JNO. SCOTT. Lines: ROBT. JOHNS, CHRISTIAN. Wit: LUNS-
FORD LOMAX JR., HENRY ROSE, HUGH ROSE. Page 360, JOHN HENDERSON & JNO.
COLES, Alb, J.P.'s certify that MARGARET SCOTT, wife of JNO., consents to
deed on 10 Mar 1772.

Page 361. 16 Nov 1767. ROBT. HAYS, AC, to JNO. COFFEY, AC, for 16 pds,
          80 acres. Lines: Creek side. Pat. 15 Aug 1764. Wit: EDMOND
COFFEY, REUBEN COFFEY, GEO. BELL. (X) of HAYS.

Page 362. 5 Sep 1768. JNO. PARKS & wife MARY, AC, to NEILL CAMPBELL,
          Alb. Co., for 110 pds, 390 acres. Lines: Crossing Thresher's
creek.

Page 363. 6 Sep 1768. GEO. CARRINGTON, Cumberland Co., to JAS. SIMMONS,
          AC, for Ł9-16, 197 acres branch of Harris. Lines: JNO. WOOD-
RUFF, JNO. OWNBY, RICH. SHELTON, ISAAC WRIGHT, THOS. WATTS, GEO. CARRING-
TON.

Page 364. 5 Sep 1768. JESSE MILLS & wife, LUCY, AC, to LUCAS POWELL,
          Alb. Co., for 90 pds, 396 acres branch of Tye. Lines: ROSE.
Wit: JACOB SMITH, WYATT POWELL, WM. FLOYD.

Page 366. 3 Sep 1768. JNO. MORRISON, AC, to SAML. SHANNON, AC, for 30
          pds, 175 acres branch of Rockfish near the Blew Mts. Lines:
THOS. SHANNON, WM. CRWO, WM. SIMPSON. Wit: ALEX. REID, JR., SAML. WOODS,
WM. LEAKEY, OWEN HERNDON.

Page 367. 5 Sep 1768. LUNSFORD LOMAX, JR., Caroline, to JNO. LOVING SR,
          AC, for Ł27-15-6, 101 acres branch of Rucker's Run. Lines:
WM. LOVING. Part of 6134 acres - see page 194.

Page 368. 16 Jul 1768. JNO. ROACH, AC, to CARTER BRAXTON, King Wm., for
          Ł66-18, 223 acres S side and next to Buffaloe - conveyed by
CARTER BRAXTON to JNO. ROACH 8 Apr 1768. Deed of Trust. Wit: THOS. REID,
THOS. WYATT, GABL. PENN.

Page 369. 5 Sep 1768. WM. PARKS to EDMUND WARE, AC, for 500 pds - WM.
          PARKS has a son by his former wife, TABITHA, daughter of ED-
MUND WARE, and has received a slave girl, Nell, as TABITHA's portion, and
thinks it most reasonable that his son, being the only child by that marriage, should have the slave and increase rather than any child or children that WM. PARKS hath or shall have by the present or any other wife.
Wit: JNO. FLOYD, JAS. DILLARD, JNO. TALIAFERRO.

Page 370. 5 Aug 1768. RICH. POWELL, AC, to EDMUND POWELL, AC, for 5 sh,
          283 acres on Buffaloe. Lines: JACOB SMITH, BALLENGER.

Page 371. 5 Sep 1768. JNO. OWNBY, JR., AC, to MARTIN TRAP, AC, consider-
          ation - 111 acres N branch of Buffaloe. Lines: JAS. WILLIAM-
SON, JOHN ROWZIE, CARTER.

Page 372. 5 Sep 1768. ROBT DAVIS, AC, to JNO. FLOYD, AC, DAVIS for par-
          ental affection for my nephew, JNO. FLOYD - 26 acres laid off
for FLOYD - E side Wilderness Creek, part of 400 acres where DAVIS lives.
Wit: JOS. GOODWIN, WM. FLOYD, JOS. LAYNE, WYATT POWELL.

Page 373. 19 Feb 1768. JNO. HOUCHIN, AC, to ALEX. SPIERS & Co, Glasgow
merchants, 35 pds, for 95 acres, branch of Harris Creek in
Graham's Cove and where he lives - HOUCHIN has not obtained pat., but has
had survey and fees sent to Secretary's office. Also, beds, pigs, horses,
etc. Deed of Trust. Wit; GEO. SEATON, WM. PENN, THOS. REID, JNO. BARRETT.

Page 374. 12 Mar 1768. ANDREW SMITH, AC, to ROBT. DONALDS & Co, for
L12-5, horse, cows, pigs, 2 blankets, and two "Ruggs", etc.
Deed of Trust. Wit: GEO. SEATON, MATT. NIGHTINGALE, WM. MITCHELL.

Page 375. 6 Sep 1768. PETERFIELD TRENT, AC, to THOS. HERD, Hanover Co,
for 25 pds, 274 acres branch of Taylor's Creek. Lines: DAVID
MERRIWETHER, JNO. TOMPSON. Land bought from NICHOLAS MERRIWETHER & RICH.
NALLY and whereon NALLY lives. Marginal notation that the original was
delivered to WM. FITZPATRICK 12 Nov 1768.

Page 376. 3 Oct 1768. GERRARD BANKS, AC, to LYNN BANKS, part of tract
bought of CARTER BRAXTON - for love borne my son, LYNN BANKS,
and his wife SARAH, 70½ acres for their lives or to the one who lives
"longest". Lines: "The Spring". They may not sell it.

Page 376. 3 Oct 1768. NATHANIEL WOODROOF, Sr., and his wife, HANNAH,
AC, to JNO. WEBB, AC, for 50 pds, 270 acres S side and joining
Tye and bought from VALENTINE BALL, rec. in AC. Wit: HENRY THOMAS, JNO.
OLD, NEILL CAMPBELL. Note: NEILL CAMPBELL certifies that the land is
mtgd. to GEO. KIPPEN & Co., and in their names relenquishes right of title.

Page 378. 3 Oct 1768. JNO. KEY, SR, AC, to wife, SUSANNAH and the children lawfully born of her body and now living - great many
items; cattle, beds, hogs, sheep, horse, pewter, iron, tin and all sorts
of vessels. Wit: WM. HANSBROUGH, JNO. REESE.

Page 378. 3 Oct 1768. NEILL CAMPBELL, Alb. Co, to AARON HIGGINBOTHAM,
AC, for 110 pds, 390 acres Thresher's creek and which CAMPBELL
bought from JNO. PARKS, rec. in AC.

Page 379. 3 Oct 1768. AARON HIGGINBOTHAM & wife, CLARA, AC, to NEILL
CAMPBELL, Alb., Co, for 150 pds, 3 parcels both sides of S
fork of Buffaloe - 489 acres in all. 1) 190 acres pat. to HIGGINBOTHAM
30 Aug 1763; 2) middle tract of 200 acres pat. 3 Mar 1760 to HIGGINBOTHAM,
3) lower tract of 99 acres pat. July 1765. Marginal notation "Sent to
WM. CAMPBELL 16 Nov 1768, by Mr. JORDAN(?)"

Page 381. 3 Oct 1768. JNO. PARKS, SR., & wife, MARY, AC, to AARON HIG-
GINBOTHAM, AC, for 40 pds, 378 acres, which PARKS bought of
JER. WADE, rec. in AC, pat. to JER. WADE 23 May 1763. Wit: NEILL CAMP-
BELL, JNO. OLD, CLOUGH SHELTON.

Page 382. 3 Oct 1768. ISAAC GIBSON, & wife, FRANCES, AC, to NEILL CAMP-
BELL, Alb. Co., for 40 pds, 250 acres branch of S fork of
Buffaloe and on the long Mt. Lines: CARNABY VEAL. Marginal notation
that it was sent to Mr. CAMPBELL 16 Nov 1768 by Mr. JORDON.

Page 383. 3 Oct 1768. JONATHAN STAMPER and wife RACHEL, AC, to JOS.
RICHARDS, AC, for 25 pds, 200 acres, crossing Stonehouse Creek.
Grantors signed with (X).

Page 384. 3 Oct 1768. JOS. HIGGINBOTHAM to CORNELIUS CAMPBELL - J.H. of
AC, and C.C. of Alb., for 20 pds, 96 acres pat. to J.H. 10 Jul
1766. Lines: ADAM REID, S side of Pedlar and crossing it. HANNAH HIG-
GINBOTHAM, wife of JOS. HIGGINBOTHAM, consents.

Page 385. 12 Sep 1768. LUNSFORD LOMAX, JR., Caroline, to RICH. PRITCH-
ARD, AC, for L11-5, 50 acres branch of Purgatory Swamp below
Fenely's Gap. Lines: ROBT. JOHNSTON, JACOB EADES. Part of 400 acres
conveyed to LL Jr. - see page 194. Wit: HENRY KEY, JACOB EADES(X), HUGH
PATRICK.

Page 386. 12 Sep 1768. LUNSFORD LOMAX, JR., Caroline, to HUGH PATRICK,
AC, for 30 pds, 119 acres branch of Purgatory Swamp below

Fenley's Gap. Lines: JACOB EADES, RICH. PRICHARD. Part of 400 acres - see page 194.

Page 387. 3 Oct 1768. LUNSFORD LOMAX, JR., CAroline, to JNO. MONTGOMERY, AC, for Ł100-16, 252 acres branch of Rucker's Run. Lines: TUGGLE. Part of 6134 acres - see page 194. Marginal notation that orig. was delivered to MONTGOMERY 3 Jul 1784.

Page 388. 7 Nov 1768. RICH. TANKERSLEY, AC, & wife, WINNIFRED, to RICH. TANKERSLEY, Jr., for 5 pds, 150 acres - a blank space where description should be. Wit: THOS. REID, HUGH ROSE, DAVID CRAWFORD.

Page 389. 13 Oct 1768. JNO. GILMORE, AC, for love borne my children & children of my wife, JUDITH, formerly the wife of THOS. OBRYAN, to my son, JNO. GILMORE, my daughter, MARY GILMORE, to WM. OBRYAN, to MARY OBRYAN, to CATH. OBRYAN, JNO. BRADY. (X) of GILMORE. Conveys to each, stock. Wit: JNO. MAYFIELD, SR, JNO. MAYFIELD JR.(X), JNO. BRADY.

Page 389. 7 Nov 1768. AMBROSE RUCKER, AC, & wife, MARY, to JNO. HOU-CHINS, AC, for 5 pds, 90 acres pat. to RUCKER, 10 Sep 1767. Wit: BENJ. POLLARD. Marginal notation: Original delivered to RICH. HAR-RISON by order of WM. HOUCHINS, Heir to JNO. HOUCHINS.

Page 390. 2 Jan 1769. JNO. THURMOND, AC, on the "won" part from LAU-RANCE SUDDETH & wife, MARTHA, AC, 35 pds for 97 acres on the Mt., and in the cove at the head of the Dutch Creek. Signed, SUDDATH and (X) of wife. Original delivered to THURMOND 24 Feb 1786.

Page 392. George the Third by the grace of God, etc, to FIELDING LEWIS, CHAS. DICK, & ROGER DIXON, Gent. PETER TALIAFERRO & wife, ANNA, on 6 Jul 1767, conveyed to WM. HANSBROUGH 400 acres - order to examine ANNA on June 6, Spotsylvania, 11 Oct 1768, returned by CHAS. DICK JR. & ROGER DIXON.

Page 393. 3 Jan 1769. JAS. BARNET JR., Augusta, to THOS. CARPENTER, AC, for 10 pds, 47 acres head branch of Corbin Creek. Lines: THOS CARPENTER. Wit: ALEX. REID, JR., WM. HENDERSON, SAML. WOODS, ANDREW LACKEY.

Page 394. 6 Sep 1768. DAVID PATTERSON, Buckingham, & wife MARY to NEL-SON & JAS. PATTERSON, orphans of JAS. PATTERSON, late of Ches-terfield. JAS. in lifetime bought 400 acres on N side of Fluvanna - sur-veyed lately by WM. CABELL, JR., surveyor for AC - no deed had been made. JAS. PATTERSON left will rec. in Chesterfield and gave NELSON the 400 acres, but with reservation that if wife thought herself with child and should bring forth a son, then this son should have equal part with NELSON. Wife after his death delivered JAS. ANDERSON PATTERSON & deed made in compliance with their FATHER's wishes. Lines: CHRISTIAN. Wit: CHAS. PATTESON, WM. PHELPS, DAVID VIA(X). Page 396, Commission to JOS. CABELL, BENJ. HOWARD, & CHAS. PATTERSON, Gent. J.P.'s of Buckingham, to examine MARY PATTERSON, Feb. 15, and done on April 3, 1769.

Page 397. 6 Feb 1769. GEO. TAYLOR, AC, to NICHOLAS WRENN, AC, for 45 pds, 170 acres. Lines: Crawley's Creek, SAML. MURPHY, DUNCAN CAMERON, HENRY TAYLOR - part of 400 acres pat. to GEO. TAYLOR on 20 Sep 1751. Memo: release by WM. MITCHELL for JAS. & ROBT. DONALDS & Co. Wit: EDMUND WILCOX & REUBEN JORDAN.

Page 397. 6 Feb 1769. JAS. BROWN & wife, JANNAT, AC, to DANL. McBANE, AC, for 30 pds, 150 acres branch of Rockfish - Lines: EDWARD MOLLY(?) - MOLLOY later - CLAPHAM(?), Col. CHISWELL. Deeded to JAS. BROWN by JNO. PLEASANTS, JR., & ROBT. ABRAHAM on 7 Jun 1760, rec. in Alb. Wit: JAS. COFFEY, HENRY KEY, LEONARD TARRANT. Mark of JANNAT BROWN.

Page 399. 6 Feb 1769. DANL. MACBAINE, AC, to GEO. CAMPBELL, for 40 pds, 162 acres both sides Piney. (X) of grantor. Wit: WM. LOVING, CHAS. BOND JR., WM. RYAN, JAS. BROWN, JNO. RYAN.

Page 400. 9 Nov 1768. GEO. BLANE, AC, to NEILL CAMPBELL, Factor for GEO. KIPPEN & Co, Galsgow merchants. Ł63-3-9 for 202½ acres.

Lines: WALTER KING, where BLANE lives. Deed of Trust to be repaid by 1
Oct 1771, with interest. Wit: HENRY BARNES(X), EDMUND WILCOX, BENJ.
POLLARD(X), RICH. TANKERSLEY(X).

Page 401. 6 Mar 1769. LAWRANCE CAMPBELL, AC, & wife, HERNITER, to HENRY
CAMPBELL, AC, for 45 pds, 300 acres. Lines: RICE MEREDITH,
CARTER BRAXTON, Geeabe(sic) line, HIGGINBOTHAM, RICH. DAVIS.

Page 402. 6 Mar 1769. HUGH ROSE, AC, attorney for DUNCAN GRAHAM, AC, to
JNO. TINSLEY, AC, for 33 pds, 152 acres. Lines: WM. MILLER,
EDWARD TINSLEY, BATTLE HARRISON.

Page 403. 6 Mar 1769. EDWARD TINSLEY & wife, MARGARET, AC, to JNO. TIN-
SLEY, son of EDWARD & MARGARET, 5 sh. for 100 acres Harris
Creek, part of tract bought by EDWARD TINSLEY from DUNCAN GRAHAM of Caro-
line. (Note: GRAHAM is styled of AC in previous deed.)

Page 404. 6 Mar 1769. DAVID HARRIS, AC, to JNO. PARSON, AC, for 15 pds,
100 acres, part of 400 acres pat. to JNO. HARRIS, 10 Sep 1755,
on Indian Creek. Lines: HENRY ROSE. (X) of HARRIS.

Page 405. 6 Mar 1769. DAVID HARRIS, Heir of JOHN HARRIS, dec'd, to
GILBERT HAYS - JNO. HARRIS sold to one THOS. WHITE & made no
deed - and WHITE sold to HAYS & DAVID HARRIS, knowing his father's inten-
tions for 5 sh. conveys to HAY. 300 acres, no description. (X) of D.H.

Page 405. 6 Mar 1768. WM. HANSBROUGH & wife, KEZIAH, to JNO. TUGGLE JR.
for Ŀ16-11-3, 98 acres on Rucker's Run. Lines: Col. LOMAX.
Wit: WM. WALTON, JNO. LOVING, JR., BARTHOLEMEW RANSAY. Dated 1768, but
proved 6 Mar 1769.

Page 406. 6 Mar 1769. PHILIP SMITH, AC, to ISAAC GIBSON, AC, for 65 pd,
216 acres on N side Buffalo, part of tract of CARTER BRAXTON.
Lines: BRAXTON, Higginbotham's Old Mill Creek. Wife of SMITH examined,
but not named.

Page 407. 7 Feb 1769. LUNSFORD LOMAX, the younger, Caroline to WM. FUR-
BUSH, Alb. Co, for 40 pds, 199½ acres on Rucker's Run. Lines:
HARMER. Part of 6134 acres - see page 194. Wit: ZACK TALIAFERRO, S.
MURPHY, THOS. LANDRUM, WM. CABELL JR.

Page 408. 6 Mar 1769. LUNSFORD LOMAX, Jr., Caroline, to SAML. SHAKEL-
FORD, Alb. Co., for Ŀ49-10, 165 acres on Horsley Creek. Lines:
PHILIP PAYTON, CHAS. TALIAFERRO. Part of 3553 acres - see p.194.

Page 409. 6 Feb 1769. JNO. OWNBY, JR., AC, to DAVID BLIZE, AC, for
Ŀ9-12, 70 acres branch Buffaloe. Lines: GERRARD BANKS, JNO.
ROWZIE, MARTIN TRAP (FRAP?), part of tract of J.O. Jr. (Note: the name
BLIZE is spelled BAIZE in one place.) Wife of OWNBY examined, but not
named. Wit: AMBROSE PORTER, GILBRID COTTRELL, WM. MAYS(X).

Page 410. 8 Apr 1768. CARTER BRAXTON, King Wm., & GEO. SEATON, AC, to
JNO. ROAIK (ROACH in margin), AC, for Ŀ66-18, 223 acres S side
and adj. Buffaloe, which SEATON lately bought of executors of AMBROSE LEE,
dec'd. and by him mtgd. to BRAXTON. Lines: crossing Huff's Creek. (Note:
ROARK & ROAK are spellings employed in deed.) Wit: CORLS. THOMAS, JOS.
CABELL, WM. CABELL JR., THOS. REID, THOS. WIATT, GABL. PENN.

Page 411. 25 Feb 1769. JNO. OWNSBY, JR., AC, to WM. MAYS, AC, for 30
pds, 178 acres branch of Buffalow (sic). Lines: JAS. WILLIAM-
SON, JONATHAN JOHNSON, CARTER BRAXTON, DAVID BLIZE, MARTIN TRAP. Part
of tract of J.O. Jr. Wit: LINN BANKS, AMBROSE CARTER, DAVID BLY(X).
Wife of J.O. Jr. consents, but not named.

Page 413. 4 Aug 1768. JOS. CREWS, AC, to JAS. ROWZEE, AC, for 10 pds,
150 acres S side Buffaloe. Lines: MOSES HIGGINBOTHAM. Pat.
to JOS. CREWS 25 Sep 1762. Wit: THOS. REID, JOHN BARRET, JNO. PHILLIPS,
WM. PENN.

Page 414.   6 Mar 1769.   JAS. STINNET & wife, ANNE, AC, to WM. CAMDEN, AC,
            for 35 pds, 152 acres, part of pat. of 227 acres to J.S. 1 Jun
1750. Grantors signed with (X).

Page 415.   6 Mar 1769.   WM. TERREL LEWIS, ST. Ann's parish, Alb. Co., to
            JEREMIAH PATRICK, AC, for 30 pds, 400 acres, pat. to PHILLIP
MORRIS on condition of paying his majors Quit rents and cultivating and
improving, but he has failed to comply, and it has since been granted to
WM. TERREL LEWIS and is in possession of PATRICK. SARAH, wife of WM.
TERREL LEWIS, consents.

Page 416.   Division under court order of AC of lands and slaves of WM.
            HORSLEY dec'd, and agreeable to will (Plat of division is on
page 417) To WM. HORSLEY, 200 acres upper end of the great bend and 400
acres on both sides of the Rich Branch. To ROBT. HORSLEY - 200 acres on
middle part of the great bent and 400 acres on Fishing Creek and branches.
To JOHN HORSLEY - 200 acres lower part of the great bent and 375 acres on
S side of Fluvanna. Slaves: To WM., to RODERICK McCULLOCH who intermarried with ELIZ. HORSLEY, to ROBT. & JOHN HORSLEY who are both underage.
WM. HORSLEY & RODERICK McCULLOCH are to pay them 5 pds. Done by committee on 2 Sep 1768, consisting of JAS. NEVIL, CORLS. THOMAS, JAS. HIGGIN-
BOTHAM. Plat made 6 Mar 1769.

Page 418.   3 April 1769.   PEYTON RANDOLPH, BENJ. GRYMES, & JNO. ROBINSON,
            Gentlemen executors of PHILIP GRYMES, and LUNSFORD LOMAX, the
Younger, Caroline, to RICHARD ALCOCK of same county. LUNSFORD LOMAX, the
elder, mtgd. on 7 Aug 1756, and rec. 21 Oct 1756, land to secure debt to
PHILIP GRYMES - 7881 acres - not repaid. L.L. Sr. & wife, JUDITH, on 13
Jan 1767, conveyed to LL Jr., for 600 pds, 1070 acres, part of tract con-
veyed by mtg. to PHILIP GRYMES and formerly granted to HARMER, KING, RAN-
DOLPH, & LOMAX by order of Council. On branch of Tye. Lines: KING,
BLAIN. WM. CABELL JR. signs as attorney for executors.

Page 420.   27 Mar 1769.   GROVES HARDING, AC, to NEILL CAMPBELL, Factor
            for GEO. KIPPEN & Co, Glasgow merchants - Deed of Trust to
secure payment of Ł205-11-7, 710 acres and which HARDING bought of NEILL
CAMPBELL - also six slaves. Wit: JNO. DAWSON, LUNSFORD LOMAX, JR.,
PATRICK ROSE, CHAS. IRVING.

Page 421.   21 Jan 1768.   WM. ROBERTSON, AC, to ALEX. PATTENT, AC, for
            Ł21-10, 174 acres on Taylor's Creek. Lines: SAML. MAN, ARCH-
IBALD WOODS. Wit: FRANS. MERIWETHER, ROGER KASEY(X), JNO. McGUER(X).

Page 422.   7 Apr 1769.   LUNSFORD LOMAX, JR., Caroline, to WM. LOVEDAY,
            Province of Maryland, for 30 pds, 200 acres on Purgatory Swamp
below Fenley's Gap. Part of 400 acres conveyed to LL Sr. by WALTER KING,
Bristol Merchant, and THOS. MANN RANDOLPH on 1 Dec 1764, and conveyed by
LL Sr. and wife JUDITH, to LL Jr. 13 Jan 1767, and rec. in AC. Wit: WM.
BIBB, RICH. TANKERSLEY, JNO. RYAN, HUGH PATRICK(X).

Page 423.   13 Apr 1769.   JNO. LOVING, AC, to NEILL CAMPBELL, Factor for
            GEO. KIPPEN & Co, Deed of Trust to secure debt of Ł327-8-3.
1) Tract in Spotsylvania, 400 acres pat. to LOVING 30 Aug 1764; 100 acres
in AC pat. to LOVING 10 Mar 1762, 400 acres in AC pat. 2 Jun 1760 to LOV-
ING. 200 acres in Lunenberg and now Halifax pat. to LOVING 10 Aug 1759.
Also, three slaves. Signed: JOHN LOVING SR. Wit: CHAS. IRVING, JNO.
OLD, REUBEN JORDAN, CLOUGH SHELTON.

Page 426.   1 May 1769.   Deed of Trust - JNO. LOVING Sr., AC, Ł51-1-6 to
            WM. MITCHELL to secure debt to JAS. & ROBT. DONALDS & Co,
Glasgow Merchants - mare, other stock, furniture and tobacco. Wit:
ANDREW LEAKEY, JNO. MacLEAN.

Page 427.   1 May 1769.   JNO. LOVING & wife, SARAH, to WM. LOVING, for 20
            pds, 101 acres, branch of Rucker's Run and joining WM. LOVING.
Conveyed to JNO. LOVING by LUNSFORD LOMAX, JR. 5 Sep 1768; rec. in AC.
Wit: JAS. NEVIL, W. HANSBROUGH, JNO. LOVING JR.

Page 428.   1 May 1769.   WM. LOVING, AC, to JNO. LOVING, AC, 136 acres pat.
            to WM. LOVING, 25 Jun 1762. Lines: LOMAX - lease during

115

natural lives of JNO. LOVING & wife, SARAH, and 5 sh. to be paid 10 Jun
annually - not to work over two tithables. Wit: JS. NEVIL, W. HANSBROUGH,
JNO. LOVING JR.

Page 429.   9 Mar 1769.   JOB. CARTER SR., & wife ANNE, AC, to THOS. REID,
            AC, for 150 pds, 406 acres where JOB now lives. Lines: WM.
CABELL SR, NATHANIEL DAVIS, LUNSFORD LOMAX JR., on Horsley Creek. Also
one slave woman and tobacco. Wit: B. POLLARD, GABL. PENN, WM. HORSLEY,
JNO. SALE, REUBEN JORDAN.

Page 430.   1 May 1769.   THOS. PARKS, AC, to NEILL JOHNSTON, AC, for 200
            pds, 400 acres. PRISCILLA, wife of THOS. PARKS, consents.

Page 431.   3 Apr 1769.   WM. CABELL SR., AC, to WM. CABELL JR., AC, love
            borne by SR for JR, his son, fishery on Woods Island in the
Fluvanna - agreeable to reservations in deed from WM. CABELL, the elder,
to his son, JNO. CABELL, 13 Apr 1763; rec. in AC. Wit: WM. WALTON, JNO.
SAVAGE, ELEONAR MILLS(X).

Page 432.   5 May 1769.   SAML. MARKSBURY, AC, to PHILIP SMITH, AC, for 25
            pds, 85 acres S side of Buffaloe, part of 740 acres pat. to
AZCHARIAS TALIAFERRO 10 Sep 1755. Lines: AARON HIGGINBOTHAM. ISBELL,
wife of SAML. MARKBURRY, consents.

Page 433.   5 Jun 1769.   JNO. WOODROOF, Bedford Co, to THOS. WRIGHT, AC,
            for 100 pds, 242 acres on Fluvanna. MARY, wife of JNO.
WOODROOF, consents.

Page 434.   3 Jun 1769.   HENRY KEY, AC, to WM. ALFORD, AC, for 45 pds, 266
            acres, pat. to KEY 5 Jun 1765, on Rucker's run and Tye on N
side of Berry's Mt. Lines: HARMER & KING.

Page 435.   9 Jun 1769.   RICH. TANKERSLEY releases CATHERINE SANDERS from
            all service as she has fairly bought and paid me for remaining
time in her transportation bill. Wit: ZACHS. TALIAFERRO, MARY TALIAFERRO.

Page 436.   Same deed as on page 353 - WADE TO BALLENGER.

Page 437.   3 Jul 1769.   LEONARD GOFF & wife ANN, Bedford Co, to PERTER
            RUCKER, JNO. RUCKER, AMBROSE RUCKER, BENJ. RUCKER, ISAAC RUCK-
ER, ANTHONY RUCKER, SARAH MARR, WINEFORD LEE, MELLA (MILDRED) HAM, PHEBE
RUCKER, AC, for 50 pds, 100 acres. Lines: JNO. BURFORD, Rucker's Run,
drinking corner in JNO. BURFORD's line, conveyed by JNO. GOFF, dec'd,
to LEONARD GOFF.

Page 438.   11 Apr 1769.   JAS. CREWS & wife MILDRED, AC, to WM. HUGHES,AC,
            for 60 pds, 375 acres, branch of Harris Creek and part of 578
acres granted to JAS. CREWS by deed from GEO. CARRINGTON & recorded in
AC. Wit: JNO. FLOYD, JOS. CREWS, JNO(?) DAWSON.

Page 440.   4 Dec 1768.   JNO. LOVING & wife, SARAH, AC, to LUCAS POWELL,
            Alb. Co, for 20 pds, 114 acres. Lines: Shoe branch of N fork
of Piney; THOS. JEFFERSON, pat. to JNO. LOVING, 20 Jul 1768. Wit: WM.
LOVING, LUNSFORD LOMAX, JR., W. HANSBROUGH, WM. MONROE.

Page 441.   3 Jul 1769. JOSIAH ELLIS, AC, to DANL. BURFORD, AC, for 60 pds,
            246 acres N branch of Brown's Creek, pat. to ELLIS 10 Sep
1767. Wit: WM. SYMMONS, ISAAC WRIGHT.

Page 442.   3 July 1768.   JNO. GOODWIN, AC, to MICAJAH GOODWIN - JNO. for
            love borne his son, MICAJAH - 200 acres on N side Fluvanna,
200 acres laid off for him on N side of river. Lines: JOS. GOODWIN, part
of tract that JNO. GOODWIN bought of ROWLAND HORSLEY BIRK. Wit: JNO.
OWNBEY, GEO. GOODWIN, JOS. GOODWIN, RICH. GOODWIN.

Page 443.   10 May 1769.   DANL. EDMUNDS, AC, to ALEX, SPEIRS, JNO. BOWMAN
            & Co, Glasgow merchants - 30 pds, paid by THOS. REID, Factor,
75 acres head branch of Huff's Creek adj. THOS. PARKS - also cattle,
hogs, mare, etc. Deed of Trust on demand. Wit: GABL. PENN, WM. PENN,
JNO. WIATT.
                        End of Deed Book B

AMHERST COUNTY, VIRGINIA DEED BOOK C

DEDICATION

This work is dedicated to my only brother, Bernard Byrd Davis. We are the only children of our late and beloved parents, John Fulton Davis and Lucy Ann Bailey Davis. Bernard is a graduate of Washington and Lee Law School; former FBI agent; Order of the Coif and is an attorney in Shelbyville, Kentucky.

Page 1.   6 Mar 1769. SAMUEL MURPHY, AC, to BARTHOLOMEW RAMSAY, AC, for
           £75, 81 acres pat. 10 Sep 1755. Lines: GEO. TAYLOR, N branch
of Piney; also 200 acres adj. Lines: Crawley's Creek, HENRY TAYLOR.
Part of a pat. of 20 Sep 1751.

Page 2.   7 Aug 1769. LUNSFORD LOMAX, JR., Caroline County, to JAMES
           STEVINS, Caroline, for £25, 216 acres branch of Lomax creek;
branch of Rucker's Run. Part of 6134 acres conveyed to LUNSFORD LOMAX,
the Elder, by BENJ. WALLER, atty. for WALTER KING, Bristol merchant, and
THOS. MANN RANDOLPH, 1 Dec 1764, and by LL Ar. and wife, JUDITH, to LL Jr,
13 Jan 1767. Wit: DUDLEY GATEWOOD, JNO. STEVENS, CLAYTON COLEMAN.

Page 3.   27 Jul 1769. LUNSFORD LOMAX, Jr., Caroline Co., to JAMES STE-
           VENS, Caroline, for £200, 1735 acres and located as above.
Lines: TUGGLE, Loving's Creek, JNO. McGOMERY(sic), FURBUSH, Lomax Creek
below the mill. Part of 6134 acres - see previous deed. Wit: CHAS. ROSE,
JNO. ROSE Jr., AL ROSE, ZACH. TALIAFERRO.

Page 5.   7 Aug 1769. WILLIAM CABELL, the Elder, to JOSEPH CABELL,
           Buckingham, for love borne by WM. for his son, JOSEPH - and
for certain promises made - 350 acres, branch of Owen's Creek. Lines:
JNO. JOSLIN. Pat. 26 Nov 1756.

Page 6.   15 Jul 1769. ALEX. PATTON, AC, to WILLIAM MONTGOMERY, Augusta
           Co., for £40, 174 acres on Taylors Creek. Lines: SAML. MANN,
ARCHIBALD WOODS. Wit: ALEX. REID, SR., MATTHEW NIGHTINGALE, ALEX. BARN-
ETT, ROBT. BARNETT.

Page 7.   7 Aug 1769. LUNSFORD LOMAX, JR., to GEORGE PURVIS, for £54-4,
           221 acres on Loving's Creek; branch of Rucker's Run, part of
6000 acres and "off" acres etc. See page 2. Wit: ZACH. TALIAFERRO,
BENJ. POLLARD, HENRY ROSE.

Page 8.   10 Aug 1769. LUNSFORD LOMAX, JR., Caroline, to THOMAS LUCAS,
           Alb. Co., for £355, 3 tracts of 1154 acres on Harris Creek.
1) 400 acres granted to LUNSFORD LOMAX SR, by deeds of 16 Aug 1756. Lines:
JNO. HARVIE, N side of Harris. 2) 398 acres granted by deeds to LL Sr.
16 Aug 1756; N side of Harris. 3) 356 acres pat. to LL Sr. 11 Jul 1761;
Harris Creek. All conveyed to LL Jr. by LL Sr. on 13 Jan 1767, and rec.
in AC. Wit: CORNL. THOMAS, WM. MITCHELL, CHAS. IRVING, JNO. RYAN, JNO.
BIBB.

Page 9.   25 Feb 1769. Bill of sale by DAVID BLY, AC, to JNO. OWENBEY,
           AC - horse and cow for £9-12. Wit: LINN BANKS, AMBROSE PORTER.

Page 10.   3 Jul 1769. RICH. KEARBY, Alb. Co., to ABNER WITT, Alb., for
           £18, 96 acres in cove of a mountain; branch of Rockfish. Lines:
JAMES LACKEY, JOHN LACKEY. Wit: RO. WRIGHT, THOS. EADS, WM. EADS.

Page 11.   19 Jul 1769. JNO. SANDIDGE, AC, Deed of Trust ot WM. MITCHELL,
           Factor for JAS. & RO. DONALDS & Co, - del. to SHEPHERD 6 Apr
1774. 5 sh., 180 acres bought by JS of JNO. ROBERTS. Also slaves, stock,
etc. Wit: EDMD. WILCOX, THOS. MITCHELL, GABL. PENN.

Page 12.   22 Jul 1769. GEO. JEFFERSON, Pitsylvania, to JOS. CREWS, AC,
           for £162, 700 acres Stoval Creek. Lines: FRY. Wit: CHAS.
REYNOLDS, MOSES CAMPBELL, JNO. HARDWICK, AARON CAMPBELL, MARY STOVALL,

JNO. BALLOW.

Page 13.   4 Sep 1769.   JOS. CREWS, AC, to ELISHA LION, Alb., for L70,
            150 acres N fork of Stovall.

Page 14.   14 Sep 1769.   JOS. CREWS, AC, to GEO. STOVALL, AC, for L37-10,
            150 acres on Stovall.

Page 15.   4 Sep 1769, WM. BICKNALL, AC, to HOWARD CASH, AC, for L10, 100
            acres, part of 400 acres formerly of CASH & granted to BICK-
NALL. HANNAH, wife of BICKNELL (also spelled BICKNELL)

Page 16.   26 Jun 1769.   JNO. TUGGLE, AC, to JAMES LYLE, Chesterfield,
            Deed of Trust, Negro, Hampton. Wit: HENRY KEY, WM. BICKNELL,
CHAS. IRVING.

Page 17.   2 Sep 1769.   JNO. MILLER, AC, to WM. OGLESBY, AC, for L160,
            260 acres Rockfish - laid off to JM out of 600 acres belonging
to SAML. BELL. Wit: MATT. NIGHTINGALE, AARON MOORE, WM. HENDERSON, FRAN-
CIS CAMPBELL.

Page 18.   15 Jun 1769.   JNO. DENNEE & wife ELIZ, Roann (sic) Co, N.C.,
            to JNO. THURMOND, AC, - rents moveing and L35, 50 acres on
branch of Dutch. Lines: SAML. STAPLES, JNO. HUNTER, N side Dutch, LOUR-
NESS(?) SUDDARTH. Wit: JNO. DEPRIEST, SAML. STAPLES, JAS. DENNE.

Page 19.   15 Sep 1769.   JNO. CABELL, Buckingham, lease to JAMES PAMPLIN,
            Buckingham - yearly rents of L2500 tobacco; plantation where
PANPLIN lives. He is to build tobacco house 40 ft. long, 20 ft. wide; 12
ft. pitch. Lease from Jan. 1 next for 5 years. L500 due for each tithable worked. To build two corne (sic) houses - 1 to be 16 ft. square.
2. to be 12 ft. wide, 16 ft. long, 8 ft. pitch. Sawed logs to be used.
To take off weather boarding and shingles on house where he lives and put
on new. Jointed and bead; new set of Cornish; 2 door frames; 3 pannell
doors; 2 twelve light window frames and sashes; lay floor above and below;
run up pair of stairs to make partition above stairs; build a chimney
with two fire places; underpin the house and one smoake (sic) house with
brick; plant an apple orchard of 100 trees and build a fence. He is also
to find diet and lodging for workmen shile they are about the tobacco
house. Wit: THOS. HUGHES, MILTON BURFORD.

Page 21.   14 Jul 1769.   PHILIP PAYTON, Sr., AC, to WM. MITCHELL for acct.
            with JAS. & RO. DONALDS & Co, merchants in Glasgow - deed of
trust. Bed, cows & calves - two bought of CARNABY VEAL and one from JAS.
SMITH; stock, dishes, furniture etc. Due Jan 1 next. Wit: JNO. WIATT,
DUDLEY GATEWOOD, RICH. MEREDITH.

Page 21.   2 Oct 1769.   ELLICK DUGGINS, AC, to FRANCIS GARNER, AC, for L8,
            60 acres on branch of Huff Creek. Lines: BENJ. STINNETT, side
of a mt. DUGGIN's wife mentioned, but not named.

Page 22.   13 Jun 1769.   JOHN DENNE & wife ELIZ., Roann Co, NC, to JOHN
            GRIFFIN (GREAFIN), AC, for L16-10, 90 acres on Rucker's Run.
Lines: Col. LOMAX. Wit: JAS. DENEY, JNO. LOVING JR., JNO. DEPRIEST.
Signed: JNO. DENEY.

Page 23.   1 Nov 1769.   JAMES EVANS, AC, to GEO. HILTON, AC, for L11-6-3,
            195 acres on branch of Elk Island. Lines: JNO. JOPLIN. Wit:
RO. CHRISTIAN, THOS. WINGFIELD, WM. RIDGWAY, HENRY BELL.

Page 24.   6 Oct 1769.   PETER RUCKER, Orange Co, to BENJ. RUCKER, AC, for
            L32-10, 526 acres. Lines: BENJ. RUCKER, ROSE's patent. Wit:
EZEK. REMEDY(?), ANTHONY RUCKER, AMBROSE RUCKER.

Page 25.   6 Nov 1769 (recorded). LEONARD TARRANT, Jr, AC, to CHAS. BUR-
            RUS, Alb., for blank sum, 433 acres both sides of Bever creek,
branch of Buffalo - part of 674 acres which TARRANT bought from WILLIAM
CABELL JR. & rec. in AC. Wife of TARRANT ment., but not named.

Page 25.   6 Nov 1769.   JOHN TARRANT, AC, to CHAS. BURRUS, Alb., blank sum, 241 acres on both sides of Bever, branch of Buffalo. Part of 674 acres which LEONARD TARRANT bought of WM. CABELL, JR., and rec. in AC. Lines: CALEB WORLEY, THOS. PARKS, RO. WHITTEN, JER. WHITTEN. Wife of TARRANT mentioned, but not named.

Page 26.   6 Nov 1769.   JOHN WEBB & wife USLEY, AC, to JOHN HARPER, Sr., and Jr., AC, for Ł50, 270 acres S side and joining Tye. Land bought by WEBB from NATHL. WOODROUGH; WOODROUGH got it from VALENTINE BALL by sale and rec. in AC. Wit: JAS. PAMPLIN, AUGUSTINE WRIGHT, WM. BICKNELL.

Page 27.   7 Nov 1769.   WILLIAM MORRISON, AC, to MICHL. MORRISON, AC, for Ł4, 125 acres on both sides of Cub, a branch of Hickory Creek. Lines: THOS. & MICHL. MORRISON.

Page 28.   6 Nov 1769.   PHILLIP PAYTON & wife, WINNEFORD, AC, to PHILLIP THURMOND, AC, for Ł75, 422 acres on branch of Horsley. Lines: CHAS. TALIAFERRO, Widow CARTER.

Page 29.   2 Nov 1769.   PETER CARTER & wife MARY ANN, AC, to WILLIAM WAUGH, AC, for Ł31-5-6, 179 acres in coves of Tobacco Row Mt. Lines: Col. LUNSFORD LOMAX.

Page 30.   4 Feb 1770.   DANIEL BURFORD, AC, to MILES BURFORD, AC, for Ł25, 166 acres waters of Fluvanna and Bolling's Creek. Lines: LYNCH. Pat. to DANL. BURFORD 10 Sep 1767. Wit: JNO. FLOYD, ELIZ. GOODWIN, VA. BURFORD.

Page 31.   5 Feb 1770.   Agreement between THOS. WRIGHT & WM. BURT, both of AC - May 13, 1765; BURT conveyed slaves to WRIGHT by deed and hereby WRIGHT agrees to maintain BURT in a "plaindecent" manner. Wit: W. HANSBROUGH, JAS. SYMMONS.

Page 31.   5 Feb 1770.   WM. BURT, AC, to THOS. WRIGHT, AC, - BURT for love and affection borne my beloved brother, THOS. WRIGHT, conveys three slaves, Jack, Mary and Ben to WRIGHT. Wit: JAS. SYMMONS, W. HANSBROUGH.

Page 32.   1 Dec 1769.   JAS. MONTGOMERY, AC, blacksmith, to JNO. LYON, AC, planter. (Orig. delivered to JNO. BAILEY by LYON's order 16 Oct 1783), for Ł50, 200 acres, land SAML. MILLER bought of JNO. BURNS 10 Apr 1755, and by MILLER conveyed to JAS. MONTGOMERY 7 Dec 1761. South of and adj. Cove creek. Part of a larger tract of 222 acres pat. to JNO. BURNS 24 Apr 1753. Lines: Capt. CHAS. LEWIS, and observed that the whole 222 acres described, but 22 acres sold to ALEX. CHISUM by BURNS. Lines: side of a mt., JAS. LEWIS. Twig and parcel delivery.

Page 33.   19 Oct 1769.   PEYTON RANDOLPH & JNO. ROBINSON, exrs. of will of PHILIP GRYMES, and LUNSFORD LOMAX, Jr., to SAML. MURPHY, AC. LUNSFORD LOMAX, Caroline Co, 7 Aug 1756, rec. in General Court on 21 Oct of that year - to secure payment of money loaned to him by PHILIP GRYMES, late of Middlesex - 7881 acres in AC - this sale is agreeable to all parties - Power of atty. to WM. CABELL, the Younger, to convey - LUNSFORD LOMAX and wife JUDITH, 13 Jan 1767, conveyed to LUNSFORD LOMAX, Jr, and now for Ł39-17-6 paid by S MURPHY, 159½ acres, land formerly granted to HARMER, KING, RANDOLPH & LOMAX by Council order. On branch of Tye. Lines: LOMAX & KING. Wit: WM. LOVING, ZACH. TALIAFERRO, WM. BIBB, JAS. YOUNG.

Page 35.   5 Feb 1770.   HUGH PATRICK & wife SUSANNA, to JNO. KEY, JR, AC, for Ł45, 59 acres on S side Fendley's Mt.; part of 400 acres late property of LUNSFORD LOMAX, JR, and by him conveyed to HUGH PATRICK. Lines: RICH. PRICHARD, JACOB EADES. Wit: HENRY KEY, JEREMIAH PATRICK, JACOB EADES, WM. CABELL JR.

Page 36.   1 Jan 1770.   TERISHA TURNER, AC, to JAS. TURNER, AC, for Ł20, 150 acres on N side of Rockfish and where JAS. TURNER now lives. Lines: old pat. line; side of a mt.

Page 37.   5 Mar 1770.   JNO. KEY, JR., & wife, AGNES, to JNO. CRAGHEAD,

AC, for Ł40, 170 acres Lackey's Thoroughfare and both sides of N branch Davis Creek. 71 acres pat. to HENRY KEY 10 Sep 1760, and by him to JNO. KEY, JR. Lines: JAS. LACKEY. 99 acres pat. to JNO. KEY 26 Jul 1765.

Page 38. 5 Mar 1770. PHILIP GRYMES exrs - for particulars see p.33 to JOHN CARGWRIGHT. Ł59-12-6 for 265 acres on Tie. Lines: RICH. ALCOCK.

Page 40. 4 Sep 1769. ZACHARIAS TALIAFERRO & wife MARY, AC, to CHAS. TALIAFERRO, AC, for Ł200, 2 tracts on borh sides of Puppie's Creek, lower tract of 400 acres. Lines: JNO. THRASHER; crossing creek; spur of Taliaferro's Mt. Other tract of 380 acres on both sides of creek and separated from the first by land of CHAS. TALIAFERRO. Wit: THOS. LANDRUM, RICH. TANKERSLEY Jr., JACOB SMITH, HENRY ROSE, FRANCIS MERIWETHER, JNO. TALIAFERRO.

Page 41. 6 Feb 1770. AMBROSE JONES to JNO. CARTWRIGHT of Province of Maryland, for Ł130, 135 acres N side of Tye, part of larger tract granted by Order of Council to RO. ROSE, Clerk, and THOS. CHEW and sold by ROSE to JONES and by JONES to JNO. GIZAGE FRAZER on 8 Oct 1768; deed from ROSE to JONES rec. in Alb. Wit: HUGH ROSE, GABL. PENN, THOS. WORTHAM, EDMD. WILCOX.

Pagd 42. 6 Nov 1769. JNO. SMALL, AC, to MW. ROBERTSON, AC, for Ł20, 100 acres Rockfish - surveyed by JNO. SMALL on 25 Apr 1754; part of tract granted to JNO. CHISWELL, Gent, of Hanover on S side of Rockfish. Lines: SAML. BELL, JOS. BARNETT. Wit: ALEX. PATTON, CHAS. YANCEY, WM. PATTON, JOS. MILLER, JAS. MAXWELL.

Page 43. 12 Dec 1769. WILLIAM PENN, AC, to JOSHUA HUDSON, St. Thomas Parish, Orange Co, for Ł100, 173 acres. Lines: GABL. PENN, JNO. BANGER, top of Turkey Mt. Wit: GABL. PENN, RICH. GATEWOOD, JNO. ROWSEY. (Note: JOSHUA HUDSON had a large family as shown by his will here. One daughter, NANCY ANN - called NANCY and ANN in various data - married here in 1777 WM. GILLESPIE. They removed to Madison Co, Ky, and GILLESPIE was killed there in a duel. They had a daughter, MARY ANN, who married HENDERSON THURMAN and my wife, MILDRED MILLER DAVIS, is a descendant of this couple. The HUDSON family is very large in present Amherst and one of them still owns land on Turkey Mt. I have located the site of the old home and graveyard. Joshua married MARY TERRELL, but we have not record save mention of her in will in Orange of RO. TERRELL who was her father. We have recently been able to trace the HUDSON family back to the Eastern shore via WESTMORELAND HUDSON who stemmed from them.)

Page 45. 20 Feb 1770. JOHN DAVIS, AC, to SAML. WOODS, AC, for Ł15, 46 acres on a branch and mt. on N side of Rockfish. Lines: JNO. MOUNTGOMERY, Col. CHISWELL. Wit: WM. HENDERSON, JNO. KEY JR., JAS. TULEY, JR.

Page 46. 4 Jul 1769. EDWARD BOLLING, Chesterfield Co., to GEO. STOVAL, AC, for Ł100, 50 acres N side Fluvanna - 3 small branches. Wit: DANL. BURFORD, WM. MITCHELL, JOS. GOODWIN, JNO. WIATT.

Page 47. 22 Jun 1769. Deed of Trust by JNO. HOWARD, Augusta, to BENJ. HOWARD & WM. LEAK, Buckingham Co, and Tillotson Parish. Slaves; Great George, Kate, Cato, Betty, Little Geo. Hannah Rockfish, Peter and Moll, and penknife. Wit: WM. LOVING, JOS. CABELL, CHAS. MAY, THOS. COBBS and JNO. COBBS.

Page 47. 1 Dec 1769. ABRAM SMITH, AC, to JOEL CRAWFORD, AC, for Ł20, 125 acres on branch of Rucker's Run and Hatt creek. Pat. at Williamsburg to ABRAHAM SMITH 10 Sep 1767. Lines: BENJ. DENNEY.

Page 49. 5 Mar 1770. WILLIAM BIBB, AC, to THOS. DICKERSON, AC, for Ł15, 97 acres pat. at Williamsbyrg to WM. BIBB 10 Sep 1760. Both sides of Indian Creek. SARY, wife of WM. BIBB.

Page 50. 9 Aug 1769. DANL. McCANE, AC, to JNO. McCLURE, AC, for Ł32, 150 acres branch of Rockfish. Lines: EDWD. MALLOY (MOLLOY), CLAPBURN, CHISWELL. Wit: FRANS. MERIWETHER, FRANCIS TURNER, JNO. HENDERSON.

Page 51.   5 Mar 1770.   JOS. MAGANN, AC, to WM. GARLAND, AC, for Ł10, 30
            acres Harris Creek and part of where MAGANN'S Ordinary now
stands. Lines: GAINES, RUCKER. Margin: Del. to D.S. GARLAND 10 Sep 1798.

Page 51.   4 Dec 1769. JNO. MONTGOMERY, AC, to MATT HARRIS, AC, for Ł80,
            98 acres branch of Rockfish. Lines: WM. WRIGHT, Col. JNO.
CHISWELL. Pat. to JNO. MONTGOMERY 25 Sep 1762. Wit: JNO. PHILLIPS, JNO.
REID, THOS. EWERS, FRANCIS MONTGOMERY.

Page 52.   4 Dec 1769. JNO. MONTGOMERY, AC, to MATT. HARRIS, AC, for Ł20,
            84 acres S branch of Rockfish. Lines: SAML. SHELTON, JAS.
MONTGOMERY. Pat. to JNO. MONTGOMERY 10 Sep 1767. Wit: Same as p.51.

Page 53.   6 Mar 1770. PEYTON RANDOLPH, BENJ. GRYMES, JOHN ROBINSON,
            Gents. and Exrs. of PHILIP GRYMES, dec'd, to JAS. & SAML. ED-
MONDS - for particulars of this tract see p.33 herein. For Ł95, 500
acres on branch of Tye. Lines: WM. BIBB, Naked Creek, Lick Branch, MUR-
PHY. Margin: orig. delivered.

Page 55.   19 Mar 1770.   JACOB EADES & wife, ANN, AC, to JAS. MATTHEWS,
            AC, for Ł20, 50 acres on branch of Purgatory Swamp below
Fendley's Gap. Lines: WM. LOVEDY. Conveyed to JACOB EADES by LUNSFORD
LOMAX, JR. 7 Dec 1767 and rec. in AC. Wit: HENRY KEY, RICH. PRICHARD,
WM. KEY, JNO. KEY, JR.

Page 57.   Same parties as p.55. 19 Mar 1770. for Ł26, 99 acres on
            branch of S fork of Rockfish. Lines: Col. LOMAX. Pat. to
EADES 25 Sep 1762. Wit: Same as above.

Page 57.   5 Apr 1770. LUNSFORD LOMAX, JR., Caroline Co, to JAS. STE-
            VENS, AC, for Ł40, 437 acres Rucker's Run. Lines: FURBUSH,
HARMER. Another tract on the Run of 88 acres and next to upper part of
437 acres. Lines: near WHITTON's Cabbin; under a mt.   Part of 6134 acres
conveyed to LUNSFORD LOMAX, JR. 13 Jan 1767, by LUNSFORD LOMAX, the Elder
and wife JUDITH 13 Jan 1767. The Elder got it from BENJ. WALLER, atty.
for WALTER KING, Bristol merchant, and THOS. MANN RANDOLPH, 1 Dec 1764,
and rec. in General Ct. Wit: ZACH. TALIAFERRO, DAVID MONTGOMERY, JNO.
MONTGOMERY, THOS. WORTHAM.

Page 59.   8 Nov 1769. JONATHAN JOHNSON, AC, to PHILIP PENN, AC, for Ł30,
            200 acres on N branch Buffalo and pat. to CHAS. PARKS at Will-
iamsburg 16 Aug 1756. Sold by PARKS to JOHNSTON (sic). Lines: BRAXTON,
JAS. WILLIAMSON. Wit: GABL. PENN, MOSES PENN & JOHNSON BEAN.

Page 60.   17 Apr 1770. PAYTON RANDOLPH, BENJ. GRYMES & JNO. ROBINSON,
            Gents., exrs. of PHILIP GRYMES, and LUNSFORD LOMAX, the
younger, Caroline Co., to GEO. GILLESPIE. (See MURPHY from GRYMES, p.33,
for details.) For Ł89-5, 875½ acres on Tye River. Lines: CARTWRIGHT,
ROSE, JONE, sapling on a mt., EDMONDS. Wit: ZACH. TALIAFERRO, RODERICK
McCULLOCH, THOS. MITCHELL, THOS. HAWKINS, THOS. REID, AMBROSE JONES.
(GILLESPIE was ancestor of my wife, MILDRED MILLER DAVIS. His son, WM.,
married NANCY ANN HUDSON and they removed to Madison Co, Ky. GEO. is
found in Albemarle when he and wife, MARY, show in a deed. This wife
was mother of his children and was probably a MOORE for the MOORE name
is used for two of GEORGE's children: one was Capt. SHEROD MOORE GILLES-
PIE who was a Revolutionary soldier. He later married a widow, MARY
FARIS, in Louisa and at least two of his children married FARIS girls.
He later made a swap with the ROSE group and moved up on Piney River. He
is buried at foot of Little Friar Mt. It took me several years to locate
the site, but I finally found a copy of the deed by AMHERST GILLESPIE
heirs wherein they sold 404 acres on Piney to DAVIS S. GARLAND and reserved cemetery site where "our father GEORGE is buried". A surveyor's
plat is with the old deed in the hands of the TAYLOR WRIGHT family.)

Page 62.   17 Apr 1770. GRYMES group above to LEONARD TARRANT, for Ł70,
385 acres on branch of Tye. Lines: WRIGHT, N side of Tye; Naked Creek;
WILCHER. Wit: ZACH. TALIAFERRO, THOS. MITCHELL, THOS. HAWKINS, AMBROSE
JONES, GEO. GALASBEY, MOSES CAMPBELL.

Page 64.   17 Apr 1770. GRYMES group to RICH. TANKERSLEY, the younger,

for Ł10-2-9, 174 acres. Lines: GALASBEY, ROSE, DILLARD. Wit: ZACH. TAL-
IAFERRO, THOS. MITCHELL, ROD. McCULLOCH, THOS. REID, GEO. GALASBY.

Page 66.   17 Apr 1770. GRYMES exrs. to MOSES CAMPBELL for Ł30, 199 ac-
            res on branch of Tye. Lines: WILTSHIRE. Wit: ZACH. TALIAFERRO,
ROD. McCULLOCH, GEO. GALASBY, THOS. HAWKINS.

Page 69.   17 Apr 1770. GRYMES exrs. to AMBROSE JONES, AC., for Ł84-3,
            374 acres branch of Tye. Lines: CARTWRIGHT, ALCOCK, BLAIN.
Wit: ZACH. TALIAFERRO, CHAS. IRVING, JNO. SALE, THOS. MITCHELL, GEO.
GALASBY, MOSES CAMPBELL, THOS. HAWKINS.

Page 71.   17 Apr 1770. GRYMES exrs. to WILLIAM BIBB for Ł73-8-9, 587½
            acres on Tye. Lines: SAML. MURPHY. Wit: ZACH. TALIAFERRO,
THOS. MITCHELL, THOS. HAWKINS, AMBROSE JONES, GEO. GALASBEY, MOSES
CAMPBELL.

Page 74.   17 Apr 1770. LUNSFORD LOMAX, Jr., Caroline, to JESSE MILLS,
            for Ł60, 297 acres branch of Rucker's Run and part of 6134
acres etc. - see p.57 herein - LOMAX to STEVENS. Wit: ZACH. TALIAFERRO,
THOS. MITCHELL, ROD. McCULLOCH, THOS. REID, RICH. TANKERSLEY, RICH.
TANKERSLEY, JR.

Page 75.   2 Apr 1770. WM. BRAVES ASHBURN, late of Spotsylvania, to
            CALEB COLEMAN Ł9 for four years as apprentice to learn art of
carpenter and joiner.

Page 76.   17 Apr 1770. GRYMES Exrs. to THOS. WILSHER - see p.33 for de-
            tails of GRYMES - for Ł8-15, 174 acres on branch of Tye. Lines:
WILSHER, CAMPBELL, EDMONDS. Wit: ZACH. TALIAFERRO, ROD. McCULLOCH, THOS.
REID, RICH. TANKERSLEY SR. & JR.

Page 78.   17 Apr 1770. GRYMES exrs. to WM. LAVENDER - see p.33 for
            GRYMES - for Ł25, 546½ acres on branch of Tye. Lines: MILLS,
ALCOCK, KING. Wit: ZACH. TALIAFERRO, THOS. MITCHELL, THOS. HAWKINS,
AMBROSE JONES, GEO. GALASBEY, MOSES CAMPBELL.

Page 80.   7 Apr 1770. GRYMES exrs. to THOS. WORTHAM, AC,-see p.33 for
            GRYMES - for Ł10, 179 acres on Rucker's Run. Lines: BARNES,
KING, JAS. STEVENS, Wit: JAS. STEVENS, BENJ. TALIAFERRO, ZACH. TALIAFERRO,
FRANCIS GRAVES, JNO. GRIFFIN.

Page 81.   22 Jan 1770. JAS. WILLIAMSON to JAS. GATEWOOD. Bond for Ł200
            for 310 acres. Lines: EDWD CARTER, MARTIN TRAP, PHILLIP PENN,
WM. MAYS, JNO. KENADY. Pat. to WILLIAMSON at Williamsburg 16 Aug 1756.
Bond is null when fee simple conveyance is made. Wit: GABL. PENN, JESSE
KENNEDY.

Page 82.   4 Jun 1770. GEO. BLAIN, AC, to JNO. LYON, for Ł80, deed of
            trust - 5 sh. to secure payment - 202½ acres bought of LUNS-
FORD LOMAX, JR., by BLAIN. Wit: EDMD. WINSTON, WM. LOVING, HENRY KEY.

Page 84.   4 Jun 1770. WM. WHITESIDES, AC, to WM. MARTIN, AC, for Ł40,
            200 acres on N fork Davis Creek and branch of Rockfish. Lines:
WM. TROTTER. Half of a tract bought of WM. WRIGHT. Wit: JO. MEGANN,
MARTIN DAWSON, JAS. McNEEL(?). Signed WHITESIDES, but clerk has inserted
name of WM. WHITSETT. ELLINER, wife of WW.

Page 85.   1 Jun 1770. WM. COFFEE to DAVID BARNETT for Ł64-10, 120 acres
            where BARNETT lives on Cokse's Creek. Bought by WM. COFFEE &
his brother, JAMES COFFEE - fork of Elk Creek and both sides of Tye.

Page 87.   4 Jun 1770. AMBROSE JONES, AC, to THOS. GOLDSBY, Alb. Co, for
            Ł20, 98 acres pat. 10 Sep 1760, to JONES. N fork of Piney.
Wit: CHAS. IRVING, WM. WALTON, WM. MARTIN, WM. MONROE.

Page 88.   2 Jun 1770. SIMON DEHART & wife RACHEL, AC, to AARON DEHART,
            AC, for 5 sh., 108 acres both sides Porridge Creek. Lines:
WM. BROWN, part of tract of SIMON bearing date of 6 Sep 1762. Wit: DANL.
GAINES, JO. MORGAN, BATTAILE HARRISON, JNO. HARDWICK.

Page 89.   6 Aug 1770. GEO. STOVALL, AC, to EDWARD BOLLING, Chesterfield
            Co., for Ł100, 249 acres N side of Fluvanna. Lines: EDWARD
BOLLING. Signed: GEO. STOVALL JUNIOR.

Page 90.   12 Jul 1770. WM. STATON, AC, to CHRISTOPHER LYNCH, Bedford Co,
            for 5 sh., 59 acres and part of 400 bought by STATON of ROU-
LAND HORSELEY BIRKS on ---17--. Bank of Harris Creek. Lines: WAILES,
bank of Fluvanna. Wit: GEO. STOVALL, JR, BENJ. RUCKER, ANTHONY RUCKER,
JAS. FRANKLIN.

Page 92.   12 Jul 1770. WM. STATON, AC, to CHRISTOPHER LYNCH, Bedford Co,
            for Ł25-10, 59 acres and part of 400 acres. Release of inden-
ture upon payment of debt. Land described on page 90. Wit: same as p. 90.

Page 94.   6 Aug 1770. JOHN BALLEW & wife, MARY, AC, to ROBT. BALLEW,
            AC, for Ł50, 160 acres.

Page 95.   6 Aug 1770. LAWRENCE CAMPBELL & wife - not named - to VALEN-
            TINE COX for Ł10, 27 acres. Lines: GABL. PENN.

Page 95.   1 Jan 1770. WM. CABELL to JOSEPH MILSTEAD - lease of planta-
            tion where MIRTY CONNEL lived on Horsley Creek. From 1 Jan.
last, for 8 years. Yearly rent of Ł3-10 to work himself and children
only. Wit: WM. WALKER, JR. Memo: JOS. MILSTEAD is to plant 500 peach
trees and 100 apple trees and keep them from being destroyed by horses
and cattle.

Page 97.   28 May 1770. GEO. JEFFERSON, Pittsylvania, to BENJ. RUCKER,
            AC, for Ł65, 200 acres on Stovall Creek. Wit: ANTHONY RUCKER,
JAS. FRANKLIN, JNO. HARDWICK.

Page 98.   31 Mar 1770. JOEL FIELDS, AC, to NEIL CAMPBELL, Henrico, for
            Ł35, 150 acres and part of 450 acres pat. to Col. WM. CABELL
at Williamsburg 23 May 1760. Bought by FIELDS of JOHN PETER and rec. in
AC. Branch of Harris between the Bear and Cedar Mts. Lines: CABELL.
Wit: JOHN OLD, THOS. WORTHY, CLOUGH SHELTON, CHAS. IRVING.

Page 100.   6 Aug 1770. JNO. ROWZIE & wife MARY, to JNO. WRIGHT for Ł27,
            124 acres Head of branches on N side of Buffalo. Lines: EDWD.
CARTER. Signed: ROWSA.

Page 101.   6 Aug 1770. RICH. GATEWOOD & wife, ELIZ., to JOSHUA HUDSON for
            Ł60, 115 acres on N branch of Buffalo and part of tract of
CARTER BRAXTON; where GATEWOOD now lives. Lines: BANKS, GABL. PENN.

Page 102.   1 Sep 1770. CHAS. PATTERSON & wife, MARY, Buckingham, to WM.
            CABELL, the Elder, for Ł55, 37 acres N side and joining Flu-
vanna. Upper part of tract STEPHEN TURNA (sic) bought of JNO. HOWARD
and sold to PATTERSON; of record in AC. Wit: JOS. CABELL, GEO. BARCLAY,
RO. HORSLEY, JNO. HORSLEY.

Page 104.   - --- 1768. AUGUSTINE WRIGHT & wife, ALICE, AC, to THOS. WIL-
            SHER, AC, for Ł20, 150 acres, part of 341 acres bought by
WRIGHT of exrs. of PHILIP GRYMES & LUNSFORD LOMAX, JR. Wit: MINOS WRIGHT,
KILLIS WRIGHT, ALEX. CHISNAL.

Page 105.   3 Sep 1770. LEONARD TARRANT, JR. & wife, MARY, AC, to JOS.
            MAYS, AC, for Ł110, 385 acres on branch of Tye and Naked
Creek. Part of LOMAX tract.

Page 106.   11 Aug 1770. JNO. GRIFFIN, AC, to HENRY BARNS, AC, for Ł18-10,
            90 acres bought by GRIFFIN of JNO. DENNEY on branch of RUCKERS
Run. Wit: WM. DEAVER, WM. LOVING, THOS. PARRICK, THOS. WORTHAM.

Page 106.   25 Jun 1770. RO. BALLEW, AC, to EDWD. BOLLING, Chesterfield
            Co, for Ł20, 143 acres both sides Juniper Creek and N side of
Fluvanna. Lines: COL. JNO. BOWLING, another survey.

Page 107.   8 Sep 1770. GEO. JEFFERSON, Pittsylvania Co., to SAML. BAILEY,
            AC, for Ł15, 180 acres Stoval's Creek. Lines: BENJ. RUCKER.

Wit: BENJ. RUCKER, JOS. CREWS, JNO. HARDWICK, WM. FOWLER. (Original delivered to BENJ. RUCKER 7 Jun 1791 on order.)

Page 109. 8 Sep 1770. GEO. JEFFERSON, Pittsylvania Co., to JNO. HARD-
WICK, AC, for Ł145, 470 acres on Stoval's Creek. Lines: near
Lynch's Ferry Road. Wit: BENJ. RUCKER, JOS. CREWS, SAML. BAILEY, WM.
FOWLER, WM. WILLIS.

Page 110. 8 Sep 1770. GEO. JEFFERSON, Pittsylvania Co., to JOS. CREWS,
AC, for Ł50, 461 acres Stoval's Creek. Lines: FRY, SAML. BAI-
LEY. Wit: BENJ. RUCKER, WM. WILLIS, JNO. HARDWICK, SAML. BAYLEY (X),
WM. FOWLER (X).

Page 111. 18 Jun 1770. CARTER BRAXTON & wife, ELIZ., King Wm. Co., to
JOS. CABELL, Buckingham Co., for Ł300, 1200 acres N side &
joining Buffalo. Part of 25,000 acres pat. to GEO. BRAXTON 21 Nov 1743.
Lines: AMBROSE LEE, Dec'd, Glebe line, late JOHN BENGER, GABL. PENN, CAR-
TER BRAXTON. Wit: WM. CABELL, JR., BENJ. HOWARD, CORNL. THOMAS, CHAS.
LYNCH, JNO. TALBERT.

Page 113. 27 Sep 1770. THOS. REID, AC, to PETER CARTER, AC, for Ł80,
400 acres N side of a branch of Horsley. Lines: NATHL. DAVIS,
WM. CABELL, Col. LOMAX. REID bought it of JOB CARTER. Wit: ALEX. GOR-
DON, ABRAHAM NORTH, JOS. BANGON (X), SOLOMON CARTER.

Page 114. 5 Nov 1770. HUGH ROSE, AC, atty. for DUNCAN GRAHAM, Caroline
Co, to JNO. TINSLEY, AC, for Ł21-10, 86 acres Harris Creek.
Lines: SHELTON, MILLER, HARRISON, TINSLEY.

Page 115. 5 Nov 1770. HUGH ROSE, AC, atty. for DUNCAN GRAHAM, Caroline
Co, to RICH. SHELTON, AC, for Ł90-18, 697 acres Harris Creek.

Page 116. 5 Nov 1770. HUGH ROSE, AC, atty. for DUNCAN GRAHAM, Caroline
Co, to RICH. POWELL, AC, for Ł112-10, 320 acres Harris Creek.

Page 116. 5 Nov 1777(sic) RICH. PETER, AC, to CHAS. REYNOLDS, AC, for
Ł65, 179 acres Harris Creek. Lines: JAS. CREWS, PEARCE WADE.
(Orig. delivered to JNO. REYNOLDS July court, 1788, but line is drawn
through notation.)

Page 118. 5 Oct 1770. WM. MILLS, North Carolina, to JNO. LEWIS, AC,
for Ł25, 330 acres branch of Buck Creek of Pedlar. Lines:
THOS. MILLS, JNO. DAVIS, ISHAM DAVIS. Wit: DAVID CRAWFORD, ALEX. REID
JR., RICH. POWELL.

Page 119. 14 Apr 1770. THOS. HODGES to PHILIP SMITH waggon (sic) and 6
horses. Wit: ZACH. TALIAFERRO, DAVID CRAWFORD, CHAS.TALIAFERRO.

Page 119. 5 Nov 1770. WM. PHELPS & wife SARAH, Tilotson Parish, Buck-
ingham Co, to JAS. MARTIN, St. Ann's Parish, Albemarle, for
Ł100, 170 acres both sides of Raven Creek. Bought by PHILPS from Dr.
WM. CABELL.

Page 121. 5 Nov 1770. HENRY BELL & wife, SARAH, AC, to WM. DUVAL, AC,
for Ł20, 80 acres Lime Kill Creek. Lines: JAS. CHRISTIAN,
DAVID PATTERSON.

Page 122. 27 Aug 1770. HENRY CHILDRES & wife SUSANNA to WM. HIX, AC,
for Ł65, 138 acres branch of Huff and E side of Tobacco Row
Mt. Part of 276 acres which HC bought of WM. CABELL JR. Lines: Line of
marked trees to divide the 276 acres between HENRY & JNO. CHILDRES;
BENJ. STINNETT. Wit: JOS. CHILDERS, JNO. GOOLSBY, JOS. CHILDERS JR.

Page 123. 5 Nov 1770. WILLIAM GATEWOOD & wife ANN, AC, to DAVID BLY,
AC, for Ł25, 130 acres both sides Buffalo. Lines: JAS. FREE-
LAND, STANHOPE EVANS, JNO. FRY, JOHN HARVEY. Pat. to GATEWOOD - no date.

Page 124. 5 Nov 1770. DAVID BLY, AC, & wife MARY to LINN BANKS, AC, for
Ł15, 70 acres branch of Buffalo. Lines: GERRARD BANKS, JNO.
ROWZIE, MARTIN TRAP. Part of tract of JNO. OWNBEY JR. Wit: JAMES

HIGGINBOTHAM, JAS. GATEWOOD, RICH. GATEWOOD.

Page 126. 5 Oct 1770. JNO. SCOTT & wife MARGARET, St. Ann's Prish, Al-
             bemarle, to TERISHA TURNER, AC, for Ƚ155-14, 1557 acres branch
of Porrage, part of 2018 acres pat. to MARGARET FRY who has since married
JNO. SCOTT. Lines: Licking hold branch, JAS. LONDON. Wit: WM. CABELL,
CHAS. IRVING, PETER DAVIS.

Page 127. 7 Apr 1770. CHAS. IRVING, Factor for GEO. KIPPENS & Co, Glas-
             gow merchants, to JOHN RYAN. Deed of trust by RYAN to secure
his debt to KIPPENS & Co. 5 sh. from IRVING - land on Tye at mouth of
Cub creek. Lines: Col. JOHN ROSE, GEO. MONROE, WM. MOORE. Bought from
Col. JNO. SIMMS, Hanover, and rec. in AC. Also two slaves: Henry, a fel-
low about 22 and Danl. a boy about six. Debt due 1 Jun 1771. Wit:
REUBEN JORDAN, JNO. DIGGE, JNO. OLD, CLOUGH SHELTON.

Page 128. 9 Apr 1770. HUGH PATRICK & wife SUSANNA, to WM. LOVEDAY for
             Ƚ15, 60 acres branch of Purgatory. Part of 119 acres which
PATRICK got of LUNSFORD LOMAX, JR. Lines: RICH. PRICHARD, JACOB EADES.
Wit: JNO. FRY JR., HENRY KEY, JAS. MATTHEWS, RICH. PRICHARD, MARY PRICHARD.

Page 130. 5 Nov 1770. GEO. CARRINGTON, Cumberland Co, to DAVID WOODROOF,
             AC, for Ƚ10, 320 acres. Lines: JNO. OWNBY. Part of 6750 acres
pat. to GC 20 Jun 1753.

Page 130. 5 Nov 1770. GEO. CARRINGTON, Cumberland Co, to PETTIS THACK-
             ER, AC, for Ƚ14, 100 acres branch of Harris Creek. Lines:
THOS. WILLIAMS. Part of pat. of 6750 acres of 20 Jun 1753 to GC.

Page 131. 3 Dec 1770. JAS. MARTIN JR., AC, to SAML. FOX, AC, for Ƚ15,
             100 acres Pounder branch, part of 200 acres pat. to MARTIN,
no date. Lines: Top of Pounder Branch Mt.

Page 132. 8 Nov 1770. JNO. PARKS, AC, to MATT. TUCKER, AC, for Ƚ65,
             223 & 1/8 acres. Lines: E side of Piney Mt., top of Taliaferro
Mt. Wit: JOF(?) TUCKER, GEO. PENN, DRURY TUCKER. ANN, wife of PARKS.

Page 133.   Nov 1770. JOHN PARKS & wife ANN, AC, to MATT. TUCKER, AC,
             for Ƚ35, 266 acres both sides of Long branch of Buffalo.
Lines: EDWD. WARE, AARON HIGGINBOTHAM. Wit: JOF(?) TUCKER, GEO. PENN,
DRURY TUCKER.

Page 135. 8 Nov 1770. WILLIAM CARRELL & SAML. MARKSBURY to MATT TUCKER,
             AC, for Ƚ45, 276 acres Buffalo. Lines: JNO. PARKS, JR.,
Horsley Creek. Wit: JOF(?) TUCKER, GEO. PENN, DRURY TUCKER.

Page 136. 5 Nov 1770. HUGH ROSE, AC, atty for DUNCAN GRAHAM, Caroline
             Co., to ANTHONY STREET, AC, for Ƚ55-10, 372 acres. Lines:
POWELL, DAVIS.

Page 137. 3 Dec 1770. PETER FARRAR, AC, to ELIOT ROBERTS, AC, for Ƚ40,
             236 acres on both sides of Ivey Creek of Rockfish.

Page 138. 14 Nov 1770. LUNSFORD LOMAX JR., Caroline, to SAML. SHACKLE-
             FORD, AC, for Ƚ45, two tracts: 1) 1632 acres. Lines: THURMAN'S
gum on top of a mt., CHAS. TALIAFERRO. Part of 3553 acres on Horsley and
branches; pat. to LUNSFORD LOMAX SR. in 1764, and by Sr. and wife, JUDITH
to Jr., 13 Jan 1767. 2) 3 acres. Lines: CHAS. TALIAFERRO, Horsley. Title
from LL Sr. Wit: ZACH. TALIAFERRO, THOS. WORTHAM, JAS. STEVENS, HENRY
BARNS.

Page 139. 10 Nov 1770. JOEL WATKINS, Prince Edward Co, to RICH PETER,
             AC, for Ƚ42-10, 480 acres Cedar Creek. Lines: MARVEL STONE,
MICAJAH CLERK. Wit: CHAS. BURKS, DAVID BURKS, MATT. WILLSON.

Page 141. 10 Nov 1770. JOEL WATKINS, Prince Edward Co, to DAVID BURKS,
             AC, for Ƚ42-10, 392 acres on Cedar Creek. Lines: Davis road;
excepting the church with one acre. Wit: CHAS. BURKS, RICH. PETER, MATT.
WILLSON.

Page 142.   3 Dec 1770.   JNO. LOVING JR. & wife AMEY to JNO. TUGGLE for
Ł12, 42 acres. Lines: Col. LOMAX.

Page 143.   3 Dec 1770.   JNO. TUGGLE JR. to ABRAHAM SEAY JR. for Ł35, 98
acres on Rucker's Run. Lines: Col. LOMAX.

Page 144.   28 Nov 1770.   THOS. McLEAN, son of HENRY McLEAN, AC, apprentice
bond of self to OWEN HERNDON, AC, for 3½ years. Wit: SAML.
WOODS, WM. PATTON, JOS. HIGGINBOTHAM MORRISON, ROBT. JOHN KNIGHT.

Page 145.   4 Mar 1771.   GEO. McDANIEL & wife MARGARET, AC, to ABRAHAM
PENN, AC, for Ł5, 165 acres S branch Harris Creek and E side
of Tobacco Row Mt.

Page 146.   3 Nov 1770.   Marriage contract between JOHN SORRELS, AC, to
MARY COALMAN ELLICE (Probably ELLIS. BFD.) He covenants to
maintain her until death and then his erors. are to pay her Ł60 or Ł10
annually as long as she has been his wife. She may elect which payment,
but otherwise, 12 monts after his death she has no other dower claim except what he chooses to leave her by will. She promises to be a kind,
loving and obedient wife and "to be chaste and faithful to his marriage
bed until death and to demean myself as a wife ought to do according to
my Station in the world until death and agrees to abide by financial
covenant." If he outlives her, she loses right to will money as she
chooses, but if reverse is true, she may will it at her pleasure. Wit:
CALEB COLEMAN, JNO. DAWSON, SAML. GAY. (Note: This is one of several
marriage contracts which I have found in the deed books and which SWEENY
did not include in his excellent marriage data on Amherst marriages up to
1801. It is evident that he made no attempt to look for deed data on
marriages. Mary outlived her husband and data in Nelson is extant on her.)

Page 147.   4 Mar 1771.   ELISHA LYON & wife, MARY AC, to JOSEPH CREWS, AC,
for Ł70, 150 acres N fork of Stoval's Creek. Lines: FRY.

Page 148.   4 Mar 1771.   JOS. CREWS, AC, to ELISHA LYON, AC, for Ł125, 400
acres on both sides of N fork of Stoval.

Page 150.   4 Mar 1771.   JOS. CREWS, AC, to BENJ. RUCKER, AC, for Ł7-10,
130 acres. Lines: the creek. (Note: JOS. CREWS left a will and
in it stated that he has reason to believe that his son, JOS., is dead.
There are CREWS recorded in Madison Co, Ky., and I wonder if they tell
anything of this son. BFD.)

Page 151.   17 Jan 1771.   HENRY TENISON, AC, to NEILL CAMPBELL, Merchant
of Richmond - deed of trust to secure debt of Ł44-9-3, for 5
sh., 200 acres on Porridge. Wit: DANL. GAINES, JO. MAGANN, JAS. FRANKLYN.

Page 152.   4 Mar 1771.   JNO. JOPLIN (JOSLIN?), AC, to GEO. HILTON, AC,
for Ł25, 200 acres branch of Elk Island Creek, upper part of
400 acres. Wit: WM. HORSLEY, SAML. ALLEN, JESSE ALLEN.

Page 154.   4 Mar 1771.   HUGH ROSE, atty. for DUNCAN GRAHAM, Caroline Co,
to NICHL. DAVIS, Bedford, for Ł35, 200 acres on Fluvanna below
Tobacco Row Mt. and joining DAVIS. (Note: This is one of the common errors found here as to spelling of DAVIS & DAVIES. This man shows in
marriages as NICHL. CLAYTON DAVIES. It took me some time to straighten
out the errors in the will books for the indexer seemed to make no effort
to separate them and many of each family of DAVIS & DAVIES are incorrect-
ly indexed. I have not got them separated and corrected in my will note-
books for I have finished abstracting all will books from 1761 to 1919.
BFD.)

Page 155.   Commission to quiz MARGARET WHITE, wife of THOS. WHITE as to
deed to GILBERT HAY, 11 Nov 1766 deed. Done 28 Oct 1770, by
JNO. & HUGH ROSE & ZACH. TALIAFERRO.

Page 156.   11 Apr 1769.   JAMES CREWS & wife MILICENT, AC, sold to WM.
HUGHS 375 acres. Order to quiz MILICENT apart from husband.
Done by DANL. GAINES & AMBROSE RUCKER 28 Jul 1770.

Page 157.   6 May 1771.   JEREMIAH PATRICK & wife SARAH, AC, to ENOCH NASH
for £45, 400 acres which PATRICK bought from WILLIAM TERREL
LEWIS.

Page 158.   1 Apr 1771.   JOHN EASTAINS, Bedford Co, to BENJ. WRIGHT of AC
for £100, 137 acres on branch of Beaver Creek. Lines: HENRY
CHILDRESS (CHILDERS), RO. WHITTEN. Part of 400 acres belonging to RO.
WHITTEN by deed from WM. CABELL JR. Wits: ISAAC WRIGHT, GABL. PENN, JNO.
KENNEDY, WM. JOHNS, JOHN BURRES.

Page 159.   8 Apr 1771.   JOS. ALLEN & wife SARAH, AC, to JNO. HITE of AC,
for £23, 50 acres on S side and joining Money Run, a branch of
Tye. Pat. to ALLEN 20 Jul 1768. Lines: Stoney Run. Wit: JNO. ROSE,
STEPEHN JOHNSON, WM. HOUTCHINS.

Page 160.   6 May 1771.   DAVID WOODROOF, AC, to THOS. MERRITT, AC, for £19,
326 acres. Lines: CARRINGTON, RICH. SHELTON, D. WOODROOF, JNO.
OWNBEY. Part of 6750 acres pat. to GEO. CARRINGTON 20 Jun 1750.

Page 161.   4 May 1771.   JNO. HITE, AC, to JNO. ROSE, LEONARD TARRANT &
STEPHEN JOHNSTON - they are bond for HITE to JOSEPH ALLEN for
purchase of 50 acres. Wit: WM. WILSON, CHAS. SAUNDERS, JNO. DAVIS.

Page 161.   26 Apr 1770.   JOHN BROWN pedlar (so signed, but I am of opinion
that this is to locate him as living on Pedlar River.   JNO.
CHRISTIAN on Buffalo always signed as JNO. CHRISTAIN, B., to denote his
residence. BFD.) of AC - deed of trust - to GEO. KIPPEN & CO, merchants,
for £00 5 sh, 300 acres on branch of S Pedlar and next to JACOB BROWN.
Wit: WM. WILSON, NEILL JOHNSON, THOS. KEY.

Page 163.   12 Nov 1770.   LUNSFORD LOMAX, JR., of Caroline, to CHAS. TAL-
IAFERRO, AC, for £41, 732 acres. Lines: SHACKLEFORD, THERMON,
PAYTON. Part of 3553 acres on Horsley. Pat. to LOMAX SR. in 1764 and by
him and wife JUDITH, to Jr., 13 Jan 1767. Wit: ZACH. TALIAFERRO, HENRY
BARNS, RICH. TANKERSLEY, STEPHAN WATTS, WM. CRISP. Original delivered to
TALIAFERRO 2 Apr 1785.

Page 164.   12 Nov 1770.   LUNSFORD LOMAX JR., Caroline, to PHILIP PAYTON,
AC, for £57-10, 341 acres. Derivation of title as above.
Wit: ZACH. TALIAFERRO, and others as above.

Page 165.   12 Nov 1770.   LUNSFORD LOMAX JR., Caroline, to JNO. BROWN, AC,
for £139-7-7. Derivation of title as above, 500 acres. Wit:
Same as above. Margin: Delivered to BROWN.

Page 167.   12 Nov 1770.   Exrs. of PHILIP GRYMES - see MURPHY, p.33 - and
LUNSFORD LOMAX Jr. to WILLIAM CRISP for £27, two tracts on Tie
River. 1) 200 acres. Lines: TANKERSLEY, DILLARD, TARENT, WILCHER, EDMUNDS,
GALASPIE.   2) 71 acres. Lines: DILLARD, RICH. TANKERSLEY SR. & JR, ROSE,
LOMAX. Wit: ZACH. TALIAFERRO, STEPHEN WATTS, RICH. TANKERSLEY JR., HENRY
BARNS.

Page 169.   12 Feb 1771.   RICH. HARVIE, Albemarle Co., to WM. PENN, AC,
for £65, 329 acres both sides of the road; N side Buffalo
ridge; FRY. Pat. to HARVIE 5 Sep 1749 in Albemarle. Wit: GABL. PENN, WM.
WILSON, THOS. MITCHELL.

Page 170.   12 Oct 1770.   HENRY FRY to GEO. STOVALL for £100, 334 acres
near head of Bolling's Creek. Wit: PATRICK ROSE, WM. PENN,
JNO. HARVIE.

Page 171.   25 Mar 1771.   JNO. MURRELL, AC, to JNO. MARTIN, St. Ann's Parish, Albemarle Co, for £172, 172 acres, part of 207 acres pat.
to MURRELL at Williamsburg 26 Jul 1765. Head of Davis Creek. Lines: RO.
WRIGHT. Orig. del. to MARTIN.

Page 173.   4 Mar 1771.   NATHL. DAVIS & wife ELIZ., to JOSEPH EDWARDS, AC,
for £110, 331 acres on N branch of Horsley. Lines: Col. LOMAX.
Pat. to DAVIS 1 Jun 1750. Wit: FRANCIS WAINWRIGHT, LEA, NANCY SANDERS,
ELIZ. DAVIS.

Page 174. 4 Mar 1771. JOSEPH BALLINGER & wife SARAH, AC, to CORNL. SAIL
          (sic: actually SALE in most AC data.) for Ŀ100, 279 acres Bea-
ver Creek, part of tract and deed in AC. Lines: WM. MITCHELL. Wit: HENRY
FRANKLYN SR, JNO. FRANKLYN, JNO. SMITH.

Page 175. 6 May 1771. STEPHEN GOLDSBY & wife MARTHA, AC, to JNO. WEBB,
          AC, for Ŀ100, 150 acres branch of Harris between the Bair(sic)
and Cedar Mts. Lines: GOLDSBY, JOS. CHILDRESS.

Page 176. 12 Nov 1770. PHILIP GRYMES' exrs - see MURPHY, p.33 - to
          JOSEPH DILLARD for Ŀ40-17-6, 327 acres on branch of Tye. Lines:
TARRANT, DILLARD. Wit: ZACH. TALIAFERRO, HENRY BARNS, RICH. TANKERSLEY,
STEPHEN WATTS, THOS. WIATT, RODERICK McCULLOCH, Capt. AMBROSE RUCKER.

Page 178. 14 Jun 1770. JESSE MILLS, AC, to THOS. LUMPKIN, AC, for Ŀ100,
          297 acres bought by TL of LUNSFORD LOMAX JR. and rec. in AC.
Wit: GEO. PENN, ISAAC TINSLEY, GEO. McDANIEL, GEO. GALASPIE.

Page 181. 10 Jun 1770. JAS. DICKIE, King & Queen Co, to SAML. WOODS,
          AC, for Ŀ120, 123 acres. Lines: Mt. at the head of the creek,
Elk, Ivy thicket. Wit: JAS. BROWN, STEPHEN JOHNSON, THOS. BROWN.

Page 182. 24 Jun 1771. THOS. WIATT, AC, & wife SUCKIE to GABL. PENN,
          AC, for Ŀ21-5, 47½ acres. Lines: CHEWS old line, LAURANCE
CAMPBELL, GABL. PENN.

Page 183. 1 May 1771. JAMES KENNEDAY & wife SARAH, Albemarle, to WM.
          STEPHENSON, AC, for Ŀ30, 62 acres on Lynch's Creek. Lines: JNO.
ROBERTSON, Dec'd. Part of 123 acres "granted by deed" to JK. Wit: RICH.
and SAML. WOODS.

Page 184. 1 May 1771. JAS. KENNEDY & wife SARAH, Albemarle, to ROBT.
          STEPHENSON, for Ŀ22-10, 61 acres on Lynch Creek. Lines: JNO.
ROBERTSON dec'd, WM. STEPHENSON. Part of 123 acres granted by deed to
grantor.

Page 185. 1 Jul 1771. WM. CRISP & wife LUCY, to JOS. MAYS for Ŀ155, 200
          acres branch of Tye. Lines: TANKERSLEY, DILLARD, TARRANT,
WILSHER, EDMONDS, GALASPIE. Also 70 acres. Lines: DILLARD, RICH. TANKER-
SLEY, ROSE, LOMAX, old pat. line near a branch, RICH. TANKERSLEY JR.

Page 187. - -- 1771. MICHL. MORRISON, AC, to ELIOT ROBERTS, AC, for
          Ŀ40, 100 acres N branch of Rockfish, part of pat. of Col. CHAS.
LEWIS on ---. Lines: ELIOT ROBERTS, WM. MORRISON. Del. 7 Mar 1788.

Page 189. 28 Mar 1771. NEILL CAMPBELL, Henrico, to JOS. CHILDERS of AC
          for Ŀ35, 150 acres, part of 450 acres pat. to Col. WM. CABELL
at Williamsburg 23 May 1760. Bought by CAMPBELL from JOEL FIELDS and
rec. in AC. Branch of Harris between the Bar(sic) and Cedar Mts. Lines:
CABELL. Wit: WM. WILSON, WM. MITCHELL, CHAS. IRVING.

Page 190. 1 Jul 1771. WILLIAM HARRIS; Albemarle, to JOHN DIGGS, AC, for
          Ŀ50, 150 acres on N side of Rockfish. Part of tract bought by
WM. HARRIS from JACOB WRIGHT. Lines: WM. HARRIS, N side of the main road;
crossing Buck Creek. Wit: WM. HARRIS JR., JNO. MONTGOMERY, JOSIAH JOPLING.

Page 192. (We now begin a list of surveys made by WM. CABELL from 20 Jun
          1761 to 27 Jun 1771, inclusive. They show no locations, but
merely date and acres. I have never had time to work on the several old
plat books and surveys in the office. I have made no attempt to correct
variations in spellings of names, but simply copied them as written. The
columns are headed by dates, names and acres.) Line dividing Amherst Co.
from Albemarle Co. from the mouth of Green Creek to the Blue Ridge N 23,
30 West 21 miles and 296 poles. Dated 20 Jun 1761. (a = acres)

17 Dec 1761. CHAS. McANALLY 13 a.	9 Mar 1762 ELLICK DUGGINS 60 a.
2 Feb 1762 JACOB BROWN 90 a.	10 Mar " JAMES BIAS 230 a.
23 Feb " JOSEPH KINKEAD 60 a.	11 Mar " JNO. HOGG 63 a
8 Mar " ROBT. WHITTEN 32 a.	" " " WM. KIPPERS 82 a.
9 Mar " BENJ. NOEL 150 a.	12 Mar 1762 BENJ. HIGGINBOTHAM 236a.

13 Mar 1762 ISAAC MAYFIELD 200a.
" " " JOS. HIGGINBOTHAM 385a.
15 " " AARON HIGGINBOTHAM 190a.
16 " " CARNABY VEAL 215 a.
" " " ISAAC GIBSON 250 a.
17 " " WM. FLOYD 125 a.
" " " JNO. HIX 77 a.
19 " " HUGH MORRIS 200 a.
" " " CORNL. THOMAS 180 a.
20 " " CHAS. TULEY 63 a.
16 Apr " ROBT. JOHNSTON 99 a.
7 Oct " WILLIAM DIUGUID 116 a.
17 Jan 1763 HENRY KEY 82 a.
18 Jan " RICH. PRICHARD 80 a.
" " " JNO. SUTTEN FIELD 160 a.
19 " " WM. WATTS 70 a.
20 " " WM. WATTS 50 a.
" " " THEOPHILUS FAVERS 170a.
21 " " JNO. DENNY 142 a.
22 " " THEOPHIS FAVERS 170a.
14 Feb " ANNE NEAL 58 a.
" " " DAVID MONTGOMERY 22 a.
17 " " JAS. BARNETT 47 a.
18 " " RO. WRIGHT 20 a.
17 Mar " JAS. DILLARD 30 a.
" " " " " 400 a.
18 " " ANDREW TURNER 350 a.

Page 193 - Surveys continued
21 Mar 1763 RO. CAMPBELL 140 a.
" " " EDWARD EIDSON 180 a.
22 " " JOSEPH FROST 170 a.
" " " PETTIS THACKER 210 a.
23 " " MICAJAH TERRILL 32 a.
" " " " " 46 a.
24 " " JAS. WARREN JR. 30 a.
" " " WM. TACKET 244 a.
25 " " HENRY BELL 80 a.
1 Apr " HENRY KEY 97 a.
2 " " " " 400 a.
5 " " AARON HIGGINBOTHAM 99a.
" " " BENJ. HIGGINBOTHAM 130a.
6 Apr " JNO. ROBERTS 200 a.
" " " BENJ. HIGGINBOTHAM 200a.
7 " " JACOB BROWN 300 a.
" " " JNO. BROWN 120 a.
8 " " NICHL. PRIOR 330 a.
9 " " EDWD. WARE 250 a.
19 " " JNO.VALENTINE EATON 31a.
" " " DANL. ARON 25 a.
21 " " HENRY KEY 400 a.
" " " " " 266 a.
" " " " " 300 a.
15 Oct " JNO. RYON 60 a.
20 Feb 1764 ISHAM DAVIS 60 a.
" " " JNO. EDMANDS 197 a.
27 " " WM. CABELL JR. 99 a.
28 " " " " 480 a.
1 Mar " NICOLAS CABELL 190 a.
2 Apr " MOSES RAY 80 a.
4 " " JNO. LOVING JR. 42 a.
11 " " WM. HANSBROUGH 98 a.
16 " " THOS. DOSWELL and
JNO. DRUMMOND 3980 a.
21 Feb 1765 GEO. McDANIEL 330 a.
22 " " RICH. PETER 350 a.
23 " " AMBROSE RUCKER 90 a.
25 " " JOS. FROST 50 a.
27 " " JNO. SPEARS 345 a.
28 " " GEO. HELTON 223 a.

11 Mar 1765 CHAS. TULEY 220 a.

Page 194 - Surveys continued
12 Mar 1765 JOS. HIGGINBOTHAM 300a.
13 " " JAS. SMITH 200 a.
14 " " " " 322 a.
15 " " JAS.COLBARD BLAIR 166a.
" " " " " 154a.
16 " " JOS. HIGGINBOTHAM 70a.
" " " " " 96a.
18 " " BENJ HIGGINBOTHAM 54a.
19 " " THOS. POWEL 354a.
20 " " HENRY McGUFFEY 35a.
28 " " JNO. PHILLIPS 400 a.
11 Apr " THOS. SHANNON 60 a.
" " " HENRY McCLAIN 137 a.
12 " " RACHAEL MORRISON 32 a.
" " " JNO. KEY 185a.
13 " " JNO. KEY 35a.
9 Oct " NATHL. WOODROFF 126a.
25 " " FRANCIS MERRIWETHER 18
26 " " SAML. SHANNON 48 a.
29 " " JAS. BROWN 50 a.
" " " ZACHARIAS TALIAFERRO 62
30 " " JNO. PARSONS 50 a.
31 " " ZACH. TALIAFERRO 139 a.
2 Nov " WM. MONTGOMERY 38 a.
6 " " PHILIP WALKER 154 a.
" " " SAML. MARKSBURY 73 a.
8 " " EDWD. WARE 351 a.
11 " " ROBT. DAVIS 98 a.
13 " " JOSIAH ELLIS 254a.
14 " " WM. PRYOR 395 a.
15 " " " " 66 a.
16 " " JNO. BROWN 64 a.
18 " " JNO. BEAZLY 150 a.
20 " " SOLOMON CARTER 254 a.
29 " " ROWLAND ATKINS 95 a.
2 Dec " RICH. PETER 81 a.
3 " " RICH. ELLIOT 145 a.
5 Nov " ABRAHAM CHILDERS 47 a.

Page 195 - Surveys continued
5 Dec 1765 STEPHEN GOOLSBY 38 a.
13 " " ABRAHAM SMITH 125 a.
14 " " WM. DENNY 82 a.
" " " ALEX. McGLOHLIN 120 a.
16 " " WM. BIBB 170 a.
18 " " ANGUS FORBUS 45 a.
19 " " JNO. MOUNTGOMERY 84 a.
20 " " DAVID MOUNTGOMERY JR 71
" " " DANIEL CONNER 98 a.
9 Jan 1766 NATHL. WOODRUFF 318 a.
6 Feb " ZACH. TALIAFERRO 14 a.
7 " " JOSEPH BLAIN 166 a.
11 " " LEONARD TARRANT 191 a.
12 " " SAML. POE 48 a.
" " " JOSEPH ALLEN 50 a.
13 " " THOS. HAYS 50 a.
27 " " NATHL. WOODRUFF 70 a.
" " " GEO. JEFFERSON 400 a.
1 Mar " DANL. BUFORD 370 a.
" " " " " 377 a.
12 " " WM. FOWLER 147 a.
13 " " SAML. BAUGHN 230 a.
14 " " JNO. LAMASTER 67 a.
24 " " SAML. SHANNON 5 a.
27 " " JNO. McGUIRE 54a
28 " " JNO. MOUNTGOMERY 37 a.
29 " " JNO. SMALL 149 a.

Surveys continued
31 Mar 1766 JAMES THURSLER 95 a.
 3 Apr "   JAMES BARNETT 40 a.
 "   "   "   JAMES McALEXANDER 39 a.
 "   "   "   THOS. WEST 18 a.
 7   "   "   CHAS. TATE 54 a.
 8   "   "   JNO. LEVISTON 50 a.
 9   "   "   CHAS. WHITTEN 76 a.
10   "   "   WM. MUSTARD (?) 37 a.
28   "   "   JNO. NITE 192 a.
30   "   "   JNO. VICKERS 70 a.

Page 196 - Surveys continued
 1 May 1766 GEO. TAYLOR 70 a.
 2   "   "   JNO. PARSONS 128 a.
 3   "   "   CHAS. TYLER 95 a.
 3   "   "   JAS. TOLLY 66 a.
 3   "   "   DANL. ROYALTY 65 a.
 5   "   "   JNO. WILLIAMS 200 a.
22 Oct   "   WM. PENDLETON 64 a.
23   "   "   AMBROSE RUCKER 160 a.
27   "   "   ROBT. JOHNSTON 325 a.
28   "   "   JOSIAH ELLIS 32 a.
29   "   "   ROBT. JOHNSTON 98 a.
30   "   "   JOHN BELL 185 a.
31   "   "   BENJ. STINNETT JR. 400a.
 4 Nov   "   JOS. HIGGINBOTHAM JR 250
 4   "   "   FREDERICK HAYS 50 a.
 5   "   "   WALTER POWER 46 a.
 5   "   "   JNO. BLAN 154 a.
13   "   "   ZACH. TALIAFERRO 196 a.
15   "   "   WM. CARR 54 a.
17   "   "   HUGH MEANS 97 a.
18   "   "   ROBT. HAYS 143 a.
18   "   "   HENRY STRATTON 77 a.
20   "   "   WM. TROTTER 76 a.
21   "   "   WM. WRIGHT 97 a.
25   "   "   MILES RAILY 20 a.
25   "   "   THOS. BICKNELL 373 a.
26   "   "   ELLIOT ROBERTS 40 a.
28   "   "   CHAS. EVANS 90 a.
 1 Dec. "   JNO. MILLER 53 a.
 2   "   "   ALEX. REID JR. 80 a.
 3   "   "   JNO. LOVING 32 a.
 4   "   "   WM. LOVING 92 a.
 8   "   "   JAS. DILLARD 98 a.
12   "   "   PHILIP DAVIS 114 a.
15   "   "   THOS. CRAWLEY 71 a.

Page 197 - Surveys continued
16 Dec 1766 DAVID DAVIS 238 a.
17   "   "   SAML. POE 200 a.
19   "   "   JNO. ROSE 70 a.
26 Jan 1767 JOHN JOHNSTON 53 a.
28   "   "   BENJ. HIGGINBOTHAM 390a.
 6 Feb   "   JAS. CHRISTIAN 253
 7 Feb   "   "   "   250
20   "   "   JOEL CRAWFORD 38 a.
21   "   "   JNO. COFFEE 99 a.
21   "   "   JULIUS WEBB 133 a.
23   "   "   FRANCIS STEEL 60 a.
 4 Mar   "   RO. JOHNSTON 236 a.
 5   "   "   AMBROSE RUCKER 262 a.
 9   "   "   WM. CARREL 266 a.
11   "   "   JNO. BRYANT 220 a.
12   "   "   HENRY HARPER 235 a.
12   "   "   JNO. DUNCAN 265 a.
14   "   "   JAS. SMITH 54 a.
16   "   "   JACOB SMITH 33 a.
17   "   "   BENJ. ASBURY 237 a.

17 Mar 1767 JOS. HIGGINBOTHAM 99 a.
18   "   "   LEONARD BALLOWE 400 a.
19   "   "   "   "   390 a.
24   "   "   DANL. McBANE 23 a.
25   "   "   JNO. SMITH 49 a.
27   "   "   EDMUND COFFEY 200 a.
27   "   "   REUBIN COFFEY 78 a.
31   "   "   ALEX. REID JR. 84 a.
31   "   "   ALEX. REID 30 a.
 3 Apr   "   THOS. PHILLIPS 182 a.
10   "   "   BENJ. DENNEY 100 (199?)
13   "   "   JAS. MONTGOMERY 66 a.
14   "   "   JNO. SORREL 95 a.
15   "   "   ANGUS FORBUS 72 a.
17   "   "   JNO. BELL 84 a.

Page 198 - Surveys continued.
17 Apr 1767 LEONARD PHILIPS 98 a.
18   "   "   JOS. TURNER 315
20   "   "   HUGH WILLOUGHBY 300 a.
21   "   "   THOS. EADS 50 a.
22   "   "   ROBT. MONTGOMERY 60 a.
24   "   "   PAUL ABNEY 76 a.
25   "   "   THOS. MORRISON 124 a.
27   "   "   JAS. McALEXANDER 76 a.
 7 May   "   JNO. BLAN 99 a.
 7   "   "   CHAS. BLAN 200 a.
 8   "   "   WM. TAYLOR 276 a.
 9   "   "   ANGUS McDANIEL 99 a.
 9   "   "   JOSEPH KING 77 a.
 7 Oct   "   THOS. DOSWELL 204 a.
 8   "   "   "   "   178 a.
 9   "   "   ABRAHAM SMITH 890 a.
13   "   "   JAS. JONES 204 a.
14   "   "   "   "   320 a.
 6 Nov   "   THOS. DICKERSON 98 a.
11   "   "   JOS.HIGGINBOTHAM JR 396
13   "   "   WM. HIX 284 a.
16   "   "   WM. FLOID 300 a.
17   "   "   WM. PRYOR 90 a.
19   "   "   WM. HIX 320 a.
20   "   "   WM. TAYLOR 80 a.
21   "   "   JNO. HIX 90 a.
25   "   "   JNO. BROCK 99 a.
27   "   "   JAS. BRUMMIT 15 a.
27   "   "   JNO. MAYFIELD 60 a.
28   "   "   JNO. PHILLIPS 96 a.
 3 Dec   "   ANTHONY ROGERS 99 a.
 4   "   "   THOS. GRISSOM(UM) 123a.
 5   "   "   ABRAHAM PENN 16 a.
10   "   "   MATT. MOORE 50 a.
11   "   "   GILBERT HAY 46 a.

Page 199 Surveys continued
12 Dec 1767 PHILIP DAVIS 99 a.
28 Jan 1768 NATHL WOODRUFF 254 a.
28   "   "   THOS. EVANS 54 a.
17 Feb   "   JAS. DILLARD 99 a.
19   "   "   GEO. STOVAL JR. 240 a.
20   "   "   "   "   "   178 a.
22   "   "   JOS. CREWS 120 a.
22   "   "   BOYCE EIDSON 300 a.
 5 Mar   "   LEONARD BALLOWE 48 a.
 8   "   "   BENJ. HIGGINBOTHAM 75a.
 8   "   "   JOS. HIGGINBOTHAM 300a.
 9   "   "   AARON HIGGINBOTHAM 200
 9   "   "   SAML. MARKSBURY 99 a.
11   "   "   LEONARD BALLOWE 200 a.
12   "   "   ISAAC MAYFIELD 228 a.
14   "   "   NEILL CAMPBELL 115 a.

130

Surveys continued.
14 Mar 1768 ANGUS McDANIEL 82 a.
16 " " BENJ. MURRY 90 a.
17 " " ISON MATLOCK 350 a.
18 " " JNO. HIX 320 a.
31 " " JAS. MOBLEY 227 a.
1 Apr " PETER BIBY 99 a.
2 " " REUBEN TYREE 86 a.
12 " " WM. MARTIN 95 a.
13 " " JNO. CAMPBELL 54 a.
16 " " ROGER CASEY 28 a.
18 " " ROBT. JOHNSTON 300 a.
20 " " EDWD. MOSELEY 185 a.
22 " " ROBT. PAGE 54 a.
22 " " DANL. ROSS 46 a.
25 " " JOS. MORRIS 50 a.
25 " " ROBT. DAVIS 54 a.
27 " " JNO. PRICE 70 a.
30 " " JAS. TILFORD 93 a.

Page 200 Surveys continued
2 May 1768 JAMES BROWN 54 a.
3 " " JAS. BROWN 54a.
5 " " JOSEPH MAGANN 95 a.
9 " " ADAM REID 99 a.
9 " " CHAS. BOND 90 a.
10 " " NATHAN NUCKULS 54 a.
16 " " GEO. McDANIEL 54 a.
2 Sep " GEO. HILTON 350 a.
8 Nov " JNO. VIA 290 a.
15 " " RALPH BOWMAN 117 a.
16 " " JNO. LACKEY JR. 53 a.
16 " " WM. MORRISON JR. 66 a.
29 " " ROBT. JOHNSTON 195 a.
2 Dec " JNO. FLOYD 26 a.
3 " " JNO. ROBERTS 164 a.
12 " " TURNER CHRISTIAN 370 a.
13 " " WM. HENSON 86 a.
19 " " FRANCIS WEST 70 a.
20 Jan 1769 JNO. CHRISTIAN 400 a.
21 " " JAS. CHRISTIAN 47 a.
25 " " STANHOPE EVANS 350 a.
25 " " WM. GATEWOOD 130a
26 " " WM. BRUMMIT 35 a.
13 Mar " CHRISTOPHER LYNCH 40 a.
14 " " JNO. HARDWICK 340 a.
16 " " JONATHAN JOHNSON 350 a.
16 " " MICAJAH TERRELL 400 a.
17 " " HENRY HARPER 345 a.
17 " " MICAJAH MOREMAN 125 a.
18 " " MICAJAH TERREL 99 a.
20 " " SAML. BAUGHN 170 a.
20 " " WM. GUTTRY 99 a.
21 " " DANL. & JNO. BURFORD 400
22 " " GEO. STOVAL 40 a.
23 " " ABRAHAM EADS 154 a.

Page 201 - Surveys continued.
27 Mar 1769 JAS. MATTHEWS 92 a.
3 Apr " DAVID CHRISTIAN 99 a.
3 " " JNO. COTTRIL ½ a.
8 " " ZACH. TALIAFERRO 99 a.
10 " " JAMES WRIGHT 63 a.
11 " " PETER MARTIN 34 a.
13 " " JNO. MATTHEWS 46 a.
14 " " JNO. McGUIRE 99 a.
18 " " WM. STAPLES 220a
19 " " RACHEL MORRISON 32 a.
21 " " JNO. PRICE and
        JNO. McANALLY 70 a.

21 Apr 1769 JNO. PRICE and
        JNO. McANALLY 237a.
22 " " THOS. PANNAL 60 a.
25 " " GEO. MONROE 20 a.
4 May " JOSEPH LAYNE 90 a.
5 " " WM. LILLY 70 a.
6 " " JACOB BROWN 99 a.
8 " " THOS. TUNGET 165 a.
12 " " ROBT. WOOD 44 a.
13 " " SIMON DEHART 146 a.
17 " " MICAJAH TERREL 376 a.
9 Nov. " LUKE BINNION 164 a.
10 " " LEE HARRIS 62 a.
11 " " ROBT. MOUNTGOMERY 70 a.
13 " " JOEL CRAWFORD 184 a.
14 " " JNO. REID 200 a.
15 " " JAS. McALEXANDER 99 a.
17 " " ALEX. REID JR. 99 a.
18 " " WM. BARNET 47 a.
22 " " THOS. HEARD 40 a.
23 " " FRANCIS TURNER 86 a.
25 " " ALEX. REID 136 a.
27 " " SAML. WOODS 213 a.
7 Dec " CARNABY VEAL 50 a.
12 " " ROBT. JOHNSTON 140 a.
14 " " " " 328 a.

Page 202 Surveys continued.
15 Dec 1769 JNO. DUNCAN 126 a.
8 Feb 1770 JNO. CHRISTIAN and
        HENRY BELL 126 a.
9 " " WM. DUVAL 180 a.
20 " " DANL. BURFORD JR. 300 a.
21 " " GEO. McDANIEL and
        BATTLE HARRISON 127 a.
21 " " GEO. DAVIS 47 a.
22 " " JNO. COLEMAN 87 a.
22 " " JOS. CHILDRES 125 a.
23 " " THOS. LUCAS 37 a.
23 " " MOSES SWINEY 18 a.
27 " " THOS. EVANS 99 a.
9 Mar " JONATHAN JOHNSTON 340
10 " " JNO. HARDWICK 345 a.
14 " " ROBT. CHRISTIAN 279 a.
14 " " DRURY CHRISTIAN 96 a.
21 " " MATT. HARRIS 280 a.
22 " " DAVID MONTGOMERY 40 a.
23 " " HENRY WOODY 53 a.
24 " " WM. MARTIN 54 a.
27 " " WM. MAXWELL 38 a.
27 " " DAVID MERIWETHER 50 a.
28 " " ROBT. WEAR 18 a.
29 " " SPENCER RAYFIELD 70 a.
31 " " CHAS. TATE 70 a.
3 Apr " EZRA MORRISON 180 a.
7 " " WM. PRYOR 247 a.
9 " " JNO. JARVIS 99 a.
11 " " JOS. HIGGINBOTHAM 204a.
12 " " RICH. ELLIOT 50 a.
12 " " WM. EVANS 35 a.
17 " " JNO. OWNBY JR. 76 a.
23 " " JNO. ROUSY 130 a.
25 " " JNO. HOUTCHIN 114 a.
28 " " ANGUS McDANIEL 162 a.
1 May " JAS. MURRY 54 a.

Page 203 - Surveys continued.

1 May 1770 WM. FORBES 86 a.
2 " " EDMUND COFFEE 98 a.

Surveys continued
3 May 1770 ELIAS SMITH 99 a.
4 "   "   JNO. HITE 47 a.
5 "   "   PHILIP DAVIS 84 a.
10 "   "   JNO. LOVING JR. 65 a.
3 Jul "   JNO. COLEMAN and
              THOS. LUCAS 367 a.
16 "   "   JNO. COTTRIL 270 a.
26 Oct "   JNO. DAVIS 90 a.
27 "   "   WM. McBEAN 54 a.
7 Nov "   JNO. LOVING 20 a.
7 "   "   HENRY BARNS 30 a.
8 "   "   JNO. TUGGLE 82 a.
13 "   "   JOS. KING 96 a.
14 "   "   ALEX. LYALL 92 a.
15 "   "   "   " 46 a.
16 "   "   GEO. TAYLOR JR. 144a
16 "   "   WALTER POWER 99 a.
17 "   "   THOS. ROBERTSON 122a.
26 "   "   JNO. RYAN 140 a.
5 Dec "   LEONARD PHILLIPS 87 a.
6 "   "   ELLIOT ROBERTS 46 a.
7 "   "   THOS. JOPLIN 294 a.
10 "   "   GEO. CAMPBELL 54 a.
10 "   "   WM. HUMPHREY 204 a.
12 "   "   CHAS. TYLER 23 a.
13 "   "   AARON HIGGINBOTHAM 54 a.
22 "   "   WM. GATEWOOD 388 a.
14 Jan 1771 JNO. GREGORY 197 a.
14 "   "   CHAS. TRAYL 60 a.
7 Mar "   ABRAHAM SEAY JR. 45
12 "   "   THOS. FARRAR 54 a.
14 "   "   ELIOT ROBERTS 204 a.
16 "   "   JAS. BICKNELL 52 a.
16 "   "   THOS. MATTHEWS 64 a.

Page 204 - Surveys continued
18 Mar 1771 ANGUS FORBES 54 a.
20 "   "   DAVID DONAHOE 29 a.
28 "   "   ROBT. FREELAND 150 a.
29 "   "   WM. MIGGINSON 92 a.
4 Apr "   JAS. BIAS 53 a.
5 "   "   WM. HIX 74 a.
9 "   "   ROBT. JOHNSTON 294 a.
10 "   "   JOSEPH LAYNE 297 a.
11 "   "   BENJ. ASBURY 258 a.
12 "   "   WM. PRYOR 229 a.
15 "   "   JNO. THOMSON 219 a.
18 "   "   EDWARD BIGGS 65 a.
18 "   "   THOS. PANNELL 39 a.
20 "   "   LUKE PANNELL 134 a.
20 "   "   JNO. PANNELL 117 a.
22 "   "   JNO. REID 137 a.
23 "   "   LAURENCE SUDDETH 40 a.
24 "   "   WM. HORRALL 98 a.
24 "   "   JNO. WAID 17 a.
25 "   "   SAML. STAPLES 128 a.
27 "   "   WM. BICKNALL 160 a.
1 May "   JOS. HIGGINBOTHAM 275a.
3 "   "   THOS. GOOLDSBY 50 a.
4 "   "   HENRY CHILDERS 170 a.
6 "   "   WM. PAYTON 270 a.
8 "   "   ROBT. JOHNSTON 197 a.
9 "   "   "   "   204 a.
10 "   "   "   "   404 a.
10 "   "   "   "   280 a.
11 "   "   VALENTINE PAYTON 54 a.
13 "   "   PETER CARTER 50 a.
27 Jun "   WM. CABELL JR. 120 a.

Signed: W. CABELL JUNR, Sur. A Cty.

Page 205. 28 Nov 1770(?). Order to HUGH INNIS & PETER COPELAND to quiz
ELIZ. JEFFERSON, wife of GEO. JEFFERSON, Pittsylvania Co, as
to deed to JOS. CREWS on 20 Jul 1769, for 700 acres. Done 30 Mar 1771.

Page 206. 5 Aug 1771. RICH. FARRAR & wife SUSANNAH, Albemarle and St.
Anne's Parish, to THOS. FARRAR, same county and parish, for
Ł100, 189 acres, part of pat. of ABRAHAM WHITNEORTH on both sides of Rock-
fish, south side being sold and where THOS. now lives.

Page 207. 11 May 1771. ANTHONY STREET & wife ELIZ., AC, to NICHL. DAVIS,
AC, for Ł25-10, 170 acres on branch of Fluvannah or James
(Note: This river was first called the Fluvanna(h) and then deeds begin
to use both names. It is now known only as the James in AC and many do
not know of the first name by which it was called. BFD) Lines: RICH.
POWELL, THOS. MERRET. Wit: DANL. BURFORD, FICH. POWELL, JER. TAYLOR, FRAN.
GOODWIN, JOS. GOODWIN.

Page 208. 5 Aug 1771. THOS. MONTGOMERY & wife ANN; JAMES MONTGOMERY &
wife MARY to LEE HARRIS for Ł150, 500 acres on S side Rockfish.
Part of 11,140 acres pat. to JNO. CHISWELL at Williamsburg in 1739. By
BHISWELL to MICHL. MONTGOMERY and devised by MICHL. as father of the
above grantors. Lines: Davis Creek; S side of Rockfish, JOS. BARNETT,
FRANCIS WRIGHT.

Page 210. 17 Jul 1771. WM. BIBB & wife SARAH, AC, to WILLIAM DEAVER, AC,
for Ł12-10, 188 acres Rucker's Run. Lines: Col. LOMAX. Pat.
12 May 1770.

Page 212. 3 Aug 1771. WM. DEPRIEST & wife ANN, AC, to WM. CLARKE, AC,
for Ł80, 144 acres branch of Linch Creek - word Cold there-
after - Long branch on N side of Rockfish. Lines: LANGDON DEPRIEST, WM.
CLARK, MARGET BELL, JNO. ROBINSON, dec'd., WM. STEPHENSON. Wit: WM.
HENDERSON, SAML. WOODS, EDWD. STEPHENSON.

Page 213. 3 Aug 1771. LANGDON DEPRIEST & wife ANN, AC, to DAVID CLARK,
          AC, for £65, 128 acres Lynch Creek and N side Rockfish. Lines:
LANGDON DEPRIEST, WM. CLARK, JNO. ROBINSON, dec'd.

Page 215. 5 Aug 1771. JOS. MAYS (MAISE) and wife SARAH, to JAMES MOBLEY
          for blank sum, 400 acres Ballenger's Mt., Sycamore Longround
Creek, EDWD CARTER.

Page 216. 4 Feb 1771. JNO. LAIN, AC, to JNO. EDMONDS & THOS. WILSHER
          for £11-14-6, one bay horse branded "FB", one "rifle gun".
Wit: WM. HANSBROUGH, MENOS WRIGHT.

Page 216. 2 Sep 1771. WM. ROBERTSON, AC, to JNO. PUCKETT, AC, for £50,
          100 acres S side and joining Rockfish. Part of tract pat. to
JNO. CHISWELL and surveyed for JNO. SMALL 1 Apr 1754. Lines: SAML. BELL
on S side of river; JOS. BARNETT. Wit: EDMD. WILCOX, G. WALKER JR., JNO.
WIATT.

Page 217. 16 Aug 1771. JNO. SMALL, AC, to JAS. WOODS, AC, for £50, 150
          acres on N side & joining Rockfish. Lines: Col. JNO. CHISWELL,
JNO. LYONS. Wit: SAML. WOODS, OWEN HERNDON, GEO. DIVERS. MARGARET, wife
of JNO. SMALL.

Page 219. 16 Aug 1771. JNO. SMALL, AC, planter, and wife MARGARET, to
          JAS. WOODS, AC, for £50, 156 acres N branch of Rockfish. Lines:
JNO. LYON, JAS. LYON, JNO. FARROR. Part of 400 acres bought by SMALL of
Col. JNO. CHISWELL and rec. in Albemarle; where SAMLL now lives. Wit:
same as previous deed.

Page 220. 3 Sep 1771. ELIAS SMITH, AC, to WM. GARLAND for £70, 84 acres
          N side of Cub Creek. ANN, wife of SMITH. Margin: Orig. del.
to D.T. GARLAND, Aug 1788.

Page 221. 25 Mar 1771. JOS. BALLENGER, AC, to SAML. HANCOCK, AC, for
          £5, 247 acres in two parcels: 1) 114 acres top of Smith's Mt.
and coves on side. Lines: WM. CABELL, JR., JON BALLENGER. 2) 133 acres.
Lines: a branch, FRANKLYN. Wit: HENRY FRANKLYN SR., RICH. BROOKS, JEAN
SALE, JEAN GARRASON, CORNL. SALE.

Page 222. 2 Sep 1771. PATRICK MORRISON & wife BETTY, AC, to NICHL.
          MORAN, for £25, 50 acres on small branch of Piney River.
Lines: PHILLIP DAVIS, ROSE.

Page 223. 2 Sep 1771. MARTIN TRAP & wife MARY, AC, to VALENTINE COX &
          JNO. SWANSON, AC, 111 acres on N branch of Buffalo. Lines:
JAS. WILLIAMSON, JNO. ROWZIE, CARTER.

Page 224. 7 Oct 1771. JOS. RICHARDS & wife MARY, Pittsylvania, to ROBT.
          MAYS, AC, for £25, 200 acres; crossing Stone House Creek.
Wit: EDMD. WILCOX.

Page 226. 5 Oct 1771. MICAJAH CLARK, Albemarle, to NEILL McCANN, AC,,
          for £50, 400 acres N fork of Maple Creek. Lines: MARVEL STONE,
MARGARET STONE. Wit: JNO. HARVIE, ROBT. HART, MICAJAH CLARK JR., RICH.
HARVIE.

Page 227. 1 Oct 1771. WM. LOVING & wife BETTY, AC, planter, to JNO.
          JOHNSON, AC, carpenter, for £30, 98 acres. Lines: JNO. LOVING
JR. Bought by WM. LOVING of JNO. LOVING 6 Jun 1768. Margin: Del. to JOHN
JOHNSON 2 Apr 1774.

Page 228. 7 Oct 1771. SAML. MARKSBURY, AC, to ZACH. TALIAFERRO, AC, for
          £100, 99 acres Tie River. Lines: ZACH. TALIAFERRO, ROSE. Part
of tract granted JAS. CHURCHILL and by him sold to SAML. MARKSBURY, the
Elder, dec'd, and it fell to SAML. MARKSBURY, the younger, as heir at law.
Wit: JNO. ROSE, WM. HIGGINBOTHAM, ISAAC MAYFIELD, JOS. HIGGINBOTHAM JR.,
JNO. HIGGINBOTHAM, JR.

Page 230. 18 Sep 1771. WM. HUMPHREY, AC, to THOS. MITCHELL, Factor for
          JAS. & RO. DONALDS & Co, Glasgow merchants, for £52, 204 acres

S side of Depriest Mt. and next to Dr. WM. CABELL, HENRY KEY, JAS. DICKEY and PHILIP DAVIS. Also cattle & furniture. Deed of trust. Wit: DAVID SHEPHERD, JNO. McKINDLEY, AARON HIGGINBOTHAM.

Page 231.   7 Oct 1771.   JNO. ROARK & wife CATHERINE, AC, to JNO. PENN, AC, for Ƚ28-13-6, 31 acres S bank of Huff creek and S branch of Buffalo. Wit: CHAS. STATHAM, EDMD. HODGE.

Page 233.   19 Jun 1771.   MARY SHANNON, AC, to JNO. STRATTON, AC,- horse, cows, hogs, furniture, pewter, iron puts etc. Wit: ABRIM STRATTON, WM. LEAN, JAS. SHANNON.

Page 233.   18 Nov 1770.   Order to King William J.P.'s: JNO. QUARLES & WM. BURNETT BROWN, to quiz ELIZ. BRAXTON, wife of CARTER BRAXTON, as to deed on 18 Jun 1770 to JOS. CABELL; 1200 acres. Done 13 Sep 1771.

Page 234.   15 Aug 1771.   AMBROSE PORTER & wife JIMIMIA, to JNO. SCOTT for Ƚ130, 310½ acres on S branch of Buffalo. Lines: DRURY TUCKER. Wit: GABL. PENN, THOS. LUMPKIN, BENJ. TALIAFERRO, AARON HIGGINBOTHAM.

Page 236.   2 Sep 1771.   WM. FOWLER & wife MARY, AC, to SAML. BAILEY, Albemarle and St. Ann's Par., for Ƚ30, 147 acres on head branch of Stoval. Lines: MICAJAH CLARK, Lynch road, GEO. JEFFERSON.

Page 237.   4 Nov 1771.   JNO. FITZPATRICK & wife FRANCES, Albemarle, to WM. FITZPATRICK, AC, for Ƚ25, 170 acres on head branch of N fork of Nassau and part of where WM. lives. (Note: Nassau and Dutch Creek are names used for the same creek with is now generally known as Dutch in present Nelson county BFD.)

Page 238.   4 Nov 1771.   WM. FITZPATRICK & wife REBECCA, AC to JOSIAH WOOD for Ƚ5, 50 acres. Lines: FITZPATRICK, WOODS, top of the Mt.

Page 239.   23 Oct 1771.   MATT. ROBERTSON, Augusta Co, to JAS. HENDERSON, AC, for Ƚ40-10, 240 acres on branch of Rockfish. Lines: RO. WARE, JNO. HENDERSON, EDWD. STEPHENSON. Wit: GEO. DIVERS, JOS. ROBERTS, JNO. HENDERSON, WM. HORRALL.

Page 241.   2 Nov 1771.   EDWD. TINSLEY, AC, to his son, JNO. TINSLEY, AC, for five shillings and love borne for son - 115 acres on both sides of Harris Creek. Part of tract bought by EDWD. from DUNCAN GRAYHAM, Caroline Co, and rec. in AC. Lines: JNO. TINSLEY, ROSE, MILLAR. Wit: JNO. COLEMAN, JNO. WEB, JOS. MAGANN, GEO. McDANIEL, THOS. LUMPKIN.

Page 242.   3 Nov 1771.   EDWD. TINSLEY & wife MARGARET, AC, to their son, DAVID TINSLEY, AC, for five shillings & love - 122 acres on both sides of Harris. Derivation of title as above. Wit: same as above.

Page 243.   4 Nov 1771.   SAML. BURK JR., and wife ELIZ, AC, to EZEKIAH HARTGROVE, AC, for Ƚ20, 100 acres. Lines: VALENTINE BALL, Tye River. Pat. to BURK 7 Nov 1764.

Page 244.   4 Nov 1771.   WM. PARKS & wife MARY, AC, to JNO. WEBB, AC, for Ƚ110, 180 acres Thresher's Creek. Lines: PEARCE WADE, JNO. BISWELL. Wit: WM. PARKS.

Page 245.   4 Nov 1771.   CORNL. THOMAS, AC, to MATT. WILSON, AC, for Ƚ21, 169 acres bought by CT of ROBT. DAVIS on branches of Maple Creek. Lines: MARVELL STONE, SAML. BURKS, JR., ARTHUR TOOLEY, MICAJAH CLARK.

Page 246.   4 Nov 1771.   THOS. WIATT & wife SUCKEY, AC, to JNO. WIATT, AC, for Ƚ250, 1100 acres. Lines: HUGH ROSE, PATRICK ROSE, EDWD. CARTER, JOSHUA HUDON, GABL. PENN, LAURENCE CAMPBELL. Margin: Orig. del. to RO. M. BROWN for SARAH DAVIS.

Page 248.   4 Nov 1771.   THOS. WIATT, AC, to JNO. DAVIS, AC, for Ƚ32-10, 108 acres on branch of Rutledge. Lines: JAS. MANEES. Margin: Orig. Del. to DAVIS 1 Oct 1785.

134

Page 248.   4 Nov 1771.   THOS. POWELL, AC, to JAS. POWELL, AC, for Ŀ48-12-
                  6, 162 3/4 acres branch of Horsley. Lines: SOLOMON CARTER.
Wit: THOS. WAUGH.

Page 250.   4 Nov 1771.   HENRY KEY, AC, to GEO. CAMPBELL, AC, for Ŀ102-10,
                  228 acres, formerly land of PATRICK MORRISON on N side of
Piney.

Page 251.   24 Aug 1771.   JNO. ROARK, AC, to WM. WILSON, AC, for Ŀ100, 223
                  acres, except a small quantity of same - about 16 acres and if
it exceeds 20 acres sold to JNO. and GEO PENN - N side of Huff Creek,
ROARK will pay 18 sh. per acres for difference; S side and joining Buffalo and bought by ROARK from GEO. SEATON & CARTER BRAXTON.   CATHERINE,
wife of ROARK.   Wit: JAS. WILLS, JOHNSON BEEN, JAS. FRANKLIN.

Page 252.   5 Jul 1771.   JESSE MILLS to ALEX. SPIERS, JNO. BOWMAN & CO -
                  Deed of Trust - 5 sh.   297 acres which Mills bought of LUNS-
FORD LOMAX.   Also one Va. born negro wench named PHEOBE; stock, tobacco.
Wit: THOS. JONES, JAS. PENDLETON, MARTIN BIBB.

Page 254.   20 Sep 1771.   JESSE MILLS to THOS. MITCHELL, Factor for JAS.
                  & RO. DONALDS & CO, Glasgow merchants - all household furni-
ture, stock and all book debts after paying WM. WATSON his demands vs.
me.   Memo: Trunk and table mentioned in fifth line delivered in lieu of
the whole.   Wit: EDMD. WILCOX, NATHL. TILMAN.

Page 255.   4 Nov 1771.   Shff. bond for JAMES DILLARD.   Appointed by gov-
                  ernor 15 Oct last.   To King Geo. III for Ŀ500. Bondsmen: JOS.
CABELL, DAVID CRAWFORD, CORNL. THOMAS, DUDLEY GATEWOOD, JAS. GATEWOOD,
RICH. GATEWOOD, HENRY BELL, JAS. CHRISTIAN, GEO. HILTON, DRURY CHRISTIAN,
THOS. JOPLIN, JAS. PAMPLIN, WM. HORSLEY, JOS. TUCKER, JNO. DILLARD.

Page 256.   Same men and date for additional bond for other duties as shff.

Page 257.   11 Feb 1772.   WM. CABELL, AC, to WM. CABELL JR., for Ŀ50, 150
                  acres N side and joining Tye just above mouth of Joe's Creek.
Pat. to WM. MATTHEWS 12 Jan 1746 and by MATTHEWS & wife HANNAH, to WM.
CABELL in Albemarle in Jan. court, 1749. Lines: WM. CABELL JR.   Wit: WM.
WALTON, JOS. CABELL, NICHL. CABELL.

Page 258.   2 Mar 1772.   JAS. NEVIL & wife MARY, to WM. CABELL JR., for
                  Ŀ40, 400 acres N side and joining Tye; both sides of Rucker's
Run.   Pat. to JAS. NEVIL, father of JAS. NEVIL, 25 Dec 1746, and by him
devised to his son, JAS. NEVIL. Lines: WM. MATTHEWS. Wit: WM. KEY, JAS.
MATTHEWS, JNO. KEY, JAS. WARD.

Page 260.   18 Dec 1771.   JOSEPH MAGANN, AC, to JAS. & RO. DONALDS, Glas-
                  gow merchants, for Ŀ160, 175 acres whereon I now live; also
negro wench, Jane and two negro girls, Moll and Cate; stock, furniture,
etc.   Deed of trust.   Wit: GABL. PENN, EDMD. WILCOX, DAVID SHEPHERD.
Memo: knife delivered in lieu of the whole.

Page 261.   4 Nov 1771.   WM. KEAINES (signed CAINES), AC, to EDMD. TILLEY,
                  AC, Deed of trust - stock. Wit: WM. RYAN, JNO. CAMPBELL, GEOR-
GE CAMPBELL.   Clerk records it as WM. KEARNS, so note three different
spellings for this man.

Page 262.   2 Mar 1772.   JNO. WEBB & wife URSLEY, AC, to JOS. CHILDRESS,
                  AC, for Ŀ110, 150 acres, part of 450 acres granted to WM.
CABELL - branch of Harris Creek between Bear and Cedar Mts. Lines: JNO.
WEBB, JOS. CHILDRESS.

Page 263.   19 Jun 1771.   MILES BURFORD, AC, to NEILL CAMPBELL, Richmond
                  merchant, for GEO. KIPPEN & Co, Deed of Trust - 5 sh. 136-18-
3½ debt.   By pat.   377 acres (now reduced between 80 and 90 acres because
of mistake in survey) a former pat. having been obtained for that quantity of land prior to his by JOS. ANTHONY and which he has given up. N side
and joining Fluvannah. Lines: JOS. ANTHONY, LYNCH. Wit: WM. WILSON, JNO.
JOPLING, JAS. FRANKLYN.

Page 265. 23 Nov 1771. JOB CARTER JR., AC, to ROBT. DONALDS, Glasgow
merchant, with JAS. DONALDS parter - 5 sh. - Deed of trust.
157 acres on Pedlar and Horsley and where I live. Formerly that of CHAS.
ELLIS; also stock. Wit: JNO. McKINDLEY, JOS. EDWARDS, DAVID SHEPHERD.

Page 267. 2 Mar 1772. JNO. TULEY, AC, to NATHL. DAVIS, for Ł50, 350 acres on Pedlar. Lines: WM. MILLS, crossing Maple Creek, EDWD.
WATTS, JR., STONE.

Page 268. 11 Jan 1772. ALEX. PATTON, AC, to WM. PATTON, AC, for Ł75,
192 acres S side and joining S fork of Rockfish. Part of
larger tract. Lines: JNO. MORRISON, ALEX. PATTON, JAS. WOODS, JNO.
THOMSON. Wit: JAS. HIGGINBOTHAM, SAML. WOODS, EDWD. STEPHENSON, MATTHEW
NIGHTINGALE.

Page 270. 11 Jan 1772. ALEX. PATTON, AC, to THOS. PATTON, AC, for Ł65,
164 acres both sides Rockfish and part of larger tract. S bank
of S fork of Rockfish. Lines: ALEX. PATTON. Wit: JAS. HIGGINBOTHAM, SAML.
WOODS, EDWD. STEPEHNSON.

Page 272. 2 Mar 1772. JAS. BROWN, AC, to BENJ. WRIGHT, AC, for Ł122-10,
200 acres Castle Creek and branch of Tye. Lines: JAS. DICKIE,
JNO. ROSE, late Rev. ROBT. FOSE. JENNET, wife of BROWN. Margin: Orig.
del. to JNO. HOUCHIN by order of WRIGHT on 2 Dec 1786.

Page 273. 11 Oct 1771. JOSEPH EATON & wife REBECCA, AC, to MATTHEW
NIGHTINGALE, AC, for Ł46, 150 acres Cuffy Creek. Lines: GEO.
MORRISON(?), Col. JNO. HENRY. Wit: JNO. RYAN, ROBT. CAWTHON, WM. DEMPSEY,
WM. KEARIES, GEO. CAMPBELL, JAS. ROSE.

Page 274. 23 Jan 1772. JAMES BROWN & wife JENNETT, AC, to JNO. THOMSON,
AC, for Ł88-12, 200 acres branch of Tye. Lines: ZACH. TALIA-
FERRO. Wit: ZACH. TALIAFERRO, JAS. COFFEY, WM. RYAN.

Page 276. 22 Oct 1771. THOMAS LOMAX, Caroline Co, to JNO. DEPRIEST, AC,
for Ł70-1. 1054 acres/ lines: HARMEN, LOMAX, PURVIS, STEPHENS,
FURBISH. Wit: ZACH. TALIAFERRO, JNO. ROSE, GEO. PURVIS.

Page 278. 7 Dec 1771. ISAAC WRIGHT, AC, to PETER CARTER, for Ł48, negro
girl, Hannah. Wit: JOSIAH ELLIS, DEVORIX GILLAM.

Page 279. 1 Mar 1772. JNO. SLED, to JOS. EDWARDS - Deed of Trust -
horse, furniture and bond due SLED from RICH. LAWLESS to satisfy an execution and cost of EDWARDS. Wit: JNO. DILLARD.

Page 280. 23 Sep 1771. LAURANCE SMALL, AC, to ABNER WITT, AC, for Ł220,
200 acres branch of Corban Creek. Lines: JAS. BARNETT, JNO.
REID, where SMALL liveth. Wit: JNO. WITT, SAML. LEAKEY, WM. SMALL. Orig.
del. to ABNER WITT.

Page 281. 26 Mar 1772. WM. TROTTER, AC, to WM. HORRAL, AC, for Ł210,
333 acres both sides Davis Creek - 200 acres, part sold by JNO
WADE and wife ELIZ, to WM. TROTTER in Albemarle on 9 Apr 1761; 133 acres
adj. pat. to TROTTER 1 Jun 1750. Wit: JAS. McALEXANDER JR., SAML. McAL-
EXANDER, WM. DEVER, JNO. McALEXANDER.

Page 283. 20 Jul 1771. NICHL. PRYOR, AC, to THOS. MITCHELL, Factor for
JAS. & RO. DONALDS, Glasgow merchants, Deed of Trust. Ł30.
338 acres Lovelady Creek where PRYOR lives. Lines: WM. PRYOR, SAML. GUEST,
also stock. Wit: PETER DAVIE, JNO. WIATT, DANL. GAINES.

Page 284. 16 Nov 1771. THOS. WORTHAM & wife ELIZ., AC, to THOS. GRIFFIN,
AC, for Ł20, 179 acres branch of Rucker's Run. Lines: BARNES,
KING, JAS. STEPHENS. Part of 6134 acres conveyed by BENJ. WALLER, atty.
for WALTER KING, British merchant, and THOS. MANN RANDOLPH and rec. in
General Court to LUNSFORD LOMAX SR. and by him and wife JUDITH, to LUNS-
FORD LOMAX JR, 13 Jan 1767, and by JR. to WORTHAM on 7 Apr 1770. Wit:
ZACH. TALIAFERRO, JAS. STEVENS, JESSE MILLS, WM. HAREGROVE. Margin: Orig.
delivered to GRIFFIN March 1785.

Page 285. 7 Oct 1771. ELISHA LYON, AC, to NICHL. LYON, Albemarle and
        St. Ann's Parish, for Ŀ30, 100 and ---acres Stovall's Creek.
MARY, wife of ELISHA LYON.

Page 286. 6 Apr 1772. WM. DEAVER & wife SUSANNA, AC, to THOS. HAWKINS
        for Ŀ35-1, 188 acres Little cove at a branch of Rucker's Run.
Line of Col. LOMAX.

Page 288. 23 Mar 1772. THOS. TUNGATE (TONGATE), AC, to ALEX. SPIERS,
        JNO. BOWMAN & CO, Glasgow Merchants - Deed of Trust - Ŀ7-6-1
debt. 5 sh. - cows, pots, etc. Wit: WM. TAYLOR, GEO. WEIR, PETER HART.

Page 290. 4 Dec 1772. ARCHIBALD BURDEN to ALEX. SPIERS, JNO. BOWMAN &
        CO., Glasgow merchants - Ŀ27-9-8 debt - Deed of Trust - 5 sh.
280 acres bought by BURDEN from RICH. ELLIOTT. Lines: WM. WRIGHT CLEMENTS,
RICH. DAVIS, CARNABY VEALE, THOS. WAUGH & EDWD WARE, Horsley Creek, also
horse, other stock, furniture etc. Wit: GABL. PENN, ALEX. GORDON, WM.
WARNACKS, THOS. REID.

Page 292. 8 Oct 1771. JNO. CONNELLY, late of AC, to ALEX. SPIERS, JNO.
        BOWMAN & CO, Glasgow merchants. Deed of Trust - Ŀ78-18-8 debt;
5 sh. negro slave, Pompey; furniture furniture, stock etc. Wit: WM. PENN,
JOHNSON BEAN, ALEX. GORDON, THOS. REID. Margin: Examined & del. to PAT.
HART.

Page 294. 20 Sep 1771. THOS. HODGES, AC, to PHILIP SMITH, AC, for Ŀ25-10,
        deed of trust - stock. Wit: THOS. COTTRILL, JAS. COTTRELL.

Page 295. 12 Nov 1771. WM. ALLEN, AC, to JNO. HARDWICK, one mare. Wit:
        THOS. LUMPKIN, MOSES WRIGHT.

Page 295. 6 Aug. 1771. WM. WALTON to HUGH ROSE for Ŀ610 debt - Deed of
        trust 5 sh. - many slaves named: Will, Siesor, Dick, Quillar,
Aquire, Seros, Stephen, Punch, Chas. Will, Lewis, Matt., Sarah, Rose,
Nann, Hannah, Rachel, Annica. Wit: JAS. PAMPLIN, ANDREW LACKEY, JNO.
JACOBS.

Page 297. 6 Aug 1771. Order to Albemarle J.P.'s: JNO. HENDERSON & JNO.
        COLES to quiz MARGARET SCOTT, wife of JNO. SCOTT, as to deed
of 1 Oct 1770 to TERISHA TURNER - 1557 acres. Done 10 Mar 1772.

Page 298. 7 Mar 1772. JESSE MILLS Deed of Trust to ALEX. SPIERS, JNO.
        BOWMAN & Co., Dect of Ŀ255-8-2 - 5 sh - one negro girl, Letty,
about 30; one boy Harry, about 12; other slaves, stock, tobacco-land on
head of Tye - 200 acres. Wit: GEO. WALKER, JR., GEO. WEIR, THOS. WRIGHT,
THOS. REID.

Page 300. 20 Mar 1772. JNO. KENNADY, AC, Deed of Trust to ALEX. SPIERS,
        JNO. BOWMAN & Co. Debt of Ŀ35-16-11 - 5 sh. for 96 acres on
Buffalo and three tracts belonging to PHILLIP PENN, MATT TUCKER & JAS.
GATEWOOD. Also stock, furniture etc. Wit: THOS. REID, ALEX. GORDON, GEO.
WEIR.

Page 302. 17 Jan 1772. JEREMIAH WHITNEY, Buckingham Co, to WM. WILSON,
        Factor for GEO. KIPPEN & Co, Glasgow merchants, Deed of Trust.
3 slaves, males, and 2 females and children. Also Buckingham land, 100
acres, where he lives. Wit: WM. POWELL, THOS. POWELL, Jr., BENJ. CASH.

Page 304. 4 Mar 1772. JNO. ROWZIE, AC, Deed of trust to SPIERS & BOWMAN
        as above - 5 sh. 100 acres where ROWZIE lives. Lines: CARTER
BRAXTON, MOSES HIGGINBOTHAM, JNO. OWENBY JR. - also stock and furniture.
Wit: WM. MITCHELL, GEO. WEIR, THOS. REID.

Page 306. 31 Mar 1772. JNO. WHITEHEAD, AC, to SPIERS & BOWMAN as above,
        Deed of Trust - 5 sh. Slave, Sam; land where WHITEHEAD lives.
Wit: MATT. TUCKER, JOS. (?) TUCKER, ALEX. GORDON.

Page 308. 11 Apr 1772. ANGUS McDANIEL (Margin has it McDONALD and
        scratched) to GEO. KIPPEN & Co, Glasgow merchants - 5 sh. Deed
of trust - 72 acres S side Buffalo and where McDANIEL lives; also 84 acres

on Black Water on NE side of Mt...This has been surveyed, but no pat. or
fee paid although the works have been returned. Wit: OBEDIAH HENDERSON,
BENJ. CASH, WM. WILSON.

Page 310. 30 Mar 1772. JNO. COTTRILL, AC, to SPIERS & BOWMAN, Deed of
trust - 400 acres for 5 sh. on Stovall Creek which COTTRILL
got by deed from JOS. CREWS. Wit: WM. LEE, THOS. REID, GEO. WEIR.

Page 312. 23 Mar 1772. SAML. SHANNON, AC, Shoemaker, to Rev. WM. IRVIN,
preacher of the gospel at Rockfish, AC, for Ł127-10, 175 acres
on branches of Rockfish near the Blue Mts. Lines: THOS. SHANNON, WM.
CREWS, WM. SIMPSON. JEAN, wife of SHANNON. Wit: SAML. LEAKEY, SAML.
WOODS, ALEX. REID JR., THOS. WOODY.

Page 315. 4 May 1772. GEO. CARRINGTON, Cumberland Co, to JNO. HARDWICK,
AC, for Ł6, 100 acres branch of Harris creek. Lines: on S by
MOSES HIGGINBOTHAM, W by JAS. CREWS, E by other lands of JNO. HARDWICK.

Page 316. 3 May 1772. HUGH ROSE, AC, to JAS. DICKIE, King and Queen Co,
for Ł23, no acres set forth. Lines: JAS. DICKIE, Castle Creek.

Page 316. 8 Oct 1771. JESSE MILLS, AC, to EDWD. TILMAN, for Ł12, stock.
Wit: ANN NBAS(?) JONES, LEDE JONES.

Page 317. 4 May 1772. JAS. DILLARD - Shff. bond to collect levies - to
King Geo. III - Ł1000. Bondsmen: GABL. PENN, WM. LOVING, MATT
TUCKER, JNO. DILLARD, EDMD. WILCOX.

Page 318. 1 Jun 1772. CHAS. TALIAFERRO & wife ISBELL, AC, to PHILIP
THURMOND, AC, for Ł35, 104 acres both sides of Horsley.

Page 319. 1 Jun 1772. CHAS. TALIAFERRO & wife ISBELL, AC, to JOHN PAY-
TON, AC, for Ł20, 267 acres Horsley Creek and branches. Lines:
LUNSFORD LOMAX, JNO. POWELL, PHILIPP THURMOND, PHILIP PEYTON.

Page 321. 1 Jun 1772. CHAS. TALIAFERRO & wife ISBELL, AC, to WM. LILLEY,
AC, for Ł8, 65 acres Horsley Creek. Lines: SAML. SHACKLEFORD.

Page 322. 1 Jun 1772. CHAS. TALIAFERRO & wife ISBELL, AC, to JNO. POW-
ELL, AC, for Ł75, 400 acres both sides Horsley. Lines: CHAS.
TALIAFERRO, PHILIP THURMOND.

Page 324. 8 May 1772. RICH. ALLCOCK, AC, to JAS. & RO. DONALDS & Co,
Glasgow merchants. Deed of Turst - Ł100, slaves. Wit: G.
WALKER JR., DAVID SHEPHERD, JNO. McKINDLEY.

Page 324. 1 Jun 1772. JAS. SIMMONS, AC, to JNO. DAVIS, AC, for Ł20, 197
acres branch of Harris Creek. Lines: JNO. OWNBY, RICH. SHELTON,
ISAAC WRIGHT, THOS. WATS, GEO. CARRINGTON, JNO. WOODRUFF. Deeded to SIM-
MONS by GEO. CARRINGTON. Wit: JOSHUA FOWLER, CALEB WATTS, BALLENGER WADE.

Page 326. 4 Nov 1771. JNO. MURRIL, AC, to JOSIAH WOOD, AC, for Ł35, 125
acres on Horse Shoe Mt.

Page 327. 30 May 1772. THOS. WATS, AC, to JOS. DAWSON, AC, for Ł40-1,
73 acres Harris Creek. Lines: JAS. CREWS, ISAAC WRIGHT. Wit:
DAN. BURFORD JR., JNO. HARDWICK, WM. McFRAW, JNO. STOAKES, THOS. LUMPKIN.

Page 329. 30 May 1772. THOS. WATS, AC, to JNO. DAWSON, AC, for Ł94-19,
170 acres on Harris Creek. Wit: same as above.

Page 331. 1 Jun 1772. THOS. LUMPKIN, AC, to LUCAS POWELL for Ł133-10,
297 acres on branch of Rucker's Run. Bought by LUMPKIN from
JESSE MILLS. Wit: WM. WILSON, THOS. POWELL JR., ALEX REID. Ordered del.
to THOMAS HAWKINS for POWELL 19 Apr 1791.

Page 332. 3 May 1772. RICH. ALLCOCK & wife FRANCES, AC, to WM. CABELL,
JR, AC, for Ł800, 1070 acres N branch of Tie. Part of 7881
acres mortgaged by LUNSFORD LOMAX to late PHILIP GRYMES, 7 Aug 1756, and
land whereon Amherst Courthouse now stands. Lines: WALER, KING, a mt.,

ALLCOCK, top of a mt., crossing 2 branches, LUCAS POWELL, EDMD. WILCOX,
JNO. CARTWRIGHT, GEO. BLAIN. Wit: ZACH. TALIAFERRO, EDMD. WILCOX, JOS.
TUCKER, THOS. HAWKINS, JAS. STEVENS, JOS. CABELL, JNO. SALE, RICH.
TANKERSLEY.

Page 335. 9 Apr 1772. JNO. HOUCHINS to SPIERS & BOWMAN CO. Deed of Trust
            5 sh. 90 acres Graham's Creek. Lines: DUNCAN GRAHAM; whereon
HOUCHINS lives; beds, stock. Wit: JNO. ROSE, JR., GEO. WIER, JOSHUA
FOWLER, JNO. WIATT.

Page 337. 21 Mar 1772. FRANCIS GARDINER, AC, to SPIERS & BOWMAN, Deed of
            trust. 5 sh. 100 acres Huff Creek. Bounded by 6 several
tracts of BENJ. STINNETT, JNO. COLEMAN, JNO. WHITEHEAD, JNO. WARD, WM.
HIX, BENJ. NOWELL (NORVELL?), stock, beds. Wit: WM. JOHNS, GEO. WIER,
THOS. REID.

Page 339. 1 Jun 1772. JNO. DEPRIEST, AC, & wife ELIZ., to WILLIAM LOV-
            ING, AC, for Ł25-7, 169 acres branch of Rucker's Run and join-
ing WM. LOVING. Lines: GEO. PURVIS, JAS. STEPHENS, Part of land DEPRIEST
bought from THOS. LOMAX.

Page 341. 1 Jun 1772. JNO. DEPRIEST & wife ELIZ, AC, to ABRAHAM WARWICK,
            AC, for Ł76-8, 382 acres branches of Horsley. Lines: HARMER,
FURBUSH, MILLS, LOMAX. Part of 6134 acres conveyed by LUNSFORD LOMAX SR.
and wife JUDITH, to LUNSFORD LOMAX, JR. Senior got it from BENJ. WALLER,
atty. for WALTER KING, Bristol merchant. and THOS. MANN RANDOLPH. Orig.
delivered Dec, 1799.

Page 343. 1 Jun 1772. JNO. DEPRIEST & wife ELIZ., AC, to WM. CRISP of
            AC, for Ł65, 200 acres branch of Rucker's Run. Lines: Col.
LOMAX.

Page 344. 1 Jun 1772. WM. BIBB & wife SARAH, AC, to LUCAS POWELL, AC,
            for Ł10, 170 acres branch of Rucker's Run. Lines: WALTER KING,
Col. LOMAX, LOMAX & CO. Pat. to WM. BIBB 27 Aug 1770. Wit: JNO. REID,
WM. WILSON, NICHL. MORAN. Margin: 16 Nov 1807, del. to CRISP's admr.

Page 346. 1 Jun 1772. WM. GARRISON, AC, to WM. WILSON - sundries: bed,
            etc., Ł500 tobacco in care of HENRY FRANKLYN on plantation of
SAML. HANCOCK. Wit: JAS. FRANKLYN.

Page 346. 21 Dec 1771. HENRY KEY, AC, to JNO. GREGORY, AC, for Ł30, 100
            acres, part of 258 acres pat. to KEY at Williamsburg 20 Sep
1759. Lines: JNO. HARMOND, HENRY KEY. Wit: WM. MARTIN, SAML. STAPLES;
marks of JNO. & PETER, but no last names.

Page 348. 6 Jul 1772. JNO. ROBERTS, AC, to HENRY ROBERTS, Albemarle,
            for Ł10-8-1, cows, calves etc. Wit: DAVID SHEPHERD, JNO.
McKENDLEY.

Page 348. 6 Jul 1772. JOSIAS WOOD & wife RODE, AC, to THOS. MATHEWS, AC,
            for Ł20, 200 acres both sides Nassau Creek. Part of 400 acres
pat. to JNO. HUNTER 15 Dec 1757. Lines: JNO. HUNTER, crossing Creek.
Wit: ROBT. WRIGHT, WM. TILLAR, JNO. WRIGHT. Margin: Orig. del. to JNO.
MATTHEWS 27 Apr 1791.

Page 350. 6 Jul 1772. JOSIAS WOOD and wife RODE, AC, to THOS. HOPPER,
            AC, for Ł20, 200 acres. Description of title as above. Lines:
THOS. MATTHEWS, JNO. HUNTER, WALTER KING. Wit: Same as above.

Page 351. 12 Nov 1771. THOS. HODGES, AC, to SPIERS & BOWMAN, Glasgow
            merchants. Deed of Trust. 5 sh. Wagon and stock. Wit: LEONARD
TARRANT, PHILIP SMITH, JAS. TARRANT, THOS. REID.

Page 353. 1 May 1772. WM. CLARKE, AC, to CARTER & TRENT. Deed of Trust.
            Ł50 debt. 148 acres. Wit: WM. GAY, THOS. SMITH, THOS. BOWEN,
JNO. REID, ALEX. REID JR., WM. HARRIS, GEO. DIVERS, WM. LOVING.

Page 354. 18 Nov 1771. JAS. ROSE, AC, to ALEX. BARNETT, AC, for Ł3-10,
            Deed of Trust. cow and calf. Wit: ROBT. & JAS. BARNETT.

Page 355.   10 Jun 1772.   MARK WARE, AC, Deed of Trust to JAMES & ROBT.
DONOLDS & Co, Glasgow, 5 sh. one mare, cow and calf, bed etc.
and all other estate that I possess. Wit: JNO. LAMANT, WM. PENN, DAVID
SHEPHERD. (Note: Does anyone have data on MARK WARE in Kentucky? My
brother, BERNARD BYRD DAVIS, Shelbyville, Kentucky, married SARAH WARE.
She is the daughter of the late HARRY WARE who was from northern Kentucky.
The family states that they descend from a MARK WARE who was a Virginian,
but I am unable to find anyone who knows the data on this man. He dis-
appears from Amherst and could easily have gone to northern Kentucky. In
Will Book 3:9 is the will of Edward Ware - 1 Jun 1779; 3 Jul 1786. Wit:
PETER CARTER, RODERICK McCULLOCH, ELIZ. McCULLOCH. He does not call
these legatees his children, but it is presumptive. He names MARK WARE
and his children, JAMES POWELL - 400 acres where he lives; WM. POWELL,
214 acres where he lives; JOHN POWELL - 400 acres whre he lives; EDWARD
POWELL - 200 acres where I live and 351 acres on Pedlar on Rich. Mt.;
ELIZ. JOPLIN - 200 acres next to M.(?) HIGGINBOTHAM; ANNE CAMPBELL - land
next to GORDON; SARAH WARE - land next to GORDON; my wife, LETTIS; EDMD.
(EDWD. above) POWELL. Exrs: JAS. WILLIAMS & EDWD & JNO. POWELL. EDWARD
WARE must have acquired most of this land prior to the formation of Amherst for there is only one deed in Book B showing purchase from LOMAX of
a tract of a bit over 200 acres on Horsley. If these POWELLS are sons-in
law, their marriages took place prior to Amherst settlement or were unre-
corded. There is no marriage data extant here for MARK WARE, but he is
listed as a Revolutionary soldier from Amherst. The WARE family still in
the county claims that Gloucester County was the place from whence their
branch came into Amherst. I have done no work on POWELL or WARE families
prior to Amherst, but have noted a group of WARES in Culpeper and it may
be that MARK came from that area. BFD)

Page 356.   6 Jul 1772.   JACOB BROWN & wife SUSANNA, AC, to WM. PRYOR, AC,
for Ŀ50, 93 acres on N branch of Brown's Creek, and S branch
of Inchanted Creek. Lines: JOSIAH ELLIS.

Page 358.   22 Jun 1772.   WM. PRYOR & wife MARGARET, AC, to JACOB BROWN,
AC, 350 acres on both sides of Pedlar River. Lines: WM.
MATTHEWS.

Page 359.   9 Dec 1771.   BENJ. ASBURY to SPIERS & BOWMAN, Deed of trust.
5 sh. 175 acres on CARTER's Mill Creek. Bought by ASBURY
from JAS. GRAY; also a survey of about 300 acres next to NEILL CAMPBELL &
BENJ. HIGGINBOTHAM; tobacco, horse, cattle and furniture. Wit: GABL. PENN,
WM. CAMDEN, ADDISON DAY, JNO. NOEL, THOS. REID.

Page 361.   29 Feb 1772.   JAS. WARREN, AC, to SPIERS & BOWMAN, Deed of
trust, 5 sh. 99 acres on Owen's Creek. Bought by WARREN from
THOS. BIBEE; cow, hogs, bed, 2 blankets, one handkerchief. Wit: THOS.
REID, GEO. WEIR, JESSE EVANS.

Page 363.   14 Oct 1771.   DUNCAN CAMRON, AC, to SPIERS & BOWMAN - Deed of
trust - 5 sh. Land in fork of Piney River. Lines: HENRY ROSE,
NICHL. WREN. Wit: WM. LEE, ADDISON DAY, JNO. DAWSON, THOS. REID.

Page 365.   6 Jul 1772.   JAS. NOWLIN & wife BETHINEAH, AC, to WM. McCRAW,
AC, for Ŀ80, 200 acres bought by NOWLIN from AMBROSE GATEWOOD
and wife MARGARET - branch of Harris Creek. Part of 400 acres pat. to
PATRICK NOWLING on 19 Aug 1758, and where MCCRAW lives. Lines: MOSES
SWINNEY, JNO. HARVIE, JAS. WRIGHT, JNO. DAVIS, JNO. COLEMAN. AMBROSE
GATEWOOD & wife MARGARET, also sign.

Page 366.   1 Feb 1772.   JNO. HEARD, AC, apprentices himself to GEO. BLAIN,
sadler, Ŀ50 for 2 years and 3 months. Wit: JNO. REID, NATHAN
REID, ALEX. REID, JR.

Page 367.   3 Dec 1771.   Order to ARCHIBALD ALEXANDER & SAML. McDOWELL,
Augusta Co. J.P.'s, to quiz ELIZ, wife of MATT ROBINSON, as to
deed of 23 Oct 1771, to JAS. HENDERSON for 240 acres. Done 18 May 1772.

Page 368.   3 Aug 1772.   MATT NIGHTINGALE & wife LUCY, to JNO. MERRILL
(MURRELL) for Ŀ200, 333 acres S side Rockfish and both sides
of Corban Creek. Lines: JNO. SMALL, line that is now PUCKETT's(?) on Rock-

140

fish, DAVID REID, late Col. JNO. CHISWELL, MICHL. MONTGOMERY, ALEX. REID, FRANCIS MERIWETHER.

Page 369. 3 Aug 1772. RICH. TANKERSLEY & wife WINNEFORD, AC, to STEPHEN WATTS, AC, for Ŀ55, 182 acres N side Tye & opposite mouth of Piney. Part of RICH. TANKERSLEY SR., land which he gave to his son, Jr., and joins CHAS. ROSE. Wit: HUGH ROSE, AUGUSTIN WRIGHT, THOS. WORTHAM.

Page 370. 1 Aug 1772. GILBERT COTTRELL, AC, to JAS. & RO. DONALDS & Co, Deed of trust - 5 sh. mare, cow, furniture and "tobacco he makes with WM. BIBB". Wit: WM. BICKNELL, JR., WM. PENN, PETER HART, JNO. McKINDLEY. Penknife del. in lieu of whole.

Page 372. 23 Mar 1772. GROVES HARDING, AC, to GEO. KIPPEN & Co, Deed of Trust - also to JAS. BUCHANAN, merchant in Richmond - 5 sh. 710 acres which HARDING bought of NEILL CAMPBELL, Factor for KIPPEN; 6 slaves; Wit: CHAS. IRVING, JNO. OLD, JAS. McCAUL.

Page 374. 3 Aug 1772. GEO. McDANIEL, AC, to DRURY TUCKER, AC, for Ŀ3, 54 acres on Tobacco Row Mt. Lines: ABRAHAM PENN. Margin: or. del. to JOS. TUCKER 30 Oct 1779, and someone has put note in pencil and the name of DRURY TUCKER so I don't think it is clerk notation.

Page 375. 3 Aug 1772. DRURY BOWMAN & wife MILDRED, AC, to RICHARD ALL-COCK, AC, for Ŀ150, 400 acres S side Tie on Camp Creek. Lines: JNO. McKENNIES(?), JNO. PEARTREE BURKS, WM. ROSE. (X) of BOWMAN and signature of WM. CABELL.

Page 377. 3 Aug 1772. JACOB TYRE, AC, and wife MARY to ENOUCH NASH, AC, for Ŀ32, 150 acres both sides of Nassau. Line of JNO. HARMER.

Page 378. 27 Aug 1771. DAVID ENIX, AC, to GEO. KIPPEN & CO, Deed of trust, 5 sh. 400 acres Gladie and Bririe Creek. Lines: PERRIN FARRAR, THOS. JOPLING. Bought by ENIX from THOS. JOPLING and rec. in Albemarle. Wit: CHAS. IRVING, DAVID KIPPEN, WM. MITCHELL, CLOUGH SHELTON.

Page 380. 7 Sep 1772. JNO. BRYAN & wife JUDITH, AC, to JNO. HARRIS, AC, for Ŀ22, 46 acres branch of Davis Creek. Lines: WM. WRIGHT. Wit: WM. HORRALL. Margin: Orig. del. Mar 1785 to JNO. HARRIS.

Page 381. 5 Sep 1772. WM. MONTGOMERY (Jr. in one item) to DAVID MERIWE-THER, AC, for Ŀ50, 174 acres on Taylor's Creek. Lines: SAML. MANN, ARCHIBALD WOODS. Wit: WM. MONTGOMERY, JAS. HENDERSON. Margin: Orig. del. to BENJ. TALIAFERRO.

Page 383. 15 May 1772. JNO. LEWIS & wife MILDRED, Pittsylvania Co, to JNO. ROSE, AC, for Ŀ750, 925 acres. Lines: Hillside on lines of LEWIS & ROSE; east side of Tye, Piney woods on W side of Tye; Roseisle at mouth of a creek formerly called Learses(?); western branch of Hatt Creek. Surveyed by ZACH. TALIAFERRO; upper part of tract granted to CHAS LEWIS, father to JOHN LEWIS, by pat. 25 Jul 1741, and afterwards vested in CHAS. LEWIS in Tail in lieu of land in New Kent - Act of Assembley obtained by CHAS. LEWIS and then again vested in JNO. LEWIS in fee simple by another act in 1769 in lieu of a tract in Pittsylvania. Wit: ZACH. TALIAFERRO, JNO. TALIAFERRO, WM. TUGGLE, EDMD. WILCOX.

Page 385. 16 May 1772. Order to WM. THOMAS, RO. PAYNE & JNO. DICKS, Pittsylvania J.P.'s, to examine as to dower rights MILDRED LEWIS for deed above. Returned by PAYNE & THOMAS.

Page 386. 15 May 1772. JNO. LEWIS & wife MILDRED, Pittsylvania, to EDMD. WILCOX, AC, for Ŀ750, 925 acres. Lines: W side of Tye, LEWIS, ROSE, JACKSON's old field, surveyed by ZACH. TALIAFERRO; lower part of tract of CHAS. LEWIS - see above deed. Wit: Same as above, but add JNO. ROSE. Margin: Orig. del. to WILCOX.

Page 388. 16 May 1772. Order to same Pittsylvania J.P.'s to quiz MIL-DRED LEWIS, wife of JNO. Done by same men.

Page 389. 3 Sep 1772. WM. STINNET, AC, to SPIERS & BOWMAN, Glasgow

merchants in North Britain - Deed of Trust - 5 sh. cattle, furniture etc.
Wit: JNO. DILLARD, JAS. DILLARD JR., GEO. WEIR.

Page 391. Entry of WM. CABELL JR., AC surveyor, with HUGH ROSE, J.P.
CABELL enters 400 acres on a N branch of Tye known as the
Great Branch. Lines: Dr. CABELL, SPENCER, WM. LAINE, Poplar Holler.
Dated 7 Sep 1772.

Page 392. 7 Sep 1772. CHAS. TULRY, AC, to STEPHEN GOOLSBY, AC, for Ł100,
400 acres pat. to ARTHUR TULEY, dec'd, 3 Nov 1750. Branch of
Pedlar. Lines: RO. DAVIS, Maple Creek, EDWD. WATTS. Wit: RICH. PETER,
JER. TAYLOR, WM. FLOYD. ELIZABETH, wife of TULEY.

Page 394. 13 Mar 1772. THOS. MORRISON, AC, planter, to JAMES TULEY SR,
Albemarle, for Ł50, 73 acres on Long Meadow a branch of Rock-
fish. Lines: Col. JNO. CHISWELL. Wit: ABNER WITT, JAS. TULEY JR., SAML.
LACKEY, FRANCIS NEW, CHAS. TULEY.

Page 395. 5 Sep 1772. ABNER WILL, AC, to LAURENCE SMALL, AC, for Ł100,
100 acres branch of Corbin Creek. Lines: JNO. LACKEY, JAS.(?)
BARNETT. Wit: CHAS. WITT, JNO. WITT JR., LITTLEBERRY WITT.

Page 397. 20 Aug 1772. ABNER WITT, AC, to JNO. WITT JR. & SR., Deed of
Trust - 5 sh. 200 acres. Lines: JAS. BARNETT, JNO. REID, also
slaves, furniture etc. Wit: LAURENCE SMALL, CHAS. WITT, CHAS. BARNERD,
LITTLEBERRY WITT, WM. SMALL. Or. del. to JNO. WITT.

Page 399. 18 Jul 1772. RICH. ALLCOCK, AC, to HENDERSON & McCAUL & Co,
merchants in Glasgow. Deed of Trust - 5 sh. Slaves.

Page 401. 31 Aug 1772. Rec'd. of JNO. GILLILAND Ł8-15-10 in full for
debt to GEO. KIPPEN & Co, Glasgow Merchants for which HENRY
TENNISON mtgd. his land. By WM. WILSON, Factor. Wit: JAS. MANEES JR.,
GEO. McDANIEL.

Page 402. A list of surveys made in AC from 27 Jun 1771 to 20 Jun 1772
and signed by WILLIAM CABELL JR., AC surveyor.

28 Oct 1771	THOS. BIBEY 220 a.	9 Mar 1772	WM. WALKER	2000 a.
2 Nov "	SOLOMON CARTER 72 a.	23 " "	OWEN HERNDON	400 a.
6 " "	RO. JOHNSTON 400 a.	24 " "	JNO. REID	77 a.
6 " " " "	200 a.	25 " "	FRANCIS MERIWETHER	99a.
7 " " " "	400 a.	26 " "	JNO. SMALL	115 a.
7 " " " "	218 a.	27 " "	CHAS. YANCEY	140 a.
11 " "	WM. FLOYD 400 a.	30 " "	RO. PAGE	22 a.
13 " "	RO. JOHNSTON 120 a.	31 " "	" "	87 a.
14 " " " "	170 a.	8 Apr "	THOS. JOPLING	400 a.
18 " "	CHAS. MOSS 48 a.	9 " "	" "	400 a.
26 " "	JOSHUA FOWLER 92 a.	9 " "	" "	30 a.
28 " "	JNO. COLEMAN 322 a.	10 " "	DAVID MONTGOMERY	98 a.
29 Dec "	" " 54 a.	11 " "	ABRAHAM WARWICK	45 a.
9 " "	RO. JOHNSTON 125 a.	13 " "	JNO. TUGGLE JR.	98 a.
9 " " " "	324 a.	14 " "	RICH. HARVEY	92 a.
17 " "	HESEKIAH STRATTON 80 a.	15 " "	JAS. STEPHENS 53 a.
18 " "	JNO. SHIELDS 50 a.	24 " "	JNO. BALLOWE 200 a.
19 " "	RO. DUNWOODY 154 a.	25 " "	JNO. BAILEY 39 a.
21 " "	JNO. HENDERSON 20 a.	25 " "	DANL. BURFORD 174 a.

Page 403. 29 Aug 1772. RICH. ALLCOCK, AC, to PETER HART & JAMES FRANK-
LYN, AC, Deed of Trust - 2 slaves & penknife for 5 sh. Wit:
GEO. LAMBERT, LINN BANKS, JOELL CASH.

Page 404. 6 Oct 1772. JNO. HENDERSON & wife MARY, AC, to JAS. JOHNSON,
AC, for Ł110, 162 acres. Lines: DAVID MERIWETHER, CHAS. YANCEY,
THOS. ROBERTSON, on the road, ELEXANDER HENDERSON.

Page 406. 11 Aug 1772. GEO. CAMPBELL, AC, to JAS. & RO. DONALDS, merchants, Deed of Trust. 5 sh. 170 acres whereon I live; cattle
etc. Also entry of 50 acres adj. and tobacco now growing. Wit: DAVID
SHEPHERD, JAS. FRANKLYN, JAS. MASTERS.

Page 408.   7 Sep 1772.   DANL. & MILES BURFORD, AC, to GEO. LOVELL, AC,
            for L25, 300 acres on Lynch road. Lines: JO. FROST. Wit:
JAMES SYMONS, JNO. WARTERS(?), WM. BROWN, DAN BURFORD JR.

Page 409.   5 Oct 1772 (rec. 6 Oct 1772.) HENRY KEY, AC, to BARTHOLOMEW
            RAMSEY, AC, for L30, 73 acres S side of N branch of Piney.
Lines: ROSE.

Page 412.   5 Oct 1772.   GEO. DOUGLAS & wife MARY, and JAS. DOUGLAS, Albe-
            marle and AC to GEO. BLANE, AC, - one deed to GEO. DOUGLAS by
CHAS. LEWIS (Jr. or Gent.?) 400 acres on Hickory and rec. in Albemarle;
also one small tract pat. to JAS. DOUGLAS on 10 Sep 1767(?) -5- on small
branch of Hickory. JAS. is called son of GEO. L80-1 and part of 229
acres which are part of these tracts of 458 acres. Orig. del. to BLAIN.

Page 414.   21 Apr 1772.   JACOB EADES & JAS. MATTHEWS to RICHARD MURRY for
            L27, 99 acres branch of S fork of Rockfish. Lines: Col. LUNS-
FORD LOMAX; pat. to JACOB EADES. Wit: JAS. NEVIL, JNO. PETER, MARGARET
REES, WM. SCRUGGS, RO. EASLEY, WM. KEY.

Page 416.   21 Apr 1772.   JACOB EADES & JAS. MATTHEWS, AC, to RICH. MURRER
            (margin has MURRAH), AC, for L13, 50 acres branch of Purgatory
Swamp below Fenley's Gap. Lines: JOHNSTON, part of 400 acres granted to
JACOB EADES by LUNSFORD LOMAX, the Younger. Wit: JAS. NEVIL, JNO. PETER,
MARGARET REES, RO. EASLEY, WM. SCRUGGS, WM. KEY.

Page 417.   5 Oct 1772.   GEO. DOUGLAS, SR, Albemarle, & wife MARY, to
            WILLOUGHBY PUGH, AC, for L100, 200 acres both sides of Hickory
Creek, on Rockfish. Part of survey for Capt. CHAS. LEWIS by JOSHUA FRY
on 24 Oct 1748.

Page 418.   5 Oct 1772.   JAS. DOUGLAS, Albemarle Co, to JOHN PUGH, Orange
            Co, for L13-15, 29 acres, part of survey made for JAS. DOUGLAS
next to GEO. DOUGLAS SR. & EDWD. MOUZLEY. Pat. to JAS. DOUGLAS.

Page 420.   5 Oct 1772.   EDWD MOUSLEY, AC, to JNO. PUGH, Orange Co, for
            L13-15, 92 acres head branch of Hickory; part of pat. to MOUS-
LEY 12 May 1770. Lines: GEO. DOUGLAS. Wit: CHAS. YANCEY, JNO. HENDERSON,
JOEL CRAWFORD, JAS. HENDERSON, JOS. ROBERTS, ELIJAH MORAN.

Page 422.   29 Jul 1772.   JAS. & RO. DONALDS, Glasgow merchants, from JOHN
            BLAND, AC, Deed of Trust - 5 sh. - horse, beds, hogs, furni-
ture, mare and tobacco. Wit: WM. PENN, JNO. HOUCHIN, JAS. McKINDLEY,
PETER HART.

Page 423.   5 Oct 1772.   THOS. FITZPATRICK, Albemarle, to his son, ALEX.
            FITZPATRICK, AC, for love and 20 sh., 183 acres on Rich Cove.
Lines of the 183 acres - Courthouse road. Wit: GEORGE BLAIN, JR., JNO.
BIBB, WM. FITZPATRICK. ELIZABETH, wife of THOS.

Page 425.   5 Oct 1772.   THOS. FITZPATRICK & wife ELIZ., Albemarle, to
            son, ALEX. FITZPATRICK, AC, love and 20 sh., 75 acres on head
branch of Kerby's Creek. Lines: JNO. BURUS. Wit: Same as above.

Page 427.   29 Jul 1772.   WM. HARRIS, Albemarle, to WM. HARRIS JR., AC,
            for L100, 500 acres, two tracts. 1) Part of land bought of
JACOB WRIGHT.   2) Land bought of WM. MAXWELL. N side of Rockfish. Lines:
JACOB WRIGHT. Wit: JNO. DIGGS, MATT. HARRIS, JNO. GRIFFIN.

Page 429.   21 Sep 1772.   ABRAHAM PENN, AC, to DRURY TUCKER, AC, for L150,
            301 acres S side branch of Harris Creek and E of Tobacco Row
Mts. Bought by PENN from BAYLOR WALKER of King and Queen and two deeds
in AC. 1) From WALKER on 5 Oct DCCLXVII - 136 acres. Lines: JNO. HARRIS.
2) Bought from GEO. McDANIEL 4 Mar 1771 - 165 acres. Wit: EDMD. WILCOX,
BENJ. TALIAFERRO, THOS. LUMPKIN, JOS. CABELL, MATT. TUCKER, GABL. PENN.
Margin: Orig. del. to JOS. TUCKER 30 Oct 1779.

Page 430.   4 Nov 1771.   CHAS. ELLIS & wife SARAH, AC, to JOBE CARTER of
            AC for L34-13, 86 acres 10/16, Horsley Creek, Pedlar River,
the Plantation on the bank of said river.

Page 431.   13 May 1772.   MARY GREGORY, widow of RICH. F. GREGORY; EDWD.
           GREGORY & FLETCHER GREGORY "his sons", AC, to HENDERSON McCAUL
& Co, Glasgow merchants.   Deed of Trust - 5 sh.   400 acres on S fork of
Fishing Creek whereon a "chapple" has been lately built and "whereon they
now live".   Also 200 acres called Lick land and within a mile of and on
the road to Migginson's ferry; also cattle with mark in one ear of "a
flower delous"; horse, beds, blankets, rugs etc.

Page 433.   4 Aug 1772.   MATT. NIGHTINGALE, AC, to JAS. & RO. DONALDS & Co,
           Deed of Trust - 5 sh.   Slave man and woman; land in Goochland
on Broad branch - 90 acres adj. THOS. WADLEY & WM. EAVES; beds etc. Wit:
BENJ. TALIAFERRO, WM. PENN, DAVID SHEPHERD.

Page 435.   9 Oct 1772.   OBEDIAH HENDERSON, AC, to HENDERSON McCAUL & Co,
           Glasgow merchants, Deed of Trust - 5 sh.   112 acres both sides
of Porrage Creek, formerly that of ELIAS DEHART; also female slave bought
of the county last March; horses etc.   Wit: MORDECAI BROWN, EDMD. POWELL,
WM. WILSON.

Page 436.   26 Oct 1772.   GILBERT HAY, AC, to HENDERSON McCAUL - Deed of
           Trust - 5 sh.   300 acres on Indian Creek; also 136 acres adj.
On first he has pat. and on second a deed.   Formerly that of THOS. WHITE,
late of AC.   Also a negress. Wit: WM. WILSON, WM. AALTON, JNO. PARSONS.

Page 438.   2 Nov 1772.   ROBT. CAUTHON, AC, to HENDERSON McCAUL & Co, Deed
           of Trust - 5 sh.   Six Slaves.

Page 440.   2 Nov 1772.   ROBT. JOHNSTON, AC, to JNO. HOGG, AC, for Ł40,
           392 acres on S side of Maple Creek. Lines: HUGH MORRIS.

Page 441.   4 Dec 1772.   EDWARD WARE, AC, to MATT. TUCKER, AC, for 20 sh.,
           4 acres on Horsley Creek. Lines: WM. CARRELL; bought from him.
Wit: JOS. TUCKER, THOS. LUMPKIN, JOS. CABELL.

Page 442.   4 Nov 1772.   RO. JOHNSTON, AC, to ALEX. GORDON, Deed of Trust.
           5 sh.   328 acres on Buffalo Spur and adj. Tobacco Row Mts.
Also 125 acres adj. LOMAX, McCULLOCH & DAVID CRAWFORD on head branch of
Pedlar; two negro fellows, Phil and Driver.   Wit: JAS. FRANKLYN, WM. POW-
ELL, JNO. McKINDLEY, EDMD. WILCOX, BENJ. TALIAFERRO.   Margin: 6 Jan 1812,
delivered to GORDON agent.

Page 445.   14 Nov 1772.   ROBT. JOHNSTON, AC, to SPIERS & BOWMAN, Deed of
           Trust - 5 sh.   404 acres next to James River; Otter Creek &
Capt. THOMAS' lines at the Stone Chimney; also 280 acres adj. on James;
also 294 acres joining the 280; also 170 acres adj. the 294 - above Otter
Creek.   Wit: WM. PENN, DAVID SHEPHERD, PAT. HART, JNO. McKINDLEY.   (Note:
Much of the Otter Creek area is now in the National Forest and the last
gap of about six miles of the Parkway Drive was opened a few years ago
when a bridge was built across James River.   There is a beautiful spot
called Otter Creek where one can camp and there is also a restaurant for
tourists.   It is about the lowest point in altitude on the Parkway, but
soon after crossing the James one begins the steep climb to the famed
Peaks of Otter.BFD)

Page 447.   9 Apr 1772.   MICAJAH CLARK, Albemarle Co, to CALEB WATTS of
           AC for Ł160, 350 acres. Lines: WM. WATTS, PETER BAY; also 250
acres. Wit: PETER DAVIE, JNO. HARVIE, MICAJAH CLARK JR.

Page 448.   29 May 1772.   FRANCIS NEW, AC, to CHAS. IRVING & JAS. TULEY SR,
           Albemarle Co, Deed of Trust - 5 sh.   76 acres on branch of
Short's Creek (which makes into Rockfish); also 3 slaves. Wit: JNO. OLD,
JNO. COBBS, JAS. McCAUL.

Page 450.   29 May 1772.   FRANCIS NEW, AC, to RICH. HARVIE, CHAS. IRVING
           & WM. MITCHELL, Albemarle Co, Deed of Trust - 5 sh.   76 acres
where he lives on Short Creek branch.   Also slaves. Wit: as above, but
put JAS. TULEY in room of JAS. McCAUL.

Page 452.   7 Dec 1772.   JAS. BROWN & wife JANNETT, Bedford Co, to JNO.
           HIGHT, AC, for Ł30, 248 acres on Stoney Run a branch of Ty(sic)

Lines: SAML. PO(?). Wit: JNO. SALE, WM. CAMPBELL, JNO. TILFORD.

Page 454. 7 Dec 1772. BENJ. DENNEE, AC, to HENRY HARPER, AC, for Ł45,
150 acres pat. to DENNEE Sep. 1764. Lines: Late Rev. ROBT.
ROSE. Wit: WM. MARTIN, MARTIN BIBB, GEO. CAMPBELL. Margin: Orig. del. to
WM. HARPER March 1786.

Page 455. 7 Dec 1772. MATT. TUCKER, AC, to ALEX. GORDON, AC, for Ł200,
4 tracts: 1) 223 acres 1/8, E side of Piney Mts., top of TAL-
IAFERRO Mts. 2) On Buffalo - 276 acres. Lines: JNO. PARKS, JR., branch
of Horsley. 3) 4 acres. Lines: WM. CARROLL, line where MATT. TUCKER
bought of CARROLL; branch of Horsley. 4) 266 acres on both sides of Long
branch of Buffalo. Lines: EDWD. WARE, AARON HIGGINBOTHAM, Long Branch.
Wit: JAS. HIGGINBOTHAM, ALEX. REID, CHAS. ELLIS. Margin: 6 Jan 1812,
orig. del. to GORDON, agent.

Page 459. 7 Dec 1772. WM. HIX, AC, to EDWARD BOWMAN, AC, for Ł65, 138
acres on branch of Huff and E side of Tobacco Row Mts. Part of
276 acres bought by HENRY CHILDRESS from WM. CABELL JR. Marked trees between HENRY & JNO. CHILDRESS and lines of BENJ. STINNETT & WM. HIX.

Page 460. 7 Jun 1772. WM. BICKNALL JR., AC, to WM. WILSON - horse and
other stock. Wit: JAS. FRANKLYN, WM. POWELL.

Page 461. 7 Dec 1772. JNO. BURROWS, Bedford Co, to HENDERSON McCAUL &
Co, Deed of Trust to secure debt of Ł10-14-10. Mare, bed, etc.
Wit: WM. WILSON, JNO. BROWN.

Page 462. 17 Nov 1772. THOS. DICKERSON, AC, to JAS. & RO. DONALDS & Co,
Deed of Trust - 5 sh. 3 tracts on Indian Creek; where I live;
slaves. Wit: BENJ. TALIAFERRO, DAVID SHEPHERD, JNO. McKINDLEY, JAS.
FRANKLYN.

Page 464. 5 Dec 1772. RICH. GATEWOOD to JAS. & RO. DONALDS & Co, Deed
of Trust - 5 sh. 70 or 80 acres on Buffalo. Lines: WM. GATE-
WOOD; where I now live; also bed, slave etc. Wit: EDMD. WILCOX, BENJ.
TALIAFERRO, DAVID SHEPHERD.

Page 466. Release by NEILL CAMPBELL, Factor for GEO. KIPPEN & Co. of
mortgage of Ł1559-11-9 of lands and slaves by Capt. HENRY KEY,
AC, in 1764. Release on 18 Apr 1770. Wit: WM. WILSON, JNO. STRATTON, WM.
LAYNE. Margin: Orig. del. to HENRY KEY's exrs. 14 Feb 1790.

Page 466. 1 Mar 1773. FRANCIS MERIWETHER, AC, to SAML. DAVIS, AC, for
Ł110, 400 acres on Rockfish. Lines: JNO. MILLION, MELOY, WOODS,
MORRILL, SAML. BELL.

Page 468. 9 Dec 1772. WM. FARRER to ELIOT ROBERTS, both of AC for Ł40,
200 acres on Ivey Creek. Lines: ELIOT ROBERTS. Wit: RICH.
FARRAR, HENRY ROBERTS, THOS. FARRAR.

Page 470. 28 Dec 1772. JAS. LYONS & wife AGNES, planters, to JAS. WOOD,
planter, for Ł70, 200 acres on Rockfish. Lines: CHISWELL's
line at the foot of the Mt. Bought by LYON of JOHN WEBB. Wit: MICHL.
McNEELEY, SAML. WOODS, WAML. LACKEY, JNO. FARRAR.

Page 473. 21 Nov 1772. THOS. MERRITT, Bedford Co, to DAVID WOODROOF, AC,
for Ł40, 321 acres branch of Harris and John Creek. Lines:
RICH. SHELTON, JNO. OWNBY, my own line, CARRINGTON's old order line. Wit:
JNO. GOODWIN, HEN. TRENT, JOS. GOODWIN, OBEDIAH TRENT, JO. MAGANN.

Page 474. 1 Mar 1773. WM. GILLAM & wife ELIZ., Bedford Co, to BENJ.
WASH, AC, for Ł55, 121 acres on N branch of Horsley. Line of
DAVID CRAWFORD.

Page 476. 1 Mar 1773. MARTIN DAWSON, AC, to his son, THOS. DAWSON, a
gift of 174(5?) acres.

Page 477. 4 Nov 1772. ROBT. JOHNSTON, AC, to GEO. KIPPEN & Co, Deed of
Trust - 5 sh. 400 acres and 200 acres adj. Under Rockey Row

Mt. on Rockey Row Creek. Also 140 acres on Irish Creek next to WM. PRYOR at the top of the blue ledge. Wit: WM. WILSON, JOS. GOODWIN, JOHNSTON BEEN. Margin: Del. to CHAS. IRVING 22 Mar 1774.

Page 479. 1 Mar 1773. JNO. SNYDER, AC, to GEO. COCKBURN, AC, deed of gift for tender love of SNYDER for his daughter, ELIZABETH, and her husband, GEORGE COCKBURN - 150 acres - old survey whereon NICHL. NEAL formerly lived. Part of 247 acres pat. to WM. CABELL 30 Mar 1759, and by CABELL sold to JULIAN NEAL by by NEAL sold to SNYDER.

Page 480. 31 Aug 1772. HENRY TENNISON, AC, to JNO. GILLILAND, AC, for Ŀ120, 200 acres on Porridge Creek. Lines: JNO. TENNISON. Wit: WM. WILSON, GEORGE McDANIEL, JNO. MANEES, JR.

Page 483. 30 Jan 1773. DANL. BURFORD for love of his daughter, FRANCES GOODWIN, AC, and children lawfully begotten - if either of children shoudl die before lawful age; or lawful issue - negress slave and increase. Wit: GABL. PENN, THOS. LUMPKIN, JAS. CREWS. To children at death of their mother.

Page 484. 1 Mar 1773. ABNER WITT, AC, to DAVID WITT for Ŀ30, 76 acres in a cove of a mt. on a branch of Rockfish. Lines: ANDREW REID, JAS. HERD, THOS. WEST. Wit: CHAS. WITT, LITTLEBERRY WITT, JNO. BABER. Margin: Or. del. to JNO. WITT.

Page 486. 1 Mar 1773. THOS. WILSHER & wife ANNE, AC, to AMBROSE CAMP- BELL, AC, for Ŀ30, 174 acres on branch of Tye. Lines: WILSHER & CAMPBELL pointers; WILSHER's old survey; EDMANDS, TARRANT. Wit: JOS. CABELL, JNO. CABELL, LARKIN GATEWOOD.

Page 488. 4 Nov 1772. JAS. BUSH, AC, to HUGH McCABE, AC, for Ŀ20, 130 acres Huff Creek. Lines: AMBROSE PORTER, JNO. WHEELER, GEO. BRAXTON, gent. Wit: HENRY FRANKLYN SR, RICH. BALLENGER, CORNL. SALE.

Page 489. 20 Feb 1773. JOB CARTER JR., AC, to JAS. & RO. DONALDS, Deed of Trust - 5 sh. paid to DAVID SHEPHERD, Factor - Ŀ1500 unin- spected tobacco; 50 "Barrells" of Indian corn; many other items. Wit: GEO. WEIR, DAVID SHEPHERD, JNO. McKINDLEY, THOS. LANDRUM.

Page 492. 24 Jul 1772. GEO. CAMPBELL, AC, to CARTER & TRENT, Deed of Trust - 5 sh. 228 acres on main fork of Piney which CAMPBELL bought of HENRY KEY; also stock etc. Wit: WM. LOVING, JAS. TARRANT, JAS. CAMPBELL, ELIZ. CAMPBELL, STEPHEN JOHNSON, LEONARD TARRANT.

Page 493. 2 Nov 1772. JNO. THOMPSON, AC, to CARTER & TRENT for Ŀ48-10, 219 acres on Rockfish. Pat. in Aug. of 1771. Wit: WM. LOVING, RO. WOODSON, WM. DEAVER.

Page 495. 1 Aug 1772. MATT. NIGHTINGALE, AC, to CARTER & TRENT, Deed of Trust - 5 sh. 150 acres. Lines: JNO. RYAN, bought by NIGHTIN- GALE of JOS. EATON; also one negress. Wit: WM. LOVING, RO. WOODSON, JAS. REID.

Page 496. 5 Mar 1773. GEO. STOVALL SR. & wife ELIZ, Bedford Co, to LEE ROY UPSHAW, Bedford, for Ŀ100, 400 acres on N side of Fluvanna on Stovall's Creek. (Note: It is queer to relate, but not a single person with last name beginning with "U" is to be found in the will books here from 1761 to 1919 Master Index. However, there are many in deeds for that period. BFD)

Page 499. 9 Jul 1772. JNO. BELL, AC, to HENDERSON McCAUL & CO, Deed of Trust - 5 sh. 200 acres on S side of Pedlar. Lines: NATHL. DAVIS, JNO. LEWIS, Buck branch. Wit: WM. POWELL, GEO. LAMBERT, JNO. STRATTON.

Page 501. 1 Jan 1773. JNO. MORRAL (signed MURRILL), AC, to SAML. WOODS of AC, merchant, for Ŀ80, negress, Dinnia, about 18, and her child, Isaac, about 2 months old. Wit: JAS. WALSH, JAS. WOODS, THOS. PATTON. Bill of sale.

Page 502. 26 Aug 1772. LUKE PANNALL, AC, to SAML. WOODS, AC, merchant,
for Ŀ12, black mare, gun, tobacco at JAMES HUSLEY's - except
Ŀ2-17 due HUSLEY out of crop. Wit: JAS. WALSH, JAS. STEPHENS, THOS.PATTON.

Page 502. 29 Oct 1772. JNO. RUCKER & wife ELENOR, AC, to AMBROSE RUCKER,
AC, for Ŀ5, 9 acres. Wit: THOS. LUMPKIN, MOSES PENN JR., ARCH-
ELAUS COX, ADAM BROWN. Margin: Or. del. to JNO. RUCKER for AMBROSE RUCKER
Feb 1791.

Page 506. 13 Mar 1773. ROBT. JOHNSTON, AC, to SPIERS & BOWMAN, Deed of
Trust - 5 sh. 1) Entry of 120 acres on S side of Otter Creek.
2) Entry of 404 acres on Otter & Fluvannah. 3) Entry of 218 acres on S
side of Cashaw Creek and on Chestnut Mt. 4) 500 acre survey on S side of
Cashaw; also penknife. Wit: GEO. WEIR, JNO. BIBB, JNO. McKINDLEY.

Page 508. 6 Jan 1773. STEPHEN HAM & wife MILDRED, AC, & AMBROSE GATE-
WOOD, AC, to EDWARD TINSLEY, AC, for Ŀ64, 126 acres on head
branch Rutledge Creek. Lines: JAS. MANEES, AMBROSE RUCKER, JNO. HARVIE,
JNO. DAVIS. Wit: MOSES PENN JR., AMBROSE RUCKER, WM. PATTERSON, JNO.
RITCHIE, JAS. WHITE.

Page 510. 18 Feb 1773. AMBROSE CAMPBELL & wife --- & AARON CAMPBELL, AC,
to JOS. CABELL, AC, for Ŀ100, 200 acres branch of Higginbotham
Mill Creek. Lines: VALENTINE COX, Glebe, MOSES HIGGINBOTHAM, JNO. BROWN,
LAURENCE CAMPBELL. Wit: GABL. PENN, WM. HORSLEY, JNO. HORSLEY, PAT. HART,
JNO. McKINDLAY.

Page 512. 16 Feb 1773. THEODORICK WEBB, Buckingham, to CUTHBERT WEBB,
Albemarle, for Ŀ100, 304 acres (150 of it pat. to WM. BRUSSE?)
Lines: HENRY KEY. 154 acres of it granted to THEODORICK WEBB. Wit: JAS.
MATTHEWS, JAS. HIGGINBOTHAM, JNO. GREGORY, JOSIAS WOOD, JNO. MOORE.

Page 515. 11 Dec 1772. JAS. MURRAH (mark of JAS. MURRAY) AC, to HENDER-
SON McCAUL & Co., Deed of Trust - 5 sh. Slave, cattle, 66
acres in fork of Cox Creek. 55 acres on branch of same creek; beds, etc.
Wit: WM. POWELL, DAVID KIPPEN, WM. GARLAND.

Page 517. 17 Mar 1773. SAML. CRAWLEY, AC, to GEO. KIPPEN & Co, Deed of
Trust. Cattle, etc. Wit: WM. WILSON, JAS. DILLARD JR.

Page 518. 13 Nov 1772. JNO. WARD, AC, to HENDERSON McCAUL & Co, Deed of
Trust - mare, etc. Wit: JNO. WHITEHEAD, WM. WILSON, DAVID
KIPPEN.

Page 519. 8 Mar 1773. JNO. SWANSON to THOS. BANKS, Deed of Trust - 5 sh.
11 acres adj. Turkie Mts. which SWANSON & VALENTINE COX bought
of THOS. REID, trustee of MARTIN TRAP; all working "tooles", carpenter's
and joiner's of SWANSON. Wit: GABL. PENN, WM. BANKS, JAS. DILLARD JR.

Page 521. 31 Mar 1773. JNO. RYAN, planter, AC, to MOSES HUGHES, AC, for
Ŀ100, 327 acres on Tye. UNITY, wife of RYAN.

Page 523. 21 Sep 1772. JNO. REID to ALEX. REID JR., both of AC, for Ŀ20,
S branch of S fork of Rockfish. Lines: EZRA MORRISON, WM. BAR-
NET. Wit: NATHAN REID, ALEX. REID, WM. WATERSON(?). Margin: Orig. del. to
ALEX. REID JR. 13 Apr 1785.

Page 524. 3 May 1773. JNO. RUCKER & wife ELENOR, AC, to JNO. RUCKER,
their son - love and 5 sh. 202 acres. Lines: DANL. GAINES.

Page 525. 8 Jan 1773. JNO. MURRIL SR, AC, to CHAS. IRVING, Factor for
HENDERSON McCAUL & Co, Deed of Trust - 5 sh. 343 acres on
Rockfish. Lines: ALEX. REID, DAVID MERIWETHER, JNO. PUCKET, DAVID REID.
MURRIL bought it from MATT. NIGHTINGALE; slaves, etc. Wit: CLOUGH
SHELTON, REUBIN JORDEN, JAS. McCAUL, ALEX. ROSE.

Page 528. 29 Oct 1772. AMBROSE RUCKER & wife MARY, AC, to JOHN RUCKER
SR, AC, for Ŀ5, 9 acres on a branch. Wit: THOS. LUMPKIN, JNO.
ROUZIE, MOSES PENN JR., ADM. BROWN. Margin: Orig. del. to JNO. RUCKER
Feb. 1791.

Page 531.   27 Mar 1773.   THOS. CRAWLEY, AC, to SPIERS & BOWMAN, Deed of
          Trust - 5 sh.   167 acres on branch of Piney - where he now
lives; also 99 acres on brnach of Piney. Wit: WM. PENN, DAVID SHEPHERD,
GEO. WEIR.

Page 533.   29 Apr 1773.   JNO. SWINNEY, AC, to RUTH CASH, BENJ. CASH and
          THOS. POWELL, JR., AC, - Deed of Trust. 5 sh.   Negress; bed,
stock, etc., and 64 acres on Pedlar. Wit: PAT. HART, RICH. BALLENGER,
ADAM BROWN, BENJ. TALIAFERRO.

Page 535.   10 Mar 1773.   JNO. GREGORY, AC, to CHAS. IRVING, Factor for
          HENDERSON McCAUL & Co, Deed of trust - 5 sh.   land on Rucker's
Run where he lives. Lines: HENRY KEY, JNO. HARMER; bought of HENRY KEY.
Wit: CLOUGH SHELTON, JAS. McCAUL, ALEX. ROSE, JNO. OLD.

Page 537.   3 May 1773.   JNO. REID, AC, to CHAS. SIMS, Albemarle Co, for
          Ŀ75, 137 acres on Hatt Creek. Line of THOS. MANN RANDOLPH.
Margin: Orig. del. to LEE HARRIS' son.

Page 540.   3 May 1773.   JNO. REID, AC, to CHAS SIMS, Albemarle Co, for
          Ŀ75, 200 acres on branch of Hatt Creek. Lines: FRANCIS STEELE
(or is it FRANCES?), his own line. Margin: as deed above.

Page 543.   3 May 1773.   JNO. COLEMAN, AC, to THOS. LUCAS, AC, for Ŀ130,
          183½ acres on Harris - half of land surveyed by COLEMAN &
LUCAS. Lines: N side of Cedar Mts. against the head of a branch; S side
of Tobacco Row Mt. Margin: Orig. del. to LUCAS July 1788.

          This book compared through and Memorials Transmitted.

                              BENJAMIN POLLARD

                                   Clerk

                         End of Deed Book C

148

DEDICATION

This work is affectionately dedicated to the recently reorganized Amherst Chapter of DAR. My good friend and church member, Mrs. Walter H. Carter, is the Regent.

Page 1.   17 Oct 1772.   JNO. THOMPSON, AC, to JOS. CABELL & JAS. HIGGIN-
           BOTHAM, AC, Deed of Trust - to secure debt of Ŀ88-12 - delivers
two tracts: 1) 200 acres, Lines of ZACH. TALIAFERRO and bought by "THOM-
SON" of JAS. BROWN on branch of Tye. 2) 194 acres on head branches of
Buck Creek and where TOMSON now lives. Lines: RO. BARNETT which he sold
to JNO. MONTGOMERY, "waggon Maker" can redeem after 10 Nov 1772. Wit: GEO.
LAMBERT, DAVID KEPPEN, JNO. HIGGINBOTHAM, WM. PENN, RICH. SHELTON, JNO.
CABELL. Proved 3 May 1773 by LAMBERT & PENN and on 7 Jun 1773, by JNO.
HIGGINBOTHAM. EDMD. WILCOX, Clk.

Page 3.   7 Jun 1773.   SAML. CULWELL (CALDWELL) & wife ANN, AC, to THOS.
           STEPHENSON, AC, for Ŀ160, 200 acres branch of Rockfish. Lines:
CHISWELL. Signed: CALDWELL.

Page 5.   3 Jun 1773.   WM. CABELL to his son, NICHL. CABELL, all jewels,
           leases, etc.--except 8 working slaves; my druggs (sic), books,
tobacco, furniture, stock. Wit: JOHN GOODE, CHAS. CREASY, WM. JOHNSON,
JAS. BOATWRIGHT. Receipt ack. of delivery of one punch ladle of silver.

Page 6.   3 Jun 1773.   WM. CABELL to his son, NICHL. CABELL (Margin: Del.
           to JOS. CABELL 5 May 1774), for 5 sh, 1400 acres bought and re-
covered of DANL. MAYO's exrs. 37 acres bought of CHAS. PATTERSON; 500
acres below Swann's Creek; 450 acres where I now live; 693 acres on Castle Creek of Tye; 1400 acres on Horsley; 430 acres on the Ginsang(?)
branch, a branch of Hatt Creek; 200 acres where WM. TYRE lately lived;
100 acres where THOS. LANGIN lives; 200 acres bought of JNO. EDMONDS.
Last 4 tracts on the branches of Tye; 400 acres late in possession of
JERRY WHITTEN near the Tobacco Row Mts. and now in possession of WM.
Reserves uses of plantations on the river below JOS. CABELL's ferry and
liberty to clear a plantation at the Red Land near FRANCES WEST and timber for support of the plantations during lives of self and wife, if he
should marry; and if he dies before her, reserves use of the new dwelling
house and partial use of office houses belonging thereto. Wit: Same as
previous deed.

Page 8.   14 Apr 1773.   WM. TYRE to HENDERSON McCAUL, Deed of Trust - to
           secure Ŀ24-3-3-5 sh. One entry where WM. TYREE now lives - 150
acres on Buffalo; stock. Wit: WM. WILSON, OBEDIAH HENDERSON, THOS.WRIGHT.

Page 10.   23 Apr 1773.   JOS. LAYNE, AC, to ALEX. SPIERS, JNO. BOWMAN &
           Co., Glasgow merchants, Deed of Trust - Ŀ35 debt- 5 sh. where
he lives on Otter branch. Lines: NATHL. DAVIS, RO. JOHNSTON. Wit: WM.
PENN, THOS. LUMPKIN, DANL. BURFORD JR. (SR?).

Page 12.   25 May 1773.   CARNABY VEAL, AC, to SPIERS & BOWMAN - Deed of
           Trust - WM. PENN, factor - a tract where he lives and lines of
SOLOMON CARTER & THOS. WAUGH; another tract on Tobacco Row - lines of
RICH. DAVIES and now cultivated by VEAL. Furniture, stock etc. Wit:
WM. PENN, PETER CARTER, MARY ANN CARTER.

Page 15.   12 Jan 1773.   PERRIN FARRAR, AC, to RICH. FARRAR, Albemarle Co,
           for Ŀ150, 189 acres S side Rockfish River. Lines: THOS. FARRAR.
Wit: SAML. SHELTON, THOS. FARRAR, WM. FARRAR, MICHL. THOMAS.

Page 16.   9 Nov 1772.   SAML. HANCOCK, AC, to MARTIN DAWSON, AC, for Ŀ100,
           277 (5?) acres top of Smith's Mt. and coves on side of same.
Lines: WM. CABELL JR., JOS. BALLINGER, WM. CABELL. Wit: WM. DAWSON,
NATHL. HILL, JOS. DAWSON, RO. DAWSON. Margin: Del. to JAS. FRANKLYN.

Page 19.   11 Jan 1773.   LEONARD GOFF, AC, to WM. GUTTRY for Ŀ30, 100 ac-
           res branch of Stovall Creek. Lines: Orphins. ANN GOFF, wife of

LEONARD. Wit: JNO. FORQUERAN, JNO. GOFF, MARY GOFF. Proved by the 3 wit. 5 Jul 1773.

Page 21. 18 Nov 1772. JAS. BYOUS to JAS. MANEES - Deed of Trust - 5 sh. cows, pigs, dishes, etc. Wit: THOS. HARGET, JAS. MANEES. Rec. 5 Jul 1773.

Page 23. 3 Jul 1773. STEPHEN GOLDSBY, AC, to MATT. WILSON, for Ł35, 100 acres. Lines: CHAS. BURKS, SARAH NEWTON's ford (This is on two lines and a bit difficult to decipher) so called. Branch above RUSSELL's Cabbin (sic). Wit: CHAS. BURKS, MOSES SWEENEY, DAVID BURKS, NEAL McCANN.

Page 25. 2 Jul 1773. JNO. WEBB, AC, to HENDERSON McCAUL & Co, Deed of Trust to secure Ł123-102 - 5 sh. One mare and colt; two slaves Mariah and Jean; black horse which he had of JNO. D. COLEMAN; furniture and tobacco crop. Wit: NOELL JOHNSTON, RICH. BALLENGER, CHAS. BURRUS, RO. MAYS.

Page 27. 2 Jul 1773. JNO. WEBB & wife URSULA, for Ł90, 180 acres on Thresher's Creek. Lines: PEARCE WADE, JNO. BOSWALL. Wit: WM. WILSON, CHAS. BURRUS, NOELL JOHNSON.

Page 29. 27 Oct 1772. LEANDER HUGHES, Cumberland Co, to DAVID CRAWFORD, AC, for Ł65, 400 acres N branch Horsley. Lines: Side of a mt., in a valley. Wit: JNO. CRAWFORD, JAS. ALLEN, WM. WOMACK, JNO. WATKINS.

Page 31. 14 Nov 1772. Marriage contract between SAML. AYRES & RACHEL MORRISON, both of AC, makes over all land and 6 slaves with increase to her. To go to any heirs begotten by me of RACHEL. If no heirs, then to heirs of RACHEL begotten by late WM. MORRISON, dec'd. Wit: THOS. MORRISON, WM. PATTON, JOS. H. MORRISON.

Page 31. 4 Aug 1772. Agreement between WM. CABELL JR. and JOS. CABELL, both of AC. JR. has lately bought the ordinary at Amherst Courthouse from RICH. ALLCOCK and 1070 acres adj. for Ł800. JOSEPH wishes to become partner & obligates himself for one half of purchase money and same for conveniences at ordinary. Wit: HUGH ROSE, GABL. PENN, EDMD. WINSTON. (Note: This courthouse was in present Nelson and near hamlet of Colleen on U.S. highway 29.)

Page 32. List of surveys made by WM. CABELL JR., county surveyor, from 20 Jun 1772 to 20 Jun 1773. Dates and acreage are given, but no location of land.

12 Mar 1773			66 a.	20 Apr 1773 JAS. KITCHEN	136 a.
8 "	DAVID BARRET		54 a.	3 Dec 1772 RICH. LAURENCE	49 a.
27 Apr "	GEO. BLAINE		26 a.	22 Feb 1773 Resurveyed for THOS.	
5 Mar "	JNO. BROWN JR.		182 a.	LUCAS & AMBROSE RUCKER	
25 Mar "	JOS. CABELL		188 a.	by order of Gen Court	
10 May "	NICHL. CABELL		300 a.		272 a.
11 May "	" "		450 a.	11 Nov 1772 PETER MARTIN	148 a.
18 "	" "	"	450 a.	17 Feb 1773 JAS. MATHEWS	230 a.
19 "	" "	"	5176 a.	26 Mar 1773 DAVID McANALLY	170 a.
21 "	" "	"	400 a.	28 Apr 1773 RICH. McCARY	190 a.
29 Mar "	WM. CALBREATH		180 a.	15 Apr 1773 RODERICK McCULLOCH	11 a.
28 Nov 1772	GEO. CAMPBELL		48 a.	2 Dec 1772 MICHL. MORRISON	48 a.
30 Mar 1773	MOSES CLACK		54 a.	5 Dec 1772 WM. MORRISON JR	53 a.
10 Mar 1773	EDMUND COFFEE		197 a.	30 Apr 1773 JAS. NEVIL	69 a.
29 Mar 1773	WM. CRIBBON		53 a.	22 May 1773 JNO. PHILLIPS	203 a.
12 Apr 1773	NICHL. DAVIES		383 a.	27 Nov 1772 WM. RAMSEY	33 a.
	"	390,	324 a.	13 Nov 1772 ALEX. SMITH	53 a.
7 Nov 1772	" "		38 a.	16 Dec 1772 GEO. STOVAL JR.	140 a.
20 Apr 1773	RO. DAVIS		380 a.	18 Nov 1772 WM. TILLAR	36 a.
26 Apr 1773	JNO. DAWSON		146 a.	26 Nov 1772 THOS. TYLER	134 a.
17 Dec 1772	JAS. DILLARD		400 a.	16 Mar 1773 EDWARD WARE	54 a.
10 Mar 1773	JNO. DURHAM		46 a.	15 Feb 1773 CUTHBERT WEBB	229 a.
3 Nov 1773	WM. EVANS		360 a.	6 May 1773 FRANCIS WEST	110 a.
3 Mar 1773	SAML. HIGGINBOTHAM		140a.	17 Nov 1772 JNO. WOOD	76 a.
24 Apr 1773	RALPH JOPLING		400 a.	Signed by WM. CABELL JR., Amherst	
16 Feb 1773	THOS. JOPLING		391 a.	Co. Surveyor, 20 Jun 1773.	

Page 34.   3 Feb 1773.   THOS. CARPENTER, AC, & Parish to SAML. WOODS for
Ł140, slave, Bob, about 6; negro wench Hannah, about 30; cows,
calves, stock, dishes, corn, tobacco etc. Wit: JAS. WALSH, THOS. CARPEN-
TER, Jr.

Page 35.   2 Aug 1773. WM. PATTON, AC, to THOS. MORRISON, Jr., AC, for
Ł75, 192 acres on S side and joining S fork of Rockfish. Lines:
JNO. MORRISON, ALEX. PATTON, WM. PATTON JAS. WOODS, JNO. THOMSON. JEAN,
wife of WM. PATTON.

Page 37.   2 Aug 1773.   JNO. CRAWFORD & wife ELIZ, AC & Parish, to LAUR-
ENCE LONG, St. Ann's Parish of Albemarle, for Ł20, 92 acres
on Meloy's Creek.

Page 38.   7 May 1773.   DAVID BARNETT, AC, to CARTER & TRENT - Deed of
Trust to secure debt of Ł77-3-6, 120 acres on Tye and Cockses'
Creek and Elk Creek. Bought by BARNETT from WM. COFFEE 1 Jun 1770. Also
cattle, dishes etc. Wit: WM. LOVING, JAS. COFFEE, PATTY COFFEE.

Page 40.   5 Jul 1773. WM. McCRAW, Pittsylvania Co, to THOS. LUMPKIN,
AC, for Ł95, 200 acres which McCRAW bought of JAMES NOWLIN
and part of 400 acres pat. 19 Aug 1758 to PATRICK NOWLIN. Lines: MOSES
SWEENEY, JNO. HARVIE, EDWD. TINSLEY - formerly that of WM. MORRAN; JNO.
DAVIS, JNO. COLEMAN. Wit: W. CABELL JR., EDMD. WILCOX, BENJ. TALIAFERRO,
MOSES SWEENEY.

Page 43.   20 Jan 1773.   JNO. LOVING, AC, to WM. HANSBROUGH, RO. WRIGHT,
RO. MONTGOMERY, JNO. JOHNSON, JNO. TUGGLE - Deed of Trust for
debt of Ł17-10 - stock, furniture, etc. Wit: WM. LOVING, JNO. LOVING JR.,
WM. KEY.

Page 44.   21 Jul 1773.   WM. CAMPBELL, AC, to JNO. ROSE, AC, for Ł30,
mare, cow, hogs, etc. and tobacco now in CAMPBELL's warehouse.
Wit: JOHN RYAN, ZACH. TALIAFERRO.

Page 45.   20 Apr 1773.   ADAM BROWN to WM. GATEWOOD - horse I had of
PHILL THURMOND - Deed of Trust. Wit: GABL. PENN, DUDLEY GATE-
WOOD.

Page 46.   11 Aug 1773.   RICH. ALLCOCK, AC, to EDMD. WILCOX, AC, Deed of
Trust for debt of Ł26-16-7; 5 sh. - stock, furniture, knife
etc. Tobacco fees due WILCOX. Wit: JNO. DILLARD, BENJ. TALIAFERRO. Knife
delivered.

Page 47.   25 Mar 1773.   JNO. LIVINGSTONE, AC, to THOS. LIVINGSTONE, AC,
Deed of Trust for debt of Ł10-5; stock, furniture. Wit: BENJ.
MANEES, JAS. MANEES, SR. (?).

Page 48.   10 Apr 1773.   RICH. PETER, AC, for love borne his son, SAML.
PETER, AC, 280 acres on Cedar Creek where RICH. now lives. Lines:
NEAL McCANN, EDWD BARNET. Wit: EDWD BARNET, CHAS. BARNET, CHARITY BARNET.

Page 50.   6 Sep 1773.   ALEX. BAGGS & wife SARAH, AC, to JNO. MARCHALL,
AC, for Ł30 paid to WM. TAYLOR by MARCHALL. One year of in-
denture - 166 acres both sides of S branch of middle fork of Pedlar.
Pat. to JAS. COLBERT BLAIR 10 Jul 1766. Margin: Orig. del. Oct. 1779.

Page 52.   6 Sep 1773.   JNO. SIMS TENNISON, AC, to HUGH GILLILAND, AC,
for Ł30, 100 acres on Porage Creek. Lines: HENRY TENNISON JR.
Wit: JAS. HIGGINBOTHAM, MERRITT MAGANN, JAS. MANEES, JR.

Page 54.   11 Aug 1773.   RICH. ALLCOCK, AC, to SPIERS & BOWMAN, Glasgow
merchants, Deed of Trust. Debt of Ł44-1-1. 5 shillings. 400
acres. Lines: WM. SPENCER, HUGH ROSE, Gent., WM. CABELL SR., WM. CABELL
JR., Gent. Bought of DRURY BOWMAN and now ALLCOCK lives on tract; also
slave, Davey; knife. Wit: GEO. WEIR, WM. PENN, PATRICK HART.

Page 57.   16 Jul 1773.   THOS. GRIFFIN, AC, to JAS. STEPHENS, Deed of
Trust for debt of Ł62-3-7½. 5 sh. 160 acres and slaves.
Lines: WALTER KING, HENRY BARNS, JAS. STEPHENS and where GRIFFIN lives.

Wit: GEO. WEIR, JNO. LAMONT, PATRICK HART.

Page 60.   Recorded 2 Sep 1773. Order to DANL. GAINES & AMBROSE RUCKER,
            AC, J.P.'s, to quiz REBEKAH TENNISON, wife of HENRY, as to
dower wishes in deed to JNO. GILLILAND on 31 Aug 1772. Done and rec. as
above.

Page 62.   4 Oct 1773. JAS. TULEY SR. & Wife, JUDEY, AC and Parish, yeo-
            man, to ASHCRAFT ROACH, AC, yeoman, for Ł100, 200 acres on
Wilderness Creek. Lines: RO. DAVIS, JR.

Page 64.   4 Oct 1773. EDWD. STEPHENSON & wife PHEBE, AC and Parish, to
            SAML. WOODS, AC & Parish, for Ł140, 113½ acres on both sides
Taylor Creek. Lines: ELIZ. STEPHENSON, FRANCIS MERIWETHER, REBECCA RO-
BERTSON, RO. STEPEHNSON; near the mill and door thereof; peach trees.
Margin: Orig. del. to WM. WOODS 16 May 1782.

Page 66.   4 Oct 1773. LANGSDON DEPRIEST & wife ANN; DAVID CLARK & wife
            SARAH; and WM. CLARK & wife FRANCES, all of AC & Parish, to
SAML. WOODS, AC, & Parish, for Ł215, 400 acres both sides Lynch Creek and
N side Rockfish. Lines: JAMES BELL. Margin: Orig. del. to WM. WOODS 16
May 1782.

Page 68.   2 Oct 1773. DAVID WOODROOF & wife CLARY, AC, to NICHL. DAVIS,
            Bedford Co, for Ł20, 200 acres head of John's Creek and branch
of Fluvanna or James. Lines: JNO. OWNBEY, RICH. POWELL, NICHL. DAVIS.
Wit: ELIAS LEMASTER, JOS. GOODWIN, RICH. POWELL, OBEDIAH H. TRENT. Del.
to H. LANDON DAVIES, 5 Jun 1774.

Page 70.   21 Jul 1773. SAML. CROUTCHER to GEO. PENN, Exr. of AMBROSE
            LEE, dec'd., for Ł30 debt due estate - 5 sh. - slave lad Taff
(?), formerly property of LEE. Wit: GABL. PENN, BENJ. TALIAFERRO.

Page 72.   17 Aug 1773. MICAJAH GOODWIN to ALEX. SPIERS, JNO. BOWMAN &
            Co, Deed of Trust - debt of Ł35-16-2; 5 sh. 200 acres given
him by deed from his father, JOHN GOODWIN on James river, between lands
of JOS. GOODWIN & NICHL. DAVIS. Also pair of shoe buckles. Wit: THOS.
LUMPKIN, JOHN RITCHIE, WM. PENN. Buckles delivered.

Page 75.   3 Sep 1773. JNO. GRAYHAM, AC, to RICH. HARVIE, Merchant, for
            Ł250, slaves named - seven in all; horse, etc. Deed of Trust.
Wit: DANL. HARVIE, JNO. FRANKLIN, JNO. HARRISON. Margin: Orig. del. to
RICH. HARVIE by his Boy, 22 Aug 1778.

Page 76.   23 Jun 1769. JNO. HOWARD, Augusta Co, to BENJ. HOWARD & WM.
            LEAK - Did yesterday sell them slaves named to satisfy two
executions sent out by McALEXANDER BAIN vs. JOHN HOWARD. Two sums due:
Ł271-16-5 and Ł5-3-10. Wit: JOS. CABELL, CHAS. MAY. Receipt by BENJ.
HOWARD for self and LEAK.

Page 77.   Shff. bonds for various duties for ZACHARIAH TALIAFERRO, 1 Nov
            1773. Bondsmen: WM. SPENCER, JOS. DILLARD, JAS. STEPHENS,
HUGH ROSE, GABL. PENN, WM. WALTON, JAS. DILLARD, CHAS. ROSE, JNO. HARVIE,
CHAS. STATHAM, JOELL CRAWFORD, DANL. GAINES. Bond of Ł1000 and appointed
by Gov. of Colony 25 Oct last. Two bonds.

Page 79.   5 Jun 1773. GEO. LOVELL & wife ELIZ., AC, to THOMAS WRIGHT,
            AC, for Ł18, 300 acres Lynch Road and line of JOSEPH FROST.
Wit: JAS. SIMMONS, WM. WRIGHT, THOS. DAWSON, WM. BROWN. SIMMONS also
spelled SYMONS. ELIZ. signed as BETTY.

Page 81.   30 Oct 1773. EDWD MOUSLEY to CHAS. YANCEY, both of AC, for
            Ł15, 93 acres on Rockfish and head branch of Hiccory and Tay-
lor Creeks. Lines: MOUSLEY. Wit: JOELL CRAWFORD, NATHL. BARNETT, JNO.
JACOBS.

Page 83.   29 Oct 1773. RO. STEPHENSON & WM. STEPHENSON, AC, to SAML.
            WOODS, AC, for Ł187-10, 334 acres Lynch Creek on N side of
Rockfish. Lines: JAS. MARTIN, LANGSDON DEPRIEST, JAS. ROBERTSON, FRANCIS
MERIWETHER. Wit: ALEX. REID JR., JNO. HENDERSON, MATT. MONTGOMERY. MARY,

wife of RO. STEPEHNSON. EDMD. WILCOX, Clk, by WM. LOVING, deputy.

Page 84.   5 Oct 1773. WM. MILLER, SR., AC, (McCULLAR in deed) to DANL.
            GAINES - Debt due JAS. & RO. DONALDS & Co. and GAINES is
MILLER's special bail for Ŀ25-8-1 due WM. CUNNINGHAM & Co, Deed of Trust
to secure GAINES - 5 sh. 227 acres on Harris Creek which MILLER bought
of GEO. CARRINGTON. Lines: HUGH ROSE, JNO. TINSLEY, RICH. SHELTON, ISAAC
WRIGHT; also stock, furniture etc. Also CHARLES MILLER's part of tobacco
at HOUCHEN's. Wit: THOS. LUMPKIN, GEO. McDANIEL, JNO. McDANILE, WM.
MILLER, JR.

Page 87.   28 Oct 1773. GEO. TAYLOR to his daughter, BETTY BOND, wife of
            CHARLES BOND, and my grandchildren: CHAS, ZACH. & ANN BOND -
150 acres where CHAS. BOND now lives on Crawley's creek. Lines: SAML.
MURPHY, HENRY TAYLOR, DUNCAN CAMMERON, pat. line - granted to GEO. TAYLOR
20 Sep 1751, by pat. Also stock to grandchildren.

Page 88.   1 Oct 1773. WM. HORRAL & wife MARY, AC, to THOS. FONTAINE, AC,
            for Ŀ80, 262 acres on Head branch Davis Creek and head of Ruck-
er's Run. Part of 3 "survies". Lines: JNO. WADE, CHAS. TATE, JOELL CRAW-
FORD, LAURENCE SUDDARTH. Wit: ABRAHAM SEAY, JNO. THURMOND.

Page 89.   1 Nov 1773. HENRY KEY, AC, to JNO. BUSH, Buckingham Co, for
            Ŀ33-1, 158 acres S side Peavine Mt. Part of pat. to KEY on
20 Sep 1759. Lines: JNO. HARMER, Rucker's Run. MARY, wife of KEY. Del.
to CARROL EADES 30 Jan 1794. (Note: This deed has been damaged and seemingly some later scribe has gone over parts of it to make it more legible)

Page 91.   1 Nov 1773. Same parties as above Ŀ59-5 (blurred?) 298 acres
            in same area as land just above. This deed has also had some
later writing done by someone.

Page 92.   Same date and parties as above two deeds - Ŀ55-7, 278 acres on
            both sides of N branch of Rucker's Run. Line of JNO. HARMER.
Margin as above for del. to CARROL EADES.

Page 94.   Same date and parties as above - Ŀ16-5, 82 acres on Naked Run
            and pat. to KEY 5 Jun 1765. Lines: JNO. HARMER, BUSH. Del.
to EADES as above.

Page 95.   1 Nov 1773. SAML. MARKSBURY, AC, to his children: JOHN,SAML.
            & RACHEL MARKSBURY, AC - JOHN gets land & furniture; SAML.
gets a negress; RACHEL "of these presents which I have delivered". My
wife ISBELL, and I are to enjoy estate during our lives. Wit: AARON HIGG-
INBOTHAM JR., RICH. PETERS, PHILIP OWEN. (I have noted that these people
are found later in Garrard and Shelby counties in my native Kentucky. I
am not prepared to state which ones went, but it is the same family. BFD)

Page 96.   6 Dec 1773. WM. McQUERRY & wife ANNDORE, AC, to HENRY KIRBY,
            AC, for Ŀ80, and KIRBY is discharged of Ŀ36-10, 150 acres on
head of Franklyn's Creek. Wit: WM. CRAWFORD, WM. WELCH.

Page 98.   6 Dec 1773. JNO. FARRAR,AC, to JNO. LYON, AC, for Ŀ25, 103
            acres on N branch Rockfish. Part of tract of JNO. FARRAR's
and got by recorded deed. Lines: JNO. FARRAR, REUBEN JORDAN, JNO. MONT-
GOMERY.

Page 100.   12 Oct 1773. DAVID DUNCAN, AC, to GABL. PENN, AC, for Ŀ105,
            Deed of Trust for debt due JAS. & RO. DONALDS & Co, Glasgow
merchants - slaves, tobacco on plantation where I live. DAVID SHEPHERD
factor for company. Wit: BENJ. TALIAFERRO, JO. TUCKER.

Page 102.   24 Nov 1773. CARTER BRAXTON, King William county, to WM. WIL-
            SON, AC, for Ŀ297-10, 850 acres on N side and joining Buffalo
River - part of a tract. Lines: MATT. TUCKER on N side of Buffalo; CARTER
BRAXTON, GERRARD BANKS, JOSHUA HUDSON, JOS. CABELL. Wit: JO. TUCKER, JNO.
DILLARD, GABL. PENN.

Page 104.   6 Dec 1773. JNO. CRAGHEAD & wife JENNY, AC, to JOHN BOLES,
            Buckingham Co, for Ŀ67-10, 4 surveys of 309 acres on both

sides of Lackey's Mt. & Corbin Creek and N side of Davis Creek. Lines: JAS. LACKEY, WM. HORRAL, top of the mt. Wit: WM. HORRALL, JAS. W.(H?) BUNTON.

Page 106. 12 Jul 1773. JNO. VICKERS, Orange Co, N.C., to JAS. EDMESTON, AC, for 5 sh, 70 acres S branch of Middle Fork of Pedlar and blue ridge. Lease for 1 year - one ear of Indian corn due on Lady Day next. Wit: GEO. TAYLOR, ABRAHAM SMITH, CHAS. ISON. 70 acres leased, but next day it was sold. See next deed.

Page 107. 13 Jul 1773. JNO. VICKERS & wife EALS, Orange Co, N.C. to JAS. EDMISTON, AC, for Ŀ20, 70 acres. Same witnesses.

Page 110. 5 Dec 1773. WM. DUIGUID, Buckingham Co, to OBADIAH HENDERSON, AC, for Ŀ25, 112 acres both sides Porrige Creek. Lines: WM. DUIGUID, WM. TACKET, ELIAS DEHART's old line. Part of 300 acres pat. to ELIAS DEHART, 20 Aug 1760. Wit: JAS. PATTISON, THOS. RIDGWAY, JNO. CHRISTIAN.

Page 111. 6 Dec 1773. WM. HAYNES & wife HANNAH, AC, to DAVID CRAWFORD, AC, for Ŀ27, 121 5/8 acres on N side Tobacco Row Mt. and coves. Wit: ISAAC WRIGHT, DEVORIX GILLIAM, PETER CARTER. Orig. del. JO(?) BARNES Jan 1792 per order.

Page 113. 1 Dec 1773. HENRY KEY & wife MARY, AC, to CHAS. IRVING & MARTIN KEY, Albemarle (Margin: Orig. del. to CHAS. IRVING 22 Mar 1774) HENRY & wife are about to remove to South Carolina and most of goods sent on to new habitation. Ŀ5, 97 acres pat. to KEY, 5 Jun 1765. Lines: KEY, Finley's Gap, and 160 acres pat. in 1771. 400 acres pat. 15 Aug 1764. Lines: JNO. HARMER, KEY. Tract of 273 acres bought of THOS. PHILLIPS on W side of Cub Creek. 150 acres pat. to MARTIN TRAP 10 Sep 1744. Lines: JNO. DAVIS. 400 acres in Albemarle pat. to KEY 16 Jun 1759. 400 acres in AC on branch of Tye on N side Berry's Mt. 300 acres in AC on branch in same location as 400. Lines: HARMER, KING, Col. FRY, KEY. Power of atty. to them to sell and to pay debt due GEO. KIPPEN & Co, CHAS. IRVING is factor; many evil disposed persons might otherwise seize land. Wit: WM. CABELL JR., JAS. NEVIL, WM. SCRUGGS, JAS. MATTHEWS, CORNL. THOMAS, JNO. STRUTTON. Page 117 is order to AC JP's WM. CABELL JR., JAS. NEVIL & CORNL. THOMAS to quiz MARY as to total of 2180 acres conveyed above in AC and Albemarle. Order of 4 Dec 1773; done 6 Dec 1773 by CABELL & THOMAS.

Page 118. 6 Dec 1773. WM. HANSBROUGH to JAS. NEVIL for Ŀ7-10, 100 acres Line of NEVIL. (Here again I should like to point out that at least on descendant went to Shelby County, Kentucky, where I was reared. A will in Nelson County Va. shows this when a widow of this same family has remark showing that a son is living in the Kentucky County mentioned. She "baits" him to get him to return. I have found several such lures in Nelson County wills. The "western" country was just not a "Fitten" place for one to live from the tone of such documents. BFD)

Page 119. 11 Dec 1773. WM. LAVENDER & wife MILDRED, AC, to EDMD. WILCOX, AC, for Ŀ100, 546½ acres bought by WM. LAVENDER from exrs. of PHILIP GRYMES & LUNSFORD LOMAX, JR., 17 Apr 1770. On branch of Tye. Lines: MILLS, ALLCOCK, KING. Wit: PATRICK HART, BENJ. TALIAFERRO, WM. POWELL, GABL. PENN, AARON CAMPBELL, RICH. ALCOCK.

Page 121. 11 Dec 1773. RICH. ALCOCK, AC, to EDMD. WILCOX, AC, Deed of Trust, debt of Ŀ65. 5 sh. 400 acres. Lines: WM. SPENCER, HUGH ROSE, WM. CABELL SR, WM. CABELL JR. Bought of DRURY BOWMAN and where ALCOCK now lives; one snuff box. Wit: GABL. PENN, BENJ. TALIAFERRO, JNO. WIATT, THOS. POWELL JR., WM. McQUERRY.

Page 123. 8 Jul 1773. WM. CAMDEN, AC, to ALEX. SPIERS, JNO. BOWMAN, Merchants of North Britain. Deed of Trust. 5 sh. 152 acres. Lines: NOELL JOHNSTON, JNO. HIGGINBOTHAM, WM. STINNETT, BENJ. NOELL. On Huff Creek, where he lives. Wit: WM. POLLARD, JESSE MILLS, GEO. WEIR.

Page 125. 8 Dec 1773. RICH. ALCOCK, AC, to EDMD. WILCOX, AC, for Ŀ65, household furniture, stock, smith's tools, bellows & snuff box.

Wit: BENJ. TALIAFERRO, PATRICK HART, MATT. NIGHTINGALE (Note: This man went to Kentucky, too.)

Page 125. 22 Dec 1773. RICH. ALCOCK to JOS. CABELL, EDMD. WILCOX, WM. SPENCER - 5 sh. to secure them on replevy bond to DONALDS & Co. - slave, Davie. Wit: DAVID SHEPHERD, GABL. PENN, JOS. MAYS.

Page 126. 20 Dec 1773. JNO. LONDON, Halifax Co. and Parish of Antrom (sic) to JOS. WILSURE, AC, for Ь14, 185 acres branch of Buffalo, branch of Tye. Lines: Col. JOSHUA FRY. Wit: JNO. OWNBY JR., JAS. OWENBY, HENRY TUGGLE.

Page 128. 4 Mar 1774. Entry of WM. CABELL, AC Surveyor (Junior), 400 acres between his own lines; Joe's Creek - about ½ mile from the mouth; Pounding Mill Creek. Also 400 acres - his own line; same creek; S fork of Fendley's Creek. 400 acres - Lines: his own; WM. HANSBROUGH, between S and N forks of Fendley's Creek. 400 acres between his own line and MOSES RAY, NICHL. CABELL, WM. RAY - branches of Stephen's and Mayo's Creek. 400 acres on branch of Fendley's Creek. Lines: WM. HANSBROUGH's upper line, creek. Small island in Fluvanna River, just above Wood's Island; nearly adjacent to Pounding Mill creek. Another small island in Fluvanna River and just below Wood's Island and adjacent to his own plantation on Watt's Creek. Certified by JAS. NEVIL, J.P.

Page 129. 20 Aug 1773. ABNER WITT, AC, to EDWD. CARTER & RO. TRENT - Deed of Trust to secure debt of Ь126-5-7, 100 acres where I live. Lines: ALEX. REID JR., JNO. LACKEY, slaves (3), cattle. Wit: WM. LOVING, CHAS. WITT, LITTLEBERRY WITT, JOS. GRAYSON. Margin: Del. to WM. LOVING.

Page 130. 27 Sep 1773. GEO. BLAIN, AC, sadler, to JNO. MONTGOMERY & WM. WALTON, AC, - various items - slave, mare, cows etc; formerly property of WM. BOWEN & JAS. MATTHEWS; tobacco - 5000 pds. of crop for year; corn, furniture, horse which was that of THOMPSON DICKERSON formerly; cow and calf once belonging to JOHN LOVING; 9 pigs - formerly those of WM. BARNET; sow and pigs formerly those of ABRAHAM LEA. Wit: JAS. CULL, THOS. & RO. MONTGOMERY.

Page 131. 24 Feb 1774. JOS. CABELL & wife MARY, AC, to WM. CABELL JR. of AC,- Ь450 their interest in ordinary at Amherst Courthouse and 1070 acres adjoining; held in common with WM. CABELL JR. Wit: FRANCIS WEST JR., BRANSFORD WEST, HEZEKIAH EADS, FRANCIS WEST, WM. CABELL.

Page 133. 1 Jan 1774. THOS. MANN RANDOLPH & wife ANN, Goochland Co, to DAVID MONTGOMERY JR., for Ь67-10, 226 acres on branch of Nassau Creek. Pat. to RANDOLPH 16 Aug 1756. Wit: DAVID MONTGOMERY, WM. WRIGHT, JAS. MONTGOMERY.

Page 134. 17 Mar 1774. AMBROSE JONES, AC, to WM. CABELL JR., AC. for Ь150, 374 acres on N side Tye; branch of Black Creek. Part of tract formerly that of LUNSFORD LOMAX. Lines: JNO. CARGWRIGHT, WM. CABELL JR., small mt., GEO. BLAIN. Wit: BENJ. TALIAFERRO, WM. LOVING, JOS. CABELL, JAS. NEVIL, CORNL. THOMAS, RO. POLLARD.

Page 136. 1 Sep 1773. EDWD CHEATHAM, AC, to CARTER & TRENT - Deed of Trust - Ь45 debt. 5 sh. 197 acres N side Rockfish and head branch of Lynch Creek. Lines: WM. MORRISON (formerly that of Col. LEWIS). Wit: WM. LOVING, LEONARD PHILLIPS, FRANCIS WRIGHT, JACOB WRIGHT.

Page 138. 4 Apr 1774. Agreement between STEPHEN HAM and DANL. GAINES, both of AC and Parish - GAINES leases 298 acres to HAM to farm on head branch of Rutledge. Lines: ANTHONY RUCKER. MILLEY, wife of HAM. Lease runs for 17 years from Jan 1 next. During last 15 years HAM is to pay GAINES Ь10 per year for each tithable employed on farm or in Taylor (sic) business. HAM is to plant 100 apple or peach trees - or 150 and 50 of each - and is to leave land under good fence and is to erect houses.

Page 140. 30 Aug 1773. THOS. LOMAX, Caroline, to MATT. CARTWRIGHT of AC, for Ь17-18-2, 98 3/4 acres. Lines: AMBROSE JONES, BLAIN, BIBB, GILLESBIE. Wit: JNO. ROSE, ZACH. TALIAFERRO, HUGH ROSE.

Page 141.   13 Jul 1773.   RICH. PETER, AC, to WM. PETER, AC, for Ŀ30, cows, calves, sheep, horse & bed. Wit: WM. HIX, JOSEPH CHILDRESS.

Page 142.   4 Mar 1774.   ABNER WITT, AC, to JNO. WITT, SR., for Ŀ20, 96 acres Mt. cove on branch of Rockfish. Lines: JAS. LACKEY, JNO. LACKEY. Wit: JNO. WITT, JR., GEO. WITT, LITTLEBERRY WITT.

Page 144.   15 Apr 1774.   MERRITT MAGANN, AC, to SAML. BAUGHAN (BAUGHN), AC, - horse of 6 years age - no price set forth. Wit: JNO. HARDWICK, JNO. MERRIT.

Page 144.   2 May 1774.   JNO. GOODWIN, AC, to his "Sun" RICH. GOODWIN, AC, for love, 105 acres on Harris Creek. Wit: JOS. GOODWIN, JAS. CREWS, JNO. HENRY GOODWIN, JNO. BLAKE TRENT.

Page 145.   18 Apr 1774.   JNO. MERRY GRIFFIN, AC, to JNO. DEPRIEST - no sum for stock. Wit: JNO. DICKINSON, REUBEN GRIFFIN.

Page 146.   4 Apr 1774.   JOS. GOODWIN, AC, to THOS. LUMPKIN, AC, Deed of Trust for amount due WM. CUNNINGHAM & Co, Glasgow merchants. 5 sh. slave, Brunswick; woman, Alse; penknife. Wit: LINDSEY COLEMAN, JNO. RITCHIE, GEO. COLEMAN, CALEB COLEMAN.

Page 148.   2 May 1774.   BENJ. WRIGHT, AC, & wife ELIZ, to GABL. PENN, AC, for Ŀ100, 137 acres on branch of Beaver Creek. Lines: HENRY CHILDERS, RO. WHITTEN.

Page 151.   15 Jan 1774.   EZEKIEL KENNIDY, AC, to DANL. GAINES, AC. KENNIDY arrested "some past" for debt due WM. CUNNINGHAM & Co. and GAINES became his bondsman; 5 sh. Deed of Trust. very interesting list - pewter plates, 6 spoons, 2 qt. basons, 1 dish, iron pot, frying pan, 1 butter pat, tools, clothes etc. Wit: ARCHELAUS MITCHELL, HAWKINS KEARBY, HANNAH MITCHELL.

Page 152.   2 May 1774.   WM. EVANS (EVINS), AC, to JAS. THOMPSON, AC, Parish of Amherst - for Ŀ29-10, 360 acres S branch of Elk Island Creek. Lines: JNO. CHRISTIAN, BENJ. POLLARD, Clk. (Deputy.)

Page 154.   10 Dec 1773.   HENRY DUVAL, AC, to LAURENCE CAMPBELL, AC, Deed of Trust - 5 sh. CAMPBELL is bondsman on debt of DUVAL due SPIERS & BOWMAN - "I am this instant sueed" - Ŀ93-12-8 - negro, Caeser; horse, penknife, etc. Wit: EDMD. WILCOX, GABL. PENN.

Page 155.   19 May 1774.   RO. CAWTHON, AC, to HENDERSON McCAUL, Glasgow merchants, 5 sh. Seven negroes named. Wit: PATRICK HART, GABL. PENN, CLOUGH SHELTON.

Page 157.   8 Apr 1774.   RO. JOHNSTON, AC, grants power of atty. to EDMD. WILCOX, GABL. PENN, HUGH ROSE & NATHL. DAVIS, AC, to sell all my lands except on waters of Maple Creek; Rockfish and Meriwether's Branch. Wit: MOSES PENN JR., BENJ. POLLARD, THOS. POWELL JR.

Page 158.   13 Oct 1773.   JNO. DAWSON, AC, to JOS. DAWSON, AC, Deed of Trust to secure debt of Ŀ27-1-1. 5 sh. 170 acres on Harris Creek. JOHN bought it of THOS. WATTS. Also penknife. Wit: THOS. LUMPKIN, BALLENGER WADE, PETTIS THACKER.

Page 161.   10 Jul 1774.   JOB CARTER, AC, to DAVID CRAWFORD & GABL. PENN, power of atty. to sell land on Pedlar and Horsley - 190 acres, where I live. Also furniture, stock etc., so as to pay Ŀ71-10 due on execution of CHAS. ELLIS vs. JAS. & RO. DONALDS & Co, DAVID SHEPHERD and myself. SHEPHERD is due Ŀ33-11-8. Wit: BEN. POLLARD, PATRICK HART, MOSES PENN, Jr. (Note: Here is $64.00 question: Where are the original chancery papers for Amherst from 1761 to about 1825? Mrs. Sweeny told me that a friend got a court order and had them removed to Richmond on grounds that they were not properly stored. I am unable to find the order as of today. I have visited Richmond and they know nothing of the papers. The chancery data after about 1825 contains much material which throws light on persons and the litigation of those days, but it is too bad that we can not locate the data prior to this time. BFD.)

156

Page 162. 1 Apr 1774. BATTAILE HARRISON, AC, to GEO. WEIR for SPIERS &
BOWMAN - Deed of Trust to secure Ł274-18-6. 5 sh. 260 acres
bought from DUNCAN GRAHAM and where I live; also six slaves. Wit: EDMD.
WILCOX, THOS. HAWKINS, PAT. HART.

Page 165. Surveys by WM. CABELL JR., County Surveyor, from 20 Jun 1773
to 15 Jun 1774.

19 Apr 1774	JNO. BIGGS	36 a.		13 Dec 1773	RICH. McCARY	174 a.
2 Dec 1773	NICHL. CABELL	227 a.		22 Jan 1774	"	230 a.
18 Nov 1773	WM. CABELL JR.	3200 a.		9 Jun 1774	GEO. McDANIEL	164 a.
12 Mar 1774	JNO. COTTERAL	240 a.		18 Apr 1774	CHAS. NUCKOLS	149 a.
18 Mar 1774	NATHL. DAVIS	124 a.		30 Nov 1773	CHAS, HUGH, JNO.	
17 Mar 1774	RO. DAVIS	250 a.			& PATRICK ROSE	167 a.
26 Nov 1773	ALEX. FORBUS	20 a.		14 Mar 1774	AMBROSE RUCKER	375 a.
6 Apr 1774	DANL. GAINES	38 a.		3 Mar 1774	WM. SMALL	47 a.
20 Apr 1774	JNO. GILMORE	135 a.		16 Dec 1773	SAML. STAPLES	17 a.
21 Jan 1774	JNO. GRIFFIN	99 a.		14 Apr 1774	CORNL. THOMAS	320 a.
18 Nov 1773	WM. HANSBROUGH	30 a.		11 May 1774	" "	280 a.
7 Apr 1774	" "	112 a.		19 Nov 1773	WM. TYREE	180 a.
24 Feb 1774	JNO. HARGROVE	20 a.		11 Mar 1774	BALLENGER WADE	94 a.
4 Mar 1774	OWEN HERNDON	182 a.(?)		17 Dec 1773	ABRAHAM WARWICK	50 a.
21 Apr 1774	" "	50 a.		24 Jan 1774	CUTHBERT WEBB	230 a.
23 Mar 1774	WM. HORSLEY	275 a.		14 Dec 1773	JAS. WILLOUGHBY	116 a.
26 Mar 1774	" "	300 a.		25 Feb 1774	JESSE WRIGHT	70 a.
26 Mar 1774	" "	250 a.		20 Nov 1773	MENOS WRIGHT	84 a.
7 Apr 1774	RALPH JOPLING	224 a.		25 Nov 1773	WM. WHITE VAUGHAN	
25 Nov 1773	HENRY LAWHORN &				& HENRY LAWHORN	48 a.
	WM. WHITE VAUGHAN	48 a.				

Page 166. 3 Jan 1774. WM. PRYOR & wife MARGARET, AC, to PHILIP THURMOND,
AC, for Ł114-11, 395 acres on the blue ridge; branch of Irish
Creek. Wit: RODERICK McCULLOCH, DAVID CRAWFORD, ISAAC WRIGHT, WM. CRAW-
FORD.

Page 168. 4 Jul 1774. BENJ. HIGGINBOTHAM, AC, to JAS. HIGGINBOTHAM, AC,
for Ł20, 75 acres N branch of S fork of Buffalo. Lines: BENJ.
HIGGINBOTHAM, AARON HIGGINBOTHAM, Pounding Mill Creek; JAS. HIGGINBOTHAM.
Pat. to BENJ. HIGGINBOTHAM at Williamsburg on 14 Jul 1769.

Page 169. 6 Jun 1774. SAML. AYRES & wife RACHEL, late MORRISON, & JOS.
HIGGINBOTHAM MORRISON, eldest son of RACHEL, by her first
husband, WM. MORRISON, dec'd, of Amherst Co. and Parish - to JNO. DILLARD
of AC. Reference to marriage contract between AYRES & RACHEL, 14 Nov 1772.
This tract was sold prior to contract, for Ł100, 250 acres on branch of
Beaver. Part of 2700 acres pat. to WM. CABELL JR. and on E side and adj.
Tobacco Row Mt. Liens: WM. CABELL JR., Smith's Mt., Tobacco Row Mt.
Wit: CHAS. ROSE, PHILIP THURMOND, EDMD. POWELL.

Page 172. 17 Aug 1773. THOS. LOMAX, Caroline, to JNO. BROWN, AC, for
Ł20, 340 acres. Lines: BROWN, WARE. Wit: ZACH. TALIAFERRO,
JNO. ROSE, GEO. PURVIS, HUGH ROSE. Margin: Del. to JNO. BROWN.

Page 176. 25 Jan 1774. JNO. MURRELL (signed MURRILL) and wife RACHELL,
AC, to CHAS. IRVING, for Ł200, 333 acres on S side of Rockfish.
and both sides of Corbin Creek. Lines: JNO. SMALL (now RUCKER) on Rock-
fish; DAVID REID at mouth of Corbin Creek; late Col. JNO. CHISWELL;
MICHL. MONTGOMERY, ALEX. REID (READ); FRANCIS MERIWETHER, PUCKETT. Wit:
JNO. OLD, CLOUGH SHELTON, ALEX. ROSE, WM. HENDERSON, JAMES McCAUL.

Page 178. 29 Nov 1773. JNO. FARRAR & wife ELIZ, AC, to REUBEN JORDAN,
Albemarle, for Ł280, 260 acres on Rockfish. Lines: JNO. WRIGHT,
WM. MONTGOMERY, JNO. SMALL. Part of pat. of JNO. CHISWELL on 26 Mar 1739,
and by him sold to ALEX. MONTGOMERY 25 Apr 1745, and by ALEX. MONTGOMERY
sold to ROB. BARNET on 4 Aug 1759, and by BARNET to FARRAR on 5 Jul 1762.
Also 163 acres on N branch of Rockfish, part of FARRAR's tract and rec.
in AC. Lines: JNO. FARRAR, JOSIAH JOPLING, JNO. MONTGOMERY. Wit: CHAS.
IRVING, JOSIAH JOPLING, JAS. LYON, ALEX. REID JR. On page 180 is order
to quiz. ELIZ. FARRAR as to this deed. Rec. 3 Jan 1774, and done by CHAS.
RODES & ALEX. REID JR.

Page 181.   2 Apr 1774.   JNO. JOHNSTON, AC, to GEO. WEIR, Factor for
            SPIERS & BOWMAN, Deed of Trust - 5 sh.   100 acres bought by
JOHNSTON from WM. LOVING and where JOHNSTON lives; also one "hatt". Wit:
PATRICK HART, JAS. BIBB, THOS. WORTHAM.

Page 184.   17 Jan 1774.   NATHAN NUCKOLS (signed NUCKOLLS), AC, to HENRY
            TRENT, AC, for Ł10, attachment - stock, furniture, tobacco now
on TRENT's plantation; one knife. Wit: THOS. LUMPKIN, RICH. SHELTON.

Page 185.   30 Aug 1774.   JAS. LACKEY & wife MARY, AC, to JNO. HARDY, AC,
            for Ł60, 100 acres on the mts. and amongst ye head of ye Rock-
fish. Lines: JAS. LACKEY, THOS. CARPENTER. Wit: ABNER WITT, ANDW. SMITH,
RO. HARDIE.

Page 186.   3 Oct 1774.   AARON HIGGINBOTHAM & wife CLARA, AC, to JACOB
            TYREE, AC, for Ł200, 400 acres on both sides & joining N side
of Buffalo and N side of Fluvanna. Lines: BRAXTON & Co.

Page 188.   1 Oct 1774.   JNO. JOSLIN (signature seems to be mark of JOP-
            LING), AC and Parish, to GEO. HILTON, AC & Parish, for Ł65,
200 acres, lower part of 400 acres on branch of Elk Island Creek. Wit:
RO. CHRISTIAN, JESSE ALLEN, VALENTINE SCRUGGS, SAML. ALLEN, JAS. PAMPLIN.

Page 191.   2 May 1774.   JNO. SWANSON, AC, to SPIERS & BOWMAN, Glasgow
            merchants, Deed of Trust - 5 sh.   111 acres belonging jointly
to SWANSON & VALENTINE COX. Lines: JNO. WRIGHT, WM. MAYS, EDWD CARTER.
6 acres where SWANSON lives; carpenter's tools. Wit: GEO. WEIR, JNO.
LAMONT, PATRICK HART. Margin: Del. to JNO. TALIAFERRO, Factor, for SPIERS
etc.

Page 193.   5 Jul 1774.   JNO. WHITEHEAD, AC, to GEO. WEIR, Factor for
            SPIERS & BOWMAN, Deed of Trust - 5 sh.   150 acres Huff Creek
and bought of HENRY CHILDERS & where WHITEHEAD lives; slave, "hatt". Wit:
PATRICK HART, JNO. LAMONT, NOELL JOHNSON, GEO. BURKS. Del. to JNO. TALIA-
FERRO 8 Feb 1797.

Page 195.   20 Apr 1774.   JAS. STEVENS & wife BEHETHLAND, AC, to WM. LOV-
            ING, AC, for Ł55-8, 216 acres N branch Rucker's Run. Lines:
Courthouse Road, LOVING, STEVENS.   Bought of LUNSFORD LOMAX JR. 7 Aug
1769. Wit: GEO. WORTHAM, THOS. GRIFFIN, BENJ. TALIAFERRO. Orig. del. to
WM. LOVING.

Page 197.   6 Jun 1774.   DEVERIX GILLIAM & wife EDITH, AC, to ISAAC WRIGHT,
            AC, for Ł50, 91 acres on N side Tobacco Row Mts. Orig. del.
to ISAAC WRIGHT 12 Mar 1790.

Page 199.   3 Oct 1774.   THOS. LUCAS & wife ANN, AC, to THOS. COLLINS of
            Albemarle Co, for Ł95, 300 acres on both sides of Harris Creek.
Lines: THOS. LUCAS. Orig. del. to THOS. GARLAND.

Page 200.   9 Jul 1774.   WM. PENN, AC, to his brother, MOSES PENN, for Ł50,
            and Ł20 advanced by MOSES for him to HENDERSON McCAUL Co. Ł20
to JAS. & RO. DONALDS & Co.,Ł10 to SPIERS & BOWMAN. My brother, GABL.
PENN, is also bound.   Seven slaves & knife. Wit: DAVID SHEPHERD, JNO.
PHILLIPS, BENJ. POLLARD.

Page 201.   3 Jan 1774.   PETER CARTER & wife MARY to ISAAC WRIGHT for Ł30,
            121 5/8 acres on N side Tobacco Row and coves. Orig. del. to
ISAAC WRIGHT 12 Mar 1790. (Note: PETER CARTER died testate here and later
his heirs moved to Kentucky. There are many deeds showing the transac-
tions of the family in later deed books. BFD)

Page 203.   2 Oct 1774.   JNO. BROWN & wife RACHEL, AC, to RICH. DAVIS, AC,
            for Ł200, 500 acres and 340 acres adj.   Lines: BROWN, WARE.

Page 204.   3 Oct 1774.   RICH. DAVIS & wife ELIZ, AC, to JNO. BROWN, AC,
            for Ł200, 204 acres on branch of Higginbotham's Mill Creek.
Bought by DAVIS and of record in AC. Orig. del. to BROWN July 1785.

158

Page 206.   15 Aug 1774.   JNO. CONNOR & wife ELEANOR, AC, to JNO. ROWSEY
            (ROWZIE) for Ь20, 100 acres on branch of John's branch and a
N branch of Buffalo. Part of 254 acres pat. to CONNOR 5 Jul 1774. Lines:
CONNOR, JAS. MAYFIELD. Wit: JOS. CABELL, JAS. GARLAND, WM. & AMBROSE
GATEWOOD.

Page 208.   10 Sep 1774.   JNO. HARRISON & wife SARAH; DEVERIX GILLIAM &
            wife EDITH (EDY), AC, to WM. HAYNES, AC, for Ь75, 150 acres -
left to them by CHAS. ELLIS, dec'd; N side of tobacco Row Mts. and 30
acres of it on Rocky Branch. Lines: ISAAC WRIGHT, cove in Tobacco Row.

Page 210.   7 Nov 1774.   DAVIS TINSLEY, AC, to JNO. TINSLEY, AC, for Ь30,
            71 acres adj. DAVID TINSLEY; also 122 acres on Harris Creek.

Page 211.   11 Jul 1774.   WM. PENN, AC, to DAVID CRAWFORD, AC, for Ь125,
            329 acres both sides of road on N side Buffalo Ridge. Lines:
FRY. Pat. to JNO. HARVIE 5 Sep 1749 in Albemarle and since conveyed to
WM. PENN by RICH. HARVIE. Wit: DAVID SHEPHERD, GEO. PENN, GEO. WEIR,
BEN. POLLARD, MOSES PENN JR.

Page 212.   3 Oct 1774.   MARTIN DAWSON, AC, to JNO. FRANKLYN, AC, for Ь80,
            368 acres. Lines: THOS. DAWSON, NUTON (NEWTON). Wit: JNO.
THURMOND, GEO. PENN, JNO. DAWSON.

Page 214.   5 Nov 1774.   Order to CHAS. RODES & ALEX. REID JR. to quiz
            MARTHA MERIWETHER, wife of FRANCIS, as to deed to SAML. DAVIS
1 Mar 1773. EDMD WILCOX, Clerk. Done on same day. Margin: Orig. del. to
DAVIS 31 Jul 1778.

Page 215.   3 Oct 1774.   HENRY McDANIEL & wife MARTHA, AC, to ISAAC TINS-
            LEY, AC, for Ь75, 142 acres branch of Harris and S side of
Tobacco Row. Lines: JNO. HARVIE, JNO. BURFORD.

Page 217.   4 Nov 1774.   FRANCIS NEW, planter of AC & Parish, to JAS.
            TULEY (TOOLEY) SR, planter of St. Ann's Parish of Albemarle,
for Ь40, 70 acres and part of a tract. Pat. to NEW. Lines: JNO. CHISWELL.

Page 219.   7 Nov 1774.   JAS. SMITH & wife MARY, AC, to GEO. McDANIEL, AC,
            for Ь100, 322 acres on Pedlar.

Page 220.   5 Nov 1774.   THOS. PATTON, AC, to SAML. WOODS, AC, for Ь130,
            154 acres on both sides of Rockfish. Part of tract. S fork of
S branch. Lines: ALEX. PATTON. Margin: Del. to WM. WOODS 16 May 1782.

Page 222.   7 Nov 1774.   Decree of AC court, 7 Dec 1773 - an inventory of
            estate of WM. HOWARD who lived in the several counties of
Amherst, Albemarle, Buckingham and Cumberland. One fourth of known property to his wife JEAN HOWARD. One tract in Cumberland on Deed Creek;
slaves, stock etc. Committee: JNO. BERNARD, HARDIN PERKINS, NICHL.
CABELL.

Page 223.   7 Nov 1774.   ALEX. PATTENT, AC, to JNO. PATTENT, AC, for Ь30,
            170 acres, branch of Rockfish near Blue Mts. Lines: EDWD.
MALLOY, EDWIN HIEMAN, JAS. HENDRICK, JOSIAS CLAPHAM. Wit: SAML. WOODS,
WM. PATTON, THOS. PATTON.

Page 224.   10 May 1774.   AMBROSE CAMPBELL to JOS. DILLARD & HUGH ROSE for
            Ь38, 175 acres, furniture, working tools - Deed of Trust. Wit:
JNO. KENNIDY, WM. LAWSON.

Page 225.   7 Nov 1774.   EDWD. CHEATHAM & wife MARY, AC, & Parish, to
            ELIOT ROBERTS, AC, & Parish, for Ь40, 197 acres N side of
Rockfish and head branch Lynch Creek. Pat. to CHEATHAM 3 Mar 1760. Lines:
Col. LEWIS. Orig. del. to WM. HARRIS for ROBERTS, 7 Mar 1788. Memo:
Sometime past conveyed to CARTER & TRENT by CHEATHAM, WM. LOVING, factor.
He had rec'd. payment and released lien.

Page 227.   4 Jul 1774.   JOB CARTER & wife SARAH, AC, to GEO. COLEMAN, AC,
            for Ь80, 86 acres Pedlar bank. Lines: Horsley Creek. Also
104 acres adj. Wit: W. POLLARD, LUCAS POWELL, JNO. DILLARD. Order

follows to quiz SARAH, wife of CARTER, by DAVID CRAWFORD & RODERICK Mc-
CULLOCH. Done 9 Nov 1774.

Page 230.   15 Jul 1774.   HUGH GILLILAND, AC, to JAS. MENEES, JR., AC,
            Deed of Trust - Ł66 debt.   5 sh.   Wagon, stock. Wit: JAS.
McNEES SR., BENJ. MENEES, JNO. BROWN.

Page 232.   6 Oct 1774.   CARTER BRAXTON, King William Co, to JOHN PENN,
            AC, for Ł413, 472 acres S side and joining Huff Creek. Part of
tract. Lines: JAS. GATEWOOD, BAYLOR WALKER, JNO. PENN.   Wit: HENRY GIL-
BERT, WIATT GILBERT.   ELIZ., wife of BRAXTON. Margin: 15 Aug 1808, del.
to JNO. PENN Jr. as also the Relqt (sic).   Commission to King William
JP's: JNO. QUARLES, WM. AYLETT & JO. ROANE, 10 Oct 1774, to quiz ELIZ,
wife of CARTER BRAXTON. Done 29 Oct 1774 by QUARLES & AYLETT.

Page 234.   7 Mar 1775.   RO. HORSLEY & wife JUDITH, AC & Parish, to JAS.
            PAMPLIN, AC, & Parish, for Ł260, 392 acres on Elk Island
Creek, conveyed to HORSLEY by NICHL. CABELL dec'd, 30 Sep 1760. HORSLEY
has lately broken intail by an inquisition by virtue of a writ. Lines:
WM. HORSLEY. Wit: JESSE ALLEN, SAML. ALLEN, JAS. THOMPSON.

Page 235.   1 Apr 1774.   WM. MITCHELL, Richmond merchant to RICH. OGLESBY,
            planter of Goochland - for Ł350, 800 acres S side Buffalo.
Lines: EDWD. CARTER - 400 acres sold to GEO. SEATON by JER. WADE, JOS. &
RICH. OGLESBY and 400 acres adj. other 400 acres sold to GEO. SEATON by
PEARCE WADE et al. Orig. del. to OGLESBY, June 1778.   Sold to WM. MIT-
CHELL by SEATON.   Wit: CHAS. & PATRICK ROSE, CHAS. IRVING, JNO. ROSE.

Page 237.   16 Jan 1775.   SAML. WOODS, AC, & Parish, to JNO. HENDERSON for
            Ł28-3-6, three tracts of 355 acres. 1) 100 acres on branch of
Hughes Creek. Lines: OWEN CRAWFORD, Capt. JAS. MARTIN.   2) 115 acres.
Lines: Capt. MARTIN, DANL. LATTIMORE.   3) 140 acres S of Meriwether's
Creek. Lines: DANL. LATTIMORE.

Page 239.   3 Mar 1775.   THOS. PANNELL, AC, to HUGH PEASLEY, AC, both
            of Amherst Parish, for Ł20, 60 acres N branch of Rodes' Creek.
Surveyed for PANNELL 22 Apr 1769 by JAS. HIGGINBOTHAM. Lines: CHAS. RODES.

Page 240.   2 Jan 1775.   Deed of gift by JAS. MARTIN Senior, planter of
            AC & Parish, to his son, DAVID MARTIN, same county and parish,
3 slaves. Wit: CHAS. RODES, FRANS. MERIWETHER, THOS. PANNELL.

Page 241.   2 Jan 1775.   Deed of gift by JAS. MARTIN SR, planter of AC &
            Parish, to his son, AZARIAH MARTIN his youngest son - slaves,
stock and furniture. Wit: Same as above.

Page 241.   2 Jan 1775.   JAS. MARTIN SR, as above, to his son, JAS. MARTIN,
            slaves. Wit: as above.

Page 242.   2 Jan 1775.   JAS. MARTIN SR, as above, to his son, WM. MARTIN,
            slaves. Wit: as above.

Page 243.   2 Jan 1775.   JAS. MARTIN SR, as above, to his son, JOHN
            MARTIN, slaves. Wit: as above.

Page 243.   3 Mar 1775.   JAS. BARNETT & wife ANN, AC, to WM. BARNETT, AC,
            for Ł200, 235 acres S branch of Rockfish. Lines: LAURENCE
SMALL, THOS. CARPENTER, JAS. LACKEY, ALEX. REID JR. & WM. BARNETT.
"Whole of lands of JAS. BARNETT IN AC". Wit: ALEX. REID JR., JOEL CRAW-
FORD, JAS. REID, and two more ALEX. REID signatures.

Page 245.   7 Mar 1775.   JNO. WADE, AC, to SAML. DENNY, AC, for Ł60, 80
            acres where DENNY lives. Lines: old survey, Butler ridge.

Page 248.   7 Mar 1775.   JNO. WADE, AC, to JAS. CULL, AC, for Ł40, 50 ac-
            res, part of place where WADE "liveth". Lines: CHAS. TATE.

Page 250.   5 Mar 1775.   JNO. PATTON, AC, to WM. PATTON, AC, for Ł30, 170
            acres branch of Rockfish and near Blue Ridge. Lines: S side
Rockfish, EDWD MOLLOY, EDWIN HICKMAN, JAS. HENDRICK, JOSIAH CHAPHAM. Wit:

JOS. ROBERDS (ROBERTS), SAML. WOODS, MICHL. McNEALY, ALEX. REID JR., JOEL CRAWFORD.

Page 251. 16 Jan 1775. JNO. TINSLEY, AC, to DAVID TINSLEY, AC, consists of 120 acres, part of it: 71 acres. Lines: SHELTON, ROSE. Wit: JAS. RITCHIE, AMBROSE RUCKER, MATT. LIVELY, GEO. McDANIEL, JAS. FRANKLYN.

Page 252. 7 Apr 1775. WM. MILLER & wife ISBELL, AC, to DANL. GAINES & DAVID TINSLEY, AC,. MILLER conveyed to GAINES 5 Oct 1773, 227 acres on Harris which MILLER bought of GEO. CARRINGTON. Lines: HUGH ROSE, JNO. TINSLEY, RICH. SHELTON, ISAAC WRIGHT. DAVID TINSLEY has now bought bract. Ƚ79. Orig. del. to TINSLEY.

Page 253. 5 Nov 1774. LEONARD TARRANT & wife MARY, AC, to JOHN ROSE of Roseisle, AC, for Ƚ15, 191 acres Tye river and Priest Mt. Lines: JNO. ROSE, Hay's creek or Priest's run. Pat. to TARRANT 10 Sep 1767. Wit: ZACH. TALIAFERRO, JESSE BOULWARE, BENNETT C(?) PHILLIPS or BENNETT C. (his mark) PHILLIPS, WM. LUNSFORD. Order to WM. CABELL, HUGH ROSE & DANL. GAINES to quiz MARY, wife of LEONARD TARRANT, and rec. 5 May 1775, by ROSE & GAINES. Orig. del. to JNO. ROSE.

Page 256. 3 Apr 1775. JACOB MORRIS, yeoman of Albemarle, & wife MARY, to JNO. TULEY, JR., AC, yeoman, for Ƚ30, 200 acres. Lines: RO. DAVIS' Mill Creek; JACOB MORRIS, NATHL. DAVIS, RO. DAVIS.

Page 258. 30 Sep 1774. ALEX. REID SR, AC, to ALEX. REID JR., AC, - father to son, for Ƚ30, 398 acres, part of where Sr. now lives. Branch of Rockfish. Lines: THOS. MORRISON, ALEX. REID SR. Wit: JAS., ANNIE, & SAML. REID. Orig. del. 4 Oct 1779.

Page 259. 30 Sep 1774. ALEX. REID SR, to his son, SAML. REID, both of AC, for Ƚ30, 136 acres, same location as deed above. No adj. owners named. Wit: same as above.

Page 261. 22 Mar 1775. CARTER BRAXTON, King Wm. county, to DAVID SHEPHERD, AC, for Ƚ212-16, 304 acres S side Tribulation Creek and part of tract. Lines: GABL. PENN at Lynch road, JAS. GATEWOOD, HENRY GILBERT, bridge, Tribulation at Parker's road. Wit: JOS. CABELL, CORNL. THOMAS, GABL. PENN; 23 Mar 1775. W. CABELL & PATRICK ROSE. Orig. del. to GABL. PENN, July 1784.

Page 263. 6 Mar 1775. RICH. BALLENGER & wife ELIZ, AC, to ABRAHAM MOORE, AC, for Ƚ65, 232 acres, part of pat. to JOS. BALLENGER and by him conveyed to RICH. Lines: BALLINGER's Mt., JOS. MAYS. Wit: HUGH ROSE, EDMD. WILCOX, JNO. PHILLIPS.

Page 264. 22 Mar 1775. CARTER BRAXTON & wife ELIZ, King Wm. Co, to GABL. PENN, AC, for Ƚ383-8, 562 acres N side & joining Rutledge Creek, part of tract. Lines: Lynch Road, HENRY GILBERT at PARKER's road; JNO. STEWART. Wit: JOS. CABELL, CORNL. THOMAS, WM. CABELL, PATRICK ROSE. Orig. del. PENN, July 1784. (Note: HENRY GILBERT bought two tracts from BRAXTON and the line referred here to as being at PARK's road was the tract whereon is an old house called Hunting Tower in later deeds. It is not too far from my home. It is now owned by one of my members, MADISON SETTLES. The other tract was on Tribulation and the west side of Main Street here in the Village is built in part on part of this tract. This deed to GILBERT will be shown on page 271 herein. BFD)

Page 268. 3 Apr 1775. JNO. MacLURE (signed McCLURE) & wife ELIZ, AC, planter, to DAVID SIMPSON, AC, planter, for Ƚ52-10, 150 acres branch of Rockfish. Lines: EDWD. MOLLY, CLAPUM, CHISWELL.

Page 270. 1 Dec 1774. SAML. MILLER, AC, to JAMES HENDERSON, AC, for Ƚ5, horse and cow. Wit: ANDREW & JOS. HENDERSON.

Page 271. 22 Mar 1775. CARTER BRAXTON & wife ELIZ, King Wm., to HENRY GILBERT, Hanover Co, for Ƚ1787-10, 2 tracts. 1) S side of & joining Rutledge Creek and Crooked Run, 1113 acres, part of BRAXTON's tract. Lines: HIGGINBOTHAM, Roleing(sic) road (see historical works on Amherst by ALFRED PERCY, JR. for good descriptions of these rolling roads

and tobacco industry in early Amherst) pat. line, Cabbin Branch, Park's
Road. 2) plantation called Round Top (Note: There is still a hill in
vicinity called by this name.), both sides and joining Tribulation (still
known as such) Creek and on branch of Rutledge - 1440 - part of the above
tract. Lines: Lynch Road, BALER WALKER dec'd, JAS. MENEES, Tribulation,
JNO. PENN, Park's Road, JAS. GATEWOOD, bridge on Tribulation at Park's
Road, surveyed by JAS. HIGGINBOTHAM and containing 2553 acres. Wit:
CORNL. THOMAS, GABL. PENN, JOS. CABELL, NICHL. CABELL, JNO. HARVIE. (Note:
GILBERT died testate here and devised this land to several sons.)

Page 274. 6 Feb 1775. CLADIUS BUSTER, Albemarle Co, to FRANCIS WATHERED
           of Albemarle, for Ŀ27-10, 70 acres on branch of Rockfish, part
of tract belonging to JNO. ROBINSON. Lines: W side Bever Creek, branch of
Rockfish; old Scool(sic) house on S side of road leading to MECHAIL
CRAFT's; old line of JNO. ROBINSON, JNO. PATRICK. BUSTER acquired it "by
deed". Also line of MOSES CLACK. Dividing line between BUSTER & WEATH-
ERED - all that BUSTER owns on W side Bever. Two acres on E side of
"same branch" for a mill seat at fork leading to THOS. RAY's old plantation. Wit: AMBROSE RUCKER, JNO. SCOTT, ALEX. REID JR.

Page 276. 22 Mar 1775. CARTER BRAXTON & wife ELIZ, King Wm., to RICH.
           JONES, Cumberland, for Ŀ210, 300 acres N branch Rutledge; part
of tract. Lines: Lynch Road, HENRY GILBERT, JAS. MENEES, JNO. STEWART.
Wit: JOS. CABELL, CORNL. THOMAS, GABL. PENN, NICHL. CABELL, JNO. HARVIE.

Page 277. 20 Apr 1775. HUGH McCEEBES (mark of McCEEB) to WM. BANKS for
           Ŀ25, 130 acres Huff Creek. Lines: JNO. SCOTT, DAMMERON's or-
phans, BRAXTON. Wit: GABL. PENN, GEO. WEIR, DAVID SHEPHERD.

Page 278. 1 May 1775. WM. BIBB & wife SARAH, AC, to WM. HENDERSON, AC,
           for Ŀ65, 193 acres - coves on the ridge at head of middle fork
of Rucker's Run. Orig. del. to JOELL PONTON, 7 Feb 1789.

Page 280. 21 Nov 1774. JOS. CABELL & wife MARY, AC, to WM. HORSLEY, AC,
           for Ŀ125, 350 acres on Owen's Creek. Lines: JNO. JOSLIN. Wit:
GEO. COLEMAN, JNO. CABELL, LINDSEY COLEMAN.

Page 281. 29 May 1775. Deed of gift by CORNL. THOMAS, AC, to his child-
           ren: JOHN, NORBORNE, CORNL., ELIZ., LUCY & SALLY THOMAS; about
16 slaves named; 6 feather beds, 2/3 of stock - CORNL. reserves life
interest. Wit: LINDSEY COLEMAN, NICHL. CABELL, RALPH JOPLING, JAS. NEVIL.
Memo: one gold ring del. to children. (It will be seen by next item that
CORNL. intended to re-marry.)

Page 282. 1 Jun 1775. Marriage contract between CORNL. THOMAS, AC, to
           HANNAH SCOTT, Buckingham, soon to be solemnized - joint use
and to her and any issue, if he dies first. If no issue, then by terms
of any will made by him. Wit: NICHL. CABELL, SAML. JORDAN CABELL, JNO.
NICHOLAS JR., THOS. MARTIN JR., BENJ. JORDAN, WM. CABELL. (Note: This is
another of the marriage data not found in SWEENY. I have pointed out in
a prior statement that SWEENY did an excellent piece of work in finding
the Order Book items to put with the bonds, but he seemed to have made no
effort to locate the contracts in the deed books. BFD)

Page 284. 25 Jan 1775. JAS. HEARD, AC, to JNO. HEARD, AC, for Ŀ10, 128
           acres branch of Rockfish. Lines: ANDREW REID, dec'd, WM.
HEARD. Pat. to JAS. HEARD, 1 Aug 1771. Wit: ALEX. REID, ALEX. REID,
miner(sic), JNO. BORDEN, ROLEN LANESTER, WM. BROOKS, JAS. REID.

Page 286. 20 Jun 1775. GEO. LEE & wife ELIZ, to ARCHELAUS MITCHELL,
           Bedford Co, for blank sum, 200 acres on N side Buffalo; part
of 1370 acres formerly that of CARTER BRAXTON. Lines: GEO. PENN on
Buffalo. Orig. del. to GABL. PENN.

Page 287. 5 Dec 1774. WM. PENN, AC, to GEO. WEIR, Factor for SPIERS &
           BOWMAN, and DAVID SHEPHERD, Factor for JAS. & RO. DONALDS,
Deed of Trust - 5 sh. Slave and her children. Wit: BENJ. POLLARD, PAT-
RICK HART, ALEX. ROSE. Del. to PAT. HART.

Page 289. 1 Jul 1775. RO. BALLEN, AC, to WM. EVINS, AC, for Ŀ45, 160

162

acres both sides Stovall's Creek.

Page 291. 20 Aug 1774. DAVID DUNCAN, AC, to THOS. LUMPKIN, factor for
WM. CUNNINGHAM & Co, Deed of Trust - 5 sh. Negress & horse.
Wit: JNO. RITCHIE, HENRY KERBY, THOS. EDWARDS.

Page 294. 17 Jun 1775. CARTER BRAXTON & wife ELIZ, King Wm., to JNO.
STEWART, Cumberland Co, for Ł364, 520 acres N side Rutledge
and Crooked Run. Part of tract. Lines: Lynch road, HENRY GILBERT, JAS.
MENEES, DANL. GAINES, HIGGINBOTHAM, CAPT. HENRY GILBERT at Crooked Run.
Wit: JNO. WEST, THOS. LUMPKIN, JOS. CABELL, JAS. CALLAWAY, RO. BURTON,
W. CABELL, SAML. CABELL.

Page 296. 7 Aug 1775. ALEX. MILLER, AC, to SAML. WOODS, AC, for Ł30, 90
acres S side and joining Rockfish - part of tract pat. to JNO.
CHISWELL and conveyed by JNO. ROBINSON to JOS. MILLER and now property
of ALEX. MILLER. Lines: LEE HARRIS, CLUFF SHELTON. Orig. del. to ABNER
WITT.

Page 297. 14 Jul 1775. AMBROSE GOFF & wife ANN, Bedford Co, to HENRY
McDANIEL, AC, for Ł50, 112 acres. Wit: AMBROSE RUCKER, JNO.
RITCHIE, MATT. LIVELY, JNO. RUCKER, GEO. McDANIEL.

Page 298. 7 Aug 1775. HUGH ROSE, AC, to CHAS. IRVING, Albemarle, for
Ł400, 600 acres on upper Davis Creek. Part of pat. to RO. ROSE,
Clerk, by order of Council. Lines: HIGGINBOTHAM, PHILLIP DAVIS, Rolling
Road, PATRICK ROSE, CARTER. Also entry bought by RO. ROSE, Clerk, of
THOS. HIGGINBOTHAM - 200 acres and adjoining. Lines: EDWD. CARTER,
PATRICK ROSE, ROSE Common.

Page 300. 28 Jul 1775. CARTER BRAXTON & wife ELIZ, King Wm., to WM.
JOHNS, AC, for Ł202-16, 243 acres N side and joining Rutledge.
Part of tract of BRAXTON. Lines: N branch of Rutledge, GABL. PENN. Wit:
W. CABELL, JNO. HARVIE, SAML. CABELL, JOS. CABELL.

Page 201. (Numbered page 310 in book, but pages before and after are
correct) 4 Feb 1775. JAS. LACKEY, AC, to SAML. WOODS, AC,
merchant, for Ł195, 248 acres S branch of Rockfish and on Mts. Lines:
JNO. LACKEY, JAS. BARNETT, JNO. REID. Wit: EDWD. STEPHENSON, JAS. CONNER.

Page 303. 4 Feb 1775. JAS. LACKEY, AC, to SAML. WOODS, AC, merchant,
for Ł195, mare, natural pacer; stock, furniture etc. Wit:
EDWD. STEPEHNSON, JAS. WALSH, JAS. CONNER.

Page 304. 1 Feb 1775. JACOB WRIGHT & wife ELIZ, AC to WM. HARRIS, AC,
for Ł90, 400 acres N side and joining Rockfish and where
WRIGHT lives. Wit: DAVID SHELTON, EDWD. STEPHENSON, JOSIAH JOPLING, FRANK
WRIGHT. Orig. del. to HARRIS Nov 1785.

Page 306. 29 Sep 1775. NICHL. CABELL & wife HANNAH, AC, to WM. LAYNE
for Ł50, 157 acres on both sides Ravin Creek. Part of tract.
Lines: WM. CABELL; at Rolling Road, NICHL. CABELL. Wit: JOS. CABELL, JNO.
HORSLEY, WM. MEGGINSON.

Page 308. 2 Sep 1775. JNO. CONNER & wife ELEANOR, AC, to PETER HENDRIX-
SON, AC, for Ł15, 54 acres branch of Buffalo. Lines: JNO.
CONNER, JAS. MAYFIELD. Part of tract pat. at Williamsburg to JNO. CONNER.

Page 310. 4 Feb 1774. JNO. CONNER & wife ELEANOR, AC, to JAS. MAYFIELD,
AC, for Ł30, 100 acres branch of John's Branch and N branch of
Buffalo. Part of CONNER's. tract. Wit: CORNL. THOMAS, RO. HORSLEY, JOS.
CABELL, BENJ. MEGGINSON.

Page 312. 5 Apr 1775. JNO. HARDWICK, AC, to DANL. MEHONE, AC, for Ł35,
no acres set forth. Lines: JNO. KNIGHT. Wit: NICHL. LYON,
ELISHA LYON, JNO. MERRITT, CHAS. HUDSON, ROWLAND JONES.

Page 313. 29 Set 1775. NICHL. CABELL & wife HANNAH, AC, to GILBERT BOW-
MAN, AC, for Ł40, 150 acres on both sides Raven Creek. Part of
tract. Lines: Rolling Road, WM. LAYNE, NICHL. CABELL, JAS. MARTIN, WM.

CABELL. Wit: JOS. CABELL, JNO. HORSLEY, WM. MEGGINSON.

Page 316.   1 Sep 1775.   WM. MARTIN, AC, to JNO. WITT JR., AC, for Ł10, 54
            acres S branch Rockfish. Lines: ABNER WITT. Wit: ABNER WITT,
CHAS. WITT, JNO. WITT. (Note: Members of the WITT family went to Estill
Co., Ky.; see SWEENY on AC in the Revolution. I have a ms. done on the
Ky. descendants by one of them. BFD)

Page 317.   30 Sep 1775.   DANL. BURFORD, SR., AC, to DANL. BURFORD JR, AC,
            for Ł50, 95 acres. Lines: GEO. CARRINGTON, DANL JR., HUGH ROSE,
SAML. THOMAS, JNO. BURFORD, MARTIN DAWSON. Wit: DANL. GAINES, GABL. PENN,
JNO. RITCHIE, AMBROSE RUCKER. Margin: Del. to E. WILLS, admr.

Page 319.   Survey List by WM. CABELL, Surveyor of County, between 15 Jun
            1774, and 20 Jun 1775.

7 Apr 1775	STEWARD BALLOW	340 a.		2 Dec 1774	JNO. LEMASTER	265 a.
10 Feb 1775	JNO. BRADY	64 a.		20 Mar 1775	JNO. MARTIN	127 a.
13 Apr "	NEILL CAMPBELL	114 a.		8 Apr 1775	JAS. MATHEWS	90 a.
11 " "	MATT. CARTWRIGHT	296 a.		11 Feb 1775	JNO. MAYFIELD	116 a.
15 " "	WM. CLARK	72 a.		10 Mar "	ANGUS McDANIEL	250 & 110
12 Jul 1774	NICHL. DAVIS	64 a.		10 Apr "	JNO. McDANIEL	324 a.
15 Apr 1775	ALEX. DUGGIN	110 a.		23 Mar "	EDWD MOSELY	26 a.
11 " "	JAS. FRAZIER	366 a.		17 Nov 1774	JACOB PHILLIPS	190 a.
14 " "	JOS. HIGGINBOTHAM	290 a.		11 Mar 1775	WALTER POWER	154 a.
12 " "	WM. HIGGINBOTHAM	154 a.		14 Apr "	" "	380 a.
13 Sep 1774	RO. HORSLEY by writ AQD	392 a.		8 Feb 1775	JNO. WARREN	166 a.
15 Mar 1775	WM. HORSLEY	245 a.		1 Dec 1774	JAS. WEBB	70 a.
18 Mar "	JNO. JOSLIN	400 a.		25 Mar 1775	SAML. WOODS	146 a.
20 Apr "	THOS. LAYNE	385 a.				

Page 320.   30 Sep 1775.   DANL. BURFORD, SR. to JNO. BURFORD, AC, for Ł50,
            95 acres. Lines: SAML. THOMAS, MARTIN DAWSON, Harris Creek,
JNO. BURFORD. Wit: DANL. GAINES, GABL. PENN, JNO. RITCHIE, AMBROSE RUCKER.

Page 321.   7 Nov 1775.   PATRICK ROSE to his brother, HUGH ROSE, for bene-
            fit of PATRICK's son, ROBT. ROSE - my half of tract called
Rose Mount - formerly that of HENRY ROSE, dec'd, in trust for 19 years -
if ROBT. dies before age or marries and has no legitimate children, it
then returns to PATRICK, if alive. If not, to my eldest son. If I have
no son, then to my daughters in common. Slave, Dinal, received of Rev.
MILES SELDON as part of the fortune of his daughter - to ROBT. on same
condition as land. If he dies, then to REBECCA SELDON, daughter of Rev.
MILES SELDON. Repeats desires since men of law disagree as to interpretations. Wit: CHAS. IRVING, JOSHUA FRY, EDMD. WILCOX, WM. LEE, CHAS. ROSE.

Page 323.   -- Dec 1775.   PATRICK ROSE, AC, to EDMD. WILCOX, AC, for Ł20,
            20 acres on Tye. Lines: Jackson Creek, LEWIS, EDMD. WILCOX.
Orig. delivered.

Page 324.   4 Dec 1775.   PETER BIBY & wife ELIZ, Albemarle Co, and Parish
            of St. Ann, to ELIZ. EVANS, AC, and Parish of Amherst, for
Ł16-10, 99 acres on S branch of Owen's Creek. Lines: JNO. JOSLIN. ELIZ.
& PETER are also called BIBEE.

Page 326.   6 Oct 1775.   ROBT. HOWARD CASH & wife TAMASAN, AC, to STEPHEN
            CASH, AC, for Ł30, 95 acres, part of 440 acres pat. to ROBT.
3 Mar 1760. Lines: BENJ. CASH.

Page 328.   4 Dec 1775.   BENJ. HIGGINBOTHAM & wife ELIZ, AC, to CALEB
            HIGGINBOTHAM, AC, for 5 sh., 355 acres. Lines: BRAXTON & Co.

Page 330.   9 Dec 1774.   WM. GOLDSBERY (signed GOLSBY) Albemarle Co, to
            GEO. DOUGLAS, AC, for Ł30, 148 acres - coves of Tobacco Row.
Lines: WM. CABELL. Wit: MATT. TUCKER, AMBROSE RUCKER, THOS. LUMPKIN, JNO.
MERRITT.

Page 331.   22 Nov 1775.   JAS. SMITH, AC, & wife MARY, to NEILL CAMPBELL,
            Henrico merchant, for Ł400, 385 acres on E side Pedlar and

164

both sides of Camp Creek. Lines: WM. CABELL. Pat. to JAS.SMITH 11 Nov
1761. Wit: DAVID TINSLEY, JOS. HIGGINBOTHAM, JACOB SMITH, JNO. MATTHEWS.
Orig. del. to NICHL. VANSTAVERN on written order 18 Jan 1803.

Page 334. 14 Dec 1775. JNO. KNIGHT to JAS. LIVELY for ₺40, 192 acres.
            Lines: BENJ. HIGGINBOTHAM, PATRICK NOWLAND, JNO. COLEMAN,
Huff Creek.

Page 336. 4 Dec 1775. CALEB HIGGINBOTHAM & wife MARY ANN, to JAS.
            LIVELY, for ₺5, 13 acres next to LIVELY.

Page 337. 1 Jan 1776. WM. LOVDAY & wife SARAH to NATHAN WARD for ₺30,
            60 acres branch of Purgatory. Lines: RICH. PRITCHARD, JACOB
EADES, JNO. KEYS. Wit: WM. KEY, JAS. MATTHEWS, SAML. WARD, JAS. WARD.
Orig. del. to WARD, 27 Feb 1786.

Page 339. 4 Oct 1775. NICHL. CABELL & wife HANNAH, AC, to JOS. CABELL,
            AC, for ₺200, 2 tracts: 1) 199 acres pat. and part of 5176
acres. Lines: N bank of Buffalo; JAS. FREELAND, dec'd, NICHL. CABELL,
Freeland's Creek, Higginbotham's Road, Raven Creek, THOS. BALLOW, S bank
of Tye. 2) 93 acres, part of 400 acres on N branch of Raven Creek. Lines:
JAS. MARTIN, GILBERT BOWMAN, NICHL. CABELL, RICH. ALLCOCK, WM. CABELL.
Wit: HUGH ROSE, WM. HORSLEY, JNO. STRATTON.

Page 341. 10 Jun 1775. CARTER BRAXTON & wife ELIZ, King Wm. Co, to SAML.
            ALLEN, AC, - at request of JAMES HIGGINBOTHAM,atty. for heirs
of THOS. HIGGINBOTHAM, dec'd, late of province of Georgia - ₺54-2-5 -
which was due BRAXTON from THOS. HIGGINBOTHAM - paid by SAML. ALLEN -
475 acres on N branch of Buffalo. Part of 25,000 acres pat. to GEO.
BRAXTON 25 Nov 1743; N side of Buffalo. Lines: ISAAC GIBSON, WM. CABELL.
Wit: GABL. PENN, W. CABELL, RICH. HARVIE.

Page 343. 18 Aug 1775. CARTER BRAXTON & wife ELIZ, King Wm. Co, to JOS.
            CABELL, AC, for ₺180, grist mill on Buffalo and 50 acres land
on S side of river. Surveyed by WM. CABELL, AC surveyor. Lines: JOS. CA-
BELL; part of BRAXTON tract. Wit: JNO. HARVIE, BENJ. POLLARD, PATRICK
ROSE, W. CABELL, THOS. MILLER, RICH. HARVIE. Orig. del. to CABELL.

Page 344. 16 Nov 1775. VALENTINE COX, & wife ANNE, AC, to GABL. PENN,
            AC, for ₺45, 27 acres. Lines: GABL. PENN, CAMPBELL. Wit: PAT-
RICK HART, GEO. WEIR, JNO. PHILLIPS, JNO. SALE, WM. PENN, JNO. McKINDLEY,
EDMD. WILCOX, ISAAC RUCKER, GEO. McDANIEL.

Page 348. 4 May 1776. NICHL. CABELL & wife HANNAH, AC, to STEPHEN TURN-
            ER, AC, for 5 sh, 450 acres on both sides of Ivey Creek. Lines:
WM. HOWARD, STEPHEN TURNER, EDWD. BOWMAN. Wit: SAML. FARGUSON, TERISHA
TURNER, SAML. TURNER, EDWD. HARDING. Orig. del. to CHAS. IRVING, 29 Sep
1778.

Page 349. 21 May 1776. NICHL. CABELL & wife HANNAH, AC, to ARTHER RO-
            BINSON, AC, for ₺35, 200 acres N side Tye. Lines: side of
Berry's Mt. Wit: SAML. FARGUSON, TERISHA TURNER, EDWD. HARDING, SAML.
TURNER. Orig. del. to ROBINSON.

Page 350. 14 Oct 1775. MATT. CARTWRIGHT & wife MARGET, AC, to JNO.
            BOWLING, AC, for ₺41, 198½ acres. Lines: AMBROSE JONES, BLAIN,
BIBB, GILISPIE; on a mt. Wit: JNO. CARTWRIGHT, RICH. TANKERSLEY, GEO.
GALASBY.

Page 352. 1 Jul 1776. JNO. SIMS TENISON & wife ANNE, AC, to WM. MILLER,
            AC, for ₺35, 100 acres on Porrige Creek. Lines: JAS. CHRISTIAN.
Part of 400 acres taken up by EDWD. EIDSON and conveyed by him to HENRY
TENISON SR.

Page 353. 1 Jul 1776. GILBERT BOWMAN & wife ELIZ, AC, to JNO. STRUTTEN,
            AC, for ₺75, 150 acres both sides Raven Creek. Lines: CABELL
at Rolling Road, WM. LAIN, JAS. MARTIN.

Page 354. 10 Oct 1775. RICH. JONES & wife NANNY, Cumberland Co, to
            JACOB COOLEY, Cumberland Co, for ₺70, 100 acres on E side

Rutledge Creek. Lines: Lynch Road, HENRY GILBERT, JAS. MENEES, N fork
Rutledge; bridge across road. Wit: HENRY GILBERT, JNO. STEWART, NICHL.
RICE, DANCY(?) McCRAW, THOS. GOOD.

Page 357.   3 Feb 1776.   MATT. TUCKER, AC, to JESSE KENNEDY, AC, for Ł7,
             80 acres N side Buffalo. Lines: Col. EDWD. CARTER's mill
creek, Col. BRAXTON, TUCKER, CHAS. PARKS, now in possession of JAS. GATE-
WOOD. Orig. del. to RICH. FULCHER agreeable to order from KENNEDY, 17 Dec
1790. Wit: DRURY, FRANCIS & JNO. TUCKER.

Page 358.   13 Oct 1775.   CHAS. CHRISTIAN SR, Goochland Co, for love borne
             his son, ELIJAH CHRISTIAN, AC, 400 acres where ELIJAH lives &
next to plantation belonging to MATT. WHITTLE and tract "paternd" to
JAMES CHRISTIAN, JNO. CHRISTIAN & WM. BROWN. Wit: ABRAHAM LEMASTER, DAVID
LONDON, JNO. OWENBY JR., JNO. CHRISTIAN.

Page 359.   4 Aug 1776.   JACOB MORRIS, Albemarle Co, & wife MARY, Parish
             of St. Ann, to JNO. TULEY JR., AC and parish - for Ł25, 200
acres branch of Thomas Mill Creek. Lines: DAVENPORT. Wit: EDMD. WILCOX,
WM. BANKS, RICH. BALLENGER, THOS. JOPLING, JNO. SALE.

Page 360.   8 Jan 1776.   ICHABOD CAMP & wife ANN, AC, to PETER JOYNER
             (JOINER), Louisa Co, for Ł70, 205 acres both sides of Rockey
Run a branch of Buffalo. Lines: WM. DILLARD. Wit: ANTHONY RUCKER, JOS.
PENN.   (Note: CAMP was a rector and Mrs. SWEENY treats him in her book.
ANTHONY RUCKER was the inventor of the river craft which facilitated
tobacco transportation.   See ALFRED PERCY's work for details.   He, RUCKER,
goes into some detail in his AC will about his craft. BFD)

Page 362.   6 May 1776.   JNO. PUCKETT, AC, & parish, to JACOB PUCKETT, AC
             & parish, for Ł50, 50 acres S side and joining Rockfish. Lines:
WM. OGLESBY. Wit: ALEX. REID JR., JOS. ROBERDS, THOS. FITZPATRICK JR.

Page 363.   27 Jan 1776.   THOS. BALLOW(EW), AC & Parish, to NATHL. WOOD-
             RUFF, AC, & Parish, for Ł25, 100 acres, part of 400 acres pat.
to BALLOW at Williamsburg 12 May 1759. S side Tye. Lines: BALLOW; where
WOODRUFF now lives, main road, top of Brushey Mt. Wit: KILLIS WRIGHT,
CHAS. LAVENDER, ALEX. CHISNELL.   Orig. del. to WM. MEREDITH, Aug 1793,
by order of DC(?).

Page 365.   6 May 1776.   GEO. CARRINGTON, Cumberland Co, to JOS. GOODWIN,
             AC, for Ł14, 500 acres branch of Harris Creek. Lines: PETTUS
THACKER, CARRINGTON, RICH. PETERS, JAS. CREWS, THOS. WILLIAMS. Wit: DANL.
GAINES, JACOB SMITH, HENRY GILBERT, SAML. WOODS, RICH. McCARY.

Page 367.   3 Feb 1776.   WM. PRIOR(PRIER), AC, to DANL. BURFORD, AC, for
             Ł20, 99 acres.   Lines: JOSIAH ELLIS.   Tract taken up by JACOB
BROWN and to PRIOR by deed. N branch of Brown's Creek and S branch of
Inchanted Creek. Wit: MICAJAH GOODWIN, VA. BURFORD, EDWAR(sic) STEVENS.

Page 369.   5 Aug 1776.   DANL. BURFORD to VA. TAYLOR, his daughter, for
             love of her - a slave, Daphney, for daughter's children at
death of daughter, VA. Wit: JAS. CREWS, GABL. PENN.

Page 369.   27 Apr 1776.   JAS. GATEWOOD, AC, to JAS. WATSON, AC, for Ł250,
             400 acres where I live. Lines: JNO. PENN, HENRY GILBERT,
DAVID SHEPHERD, land WATSON bought of CARTER BRAXTON; Buffalo River. Wit:
GABL. PENN, DAVID SHEPHERD, GEO. PENN, DUDLEY GATEWOOD.

Page 372.   30 Sep 1776.   PATRICK ROSE & wife MARY to CHAS. IRVING and
             orig. del. to him - for Ł700, tract called Gray's Point - 894
acres. Lines: N side of Piney.   Another tract adj. upper part and bought
of THOS. HIGGINBOTHAM by Rev. ROBT. ROSE - 200 acres. Wit: EDMD. WILCOX,
JOS. ALLEN, JAMESTOUN PATTERSON. Twig and turf delivery.   Memo: JNO. SALE
is to remain on place where he lives as a tenant and to pay IRVING 40
shillings per year for 6 years for each laboring tithable. Wit: EDMD.
WILCOX.

Page 373.   1 Oct 1776.   NATHAN CRAWFORD, AC, to BENJ. MOOR, both of AC
             and parish - for Ł140, 200 acres in Rich Cove and both sides

166

of Cove Creek. Lines: BENJ. MOOR, TERISHA TURNER, JNO. DAWSON, JNO. SOR-
RELS. Orig. del. 27 Jul 1804 to J. MOORE.

Page 374. 1 Apr 1776. MICHL. MONTGOMERY & wife MARY, AC, to SAML. WOODS,
AC, for Ŀ130, 200 acres branch of Rockfish and Short's branch.
Part of tract pat. to Col. JNO. CHISWELL, dec'd. and was property of MICL.
MONTGOMERY by deed. Lines: JOS. BARNETT. Wit: ALEX. REID JR., MICHL. Mc-
NEELY, J.H. MORRISON, ALEX. REID.

Page 376. 7 Oct 1776. GEO. COLEMAN, AC, to THOS. WAUGHT, for Ŀ220, 86
acres where COLEMAN lives. BAnk of Pedlar and Horsley Creek.
Adj. tract of 104 acres and this is set forth as where COLEMAN now lives.

Page 377. 7 Oct 1776. EDWD. BOWMAN, AC, to RALPH JOPLING, Albemarle &
parish of St. Ann, for Ŀ20, 117 acres on branch of Tribble
fall and Dutch Creek. Lines: THOS. BICKNELL.

Page 378. 4 Nov 1776. JNO. STEWART & wife ANN, AC, to BARTLETT CAULEY,
Cumberland Co, for Ŀ244 (or 245 - blurred) 260 acres on N side
& joining Crooked Run; part of tract. Lines: JNO. STEWART; up the road,
JAS. MENEES, DANL. GAINES, HIGGINBOTHAM.

Page 380. 4 Nov 1776. THOS. GILLENWATERS & wife MARTHA, AC, to JNO. Mc-
DANIEL, AC, for Ŀ70, 100 acres on Harris Creek. Lines: EDWD.
TINSLEY, HUGH ROSE, ANTHONY RUCKER, SUSANNAH RUCKER, GEO. McDANIEL.

Page 381. 4 Oct 1776. ABRAHAM NORTH & wife SUSANNAH, AC, to THOS. GILL-
ENWATERS, AC, for Ŀ150, 278 acres on Boling's Creek and where
NORTH lives. 200 acres of it bounded by pat. of 7 Jul 1755 and 46 acres
of it pat. 24 Mar 1767. 4 acres pat. 24 Mar 1767. SUSANNAH consented to
deed on 4 Nov 1776.

Page 383. 4 Nov 1776. JAS. HENDERSON, AC, to ALEX. HENDERSON, AC, for
Ŀ50, 240 acres on branch of Taylor's Creek. Lines: RO. WARE,
JNO. HENDERSON, EDWD. STEVENS, RO. STEVENSON. Del. to ALEX. HENDERSON
Nov. 1787.

Page 385. 4 Nov 1776. ALEX. HENDERSON, AC, to JAS. HENDERSON, for Ŀ50,
130 acres on branch of Rockfish. Lines: ALEX. HENDERSON, CLAP-
HAM. Orig. del. to JAS. HENDERSON 12 Jan 1786.

Page 387. 3 Feb 1777. NICHL. CABELL & wife HANNAH, AC, to WM. SPENCER,
AC, for 5 sh. 867 acres on Raven's Creek. Lines: NICHL.
CABELL, JAS. MARTIN, RICH. ALCOCK, WM. SPENCER, THOS. BALLEW.

Page 388. 3 Feb 1777. JOSIAS WOODS & wife RHODA, AC, to JAS. HOPKINS,
Albemarle and Par. of St. Ann, for Ŀ273, several adj. tracts,
pat. to several persons at different times. 1) 190 acres pat. to JOS.
CABELL 20 Sep 1759. Lines: JNO. HUNTER, WM. BURNS. 65 acres - part of
tract - passing through several proprietors' hands and having been forfeited for want of Quitrents and cultivation and by virtue of an assignment from JNO. LOVING granted by pat. to WOODS 16 Feb 1771. 2) Tract pat.
to JOSIAS WOODS, 27 Aug 1770, 315 acres, but 100 acres of it on N side of
the Mt. adj. LEE HARRIS and separated by marked line beginning at JOS.
CABELL's on GREGORY MATTHEWS' line; Rockey Mt. Retained for use of JO-
SIAS & wife, RHODA. Remaining 215 acres sold to HOPKINS. Lines: LEE HAR-
RIS, ABRAHAM WARWICK, WM. FITZPATRICK. 3) 50 acres bought by JOSIAS of
WM. FITZPATRICK and adj. tract 2 bought 4(?) Aug or Nov (blurred) 1771,
rec. in AC. Lines: WOODS, FITZPATRICK, fork of Creek, top of the mt. -
All except the 100 acres reserved on Horse Shoe Mt. and head branch of
Dutch Creek and Davis Creek - 455 acres. Wit: DANL. GAINES, JOS. CABELL,
JOS.TUCKER. Orig. del. to W. HOPKINS. (Note: This is doubtless Dr. JAS.
HOPKINS who died testate in AC. I regard his very long will as one of
the most interesting in the records here. He attempted to set up a
group of hospital farms in several counties and offered prizes for tuber-
cular cures, etc. He and his son-in-law were at odds and he does not
throw any bouquets at the man. In fact, he baits his grandson to part
with his father's name. This is another story, but worth commenting upon
in noting the deed to HOPKINS.

Page 393.   1 Feb 1777.   HENRY BARNES & wife SARAH, AC, to MARTIN KEY, JR,
           of AC, for Ŀ200, 306 acres on branch of Rucker's Run. BARNES
bought it from LUNSFORD LOMAX, JR. Wit: WM. LOVING, JOS. TUCKER, JOSHUA
BUSH. Orig. del. to KEY.

Page 394.   3 Feb 1777.   EDWD. BOWMAN to WM. GOOLSBEY, AC, for Ŀ70, 138
           acres on Huff Creek and E side of Tobacco Row. Part of 276 ac-
res which HENRY CHILDERS bought of WM. CABELL. Lines: Line run to divide
276 acres between HENRY & JNO. CHILDRES (or ERSS); BENJ. STINNETT, WM.HIX.

Page 397.   10 Sep 1776.   JESSE MILLS, AC, to EDMD. WILCOX, AC, for Ŀ12-8-
           11, debt, Deed of Trust. 5 sh. Two slaves, Moll and Bristol
and descended to me at death of my mother; stock, etc. Wit: GEO. GILLAS-
PIE, JAS. HIGGINBOTHAM, JOS. CABELL.

Page 398.   3 Feb 1777.   Several Shff. bonds for DANL. GAINES. Commission
           from Governor on 16 Dec last. Bond to AC JP's: WM. CABELL,
ZACH TALIAFERRO, AMBROSE RUCKER, ALEX. REID JR. Bondsmen: HUGH ROSE,
RICH. HARVIE, GABL. PENN, THOS. LUMPKIN, EDMD. WILCOX, CHAS. ROSE.

Page 401.   21 Jan 1777.   Surveyor's bond by JAS. HIGGINBOTHAM. Appointed
           by President & Masters of the College of Wm. and Mary on 3 Dec
last. Bondsmen: JOS. CABELL & EDMD. WILCOX. (Note: It will be remembered
that WM. CABELL Jr. was the official surveyor for the county from 1761
until this man took his place. All CABELL researchers know that WM.
CABELL JR. was a colonel in the Continental Army so he had to give up his
position. JAMES HIGGINBOTHAM is listed as a major in the Continental Army.
There are later surveys in books yet to be put out by the compiler, so it
will be shown just who did the work; when indicated.)

Page 402.   2 Dec 1776.   LAURENCE SUDDEATH (signed SUDDER) and wife MARTHA,
           AC, to WM. HENDEROSN, Albemarle, for Ŀ80, 94 acres on both
sides of main branch of Rucker's Run and in cove of a mt. Margin: Orig.
del. to JNO. PUGH by order. MARTHA approved deed 3 Mar 1777.

Page 405.   2 Dec 1776.   CHAS. IRVING, Albemarle, to CLOUGH SHELTON for
           Ŀ300, 333 acres on S side of Rockfish and on both sides of
Corbin's Creek. Lines: JNO. SMALL - or line that is now PUCKETT's on Rock
fish; DAVID REID at the mouth of Corbin's Creek, late Col. JNO. CHISWELL,
MICHL. MONTGOMERY, ALEX. REID, FRANCIS MERIWETHER.

Page 407.   3 Feb 1777.   WM. GOOLSBEY, AC, to DRURY BOWMAN, AC, for Ŀ40,
           66 acres on the blue ridge and branch of Pedlar.

Page 408.   3 Mar 1777.   JACOB SMITH, AC, to RUBEN HARRISON, AC, for Ŀ50,
           400 acres branch of Franklyn Creek and Moll's Creek. Lines:
JAS. SMITH, HOWARD CASH, PEARCE WADE, BENJ. TALIAFERRO. Wit: JNO. ROSE,
EDMD. WILCOX, RODERICK McCULLOCH, WM. POLLARD.

Page 410.   24 Jan 1776.   JUDITH GILMORE, AC, for love of her daughter,
           BRIDGETT MAYFIELD - 7 cattle and to her children at her death
(save those killed and male kind.) If children reach 20 before BRIDGETT's
death. Wit: GABL. PENN, WM. BRYAN. Rec. 3 Mar 1777.

Page 411.   3 Mar 1777(recorded) JNO. DEPRIEST & wife ELIZ, AC, to JNO.
           STAPLES, AC, for Ŀ58-19, 196½ acres on branch of Rucker's Run.
Lines: ABRAHAM WARWICK, THOS. HAWKINS, WM. FURBUSH. Part of tract DE-
PRIEST bought of THOS. LOMAX.

Page 412.   5 May 1777.   WM. WAUGH & MARY ANN CARTER, AC, to JAS. GOODRICH,
           AC, for Ŀ60, 179 acres in coves of Tobacco Row Mt., formerly
sold by PETER CARTER & wife to WM. WAUGH, but MARY ANN had not relinquished dower rights. Lines: Col. LUNSFORD LOMAX. Wit: JOS. EDWARDS, EDMD.
GOODRICH, PETER CARTER.

Page 414.   1 May 1777.   AARON HIGGINBOTHAM SR, AC, to his son, SAML.
           HIGGINBOTHAM, AC, for love, 300 acres both sides Buffalo.
Lines: PHILIP SMITH. Wit: HENDRICK ARNOLD, RICH. OGLESBY, AARON HIGGIN-
BOTHAM. Orig. del. to SAML. HIGGINBOTHAM by JNO. TALIAFERRO "verble"
order.

168

Page 415.   1 May 1777.   AARON HIGGINBOTHAM SR, AC, to his son, AARON
           HIGGINBOTHAM JR, AC, for love, 390 acres on Thrasher's Creek.
bought by AARON SR, of NEILL CAMPBELL. Wit: HENDRICK ARNOLD, RICH. OGLES-
BY, SAML. HIGGINBOTHAM. Del. as deed above.

Page 417.   5 May 1777.   JNO. TULEY & wife ANN, AC, to JNO. STINETT, AC,
           for Ł52-12, 200 acres on both sides of CORNL. THOMAS' Mill
Creek. Part of tract of JACOB MORRIS. Lines: JACOB MORRIS, NATHL. DAVIS.

Page 418.   5 May 1777.   JAS. JONES, Albemarle Co, to JNO. HENDERSON JR.,
           Albemarle Co, for Ł63, 634 acres, 110 acres of it pat. to
JONES 15 Jul 1760, on head branch of Piney and branch of Irish Creek.
320 acres pat. to JONES 20 Jul 1768, on N fork of Piney; 204 acres pat.
same date and in same area - in the great mts. Wit: ZACH. TALIAFERRO,
BENJ. NOWELL, HENRY HARPER.

Page 421.   22 Oct 1775.   ISAAC WRIGHT, AC, to MARTIN DAWSON, for Ł100,
           400 acres Harris Creek. Lines: SHELTON, BURFORD, DANL. BURFORD.
Wit: MOSES WRIGHT, WM. HAYNES, BENJ. GOOD, EDMD. WILCOX.

Page 422.   22 Oct 1775.   ISAAC WRIGHT, AC, to MOSES WRIGHT, AC, for Ł30,
           92 acres on Harris. Lines: JNO WATERS. Part of 446 acres which
I bought of GEO. CARRINGTON. Wit: WM. HAYNES, BENJ. GOODE, MARTIN DAWSON,
EDMD. WILCOX.

Page 424.   9 Apr 1777.   FRANCIS WEATHERED, Albemarle Co, to CLAUDIUS BUS-
           TER, Albemarle Co, for Ł27-10, 70 acres branch of Rockfish.
Part of tract belonging to JNO. ROBINSON's estate. Lines: JNO. PATRICK,
BEaver branch - all on W side of Beaver branch and which PATRICK sold to
BUSTER. 2 acres on E side of Beaver from fork to small branch below -
being for a mill seat and in possession of BUSTER. Wit: JNO. CAMPBELL,
CHAS. PATRICK, JAS. BELL, MAGRATE CAMPBELL, JNO. SHIELDS JR.

Page 426.   5 May 1777.   CALEB HIGGINBOTHAM, AC, to MOSES PENN, AC, for
           Ł125, 342 acres on both sides Huff. Lines: BRAXTON's pat,
JAS. LIVELY. Wit: LINDSEY COLEMAN, JNO. SCOTT. CALEB's wife is not
named, but relinquished dower. Orig. del. to WM. STEWART on order of
PENN.

Page 428.   May 1777.   ABRAHAM WARWICK & wife AMY, AC, to JOSIAH WOOD,
           AC, for Ł114, 218 acres.) 1) Pat. to THEOPHILUS FAVER 26 Sep.
1764 - 170 acres, but 70 of it conveyed to JNO. BIRD and separated by
marked trees and not to be considered. 100 acres of FAVER pat. conveyed.
Lines: Col. LOMAX, Rocky Mt. spur. 2) 73 acres. Lines: LOMAX. 3) Pat. to
WARWICK, 5 Jul 1774 - 45 acres. Lines: WM. MARTIN, SAML. STAPLES - all
adjoining - 218 acres. Wit: WM. MARTIN, JNO. STAPLES, JNO. DEPRIEST.

Page 431.   9 Dec 1776.   MATT. WHITTLE, AC, to his son, JOSEPH WHITTLE,
           for love, 200 acres and upper end of tract where I live. Wit:
JNO. WARREN, JAS. WARREN, PETER JOYNER.

Page 432.   5 May 1777.   MATT. WHITTLE, AC, to son, JNO. WHITTLE, AC,
           (Note: JOS. in deed above was also of AC) for love, 200 acres
with my dwelling house, my pat. of 400 acres on Buffalo Ridge, branch of
Rockey Creek and above where I now live.

Page 433.   5 Jul 1777.   ABNER WITT, AC, to JNO. WITT SR, for Ł40, 100
           "achors" on branch of Rockfish. Lines: JNO. LACKEY. Wit: JNO.
WITT JR., CHAS WITT, LITTLEBERRY WITT. Orig. del. to LITTLEBERRY WITT.

Page 434.   14 Nov 1773.   CHAS. TULEY, Botetourt Co., to BENJ. THURMOND,
           Albemarle Co, for Ł60, 300 acres S side Pedlar on Inchanted
Mt. Wit: PHILIP THURMOND, JOS. EDWARDS, NICHL. PRYOR.

Page 436.   7 Jul 1777.   JACOB COOLY & wife SARAH, AC, to WIATT POWELL, AC,
           for Ł140, 100 acres E side Rutledge. Lines: Lynch Road, HENRY
GILBERT, JAS. MENEESE, N fork Rutledge, bridge across creek at Lynch road.
Wit: DUDLEY GATEWOOD, EDMD. POWELL, RICH. POWELL.

Page 437.   24 Jun 1777.   MARTIN DAWSON & wife ELIZ, AC, and Parish, to

JAS. FRANKLIN, AC & parish, for Ⱡ85, 247 acres Top of Smith's Mt. and
coves of side. Lines: WM. CABELL JR., JOS. BALLINGER, FRANKLIN. Wit:
DANL. GAINES, JNO. FRANKLIN, THOS. LANDRUM, EDMD. WILCOX.

Page 439. 28 Nov 1776. NATHL. BARNETT, AC, Planter, Power of atty. to
        friend, NATHAN CRAWFORD, AC, to sell tract of 280 acres on S
bank Rockfish; to let or farm any lands of mine or to act in any court
matters. Wit: JNO. LANCASTER, WM. CLARK, JOEL CRAWFORD.

Page 440. 22 Feb 1777. ELIZ. WADE gives up all "hole" living and poss-
        essions to my eldest son (boy) JACOB PETTYJOHN - cattle, furn-
iture, spinning wheel (2), 2 dishes and two basons etc - interesting list
-to pay all of my debts. Wit: JNO. HENRY GOODWIN, RICH. HARRISON JR.,
GEO. BOND, WM. PETTYJOHN. Proved 4 Aug 1777.

Page 441. 1 Aug 1777. EDWD. TINSLEY, AC, to JOSHUA TINSLEY, AC, for 5
        sh., 220 acres N side and joining Harris Creek. Lines: HUGH
ROSE, EDWD. TINSLEY. Part of EDWD's tract. Wit: JAMES HIGGINBOTHAM, JNO.
& DAVID TINSLEY.

Page 442. 4 Aug 1777. WM. HORRALL & wife MARY, AC, to THOS. McDONALD,
        Albemarle, for Ⱡ130, 200 acres both sides Davis Creek.

Page 444. 22 Dec 1773. JAS. TUGGLE, Goochland Co, to JOHN TUGGLE, AC,
        for Ⱡ50, slave, Lucy, now in possession of JOHN SMITH, Pitt-
sylvania Co. Wit: WM. LOVING, JNO. BARNETT, JNO. LOVING JR.

Page 444. 4 Aug 1777. STEPHEN WATTS & wife ELIZ, AC and parish, to GEO.
        WORTHAM, AC, for Ⱡ60, 182 acres N side Tye. Lines: RICH.
TANKERSLEY, CHAS. ROSE.

Page 446. 23 Jul 1773. JAS. DOUGLAS, AC, to RICH. LAWRANCE, AC, for Ⱡ20,
        46 acres SE side Hickory Creek, branch of Rockfish. Lines:
GEO. DOUGLAS. Wit: MATT. HARRIS, JNO. LACKEY JR., JOS. LAWRANCE, JAS.
LAWRENCE. Proved 3 Jan 1774 by LACKEY & by LAWRENCES, 4 Aug 1777.

Page 447. 4 Aug 1777. WIATT POWELL & wife SARAH, AC, to JOS. LIVELY,
        AC, for Ⱡ80, 400 acres Thresher's Creek. Lines: JAS. SMITH,
PIERCE WADE.

Page 448. 1 Sep 1777. JNO. DILLARD & wife SARAH, AC and parish, to MATT.
        TUCKER, AC and parish, for Ⱡ150, 250 acres branch of Beaver
Creek and E side and adj. Tobacco Row Mt. Part of 2700 acres pat. to
WM. CABELL JR. Lines: WM. CABELL JR., Smith's Mt. Orig. del. to GARLAND
HUNT JR. on order of TUCKER, 19 Jul 1791.

Page 450. 1 Sep 1777. CHAS. IRVING & MARTIN KEY, Albemarle Co, to JOSH-
        UA BUSH, AC, for Ⱡ100, 400 acres branch of Tye and N side
Berry's Mt. 1) Deed of Trust by HENRY KEY, late of AC, to grantors, 4
Dec 1773. Lines: HARMER & KING, Col. FRY. 2) 300 acres branch of Tye and
N side Berry's Mt., their own pointers; FRY.

Page 451. 1 Sep 1777. RO. MONTGOMERY & wife EASTER, AC, to MARTIN KEY,
        Fluvanna Co, for Ⱡ300, 1) 200 acres branch of Davis Creek.
Lines: THOS. MONTGOMERY, conveyed to RO. MONTGOMERY by THOS. MONTGOMERY
& wife BRIDGET 3 Mar 1768. 2) 60 acres adj. Lines: RO. WRIGHT. Pat. 20
Jul 1768. Orig. del. to MARTIN KEY.

Page 453. 19 Aug 1777. JNO. JOHNSON (signed JOHNSTON) and wife DICEY,
        AC, to JNO. WRIGHT, AC, for Ⱡ60, 98 acres. Lines: JNO. LOVING
JR. Bought by JOHNSTON of WM. LOVING, 1 Oct 1771. Relenquishment of Deed
of Trust by GABL PENN for SPIERS & BOWMAN, 6 Aug 1777. Wit: EDMD. WILCOX,
WM. LOVING, GEO. BLAIN JR. Orig. del. to JNO. WRIGHT Dec 1786.

Page 455. 28 May 1777. JNO. MARTIN & wife MARY, AC, to SHEARWOOD MARTIN,
        Albemarle Co, for Ⱡ120, 310 acres both sides Hughes' Creek.
Wit: WM. MARTIN, ALEX. PATTON, JAS. MARTIN.

Page 456.   Oct 1777. JNO. WADE, AC, to ARCHELUS COFFEY, AC, for Ⱡ120,
        150 acres S fork of N branch of Davis Creek. Lines: WM. ALLEN,

3 Springs, the road, JAS. CULL, the Mt., SAML. DENNY, JAS. McALEXANDER.
Wit: on 6 Oct 1777. MICHL. McNEELY, ALEX. REID JR., NICHL. CABELL,
EDMD. WILCOX.

Page 461.   30 Aug 1776.   Power of stty. by JNO. CRAWFORD, AC, to his
            brother, NATHAN CRAWFORD, AC, to sell 200 acres on Cove Creek.
Wit: JOEL CRAWFORD, JAS. MONTGOMERY, AUGHSTIN SMITH. Proved 3 Mar 1777 by
JOEL CRAWFORD; proved 7 Jul 1777, by JAS. MONTGOMERY; 6 Oct 1777, by A.
SMITH.

Page 462.   5 Jun 1777.   Deed of gift by MARY RENALDS (signed RENOLDS), AC,
            to her son, PLEASANT RENALDS, and her daughter, SUBVINA RE-
NALDS, 2 feather beds, 1 pot, 1 chest, 2 spinning wheels, some pewter.
Wit: WM. & WINEFRED POLLARD.

Page 463.   3 Nov 1777.   JNO. KEY JR., & wife AGNES, AC, to JAS. TRAIL, AC,
            for Ƚ50, 59 acres S side Finley's Mt., part of 400 acres of
late property of LUNSFORD LOMAX JR. and by him conveyed to HUGH PATRICK
and by PATRICK conveyed to KEY. Lines: RICH. PRICHARD, JACOB EADES, HUGH
PATRICK. Wit: CHAS. ASHLEY, JNO. WALLER KEY. Orig. del. to TRAIL 27 Feb
1786.

Page 464.   3 Nov 1777.   WM. CAMDEN & wife SEBEL, AC, to LEVI BALDOCK,
            Buckingham Co, for Ƚ149-15, 152 acres on Huff Creek. Part of
pat. to JAS. STINNET at Williamsburg 1 Jun 1750. Rest of tract of 227
acres granted to DANL. EDMONDS by JAS. STINNET by AC deed. Wit: N. CABELL.

ge 465.·   1 Dec 1777.   THOS. BALLEW & wife ELIZ, AC, to WM. SPENCER for
            Ƚ42-10, 150 acres, S branch of Tye. Lines: THOS. BALLEW, ALEX
CHISNALL, S side and near bank of Tye, JOS. CABELL, NATHL. WOODROOF,
Spencer's Road. Part of tract. Orig. del to THOS. SPENCER by order 21
Mar 1791.

Page 467.   1 Nov 1777.   NATHAN CRAWFORD, AC, planter, to JNO. WITT, AC,
            for Ƚ150, 200 acres on branch of Rockfish near the Great Mt.
Lines: CHISWELL; also 80 acres adjoining. Wit: ABNER WITT, JAS. REID JR,
SAML. DINWIDDIE.

Page 469.   1 Dec 1777.   WM. TILLER, AC, to HENRY SORROW, AC, for Ƚ12, 74
            acres, part of TILLER's land. Lines: DAVID MONTGOMERY JR.,
N branch of Nassau Creek. Orig. del. to SORROW.

Page 470.   1 Dec 1777.   NICHL. MORAN (MORRAN) & wife WINIFRED, to CHAS.
            IRVING for Ƚ40, 50 acres. Lines: PHILIP DAVIS, ROSE. Orig.del.

Page 471.   1 Dec 1777.   JNO. HARDWICK & wife ELIZ, AC, to HENRY McDANIEL,
            AC, for Ƚ40, 115 acres. Orig. del. to PARKER Dec 1786 (1788?)

Page 472.   1 Dec 1777.   JNO. HARDWICK, AC, to JNO. PARKER, AC, for Ƚ60,
            200 acres. Orig. del. to PARKER Dec, 1788.

Page 473.   4 Nov 1777.   JNO. HARDWICK, admr. to PEARCE WADE, AC, to JNO.
            PARKER, AC, for Ƚ210, at Ƚ35 a year for 6 years - a certain
tract with plantation and mill thereon.

Page 474.   4 Dec 1777.   ABRAHAM MOORE & wife JEAN, AC, to WM. OGLESBY,
            AC, for Ƚ100, 232 acres, part of tract pat. to JOS. BALLENGER
and by him to RICH. BALLENGER by deed of fioffment. Lines: Top of Ballinger's Mt., JOS. MAYS. Wit: EDMD. WILCOX, WM. FRANKLIN, FRANCIS BUSH, JAS.
FRANKLIN, FRANCIS LEE, RICH. OGLESBY. Orig. del. to OGLESBY 4 Jul 1785.

Page 475.   5 Jan 1778.   BARTLETT CORLEY and wife,Powhatan, to JOS. MAYO,
            Powhatan, for Ƚ244-10, 260 acres. Lines: Lynch road, down
Crooked Run, JAS. MENEES, DANL. GAINES, JNO. STUART.

Page 477.   3 Dec 1778.   GEO. McDANIEL, AC, to AMBROSE RUCKER, AC, for
            Ƚ250, 253 acres Harris Creek. Wit: JNO. McDANIEL, WM. GALT,
JNO. CRAWFORD. Orig. del. to RUCKER by BARTLETT EADS Jul 1788.

Page 478.   3 Jan 1788.   ALEX. FITZPATRICK & wife SARAH, AC & parish, to

BENJ. LANHAM, AC & parish, for ₺40, 100 acres, part of where FITZPATRICK
now lives, Cosbey Creek and S end. Orig. filed 2 Mar 1805 - sent to
LANHAM.

Page 479. 2 Mar 1778. MICHL. CRAFT, AC, to WM. KYLE, Augusta, for ₺164,
369 acres on head of N fork of Rockfish. Part of pat. of DAVID
KINKHEAD. Orig. to SAML. REEVES by KYLE. DAVID KINKHEAD's pat. line
given as line.

Page 481. 2 Mar 1778. BARTHOLOMEW RAMSEY & wife MARGARET, AC, to NICHL.
WREN for ₺15, 36 acres S side of N fork of Piney; one moiety
bought of HENRY KEY. Lines: CHAS. ROSE, WM. HOUCHINGS, BARTHOLOMEW RAMSEY,
NICHL. WREN. Wit: CHAS. ROSE, JOS. HIGGINBOTHAM JR., JNO. SALE, GEO. LEE,
WM. LEE. Orig. del. to WREN.

Page 483. 2 Mar 1778. BARTHOLOMEW RAMSEY & wife MARGARET, AC, to JNO.
HOUCHIN, AC, for ₺150, 3 tracts. 1) 81 acres pat. at Williamsburg 10 Sep 1755. Lines: GEO. TAYLOR, N fork Piney. 2) 200 acres on
Piney and joining tract 1; S branch Crawley Creek, HENRY TAYLOR. 3) "Joins
the other" - 37 acres - the river, ROSE. No 2 is part of a pat. at Williamsburg 20 Sep 1751; No. 3 conveyed by HENRY KEY to RAMSEY 5 Oct 1777.
Wit: CHAS. ROSE, WM. LEE, JNO. SALE, GEO. LEE, NICHL. WREN. Orig. del.
to HOUCHIN.

Page 485. 2 Mar 1778. WM. MARTIN & wife FRANCES, AC, to HENRY MARTIN,
Fluvanna Co, for ₺400, 200 acres head of N fork of Nassau -
now called the Dutch Creek at a place called the Indian Cove. Orig. del.

Page 488. 2 Mar 1778. JNO. DEPRIEST & wife ELIZ, AC, to JOSIAS WOOD for
₺200, 305 acres. Lines: SAML. STAPLES, WM. LOVING. Orig. del.

Page 490. 2 Mar 1778. JOSIAS WOOD & wife RHODA, AC & Parish to JAS.
HOPKINS, now of the same county & parish, for ₺40, 100 acres
on head branch of Davis Creek - 315 acres pat. to WOOD 27 Aug 1770.
Whole tract with contiguous lands - except the 100 acres already conveyed
to HOPKINS in Feb 1776. The 100 acres is separated from rest by line
along top of the Mt. and on other side joins tract which HOPKINS lately
bought of LEE HARRIS and where HENRY LAWHORN recently lived.

Page 493. 2 Mar 1788. JOSIAS WOOD, & wife RHODA, AC, to HENRY MARTIN,
Fluvanna, for ₺200, 218 acres. Lines: Land HENRY MARTIN recently bought of WM. MARTIN on Dutch Creek - several contiguous tracts. Lines:
SAML. STAPLES, dec'd, JNO. BYRD. Bought by WOOD from ABRAHAM WARWICK &
wife AMY, 5 May 1777.

Page 495. 28 Feb 1778. MATT. HARRIS, AC & parish, to JAMES HOPKINS, AC
& parish, for ₺44-17, 80 acres on head branch Davis Creek.
Lines: JAS. HOPKINS, ZACHARIAS PHILLIPS, MATT. HARRIS. Part of survey of
280 acres and line is visible. HOPKINS (formerly LEE HARRIS') pat. to M.
HARRIS, 3 Aug 1771. Wit: HENRY & JNO. MARTIN, JNO. BIRD.

Page 498. 5 Sep 1775. HENRY TUGGLE, Goochland planter, power of atty.
to his brother, JNO. TUGGLE, AC, to receive from JNO. SMITH,
Pittsylvania, my part in slave, Luce. She was bought by JNO. SMITH from
DANL. BASKETT. Wit: JNO. HOPKINS, JAS. HOUCHINS, JOSHUA TUGGLE.

Page 499. 2 Mar 1778. DAVID BARNETT, AC, to NICHL. MORAN, AC, for ₺75,
125 acres BARNETT bought from WM. COFFEY; WM. COFFEY bought
from JAS. COFFEY, and part of land JAS. COFFEY bought of Col. PETER JEFF-
ERSON, Albemarle - on both sides of Tye. Lines: Elk Creek, JAS. COFFEY,
Cox creek. Release by THOS. STAPLES for CARTER & TRENT 2 Mar 1778.

Page 501. 6 Apr 1778. JNO. GILMER, AC, to JAS. JOHNSON, AC, for ₺240,
160 acres both sides Taylor Creek. Lines: DAVID MERIWETHER,
CHAS. YANCEY, THOS. ROBERTSON, ALEX. HENDERSON. Wit: BENJ. TALIAFERRO.
Orig. del. to BENJ. TALIAFERRO.

Page 502. 2 Mar 1778. JNO. WRIGHT & wife ELIBETH, AC & parish, to JAS.
HALLEY BURTON, yeoman, of AC & parish, for ₺145, 230 acres
both sides Davis Creek on Rockfish. Lines: SAML. SHELTON. Wit: DAVID &

THOS. MONTGOMERY. Original sent, 19 Nov 1839, to ALEX. BROWN, exr. of J.H. HALLEYBURTON.

Page 504. 30 Jan 1778. DUDLEY GATEWOOD, AC, to GEO. COLEMAN, AC, for Ƚ500, 370 acres on N side Buffalo, where GATEWOOD liveth and he bought it of CARTER BRAXTON. Lines: GEO. PENN, GEO. LEE, Glebe line, late AMBROSE LEE. Wit: GABL. PENN, EDMD. WILCOX, JOS. CABELL, GEO. GILBERT.

Page 505. 28 Feb 1778. JNO. GOODWIN & wife MARY, AC, to WM. LEE for Ƚ125, 100 acres. Lines: JAS. RIVER, GEO. GOODWIN. Wit: JNO. MERRITT, CORNL. SALE, JNO. DAWSON.

Page 507. 2 Feb 1778. NICHL. CABELL, AC, to JOS. EDWARDS, AC, for Ƚ70, 550 acres branch of Horsley. Lines: NICHL. CABELL, JOS. EDWARDS, JOS. MILSTEAD. Wit: GEO. McDANIEL, ADAM BROWN, PETER CARTER, JOS. CABELL.

Page 509. 1 Dec 1777. WM. GOOLSBY, AC & parish, to HENRY CHILDRES for Ƚ40, 284 acres, pat. to THOS. GOOLSBY at Williamsburg 16 Feb 1771. Branch of Roberts' Creek and S branch of Pedlar. Lines: WM. PRYER. THOMAS' name is used in deed, but signed by WM. Wit: CHAS. BURNES, NEILL JOHNSON, WM. HIX, JNO. CHILDRES.

Page 511. 30 Mar 1778. THOS. RICKETS, AC, to GEO. WILKINSON, AC, for 20 sh., 1 acre.

Page 512. 24 Nov 1777. WM. GOOLSBY & wife FRANCES, AC, to JOS. CHILD-RESS for Ƚ140, 138 acres branch of Huff and E side of Tobacco Row. Part of 276 acres which HENRY CHILDRESS bought of WM. CABELL. Lines; HENRY & JNO. CHILDRESS, BENJ. STINNETT, JNO. WHITEHEAD, NOELL JOHNSON. Orig. del. to WM. CAMDEN 4 Jul 1778.

Page 513. 1 Apr 1778. THOS. MATTHEWS, AC, to JAS. TURNER, AC, for Ƚ32, 64 acres on N branch Dutch on Marrowbone Mt. Wit: LEONARD PHILLIPS, THOS. HOPPER, WM. MATTHEWS. Orig. ded. to TURNER.

Page 514. 6 Apr 1778. RO. DINWIDDIE, AC, to SAML. DINWIDDIE, for love borne SAML., 180 acres on N branch Rockfish. Lines: JAS. DIN-WIDDIE; part of whereon is dwelling house. Orig. del. to JAS. HENLEY.

Page 515. 10 Nov 1777. LEE HARRIS & wife, WINNIFRED, AC & parish, to JAS. HOPKINS, St. Ann's Par. of Albemarle, for Ƚ391-6, 602 acres in 3 contig. tracts. Davis Creek and branches & pat. to HARRIS. 1) 326 acres. 2) adjoining - 214 acres. Lines: his own, both pat. 3 Mar 1760. 3) Adjoining and pat. 16 Feb 1771. Lines: his own, ZACH. PHILLIPS. Wit: JNO. DIGGS, JOSIAH JOPLING, WM. HARRIS, JR, HENRY MARTIN. Orig. del. to W. HOPKINS.

Page 519. 4 May 1778. WM. LILLIE & wife ADEDIAH, AC, to JNO. PAYTON, AC, for Ƚ20, 70 acres on branch of Horsley. Lines: JOB CARTER, LUNSFORD LOMAX. Surveyed by JAS. HIGGINBOTHAM 5 May 1769 and pat. to grantor.

Page 520. 3 May 1778. JAS. LACKEY, AC, to JOS. ROBERTS, AC, for Ƚ262, 262 acres on branch of Corbin's Creek of Rockfish, part of tract. Lines: JNO. LACKEY, WM. BARNETT, JAS. LACKEY, THOS. CARPENTER, JNO. HARDY, top of a ridge.

Page 522. 4 May 1778. MATT. MONTGOMERY & wife ELSE, Albemarle, to WM. HITCHCOCK, AC, for Ƚ60, 172 acres - sides of a mt., S side Rockfish. Lines: DAVID MONTGOMERY, WM. BELL.

Page 524. 2 Feb 1778. NICHL. CABELL, AC, to PETER CARTER, AC, for Ƚ215, 376 acres on branch of Horsley. Lines: JOS. EDWARDS. Wit: JOS. EDWARDS, ADAM BROWN, GEO. McDANIEL, JOS. CABELL.

Page 525. 4 May 1778. NICHL. CABELL, AC, to JOS. MILSTEAD, AC, for Ƚ215, 890 acres on branch of Horsley. Lines: JOS. EDWARDS, PETER CARTER, NICHL. CABELL. Part of tract. Wit: JOS. EDWARDS, ADAM BROWN,

JOS. CABELL, GEO. McDANIEL.

Page 526. 5 Dec 1777. JNO. SYME, Esqu. of Hanover, & WM. HENRY Esq. of
        Fluvanna, heir at law to Col. JNO. HENRY, Hanover, dec'd, to
MOSES MARTIN, AC. JNO. HENRY in life owed JNO. SYME about Ŀ500 and exe-
cuted mortgage on AC land - about 1200 acres. JOHN HENRY later sold to
WM. MOORE, now dec'd, 300 acres, but died before conveyeance was made.
WM. MOORE devised it to his sons, JNO. & JAS. MOORE, and MOSES MARTIN
hath purchased it - Ŀ48, 300 acres. Lines: Cub Creek. Wit: WM. CABELL,
EDMD. WINSTON, HUGH ROSE. (Note: Those conversant with the genealogy of
the HENRY family know that this JOHN HENRY was the father of PATRICK
HENRY. SARAH HENRY, mother of PATRICK, lived later in Amherst county and
her will is in the courthouse here. She is buried at Winton which is one
of the beautiful estates of the county and it is located at Clifford;
once called New Glasgow. The bed in which SARAH HENRY died is still
owned by a descendant of the family, Mrs. FRANCIS HAMILTON, who owns the
old LINDSEY COLEMAN home which is named Mountain View. This home is
back of the courthouse and the lot for the courthouse was sold to the
county by LINDSEY and other sons of GEO. COLEMAN, dec'd, for a nominal
sum. This purchase became necessary when Nelson county was formed in
1808 and a new courthouse had to be built since the old one was in present Nelson County. Mountain View is just across the street from my home
in the Baptist parsonage. BFD)

Page 528. 18 Nov 1777. RICH. LAWRANCE & wife ISABELL, AC, to THOS. JOHN-
        SON for Ŀ20, 46 acres on SE side of Hickory Creek. Lines: GEO.
DOUGLASS. Wit: JNO. DAWSON, JOS. MORRISS, JNO. LACKEY JR., WM. HARRIS Jr.

Page 530. 18 Nov 1777. RICH. LAWRANCE & wife ISABELL, AC & parish, to
        JOS. MORRIS, AC & par., for Ŀ130, 200 acres, part of 400 acres
pat. to CHAS. SMITH and by him deeded to LAWRANCE. On both sides of
Hickory. Divided from other part of tract which is now property of JNO.
LACKEY JR., by line of marked trees. Lines: WM. MORRISON. Wit: JNO.
DAWSON, THOS. JOHNSON, JNO. LACKEY JR.

Page 531. 2 Mar 1778. REUBIN HARRISON & wife PEGGY, AC, to RICH. BALL-
        INGER, AC, for Ŀ50, 250 acres on Thresher's creek and N side
of Moll's Mt. Line of AARON HIGGINBOTHAM.

Page 533. 5 Nov 1777. Commission to AMBROSE RUCKER & BENJ. RUCKER to
        quiz NANCY JONES, wife of RICH. JONES, as to deed of 10 Oct
1775, to JACOB COOLEY for 100 acres. Done Nov 1777.

Page 534. 8 Apr 1778. Commission to ALEX. REID JR., JNO. DAWSON & JNO.
        DIGGS to quiz ELIZ. JOHNSTON, wife of JAS. JOHNSON, as to
deed to JNO. GILMER for 160 acres. Done 25 Apr 1778 by REID & DIGGS.

End of Deed Book D

AMHERST COUNTY, VIRGINIA DEED BOOK E

DEDICATION

This work is dedicated to my brother-in-law, CLARENCE LUDLOW MILLER, Shelbyville, Kentucky; an Assistant Secretary in the Department of Agriculture under DWIGHT D. EISENHOWER.

BAILEY FULTON DAVIS
1963

Page 1.   6 Jul 1778. JNO. CHILDRESS, Albemarle Co., to WM. CAMDEN, AC, for Ŀ120, 138 acres on a branch of Huff; pat. of 276 acres which HENRY CHELDRESS bought of WM. CABELL JR. Lines: HENRY CHILDRESS, BENJ. STINNETT, RO. WHITTEN. Orig. del. to CAMDEN 3 Aug 1782.

Page 2.   6 Jul 1778. PHILLIP SMITH & wife SUSANN, AC & parish, to CALEB HIGGINBOTHAM, AC & parish, for Ŀ100, 244 acres on both sides Buffalo. SMITH bought it of JAS. SMITH. Lines: JACOB SMITH, Puppie Creek. Orig. del. to CHAS. TALIAFERRO per order, May, 1791.

Page 3.   15 Jun 1777. DUNCAN GRAHAM & wife MARY, Acroline Co., to GEO. LEE, AC, for Ŀ150, part of 503 acres. Wit: HENRY GILBERT JR, JUDITH GILBERT, ELIZ. CRENSHAW, GO. McDONALD. Orig. del. to LEE.

Page 3.   30 May 1778. RO. DOAKES, Augusta Co., to GEO. WITT, AC, for Ŀ100, 200 acres on branch of Stoney Creek of Rockfish. Lines: JAMES HORD, WM. HIRD, HUGH WILLOUGHBY. Wit: ABNER WITT, JNO. WITT JR., JNO. DINWIDDIE, ELISHA WITT.

Page 5.   6 Jul 1778. GEO. McDANIEL & wife MARGARET, and REUBIN HARRISON & wife PEGGY, AC, to AMBROSE RUCKER, AC, for Ŀ15, 127 acres on N branch Harris. Lines: AMBROSE RUCKER, THOS. LUCAS, STEPHEN GOLDSBY, WM. HICKS. Orig. sent to AMBROSE RUCKER July, 1788.

Page 6.   10 Mar 1778. DUNCAN GRAHAM, Caroline Co, to GEO. McDANIEL, AC, for Ŀ1105, 710 acres. Wit: JNO. CHICK, RO. GRAHAM, JNO. PENN. Orig. del. to McDANIEL.

Page 7.   6 Nov 1777. JNO. WRIGHT & wife SARAH, to NATHL. MANTIPLY for Ŀ30, 124 acres on N side Buffalo. Lines: EDWD. CARTER. Wit: DAVID SHEPHERD, VALENTINE COX, JNO. McKINDLEY, SAML. WOODS, PAT. HART, WM. BANKS. Orig. del. 19 Apr 1821, to N. MANTIPLY's exr.

Page 8.   6 Jul 1778. JOS. CHILDRESS & wife MARY, AC, to WM. CAMDEN for Ŀ180, 138 acres on branch of Huff and E of Tobacco Row Mts. Part of 276 acres which HENRY CHILDRESS bought of WM. CABELL JR. Lines: Dividing line between JNO. & HENRY CHILDRESS, BENJ. STINNET, WM. HIX.

Page 9.   9 Mar 1778. RICH. OGLESBY, AC, to his son, WM. OGLESBY, for 5 sh, 300 acres from lower end of survey. RICH. bought it from WM. MITCHELL. Lines: EDWD. CARTER. Also slave Jacob. Wit: HENRY FRANKLIN, CORNL. SALE, DANL. TUCKER.

Page 10.   6 Jul 1778. CHAS. PATTERSON & wife MARY, Buckingham Co, to JNO. JOPLING, AC, for Ŀ150, 500 acres on S side Berry's Mt. & S side Rucker's Run. Part of 2000 acres granted to SAML. SPENCER SR, and by him conveyed to CHAS. PATTERSON & wife MARY, 20 Apr 1765. Wit: EDMD. WINSTON, WM. SPENCER, WM. HORSLEY, CHAS. IRVING.

Page 11.   28 May 1778. EDWD. MOUSLEY, AC, to DAVID MERIWETHER for Ŀ300, 247 acres. Lines: ARCHIBALD WOODS, top of the Mt., ARCHY McDANIEL. Wit: FRANCIS MERIWETHER, JNO. LANCASTER, JAS. MOZLY. Orig. del. to BENJ. TALIAFERRO.

Page 13.   3 Aug 1778. Commission to ALEX. REID Jr, JNO. DAWSON, JNO. DIGGS to quiz MARY, wife of EDWD. MOUSLEY, as to above deed. Done 9 Oct 1778 by REID & DIGG (sic).

Page 14. 1 Jun 1778. JAS. FRANKLIN, AC, to MATT. TUCKER, AC, for Ł300,
247 acres on Buffalo & Beaver Creek and at foot of Tobacco Row
and coves thereof. Lines: WM. CABELL, JOSEPH BALLINGER, FRANKLIN. Orig.
del. to SAML. CAMP.

Page 15. 2 Jan 1778. JNO. HARDWICK, AC, to DANL. BURFORD SR, AC, for
Ł250, ---acres. Wit: JNO. MERRITT, JNO. BURFORD, JAS. CREWS,
DANL. BURFORD JR. Orig. del. to JNO. STEWART, Exr. of DANL BURFORD,
Jan 1789.

Page 16. 3 Aug 1778. SAML. DAVIS, AC, to SAML. RICHARDSON, Louisa Co,
for Ł475, 400 acres on Rockfish. Lines: GEO. DUNCAN, MOLOY
(now JNO. THOMPSON's), MORRELL, SAML. BELL. Bought by DAVIS from FRANCIS
MERIWETHER. ANNIS, wife of DAVIS.

Page 17. 7 Mar 1778. RICH. GOODWIN, JNO. GOODWIN & MARY GOODWIN, AC,
to WM. LEE, AC, for Ł100, 105 acres Harris Creek. Wit: JNO.
DAWSON, WM. GUTTRY, JNO. MERRITT. Committee to quiz MARY GOODWIN, wife
of JNO.; done 31 Oct 1778 by DANL. GAINES & BENJ. RUCKER.

Page 19. 3 Aug 1778. ALEX. HENDERSON, Sr, AC, to JAS. HENDERSON, AC,
for Ł60, 100 acres head of Long Branch. Lines: ALEX. HENDERSON.
Wit: ALEX. REID JR., NATHAN CRAWFORD, RICH. DAVIS. Orig. del. to JAS.
HENDERSON 12 Jan 1786.

Page 20. 31 Jul 1778. THOS. BELL, AC & Parish, to JNO. & JAS. McCLORE,
AC & Parish, for Ł160, 166 acres on branch of Rockfish. Lines
of Col. CHISWELL.

Page 22. 3 Aug 1778. JNO. WIATT GILBERT, AC, & wife SALLY, to WM.
POLLARD, AC, for Ł740, 360 acres on branch of Tribulation.
Lines: Lynch road, BALER WALKER dec'd, EZEK. GILBERT. Tract given to
JOHN W. GILBERT by HENRY GILBERT, dec'd.

Page 23. 3 Aug 1778. RICH. ALCOCK & wife FRANCES, AC, to EDWD. WARE,
AC, for Ł350, 400 acres on Tye. Tract granted to WM. CABELL
at Williamsburg 25 Sep 1746, and by CABELL conveyed to DRURY BOWMAN and
by BOWMAN to ALCOCK. Orig. del. to WARE.

Page 24. 3 Aug 1778. SAML. DOAK, Augusta Co, to LUKE HAMBLETON, AC,
for Ł100, 190 acres. Lines: Capt. JNO. JACOBS.

Page 25. 3 May 1778. JAS. LACKEY, AC, to JOS. ROBERTS, AC, for Ł262.
(This deed has big X through it and is incomplete; a page has
been torn out, but next page is correctly numbered. Comm. to quiz MARY,
wife of JAS. LACKEY, is on page 26 for this deed and 262 acres mentioned
in comm.)

Page 27. 30 Oct 1777. JNO. & CHAS. CHRISTIAN, Charles City, to JAS.
GRISHAM, Cumberland Co, for Ł300, 933 acres on branch of Rockey
Run. Lines: HENRY CHRISTIAN, JNO. & CHAS. CHRISTIAN. Part of larger
tract of JNO. & CHAS. obtained by General Court decree "for of" WM. BROWN.
Wit: JAS. HIGGINBOTHAM, HENRY CHRISTIAN, ELIJAH CHRISTIAN.

Page 28. 3 Aug 1778. JOS. MAYS, AC, to JAS. MAYS, AC, for 5 sh, 110
acres N branch Tye. Lines: JAS. EDMONDS, GEO. GALASPIE, RICH.
TANKERSLEY, JOS. DILLARD, LEONARD TARRANT, JNO. MAYS. Part of 200 acres
deeded to JOS. MAYS in AC. SARAH, wife of JOS. MAYS.

Page 29. 3 Aug 1778. JOS. MAYS & wife SARAH, AC, to JNO. MAYS, AC, for
5 sh, 90 acres N branch Tye. Lines: LEONARD TARRANT, THOS.
WILTSHIRE, JAS. EDMONDS. Part of 200 acres as above. Both of these
deeds bear note that they were del. to grantees; no date.

Page 30. 3 Aug 1778. JOS. MAYS & wife SARAH, AC, to JAS. WALTERS, AC,
for 5 sh, 71 acres on N branch Tye. Lines: JOS. DILLARD, RICH.
TANKERSLEY. Granted by deed in AC to MAYS. Orig. del. to JNO. MAYS.

Page 32. 22 Jul 1778. JOS. CABELL & wife MARY, AC, to RICH. ALCOCK, AC.
for Ł60, 93 acres on N branch Raven Creek. Lines: JAS. MARTIN,

GILBERT BOWMAN, NICHL. CABELL, RICH. ALCOCK, WM. CABELL. Wit: JOS.
STARK, THOS. SHANNON, NANCY BURKS, WM. HORSLEY, JNO. WILKINSON.

Page 33. 3 Aug 1778. LAWRANCE LONG, Albemarle, to WM. BRYAN, AC, for
Ł33, 92 acres on head of Maloy Creek. Lines: a spring.

Page 34. 3 Aug 1778. ANGUS FORBUS, AC, to JNO. TOMMERSON (THOMASON) for
Ł20, 25 acres on branch of Davis Creek. Part of 45 acres pat.
to FORBUS 10 Sep 1767, and where he lives. Orig. del. to THOMASON.

Page 35. 3 Mar 1778. Commission to examine as to dower rights ANN CAMP,
wife of ICHABOD CAMP, as to 8 Jan 1776 deed to PETER JOYNER,
Louisa. Done 7 Mar 1778. Orig. del. to JOYNER.

Page 36. 7 Sep 1778. BENJ. HIGGINBOTHAM, AC, to JNO. MATTHEWS, AC,
(blank sum) 54 acres. Lines: JAS. HIGGINBOTHAM, ISAAC MAYFIELD,
AARON HIGGINBOTHAM.

Page 37. 7 Sep 1778. WM. MARTIN, AC & Parish, to JNO. GRIFFIN of same,
for Ł50, 82 acres on S branch Nassau. Lines: JNO. HAMNER. Wit:
JAS. REID. Orig. del. to ALLEN BLAIR for JNO. GRIFFIN Aug. 1790.

Page 38. 7 Sep 1778. RO. HOWARD CASH & wife TAMSEY, AC, to HENDRICK
ARNOLD, AC, for Ł150, 545 acres willed to the said RO. CASH by
his father, RO. HOWARD CASH, dec'd. Pat. to RO. CASH 3 Nov 1750 at
Williamsburg. Orig. del. to ARNOLD 30 Sep 1783.

Page 39. 29 Aug 1778. WM. DUIGUID, Buckingham Co. & Tillotson Parish,
to GEORGE HILTON, AC, for Ł50, 116 acres on both sides of Elk
Creek. Lines: JAS. FREELAND, JAS. EVANS. Wit: WM. HORSLEY, JESSE ALLEN,
JNO. WILKINSON, SAML. MEGGINSON.

Page 41. 20 May 1778. JNO. COLEMAN, AC, to TYREE SLADING, AC, for blank
sum, 100 acres. Lines: near Huff Creek, top of the Mt., JNO.
COLEMAN, BENJ. NOWEL, JAS. BYAS. Wit: JNO. DANIEL COLEMAN, WM. PETER,
MOSES SWEENEY. Orig. del. to SLADING.

Page 41. 4 May 1778. WM. GOLDSBY (signed GOOLSBY), AC, to JNO. DANL.
COLEMAN, AC, for Ł25, 98 acres; pat. to AMBROSE JONES at Williamsburg 10 Sep 1760; N fork Piney. Also 50 acres at head of S branch
Piney. Lines: JNO. MANION. This was surveyed for THOS. GOOLSBY, father
of WM., 3 May 1771. Wit: ROBERT CHRISTIAN, JOS. TUCKER, CHAS. BURRUS.

Page 43. 7 Sep 1778. RO. BARNETT, AC, to JNO. MONTGOMERY, AC, for Ł50,
250 acres on both sides Buck Creek. Part of 450 acres pat. to
ALEX. MONTGOMERY 25 Jun 1747, and by him sold to RO. BARNETT. Orig. del.
to MONTGOMERY.

Page 44. 8 Aug 1778. DANL. GAINES & wife MARY, AC, to STEPHEN HAM, AC,
for Ł150, 298 acres on head branch of S fork of Rutledge. HAM
holds under unexpired lease. Wit: EZEK. GILBERT, JOSEPH STARKE, JOSIAS
GILBERT.

Page 45. 16 Mar 1778. JNO. THOMSON, AC, to JOS. MONTGOMERY, AC, for
Ł150, 194 acres on both sides Buck Creek of Rockfish. Lines:
ALEX MONTGOMERY. Wit: WM. HARRIS JR, WM. MONTGOMERY, JAS. THOMSON.
Orig. del. to MONTGOMERY.

Page 47. 28 Feb 1778. GEO. REEVES, Henry Co, to HENRY HARTLESS, AC, for
Ł35, 215 acres on branch of S fork of Buffalo and on Long Mt.
Wit: RODERICK McCULLOCH, RICH. DAVIS, FRANCIS VEALE, CARNABY VEALE. Orig.
del. to H. HARTLESS JR, Exr. of H. HARTLESS, dec'd, 29 Mar 1805. (Note:
Long Mt. is still known by the same name and is west of Amherst. There
is a state picnic table at top and in years past various churches have
ehld sunrise Easter services at this site. I make this comment for there
are some names of mountains and branches in some deeds which are unknown
to me. BFD)

Page 48. 7 Sep 1778. JNO. TUGGLE & wife MARY, AC, to WM. WALTON, AC,
for Ł140, 3 tracts adjoining, but in three parcels on N branch

Rucker's Run and Ragged Mts. 1) 42 acres pat. to JNO. LOVING JR. 5 Jun
1765. Lines: Col. LOMAX. Conveyed by LOVING to TUGGLE. 2) 40 3/3 acres
bought by TUGGLE from LUNSFORD LOMAX JR. 5 Oct 1767. Lines: LOMAX; top of
a Mt. 3) 82 acres pat. to JNO. TUGGLE 1 May 1775. Lines: JNO. MONTGOMERY,
JNO. LOVING JR., ABRAHAM SEAY JR, LUNSFORD LOMAX.

Page 49. 7 Sep 1778. ABRAHAM SMITH & wife ELIZ, AC, to THOS. PARROCK,
        AC, for Ł50, 170 acres. Lines: REV. RO. ROSE, dec'd. Pat. to
SEAY 15 Jun 1773. Orig. del. to JNO. PARROCK 25 Jul 1787.

Page 51. 5 Oct 1778. JNO. DURHAM & wife MABELL, AC, to JONATHAN WATERS,
        Augusta Co, for Ł30, 78 acres on Tye. Lines: ZACH. TALIAFERRO,
MOSES HUGHES, JNO. HATTER, HEZEKIAH JONES. (Note: It is interesting to
note that one can still see HATTER names on mailboxes and also on one or
two country stores in Nelson County near Tye. BFD)

Page 52. 5 Oct 1778. ARCHELAUS COFFEY, AC, to JAS. McALEXANDER JR., AC,
        for Ł200, 100 acres S branch of N fork of Davis Creek. Lines:
WM. ALLEN, 3 springs, JNO. WADE, JAS. McALEXANDER. ELEANOR, wife of
COFFEY.

Page 54. 5 Oct 1778. ARCHELAUS COFFEY & wife ELEANOR, AC, to JNO. WADE,
        AC, for Ł70, 50 acres S branch of N fork of Davis. Lines: JAS.
CULL, WM. ALLEN, SAML. DENNY, mountain line.

Page 55. 2 Feb 1778. ZACHARIAS TALIAFERRO, AC, to JAS. COLEMAN, Albe-
        marle, for Ł40, 139 acres pat. to TALIAFERRO 22 Aug 1770 on S
side Tye and near the fork. Wit: WM. COFFEY, JNO. B. TALIAFERRO, GEO.
MUNROE.

Page 57. 8 Sep 1778. JAS. MAYFIELD & wife ELLENDER, AC, to JNO. ROWSEY,
        AC, for Ł100, 100 acres N branch Buffalo. Lines: WM. GATEWOOD,
by deed in AC to MAYFIELD. Wit: RICH, AMBROSE & WM. GATEWOOD, SUTHERLIN
MAYFIELD.

Page 58. 7 Sep 1778. GEO. McDANIEL & wife MARGET, AC, to RO. HOWARD
        CASH, AC, for Ł500, 322 acres. McDANIEL bought it from JAS.
SMITH and rec. in AC. Pat. to SMITH at Williamsburg 10 Jul 1766.

Page 59. 5 Oct 1778. NICHL. WREN, AC, & wife ELIZ., to RICHARD HARRISON,
        AC, for Ł125, 2 tracts. 1) 170 acres on Crawley's Creek. Lines:
SAML. MURPHY, DUNCAN CAMERON, HENRY TAYLOR. Part of 400 acres pat. to
GEO. TAYLOR at Williamsburg 20 Sep 1751. 2) 36 acres on S side of N
fork Piney and bought of HENRY KEY. Lines: CHAS. ROSE, WM. HOUCHINS,
BARTHOLOMEW RAMSEY, NICHL. WREN. Orig. del. to MOSES WRIGHT per order
in July 1784.

Page 60. 5 Oct 1788(sic) MATT. NIGHTINGALE & wife LUCY, AC, to NICHL.
        WREN, AC, for Ł135, 150 acres Coffey's (otherwise RACON) Creek.
Lines: JNO. RYAN. NIGHTINGALE bought it of JOSEPH EATON and rec. in AC.
Release of mtg. to CARTER & TRENT by THOS. STAPLES, factor, 5 Oct 1778.
Orig. del. to WREN, Feb of 1788.

Page 61. Order to DANL. GAINES & BENJ. RUCKER, AC, to quiz MARY GOODWIN,
        wife of JNO. GOODWIN, as to deed of 8 Feb 1778, to WM. LEE.
Done 31 Oct 1778.

Page 62. 1 Nov 1778. WM. MORRELL, Burk Co. N.C., to MOSES HUGHES, AC,
        for Ł100, 217 acres on branch of Rockfish. Lines: THOS. ADAMS,
WM. MORREL. Wit: JAS. TILFORD JR, JAS. PAMPLIN, JNO. TILFORD.

Page 64. 26 Aug 1778. JAS. REID, SR, AC, to GEO. JUDE, Goochland, for
        Ł400, 200 acres, part of pat. of 400 acres to GEO. HERD 1 Feb
1748. Lines: THOS. ADAMS (formerly that of ANDREW REID), JNO. & CHAS.
WITT; pat. line formerly that of WILLIAM MEHO(?), Gent., JNO. HERD. Wit:
WM. LOVING, MOSES HUGHES, WM. RYAN, JAS. REID JR., MATT. NIGHTINGALE.

Page 65. 2 Nov 1778. JOS. CABELL, AC, to JAS. DILLARD, Louisa Co, for
        Ł1355, 1020 acres on fork of Tye and Buffalo. Lines: Mouth of
Raven Creek; STEPHEN WATTS, WM. SPENCER, JOS. CABELL. Part of 1990 acres

by deed to CABELL in AC. Wit: WM. HORSLEY, GEO. STOVALL, minor, JNO.
PENN, RICH. HARVIE. Memo: HENRY STRATTON to have peaceable possession of
plantation whereon he now lives and part of the tract until 25 Dec 1779;
same for WM. HOLLANDSWORTH & EZEK. STRATTON until 25 Dec 1778, as to
their tenements.

Page 67. 8 Oct 1778. THOS. LUMPKIN, Bedford Co, to JAS. THOMAS, AC -
          consideration - tract in Bedford which THOMAS bought of GEO.
WALTON - 300 acres - Lines: THOS. LUMPKIN (late HENRY GUTTREY), JNO.
WARD, JNO. CALLAWAY (late WM. GIBBS), Oak Mt. Creek, for 175 acres in AC.
Lines: MOSES SWENEY, JNO. HARVIE, EDWD. TINSLEY, JNO. DAVIES, JNO. COLE-
MAN, dec'd. Wit: DANL. GAINES, WM. GALT, JNO. McDANIEL, JAS. MENEES JR.

Page 67. -- Oct 1778. (Rec. 2 Nov 1778) JNO. FRANKLIN & wife, MARGRETT,
          AC, to JNO. COTTRELL, Bedford Co, for Ł450, 368 acres. Lines:
THOS. DAWSON, the creek, between THOMAS. Wit: BALLINGER WADE, WM.
WRIGHT, ELIZ. FOWLER.

Page 68. 6 Feb 1775. THOS. SHANNON, Fincastle, to SIMON RAMSEY, AC, for
          Ł60, 75 acres branch of Rockfish near the Blew Mts. Lines: WM.
IRVIN. Wit: WM. SIMPSON, JNO. MURRELL, DAVID SIMPSON, ALLEN SIMPSON.
Orig. del. to RAMSEY 27 Sep 1790. Final proof 2 Nov 1778, by JNO. MUR-
RELL; 3 Apr 1775 by WM. & ALLEN SIMPSON.

Page 70. 2 Nov 1778. HENRY WOODS, AC & parish, yeoman, to ANGUS FORBUS,
          yeoman, AC, for Ł30, 53 acres branch of Davis Creek. Lines:
ANGUS FORBUS. Pat. to WOODS at Williamsburg. Orig. del. to FORBUS.

Page 71. 10 Sep 1778. HUGH R. MORRIS, Albemarle, to WM. CAMDEN. MORRIS
          under power of atty. from CHAS. DAWSON and rec. in Albemarle -
for Ł100, 374 acres Huff Creek. Pat. to JNO. WHEILER at Williamsburg
10 Sep 1755. Wit: TH. MILLER, CHAS. IRVING, WM. HORRALL. Orig. del. to
CAMDEN 3 Aug 1782.

Page 72. 9 Dec 1777. JNO. & CHAS. CHRISTIAN, Charles City, to HENRY
          CHRISTIAN, AC, for 5 sh., 507 acres on both sides Porage Creek.
Lines: On east by JNO. CHRISTIAN, S by AARON DEHART, W. by JOS. HIGGIN-
BOTHAM, N by CHAS. CHRISTIAN. Wit: JNO., EDMD., & TURNER CHRISTIAN.
Orig. del. to LARKIN GATEWOOD by CHRISTIAN's order.

Page 73. 24 Sep 1778. JNO. CHRISTIAN, New Kent, and CHAS. CHRISTIAN,
          Charles City, to CHAS. CHRISTIAN, JR., Goochland, for Ł150,
507 acres. Lines: JAS. GRESHAM, HENRY CHRISTIAN. Part of tract of 3927
acres taken up by JAS. CHRISTAIN, JNO. CHRISTIAN, & WM. BROWN. (Note:
Signed by wit: WM. BROWN CHRISTIAN) and other witnesses were EDMD. &
TURNER CHRISTIAN. Orig. del. to CHAS. CHRISTIAN JR.

Page 74. 17 Aug 1778. RICH. OGLESBY, AC, to his daughter, ANN MORELAND,
          Powhatan Co. a slave, Sarah. Wit: JNO. CURD, ROBIN POOR, JAS.
CURD, JNO. CURD JR.

Page 75. 17 Aug 1778. RICH. OGLESBY, AC, to his daughter, ELIZ. TOURMAN,
          Henrico Co, a slave, Aggy. Wit: JNO. CURD SR, JNO. CURD, ROBIN
POOR, JAS. CURD.

Page 75. 7 Dec 1778. JAS. McALEXANDER, SR, AC & parish, to JAS. McALEX-
          ANDER JR, AC & parish, for 20 sh, 78 acres S branch of N fork
Davis Creek. Lines: JAS. McALEXANDER SR., and pat. to him at Williamsburg.

Page 76. 15 Oct 1778. JOS. GOODWIN & wife FRANCES, AC, to CHAS. REY-
          NOLDS, AC, for Ł200, 500 acres on Harris Creek. Lines: PETER
THACKER, GEO. CARRINGTON, RICH. PETERS, JAS. CROUSE, PETTIS THACKER. Part
of 6750 acres pat. to GEO. CARRINGTON 20 Jun 1763. Wit: OBEDIAH TRENT,
HENRY TRENT, DUDLEY CALLAWAY, JNO. B. TRENT. (Note: middle initial of
OBEDIAH is given as H.) Orig. del. to JNO. REYNOLDS.

Page 77. 26 Jan 1778. JOS. MORRISS, AC, to JNO. STRANGE, Fluvanna Co,
          for Ł200, 133 acres in AC & Albemarle. Lines: JNO. LACKEY,
JOS. MORRISS. On N fork Hickory and where JOS. MORRISS lived last year.
Wit: LEONARD THOMPSON, JNO. BIBB, GEO. THOMPSON.

Page 78. 24 Nov 1778. SAML. BELL, AC & parish, to CLAUDIUS BUSTER, AC
& parish, for Ł375, 320 acres on Lynch Creek. Part of 640 acres bought of Col. JNO. CHISWELL in Albemarle on 25 Apr 1740. Part of
16,400 acres pat. to CHISWELL at Williamsburg 26 Mar 1739. Lines: CHIS-
WELL. Wit: WM. HARRIS JR, SAML. DINWIDDIE, SAML. WOODS, MICHL. McNEALY,
JAS. HENDERSON, ABNER WITT, JAS. REID, JR.

Page 79. "Last day of April, 1778." LEONARD PHILLIPS, AC, to WM. MAT-
THEWS, AC, for Ł40, 80 acres. Lines: JNO. FARRAR, a branch fork,
pat. line, Ivey Creek. Pat. to PHILLIPS 3 Mar 1760. Wit: JAS. TURNER,
THOS. MATTHEWS, THOS. HOPPER, JOS. LANHUM.

Page 80. 29 Jul 1778. WM. THOMPSON & wife SARAH, to GIDEON PULLIAM, all
of Louisa Co. for Ł150, 375 acres head of Rockfish. Lines: GEO.
CAMPBELL, MICHL. CROFT, JAS. GLENN, MOSES CLACK and land granted to Col.
CHISWELL, dec'd. Wit: JOS. BUNCH, ISHAM PULLIAM, THOS. PULLIAM. Proved
in AC 7 Dec 1778. Orig. del. 2 Feb 1790.

Page 81. 1 Mar 1778. JOS. TUCKER & wife KATEY, AC, to JNO. ENNIS, AC,
for Ł100, 133 acres on Rucker's Run. Lines: WM. LOVING, JOSIAS
WOOD, THOS. HAWKINS, WM. CRISP. Orig. del. to ENNIS.

Page 82. 7 Dec 1778. GEO. CAMPBELL, AC, to JNO. CAMDEN JR, AC, for Ł200,
228 acres bought of HENRY KEY on branch of Piney (north branch).
Memo: THOS. STAPLES, factor for CARTER & TRENT, releases lien upon property. Orig. del. to CAMDEN. CAMDEN has paid debt of CAMPBELL.

Page 84. 24 Aug 1778. JNO. BALLOW & wife MARY, AC & Parish, to WM.
BOOTH, AC & parish, for Ł150, two tracts on N side of Fluvanna
and both sides of Stovall Creek; adj. tracts. 1) 200 acres of 260 acre
tract. 60 acres sold to RO. BALLOW. Surveyed by JAS. BOND's request and
he was formerly of AC. Lines: GEO. STOVALL. 2) 99 acres. Lines: JAS.
BOND, THOS. JEFFERSON. Wit: JAS. DILLARD, THOS. BALLOW, HENRA TURNER,
JOS. CREWS.

Page 86. 7 Dec 1778. WM. OGLESBY, AC, to RICH. PERKINS, Fluvanna Co,
for Ł300, 260 acres on Rockfish. LInes: Formerly SAML. BELL's
corner. OGLESBY got it by AC deed.

Page 87. 7 Dec 1778. JACOB MORRIS, Fluvanna Co, to JNO. SLEAD, AC, for
Ł80, 200 acres. One half of survey of JEA ADKINS on ROBT.
DAVIS's mill creek. Lines: NATHL. DAVIS.

Page 88. 7 Dec 1778. JNO. McDANIEL, AC, to ISAAC RUCKER for Ł140, 100
acres. Lines: ANTHONY RUCKER, HUGH ROSE, JOSHUA TINSLEY, EDWD.
TINSLEY, AMBROSE & SUSANNAH RUCKER.

Page 89. 7 Dec 1778. STEPHEN HAM, AC, to ISAAC RUCKER, AC, for Ł15,
30 acres.

Page 90. 14 Nov 1778. Third year of the Commonwealth. WM. MORRELL,
Burke Co, N.C. - power of atty. to friend, ROBT. WRIGHT, AC, to
get possession of 69 acres now in possession of ROBT. M.KNIGHT and next
to JAS. WOODS. He is to sell it and convey it and to collect any tres-
pass damages. Wit: PETER PARRISH, SAML. KING, THOS. EADES. Proved in
AC 7 Dec 1778.

Page 91. 10 Sep 1777. JNO. TURNER & wife ELIZ, Charles Town, S.C., to
ASHCRAFT ROACH, AC, for Ł150, 335 acres on branch of Bader(sic)
River. Lines: RO. DAVIS, ATTHUS TULEY, EDWD. WATTS. Pat. to THOS. MILLS
10 Mar 1756. Wit: GABL. PENN, THOS. LUMPKIN, WM. VANNERSON.

Page 92. 25 Jun 1778. SHADRACK INMAN, Burk Co, N.C., to MOSES HUGHES,
AC, for Ł100, 217 acres branch of Rockfish. Lines: THOS. ADAMS,
WM. MAYO. Wit: SAML. DINWIDDIE, JAS. DUNWOODY, RO. DINWIDDIE.

Page 93. 1 Feb 1779. JOSHUA BUSH & wife FRANCES, AC, to WM. HOLLANDS-
WORTH, AC, for Ł420, two tracts. 1) 400 acres branch Tye and
N side Berry. One of tracts made over by HENRY KEY, late of AC, to CHAS.
IRVING & MARTIN KEY 1 Dec 1773. Lines: HARMER & KING, Col. FRY. 2) 300

acres branch of Tye and N side Berry's Mts. - derived as #1. Lines: FRY, their own (formerly HENRY KEY's). Wit: KILLIS WRIGHT, STEPEHN WATTS, ALEX. CHISNAL.

Page 95.   1 Feb 1779. GEO. COCKBURN, AC, to SAML. WARD, AC, for L150,
            150 acres both sides Rockfish. Surveyed for NICHL. NEAL and
where he formerly lived. Part of 247 acres pat. to WM. CABELL 20 Mar 1759 and by CABELL by deed to JULIAN NEAL (NAIL). JULIAN NAIL deeded it to JNO. SNIDER, dec'd, and SNIDER conveyed to COCKBURN. Wit: EZEKIAH BAILEY, JAS. WARD.

Page 96.   23 Dec 1778. PERRIN FARRAR, louisa Co, to NATHAN BOND, AC,
            for L35, 300 acres Stone House Creek and branch thereof. Wit:
FRANCIS SATTERWHITE, JOS. BOND, FRANKLIN BOWLLEN.

Page 97.   1 Feb 1779. JNO. BARNETT & wife REBECCA, AC, to JNO. BONES,
            AC, for L10, 38 acres on S bank Hatt Creek.

Page 98.   1 Feb 1779. EZEK. GILBERT, AC, to DAVID SHEPHERD, AC, for L60,
            400 acres N side and joining Tribulation Creek. Part of a
tract. Lines: bridge on Creek at Park's Road, JNO. PENN, JAS. WATSON, N branch Tribulation. Wit: GABL. & GEO. PENN, GEO. COLEMAN. Orig. del. to GABL. PENN July 1784.

Page 99.   1 Feb 1779. STANHOPE EVANS, AC, to THOS. PENN, AC, for L9,
            100 acres N branch Buffalo. Lines: THOS. POWELL, STANHOPE
EVANS, JAS. FREELAND, dec'd. Part of a tract of EVANS. Wit: JNO. CHRISTIAN, TURNER CHRISTIAN, JNO. EDMONDS, JR.

Page 101.   8 Feb 1779. CHAS. SIMS, Albemarle Co, to LEE HARRIS, AC, for
            L1000, 487 acres on branch of Hatt and Davis Creeks. Pat. to
JNO. REID and now property of SIMS. Lines: W by PETERFIELD TRENT & FRAN-CIS STEEL. Known as Spring Hill. Wit: ALEX. REID JR, SAML. WOODS, JNO. DIGGS, JNO. DAWSON.

Page 102.   1 Mar 1779. SAML. WOODS & wife MARY, to DAVID WITT for L30,
            30 acres Short's Creek. Lines: JNO. WITT, CLUF SHELTON, "feet
of the Mts." in MONTGOMERY's old line, DAVID WITT. Wit: LITTLEBERRY WITT, JNO. & ELISHA WITT. Orig. del. to WITT.

Page 103.   1 Mar 1779. THOS. MORRISON, AC, to WM. CLARK, AC, for L30,
            127 acres branch Rockfish. Called the Cermadean. Orig. del.
to WM. CLARK JR., 4 Feb 1789.

Page 104.   1 Mar 1779. JACOB BROWN, The Elder, and wife SUSANNAH, AC, to
            his son, JNO. BROWN, AC, for L100, 140 acres S side Bedler
(Pedlar?) River. Pat. to JACOB BROWN, The Elder, 15 Jul 1760. Orig. del. to RO. HOLLOWAY for JNO. BROWN.

Page 105.   1 Mar 1779. SAML. WOODS, & wife MARY, to JAS. LITTREL and
            BENJ. CARPENTER, for L140, 140 acres Short's Creek. Lines:
CLUFF SHELTON, DAVID WITT, JNO. WITT, FRANCIS NEW, CHISWELL's old pat. line. Wit: ELISHA, LITTLEBERRY & DAVID WITT. Orig. del. to DAVID WITT.

Page 106.   1 Mar 1779. SAML. WOODS, & wife MARY, to JNO. WITT for L30,
            30 acres Short's Creek. Lines: JNO. WITT, DAVID WITT. Wit:
Same as above.

Page 107.   14 Jan 1779. JNO. WITT SR. to DAVID WITT, both of AC, for L34,
            34 acres head of Short's branch; joining of the Mt., Rockfish.
Lines: MICHL. MONTGOMERY's old line. Wit: ABNER, ELISHA & LITTLEBERRY WITT.

Page 107.   1 Mar 1779. JNO. WITT, AC, to LITTLEBERRY WITT, for L16, 16
            acres Short Creek. Lines: SAML. LACKEY, DAVID WITT, top of the
Mt. Wit: ABNER WITT, DAVID WITT, JNO. CARPENTER.

Page 108.   9 Feb 1779. STANHOPE EVANS, AC, to JNO. UPSHAW, AC, for L65,
            200 acres N branch Buffalo. Lines: S. EVANS, JAS. FREELAND,
dec'd, THOS. EVANS. Part of tract. Wit: RICH., WM. & LARKIN GATEWOOD.

Page 110.   1 Mar 1779.   HEZEKIAH STRATTON & wife SUSANNA, AC, to RO. BAR-
NETT, AC, for Ⱡ25, 94 acres S branch Hatt and Racoon. Lines:
Col. MW. RANDOLPH, JNO. ROSE. Pat. to STRATTON 1 Aug 1772.

Page 111.   18 Dec 1778.   THOS. JOHNS to RO. JOHNS - THOS. for love of his
brother, ROBT, " and to fulfill desire of his late father,
ROBT. JOHNS" - 100 acres both sides Porrage Creek. Part of 218 acres
granted to my father, RO., who died without will.   Upper end of tract.
Lines: JOSHUA FRY. Wit: JAS. DILLARD, JNO. CHRISTIAN, JNO. STEWART.
MARY JOHNS, mother of THOS, appeared and relinquished dower.

Page 113.   18 Sep 1778.   CHAS. YANCEY & wife MARY, Louisa Co. and Trinity
Parish, to JNO. GILMER, AC, for Ⱡ312, 484 acres on Taylor
Creek. Lines: Side of the land from off the Pilate Mt., SMALL's, ARCHI-
BALD WOODS, DAVID MERIWETHER, JAS. JOHNSON, RICH. ROBERTSON. Wit: WM.
HARRIS JR., NATHAN CRAWFORD, RICH. DAVIS, JOELL CRAWFORD, LEE HARRIS.
Orig. del. to B. TALIAFERRO.

Page 114.   2 Apr 1779.   Commission to THOS. JOHNSON JR, WM. WHITE, WADDY
THOMSON, Louisa Co, J.P.'s, to quiz MARY YANCY, wife of CHAS,
as to deed to JNO. GILMER on 18 Sep 1778.   Done 13 Apr 1779 by JOHNSON
& WHITE.

Page 115.   1 Mar 1779.   JNO. RYAN, AC & parish, to Society of Baptists
on Tye River, AC & parish.   20 sh. for one half acre on Tye.
Lines: ROSE.

Page 117.   15 Oct 1778.   JOELL CRAWFORD & wife FRANCES, AC, to JNO. POGE
JR, Henrico Co, for Ⱡ400, 3 tracts. 1) Where JOEL lives.   2)
Rucker's Run and Hatt. Line: BENJ. DENNY.   3) Head of N fork of Davis.
Lines: THOS. WEST. All - except 35 acres. Part of 400 acres which ANN
CRAWFORD, mother of JOEL, is to have for her life.   She is to choose the
35 acres at upper end of tract. Wit: NATHAN CRAWFORD, JNO. MONTGOMERY,
LANDGON DEPRIEST, ALEX. MILLER.

Page 119.   1 Mar 1779.   SAML. AYRES & wife RACHEL, AC, to ROBT. LASTLY
(LASLEY) and DAVID CLARK, JR., AC, for Ⱡ60, 53 acres, both
sides of Bermuding of Rockfish.

Page 120.   13 Feb 1779.   THOS. WILSHIRE & wife ANNE, AC, to GEO. STONEHAM,
AC, for Ⱡ700, 150 acres bought by WILSHIRE of AUGUSTINE WRIGHT
and wife ALICE, and part of 341 acres which WILSHIRE bought of exrs. of
the Hon. PHILIP GRYMES, dec'd, and LUNSFORD LOMAX JR. Wit: DANL. GAINES,
GABL. PENN. Orig. del. to STONEHAM. (Note: GEO. STONEHAM was in the cut-
off which became Nelson County.   His descendants are fortunate in that
the clerk inserted in the will book the family data from the family
prayer book.   It shows birth dates of children and also data on GEORGE
prior to Amherst and wife's family in part.   I have abstracted this will
book of Nelson and hope to publish it someday.   I have previously stated
that Nelson took half of our area so the researcher meets many "old
friends" from early Amherst in the will and deed books of Nelson.   I have
not made a search for the original papers from which this book was copied,
but two pages of Stoneham data are missing from the book.   A notation has
been entered to cite this, but no explanation is given as to the reason.
I am hoping that I can find the original documents and supply the missing
pages. BFD)

Page 121.   30 Jan 1779.   NICHL. CABELL, AC, Esquire, and wife HANNAH, to
EDMUND WILCOX for Ⱡ3000, 2325 acres S side of and joining
Buffalo and Tye. Lines: JNO. HARPER, Roling (sic) Road, JNO. NICHOLAS,
Punch Creek, JAS. FREELAND, dec'd, confluence of Buffalo and Tye, CHAS.
LAVENDER - excepting only that M (Mr?) JNO. NICHOLAS or estate of JNO.
FRY, dec'd. may possibly be entitled to - a small part of the upper end
of the land; may be entitled to it by prior right. Wit: FRANCIS SPENCER,
SAML. BURKS, SARAH JOHNSON, JOHANES JONES. (Note: These Rolling Roads
are well treated by ALFRED PERCY in his splendid works on Amherst County.
His Piedmont Apocalypse and The Amherst County Story are but two of
several fine compilations. BFD)

Page 123.   1 Mar 1779.   JAS. COFFEY, AC, to JNO. CLARKSON, AC, for ₺1200,
            244 acres Tye River.   Lines: WM. GARLAND, Cox Creek, mouth of
Elk Creek.

Page 124.   7 Dce 1778.   THOS. POWELL, AC, to JNO. TURNER, AC, for ₺100,
            250 acres.   Lines: down James River.

Page 125.   6 Sep 1779.   CORNL. VAUGHAN, eldest son of MARTIN VAUGHAN,
            dec'd, now in AC, but planning to join the Continental Army as
a soldier under Gen. Washington - power of atty. to PETER CARTER, AC, to
sell tract in Onslow Co, N.C., which was pat. to JNO. WALLACE 20 Apr 1745
at Newbern.   100 acres held since that time by my father, MARTIN VAUGHAN,
and at his death it descended to me.   CARTER is also to obtain a pat. to
400 acres adjoining this tract and may sell for me.   Orig. del. to CARTER.

Page 126.   18 Oct 1778.   THOS. MANN RANDOLPH, Goochland, to PETERFIELD
            TRENT, Chesterfield, for ₺3750, 2790 acres in AC.   2500 acres
of it pat. in name of RANDOLPH, HARMER, & KING.   120 acres of it pat. in
name of JNO. DEPRIEST.   50 acres of it pat. in name of JAS. McGUIRE.
Lines: JNO. ROSE, RO. BARNETT and where WM. BRITT now lives as my over-
seer; 32 negroes named as slaves.   Wit: THOS. RANDOLPH, PEYTON RANDOLPH,
MARY CARY, THOS. ANDERSON (3 Nov 1778), GABL. PENN (Nov. 1778), WM. CA-
BELL (Nov. 3, 1778.)   Memo: Slaves named.   Proved 1 Feb 1779 by CABELL &
PENN and 3 May 1779 by THOS. ANDERSON.

Page 128.   22 Apr 1779.   JOS. CABELL, AC, bought of WM. MITCHELL, factor
            for HENDERSON McCAUL & Co. for ₺126-14, land formerly that of
WM. WILSON.   MITCHELL has removed from this state and no deed obtained.
I have sold my right to land to Dr. JNO. POWELL, Richmond Town and will
do my best to get deed from McCAUL (McCALL)& Co. or someone of their fac-
tors.   Bond of ₺253-10 which is same as that of WM. MITCHELL.   Wit: CHAS.
ROSE, EDMD. WILCOX, GABL. PENN.

Page 128.   5 Feb 1779.   JOS. CABELL & wife MARY, AC, to JNO. POWELL, Hen-
            rico, for ₺1500, 970 acres N side Buffalo and joining.   Part of
former tract of NICHL. CABELL.   Lines: N bank Buffalo, JAS. FREELAND,
dec'd.   Wit: WM. HORSLEY, CHAS. ROSE, N. CABELL, EDMD. WILCOX, GABL. PENN.
Commission follows on page 129 for HUGH ROSE, GABL. PENN, & DANL. GAINES
to quiz MARY CABELL.

Page 130.   21 Apr 1779.   JOS. CABELL & wife MARY, AC, to JNO. POWELL,
            Henrico, for ₺10,000, 1450 acres on Buffalo or branches in 3
tracts.   1) 1200 acres bought of CARTER BRAXTON and rec. in AC.   Lines:
AMBROSE LEE, Glebe, late JNO. BENGER, GABL. PENN, CARTER BRAXTON.   2) 200
acres bought of AMBROSE & AARON CAMPBELL.   Lines: VALENTINE COX, Glebe,
MOSES HIGGINBOTHAM, JNO. BROWN, LAURANCE CAMPBELL.   3) Distinguished by
CARTER BRAXTON's Mill tract of 50 acres and bought of him by CABELL and
rec. in AC.   Wit: EDMD. WILCOX, GABL. PENN, CHAS. ROSE, WM. HORSLEY.
Note: The Glebe is mentioned herein and it shows earlier when the Amherst
Parish Church Wardens bought it.   The house still stands and I have recently made a tour of it.   It is not far from Winton where PATRICK HENRY's
mother, SARAH HENRY, is buried.   It has been beautifully restored and it
is now called Minor Hall.)   Page 132 has order to AC J.P.'s to quiz MARY
as to this deed by her husband, JOS. CABELL.   Rec. 18 Nov 1779.

Page 133.   22 Apr 1779.   JNO. POWELL, Henrico, Gent., to JOS. CABELL, AC,
            Gent, for 5 sh., ₺9000 debt and interest for three tracts.
Deed of Trust for 1450 acres and 192 acres which CABELL bought of WM.
MITCHELL, factor for HENDERSON McCALL & CO.   POWELL now has two deeds of
22 Apr.   Wit: WM. HORSLEY, GABL. PENN, EDMD. WILCOX, CHAS. ROSE.

Page 134.   3 May 1779.   WM. BANKS & wife TOMZEN, AC, to WM. CAMDEN, AC,
            for ₺40, 130 acres Huff Creek.   Pat. to JAS. BUSH at Williams-
burg 3 Aug 1771.

Page 135.   20 Jan 1779.   JAS. MENESS, AC, for love of son, JAS. Jr. and
            his daughter, JANE MENEES - a negro boy, Isaac.   To his son,
JAMES, JR, and at his death to his other child, JANE MENEES.   Wit: DANL.
GAINES, JOSIAS GILBERT, AMBROSE RUCKER.   Orig. del. to BENJ. MENEES.

Page 135.   18 Dec 1778.   JAS. MENEES, AC, to his children: son BENJ. ME-
NEES, and his daughter, ELENOR MENEES - slave, Caeser.   To
JAMES' son, BENJ., and wife MARGARET, and at BENJ's death to ELENOR. Wit:
as above. Orig. del. to BENJ. MENEES.

Page 136.   3 May 1779.   MARTIN KEY, Fluvanna Co, atty for WALTER KING,
Kingdom of Great Britain, to WM. BIBB, AC, for Ł1000, 800 acres N branches of Tye River. Lines: BIBB, Naked Creek, WALTER KING, Court
house road. Part of KING's tract. Orig. del. to CHAS. PERROW, atty. for
the heirs of WM. BIBB, 15 Feb 1830.

Page 137.   3 May 1779.   WM. BIBB, AC, to WALTER KING, Kingdom of Great
Britain, Ł100 paid by MARTIN KEY as KING's atty. and agent.
Two tracts: 1) 192 acres head of S fork of Rucker's Run. Lines: KING;
great point of rocks. Conveyed to WM. BIBB by LUNSFORD LOMAX 22 Oct 1764
and rec. in AC. 2) Adj. tract of 70 acres pat. to WM. BIBB 14 Jul 1769.

Page 138.   3 May 1779.   WM. HOLLANDSWORTH, AC, to WM ALFORD, AC, for Ł60,
100 acres N branches of Tye. Part of 400 acres of grantor.
Lines: his own, HARMER & KING. Wit: KILLIS WRIGHT, JAS. MAYES, JAS.
WATERS.

Page 139.   1 May 1779.   ALEX HENDERSON SR, AC & Parish, to ALEX. HENDER-
SON JR, for Ł100, 150 acres both sides Rockfish. Lines: JAS.
HENDERSON, mt. spur, FRANCIS MERIWETHER, WM. SIMPSON, ALEX. PATTON; all
houses etc. Wit: JAS. & ANDREW HENDERSON, JAS. DINWIDDIE. Orig. del. to
HENDERSON JR. 23 Aug 1786.

Page 141.   3 May 1779.   JNO. DAWSON, AC, and wife CHARITY, AC, to MARTIN
DAWSON, AC, for Ł300, 236 acres on Harris Creek.

Page 142.   3 May 1779.   Sheff's bond by AMBROSE RUCKER to GEO. WEBB,
Treasurer of Commonwealth of Va. under commission from Gover-
nor of 16 Mar 1778 and under Act of Assembly. Bondsmen: JNO. PENN, JAS.
FRANKLIN, WM. LEE, WM. LOVING, JNO. LOVING, JOS. PENN, JOS. CABELL, DANL.
GAINES, HUGH ROSE, ISAAC RUCKER, BENJ. RUCKER.

Page 142.   1 May 1779.   DAVID CRAWFORD, AC, to WM. GOLDSBY, AC, for Ł8000
tobacco, 329 acres N side Buffalo. Lines: FRY, crossing the
road. Wit: WM. HORSLEY, CHAS. BURRAS, JNO. HARGROVE.

Page 143.   7 Jun 1779.   WM. TILLER & wife ANNE, AC, to DAVID MONTGOMERY
JR, AC, 74 acres and part of 144 acres pat. to ZACHARY PHIL-
LIPS on 30 Jun 1760, and by PHILLIPS conveyed to TILLER. 70 acres was
again conveyed to HENRY SORROW and remainder is separated from SORROW by
marked trees. Lines of whole tract: LUMSFORD LOMAX, first part is where
TILLER & wife lately lived.

Page 145.   5 Dec 1778.   THOS. COTTRELL, GILBERT COTTRELL & wife ELIZ., &
JAS. COTTRELL, AC, to AARON HIGGINBOTHAM SR, AC, for Ł425, 300
acres - sides of Buffalo where THOS. COTTRELL, dec'd. lived and willed to
his five sons. Lines: State Sect. CARTER near the road of S side Stone
House Creek, Buflow(sic) River, AARON HIGGINBOTHAM. Wit: as to THOS.
COTTRELL. - WM. LOVING, AARON HIGGINBOTHAM, EDWD. COX, JNO. LOVING JR.
Orig. del. to grantee.

Page 147.   14 Jan 1779. Proved 7 Jun 1779 by wits. Power of atty. by
JAS. CONNOR - to COL. JOS. CABELL - will be away from family
for some time as a soldier. Wit: CHAS. ROSE, WM. LEE, RICH. BALLINGER.

Page 147.   17 May 1779.   WM. HOLLANDSWORTH, AC, to KILLIS WRIGHT, AC, for
Ł100, 100 acres N side and joining Great Branch of a N branch
of Tye. Part of 300 acres of grantor. Lines: grantor. Wit: WM. WALTON,
GEO. GILBERT, GEO. DIVERS. Orig. del. to WRIGHT.

Page 148.   7 Jun 1779.   VALENTINE COX & JNO. SWANSON, AC, to WM. - a
name erased - MAYS, AC, for Ł37-10, 50 acres N branch Buffalo
on part of the Turkey Mts. Lines: Near top of Turkey Mt., JNO. SWANSON,
LINN BANKS. Part of larger tract of grantors. (Note: Turkey Mt. is back
of Clifford and close to Winton.)

Page 149.   6 Apr 1778.   Certificate that JNO. ROSE, NICHL. CABELL, & JAS.
            HIGGINBOTHAM "was duly elected" commissioners of the Tax for
present year. AMBROSE RUCKER, ALEX. REID JR. & WM. LOVING deputy Shffs.
Returned 7 Jun 1779 by AMBROSE RUCKER, Shff. EDMD. WILCOX, Clerk.

Page 150.   9 Mar 1779.   Election held at courthouse on second Tuesday in
            March. WM. LOVING, ZACH. TALIAFERRO & CHAS. BURRES elected Tax
commissioner. Certified by AMBROSE RUCKER. Ret. 7 Jun 1779.

Page 150.   9 Jun 1779.   HENRY CHRISTIAN, AC, to AARON DEHART, AC, for Ŀ30,
            56 acres next to DEHART. Wit: JAS. RUCKER JR, J. MAGANN, THOS.
POWELL. Orig. del. to CHAS. CHRISTIAN 25 Nov 1799.

Page 151.   5 Jul 1779.   PETER MARTIN, AC, to JNO. HARRIS, AC, for Ŀ10,
            34 acres N branch Davis. Line of WM. MARTIN.

Page 152.   23 Dec 1778.   JAS. MOORE, N.C., to MOSES MARTIN, AC. WM.
            MOORE, late of AC, did in lifetime bargain with JNO. HENRY,
Hanover, for tract on Cub Creek, branch of Tye. 300 acres. Lines: JNO.
JACOBS, under Three Ridged Mt. WM. MOORE gave bond to HENRY and rec'd.
bond from his obliging HENRY to Convey. WM. MOORE did depart this life
about 1766 without getting deed. (MOORE's will was probated in 1767.) In
his will he devised one moiety to son, JNO. MOORE, and one to his son,
JAS. MOORE.   JAS. has bought JOHN's part. MARTIN paid Ŀ125 for 300 acres.
Wit: JNO. ROSE, WM. MURRAY. (Note: These names still are used for Cub and
the mt. Rev. LAWSON COX, Episcopal rector in Amherst, and wife HARRIET,
have bought a tract "under the mt." and on Cub. They have erected a
splendid home and the view from their place is one of the most beautiful
seen by this visitor to their home. My wife and I walked down to Cub Run
with them while spending an afternoon recently with them. BFD)

Page 153.   Blank date, but rec. 5 Jul 1779. EZEK. GILBERT to JNO. WIATT
            GILBERT, both of AC - blank sum - 150 acres both sides Tribu-
lation and part of a tract. Lines: Parks' road, WM. POLLARD, BALOR WALKER,
dec'd, JNO. PENN. Wit: DANL. GAINES, DAVID WOODROOF, WM. HORSLEY. (I
have spoken of this GILBERT land before. The tract was one of two bought
by their father, HENRY, from CARTER BRAXTON and the village of Amherst
is built in part on part of the GILBERT land which BRAXTON called Round
Top Plantation. This pertains to at least part of Main Street - southern
end - but I have not worked out details of north Main and the east side
of Main Street. However, Hunting Tower, also mentioned in work on deeds,
is east of the village. BFD)

Page 154.   31 Jul 1779.   THOS. PANNELL, AC, to his son, BENJAMIN PANNELL,
            AC, for love, 100 acres and part of 233 acres which THOS.
bought of JNO. ROBINSON Esq. S side of Shingle hollow branch -(this is
an unknown one to me.BFD) Lines: JNO. ROBINSON, SAML. CALDWELL or MARTIN.
Wit: WM. GALBRITH, WM. PANNELL, CHAS. RODES.

Page 156.   31 Jul 1779.   CHAS. RODES, SR, AC, to JNO. PANNELL, AC, for
            Ŀ12, 79 acres on the mt. at head of Patton's branch. Wit: WM.
PANNELL, CHAS. RODES JR., WM. GALBRITH.

Page 157.   2 Oct 1779.   THOS. PANNELL, Augusta, to WM. PANNELL, AC, for
            Ŀ80, mare, cattle, and furniture. Wit: RO. HAMILTON, JAS. HAM-
ILTON, CHAS. RODES, WM. GALBRITH, DAVID McANALLY, WM. DEPRIEST. Del. to
PANNELL.

Page 157.   2 Aug 1779.   RO. DAVIS & wife JENNY, AC, (signed JEAN) to
            PHILLIP THURMOND, AC, for Ŀ2000, 375 acres both sides Wilder-
ness Run. Lines: RO. DAVIS, JNO. FLOYD. Wit: THOS. JOPLING, EDMOND POW-
ELL, RO. DAVIS JR. Orig. del. to grantee.

Page 159.   2 Aug 1779.   RO. DAVIS & wife JENNY, AC, to PHILIP THURMOND,
            AC, for Ŀ2000, 98 acres on Davis' Spring Branch. Lines: RO.
DAVIS. Wit: THOS. JOPLING, EDMOND POWELL, RO. DAVIS JR.

Page 160.   2 Aug 1779.   THOS. HERD, AC, to ARCHIBALD McDONALD, AC, for
            Ŀ25, 164 acres. Lines: ARHCIBALD WOODS. "I acknowledge my
right of dower - ELIZ. HEARD (sic)." Wit: JAS. MOSLEY, WM. MONTGOMERY,

JNO. MONTGOMERY, WM. FITZPATRICK, JOS. FITZPATRICK, BOUTH WOODSON FITZ-
PATRICK.

Page 161.   16 Jul 1779.   "In the fourth year of the Commonwealth of the
United States of America" JNO. THOMAS, AC & parish, to WM.
NEWTON, AC, and parish, for Ł16, 63 acres, formerly that of CORNL. THOMAS,
on a branch of Otter Creek near the stone chimney. Wit: DAVID SHELTON,
SAML. ALLEN, N. CABELL.

Page 162.   29 Mar 1779.   JNO. WITT JR, AC, to LITTLEBERRY WITT and JNO.
WITT SR, AC, for Ł96, 96 acres branch of Rockfish. Lines: JAS.
LACKEY, JNO. LACKEY. Wit: JAS. LITTRELL, BENJ. CARPENTER, ELISHA ABNEY,
DAVID WITT. Orig. del. to DAVID WITT.

Page 163.   6 Sep 1779.   WM. MARTIN, Bedford Co, to DAVID SHELTON, AC, for
Ł200, 195 acres S side Rockfish. Lines: WM. WHITSITT, JAS.
HALLEY BURTON. SUSANNAH, wife of MARTIN. Wit: WM. HORRALL, THOS. FORTUNE,
JNO. HARRIS. Orig. del. to JNO. HARRIS 3 Mar 1785.

Page 164.   6 Sep 1779.   WM. MARTIN (scribe put MORTON, but signed MARTIN)
and wife SUSANNAH, Bedford Co, to JNO. HARRIS, AC, for Ł21, 75
acres S side Rockfish. Lines: JAS. HALLEY BURTON, THOS. McDONALD, Savan
Tree Brnach. Wit: WM. HORRALL, THOS. FORTUNE, DAVID SHELTON.

Page 165.   6 Sep 1779.   MICHL. MORRISON, AC, to JNO. THURMOND, Albemarle,
for Ł600, 250 acres on Cub Creek. Lines: JNO. MORRISON.

Page 166.   6 Sep 1779.   LEROY UPSHAW & wife ---, AC, to JOS. CREWS, AC,
for Ł2000, 400 acres N side Fluvanna on Stovall Creek.

Page 168.   5 Aug 1779.   WM. MILLER & wife ISABELLA, AC, to THOS. WILCOX,
AC, for Ł500, 100 acres Porridge Creek. Lines: CHRISTIAN. Wit:
DANL. GAINES, THOS. POWELL, REUBIN COLEMAN.

Page 169.   6 Sep 1779.   WM. FLOYD & wife ABIDIAH, AC, to CHAS. BURKS, AC,
for Ł2000, 310 acres both sides Maple Creek, branch of Pedlar.
Lines: ARTHUR TULEY. Orig. del. to grantee.

Page 170.   6 Sep 1779.   MATT. TUCKER, AC, to DRURY TUCKER, for Ł1000,
170 acres both sides Buffalo, part of a tract. Lines: DRURY
TUCKER, JNO. SCOTT, CARTER's Mill Creek, EDWD. CARTER. Wit: JOS. TUCKER,
JNO. IRVIN, JNO. TUCKER.

Page 171.   6 Sep 1779.   MATT. TUCKER, AC, to WM. TUCKER, AC, for Ł200,
170 acres both sides Buffalo. Lines: WM. BURTON, dec'd, JNO.
PENN, JNO. SCOTT, JESSE KENNADY, PHILLIP PENN, LINDSAY COLEMAN. Wit: same
as previous deed.

Page 172.   6 Sep 1779.   WM. LOVEDAY and wife SARAH, late of AC, to WM.
CABELL for Ł610, 200 acres branch of Purgatory Swamp and branch of Joe's Creek below Fendley's Gap. Part of 400 acres pat. to WALTER
KING 10 Apr 1751. Conveyed by KING to LUNSFORD LOMAX, the Elder, 1 Dec
1764, and proved in General Court; by LL to LL JR, - SR's wife JUDITH -
13 Jan 1767; JR. to LOVEDAY by deed 7 Apr 1769. Wit: WM. NEWTON, GROVES
HARDING, THOS. JOPLING, JAS. WARD, JNO. BIBB, ABRAHAM WARWICK.

Page 174.   6 Sep 1779.   EDWD. BOWMAN, AC, to WM. BOWMAN, Albemarle and
Parish of St. Ann, for Ł500, 150 acres S side Rockfish. Pat.
to MICHL. THOMAS 10 Jul 1775, and by him to WM. BLAIR, by deed; by BLAIR
to EDWD. BOWMAN. Part of 200 acres pat. to THOMAS. Wit: JNO. SNIDER,
WM. JOHNSON, WM. BOWMAN.

Page 175.   20 Aug 1779.   PETER CARTER, AC, to CORNL. VAUGHAN, AC, for
Ł100, 100 acres. Orig. del. to EDWD. CARTER.

Page 176.   5 Jun 1779.   CORNL. VAUGHAN, AC, to PETER CARTER, bond of
Ł2000 VAUGHAN has agreed to exchange 100 acres in Onslow Co,
N.C., pat. 20 Apr 1745, to JNO. WALLACE at Newbern; also entry adj. of
400 acres - for 100 acres and part of tract where PETER CARTER now lives.
Wit: RODERICK McCULLOCH, JNO. WARE.

186

Page 176.   2 Aug 1779.   MARTIN KEY & CHAS. IRVING, both of Albemarle and
            St. Ann's Parish, attys. for HENRY KEY, to ABRAHAM WARWICK, AC,
and parish, for £1000, 1) 97 acres at Fendley's Gap. Lines: attornies;
Fendley Gap, RO. JOHNSON.   2) 160 acres.   3) 400 acres near the gap.
Lines: JNO. HARMER, attornies.   4) 400 acres in the gap. Total of 1057
acres. Reference to Power of Atty. in 1773. Wit: N. CABELL, WM. SPENCER,
JAS. NEVIL, JNO. LOVING, JR.   Proved 6 Sep 1779 by N. CABELL, WM. WALTON
& THOS. GRIFFIN.

Page 178.   6 Sep 1779.   WM. PATTON, AC, to SAML. WOODS for £900, 170
            acres branch of Rockfish near the Blew Mts. Lines: S side of
Rockfish, EDWD MALLOY, EDWIN HICKMAN, JAS. HENDRICK, JOSIAS CLAPHAM.
Orig. del. to WM. WOODS 16 May 1782.

Page 179.   4 Oct 1779.   JAS. MARTIN & wife SARAH, AC, to WM. WILSON, AC,
            for £8, 100 acres S side dividing ridge between Meriwether's
branch and Pounder Branch. Lines: Wallowing hole branch, line made by
JAS. MARTIN, WM. WILSON, & SAML. FOX. Line divides 200 acres between
WILSON & FOX. Orig. del. to WILSON 25 Mar 1783.

Page 180.   4 Oct 1779.   WM. WILSON, AC, to JAS. TRUSLER, AC, for £30, 40
            acres, part of 100 acres which WW bought of JAS. MARTIN - near
the Indian branch on the S side. Lines: SAML. FOX.

Page 181.   4 Oct 1779.   THOS. LEFTWICH & wife BETHEANY, Bedford Co, to
            EDWARD or EDMUND GOODRICH - both spellings are employed in
document - of AC, for £90, 121 5/8 acres N side of Tobacco Row Mts. Orig.
del. to THOS. GOODRICH 4 Jan 1820 (it is impossible to read word - order
or admr. Note: I have stated that I have abstracts of all will books
from 1761 to 1919 so I checked G's to see just what the name of this man
should be. There is an administrators' acct. by three admrs. in 1825 and
THOS. GOODRICH was one of them. The estate was that of EDMOND GOODRICH.)

Page 182.   18 Jul 1779.   NICHL. DAVIES, Bedford Co, - lease to THOS.
            STREET, AC, 100 acres on Harris. Lines: DAVIES, ANTHONY STREET
on road called Pedlar Tract; GEO. McDANIEL SR, towards Tobacco Row Mts.
14 year lease from 25 Nov next. On last day of Mar 1781, STREET or heirs
to pay "4 barrels of merchantable Indian corn" and then to pay same each
year of lease. Within two years STREET is to plant 200 peach trees and
100 apple trees and put under fence; not to sell any trees or timber, or
use more than is sufficient. Wit: DAVID WOODROOF, H. DAVIES, RICH. POWELL,
JER. TAYLOR.

Page 183.   23 Sep 1779.   Committee under Act of General Assembly "Con-
            cerning Escheats and Forfeitures from British Subjects" sum-
moned by DAVID SHEPHERD, Esq, AC Escheator, do find that JNO. HARMER was
and remains a subject of the British King - has in AC 7080 acres on
Rucker's Run and Dutch Creek whereon is growing corn and tobacco; also
81 slaves in AC; 10 horses, 95 cattle, 171 hoggs(sic), 137 hoes, 11
plough hoes, 31 axes, 17 iron potts, 12 frying pans, six pair wedges, six
flax wheels, and some other plantation tools - old iron of little value-
also six grind stones, 18 reap hooks. Our verdict is that lands etc. be
forfeited to the Commonwealth. Committee: CHAS. ROSE, WM. WALTON, THOS.
HAWKINS, WM. FURBUSH, ABRAHAM WARWICK, GEO. BLAIN, LUCAS POWELL, JNO.
CARTWRIGHT, JOS. DILLARD, JOS. MAYS, SAML. EDMONDS, WM. SPENCER, JAS.
HIGGINBOTHAM, JAS. STEPHENS, WM. LEE, THOS. GRIFFIN, PATRICK ROSE, ABRA-
HAM SEAY, RO. WRIGHT, JNO. WRIGHT, & WM. CRISP, AC Freeholders.

Page 183.   Same committee and date as to land of WALTER KING a British
            subject. He had 7839 acres - 6241 of it commonly called
Nassau - on head branches of Rucker's Run; 800 acres on Hatt Creek and
next to JNO. ROSE & ROBERT BARNETT. 800 acres on Dutch adj. JNO. HARMER.
Corn and tobacco growing on land, 43 slaves, 10 horses, 36 cattle, 65
hoggs, 49 narrow and broad hoes, 11 axes, 8 plough hoes, 6 sickles, 1
currying knife, 7 hides in tan and two untanned, small parcel of old
iron; 9 iron pots, 1 hogshead of tobacco. One seventh claimed by JOSHUA
BUSH, overseer. Same decision as to the disposition of the property.

Page 184.   10 Jul 1776.   JOS. DILLARD & wife MARY, AC, to IGNATIUS RAINS,
            AC, for £25, 150 acres. Lines: Long Branch where a path

crosses leading from JOS. DILLARD to where JOS. MAYS formerly lived; JOS. MAYS - near his fence. Wit: BALDWIN BAIN, ZACH. TALIAFERRO, JAS. HIGGIN-BOTHAM. Ack. by grantors 4 Oct 1779.

Page 185. 7 Aug 1779. WM. HIBBITS & wife JANE, AC, to THOS. WILSHIRE, AC, for Ł300, 100 acres. Lines: WM. WRIGHT. Bought by grantor from WM. WRIGHT 23 Mar 1768.

Page 186. 13 Sep 1779. JNO. LEMASTER, AC, to RALPH LEMASTER, AC, for 5 sh, 230 acres. Lines: OBEDIAH HENDERSON on N, HENRY TURNER on S, JNO. CHRISTIAN on E, JNO. TURNER on W. SARAH, wife of LEMASTER. Wit: JAS. LONDON, HENRY & JNO. TURNER.

Page 186. 1 Nov 1779. JNO. PAYTON SR, & wife SUSANNAH, AC, to WM. PAY-TON SR, AC, for Ł5, 94 acres on Horsley. Lines: JNO. PAYTON SR, JNO. PAYTON, PHILLIP PAYTON. Wit: CHAS. & ISABELL TALIAFERRO.

Page 187. 1 Nov 1779. JNO. PAYTON SR, & wife SUSANNAH, AC, to JOS. ED-WARDS, AC, two tracts. 1) 70 acres branch of Horsley. Lines: PETER CARTER, LOMAX, surveyed by JAS. HIGGINBOTHAM 5 May 1769. 2) 300 acres on both sides Horsley. Lines: PHILLIP & WM. PAYTON(PEYTON), JNO. POWELL, JNO. PEYTON. Surveyed by JAS. HIGGINBOTHAM 20 Oct 1779. Pat. to JOHN PAYTON SR, Orig. del. to ISAAC WRIGHT Oct 1784.

Page 189. 1 Nov 1779. EZEK. GILBERT, AC, to DAVID SHEPHERD, AC, for Ł1600, 160 acres both sides Tribulation Creek. Lines: Lynch Road, WM. POLLARD, WIATT GILBERT, Parks' Road. Orig. del. to GABL. PENN. July 1784.

Page 189. 1 Nov 1779. RODERICK McCULLOCH & wife ELIZ., AC, to AMBROSE EUBANK, AC, for Ł500, 104 acres on N side and joining Horsley. Surveyed by JAS. HIGGINBOTHAM.

Page 190. 1 Nov 1779. RODERICK McCULLOCH & wife ELIZ, AC, to EDMUND GOODRICH, AC, for Ł900, no acreage stated, both sides Buffalo Spur. Orig. del. to E. GOODRICH's admr., 20 Jan 1820.

Page 191. 1 Nov 1779. RODERICK McCULLOCH & wife ELIZ, AC, to CHAS. ELLIS, AC, for Ł10, 23 acres S side and joining Horsley, surveyed by JAS. HIGGINBOTHAM. Lines: R. McCULLOCH.

Page 192. 1 Nov 1779. RODERICK McCULLOCH & wife ELIZ, AC, to RICH. TALIAFERRO, for Ł1000, 369 acres on Stone Creek and N side of Tobacco Row Mt.

Page 193. 1 Nov 1779. PHILIP THURMOND & wife JUDITH, AC, to JNO. PAYTON, AC, for Ł1000, 395 acres on Blue Ridge and branch of Irish Cr.

Page 194. 20 Oct 1779. BENJ. THURMOND, Fluvanna, to THOS. TUCKER, AC, for Ł25 - no acres- S side Pedlar on Inchanted Mt. Wit: PHILIP THURMOND, WM. GLASBY, JUDITH THURMOND. (Note: The names herein present one of my long-time enigmas. My wife, MILDRED MILLER DAVIS, is descended from this WM. GLASBY (WM. GILLESPIE) who married here in 1777 ANN HUDSON. WM. & wife moved to Madison Co, Kentucky about 1784, for the last deed in this book is the one wherein he and wife, called NANCY therein and some-times so called in Ky. (Her father, JOSHUA HUDSON, calls her ANN in his will.) WM. carried mail from Kentucky to Charlottesville and there are deeds shown in these books to indicate that he was in Kentucky from time to time. However, the enigma deals with the marriage of his daughter, MARY GILLESPIE, to HENDERSON THURMAN in Madison Co, Ky, on 20 Nov 1809. Her father had been killed in a duel in 1794. Her mother names her in her Madison county will. The unanswered question is the identity of this HENDERSON THURMAN. The Miller manuscript in the Eastern Ky. State Col-lege Library says that he was a son of BENJ. THURMAN, but I am unable to locate the right BENJ. There is one who went to Georgia and I have data on him. Here we find WM. GILLASPIE witnessing a deed for PHILIP THURMOND - spellings of families are different for wife's line and this one, but not too vital a difference. The early spelling in Louisa is THURMAN, but I am told that PHILIP SR, Albemarle, is the one who changed the spelling. I can not vouch for this, though. BFD)

188

Page 195.   1 Nov 1779.   JNO. THOMAS & wife FRANCES, Albemarle, to THOS.
            WAUGH, AC, for Ł1400, 200 acres N side and joining Fluvanna.
Lines: Back line of river tract of 400 acres sold by THOMAS to WAUGH &
RODERICK McCULLOCH, JNO. THOMAS, Thomas Mill Creek.

Page 196.   1 Nov 1779.   JNO. THOMAS & wife FRANCES, Albemarle, to RODER-
            ICK McCULLOCH, AC, for Ł1600, 600 acres in 4 tracts.   1) 200
acres N side and joining Fluvanna. Lines: THOS. WAUGH, JNO. THOMAS.   2)
Island in Fluvanna - 16 acres - little below first tract and known as
Thomas' Island; oppoiste lands of NICHL. DAVIES, Esq.   3) 204 acres on
branches of Wilderness and Lawrence Creeks. Lines: DAVID DAVENPORT, RO.
DAVIS, NICHL. DAVIES.   4) 180 acres on branches of Wilderness Creek and
Thomas Mill Creek. Lines: HUGH MORRIS, DAVENPORT, THOS. MATTOCK, in the
road, NICHL. DAVIES, Hocket's Bottom in HUGH MORRIS' line.

Page 197.   1 Nov 1779.   BENJ. MANEES & wife ANN, Pittsylvania, to WM.
            WHITSITT, AC, for Ł700, 300 acres. Lines: WHITSITT.   Orig. del.
to WHITSITT.

Page 198.   1 Nov 1779.   THOS. WAUGH & wife FRANCES, AC, to CHAS. ELLIS,
            for Ł800, 190 acres on N side Pedlar.

Page 199.   1 Nov 1779.   On 10 Apr 1750, ROBT. ROSE, Clerk, did lease to
            JNO. PARKS and covenanted that if WM. PARKS or JNO. PARKS JR.
should die before 25 Dec 1780, then said PARKS to hold lease for life of
any other person nominated by him.   JOHN PARKS assigned lease to EDWARD
MANION who assigned it to THOS. LANDRUM in 1763. WILLIAM PARKS has departed this life. THOS. LANDRUM niminated ELIZ. ROSE in stead of WM.
PARKS, dec'd. CHAS. ROSE received nomination and of record in Albemarle.
Signed by CHAS. ROSE & THOS. LANDRUM in AC on 1 Nov 1779.

Page 200.   3 Dec 1779.   JAMES MOBLEY, AC, to DRURY TUCKER, AC, for Ł1000,
            400 acres which MOBLEY bought of JOS. MAYS on Buffalo. Lines:
EDWD. CARTER, Esq, WM. OGLESBY, Minor, WM. OGLESBY JR, CHAS. BURRAS,
DRURY TUCKER. ANN, wife of MOBLEY. Wit: JOS., WM. & DANL. TUCKER & JNO.
GRIGGORY.

Page 201.   6 Dec 1779.   JNO. POWELL, AC, to his son, FRANCIS POWELL, AC,
            for Ł500, 100 acres on branch of Horsley. Lines: CHAS. TALIA-
FERRO. Wit: RODERICK McCULLOCH, RICH. TALIAFERRO, JOS. PENN.

Page 201.   13 Nov 1778.   JNO. BARNES & wife ANN, Dutchess Co., N.Y., to
            GABL. PENN, AC, Gent., for Ł140, 263 acres on both sides Bea-
ver Creek. Lines: Formerly NICHL. EASTON, NICHL. CABELL & formerly JER.
WHITTEN, WM. CABELL's order of Council Tract, WM. STINNETT (formerly BENJ.
STINNETT).   JNO. BARNES bought it from HECTOR McALASTER who bought it
from ROBT. WHITTEN - ref. to AC deeds. Wit: Two Dutchess Co, N.Y. JP's,
ZACCHEUS NEWCOMB & PETER TAPPEN.

Page 204.   10 Dec 1779.   JAS. TULEY & wife JUDITH, Albemarle, to ABNER
            WITT, AC, for Ł500, 70 acres branch of Short's Creek. Lines:
NEWS, THOS. MORRISON, FRANCIS NEWS. Wit: FRANCIS NEWS, LEWIS WITT, JOS.
ROBERDS. Orig. del. to WITT.

Page 205.   10 Dec 1779.   FRANCIS NEW & wife SARAH, AC, to ABNER WITT, AC,
            for Ł500, 76 acres. Lines: JNO. CHISWELL. Wit: DAVID, ELISHA,
LITTLEBERRY & WM. WITT. Orig. del. to WITT.

Page 206.   20 Jan 1780.   SAML. WOODS & wife SARAH, AC, to ABNER WITT, AC,
            for Ł800, 90 acres S side Rockfish. Lines: LEE HARRIS, CLUFF
SHELTON. Wit: JAS. LITTRELL, BENJ. CARPENTER, JNO. DINWIDDIE, LEWIS WITT.
Orig. del. to WITT.

Page 207.   19 Nov 1779.   JNO. LACKEY JR, AC, to ARCHELAUS CALLAWAY
            STRANGE, AC, for Ł1200, 260 acres Hickory Creek. Lines: GEO.
BLAIN, JNO. STRANGE, JOS. MORRIS, WM. MORRISON. Wit: JNO. DAWSON, JOS.
MORRIS, MARY MORRIS, JESSE MORRIS. Orig. del. to JOSEPH MORRIS for
STRANGE.

Page 208.   7 Feb 1780.   JNO. LACKEY JR, AC, to WM. MORRISON, AC, for Ł10,

68 acres Hickory Creek. Lines: JOS. MORRIS.

Page 209. 6 Mar 1780. DAVID MERIWETHER, AC, to SHEROD MARTIN of Albemarle for Ł3000, 200 acres both sides Rockfish. Part of tract
of JAMES MARTIN and conveyed by him to his son, WILLIAM MARTIN and by WM.
to MERIWETHER. Lines: MARTIN.

Page 210. 24 Feb 1780. JNO. HANSFORD, AC, to JNO. HENRY GOODWIN, AC,
for Ł500, 70 acres Bollings' Creek. Lines: MILES BURFORD, JNO.
LYNCH. ANN, wife of HANSFORD. Wit: JNO. MERRITT, SNELLING JOHNSON,
ELIJAH GILLENWATER, WM. HARRISON.

Page 211. 6 Mar 1780. HUGH ROSE & DANL. GAINES, Commissioners appointed
by Act of Assembly for disposing of the late Glebe of Amherst
Parish, to AMBROSE RUCKER, AC, and Lexington Parish, for Ł3000-5 and
whereon GABL. PENN now lives, 254 acres; 204 acres of it bought of AARON
HIGGINBOTHAM and by him conveyed to WM. CABELL JR. & CORNL. THOMAS,
Church Wardens of Amherst Parish on 6 Sep 1762. The other 50 acres was
bought of CARTER BRAXTON who conveyed to the above wardens on 14 Aug 1762.
(Note: I have made comments on the glebe before so it suffices to state
that it still stands near Winton. Of the division of the parish I have
also commented. It took place in 1779 and prior to the division of
Nelson from Amherst. What is now Amherst Parish is in present Nelson, and
Lexington Parish is what is now Amherst County. BFD)

Page 212. 27 Sep 1779. JNO. GOFF, Bedford, to RICH. WEBSTER, AC, for
Ł30, 103 acres on branch of Stovall Creek. Wit: JAS. SYMONS,
JNO. H. GOODWIN, AARON DEHART, SNELLING JOHNSON.

Page 213. 31 Oct 1779. JOS. WHITTLE, AC, to JNO. WHITTLE, AC, for Ł500,
· 200 acres Rocky Run. Wit: CHAS. WINGFIELD SR, CHAS. WINGFIELD,
PETER JOINER.

Page 214. 17 Oct 1779. GEO. MUNROE, AC, to WM. COFFEY, AC, for Ł1250,
a tract on Tye. One tract of 355 acres next to HENRY. Adj.
tract of 20 acres and pat. to grantor on 3 Nov 1770, and 27 Aug 1770.
Wit: ZACH. TALIAFERRO, DANL. McDONALD, NICHL. MORAN.

Page 215. 21 Jan 1780. JNO. WHITTLE & wife SARAH; MATTHEW WHITTLE &
wife ELIZ., AC, to CHAS. WINGFIELD SR, Albemarle, for Ł1000,
400 acres pat. to MATT. WHITTLE under letters pat. and Lees(?) under
Buffalo Ridge; branch of Rockey Creek and Christian's path to MOSES HIG-
GINBOTHAM's mill. Conveyed by MATT. to his sons, JOSEPH & JNO. WHITTLE.
JNO. bought 200 acres of his brother, JOSEPH. Lines: Col. CHISWELL, JNO.
WARREN, PETER JOINER, TURNER CHRISTIAN, ELIJAH CHRISTIAN. Wit: PETER
JOYNER, WM. WILDAY, CHAS. WARREN, RICH. HARPER.

Page 217. 17 Sep 1779. JUDITH GILMORE, AC, to RICH. GATEWOOD, AC, for
Ł1200, 200 acres on branch of Rutledge. Lines: MOSES HIGGIN-
BOTHAM, HENRY GILBERT, dec'd. Wit: DRURY CHRISTIAN, JNO. WHITTLE, MOSES
PENN.

Page 218. 6 Mar 1780. AMBROSE RUCKER, AC & Lexington Parish, to GABL.
PENN of same, for Ł4000, 254 acres - 204 of it bought of AARON
HIGGINBOTHAM who conveyed to church wardens on 6 Sep 1762; 50 acres of it
bought of CARTER BRAXTON who conveyed to wardens, 14 Aug 1762.

Page 218. 6 Mar 1780. JOS. LIVELY & wife MARY, AC, to ROBT. CASH, AC,
for Ł1800, 400 acres on Thrasher's Creek. Bought by the grant-
or of WIATT POWELL. Pat. to RICH. POWELL, SR, at Williamsburg 1 Jun 1750.

Page 220. 25 Dec 1779. ABRAHAM WARWICK & wife AMY, AC, to JNO. BIBB,
AC, for Ł1500, 382 acres on N branch of Rucker's Run. WARWICK
bought it from JNO. DEPRIEST 1 Jun 1772. Lines: HARMER(HAMNER?), WM. FUR-
BUSH, THOS. HAWKINS, but formerly MILLS, LOMAX old line. Wit: JESSE
MARTIN, MICAJAH BECKNALL.

Page 221. 7 Oct 1779. MARTHA HEARD, widow of JAMES HEARD dec'd, to JNO.
HEARD, AC, for Ł160, all dower rights in the estate of JAS.
HEARD. Wit: JAS. REID JR, JNO. LANCASTER, ALEX. MILLER.

Page 221. 1 Jun 1779. DAVID MOORE, Rockbridge, to RICHARD BALLENGER, AC, for Ⱡ50, 99 acres S branch of S fork Pedlar. Wit: JAS. FRANK-LIN, ANGUS McDONALD, WALTER POWER.

Page 222. 6 Dec 1779. PHILIP PEYTON & wife WINNIFRED, AC, to VALENTINE PEYTON, for Ⱡ200, 142 acres both sides Horsley and part of a tract. Lines: PHILIP PEYTON.

Page 223. 3 Apr 1780. WM. HOLLANDSWORTH, AC, to YOUNG LANDRUM, AC, for Ⱡ1200, 500 acres branch Tye and N side Berry's Mt. Lines: WM. ALFORD (WALTER KING of Gr. Britain), GEO. STONEHAM, MENOS WRIGHT & KILLIS WRIGHT. Remainder of two tracts of grantor's land of 400 acres and 300 acres; reference to deeds of BUSH in AC. Grantor has sold 100 of the 400 acres to WM. ALFORD and 100 acres of 300 acres to KILLIS WRIGHT. Orig. del. 20 Jul 1796, on written order to JNO. CONDUITT(?).

Page 224. 1 Jan 1780. Commission to quiz HANNAH CABELL, wife of NICHL. CABELL, as to deed of 30 Jan 1779, to EDMD. WILCOX. Done 21 Apr 1780 - 2325 acres.

Page 225. 13 Apr 1780. JNO. HARPER, AC, to EDMD. WILCOX, AC, for Ⱡ1000, 270 acres S side Tye, small Ivy Island. Bought by grantor from JNO. WEBB and rec. in AC. Wit: JOHN PHILLIPS, SALLA KILBON, JESSE WRIGHT. Orig. taken out.

Page 226. 3 May 1780. JNO. ALLOWAY STRANGE & wife ANN, Fluvanna, to THOS. SOWELL, Fluvanna, for Ⱡ5000, 233 acres in AC and Albe-marle on Hickory Creek. Lines: JOS. MORRIS, ARCHELAUS STRANGE. Orig. del. to JOS. MORRIS for SOWELL.

Page 226. 3 Apr 1780. ROBT. CASH, AC, to REUBIN RUCKER, AC, for Ⱡ500, 322 acres on Pedlar. TAMSIN, wife of CASH.

Page 227. 3 May 1780. HEZEKIAH HARGROVE & wife SUSANNAH, AC, to EDMD. WILCOX, AC, for Ⱡ500, 100 acres. Lines: JNO. FIDLER (alias LOVING), Tye river on S side. Wit: WM. EDMONDS, RO. WRIGHT. Orig. taken out of office.

Page 228. 6 Nov 1779. ALEX. FITZPATRICK, AC, to BENJ. MOOR, AC, for Ⱡ600, 183 acres head of Kerbey's Creek and where grantor now lives. Lines: BENJ. MOOR, BENJ. LANNUM, small part is in Albemarle, DAVID COOK. Wit: WM. PEARCE, CHAS. MARTIN, TERRISHA TURNER, WM. HARRIS. Orig. del. to J. MOORE, 27 Jul 1804.

Page 229. 27 Mar 1780. JNO. TOMMERSON, Bedford, to RO. MAYO, AC, for Ⱡ100, 25 acres on branch of Davis Creek. Part of 45 acres pat. to ANGUS FORBUS 10 Sep 1767, and where JNO. TOMMERSON lately lived; bought of FORBUS. Wit: JAS. HOPKINS, EDMD. BYBEE, ANGUS FORBUS. Del. to MAYO, 15 May 1786.

Page 230. 24 Dec 1779. JNO. NICHOLAS & wife MARTHA, Buckingham; JNO. SCOTT & wife MARGARET, Albemarle, to JNO. CHRISTIAN, AC, for Ⱡ145, 1160 acres pat. to MARTHA & MARGARET FRY who married JNO. NICHOLAS & JNO. SCOTT. Lines: JAS. WARREN; crossing Rockey Run of Buffalo; cross-ing Buffalo; JOSHUA FRY. 400 & 360 acres pat. to MARTHA & MARGARET, 3 Nov 1752, and 400 acres pat. 7 Jun 1764. Wit: JAS. GREHSAM, ELIJAH CHRISTIAN, WM. WELDAY. Orig. taken out of office.

Page 232. 22 Mar 1780. SAML. WOODS, AC, to JAS. BREADEN, AC, for Ⱡ300, 173 acres pat. to grantor 20 Aug 1760. South Mt. on head of Elk Creek.

Page 233. 5 Jun 1780. RICH. GATEWOOD & wife BETTY, AC, to JNO. CHRIS-TIAN, AC, for Ⱡ500, 32 acres. Lines: S side Buffalo, JNO. CHRISTIAN, THOS. PENN near the Mill Pond, Rockey Run. Wit: THOS. PENN, GEO. CHRISTIAN, WM. GATEWOOD. Sent to JNO. CHRISTIAN by order 10 May 1817.

Page 234. 5 Jun 1780. RICH. GATEWOOD & wife BETTY, AC, to THOS. PENN, AC, for Ⱡ2000, 3 acres (sic) on Rockey Run. Lines: CHAS. CHRIS-TIAN JR; across the Mill Pond; JNO. CHRISTIAN. Wit: GEO. & JNO. CHRISTIAN,

WM. GATEWOOD.

Page 235. 5 Jun 1780. WM. GATEWOOD, JR, & wife SARAH, AC, to THOS. PENN, AC, for Ł500, 145 acres W side of Rocky Run. Lines: CHAS. CHRISTIAN JR, Stoval's road, Buffalo River, mouth of Rocky Run. Wit: GEO. & JNO. CHRISTIAN, RICHARD GATEWOOD. Grantor & Grantee both of Lexington Parish.

Page 236. 29 Apr 1780. GABL. PENN, AC, to JOSHUA HUDSON, AC, for Ł100, 20 acres N branch Buffalo; part of a tract. Lines: PENN, formerly LARKIN GATEWOOD, JNO. ROWSAY - now JOSHUA HUDSON, Col. SAML. MEREDITH, LINDSEY COLEMAN. Wit: JNO. PHILIPS, GEO. PENN, I. CAMP.

Page 237. 29 Apr 1780. JOSHUA HUDSON, AC, to GABL. PENN, AC, for Ł100, 20 acres, part of a tract. Lines: PENN, HUDSON, known as GATEWOODS and ROWSEYS, JNO. WIATT, old CHEWS' line, WIATT's old field, line of land PENN bought of THOS. WIATT. Wit: GEO. PENN, JNO. PHILLIPS, I.CAMP.

Page 238. 23 May 1780. JOSHUA HUDSON, AC, to JNO. WIATT, AC, for Ł1000, 41 acres on S branch of Naked Creek. Lines: GABL. PENN, JNO. WIATT, JOSHUA HUDSON.

Page 239. 29 May 1780. JNO. WIATT, AC, to JOSHUA HUDSON, AC, for Ł1000, 115 acres on branches of Naked Creek and Maple Run. Lines: PATRICK ROSE, EDWD. CARTER, JNO. WIATT, REUBIN BANKS, JOSHUA HUDSON.

Page 240. 5 Jun 1780. WM. WRIGHT SR, & wife ESTHER, AC, to ANDREW WRIGHT, AC, for Ł5, 200 acres both sides S fork Davis Creek, part of a tract. Lines: WM. WRIGHT, JAS. HALLEY BURTON. Wit: JOS. ROBERDS, PETER MARTIN, JNO. SCRUGGS, JAS. WOODS. Orig. del. 17 Mar 1816 to A. WRIGHT per RO. GARLAND.

Page 241. 5 Jun 1780. WM. WRIGHT SR. & wife ESTHER, AC, to WM. WRIGHT JR, AC, for Ł5, 420 acres both sides S fork Davis Creek. Lines: JAS. HALLEY BURTON, ANDREW WRIGHT, WM. HIBBIT, JAS. WRIGHT, THOS. MONTGOMERY. Wit: Same as above. Orig. del. to grantee.

Page 242. 26 Mar 1780. Power of atty. by ROBT. JOHNSTON, Caroline Co, to EDMD. WILCOX, DAVID CRAWFORD, & JAS. HIGGINBOTHAM to sell, convey or dispose etc. in AC. Memo: Gentlemen: my land on waters of Rockfish-Meriwether's Branch I desire my land there not to be sold nor the entries adjoining thereto. Wit: WM. PAYTON, NELSON CRAWFORD, ISAAC WRIGHT, JNO. GOODRICH.

Page 243. 24 Mar 1780. JONATHAN WATERS, Botetourt Co, to ZACH. TALIAFERRO, AC, for Ł100, 78 acres N fork Tye. Lines: EDMD. COFFEY. Wit: KETURAH CAWTHON, ZACH. TALIAFERRO JR, JNO. TALIAFERRO, THOS. DURHAM, JAS. TALIAFERRO JR.

Page 244. 23 Oct 1779. ALEX. REID, Minor, planter, AC, to NATHL. CLARKE, Henrico, for Ł3000, 398 acres on a branch of S fork Rockfish. MARY REID, wife of grantor. Wit: ALEX. REID JR, WM. CLARKE, JNO. CARPENTER, LITTLEBERRY WITT.

Page 245. 20 May 1780. JOS. CREWS, AC, to JOS. MAYO, Powhatan, for Ł6000, 331 acres middle fork Stovall Creek. Lines: BENJ. RUCKER, STOVAL, ROBT. JOHNSON. Wit: CHAS. CHRISTIAN JR, JAS. DILLARD JR, GEO. CHRISTIAN, ELIJAH CHRISTIAN, JNO. WHITTLE. Orig. del. to WM. MAYO.

Page 246. 2 Aug 1779. ADAM REID, Rockbridge, to RICHARD BALLINGER, AC, for Ł250, 250 acres three forks of Pedlar. Wit: JAS. FRANKLIN, ANGUS McDONALD, WALTER POWER. Proved by FRANKLIN 6 Mar 1780, and others Monday, 3 Apr 1780. Page 247, Order to WM. PAXTON, DAVID GRAY, & SAML. LYLE, Rockbridge JP's to quiz BARBARY, wife of REID. Done by GRAY & LYLE 2 May 1780.

Page 248. 4 Mar 1780. JNO. BONES, AC, & wife BARSHA, to SOLOMON LEVY, AC, for Ł250, 38 acres S branch Hatt Creek. Wit: JNO. SHIELDS, THOS. & ALEX. SMITH.

Page 250. 26 Aug 1779. CHAS., JNO., & CHRISTOPHER LYNCH, Bedford Co, to
           SNELLING JOHNSON, AC, for Ł500, 75 acres by the Creek. Wit:
JNO. MEREDITH, STARK BROWN, WM. HARRISON, JNO. H. GOODWIN, ELIJAH
GILLENWATERS.

Page 251. 26 Aug 1779. CHAS., JNO., & CHRISTOPHER LYNCH, Bedford Co, to
           PHILLIP JOHNSON, AC, for Ł500, 315 acres. Wit: Same as above.
These two deeds were finally proved by buyers 5 Jun 1780.

Page 252. 7 Aug 1780. STEPHEN HAM, AC, to JAS. HILL, AC, for Ł500, 268
           acres. Lines: RUCKER.

Page 253. 3 Jul 1780. CLAUDIUS BUSTER & wife DARKUS(DARKAS), Augusta
           Co., to NATHL. HARLOE, AC, for Ł4000, 320 acres Rockfish. Part
of pat. of Col. JNO. CHISWELL at Williamsburg and by him conveyed to JAS.
BELL SR, and by SR. to JAS. BELL JR. It fell to SAML. BELL, son and heir
or JAS. BELL JR. and by SAML. BELL was conveyed to BUSTER.

Page 254. 26 Jul 1780. THOS. STEPHENSON, AC, to WM. ELLIOT, AC, for
           Ł250, 200 acres branch Rockfish. Lines: S side of river, CHIS-
WELL's old line. Wit: THOS. BELL, WM. DEPRIEST, NATHL. HARLOW.

Page 255. 7 Aug 1780. CALEB HIGGINBOTHAM & wife MARYAN, AC, to WM.
           HIGGINBOTHAM, for Ł20, 181 acres both sides Buffalo. Part of
244 acres bought by CALEB from PHILLIP SMITH - crossing Puppies' Creek
and joining JACOB SMITH.

Page 257. 10 Mar 1780. MOSES CLACK & MOSES CLACK JR., AC, to SAML.
           WOODS, AC, for Ł1100, 105 acres head branch Beaver Creek.
Lines: PULLUM COOPER. Wit: ALEX. REID JR, JAS. McCLAIN, WM. CLARK, WM.
WOODS, JNO. POPE JR, JAS. WOODS.

Page 258. 1 Aug 1780. MARTIN KEY JR, & wife NANCY, AC, to HEZEKIAH HAR-
           GROVE, AC, for Ł1000, 306 acres branch Rucker's Run. Bought
by KEY from HENRY BARNES 1 Feb 1777. Orig. del. 16 (26?) Jun 1811 to
grantee per S. GARLAND.

Page 259. 16 Mar 1780. JNO. WIATT GILBERT, AC, to DAVID SHEPHERD for
           Ł1000, 50 acres, part of tract bought by grantor from EZEKIEL
GILBERT. Lines: WM. POLLARD, SHEPHERD, S side of N fork of Tribulation -
all he possesses on N side. Wit: HENRY GILBERT, JAS. FRANKLIN, JNO.
STEWART, JOSIAS GILBERT.

Page 260. 25 May 1780. JNO. WIATT GILBERT, AC, to JNO. SAVAGE for Ł645,
           five slaves: London, Darcus, Lidia, Cloe, & Findall. Deed of
Trust to secure Ł1057 tobacco or Ł645 inspected tobacco at Shochoe or
BYRD's Warehouses. Wit: GABL. PENN, JOSIAS GILBERT.

Page 261. 26 May 1780. JNO. CHRISTIAN, AC, to WM. GATEWOOD, AC, for
           Ł750, 150 acres branches Rockey Run. Lines: Stovall's road,
WILLIAM DILLARD, Mixon's Road, CHAS. CHRISTIAN. Wit: JOS. DAVENPORT,
THOS. PENN, CHAS. CHRISTIAN JR.

Page 262. 4 Sep 1780. PETER HENDRIXSON, AC, to JNO. ROWZIE, AC, for
           Ł300, 54 acres branch Buffalo. Lines: grantor, JNO. ROWZIE.
Part of a tract pat. to JNO. CONNER at Williamsburg. DOROTHY, wife of
grantor.

Page 263. 7 Aug 1780. Plat of PATRICK ROSE's land on his motion - 3037
           acres on Naked Creek - cut by Piney River; Allen's Creek, sev-
eral courses of Tye, Jackson Creek. Land of PETER ROSE. Certified by
EDMD. WILCOX, Clk.

Page 265. 8 May 1780. WM. PRESTON & THOS. PROSSER, Trustees of JNO.
           HOWARD, late of Botetourt, and the said JNO. HOWARD & wife,
MARY, to THOS. ANDERSON, Buckingham Co, for Ł7000 and Ł50,000 tobacco,
"about 1100 acres" - land on James River known as Fishpond Tract - now
owned by HOWARD, and great Sycamore Island - all by 4 acres willed by
Col. ALLEN HOWARD, dec'd, to JNO. HOWARD, and which JOHN HOWARD sold to
Mr. STEPHEN TURNER. This is from the Clouded Marble Rock in the river

line up to Col. NICHL. CABELL's Corner Rock. Mention of WM. HOWARD's line
opposite head of an Island in James and first of note after passing mouth
of Rockfish river; STEPHEN TURNER's line, Jas. River on S side. Wit: to
THOS. PROSSER: NICHL. CABELL, JOS. CABELL, THOS. PATTESON, HUGH ROSE, JNO.
CABELL, THOS. MATHEWS. Other wit: DAVID PATTESON, SAML. SPENCER, SAML.
BURKS.

Page 266. 28 Sep 1780. ZACH. TALIAFERRO, AC, to JNO. CLARKSON, AC, for
           Ь6750, two tracts pat. 24 Mar 1767, on both sides of Tye, and
14 acres pat. 10 Sep 1767. Line of JAS. BROWN; other tract of 62 acres
and line of ELIAS SMITH. Wit: JNO. LOVING JR, WM. BIBB, ISAAC TINSLEY.

Page 268. 6 Mar 1780. ROBT. JOHNS, AC, to JAS. LONDON, for Ь1200, 100
           acres both sides Porridge Creek. Part of 218 acres which RO.
had of his brother, THOS. JOHNS. Lines: JOSHUA FRY. ELIZA, wife of
grantor. Wit: CHAS. CHRISTIAN, JNO. CHRISTIAN(B), JNO. TURNER. (Note:
I have called attention to this B for this JOHN CHRISTIAN, I believe. He
thus showed that he lived on Buffalo River. BFD)

Page 269. 2 Oct 1780. ZACH. TALIAFERRO, AC, to JNO. SMITH, AC, for Ь20,
           400 acres pat. to grantor 20 Nov 1779. On Franklyn Creek and
next to JAS. SMITH. Orig. del. to grantee.

Page 270. 2 Oct 1780. JNO. BOWLING, AC, to WM. OGLESBY, AC, for Ь500,
           198½ acres and bought by grantor from MATT. CARTWRIGHT. Lines:
WM. CABELL (formerly AMBROSE JONES), BLAIN, BIBB, GALESPIE's pointers in
BIBB line. Orig. del. to JNO. THOMPSON 15 Apr 1788, by grantee's order.

Page 271. 2 Oct 1780. An agreement between WM. GATEWOOD and WM. WEST.
           WEST is to have "makeing, mending, washing, & milking" done
for GATEWOOD, wife, and two sons during their "lifetimes". If done, WEST
is to have - along with his wife (not named) - 50 acres for lives and
part of where WM. GATEWOOD now lives. Lines: The branch, the great road,
WM. DILLARD. Wit: PETER JOINER, ANN JOINER.

Page 272. 2 Oct 1780. SAML. AYRES & wife RACHEL, AC, to ELISHA ABNEY,
           AC, for Ь250, 150 acres on branch of Stoney Creek of Rockfish.

Page 273. 2 Oct 1780. GEO. CARRINGTON, Cumberland Co, to MARTIN DAWSON,
           AC, for Ь4, 343 acres on Harris Creek. Lines: DANL. BURFORD,
WM. MILLER, RICH. SHELTON, ISAAC WRIGHT, White Oaks. Wit: JNO. & JAS.
OWNBEY, ZACH. DAWSON.

Page 274. 2 Oct 1780. GEO. CARRINGTON, Cumberland, to JOHN OWNBEY, AC,
           for Ь18-12-2, 290 acres on branch of Harris. Lines: RICH.
SHELTON, part of 6750 acres pat. to grantor 20 Jun 1753. Wit: MARTIN
DAWSON, ZACH. DAWSON, JAS. OWNBEY.

Page 275. 30 Sep 1780. WM. VEALE, AC, to DRURY BOWMAN, AC, for Ь50, 81
           acres N branch Horsley. Lines: Col. LOMAX. Wit: JOS. DILLARD,
JOS. EDWARDS, JNO. GOODRICH.

Page 276. 31 Oct 1780. WM. GOOLSBY, AC, to JNO. NICHOLAS, Buckingham Co,
           for Ь1400 tobacco, 329 acres N side Buffalo. Lines: FRY, cross-
ing road. Wit: JNO. WIATT, THOS. POWELL, JNO. PENN, JAS. FRANKLIN. Orig.
del. to GEO. NICHOLAS, 1792.

Page 277. 6 Nov 1780. MARTIN DAWSON, AC, to RICH. SHELTON, AC, for Ь225,
           76 acres on Harris Creek.

Page 277. 6 Nov 1780. JOS. GOODWIN & wife FRANCES, AC, to ARCHELAUS
           MITCHELL, AC, for Ь6500, two tracts. 1) 313 acres "both sides".
Lines: RICH. BURKS, mouth of John's Creek, bank of Fluvanna. 2) 113 acres
N side and joining John's Creek. Line: HENRY TRENT.

Page 279. 9 May 1780. CHAS. CHRISTIAN, Goochland, to his son, TURNER
           CHRISTIAN, AC, for love and better support, 400 acres by pat.
where TURNER lives on Rockey Creek of Buffalo. Lines: CHAS. WINKFIELD,
JNO. WARREN, PETER JOINER, CHAS. CHRISTIAN JR. Another tract or survey
"of mine" bought of JAS. LONDON, another bought of JNO. WARREN. Line of

ELIJAH CHRISTIAN. Wit: CHAS. CHRISTIAN JR, ELIJAH CHRISTIAN, JAS. GRESHAM.

Page 280. 15 Dec 1780. THOS. DICKERSON & wife TEMPERANCE, AC & Lexington Parish, to JNO. PHILLIPS, of same, for 50 barrels of corn and Ⱡ4000, several tracts: pat. from Dr. WM. CABELL, dec'd - 145 acres; 97 acres from WM. BIBB; 178 acres pat. in my name, 420 acres in all including whole pats. mentioned and pat. to THOS. DICKERSON at Williamsburg 16 Sue 1756; one pat. of 10 Sep 1760; one of 27 Aug 1770. All on Indian Creek. Wit: JNO. HILL, WM. BANKS, JAS. HAY. Del. to JOHNSON PHILLIPS Nov. 1791.

Page 281. 4 Dec 1780. BARTLETT CASH to BENJ. ROGERS for Ⱡ1600, 100 acres. Lines: PATRICK & CHAS. ROSE. Part of 400 acres pat. to HOWARD CASH 12 Jul 1750. Orig. del. to grantee.

Page 281. 15 Feb 1781. Sheriff bond for ALEX. REID JR. to GEO. BROOKE, Treasurer of Commonwealth of Virginia: Bondsmen: JAS. NEVIL, JAS. DILLARD, GABL. PENN, RODERICH McCULLOCH, JNO. POPE, EDMD. WILCOX, WM. SPENCER, JNO. LOVING JR, JOS. HIGGINBOTHAM MORRISON, HUGH ROSE, SAML. HIGGINBOTHAM.

Page 282. 5 Feb 1781. ALEX. REID, AC, to THOS. ADAMS, Augusta Co, for 5 sh, 237 acres; 100 acres of it is part of pat. of 200 acres on Hatt Creek Gap; pat. 10 Sep 1767. Surveyed by ALEX. MILLER. 137 acres on Inman's Mt. and part of another pat. to REID on same date - 223 acres. Lines: WM. MORRALL. Wit: ALEX. REID JR, ALEX. MILLER, JONATHAN REID.

Page 283. 3 Feb 1780. JNO. LYON, AC, to WM. PEARCE, AC, for Ⱡ30, 100 acres. Lines: Mouth of TERISHA TURNER's Spring Branch; Cove Creek. Wit: JNO. DAWSON, BENJ. MOOR, WM. MOORE. Orig. del. to OBEDIAH PEARCE, 18 Oct 1798.

Page 284. 5 Mar 1781. JAS. CULL & wife MARY, AC, to BOND BURNETT, AC, for Ⱡ55, 50 acres S fork Davis Creek. Lines: CHAS. TATE, JNO. WADE, spur of the mt., to the road, orchard fence, WM. ALLEN, JNO. WADE's old line.

Page 285. 5 Mar 1781. DAVID MONTGOMERY SR, AC & Parish, to DAVID MONTGOMERY JR, & JAS. MONTGOMERY, of same, his two sons, 22 acres. Lines: Col. LOMAX; pat. to Sr. on 6 Jul 1765.

Page 286. 5 Mar 1781. DAVID MONTGOMERY & wife ELIZ, AC, to their son, JAS. MONTGOMERY, 155 acres on Davis Creek, pat. to DAVID, 30 Aug 1763. W side of line on Creek. 40 acres of it granted by Commonwealth 12 Jul 1780. Lines of DAVID MONTGOMERY JR.

Page 287. 1 May 1780. DANL. GAINES, Shff. bond. Bondsmen: ZACH. TALIAFERRO, HUGH ROSE, CHAS. ROSE, GABL. PENN, AMBROSE RUCKER.

Page 288. 20 Apr 1781. JOSIAS WOOD & wife RHODA, AC, to WILLIAM GALASPIE, AC, for Ⱡ30,000 tobacco, 305 acres. Lines: SAML. STAPLES, WM. LOVING. Wit: WM. POWELL, WM. WALTON, GEO. GALASPIE.

Page 289. 3 Apr 1781. JNO. BELL & wife ELIZ, Orange Co, to DAVID PHILLIPS, AC, for Ⱡ450, 539 acres Rockfish. Lines: LEONARD PHILLIPS JR, HUNTER BURRESS. Wit: LEONARD PHILLIPS, MATT. PHILLIPS, LEONARD PHILLIPS JR, WM. HITCHCOCK, ELIZ. PHILLIPS, LESE(?) DAVIS.

Page 291. 7 May 1781. MARTIN DAWSON & wife ELIZ, AC, to VALENTINE COX, AC, for Ⱡ20, 243 acres. Lines: RICHARD SHELTON, S head of a branch.

Page 292. 24 Nov 1780. TURNER CHRISTIAN, AC, to WM. GOODE, Powhatan Co, for Ⱡ33,000 tobacco, 400 acres Buffalo. Lines: MATT. WHITTLE, JNO. WARREN. Wit: H. CHRISTIAN, JAMES GRESHAM, THOS. GRESHAM.

Page 293. 1 Jun 1781. RICH. BALLINGER, AC, to THOS. HILLEY for Ⱡ7000 tobacco, 250 acres pat. to ARTHUR TULEY.

Page 294. 7 May 1781. Shff. Bond for ALEX. REID JR. Bondsmen: ZACH.

TALIAFERRO, WM. WALTON, SAML. HIGGINBOTHAM, JNO. LOVING JR, HUGH ROSE, GABL. PENN, EDMD. WILCOX.

Page 295.   26 Sep 1780.   SAML. ALLEN & wife HANNAH, AC, to WM. POWELL,
            AC, for Ł2500, 475 acres N branches Buffalo. Lines: ISAAC GIB-
SON, WM. CABELL, pat. line. Grantor bought it of CARTER BRAXTON, 10 Jun
1775, and rec. in AC. Wit: JNO. HARGROVE, JOS. DILLARD, DANL. PERROW.

Page 296.   2 Oct 1780.   GEO. CARRINGTON, Cumberland, to ARCHELAUS COX, AC,
            for Ł20, 200 acres. Wit: MARTIN DAWSON, ZUCHARIAH(sic) DAWSON,
JNO. OWNBEY. Final proof on 6 Aug 1781, by OWNBEY.

Page 297.   6 Aug 1781.   Shff. bond. ALEX REID, JR. Bondsmen: DAVID SHEL-
            TON, JAS. MONTGOMERY, WM. SPENCER, WM. BIBB, WM. HARRIS JR,
J.H. MORRISON, WM. WALTON.

Page 298.   15 Jan 1781.   DANL. CONNER, AC, to HENRY MARTIN, AC, for Ł1200,
            30 acres Duck Creek under the Rockey Mt. Lines: MARTIN's own,
PAGE. Wit: WM. FITZPATRICK, ALLEN BLAIR, GEO. BODINGHAM, JNO. MARTIN JR,
DAVID MONTGOMERY.

Page 299.   3 Sep 1781.   WM. MATTHEWS & wife JIMMIMY, AC, to WM. WHITTEN,
            AC, for Ł20, 190 acres. Lines: RO. JOHNSTON, HUGH MORRIS.

Page 300.   3 Sep 1781.   WM. MATTHEWS & wife JIMMIMY, AC, to JANE DAVIS,
            AC, for Ł1000, 250 acres S side and joining Dancing Creek.
Lines: JOS. CABELL, ROBT. PEYTON.

Page 302.   3 Spe 1781.   BENJ. HIGGINBOTHAM, AC & Lexington Par., to
            PULLIAM SANDIDGE, of same, for Ł1000, 280 acres head branch of
Horsley. Lines: JNO. SANDIDGE.

Page 303.   3 Spe 1781.   JOHN BROWN & wife RACHEL, AC, to RICH. DAVIS SR,
            for Ł50, 340 acres. Lines: BROWN's old line; WARE.

Page 304.   1 Oct 1781.   JOS. CREWS, AC, to STEPHEN HAM, AC, for Ł5770 to-
            bacco, 200 acres. Lines: STOVALL's old pat. line; at lower
end; crossing creek. Wit: BENJ. RUCKER, ISAAC RUCKER, JNO. TURNER, BENAM-
MI STONE. Orig. del. 31 Dec 1823 to JESSE BECK, Exr. of STEPHEN HAM.

Page 305.   1 Oct 1781.   CHAS. DAVIS, AC, to JNO. SALE, AC, for Ł300, two
            tracts. 1) 400 acres on Davis Mill Creek. 2) 124 acres. Lines:
CORNL. THOMAS, NICHL. DAVIES, HUGH MORRIS. Wit: GEO. CHRISTIAN, AMBROSE
RUCKER, DAVID CRAWFORD, GEO. PHILLIPS, JAS. FRANKLIN, J.H. MORRISON.

Page 307.   27 Aug 1781.   HENRY GILBERT, AC, to EDWD. WATSON, AC, for
            Ł3000, land on Tribulation; part of former tract of CARTER
BRAXTON. Lines: Lynch Road, BAYLOR WALKER, dec'd, WM. POLLARD. Wit: JNO.
PENN, JAS. WATSON, AUGUSTIN STEEL.

Page 308.   17 Dec 1781.   BENJ. COX, AC, Deed of Trust - owes JNO. WHITE-
            LEY, AC, Ł27-12 - a negro fellowm MATT, about 25 and now in
possession of WM. INGLES, Montgomery Co. Wit: CALEB HIGGINBOTHAM, JACOB
BROWN, WM. HIGGINBOTHAM.

Page 308.   2 Mar 1782.   DANL. CONNER, AC, to HENRY MARTIN, AC, for Ł40,
            98 acres Dutch Creek. Lines: DAVID MONTGOMERY. Pat. to grantor
20 Jul 1768. Wit: WM. & HUDSON MARTIN.

Page 310.   4 Mar 1782.   LUKE HAMILTON, AC, to JAS. HAMILTON, AC, for Ł53,
            53 acres Thoroughfare on head of Cub Creek. Lines: LUKE HAMIL-
TON, JNO. JACOBS. (A sentence has been written in heavier ink and it
does not make sense, but the name or word "Poll" is therin. I am unable
to state that it is for wife of grantor, but could be a later addition.)

Page 311.   5 Dec 1781.   WILLOUGHBY PUGH & wife SARAH, AC, to JNO. COLE,
            Fluvanna, for Ł200, 200 acres pat. to CAPT. CHAS. LEWIS, 24
Oct 1748. Lines: GEO. BLAIN, JNO. MORRIS, BENJ. HARRIS JR(?), JNO. PUGH,
part of LEWIS pat. Wit: ABRAHAM STRANGE, ARCHELAUS STRANGE, JNO. MORRIS,
JAS. FOSTER.

196

Page 312.   2 Jun 1781.   NATHAN CRAWFORD & wife JUDITH, AC, to JOSIAS
             DODD, AC, for Ŀ2000, 95 acres S branch of Stoney Creek of
Rockfish. Wit: ALEX. REID JR, WM. CLARK JR, JNO. POPE JR, JAS. WOODS,
JNO. HALL.

Page 313.   --Jan 1782. (Rec. 4 Mar 1782.) MATT. NIGHTINGALE, AC, to ED-
             MD. WILCOX, AC, for Ŀ3053 tobacco at BYRD's or Shockhoe Ware-
houses - Deed of Trust - 5 sh. A slave, Moll, and her child, Jesse, a
boy; stock. Wit: JAS. WELLS, MILLY WELLS.

Page 314.   16 Oct 1781.   THOS. MONTGOMERY & wife BRIDGET, AC, to JNO.
             HOPKINS, Goochland, for Ŀ300, 285 acres on Davis Creek - 85
of it pat. to THOS. MONTGOMERY 14 Feb 1761; 200 acres of it by deed from
WM. WRIGHT in Albemarle. Lines: WM. WIRGHT's old pat. line, MARTIN KEYS
(formerly RO. MONTGOMERY), THOS. MONTGOMERY, and his son, ROBT. MONTGOM-
ERY. Wit: HEN. MARTIN, JAS. MONTGOMERY, WM. MARTIN. Orig. del. to Mr.(?)
HOPKINS in Mar 1791.

Page 316.   9 Feb 1782.   JNO. WHITLEY & wife ANNEY, AC, (WHITSE in deed,
             but signed WHITLEY) to JNO. MATTHEWS, AC, for Ŀ5, 8 acres on
head of Lively's Spring Branch; part of tract sold by BALLENGER WADE to
WHITTSE(sic). Lines: RO. CASH, HENDRICK ARNOLD, WADE's old road. Wit:
R. MAYS, JNO. SWINNEY, FRANCES HIGGINBOTHAM (her mark).

Page 316.   28 Jan 1782.   WM. HORSLEY & wife MARTHA, AC, to JNO. WHITTLE,
             AC, for Ŀ69, 69 acres S branch Owen's Creek; part of a tract.
Lines: JNO. JOSLIN, WM. HORSLEY. Orig. del. to WHITTLE 6 Nov 1787.

Page 317.   1 Oct 1781.   WM. WHITSETT, AC, to CHAS. STEWART, AC, for Ŀ60,
             100 acres. Lines: Col. DANL. GAINES, JOS. CREWS, JAS. McNEESE.
Wit: BENAMMI STONE, BENJ. RUCKER, ISAAC RUCKER. Note: I am inclined to
think that WHITSITT was the owner of what was to become Sweet Briar College many years later. The beautiful home of the president is known as
Sweet Briar House. ELIJAH FLETCHER bought up a huge tract and left the
Sweet Briar Plantation (his will is headed as having been written there)
to his daughter, INDIANA FLETCHER. He sets forth the various tracts
which made it up and one was acquired from JOHN CROUSE(sic). Tradition
has it that the house, enlarged by FLETCHER, was originally built by a
man named CREWS. If so, it would probably be the JOS. CREWS mentioned
herein as an adjoining owner. JOS. also got a tract from WHITSITT. I
have pointed out in an earlier note that this WHITSITT was the ancestor
of the WM. WHITSITT who became president of my theological alma mater,
Southern Baptist Theological Seminary, Louisville, Ky. I have not tried
to tract the tract whereon the college is located for I am told that a
fine title lawyer in Lynchburg was once employed to do so and gave it up
as a hopeless task. I have only given the problem a casual survey and
saw that it meant checking a number of suits here and in Lynchburg for
FLETCHER shows that it was acquired by foreclosures on his part of several folk. A look at some of these names showed that various parcels had
been broken up along the way. It may be that I can slip up on the story
from this angle in an easier way than by beginning with FLETCHER's trans-
actions in the 1840's and 1850's. It is, of course, to be remembered that
not all deeds were recorded and one sometimes comes to a dead end in
tracing a title. BFD.)

Page 318.   25 Feb 1782.   BENJ. CARPENTER & wife SAREY, AC, to JAS. LIT-
             TRELL, for Ŀ40, 70 acres branch of Short Creek and joining
LITTRELL. Lines: CHISWELL. Wit: ABNER WITT, CHAS. EADES, JNO. WITT JR.

Page 319.   27 Jan 1780.   MANUS BURGER, Albemarle, to CLAUDIUS BUSTER,
             Augusta, for Ŀ150, 137 acres - Top of Blue Ridge and head
branches Rockfish. Pat. to WM. ROGERS at Williamsburg 31 Oct 1764, and
conveyed by ROGERS to BURGER. Wit: AZARIAH MARTIN, THOS. BELL, WM. DE-
PRIEST, ELIZ. & BENJ. BURGER.

Page 320.   27 Jan 1780.   MANUS BURGER, Albemarle, to CLAUDIUS BUSTER,
             Augusta, for Ŀ150, 143 acres in same territory as deed just
cited. Pat. to WM. ROGERS 20 Aug 1760. Wit: Same as above.

Page 321.   1 Oct 1781.   WM. WHITSITT, AC, to JOS. CREWS, AC, for Ŀ500,

500 acres branch of Rutledge. Lines: Col. DANL. GAINES, JAS. McNEES, JNO.
McDONALD, JAS. McNEES JR, GEO. GILBERT, WYATT POWELL, JONES' orphans, JOS.
MAYO. Conveyed to grantor in two deeds from JAS. McNEES for 300 acres,
7 Sep 1767; other from BENJ. NcNEES for 300 acres 1 Nov 1779. Wit: BENJ.
& ISAAC RUCKER, CHAS. STEWART, JNO. TURNER, BENAMMI STONE.

Page 322. 4 Mar 1782. JNO. WHITLEY & wife ANNY, AC, to HENDRICK ARNOLD,
         AC, for L30, 100 acres branch of Stone House and pat. to gran-
tor at Richmond, 20 Jul 1780. Lines: RICH. POWELL, HOWARD CASH, JER. WADE.

Page 324. 10 Sep 1781. MATT WILSON, AC, to JOS. TUCKER for L200, 300
         acres on Pedlar; branch of Cedar. Lines: RO. JOHNSON, SAML.
GUEST, WM. CLOPTON.

Page 324. 15 Feb 1782. EDWD TINSLEY, AC, to JNO. McDANIEL, AC, for L50,
         126 acres which grantor bought of JAS. WHITE dec'd. Lines:
JAS. THOMAS, JNO. DAVIES, JNO. McDANIEL, BENEMMI STONE, JAS. MORTON, EDMD.
WINSTON. Wit: DAVID TINSLEY, WM. GALT, JOSHUA TINSLEY, AMBROSE RUCKER,
GEO. McDANIEL. Orig. del. to JNO. McDANIEL.

Page 325. 4 Dec 1781. LUCY JOHNSON, widow of RO. JOHNSON, dec'd, of
         Louisa - power of atty. to friends: DAVID CRAWFORD, EDMD. WIL-
COX, WM. BIBB, and CHAS. BURRAS, AC - to sell AC lands under the will of
late husband. Wit: WM. LOVING, JNO. WRIGHT, HEZ. HARGROVE. Orig. del.
to D. CRAWFORD, Nov. Court, 1789.

Page 326. 3 Sep 1781. MOSES RAY, AC, to WM. BRABHAN, AC, one bay horse
         as consideration - 100 acres on Fluvanna next to Swift Islands.
Lines: Col. NICHL. CABELL, Col. WM. CABELL. Wit: WM. CABELL, WILL CABELL
JR, SAML. J. CABELL, LANDON CABELL.

Page 327. 14 Mar 1782. GABL. PENN & wife SARAH, AC, to SMYTH TANDY,
         Augusta, for L1000, 317 acres N branch Buffalo and known as
New Glasgow. Lines: LAURENCE CAMPBELL; JNO. WIATT; JOSHUA HUDSON; SAML.
MEREDITH. Reservation of 36 feet square graveyard to PENN; some of
family already buried there. Wit: JAS. FRANKLIN, WIATT POWELL, THOS.
POWELL, SAML. HILL.

Page 329. 1 Apr 1782. WM. CABELL & wife MARGARET, AC, to WM. CABELL JR,
         AC, for love of son - 2200 acres branch of Buffalo and Tye.
Part of 25,000 acres pat. to GEO. BRAXTON 25 Nov 1743. 2000 acres of
BRAXTON tract was conveyed to WM. WALKER & wife ELIZ, and WM. PRICE in
General Court 6 May 1749. WM. WALKER, son and heir of WM. WALKER, con-
veyed to WM. CABELL in General Court 10 Apr 1772. 200 acres was conveyed
by CARTER BRAXTON to WM. CABELL 21 Oct 1778. Lines: RICE MEREDITH, JNO.
BROWN, Higginbotham's Mill Creek, ISAAC GIBSON, HUGH ROSE.

Page 330. 1 Apr 1782. FRANCIS SPENCER & wife MARY, Buckingham Co, to
         DAVID PROFITT, AC, for L3000 tobacco, 250 acres S branch Ruck-
er's Run and S side Berry's Mt. Lines: JNO. JOPLING, WM. CABELL, SPENCER.
Part of a tract.

Page 331. 1 Apr 1782. GEO. LEE, AC, to RICH. SHELTON, AC, for L20, 31
         acres on Harris Creek. Lines of JONES.

Page 331. 1 Apr 1782. RICH. SHELTON & wife MARY, AC, to RICH. LEE, AC,
         for L50, 46 acres S side Harris; next to land GEO. LEE bought
of DUNCAN GRAHAM. Orig. del. to M(?) LEE, June, 1790.

Page 332. 4 May 1782. GABL. PENN & wife SARAH, AC, to GEO. COLEMAN, AC,
         for L800, 562 acres N side and joining Rutledge Creek. Lines:
Lynch Road, HENRY GILBERT at Park's road; JNO. STEWART, N branch Rutledge.
Wit: WIATT POWELL, WM. GALT, NOELL JOHNSON, THOS. POWELL.

Page 333. 4 May 1782. GEO. COLEMAN & wife JUDITH, AC, to GABL. PENN of
         AC, for L800, 370 acres N side Buffalo and where COLEMAN now
lives. COLEMAN bought it of DUDLEY GATEWOOD 30 Jan 1778. Lines: GEO. PENN,
former glebe line, Col. SAML. MEREDITH. Wit: THOS. POWELL, NOELL JOHNSON,
WM. GALT, WIATT POWELL.

198

Page 334.   6 May 1782.   FRANCIS WEST & wife ELIZ., AC, to WM. CABELL, AC,
             for ₺15, 110 acres Mayo Creek and pat. to WEST by Commonwealth
on 20 Jul 1780. Lines: MOSES GOING. Wit: JNO. MARTIN JR, ABRAHAM WARWICK,
THOS. JOPLING.

Page 335.   6 May 1782.   NICHL. CABELL, AC, to MATT TUCKER, AC, for ₺62-10,
             200 acres and joins where TUCKER now lives and CHAS. BURRUS.
Part of 400 acres formerly that of Dr. WM. CABELL, dec'd. and separated
from remainder (200 acres) by new line of marked trees beginning at Capt.
CHAS. BURRUS; Punch Ridge.

Page 336.   6 May 1782.   NICHL. CABELL, AC, to GABL. PENN, AC, for ₺62-10,
             200 acres on headwaters of Beaver. Lines: CHAS. BURRUS; land
GABL. PENN bought of JNO. BARNES & BENJ. WRIGHT on the west; Punch Ridge;
separate 200 acres NICHL. CABELL sold to MATT. TUCKER.

Page 337.   15 Mar 1782.   SMYTH TANDY, Augusta Co, to GABL. PENN, AC, for
             5 sh, Deed of Trust to secure debt - 317 acres known as New
Glasgow and which TANDY recently bought of PENN. Wit: WIATT POWELL, THOS.
POWELL, JAS. FRANKLIN, SAML. HILL.

Page 338.   9 Jan 1782.   EDWD. TINSLEY, AC, to his sons: JOHN, ISAAC,
             DAVID, & JOSHUA TINSLEY - they are to rebuild mill on Harris
Creek - 20 acres. Lines: JNO, DAVID, & JOSHUA TINSLEY, HUGH ROSE. Part of
a tract EDWD. bought of DUNCAN GRAHAM of Caroline. Wit: JO. MAGANN, VA-
LENTINE COX, JAS. LIVELY, AMBROSE RUCKER.

Page 339.   4 Feb 1782.   PETER STONER & wife FRANCES, at present of AC, to
             THOS. ANDERSON, Buckingham Co, for ₺3000 tobacco at inspec-
tions at Page, Meriwether, or Pamunkey in Hanover; Byrd's or Shockoe on
James in Henrico - or either at Manchester on James in Chesterfield and
one hogshead of good rum; 30 gal. of good wine and $30,000 - 1200 acres
on Fluvanna known as Fish Pond; includes part of an island known as Sycamore. Bought by said THOMAS of JOHN HOWARD and reference to deed from
HOWARD and wife to said THOMAS; and then sold by said THOMAS to said
PETER, 31 Jan 1782, and excepts 4 acres on Sycamore claimed by DAVID
PATTESON. Lines: WM. HOWARD, STEPHEN TURNER; articles of agreement "test-
ed" by JNO. COBBS SR, and DAVID PRYOR, 20 Apr 1781, and annexed (not with
deed). Wit: SAML. FARGUSON, SAML. ANDERSON, WM. PERKINS, SR, JOHN BOCOCK.
(Note: The agreement may be with original deed in box since there is no
margin noted for a delivery to anyone.)

Page 341.   1 Jun 1782.   WM. TYREE, AC, to WM. WEST, AC, for ₺35, 50 acres
             N side Tye. Part of 180 acres granted to grantor at Richmond
20 Jul 1780.

Page 342.   31 Dec 1781.   JNO. BAILEY & wife ELIZ., AC, to EDWARD HARPER,
             AC, for ₺1000, 143 acres. Wit: JNO. TURNER, NICHL. LYON, EDWD.
LYON, JESSE WOOD.

Page 343.   2 Jun 1782.   JOS. HIGGINBOTHAM to GEO. LEE, both of AC and
             Lex. Parish, for ₺13,000 tobacco. Branch of Buffalo; 204 acres.
Lines: JAS. HIGGINBOTHAM, S side Mill Creek.

Page 344.   5 Mar 1782.   JNO. MARTIN & wife NANCY, Albemarle, to JOSIAS
             WOOD, AC, for ₺6000, 172 acres. Lines: RO. WRIGHT. Wit: WM.
LOVING, WM. FITZPATRICK, MOSES HUGHES. Orig. del. to WOOD 20 Sep 1789.

Page 345.   3 Jun 1782.   JNO. DAVIS, AC, to GEO. GILBERT, AC, for ₺32-10,
             44 acres N branch Rutledge. Lines: JAS. MANEES, GEO. GILBERT,
BENJ. HIGGINBOTHAM, a road; part of 90 acres pat. to DAVIS.

Page 346.   23 Jan 1782.   NATHAN BOND for love borne to his four children:
             JOS. BALLINGER BOND, RICH. COX BOND, MARY WALKER KELLEY, &
NATHAN BOND - 600 acres where I live - to be divided - on Stone House
Creek. Reservation for life for my wife ELIZ., and self. Wit: JOS. BALL-
INGER, MARY PARSONS, JNO. GURTIS (mark).

Page 346.   3 Jun 1782.   DAVID CRAWFORD & CHAS. BURRAS, AC, as attornies
             for LUCY JOHNSON, widow of RO. JOHNSON, dec'd. and also his

exrx. - to PHILLIP THURMOND, AC, for Ł30, 328 acres on S branch Horsley.
Lines: orphans of CHAS. ELLIS.

Page 348. 18 Nov 1780. Marriage contract between ANGUS FORBUS, AC, and
MARY LEE, AC - if she marries me, lands and possessions; two
calves mentioned. Wit: ELIZ. AARON, NEO.(?) LOVING (her mark), JNO. LOV-
ING SR. Rec. 5 Aug 1782, upon final proof of ELIZ. AARON. It appears to
be JOHN LOVING SR. in signature, but clerk has recorded it as JOHN LOVING
JR. Rev. W. IRVINE made a return for the marriage of ANGUS FORBES (sic)
and MARY LEE, 20 Nov 1780, and it is recorded in the Order Book for 1773
-1782, page 511. In my abstracts of will books from 1761 to 1919 (complete) I note that MARY, as admrx., and testator, ANGUS, are spelled
FORBUSH, FORBUS, & FARBUSH in data. There is also data on a man named
WM. FURBUSH (will), but no mention of an ANGUS in the several items re-
lating to WILLIAM's estate - administrator, inventory, & guardian bond
for two of his orphans.

Page 348. 5 Aug 1782. JNO. HOGG, AC, to JOS. CHILDRESS, AC, for Ł50, 63
acres on branch of Harris and between the Bear and Cedar Mts.
Line of JNO. PETERS. Wit: WM. PETER, ZACHARIAS TAYLOR, RICHARD WHITEHALL.

Page 349. 5 Aug 1782. JAS. MANEES, JR, Henry Co, to JNO. McDANIEL, AC,
for Ł200, 185 acres on branch of Rutledge. Lines: BENEMMI
STONE, JOS. CREWS, JAS. PENDLETON, JAS. THOMAS, JAS. MORTON.

Page 350. 5 Aug 1782. JAS. MANEES, JR., Henry Co., to JAS. PENDLETON,
AC, for Ł100, 115 acres. Orig. del. to CHAS. STEWART for
PENDLETON, May 1785.

Page 350. 18 May 1782. JNO. JACOBS, AC, to NATHAN CRAWFORD, AC, negroes
named; stock. Wit: JNO. POPE, ZACH. TALIAFERRO, MOSES MARTIN,
MATT. NIGHTINGALE, THOS. MORRISON JR, EZRA MORRISON.

Page 351. 8 Dec 1781. MOSES HUGHES & wife ELIZ., AC, to THOS. H. TAL-
BOTT, AC, for Ł100, 5 acres on Rockfish. Lines: Stoney Creek,
BALDING, JNO. WITT. Wit: JNO. WITT JR, THOS. BALL, JAS. BROWN, GEO.
JUDE, WM. BALL.

Page 352. 13 Feb 1782. JAS. MANEES, SR, AC, to BENAMMI STONE, AC, for
Ł160, 100 acres. Lines: Col. DANL. AINES, JAS. MELTON(?),
JNO. McDANIEL, JOS. CREWS, CHAS. STEWART. Wit: A.Y. RUCKER, JNO. McDANIEL,
W. POLLARD, JOS. CREWS, JNO. STEWART.

Page 352. (two pages so munbered) 5 Aug 1782. HUGH ROSE, PATRICK ROSE,
& CHAS ROSE some years ago built a mill on Piney on public
road from Amherst Courthouse to Lynch's ferry and held it in common until
Oct 1780. At that time CHAS. sold to PATRICK, but reserved right to have
grain ground without toll as long as present works stand. PATRICK received no title and has now sold to HUGH ROSE. 5 sh. paid by HUGH for
land next to mill. S side of River. Also reservation of timber rights.
HUGH may build a tavern, but must have PATRICK's consent. PATRICK does
not object to a canal. Mention of ford above McGEEHEE's Tavern. Orig.
del. to HUGH ROSE by JOS. OGLESBY, Oct 1788.

Page 353. 5 Aug 1782. ASHCRAFT ROACH & wife MARY MAGDALIN, AC, to REZIN
PORTER, Albemarle, for Ł200, 335 acres on branch of Pedlar.
Lines: RO. DAVIS, ARTHUR TULEY, EDWD. WATTS.

Page 354. 1 Aug 1782. EDMD. POWELL, AC, to RICH. POWELL, AC, for Ł7000
tobacco, 321 acres on Harris which RICH. POWELL, dec'd. bought
of DUNCAN GRAHAM. Lines: MAGAN, DAVIS, STREET, JONES, SHELTON. Wit:
DAVID WOODROOF, RICH. WOODROOF, JNO. WOODROOF.

Page 355. 1 Jun 1782. GABL. PENN, AC, to GEO. LEE, AC, for Ł23, 23
acres both sides Higginbotham Mill Creek; part of tract of
PENN. Lines: GEO. LEE, JAS. HIGGINBOTHAM. Sent to RICH. POWELL per order
Jan 1812.

Page 356. 2 Jul 1782. WM. POWELL & wife MARY, AC, to GABL. PENN, AC,
for Ł30,000 tobacco, 475 acres N branch Buffalo. Lines: ISAAC

GIBSON, WM. CABELL. Bought by grantor of SAML. ALLEN 26 Sep 1780. Wit: EDMD. WILCOX, GEO. MUTER, TH. MILLER. Orig. del. to O(?) HASKINS for G. PENN.

Page 357. 5 Aug 1782. JNO. OWNBEY, AC, to JEREMIAH TAYLOR, AC, for Ł150, 290 acres Harris Creek. Lines: RICH. SHELTON. Bought by grantor of Col. CARRINGTON. Another tract of 132 acres joining and bought of JAS. WOODROOF. Line of DAVID WOODROOF.

Page 358. 2 Sep 1782. JNO. KIPPENS, AC, to WM. PETER, ac, for Ł70, 82 acres Harris Creek between Bear and Tobacco Row Mts. Lines: WM. PETER, Col. LOMAX.

Page 359. 31 Aug 1782. EDMD. POWELL & wife LUCY, AC, to JACOB SMITH, AC, for Ł80, 283 acres S side Buffalo. Lines: JAS. SMITH, BALLENGER. Wit: JNO. FRANKLIN, JNO. SMITH, CORNL. SALE.

Page 360. 2 Sep 1782. PHILLIP THURMOND & wife JUDITH, AC, to JNO. EUBANK, AC, for Ł3000, 2 tracts. 1) 270 acres on both sides Wilderness Run. Lines: RO. DAVIS, JNO. FLOYD. 2) 98 acres on Davis Spring Branch. Lines: RO. DAVIS. Both tracts bought by grantor from RO. DAVIS 2 Aug 1779.

Page 361. Order to quiz JUDITH GILBERT, wife of HENRY GILBERT, as to sale of Tribulation tract on 27 Aug 1781, to EDWD. WATSON. Done by DANL. GAINES & AMBROSE RUCKER, AC J.P.'s, and rec. 2 Sep 1782.

Page 362. 26 Aug 1782. DAVID BLYES, AC, to WM. GATEWOOD JR, AC, for Ł35, 30 acres S side Buffalo. Lines: FRY on Water Million (sic) Branch. Wit: CHAS. CHRISTIAN JR, JUDITH CHRISTIAN, JOHN CHRISTIAN(B). I have noted before that this B stands for the JOHN CHRISTIAN who lived on Buffalo.

Page 363. 3 Feb 1781. JNO. PHILLIPS to JAS. HAY for Ł500, 8 acres on both sides Indian Creek. Lines: GILBERT HAY. Part of 145 acres granted WM. CABELL, dec'd, by pat. 16 Aug 1756. CABELL's line mentioned. Wit: WM. HAY, CHAS. HAY, DANL. RYALTY. This is doubtless ROYALTY and some of them went into Kentucky.

Page 363. 6 Feb 1782. JNO. PHILLIPS to CHAS. TYLER for Ł8000 tobacco. 131 acres on both sides Indian Creek. Part of 145 acres as above. Lines: JAS. HAY; also 75 acres on both sides of Indian Creek. Part of 178 acres pat. to THOS. DICKERSON 27 Aug 1770. Lines: GEO. FITZGERALD. AVLA, wife of grantor.

Page 364. 4 Nov 1782. PHILLIP PENN & wife MARTHA, to AUGUSTINE STEEL for Ł200, 200 acres N branch Buffalo. Lines: BRAXTON & Co, JAS. WILLIAMSON (now JAS. GATEWOOD); where grantor now lives and pat. to CHAS. PARKS, 16 Aug 1756, at Williamsburg.

Page 365. 9 Sep 1782. NEAL McCANN, AC, to THOS. MORRIS, Rockbridge Co, for Ł200, 400 acres N fork "of creek". Lines: MARVEL STONE. Wit: JOS. PENN, JOS. BURRESS, RICH. PETER, WM. PETER.

Page 367. 9 Sep 1782. SAML. PETER, AC, to WM. PETER, AC, for Ł40, 280 acres on Cedar Creek. Lines: SAML. PETER, NEAL McCANN; upper part of 480 acres pat. to JOEL WATKINS 15 Jul 1760. Takes in plantation where RICH. PETERS now lives. Wit: RICH. PETERS, JOS. PENN, JOS. BURRUS, THOS. MORRIS.

Page 368. 1 May 1782. RICH. WEBSTER, AC, to JNO. MERRITT, AC, for Ł500, 103 acres branch of Stovall. Lines: WM. GUTTRY. Wit: SNELLING JOHNSON, WIATT STARK, HENRY McDANIEL, WM. HUGHES, WM. GUTTRY.

Page 369. 2 Nov 1782. HENRY KEY, South Carolina - District 96, to WM. ALFORD, AC, for Ł40, 171 acres, part of 371 acres pat. at Williamsbyrg to HUGH WILLOUGHBY 7 Aug 1761, on S branch of Rockfish. Lines: Pat. lines, WALTER KING. 100 acres of it sold to CHAS. McANALLY and 100 acres sold to CHAS. TATE. Rest of 171 acres included plantation whereon HUGH WILLOUGHBY formerly lived. Wit: JNO. ALFORD. Orig. del to

ALFORD, Mar. 1791.

Page 371.   23 May 1782.   ARCHELAUS ALLAWAY STRANGE, AC, to ABRAHAM ALLA-
            WAY STRANGE, AC, for Ŀ15000 tobacco, 260 acres on Hickory
Creek. Lines: GEO. BLAIN, himself, JOS. MORRIS, WM. MORRISON.

Page 371.   9 Aug 1780.   Order to MICHL. THOMAS & WM. HUGHES, Albemarle
            J.P.'s to quiz MARGARET SCOTT, wife OF JOHN SCOTT, as to deed
on above date. Done 4 May 1782. JOHN NICHOLAS & wife, MARTHA, were also
parties to the deed executed 24 Dec 1779, to JNO. CHRISTIAN. 1160 acres.

Page 371.   9 Aug 1780.   Order to CHAS. MAY, HENRY BELL, & DOLPHIN DREW,
            Buckingham J.P.'s to quiz MARTHA NICHOLAS, wife of JNO. NICH-
OLAS, as to above deed to JNO. CHRISTIAN on 24 Dec 1779. Done by MAY &
BELL 14 Mar 1781.

Page 372.   2 Dec 1782.   JAS. HIGGINBOTHAM, AC, to DANL. GAINES, AC, for
            Ŀ400, 200 acres S and middle branches of Rutledge. Lines: DANL.
GAINES, JOS. HIGGINBOTHAM. Wit: GABL. PENN, THOS. WATT, THOS. BAILEY.

Page 374.   2 Dec 1782.   WM. BOOTH, Bedford Co, to WM. SCOTT, AC, for Ŀ200,
            41 acres Stovall's Creek.

Page 374.   2 Dec 1782.   GEO. LEE, AC, to RICH. HARRISON, AC, for Ŀ500,
            303 acres. Lines: HARVIE or HARRIS(?).

Page 375.   22 Oct 1782.   JNO. COTTRELL, Bedford, to JNO. WARD, Bedford,
            for Ŀ150, 368 acres. Lines: up Nuton Creek. Wit; JNO. H. GOOD-
WIN, SNELLING JOHNSON, WM. BROWN, WM. GUTTRY, POWELL OWNBY.

Page 376.   21 May 1782.   Order to WM. CALLAWAY, WM. MEAD, & CHAS. WATKINS,
            Bedford J.P.'s, to quiz SARAH COTTRELL, wife of JNO. COTTRELL,
as to deed above. Done May 25 1782.   (There is a contradiction in dates
therein, but so recorded.)

Page 377.   3 Jan 1783.   REBECCA BURTON sets forth that some time past she
            executed writing and refers to dec'd. husband's will. She
thereby gave up all claims against her father's estate except for one
negro wench which my children shall lend me for life.   Intended that my
son, JESSE BURTON, shall execute purpose - mentions a suit in chancery on
the estate of my late father, JOHN COBBS.   She releases all rights since
her son, JESSE, so desires in estate of JNO. COBBS. This makes it possible for the will of WILLIAM BURTON to be "thus carried out". Wit: PHILLIP
PENN, WM. TUCKER, GEO. PENN.

Page 378.   6 Jan 1783.   Shff. bond for RODERICK McCULLOCH. Bondsmen: CHAS.
            ROSE, DANL. GAINES, EDWD. WARE, GABL. PENN. ALEX. REID JR.
was appointed, but failed to give security in 1782.

Page 379.   9 Nov 1782.   JNO. RICHESON, AC, to his daughter, MARY, for 1
            sh, 3 negroes, etc, but he retains John for his lifetime and
then to MARY. Wit: DANL. GAINES, WM. STEWART, BERNARD GAINES.   Proved
3 Mar 1783.

Page 380.   3 Feb 1783.   ALEX. FORBES, AC, to PETER MARTIN, AC, for Ŀ80,
            88 acres branch S fork Davis Creek. Pat. 10 Jul 1767 to grant-
or. Lines: JNO. MONTGOMERY, WM. WRIGHT. Orig. del. to JAS. VAUGHN.

Page 381.   4 Nov 1782.   HUGH McCABE, AC, to THOS. STATEN, Rockbridge Co,
            for Ŀ42, 50 acres both sides middle fork Pedlar. Lines: JOS.
HIGGINBOTHAM JR.   3 Mar 1783, SARAH McCABE, widow of HUGH McCABE, appeared and relinquished dower rights.

Page 382.   19 Aug 1782.   EPHRAIM SEAMANDS (SEAMONDS), Orange Co, to MATT.
            HARRIS, AC, for Ŀ60, 78 acres head of S branch Rockfish on
Marrowbone Mt. Part of pat. to LEONARD PHILLIPS 20 Jul 1768. Wit: LEON-
ARD PHILLIPS SR, SCHUYLAR HARRIS, MATT. PHILLIPS, LEONARD PHILLIPS JR,
THOS. MATTHEWS, DAVID PHILLIPS.

Page 383.   5 Jan 1782.   JNO. PHILLIPS & wife AVEA, to GEO. FITZGERALD for

Ł5000, 103 acres both sides Indian Creek and joining his own line and part of 175 acres pat. to THOS. DICKERSON 27 Aug 1770. Wit: JAS. HAY and JNO. TYLER.

Page 384.   4 Mar 1783. Shff. bond for RODERICK McCULLOCH. Bondsmen: ZACH. TALIAFERRO, HUGH ROSE, DANL. GAINES, CLOUGH SHELTON, EDMD. WILCOX, GABL. PENN.

Page 385.   1 Oct 1782. DAVID BLY & wife MARY, AC, to JOHN UPSHAW, AC, for Ł100, 100 acres, part of tract granted to WM. GATEWOOD and by him conveyed to BLY. Lines: Water Million (sic) Branch. Wit: WM. HORSLEY, PHILLIP PENN, PETER JOINER. (I may have commented on this before, but there are no U's in Amherst wills from 1761 to 1919. However, there are U's in deeds; as in this case. This does not mean that there are no U legatees, but simply that there are no U testators. BFD)

Page 386.   5 May 1783. THOS. LUCAS to ELIZ. COLEMAN, widow of JNO. COLEMAN, DAVID CRAWFORD, JNO. DANL. COLEMAN, THOS., SAML., NANCY, JOHN, JAMES, BETSY, & MARY COLEMAN. It is set forth that JNO. COLEMAN dec'd., and THOS. LUCAS, AC, bought of LUNSFORD LOMAX JR., tracts involving 1154 acres in partnership on 10 Aug 1769. On same day JNO. COLEMAN covenanted to convey to LUCAS; partition was made, but COLEMAN died before making deed. In will of 9 Jan 1778, he devised to ELIZ., his wife, for education of his children. ELIZ. has paid LUCAS 20 sh. LUCAS sells to her two tracts of 509 acres and 353 acres. Lines: LUNSFORD LOMAX pat. line, Harris Creek, - plat - life estate to ELIZ. and then to the children: THOS., SAML., NANCY, JOHN, JAMES, BETSY, & MARY COLEMAN. (Note: The names of DAVID CRAWFORD & JNO. DANL. COLEMAN appear as bondsmen and wit. in various JNO. COLEMAN items pertaining to his estate. It might be pointed out that MARY was not born when he wrote his will. However, he refers to expected child and wishes her to be named MARY, if girl. BFD) JAMES HIGGINBOTHAM was surveyor.

Page 388.   18 Sep 1782. ZACH. TAYLOR, AC, to JNO. HOGG, AC, for Ł100, 300 acres on Maple Creek. Lines: MICAJAH CLARK, ABSALOM ATHENS! plantation where he lives. Wit: RICH. PETER, WM. SLEDD, CHAS. ELLIS, JOSHIAH ELLIS.

Page 391.   8 Nov 1782. EZEK. GILBERT to JAS. FRANKLIN & WM. GALT, Deed of Trust. 5 sh. Ł10,000 of tobacco at Richmond and Manchester; slave, Joe, unto GABL. PENN. If GILBERT does not pay by 15 Apr next, then PENN is to sell Joe. Wit: WM. CAMDEN, WM. POLLARD, WIATT POWELL. Orig. del. to GALT.

Page 392.   29 Apr 1783. JNO. HEARD & wife MARY, AC, to RO. BABER, AC, for Ł60, 128 acres branch Rockfish. Lines: ANDREW HAIRSTONE, WM. HEARD. Wit: RICH. LITTRELL SR, & JR, JNO. MASK LEAK.

Page 393.   21 Jan 1783. GEO. BLAIN, AC, to JNO. MONTGOMERY JR, for Ł6000 tobacco of Shockhoe inspection - MONTGOMERY is to board HIRAM & GEO. SHIP, the two children of MILLY SHIP, until they are of age; also one slave, Cook; cattle, beds, etc. Wit: WM. POLLARD, NICHL. PRYOR, THOS. GAY. Orig. del. to MONTGOMERY 13 Jul 1784.

Page 394.   19 May 1783. NOELL JOHNSON & wife TABITHA, AC, to WM. CAMDEN, AC, for Ł300, 400 acres which JOHNSON bought of THOS. PARKS, 1 May 1769. Wit: EDMD. WILCOX, JNO. WEST, THOS. LUCAS, PHIL. BURTON. Orig. del. to CAMDEN, Jan., 1791.

Page 395.   11 Oct 1782. JNO. THOMPSON, AC, to WM. BARNETT & JOS. HIGGINBOTHAM MORRISON, AC, for Ł54-7-1, 200 acres on branch of Tye. Lines: ZACH. TALIAFERRO. Wit: JAS. THOMSON, DAVID THOMSON, JOS. BARNETT, RO. WOOD, ALEX. BARNETT. Orig. del. to BARNETT.

Page 396.   11 Oct 1782. JNO. THOMPSON, AC, to WM. BARNETT & JOS. HIGGINBOTHAM MORRISON, AC, for Ł60, one 55 gal. still; stock. Wit: same as previous deed. (Note: I have seen the old ledger of THOMPSON wherein he kept his still accounts. It found its way to the Village of Amherst and reposed for years in old cellar of Voorheis house on South Main. Thompson operated his still in what is now Nelson, but JNO. JR, and WM. THOMPSON were descendants and WM. owned the VOORHEIS house. However, his brother, JOHN, had a lien upon it and devised it to WM's daughter who married a VOORHEIS. There is a picture of the house in ALFRED PERCY's book, The Amherst Story.

Page 397. 2 Jun 1783. JNO. SALE (SAILE), AC, to CHAS. DAVIS, AC, for Ŀ300, two tracts on Thomas Mill Creek. 1) 400 acres. 2) 124 acres. Lines: CORNL. THOMAS, NICHL. DAVIES, HUGH MORRIS.

Page 398. 24 May 1783. JNO. CARTWRIGHT, AC, to EDMD. WILCOX, AC, for Ŀ24, 15 acres N side Tye. Grantor bought it of AMBROSE JONES. Lines: AMBROSE JONES, EDMD. WILCOX, Black Creek hill, main road to Courthouse. Wit: SAML. HIGGINBOTHAM, WM. SID. CRAWFORD, WM. MEREDITH, HENRY BROWN.

Page 399. --May 1783. (Rec. 2 Jun 1783.) DANL. GAINES & wife MARY, AC, to JEREMIAH TAYLOR, AC, for Ŀ100, 124 acres Harris Creek and Rutledge and part of where GAINES now lives. Lines: GAINES, RUCKER. Wit: RICH. TALIAFERRO, RICH. FULCHER, LEVI BALDOCK, JNO. STEWART.

Page 400. 24 May 1783. DANL. GAINES & wife MARY; JOS. MAGANN & wife PHEBE, AC, to JEREMIAH TAYLOR, AC, for Ŀ100, 171 acres Harris and Porridge Creeks. Part of where J. MAGANN formerly lived and known as MAGANN's Ordinary. Mortgaged to GAINES and sold by Chancery decree and GAINES bought it. Lines: GAINES, Lynch Road. Wit: JNO. WOODROOF, THOS. POWELL, minor; JNO. MITCHELL, PTK. REYNOLDS, HUGH ROSE, GABL. PENN.

Page 401. 14 May 1783. JNO. DEPRIEST & wife ELIZ., AC, to WM. POWELL, for Ŀ30,000 tobacco, 400 acres both sides Rucker's Run, S fork. Lines: EDMD. WILCOX, LUCAS POWELL, JAS. WILLS, JAS. THOMPSON, Col. WM. CABELL. Lately that of British subject, KING, and sold by DAVID SHEPHERD, Escheator, to DEPRIEST under two acts of Assembly; pat. 1 Sep 1782. Sold by DEPRIEST to RO. HARRIS of ----County, N.C. and by HARRIS to WILLIAM POWELL. Lines: Survey belonging to KING. Wit: THOS. POWELL, T.A. (sic); ABRAM WARWICK, WM. WARWICK, CHAS. STEWART. WILLIAM POWELL objected that it would not convey to him in fee simple and "disclaimed" unless DEPREIST can pass such an estate as he claims; so recorded.

Page 402. 7 Apr 1783. SAML. SHACKELFORD, AC, to FRANCIS POWEL, AC, for Ŀ40, 14 acres S branch Horsley; part of a tract. Lines: S side of Thomas' road.

Page 403. 25 Sep 1782. OBEDIAH HENDERSON, AC, to ABRAHAM LEMASTER, AC, for Ŀ70, 112 acres where grantor liveth. Lines: On E by JNO. CHRISTIAN; W by MARY WOOD, N by AARON DEHART, S by RALPH LAMASTER. Wit: WM. B. CHRISTIAN, BENJ. HENDERSON, AARON DEHART, JNO. & RALPH LAMASTER.

Page 404. 7 Apr 1783. THOS. ANDERSON & wife SARAH, Hanover Co; PETER STONER & wife FRANCES, AC, to DAVID PATTESON, Buckingham Co, for Ŀ3150 - tract on James River known as Fish Pond and includes land of great Sycamore Island - except 84 acres which now belongs to said DAVID. Part of the land was willed by Col. ALLEN HOWARD, dec'd., to his son, JOHN HOWARD, and by him sold to the said THOMAS, 8 May 1780, and rec. in AC. Wit: SAML. SPENCER, JOS. GOODWIN, GEO. BLAKEY, JOS. BLAKEY, FRANCIS SPENCER, JNO. BAGBY.

Page 406. 7 Jul 1783. JAS. DILLARD, AC, to WM. MEREDITH, AC, for Ŀ35000 tobacco, 120 acres fork of Tye and Buffalo. Lines: Raven Creek, STEPHEN WATTS, WM. SPENCER, WM. MEREDITH.

Page 407. 7 May 1783. RICH. HARVIE, Albemarle, to ISAAC TINSLEY, AC, for Ŀ50, 49 acres S branch Harris. Lines: DUNCAN GRAHAM; part of grantor's land. Wit: WM. TINSLEY, DANL. HARVIE, THOS. GOOCH.

Page 408. 7 Jul 1783. THOS. HILLEY & wife MARY, AC, to JNO. WOOD, Albemarle, for Ŀ125, 250 acres on three forks of Pedlar. Wit: JNO. PENN, RICH. BALLENGER.

Page 409. 3 Mar 1783. GEO. LEE to GABL. PENN, AC, for Ŀ58, 58 acres Glebe tract adj. GABL. PENN. Orig. del. to PENN Jul 1784.

Page 410.   26 May 1783.   Commission to quiz MARGARET McDANIEL, wife of
           GEO., as to deed conveying 54 acres on Tobacco Row Mt. to
DRURY TUCKER. Done, 9 Jun 1783, by AMBROSE & BENJ. RUCKER.

Page 411.   26 May 1782.   Commission to Henry Co. J.P.'s: JNO. DILLARD &
           HENRY LYNE to quiz RUTH PENN, wife of ABRAHAM PENN, as to deed
of 21 Sep 1772(sic) - 301 acres to DRURY TUCKER, S branch Harris. Done
18 Jun 1783.

Page 412.   5 Jul 1783.   DRURY TUCKER & wife FRANKEY, AC, to DANL. GAINES,
           AC, for Ł50, 54 acres Tobacco Row Mt. Lines: formerly ABRAHAM
PENN, but now GAINES. Wit: GABL. PENN, SAML. MEREDITH JR, FRANCIS LEE.
Orig. del. to AMBROSE RUCKER for GAINES, 8 Jun 1784.

Page 413.   5 Jul 1783.   DRURY TUCKER & wife FRANKEY, AC, to DANL. GAINES,
           AC, for Ł300, 301 acres S side Harris Creek and E side Tobacco
Row - bought by DRURY TUCKER, Henry Co. and rec. 21 Sep 1772. Part of it
contains 136 acres from BAYLOR WALKER to ABRAHAM PENN. Lines: HARVEY;
one part - 165 acres from GEO. McDANIEL to said PENN. Wit: same as above.

Page 414.   -- Jul 1783.   GEO. BLAIN, AC, to GEO. GALASPIE, AC, for 5 sh.,
           Deed of Trust to secure Ł11,900 tobacco of Richmond or Man-
chester inspection - to PATRICK ROSE in trust; 11 horses, much stock etc.
Due 25 Dec 1784. Wit: HUGH ROSE, ELIZ. MILLER, SUSANNA DEMSEY. Rec. 7 Jul
1783.

Page 415.   10 Mar 1783.   FRANCIS BUCKNER, Caroline, to JAS. UPSHAW JR,
           Essex - for parcel of negroes received from ELIZABETH UPSHAW,
AC; also other slaves. Wit: JNO. CHRISTIAN, WILLIAM HORSLEY, JAS. DILLARD
JR.

Page 416.   21 May 1783.   MATT. NIGHTINGALE, AC, to BENJ. FORSYTHE for
           Ł11,290 tobacco of Richmond inspection - Deed of Trust, 5 sh.
slave, Moll, and son Jesse & daughter Esther. Due 21 Aug 1783. Wit: ZACH.
TALIAFERRO, CATHERINE NIGHTINGALE.

Page 417.   10 Feb 1783.   WM. AARON & wife ELIZ., AC, to WM. CABELL, AC,
           for Ł20, 150 acres both sides Cabell's Mill Creek and pat. to
grantor 20 Jul 1780. Wit: WILL CABELL JR, SAML JORDAN CABELL, MARY ORR
PRICHARD, HECTOR CABELL.

Page 419.   4 Aug 1783.   WM. TYREE & JNO. WILLIAMS, AC, to WM. AARON, for
           Ł25, 90 acres N side and joining Tye. Upper part of 180 acres
pat. to grantor (TYREE), 20 Jul 1780. Lines: Joe's Falls on Tye.

Page 420.   31 May 1783.   JAS. BIAS, AC, to WM. CAMDEN, AC, for Ł24, 60
           acres pat. to BIAS at Williamsburg 3 Aug 1771. S branch Huff
Creek. Lines: BENJ. NOELL, JNO. COLEMAN, FRYE(?) STATAIMS's(?) named Old
Cove. Wit: JOS. TUCKER, GEO. DUNCAN, JNO. DUNCAN.

Page 421.   31 May 1783.   BENJ. NOELL, AC, to WM. CAMDEN, AC, for Ł120,
           150 acres and pat. to grantor at Williamsburg 16 Feb 1770.
On branches of Huff Creek. Lines: JAS. ISON, JAS. STINNETT. Wit: JOS.
TUCKER, JNO. & GEO. DUNCAN. This and above deed del. to CAMDEN 7 Jan 1791.

Page 422.   4 Aug 1783.   GEO. WORTHAM & wife JUDAH, AC, to JAS. MAYS, AC,
           for Ł200, 182 acres N side Tye. Lines: JAS. DILLARD (formerly
RICH. TANKERSLEY JR), CHAS ROSE, N bank Tye. Bought by grantor from STE-
PHEN WATTS 4 Aug 1777.

Page 423.   24 May 1783.   DANL. GAINES, AC, about to travel to southern
           states - power of atty. to HUGH ROSE to collect and sell if
necessary. Wit: WM. GOODE, GABL. PENN, RICH. FULCHER.

Page 423.   1 Sep 1783.   RICH. TANKERSLEY & wife MARY, AC, to JAS. DILLARD,
           AC, one negro girl, Watsey, and Ł20,000 tobacco to be deliver-
ed on James River in two deliveries. Also two adj. tracts and where grantor lives. 1) 150 acres on N bank Tye. Lines: JOS. DILLARD, JOS. MAYS.
2) 174 acres. Lines: ROSE, GLASBY, DILLARD, a Stoney Hill. Orig. del. to
Capt. JAMES DILLARD 13 Jul 1797.

Page 424.   9 Sep 1783.   GEO. GILBERT, AC, to WIATT POWELL, AC, for ₺250,
            206 acres on branch of Rutledge and Tribulation Creek and part
of GILBERT's tract and where he now lives.   44 acres of it bought of JNO.
DAVIS. Lines: EDWD. WATSON, JAS. PENDLETON, JNO. DAVID; a "rode". Wit:
JAS. FRANKLIN, JAS. STEWART, MAURIES GILBERT.   (I can't be dogmatic without tracing the property, but feel almost sure that this property is the
place now owned by Mr. and Mrs. R.L PUTT. It is located on what is now
called Sunset Drive and they bought it from Mrs. NOYES. They have a copy
of the old insurance policy which is dated around 1800 and there is a
sketch of the house (still standing and in excellent state) and grounds.
At that time the place belonged to WIATT POWELL.   Mr. and Mrs. PUTT have
had a film made of the original policy. BFD)

Page 425.   3 Oct 1783.   JOS. MORRIS, AC, to ARCHELAUS ALLAWAY STRANGE, AC,
            for ₺20, 10 acres on Hickory Creek and adj. both of them.
Line: two ridges.

Page 426.   6 Oct 1783.   JAS. THOMAS, AC, to EZEKIEL GILBERT, AC, for ₺100,
            170 acres on Muddy Ass Run. Formerly that of THOS. LUMPKIN.
Lines: EDMD. WINSTON, MOSES SWENEY, JNO. DAVIS, JNO. McDANIEL. Wit:
DAVID WOODROOF, WM. OGLESBY SR, RICH. POWELL. (Note: This name of the
run intrigued me and I asked several lawyers to verify my interpretation
of it.   One of the deputy clerks said that just a few weeks prior to my
running across this item, a Mr. WOODROOF from this area had come into
the office and had asked if anyone knew that such a run was so named. It
has been a well de-emphasized secret for no one knew of such a name. However, he insisted that such was the case. It is interesting to note that
a DAVID WOODROOF was one of the witnesses to the document so the modern
WOODROOF is probably of the same clan. BFD)

Page 427.   20 Jun 1783.   JNO. MERRITT, AC, to JNO. CRITTENDON, AC, for
            ₺60, 300 acres N branch Stovall. Lines: JOS. CREWS, STOVALL's
road, GEO. JEFFERSON, Isham's branch. Wit: HENRY TURNER, EDWD. WATSON,
JNO. TURNER.

Page 429.   4 Oct 1783.   ARCHELAUS STRANGE & wife ELIZ., AC, to ELIJAH
            STONE, Fluvanna, for ₺100, 243 acres in AC and Albemarle and
where grantor and wife live on Rockfish. All that grantor had of THOS.
SOWELL (SORRELL?). Lines: JOS. MORRIS, ABRAHAM STRANGE; 10 acres of it
bought of JOS. MORRIS. Wit: ABRAHAM STRANGE, EPHRAIM BLAINE, JAS. FOSTER.
Orig. del. to STONE, Apr 1789.

Page 429.   20 Sep 1783.   SAML. SAHCKELFORD & wife NANCY (signed ANN), AC,
            to PHILLIP THURMOND, AC, for ₺1000, two tracts. 1) 632 acres.
Lines: CHAS. TALIAFERRO. Part of 3553 acres on Horsley pat. to LUNSFORD
LOMAX SR, in 1764, and by him and wife JUDITH, to LUNSFORD LOMAX, JR, on
13 Jan 1767. Wit: CHAS. ELLIS, SHEROD MORE GALASPIE, VALENTINE PAYTON,
JNO. PAYTON, ISAAC WRIGHT, PETER CARTER, JOSIAH ELLIS. Memo: 14 acres
joining FRANK POWELL sold out of the land to THOS. POWELL TAYLOR. (Note:
Here again heels of THURMONDS & GILLESPIES are seen in the same ground.
SHEROD MORE GALASPIE was a captain in the Revolution and was a son of
GEO. GILLESPIE (several variations in spelling). SHEROD was a brother of
WILLIAM GILLESPIE who married ANN or NANCY HUDSON, daughter of JOSHUA. I
have previously pointed out tha WM. & wife went to Madison County, Ky,
from Amherst. Their daughter, MARY, married in Ky. HENDERSON THURMAN and
he is my enigma. The THURMANS(MONDS) and GILLESPIES are seen to have been
closely associated in Amherst, but to date I am unable to identify the
parents of HENDERSON THURMAN.   HENDERSON is my wife's ancestor and I have
worked on this puzzle for years. BFD)

Page 431.   1 Sep 1783.   JNO. POWELL, AC, to JNO. BROWN, AC, (del. to him
            May 1787) for ₺5000 tobacco, 200 acres branch of Horsley.
Lines: JNO. POWELL, ISAAC WRIGHT; part of tract of grantor. Wit: JAS.
TURNER, RICH. OGLESBY, ABRAHAM STRANGE.

Page 432.   11 Oct 1782.   JOSHUA HUDSON & wife MARY, AC, to RUSH HUDSON,
            Orange Co, for ₺100, 150 acres N branch Buffalo. Part of
JOSHUA'a land where he liveth. Lines: REUBEN BANKS, MEREDITH, the planta-
tion. Wit: PHILLIP GOOCH, LINN BANKS, PULLIAM SANDIDGE, JOSHUA HUDSON JR.
Orig. del. 11 Oct 1782.

206

Page 433.   1 Sep 1783.   BENJ. WASH, AC, to JAS. GOODWIN for ₤1000, 121
            acres N side Tobacco Row and branch of Horsley.

Page 434.   6 Oct 1783.   JNO. JOPLING, Burk Co, NC, to JNO. EDMONDS JR, AC,
            for ₤1250, and likely young black "mair", 500 acres S side
Berry's Mt. Part of 2000 acres pat. to SAML. SPENCER Sr. Sept. 10, 1755.
Lines: S side and joining Rucker's Run. Wit: JAS. PAMPLIN, WM. HORSLEY,
JNO. PENN, MATT. TUCKER, WM. COFFEY.

Page 435.   1 Sep 1783.   JAS. GOODRICH, AC, to WM. WARE, AC, for ₤70, 101
            acres N branch Horsley; part of a tract of grantor. Lines:
JNO. GOODRICH, JAS. GOODRICH.

Page 436.   Return on 29 Aug 1783; Rec. 6 Oct 1783.   Order to Henry Co.
            J.P.'s ABRAHAM PENN & JNO. SALMON, to quiz ELLENOR WHITSITT,
wife of WM. WHITSITT, as to dower - deed of 1 Oct 1781, to JOS. CREWS
for 500 acres.

Page 437.   6 Oct 1783.   JOS. GRYMER & wife GRACE (mark of CRISSUS), AC,
            to JNO. SCOTT, Albemarle, for ₤3, 116 acres in Albemarle and
Fluvanna on S side Hardware River. Lines: County; part of 250 acres pat.
to grantor 1 Mar 1781. Wit: RO. WRIGHT, WM. KEY, HELEN HILE BURTON.

Page 439.   6 Oct 1783.   JOS. GRYMES & wife GRACE, AC, to JAS. HOPKINS,
            AC, for ₤5, 134 acres in Albemarle and Fluvanna on S side of
Hardware River. Lines: County; JNO. SCOTT, HOPKINS, crossing two roads,
JNO. MORRIS; pat. on same date as previous deed for 250 acres. Wit: Same
as previous deed.

Page 440.   6 Oct 1783.   CHAS. ELLIS & wife SALLY, AC, to RICH. WILBRON,
            AC, for ₤30, 118 acres on Horsley. Lines: EDMD. GOODRICH,
CHAS. DAVIS, WM. CLOPTON, AMBROSE EUBANK. Wit: WM. HORSLEY, EDMD. GOOD-
RICH, WM. TUCKER.

Page 441.   6 Oct 1783.   THOS. WILSHER & wife ANNE, AC, to WM. BONES for
            ₤80, 100 acres. Lines: WM. WRIGHT. Bought by grantor of WM.
HIBBITS & wife JANE, 2 Aug 1779.

Page 442.   16 Sep 1783.   JNO. CARTWRIGHT & wife MARTHA, AC, to LUCAS
            POWELL, AC, for ₤25,000 tobacco, 385 acres N side Tye. 1)
120 acres, part of tract of 135 acres bought by grantor of AMBROSE JONES
16 Feb 1770. 2) 265 acres joining and bought of LUNSFORD LOMAX JR, 5 Mar
1770. Wit: JUSTINIAN CARTWRIGHT, WM. POWELL, GEO. GALASPIE. Orig. del.
16 Feb 1812, to T. HAWKINS(?) per order. (Note: This is part of the PETER
CARTWRIGHT group and data on my wife's ancestor, GEO. GILLESPIE, shows
that he had a daughter, FANNY, who was wife of JESSE CARTWRIGHT. There
is no bond here, but deed data shows JESSE & wife in Kentucky. The CART-
WRIGHTS moved to my native state and the famous Circuit rider, PETER,
served there for some years and later went to Ill. I prize my copy of
the autobiography of PETER CARTWRIGHT. BFD)

Page 444.   Rec. 6 Oct 1783.   The dower relinquishment by MARTHA PENN,
            wife of PHILLIP PENN, as to deed to AUGUSTINE STEEL, 4 Nov
1782, to land on N branch Buffalo. AC J.P.'s.

Page 445.   5 Nov 1783.   JOSIAS GILBERT, AC, to BENJ. RUCKER, for ₤172,
            172 acres at confluence of Crooked Run with Rutledge and adj.
HIGGINBOTHAM.

Page 446.   1 Sep 1783.   WM. PETER & wife FRANCES, AC, to THOS. JENKINS of
            AC, for ₤65, 140 acres Cedar Creek and branch of Pedlar. Part
of 480 acres conveyed to RICH. PETER by JOELL WATKINS and by RICHARD
PETER to WM. PETER and of record. Lines: WM. PETER"s plantation on creek;
HUGH McCABE, JOEL WATKINS' former line; includes plantation where RICHARD
PETER now lives. Wit: none. Orig. del. to grantee 6 Jan 1791.

Page 447.   3 Sep 1783.   LEVI(Y) BALDOCK & wife ANNE, and ELIZ. BALDOCK,
            AC, to JNO. WHITEHEAD, AC, for ₤137-10, 252 acres where LEVI
lives and which he and RICH. BALDOCK bought of WM. CAMDEN. Lines: JNO.
HIGGINBOTHAM, BENJ. NOWELL, NOELL JOHNSON. Wit: JNO. PENN, NOELL JOHNSON,

WM. CAMDEN.

Page 448. 22 Nov 1782. RICH. DAVIS & wife TIRZAH, AC, to JAMES HIGGIN-
BOTHAM, AC, for Ł350, 204 acres on Higginbotham Mill Creek.
Lines: JAS., MOSES, & JNO. HIGGINBOTHAM, JNO. BROWN, WM. CABELL. It was
conveyed by MOSES HIGGINBOTHAM 14 May 1751, to WM. MORRISON. WM. MORRI-
SON, by will, gave the 204 acres to his daughter, TIRZAH. Reference to
Albemarle documents. Wit: SAML., JNO. & THOS. HIGGINBOTHAM.

Page 449. 3 Nov 1783. ABNER WITT, AC, heir at law of CHARLES WITT, decd,
5 sh. paid by JNO. WITT, AC, ABNER releases all claims to estate of his brother, CHARLES - land in partnership with JNO. & CHAS. WITT
which was bought of NATHL. BARNETT - 280 acres on S fork Rockfish.

Page 451. 7 Jul 1783. JNO. SCOTT, AC, to GEO. COLEMAN, JOS. PENN, &
GABL. PENN, as trustees, for 5 sh. and for love JNO. SCOTT has
for his wife, ELIZ., and children, 310 acres on S branch of Buffalo and
where SCOTT lives and joins DRURY TUCKER. Also 12 slaves named; furniture,
stock, etc. on plantation. SCOTT is to manage, but subject to control of
trustees. If at any time hereafter, SCOTT certifies that a happy reconciliation has taken place between his wife, ELIZ., and him and she sub-
scribes to it - then trustees are to re-convey to him. If no reconciliation takes place, then all at Scott's death goes to his children by ELI-
ZABETH. Wit: S. MEREDITH, WIATT POWELL, SAML. MEREDITH JR, WM. MEREDITH.
Note: I am unable to furnish the sequel to this sad state of affairs. It
may be that later deeds will reveal that a reconciliation took place. I
have not checked for this angle. However, there is nothing in the will
books to give us a postscript. If she was the ELIZ. DILLARD who married
JNO. SCOTT in 1772, there is nothing in DILLARD data in wills to throw
any light upon this. BFD)

Page 452. 9 Aug 1783. RICH. DAVIS, AC, to WM. WARE, for Ł100, 200 acres
N fork on N branch of Horsley. Lines: MOSES DAVIS, RICH. DAVIS.
Wit: HENRY PAYTON, DAVID JARRELL, PETER CARTER, MOSES DAVIS. Orig. del.
to WARE, 28 Oct 1787.

Page 454. 1 Mar 1784. FRANCIS MERIWETHER, AC, to JNO. COLES, Albemarle,
for Ł800, 782 acres where he lives in three surveys. West side
of Rockfish. Lines: CHISWELL, Major MERIWETHER, CLAPHAM.

Page 455. 10 Feb 1784. JNO. STEWART, SR, AC, to BENJ. RUCKER, AC, for
Ł251, 200 acres fork of Rutledge and Crooked Run. Lines: WM.
CHAPPELL on Lynch's road; JOS. MAYS to Crooked Run. ANN, wife of STEWART.
Wit: WIATT POWELL, ISAAC & ANTHONY RUCKER.

Page 456. 28 Jan 1784. JNO. STEWART & wife ANN (Sr.), AC, to WIATT POW-
ELL, AC, for Ł150, 60 acres on Rutledge. Part of tract and
where he lives. Lines: Top of hill by Lynch's road; Stewart's Spring
Branch, N fork Rutledge, main creek, GEO. COLEMAN. Wit: EZEK. GILBERT,
WM. CHAPPEL, J. STEWART JR.

Page 457. 26 Jul 1783. CARTER BRAXTON & wife ELIZ, King William Co, to
SAML. MEREDITH, AC, for Ł400, 1364 acres branch of Rutledge
and known as Old Church Tract. Lines: DANL. GAINES, pat. line, HENRY GIL-
BERT, dec'd, RICH. GATEWOOD, HIGGINBOTHAM. Wit: CHAS. IRVING, JNO. SCOTT,
JAS. FRANKLIN.

Page 459. 1 Mar 1784. WM. CABELL & wife PEGGY, AC, to their son, SAML.
JORDAN CABELL, AC, 1444 acres upon a certain promise - N branch Tye - tract whereon Amherst Courthouse now stands; 1020 acres of it
bought of RICH. ALLCOCK, 1 Jun 1772; 374 acres of it bought of AMBROSE
JONES 17 Mar 1774. Reservation of ordinary and plantation at courthouse
and as much land and timber as needed during lives.

Page 460. Shff. bond - RODERICK McCULLOCH, 1 Mar 1784. Bondsmen: PAT-
RICK ROSE RICK ROSE (for HUGH ROSE), CHAS. TALIAFERRO, GABL. PENN,
JOSIAH ELLIS, THOS. HAWKINS.

Page 460. 12 May 1783. ELISHA LYON, AC, to JNO. CRITTENDON, AC, for
Ł120, 140 acres E side of N fork Stovall Creek. Lines: NICHL.

LYON, BAILEY, MERRITT, RO. JOHNS. Wit: JNO. TURNER, RICH. HAZELWOOD CRIT-
TENDON, HENRY TURNER, JNO. KNIGHT, ABRAHAM LAMASTER.

Page 462.   1 Mar 1784.   WM. TUCKER, AC, to JNO. RICHARDSON, AC, for
            Ł12,000 tobacco, 170 acres both sides Buffalo. Lines: WM.
BURTON, dec'd, JNO. PENN, JNO. SCOTT, JESSE KENADY, PHILLIP PENN, LYNDSAY
COLEMAN. Wit: JNO. HILL, HENRY HARPER, JNO. EWERS. Orig. del. with com-
mission 24 Mar 1790, to AM. RUCKER JR.

Page 463.   1 Mar 1784.   WM. POLLARD & wife WINNIFRED, AC, to WM. GALT for
            Ł320, 360 acres on Tribulation. Lines: Lynch road; BALER WAL-
KER, dec'd, EZEK. GILBERT.   Surveyed by WIATT GILBERT and conveyed by
him and wife SARAH, to WM. POLLARD.

Page 464.   1 Feb 1784.   ELIJAH & JOELL GILLENWATERS, AC, to PLEDGE PALMER,
            AC, for Ł90, 123 acres Bolling's Creek. Lines: Duck Bill
Branch, JOHNSON, CLARK.   Wit: THOS. LUCAS, S. JOHNSON, SAML. HANDLY, ED-
MOND TYLER, JNO. MERRITT, ELIJAH GOODWIN, JAS. SIMMONDS.

Page 465.   1 Mar 1784.   SAML. MEREDITH, AC, to NOTLEY MATTUCKS, AC, for
            Ł75-18, 253 acres S branch Rutledge. Lines: JOS. HIGGINBOTHAM,
DANL. GAINES, STEWART, pat. line. Part of tract.   (Note: This is really
MADDOX and his name is usually so spelled. BFD)

Page 466.   -- 1784, Rec. 3 May 1784.   DAVID MERIWETHER, AC, to AUGUSTINE
            SHEPHERD, Albemarle, for Ł560, 723 acres both sides of Taylor
Creek. Lines: JACK GILMORE. Wit: BEN TALIAFERRO, JNO. HAGGARD, MOSES
CLARK.   (Note: A very poor scribe takes over just here and the writing
is terrible.BFD)   Orig. del. to HAGGARD per order Mar, 1791.

Page 468.   -- 1784, rec. 3 May 1784.   DAVID MERIWETHER, AC, to AUGUSTINE
            SHEPHERD, Albemarle, for Ł130, 170 acres Taylor's Creek.
Lines: SAML. MANN, ARCHIBALD WOODS. Wit: as above. Orig. del. 21 Mar
1791.

Page 469.   -- 1784, Rec. 3 May 1784.   DAVID MERIWETHER, AC, to AUGUSTINE
            SHEPHERD, Albemarle, for Ł40, 99 acres N branch Taylor Creek.
Wit: same as above. Orig. del. per order, 21 Mar 1791.

Page 471.   15 May 1784.   WM. WITT, AC, to LITTLEBERRY WITT for Ł96, 96
            acres in cove of a mt., Rockfish. Lines: JOS. ROBERTS, SAML.
LACKEY. Orig. del. to WITT 21 Jul 1786.

Page 472.   29 Mar 1784.   ABNER WITT, AC, to WM. WITT, AC, for Ł110, 111
            acres in cove of a mt., Short's Creek, head of a branch. Lines:
JNO. CHISWELL, ABNER WITT, top of the ridge. Wit: LITTLE BERRY WITT,
LEWIS WITT, JAS. LITTRELL.   Orig. del. to LITTLEBERRY WITT for WM. WITT
21 Jul 1786.

Page 473.   27 Apr 1784.   JNO. GRIGGORY & wife SARAH, AC, to WM. CABELL,
            AC, for Ł40, 100 acres N branch Rucker's Run; part of 258
acres pat. to HENRY KEY 20 Sep 1759, and conveyed by him to GRIGGORY and
rec. in AC. Lines: JNO. HARMER, HENRY KEY. Wit: WM. CABELL JR, JNO. STA-
PLES, JNO. BUSH, THOS. HOOTON.

Page 475.   29 Apr 1784.   WM. WITT, AC, to DAVID WITT for Ł27, 27 acres
            branch of Short's Creek. Lines: WM. WITT, ABNER WITT; bought
of JAS. TULEY. Orig. del. to WITT, 21 Jul 1786.

Page 476.   6 Feb 1784.   WM. ELLIOT, AC, and wife MILLEY, to JNO. THOMAS,
            AC, for Ł160, 200 acres branch Rockfish. Wit: ELLIOTT ROBERTS,
JNO. ROBERTS, HENRY ROBERTS.

Page 478.   -- 1784, rec. 3 May 1784.   IGNATIOUS RAINS & wife NANNY, AC,
            to JESSE KENEDY, AC, for Ł25, 150 acres whereon grantee lives.
Lines: Long Branch, path from JOS. DILLARD, JOS. MAYS' former residence,
MASES' fence, JAS. MAYS' Spring branch. Wit: THOS. HAWKINS, THOS. LANDRUM
JR. Signed ANN RAINS. Orig. del. to grantee 11 Nov 1788.

Page 479.   2 Apr 1784.   WM. HORRELL & wife ELIZ, Albemarle, to ABNER WITT,

AC, for Ł100, 193 acres N side N branch Davis Creek. Lines: JNO. WADE (as were) which he sold to WM. MARTIN & MARTIN to JNO. HARRIS. Wit: LITTLE-BERRY WITT, WM. & LEWIS WITT. Orig. del. to BARTLETT EADES by WITT's order.

Page 480.   5 Dec 1783.   JAS. RILEY, District of Camden, S.C., to JAS. TURNER, AC, for Ł60, 270 acres E side Rockfish below mouth of Cove Creek and above and below Jumon(?) Creek on other side. Wit: LEONARD, MATT., & DAVID PHILLIPS, JNO. TURNER.

Page 480.   22 Apr 1784.   WM. HITCHCOCK & wife MARY, AC, to JAS. TURNER, AC, for Ł50, 172 acres N side Davis and joins DAVID MONTGOMERY, MATT. HARRIS, & JAS. TURNER. Wit: DAVID & JAS. MONTGOMERY, THOS. MATTHEWS, MATT. PHILLIPS.

Page 481.   1 Mar 1784.   THOS. WRIGHT & wife CORDILIA, AC, to JNO. HENRY GOODWIN, AC, for Ł100, 22 acres on Lynch's road. Wit: JAS. SIMONS SR, JOS. CREWS, JNO. TENISON.

Page 482.   1 Mar 1784.   THOS. WRIGHT & wife CORDILIA, AC, and JNO. TENESON, AC, to JNO. WARD, Campbell Co, for Ł150, 260 acres on James River. Lines: JNO. TENNISON, S fork crossing. Wit: BALLINGER WADE, JOS. CREWS, JAS. SIMONS. Orig. del. to JNO. WARD, 7 Nov 1815.

Page 484.   11 Mar 1784.   JNO. WOOD, AC, to JAS. HOPKINS, for Ł17-10, 70 acres branch of Nassau near the Rockey Mt. Wit: JAS. WOOD, WM. BURGESS, WM. MARTIN. Orig. del. to JNO. LOVING per JAS. HOPKINS' order.

Page 486.   1 Mar 1784.   THOS. WRIGHT & wife CORDILIA, AC, to JNO. TENISON, AC, for Ł100, 30 acres N side of S fork of Frost's Creek and joining grantee. All WRIGHT holds on N side of the said fork. Wit: BALLINGER WADE, JOS. CREWS, JAS. SIMMONS, JR.

Page 487.   4 Oct 1784.   SAML. MEREDITH, AC, to WM. MAY, Jefferson Co. - power of atty. to prosecute suit, if any, to confirm my right to several tracts in Jefferson Co. as of 15 Jun 1781, and 25 Dec 1782. Entered in Surveyor's book in said county. Wit: EDMD. WINSTON, JOS. PENN. (Note: MAY's data is one of finest sources of Kentucky land items. BFD)

Page 488.   16 Sep 1783.   RICH. PETER, AC, to THOS. MORRIS, AC, for Ł30, 200 acres both sides Cedar Creek; lower part of 480 acres grantor got by deed from JOEL WATKINS. Lines: WM. PETER, a little below his mill; THOS. MORRIS, JOEL WATKINS' former line, DAVID BURKS, HUGH McCABE. Wit: JOS. GOODWIN, JNO. HOGG, EDWD. SAUNDERSON, WM. PETER.

Page 489.   15 Mar 1784.   WM. SMITH, AC, to GEO. DAVIS, AC, for Ł50, 120 acres surveyed 13 Nov 1771. S side and joining Otter Creek. Lines: RO. JOHNSON. Wit: SAML. HIGGINBOTHAM, JER. TAYLOR, BALLINGER WADE, RICH. POWELL. Orig. del. to Grantee, 24 Dec 1788.

Page 490.   1 May 1784.   WM. MATTHEWS, AC, to WM. WHITTON for Ł30, 136 acres surveyed 20 Apr 1773; N branch Otter. Lines: his own, JNO. HOGG. Wit: RODERICK McCULLOCH, JOSIAH ELLIS, THOS. WAUGH.

Page 491.   1 May 1784.   WM. MATTHEWS, AC, to WM. WHITTEN, for Ł70, 380 acres surveyed 20 Apr 1773, on branch of Thomas Mill Creek and N branch of Otter. Lines: JAS. KITCHEN, JNO. HOGG, RO. JOHNSTON. Wit: RODERICK McCULLOCH, JOSIAH ELLIS, THOS. WAUGH.

Page 492.   3 May 1784.   SARY HENRY, Sole legatee of JNO. HENRY, Hanover, and SAML. MEREDITH, Exr. of JNO. HENRY, dec'd, to PETER RIPPETO for Ł10,000 tobacco, 523 acres. Lines: MOSES MARTIN. Wit: W. GOODE, P. ROOT, EDMD. WINSTON, DAN. GAINES.

Page 493.   20 Dec 1783.   WM. GATEWOOD, JR, AC, to AMBROSE GATWEOOD, AC, for Ł200, 150 acres in Lexington Parish. Lines: WM. DILLARD, PETER JOINER, the Road, Mouth of a branch, CHAS. CHRISTIAN, Stovall's road; near OWNSBY's cabbin. Wit: PETER JOINER, CHAS. CHRISTIAN, JAS. CHRISTIAN, RICH. GATEWOOD.

Page 494. 7 Feb 1784. HENRY GILBERT, AC, - Deed of Trust - to SAML.
MEREDITH, AC, Ŀ10,000 tobacco due 1 Mar 1783 - consideration
of Ŀ232 Richmond inspection and market. Slaves, Sarah, a wench; Toby, at
Ŀ90, Stock; in possession of Capt. JNO. STEWART. Wit: WIATT POWELL, WM.
GALT, JAS. FRANKLIN.

Page 495. 3 May 1784. SAML. MEREDITH, AC, to JNO. JOHNSON, AC, for Ŀ30,
130 acres N branch Rockey Run. Lines: JOS. WILCHER, SAML. MERE-
DITH; part of a tract sold by MEREDITH to JNO. STEWART JR, and by him to
JOHN JOHNSON.

Page 496. 5 Jun 1784. WM. HORRELL & wife ELIZ., Albemarle, to ABNER
WITT, AC, for Ŀ76, 76 acres on Davis Creek and adj. JOHN
JOHNSON.

Page 497. 5 Jun 1784. JNO. WITT, AC, to ELISHA WITT, AC, for Ŀ60, 60
acres branch Rockfish. Lines: GEO. WITT, JOSIAH DODD.

Page 498. 1 Dec 1783. OBEDIAH MARTIN, Caswell Co, N.C. Province, to JNO.
MARTIN, AC, for Ŀ170, 200 acres and part of 1650 acres of Capt.
JAS. MARTIN. Wit: JAS. MARTIN, JAS. MARTIN JR, AZARIAH MARTIN SR. & JR.,
WM. MARTIN. Del. to grantee's widow - no date given.

Page 499. 24 Sep 1778. HENRY KIRBY & wife PATTY, AC, to JAS. FRANKLIN,
AC, for Ŀ100, 150 acres head of Franklin Creek. Wit: JACOB
SMITH, JNO. SMITH, JAS. FRANKLIN.

Page 501. 26 May 1784. FRANCIS MERIWETHER, AC, to JNO. LOBBIN, AC, for
Ŀ10, 99 acres N branch Rockfish and side of Pilate Mts. Lines:
ALEX. HENDERSON, ALEX. PATTON, SAML. MURRELL. Wit: THOS. EWERS, WM.
HARRIS, JNO. GILMORE, JNO. MURRELL, THOS. PATTON.

Page 502. 1 Dec 1783. DRURY TUCKER, AC, to DANL. TUCKER, for Ŀ100, 250
acres S side Mobley's Mt. on Buffalo. Part of tract of DRURY's
bought of JAS. MOBLEY. Lines: Capt. CHAS. BURRUS on the thoroughfare
branch; MICAJA OGLESBY. Wit: CHAS. ELLIS, WM. TUCKER, WM. OGLESBY JR,
RICH. HARRISON, SAML. FRANKLIN.

Page 503. 7 Jun 1784. JAS. GOODRICH, AC, to MARTHA HUDSON, AC, for Ŀ30,
68 acres on Horsley; part of a tract. Lines: WM. WARE, THOS.
GOODRICH. (Note: I am unable to tie this woman into the JOSHUA HUDSON
family from her will data etc. here. BFD)

Page 504. 7 Jun 1784. MOSES RAY, AC, to WM. CABELL, AC, for Ŀ150, two
tracts. 1) 300 acres near Fluvanna River; opposite Swift Islands and where RAY now lives. Pat. to MOSES RAY, dec'd, 10 Sep 1755.
2) 9 acres - an island in Fluvanna River whereon RAY has a fishery and
known as Swift Island. Pat. to MOSES RAY, Dec'd, 15 Dec 1749.

Page 505. 23 Oct 1783. THOMPSON GLIN, Surry Co, N.C., to WM. WOOD, Albemarle, for Ŀ65, 119 acres head waters Beaver Creek. Part of
tract pat. to THOS. THOMPSON. Wit: JESSE WOOD, GOODMAN BARKSDALE, WM.
WOOD JR.

Page 506. 13 Mar 1784. Order to JNO. DIGGS & JAS. HOPKINS to quiz MAR-
THA MERIWETHER, wife of FRANCIS, as to deed to JNO. COLES -
682 acres, 1 Mar 1784. AC J.P.'s.

Page 507. 5 Jul 1784. DANL. GAINES & wife MARY, AC, to JONATHAN WILSON,
AC, for Ŀ50, 54 acres on Tobacco Row. Next to 301 acres con-
veyed by GAINES & wife to grantee. Reference to deed by DRURY TUCKER to
GAINES, 5 Jul 1783, and acknowledged on 7th and rec. on "page 412".

Page 508. 5 Jun 1784. DANL. GAINES & wife MARY, AC, to JONATHAN WILSON,
AC, for Ŀ100, 301 acres on Harris Creek and E side of Tobacco
Row. Conveyed by DRURY TUCKER to GAINES and ref. to page 413 of deed book.

Page 509. 1 Apr 1784. ARCHILUS MITCHEL, AC, to GABL. PENN, AC, for
Ŀ400, 200 acres N side Buffalo and joining. Lines: GEORGE PENN
on Buffalo. Wit: WM. SID CRAWFORD, PHILLIP ROOTS, JAS. FRANKLIN.

Page 510. 4 Jan 1784. JAS. STEWART, AC, about to remove to Georgia - power of atty. to DANL. GAINES & JNO. STEWART JR. Wit: HENRY GILBERT, PATTRICK REYNOLDS, JUDITH GILBERT, MOURNING FLOYD.

Page 510. 13 Mar 1784. Order to AC J.P.'s to quiz ANN STEWART, wife of JOHN STEWART, as to deed of 28 Jan 1784, to WIATT POWELL. Done 20 Jun 1784, by DANL. GAINES & AMBROSE RUCKER.

Page 511. 4 May 1784. GEO. LEE, AC, to FRANCES LEE, AC, for Ь100, 88 acres N branch Buffalo. Lines: JAS. WATSON, GABL. PENN. Wit: GABL. PENN, WM. SID CRAWFORD, WIATT POWELL.

Page 512. 3 Jul 1784. SAML. MEREDITH to WM. MONTGOMERY, for Ь76, 38 acres. Lines: JOEL CAMPBELL, LAURENCE CAMPBELL, road leading from New Glasgow to JNO. BRON's shop.

Page 513. 5 Jul 1784. JNO. MONTGOMERY & wife JANE, to JNO. DEPRIEST, AC, for Ь700, 252 acres head of one of branches of Rucker's Run. Line of TUGGLE. Conveyed to grantor by LUNSFORD LOMAX JR, 3 Oct 1768. Del. to grantee; no date.

Page 514. 15 May 1784. HENRY GILBERT, AC, to JOSIAH GILBERT, AC, for Ь6, tables, etc. - an interesting and long list. Wit: CH.(?) REYNOLDS, JAS. BAILEY, MAURIS GILBERT. Orig. del. to EZEK. GILBERT, 16 Jul 1785.

Page 516. 15 Nov 1783. WM. GILLESPIE, AC, to PETER CARTER for Ь10,000 tobacco, a slave, Gloucester, about 19. Wit: WM. WALTON, SHEROD MORE GILLESPIE, THOS. WALTON.

Page 516. 24 Jul 1784. THOS. LOMAX, Caroline Co, to WM. WALTON, AC, for Ь600, two tracts on Rucker's Run. 1) 816 acres joining JAS. STEVENS, generally known as Trotter's Cove. 2) 59 acres adj. and known as Walnut Cove. 1) is bounded by STEVENS, MONTGOMERY, old line of LOMAX. 2) by LOMAX old line. Wit: ZACH. TALIAFERRO, JNO. ROSE, PATRICK ROSE, CHAS. ROSE, JNO. TUCKER.

Page 518. 16 Apr 1784. SAML. THOMAS, Essex Co, to JAS. SYMONS, AC, for Ь47-10, 225 acres on Harris Creek. Lines: DANL. BURFORD JR, SYMON's plantation. Wit: RICH. HARRISON, WM. LEE, RICH. GOODWIN, HARDIN HAINS.

Page 520. 16 Apr 1784. SAML. THOMAS, Essex Co, to DANL. BURFORD JR, for Ь47-10, 225 acres on Harris. Lines: BURFORD, JAS. SYMON's plantation, MARGARET MUSHILL(?), HUGH ROSE. Wit: Same as deed above.

Page 521. 23 Jul 1784. HENRY ROBERTS, AC, to CORNL. MURRELL for Ь30, 150 acres N side Corbey's Creek.

Page 522. 21 Dec 1783. JAS. RAY & wife MILLY, Lincoln Co, Va. to JAS. BARNETT, Botetourt Co, for Ь100, 125 acres both sides Pedlar. Willed to JAS. RAY by his father, JNO. RAY; ref. to AC records. Lines: JAS. SMITH, Camp Creek, Pedlar. Wit: ALEX. BLANE, RICH. BALLENGER, JNO. FRANKLIN, EDMD. POWELL, MOSES SWENEY.

Page 523. 5 Jul 1784. JNO. MATTHEWS & wife JANE, AC, to AARON HIGGINBOTHAM, AC, for Ь20, 8 acres at head of Lively Spring Branch; part of tract BALLENGER WADE sold to JNO. WHITLEY; surveyed for RICH. BALLINGER; sold later by MATTHEWS to A. HIGGINBOTHAM. North side Buffalo. Lines: RO. CASH, dec'd., HENDRICK ARNOLD, Wade's old road. Wit: RICH. BALLINGER, MARYAN FRANKLIN, JAS. COTTERELL.

Page 524. 3 Aug 1784. JAS. BARNETT, Botetourt Co, to EDWARD WARE, AC, for Ь100, 125 acres on Pedlar. Pat. to JNO. RAY in 1764. Lines: JAS. SMITH, Camp Creek; near Elk Rock. Wit: JNO. CRAWFORD, THOS. HAWKINS, WM. POWELL, AMBROSE CAMPBELL.

Page 526. 2 Aug 1784. JAS. BIAS & wife ELIZ, AC, to LEMASTER COOKSEY, AC, for Ь78, 170 acres S branch Huff; part of pat. to grantor at Williamsburg 3 Aug 1771. Wit: CHAS. BURRUS, JOS. LAYNE, WM. CAMDEN.

212

Page 527. 7 Jun 1784. JNO. MATTHEWS & wife JANE, AC, to LARKIN SANDIDGE of AC for Ŀ20, 54 acres, bought by grantor of BENJ. HIGGINBO-THAM on S fork Buffalo. Lines: JAS. HIGGINBOTHAM, ISAAC MAYFIELD, AARON HIGGINBOTHAM.

Page 528. 2 Aug 1784. DAVID CRAWFORD, CHAS. BURRUS, & WM. BIBB, attorn-ies in fact for LUCY JOHNSTON, Exrx. of will of ROBT. JOHNSTON dec'd, all of AC, to WM. CABELL, AC, 5 sh. and making out 16 plats and certificates of survey - formerly made for RO. JOHNSTON, dec'd, and re-turning them to Registrar's office. Land at Fendley's Gap and pat. to JOHNSTON 7 Jul 1763. Lines: WM. CABELL, top of Fendley's Mt., ABRAHAM WARWICK, crossing the road.

Page 529. 22 Jul 1784. THOS. LOMAX, Caroline Co, to RICH. LAWLESS, AC, for Ŀ40, 200 acres on Horsley Creek. Lines: COL. LUNSFORD LOMAX's old line, SOLOMON CARTER, WM. WARE, MOSES DAVIES. Wit: ZACH. TALIAFERRO, WM. WARE, CHAS. TALIAFERRO, MOSES DAVIS. Orig. del. 7 Nov 1790.

Page 531. 2 Aug 1784. RICH. BALLINGER & wife ELIZ., AC, to JNO. SALE, AC, for Ŀ200, 180 acres on Thresher's Creek; pat. 12 Jul 1750. Lines: PEARCE WADE, JNO. BISWELL, N branch of the creek. Also another tract of 250 acres on same creek and N side of Moll's Mt. and adj. AARON HIGGINBOTHAM. Orig. del. with commission "to take femes' Dower Mar,1790".

Page 532. 20 Jul 1784. Honorable THOS. LOMAX, Caroline, to GEORGE GAL-ASPIE, AC, for Ŀ20-7-4, 122 3/4 acres. Lines: GEO. BLAIN, BIBB. Wit: ZACH. TALIAFERRO, WM. BIBB, BENJ. POWELL, LUCAS POWELL, ELIZ. POWELL. Orig. del. to GEO. BLAINE.

Page 534. 2 Aug 1784. CHAS. BURKS & wife MOLLY, AC, to EDWARD SAUNDER-SON, AC, for Ŀ140, 310 acres both sides Maple Creek; branch of Pedlar. Lines of ARTHUR TOOLEY.

Page 535. 29 Jun 1784. GEO. GILBERT, AC, to EDWARD WATSON,AC, for Ŀ9, 9 acres and part of where grantor lives. Lines: Lumpkin's road; EDWD WATSON; small path leading to Watson's Mt. field. Wit: JNO. McDANIEL, JOS. SWENNEY, WM. MAYS.

Page 536. 27 Mar 1784. THOS. PENN, AC, to CHAS. CHRISTIAN, AC, for Ŀ105, 153 acres in Lexington Parish on Buffalo and Rockey Run. In-cludes the mill on Rockey Run which I bought of RICH. GATEWOOD and where-on I now live. Lines: JNO. CHRISTIAN, mill pond, CHARLES CHRISTIAN, WM. GATEWOOD, mouth of Rockey Run and up it. Wit: CHAS. WILCHER, ANY(AMY?) HOLLADY, JAS. CHRISTIAN, MARY DUKE CHRISTIAN.

Page 538. 3 Aug 1784. MATHEW WILSON & wife AMY, AC, to GEO. BURKS, Buckingham Co, for Ŀ100, adjoining tracts. 1) 169 acres pat. to RO. DAVIS, JR, 3 Mar 1760. Lines: MARVEL STONE, SAML. BURKS, JR, AR-THUR TOOLEY, MICAJAH CLARK. 2) 20 acres and line of JOSIAH ELLIS, DAVID BIRKS. 3) 100 acres conveyed to grantor by STEPEHN GOOLDSBY 3 Jul 1773. Orig. del. to SAML. BURKS.

Page 539. 5 Jul 1784. JESSE MILLS, AC, to TILMAN WALTON, AC, for Ŀ21-10, Deed of Trust - 1 sh. - slave, stock, etc. Wit: RO. WRIGHT, JNO. SWANSON, WM. WALTON.

Page 540. 3 Aug 1784. SAML. MEREDITH, AC, to DANL. GAINES, AC, for Ŀ65, 219 acres S branch Rutledge and next to where GAINES now lives. Part of CARTER BRAXTON tract known as the Old Church Tract. Lines: JOS. HIGGINBOTHAM, NOTLY MATTOX, DANL. GAINES' land bought of JAS. HIG-GINBOTHAM, old field near the old church. Wit: EZEK. GILBERT, JOSIAH GILBERT, MAURIS GILBERT, WIATT POWELL.

Page 541. 3 Aug 1784. DANL. GAINES & wife MARY, AC, to FRANCES LIPSCOMB, Louisa Co, for Ŀ300, 114 acres branches of Rutledge and Por-rage Creek - formerly that of CARTER BRAXTON and called The Old Church Tract. Part of it bought by GAINES of JAS. HIGGINBOTHAM; and part is his patrimonial estate. Lines: JOSEPH HIGGINBOTHAM, NOTLY MADDOX, BRAXTON's pat. line, WM. MAHON's fence.

Page 542. 29 Apr 1784. WM. POLLARD, AC, about to remove to South
        Carolina - power of atty. to WIATT POWELL, AC,. Wit: WM. GALT,
DANL. GAINES, JAS. POLLARD.

Page 543. 4 Sep 1784. JAS. CREWS & wife MILLY, AC, to JOS. DAWSON, AC,
        for Ł40, 38 acres Harris Creek. Lines: JAS. SYMONS, WM. HUGHS.
Wit: WM. LEE, JAS. LIVELY, JOS. CREWS, JONATHAN DAKON. Orig. del. to
PLEASANT DAWSON 28 Oct 1796.

Page 544. 2 Oct 1784. JOS. MORRIS & wife MARY, AC, to ELIJAH STONE, AC,
        for Ł100, 190 acres where I now live on HIckory Creek. Lines:
ABRAHAM STRANGE, WM. MORRISON, ELIJAH STONE. Wit: JNO. MORRIS, EPHRAIM
BLAINE, ABRAHAM A. STRANGE. Orig. del. to STONE Apr 1789.

Page 545. 1 Oct 1784. WM. HIGGINBOTHAM & wife DOLLY, AC, to THOS. POW-
        ELL (Taylor) for Ł30, 181 acres, bought by CALEB HIGGINBOTHAM
of PHILLIP SMITH and conveyed to grantor. Lines: crossing Puppie's Creek,
JACOB SMITH HORN BEAM - S side of river.

Page 546. 22 Apr 1784. THOS. WRIGHT & wife CORDELA (DILLEE in one
        place), AC, to JNO. MILLER, Campbell Co, for Ł90, 280 acres on
Lynch Ferry Road. Wit: JOS. CREWS, THOS. JOHNSON, JAS. REED, JNO.
TENNERSON.

Page 547. 11 Aug 1784. WM. RAY, AC, to NICHL. CABELL, AC, for Ł200, 2
        tracts. 1) 342 acres granted to MOSES RAY by pat. 15 Dec 1749,
and by him devised to his son, WM. RAY. Both sides Gilbert's Creek. Lines:
Col. WM. MAYO (now CABELL's). 2) 80 acres pat. to MOSES RAY 26 Jul 1765
on branch of Gilbert's Creek. Wit: LEWIS NEVIL, EZEKIAH BAILEY, DAVID
PROFFITT. Orig. del. to J. MURPHY to carry to CABELL, Mar, 1789.

Page 548. 4 Oct 1784. BENJ. HIGGINBOTHAM & wife ELIZ., AC, to JNO.
        CLARKSON, AC, for Ł610, 300 acres on Buffalo. Lines: AARON
HIGGINBOTHAM. Also 390 acres on Davis Mt. and S branch of Franklin Creek.
Pat. to grantor 14 Jul 1769. Line of JACOB SMITH. Also 236 acres on N
branch Buffalo. Pat. to grantor 30 Aug 1763. Lines: grantor, AARON HIG-
GINBOTHAM, Davis Mt. spur, JOS. HIGGINBOTHAM. Also 130 acres on N side
Buffalo and by Dinnis' Thourofare. Pat. to grantor 26 Jul 1765.

Page 551. 5 Jul 1784. AUGUSTIN SHEPHERD, JNO. SHEPHERD, & DEBARTUS
        SHEPHERD to JAS. CALLAWAY, AC, for Ł800, 554 acres. Property
of DAVID SHEPHERD and by his will devised to his three brothers above;
ref. to AC will and deeds. Line of CARTER BRAXTON. On 22 Mar 1775 for
"300 or 4 acres". Also deeds of EZEK. GILBERT, 1 Feb 1779, for 40 acres;
EZEK. GILBERT on 1 Nov 1779, for 160 acres; JNO. WIATT GILBERT, 16 Mar
1780, for 50 acres. Tracts adjoining. Wit: WM. POWELL, JESSE MILLS,
BENJ. POWELL, W. WRIGHT.

Page 552. 2 Oct 1784. RICH. TALIAFERRO & wife MILLY, AC, to DAVID CRAW-
        FORD, AC, for Ł400, 369 acres on Stone's creek and entry of
11 acres. Lines: ISAAC WRIGHT, WM. HAINES, DAVID CRAWFORD.

Page 553. 14 Feb 1784. JAS. ROWSEY & wife ELIZ., AC, to CHAS. CHRISTIAN
        for Ł61, 226 acres in Lexington Parish. Lines: CHRISTIAN, JNO.
WEST, MOSES HIGGINBOTHAM, S branch Buffalo, WM. GATEWOOD, CHAS. WILCHER.
Wit: AMBROSE GATEWOOD, JAS. CHRISTIAN, SAML. UNDERWOOD, MARY CHRISTIAN.

Page 555. 22 Sep 1784. WM. CLARK, AC, to JAS. REID, minor - I have war-
        rant Number 12360 for 1040½ acres of June 18(10?) 1782. I lent
to Col. JAS. KNOX to locate in the Kentucky country. He gets one half
for so doing and I pay expenses of locating, chain carrying and pat. Two
equal surveys, if KNOX chooses. REID is to sell my half, when surveyed,
and convey KNOX his half. Wit: WM. BRITT, NATHL. CLARK, JAS. REID. Orig.
del. to JAS. REID, Gent.

Page 556. 1 Nov 1784. ROGER KERSEY & wife MARGARET, AC, to MARBLE
        STONE, Fluvannah, for Ł140, two tracts on Taylor Creek. 1)
141 acres bought by grantor of SAML. MAN. 2) 28 acres adj. Orig. del.
to grantee 8 Nov 1786.

Page 557. 1 Nov 1784. MAURIS GILBERT, AC, to BENJ. RUCKER, AC, for Ł175,
470 acres S branch Rutledge & Buffalo. Part of 1100 acres belonging to HENRY GILBERT, dec'd. Lines: RICH. GATEWOOD, PARK's road, MEG-
GINSON's road, HENRY GILBERT. Wit: THOS. POWELL, minor, RICH. HARRISON,
WIATT POWELL, MARTIN DAWSON.

Page 558. 16 Sep 1784. SAML. MARKSBURY, AC, to JER. TUNGET for Ł5, 73
acres N side of N fork Buffalo. Pat. to grantor 5 Jul 1774.
Wit: CALEB HIGGINBOTHAM, JOS. HIGGINBOTHAM, JR, BENJ. HIGGINBOTHAM,
ABROS. TOMBLIN.

Page 559. 25 Aug 1784. ISAAC MAYFIELD, AC, to AMBROUS TOMBLIN, for Ł15,
25 acres between S and N fork Buffalo. Part of 200 acres pat.
to grantor 20 Jul 1768. Wit: THOS. GARLAND, BENJ. HIGGINBOTHAM, JOS.
HIGGINBOTHAM JR, JNO. BELEW.

Page 560. 5 Aug 1784. JNO. FRANKLIN, Lincoln Co. to JACOB SMITH, AC,
for Ł80, 150 acres Head branch Franklin Creek. Wit: JNO.,
PHILLIP & WM. SMITH.

Page 561. 25 Oct 1784. JNO. PAYTON, AC, to JOS. EDWARDS, AC, for Ł100,
395 acres on Blue Ridge and branch of Irish Creek. Lines: Top
of the Blue Ridge. Wit: JAS. WARE, ISAAC WRIGHT, PETER CARTER.

Page 562. 14 Oct 1784. WM. GOODE, Powhatan Co, to AMBROUSE RUCKER, AC,
for Ł300, 400 acres on Rockey Creek of Buffalo. Lines: MATT.
WHITTLE, JNO. WARREN, JAS. WARREN. Wit: THOS. POWELL, minor; JAS. LIVELY,
WM. WARE, JNO. RICHARDSON. Orig. sent to RUCKER by BARTLETT EADES, July
1788.

Page 564. 25 Oct 1784. MOSES RAY & wife MARY ANNE, AC, to WM. CABELL,
AC, for Ł250, two tracts of 309 acres. 1) 300 acres, part of
400 acres pat. to MOSES RAY, dec'd, 10 Sep 1755. Lines: WM. & NICHL. CA-
BELL; nearly adjacent to Swift Islands. 2) 9 acres - Island in Fluvannah
and uppermost and largest of the Swipf Islands to which appertains a val-
uable fishery. Known as Swift's Island and Ray's Fishery. Pat. to MOSES
RAY, dec'd, 15 Dec 1749. Wit: LEWIS NEVIL, THOS. POWELL, minor, WILL CA-
BELL JR, SAML. J. CABELL, HECTOR CABELL.

Page 565. 6 Oct 1784. CHAS. ELLIS & wife SARAH, AC, to JOSIAH ELLIS, AC,
for Ł610, two tracts. 1) 400 acres N side Pedlar and conveyed
to grantor by exrs. of JAS. MEREDITH, 13 Mar 1768. 2) 23 acres surveyed
for grantor by JAS. HIGGINBOTHAM. Lines: RODERICK McCULLOCH, S branch
Horsley. 423 acres. Wit: WM. LOVING, WM. WALTON, CHAS. TALIAFERRO JR.,
HENRY BROWN, JOS. GOODWIN. Orig. del. to R.S. ELLIS 30 Mar 1801.

Page 567. 13 Mar 1784. Order to AC J.P.'s, DANL. GAINES & AMBROUS RUCK-
ER, to quiz ANN STEWART, wife of JOHN STEWART, as to deed,
10 Feb 1784, to BENJ. RUCKER, 200 acres on fork of Rutledge and Crooked
Run. Done 28 Jun 1784.

Page 568. 1 Nov 1784. JOS. EDWARDS & wife ELLENER, AC, to ISAAC WRIGHT,
AC, for Ł100, two tracts. 1) 70 acres branch of Horsley. Lines:
PETER CARTER, LOMAX. 2) 300 acres both sides Horsley. Lines: PHILLIP,
WM. & JNO. PAYTON; JNO. POWELL.

Page 569. 7 Jun 1784. SAML. WARD & wife SUSANNAH, AC, to JOS. LIVELY,
AC, for Ł50, 150 acres Bear Branch and branch of Rockfish.
Part of 247 acres.

Page 570. 28 Oct 1784. JOS. EDWARDS & wife NELLY, AC, to PHILLIP THUR-
MOND, AC, for Ł300. 1) 331 acres N fork Horsley. Lines: Col.
LOMAX, a Naked Hill. 2) 450 acres on HOrsley. Lines: NICHL. CABELL, JOS.
MILSTREAD. Wit: JNO. PARKS, WM. GALASPIE, WM. THURMOND, SHEROD MORE
GALASPIE, ISAAC WRIGHT, JNO. POWELL.

Page 571. 18 Jun 1784. JNO. WIATT, AC, to JOSHUA HUDSON, AC, for Ł20,
59 acres branches of Maple Run. Lines: EDWD. CARTER, JNO.
WIATT, Top of Turkey Mt., LINN BANKS. Part of a tract. Wit: RUSH & REUBEN
HUDSON.

Page 572. 17 Aug 1784. JNO. JOSLING, AC, to ELIZ. EVANS, AC, for Ь20,
140 acres on branches of Owen Creek. Wit: WM., RO. & JNO.
HORSLEY; SAML. ALLEN, JNO. WHITTLE, WM. STEWART, NICHL. PAMPLIN. Orig.
del. to WM. HORSLEY for EVANS.

Page 573. 1 Nov 1784. Shff. bond for DAVID CRAWFORD. To JACQUALIN
AMBLER, Virginia Treasurer. Bondsmen: GABL. PENN, CHAS. ROSE,
GEO. HILTON, HUGH ROSE.

Page 574. 1 Nov 1784. DAVID CRAWFORD - bond for shff. for various
duties. Bondsmen: HUGH & CHAS. ROSE.

Page 575. 1 Nov 1784. JAS. GOODRICH & wife MARGARET, AC, to THOS. LUCAS,
AC, for Ь100, 121 acres N side Tobacco Row.

Page 576. 5 Dec 1784. RICH. WILBOURN, AC, to JNO. HEUBANK (EUBANK), AC,
for Ь20, 118 acres Horsley Creek. Lines: EDMOND GOODRICH, CHAS.
DAVIS, WM. CLAPTON, CHAS. ELLIS, AMBROUS EUBANK. Wit: WM. WARE, AMBROUS
TOMBLINSON, JNO. DANL. COLEMAN, WM. DAVIS, son of RICH. DAVIS.
Orig. del. 7 Oct 1796, to JNO. EUBANK.

Page 577. 7 Aug 1784. PULLIAM SANDIDGE, AC, to WM. CARTER, AC, for Ь60,
280 acres which grantor bought of BENJ. HIGGINBOTHAM. Head
branch Horsley. Lines: JNO. ROBERTS.

Page 578. 28 Dec 1784. DANL. GAINES, AC, to DAVID WOODROUGH, AC, for
Ь700, 693 acres on road from Rockfish Gap to Linches' Ferry
and known as DANL. GAINES Mt. Lot of Land. Plot annexed (not in book).
Wit: S. MEREDITH, GABL. PENN, THOS. POWELL, minor, JNO. WIATT, EDWD. WAT-
SON, WIATT POWELL. Orig. del. to grantee Mar 1789.

Page 579. This page is blank in the deed book.

Page 580. 13 Dec 1784. DANL. GAINES, AC, to HUGH ROSE, AC, CHAS. IRVING
of Albemarle, GABL. PENN & JAS. FRANKLIN of AC, 10 sh. Deed of
Trust - of May 14, 1783, debt of GAINES to GABL. PENN for Ь4960 tobacco
and smaller debt; also debt due JNO. WIATT & Co. for dealings at store in
AC (GABL. PENN is a partner) - to secure the above bondsmen on bond pay-
able to JOHN HOOK, Bedford, on AC judgment in Assignee of J. JONES vs.
GAINES; bond payable to JAS. MANEES; also bond due SAML. MEREDITH, AC, -
land known as Old House Lot of 606 acres. Lines: JER. TAYLOR (alias MA-
GAN's Ordinary), JAS. HILL, HENRY BELL, JNO. STEWART, CHAS. IRVIN; also
Crooked Run lot of 175 acres. Lines: JOS. MAYS, BENJ. RUCKER, JOS. HIG-
GINBOTHAM, JNO. STEWART, CHAS. IRVING, Crooked Run lot; also 92 acres on
Mobley's Mt. and pat. 13 Mar 1781; also thirty slaves, named; stock,
tools, furniture, crops. Wit: WM. SID CRAWFORD, LINDSEY COLEMAN, RICH.
OGLESBY, JOS. BURRESS. Sent to GABL. PENN, 28 Sep 1790.

Page 583. 17 Aug 1784. JNO. JOSLIN & wife DINAH, AC, to GEO. HILTON,
AC, for Ь250, 1070 acres in three tracts on branch of Owen
Creek. 1) 450 acres pat. 22 Nov 1755, on S branch Owens. 2) 220 acres
both sides of S fork Owens. Lines: JNO. JOSLIN; pat. 1 Sep 1782. 3) 400
acres N branches Owens. Lines: LOVING; THOS. BIBY; pat. 1 Sep 1783. Wit:
WM. HORSLEY, SAML. ALLEN, NICHL. PAMPLIN, JNO. HORSLEY, WM. STEWART.

Page 585. 7 Aug 1784. LAURENCE SMALL, AC & parish, to WM. SMALL of same,
for Ь10, 100 acres on Corbin Creek and branch of Owen(?).
Lines: ALEX. REID JR, NATHAN REED, WM. BARNETT, SAML. LACKEY, ROBT. HAR-
DIE. Wit: ALEX. REID JR, DAVID CLARK, JNO. TRUSLER, JNO. WOOD, MARY
SMALL.

Page 586. 27 Oct 1784. SAML. MEREDITH, AC, & wife JANE, to HENRY GIL-
BERT, AC, for Ь18,000 tobacco, 432 acres. Lines: HENRY GILBERT,
dec'd, RICH. GATEWOOD.

Page 587. 21 Jul 1784. DANL. GAINES, AC, to CHAS. IRVING, Albemarle,
for Ь1800, 1027 acres S and main branch Rutledge and includes
the dwelling house of GAINES. Lines: 30 acres which GAINES sold to JOS.
CREWS; ridge path from GAINES to St. Matthews Church; Megginson's road
at a bridge on S branch of Rutledge. Wit: HUGH ROSE, THOS. WORTHAM,

216

JNO. HALEY.

Page 588. 28 Dec 1784. Order to AC J.P.'s HUGH ROSE & GABL. PENN, to
quiz MARY GAINES, wife of DANL. GAINES, as to deed to CHAS.
IRVING - 1027 acres - 1 Jul 1784.

Page 589. 24 Aug 1784. Order to AC J.P.'s to quiz HANNAH ALLEN, wife of
SAML. ALLEN, as to 26 Sep 1780 deed of 475 acres to WM. POWELL
on N branch Buffalo. Done 5 Mar 1785 by JAS. DILLARD & WM. HORSLEY.

Page 590. 19 Sep 1784. DANL. MAHONE & wife SARAH, AC; JNO. HARDWICK &
wife ELIZ, Bedford; to NOEL BLANKENSHIP, Campbell Co, for Ŀ40,
250 acres branch Stoval Creek and Lynch road. Wit: GIDEON LEA, DAVID
BLANKENSHIP, ABEL BLANKENSHIP, FRANCIS WARD. Orig. del. to JAS. HILL 11
Oct 1794.

Page 591. 20 Dec 1784. JNO. SHEPHERD, York Co, to JOS. MAYS, AC, for
Ŀ100, 370 acres branch Juniper Creek. Pat. at Williamsburg 20
Oct 1779. Wit: JNO. MAYS, JAS. HIGGINBOTHAM, JOS. MAYS, JESSE MAYS, CHAS.
MAYS. Orig. del. to grantee 2 Oct 1788.

Page 592. 11 Oct 1783. JAS. & JNO. WILLOUGHBY, AC & parish, to PHILLIP
SMITH of same, for Ŀ3600 tobacco inspected at Byrd's, Shoccow,
or Rocky Ridge - land on head branch Dutch Creek. Lines: Capt. HENRY MAR-
TIN, JNO. STAPLES; now in possession of ALLEN BLAIR. Wit: JNO. MERRY
GRIFFIN, JOS. LIVELY, ALLEN BLAIR. Orig. del. to JNO. TALIAFERRO for
SMITH.

Page 593. 4 Sep 1784. DANL. GAINES, AC, to JOS. CREWS, AC, for Ŀ60, 32
acres Lynch Road and Crooked Run. Lines: Grantor, BINAMY STONE,
JOS. MAYS, CHAS. IRVING, Mt. Lot. Wit: WM. DAWSON, DAVID TINSLEY., GIDEON
CREWS.

Page 594. 6 Jan 1785. LEMASTER COOKSEY, AC, to WM. CAMDEN, AC, for Ŀ70,
170 acres S fork Huff Creek. Lines: BENJ. NOWELL, top of a
mt., JNO. HIGGINBOTHAM, BENJ. HIGGINBOTHAM, PATRICK NOWELL. Wit: JNO.
WATSON, WM. TUCKER, PLEDGE PALMORE, THOS. BAILEY.

Page 595. 6 Sep 1784. TYRE SLADING, AC, to WM. CAMDEN, AC, for Ŀ20, 100
acres. Lines: Near Huff Creek, JNO. COLEMAN, top of the mt.,
BENJ. NOWELL, JAS. BIAS. Wit: JNO. DANL. COLEMAN, THOS. LUCAS, SOLOMON
ELLIS. Proved 7 Mar 1785 - JNO. DANL. COLEMAN is now dead, but signature
proved by LUCAS & ELLIS under oath.

Page 596. 15 Sep 1784. JANE DAVIS, AC, to DRURY BOWMAN, AC, for Ŀ70,
250 acres S side Dancing Creek. Lines: JOS. CABELL, RO. PAYTON,
S branch Dancing Creek. Wit: JNO. GOODRICH, JOS. LANE, JNO. TOOLEY, JNO.
SALE.

Page 597. 26 Aug 1784. ISAAC MAYFIELD, AC, to JACOB PHILLIPS, AC, for
Ŀ60, 175 acres both sides S fork Buffalo. Lines: JNO. HIGGIN-
BOTHAM JR, top of a mt. Wit: CALEB HIGGINBOTHAM, ABROUS TOMBLINSON, JNO.
POWELL.

Page 598. 2 Sep 1784. JAS.MARTIN SR, AC, to CHAS. BRIDGEWATER, Henrico,
for Ŀ320, 200 acres on heads of some branches of S side of
Rockfish. Lines: N side Meriwether's Branch. Wit: JNO. MURRELL JR, JAS.
TRUSLIN, VIRGIL POE. Wit: to receipt - NATHL. CLARKE, WM. BRITT, WM.
CLARKE. Orig. del. to grantee 27 Jan 1794.

Page 600. 7 Mar 1785. JNO. HARRIS, AC, to JNO. JOHNSON, AC, for Ŀ22,
46 acres on branch of Davis. Lines: WM. WRIGHT. Wit: ABNER
WITT, ALEX. FORBUS, SAML. SCOT SCRUGGS.

Page 601. 29 Oct 1784. GEO. GILBERT to WIATT POWELL for Ŀ145, 145 acres
Rutledge Creek. Lines: Top of a mt., WIATT POWELL, EDWD. WAT-
SON, JOS. CREWS, JAS. PENDLETON. Wit: JAS. FRANKLIN; HENRY, JOSIAS, EZEK.
& JUDITH GILBERT.

Page 602. 7 Mar 1785. JNO. DEPRIEST & wife ELIZ., AC, to WM. POWELL,

AC, for Ŀ30,000 tobacco, 400 acres both sides S fork Rucker's Run. Lines:
EDMD. WILCOX, LUCAS POWELL, JAS. WILLS, JAS. THOMPSON, Col. WM. CABELL.
Former property of WALTER KING, British subject, and sold under 2 acts of
Assembly by DAVID SHEPHERD, AC Escheator. Mention of pat. of grantor
1 Sep 1782.

Page 603. 8 Dec 1784. ESTHER BALLOW, Botetourt Co, to WM. CABELL, JR,
AC, for Ŀ270, 270 acres. Lines: CABELL, HUGH ROSE, LAURENCE
CAMPBELL, JOEL CAMPBELL, JNO. BROWN. Wit: JAS. & RACHEL HIGGINBOTHAM,
GEO. SOUTHERLAND.

Page 604. 1 Jan 1785. JOSIAS GILBERT, AC, about to remove to Georgia
where I may probably reside for some time. Power of atty. to
my brother, EZEK. GILBERT. Wit: GABL. PENN, RICH. GILBERT, DANL. GAINES.
Orig. del. to EZEK. GILBERT 16 Jul 1785.

Page 604. 24 Feb 1785. JNO. DEPRIEST & wife ELIZ., AC, to WM. DEPRIEST,
Henrico, for Ŀ250, 252 acres in Amherst Parish. Wit: JOHN
MONTGOMERY, JESSE CARDIN, EDWD. HOUCHINS.

Page 605. 5 Aug 1784. DAVID BLY, Lincoln Co, to WM. GATEWOOD JR, AC,
for Ŀ15, 50 acres in Lex. Parish, S side and joining Buffalo.
Lines: FRY, WM. GATEWOOD. Wit: CHAS. CHRISTIAN, EDMOND ROWSEY, HENRY
GATEWOOD, THOS. PENN. Continued for further proof, but attested by CHAS.
CHRISTIAN & THOS. PENN.

Page 606. 1 Jan 1785. DANL. GAINES, AC, to JAS. MORTON, AC, for Ŀ100,
land on Rugledge. Creek. Lines: DANL. HARVIE, ISAAC RUCKER,
BENAMONE STONE, DANL. GAINES. Wit: SAML. HUCKSTEP, EZEKIAH GILBERT,
JNO. McDANIEL, JNO. KNIGHT.

Page 607. 5 Nov 1784. Deposition of WM. BELL of lawful age - sometime
in 1759, to best of his knowledge, he bought 400 acres of pat.
land in 3 surveys of JNO. THORNTON, lately an inhabitant of AC. 1) 136
acres. 2) 196 acres 3) 140 acres for JNO. BELL of Orange Co. THORNTON
gave him an order on Secretary's office for pat. and acres and he gave it
to GEO. WEBB to apply. One had been issued previously in name of JNO.
THORNTON, as WEBB informed him. The other pat. came out in name of JNO.
BELL and he paid THORNTON. Sworn to in Orange Co. before THOS. BARBOUR
on above date; rec. in AC on motion of DAVID PHILLIPS 7 Mar 1785.

Page 608. 18 Nov 1784. Depositions of LEONARD & ZACHARIAS PHILLIPS,
both of lawful age - they were present when WM. BELL, Orange
Co., bought the land from JNO. THORNTON. They refer to 4 tracts for use
of JNO. BELL, Orange County. WM. BELL paid THORNTON for the land and he
acknowledged payment for 400 acres. Two patents came out agreeable to the
order and 190 acres came out sometime before in THORNTON's name. Both
men deposed before JNO. HOPKINS, AC, 18 Nov 1784.

Page 608. 7 Mar 1785. DAVID SHELTON, AC, to JNO. HARRIS, AC, for Ŀ150,
190 acres S side Rockfish. Lines: WM. WHITSED, JAS. HALLY
BURTON. Orig. del. to MOLLIE HARRIS, 13 Mar 1806(1?).

Page 609. 27 Jan 1785. JNO. BROWN, AC, to ADAM BROWN, AC, for 5 sh. on
account of ALEX. SINCLAIR; also Ŀ3000 tobacco, Richmond inspection - replivin bond of WYATT POWELL. I owe JEREMIAH WADE, assignee
of JAS. MAINON(?); also owe CHAS. IRVING as surety on replivin bond to
ZACH. TALIAFERRO; to JAS. FRANKLIN, one slave. Wit: JAS. REID, THOS. LAN-
DRUM JR, THOMAS WORTHAM. Orig. del. to SAM BROWN, son of JNO. BROWN, 18
Aug 1787.

Page 611. 10 (?) Dec 1784. FRANCES SATERWHITE, AC, power of atty. to
SAML. HIGGINBOTHAM, AC, to collect sums due from "any relation"
and to conduct all business. Wit: CHAS. TALIAFERRO, JR, ZACH. TALIAFERRO
JR.

Page 611. 15 Nov 1784. WM. WRIGHT JR, to RO. WRIGHT, AC, for Ŀ176, 176
acres both sides Davis Creek. Lines: WM. BOANES, ANDREW WRIGHT,
S fork Davis, JAS. HALLEY BURTON, WM. WRIGHT JR, WM. BONES. Wit: JNO.
LOVING, JOS. ROBERTS, GEO. LOVING. Orig. del. to JOS. SHELTON for WRIGHT.

Page 613. 24 Sep 1784. ISAAC WRIGHT, AC, to VALENTINE PAYTON, AC, a
negro girl about 15. Wit: HENRY BROWN, EDMOND GOODRICH, JNO.
BROWN, WM. THURMOND.

Page 614. 8 Mar 1785. RO. THOMPSON, AC, power of atty to friend, JNO.
CARRINGTON, Orange Co, N.C. Orig. del. to THOMPSON.

Page 614. 9 Feb 1785. Order to AC J.P.'s, AMBROSE RUCKER & GABL. PENN,
to quiz MARY GAINES, wife of DANL. GAINES, as to deed for 693
acres on road from Rockfish Gap to Linch's Ferry and known as GAINES Mt.
Lot. to DAVID WOODROUGH. Done by J.P.'s 6 Apr 1785.

Page 615. 12 Jul 1784. Order to quiz MARY GAINES, wife of DANL., as to
deed to JONATHAN WILSON for 301 acres on branch of Harris and
E side Tobacco Row Mt. Done by HUGH ROSE & GABL. PENN 28 Dec 1784.

Page 616. 12 Jul 1784. Order for same men and parties for 54 acres on
Tobacco Row. Done same date.

Page 617. -- Sep 1784. (Rec. 2 May 1785.) VALENTINE PAYTON & wife MARY
of AC to ISAAC WRIGHT, AC, for L100, 142 acres Horsley Creek.
Lines: PHILLIP PAYTON. Surveyed by JAS. HIGGINBOTHAM, 20 Oct 1779, and
pat. to grantor. Wit: HENRY BROWN, WM. GALASPIE, PETER CARTER, EDMOND
GOODRICH. Proved by all but CARTER on 2 May 1785. Carried to court for
WRIGHT in Mar 1790.

Page 618. 12 Nov 1784. JACOB SMITH, AC, to JNO. MARTIN, Fluvanna, for
L125, 150 acres branch of Franklin Creek. Wit: WM. WARE, JNO.
SMITH, PHILIP & JAS. SMITH. Orig. del. to WM. MARTIN, one of the laga-
tees of JNO. MARTIN, dec'd, 20 Jul 1822.

Page 619. 2 May 1785. DRURY TUCKER, AC, to JONATHAN WILSON, AC, for L6,
6 acres. Lines: LUNSFORD LOMAX, Harris Creek, WM. KIPPERS.
Wit: DANL. TUCKER, MATT. TUCKER, JR, MILLIE(?) COLEMAN (mark).

Page 620. 2 May 1785. THOS. GRIFFIN & wife MILDRED, AC, to ALLEN BLAIR,
AC, for L120, 179 acres on branch Rucker's Run. Lines: BARNES;
JAS. STEVENS, KING. Part of 6134 acres of LUNSFORD LOMAX, The Elder,
from BENJ. WALLER, atty for WALTER KING, Bristol Merchant, and THOS. MANN
RANDOLPH, 1 Dec 1764; conveyed by the Elder to LUNSFORD LOMAX Jr. (JUDITH,
wife of the Elder) 13 Jan 1767. Conveyed by LUNSFORD LOMAX JR, 7 Apr 1770,
to THOS. WORTHAM. THOS. WORTHAM & wife ELIZ., conveyed to grantor 16
Nov 1797.

Page 622. 20 Oct 1784. Order to AC J.P.'s, HUGH ROSE & GABL. PENN, to
quiz MARTHA, wife of GEO. GILBERT, as to deed to 250 acres on
Rutledge and Tribulation - to WIATT POWELL, 9 Sep 1783. Done, 15 Apr 1785.

Page 623. 4 Dec 1784. HENRY SORROW, AC, to JNO. CESTERSON (CASTERSON),
AC, for L50, 74 acres on Nassau; part of tract in possession
of DAVID MONTGOMERY. Lines: MONTGOMERY. Wit: JOS. LIVELY, THEODORICK
WEBB, WM. TILLER.

Page 625. 6 Jun 1785. PERRIN GILES SR, and wife LUCY, to GEO. FITZJAR-
RELL, AC, for L25, land on N branch Indian Creek and pat. to
grantor 28 Dec 1784. Lines: WM. PARKS, WM. BIBB. Wit: HENDRICK ARNOLD.

Page 626. 8 Nov 1784. JOS. CANTERBURY JR, AC, to WM. NALLEY AC, for
L100, 174 acres on Dutch; pat. under the Broad Seal of the
State of Virginia. Lines: WALTER KING, WM. TILLER, THOS. HOPPER. Wit:
THOS. BECKNAL, JNO. KESTERSON, BENNETT NALLY.

Page 627. 5 Dec 1784. JNO. THOMAS & wife SARAH, AC, to AUGUSTINE SMITH,
AC, for L200, 200 acres on S side Rockfish. Lately occupied by
WM. ELLIOTT. Lines: CHISWELL. Wit: JNO. SMITH, EDWD. BIGGS.

Page 629. 1 May 1785. GABL. PENN, AC, to WM. PHILLIPS, AC, for L6000
tobacco of James River crop - 60 acres N side and joining
Buffalo. Part of 475 acres of grantor. Lines: WM. CABELL, the Younger,
JNO. PHILLIPS, JACOB TYREE, JAS. WATSON.

Page 630.   5 Feb 1785.   SMYTH TANDY, AC, to SAML. MEREDITH, HUGH ROSE,
GABL. PENN, & JNO. WIATT - they are on two replevin bonds to
JAS. CURRE(?), Richmond. Deed of Trust - tract known as New Glasgow -
370 acres - which TANDY bought of GABL. PENN on 14 Mar 1782, and mort-
gaged to PENN. Also four Irish indentured servants: THOS. SULLAVAN, WM.
HAYS, GARRETT SHAUGUNSY (?) & wife MARY. Wit: WM. MEREDITH, JAS. REED,
WM. SID CRAWFORD.

Page 632.   10 Jun 1785.   CARTER BRAXTON & wife ELIZ., King William Co, to
JESSE BURTON, exr. of WM. BURTON, dec'd, Campbell Co, for Ŀ520,
800 acres S side Buffalo. Lines: MATT. TUCKER, N branch Huff, JNO. PENN,
SAML. MEREDITH (formerly CABELL). Wit: GABL. PENN, FLEMING JORDAN, JNO.
THOMPSON, MILIDALE(?) THOMAS, JAS. HOOD.

Page 633.   24 Jan 1785.   Order to Buckingham Co, Va. J.P.'s ANTHONY WIN-
STON & --- to quiz MARY BABER, wife of GEO. BABER, as to 1785
deed to JNO. RICHERSON for 350 acres on Pedlar. Done by WINSTON & CHAS.
MAY, 19 Mar 1785.

Page 634.   18 Mar 1785.   GEO. BABER, Buckingham Co, to JNO. RICHERSON, AC,
(no sum mentioned) two adj. tracts on N branch Brown's Creek.
1) 245 acres. 2) 99 acres, S branch of Inchanted Creek; adj. JOSIAS ELLIS.

Page 635.   5 Jul 1785.   WM. OGLESBY, AC, to CHAS. JOHNSON, Goochland, for
Ŀ120, 232 acres, part of pat. of JOS. BALLINGER and by him
sold to RICH. BALLINGER. Lines: BALLINGER's Mt., JOS. MAYS. Wit: BART-
LETT EADES, WM. SCOTT, JNO. CRITTENDON.

Page 636.   1 Aug 1785.   Will and desire of ANNE ROSE, that one of my
female slaves, MARY DEAN, be freed. Wit: HUGH, PATRICK, & CHAS.
ROSE who are heirs of ANNE ROSE. Orig. del. to HUGH ROSE.

Page 636.   Alphabetical list of old surveys from 6 Oct 1783 to 6 Jul 1784;
and from 6 Jul 1784 to 6 Jul 1785. Made of record by WM.
LOVING, Clerk.

13 May 1785	JNO. CHILDRESS	400	acres
22 Apr 1785	DAVID CLARKSON	94	"
12 May 1785	ALEX. DUGGINS	300	"
13 May 1785	WM. HIX	100	"
10 May 1785	JAS. HOPKINS	36	"
1 Jun 1785	PETER LE GRAND	344	"
24 May 1785	HENRY MARTIN	40	" and 1 Mill Seat
16 Apr 1785	JOS. ROBERTS	146	"
6 May 1785	WM. SMALL	97	"
20 Apr 1785	ZACHARIAS TALIAFERRO	10	acres & 109 acres
21 Apr 1785	" "	98	"
25 Apr 1785	JAS. WELLS	150	acres
24 Apr 1784	FRANCES WEST	390	acres
14 Apr 1785	ABNER WITT	360	"

Page 637.   12 Oct 1784.   WM. GALASPIE & wife NANCY, AC, to WM. LOVING,
AC, for Ŀ140, 305 acres N branch Rucker's Run. Lines: JNO.
STAPLES, LOVING, old line. Bought by grantor of JOSIAH WOOD. Wit: PETER
CARTER, HENRY PAYTON, CHAS. STEWART. (GILLESPIE & wife went to Madison
Co, Ky - ancestors of my wife. I have much data on the family. See
COLEMAN's Kentucky Duels for his death. BFD)

END OF DEED BOOK E

220

DEDICATION

This work is affectionately dedicated to CATHERIN BARRICKMAN HELM MILLER, wife of my brother-in-law, CLARENCE MILLER. I have known her since she was a babe in Shelbyville, Kentucky. She is known as "Toddy" to her many friends.

FOREWORD

I have dubbed this abstract as "Grandfather F" since it is by far the largest one to date. This is the first time that I have attempted to put deeds in alphabetical order. I must confess that I am somewhat less than enamored with the process.

The various survey, tax and poll lists have been arranged alphabetically to avoid including each of these names in the index.

BAILEY FULTON DAVIS - 1963

Page 17.   30 Oct 1785. WM. AARON & wife ELIZ, AC, to MOSES RAY, AC, for
            Ŀ20, 90 acres N side and joining Tye. Upper part of 180 acres
pat. to WM. TYREE, 20 Jul 1780. Lines: Joe's Falls. Wit: WM. CABELL SR.
& JR, ANNE CABELL, JNO. TALIAFERRO.

Page 582.   7 Jan 1791. WM. ALFORD, AC, to WM. HOLLINGSWORTH, AC, for Ŀ50,
            93 acres S branch Rucker's Run. Part of a tract. Lines: WM.
CRISP; grantor. Wit: AUSTIN SMITH, WM. KEY, WM. TATE.

Page 174.   14 Jun 1787. RICH. ALLCOCK (ALCOCK) AC, to WM. WARE, Exr. of
            EDWD. WARE, Dec'd, for Ŀ250, Deed of Trust - 5 sh. 93 acres.
Lines: WM. SPENCER, JNO. WARE, WM. CABELL, JNO. STRATTON. Also two negroes. Wit: JAS. FRANKLIN, JNO. PENN, WM. SPENCER.

Page 179.   13 Jun 1787. Rec'd. of RICH. ALLCOCK Ŀ54 by JAS. FRANKLIN -
            bond of Ŀ40 due in July and Ŀ9 due Apr 1788 - in full for
mortgage between ALLCOCK & EDMD. WILCOX, dec'd. Signed by JNO. PENN for
SUSANNAH WILCOX, admrx. of EDMD. WILCOX. Wit: JAS. FRANKLIN, WM. WARE.

Page 285.   1 Dec 1788. RICH. ALLCOCK, AC, to HENRY SHELTON, AC, for Ŀ80,
            93 acres on Tye. Lines: JAS. MARTIN, NICHL. CABELL, CHAS. PAT-
TERSON, WM. CABELL, GILBERT BOWMAN.

Page 373.   9 May 1789. WM. ALLCOCK, AC, to THOMPSON & TEAS - Deed of
            Trust - 200 acres surveyed for JESSE KENNEDY 22 Jun 1781; part
of a tract of WM. GATEWOOD on N branch of Buffalo. Lines: WM. GATEWOOD,
JAS. FREELAND, dec'd. Wit: DAVID S. GARLAND, HENRY BIBB, JAS. BIBB.

Page 154.   1 Jun 1787. WM. ALLEN & wife HANNAH, AC, to CLEVER CORDWELL
            HORRELL, AC, for Ŀ50, part of where JNO. WADE now lives; N
fork of Davis Creek. Lines: CHAS. TATE. Wit: JAS. McALEXANDER, JR, JOHN
BORDEN, CHAS. TATE. Original Delivered to WM. TATE for HERRILL (sic).

Page 158.   2 May 1787. SAML. ANDERSON, AC, to JAS. TURNER - JNO. LYON,
            late of Cashwell (sic) Co, N.C., dec'd, by last will gave
power of attorney to SAML. ANDERSON, his son-in-law, to sell the Mill
Tract - 150 acres and will of record in N.C. county named above. Two
lines: Near a branch; BENJ. MOORE's old line; Mill Tract of ANDERSON's
own line and divided to him by another clause in the will; mouth of
TERISHA TURNER's spring.

Page 304.   7 Apr 1789. WM. ANGUS, AC, to JNO. WRENN & JAS. MARTIN, both
            of Fayette County - Power of Atty. to survey tract in (blank)
county; location made by Capt. RICH. BALLINGER. 120 acres. Wit: HUGH &
PATRICK ROSE. Orig. del. to ANGUS.

Page 124.   30 Dec 1786. BENJ. ARNOLD & wife MARY, to SAML. HIGGINBOTHAM
            & HENRY FRANKLIN JR. - consideration, 2 slaves, Jean & Matthew,

from estate of HENRY FRANKLIN, dec'd - their interest in two slaves,
Millender & Joshua, from same estate. For benefit of children of HENRY
FRANKLIN: REUBIN, AARON, JASPER, PEACHIE, ANTONY & HENRY TALTERN FRANKLIN;
also any property that would revert to us by will of AARON HIGGINBOTHAM
on death of CLARY HIGGINBOTHAM, my wife's mother. Wit: HENDRICK ARNOLD,
AARON HIGGINBOTHAM, WM. SNITH, BENJ. HORSLEY.

Page 321. 1 Nov 1788. HENDRICK ARNOLD & wife RUTH, AC, to JOHN HOLLIDAY,
          AC, for Ł80, 103 acres. Lines: The House, Long Branch. Wit:
JAMS(?) EAMMES, WM. SANDIDGE, WM. MAYS, AARON HIGGINBOTHAM, JAS. MAYS.

Page 567. 5 Jan 1791. RACHEL AYRES, JOS. H. MORRISON & wife FRANKEY,
          AC, to HAWS COLEMAN, AC, for Ł300, 210 acres S fork of Rock-
fish and N side of river; now in possession of MORRISON. Orig. sent 3
Aug 1821, to HAWS COLEMAN.

Page 456. 12 Jun(13?), 1789. WM. BAILEY & wife SARAH, AC, to JOSEPH
          NICHOLS, AC, for Ł50, 197 acres both sides Stovall's road and
branches of Stovall and Porrage Creeks. Lines: JNO. LYNE, EDWD. HARPER,
MARTIN BIBB, JNO. CRITTENDON. Wit: JER. TAYLOR, WM. TINSLEY, CHAS. ELLIS,
JNO. POWELL, JOS. MEGANN.

Page 218. 1 Oct 1787. ESTHER BALLOW & son MEREDITH BALLOW, Botetourt
          Co., to WM. CABELL JR, AC, for Ł270, 270 acres S branch of
Piney and Tye and N branch of Buffalo. Lines: grantee; HUGH ORSE, LAU-
RENCE CAMPBELL, JOEL CAMPBELL, WM. S. CRAWFORD.

Page 234. 8 Oct 1787. LINN BANKS & wife SARAH, AC, to LINDSEY COLEMAN,
          AC, for Ł40, 75 acres N branch Buffalo and where BANKS now
lives. Lines: grantee; JOSHUA HUDSON, BUGG. RUBIN BANKS relinquishes all
rights. Wit: JAS. FRANKLIN, SHEROD BUGG, JNO. LANDRUM, GARLAND HURT,
JOSHUA HUDSON. Orig. del. Mar, 1792, to grantee.

Page 234. 9 Oct 1787. LINN BANKS & wife SARY, AC, to NATHL. MANTIPLY of
          AC for Ł40, 65 acres N branch Buffalo. Lines: JOSHUA HUDSON,
NATHL. MANTIPLY, JNO. SWANSON, SHEROD BUGG, LINDSEY COLEMAN. Wit: as
above. Orig. del. 19 Apr 1821 to SAML. MANTIPLY.

Page 208. 27 Sep 1787. REUBIN BANKS & wife ANN, and ANN BANKS, AC, to
          LINDSEY COLEMAN, AC, for Ł120, 228 acres on Buffalo and Turkey
Mt. Lines: RUSH & JOSHUA HUDSON, LINN BANKS, Banks' Spring, SHEROD BUGG,
LINDSEY COLEMAN. Wit: DANL. TUCKER, WM. BANKS, RUSH HUDSON. Orig. del.
Mar. 1792.

Page 209. 1 Oct 1787. RUBIN BANKS & wife ANN, AC, to SHEROD BUGG, AC,
          for Ł85, 82½ acres N side Buffalo near Turkey Mt. and part of
tract of GERRARD BANKS, dec'd. Lines: LINDSEY COLEMAN, LINN BANKS, WM.
MAYS. Orig. del. to BUGG, 9 Mar 1796.

Page 615. 6 Jun 1791. JNO. BARCHELOT & wife MOLLEY, AC, to CHAS. McCABE,
          for Ł40, 100 acres head of Puppie Creek. Lines: WM. WARE; be-
tween Horsley & Puppie Creeks; WM. CARTER; TALIAFERRO; land SOLOMON CAR-
TER bought of TALIAFERRO - 3 acres.

Page 1.   1 Aug 1785. JAMES BARNETT & wife JANE, heir and devisee of
          JAMES MORRISON, dec'd; MICHL. McNEELY & wife REBECCA, widow
and relict of said decedent, AC, to SAML. REID, Albemarle, for 5 sh., 25
acres S fork Rockfish. SAML. REID recovered from JAS. BARNETT & wife
JANE; MICHL. McNEELY & wife REBECCA, widow and relict of decedent above
by AC court decree, 3 Nov 1784. Lines: THOS. & JAS. MORRISON, dec'd;
ALEX. REID. On page 12 is order to AC J.P.'s JNO. DIGGS & JNO. DAWSON,
to quiz JANE and issued by WM. LOVING, Clerk. Done 18 Aug 1785.

Page 80.   4 Sep 1786. JAS. BARNETT & wife JANE, AC, to JOS. MONTGOMERY,
          AC, for Ł600, 395 acres on Rockfish. Lines: THOS. ADAMS, ALEX.
REID, SAML. REID, THOS. MORRISON, EZRA MORRISON.

Page 129. 3 Feb 1787. ROBT. BARNETT, AC, to DAVID DONNAHOE, AC, for Ł20,
          94 acres branch of Hatt and Raccoon. Lines: Col. WM. RANDOLPH,
JNO. ROSE. (Note: also spelled DONOHUGH in deed.) Wit: JNO. BARNETT,

WM. BROOKS, JAS. HAMBLETON.

Page 213. 4 Jun 1787. WM. BARNETT & wife MARY; JOSEPH HIGGINBOTHAM MOR-
RISON & wife (does not sign and not named), AC, to JOS. BURGER,
AC, for Ł55, paid by DANL. McDONALD, AC, two adjoining tracts on branch
of Tye. Line of ZACH. TALIAFERRO for one of 150 acres and pat. to WM. CA-
BELL 4 Jul 1759. Other tract of 50 acres pat. to JAS. BROWN 20 Jul 1768.

Page 165. 4 Jun 1787 (recorded). HENRY BELL, AC, to FRANS. PAGETT of
AC, for Ł20, 100 acres.

Page 166. 4 Jun 1787. HENRY BELL, AC, to WM. MOON, AC, for Ł50, 240 ac.

Page 125. 26 Jun 1786. JNO. BELL & wife ELIZ., Orange Co., to JAS. TUR-
NER, AC, for Ł500, 411 acres S side Rockfish. Lines: Capt.
MATT. HARRIS; known by JNO. THORNTON's old survey; 84 acres of it known
as Mill survey. Wit: FLEMING WATKINS, JNO. TURNER, STEPHEN TURNER, DAVID
PHILLIPS.

Page 49. 6 Mar 1786. WM. BIBB, AC, to JNO. ALFORD, AC, for Ł5, 200
acres bought by grantor of LUNSFORD LOMAX and rec. in AC.
Lines: MURPHY. Wit: JNO. BIBB, JNO. THOMPSON, CHRISTOPHER BOLLING.

Page 286. 26 Nov 1788. WM. BIBB, AC, to WM. LOVING, AC, for Ł147, 294
acres Bobb's Creek, branch of Rucker's Run. Lines: WM. BIBB,
WM. CRISP, JOS. CABELL, WM. LOVING. Part of 392 acres pat. to WM. BIBB 1
Sep 1782; reference to Land Office Register. Wit: THOS. HAWKINS, JAS.
CALLAWAY, WM. TEAS, DAVID S. GARLAND.

Page 402. WILLIAM BIBB, Tobacco inspector at Swan's Warehouse - 2 Nov
1789. Bondsmen: JNO. HORSLEY, LUCAS POWELL, JAS. WILLS.

Page 492. 15 Mar 1790. WM. BIBB, WM. LOVING, SAML. J. CABELL, WM. CA-
BELL JR, CLOUGH SHELTON, ABRAHAM WARWICK & JNO. HOWARD, Trustees under Act of Assembly, 13 Nov 1788, for establishing a Town and Tobacco Warehouse on lands of NICHL. CABELL to WM. GALT & Co, for Ł31, 2½
acre lotts(sic) in Town of Warminster #3 & #5, beginning at stake on Main
Street. To build dwelling house 16 ft. square; brick or stone chimney
and fit for habitation by 20 Apr 1792. Wit: JNO. THOMPSON, TILMAN WALTON,
JAS. STEVENS, JR, N. POWELL. Orig. del. to GIDEON CREWS.

Page 226. 15 Jan 1788. GEO. BLAINE, AC, Deed of Trust to THOMPSON &
TEAS - cows etc. Wit: BENJ. POWELL, WM. HOOKER, DAVID S.
GARLAND.

Page 523. 1 Aug 1790. GEO. BLAINE & wife RACHEL, to THOMPSON & TEAS
(Orig. del. to CHAS. IRVING Aug 1791), and CHAS. IRVING, Al-
bemarle, 5 sh. Deed of Trust. 122 3/4 acres "where BLAIN lives and WM.
BIBB and THOMPSON and TEAS" (sic) has been conveyed to THOMPSON & TEAS
and rec. in AC; also two beds, stock and crops. Signed also by JNO.
THOMPSON & WM. TEAS. Wit: RO. HOLLOWAY, CALEB HIGGINBOTHAM, RO. WHYTE.

Page 519. 6 Sep 1790. ALLEN BLAIR & wife MARY ANN, AC, and JNO. MERRY
GRIFFIN & wife ELIZ, AC, to WM. CABELL, for Ł80, 180 acres S
branch Nassau and N branch of Rucker's Run. 82 acres of it sold by WM.
MARTIN to JNO. M. GRIFFIN 7 Sep 1778. 99 acres pat. to GRIFFIN 24 Jul
1787. Lines: WM. CABELL, ENOCH NASH. Orig. del. to WC, Jan 1793.

Page 505. 6 Sep 1790. JOSEPH BOND & iwfe JANE, AC, to JNO. HOLLODAY,
AC, for Ł90, 155 acres N branch Buffalo. Lines: STEPHEN CASH.

Page 587. 10 Sep 1790. NATHAN BOND & wife EDITH, Wilks Co, Georgia, to
JNO. MAYS, AC, for Ł100, 150 acres Stone House Creek. Lines:
CHAS. TUCKER on N; RO. MAYS on W; JOS. BOND on S; STEPHEN CASH on E.
Part of 600 acres pat. to NATHAN BOND SR, 10 Jun 1760. Wit: JAS. & HUGH
HAY, JAS. EDMONDS, CHAS. & JAS. MAYS. Orig. del. with commission 4 Oct
1791.

Page 275 . 16 Sep 1788. RICH. BOND, AC, to WM. TUCKER, AC, for Ł100, 179
acres Stone House Creek; N side Buffalo. Lines: JOSEPH BOND,

RO. MAYS, BALLENGER WADE, THOS. HILLEY, NATHAN BOND JR. Wit: JAS. HIG-GINBOTHAM, DANL. TUCKER, WM. PETER. Orig. del. to AMBROSE RUCKER JR, by TUCKER's order 24 Mar 1790.

Page 24. 4 Nov 1785. JNO. BOWLES, Hanover, to ABNER WITT, AC, for Ŀ100, three tracts adjoining - 205 acres both sides branch of N fork Davis Creek - taking in the Thoroughfare that leads over Lakey's Creek and over Lakey's Mt. Lines: JOSEPH ROBERTS, on over N side of Lackey's Mt. at the gap. Lines: ABNER WITT.

Page 97. 1 Jan 1787, recorded, but of blank date in 1786. DRURY BOWMAN, AC, to WM. WARE, AC, for Ŀ60, 81 acres N branch Horsley. Lines: LOMAX. Wit: SAML. MOORE, JNO. CRAWFORD, WM. GILLESPIE, WM. THURMOND, JNO. MATTHEWS, PETER CARTER.

Page 285. 1 Dec 1788. SPEARS, BOWMAN Co. release mortgage vs. RICH. ALLCOCK by factor, WM. WARE. 93 acres sold to "EDWD. WARE & JAMES exrs." (sic).

Page 98. 1 Aug 1786. CARTER BRAXTON & wife ELIZ., King William Co, to JAS. WATSON, AC, for Ŀ823-10,1205 acres S and N side of Buf-falo. Lines: JAS. GATEWOOD, DAVID SHEPHERD, GABL. PENN, WM. JOHNS, Rut-ledge Creek; pat. line; part of BRAXTON's land. Wit: WM. GALT, FRANCIS L. CAMPBELL, JOEL FRANKLIN, THOS. LUCAS.

Page 391. 24 Jun 1789. Order to Henrico J.P.'s: JNO. HARVIE & JNO. PEN-DLETON to quiz ELIZ. BRAXTON, wife of CARTER BRAXTON, as to deed to JESSE BURTON, exr. of PHILLIP BURTON - 800 acres on S side of Buffalo. Done 16 Jul 1789. (Note: This is evidently deed in F:632 for acreage is the same, but therein it is WM. BURTON's exr. and not PHILIP.)

Page 401. 5 Oct 1789. JNO. BROCKMAN & wife ELIZ., AC, to JNO. ALLEN, Albemarle, for Ŀ45, 120 acres Indian Creek. Wit: DANL. TUCKER, JNO. JOHNS, JNO. HILL. Orig. del. to ALLEN 21 Dec 1791.

Page 558. 1 Nov 1790. JAS. BROOKS, Albemarle, to DAVID WITT, AC, for Ŀ65, 140 acres Rockfish. Formerly that of MICHL. MONTGOMERY. Lines: E by CLOUGH SHELTON, S by CHISWELL, W by LITTLEBERRY WITT, N by DAVID WITT. Wits: JNO. WITT, LITTLEBERRY WITT, JOS. ROBERTS.

Page 639. 6 Jun 1791. JAS. BROOKS, Albemarle; GABL. PENN & JAS. WOODS, AG, exrs. of SAML. WOODS, dec'd, to JNO. THOMSON, AC, for Ŀ50, 159 acres on branch of Beaver. Lines: WM. RICE, SAML. WOODS, dec'd, SIMON SHROPSHIRE, FREDERICK WEAR, DAVID MOTLEY.

Page 225. 2 Jan 1788. ADAM BROWN, AC, to THOMPSON & TEAS, Deed of Trust - horse; one pair of "bellers", hammers, all of my smith's tools. Wit: BENJ. POWELL, DAVID S. GARLAND.

Page 337. 3 Nov 1788. JAS. BROWN, AC, to WM. BALL, Albemarle, for Ŀ5, 188 acres "In Dutch Thurifar". Wit: GIDEON CREWS, PLEASANT MARTIN, JNO. THOMPSON, HEZ. HARGROVE.

Page 5. 1 Aug 1785. JNO. BROWN & wife RACHEL, AC, to WM. SIDNEY CRAW-FORD for Ŀ204, 204 acres branch Higginbotham's Mill Creek; deeded in AC and recorded to JNO. BROWN. Orig. del. to WM. SID CRAWFORD 14 May 1787.

Page 362. 23 May 1789. BENJ. BRYANT to MARTIN KING SR. and JNO. BRYANT, AC and Bedford counties - sheep, cattle, furniture. Wit: WM. WILLIAMS, GILLIAM KING.

Page 355. 30 Jun 1789. JNO. BURFORD SR; DANL. BURFORD SR; JAS. CREWS SR; & JNO. STEWART, AC, to JOS. CREWS JR, AC, for Ŀ40, 140 acres. Lines: Lynch road, branch of Stovall, VA. TAYLOR. Wit: WM. HUGHES, JESSE BECK, WM. BURFORD, BENJ. PLUNKETT, REUBIN PENDLETON, RICH. GATEWOOD. Signed also by wives: MOLLEY CREWS, SARAH & MARY BURFORD.

Page 529. 26 Jun 1790. JNO. BURFORD; JNO. STEWART; JAS. CREWS and DANL. BURFORD SR, AC, to DANL. BURFORD JR, for 5 sh, 304 acres S branch Harris. Wit: JAS. CALLAWAY, ALEX. BRYDIE, CHAS. CHRISTIAN, RICH. CHANDLER.

Page 471. 17 Dec 1789. BOND BURNETT & wife ISABELL, AC, to JACOB PUCK-
ETT, AC, for Ŀ60, 50 acres Davis Creek; formerly tract of JNO.
WADE, dec'd. Lines: along the road. Wit: JAS. McALEXANDER JR, WM. BURN-
ETT, ALEX. McALEXANDER.

Page 18. 6 Sep 1785. JESSE BURTON, Campbell Co, to WM. BURTON, AC, for
Ŀ400, 400 acres S side Buffalo. Lines: PHILLIP BURTON, N bank
Hugg Creek, JNO. PENN, SAML. MEREDITH. Wit: ALEX.(?) HORSBURGH, PHIL
BURTON, WM. HENLEY.

Page 19. JESSE BURTON as above conveys to PHILLIP F. BURTON same area;
same acreage, witnesses and same date.

Page 68. 2 Sep 1786. JNO. BURTON & wife JANE, AC, to JNO. BURGER, Albemarle, for Ŀ40, 119 acres Beaver Creek. Part of pat. of
THOS. THOMPSON.

Page 59. 25 Apr 1786. PHILIP BURTON & wife JANCY, AC, to JOS. BURRUS,
AC, for Ŀ400, 400 acres Buffalo. Lines: MATT. TUCKER, Huff
Creek. On page 140 is order to quiz NANCY as to this deed. Done by
AMBROSE & BENJ. RUCKER, AC J.P.'s, 31 Mar 1786 (sic).

Page 96. 1 Jul 1786. WM. BURTON & wife FRANCES, AC, to JOS. BURRUS,
AC, for Ŀ76, 76 acres S side and joining Buffalo. Part of 400
acres of grantor. Lines: PHILLIP BURTON. Wit: JAS. FRANKLIN, RICH. LEE,
SAML. FRANKLIN, ALEX. BRYDIE, WM. & HENRY CAMDEN.

Page 467. 2 Jul 1787. WM. BURTON, AC, to LINDSEY COLEMAN, AC, for Ŀ324,
324 acres S side and joining Buffalo and Huff. Lines: CHAS.
BURRUS, JNO. PENN, SAML. MEREDITH. Wit: BEN COLEMAN, ACHILLES BALLINGER,
WM. TINSLEY, JNO. McDANIEL, JOSHUA TINSLEY, JESSEY CLEMENTS. On next
page is order to AMBROSE RUCKER & JOSIAH ELLIS to quiz FRANCES, wife of
WM. BURTON, and issued 3 Oct 1787; done 5 Nov 1787. Orig. deed delivered
to LIN COLEMAN Mar 1792.

Page 554. JNO. BUSH, tobacco inspector at Swan's Creek Warehouse, 1 Nov.
1790; Bondsmen: NELSON CRAWFORD, BEN COLEMAN.

Page 557. 4 Jan 1791. JOSEPH CABELL, The Elder, Buckingham Co, to his
daughter, ANNE HARRISON - love and 5 sh. - 2200 acres on both
sides Rucker's Run and about 4 miles above courthouse. Bought of Commonwealth and lately that of JOHN HARMER; also 17 slaves named; cattle,
tools and all houses thereon. Wit: NANCY BURKS, WM. BRECKENRIDGE, JOS.
C. MIGGINSON, NORBORN THOMAS, SAML. SPENCER JR, JOS. CABELL JR, WM.
CABELL JR. (Note: see WM. & JOSEPH CABELL as trustees of JNO. ROBINSON.)

Page 501. 6 Sep 1790. NICHL. CABELL & wife HANNAH, AC, to RO. RIVES of
AC for Ŀ20, 2 acres next to town of Warminster. Lines: Next to
Lot #36 on S side "Mane" St.

Page 350. 6 Jul 1789. WM. CABELL, The Elder, AC, to HECTOR CABELL -
love of WM. for his son, HECTOR and 5 sh., 99 acres Fendley's
Mt. and includes the Fendley Gap. Lines: ABRAHAM WARWICK, WM. CABELL;
granted to RO. JOHNSTON under the Regal Govt. Orig. del. 14 May 1828
to RO. RIVES, exr. or esq.(?).

Page 430. (This is the first of many deeds setting forth the same particulars, so I shall not repeat them in the following deeds.)
1 Jan 1790, WILLIAM & JOSEPH CABELL to CLOUGH SHELTON. They set forth
that under Act of Assembly in 1766 to vest certain lands in trustees -
JNO. CHISWELL, Gentl, 31 May 1760, to JNO. ROBINSON - 20,000 acres on
Rockfish in trust to JNO. ROBINSON. ROBINSON sold part of it and departed this life without conveying title and it is necessary to vest title of
purchase and residue. Land not conveyed was vested in PEYTON RANDOLPH,
ARCHIBALD CARY, SETH WARD, WM. & JOS. CABELL, or survivors to sell - balance to exrs. of JNO. ROBINSON - dispersed and remote situation of
trustees and "other accidents" - all are now dead but two CABELLS who are

225

situated convenient to each other and to the land. 190 acres of Rockfish
tract to CLOUGH SHELTON for Ⱡ19-4. Lines: Davis Creek, ELIZ. TULEY, JAS.
BROOKS, LEE HARRIS. Wit: GDN. CREWS, NORBORN THOMAS, JAS. NEVIL, WILL
CABELL JR, N. CABELL, JOS. C. MIGGINSON.

Page 431. 1 Jan 1790. WM. & JOS. CABELL, as above, to JNO. SHIELDS, JR,
        for Ⱡ42, 214 acres N branch Rockfish. Lines: orphans of GEO.
CAMPBELL; JNO. SHIELDS, SAML. WOODS' orphans; CHAS. PATRICK, SHEROD MAR-
TIN, top of the mt., flat ground of Beaver Creek. Wit: same as above,
plus CLOUGH SHELTON.

Page 433. 1 Jan 1790. WM. & JOS. CABELL to JOS. SHELTON - as above,
        for Ⱡ15-10, 155 acres on Davis Creek. Lines: WM. LEE HARRIS.
Wit: as above.

Page 435. 1 Jan 1790. WM. & JOS. CABELL to WM. LEE HARRIS as above, for
        Ⱡ12, 59 acres Davis Creek. Lines: "his own", JOS. SHELTON.
Wit: as above.

Page 436. 1 Jan 1790. WM. & JOS. CABELL to WM. HARRIS as above, for
        Ⱡ25, 101 acres Buck Creek. Lines: "his own". Wit: as above.

Page 438. 1 Jan 1790. WM. & JOS. CABELL to RO. HARDY & DAVID WITT as
        above, for Ⱡ5, 79 acres Corbin's Creek. Lines: DAVID WITT,
SAML. LACKEY, ROBERT HARDY, BRIDGWATER, CLOUGH SHELTON. Wit: as above.

Page 440. 1 Jan 1790. WM. & JOS. CABELL to JAS. BROOKS as above, for
        Ⱡ35-2, 234 acres both sides and joining Rockfish. Lines: WM.
PANNEL, CHAS. RODES, THOS. SHANNON, GEO. CAMPBELL's orphans, JNO. SHIELDS,
JOS. SMITH. Wit: same as above.

Page 441. 1 Jan 1790. WM. & JOS. CABELL to SHEROD MARTIN as above, for
        Ⱡ27-7, 547 acres N branch Rockfish. Lines: his own, JNO. BUR-
GER, RICH. RICHARDSON, the county, NATHL. HARLOW, SAML. WOODS' orphans,
JNO. DEPRIEST, AZARIAH MARTIN, JNO. SMITH, JNO. SHIELDS JR. Wit: as
above.

Page 443. 1 Jan 1790. WM. & JOS. CABELL to SEYMOUR SHROPSHIRE as above,
        for Ⱡ62, 310 acres N branch Rockfish. Lines: JNO. SHIELDS JR,
SAML. WOODS's orphans, GEO. CAMPBELL' orphans. Wit: as above.

Page 445. 1 Jan 1790. WM. & JOS. CABELL to CHAS. RODES JR. as above,
        for Ⱡ12-2, 242 acres N branch Rodes Creek. Lines: THOS. SHAN-
NON, JAS. GARLAND, CHAS. RODES. Wit: as above. Orig. del. to THOS.
STOCKTON 11 Aug 1794.

Page 448. 1 Jan 1790. WM. & JOS. CABELL to WM. SMITH as above, for
        Ⱡ63-18, 213 acres N branch Rockfish. Lines: Orphans of SAML.
WOODS, BENJ. HARRIS, NATHL. HARLOW. Wit: as above.

Page 449. 1 Jan 1790. WM. & JOS. CABELL to RICH. RICHARDSON as above,
        for Ⱡ5-18, 118 acres Meecham's river in AC and Albemarle.
Lines: JNO. BURGER, SAML. MUSE, his own, the county line, SHEROD MARTIN.
Wit: as above.

Page 475. 1 Jan 1790. WM. & JOS. CABELL to JNO. SMITH as above, for
        Ⱡ12-4, 244 acres N branch Rockfish. Lines: JNO. SHIELDS JR,
JNO. SHIELDS, the Elder, JOS. SMITH, AZARIAH MARTIN, SHEROD MARTIN.
Wit: as above. Orig. del. to WM. DAWSON for JNO. SMITH agreeable to
note filed.

Page 621. 9 Mar 1791. WM. & JOS. CABELL to NATHL. HARLOW as above, for
        Ⱡ28-18 (later stated as Ⱡ29-15), 289 acres on N branch Rock-
fish. Lines: orphans of SAML. WOODS, SHEROD MARTIN. Wit: PLEASANT MARTIN,
SAML. MEREDITH, GABL. PENN, JAS. CALLAWAY.

Page 242. 7 Nov 1787. AARON CAMPBELL, AC, to LAURENCE CAMPBELL, AC,
        Deed of Trust - stock, dishes, furniture etc. - to satisfy
debt due IRVING GALT & Co. of Ⱡ36. Wit: CATLETT CAMPBELL, LAURENCE CAMP-
BELL, JOEL CAMPBELL.

Page 241. 5 Apr 1788. JOELL CAMPBELL & wife PATTY, AC, to WM. SIDNEY
CRAWFORD, AC, for Ŀ25, 137 acres near town of Cabellsburg on
waters of Higginbotham Mill Creek. Lines: LAURENCE CAMPBELL, CRAWFORD,
WM. MONTGOMERY, WM. CABELL JR. Wit: HUGH ROSE, GABL. PENN, SMYTH TANDY,
ALEX. BRYDIE. Orig. del. to CRAWFORD Oct 1790. On page 272 is an order
to quiz PATTY as to dower rights. Done 25 Sep 1788, by HUGH ROSE &
GABL. PENN.

Page 513. 14 Aug 1790. LAURENCE CAMPBELL & wife HENRIETTA, AC, to WM.
CABELL, The Elder, AC, for Ŀ14, 14 acres head branch Higgin-
botham's Mill Creek and joining CABELL's New Glasgow tract. Part of CAMP-
BELL's tract. Lines: CABELL, Col. SAML. MEREDITH, JNO. SWANSON, JNO. CA-
BELL, the Road. Wit: WM. CABELL JR, RO. RIVES, HECTOR CABELL.

Page 303. 30 Dec 1788. MOSES CAMPBELL & wife JANE, AC, to JOSEPH MAYS,
Jr, AC, for Ŀ150, 199 acres N branch Tye. Lines: GEO. STONEHAM.
EDMOND CAMPBELL got land by deed from exrs. of Hon. PHILIP GRIMES. Wit:
WM. BIBB, JOS. MAYS SR, JAS. WATERS, ELIJAH MAYS, MOSES CAMPBELL JR.
Orig. del. to HENRY HOLLOWAY 29 Nov 1790.

Page 534. 1 Oct 1790. WM. CARTER & wfe CATEY, to JNO. BARCHELOT (BOUCH-
ELOT), AC, for Ŀ30, 100 acres head branch Puppie Creek. Lines:
Job's Mt., TALIAFERRO, CARTER's plantation, WARE, between Puppie and
Horsley Creek, the Main Mt.

Page 374. 8 Jun 1789. JNO. CARTWRIGHT, AC, to THOMPSON & TEAS- Deed of
Trust - slave and mare. Wit: DAVID S. GARLAND, NATHL. POWELL.
Orig. del. to BEN JOHNSON for T & T, July 1790.

Page 372. 7 Sep 1789. PETER CARTWRIGHT; WM. LAYNE & wife NANCY, AC, to
WM. CABELL, The Elder, AC, for Ŀ24, 46 acres branch of Purga-
tory below Fendley's Gap; part of 60 acres late that of NATHAN WARD.
Lines: WM. CABELL, RICH. MURROW, JESSE MARTIN.

Page 547. 4 Oct 1790. PETER CARTWRIGHT; WM. LAINE & wife NANCY, AC, to
JESSE MARTIN & wife ELIZ, AC, for Ŀ4, 10 acres S side of Fendley's Mt.; branch of Purgatory. Part of 60 acres lately bought by PETER
CARTWRIGHT from WM. LAINE. Lines: MARTIN, old road, WM. CABELL's purchase
from PETER CARTWRIGHT, JNO. BALL, WM. ALFORD, JESSE MARTIN.

Page 502. 20 Apr 1790. JAS. CARY, AC, to JAS. TINSLEY, Bedford Co, for
Ŀ70, 53 acres. Lines: NICHL. CABELL, PHILIP BURTON. Wit: RICH-
ARD HARRISON, RICH. POWELL, JNO. TINSLEY, GEO. McDANIEL, DAVID TINSLEY.

Page 258. 1 Sep 1788. HOWARD CASH & wife LUCY, AC, to JNO. BROCKMAN, AC,
for Ŀ50, 120 acres SW side of Indian Creek.

Page 188. 2 Mar 1787. JOS. CASH, AC, to TABITHA CASH, admrx. of JOEL
CASH, dec'd, for Ŀ1018-5 of tobacco - horse, cow. Wit: BART-
LETT CASH, HENRY BROWN.

Page 417. 1 Jun 1789. RICH. CHANDLER, AC, to JOS. RICHESON, Caroline Co,
Deed of Trust - 5 sh. 114 acres bought of JNO. STEWART and
PAUL TILMAN. Lines: JNO. WIATT & others. Two tracts of 414 acres and 700
acres on Tye bought of P. THILMAN(sic); 6 slaves named. Wit: JOS. ROBERTS,
JAS. LIVELY, CHAS. TUCKER.

Page 13. 5 Sep 1785. BENJ. CHILDRESS, AC, to PETER MARTIN, AC, for
Ŀ22-10, 72 acres S branch of S fork Davis Creek. Lines: MATT.
HARRIS, WM. WRIGHT, his own. Wit: TILMAN WALTON, WM. POWELL.

Page 328. 3 Sep 1788. GOOLSBY CHILDRESS & wife NANCY, AC, to BENJ. SAN-
DIDGE, AC, for Ŀ30, 66 acres top of Blue Ridge and branches of
Pedlar. Wit: STEWART BALLOW, BENJ. HIGGINBOTHAM, JNO. SANDIDGE.

Page 31. 5 Dec 1785. CHAS. CHRISTIAN, AC, to THOS. EDWARDS, AC, for
Ŀ85, 200 acres branch of Porrage. Lines: JOS. HIGGINBOTHAM,
HENRY CHRISTIAN, THOS. WILSON, WM. MALION, CHAS. CHRISTIAN. Part of tract
of grantor. Page 184 - SARAH CHRISTIAN, wife of CHAS., quizzed 20 Mar
1787.

Page 34.   5 Dec 1785.   CHAS. CHRISTIAN, AC, to MOSES PENN, AC, for Ŀ220,
            307 acres branch Porrage and Rockey Run. Lines: THOS. EDWARDS,
CHAS., JNO. & HENRY CHRISTIAN; part of a tract. Page 185, SARAH, wife of
CHAS. CHRISTIAN, quizzed on same date as above.   AMBROSE RUCKER & GABL.
PENN were J.P.'s.

Page 283.   21 Jun 1788.   CHAS. CHRISTIAN, AC, to RAWLEY PENN, AC, for Ŀ50,
            90 acres S branch Buffalo and NW side of Braxton's Ridge.
Lines: M(?) HIGGINBOTHAM, grantor, head of Wilsher's branch. Wit: WM.
PHILLIPS, DAVID BELL, CHAS. WILSHER.

Page 374.   7 Sep 1789.   CHAS. CHRISTAIN & wife SARAH, AC, to JNO. BOLLING,
            AC, for Ŀ55, 118 acres Buffalo. Lines: S side Buffalo, CHRIS-
TIAN, top of Braxton's ridge; WM. GATEWOOD dec'd - his plantation; MOSES
HIGGINBOTHAM, greater part of it bought of JAS. ROWSEY & balance of sur-
vey made by CHRISTIAN. Wit: JAS. CHRISTIAN, WM. DAVENPORT, JAS. HIGGIN-
BOTHAM.

Page 641.   19 Mar 1790.   HCAS, GEO, & WALTER CHRISTIAN, AC, to ISAIAH
            ATKINSON for Ŀ9000 Richmond inspected tobacco paid to CHAS.
CHRISTIAN - 200 acres by late survey on branch of Rockey Run and S side
Buffalo. Lines: WALTER & CHAS. CHRISTIAN, Stovall's road; Col. RUCKER;
part of tract bequeathed by CHS. CHRISTIAN, Goochland Co, to GEO. & WAL-
TER CHRISTIAN and sold by GEO. unto CHAS. CHRISTIAN and all of his claim
bequeathed to him. Wit: JAS, MARY & HENRY CHRISTIAN; JAS. HIGGINBOTHAM,
MICHL. ATKISSON. Orig. del. to I.A. 21 Dec 1794.

Page 369.   5 Nov 1787.   ELIJAH CHRISTIAN & wife ELIZ, AC, to JOELL CAMP-
            BELL for Ŀ350, 400 acres branch of Rockey Run of Buffalo.
Lines: AMBR. RUCKER JR, SACKVILLE KING, JNO. WINGFIELD and where grantor
now lives. Wit: CHAS. CHRISTIAN, PLEASANT MARTIN, JAS. HILL, LAURENCE
CAMPBELL.   Page 482, order to quiz ELIZ., wife of ELIJAH CHRISTIAN, and
done 20 Oct 1789 by AMBROSE RUCKER & BENJ. RUCKER.

Page 159.   14 Oct 1786.   HENRY CHRISTIAN, AC, to RO. WOOD, AC, for Ŀ25,
            24 acres. Lines: E by HENRY CHRISTIAN, W by JOS. HIGGINBOTHAM,
N by THOS. EDWARDS, S by HENRY CHRISTIAN. Wit: RALPH, JNO. & ABRAHAM
LAMASTER.

Page 642.   19 Apr 1791.   JNO. CHRISTIAN & wife JUDITH, AC, to CHAS.
            CHRISTIAN, AC, for Ŀ100, 420 acres S waters of Buffalo. Part
of tract bought by JNO. SCOTT, Albemarle, and JNO. NICHOLAS, Buckingham.
Lines: MEGGINSON's Ferry road; NOTLEY MADDOX, WM. DILLARD, PETER JOINER,
AMBROSE RUCKER, CHAS. CHRISTAIN, CHAS. WILSHER, WM. GATEWOOD, dec'd.,
CHAS. CHRISTIAN's Mill pond a little above the mill, Rocky Run, JNO.
CHRISTIAN, Stovall's old road. Wit: NOTLEY W. MADDOX, JNO. KENNEDY,
CHAS. WILCHER. Memo: CHAS. CHRISTIAN has been in possession of the land
since 1775, but has never had a conveyance from JOHN CHRISTIAN.   Orig.
del. to WALTER CHRISTIAN JR, 15 Dec 1798, per order.

Page 128.   30 May 1786.   WALTER CHRISTIAN, AC, to CHAS. CHRISTIAN, AC,
            for Ŀ15, 50 acres Buffalo. Lines: Parks' road, CHAS. CHRIS-
TIAN, Migginson's road. Wit: RICH. GATEWOOD, JAS. & CHAS. H. CHRISTIAN,
NOTLEY MADDOX.

Page 171.   12 May 1787.   NATHL. CLARKE & wife MOLLEY, AC, to THOMAS
            GOODWIN, Hanover Co., for Ŀ140, 360 acres. Lines: THOS. MOR-
RISON, ZACH. CLARK, THOS. ADAMS, SAML. REID. Wit: THOS. PROSSER, PAUL
TILMAN, NICHL. BUCKNER. Note: Also spelled CLARK.

Page 361.   8 Apr 1789.   NATHL. CLARK & wife MARY, to THOS. GOODWIN,
            Caroline Co, for Ŀ60, 100 acres branch Rockfish. Lines: THOS.
MORRISON, and now in possession of ZACHARIAS CLARK. Wit: NATHAN CRAWFORD,
ZACH. CLARK, JNO. McKNIGHT. Margin: MARY, gave consent as to dower
rights 6 Jun 1791.

Page 571.   12 May 1790.   NATHL. CLARK, AC, to THOS. PROSSER - Deed of
            Trust - 5 sh.   517 acres, part of tract granted DRUMMOND &
DOSEWELL (DOWELL), and CLARK bought it of THOS. GOODWIN; also 4 slaves.
Wit: CLO. SHELTON, N. CABELL, SAML. WINFREY, BENJ. JORDON, JOS. SHELTON.

Page 384. 1 Jun 1789. WM. CLARK JR. & wife LUCY, AC, to JNO. BREADEN, AC, for Ł35, 127 acres branch of Rockfish called Bermudian(?) Creek. Wit: JNO. DAWSON, CHAS. ADAMS, OBEDIAH BRITT. Page 522, order to AC J.P.'s to quiz LUCY. Done by NATHAN CRAWFORD & WM. HARRIS 16 Aug 1790.

Page 599. 23 Oct 1790. JNO. CLARKSON & wife SUSANNAH, AC, to ZACH. TALIAFERRO, AC, for Ł150, two tracts of Tye. Lines: ZACH. TALIAFERRO, JOS. BURGER, DAVID GARLAND, WM. COFFEY. 1) 62 acres on N side river. 2) 14 acres in adjoining tract and on S side of river. Wit: JNO. WARE, SAML. HIGGINBOTHAM, DAVID CLARKSON, CHAS & JNO. TALIAFERRO.

Page 325. 2 May 1789. WM. COFFEY & wife ELIZ., AC, to JAMES BROWN, AC, for Ł6000 tobacco, 50 acres on Ivy Creek; branch of Tye; also tract adj. and 50 acres in all. Lines: JAS. BROWN, HAYS. Wit: JNO. JACOBS, MOSES MARTIN, JOS. BURGER, PETER RIPPITOE, WM. & DAVID JACOBS. Orig. del. to BROWN 18 Jul 1789.

Page 362. 10 Dec 1788. THOS. COLLINS, Albemarle, to EDWD.& THOS. GARLAND, AC, for Ł150, 300 acres both sides Harris Creek. Lines: THOS. LUCAS. Wit: NATHAL. GARLAND, CLIFTON & RO. GARLAND.

Page 630. 2 Apr 1791. JNO. COOPER, AC, to NATHL. ANDERSON & HUDSON MARTIN, attornies for HENRY MARTIN & assigness, London merchants of 2nd part and NATHAN CRAWFORD & WM. HARRIS, AC, of 3rd part. Deed of Trust - 5 sh. 196 acres on top of the Great Mt., conveyed this day to him by DAVID McANALLY & JNO. PANNELL. Wit: JNO. STAPLES, JNO. HENDERSON, BARNABAS PULLIAM. Orig. del. to JAS. MONTGOMERY 20 Sep 1799 for HUDSON MARTIN.

Page 253. 30 Oct 1787. THOS. COOPER & wife SARAH, Henry County, to BENJ. RUCKER, AC, for Ł210, 320 acres Stovall's creek. Lines: JNO. SCOT, N side Main Creek, BENJ. RUCKER, N fork Stovall. Wit: THOS., AMBROSE & ANTHONY RUCKER, JOS. CREWS JR. Page 273, order to Henry Co. JP's GEO. WALLER & THOS. STOVALL, to quiz SARAH. Done 1 Sep 1788. Orig. deed del. to THOS. RUCKER, 12 Oct 1795.

Page 573. -- 1789. Rec. 4 Oct 1790. THOS. COOPER of Henry Co. to BENJ. RUCKER, AC, for Ł50, 200 acres N side and S fork Stovall Creek. Lines: bottom of Mayo Path, Posom Island road. Wit: ANTHONY, THOS., GIDEON & SOPHIA RUCKER. Orig. del. to RUCKER, THOMAS on 12 Oct 1795.

Page 29. 8 Nov 1785. DAVID CRAWFORD, Shff. bond. Bondsmen: NATHAN CRAWFORD, GEO. HYLTON, JNO. CRAWFORD, BENJ. RUCKER.

Page 133. 7 Nov 1786. DAVID CRAWFORD bonded as late shff. to collect taxes. Bondsmen: SAML. MEREDITH, GABL. PENN, HENRY L. DAVIES, NATHAN CRAWFORD, WM. SID CRAWFORD, JNO. CRAWFORD, EDMD. WINSTON.

Page 360. 30 May 1789. JOS. CREWS, AC, to PETTIS THACKER, AC, for Ł10,000 tobacco, 170 acres Stovall's Creek. Lines: STEPHEN HAM, JOS. CREWS. Wit: JNO. WIATT, GIDEON CREWS, AUGUSTINE STEEL, JOS. WILSHER, DAVID WOODROOF, WM. TINSLEY, JER. TAYLOR.

Page 70. 14 Feb 1786. JNO. CRITTENDON, AC, to PETER DAY, for Ł100, 140 acres. Lines: JNO. TURNER, JOS. GOODWIN, E by N branch Stovall Creek, W by JOS. GOODWIN & MARTIN BIBB, N by RO. JOHNS. Wit: JOS. GOODWIN, JAS. SIMMONS, JON. HARRIS, DAVID LONDON, EDWD. HARPER. Page 113, order to AC J.P.'s to quiz MARY, wife of JNO. CRITTENDON. WM. LOVING, Clerk. Done by AMBROSE & BENJ. RUCKER, 30 Dec 1786. Orig. deed del. to SOLOMON DAY, 23 Dec 1820, one of legatees of PETER DAY.

Page 613. 6 Jun 1791. JOS. CURD & wife MARY, Buckingham Co, to DANL. WHITE, Charlotte Co, for Ł150, 400 acres head branch on Buffalo. Granted to AARON TRUHART, 20 Sep 1759.

Page 335. 15 Nov 1788. GEO. DAMRON, AC, to ALEX. CHISNALL, AC, Deed of Trust - corn, blades, tobacco, stock - 90 acres. Wit: WIATT & JNO. POWELL. Orig. del. to CHISNALL, Jan 1790.

Page 464. 7 Jun 1790. JNO. DAVIS & wife MARTHY, AC, to JAS. PENDLETON,

AC, for Ŀ80, 152 acres Rutledge Creek. Lines: CHAS. STEWART, JNO. McDAN-
IEL, JAS. PENDLETON, WIATT POWELL. Orig. and commission del. to PENDLE-
TON 10 Jun 1790. Page 491, order to quiz MARTHA wife of JNO. DAVIS, done
19 Jun 1790 by AMBROSE & BENJ. RUCKER.

Page 399. 12 Feb 1789. LARKIN DAVIS & wife SALLY, AC, to WM. WARE, AC,
232 acres Horsley Creek. Lines: RICH. DAVIS, WM. DAVIS. Wit:
JNO. POWELL, MOSES DAVIS, WM. CARTER, GEO. McDANIEL, ABRAHAM CARTER, JNO.
BROWN, WM. PRYOR.

Page 533. 8 Mar 1790. MOSES DAVIS & wife MILLIFORD, AC, to WM. PRYOR,
AC, consideration: one negro boy - for 88½ acres. Lines: DAVIS,
N fork Horsley & part of DAVIS land. Wit: JAS. WADE, JNO. BROWN, JNO.
GOODRICH.

Page 579. 7 Feb 1791. MOSES DAVIS & wife MILLY, AC, to WM. WARE, AC,
for Ŀ90, 112½ acres N fork Horsley & where DAVIS lives. Lines:
PRYOR, DAVIS old line.

Page 580. 9 Oct 1790. RICH. DAVIS, AC, to WM. WARE, AC, for Ŀ150, 200
acres N branch Horsley. Lines: MOSES DAVIS, RICH. DAVIS. Wit:
WM. CARTER, FRANCIS VEALE, BENJ. LOWELL, GEO. McDANIEL, RICH. LAWLESS.

Page 233. 8 Oct 1787. THOS. DAVIS, Lincoln Co. - power of attorney to
THOS. JOPLING, AC, to receive of THOS. UPTON, Albemarle, 1400
acres in Montgomery County - S side of the great Canaway which my father,
ROBT. DAVIS, bought of JAS. MOONEY, and afterwards descended to me as
heir at law of ROBT. DAVIS - he is to convey one half in equal portions
to my seven sisters: NANNAH(HANNAH?), ABIGALE, JANE, MARTHA, LUCY, ANN &
POLLEY DAVIS and two thirds in equal portions to my two brothers, ROBT.
& OLANDER DAVIS. Wit: RICH. FARRAR, MICHL. THOMAS, THOS. JOPLING, SHER-
ROD GRIFFIN. Orig. del. to JOPLING, Sept,1788.

Page 632. 6 Jun 1791. WM. DAVIS & wife BENEDICTOR, AC, to WM. WARE, AC,
for Ŀ40, 60 acres N branch Horsley. Lines: "Between him and
tract said WARE bought from RICH. DAVIS", W by a main leading ridge that
leads from Tobacco Row Mt. down to Horsley Creek by WM. PRYOR and includes plantation whereon FRANCIS VEAL now lives.

Page 331. 20 Apr 1789. SAML. DENNY & wife ELIZ, AC, to WM. BURNETT, AC,
for Ŀ50, 70 acres late that of JNO. WADE, dec'd.; N fork Davis
Creek. Lines: the graveyard. Wit: ALEX. McALEXANDER, MICAJAH & ZACH. BUR-
NETT, JACOB PUCKETT. Page 332, order of 21 Apr 1789, to quiz ELIZ., to
AC J.P.'s. Done 25 Apr 1789.

Page 149. 16 June 1785. Commission to Campbell Co. J.P.'s, RICH. HALL,
JAS. CALLOWAY, WM. HENDERSON, JNO. WARD & JOSIAH BULLOCK to
quiz ELIZ., wife of JOHN DEPRIEST, as to deed of 7 Mar 1785, to WM.
POWELL - 400 acres on Rucker's Run. Done by WARD & BULLOCK, 3 May 1787.
See Deed Book F for this deed.

Page 447. 2 Nov 1789. JNO. DIGGS, Shff. bond. Bondsmen: NELSON CRAW-
FORD, LUCAS POWELL, JNO. CRAWFORD, JNO. THOMPSON, JAS. MONT-
GOMERY, JAS. WOODS, WM. HARRIS.

Page 646. 10 Jan 1791. JOSHUA DOSS, AC, to JNO. ROSE, AC, Deed of Trust.
Cows, hogs, horse, cart wheels, guns etc., tobacco. Wit:
HENRY ROSE, ALEX. ROSE, SAML. PARRISH. Enclosed to Col. JNO. ROSE.

Page 139. 2 Apr 1787. JNO. DUNCAN & wife SALLY TALBERT DUNCAN, AC, &
Lexington Parish, to PHILIP HOLT, same county & parish, for
Ŀ80, 265 acres N branch Cedar Creek. Lines: JOEL WATKINS.

Page 50. 27 Oct 1785. WM. DUVAL, Spotsylvania Co, to IGNATIUS RAINS,
AC, for Ŀ500, 260 acres Lime Kiln Creek. Pat. to HENRY BELL in
1754(?). Lines: JAS. CHRISTIAN, DAVID PATTERSON, remainder pat. to DUVAL
10 Nov 1779 - 180 acres. Lines: JAS. CHRISTIAN, HENRY BELL, LARKIN GATE-
WOOD; tracts adjoin - 260 acres. Wit: ELIZ. BOWLING, THOS. GRIFFIN, JNO.
BOWLING.

Page 244. 24 May 1788. BARTLETT EADS, AC, to THOS. EADS, for Ŀ15, mare
and saddle. Wit: DAVID S. GARLAND, JNO. THOMPSON. Orig. del.
to BARTLETT EADS as per order from THOS. EADS.

Page 251. May Court 1788; rec. 5 Jul 1788. BARTLETT EADES, AC, assigns
to IRVING GALT & Co., JNO. BRECKENRIDGE, atty.- all title to a
bond in suit due me of WM. BONES as assignee of JOS. ROBERTS. Deed of
Trust. Wit: NELSON CRAWFORD, RO. WILSON, ALEX. BRYDIE, factor, for GALT
& Co.

Page 466. 7 Jun 1790. THOS. EADES, AC, to his daughter JANE EADES (EADS)
5 sh. & love - female mulatto child, Hannah. Wit: WM. LOVING,
WM. MOSS.

Page 594. 8 Feb 1791. THOS. EADS to his son, BARTLETT EADS, for 5 sh.
and because of old age - several slaves - to support my wife
MARGARET and me. Wit: TILMAN WALTON, SAML. LACKEY, CHAS. CHRISTIAN. Orig.
del. to BARTLETT EADS, Apr., 1791.

Page 38. 29 Jul 1785. JOS. EDWARDS, AC, to LEROY POPE & ISAAC WRIGHT
for Ŀ13,800 tobacco - slaves named; cattle, furniture & 395
acres on top of Blue Ridge. Deed of Trust.

Page 197. 24 Aug 1787. JOS. EDWARDS & wife ELINOR, AC, to WM. PACKSTON
of Rockbridge, for Ŀ40, 395 acres on top of the main ledge.
Wit: WM. WARE, JNO. BROWN, J. CRAWFORD.

Page 217. Blank date of 1785; rec. 1 Oct 1787. JOSEPH EDWARDS, AC, to
JNO. HALL, for Ŀ30, 300 acres N branch Pedlar and adjoins CHAS.
BLAIN. Orig. del. to JNO. HALL, 10 Oct 1795.

Page 265. 6 Oct 1788. JOS. EDWARDS, AC, to WM. HARTLESS, AC, for Ŀ20,
350 acres both sides Brown Mt. Creek; N branch of Pedlar.
Lines: JNO. BEAZLEY, top of Brown Mt. Orig. sent to WM. HARTLESS per
order 27 Jan 1823.

Page 186. Order of 30 Oct 1786 to quiz SARAH ELLIS, wife of CHAS., as to
deed of 6 Oct 1784, to JOSIAH ELLIS for two tracts of 400
acres on N side Pedlar and 23 acres by survey for CHAS. by JAS. HIGGIN-
BOTHAM. Returned 3 Sep 1787 by AMBROSE RUCKER & GABL. PENN.

Page 512. 6 Sep 1790. JNO. EUBANK & wife PEGGY, AC, to ASHCRAFT ROACH,
AC, for Ŀ120, 173 acres - survey and division for EUBANK by
JOS. BARNETT; other part in possession of DAVID JARRELL (JANELL?) on
Wilderness Creek and branches of Laurinies' Creek. Lines: McCULLOCH.
Tract of 13 acres by pat. of 16 Jun 1789, on ridge between Wilderness and
Laurence's Creek. and joins No. 1. Lines: RODERICK McCULLOCH, ASHCRAFT
ROACH, NICHL. DAVIES.

Page 322. 14 Jan 1789. BENJ. EVANS, AC, to SAML. MEGGINSON, AC, for
Ŀ100, 100 acres N side Buffalo. Lines: MEGGINSON, JOHNSON,
BAIN, JESSE KENNEDY. All that EVANS owns in AC and where he lives. Wit:
WM. PHILLIPS, JNO. KENNEDY, JNO. COLLINS, EDMD. ROWSEY.

Page 157. 4 Jun 1787. WM. EVANS, AC, & wife JOYCE, to BENJ. COFLAND,
AC, 166 acres Stovall's Creek. Lines: By the path.

Page 235. 27 Oct 1787. WM. EVANS, AC, to ALEX. BRYDIE, Factor for IRV-
ING GALT & Co.- special bail in suit - WM. HAY assignee of
RICH. GATEWOOD for Ŀ92-4 in AC court; Deed of Trust - knife, negroes.
Wit: RICH. CHANDLER, JAS. McNACIN(?).

Page 327. 26 Jan 1789. WM. EVANS (EVINS) & wife JOYCE, AC, to BENJ.
MILES, AC, for Ŀ150, 200 acres Rutledge. Lines: MOSES HIGGIN-
BOTHAM, JNO. STEWART.

Page 62. 2 Sep 1785. JNO. FARRAR, JNO. WAMMOCK of Caswell Co, NC, as
exrs. of JNO. LYON, dec'd; RICH. LYON, heir at law to BENNETT
NALLEY, AC, Ŀ500, 350 acres - agreeable to tenor of will of JNO. LYON -
part of 400 acres sold to JNO. LYON by Capt. CHAS. LEWIS, Goochland, on

Rich Cove Creek. Lines: BENJ. MOORE, Capt. JNO. DAWSON, PETER LYON, JNO.
BURRESS. Exculding 50 acres sold to BENJ. MOORE. Note: RICH. LYON is
called RICH. TANKERSLEY LYON later in deed. Wit: SAML. ANDERSON, THOS.
MOOR, RICH. FARRAR, THOS. FARRAR.

Page 167.   21 Nov 1786, rec. 4 Jun 1787. JNO. WOMMACK & JNO. FARRAR as
            exrs. of JNO. LYON, dec'd. give power of atty. to friend SAML.
ANDERSON. Wit: RICHD. LYON, WM. TURNER, OBEDIAH PEARCE.

Page 122.   26 Jun 1786. THOS. FITZPATRICK SR, Albemarle, to his son-in-
            law, JOHN WILLIAMSON and wife SARAH, AC, for love - to any
children that they may have - slaves - to be divided by WILLIAMSON & wife
and my son, THOS. FITZPATRICK JR. Wit: ELIZ. STRANGE, JNO. WILKINSON,
JNO. FITZPATRICK.

Page 64.   25 Apr 1786. JAS. FITZJARRELL, AC, to WM. MAYS for Ł10, horse
            and mare. Wit: LINN BANKS.

Page 560.   25 Dec 1790. THOS. FROST, Washington Co, to JNO. HANSARD, AC,
            for Ł100, 110 acres. Wit: THOS. JOHNSON, NEHEMIAH ROZEL, PETER
ROZEL, WM. HANSARD. Orig. del. to PETER HANSARD 8 Oct 1834.

Page 14.   3 Sep 1785. DANL. GAINES, AC, to THOS. POWELL, for Ł238,
            slave, Richard; mare, Apollo, etc. Horse in possession of JAS.
FONTAINE. Powell is thus secured on bond with GAINES - WIATT POWELL &
SAML. MEREDITH to DAVID ROSS & Co. for goods.

Page 14.   3 Sep 1785. DANL. GAINES, AC, power of atty. to BERNARD
            GAINES & JNO. STEWART to dispose of my Kentucky lands in Lin-
coln, Fayette, Jefferson & Nelson and settling my partnership with EZEK.
KENNEDY. On next page, 15, Sept. 6, 1785, DANL. grants separate power to
his son, BERNARD, to attend to the KENNEDY business and to sell lands in
the counties named: "generally called Kentucky District".

Page 56.   21 Mar 1780. DANL. GAINES' receipt from SAML. ALLEN for negro
            given JNO. WYATT GILBERT, a specialty, and sold by GILBERT to
ALLEN. Recorded, 6 Mar 1786. Wit: JAS. FRANKLIN.

Page 66.   Order of 25 Aug 1784 to quiz MARY GAINES, wife of DANL., as to
            deed of 3 Aug 1784 to FRANCIS LIPSCOMB for 414 acres. Done by
AMBROSE RUCKER & GABL. PENN 12 May 1786.

Page 112.   5 Oct 1786. Order to same J.P's as above to quiz MARY GAINES,
            wife of DANL. as to deed of 8 Aug 1778 to STEPHEN HAM - 298
acres S fork Rutledge. Done, 4 Nov 1786.

Page 46.   3 Mar 1786. GEO. GILLASPIE & wife MARY, AC, to JNO. THOMPSON,
            AC merchant, for Ł240, 471 acres, part of a tract bought by
GILLESPIE of LUNSFORD LOMAX JR. Lines: Red oak stump on a mt., JONES,
BIBB, EDMUNDS, CHAS. ROSE. Wit: LUCAS POWELL, CHRISTOPHER BOLLING,
TILMAN WALTON, JNO. ALFORD.

Page 363.   6 Apr 1789. THOS. GARLAND, AC, to AMBROSE RUCKER, AC, for Ł75,
            99 acres Harris Creek. Lines: at the Road; old line; no cor-
ners nor pointers could be found; where LUCAS said the corner was.

Page 11.   5 Sep 1785. AMBROSE GATEWOOD, AC, to NOTLEY WARREN MADDOX,
            AC, for Ł120, - both of Lexington Parish - 150 acres. Lines:
Capt. CHAS. CHRISTIAN on SW; WM. DILLARD on E; Rocky Creek on W; grantor
bought it of WILL GATEWOOD, SR. Wit: CHAS. CHRISTIAN, PETER LYON, ELIJAH
MAYS.

Page 589.   6 Sep 1790. AMBROSE GATEWOOD & wife MARGARET, AC, to JESSE
            KENNEDY, AC, for Ł100, 218 acres. Lines: N side Buffalo, RICH.
BAINS, WM. PHILLIPS, GEO. PHILLIPS, JNO. ROWSEY. Wit: GEO. BLAIN, WM.
WARWICK, STEPHEN WATTS.

Page 81.   15 Apr 1786. JAS. GATEWOOD, Bedford Co, to JNO. HENRY WOOD-
            ROOF, AC, for 5 sh, 310 acres N branch Buffalo; granted to
JAS. WILLIAMSON 16 Aug 1756. Lines: Late Secretary CARTER. Wit: JNO.

JONES, RICH. GATEWOOD, JNO. MITCHELL.

Page 457. 30 Mar 1790. JAS. GATEWOOD & wife FANNY, Bedford Co, to JOS.
          PENN, AC, for Ł250, 400 acres both sides Harris. Lines: FRAN-
CES HARRISON, GEO. LEE, RICH. HARVIE, WM. HARVIE. Wit: JOS. BURRUS, CHAS.
STEWART, DAVID HUNTER, JNO. McDANIEL, BENJ. PLUNKETT.

Page 33. 5 Dec 1785. LARKIN GATEWOOD & wife CATHERINE, AC, to ISAAC
          WRIGHT, AC, for Ł150, 300 acres both sides Enchanted Creek.
Lines: PHILLIP PENN, Linchill Creek. Orig. del. to grantee April 1792.

Page 60. 23 Dec 1785. RICH. GATEWOOD & wife BETTY, AC, to WM. EVANS
          for Ł150, 200 acres branch Rutledge. Lines: MOSES HIGGINBOTHAM,
HENRY GILBERT, dec'd. Wit: HENRY & PATTEY GATEWOOD, JOS. HIGGINBOTHAM.

Page 248. 3 Nov 1787. HENRY GILBERT & wife JUDITH, AC, to SAML. MERE-
          DITH, AC, for Ł86, 432 acres Rutledge & Rockey Run. Lines:
HENRY GILBERT dec'd, RICH. GATEWOOD. Wit: JNO. SMITH, WM. HORSLEY, ABRAM
CARTER, JNO. BROCKMAN, PETER CARTER. Orig. del. to grantee 15 Sep 1798.

Page 634. 8 May 1788. PERIN GILES, SR & wife LUCY, AC, to BENJ. CARPEN-
          TER, AC, for Ł150, 190 acres Thrasher Creek. Lines: AARON HIG-
GINBOTHAM. Wit: AARON HIGGINBOTHAM, BENJ. MAYS, WM. YELTON. Orig. del.
to EATON CARPENTER 1 Nov 1836(30?).

Page 637. 8 May 1788. PERRIN GILES SR, & wife LUCY, AC, to BENJ. MAYS,
          AC, for Ł100, 85 acres SW side Thresher Creek. Wit: AARON
HIGGINBOTHAM, WM. YELTON, BENJ. CARPENTER. Orig. del. to EATON CARPENTER
12 May 1796.

Page 638. 8 May 1788. PERRIN GILES SR, & wife LUCY, AC, to JAS. YELTON,
          AC, for Ł100, 140 acres - first fork of Thresher Creek. Wit:
AARON HIGGINBOTHAM, BENJ. MAYS, WM. YELTON.

Page 20. Blank date, 1785; rec. 7 Nov 1785. Land exchange between GEO.
          GILLESPIE (this name is spelled in many ways: GLASBY, GALASPIN,
GALASPIE, etc. I have commented on this man before as he is ancestor of
my wife, MILDRED MILLER DAVIS.) and CHAS. ROSE. GEO. to CHAS: 404 acres
Lines: LUCAS POWELL, ROSE, JAS. DILLARD, JAS. MAYS. CHAS. TO GEO.: pat.
of 400 acres, but by survey - 404 acres on S side Piney; also 81 acres on
S side of little Piney. Lines: GILBERT HAYS, GEO. MONROE. JAS. BOWLING
holds 20 year lease on part of first tract and GG knows it. Also ROSE
promised a certain ELIZ. PATTERSON that she could settle and reside for
5 years from 1 Nov 1784. He did not mean to restrict her in manner and
quality of clearing the land and also to prevent her disposing of the
same for the term as he did not grant her a lease and also to keep her
dependent upon his will - she being no more than tenant at will without
paying rent or liable to be turned out at any time. This can be done at
end of any year, if just cause is shown. She remains and GG knows it.
Wit: PATRICK ROSE, BALLINGER WADE, JER. WADE. Orig. del. to JAS. HAY for
GILLESPIE. (Note: It took me three years to run down this land of GILL-
ESPIES' and it is a long story told elsewhere. He operated a mill on
Piney as later deeds show and is buried in unmarked grave at foot of
Little Friar Mt. I found the plat of the graveyard and copy of a later
deed wherein Amherst heirs reserved spot where he is buried. BFD)

Page 52. 3 Mar 1786. GEO. GILLESPIE & wife MARY, AC, - he is called
          SR. herein - to GEO. BLAIN, AC, for Ł20, 122 3/4 acres. Lines:
Grantee, BIBB. Wit: NATHL. OFFUTT, WM. BIBB, WM. LAVENDER, DAVID PARROCK.
Orig. del. to BLAINE 28 Nov 1787. (Note: This was second wife of GILLES-
PIE and not mother of his children. This second wife was a widow, MARY
FARIS, and he married her in Louisa. I am of opinion that first wife and
mother of his children was a MOORE since she named on son, SHERROD MOORE,
and used MOORE for middle name of one daughter. Two of GEORGE's sons
married FARIS step-sisters in AC. BFD)

Page 201. 1 Mar 1786. Order to AC J.P.'s RODERICK McCULLOCH and JOSIAH
          ELLIS, to quiz NANCY GILLESPIE, wife of WM., as to deed to WM.
LOVING - 305 acres on Rucker's Run, N branch. Done 31 Mar 1787.

Page 356. 11 Mar 1789. JNO. GILMER, Georgia, to WM. HARRIS for Ł230, 779 acres Taylor's Creek. 1) 484 acres bought by CHAS. YOUNG 18 Sep 1778. Lines: To Mt., SMALL, ARCHIBALD WOODS, DAVID MERIWETHER, JAS. JOHNSON, RICH. ROBERSON. 2) 160 acres joining and bought of JAMES, 6 Apr 1778 - both sides Taylor Creek. Lines: AUSTIN SHEPHERD, THOS. ROBERTSON, ALEX. HENDERSON. 3) 135 acres surveyed 20 Jun 1774 and branch of Nekles(?) Creek, waters of Rockfish and joins #1. Wit: NATHAN CRAWFORD, CHAS. CRAWFORD, JOS. MONTGOMERY, WM. BRITT. Orig. del. to JAS. HAY with commission to carry to Georgia.   Page 500, order to THOS. B. SCOTT, JNO. MOORE of Wilkes Co, Ga. 21 Dec 1789, to quiz MILDRED, wife of JNO. GILMER, as to this deed. Done, 9 Mar 1790.

Page 163. 15 Oct 1786. JNO. GOODWIN to his daughter, LUCY GOODWIN, a slave, bed, cow & calf for Ł50. Signed by JNO. GOODWIN, LEWIS DAWSON, WM. & GEO. GOODWIN. Wit: JNO. & MARY MERRITT and also proved by the others above, save JNO. GOODWIN.

Page 206. 30 Sep 1786. JNO. GOODWIN, AC, to WM. GOODWIN, AC, for Ł5, 87 acres Harris Creek. Wit: SNELLING JOHNSON, JONATHAN DAKEN(?), JNO. REYNOLDS, WM. GUTHERY, LEWIS DAWSON.

Page 324. 9 Jan 1789. JNO. GOODWIN, AC, to his son, JAS. GOODWIN, for Ł5, 131 acres. Lines: a path, LEE, WM. GOODWIN's spring. Wit: JESSE & SAML. WRIGHT, SAML. TURNER, JNO. PHILLIPS.

Page 426. 15 Oct 1786. JNO. GOODWIN, AC, to GEO. GOODWIN, AC, for Ł100, 90 acres on James River. Lines: STITH. Wit: WM. GOODWIN, JNO. MERRITT, Major MERRITT, LEWIS DAWSON.

Page 178. 22 Jun 1787. WM. GOOLSBY, AC, to THOMPSON & TEAS CO. of AC, Deed of Trust - Ł11-19, stock, etc.; one man's saddle delivered. Wit: DAVID S. GARLAND, JNO. GOOLSBY, JR. Orig. del. to D.S. GARLAND for firm, Dec, 1788.

Page 193. 21 Aug 1787. JAS. GRAYSHAM, AC, to THOS. POWELL, AC, for Ł282, 433 acres branch Rocky Run; part of tract where grantor lives. Wit: JNO. WIATT, DAVID WOODROOF, WM. EVANS, DANL. GAINES.

Page 230. 25 Sep 1787. JAS. GRESHAM, AC, to SACKVILLE KING, Campbell Co., for Ł300, 582 acres Rocky Run where grantor lives. Lines: WILL BROWN CHRISTIAN, ELIJAH CHRISTIAN, JNO. EDLON(?), THOS. POWELL. Wit: JOS. BURRUS, DANL. MAYS, DRURY & JAS. CHRISTIAN. (Note: This is undoubtedly the same man as deed above, but spelled in different fashion, for THOS. POWELL adjoins this last tract. BFD)

Page 323. 17 Jan 1789. JNO. HALL & wife ELIZ., AC, to JNO. DODD for Ł45, 150 acres branch Stoney Creek of Rockfish. Wit: THOS. A. TALBERT, JOSIAS DODD, GEO. WITT.

Page 114. 5 Oct 1786. Order to AC J.P.'s to quiz MILDRED HAM, wife of STEPHEN, as to deed of 7 Aug 1780, to JAS. HILL for 268 acres next to RUCKER. Done by AMBROSE RUCKER & GABL. PENN, 4 Nov 1786.

Page 583. 25 Oct 1790. JAS. HAMBLETON & wife NANCY, Augusta Co., to WM. LITTRELL, AC, for Ł40, 53 acres binding on the Three Ridge Mt. and S side Doak's Gap. Lines: LUKE HAMBLETON, JNO. JACOBS. Wit: THOS. H. TALBOT, JNO. WITT, WM. LITTRELL, JNO. LITTRELL.

Page 58. 30 Nov 1785. LUKE HAMILTON, AC, to WM. HUGHES, AC, for Ł80, 140 acres S fork Rockfish. Lines: OWEN HERNDON on E, S by OSBURN COFFEY, W by Three Ridge Mt., N by entry of M(?) SAML. WOOD, dec'd. Wit: JAS. BROOKS, NATHAN CRAWFORD, EZRA MORRISON, JNO. CLARKE. (Note: spelling is HAMILTON here and previous deed of JAS. is HAMBLETON. This happens with this family in various items found in books. I was up at the Three Ridge Mt. area not too long ago and stopped at an old home to get directions. The man who lived there told me that it was "The old HUGHES home", but I am unable to say that it is the same tract for I have never traced it. It is in present Nelson County. BFD)

Page 37. 6 Feb 1786. KEZIAH HANSBROUGH, exrx. and JNO. LOVING, exr.

of WM. HANSBROUGH's will, to WM. CABELL, AC, for ₤50, 156 acres both sides Cabell's Mill Creek. Pat. to WM. HANSBROUGH 26 Sep 1760. Lines: N side Creek, WM. CABELL. Orig. del. to CABELL.

Page 625. 6 Dec 1790. WM. HANSBROUGH & wife SALLY, Culpeper Co, to JNO. BALL, AC, for ₤80, 100 acres Joe's Creek. Lines: WM. CABELL, the great road. Wit: WM. LOVING, WM. LOVING JR, JNO. LOVING JR, JNO. WATSON, WM. WARE. Orig. del. with commission to JNO. BALL 14 Oct 1791.

Page 539. 4 Oct 1790. EDWD. HARPER & wife FANNY, AC, to STEPHEN SMITH, Orange Co, for ₤53, 333 acres. Bollings Creek. Lines: WILLIAMS, along a path, HARPER's old line. Orig. del. to JNO. ROBERTSON.

Page 543. 4 Oct 1790. EDWD. HARPER & wife FANNY, AC, to WILLIAM HARPER, AC, for ₤75, 93 acres; part of 187 acres S side Hatt Creek; pat. at Williamsburg & Richmond. Lines: Rev. ROBT. ROSE, DENNY.

Page 617. MATT. HARRIS & wife ELIZ, AC, to MATT. PHILLIPS, AC, for ₤35, 78 acres lately occupied by LEONARD PHILLIPS, head branch of Rockfish and Marrow Bone Mt. Wit: LEONARD PHILLIPS, HEZEKIAH PURYEAR JR, ZACH. PHILLIPS, JACOB WOOD, DAVID PHILLIPS.

Page 183. 31 May 1787. CHAS. HARRISON, Fayette Co, Pa., to son RICH. HARRISON, AC, - power of atty. Wit: GABL. PENN, WIATT POWELL, JER. FRANKLIN. Orig. del. to RICH. HARRISON, Nov 1788.

Page 346. 6 Jul 1789. JAS. HARRISON & wife MARY, AC, to RUSH HUDSON, AC, for ₤75, 118 acres N branch Buffalo on N side and joins Still House Branch. Part of larger tract of JOSHUA HUDSON. Lines: RUSH HUDSON, Church road, JNO. WIATT, SMYTH TANDY, SAML. MEREDITH. Page 551, order to NICHL. CABELL, WM. CABELL JR, & WM. HARRIS, AC J.P.'s to quiz MARY HARRISON, wife of JAS., as to this deed. Order of 13 Mar 1790; done 11 Oct 1790.

Page 556. 7 Feb 1791. REUBIN HARRISON, AC, to GEO. McDANIEL, AC, for ₤18, 236 acres head branch Miller's Creek. Orig. del. to A. RUCKER 6 Sep 1817.

Page 563. 5 Feb 1791. REUBEN HARRISON & wife PEGGY; WM. TINSLEY & wife BETTY; JNO. HARRISON & wife SALLY; RICH. HARRISON & wife SUSANNA; RICH. LEE & wife FANNY, AC, to JAS. HARRISON, Buckingham Co, for ₤150, 263 acres Harris Creek. Lines: E bank Harris Creek, JNO. AMBLER, WM. TINSLEY, RICH. SHELTON, JNO. TINSLEY. Wit: NELSON CRAWFORD, NORBORN THOMAS, G. MARTIN, GEO. McDANIEL, WM. TUCKER, CHAS. ELLIS. Orig. del. to RICH. HARRISON.

Page 564. 5 Feb 1791. Same men as above as grantor, but wives are not named, to SAML. BURKS, AC, for ₤81, 81 acres Harris Creek. Lines: GEO. LEE, BATTAILE HARRISON, dec'd., RICH. SHELTON, RICH. HARVIE. Wit: same as above.

Page 4. 1 Aug 1785. RICH. HARRISON, AC, to MOSES WRIGHT, AC, for ₤125, Two tracts. 1) 170 acres on Crawley Creek. Lines: SAML. MURPHY, DUNCAN CAMMERON, HENRY TAYLOR. Part of pat. of 400 acres to GEO. TAYLOR at Williamsburg 20 Sep 1751. 2) 36 acres S side of N fork Piney bought by HENRY KEY. Lines: CHAS. ROSE, WM. HOUCHIN, BARTHOLOMEW RAMSEY, NICHL. WREN.

Page 148. 9 Dec 1786. DANL. HARVIE, AC, to THOS. WILSHIRE, AC, for ₤600, 481 acres Harris Creek. Lines: WM. HARVIE, N bank Harris, BATTAILE HARRISON, dec'd, GEO. LEE, RICH. HARVIE. Wit: JNO. WIATT, FLEMING JORDAN, THOS. POWELL, GEO. LEE, AMBROSE RUCKER, GIDEON CREWS, CHAS. STEWART, ALLEN LAVENDER, JNO. BRADSHAW.

Page 307. 2 Mar 1789. DANL. HARVIE & wife SARAH, Rutherford Co, N.C., to GEORGE LEE, AC, for ₤600, 555 acres both sides Muddy Ass Run. Lines: N bank Harris, WM. TINSLEY, THOS. WILTSHER, WM. HARVIE, JNO. HARVIE, RUCKERS. Wit: JNO. TALIAFERRO, J. STEWART, WM. LOVING, ALEX. BRYDIE, JAS. WOODS. Page 309, 2 Mar 1789, order to AC J.P.'s NATHAN CRAWFORD & ZACH. TALIAFERRO to quiz SALLIE HARVIE, wife of DANL., as to deed to GEO. LEE for 555 acres. Done, 4 Mar 1789. (Note: We can but assume that they visited AC to see about selling land for this is the way data reads. BFD) On page 314 is order to WM. NEVIL & STEPHEN WILLS, 5 Jun 1787, J.P.'s of Rutherford Co, N.C., to quiz SARAH HARVIE, wife of DANL., as to deed to THOS. WILSHER for 481 acres on Harris. Done by them in blank month and day, 1787, in Rutherford Co, N.C.

Page 42.   5 Dec 1785, rec. 6 Mar 1786. RICH. HARVIE, AC, to WM. HARVIE,
            AC - Power of Atty. to transact all of my business in Georgia
during my absence. Wit: RICH. & REUBIN HARRISON, ISAAC TINSLEY.

Page 84.   2 Jun 1786. RICH. HARVIE, AC, to RICH. PENDLETON, AC, for
            Ł20-15, 20 3/4 acres near Tobacco Row Mts.; part of a tract.
Wit: WM. TINSLEY, REUBIN HARRISON, REUBIN TINSLEY, WM. SID. CRAWFORD,
WM. LOVING.

Page 305.   25 Sep 1788. RICH. HARVIE, AC, to THOMPSON & TEAS & Co. of
            AC, Deed of Trust - crops; furniture etc. Wit: DAVID S. GAR-
LAND, WM. ALCOCK. Del. to JNO. THOMPSON, 21 Nov. 1800.

Page 43.   5 Dec 1785. WM. HARVIE, AC, Power of Atty. to RICH. HARVIE
            to transact my Virginia business. Wit: RICHARD & REUBIN HARRI-
SON & ISAAC TINSLEY.

Page 335.   29 May 1789. THOS. HAWKINS, AC, to THOMPSON & TEAS, Deed of
            Trust - slaves named and ages given. Wit: DAVID S. GARLAND,
JNO. STAPLES. Orig. del. to JNO. THOMPSON, 21 Nov 1800.

Page 305.   11 Feb 1789. CHAS. HAY, AC, to THOMPSON & TEAS - Deed of
            Trust - stock. Wit: EDWD. BOLLING, DAVID S. GARLAND. Orig.
del. 21 Nov 1800 to JNO. THOMPSON.

Page 313.   7 Apr 1789. CHAS. HAY, AC, to STEPHEN TURNER, AC, for Ł100,
            300 acres both sides Little Piney; part of a tract. Lines:
JOS. DILLARD, top of the mt. Wit: CLOUGH SHELTON, JAS. MATTHEWS, JAS.
TURNER. Orig. del. to SAML. TURNER (sic).

Page 415.   7 Dec 1789. CHAS. HAY, AC, to WM. CAMPBELL, AC, for Ł100,
            150 acres, 46 acres of it pat. to CHAS. HAY; other pat. to
MATT. DAVIS, 10 Sep 1755; formerly that of GILBERT HAY, dec'd., on both
sides of Piney. Lines: Top of the river (Little Piney) ridge; JOS. DILL-
ARD, GEO. GALASPIE.

Page 239.   27 Mar 1788. DAVID HAY, North Carolina, & JNO. SMITH, AC, to
            EDWD. WARE, AC, for Ł100, 323 acres N of Horsley Creek. Lines:
L(?) TALIAFERRO, CHAS. TALIAFERRO, WM. CABELL. Also later survey of 54
acres adj. on SW between PETER CARTER and above tract. Wit: CHAS. TALIA-
FERRO JR, JNO. & BENJ. TALIAFERRO. Orig. del. to EDWD. WARE 4 Oct 1791.

Page 623.   6 Dec 1790. DAVID HAY & wife ANNE; JNO. SMITH & wife SARAH;
            JAMES WARE & wife MARY; WM. WARE & wife PATTY; EDWD. WARE &
wife SALLY; JOSIAH JOPLING & wife SUSANNAH, all of AC to JNO. WARE, AC,
for Ł100, 125 acres both sides Pedlar. Lines: JAS. SMITH, Swaping Camp
Creek, near Elk Rock, crossing the river. JAS. SMITH. Wit: THOS. GARLAND,
HENRY BROWN, WM. DAVIS, ABRAHAM CARTER, GEO. McDANIEL.

Page 339.   11 Oct 1788. JNO. HEARD & wife MARY, AC, to GEO. & JNO. WITT
            and JOSIAH DODD, AC, for Ł100, 130 acres, part of 530 acres
pat. to GEORGE HERD BAKER and agreeable to a deed made to JAS. HERD for
same tract on 21 Nov 1748. S branch of S fork of Rockfish. Lines: JNO.
HERD, GEO. JUDE, THOS. ADAMS, JNO. WITT. Orig. del. to JNO. WITT 22 Aug
1791.

Page 376.   21 Dec 1787. ALEX. HENDERSON, AC & parish, to BENJ. HARRIS,
            Albemarle, for Ł80, 140 acres branch Taylor Creek. Lines: JNO.
McCLURE, JNO. GILMORE, SAML. WOODS, dec'd. Wit: JOS. HENDERSON, JAS.
WOODS, JAS. SIMPSON, SARAH HENDERSON.

Page 142.   15 Sep 1786. JAS. HENDERSON, AC, to JNO. MURRELL, AC, for
            Ł150, 230 acres branch Rockfish. Lines: ALEX. HENDERSON,

CLAPHAM, JNO. LOBBAN. Wit: JOS. BARNETT, RICH. PERKINS, JOS. ROBERTS, RICH. OGLESBY, THOS. EWERS, JAS. MORRISON, GEO. McDANILE, JNO. McCLORE. Two margin notes: 1) Orig. del. to MURRELL with commission, 7 Jan 1790(?) 2) Orig. del. with commission to H. MARTIN, per order Aug of 1791. Page 498, 4 Jan 1790, order to JAS. BARNETT & JOS. KENNEDY, Gentlemen of Madison County, to quiz DOROTHY, wife of JAS. HENDERSON as to deed on date cited. JNO. MURRELL is called Jr. herein. Done, 14 Apr 1790. Orig. del. to H. MARTIN JR, per order Aug 1791.

Page 145. 4 Jul 1765(sic). JNO. HENRY & JNO. SYMS, Hanover, to JNO. RYAN, AC, for Ŀ131, 524 acres on Tye. Lines: ROSE. Wit: CHAS. McPHEARSON, WM. ANDERSON, JNO. PARKS, JNO. JACOBS, DAVID WADE. Proved 7 Oct 1765 by PARKS & JACOBS; 4 Sep 1786 by DAVID WADE.

Page 614. 4 Jun 1790. CALEB HIGGINBOTHAM & wife MARY ANN, AC, to BENJ. TALIAFERRO for Ŀ150, 62 acres, part of tract bought of PHILIP SMITH; also survey adj. and pat. to grantor 18 Mar 1784, of 36 acres. Lines for both: PHILLIP SMITH, JACOB SMITH, SAML. HIGGINBOTHAM, JNO. HURT; N side Buffalo.

Page 227. 8 Aug 1787. JNO. HIGHT, AC, to JNO. ROSE for Ŀ20-7, and Ŀ359 tobacco - beds, cows, crops etc. Wit: PATRICK HIGHT, SAML. HIGHT. Orig. del. to ROSE, July 1790.

Page 181. 15 Mar 1787. MATT. HIGHT, AC, to THOMPSON & TEAS, Deed of Trust - mare, cow with CHAS. IRVING's mark; one English fiddle etc. Wit: PATRICK HIGHT, JNO. HIGHT, DAVID S. GARLAND.

Page 364. 10 Dec 1788. THOS. HILLEY & wife MARY WALKER HILLEY, AC, to CHAS. TUCKER, AC, for Ŀ100 and 600 acres with was deed of gift by NATHAN BOND to his four children and acknowledged at AC court, 3 Jun 1782 - 156 acres on Stone House Creek and part of BOND's gift of 600 acres. Lines: TABITHA CASH. Wit: BARTLETT CASH, JOS. BOND, JOS. CASH, BENJ. ROGERS. Orig. del. to grantee 17 Feb 1803.

Page 334. 24 Apr 1789. WM. HOLLANDSWORTH, AC, to THOMPSON & TEAS, Deed of Trust - cow etc; one bought of WM. LAINE, bed, woman's saddle. Wit: DAVID S. GARLAND, BENJ. POWELL. Orig. del. to J. THOMPSON 8 Aug 1799.

Page 477. 15 Dec 1789. JNO. HOLLIDAY & wife LETTES, AC, to MOSES MARTIN, AC, for Ŀ50, 103 acres Buffalo. Lines: in the field, a house, long branch. Part of tract taken off of HENDRICK ARNOLD's for grantor.

Page 242. 18 Feb 1788. PHILIP HOLT & wife ANN, AC, to THOS. LUCAS, AC, for Ŀ80, 265 acres N branch Cedar Creek. Lines: JOEL WATKINS. Wit: THOS. GARLAND, ELIZ. RUCKER, MARY LUCAS, RIEC(?) KEY, HUGH McCABE, JAS. McCABE, AMBROSE RUCKER JR. Orig. del. to AMBROSE RUCKER JR., 1793.

Page 179. 15 May 1787. WM. HOOKER, AC, to THOMPSON & TEAS, AC, for Ŀ30, Deed of Trust - wagon bought of CHAS. STATHAM; stock. Wit: LUCAS POWELL, DAVID S. GARLAND.

Page 39. 14 Apr 1785. THOS. HOPPER & wife JUNIA (signed JANE and JUNIA in summary) AC, to THOS. MATTHEWS, AC, for Ŀ40, 140 acres N side Nassau. Lines: THOS. MATTHEWS dec'd. Wit: JNO. MATTHEWS, JNO. TURNER, BARY LANNUM(X).

Page 40. 14 Apr 1785. THOS. HOPPER & wife JUNIA, AC, to JOS. LANNUN for Ŀ60, 60 acres S side Nassau. Lines: THOS. MATTHEWS, dec'd, JNO. HUNTER, WALTER KING. Wit: same as previous deed.

Page 401. 2 Nov 1789. JNO. HORSLEY, Tobacco inspector a t Swan Creek WH. Bondsmen: WM. BIBB, GEO. HILTON, JAS. DILLARD JR.

Page 132. 6 Nov 1786. WM. HORSLEY, Shff. Bondsmen: JAS. DILLARD, NEL-SON CRAWFORD, JOS. PENN, GABL. PENN, JOS. BURRUS, SAML. MEG-GINSON, WM. SPENCER.

Page 219. 5 Nov 1787. WM. HORSLEY, Shff. Bondsmen: JAS. CALLAWAY,

NELSON CRAWFORD, GABL. PENN, JNO. LOVING, HUGH ROSE, SAML. MEREDITH, JOS.
PENN, JAS. DILLARD JR, J. STEWART, JAS. DILLARD, JOS. BURRUS.

Page 277.   WM. HORSLEY, late shff., bond to collect taxes, 3 Nov 1788.
            Bondsmen: JNO. CRAWFORD, CHAS. STEWART, GABL. PENN, RODERICK
McCULLOCH, WM. SPENCER, WM. HORSLEY, JOS. PENN, JOS. BURRUS, JAS. CALLA-
WAY, J. STEWART.

Page 584.   8 Jan 1791.   WM. HORSLEY & wife MARTHA, AC, to SAML. ARRING-
            TON, AC, for Ɫ50, 69 acres S branch Owen Creek; part of tract.
Lines: GEO. HILTON (formerly JNO. JOSLIN). Wit: GEO. HILTON, WM. HORSLEY
JR, JOS. HORSLEY. Orig. del. to grantee 1 Sep 1796.

Page 95.   15 Aug 1786.   ROBT. HUDSON & wife LUCY, AC, to JAS. HARRISON,
           AC, for Ɫ100, 118 acres N branch Buffalo, joining Still House
Branch; part of tract of JOSHUA HUDSON. Lines: RUSH HUDSON, Church rode
(sic), JNO. WIATT, SMYTH TANDY, SAML. MEREDITH. Wit: RICH. CHANDLER,
JAS. FRANKLIN, ALEX. BRYDIE.

Page 497.   5 Jul 1790.   RUSH HUDSON & wife LUCY, AC, to WM. CABELL, AC,
            for Ɫ50, 100 acres N branch Buffalo. Lines: WM. CABELL's New
Glasgow tract; JOSHUA HUDSON, SAML. MEREDITH, JAS. FRANKLIN, Church Road
and meanders to JOSHUA HUDSON. Page 552, order of 16 Jul 1790 to AMBROSE
RUCKER, GABL. PENN & WM. WARE, AC J.P.'s to quiz LUCY HUDSON as to this
deed. Done 8 Oct 1790.

Page 398.   4 Sep 1789.   JAS. HULSEY, AC planter, to SAML. FOX, AC planter
            for Ɫ40, 88 or 89 acres both sides Punder branch. Lines: Capt.
JAS. MARTIN.

Page 15.   30 Sep 1785.   Rev. WM. IRVINE, Albemarle, to THOS. WILLIAMSON,
           AC, for Ɫ116, 245 acres branch Rockfish near the Blue Ridge
Mt. Lines: THOS. SHANNON, WM. SIMPSON, WM. CROW. Wit: JNO. MURRELL JR,
JNO. DINWIDDIE (or JAS.), BENJ. POE. Orig. del. to CHAS. BROOKS per
order, 30 Sep 1790.

Page 338.   1 Jun 1789.   CHAS. IRVING & wife MILLA, Albemarle, to JNO.
            WIATT, AC, for Ɫ1300, 1027 acres S and middle branch of Rut-
ledge. IRVING bought it of DANL. GAINES. Lines: 30 acres GAINES sold to
JOS. CREWS; ridge path from dwelling house on said land; St. Matthew's
Church; MEGGINSON's road.

Page 520.   20 Apr 1790.   CHAS. IRVING & MARTIN KEY, Albemarle, under au-
            thority of power from HENRY KEY - to HENRY HARPER of AC - deed
by HENRY KEY & wife, for Ɫ4500 Richmond tobacco paid by HARPER - 270
acres both sides Cub Creek. Wit: WM. TEAS, BENJ. POWELL, CHAS. BURKS,
WM. HILL, WM. BIBB, D.S. GARLAND. Orig. del. Apr 1791 to HH.

Page 192.   3 Sep 1787.   ROBT. JOHNS, MARYAN DAY & SAML. DAY, exrs. of
            PETER DAY, dec'd, AC, to BENU. RUCKER, AC, for Ɫ85, 250 acres
main fork Stovall. Lines: MAYO; MERRITT; DAY.

Page 336.   21 Jan 1789.   PETER JOHNSON, AC, to THOMPSON & TEAS, Deed of
            Trust - stock. Wit: WM. TILLER, GEO. BLAINE.

Page 503.   6 Sep 1790.   DAVID JONES, AC, to WIATT POWELL, AC, for Ɫ30, 45
            acres S side and joining N fork Rutledge; part of tract of
RICH. JONES, dec'd. Lines: Lynch Road, S bank of N fork Rutledge, Big
Hill Spring. Wit: ALEX. BRYDIE, JAS. FRANKLIN, JAS. BALLINGER.

Page 562.   -- 1790, rec. 7 FEb 1791.   DAVID JONES to REUBEN PENDLETON, AC,
            for Ɫ65, 127 acres S side and joining N fork Rutledge. Lines:
Lynch road, WIATT POWELL, JOS. CREWS, Big Hill Spring; part of tract.
Wit: JOS. PENN, JAS. PENDLETON, JAS. COLEMAN, CHAS. CHRISTIAN.

Page 255.   28 Feb 1788.   NICHL. JONES, AC, to ZACHARIAS TALIAFERRO JR,
            6 sh, Deed of Trust - cattle, etc. Wit: JNO. TALIAFERRO,
CHAS. TALIAFERRO JR.

Page 121.   4 Jul 1786.   JOSIAH JOPLING, AC, to JNO. BAISDIN, Albemarle, for 40 sh, 2 acres N side road leading from Rockfish church to the great cove; part of JOPLING's land. Wit: WM. H. & JNO. DIGGES; ELIAS WILLS; WM. HARRIS JR.

Page 524. 4 Oct 1790. JOSIAH JOPLING & wife SUSANNAH, AC, to JOS. HIG-GINBOTHAM for Ł80, 200 acres both sides Duck Run. Lines: JOS. HIGGINBOTHAM. Orig. del. to grantee, 1 Jun 1803, to verbal order.

Page 169. 2 Jul 1787. THOS. JOPLING, AC, to JOS. SMITH, AC, for Ł40, 300 acres both sides Rockfish.

Page 380. 19 Jan 1789. THOS. JOPLING & wife HANNAH, AC, to WM. BALL of Albemarle, for Ł200, 400 acres Briery Creek on S side and joining Rockfish River. Lines: EDWD. HARDING, DAVID ENIX, THOS. FARRAR. Wit: MICHL. THOMAS, GIDEON CREWS, MICHL. THOMAS JR., RALPH THOMAS.

Page 342. 5 Sep 1786. REUBEN JORDAN, Albemarle, to PLEASANT MARTIN, AC, for Ł275, 423 acres Rockfish. Lines: JOSIAH JOPLING, JNO. MONT-GOMERY, WM. LYONS. Part of 1140 acres pat. to JNO. CHISWELL, Gent., 26 Mar 1739, and by him sold to ALEX. MONTGOMERY, 25 Apr 1745, and by MONT-GOMERY to RO. BARNETT, 4 Aug 1759, and by BARNETT to JNO. FARRAR, 5 Jul 1762, and by FARRAR to REUBEN JORDAN 29 Nov 1773. Wit: BENJ. & THOS. MOOR, G. MARTIN. Page 343, Albemarle J.P.'s NICHL. LEWIS, THOS. BELL, HUDSON MARTIN to quiz JANE, wife of REUBEN JORDAN, 8 May 1787; done 4 Nov 1787.

Page 368. 6 Jul 1789. JESSE KENNEDY & wife SUSANNAH, AC, to JOS. MAYS, AC, for Ł75, 150 acres where MAYS lives. Long Branch where a path crosses leading from JOS. DILLARD's to where JOS. MAYS SR, formerly lived; near JOS. MAYS's fence, JAS. MAYS' spring branch.

Page 170. 8 Jan 1788. JNO. KESTERSON, AC, to DAVID MONTGOMERY, AC, for Ł50, 74 acres Nassau; part of tract formerly that of DAVID MONTGOMERY and was in possession of HENRY SORROW and conveyed by AC deed to grantor. Wit: HENRY MARTIN, ALLEN BLAIR, PARMENAS BRYANT, JNO. M. GRIFFIN.

Page 236. 7 Feb 1788. MILLEY KEY, AC, to JAS. BOUSH, AC, for Ł27, 100 acres branch S fork Rockfish. Conveyed by CHAS. TATE to HENRY KEY 4 Mar 1765, and by HENRY KEY granted and conveyed to MILLEY KEY. Lines: WM. ALFORD, JAS. MATTHEWS. Wit: JNO. GREGORY, WM. CHAMBERLAIN, WM. W. BOUSH. Orig. del. to grantee 1 Jul 1789.

Page 620. 8 Dec 1790. DAVID KINCAID, Hakins (It is thus here and Hawk-ins in next deed. I can find no such county in North Carolina, but this is the way it is recorded. I must confess, though, that I know nothing of early counties in N.C. despite the fact that I had several ancestors from that fine state: ROBT. LUCKEY to Bourbon County; ABEL JOHNSON to Montgomery Co, Tenn, etc. BFD.) North Carolina to JAS. PENDLE-TON for Ł140, 290 acres head branch N fork Rockfish. Lines: WM. KELE, GEO. CAMPBELL dec'd, JNO. McANALLY, WM. KILE. Wit: HAMILTON KYLE, DAVID McANALLY, JNO. McANALLY, JAS. MONTGOMERY, DAVID MOTLEY. Orig. del. to C. PERROW, atty, 10 (18?) Nov 1845.

Page 647. 2 Oct 1790. DAVID KINKHEAD, Hawkins Co, N.C. to DAVID McANAL-LY, AC, for Ł100, 79 acres head branch Rockfish near Rockfish Gap. Lines: Col. JNO. CHISWELL's old pat. line, WM. KYLE, JNO. McANALLY. Part of 737 acres equally divided by DAVID KINKHEAD, dec'd, to his two sons, JOS. & BOROUGH KINKHEAD. DAVID is heir to BOROUGH KINKHEAD. Wit: DAVID SIMPSON, HAMILTON KYLE, JAS.(sic) MONTGOMERY, JAS. PENDLETON.

Page 200. 10 Aug 1787. JACOB KING, AC, to ALEX. BRYDIE, Factor for IRVING GALT & Co. to secure judgment against me in county court of Amherst - knife, horse, tobacco on plantation where I live - estimated at 1000 plants and corn. Wit: JEREMIAH FRANKLIN, ALEX. M. DOWELL.

Page 610. 25 Jan 1791. WM. KYLE & wife MARY, AC, to JAS. ANDERSON, Al-bemarle, for Ł214-10, 429 acres head of N fork Rockfish. Lines: JNO. McANALLY, JAS. PENDLETON, THOS. BRUMHALL, FREDERICK WEAR,

JAS. BROOKS, JNO. McCUE, JNO. RICE. Wit: JNO. THOMPSON, DAVID MOTLEY,
JOS. THOMPSON, WM. KYLE. Orig. del. to PERROW, atto, 18 Nov 1845

Page 395. 29 Aug 1789. WM. LAINE, AC, to ALEX. BRYDIE,facotr for IRVING
GALT & Co., Deed of Trust - 3 slaves, mare. Wit: RICH. CHAND-
LER, THOS. WIATT.

Page 578. 9 Jul 1790. WM. LAINE (wgn of AC) to CHAS. IRVING & Co,
Ł23-6-3, Deed of Trust; negro girl about 12, Ann. Wit: CLO.
SHELTON, LEWIS NEVIL. (Note: Mr. FLOYD BENJ. LAYNE, 2236 San Marco
Drive, Los Angeles 28, Cal., has recently published a very comprehensive
book on the LAYNE, LAIN, LANE Genealogy. It was my pleasure to furnish
data from order books here. The wgn. used here denoted that this WILLIAM
was a wagoner. There was also another WM. here who distinguished himself
from the wagoner by adding "Waterman" to his title. This signified that
he was engaged in river traffic of tobacco which was a big business here
in early days. BFD)

Page 306. 28 Sep 1788. JNO. LANCESTER, AC, to THOMPSON & TEAS, Deed of
Trust - stock, etc. Wit: JAS. BIBB, DAVID S. GARLAND and del.
to him, Apr, 1789.

Page 243. 10 Oct 1787. WM. LAVENDER, AC, to ALEX. BRYDIE, factor for
IRVING GALT & Co, Deed of Trust - 5 sh. for debt a New Glasgow
store; knife; negress. Wit: WIATE POWELL, JAS. McNAIN.

Page 16. 2 Jan 1785. THOS. LAYNE & wife MARY, AC, to THOS. WILSHER,
AC, for Ł50, 200 acres S side Berry's Mt. Lines: ARTHUR RO-
BERTSON, WM. TYREE, SAML. SPENCER, grantor. Part of 385 acres pat. to
LAYNE, 20 Jul 1788. Wit: CHAS. LAYNE, JAS. LAYNE, THOS. ROBINSON, ZACH.
TYREE.

½age 409. 23 Sep 1789. GEO. LEE & wife ELIZ., AC, to GABL. PENN, AC,
for Ł600, 365 acres N side Buffalo. Lines: GABL. PENN's Glebe
tract; Col. JAS. HIGGINBOTHAM, ISAAC GIBSON, dec'd, SMYTH TANDY, FRANCES
LEE - it is land grantor bought of JOS. HIGGINBOTHAM, ISAAC GIBSON, RICH-
ARD (sic). Wit: GEO. PENN, SAML. MEREDITH, ALEX. BRYDIE, JAS. BALLINGER.

Page 458. 9 Jan 1790. GEO. LEE & wife ELIZ., AC, to JNO. AMBLER, James
City, for Ł600, 585 acres Harris Creek, bought by grantor of
DANL. HARVIE. Lines: N side Harris, JOS. PENN, grantor. Wit: ALEX. BRYDIE,
W.S. CRAWFORD, JOEL FRANKLIN, GEO. PENN, FRANK LEE. Plat is on 460 and
shows lines of WILSHER, Col. RUCKER, JNO. HARVEY. Order to quiz. ELIZ.
and done by AMBROSE RUCKER & BENJ. RUCKER, 1 Feb 1790. Orig. sent to
JNO. AMBLER "his J.J. AMBER, his son", 19 Nov 1821.

Page 488. 5 Jul 1790. GEO. LEE, AC, to RICH. SHELTON, for Ł430, 384
acres Harris Creek. Lines: Miller's branch, the old Muster-
field. Orig. del. to ELIAS WILLS, 21 Jun 1804., As SHELTON's admr.

Page 555. 15 Sep 1790, rec. 7 Feb 1791. GEO. LEE, AC, Power of Atty to
FRANK LEE. GEO. is "about to go to Kentucky". Wit: WM. DAMER-
ON, JAS. LIVELY, RICH. LEE, JS. (sic) TINSLEY.

Page 487. 3 Jul 1790. RICH LEE & wife FRANCES, AC, to RICH. SHELTON,
AC, for Ł50, 46 acres Harris Creek; joins land GEO. LEE bought
of DUNCAN GRAHAM. Lines: The plantation. Wit: JNO. HARRISON, GEO. LEE,
JNO. SHELTON, RICH. HARRISON. Orig. del. to ELIAS WILLS, SHELTON's admr,
21 Jun 1804.

Page 511. 6 Sep 1790. RICH. LEE & wife FRANCES, AC, to GEORGE LEE, AC,
for Ł100, 200 acres N side Buffalo. Part of 1370 acres. Lines:
DUDLEY GATEWOOD, Glebe, JOS. HIGGINBOTHAM, AMBROSE & FRANCES LEE.

Page 278. 1 Dec 1788. ABRAM LEMASTER & wife SALLY, AC, to SACKVILLE
KING, Campbell Co, for Ł50-10, 112 acres N fork Porrage and
where grantor lives. Lines: SACKVILLE KING, EDLOE, AARON DEHART on west.
Orig. del. to R. NOWELL, 4 Nov 1800.

Page 161. 4 Jun 1787. RALPH LEMASTER, AC, to JNO. LEMASTER, AC, for

Ł5-10, 25 acres Porage Creek. Part of tract bought by SACKVILLE KING of
RALPH LEMASTER. Lines: SACKVILLE KING on E, MARY WOOD on W, N by SACK-
VILLE KING, S by JNO. TURNER.

Page 162. 2 Jun 1787. RALPH LEMASTER & wife LUCY, AC, to SACKVILLE KING,
    Campbell Co, for Ł54-5-6, 239 acres both sides Porrage; part
of 244 acres pat. to JNO. LEMASTER, 10 Sep 1787(sic) and part of pat. to
SIMON DEHART & remainder now belongs to ABRAHAM LEMASTER & ARON DEHART.
Lines: S side Porrage; HENRY TURNER, WM. TURNER, JNO. TURNER, JNO. LEMAS-
TER (part of grant of JNO. LEMASTER SR.), JNO. WOODS, ABRAHAM LEMASTER,
JNO. CHRISTIAN. 239 acres contains 189 acres of JNO. LEMASTER's grant
adn 50 acres of SIMON DEHART's grant.

Page 101. 5 Sep 1786. RO. LESLEY, AC, to JNO. JONES, AC, for Ł18, an
    English mare and other stock. Wit: CHAS. HAY & JAS. CAMPBELL.
Orig. del. to JNO. CAMPBELL by order of JNO. JONES.

Page 408. 23 Sep 1789. JNO. LEWIS, AC, to his son, JNO. FRANCIS PENNEY
    LEWIS - land where I live and all personal estate. All at my
death and one half now. Wit: WM. CARTER, JNO. ROACH, ARCHELAUS GILLIAM.

Page 67. 2 Sep 1786. FRANCIS LIPSCOMB & wife MARY ANN, Louisa Co, to
    JNO. STEWART, AC, for Ł300, 414 acres Rutledge & Porridge Ck,
part of former tract of CARTER BRAXTON - Old Church Tract - part of it
bought by DANL. GAINES of JAS. HIGGINBOTHAM and of DANL. GAINES' patrimonial estate. Lines: JOS. HIGGINBOTHAM, NOTLEY MADDOX, BRAXTON's pat.
line, GAINES' old line, WM. MAHON's fence. Grantor bought it of DANL.
GAINES, 3 Aug 1784. Wit: WM. LOVING, BARTLETT EADES, CHESLEY KINNEY, WM.
LOVING JR.

Page 204. 28 Feb 1787. JAS. LITTERELL & wife ELIZ., AC, to JAS. BROOKS,
    Albemarle, for Ł44-1-5, 140 acres Rockfish, formerly that of
MICHL. MONTGOMERY, dec'd. Lines: CLOUGH SHELTON on east, CHISELL on east,
LITTLEBERRY WITT on west, DAVID WITT on North. Wit: LANGSDON DEPRIEST,
HENRY McCLURE(McCLANE?), EZRA MORRISON. Orig. del. from BROOKS to DAVID
WITT Sept, 1790.

Page 180. 19 Apr 1787. RICH. LITRELL, AC, to THOMPSON & TEAS Co, for
    Ł34-19-10, deed of trust - mare, bedd(sic), etc. Wit: DAVID
S. GARLAND, ALEX. SMITH, JNO. CAMPBELL. Orig. del. to T & T through
GARLAND, Dec, 1788.

Page 260. 10 Apr 1788. RICH. LITTRELL, AC, to THOMPSON & TEAS, Deed of
    Trust - stock, furniture etc. Wit: JER. PHILLIPS, and several
flowery initials which are lavish, but illegible.

Page 633. 1 Apr 1791. JAS. LIVELY, AC, to JAS. CALLAWAY, AC, for Ł160,
    192 acres both sides S fork Huff. Lines: BENJ. HIGGINBOTHAM,
PATRICK NOWLAND, JNO. COLEMAN, also 13 acres adjoining. Lines: WM. CAMDEN,
MOSES PENN. Wit: D.S. GARLAND, JOS. BURRUS, GEO. MARTIN.

Page 110. 1 Jan 1787. JOS. LIVELY & wife MARY, AC, to WM. CABELL, AC,
    for Ł280, 400 acres both sides Dutch Fork. Part of JNO. HARMER
tract escheated and sold and granted to grantor 1 Sep 1782.

Page 216. 25 Jul 1784. THOS. LOMAX, Caroline Co, to AUSTIN SMITH of AC
    for Ł15, ---acres. Lines: WM. BIBB, WM. CRISP, WM. ALFORD,
MOSES CAMPBELL, AMBROSE CAMPBELL, SAML. EDMONDS, HEZEKIAH HARGROVE. Wit:
PATRICK ROSE, CHAS. ROSE, JNO. FULCHER.

Page 269. 3 Oct 1788. JAS. LONDON & wife MARY, AC, to LARKIN LONDON,
    both AC planters, for Ł15, 100 acres branch Porrige; part of
pat. to MARGARET FRY. Lines: CHRISTIAN. Wit: ELIZ. LAMASTER, ABRAHAM
LAMASTER, WM. LEMASTER.

Page 119. 31 Oct 1786. THOS. LOVING, Powhatan Co, to nephew, WM. LOVING,
    AC, for 12 sh, my interest in estate left by my dec'd. sister,
MARY LOVING, to her son, ISHAM LOVING. Wit: JNO. LOVING, JNO. LOVING JR,
GABL. LOVING.

Page 84.   2 Oct 1786.   WM. LOVING, eldest son of JOHN LOVING, Dec'd,
late of AC, who was eldest brother of MARY LOVING, dec'd, late
of King William county. Power of Atty. to my brother, JNO. LOVING, AC,
to apply to THOS. JACKSON, Wake Co, N.C., to recover a negro woman, Oney,
and increase - or others in lieu of her - and to settle with JACKSON for
MARY LOVING's furniture, debts, etc. Reference made to will of MARY LOV-
ING. Orig. del.

Page 64.   3 Jul 1786.   THOS. LUCAS, AC, to PHILIP THURMOND for Ⱡ300, 121
acres N side Tobacco Row.

Page 189.   9 Aug 1787.   THOS. LUCAS, AC, to AMBROSE RUCKER, for Ⱡ300, 683
acres Harris Creek. Lines: COLLINS. Wit: JNO. & THOS. WIATT,
JOS. S. GAILBRAITH, JAS. CARY, GIDEON CREWS. Orig. del. to RUCKER by
BARTLETT EADES, July 1788.   Page 220, order of 9 Nov 1787 to BENJ. RUCKER
& WM. WARE, to quiz MARTHA, wife of THOS. LUCAS, to see about dower
rights in this deed. Done, 9 Jan 1788.

Page 135.   7 Aug 1786.   WM. LUNSFORD, AC, Deed of trust to JNO. ROSE, AC.
Beds, etc. Wit: RO. WHYTE, EDMD. ROOTES.

Page 559.   16 Sep 1790.   CHAS. LYNCH, JNO. LYNCH & heirs of CHRISTOPHER
& EDWD. LYNCH, dec'd, Campbell Co, to NEHEMIAH ROZZEL, AC, for
Ⱡ100, 50 acres on James. Lines: edge of Burford's old field, Bolling's
Creek. NANCY MITCHELL also signs with CHAS. & JNO. LYNCH. Wit: WM. HAN-
SARD, ZACH. POWELL, PETER ROSZEL.

Page 351.   21 Jun 1789.   CHAS. LYNCH & wife ANNA, Campbell Co, to JNO.
LYNCH, same county, for Ⱡ10, 150 acres, formerly that of ED-
WARD LYNCH, without issue. CHAS. is heir-at-law. N side James and in-
cludes the Ferry landing which is called Lynch's. Part of 400 acres for-
merly that of MICAJAH MOORMAN. Lines: JNO. WARD, JNO. GOODWIN (formerly
MILES BURFORD), including a spring; near Ferry road, another spring on
E side of road within cleared land, JNO. LYNCH (surveyed for MICAJAH
TERRELL), Horse ford, opposite Chain Island. Wit: WM. HUGHES, ENOCH RO-
BERTS, JNO. MILLER, WM. MICKLE, CHAS. L. ADAMS. Orig. sent to JNO. LYNCH
21 Mar 1803.   (Note: Here are two men who occupy prominent places in Virginia history. CHARLES LYNCH has become the center of a controversy over
his connection with the term called the "Lynch Law" or lynching. One can
find his name connected with its origin in many reference books. It is
not my purpose to enter into the argument in this excursus, but I cite
the treatise by my good friend, ALFRED PERCY JR, on this controversial
subject to those who wish to read the other side of the story. He has
prepared a discussion on the whole matter wherein he sets forth a defense
of CHAS. LYNCH.   JNO. LYNCH was to have the city of Lynchburg named
for him.   This metropolis is now one of about 55,000 in population. It is
located just across the James river from Amherst County. Actually, one is
not out of sight of houses - save for a brief space where Sweet Briar
College owns land - as one drives from Amherst to Lynchburg.   Amherst
folk refer to their county seat of Amherst as The Village and speak of
going to "Town" when they travel to Lynchburg.   Lynchburg is a "Corporation" and therin lies a story for the genealogist who seeks data on early
Virginians.   I came here in 1957 and was used to the Kentucky custom of
my native state whereby each county has a county seat and courthouse.
Such is not the case in Virginia for there Corporations are separate en-
tities. Lynchburg, for example, has her old courthouse which is no longer
used, but she has erected a modern one just across the street. In it are
housed records dating from 1809. The city actually straddles Campbell
and a part of Bedford. However, it is possible to lose track of a person
who left, let us say, Charlotte County and then drops from sight. This
person may have come to Lynchburg and reared a family. All of them may
have lived there and married in the city. If so, all marriages after 1809
are found only in Lynchburg and not in Campbell county court data at
Rustburg. This man may have bought and sold property which was in the
limits of the city. If so, all deeds on this property are recorded in
Lynchburg and not in Rustburg. He may have left a will or may have been
in chancery and the data may show no place else save Lynchburg. I found
this a bit confusing at first, but have learned that many Amherst families left here and settled in "Town" and the trails have to be picked up
across the James river in Corporation Court data.

Page 143.   2 Apr 1787.   NOTLEY MADDOX & wife FRANCES, AC, to WM. CHAPPLE, AC, for Ł150, 253 acres S branch Rutledge. Lines: JOS. HIGGIN-BOTHAM, SAML. MEREDITH, pat. line, RICH. CHANDLER. Grantor got it by "AC deed ".

Page 135.   12 Mar 1787.   HENRY MARTIN - Commissioner in Amherst Parish. Took oath before W. CABELL.

Page 349.   29 May 1787.   HENRY MARTIN, AC, to JNO. MOSBY, AC, for Ł41, 180 acres Nassau or Dutch Creek. Lines: old line of DANL. CONNER, DAVID MONTGOMERY (now MOSBY's).

Page 451.   10 Mar 1790.   WM. MARTIN & wife PATSY, AC, to HUDSON MARTIN of AC, for Ł31-5-7, two acres Davis Creek. Lines: grantee, JAS. WRIGHT. Wit: MARTIN KEY JR, RICHARD NASH, JNO. LOVING.

Page 10.   5 Sep 1785.   JAS. MATTHEWS, AC, to THOS. JOPLING, AC, for Ł40, 92 acres head branch of S fork Rockfish. Lines: ABRAHAM EADES JR. Pat. to grantor 15 Jun 1773.

Page 75.   18 May 1786.   RO. MAYO, AC, to PETER MARTIN, AC, for Ł15, 25 acres S branch Davis; part of pat. of 45 acres to ANGUS FORBUS 10 Sep 1767, and where TOMMERSON lived and which TOMMERSON bought of FOR-BUS. Wit: WM. MARTIN, HUDSON MARTIN JR, WM. WRIGHT. Orig. del. to JAS. VAUGHAN.

Page 77.   18 May 1786.   RO. MAYO, AC, to RO. MARTIN, AC, for Ł15, 26 acres S branch Davis; part of grantor's pat. land, assignee of JNO. TOMMERSON, who was assignee of ANGUS FORBUS. New line made in pre-sence of WM. MARTIN & WM. WRIGHT. Lines: BENJ. CHILDRESS, ANGUS FORBUS' former line, E part. Wit: as on page 75. Orig. del. to JAS. VAUGHAN.

Page 78.   18 May 1786.   RO. MAYO, AC, to MARY FORBUS, AC, for Ł20, 26 acres S branch Davis; data as above and wits. as p.75.

Page 348.   6 Feb 1789.   WM. MAYO, son and heir of DANL. MAYO, late of Cumberland Co, who was eldest son and heir of WM. MAYO, late of Goochland, dec'd, to NICHL. CABELL, AC, - WM. CABELL, dec'd. at Cum-berland court, 23 Jun 1767 - between W. CABELL, pltff. and MARY MAYO and GEO. CARRINGTON, exrs. of will of DANL. MAYO, and WM. MAYO, infant orphan of DANL. MAYO, by GEO. CARRINGTON JR, guardian - CABELL obtained decree on 400 acres and 200 acres on N side Fluvanna. Pat. to WM. MAYO, grand-father of WM. MAYO, and 100 acres on S side of Fluvanna and now in Buck-ingham. Ł600 for 800 acres; remainder of 1400 acres as well as 400, 200 and 100 acres. WM. CABELL, by will, devised the 1400 acres to NICHL. CA-BELL & heirs. 10 sh. paid. Wit: CLO. SHELTON, HECTOR CABELL, COD(?) CARRINGTON, PEYTON HARRISON, WM. R. BERNARD, NELSON ANDERSON.

Page 378.   7 Sep 1789.   JNO. MAYS & wife FRANCES, AC, to JAS. EDMONDS, AC, for Ł45, 90 acres N branch Tye. Lines: LEONARD TARRANT, THOS. WILSHER, JAS. EDMONDS. Part of 200 acres of JOS. MAYS, SR.

Page 207.   1 Oct 1787.   WM. MAYS & wife SARAH, AC, to LINDSEY COLEMAN, AC, for Ł50, 178 acres N branch Buffalo. Lines: JAS. WILLIAMSON, JONATHAN JOHNSON(JOHSON), CARTER BRAXTON, DAVID BLY, MARTIN TRAP, top of Turkey Mt., JNO. SWANSON, LINN BANKS - last 3 for 50 acre tract, too. Wit: JNO. PENN, DAVID TINSLEY. Orig. del. to LC, Mar 1792.

Page 262.   10 Jul 1788.   JAS. McCALL, AC, to ALEX. BRYDIE, Factor for IRVING GALT & Co. - Deed of Trust - stock, furniture, etc. Wit: JAS. McNAIN, ANDREW McDOWALL.

Page 188.   2 May 1787.   WM. McCRAW, of North Carolina, to JNO. SCOTT, AC, for Ł10, 54 acres adj. where SCOTT now lives; pat. at William-sburg 1 Aug 1772. Wit: WM. BURTON, DAVID HUNTER, LINDSEY COLEMAN, JOS. PENN, GABL. PENN.

Page 408.   3 Dec 1789.   JNO. McCUE, AC, to his children, DAVID & MARY McCUE, AC, 71 acres on branch of Rockfish near Blue Mts. It is signed CUE. Wit: JAS. BROOKS, THOS. WILSON, GEO. CAMPBELL.

Page 24.   7 Nov 1785. GEO. McDANIEL & wife MARGARET, AC, to PHILIP BUR-
TON, AC, for Ł300, 300 acres Harris Creek. Lines: McDANIEL.
Part of 710 acres formerly that of DUNCAN GRAYHAM.

Page 252.   7 Jul 1788. GEO. McDANIEL (so signed, but McDONALD at beginning of deed) and wife MARGARET, AC, to JAS. CARY, AC, for Ł53,
53 acres. Lines: NICHL. DAVIES, ANTHONY STREET, PHILIP BURTON.

Page 152.   23 Dec 1786. HENRY McDANIEL, AC, to SNELLING JOHNSON, AC, for
Ł260, 200 acres. Lines: GUTTRY. Wit: ARCHELAUS COX, JESSE BECK,
WILL GUTTRY, PHILLIP JOHNSON, JNO. GUE, JNO. MERRITT, JNO. JOILES. Orig.
del. to PHILLIP JOHNSON 12 Dec 1815.

Page 126.   27 Sep 1786. JNO. McMAHON & wife ROSOMOND MARY, & MOSES RAY,
AC, to WM. CABELL, for Ł20, 100 acres N side and joining Flu-
vanna; nearly adjacent to upper end of Swift Island. Lines: NICHL. CABELL,
WM. CABELL. Part of 400 acres to MOSES RAY, 10 Dec 1755, and late the
property of WM. BRABBIN, dec'd, and now in CABELL's possession. Wit: WILL
CABELL JR, SAML. J. CABELL, JER. PHILLIPS, JOS. PAGE.

Page 551.   7 Aug 1783. JAS. MENEES, Nashborough on Cumberland River,
Power of Atty to friend, JNO. McDANIEL, AC, to transact any
AC business. Wit: AMBROSE RUCKER, GEO. McDANIEL.(Note: Mrs. BEULAH H.
BLAIR of 1010 12th St, Apt. 7, Boulder, Colorado, has much Tennessee data
on this MENEES family. BFD)

Page 56.   22 Nov 1785. SAML. MEREDITH, AC, to THOS. MAN, Louisa Co, for
Ł100, 100 acres Rockey Run and Rutledge; part of middle lot
formerly that of CARTER BRAXTON; known as the Old Church Tract. Lines:
JOS. WILTSHIRE, JNO. JOHNSON, HIGGINBOTHAM, SAML. HILL. Orig. del. to
WM. CRAWFORD.

Page 194.   28 Jul 1787. SAML. MEREDITH, AC, to JOS. HIGGINBOTHAM, AC,
for Ł30, 119 acres Rutledge Creek. Lines: WM. CHAPPEL, MIGGIN-
SON road, JNO. STEWART, HIGGINBOTHAM. Wit: SAML. MEREDITH JR, JAS. DILL-
ARD, SALLY MEREDITH.

Page 413.   12 Nov 1789. SAML. MEREDITH, JNO. STEWART & JOS. WILSHER, AC,
to JAS. OWEN, AC, for Ł70, 95 acres - 9 acres of it is MERE-
DITH's. Lines: his own; JNO. STEWART, BRAXTON's old order line; 30 acres
of it is STEWART's; Lines: SAML. MEREDITH, JOS. WILSHER; 56 acres is that
of WILSHER. Lines: CHRISTIAN, SAML. MEREDITH (formerly BRAXTON). Wit:
NELSON CRAWFORD, LINDSEY COLEMAN, JAS. CALLAWAY, JAS. BALLINGER.

Page 484.   1 Jul 1790. SAML. MEREDITH & wife JANE, AC, to REUBIN THORN-
TON, AC, for Ł500, 979 acres N side and joining Buffalo. For-
merly that of NICHL. CABELL. Lines: JAS. FREELAND, dec'd, N bank Raven
Creek and confluences with Buffalo.

Page 150.   20 May 1787. JNO. MERRITT, AC, to DANL. MAHONE, AC, for Ł150,
436 acres (hard to decipher; could it be 236?) on Lynch Road.
Wit: JESSE BECK, NATHL. GUTTRY, WM. GUTTRY, J. ROBINSON, WM. WILSON,
PHILIP JOHNSON.

Page 151.   29 May 1787. JNO. MERRITT, AC, to CHAS. PORLEY (PERLEY?), AC,
for Ł35, 73 acres W side Lynch Road; HIGGINBOTHAM's line. Wit:
WILL GUTTRY, JESSE BECK, WM. MOON, DANL. MAHONE, NATHL. GUTTRY, PHILIP
JOHNSON. Orig. del. to WM. HANSARD.

Page 238.   2 Apr 1788. DABNEY MINOR & wife ANN, Richmond in Henrico Co,
to WM. LOVING, AC, for Ł350, two tracts of 400 acres each on
S branch Rucker's Run. 1) Line of JOS. CABELL, Spencer's Road, WM. BIBB
(formerly W. KING). 2) Adjoins and lines of CABELL & KING; crossing
Courthouse road, HEZEKIAH HARGROVE (formerly LOMAX). DABNEY MINOR bought
it of JNO. HARVEY 8 Sep 1786, and rec. in General Court. Wit: JNO. LOVING,
NELSON CRAWFORD, JOS. BURRUS. Page 251, order to Henrico J.P.'s JNO.
HARVIE & JNO. PENDLETON, to quiz ANN, wife of DABNEY MINOR, and issued
6 Jun 1788; done, 11 Jun 1788.

Page 268.   15 Apr 1788. DAVID MONTGOMERY & wife ELIZ, AC, to MATT HARRIS,

AC, for Ŀ155, 195 acres Davis Creek; S branch Rockfish and W end of Mar-
rowbone Mt. Lines: DAVID PHILLIPS, JNO. MATTHEWS, MATT. HARRIS, DAVID &
JAS. MONTGOMERY, DAVID MONTGOMERY JR, ZACHARIAH PHILLIPS, JNO. CHISWELL,
JAS. TURNER. Wit: BENJ. POWELL, JAS. TURNER, WM. WRIGHT, ANDREW WRIGHT,
WM. TILLER.

Page 270.   6 Oct 1788.   DAVID MONTGOMERY & wife MARY, AC, to DANL. MOSBY,
            Albemarle, for Ŀ300, 641 acres, five surveys adjoining on
Nassau or Dutch.   270 acres pat. to THOS. MANN RANDOLPH, 16 Aug 1756;
144 acres pat. to ZACH. PHILLIPS, 13 Jun 1760; 71 acres pat. to DAVID
MONTGOMERY 14 Jul 1769; 98 acres pat. to DAVID MONTGOMERY, 20 Jul 1780;
58 acres pat. to DAVID MONTGOMERY, 20 Jul 1780.   Orig. del. to JNO. MOSBY.

Page 590.   21 Sep 1790.   Order to WM. TERRELL & HENRY MOUNGER, Wilkes Co,
            Ga, J.P.'s, to quiz ELIZ., wife of DAVID MONTGOMERY, as to
deed above on page 268; here it is set forth as 295a. Done, 7 Dec, 1790.

Page 506.   6 Apr 1788.   JAS. MONTGOMERY & wife REBECCAH, AC, to JNO.
            THOMAS, AC, for Ŀ150, 115 acres where grantor lives in "Patton"
to DAVID MONTGOMERY; Davis Creek. Lines: ZACH. PHILLIPS, the Gap of the
Thoroughfare, DAVID MONTGOMERY, another adjoining tract with lines of
DAVID MONTGOMERY JR; his own. Wit: MATT. PHILLIPS, WM. NALLEY, JNO. KES-
TERSON.   Orig. del. to THOMAS, 15 Nov 1791.   Page 591, 21 Sep 1790,
order to Wilks Co, Ga. J.P.'s WM. TERRELL, HENRY MOUNGER & RICH. WORSHAM
to quiz REBECCA, wife of JAS. MONTGOMERY, as to deed to JNO. THOMAS, and
done, 19 Nov 1790.

Page 164.   2 Jun 1787.   JOS. MONTGOMERY & wife ELIZ., AC, to ELLIOTT
            ROBERTS, AC, for Ŀ300, 194 acres - pat. of JNO. THOMPSON -
both sides head of Buck Creek and N side Rockfish. Lines: ALEX. MONTGOM-
ERY. Adjoining tract of 215 acres; adjoining tract of 46 acres on SE side
and pat. to JNO. MONTGOMERY, dec'd.   Orig. del. to ZACH. ROBERTS, Dec.
1788.

Page 257.   20 Aug 1788.   JOS. MONTGOMERY, AC, to JNO. ROBERTS, AC, for
            Ŀ20, 40 acres; lately occupied by THOS. HERD, head branch Buck
Creek. Lines: JNO. THOMPSON.   Orig. del. to Z. ROBERTS for JNO. ROBERTS,
9 Dec 1788.

Page 17.   3 Oct 1785.   JAS. MORRISON, AC, Power of Atty. to WM. PATTON,
           Lincoln Co, to recover and receive for me 850 acres on Lick
Creek and located for me by SAML. BELL. ADAMS also contends for it.
Ky. Dist.

Page 495.   26 Jan 1790.   JOS. H. MORRISON & EZRA MORRISON, AC, to JOS.
            MONTGOMERY, AC, for Ŀ70, 240 acres S branch Rockfish. Lines:
grantee, EZRA MORRISON. Wit: JAS. BROOKS, JAS. MONTGOMERY, JAS. McCLAIN.

Page 310.   7 Apr 1789.   THOS. MORRISON & wife FRANCES, and RACHEL AYRS,
            AC, to HAWES COLEMAN, Spotsylvania - sent to him by REUBEN
COLEMAN's order - for Ŀ800, 420 acres Rockfish. Lines: ALEX. REID, JAS.
MORRISON (now SAML. REID's), JOS. MONTGOMERY, WM. MORRISON (now EZRA &
JOS. MORRISON).

Page 48.   6 Feb 1786.   BENNETT NALLEY, AC, to JNO. SORRELL DAWSON, AC,
           "full satisfaction" 131 acres both sides Cove creek. Lines:
BENJ. MOOR, JNO. DAWSON, PETER LYONS.   Orig. del. to M. DAWSON per order
filed, 12 Sep 1799.

Page 191.   25 Jun 1787.   JAS. NOWLAND & wife BATHANEAH, AC, to PHILIP
            PENN, AC, for Ŀ50, 279 acres on N side and joining Fluvanna;
mouth of "Orter" (Otter) Creek. Lines: NATHL. DAVIES, BENJ. STINNETT JR.
Wit: GEO. DAVIS, BENJ. BRYANT, EDWD. ROWZEE.

Page 616.   31 Dec 1790.   RICH. OGLESBY & wife NANCY, AC, to HENRY FRANK-
            LIN, AC, for Ŀ10, 10 acres S branch Buffalo. Part of a tract.
Lines: grantor, WM. OGLESBY.

Page 244.   2 Jun 1788.   WM. OGLESBY, AC, to JNO. THOMPSON, AC, and WM.
            TEAS, AC, Merchants, for Ŀ112, 198½ acres - bought by grantor

of JNO. BOWLING(BOLING). Lines: WM. CABELL (formerly AMBROSE JONES), BLAINE, BIBB, GALASPIE, WM. CABELL "on a mt." Wit: CALEB HIGGINBOTHAM, D.S. GARLAND.

Page 462. 24 Sep 1789. WM. OGLESBY & wife MARTHA, AC, to LEONARD HENLEY, Fluvanna Co, for Ŀ274, 274 acres S side and joining Buffalo. Lines: EDWD. CARTER, RICH. OGLESBY, Beaver Creek. Wit: JAS. HIGGINBOTHAM, RICH. OGLESBY, ISREL DAVIS. Page 464, order to quiz MARTHA 7 Oct 1789; done, 2 Dec 1789, by WM. WARE & RODERICK McCULLOCH.

Page 30. 23 Apr 1785. JNO. OLD, Albemarle Co, to DAVID ROSS, Chester-field, for Ŀ267, 120 acres "Great Bent" of James River and bought by OLD of GEO. HILTON with the mill works and adj. tract bought of HILTON; commonly known as The Mine Bank - 5 acres. Deed of Trust. Wit: GEO. NICHOLAS, RO. DRAFFIN, THOS. BELL. Orig. del. to RO. REEVES per order, July, 1794.

Page 141. 14 Nov 1785. OLLIVER ORR (OAR), AC, to RICH. PERKINS, AC, for Ŀ10, 46 3/4 acres S side Rockfish. Lines: THOS. EWERS, SAML. MILLER, PERKINS. Wit: PHILIP BAILEY, JAS. McCLAIN, JESSE OGLESBY.

Page 119. 2 Oct 1786. JAS. PAMPLIN, AC, to JNO. HORSLEY, AC, Deed of Trust. One negro, Jack. Wit: WM. HORSLEY, MICAJAH PENDLETON.

Page 176. 23 May 1787. JAS. PAMPLIN & wife RACHEL, AC, to DANILE PERROW, AC, for Ŀ32, 32½ acres S side Elk Island Creek. Lines: grantor. Wit: GEO. HILTON, JNO. WHITTLE, JOSIAH WINGFIELD.

Page 570. 5 Feb 1791. JAS. PAMPLIN, AC, to NICHL. PAMPLIN, AC, for Ŀ100, 150 acres, part of tract on both sides Elk Island Creek. Lines: SAML. ALLEN, W side Buck Mt., mouth of Chickeyhominy branch, GEO. HYLTON, WM. HORSLEY, DANL. PERROW. Includes all land owned by grantor on Elk Is-land, except 2 acres where the mill stands. Wit: JNO. PENN, ISAIAH ATKIS-SON, REUBIN PENDLETON.

Page 198. 9 Jul 1787. SAML., JNO SR., GEO. & BENJ. PARKS, son of JNO. PARKS JR, Wilks Co, N.C. - 5 sh. - to legally born children of WM. PARKS, formerly resident of Virginia and since killed by Indians in Powell's Valley - all of interest in estate of JNO. PARKS, JR., dec'd, and late of AC. Wit: JESSE DAWSON, PATRICK McCARY(COY), EDWD. TINSLEY.

Page 223. 26 Jul 1787. THOS. PARROCK, AC, to THOMPSON & TEAS, AC, Deed of Trust - 160 acres. Lines: Rev. RO. ROSE, dec'd. Wit: NATHAN POWELL, BENJ. POWELL, DAVID S. GARLAND. Del. to GARLAND, 7 Dec 1788, for grantees.

Page 54. 25 Aug 1785. PHILIP PAYTON & wife WINNEFORD, AC, to JNO. PAY-TON, AC, for Ŀ95, 200 acres Horsley Creek. Wit: PHILLIP THUR-MOND, BENJ. COLEMAN, JOS. EDWARDS, HENRY BROWN, LEROY POPE, WM. GILLESPIE. Orig. del. to Court PAYTON 1790 crossed out. Is this Court of AC?

Page 644. 13 Sep 1790. VALENTINE PAYTON, Lyncoln & State of Virginia, to JNO. BROWN, JR, Power of Atty. to act in AC for him. Wit: WM. WARE, HENRY BROWN, THOS. GARLAND.

Page 137. 2 Aug 1786. WM. PAYTON & wife MARGARET, AC, to JNO. BROWN, AC, for Ŀ100, 94 acres both sides Horsley. Lines: JNO. PAYTON, PHILIP PAYTON. Wit: PHILIP THURMOND, PHILIP GOOCH, ISAAC WRIGHT, PHILIP HOLT(?).

Page 115. 24 Jan 1787. GABL. PENN & DANL. GAINES, exrs. of HENRY GIL-BERT, dec'd, AC, to JNO. STEWART - appointed under will of record, 4 May 1778 - "lend my land where I live" 450 acres to wife MARY for life; at her death, to be sold and divided to sons, THOS. & RICH. GILBERT or heirs. May it be noted that on 15th day of present instance, MARY GILBERT, did deliver to JNO. STEWART, a writing relinquishing claims - Ŀ525 includes mansion house wherein HENRY GILBERT died - 450 acres in tract. Wit: JAS. CALLAWAY, JAS. FRANKLIN, WM. BRECKENRIDGE, WIATT POWELL, WILL TANDY, SAML. MEREDITH JR, RICH. CHANDLER, JOS. PENN, JOS. BURRUS. Will cited for description of tract.

Page 554.   1 Nov 1790.   GABL. PENN, Shff. Bond. Bondsmen: SAML. MEREDITH,
            HUGH ROSE, SAML. HIGGINBOTHAM, WM WARE, JNO. PENN, LINDSEY
COLEMAN, JOS. PENN, AMBROSE RUCKER, PLEASANT MARTIN, JAS. CALLAWAY, JOS.
BURRUS.

Page 320.   29 May 1789.   JNO. PENN & wife ELIZ., AC, to JOS. PENN, AC,
            for Ł474, paid in Jan, 1779; 324 acres both sides Huff Creek;
part of JOHN's tract. Lines: School House branch, Parks' road, JNO. PENN's
mill pond, BAILER WALKER, old order line. Wit: ALEX. BRYDIE, GIDEON
CREWS, JAS. BALLENGER, ANDREW McDOWELL, WIATT POWELL, FRANK LEE. Page
340, order to HUGH & CHAS. ROSE & GABL. PENN to quiz ELIZ, 3 Jun 1789;
done, same day, by HUGH ROSE & GABL. PENN.

Page 421.   7 Dec 1789.   MOSES PENN & wife FRANCES, AC, to JNO. & BEVERLY
            PADGETT, AC, for Ł75, 307 acres branches of Porrage and Rockey
Run. Lines: EDWARDS; CHAS. CHRISTIAN, JNO. CHRISTIAN, HENRY CHRISTIAN.
Part of tract of CHAS. CHRISTIAN. Orig. del. with commission, 3 Oct 1791.

Page 480.   22 Dec 1789.   PHILIP PENN & wife MARTHA, AC, to NICHL. DAVIES,
            Bedford, for Ł25, 279 acres Otter Creek near the mouth. Lines:
N bank Fluvanna, NATHL. DAVIES, BENJ. STINNETT. Wit: H.L. DAVIES, CHAS.
ELLIS JR, CHAS. DAVIES, JOS. PENN, NELSON CRAWFORD, ARTHUR L. DAVIES.
Orig. del. to H.L. DAVIES.

Page 535.   15 Sep 1790.   JACOB PETTYJOHN, LUCY STATON, REBECCA & MARY
            STATON, & JACOB PETTYJOHN, gdn. for NANCY STATON, AC, to WM.
DAMRON, AC, for Ł100, 200 acres Harris Creek. Lines: A hornbeam at creek,
mouth of Polecat. Wit: JNO. ROBINSON, JESSE BECK, ALLEN HEADEN.

Page 609.   1 Jun 1791.   HENRY PEYTON(PAYTON) & wife ELIZ., AC, to CHAS.
            TALIAFERRO JR, AC, for Ł30, 167 acres on Puppy Creek; S branch
of Buffalo. Lines: CHAS. TALIAFERRO, EDWD. WARE, WM. CLEMENTS , WM. HOW-
ARD. Part of land willed to ELIZ. PEYTON by THOS. POWELL, 18 Mar 1783,
and recorded in AC.

Page 453.   10 Sep 1789.   JER. PHILLIPS, AC, to WM. LEE HARRIS, AC, 5 sh.,
            deed of trust - for bond due PATRICK HIGHT on judgment -
slaves named - 4: Geo., Peter, Nelley & Daphney. Wit: C. KINNEY, P.
REYNOLDS. Orig. del. to HARRIS, 7 Jun 1790.

Page 134.   8 Aug 1787.   JNO. PHILLIPS, AC, to JNO. ROSE, AC, Deed of
            Trust - slave, furniture, etc. Wit: BARTLETT CASH, MATT. HIGHT.

Page 394.   12 Mar 1789.   JNO. PHILLIPS, AC, to GEO. PHILLIPS, AC, for 5
            sh., 167 acres N side Buffalo and S side Aaron's Branch. Lines:
WM. PHILLIPS, old pat. line. Wit: THOS. FARRAR, GABL. PHILLIPS, BETSY
PHILLIPS, WM. PHILLIPS, JACOB TYREE JR.

Page 211.   1 Oct 1787.   REASON PORTER & wife ELIZ, Albemarle, to JNO.
            GILLIAM, for Ł200, 201 acres branch of Wilderness Run. Lines:
RO. DAVIS, ARTHUR TULEY, EDWD. WATTS, ARCHELAUS GILLIAM.

Page 588.   3 Jan 1791.   FRANCIS POWELL & wife NANCY, & ELIZ. POWELL to
            JAS. CHAPMAN for Ł100, 100 acres surveyed out of larger tract
by HIGGINBOTHAM; belonged to JNO. POWELL and bought off of larger tract
of SAML. SHACKLEFORD. Orig. del. to grantee on 7 Dec 1798.

Page 160.   7 Oct 1786.   JNO. POWELL SR & JR, AC, to OBEDIAH POWELL, AC,
            for Ł500, 100 acres S branch Horsley. Lines: TALIAFERRO. Wit:
GEO. GALASPIE, FRANCIS POWELL. Orig. del. to SAML. GOODRICH per order
from Mr. O. POWELL, 7 Jan 1790.

Page 223.   14 Jan 1788.   JNO. POWELL, AC, to THOMPSON & TEAS - Deed of
            Trust - cow, furniture etc; shoemaker's tools. Wit: DAVID S.
GARLAND, PARMENAS BRYANT. Del. to GARLAND for T & T, Dec., 1788 (sic).

Page 172.   2 Jul 1787.   LUCAS POWELL & wife ELIZ, AC, to WM. POWELL, AC,
            for 5 sh, part of 170 acres grantor bought of WM. BIBB, 1 Jun
1772. Lines: WM. POWELL, LUCAS POWELL, head of Bly's Hollow.

Page 532. 4 Oct 1790. OBEDIAH POWELL & wife MARY, and ELIZ. POWELL, AC, to JAS. GOODRICH, AC, for ₤200, 50 acres on S branch Horsley. Lines: TALIAFERRO.

Page 6. 1 Aug 1785. THOS. POWELL & wife ANN, AC, to JESSE KENNEDY, AC, for ₤30, 388 acres N side and joining Buffalo. Lines: THOS. EVANS, STANHOPE EVANS, John's branch, JAS. FREELAND, dec'd. Pat. to THOS. POWELL, 20 Apr 1784. Wit: RODERICK McCULLOCH, CHAS. TALIAFERRO JR.

Page 483. 31 Oct 1789. THOS. POWELL to JNO. ROSE, Deed of Trust - ₤7; named slaves, furniture, tobacco, etc. Wit: LUCAS POWELL, PATRICK ROSE.

Page 572. 7 Feb 1791. THOS. POWELL (Taylor) and wife NANCY, AC, to JNO. HURT, AC, for ₤300, 181 acres Buffalo. POWELL bought it from WM. HIGGINBOTHAM, 1 Oct 1784 - crossing Puppy Creek. Signed by grantor's wife as ANN. Orig. del. to CHAS. TALIAFERRO JR, per order, May 1791.

Page 173. 2 Jul 1787. WM. POWELL & wife MARY, AC, to JAS. WILLS, AC, for ₤225, 611 acres. 1) 400 acres. Lines: EDMD WILCOX, LUCAS POWELL, pat. line; WALTER KING's former survey and now JAS. WILLS, N branch of Rucker's Run, Col. WM. CABELL. Granted to JNO. DEPRIEST 1 Sep 1782, and to WM. POWELL by deed on ---. 2) 136 acres. Lines: JAMES WILLS; pat. to WM. POWELL 2 Dec 1785. 3) 75 acres. Lines: LUCAS POWELL. Given by LUCAS POWELL to WM. POWELL by deed of gift this day.

Page 299. 24 Dec 1788. JNO. PRICHARD & wife UNIS, and MARY PRICHARD, widow of RICH. PRICHARD, dec'd, AC, to WM. CABELL, The Elder for ₤30, 50 acres Purgatory Swamp - S branch Joe's creek below Fendley's Gap. Part of 400 acres to LUNSFORD LOMAX SR, by WALTER KING, Bristol merchant, and THOS. MANN RANDOLPH, 1 Dec 1764, and recorded in General Court. LUNSFORD LOMAX JR, got it from LUNSFORD LOMAX SR, and wife JUDITH, 13 Jan 1767, and RICH. PRICHARD got it from LUNSFORD LOMAX JR. 3 Oct 1768. Lines: WM. CABELL, RICH. MURROW. Wit: JNO. BOUSH, WM. BOUSH, HECTOR CABELL, JOS. PAGE, CAROL EADES, HENRY REID. Orig. del. to WM. CABELL 7 Jan 1790.

Page 359. 16 Jun 1789. JNO. PRICHARD & wife UNICE, AC, to CARROL EADES, AC, for ₤25, 172 acres branch of Naked Run and head of a branch of S fork Rockfish. Lines: JAS. MATTHEWS, Mrs. WEBB, JNO. BOUSH, ABRAHAM WARWICK, WM. CHAMBERLAINE. 92 acres of it pat. to RICH. PRICHARD 7 Jul 1763, and rest, 80 acres, pat. to RICHARD 10 Jul 1766. Wit: WM. & HECTOR CABELL, RICH. MURROW.

Page 494. 1 Jun 1790. JACOB PUCKETT & wife MARY, AC, to ISAAC BURNETT, AC, for ₤50, 50 acres Rockfish. Lines: JNO. WILLIAMS, CLOUGH SHELTON, RICH. PERKINS. Inclosed(sic) to JAS. WOODS, 18 Aug 1795.

Page 469. 6 Feb 1790. GIDEON PULLIAM & wife FRANCES, Albemarle, to FREDERICK WEAR, Albemarle, for ₤140, 375 acres head of Rockfish. Lines: JNO. HENDERSON, WM. KYLE, JNO. BURGY, JNO. THOMPSON & SEYMOUR SHROPSHIRE. Wit: JNO. MARTIN JR, WM. RAMSEY, JAS. ANDERSON.

Page 595. 2 Nov 1790. IGNATIUS RAINS & wife ANN, AC, to JACOB KINNEY, Augusta Co, for ₤100, 2 tracts on branch Lime Kiln Creek. 1) 80 acres. Lines: JAS. CHRISTIAN, DAVID PATTERSON. 2) 180 acres. Lines: JAS. CHRISTIAN, HENRY BELL, LARKIN GATEWOOD. Wit: CHESLEY KINNEY, WM. KNIGHT, SAML. HILL, PETER BIBEE, JNO. FULCHER. Orig. del. to grantee Apr 1792. Page 596, order to AC J.P.'s NATHAN CRAWFORD & WM. WARE, to quiz ANN; done 2 Nov 1790.

Page 531. 2 Oct 1790. SIMON RAMSEY & wife RACHEL, AC, to ALEX. HENDERSON, for ₤60, 75 acres branch Rockfish near Blue Ridge of Mts. Lines: THOS. WILLIAMSON.

Page 74. 4 Apr 1786. MOSES RAY & wife MARY ANN, AC, to GEO. DAMRON, AC, for ₤28, 90 acres N side Tye. Lines: ARTER ROBINSON, RAY's plantation, THOS. WILLSHER.

Page 44. 9 Jan 1786. WM. RAY, State of Georgia, owns 400 acres in Buckingham on branch of Rock Island. Pat. to MOSES RAY 15 Dec 1749, and late property of THOS. RAY. Power of Atty. to my brother,

MOSES RAY, AC, to see to sale of tract. Wit: WM. CABELL, WM. CABELL JR, JNO. MIKIE.

Page 333. 11 Dec 1788. WM. & CHAS. RAY to JOS. DILLARD, all of AC, for Ł100, 400 acres pat. to GILBERT HAY 10 Sep 1755; also part of two other adj. tracts: one pat. to MATT. DAVIS on same date and one pat. to CHAS. HAY - 195 acres. Lines: GEO. GILLESPIE on the river, Col. PETER ROSE, JNO. PARSON, River Hill. Two acres excepted to GEO. GILLESPIE for his mill seat on the river - Little Piney and N branch Indian Creek. Wit: GEO. GILLESPIE, JAS. DILLARD, GEO. WORTHAM, WM. HILL. Orig. del. to GEO. GILLESPIE - scratched out - NOTLEY W. MADDOX.

Page 100. 7 Dec 1786. ALEX. REID, JR. & wife ANNE, AC, to JONATHAN BRIDGWATER, AC, for Ł350, 400 acres both sides Corbin Creek, branch of Rockfish. Lines: WM. SMALL, NATHAN REID, RO. HARDIE, CLOUGH SHELTON, JNO. WILLIAMSON. Wit: WM. BARNETT, RO. HARDEY, WM. SMALL, JAS. BARNETT, WM. BRIDGWATER, SAML. BRIDGWATER. Page 465, 5 Jan 1787, order to Bedford Co. J.P.'s, HENRY BUFORD & THOS. LUMPKIN, to quiz ANN. Done 10 Nov 1789.

Page 419. 16 Apr 1789. ALEX. REID & wife ANNE, Bedford, to RO. HARDY, AC, for Ł35, -- acres. Lines: EZRA MORRISON, WM. BARNETT. Wit: JNO. N. REID, WM., SAML., & JONATHAN BRIDGWATER.

Page 611. 6 Aug 1790. ALEX. REID JR, Bedford, to RO. HARDY, AC, for Ł21, 80 acres branch Corbin Creek of Rockfish. Lines: WM. SMALL, THOS. FITZPATRICK, WM. BARNETT. Wit: JONATHAN BRIDGWATER SR, JOS. ROBERTS, JONATHAN BRIDGWATER, JNO. FITZPATRICK, JNO. CARPENTER.

Page 144. 9 Feb 1787. JNO. REID, AC, Power of Atty. to friends SAMUEL SHANNON & ALEX. REID, District of Ky. - to secure land and divide equally with SHANNON - 400 acres on Green River. Wit: WM. BRITT, JNO. N. REID, JNO. SHANNON, ANDW. WEIR. Orig. del. to JONATHAN REID 24 Oct 1791.

Page 344. 8 Apr 1789. JNO. RICHARDSON & wife MARY, AC, to LINDSEY COLE-MAN, AC, for Ł150, 173 acres both sides Buffalo. Lines: DRURY TUCKER, JNO. SCOTT, JNO. PENN, JOS. BURRUS, LINDSEY COLEMAN, AUGUSTIN STEEL, ELISHA DENNIS. RICHARDSON bought it of WM. TUCKER. Wit: THOS. TUCKER, ZED. SHEWMAKER, JOS. EDWARDS, JNO. JOHNS. Orig. del. to LIN COLEMAN Mar 1792.

Page 382. 20 Mar 1789. HENRY ROBERTS, AC, to BENDICK LANNUM, AC, for Ł75, 263 acres lately occupied by LANNUM on Corby's Creek. Lines: THOS. JOPLING, JOS. SMITH, CORNL. MURRELL, JOS. MATTHEWS.

Page 214. 1 Oct 1787. JOS. ROBERTS & wife SALLY, AC, to CLOUGH SHELTON of AC for Ł18, 50 acres. Lines: JACOB PUCKETT, RICH. PERKINS, JONATHAN BRIDGWATER, CLOUGH SHELTON, Corbin Creek. Wit: JNO. SMITH, WM. DAWSON, ABRAHAM CARTER.

Page 72. 4 Sep 1786. JNO. ROBINSON, AC, to THOS. STOVALL, Henry Co, for Ł200, 540 acres on Stovall Creek and where grantor now lives. Wit: JNO. MERRITT, JAS. STOVALL, JAS. MERRITT.

Page 104. 8 Nov 1786. JNO. ROBINSON & wife LUCY, AC, to THOS. COWPER, Henry Co, for Ł250, 540 acres Stovall Creek. Lines: Possom Island Road and Mayo's Path. Wit: CALEB HIGGINBOTHAM, NATHAN CRAWFORD, WM. HORSLEY, AMBROSE RUCKER JR., FLEMING WATKINS, THOS. STOVALL.

Page 403. 2 Sep 1789. CHAS. RODES SR, AC and Parish, to his son, CHAS. RODES JR, of same, for love and 5 sh, 95 acres both sides Rodes' Creek. Lines: JNO. BIGGERS, S fork of Creek. Wit: WM. MARTIN, JAS. WOODS, JAS. GARLAND.

Page 577. 31 May 1790. PHILIP ROOTS, AC, plans shortly to leave and re-side for sometime in District of Kentucky - Power of Atty to JNO. PENN, AC, to transact AC business. Wit: SAML. MEREDITH, JAS. FRANK-LIN, BALLINGER(sic), JOEL FRANKLIN. Orig. del. to JNO. PENN 13 Oct 1791.

Page 530. 7 Sep 1790. HUGH ROSE & wife CAROLINE MATILDA, AC, to THOS.
          LLEWELLYN LEEHMEN(MERE?) WALL, AC, for Ł50, 50 acres S branch
Tye & Stovall's road. Part of grantor's tract. Lines: Stovall's old road,
Col. WM. CABELL, crossing Camp Creek, Stovall's new road; - since discontinued by court order. Wit: BENJ. RUCKER, THOS. WORTHAM, RO. HENRY ROSE,
CHAS. CRAWFORD. Deed and commission to WALL, 21 Dec 1790. Page 598,
order to AC J.P.'s to quiz CAROLINE MATILDA, 26 Oct 1790; done 9 Feb
1790, by BENJ. RUCKER, WM. HARRIS, & SAML. MEREDITH.   WM. CABELL, JR,
herein for lines.

Page 546. 3 Oct 1790. JNO. ROWSEY & wife MARY, AC, to CHAS. LAVENDER
          for Ł50, 92 acres - granted CHAS. WINGFIELD, assignee of JOS.
WHITTLE by Commonwealth of Va. - 10 sh. paid to "Treasury of Comm." by
CHAS. WINGFIELD - N side Buffalo ridge and coves. Lines: CHISWELL,
MATT. WHITTLE, JAS. KLAIN(KLINE?). Wit: JNO. COURNEY, WM. EDMONDS, AUSTIN
SMITH.

Page 548. 6 Sep 1790. JNO. ROWSEY & wife MARY, AC, to CHAS. STEWART,
          AC, for Ł50, 200 acres. Lines: JESSE KENNDEY, GEO. PHILLIPS,
JAS. ROWSEY. Wit: JNO. CHRISTIAN(B), STEPHEN WATTS, WM. HARRIS, WM. LOV-
ING, WM. TEAS.

Page 586. 6 Sep 1790. JNO. ROWSEY & wife MARY, AC, to JAS. ROWSEY, AC,
          for Ł30, 50 acres. Grantor got it by deed of PETER HENDRICKS.
Lines: JESSE KENNDEY, SMYTH TANDY, GEO. PHILLIPS, JNO. ROWSEY. Wit:
LEROY BAYNE, WM. LOVING, WM. HARRIS, WM. TEAS. Orig. del. to J. ROWSEY
14 Nov 1802.

Page 126. 6 Nov 1786. JNO. RYAN, AC, Power of Atty. to friends, WM.
          BIBB, SR, & GEO. GILLESPIE, SR, AC, to dispose of property
left to me by my father, JNO. RYAN, dec'd; also to transact any business.
Wit: WM. TEAS, JOS. ROBERTS, GEO. WRIGHT, C. KINNEY.

Page 155. 31 Jan 1787. JNO. RYAN, AC, to ZACH TALIAFERRO, AC, for Ł8000,
          327 acres Tye. Lines: ZACH. TALIAFERRO, MOSES HUGHES, THOS.
SNEED, Col. JNO. ROSE - N side Tye which is boundary of TALIAFERRO's
original tract. Wit: RICH. SHELTON, THOS. WIATT, SALLY SHELTON, NANCY
SHELTON, JNO. WIATT, GIDEON CREWS, JOS. PENN, JNO. WATSON, WM. TURNER,
AND. McDOWALL.

Page 490. 3 Jul 1790. JNO. SCOTT, AC, to DRURY TUCKER, AC, for Ł10, 10
          acres Buffalo; part of tract where DRURY TUCKER now dwells.
Wit: JESSE TUCKER, DAVID SNODGRASS, DANL. TUCKER, MATT. TUCKER JR.

Page 549. 4 Oct 1790. JNO. SCOTT & wife ELIZ., to HENRY CAMDEN for Ł150,
          364½ acres S branch Buffalo. Lines: JNO. PENN, Spring branch,
DRURY TUCKER's Spring branch, WM. CAMDEN. (Note:This seems to answer the
problem posed in Deed Book E, page 451. The acreage is not exactly the
same, but it looks as if JNO. & wife ELIZ., had become reconciled. Let us
hope that this is the happy ending of a sad story and that no later deeds
will prove us wrong in this conclusion. BFD.)

Page 392. 5 Oct 1789. WM. SCOTT & wife MARGARET, AC, to BENJ. PLUNKETT,
          AC, for Ł150, 161 acres Stovall Creek. Lines: JNO. BALLOW,
Isham's Branch.

Page 329. 20 Apr 1789. JESSE SHASTEEN & wife ELINOR, & ELIZ. WADE, AC,
          to JACOB PUCKETT, AC, for Ł35, 50 acres "formally" that of JNO.
WADE, dec'd; N fork Davis. Lines: JAS. CULL, an old road, WM. ALLEN's
gate, The Three Springs on ARCHELAUS COFFEY's line, SAML. DENNY, the
grave yard. Wit: ALEX. McALEXANDER, MICAJAH BURNETT, ZACH. BURNETT, WM.
BURNETT. Page 330, 21 Apr 1789, order to JNO. DAWSON, WM. HARRIS &
NATHAN CRAWFORD, AC J.P.'s to quiz ELINOR. Done, 25 Apr 1789, by CRAWFORD
& HARRIS.

Page 136. 19 Jan 1787. SAML. SHELTON SR, Albemarle, to JOSEPH SHELTON,
          AC, for Ł300, 400 acres Davis Creek - The Great Road; road
from it that leads to widow CHILDRESS. Wit: PETER DAVIS, JNO. HARRIS,
JNO. CARTER SCRUGGS, PETER MARTIN.

Page 645. 6 Jun 1791. SEYMORE SHROPSHIRE (signed SAMAIR) & wife ELIZ.,
AC, to SHEROD MARTIN, AC, for Ł62, 310 acres N fork Rockfish
near Rockfish Gap. Lines: JNO. SHIELDS, JR, SAML. WOODS, his orphans,
orphans of GEO. CAMPBELL, the pat. line.

Page 454. 26 Sep 1789. AGNES SIMPSON, DAVID SIMPSON & wife MARGARET, AC,
to HUDSON MARTIN, Albemarle, for Ł1100, 550 acres Rockfish,
where "DAVID & AGNES" now live. Lines: Col. JNO. COLES on NE, SHEROD MAR-
TIN on N, THOS. WILLIAMSON on W, THOS. PATTON on S. Two surveys: 1) 400
acres bought by WM. SIMPSON of JOSIAH CLAPHAM. 2) 150 acres by deed from
JNO. McLURE to DAVID SIMPSON. Wit: NAT. CLARK, JAS. SIMPSON, NICHL. M.
LEWIS, WM. MILLER, JOS. SIMPSON. Page 455, order to NATHAN CRAWFORD, WM.
HARRIS, & JOHN DAWSON to quiz MARGARET, wife of DAVID SIMPSON, 7 Oct 1789;
done, 28 Oct 1789. Orig. del. to grantee, 22 Aug 1805, per order.

Page 112. 5 Feb 1787. DAVID SIMPSON (signed DANL., but DAVID in all
other places) to friend, ALEX. PATTON, Lincoln Co, Dist. of
Ky, to convey to THOS. KENADY a tract on Paint Lick, 400 acres in two
pats. (Note: This was "Fighting TOM" KENNEDY who killed WM. GILLESPIE,
my wife's ancestor who went to Madison Co, Ky, for purpose of starting
life in the west. WM. GILLESPIE was killed in a duel fought in the front
yard of KENNEDY's home. There is now a marker in front of the house
which is the setting of Uncle Tom's Cabin. There is a hamlet in the
county of Garrard which is called Paint Lick. One drives into Madison
County and out in a field on a farm is the site of two grave stones for
two more ancestors of my wife. JOHN MAUZEY & wife MARY KEHOE, came from
Fauquier and died in Madison. BFD)

Page 479. 16 Feb 1790. DAVID SIMPSON, AC, Power of Atty. to JAS. MONT-
GOMERY, AC. Wit: CHAS. BROOKS, JAS. WOODS.

Page 274. 26 May 1788. JNO. SMALL, Henry Co, by atty, JAS. DENNEY to
MATT. HARRIS, AC, for Ł20, 115 acres N branch Rockfish and S
side of Pilate Mt. Lines: JAS. WOODS. Wit: JNO. THOMAS, MATT. PHILLIPS,
DAVID PHILLIPS, JAS. TURNER, STEPHEN TURNER, ZACH. ROBERTS, MATT. HARRIS
JR.

Page 648. 6 Jun 1791. AUGUSTINE SMITH, AC, to JNO. SMITH, AC, for Ł100,
200 acres Rockfish. Lines: on E by JOS. SMITH & AZARIAH MARTIN;
S by CHAS. BRIDGWATER, W by SAML. FOX & BENJ. PANNELL, N by PANNELL.

Page 541. 3 Oct 1790. AUSTIN SMITH & wife NANCY, AC, to JAS. LANDRUM,
AC, for Ł50, -- acres. Lines: WM. BIBB, JOS. MAYS, JR, AMBROSE
CAMPBELL, SAML. EDMONDS, HEZEKIAH HARGROVE. Wit: JNO. ALFORD, JESSE MAR-
TIN, WM. ALFORD.

Page 542. 1 Sep 1790. AUSTIN SMITH & wife NANCY, AC, to WM. ALFORD, AC,
for Ł25, 103 acres Tye. Lines: WM. BIBB, AUSTIN SMITH, JOS.
MAYS JR, JAS. LANDRUM.

Page 635. 17 Dec 1790. JNO. STAPLES & wife AGGEY, AC, to WM. GALASPIE,
Lincoln Co, for Ł20, 81 acres branch Dutch Creek. Lines: THOS.
EADES, JNO. STAPLES, top of ridge that divides the waters that come from
where JNO. THURMOND formerly lived from where WM. FITZPATRICK now lives.
Part of 116 acres pat. to JNO. STAPLES, 7 Aug 1789. Wit: WM. LOVING.
(Note: I have just mentioned WM. GILLESPIE in DAVID SIMPSON data above.
WM. was mail carrier between Ky and Charlottesville, but had taken his
family to Madison Co. in Ky. His daughter, MARY ANN, married HENDERSON
THURMAN in that county and I have commented on THURMAN in deed books. BFD)

Page 73. 6 Mar 1786. WIATT STARK, Rockbridge Co, to DANL. BURFORD of
AC, for Ł100, 306 acres Lynch Road. Lines: PETER RUCKER, Bur-
ford's Ridge. Wit: VA. TAYLOR, J. STEWART, JESSE BECK, SUSANNAH GILLILAND,
JNO. CREWS, JAS. DILLARD JR.

Page 79. 4 Sep 1786. AUGUSTINE STEEL, AC, to WM. WILLIAMS, AC, for Ł10,
70 acres branch Bolling's Creek. Lines: HENRY HARPER, GILLEN-
WATER, LYNCH, HARRIS. Wit: JNO. PENN. Del. in 1799 to WILLIAMS.

Page 504. 26 Dec 1789. AUGUSTINE STEEL, AC, to SAML. MEREDITH, AC, for

Ҍ75, 400 acres both sides of N & S forks Bolling's Creek. Lines: LYNCH, DANL. BURFORD. Wit: WM. CRUTCHER, NATHL. MANTIPLY, ELISHA DENNIS.

Page 397.   12 Aug 1789.   CHAS. STEWART, AC, to ALEX. BRYDIE, factor for IRVING GALT & Co, Deed of Trust - five slaves and 1 horse. Wit: THOS. WIATT, ANDR. McDONALD.

Page 29.   7 Nov 1785.   JNO. STEWART, AC, Power of Atty. to PHILIP BUR-FORD & ROBT. FLOYD - to settle my Ky. business; Jefferson County, Lincoln, Fayette & Nelson - until 1 Apr 1786.

Page 35.   6 Feb 1786.   JNO. STEWART, AC, Power of Atty. to SAML. SHACK-LEFORD, Lincoln Co, District of Kentucky, to act for him there.

Page 108.   1 Jan 1787.   JNO. STEWART & wife MOURNING, AC, to SMYTH TANDY, AC, for Ҍ470, 470 acres both sides Buffalo; part of JAS. WAT-SON tract. Lines: S side Buffalo, JAS. WATSON, JAS. FRANKLIN, Rutledge Creek, MOSES HIGGINBOTHAM, WM. PHILLIPS, Higginbotham mill creek; GABL. PENN, AMBROSE LEE, dec'd.   Page 232, order of Nov 21, 1787, to quiz MOURNING; done, 4 Dec 1787, by AMBROSE RUCKER & GABL. PENN. Orig. del. to JNO. WATSON for TANDY, 17 Nov 1787.

Page 289.   5 May 1788.   JNO. STEWART, AC, to WM. PHILLIPS, AC, for Ҍ70, 50 acres S side Buffalo. Lines: JACOB TYREE; part of grantor's land. Wit: JNO. & MOSES PENN.

Page 352.   8 Mar 1789.   JNO. STEWART & wife MOURNING, AC, to JAS. FRANK-LIN, AC, for Ҍ180, 180 acres Rutledge Creek. Lines: JAS. WAT-SON. Wit: ALEX. BRYDIE, JAS. CALLAWAY, JNO. LAMONT, R. WALKER, WM. STEW-ART, JNO. FLOYD.

Page 400.   5 Oct 1789.   JNO. STEWART & wife MOURNING, AC, to RICH. CHAND-LER, AC, for Ҍ300, 414 acres Rutledge Creek. Lines: JNO. WIATT, DANL. GAINES, WM. CHAPELL, EVE LACKEY, WM. MAYS - bought by grantor of FRANCIS LIPSCOMB.

Page 414.   25 Aug 1789.   JNO. STEWART & wife MOURNING, AC, to CHAS. STEW-ART & BENAMMI STONE for 5 sh, 450 acres lately bought from GEBL. PENN & DANL. GAINES, exrs. of HENRY GILBERT. Deed of Trust - named slaves, stock furniture etc. Wit: JOS. BURRUS, RO. WALKER, JNO. McDANIEL, WM. TYREE. Orig. sent to STONE, Dec. 1790.

Page 515.   5 Sep 1790.   JNO. STEWART & wife MOURNING, AC, to BENAMMIE STONE, AC, for Ҍ468-6-8, 471 acres Rutledge Creek - bought by grantor of Capt. GILBERT's exrs. Lines: Parks' road, Crooked Run a small branch, BENJ. RUCKER, BENJ. MILES.

Page 566.   6 Dec 1790.   JNO. STEWART & wife MOURNING, JNO. & SARAH JOHN-SON to SAML. HUCKSTEP, AC, for Ҍ150, 200 acres branch Rutledge and Rocky Run. Lines: SAML. MEREDITH, James River, MILES, JOS. HIGGIN-BOTHAM, JOS. WILSHER, JAS. OWEN - other 80 acres by JNO. STEWART to SAML. HUCKSTEP. Wit: JOS. HIGGINBOTHAM, RICH. FULCHER, JOS. BURRUS.

Page 575.   30 Dec 1790.   JNO. STEWART & wife MOURNING, AC, to JAS. WATSON of AC - 1400 acres in Kentucky in Jefferson & Nelson Counties. Grantors vested with Power under will of JNO. FLOYD. Reference to FLOYD's covenant with JNO. & GEO. MAY, 5 Dec 1782; power of atty. to RO. BRECKIN-RIDGE & GEO. NICHOLAS, our friends, to convey the 1400 acres. Wit: JAS. FRANKLIN, LINDSEY COLEMAN, LEROY POPE JR, EZEK. GILBERT, ANDR. McDOWALL.

Page 476.   24 Dec 1790.   JNO. STEWART & wife MOURNING BURFORD STEWART, AC, give Power of Atty. to CHAS. SCOTT, JNO. FOWLER, HORATIO TUR-PIN & JNO. CRITTENDEN to transact business for them as to any lands lying on the western waters of this state. Wit: JAS. CALLAWAY, JOS. BURRUS, THOS. JOHNSON.

Page 577.   4 Jan 1791.   JNO. STEWART, AC, about to remove to Georgia - Power of Atty. to friend, JNO. PENN, to collect from SMYTH TANDY; to pay JAS. MAYS - TANDY's deed of trust. Wit: WIATT POWELL, JAS. CALLAWAY, JNO. WATSON, JOS. BURRUS. Orig. del. to PENN 12 Sep 1791.

252

Page 544.   4 Oct 1790.   BENAMMI STONE & wife ELIZ.; CHAS. STEWART & wife
          SALLY, AC, to GIDEON CREWS, AC, for Ł250, 2 tracts of Rutledge.
1) 81 acres of CHAS. STEWART. Lines: JOS. CREWS, DAVID WOODROOF, Lynch
Road, STEWART, JOS. CREWS.   2) 174 acres of STONE's. Lines: CHAS. STEWART,
DAVID WOODROOF, JNO. RUCKER, JNO. McDANIEL, an old fence, JOS. CREWS.

Page 525.   HEZEKIAH STONE & wife JANE, Fluvanna Co.; MARBEL STONE & wife
          MARY, AC, to DUNCAN McLACKLAN & Co, for Ł170, 169½ acres where
MARBEL STONE lives - Taylor Creek. Lines: RO. PAGE & AUGUSTINE SHEPHERD.
Wit: JNO. NAPIER, NATHAL. W. PRICE, JNO. NAPIER JR, JNO. WILLIAMSON.
Orig. del. to RO. JOUETT to carry to Fluvanna, Oct, 1791.

Page 35.   7 Sep 1785.   MARY STOVALL, admrx., & JAS. & THOS. STOVALL,
          admrs. of GEO. STOVALL, JR, dec'd, Henry Co, to WM. GALT for
Ł300, James River. 1) 340 acres. Lines: MAYO, Stovall Creek. 2) 50 acres.
Lines: GEO. STOVALL JR, dec'd, bought it of EDWD. BOLING, 4 Jul 1769.
Lines: Lower corner of EDWD. BOLING's lower tract; N side Fluvanna; ex-
cept 4 acres on which is a mill; reference to deed: GEO. STOVALL SR, to
GEO. STOVALL JR, in Albemarle in 1759. Wit: J. STEWART, JOEL FRANKLIN,
JAS. FRANKLIN.

Page 71.   4 Sep 1786.   THOS. STOVALL & wife ELIZ, Henry County, to JNO.
          ROBINSON, AC, for Ł250, 540 acres Stovall Creek - E side of N
fork; on Possom Island road, Mays' path. Page 103, order to Henry Co.
J.P.'s, GEO. WALLER, HENRY LYNE & JNO. SALMON to quiz ELIZ. 22 Oct 1786;
done, 30 Oct 1786.

Page 122.   7 Nov 1786.   THOS. & JAS. STOVALL, exrs. of GEO. STOVALL JR,
          dec'd, AC, to BENJ. COFFLIN, AC, for Ł12, 140 acres S branch
Stovall Creek. Lines: RO. BALLOE, wolf branch - S bank; THOS. RICKETS,
RO. BOWLING. Wit: JNO. WILSHER, JAS. HILL, RICH. GATEWOOD, NATHL. POWELL.

Page 299.   27 Aug 1788.   MOSES SWEENY, Kentucky, to PETER WATERFIELD, AC,
          for Ł30, Pedlar tract - part of pat. of THOS. GOOLSBY. Lines:
WM. PRYOR, former tract divided by mutual consent - 184 acres and is
whole tract of 284 acres divided - 184 conveyed. Wit: WM. CAMDEN, BURCHER
WHITEHEAD, MICAJAH CAMDEN.

Page 69.   4 Sep 1786.   ZACH. TALIAFERRO, AC, to JOS. NICHOLAS, AC, for
          Ł25, 156 acres branch Thrasher Creek. Lines: grantor; part of
a tract. Wit: JNO. B. TALIAFERRO, JNO. POWELL, ZACH. TALIAFERRO JR, JNO.
BURGER, JOS. BURGER, AZARIAH MARTIN. Orig. del. to Capt. JNO. SALE, 15
Apr 1795.

Page 228.   4 Feb 1788.   WM. TANDY, AC, Power of Atty to THOS. FREDERICK
          TANDY, Dublin, Ireland - to recover of JNO. TANDY of said
kingdom - Ł100 Irish Sterling due me - part of larger sum due me by virtue of will of my father, THOS. TANDY, dec'd.

Page 263.   6 Sep 1788.   SMYTH TANDY & wife JOYCE, AC, to WM. GALT, part-
          ner and factor for IRVING GALT & Co, Merchants, Deed of Trust.
1 acre in town of Cabellsburgh; part of tract. Lines: lumber house in
front of Main road; RICH. CHANDLER's lot; burying ground. Wit: ALEX.
BRYDIE, WIATT POWELL, ANDREW McDOWELL. Release of interest and rights by
HUGH ROSE, SAML. MEREDITH, GABL. PENN, JNO. WIATT.

Page 294.   25 Nov 1788.   SMYTH TANDY to GABL. PENN, agent for JAS. DICKIE
          deed of trust - tobacco of Shockhoe or Byrd inspection; bonds
from 1 Dec 1783 - blacksmith tools, tables, silver, slaves, stock - long
and interesting list. Wit: T. or J. HIGGINBOTHAM, WILL TANDY.

Page 370.   22 Aug 1789.   SMYTH TANDY & wife JOICE, AC, to JNO. McHENRY &
          Co, Baltimore merchants - 5 sh. Deed of Trust. 470 acres both
sides Buffalo. Lines: JAS. WATSON, JAS. FRANKLIN, N bank Rutledge, MOSES
HIGGINBOTHAM, WM. PHILLIPS, Higginbotham mill creek; GABL PENN, AMBROSE
LEE dec'd. Bought by TANDY of Capt. JNO. STEWART and whereon is grist
mill and saw mill; distillery, and dwelling house. Also slaves, still,
etc. Claim also of CAMPBELL & WHEELER, trustees of RO. GILMORE & Co.
and JNO. STEWART. Wit: WIATT POWELL, THOS. WIATT, GABL. PENN.

Page 385. 17 Jul 1789. SMYTH TANDY & wife JOYCE, AC, to JAS. CAMPBELL
& LUKE WHEELER of Prince George and Town of Petersburgh, Deed
of Trust. 10 sh. debt due RO. GILMORE & Co, Baltimore merchants - 470
acres Buffalo. Lines: S bank Buffalo, JAS. WATSON, N bank Rutledge - rest
as above in 370. Wit: W.S. CRAWFORD, THOS. WIATT, JAS. MURRAY BROWN,
GABL. PENN.

Page 387. 21 Jul 1789. SMYTH TANDY & wife JOYCE, AC, to WM. CABELL, AC,
for Ł630, 317 acres N branch Buffalo and known as New Glasgow.
Lines: LAURENCE CAMPBELL, JAS. FRANKLIN, JOSHUA HUDSON, SAML. MEREDITH,
JNO. SWANSON - except 30 ft. square in center of which is a graveyard
fully reserved to GABL. PENN and heirs - some of his family are buried
there and 10 ft. square where TANDY has a child buried. Also 1 acres
reserved where IRVING GALT & Co. have a store and ½ acre adjacent to RICH.
CHANDLER. Wit: WM. PHILLIPS, W.S. CRAWFORD, JAS. FRANKLIN, GABL. PENN,
SAML. MEREDITH. Orig. del. to CABELL, Jan 1790. Page 390, order to quiz
JOYCE, 21 Jul 1789; done same day by AMBROSE RUCKER & GABL. PENN. (Note:
This is now Clifford and I am not able to identify this cemetery as such.
However, I am wondering if it is the one around the little Episcopal
Church in the village. I have been there many times and there are
ancient markers in it. BFD.)

Page 526. 28 Jul 1789. SMYTH TANDY & wife JOYCE, AC, to JNO. STEWART,
AC, 10 sh. Deed of Trust. 470 acres on both sides of Buffalo.
Lines as described in previous deeds herein. Subject to prior claim of
RO. GILMER & Co., Baltimore merchants, as well as 3 slaves, ox cart etc.
Wit: THOS. DILLON, JAS. BALLINGER, GABL. PENN, WM. TANDY. Page 640,
order to J.P.'s to quiz JOYCE as to 1 acre to WM. GALT for IRVING GALT &
Co, 19 Nov 1788; done 1 Jan 1791.

Page 97. 7 Sep 1786. JEREMIAH TAYLOR, AC, to JNO. WIATT, factor for
IRVING GALT & Co, Deed of Trust - negro girl, Betty.

Page 259. 4 Aug 1788. JEREMIAH TAYLOR & wife NANCY, AC, to JAMES CALLO-
WAY, AC, for Ł140, 108 acres N side of N fork Tribulation
Creek. Lines: Parks' road, JAS. CALLOWAY, WM. GALT, RO. WALKER, JNO. PENN.
Wit: JNO. WATSON, LUCAS POWELL, JOS. PENN, JOS. BURRUS.

Page 302. 17 Jun 1789. JEREMIAH TAYLOR, AC, to ARCHELAUS MITCHELL of
AC, for Ł200, 200 acres Harris Creek. Lines: MEGAN by ridge
path, R. SHELTON, THOS. POWELL, Schoolhouse branch, TAYLOR's fence across
branch. Wit: DAVIS WOODROOF, BETSY MITCHELL, FRANCIS HARDWICK.

Page 254. 5 Feb 1788. WM. TAYLOR, AC, to JNO. ROSE, AC, for Ł25, stock,
furniture, etc. and crops on my plantation Wit: D. McDOWAL,
CHAS. ISOM.

Page 3. 29 Jun 1785. ZACH. TAYLOR, Lincoln Co, Ky, to JNO EUBANK, AC,
for Ł50, 120 acres on N branch Maple Creek. Lines: Col. JOS.
CABELL. Wit: RICH. & HENRY BALLINGER, JNO. SHOEMAKER.

Page 202. 6 Aug 1787. JNO. TENESON & wife ANN, AC, to WM. HANSFORD, AC,
for Ł50, 73 acres. Orig. del. to grantee, 1792.

Page 63. 1 May 1786. RICH. THOMPSON to JNO. B. TALIAFERRO for Ł50,
Deed of Trust - 1 waggon (sic), 4 horses - one bought of JAS.
CALLAWAY, and one of WM. HOOKER. Wit: HENRY HARPER, WM. CLARK, ZACH. TAL-
IAFERRO JR, and delivered to him.

Page 183. 3 Sep 1787. RO. THOMPSON to JNO. CRAWFORD - Power of Atty. to
sell lands to which I am entitled in the Kentucky country.

Page 21. 7 Nov 1785. JNO. THURMOND, Albemarle, to JNO. THURMOND JR,
AC, for 20 sh, 125 acres - part of 250 acres Cub Creek, branch
of Hickory. Lines: Col. CHAS. LEWIS - divided by consent between GOORAG
& JNO. THURMOND JR. - line chopt by JNO. THURMOND. (Note: GOORAGE or
GOORAG is GUTRIDGE - see next item.)

Page 22. 7 Nov 1785. JNO. THURMOND, Albemarle, to GUTRIDGE THURMOND
of AC, 20 sh, 125 acres and part of 250 acres as above.

254

Page 41.   6 Mar 1786.   JNO. THURMOND & wife MOLLY, Campbell Co, to WM.
           GALASPIE, AC, for Ƚ100, 97 acres Head of Dutch Creek and gran-
tor got it from LAURENCE SUDDART. Orig. del. to grantee, 7 Dec 1790. On
samw page is another deed between them and same date, for Ƚ100, 50 acres
Br. Dutch. Lines: JNO. STAPLES (formerly SAML. STAPLES), JNO. HUNTER, and
bought by THURMOND from JNO. DENNEY. (Note: WM. GILLESPIE was killed in a
duel in Kentucky in 1794, and deeds here for estate of his father, GEO.
GILLESPIE, after 1800 show his family in Madison Co, Ky. Just when he
took them there is still an unknown answer, but he was carrying mail between Kentucky and Charlottesville for an undetermined time. His daughter, MARY, was to marry HENDERSON THURMAN in Madison after 1800, and HEN-
DERSON THURMAN is a party to the Kentucky heirs and their deed to DAVID
S. GARLAND when they sold land of GEORGE GILLESPIE. This JOHN THURMOND
married MOLLY DICKERSON and later appears in Lincoln County, Ky. He had
a son, BENNETT, and so did HENDERSON THURMAN in neighboring Madison. JOHN
was a son of PHILIP THURMOND SR, & wife MARY HENDERSON, of Albemarle, and
it is logical to think that HENDERSON THURMAN got his first name from
some connection with MARY HENDERSON THURMOND(sic), but I am unable to
make the documented picture. BFD.)

Page 8.   5 Sep 1785.   PHILLIP THURMOND & wife JUDITH, AC, to CALEB
          RALLS, AC, for Ƚ20,000 tobacco, 632 acres. Lines: Top of a mt.,
grantor. 165 acres also - Lines: grantor, part of 3553 acres on Horsley
and pat. to LUNSFORD LOMAX in 1764, and by him and wife JUDITH, to LUNS-
FORD LOMAX JR, 13 Jan 1767. Memo: 14 acres joins FRANK POWELL and sold
to THOS. POWELL TAYLOR. Wit: WM.THURMOND, PATRICK ROSE. Orig. del. to
RODERICK McCULLOCH, 26 May 1797.

Page 9.   5 Sep 1785.   PHILLIP THURMOND & wife JUDITH, AC, to NELSON
          CRAWFORD, AC, for Ƚ300, 331 acres N fork Horsley. Lines: Col.
LOMAX; 550 acres as well on branch of Horsley and part of NICHL. CABELL
tract. Joins JOS. MILSTREAD.

Page 379.   7 Sep 1789.   DAVID TILFORD, AC, to JAS. FOREST, AC, - DAVID as
            devisee of JAMES TILFORD, dec'd, for Ƚ40, 93 acres pat. to JAS.
TILFORD 14 Jul 1769, under signature of Baron De Botourte. Head branch
N fork Tye. Lines: his own, top of the Blue Ridge. Orig. del. to JACOB
LUALLOW(?) of Augusta, March, 1797.

Page 423.   19 Sep 1789.   DAVID TILFORD to ARCHIBALD RHEA for Ƚ20, 126
            acres S Mt. on W side of Main ridge of Mts. Lines: JAS. TIL-
FORD. Wit: DAVID WILSON, WALTER SMILEY, RICH. COATES, ANDREW KENNEDY.
Page 425 - same date and parties - for Ƚ20, 98 acres - Augusta land when
first surveyed but now in AC - South Mt. on W side of Main ridge of Mts.
Line: Spring of Tye, a level hill. Wit: same as above deed.

Page 366.   4 Dec 1788.   PAUL TILMAN & wife MARY, Hanover, to RICHARD
            CHANDLER, AC, for Ƚ500, 700 acres on Tye - part of tract - by
order of Council to Mr. THOS. DOSWELL. Wit: J. STEWART, JAS. FRANKLIN,
WM. HORSLEY JR, JNO. FLOYD.

Page 420.   20 Dec 1788.   PAUL TILMAN (THILMAN), Hanover, to NATHL. CLARK,
            AC, for Ƚ140, 500 acres head branch of S fork Tye. Lines: HEN-
LEY DRUMMOND, part of order of Council grant to JNO. DRUMMOND. Wit: THOS.
GOODWIN, HENLEY DRUMMOND, PETER HUGHES.

Page 210.   1 Oct 1787.   JAS. TRAIL & wife SUSANNAH, AC, to JESSE MARTIN,
            AC, for Ƚ16, 59 acres S side Fendley's Mt.; part of 400 acres
late that of LUNSFORD LOMAX Jr, and by him sold to HUGH PATRICK and by
him to JNO. KEY, JR, and by him to TRAIL. Lines: RICH. PRICHARD, JACOB
EADES. Orig. del. 25 Jan 1794.

Page 383.   20 Mar 1789.   PETERFIELD TRENT, Chesterfield Co, and wife AN-
            GELICA, to JNO. DOBSON, late of Liverpool, Great Britain, but
now of Richmond, Va., for 5 sh., 2790 acres conveyed to TRENT by THOS.
MANN RANDOLPH, Goochland, 18 Oct 1778 - known as Hat Creek tract. Wit:
JNO. BAKER, ADDISON DAY, WADDY THOMPSON, JERMAN BAKER, W. FREINCE, DOUG-
ALD FERGUSON, THOS. PAGAN, JNO. CAMPBELL.

Page 410.   21 Nov 1789.   PETERFIELD TRENT, Chesterfield, to PETER DANIEL,

Albemarle, for Ł60-10, 237 acres both sides Rockfish. Bought by grantor
of JOS. SMITH. Wit: CHAS. IRVING, WM. HARRIS, JAS. TURNER, RO. LOGAN.
Orig. del. to PD 7 Apr 1790.

Page 428. 13 Nov 1789. PETERFIELD TRENT, Chesterfield, to THOS. MORRI-
SON, AC, for Ł56, 219 acres Rockfish; pat. to JNO. THOMPSON
Aug 1771, and by him mortgaged to TRENT and sold by AC decree. Wit: JER.
PHILLIPS, THOS. STAPLES, N. CABELL, SAML. J. & WM. CABELL JR. Orig. del.
to TM., June, 1790.

Page 301. 20 Aug 1788. MATT. TUCKER & wife ESTHER, AC, to ARCHIBALD
HAMLETT, AC, for Ł60, 116 acres Branch Dutch Creek. Lines:
JNO. THURMOND, THOS. EADS. Wit: CHAS. BURRSU, WM. GILLESPIE, WM. CAMDEN,
MICAJAH CAMDEN. Orig. del. to AH, 13 Jan "onet".

Page 396. 12 Aug 1789. MATT. TUCKER, AC, to ALEX. BRYDEE, factor for
IRVING GALT & Co, Deed of Trust - 5 slaves and 1 horse. Wit:
THOS. WIATT, ANDR. McDONALD.

Page 472. 17 Mar 1790. MATT. TUCKER, AC, to his son, ISAIAH TUCKER -
love and 5 sh., slave, Joel. Wit: GABL. PENN, CHAS. BURRUS,
JAS. FRANKLIN.

Page 473. 17 Mar 1790. MATT. TUCKER, AC, to his son, JESSE TUCKER, love
and 5 sh, - slaves, Henry and Aggey. Wit: as above.

Page 473. 17 Mar 1790. MATT. TUCKER, AC, to his son, WHITEFIELD TUCKER,
love and 5 sh, - slaves, Ralph & Jenny. Wit: as above.

Page 474. 17 Mar 1790. MATT. TUCKER, AC, to his daughter, SEENE - so
indexed, but could be IRENE - love and 5 sh., slaves, Molley
and Adam. Wit: as above.

Page 475. 17 Mar 1790. MATT. TUCKER, AC, to his daughter, BETEY ANN
HURT, love and 5 sh., slaves, Psukey and Betsy. Wit: as above.

Page 478. 5 Apr 1790. WM. TUCKER, AC, to RO. MAYS, AC, for Ł100, 179
acres Stone House Creek and N side Buffalo. Lines: JOS. BOND,
RO. MAYS, BALLENGER WADE, THOS. HILLEY. Wit: WM. WARE, JOS. BALLINGER,
WM. HIGGINBOTHAM, CHAS. TALIAFERRO JR.

Page 497. 6 Jan 1779. Letter by WM. TUCKER to his father, DRURY TUCKER,
AC, addressed to Dear Father. He states that the purpose of
the letter is to remove and suspicion, founded on false reports - that I
meant to demand of you a part of your estate as a promise of a marriage
contract. He renounces any promises made in his favor by his father as he
never meant to claim them - nor anything in future. He only expects
what his father, as a father, thinks proper to "bestow me". He ends with
"Dear Father, your affectionate son". Wit: GABL. PENN, AARON CAMPBELL.
Addressed to Mr. DRURY TUCKER. Motion made to record by DRURY TUCKER,
5 July 1790.

Page 177. 4 Dec 1786. JAMES TULEY & wife ELIZ., AC, to ASHCRAFT ROACH,
AC, for Ł200, 400 acres - pat. 12 Jan 1746 - both sides Wil-
derness Run. Lines: RO. DAVIS JR. Wit: RODERICK McCULLOCH, JNO. WHITTEN,
GEO. EBANK (sic), DAVID JARRELL.

Page 619. 13 May 1791. JOHN TULEY JR, AC, to RODERICK McCULLOCH, AC,
for Ł200, 200 acres, branches Thomas Mill Creek. Lines: Pat.
of HUGH MORRIS; DAVENPORT; crossing the road. Wit: ZACH. TALIAFERRO,
BENJ. & WM. TALIAFERRO.

Page 412. 7 Dec 1789. JAMES TURNER & wife REBECCA, AC, to DANL. DUNAKIN,
AC, for Ł32, 64 acres N branch Dutch Creek. Pat. to THOS.
MATHEWS, 1 Aug 1772, and bought by TURNER, Lines: JOSIAH WOOD. Del. to
MARTIN DAWSON, per order, 11 Jun 1796.

Page 508. 5 May 1790. JAMES TURNER, AC, to SAML. HAMNER, Albemarle,
WM. HARRIS, JNO. DAWSON, & JOS. SHELTON, AC, for 6 sh., Deed
of Trust - HAMNER is bound with TURNER on bond to WM. DUVAL and assigned

256

to BUCHANAN & PATTERSON; suit filed and judgment was appealed and others named above became bound with them. Sixteen slaves named; stock, furniture, etc. Wit: JOSEPH BURRUS, P. GOOCH, STEPHEN TURNER, JAS. TURNER JR.

Page 266. 7 Oct 1788. WM. TURNER & wife SALLY, AC, to STEPHEN HAM, AC,
           for ₺50, 103 acres on branch Stovall between Prize and Plank
branches. Orig. del 31 Dec 1823, to JESSE BECK, exr. of STEPHEN HAM.

Page 267. Same date and parties as above - ₺15, 30 acres on branch of
           Stovall and S side Plank Branch.

Page 43.   3 Mar 1789. H.(?) CHAS. TYLER, AC, to HOWARD CASH, AC, for
           ₺4000 tobacco, 120 acres S and W side Indian Creek of Rivenna
(sic), bought by CHAS. TYLER of JOHN PHILLIPS. Wit: CHAS. HAY, AMBROS
CAMERON, JNO. TYLER.

Page 32.   21 Oct 1785. JNO. UPSHAW & wife AMEY, AC, to SAML. MEGGINSON,
           AC, for ₺160, 300 acres Buffalo - UPSHAW bought it of STANHOPE
EVANS - part of a tract. Lines: STANHOPE EVANS, JAS. FREELAND, dec'd,
THOS. EVANS. 100 acres bought of DAVID BLY by grantor. Wit: JOHNSON
BEANE, PHILLIP PENN, WM. HORSLEY. Orig. del. to grantee June, 1788.

Page 631. 10 Mar 1791. JAS. VAUGHAN, AC, to WM. TATE - Deed of Trust -
           to secure debt due JNO. DOBSON, SUSANNAH WILCOX and TATE -
slaves, horses, furniture. Wit: OLIVER HARRELL, CHAS. TATE.

Page 117. 25 Apr 1786. JNO. VIA (VIE) & wife MARY, AC, to ABSALOM
           STINCHCOMB, AC, for ₺10-17-6, 72½ acres both sides N fork Elk
Isalnd Creek. Lines: JNO. VIA. Wit: JOEL WALKER, CHAS. WINGFIELD, WM. VIA.

Page 626. 13 Aug 1799. BALLENGER WADE & wife SARAH, and DAVID WADE SR.
           & wife of Fluvanna - BALLENGER of AC - to PERRIN GILES, AC,
for ₺40, 400 acres both sides Thresher's Creek. Lines: PEARCE WADE. Wit:
CHAS. ELLIS, ASHCRAFT ROACH, JNO. GILES. Proved 6 Mar 1780, by ROACH &
GILES; BALLINGER WADE, 2 Oct 1786, and by CHAS. ELLIS, 6 Jun 1791.

Page 203. 1 Oct 1787. WM. WALTON, AC, to ABRAHAM SEAY, for ₺45, 45 acres
           branch Rucker's Run; part of a survey. Lines: WALTON, SEAY,
LOMAX's old line. Del. to JAS. SEAY.

Page 341. 3 Jul 1789. WM. WALTON, AC, to ABRAHAM SEAY, AC, for ₺50, 76
           acres Rucker's Run. Del. to SEAY, 9 Feb 1794.

Page 493. 6 Jul 1790. WM. WALTON, AC, to ABRAHAM SEAY, AC, for ₺50, 47
           acres Rucker's Run; part of a tract. Lines: grantor, JOELL
PONTON, ABRAHAM SEAY. North fork of Rucker's Run. Del. to grantee, 25
feb. 1794.

Page 516. 6 Jul 1790. WM. WALTON, AC, to JOEL PONTON, AC, for ₺100, two
           tracts on Rucker's Run; part of his land. 1) 59 acres known
as Walnut Cove and joins grantor and THOS. FORTUNE. 2) 132 acres adjoining. Lines: grantor and ABRAHAM SEAY.

Page 517. 5 Aug 1790. WM. WALTON, AC, to THOS. FORTUNE, AC, for ₺170,
           769 acres Rucker's Run - Trotter's Cove; survey by JNO. LACKEY
asst. surveyor. Lines: grantor, ABRAHAM SEAY, JAS. WRIGHT, grantee.
Orig. sent to THOS. FORTUNE, 27 Apr 1816.

Page 85.   2 Oct 1786. NATHAN WARD & wife SARY, to WM. LAYNE, waggoner,
           for ₺20, 60 acres branch Purgatory. Lines: RICH. PRITCHET,
JACOB EADS, JNO. KEY.

Page 624. 11 Apr 1791. Power of atty by JAS. WARE, AC, to WM. WARE, AC,
           to sell my AC lands. Wit: THOS. GARLAND, HENRY BROWN, WM.
DAVIS, ABRHAAM CARTER, GEO. McDANIEL.

Page 311. 6 Apr 1789. JNO. WARE & wife ELIZ., AC, to STEPHEN TURNER of
           AC for ₺300, 400 acres Tye. Lines: HUGH ROSE, WM. CABELL JR,
HENRY SHELTON, WM. SPENCER, JOS. DILLARD. Orig. del. to SAML. TURNER.

Page 285. 1 Dec 1788. WM. WARE, factor of SPEARS BOWMAN & Co., releases
lien to RICH. ALLCOCK. He sold to EDWARD WARE "and JAMES exr."
(sic). 93 acres.

Page 581. 7 Feb 1791. WM. WARE to RICH. DAVIS, AC, for ₤100, Negress
Jude and boy, George - for land payment. WARE is to lend them
to DAVIS for life and they may not be removed from Virginia without WARE's
consent.

Page 116. 20 Oct 1786. JNO. WARREN, AC, to PETER JOYNER, AC, for ₤18,
50 acres. Lines: grantee, Spring Branch, BEN. WARREN's spring,
new road on the Glades, JNO. WINGFIELD, RUCKER. Wit: JNO. WHITTLE, JNO.
HUTCHERSON, EDMOND ROWSEY.

Page 120. 20 Oct 1786. JNO. WARREN, SR, AC, to JNO. HUTCHESON, AC, for
₤25, 100 acres New road on the Glades; JNO. WINGFIELD on South
side; CHISWELL, near Buffalo Ridge, HARVIE. Wit: JNO. WHITTLE, PETER
JOYNER, EDMOND ROWSEY.

Page 205. 20 Oct 1786. JNO. WARREN SR, AC, to BENJ. WARREN, AC, for ₤7,
25 acres. Lines: HARVEY, new road, WM. DILLARD, Spring Branch.
Wit: JNO. WHITTLE, JNO. HUTCHERSON, PETER JOINER.

Page 345. 30 May 1789. ABRAHAM WARWICK, AC, to HENRY MARTIN, AC, for
₤10, 50 acres Nassau or Dutch. Lines: HUGH WILLOUGHBY, dec'd.,
ENOCH NASH. Wit: HUDSON MARTIN, BEVERLY WARWICK, SALLY WARWICK.

Page 287. 1 Dec 1788. BEVERLY WARWICK & wife ELIZ., AC, to SMYTH TANDY,
of same, for ₤40, 400 acres N branch Buffalo. Lines: SAML.
MEREDITH, JNO. ROWSEY, JNO. PHILLIPS, WM. LAINE, JNO. STRATTON, WM.
SPENCER, STEPHEN WATTS. Orig. del. to TANDY by JNO. POWELL, son of
WYIATT POWELL.

Page 403. 7 Dec 1789. WM. WARWICK, tobacco inspector at Swan's WH
Bondsman: ABRAHAM WARWICK.

Page 106. 1 Jan 1787. JAS. WATSON & wife PATTY, AC, to JNO. STEWART
for ₤500, 700 acres both sides Buffalo. Lines: JAS. FRANKLIN,
JAS. WATSON, N bank. Rutledge, MOSES HIGGINBOTHAM, JACOB TYREE, Higginbotham Mill Creek, GABL. PENN, AMBROSE LEE, dec'd, estate.

Page 461. 6 Apr 1789. FRANCIS WEST & wife ELIZ., AC, to FRANCIS WEST JR,
love and 5 sh, 107 acres Mayo creek. Lines: PETER LEGRAND,
BRANSFORD WEST, NICHL. CABELL. Wit: N. CABELL, H. CABELL, THOS. BADDER.
Orig. del. to FRANCIS WEST, 10 Oct 1817, per order.

Page 536. 6 Apr 1790. FRANCIS WEST & wife ELIZ., AC, to JNO. WEST, AC,
for love and 5 sh, 107 acres branch Mayo creek. Lines: WM. &
NICHL. CABELL, PETER LEGRAND, NICHL. WEST. Orig. del. to JNO. WEST, 12
Oct 1796. Wit: N. & H. CABELL, THOS. BADDER.

Page 537. 6 Apr 1790. FRANCIS WEST & wife ELIZ., AC, to NICHL. WEST, AC,
for love and 5 sh, 107 acres branch Mayo Creek. Lines: PETER
LEGRAND, JNO. WEST, NICHL. CABELL. Wit: as above.

Page 538. 6 Apr 1790. FRANCIS WEST & wife ELIZ., AC, to BRANSFORD WEST,
AC, for love and 5 sh., 107 acres branch Mayo creek. Lines:
FRANCIS WEST, JR, NICHL. CABELL, PETER LEGRAND. Wit: as above.

Page 246. 11 Oct 1787. THOS. WEST, Albemarle, to ALEX. McALEXANDER of
AC, for ₤60, 150 acres NW cove and N branch of North fork
Davis. Private line drawn by DAVID CLACK and his father, BENJ., when in
possession. Wit: JAS. WOODS, JAS. BROOKS, DAVID CLACK. OD to grantee 1801.

Page 248. 11 Oct 1787. THOS. WEST, Albemarle, to HENRY HUGHS, AC, for
₤30, 50 acres branch Davis. Lines: LEE HARRIS, DANL. DUVAL,
ALEX. McALEXANDER. Part of 150 acres. Wit: JAS. BROOKS, JAS. WOODS, DAVID
CLACK. Orig. del. to WATKINS, Dec., 1790 (?).

Page 249. 11 Oct 1787. THOS. WEST, Albemarle, to JNO. WATKINS, AC, for

Ł45, 95 acres N branch Davis. Lines: JAS. McALEXANDER. Wit: JAMES WOODS, JAS. BROOKS, DAVID CLACK.

Page 221.   5 Nov 1787.   JNO. WHITTLE & wife SARAH, AC, Parish of Amherst,
          to WM. HORSLEY, AC, for Ł69, 69 acres Owens Creek.   WHITTLE
bought it of WM. HORSLEY. Wit: JNO. WILLIAMSON, ZACH. TALIAFERRO, JAS.
CALLAWAY, RICH. FULCHER.

Page 26.   1 Sep 1785.   JNO. WIATT, AC, to REUBEN BANKS, AC, for Ł20, 50
          acres N branch Buffalo; side of Turkey Mt.; part of tract.
Lines: JOSHUA HUDSON, LINN BANKS. Part of tract bought by REUBIN BANKS
of JNO. WIATT.

Page 228.   9 Nov 1787.   Order to quiz MINA, wife of JNO WIATT, as to deed
          to JOSHUA HUDSON - 315 acres. Lines: PATRICK ROSE, EDWD. CAR-
TER, JNO. WIATT, REUBEN BANKS, JOSHUA HUDSON.   Done, 1 Mar 1788 by AM-
BROSE & BENJ. RUCKER.

Page 489.   4 Apr 1790.   JNO. WIATT, AC, to JOS. CREWS, AC, for Ł100, 102
          acres N branch Crooked Run; part of a tract. Lines: DAVID
WOODROOF, JNO. WIATT. Wit: BENJ. RUCKER, PLEASANT MARTIN, CHAS. CRAWFORD,
W.S. CRAWFORD, GDN. CREWS.   Orig. del. 16 Apr 1807 to THOS. CREWS.

Page 7.   1 Aug 1785.   JNO. WILLIAMSON & wife SALLY, AC, to RICH. PER-
          KINS of AC for Ł75, no acreage mentioned - on Rockfish. Lines:
his own, JNO. WILLIAMSON, OLIVER ORR, JNO. THOMPSON. Wit: PATRICK WILL-
IAMSON, THOS. FITZPATRICK, HEZ. STONE.

Page 569.   7 Feb 1791.   THOS. WILLIAMSON & wife JUDITH, to ALEX. HENDER-
          SON, all of AC, for Ł130, 245 acres branch of Rockfish near to
the Blue Mts. Lines: THOS. SHANNON, HUDSON MARTIN, WM. CROW's old line.

Page 25.   26 Oct 1785.   JAS. WILLOUGHBY & JNO. WILLOUGHBY, AC, to PHIL-
          LIP THURMOND, AC, for Ł6000 tobacco, 172 acres branch Dutch.
Lines: SAML. STAPLES, top of a mt. Wit: SHEROD MORE GALASPIE, LUCY THUR-
MOND, ELISHA THURMOND, WM. GALASPY.

Page 181.   2 Jul 1787.   THOS. WILSHER & wife ANNEY, AC, to FRANCIS HARRI-
          SON, AC, for Ł81, 81 acres Harris Creek. Lines: GEO. LEE,
BATTAIL HARRISON, dec'd., RICH. SHELTON, RICH. HARVIE.   Orig. del. to
RICH. HARRISON for grantee.

Page 279.   4 Nov 1788.   THOS. WILSHER & wife ANNE, AC, to JAMES GATEWOOD
          of Bedford, for Ł50, 200 acres S side Berry's Mt.   Lines:
ARTHER ROBERTSON, WM. TYREE, SAML. SPENCER, THOS. LAIN (LAYN), grantor,
top of Mt.   Part of 385 acres pat. 20 Jul 1780, to THOS. LAYN and by him
conveyed to grantor on 2 Jan 1785. Wit: CHAS. LAIN, THOS. ROBERTSON, JOS.
MAYS, DAVID PROFFITT, GEO. & KILLIS WRIGHT (KILLIS).

Page 280.   4 Nov 1788.   THOS. WILSHER & wife ANNE, AC, to JAMES GATEWOOD,
          Bedford, for Ł500, 400 acres both sides Harris Creek. Lines:
FRANCES HARRISON, GEO. LEE, RICH. HARVIE, WM. HARVIE. Wit: as previous
deed.

Page 404.   27 Jun 1789.   CHAS. WINGFIELD & wife RACHEL, Albemarle, to
          NATHAN WINGFIELD, AC, for Ł100, 392 acres Rocky Creek. Lines:
JOHN WARREN, a bridge over a branch of creek. Wit: JNO. WINGFIELD JR,
WM. DAVENPORT, JOS. BENJ. WINGFIELD.

Page 406.   27 Jul 1789.   CHAS. WINGFIELD & wife RACHEL, Albemarle, to JNO.
          ROWSEY, AC, for Ł50, 99½ acres N side Buffalo Ridge. Lines:
CHISWELL, MATT. WHITTLE, JAS. CHRISTIAN. Wit: as above.

Page 2.   4 Jun 1784.   ABNER WITT, AC and Parish, to ROBT. HARDIE, AC &
          Parish, for Ł200, 100 acres Corbin Creek, branch of Rockfish.
Lines: WM. SMALL, SAML. LACKEY, ALEX. REID, ROBINSON.

Page 86.   4 Mar 1786.   ABNER WITT, AC, to JOS. ROBERTS, AC, for Ł50, 76
          acres branch of Corbin that heads near Lackey's Gap.   Line for-
mally agreed upon by JNO. WITT SR, and ABNER WITT.   Lines: JNO. BOLSE on

top of Lackey's Mt., LITTLEBERRY WITT, KEYS' old corner, JOS. ROBERTS.
Wit: RO. HARVEY, WM. DAWSON, ALEX. ROBERTS. Orig. sent to ROBERTS 1801.

Page 87. 5 Jul 1786. ABNER WITT, AC & Parish, to JOS. ROBERTS of same,
           for Ł30, 100 acres N side Lackey's Mt. in the gap. Lines: JOS.
ROBERTS, exactly on top of the mt., former line of JAS. LACKEY. Wit: BENJ.
CARPENTER, WM. FORBUS, JAMES LITTERELL, ALEX. McALEXANDER. Orig. sent to
ROBERTS 24 Oct 1801.

Page 101. 22 Jul 1786. ABNER WITT, AC, to JNO. WITT, BENJ. CARPENTER,
           LITTLEBERRY WITT & WM. WITT, AC, for 5 sh, Deed of Trust -
Ł130 - grantees are bound to MATT. HARRIS & JNO. GRIFFIN for bond to WM.
HORRELL by ABNER WITT - suit has been instituted; suit vs. BENJ. CARPEN-
TER by WM. RUSSELL and COUCH, assignees of JAS. TAYLOR va. ABNER WITT;
also suit for 1000 pds. tobacco by JAS. WOODS vs. ABNER WITT. Also 4
negroes and stock. Orig. del. to WM.WITT 13 Feb 1787.

Page 138. 1 Mar 1787. ABNER WITT, AC, to JNO. WITT, AC, for Ł300, 209
           acres Davis Creek. Lines: JAS. McALEXANDER, THOS. McDANIEL.
Also 111 acres head of Short's Creek. Lines: JAS. LITTRELL, LITTLEBERRY
WITT. 90 acres on Rockfish, mouth of Short Creek. Lines: LEE HARRIS,
CLOUGH SHELTON. 360 acres adj. BOLES tract and JAS. McALEXANDER on Rock-
ey Brnach and joining my old tract that was HORRILS. Wit: LITTLEBERRY
WITT, DAVID WITT, THOS. H. TALBERT. Orig. sent to JNO. WITT by WM. WITT.

Page 367. 6 Jul 1788. JNO. WITT, AC, to CLOUGH SHELTON, AC, for Ł18-5,
           90 acres S side and joining Rockfish. Lines: LEE HARRIS,
CLOUGH SHELTON. Wit: THOS. WIATT, J. SHELTON, BARTLETT CASH.

Page 470. 5 Mar 1790. JNO. WITT, AC, to CLOUGH SHELTON, AC, for Ł18-5,
           90 acres as above located. Lines: LEE HARRIS, grantee. Wit:
WM. MARTIN, LEWIS NEVIL, JNO. LAMONT.

Page 450. 20 Feb 1790. JNO. WITT, AC, to WM. WITT, AC, for Ł130, 774
           acres N fork Davis. Lines: JAMES McALEXANDER, JOS. ROBERTS,
THOS. McDANIEL, JNO. JOHNSON. Orig. del. to BARTLETT EADES, 22 Jun 1794.

Page 453. 19 Mar 1790. JNO. WITT, AC, to WM. ABNEY, AC, for Ł25, 111
           acres on one of branches of Short's Creek. Lines: JAS. WOODS,
ELIZ., TULEY, DAVID & LITTLEBERRY WITT.

Page 93. 1 Nov 1786. WM. WITT, AC, to LITTLEBERRY WITT, AC, for Ł80,
          80 acres on branch Rockfish. Lines: SAML. LACKEY, CHISELL's
grant line, JAS. LITTRALL, SHORT's branch. Wit: ZACH. BURNETT, DONNEL
ABNEY WITT, DAVID WITT. Orig. del. to grantee, Mar 1789.

Page 94. 28 Dec 1786. WM. WITT, AC, to DAVID WITT, AC, for Ł52, 81
          acres in cove of a mt. on Head of one of branches of Short's
Creek. Lines: JNO. CHISEL, WM. WITT. Wit; ZACH. BURNETT, DENNETT ABNEY
WITT (DONNEL above), WM. ABNEY. Orig. del. to grantee in Mar, 1789.

Page 256. 1 Sep 1788. JNO. WOOD & wife MARY, AC, to THOS. GRIMES, AC,
           for Ł150, 250 acres Three forks of Pedlar. Page 284, order of
4 Sep 1788, to quiz MARY. Done by BENJ. RUCKER, 5 Nov 1788.

Page 393. 5 Oct 1789. JOSIAH WOOD, Union Co, S.C., to JESSE THOMAS, AC,
           for Ł6000, 172 acres. Lines: RO. WRIGHT, entry adjoining of
127 acres; grantor, LUKE BINNION.

Page 57. 2 Jun 1786. WM. WOOD & wife MARTHA, Albemarle, to JNO. BURTON
          of AC for Ł65, 119 acres Headwaters Beavour and part of pat.
of THOS. THOMSON. Lines: Pat. line of THOMSON.

Page 353. 27 Jun 1789. DAVID WOODROOF & wife CLARY, AC, to NICHL.
           DAVIES, Bedford Co. THOS. POWELL, in lifetime, bought of
DAVID WOODROOF and died in possession, but title was still in WOODROOF's
name. POWELL agreed with DAVIES to exchange and swap part of the land
bought of WOODROOF for lands of DAVIES next to POWELL. 100 acres was so
exchanged and POWELL got 80 acres contiguous to him and 100 acres to be
conveyed when he got title. DAVIES has conveyed title to 80 acres to

daughters of POWELL through guardian since they are infants. Herein
WOODROOF conveys title to 100 acres on John's Creek. Lines: CARRINGTON &
Co., old line which separates POWELL and DAVIES and in occupation of JNO.
HARRISON; Widow POWELL's house and plantation occupied by JNO. HARRISON
TAYLOR; DAVIES. Wit: P. GOOCH, JNO. & RICH. HARRISON. Orig. del. to
DAVIES agreeable to note by JNO. HUMPHREYS.

Page 416. 20 May 1789. JNO. WOODROOF & wife AMEY, AC, to RO. HUDSON,
            AC, for ₤60, 310 acres N branch Buffalo. Lines: Corner of the
late Secretary. Page 593, order to AC J.P.'s to quiz AMEY, 21 Dec 1789,
and done on 25 Dec 1790 (sic). AMBROSE & BENJ. RUCKER.

Page 187. 20 Dec 1784. NATHL. WOODROOF & wife SUSANNAH, Surry Co, N.C.,
            to WM. MEREDITH,AC, for ₤40, 100 acres. Lines: WM. SPENCER,
road from FLOYD's to New Glasgow; STEPHEN WATTS. Wit: HUGH ROSE, SAML.
MEREDITH JR, STEPEHN WATTS, S. MEREDITH.

Page 312. 10 Aug 1787. GEO. WORTHAM, AC, to THOMPSON & TEAS - Deed of
            Trust - slaves. Wit: EDWD. BOLLING, DAVID S. GARLAND.

Page 281. 7 Apr 1788. NICHL. WREN & wife ELIZ., AC, to JOS. TILFORD, AC,
            for ₤90, 150 acres Coffey's (otherwise Raccoon Creek). Lines:
GEO. MORROW, Col. JNO. HENRY. Wit: JAS. TILFORD, THOS. JONES, JNO. WREN,
NICHL. MORAN, JESSE CLARKSON.

Page 195. 2 Jul 1787. BENJ. WRIGHT & wife ELIZ, AC, to NATHL. HILL, AC,
            for ₤239-2-7, 200 acres Castle Creek and branch of Tye. Lines:
JAS. DICKIE, JNO. ROSE, late Rev. RO. ROSE and now that of JNO. ROSE.
Conveyed to grantor by JAS. BROWN on 2 Mar 1772(?). Wit: ZACH. TALIAFERRO,
BARTLETT CASH, JNO. BROCKMAN, THOS. BROCKMAN. Orig. del. to WM. HILL by
order of WM. HILL, Oct. 1790.

Page 224. 10 Aug 1787. BENJ. WRIGHT, AC, to THOMPSON & TEAS, Deed of
            Trust - slaves, stock, beds, etc. Wit: GEO. GALASPIE, JR,
MOSES WRIGHT, DAVID S. GARLAND., and delivered to him for grantees in
Dec. 1788.

Page 649. 10 Mar 1791. BENJ. WRIGHT to JESSE WRIGHT, AC, for ₤160, two
            tracts on N fork Piney. 1) 81 acres pat. at Williamsburg, Sep
10, 1755. Lines: GEO. TAYLOR, N fork Piney. 2) 87 acres. Lines: by the
river, pat. line, JNO. MASSEY, Crawley's Creek. Orig. del. to JESSE
WRIGHT, 11 July 1795.

Page 650. 10 Mar 1791. BENJ. WRIGHT to JESSE WRIGHT, AC, for ₤300, two
            negroes; horses, cattle, furniture, etc. and my right to a
tract on Piney acknowledged to me by mortgage by WM. HOUCHIN. Orig. del.
as above. This is the last deed in the book.

Page 240. 30 Nov 1787. ISAAC WRIGHT & wife SUSANNAH, AC, to EDWD. CAR-
            TER, for ₤20, 50 acres Horsley Creek. Lines: CARTER, MOSSES
old field, Ridge road, WRIGHT'S upper line, NELSON CRAWFORD, PETER CARTER.
Wit: JNO. CRAWFORD, ABRAHAM CARTER, JOS. PENN, JNO. TALIAFERRO. Orig.
del. to EDWD. CARTER 31 Oct 1805.

Page 290. 29 Nov 1788. JNO. WRIGHT & wife ELIZ., AC, to JNO. LOVING, AC,
            for ₤46-10, 98 acres. Lines: LOVING. Grantor bought it of
JNO. JOHNSTON and he bought it of WM. LOVING, 1 Oct 1771. Wit: HENRY
MARTIN, JAS. STEVENS, JR, CHAS. PURVIS, BENJ. PAYNE.

Page 510. 11 Mar 1790. MINOS WRIGHT, AC, to SAML. EDMONDS, AC, for ₤60,
            150 acres on Tye and part of where WRIGHT lives. Lines:
ACHILLES WRIGHT, YOUNG LANDRUM. Wit: WM. SPENCER, JAS. FRANKLIN, JESSE
MAYS.

Page 45. 6 Feb 1786. MOSES WRIGHT & wife ELIZ., AC, to JNO. CAMPBELL
            of AC, - orig. del. to JC Mar, 1789 - for ₤50, 128 acres S
side and joining Crawley creek. Lines: GEO. GALASPIE, BENJ. WRIGHT; part
of tract. Wit: JNO. MASSEY, GEO. CAMPBELL, JR, JAS. DEMASTERS.

Page 486. 28 Nov 1789. MOSES WRIGHT, Union Co, S.C., to HENRY GOSNEY,

AC, for ₺63-7, 92 acres Harris Creek. Lines: VALENTINE COX, MARTIN DAWSON, part of tract whereon MARTIN DAWSON lives. Granted to MOSES WRIGHT by ISAAC WRIGHT and of record in AC. Wit: BENJ. WHITE, JNO. SIMMONDS, JNO. SLEDD, JAS. SIMMONS, JAS. ALEXANDER, RICH. SIMMONS.

Page 168. 4 Jun 1787. RO.WRIGHT, Heir-at-law of AUGUSTIN WRIGHT, and wife KEZIAH, AC, to SAML. EDMONDS, AC, - original sent by order to SAML. EDMUNDS, 8 Oct 1817 - for ₺150, 191 acres on Tye. Part of 341 acres which Augustin bought of exrs. of PHILIP GRYMES. Lines: JOSEPH MAYS, AMBROSE CAMPBELL, GEO. STONEHAM, MENUS WRIGHT.

Page 377. 13 Aug 1789. RO. WRIGHT, AC, to JOS. SHELTON, AC, for ₺176, 176 acres both sides of Dutch; part of land of WM. WRIGHT. Lines: WM. BONES, ANDREW WRIGHT, JAS. HALLY BURTON, WM. WRIGHT JR. Wit: JOS. ROBERTS, JAS. JOPLING, STEPHEN CLEMENTS.

Page 27. 7 Nov 1785. WM. WRIGHT, AC, to WM. & HUDSON MARTIN, AC, (orig. del. to MARTIN, June, 1786) for ₺3-15, 3 acres Davis Creek. Lines: WRIGHT, JAS. WRIGHT, Great Road. Wit: WM. TEASE, JESSE MAYS, JNO. STAPLES.

Page 198. 1 Sep 1787. WM. WRIGHT, SR, AC, to JAS. WRIGHT, AC, for ₺5, 99 acres Davis Creek and joins where grantor now lives. Wit: WM. MARTIN, CHAS. STATHAM, WM. WRIGHT.

Page 628. 4 Oct 1790. CHAS. YANCEY, Louisa Co, and wife MARY, to JOHN PUGH, AC, for ₺4000 tobacco, 224½ acres description by patent on July 25, 1780, by THOS. JEFFERSON. Head branches Hickory and Taylor. Lines: EDWD. MOSELY, JNO. COLE, BENJ. HARRIS, late CHAS. EVANS. Other 92½ acres is moiety of tract of EDWD. MOSELEY's pat. of 12 May 1770, signed by BOTOTOURT, and bought by YANCEY. WM. SID CRAWFORD acted as atty. for YANCY and wife.

The following indentures are separated from deeds since they are of more than passing interest. These men all set forth same fact of arrival on the ship, Washington, and ENOCH STICKNEY was Master. The term of service was to run from first day of arrival at Alexandria, Virginia. STICKNEY was to furnish them with food, meat and drink. They were assigned to TILMAN WALTON by FITZGERALD and MURRY or others to be noted. One assignment was to SMYTH TANDY.

Page 90. 10 May 1784. WM. HAYES, of Bandon County Cork, Taylor, voluntary servitude to STICKNEY for 3 years. Wit: WM. ABBOTT, JAN(?) HANNAH. Assigned by JNO. LORDAN, LONDON(?), to SMYTH TANDY, 2 Oct 1786.

Page 88. 22 May 1784. JNO. LANDERAGIN (LANDERGAN) of Cork, Shoemaker - to STICKNEY for 3½ years from first day of arrival. Wit: JA HANNAH, SAML. GARDNER. Assigned by FITZGERALD and MURRY, 28 Sep 1784, by JNO. LORDAN (note different spellings). Rec. AC 2 Oct 1786, by motion of JNO. LONDERAGIN's atty.

Page 130. 10 May 1784. JNO. McDONALD (signed McDANIEL) of Cork, cooper. Indenture to STICKNEY for 4 years. Wit: WM. ABBOTT, RICH. HARRISON, JON HANNAH. Made over to TILMAN WALTON, 25 Sep 1784, for FITZGARRELL & MURRY; JNO. LONDON (LORDAN).

Page 91. 22 May 1784. EDWARD NOONAN, Cork, shoemaker - 3½ years. Assigned to TILMAN WALTON, 2 Oct 1786, recorded. Wit: RICH. HARRISON.

Note: See APPENDIX for various survey, tax and pole lists contained in Deed Book F.

262

DEDICATION

This deed book abstract of Amherst County, Virginia, is dedicated to the memory of JOHN & ROBERT LUCKEY who were paternal ancestors of mine. They were prominent in Cane Ridge Church, Bourbon County.

FOREWORD

This work completes another in my deed book abstract series on Amherst County, Virginia. They seem to be more popular than my abstracts of the wills of Amherst in alphabetical series. Those owning this deed series now have a clear picture of all property owners in the books. I feel that I am just getting into the really interesting sections of books as far as out-of-state persons are concerned. It will be noted that this book contains much valuable information on people in other states and I note more and more such items in later books of deeds. It will be noted that two marriage contracts are found herein and they are not in the marriage register.

                                                    BAILEY FULTON DAVIS
                                                    1964

Page 1.   29 Oct 1790. Order to AC J.P.'s to quiz LUCY HUDSON, wife of
           RO. HUDSON - 15 Aug 1786, deed to JAS. HARRISON - 118 acres on
N branch of Buffalo. Done by HUGH ROSE & SAML. MEREDITH, 4 Jul 1791.

Page 2.   27 Dec 1790. THOS. FROST, Washington Co., to JNO. MILLER, AC,
           for ₺50, 110 acres - no description. Wit: THOS. JOHNSON, WM.
HANSARD, NEMIAH ROZEL, PETER ROZEL.

Page 3.   14 Jun 1791. JER. TAYLOR and wife ANN, to HENRY LANDON DAVIS
           (sic, but DAVIES), all of AC, (Orig. del. to SAML. B. DAVIES),
₺300 debt - 5 sh. Deed of Trust. 200 acres where TAYLOR lives. Lines:
ARCHELAUS MITCHELL SR, estate of THOS. POWELL, dec'd, NICHL. DAVIS, JOS.
MEGANN. Also 365 acres bought by TAYLOR of JAS. EATON in Henry Co. on
Mayo River. Lines: JAS. TAYLOR, formerly SEDDUCH(?) SMITH, and part adj.
Balle Mt. Also slave woman - HENRY LANDON DAVIS is my trustee - debts
due estate of JNO. WEST, SACKVILLE KING, JOS. BURRUS, DOC(?) EDMD. WILCOX,
HUBBARD & CO. Wit: WM. S (L) LANE, FRANCES LANE, NELSON CRAWFORD.

Page 5.   9 Jun 1791. LUCAS POWELL & wife ELIZ., AC, to WM. JOHNSON,
           AC, for ₺250, 297 acres Rucker's Run - except 13 acres sold to
JNO. INNIS on --- and rec. in AC. Wit: MATT. HARRIS, WM. LEE HARRIS,
JAS. MAYS.

Page 7.   22 Jan 1781. (sic) PETER RUCKER, JAS. RUCKER as exr. of JNO.
           RUCKER, dec'd., ALEX. MARR, AMBROSE RUCKER, JNO. LEA, BENJ.
RUCKER, ISAAC RUCKER, ANTHONY RUCKER, STEPHEN HAM, & JAS. MORTON, AC, to
ANTHONY RUCKER, AC, for ₺65, 100 acres. Lines: ISAAC RUCKER, Drinking
corner. Wit: JNO., AMBROSE & WM. RUCKER, GEO. GILBERT (for JAS. RUCKER),
ISAAC TINSLEY (for I. RUCKER).

Page 8.   7 Jan 1791. JNO. STEWART to sisters: BETSY, NANNY & SALLY
           STEWART and my brother, DAVID STEWART - whole estate of my
father - I bought at sale by law to pay debts - as long as my mother
lives, she is to enjoy use of estate; at death to go to above grantees.
Wit: CHAS. & THOMAS STEWART.

Page 9.   22 Jun 1791. CHAS. ROSE & wife SALLY, AC, to CHAS. IRVING,
           PATRICK ROSE, WM. SIDNEY CRAWFORD, & EDMOND FONTAIN, AC, (Orig.
del. to W.S. CRAWFORD) for ₺5, Deed of Trust - to support self and family
and to educate my children - all real and personal property - 4 tracts
in AC. 1) Bellevitt - where I live, 171 acres. 2) Claypoole.* 3) 400
acres bought of GEO. GILLESPIE and adjoins THOMPSON & TEAS; JAS. DILLARD
& others. 4) Commonly called Ewers - formerly that of my brother HENRY
dec'd, 122 acres.(*Claypoole - 1693 acres.)   Also all of my slaves,

stock, tools, and crops. To revert to ROSE when all debts are paid by
above as his trustees. Wit: ROBT. ROSE, J.W. HUNTER, JNO. PHILLIPS, PETER
SAUNDERS.

Page 12.   4 Jul 1791.   HUGH, PETER, & CHAS. ROSE, AC, to JAS. ROBERTS,
            AC, for Ł10, 81 acres both sides S fork Piney. Lines: GILBERT
HAYS, GEO. MONROE. The name of PETER is not used in signature, but those
of PATRICK & HUGH appear. Wit: J.W. HUNTER, SAML. MEREDITH, RO. & HENRY
ROSE.

Page 13.   4 Jul 1791.   JNO. SHIELDS, JR, AD, to ALEX. SHIELDS, Lexington
            in Rockbridge Co, for Ł80, 214 acres N branch Rockfish; part
of tract of late Speaker ROBERTSON. Lines: GEO. CAMPBELL, dec'd, JNO.
SHIELDS, SR, SAML. WOODS, dec'd, his orphans, CHAS. PATRICK, SHERROD
MARTIN, top of the mt., flat ground of Beaver Creek.

Page 15.   5 Sep 1791.   WM. DAMRON, AC, to WM. MICKLE, Campbell Co, for
            Ł200, 214 acres Harris Creek. Bought by PEARCE WADE of WM.
STATON, dec'd. and sold by WADE to DAMRON. Lines: mouth of Pole Cat.
(Two marginal items: Orig. carried to court; del. to E. FONTAIN for MICK-
LE, Jan. 1792, and Orig. del. to JAS. HANNY for MICKLE 3 Jul 1792.)

Page 16.   10 Jun 1791.   RACHEL AYRES, AC, to RICH. LEE, AC, for Ł12, 110
            acres S fork Rockfish. Lines: NATHL. CLARK JR, JOSIAH DOOD
(sic). Wit: JAS. MONTGOMERY, JOS. MONTGOMERY, OSBON COFFEY. Orig. del.
to R. LEE.

Page 17.   2 Jul 1787.   DAVID CRAWFORD, WM. BIBB & CHAS. BURRUS, attys.
            for LUCY JOHNSTON, Caroline (Margin scratched, but reads: 7
Jul 1807, sent to H.L. DAVIES by JNO. ELLIS) to GEO. DAVIS, AC, for Ł28,
170 acres pat. to LUCY JOHNSTON 20 Nov 1784, by survey of 14 Nov 1771.
Both sides Tarrapin Creek. Lines: His own. Wit: JNO. CRAWFORD, THOS.
GRISSOM, NELSON CRAWFORD.

Page 18.   6 Aug 1791.   THOS. PENN & wife WINNEY, Wilks Co, Ga., to SAML.
            MIGGINSON, AC, for Ł200, 100 acres Buffalo River. Part of
tract formerly that of STANHOPE EVANS and bought by THOS. PENN of THOS.
EVANS. Lines: JAS. FREELAND, dec'd, THOS. POWELL, STANHOPE EVANS. Wit:
RICH. GATEWOOD, WM., JOS. & FRANCES HIGGINBOTHAM.

Page 19.   5 Sep 1791.   PHILIP BAILEY & wife MARY, AC, to JAS. McCLAIN,
            AC, for Ł150, 150 acres. Lines: HENRY McCLAIN, JNO. WILLIAMSON,
JONATHAN BRIDGEWATER. Part of tract formerly that of SAML. RICHARDSON and
title made by him to grantor. Wit: NATHL. OFFUTT, MOSES MARTIN, MARK
LIVELY.

Page 20.   17 Jun 1790.   DAVID WOODROOF, AC, to JOS. MAGANN, AC, for Ł16,
            66 acres.

Page 22.   15 Sep 1790.   JOS., JNO. & JAS. MONTGOMERY, exrs. of JNO.
            MONTGOMERY, AC, to LEE HARRIS, AC, for Ł400, 650 acres Buck
Creek. Lines: PLEASANT MARTIN, JOSIAH JOPLING; also 35 acres adj. which
JNO bought of RO. BARNETT. Orig. del. 6 Jul 1797, to JNO. DIGGS. Wit:
LANDON BRENT, PHILIP BAILEY, JAS. MORRISON.

Page 23.   1 Aug 1791.   Order to EDWD. STEVENS, DAVID JAMISON, & RO.
            COWNE, J.P.'s of Culpeper, to quiz SALLY HANSBROUGH, wife of
WM. - 6 Sep 1790 deed to JNO. BALL. Done, 17 Aug 1791, by JAMISON who
signs JR., and STEVENS.

Page 24.   5 Sep 1791.   LUCAS POWELL & wife ELIZ, AC, to JENNY INNIS, AC,
            for Ł13, 13 acres, part of tract where THOS. HAWKINS now lives,
Rucker's Run. Wit: SEYMOUR POWELL, NATHL. OFFUTT, EZEK. HILL.

Page 26.   5 Sep 1791.   THOS. JENKINS & wife TABITHA, AC, to GEO. DAVIS,
            AC, for Ł150, 187 acres surveyed by SAML. HIGGINBOTHAM, both
sides of Cedar Creek; part of former tract of RICH. PETER. Lines: THOS.
MORRIS; DAVIS.

Page 27.   5 Sep 1791.   GEO. DAVIS & wife THANEY (signed THEAR), AC, to

264

THOS. JENKINS of AC for "value rec'd" 100 acres pat. 1 Dec 1779; S side and joining Cashaw Creek - on Chestnut Mt. Lines: his own; also 120 acres pat. 20 Jul 1780. Lines: his own, S branch Otter Creek.

Page 29.   20 Dec 1790. WM. GILLESPIE, Linchorn (sic: Lincoln), to ALEX. MOSS, Georgia (Orig. del. to FLEMMING MOSS) for Ł200, 2 tracts. 1) 50 acres on branch of Dutch. Lines: JNO. STAPLES, JNO. HUNTER on N side. 2) 97 acres at the head of Dutch. Lines: tree on the mt. Wit: GEO. GILLESPIE JR & SR, LEWIS GILLESPIE. (Note: I have commented many times on this ancestor of my wife's. He married ANN HUDSON here in 1777 and they removed to Madison Co, Ky. He carried the mail between Danville and Charlottesville and was killed in a duel in Garrard Co, Ky. The witnesses were his father, GG Sr, and brothers. BFD)

Page 30.   14 Feb 1791. GEO. FITZGERALD and THOMPSON & TEAS to WM. EVANS for Ł60, 103 acres both sides Indian Creek. Lines: his own. Wit: JAS. LOVING, JESSE THOMPSON, JESSE BIBB. Orig. del. to JNO. THOMPSON 2 Aug 1796.

Page 32.   1 Aug 1791. HUGH ROSE on own and as atty. for DANL. GAINES, AC, to ZACH. TALIAFERRO, for Ł30, Mobley's Creek near Jas. River. 1) 92 acres surveyed by WM. MIGGINSON 22 Mar 1771, and granted to grantors as tenants in common by pat., 10 Mar 1781. Lines: GEO. HILTON, N bank of Mobley, RO. FREELAND. 2) 38 acres by survey of 6 Apr 1775, S side and joining Mobley's Creek. Lines: JAS. FREELAND, dec'd, WM. MIGGINSON. Wit: RO. HO. ROSE, JNO. FITZHUGH, THOS. DAVIS, JAS. WILSON, JR. Orig. del. to Capt. ZACH. TALIAFERRO.

Page 33.   2 Sep 1791. NELSON CRAWFORD, AC, to JNO. SANDIDGE, AC, (Orig. del. to LARKIN SANDIDGE) for Ł30, "to 100 acres" N branch of Horsley; part of a tract of grantor. Lines: my own, JOS. MILSTED.

Page 34.   1 Oct 1791. WM. WITT, AC, to RO. GRANT, AC, (Orig. del. to ALEX. McALEXANDER, 4 Aug 1796) for Ł10, 45 acres N fork Davis Creek; part of tract surveyed by WM. HORRELL. Lines: THOS. McDANIEL's old line, mt. ridge, line made in presence of MARTIN KEY, JAS. VAUGHAN, and SAML. SCOTT SCRUGGS. Lower part and adjoins ELIZ. JOHNSON. Wit: JAS. VIGUS, BARTHOLOMEW MERION, THOS. ELLIOT CRUTCHFIELD.

Page 36.   22 Sep 1791. JNO. PANNELL to WM. RICE, both of AC, (Orig. del. to C. PERROW, atto., 18 Nov 1845) for Ł70, 200 acres. Lines: JNO. McANALLY, Col. CHISWELL, BORROM RINKEAD, JAS. PENDLETON. Wit: DAVID McANALLY, WM. McANALLY, THOS. VINES.

Page 38.   25 Sep 1791. LUKE PANNEL to SAML. MOSES, both of AC, (del. as deed above in 1845) for Ł25, 134 acres branch of Rode Creek. Lines: THOS. PANNELL. Wit: as above.

Page 39.   3 Oct 1791. EDWD. POWELL alias EDWD. WARE & wife, SARAH, to CHAS. TALIAFERRO JR, (orig. del. to grantee) for Ł155, 420 acres Puppie's Creek. Lines: CHAS. TALIAFERRO, top of Tobacco Row. Mt. Signed: POWELL.

Page 40.   3 Oct 1791. EDWD. POWELL & wife SARAH, AC, to JNO. TALIAFERRO, AC, (orig. del. to CHAS. TALIAFERRO JR) for Ł8, 45 acres Puppies Creek (This is still so known); part of tract formerly surveyed and pat. to EDWD. WARE. Lines: GORDEN; CHAS. TALIAFERRO, WM. CARTER.

Page 42.   3 Oct 1791. EDWD. POWELL & wife SARAH, AC, to JNO. CLARKSON, AC, (Orig. del. to JC 7 Dec 1798) for Ł12, 30 acres on Tobacco Row. Mt.; part of 250 acres pat. to EDWD. WARE. Lines: CLARKSON & WARE.

Page 43.   3 Oct 1791. EDWD. WARE & wife SALLY, to JNO. WARE, AC, for Ł100, 351 acres S side and joining Pedlar. Lines: JNO. HIX, N fork Irish Creek, & WM. FLOYD.

Page 44.   5 Sep 1791. WM. CARTER, AC, to ZACH. & BENJ. TALIAFERRO, AC, Deed of Trust - certified entry willed to WM. CARTER by SOLOMON CARTER - surveyed 2 Nov 1771 - 72 acres branch of Puppie's Creek. Lines: his own, CHAS. TALIAFERRO, EDWD. WARE. Also rest of tract by will of SOLOMON CARTER; pat. 24 Mar 1767; other part sold to JNO. BARSHLOT and now in possession of CHAS. McCABE; whereon CARTER now lives. Lines: CHAS. TALIAFERRO, CHAS. McCABE, and above entry. Wit: JNO, WM. & RODERICK TALIAFERRO.

Page 46.   2 Sep 1791.   JNO. MURRILL, AC, to WM. BRIDGWATER, AC, for Ŀ100, 230 acres on branch of Rockfish. Lines: ALEX. HENDERSON, CLAP-HAM; JNO. LOBBAN.   Wit: HUDSON MARTIN, THOS. EWERS, JAS. EWERS, RO. WEIR.

Page 48.   7 Sep 1791.   JNO. McANALLY & wife RUTH, AC, to WM. SHELTON, AC, (Orig. del. to JAS. MONTGOMERY per order) for Ŀ25, 50 acres Rockfish. Lines: KINKADE's old line. Wit: JAS. MONTGOMERY, DAVID SIMPSON, GEORGE PERRY, JNO. STAPLES.

Page 49.   7 Sep 1791.   WM. CALBREATH, AC, to WM. SHELTON, AC, for Ŀ25, 180 acres CHILTON's(?) and McANALLYS' branches and S sdie Blue Ridge. Lines: DAVID McANALLY, MANUS BURGER, JNO. McANALLY. Pat. to grantor. Wit: DAVID SIMPSON et al as above.

Page 50.   7 Sep 1791.   WM. SHELTON, AC, of 1st part; NATHAN CRAWFORD & WM. HARRIS, 2nd part and NATHL. ANDERSON & HUDSON MARTIN, atto's for HENRY MARTIN & assignees, 3rd. part - Deed of Trust to secure ANDERSON & MARTIN - 5 sh. paid by 3rd parties - 230 acres at foot of Blue Ridge. Lines: JNO. McANALLY and conveyed this day to SHELTON by WM. CALBREATH & JNO. McANALLY. (Orig. del. to SHELTON, 27 Jan.) Wit: JAMES MONTGOMERY, DAVID SIMPSON, GEO. PERRY, JNO. STAPLES.

Page 52.   7 Sep 1791.   JNO. McANALLY, AC, and parties as above - 5 sh., 100 acres - Deed of Trust - at foot of Blue Ridge. Lines: JAS. PENDLETON. Wit: same as above. Orig. del. to JNO. MURREL per order, 27 Jan 1794.

Page 54.   23 Sep 1791.   SAML. MIGGINSON & wife ELIZ, AC, to THOS. APLING, AC,(Orig. with comm. del. to TA, 31 Oct 1791) for Ŀ200, 300 acres Buffalo and branches - one part bought by SM. of JNO. UPSHAW and other from AMBROSE GATEWOOD - part from GATEWOOD by deed made by THOS. PENN. Lines: WM.ALCOCK, John's Branch, AMBROSE GATEWOOD's line run for 100 acres from MIGGINSON to GATEWOOD, JNO. CHRISTIAN, JAS. FREELAND, dec'd; as agreeable to deed from JNO. UPSHAW to MIGGINSON. Wit: THOMAS WORTHAM, WM. PHILLIPS, GEO. PHILLIPS.

Page 55.   14 Feb 1791.   JAS. MATTHEWS to JOS. BALLENGER, AC, for Ŀ3, 90 acres both sides Swaping Camp Creek. Lines: JAS. SMITH, NEILL CAMPBELL. Wit: SAML. & REUBIN FRANKLIN, JANE MATTHEWS.

Page 56.   8 Dec 1788.   JNO. LAMASTER, AC, to WM. EVANS, AC, for Ŀ20, 25 acres Porrage Creek. Lines: SACKVILLE KING & JNO. TURNER. Wit: CHAS. CHRISTIAN, JAS. VIGUST, GEO. EVANS, JAS. LONDON. Orig. del. to CALEB CHENAULT per order filed.

Page 58.   2 Oct 1791.   GEO. PHILLIPS & wife MARY, AC, to JAS. ROWSEY, AC, for Ŀ10, 10 acres; part of my last survey; adjoins grant-ee, SMITH TANDY. Wit: EZ. GILBERT, JAS. & DRURY CHRISTIAN.

Page 59.   3 Oct 1791.   GEO. PHILLIPS & wife MARY, AC, to JAS. SAVAGE (orig. del. to JNO. SAVAGE, 11 Oct 1794) for Ŀ100, 213 acres. Lines: JNO. PHILLIPS, CHAS. STEWART - all of grantor's land save 10 acres. Wit: as above.

Page 60.   2 Sep 1791.   THOS. JOPLING, AC, to WM. MARTIN, AC, (Margin has been scratched: 22 May 1797, del. per order to CHS. STATHAM) for Ŀ12, 52 acres S branch Rockfish; part of tract given him by his father. Lines: JAS. JOPLING, JOSIAH JOPLING, MARTIN KEY, CHAS. STATHAM, WM. ALLEN - wits. to line run between ourselves. Wit: JNO. GREGORY, WM. GRIGORY, JOSHUA WILLOUGHBY.

Page 62.   15 Jan 1788.   GEO. BLAIN, AC, to THOMPSON & TEAS, AC, (del. to JNO. THOMPSON) Deed of Trust - debt of Ŀ45-19-5 and Ŀ1000 tobacco. 122 3/4 acres. Lines: grantor, BIBB, old line. Wit: BENJ. POW-ELL, WM. HOOKER, D.S. GARLAND.

266

Page 63.   3 Oct 1791. WM. CABELL JR. & wife ANNE, AC, to WM. S. CRAW-
            FORD, AC, (Orig. del. with comm. to WC, Nov, 1791) for Ł60, 50
acres N branch Higginbotham Mill Creek. Lines: WM. S. CRAWFORD, WM. CA-
BELL JR, LAURENCE CAMPBELL.

Page 64.   3 Oct 1791. GEO. FITZGERALD & wife MARGARET, AC and Lexington
            Parish, to JAS. MANN, Campbell Co, for Ł50, 400 acres branches
of Mill Creek and Porrage. Lines: JAS. DILLARD, JAS. CHRISTIAN, RO. JOHNS,
dec'd. Wit: JAS. DILLARD, MATT. TUCKER JR., JAS. DILLARD JR.

Page 66.   26 Jul 1791. CORNL. SALE & wife JANE, AC, to CHAS. BURRUS,
            AC, for Ł220, 279 acres. Lines: GEO. SEATON. Wit: JAS. BALL-
INGER, JOS. PENN.

Page 68.   5 Dec 1791. JNO. CLARKSON & wife SUSAN, AC, to JOS. DODD, AC,
            (Orig. del. to JD, 1792) for Ł50, 130 acres N side Buffalo in
Denes Thoroughfare and conveyed to JC by BENJ. HIGGINBOTHAM 4 Oct 1784.

Page 69.   27 Oct 1791. THOS. SHANNON & wife MARY, AC, to JAS. BISHOP,
            AC, for 5 sh, 150 acres; part of 400 acres surveyed, on Pat-
ten's branch. Lines: JNO. NOWL. Wit: JNO. HENDERSON, ARCHD. CAMPBELL,
JNO. THOMPSON, WM. BARNETT. Del. to JB JR, 29 Aug 1797.

Page 70.   27 Oct 1791. THOS. SHANNON, & wife MARY, AC, to JNO. NOWL,
            Augusta Co, (del. to JAS. MONTGOMERY, 15 Jan) for Ł93, 257
acres Patten's branch. Lines: CHAS. RODES. Wit: as above.

Page 71.   7 Nov 1791. JNO. HEARD, State of Ga, Power of Atty. to friend
            JAS. REID of Greenbrier Co, Va., to lay off and divide the 3rd
part of 1200 acres out of a survey made for TH on Cooper's Creek, a
branch of Gawley River - containing 1000 acres by pat. 23 Aug 1787; to
make a fee simple deed to EDWD. McCLUNG who located the land and to sell
balance (Note taken of discrepancy of acreage BFD) Wit: W.L. CRAWFORD,
RO. JOUETT, WILL LOVING JR, WM. LOVING. (Just why this is of record in
AC is a mystery to me. BFD)

Page 71.   11 Nov 1791. Agreement between BENJ. PARKS, son of JNO. PARKS
            JR, dec'd - supposed to be lawful heir of JNO. PARKS, minor,
dec'd and son of WM. PARKS, dec'd. - to MARTIN PARKS, WM. PARKS, SALLA
TINSLEY, SAML. BURKS who married PEGGY PARKS, ZACH. DAWSON as gdn. of
BETSY PARKS -- BENJ. supposing himself lawful heir of JNO. PARKS, son of
WM. PARKS - suit in chancery to recover from aforesaid orphans of WM.
PARKS, dec'd, by his 2nd wife - the estate of WM. PARKS and his son, JNO.
PARKS, who are dec'd, and orphans by themselves and gdns. have compro-
mised and contracted with BENJ. PARKS to give him 1st choice of any of
the negroes that may fall to orphans' lot out of estate of JNO. PARKS,
dec'd, son of WM. PARKS - Ł5 to BENJ. PARKS, and BENJ. PARKS, supposed
heir of JNO. PARKS, son of WM. PARKS, makes over all his rights to estate
of JNO. PARKS, dec'd. SALLA TINSLEY signed as SARAH. Wit: ISAAC TINSLEY,
NICHL. WEST, JAS. & RICH. TINSLEY.

Page 72.   5 Dec 1791. MOSES PENN & wife FRANCES, AC, to JOS. BURRUS,
            AC, (Orig. del. to JB, 13 Jan 1804) for Ł261, 342 acres both
sides S fork of Huff Creek. Lines: BRAXTON's pat.; JAS. LIVELY.

Page 74.   5 Nov 1791. SAML. HIGGINBOTHAM & wife JANE (JEANE) and PHILIP
            SMITH, AC, to ZACH. TALIAFERRO, JR, AC, (Orig. del. to BART-
LETT EADES) for Ł450, 300 acres both sides Buffalo; pat. to AARON HIGGIN-
BOTHAM, 15 Dec 1749, and by deed of 5 May 1777, to SAML. HIGGINBOTHAM.
Lines: JNO. HURT, crossing river, BENJ. TALIAFERRO, JACOB SMITH, JNO.
CLARKSON, himself. Also adjoining tract of 262 acres pat. to AARON HIG-
GINBOTHAM 3 Mar 1760, and by him willed to SAML. HIGGINBOTHAM. Lines:
himself, PHILLIP SMITH, JNO. CLARKSON. Also 85 acres by deed from SAMUEL
MARKSBURY to PHILIP SMITH, 5 May 1769. Lines: ALEX. GORDON, CHAS. TALIA-
FERRO, SAML. HIGGINBOTHAM. Wit: JNO. TALIAFERRO, BENJ. TALIAFERRO, PETER
P. THORNTON, RODERICK McCULLOCH, JNO. LOVING JR.

Page 76.   5 Dec 1791. PHILLIP SMITH, AC, to SAML. HIGGINBOTHAM, AC,
            Deed of Trust to secure 85 acres sold to me and said to be
mortgaged; sold by me to SAML. HIGGINBOTHAM - 500 acres on both sides

Franklin Creek and whereon I live. Lines: JNO. TALIAFERRO, JACOB SMITH, AARON HIGGINBOTHAM, ZACH. TALIAFERRO; also negress, Cate, and increase - the 85 acres sold by SMITH to HIGGINBOTHAM and by SH to ZACH. TALIAFERRO, and by joint deed, 5 Nov 1791, to TALIAFERRO.

Page 77.   5 Dec 1791.   SAML. HIGGINBOTHAM & wife JEANE, AC, to JACOB
            PHILLIPS, AC, for Ƚ20, 2 tracts on Buffalo. 1) 200 acres pat.
to AARON HIGGINBOTHAM, 10 Apr 1781, and by him willed to SAML. HIGGIN-
BOTHAM. Lines: AMBORSE TOMLINSON, formerly PHILLIP WALKER's; S branch of
N fork of Buffalo.   2) 140 acres on S side of Cold Mt. (This is still a
landmark and Cold Mt. cabbage is "out of this world". BFD)   and S branch
of N fork of Buffalo. Pat. to SAML. HIGGINBOTHAM, 10 Apr 1781. Wit: JNO.
TALIAFERRO, RODERICK McCULLOCH, JNO. LOVING JR.

Page 79.   8 Dec 1791.   EDWD. GARLAND & wife SARAH, Albemarle; THOS. GAR-
            LAND & wife MARY, AC, to ELIZ. COLEMAN, AC, for Ƚ140, 200
acres both sides Harris Creek. Lines: THOS. LUCAS, the road. Wit: DAVID
JONES, SAML. COLEMAN, DANL. TUCKER. Del. to THOS. COLEMAN 21 Nov 1799.

Page 80.   26 Dec 1791.   THOS. GILLENWATERS, Spartinsburg (sic) S.C., to
            GEO. McDANIEL, AC, for Ƚ135, 156 acres both sides Boling's
Creek.   Tract willed to TG by THOS. GILLENWATERS, dec'd, formerly of AC.
Lines: On Duck Bill, CHAS. CLARKE, dec'd, JNO. MILLER, THOS. JOHNSON.
Wit: THOS. HAYS, NEHEMIAH ROZWELL, PLEDGE PARMER, JAS. LASHELL, MICAJAH
CLARK, WM. WILLIAMS.

Page 81.   16 Sep 1791.   PETER CARTER & wife BETIE(?), AC, and Lexington
            Parish, to JESSE CARTER, AC and parish, for Ƚ25, 63½ acres
Horsley Creek. Lines: CHAS. McCABE. Wit: WM. SANDAGE, ABRAHAM CARTER,
BENJ. HIGGINBOTHAM, LUKE WRAY, PETER CARTER, JOS. MILSTEAD.

Page 82.   14 Sep 1791.   DANL. GAINES & wife MARY, Wilks Co, Ga.; HUGH
            ROSE, GABL. PENN, JAS. FRANKLIN, AC, CHAS. IRVING, Albemarle
Co., to JAMES LIVELY, AC, - GAINES executed deed on -- 17, ---, to ROSE,
PENN, IRVING, & FRANKLIN - Deed of Trust - slaves, etc. and rec. in AC;
GAINES with consent of trustees sold 594 acres, Ƚ300, all land in Deed of
Trust known as the old house tract - 594 acres, S branch of Rutledge.
Lines: JNO. WIATT, RICH. CHANDLER, on Migginson's Road, mouth of a branch,
JAS. HILL, WM. MOHON. GAINES holds by certain Acts of Va. Assemble and
trustees by Deed of Trust. Wit: SAML. MEREDITH.   14 Sep 1791, H. OSBORNE,
one of Superior Ct. judges of Ga., certified that GAINES & wife appeared
before him; BENJ. CATCHING, Wilkes Co, Ga., Clerk of Superior Court.

Page 84.   18 Feb 1792.   ABRAHAM WARWICK, AC, to WM. WARWICK, AC, for Ƚ5,
            400 acres on Rucker's Run. Lines: JNO. HARMER, MARTIN KEY &
CHAS. IRVING as atty. for HENRY KEY. Orig. del. to DANL. WARWICK, 16
Sep 179-.

Page 86.   12 Jul 1791.   DAVID CLARKE, AC, to CHAS. BRIDGWATER, AC, for
            Ƚ30, three beds, etc; long list. Wit: SAML. BRIDGWATER, WM.
CLARK.

Page 87.   21 Oct 1791.   GEO. FITZGERALD & wife MARGARET, AC, & Lexington
            Parish, to JAS. DILLARD, AC, & Parish, for Ƚ75, 200 acres N
branch Indian Creek. Lines: WM. PARKS, WM. BIBB. Wit: LARKIN LONDON,
THOS. JOHNS, JAS. CHRISTIAN JR, JNO. CASH, BARTLETT JOHNS.

Page 88.   29 Nov 1791.   MATT. TUCKER & wife EASTER(ESTHER), AC, to JNO.
            DUNCAN, AC, (Orig. del. to JNO. IRVINE, Campbell Co, comm.
annexed) for Ƚ300, 697 acres Buffalo and Beaver Creeks - E side and adj.
Tobacco Row - where MT lives; includes 200 acres bought of NICHL. CABELL,
250 acres bought of JNO. DILLARD, 247 acres bought of JAS. FRANKLIN; rec.
in AC. Wit: JAS. FRANKLIN, HENRY CAMDEN, WM. CAMDEN.

Page 89.   4 Oct 1791.   AMBROSE RUCKER & JAS. MORTON, AC, to JESSE WOOD-
            ROOF, AC, for Ƚ50, 100 acres Harris Creek. Lines: DAVID WOOD-
ROOF, top of Paul Mt., the Thoroughfare. Wit: JNO. JONES, ISAAC RUCKER,
DAVID WOODROOF, ISAAC RUCKER JR, WIATT WOODROOF, JNO. RUCKER JR.

Page 89.   12 Oct 1791.   PHILLIP THURMOND & wife JUDITH, AC, to ELIAS

268

WILLS, AC, for Ł130, 120 acres N side Tobacco Row and S branch Horsley.
Lines: N & E by DAVID CRAWFORD, S by BURFORD's entry; W by grantor; PT
bought of THOS. LUCAS and commonly known as BENJ. WASH place and where
ELIAS WILLS now lives. Wit: WM. HAYNES, THOS. WILLS, ELIAS WILLS JR,
POLLY THURMOND.

Page 91.   16 Spr 1791.   FRANCIS W. SPENCER to CHAS. W. YANCEY, JR, for
            5 sh, 250 acres on Tye (Orig. del. to CY 28 Mar 1796). Lines:
DAVID PROFIT, Rucker's Run, SAML. SPENCER. Part of 2000 acre survey en-
tered by my father, SAML. SPENCER. Wit: WM. B. HARE, REUBEN THORNTON,
POWHATAN BOLLING.

Page 92.   22 Dec 1791.   DAVID DONOHOE, Rockbridge Co, to JNO. BARNETT,
            AC, for Ł22-10, 94 acres S branch Hatt & Raccoon Creeks.
Lines: JNO. DOBSON, JNO. ROSE. Wit: JNO. MORAN, JNO. WREN, PATRICK
HIGHT, JER. PHILIPS.

Page 93.   16 Apr 1792.   JNO. BARNETT, AC, to JNO. MORAN, AC, for Ł80,
            200 acres Hatt Creek. Lines: JNO. DOBSON on upper side of ck.

Page 94.   16 Apr 1792.   CHAS. CHRISTIAN & wife SARAH, AC, to son JAS,
            AC, (del. 10 Oct 1810 to JAS. GARLAND) for paternal love -
125 acres S waters Buffalo and E side Braxton's ridge. Lines: Wilcher's
Branch, WM. GATEWOOD, dec'd, ROLLY PENN, LEN CLARK. Wit: SAML. WRIGHT,
MARY DUKE BELL, ELIZA CHRISTIAN.

Page 94.   3 Oct 1791.   BENJ. EVANS, AC, to JNO. CHRISTIAN, AC, for Ł10,
            20 acres, part of tract by BE to SAML. MIGGINSON (he rel. all
claims). Lines: CHRISTIAN, SAML. MIGGINSON, path called Scool(sic) Path.
Wit: NOTLEY W. MADDOX, JNO. KENADY, PETER JOINER, THOS. ROWSEY, JNO.
HUTCHERSON, CHAS. CHRISTIAN. Orig. taken out by JNO. CHRISTIAN 1 May
1817.

Page 95.   16 Apr 1792.   JNO. CLARKSON & wife SUSANNAH, AC, to DAVID
            CLARKSON, AC, for Ł18,000 Richmond inspected tobacco, 244
acres; part of tract surveyed for JAS. COFFEY 24 Mar 1756, and includes
364 acres, both sides of Tye and includes forks and mouth of Cox Creek.

Page 97.   24 Sep 1791.   WM. DAVIS, AC, to ZACH. & BENJ. TALIAFERRO, AC,
            Deed of Trust - 150 acres N branch of N fork Horsley and where
DAVIS lives. Part of survey of 200 acres of 12 Mar 1782. Lines: RICH.
DAVIS, MOSES DAVIS. Wit: WM. PRYOR, RO. TUCKER, JNO. GROOME, CHAS. HAYNES.

Page 98.   12 Dec 1791.   RO. CARTER HARRISON, Cumberland Co, and wife
            ANN, to WM. LOVING, AC, for Ł35, 105 acres Bob's Creek and
branch of Rucker's Run. Lines: LOVING, across Spencer's road; HARRISON;
WM. CRISP; part of tract conveyed to ANN HARRISON by JOS. CABELL, Buckingham, 4 Jan 1791. Wit: WM. LOVING JR, PARMENAS BRYANT, JNO. TOOL,
ANDREW McDOWELL. Orig. del to WM. LOVING, 11 Apr 1794. Page 99, Order
to quiz ANNE HARRISON sent to JOS. CABELL JR. & JOSIAS JONES, 12 Dec 1791,
done next day, ret. to AC 16 Apr 1792.

Page 100.   21 Jan 1792.   JNO. HIGHT & wife MARY, AC, to WM. COFFEY, AC,
            (Orig. del. to LANDY or SANDY ROSE per order, 12 Nov 1795)
for Ł45, 298 acres Stony Run of Tye, 3 pats. 1) 20 Jul 1768, for 50
acres. Lines: S side Stony. 2) Others pat. 16 Feb 1770 - one for 200 acres and lines of SAML. POE on bank of S fork of Stony; other for 48 acres
and adjoins JOSEPH ALLEN. Wit: DANL. McDANIEL, NATHL. HILL, SAML. COLEMAN.

Page 103.   18 Jun 1792.   WIATT POWELL & wife SARAH, AC, to GEO. McDANIEL,
            AC, for Ł200, 250 acres Rutledge Creek. Lines: EDWD. WATSON,
top of a hill, a road.

Page 104.   18 Jun 1792.   JNO. PAYTON & wife SARAH, AC, to JNO. BROWN, AC,
            for Ł23-12, 59 acres N fork Horsley; part of a tract. Lines:
my own, BROWN. Wit: NELSON CRAWFORD, HENRY BROWN, ISAAC WRIGHT, THOS.
GARLAND.

Page 105.   23 Aug 1791.   RICH. CHANDLER, AC, to JOEL FRANKLIN, AC, (orig.
            del. to JAS. FRANKLIN) for Ł300, 414 acres. Lines: WM. CHAPEL,

JNO. WIATT, JOS. HIGGINBOTHAM, son of MOSES, EVE LACKEY, WM. MAYO, JAS. LIVELY, WM. MOON, JNO. & BEV. PADGETT. Bought by RC of JNO. STEWART. Wit: JAS. FRANKLIN, BENAMIMI STONE, JAS. BALLINGER.

Page 107.   27 Dec 1791.   JNO. DUNCAN & wife SARAH, AC, to JNO. F.P. LEWIS, AC, for Ł200, 200 acres branch of Pedlar. Lines: Maple Creek, NATHL. DAVIS dec'd, JNO. BURKS, DAVID BURKS, water grist mill - 1 acre on E or opposite side of river. Wit: ISHAM DAVIS, BENJ. HENSLEY, JAS. DAVIS, JNO. BURKS.

Page 108.   30 Jul 1791.   SMYTH TANDY, AC, to JAS. CALLAWAY, AC, (Orig. del. to LINDSEY COLEMAN) for 10 sh, Deed of Trust - to secure LINDSEY COLEMAN, AC, bal. due on judgment in Co. Ct. by JNO. STEWART vs. TANDY and assigned to LC. 2 copper stills - 140 and 120 gal. Wit: EDMD. TATE, THOS. CREWS, WM. TANDY.

Page 110.   29 Oct 1791.   JNO. HARDWICK, Bedford Co, to DANL. BURFORD JR, AC, for Ł25, 99 acres N branch Harris. Lines: MOSES HIGGINBO- THAM, Col. GEO. CARRINGTON. Wit: JOS. CREWS JR, JER. WADE, JONATHAN DAKIN.

Page 111.   18 Jun 1792.   Power of Atty by WM. HARRIS, AC, to LOWYEL(?) WOODFOLK, Woodford Co, Ky, to sell my Ky. land. Orig. del. to PLEASANT MARTIN.

Page 111.   21 Mar 1792.   AMBROSE RUCKER, AC, admr. of THOS. LUCAS (orig. del. to JAS. SHELTON) Widow, MARTHA LUCAS, has rel. dower rights; admr. has del. 2 slaves which were hers before marriage. Heirs referred to, but not named. 2 bonds of NICHL. PRYOR & ISAAC WRIGHT. Wit: WM. SPENCER, JAS. MURRAY BROWN.

Page 113.   26 Oct 1791.   CHAS. ISON & wife PEGGY, Mercer Co, Ky, to FRAN- CES STEPHENS, AC, for Ł50, 122 acres. Lines: WALTER POWER, ALEX. BAGGS. Wit: HENRY BALLINGER, JNO. NEW, SAML. RENSHAW.

Page 114.   19 May 1792.   SAML. HILL, AC, to JNO. ROSE & CHESLEY KINNEY, AC. (Sent to JNO. ROSE on written order, 12 Feb 1812) Deed of Trust - debt due trustees of CHAS. ROSE and to HUGH ROSE - named slaves. Wit: PATRICK ROSE, SAML. McGEHEE.

Page 115.   14 Jun 1792.   JONATHAN DAKIN, AC, to JNO. HANSARD, AC, (Orig. del. to PETER HANSARD, 8 Oct 1834) for Ł50, 42 acres on Lynch Road. With own lines and CLARK.

Page 116.   19 Mar 1792.   WM. WALTON, AC, to JAS. WILLS, AD, for Ł250, 230 acres both sides N fork of Rucker's Run. Lines: WM. WALTON, WM. DEPRIEST, JAS. STEPHENS, old line of LOMAX, side of the mt., Walton Spring. Wit: WILL LOVING, PLEASANT MARTIN, GEO. BLAIN.

Page 118.   23 Dec 1791.   JNO. PANNELL, AC, to JAS. GARLAND, AC, for Ł13, 53 acres head of S fork Patten's branch. Lines: JAS. GARLAND, his own. Wit: CHAS. RODES, HENRY PASLEY(?), JAS. ANDERSON, ARCHIBALD CAMPBELL.

Page 119.   17 Jun 1791.   JONATHAN DAKIN, AC, to PLEDGE PARMER, AC, for Ł50, 31 acres on the road.

Page 120.   18 Jun 1792.   WM. CHAPPELL & wife ANN, AC, to REUBEN PENDLETON, AC, for Ł65, 127 acres SS and joining Rutlege N fork. Lines: Lynch road, WIATT POWELL, JOS. CREWS, mouth of the big hill spring branch. Wit: JNO. LACKEY, JNO. MORTON, DAVID JONES, DAVID HUNTER.

Page 121.   4 Jun 1792.   WM. WALTON, AC, to ABRAHAM SEAY, AC, for Ł2, 10 acres N branches of Rucker's Run and Ragged Mts. Part of tract formerly that of JNO. TUGGLE and by him conveyed to WW, 7 Sep 1778. Lines: top of a mt., ABRAHAM SEAY, WM. WALTON, LOMAX's old line, near a branch.

Page 122.   17 Jun 1792.   JONATHAN DAKIN, AC, to JAS. LASHELL, AC, for Ł30, 15 acres. Lines: the road, JNO. WARD, JNO. HANSARD.

Page 123. 11 Aug 1791. JONATHAN WILSON, AC, to AMBR. RUCKER, Deed of
Trust - 10 sh. Where JW lives; 3 smaller tracts bought of
DANL. GAINES; to secure RICH. PENDLETON on bond with JW to WM. GOODE. Wit:
CORNL. POWELL, JOSEPH DAVENPORT, DAVID WOODROOF, DAVID JONES.

Page 125. 27 Jan 1792. JNO. LEWIS & JNO FRANCIS PENNY LEWIS, AC, to
HENRY LANDON DAVIES for Ŀ150, 330 acres branches of Pedlar.
Lines: NICHL. DAVIES, ASHCRAFT ROACH, ARCHELAUS GILLIAM, NATHL. DAVIES,
dec'd. Wit: LEROY POPE SR, BENJ. HENSLEY, JNO. BAGBY (or BAGLEY), ISHAM
DAVIS, JNO. BURKS.

Page 126. 12 Jun 1792. JNO. LOCKER AC, to ZACH. FORTUNE, for Ŀ20, 100
acres pat. to JNO. LOCHKER, 16 Mar 1792. Lines: NICHL. CABELL,
WM. WALTON.

Page 127. 6 Mar 1792. WM. COFFEY & wife ELIZ, AC, to GEO. HIGHT, AC,
(Orig. del. to SANDY or TANDY ROSE per order 12 Nov 1793) for
Ŀ6000 Richmond tobacco - Stony Run, branch of Tye. 1) 50 acres S side
Stoney Run; pat. 20 Jul 1768 to JOS. ALLEN and by him conveyed to JNO.
HIGHT. 2) 200 acres. Lines: SAML. POE, S & N fork Stoney Run, JOS. ALLEN;
pat. 16 Feb 1771 to JAS. BROWN. 3) 48 acres S fork Stony, pat. as 2 and
both conveyed to JNO. HIGHT - 298 acres conveyed from JH to WC.

Page 130. 20 Oct 1791. ARCHIBALD, GEO. & AUDLEY CAMPBELL and JNO. DE-
PRIEST to JNO. HENDERSON, all of AC for Ŀ20, 100 acres head
branches Rockfish; part of tract of GEO. CAMPBELL, dec'd. and held by
JNO. HENDERSON in right of wife's dower; all grantors' interest at death
of MARGARET, wife of JNO. HENDERSON. Wit: JOS. THOMPSON, WM. KYLE, JNO.
THOMPSON, JAS. ANDERSON.

Page 131. 21 Nov 1791. JAS. CREWS & wife MILDRED, AC, to HARRISON
HUGHES, AC, for Ŀ40, 40 acres. Lines: HUGHES, DAWSON, the path.
Wit: WM. HUGHES SR & JR, JOS. CREWS, JR, JONATHAN DAKIN. She signed
MILICENT.

Page 133. 21 Mar 1792. Order to Alb. J.P.'s, SAML. MURRELL & RICE GAR-
LAND - deed of EDWD. GARLAND to ELIZ. COLEMAN, 8 Dec 1791 -
200 acres Harris Creek. Sarah, wife of EG as to dower rights. Done 27
Mar 1792.

Page 134. 5 Oct 1791. Order to Fluvanna J.P.'s, JNO. THOMPSON, JNO.
PAYNE & JAS. PAYNE - MARY, wife of MARBEL STONE, JANE wife of
HEZ. STONE - deed to DUNCAN McLAUCHLAN & Co, Taylor Creek. Done by JT
and JNO. PAYNE, 11 Nov 1791.

Page 136. 2 Dec 1791. SAML. BAILEY & wife UNITY, to BENJ. RUCKER, all
of AC - for Ŀ50, 180 acres Stovall Creek. Lines: BENJ. RUCKER.

Page 137. 7 Dec 1791. CHAS. WILLSHER & wife ELIZ, AC, to LENARD CLARK
GEORGE, AC, for Ŀ60, 92½ acres. Lines: CHAS. CHRISTIAN; WEST
(?); HENRY IZABEL. Wit; JNO. LONAGAN, RICH. FULCHER, JACOB TYREE JR,
JNO. LAMONT.

Page 138. 16 Jan 1792. JNO. ALLEN & wife MARTHA, AC, to JNO. CAMPBELL,
AC, for Ŀ60, 120 acres Indian Creek. Orig. del. to JC 12 Dec
1795.

Page 140. 29 Sep 1791. JNO. & CHAS. WILCHER, AC, to CHAS. CHRISTIAN,
AC, for Ŀ50, 92 acres. Lines: CC; WM. GATEWOOD, dec'd, near
Braxton's ridge. Part of 185 acres bequeathed to JNO. & CHAS. by their
father, JOSEPH, dec'd. 92 acres sold by JNO. to CHAS., but never conveyed. Wit: JNO. CHRISTIAN, PETER JOINER, NOTLEY MADDOX.

Page 141. 16 Jul 1792. THOS. HAWKINS & wife ELIZ, AC, to JAS. WILLS,
AC, for Ŀ50, 188 acres Little Cove at head of branch of Ruckers Run. Lines: Col. LOMAX (formerly), WM. WALTON.

Page 143. 16 Jul 1792. HUGH ROSE & wife CAROLINE MATILDA, AC, to JOSHUA
TINSLEY (Orig. del. to JT) for Ŀ122, 122 acres Harris Creek,
part of tract. Lines: TINSLEY's Mill, mouth of a branch, SHELTON's road,

271

BENJ. RUCKER, MOSES RUCKER. Wit: DAVID TINSLEY, GEO. McDANIEL, PHILL BURFORD.

Page 144.   23 Feb 1792.   ZACH. TALIAFERRO to grandson, ZACH. TALIAFERRO DRUMMOND, son of HENLEY DRUMMOND - slave girl, Deophey - if ZTD dies, then to his brother, JNO. DRUMMOND. Wit: JNO. CLARKSON, WM. COFFEY, MOSES MARTIN, WM. HORSLEY. Orig. del. to BOUTWELL TALIAFERRO per order filed.

Page 144.   16 Jul 1792.   HUGH ROSE & wife CAROLINE MATILDA, AC, to PHIL-LIP BURFORD, AC, for Ł104, 104 acres (Orig. del. to JOSHUA TINSLEY). Lines: DAVID TINSLEY, Harris Creek, VALENTINE COX. Wit: DAVID TINSLEY, GEO. McDANIEL, WM. DAVENPORT.

Page 145.   Orig. del. to WM. HORSLEY, 7 May 1795.   1792 item - PLEASANT MARTIN, depty. shff, exposed to sale on May 13 last, negroes of estate of WM. HORSLEY, to satisfy execution of IRVING GALT & Co. vs. estate - slaves named - WM. CABELL bought them and rec'd receipt. Widow of WM. HORSLEY, MARTHA, in distressed condition. His children are WM., MARY, JOS, JUDITH, ROBT, MARTHA, SAMLL, ELIZ, JNO. & NICHL. HORSLEY. CABELL gives slaves to MARTHA for education of children and to support family. When NICHL. HORSLEY is of age or dies, when next youngest is 21, then division among widow and children. Wit: GIDEON CREWS, WM. BIBB.

Page 146.   16 Jul 1792.   HUGH ROSE & wife CAROLINE MATILDA, AC, to DAVID TINSLEY, AC, for Ł145, 145 acres Harris Creek. Part of tract. Lines: DAVID TINSLEY, Tinsley's Mill. Wit: PHILIP BURFORD, WM. DAVENPORT, GEO. McDANIEL.

Page 148.   9 Dec 1791.   WM. KNIGHT, AC, to SAML. MEREDITH, for Ł20, horse and saddle, stock, crop etc. Wit: JAS. McCAUL, SALLY MEREDITH, SARAH MEREDITH (sic).

Page 149.   6 Jul 1792.   EZRA MORRISON, LIncoln Co, Ky, to JOS. MONTGOMERY, AC, for Ł500, 400 acres Rockfish. Lines: JNO. FITZPATRICK, THOS. PRATT, JOS. MONTGOMERY, HAWES COLEMAN. Wit: HUDSON MARTIN, DAVID SIMPSON, JNO. STAPLES.

Page 150.   16 Jul 1792.   HENRY LANDON DAVIES, trustee of GEO. DAVIES, AC, to NICHL. DAVIES, Bedford Co. (Orig. del. to ND agreeable to note) for Ł65, 170 acres both sides Terrapin Creek. Lines: line formerly surveyed for RO. JOHNSON.

Page 151.   21 Mar 1792.   Order to AC J.P.'s as to deed of THOS. GARLAND & wife MARY, to ELIZ. COLEMAN, 8 Dec 1791 - 200 acres Harris Creek. To quiz MARY as to dower rights. Done, 14 Jul 1792, by DAVID CRAWFORD & WM. WARE.

Page 153.   3 Dec 1791.   THOS. MORE, AC, to HENRY LANDON DAVIES, AC, trustee of JER. TAYLOR, AC, (Orig. del. to TM with comm, 31 Oct, 1805) for Ł130, 222 acres where TAYLOR lives. Lines: ARCHELAUS MITCHELL, JOS. MEGANN, NICHL. DAVIES SR. and estate of THOS. POWELL dec'd. Wit: ANTHONY NORTH, JNO. HARRISON, NATHAN CRAWFORD JR.

Page 154.   17 Sep 1792.   SAML. HIGGINBOTHAM & wife JANE, AC, to AARON HIGGINBOTHAM, AC, for Ł100, 339 acres in 3 tracts. 1) 300 acres. Lines: EDWD. CARTER, near the road, AARON HIGGINBOTHAM, Stone House creek. 2) 31 acres. Lines: his own, RICH. OGLESBY, AARON HIGGIN-BOTHAM. 3) 8 acres. Lines: RO. CASH, dec'd, HENDRICK ARNOLD. Orig. del. to ROD. McCULLOCH with rel. and order.

Page 156.   17 Sep 1792.   CHAS. STEWART & wife SALLY, to RICH. ALCOCK for Ł60, 200 acres. Lines: JESSE KENNEDY, GEORGE PHILLIPS, JAS. ROWSEY.

Page 157.   29 Jul 1792.   DAVID WITT, AC, to LITTLEBERRY WITT, AC, for Ł60, 111 acres branch Rockfish; N side of the Mt. in a cove which formerly belonged to FRACES(sic) NEW. Lines: SAML. LACEY, LITTLE-BERRY WITT, WM. ABNEY, CHISEL's old line.

Page 158.   14 Jul 1792.   GEO. WITT & wife BETSY; JNO. WITT & wife ELIZ.;
            JOSIAH DODD & wife MARY, AC, to JOS. STRICKLAND, AC, for Ł100,
130 acres; part of 430 acres granted to GEO. HERD BAKER and deed by JAS.
HERD 21 Nov 1748. S branch Rockfish. Lines: GEO. & JNO. WITT, JOSIAH
DODD, GEO. JUDE, THOS. ADAMS. Wit: BARTLETT EADES, LITTLEBERRY & DAVID
WITT. Orig. del. to JS, 16 Jun 1797.

Page 160.   17 Jul 1792.   RO. BABER, AC, to DENNET WITT, AC, (Orig. del.
            to DW 96 Oct 1821) for Ł50, 128 acres branch of Rockfish.
Lines: ANDREA HARSTON, WM. HEARD. Wit: EZEK. CAMPBELL, DAVID WITT, BUMPAS
BABER.

Page 161.   17 Jul 1792.   RO. BABER, AC, to DAVID WITT - all of my personal
            property - horse, cow, hogs, furniture, etc. to dispose of as
he sees cause. Wit: LITTLEBERRY WITT, DENNET WITT, BUMPUS BABER.

Page 162.   17 Sep 1792.   JNO. THOMAS & wife SARAH, to WM. H. MOSBEY, all
            of AC, "residentures" for Ł80, 155 acres; last bought of JAS.
MONTGOMERY. 2 tracts pat. to DAVID MONTGOMERY SR; Davis Creek. Lines:
ZACH. PHILLIPS, Dutch Thurefair(sic), DANL. MOSBY, MATT. HARRIS, 2 sur-
veys, DAVID MOSBEY, his own.

Page 164.   15 Oct 1792.   JOS. MILSTEAD, AC, to BETSY SCOFFIELD, widow of
            WM. SCOFFIELD, in behalf of grandchildren of said WM.---sum;
100 acres on Horsley. Lines: MOSES HALL, JNO. SANDIDGE.

Page 165.   5 Sep 1792.   WM. LITTRELL SR, AC, to WM. EDMONS, AC, for Ł40,
            53 acres Head of Cub Creek. Lines: MOSES HUGHES, Capt. JNO.
JACOB, Thouroughfare. Wit: MOSES HUGHES, LEWIS BALL, WM. LITTRELL.

Page 167.   15 Oct 1792.   WM. PENN & wife MARTHA, AC, to TERISHA TURNER,
            AC, for Ł100, 214 acres branch Rockey Run. Lines: JNO. EDLOE,
dec'd., THOS. POWELL, dec'd, Stovall's old road. Wit: JAS. STEVENS JR(?),
STEPHEN WATTS, GIDEON CREWS. Orig. del. to WM. GREGORY 2 Aug 1794.

Page 168.   15 Sep 1792.   SAML. SHELTON JR. as atty. for THOS. McDANNEL,
            AC, to JNO. SHELTON, RO. GRANT, BARTHOLOMEW MURREN(?) & WM.
HARRIS, AC, for Ł140, 200 acres N fork Davis Creek. Lines: JNO. SKELTON,
BARTHOLOMEW MERREN, RO. GRANT, Mrs. ELIZ. JOHNSON, SAML. MERREN, WM.
HARRIS. Surveyed by JNO. LACKEY accompanied by JNO. SKELTON & RO. GRANT.
200 acres joins JAS. HALLEY BURTON, ELIZ. JOHNSON, WM. WITT & WM. HARRIS.
Orig. del. to ALEX. McALEXANDER 4 Aug 1796(?).

Page 170.   15 Oct 1792.   JNO. PEYTON & wife SARAH, AC, to NELSON CRAWFORD,
            AC, for Ł56-8, 141 acres N fork Horsley. Wit: WM. WARE, ABRA-
HAM CARTER, THOS. GARLAND, JESSE CARTER, RICH. OGLESBY, MOSES HALL. Orig.
del. to NC, 18 Sep 1798.

Page 171.   13 Mar 1792.   DAVID PHILLIPS & wife MARY, AC, to JOS. ROBERTS,
            AC, (Orig. del. to ALEX. ROBERTS, 3 Mar 1806, per order) for
Ł200, 190 acres lately occupied by JNO. THORNTON, S side Rockfish; ano-
ther tract adjoining of 136 acres, head of Wolf branches. Lines: JNO.
HUNTER, WM. BURNS, JNO. THORNTON. Wit: JNO. THOMAS, ALEX. ROBERTS, LEON-
ARD PHILLIPS, JAS. TURNER.

Page 173.   15 Oct 1792.   ABRAHAM CARTER & wife MARY, AC, to WM. HALL, AC,
            for Ł3600 tobacco, 254 acres Buffalo River & Luck Mt. Lines:
ISAAC MURPHY.

Page 174.   15 Oct 1792.   JNO. CLARKSON & wife SUSANNAH, AC, to CHAS.
            WATTS, AC, for Ł450, 3 tracts on Buffalo. 1) 300 acres. Lines:
SAML. HIGGINBOTHAM, crossing river. 2) 390 acres Davis Mt. S branch
Franklin Creek. Lines: JACOB SMITH, his own. 3) 236 acres N branch Buff-
alo. Lines: SAML. HIGGINBOTHAM, Davis Mt., JOS. HIGGINBOTHAM, his own.

Page 176.   15 Oct 1792.   CHAS. DAVIS & wife ROSANNA, AC, to JNO. EUBANK,
            AC, for Ł4000 hemp, 121 5/8 acres devised to ROSANNA ELLIS
(now DAVIS) by her father, CHAS. ELLIS - Horsley Creek and where EUBANK
now lives. Lines: EDMD. GOODRICH, JNO. EUBANK, the tract which formerly
belonged to RICH. WELBURN, WM. CLAPTON, CALEB RALLS, WM. HAYNES. Orig.

del. to JE, 2 Oct 1796.

Page 177. 11 Aug 1792. THOS. CARPENTER, AC, to JAS. & GEO. CARPENTER,
AC, for love for his 2 sons and 5 sh., 250 acres Rockfish
where I live. Lines: WM. BARNETT, HENRY SMITH, JOS. ROBERTS; cattle, hogs,
furniture. Wit: JNO. CARPENTER, THOS. PRATT, ALEX. BARNET, WM. BARNETT JR.

Page 178. 8 Sep 1792. JAS. GOOLSBY, AC, to JOS. CHILDRESS, AC, for Ŀ6,
38 acres S branches of N fork Harris. Lines: HEAVEN GOOLSBY's
former lines. Wit: SAML. COLEMAN, JESSE CHILDRESS, ALEX. DUGINGS, THOS.
MORRIS.

Page 180. 6 May 1792. RICH. CHANDLER, AC, to ALEX. BRYDIE & Co, Richmond, Deed of Trust - also penal note due WM. GALT & Co. -
knife and negroes, Sam & Sarah, at present in possession of JOEL FRANKLIN
as hirelings until 25 Dec next. Orig. del. to GEO. DILLARD. Wit: GIDEON
CREWS, GEO. DILLARD.

Page 181. 15 Oct 1792. GEO. DOUGLAS & wife MARY, AC, to WM.LEACH, AC,
for Ŀ30, 148 acres Hoop Creek.

Page 182. 24 May 1792. GEO. PERRY & wife SUSANNAH, AC, to DAVID WITT,
AC, for Ŀ40, slave, Hannah. Wit: JNO. BELL, DENNET WITT, EZEK.
CAMPBELL. 16 Oct 1821, orig. del. to DENNET WITT, admr. of DAVID WITT.

Page 183. 15 Oct 1792. EDWD. HARPER & wife FANNY, AC, to SUSANNA MARTIN,
AC, for Ŀ90, 314 acres branch Stoval and Porrage Creeks. Lines:
JOS. HIGGINBOTHAM, Stovall road, JNO. TURNER, JOS. NICHOLAS, BENJ. RUCKER,
VA. TAYLOR, JNO. KNIGHT. Wit: P. MARTIN, JNO. THOMPSON, WM. GRIFFIN.

Page 184. 15 Oct 1792. WM. BIBB, AC, to RO. WRIGHT & wife KEZIAH, AC,
for Ŀ20, 123 acres branch of Tye; part of a tract. Lines: JOS.
LIVELY, WM. BIBB, WM.LOVING, dec'd.

Page 185. 7 Jul 1792. WM. MICKLE & wife RUTH, Campbell Co, to THOS.
KEENE, Richmond - Deed of Trust. Ŀ1445-3-6 due by MICKLE to
JAS. WARRINGTON and KEENE; CHAS. HODGES on note with MICKLE.(Orig. del.
to ALEX. STEWART.) Harris Creek - 214 acres. Lines: Pole Cat at the
mouth. Wit: JNO. DABNEY, ALEX. STUART, JAS. TRICE.

Page 187. 10 Jul 1792. AARON DEHART & wife ELLENDER, AC, to SACKVILLE
KING or Campbell (Orig. del. to JNO. POWELL) for Ŀ37-10, 99
acres both sides Porrage. Lines: S & W by KING, N by AARON DEHART, E by
CHAS. CHRISTIAN (scratched as to CHAS); Part of tract and surveyed by
JNO. MERRITT, 4 Jun 1792. Wit: JAS. LONDON, JNO. POWELL, HENRY CHRISTIAN,
JNO. DEHART, JNO. F. POWELL.

Page 189. 14 Dec 1792. JNO. H. GOODWIN & wife MARY, AC, to SACKVILLE
KING, Lynchburg (Orig. del. to JNO. POWELL) for Ŀ20, 2 acres
main road to Madison and where KING & Co. have erected a tanyard. Wit:
AMB. RUCKER JR, ZACH. DAWSON, AMBR. RUCKER, PHIL JOHNSON, WIATT WOODROOF.

Page 190. 14 Nov 1792. ANN JOHNSON; JNO. H. GOODWIN & wife MARY; FRAN-
CES JOHNSON; WM. BUSTER & wife MARY, & ANN MOFFITT to PHILLIP
JOHNSON for 5 sh., 70 acres Bolling Creek; part of tract devised to
PHILLIP JOHNSON by his brother, WM. JOHNSON, and taken and possessed by
SNELLING JOHNSON, dec'd. Wit: JNO. MERRITT, WM. HANSARD, JAS. WARREN,
PLEDGE PARMER, JNO. HANSARD.

Page 192. 6 Nov 1792. ELIJAH STONE, AC, to SAML. PERKINS, AC, (Orig.
del. to S.H. LOVING for Dr. D.P.(?) WATSON, present owner, 25
Mar 1855) for Ŀ120, 243 acres in AC and Albermarle and where STONE lives,
on Rockfish - all that STONE had of ARCHELAUS STRANGE. Lines: JOS. MORRIS,
ABRAHAM STRANGE - 10 acres of it bought of JOS. MORRIS. Wit: JNO. PUGH,
WM. FARRAR, RICH. HARES.

Page 193. 22 Oct 1792. ISAAC DARNEILLE, AC, to THOS. ANDERSON, Bucking-
ham Co., for Ŀ70, 2 acres whereon he lives - houses and garden.
Wit: RICH. POLLARD, STITH WILIINSON(?), JNO. LEIGH, PLEASANT MARTIN,
AUGUSTINE SHEPHERD JR, LEWIS NEVIL.

274

Page 194.   10 Dec 1792.   CHAS. TYLER, AC, to JNO. ARRINGTON, AC, for Ł35,
            115 acres both sides Little Indian Creek. Lines: JNO. PARSON,
said WILSFORD in his old plantation - this is confusing for grantee is
called ARRINGTON - ref. to JNO. WILSFORD's line, JNO. ARRINGTON. Bought
by JNO. WILSFORD of CHAS. TYLER. Wit: JNO. ALLEN, ALLEN CAMREL.

Page 195.   15 Dec 1792.   JAS. DILLARD, AC, to SACKVILLE, Campbell Co,
            (Del. to REUBEN NORVELL, 4 Nov 1800) for Ł72, 360 acres by
survey, 17 May 1788.   Branches of Fluvanna and near Stovall's ferry.
Lines: WM. GALT, JOS. MAYS.

Page 196.   15 Dec 1792.   Same parties as above for Ł34, 400 acres by sur-
            vey of 17 Dec 1772; S branch Porrage and head of another
branch of Stovall's Creek. Lines: DAVID CHRISTIAN, dec'd, TERISHA TURNER.
JAS. DILLARD grantor as above and KING, grantee.

Page 197.   17 Dec 1792.   GEO. GILLESPIE & wife MARY, AC, to WM. WIDDIBURN,
            AC, (Orig. del. to WM. WEDDERBURN (note variation)) for Ł10,
164 acres Piney River, crossing N fork.   Ref.to Land Office at Richmond.
Wit: JNO. LOVING, JR, OWEN HASKINS.

Page 198.   5 Oct 1792.   GEO. GILLESPIE & wife MARY, AC, to JAS. ROBARDS,
            Goochland Co, (Orig. del. to HENRY or HOUNY(?) MASSIE) for
Ł20, 81 acres both sides S fork Piney. Lines: GILBERT HAYS, GEO. MUNROE.
Wit: JNO. LOVING JR, OWEN HASKINS, W. WEDDERBURNE.

Page 200.   4 Jun 1782 (sic) THOS. JOHNS & wife ---, Cumberland Co, to
            JAS. FRANKLIN, AC, for Ł430, whereon WILL--ON BRUMMEL(T?)
lived as overseer for WM. JOHNS. Lines: N bank Rutledge, GEBL. PENN. Wit:
JNO. STEWART, JNO. JOHNS, JAS. POLLARD, JNO. RICHERSON, EDMD. WILCOX,
WIATT POWELL, THOS. POWELL.   Final proof 17 Dec 1792.   Proved 4 Nov 1782
by THOS. & WIATT POWELL & RICHERSON on 17 Dec 1792.

Page 201.   18 Nov 1792.   WM. ALFORD, AC, to ELIJAH MAYS, AC, (Orig. del.
            to E.M., 17 Apr 1826) for Ł50, 103 acres on Tye. Pat. of AU-
GUSTINE SMITH. Lines: WM. BIBB, MOSES CAMPBELL.

Page 201.   19 Jul 1792.   ROY ROBERTSON, AC, to WM. GRIFFIN - Power of
            Atty to WG as my legal atty. and to sell my tract in Caroline
on Robertson's Branch. Wit: JAS. STEVENS JR, THOS. GRIFFIN, WM. TURNER.

Page 202.   15 Oct 1792.   JOS. STAPLES, Tob. Inspector at Swan Creek W.H.
            Bondsman: WM. WARWICK.

Page 203.   29 Nov 1792.   Deed of Trust by WM. LANE to JAS. FRANKLIN.
            Debt of Ł120. 5 sh. for 8 slaves named. Wit: SAML. BROWN, JNO.
STRATTON, WM. LAVENDER.

Page 204.   4 Jul 1792.   WM. BALL to AMBROSE BABER, Buckingham Co, for
            Ł125, 250 acres Tye River.

Page 205.   21 Jan 1793.   HUGH ROSE & wife CAROLINE MATILDA, to PHILIP
            BURFORD (Orig. del. to ISAAC TINSLEY) for Ł48, 48 acres, part
of a tract. Lines: BURFORD, SHELTON, VAL. COX, BURFORD's former line,
SHELTON's road.

Page 206.   21 Jan 1793.   HUGH ROSE & wife as above, to JOSHUA TINSLEY,
            AC, (Orig. del. to ISAAC TINSLEY) for Ł37, 37 acres Harris
Creek. Part of ROSE tract. Lines: SHELTON's road, Mill pond, JOSHUA TINS-
LEY.

Page 207.   21 Jan 1793.   HUGH ROSE & wife, as above, to JNO, ISAAC, DAVID,
            & JOSHUA TINSLEY (Orig. del. to JOSHUA TINSLEY) for Ł115, 23
acres Harris Creek. Includes the mill and plantation known as PAUL WOODS.
Lines: The bank of Mill pond, PHILIP BURFORD, SHELTON's road.

Page 208.   22 Jan 1793.   PHILIP LOCKHART, AC, to CHAS. TUCKER, AC, (Orig.
            del. to TUCKER 17 Feb 1803) for Ł15, 54 acres branch of Stone-
house Creek. Lines: WM. BECKNELL, JOS. LIVELY, PERRIN FARRAR.

Page 209. 17 Oct 1792. JNO. WEST, Warwick Co, to JAS. FRANKLIN, AC, for
Ƚ550, 500 acres S side and joining Rutledge; part of est. of
JNO. WEST, dec'd. Lines: PARKS' Road, COX's Cabin Branch. Wit: WIATT
POWELL, JOEL FRANKLIN, SHEROD BUGG.

Page 210. 17 Jan 1792. Order to J.P.'s of Elbert Co, Ga., JNO. CUNNING-
HAM & RALPH BANKS, to quiz SUSANNAH BONDS, wife of RICH. BONDS,
as to deed to WM. TUCKER, 16 Sep 1788 - 179 acres Stonehouse and N side
of Buffalo. Done, 29 Mar 1792.

Page 211. 21 Jan 1793. WM. WITT, AC, to WM. WOOD, AC, for Ƚ30, 150 acres Davis Creek, branch of Rockfish. Lines: SAML. MURRIN, JNO.
ABNERY, JOS. ROBARDS, THOS. CARPENTER, WM. WITT. Wit: JOS. ROBERTS.

Page 212. 29 Sep 1792. THOS. H. TALBOT (TABOTT) & wife MARY, AC, to
MOSES HUGHES, AC, for Ƚ100, 100 acres both sides Stoney Creek,
branch of Rockfish. Lines: Said MOSES on E., JNO. WITT on S, JNO. LITT-
RELL on W., Major ALEX. READ on N. Part of tract known as Banden's
Entry with mill lot. Wit: JNO. E. FITZPATRICK, GEO. PERRY, THOS. FITZ-
PATRICK, JOS. WEAVER.

Page 213. 21 Jan 1793. WM. ALFORD & wife LETTIS, AC, to JESSE MARTIN,
AC, for Ƚ4-10, 8½ acres S side and N branch of Joe's Creek.
Lines: JAS. MATHEWS; part of a tract conveyed to WA by HENRY KEY. Wit:
WM. & TILMAN WALTON. Orig. del. to JM, 25 Jan 1794.

Page 214. 21 Jan 1793. WM. ALFORD & wife, as above, to THOS. KEY, AC,
for Ƚ22-10, 60 acres S branch Rockfish. Lines: JAS. NEVIL,
dec'd, JNO. BOUSH, JAMES MATTHEWS. Part of tract from HENRY KEY by deed.

Page 215. 21 Jan 1793. WM. ALFORD & wife as above, to WM. W. KEY, AC,
for Ƚ36, 140 acres S branch Rockfish. Lines: THOS. KEY, JESSE
MARTIN, Joe's Creek, JAS. MATTHEWS, JNO. BOUSH. Title derived as above
from HENRY KEY.

Page 215. 13 Nov 1792. GEO. JUDE, Charlotte Co, to JOS. WEAVER, AC,
(Orig. del. to JOS. DODD, with comm, 22 Feb 1793) for Ƚ50, 200
acres, part of 400 acres pat. to GEO. HEARD, 15 Feb 1748. Lines: ANDREW
READ, formerly JNO. CHISNELL's, NATHL. BARNETT(BURNETT?), formerly WM.
MAYO's, JAS. HEARD. Wit: LUCAS POWELL, CARY BIBB, ADAM BROWN, JNO. M.
GRIFFIN, PETER CAMPBELL, JOS. DILLARD.

Page 217. 14 Sep 1792. RICH. CHANDLER, AC, to brother, SAML. CHANDLER
for Ƚ50, Deed of Trust - negro woman, Patt; to secure SAML. on
bond to NELSON CRAWFORD. Wit: REUBEN PENDLETON, FRANCES PENDLETON. Memo:
Del. to JOS. BURRUS, aft. for SC.

Page 218. 21 Jan 1793. WM. BIBB & GEO. GILLESPIE, attys. for JNO. RYAN,
son and heir of JNO. RYAN,dec'd, AC, to CHESLEY KINNEY (KENNEY)
AC, for Ƚ75, 200 acres S fork Hatt Creek. Part of 400 acres belonging to
WM. BIBB and GG as attys in fact for JNO. RYAN etc. Lines: JNO. ROSE,
CHAS. JONES, THOS. JONES.

Page 219. 1 Oct 1792. THOS. H. TALBOTT, AC, & wife MARY, to JNO. LITT-
RELL, AC, for Ƚ34, 150 acres N fork Stony Creek, branch of
Rockfish. Lines: RICH. LEE, MOSES HUGHES, on E by line of marked trees
made by GEO. WITT; known as CROWDER's entry. Wit: JOS. STRICKLAND SR,
JNO. WITT, JOS. STRICKLAND JR, LEWIS BALL. Orig. del. to JAS.(?) LITT-
RELL, 17 Oct 1795.

Page 219. 21 Jan 1793. JOSHUA SHELTON, AC, from a conviction that all
mentioned by nature equally free and that it is contrary to
the law of the blessed JESUS to hold any part of the human species in
slavery, and in pursuance of an Act of Assembly for manumission of slaves,
freely liberates the following negroes as of this date: Benj., Jean, and
Cate - rel. all right to them.

Page 220. 6 Jun 1791. Correction of description of deed, 3 Oct 1791.
WM. CABELL JR, and wife ANN, sold and rec. in AC. to WM. S.
CRAWFORD, AC, 50 acres on N branch Higginbotham Mill Creek. Error since

discovered in bounds, courses, and Quantity and not the parcel intended. Ŀ67, 56 acres, branches of same creek in lieu of 50 acres. Wit: RO. RIVES.

Page 221. 7 Feb 1793. JNO. THOMPSON & wife JEAN (JANE) AC, to JOS. THOMSON, AC, for Ŀ20, 60 acres Headwaters Rockfish. Lines: Beaver Creek. Wit: WM. SHELTON, JAS. ANDERSON, JNO. NOWLS, MATT. MAKEMI(?) RO. HAISLET, ARCHIBALD CAMPBELL, FREDERICK WEIR.

Page 222. 6 Oct 1792. DAVID McANALLY to THOS. BRUMHALL, both of AC, for Ŀ50, 85 acres N fork Rockfish and newar Rockfish Gap. Lines: JAS. PENDLETON on W, CHISWELL's old line on S, FRED WARE on E, JAS. ANDERSON on N. Wit: ARCHIBALD CAMPBELL, WM. SHELTON, FREDERICK WEIR.

Page 222. 15 Mar 1793. LAURENCE LONG & wife PRISCILLA, AC, to GEO. MUTER of Ky, for Ŀ122, 400 acres in Woodford Co, Ky., formerly Fayette; surveyed on 2 Nov 1784. Lines: 1st branch below Rock House, up the river, Row's Run. Memo. This tract sold by JNO. CRAIG(?) and myself in expectation - to MUTER- that 50 acres might "profittibly" be taken from tract by better title than ours. This endorsement to show only 350 acres warranted.

Page 224. 19 Mar 1793. FRANCIS W. SPENCER & SAML. J. CABELL to Gov. HENRY LEE for FWS as tob. insp. at Swan Creek W.H.

Page 225. 16 Apr 1793. WM. CABELL, AC, to RO. RIVES & wife PEGGY, AC, for love borne by CABELL for his daughter, PEGGY and to place her in comfortable circumstances which profidence has put in his power, 800 acres both sides Rucker's Run and branches. Part of grant of 19 Oct 1784, from Commonwealth - Numbers 7 and 9. Lines: LOMAX; in possession of grantees.

Page 226. 12 Mar 1793. JNO. HAGGARD, AC, to trusty friend, MARTIN HAGGARD, Fayette Co, Cantucky(sic), Power of Atty to sell 1800 acres to JAS. FRENCH. Wit: AUGUSTINE SHEPHERD, JNO. COLE, REBEKAH COLE.

Page 227. 11 Feb 1793. JNO. WILLIAMSON, Fluvanna Co, to WM. FITZPATRICK, AC, for Ŀ190, 337 acres Rockfish. Lines: THOS. MORRISON, HENRY McCLIAN JR, JAMES McCLAIN, SAML. BRIDGWATER, CLOUGH SHELTON, ISAAC BURNETT, RICH. PERKINS. Wit: JNO. E. FITZPATRICK, THOS. WILLIAMSON, JNO. FITZPATRICK.

Page 228. 17 Jun 1793. RUSH HUDSON & wife LUCY, AC, to GERARD HOTCHKISS for Ŀ90, 130 acres, part of CARTER BRAXTON pat. and since conveyed to others. JOSHUA HUDSON bought it of RICH. GATEWOOD and by deed of gift to his son, RUSH HUDSON. Lines: JOSHUA HUDSON, WM. CABELL, SAML. MEREDITH, LINDSEY COLEMAN.

Page 229. 17 Jun 1793. THOS. JOHNS & wife NANCY, AC, to JNO. JINKINS, AC, for Ŀ35, 200 acres (Orig. del. to REUBEN NORVELL 22 Sep 1795) N branch Stoval. Lines: his own, GEO. STOVAL, JOS. CREWS. Wit: CHAS. CHRISTIAN, JNO. & JAS. CHRISTIAN, JOHNSON BAINE.

Page 230. 26 Apr 1793. JAS. SIMMONS (signed SIMONS) to JOS. SHIPS, AC, (sent to JS by order, 17 Feb 1801) Ŀ180, 125 acres Harris Creek. Lines: DANL. BURFORD, JAS. SIMONS, a spring, olf pat. line. Wit: PLEASANT DAWSON, ELIJAH SHIPS, GEO. KNIGHT, JNO. KNIGHT.

Page 232. 22 May 1793. CHAS. IRVING, Alb., to JNO. THOMPSON, AC, (Del to JT 22 Mar 1795) for Ŀ60, 122 3/4 acres. Lines: GEO. BLAINE, WM. BIBB, THOMPSON & TEAS - conveyed to IRVING by Deed of Trust by GEO. BLAINE & wife RACHEL and JNO. THOMPSON & WM. TEAS, merchants & Partners. Public sale on 21 Aug last at home of BLAINE, near premises and advertised for some time previously in the public Gazette; JNO. THOMPSON became buyer. Wit: LUCAS POWELL, BENJ. POWELL, N. POWELL.

Page 233. 17 Jun 1793. WM. WALTON & wife MILDRED, AC, to JAS. WALLS, AC, for Ŀ150, 75 acres Rucker's Run. Lines: JOEL PONTON, ABRAHAM SEAY, WM. DEPRIEST, JAS. WILLS. Part of tract by deed to WW from THOS. LOMAX, 24 Jul 1784.

Page 234.   8 Feb 1793. DAVID SIMPSON, AC, of 1st part, NATHL. ANDERSON &
             HUDSON MARTIN, as attys. for W(?) HENRY MARTIN and assignees,
London, England - ₤500, 6 slaves named. Deed of Trust. Wit: J. MONTGOMERY,
JNO. STAPLES. Orig. sent 11 Jul 1805, to H. MARTIN by N. HARLOW, JR, per
his memo at June Court past.

Page 235.   18 Dec 1792. HEZ. MARTIN to JNO. STRATTON for ₤50, waggon(sic)
             and horses. Wit: JOEL FRANKLIN, JAS. BALLINGER.

Page 236.   13 Sep 1786(sic). THOS. WALLS, AC, to FRANCIS WATERS, AC, (orig
             del. to WATERS per order, Jan 1796(?)) for ₤15 and ₤50 in con-
sequence due WATERS by an agreement on acct. of his marriage with my
daughter, MARY - 2 slaves - man Tobey and boy Sampson. Wit: HENRY L.
DAVIES, NELSON CRAWFORD, 2 illegible signatures. Held over and proved by
CRAWFORD, 5 Feb 1787, and ARTHER DAVIS, 17 Jan 1793.   Other names may be
WM. COY and WM. ST----MP.

Page 237.   16 May 1793. MATT. VAUGHAN, Goochland, to HUDSON MARTIN, AC,
             for ₤10, 2 slaves lent to my son, JAS. VAUGHAN, AC; Stephen &
Chas.; now hired by MARTIN to WM. WRIGHT & LEWIS BALL. Son, JAS., is
bound by bond to POLLARD & MARTIN for goods. MARTIN is partner in firm.
Deed of Trust. Wit: JNO. STAPLES, JAS. BROOKS.

Page 238.   15 Apr 1793. WM. BONES, AC, to JOS. SHELTON, AC, for ₤90, 100
             acres. Lines: WM. WRIGHT. Bought by BONES from THOS. WILCHER,
6 Oct 1783. Wit: PLEASANT MARTIN, WM. LEE HARRIS, SAML. CHILDRESS. Page
239, order to AC J.P.'s to quiz FRANCES, wife of BONES, 7 Apr 1793 (discrepancy noted in the dates); done, 15 Apr 1793 by JNO. DIGGS & WM. HARRIS.

Page 240.   4 Mar 1793. Order to Campbell Co. J.P.'s JNO. IRVINE & JNO.
             MORRIS, to quiz ESTHER, wife of MATT TUCKER - deed of 29 Nov
1791, to JNO. DUNCAN - 197 acres. Done, 25 Mar 1793.

Page 241.   12 Oct 1791. PHILIP THURMOND & wife JUDITH, AC, to ELIAS
             WILLS, AC, for ₤130, 121 acres N side Tobacco Row and S branch
Horsley. Lines: DAVID CRAWFORD, BURFORD's Entry. Bought by PT of THOS.
LUCAS & commonly known as BEN WASH place and where WILLS now lives. Wit:
WM. HAYNES, THOMAS WILLS, ELIAS WILLS JR, POLLY THURMOND.

Page 242.   9 Apr 1793. WM. & THOS. STREET; WM. SMITH, HOWSEND (HOWSAN)
             HORRILL, North Carolina, to NICHL. DAVIES, SR, Bedford Co, for
₤188-5, 200 acres. Lines: RICH. POWELL, PHILIP BRAXTON, JAS. TINSLEY,
NICHL. DAVIS - later 220 acres. Wit: JNO. CLAYTON, ARTHUR L. DAVIES,
NICHL. C. DAVIES, CHAS. STEWART. Orig. del. to NICHL. DAVIES, agreeable
to note - by JNO. HUMPHREYS.

Page 243.   15 Jun 1793. Rental agreement between NICHL. DAVIES & JNO.
             CLAYTON, both of Bedford - 100 acres, part of land JC bought
of STREETS' legatees for ND in AC - ₤10 per year - CLAYTON & wife to have
lifetime possession - to plant 100 apple trees and 200 peach trees; fence,
keep in repair; 2 good sound cabbins, 16 ft. square, for white people to
live in. Orig. del. to JAS. CLARK, 26 Apr 1794. JC may not sell without
ND's consent nor work more than 4 tithables, except his own children.
Wit: JAS. SCOTT, JNO. W. CLAYTON, JOS. SLAUGHTER.

Page 244.   17 Jun 1793. SARAH DUNCAN, wife of JNO., appeared and rel.
             dower - 27 Dec 1791, deed to JNO. F.P.LEWIS - 200 acres on
branches of Pedlar; near Maple Creek. Lines: NATHL. DAVIS dec'd. Wit:
ISHAM DAVIS, BENJ. HENLEY or HENSLEY, JNO. BURKS.

Page 245.   7 Jan 1793. JNO. HURT & wife SARAH, AC, to BENJ. TALIAFERRO,
             AC, (Orig. del. to BT by JS. BALLENGER) for ₤250, 181 acres
Buffalo where JH lives. Lines: Puppie's Creek, JACOB SMITH, S side of
river. Wit: JNO. SMITH, SAML. GOOLSBY, JOS. HIGGINBOTHAM JR., JNO. & ZACH.
TALIAFERRO.

Page 246.   15 Jul 1793. REUBEN HARRISON & wife PEGGY, AC, to JNO. SALE,
             AC, for ₤200, "three two hundred and eight acres" Franklin
Creek and both sides of Moll's Creek. Lines: his own, JNO. SMITH, JACOB
SMITH, PHILIP SMITH. Wit: JNO. HORSLEY, THOS. GARLAND, JOEL FRANKLIN.

Page 247.   15 Jul 1793.   JOS. CREWS & wife MARTHA, AC, to ROBT. CAMPBELL,
            (Orig. del. to Z. DAWSON, 11 Oct 1794) for Ŀ50, 135 acres E
side Lynch road and next to TAYLOR. Wit: JAS. BALLINGER, JAS. PENDLETON,
REUBEN PENDLETON, JNO. RYAN, WM. CAMDEN.

Page 249.   15 Jul 1793.   HUGH ROSE & wife CAROLINE MATILDA, to WM. MOSS,
            for 5 sh, 204 acres both sides Rocky Branch, S branch of Piney,
part of ROSE tract. Lines: CHAS. & PATRICK ROSE. (Orig. del. to WM with
commission, 18 Mar 1796) Wit: THOS. DILLON, ANDERSON MOSS, GEO. WORTHAM
JR, JOS. BURRUS.

Page 250.   14 Jan 1793.   ZACH. TALIAFERRO to his son, JNO. BOUTWELL TAL-
            IAFERRO (orig. del. to BEN. TALIAFERRO) 2 tracts S branch Tye.
1) 196 acres. Lines: JAMES BROWN, JNO. ROSE, his old line. 2) 109 acres
next to JNO. ROSE. Wit: NICHL. PAMPLIN, WM. HORSLEY, CHAS. TALIAFERRO,
RICH. TALIAFERRO, WARREN TALIAFERRO, JNO. HORSLEY, N. CABELL.

Page 252.   15 Jul 1793.   ZACH. TALIAFERRO to AARON HIGGINBOTHAM, both of
            AC, for Ŀ50, 120 acres branch of Thrasher. Lines: grantee, JOS.
NICHOLAS.   Orig. del. to AH on 25 Jan 1794.

Page 253.   4 Feb 1793.   MARTIN MILLER, Halifax - Power of Atty to JOS.
            LANE, AC, to handle my father's estate of which I am an exr. in
AC. Wit: WM. P. MARTIN, ELIZ. MARTIN, WM. SMITH, JNO. MATTHEWS, WM. LAINE.

Page 254.   15 Jul 1793.   WM. LAVENDER & wife SARAH: WM. WALTON & wife
            MILDRED, AC, to LEWIS TINDALL, Buckingham Co, (Orig. del. 27
Aug 1800, to LT) for Ŀ160, 200 acres S side Tye. Lines: EDMD. WILCOX,
dec'd. Pat. to CHAS. LAVENDER, the elder, 12 Jan 1746, adjoins JNO. PAR-
TREE BURKS.

Page 255.   15 Apr 1793.   JAS. MASTERS, AC, to JNO. ROSE for Ŀ600 Richmond
            tobacco; 1 grey mare. Wit: D. McDONALD, WM. HILL JR.

Page 256.   28 Jan 1793.   JAS. WARE & wife MARY, Elbert Co, Ga., to JNO.
            CLARKSON, AC, (Orig. del. to Col. WM. WARE; Orig. del. to
JNO. CLARKSON, 7 Dec 1798 - 2 notations) for Ŀ300, 400 acres branches
Puppies Creek. Lines: CHAS. TALIAFERRO, JNO. WATKINS, top of the Mt.,
CABELL's line, Tobacco Row Mt., WM. CABELL. Wit: JONATHAN WILSON, JNO.
McCABE, HUGH McCABE, WM. WARE, RO. HOLLOWAY, CHAS. TALIAFERRO JR.   Mark
at bottom for what appears to be STEPHEN COY.

Pages 257-262.   See Appendix for a list of voters to elect a member to
            Congress on 18 March 1793.

Page 262.   16 Sep 1793.   GEO. McDANIEL, Tob. Insp., Amherst W.H.   Bonds-
            man: ZACH. DAWSON.

Page 263.   19 Apr 1793.   THOS. BARRET & wife ELIZ., to WM. BARRET for
            Ŀ500, and love for ELIZ. by THOS. bacause of marriage - Deed
of Trust to WM. for ELIZ. and at death of THOS. to be divided to ELIZ.
and children. No acreage - Long Mt.; formerly that of NEILL CAMPBELL,
dec'd.; slaves, stock, and tools. Wit: JOS. BALLENTER, ACHILLES BALLINGER,
JNO. WARE.

Page 264.   15 Jan 1793.   WM. BOOTH, Bedford Co, to BENJ. PLUNKET for Ŀ50,
            26 acres Stoval Creek. Wit: NATHL. GUTTRY, JNO. BURFORD, THOS.
JOHNS.

Page 265.   16 Sep 1793.   JNO. LOVING, agt. for WM. DEVER, AC, to JOEL
            PONTON for Ŀ24, 190 acres by pat. N branch Rucker's Run. Lines:
WM. BIBB, LAURENCE SUDDERTH, LUNSFORD LOMAX. Wit: HUDSON MARTIN, ABRAHAM
SEAY, WM. WALTON.

Page 267.   16 Sep 1793.   JNO. RUCKER & wife SARAH, AC, to AMBR. RUCKER,
            AC, for Ŀ280, 202 acres N branch Harris. Lines: AMBR. RUCKER
on Harvey's road; ANTHONY RUCKER, DAVID WOODROOF, ISAAC RUCKER JR, near
the old store.

Page 268.   15 Jan 1793.   WM. BOOTH & wife JUDA, Bedford Co.; BENJ.

PLUNKET, AC, to JNO. BURFORD, Junior, AC, for Ł100, 2 tracts. 1) Stoval
Creek, 132 acres from BOOTH & wife. Lines: BENJ. PLUNKET. 2) 37 acres
from BENJ. PLUNKET. Wit: NATHL. GURTAY(GUTTRY) STEPHEN HAM, THOS. JOHNSON.

Page 269. 16 Sep 1793. WM. EVANS & wife JOICE, AC, to SACKVILLE KING,
TURNER.   Campbell Co, for Ł10, 25 acres Porage Creek. Lines: KING, JNO.

Page 270. 5 Mar 1793. ALEX. HENDERSON JR, & wife SARAH, AC, to JNO.
          MURRILL JR, for Ł250, 320 acres branch Rockfish near the Blue
Ridge mts. Lines: THOMAS WILLIAMSON, SIMON RAMSEY, HUDSON MARTIN, WM.
CREWS. Wit: WM. BRIDGWATER, RO. WEIR, WM. LOBBAN, JESSE MURRILL, JNO.
MURRILL, CHAS. BAILEY, THOS. ROBERTSON, RO. DINWIDDIE, WM. BALLARD.

Page 271. 18 Mar 1793. To AC J.P.'s to quiz SARAH HENDERSON, above, as
          to deed. Done 6 Apr 1793 by NATHAN CRAWFORD & HUDSON MARTIN.

Page 272. 5 Mar 1793. ALEX. HENDERSON JR & wife SARAH, AC, to RO. WEIR,
          AC, for Ł100, 150 acres both sides Rockfish. Lines: WM. BRIDG-
WATER, JNO. COLES, HUDSON MARTIN, THOS. PATTON. Conveyed to AH Jr. by
ALEX HENDERSON SR. Wit: same as for page 270. Page 273, order to quiz
SARAH, 18 Mar 1793. Done 3 Apr 1793.

Page 274. 16 Sep 1793. JNO. BURFORD & wife SARAH, AC, to PETTIS THACKER,
          AC, for Ł100, 169 acres Stoval Creek. Lines: ELIZ. COFLAND,
JAME or JANE CREWS, BENJ. PLUNKET.

Page 275. 16 Sep 1793. BENJ. PLUNKET & wife FRANCES, AC, to JESSE BECK,
          AC, for Ł200, 380 acres Stoval Creek. Orig. del. 6 Apr 1803
to JB with comm.

Page 276. 16 Sep 1793. DAVID WOODROOF, AC, to WIATT WOODROOF, AC, for
          5 sh, 123 acres Crooked Run. Lines: Col. Wiatt, Lynch road,
Meginson Road, JAS. HILL; LIVELY. Orig. del. to DAVID WOODROOF 21 Apr
1796.

Page 277. 14 Sep 1793. JNO. H. GOODWIN & wife MARY, AC, to NEH. ROYSEL
          (orig. del. to C. DABNEY, 29 Apr 1827) for Ł12, 6 acres N side
Lynch Road. Lines: grantor, SACKVILLE KING, JNO. WARD. Wit: ANTHONY RUCK-
ER, GEO. McDANIEL, ABRAHAM WARREN, PETER ROYSEL.

Page 278. 14 Spe 1793. Same grantors and grantee as above, Ł10, 1/2 ac-
          re N side Lynch Road. Lines: GOODWIN. Wit: same as above.

Page 281. 14 Sep 1793. Same grantors and grantee - for Ł6, 1/2 acre
          S side Lynch Road. Lines: grantor. Wit: as above.

Page 282. 14 Sep 1793. JOS. CREWS to ABEL BLANKENSHIP, both of AC, for
          blank sum, 10 acres. Lines: Lynch Road on E; part of tract
surveyed for CREWS. Signed: JAS. CREWS JR, but summary calls him JOS.
Wit: DANL. MEHONE, NEH. ROYSEL, NATHL. GUTTRY.

Page 283. 14 Sep 1793. JOS. CREWS, JR, to WM. DEMRON (Margin: F(?) DAM-
          RON) both of AC, for Ł40, 60 acres Lynch road; part of survey
and pat. and part taken off in 2 "seprate parcels"; bal. conveyed. Wit:
MEHONE, NATHL. GUTTRY.

Page 284. 24 Aug 1793. JOS. CREWS JR & wife MARTHA, AC, to THOS. HUM-
          PHREYS, Campbell Co. - 5 sh. Contiguous to Lynch road leading
from ferry of that name to New Glasgow - about 6 miles from Madison - 83
acres. Lines: RO. CAMPBELL, on E side of road, N by ABEL BLANKENSHIP, WM.
DAMERON, W. by BENJ. RUCKER, S by DANL. BURFORD JR., W by BENJ. RUCKER,
S by DANL. BURFORD JR. Wit: NEH. ROYSEL, DANL. MEHONE, NATHL. GUTTRY.

Page 286. 14 Sep 1793. JNO. H. GOODWIN & wife MARY, AC, to ABRAHAM
          WARREN, AC, for Ł6, 1/2 acre N side Lynch. Lines: JAS. LASHELL,
GOODWIN. Wit: ANTHONY RUCKER, GEO. McDANIEL, NEH. & PETER ROYSEL.

Page 288. 14 Sep 1793. JNO. H. GOODWIN & wife MARY, AC, to JAS. LASH-
          WELL, AC, for Ł6, 1/2 acre N side Lynch Road. Lines: ROYSEL.

Wit: GEO. McDANIEL, ABRAHAM WARREN PETER ROYSEL.

Page 289.   14 Feb 1793.   JNO. DILLARD & REUBEN THORNTON, exrs. of JOSEPH
DILLARD, dec'd (orig. del. to WM. MOOR, 29 Dec 1800) to NOTLEY
W. MADDOX of AC, for Ł200, 400 acres by deed to JOS. DILLARD 11 Dec 1788;
part of two adjoining tracts by deed of same date - 195 acres. Lines: GEO.
GILLESPIE on the river; Col. PETER ROSE, JNO. PARSONS; except 2 acres
laid off for GEO. GILLESPIE opposite to his mill seat on the river;
Little Piney and N branch Indian Creek. Wkt: AMBR. RUCKER, JAS. CALLAWAY,
OWEN HASKIN, RO. HOLLOWAY.

Page 291.   23 Aug 1793.   Rev. A(E)LEXANDER BLAIN from MICAJAH BECKNALL,
both of AC & parish, for Ł70, 140 acres in two tracts and 160
acres.   1) 140 acres S side of a Mt. at head of Rucker's Run. (Orig. del.
to JNO. LOVING, 26 Jan 1796, by order) Lines: DANL. ADAMS, JNO. HARMER,
AARON.   2) 160 acres adjoining. Lines: WM. BECKNELL, JAS. HARMER, LUNS-
FORD LOMAX, DANL. AARON.   PHEBE, wife of BECKNELL(NALL)

Page 292.   16 Sep 1793.   CLEAVER CARDWELL HARRALL & wife MARY, AC, to JAS.
McALEXANDER JR, for Ł40, 50 acres formerly that of JNO. WADE,
dec'd. N fork Davis, branch of Rockfish. Lines: the road, CHAS. TATE,
THOS. FORTUNE.

Page 293.   16 Sep 1793.   RO. EDMINSTON & wife ALSE, Wilks Co, N.C. to JNO.
COOPER, AC, for Ł70, 70 acres Pedlar. Lines: Top of the Blue
Ridge. Wit: JNO. CORMEY, JNO. E. FITZPATRICK, JNO. DAVIS.

Page 293.   16 Sep 1793.   JNO. WATKINS & wife CATREN, AC, to JAS. THORP,
AC, for Ł22, 50 acres N fork Davis. Lines: his own, NATHL.
CLARK. Wit: HENRY SMITH, WM. BURNETT, WM. DAWSON.

Page 294.   4 Jun 1792.   Order to J.P.'s of City of Richmond: JNO. BARROTT,
DAVID LAMBERT, JNO. LYNE to quiz ELIZ., wife of CARTER BRAXTON
as to deed of 22 Mar 1775, to DAVID SHEPHERD - 304 acres S side and joining Tribulation. Done by BARROT & LAMBERT, 4 Jun 1793. Rec. 16 Sep 1793.

Page 295.   5 May 1792.   Order to JNO. PAYTON, RO. QUARLES, JNO. CRAETMILL
& JNO. BEALE - Gentlemen of Fluvanna & Botetourt to quiz wives
of AUGUSTINE, JNO. & DUBARTIS SHEPHERD by 3 deeds of 5 Jul 1784, to JAMES
CALLAWAY - 554 acres; land owned by DAVID SHEPHERD at death. ----, wife
of AUGUSTINE, MARY wife of JNO. SHEPHERD, and ----, wife of DUBARTUS
SHEPHERD, 29 Oct 1792.   Botetourt J.P.'s, JNO. CARTMILL & JNO. BEALE, as
to ELIZ, wife of DUBARTUS SHEPHERD. Footnote, AC court, 16 Sep 1793,
SARAH, wife of AUGUSTINE SHEPHERD, rel. dower.

Page 297.   16 Jul 1793.   Order to GEO. SWAIN & JNO. LUMPKIN, J.P.'s of
Wilkes Co, Ga, as to MARY, wife of SAML. STREET, deed 9 Apr
1793, to NICHL. DAVIES - 220 acres. Done, 29 Aug 1793.   Rec. AC 21 Oct
1793.

Page 297.   17 Aug 1793, Order to J.P.'s of Rutherford Co, N.C. to quiz
wives of THOS. STREET, WM. SMITH, & HOWSEND HARRELL, 9 Apr
1793, deed to NICHL. DAVIES - 220 acres. Done, 17 Aug 1793, by JNO.
BIGGS & ADAM WHITESIDES. "The wives" are not named. The writing is very
poor in this part of the book.

Page 298.   25 Oct 1793.   REUBEN THORNTON & wife MILDRED, AC, to JOS. STA-
PLES, AC, for Ł250, 588 acres on Buffalo. Lines: LUCAS(?);
FREELAND; JNO. SNEAD.

Page 300.   21 Oct 1793.   JNO. STAPLES & wife AGNES, AC, to HENRY MARTIN,
AC, (Orig. del. to JOSHUA WILLOUGHBY per order, 9 Jan 1796)
for Ł60, 200 acres Nassau Dutch Creek. Pat. 2 Jun 1760. Lines: LUNSFORD
LOMAX. Also 60 acres adjoining - part of survey of 128 acres and pat. to
JNO. STAPLES, 20 Jul 1780. Lines: STAPLES' old line, WM. GILLESPIE, WM.
FITZPATRICK, up the mt., HENRY MARTIN.

Page 302.   21 Oct 1793.   JNO. STAPLES & wife AGNES, AC, to WM. FITZPAT-
RICK, AC, for Ł50,130 acres Nassau or Dutch Creek. Lines: WM.
FITZPATRICK, HENRY MARTIN. Part of 2 grants on 20 Jul 1780 & 19 Aug 1789.

Page 303. 21 Oct 1793. CHAS. TATE & wife CHARITY, AC, & parish, to JNO.
WATKINS, AC & Parish, for Ƚ50, 3 adjoining tracts - 184 acres
S branch N fork Davis. Lines: JNO. WADE, his own, middle fork Davis Ck.

Page 305. 21 Oct 1793. JNO. DUNCAN & wife SARAH, AC, & Lexington Parish,
to JOSIAH ELLIS, AC & Lexington Parish, for Ƚ75, 126 acres on
branches of Pedlar. Lines: DAVID BURKS, RO. JOHNSON. Orig. del. to ELLIS.

Page 306. 21 Oct 1793. JNO. DUNCAN & wife SARAH, as above, to JOSIAH
ELLIS, as above, for Ƚ240, 2 surveys of 308 acres - 1 acre
excepted - on Pedlar. Lines: opposite JNO. FRANCES PENNY LEWIS' Mill, S
side Pedlar, Clark's Creek, WATTS, RODERICK McCULLOCH.

Page 308. 21 Oct 1793. JESSE THOMAS & wife NANCY, AC, to JNO. MILTON,
AC, for Ƚ85, 334 acres S branch Davis. Lines: RO. WRIGHT. Also
127 acres. Lines: JNO. MURRALL, RO. WRIGHT, THOS. EADES, JAS. HOPKINS,
JNO. HOPKINS.

Page 309. 21 Oct 1793. JNO. HOLLODAY & wife LETTICE, AC, to WM. STATON,
AC, (orig. del. to grantee, 27 Oct 1795) for Ƚ100, 155 acres
N bank Buffalo. Lines of STEPHEN CASH.

Page 311. 21 Oct 1793. WM. PETER & wife FANNEY, AC, to THOS. MORRIS,
AC, for Ƚ60, 100 acres, part of 293 acres. Lines: the old
line, GEO. DAVIS, the pat. line, JNO. HOGG.

Page 312. 21 Oct 1793. JNO. CAMDEN, AC, to ANN MORRIS, AC, for Ƚ50, 100
acres Pegg's Creek. Line of HUGH MORRIS.

Page 313. 21 Oct 1793. JNO. HIGGINBOTHAM JR, AC, to REUBEN NORVELL &
SACKVILLE KING, Merchants, NORVELL & KING Firm - (Orig. del.
to RN 22 Sep 1795) for Ƚ30, 100 acres S branch Porrage Creek. Lines: JAS.
DILLARD. Pat. to JH 12 Apr 1793. Wit: JAS. PENN, JNO. PENDLETON, BARTLETT
JOHNS.

Page 314. 15 Jul 1793. DANL. McDONALD, AC, to WM. GILES & NELSON MONROE,
AC, for Ƚ4000 Richmond inspected tobacco - 76 acres Tye.
Survey of 15 Sep 1788. Lines: JNO. JACOBS, MOSES MARTIN.

Page 315. 17 Jul 1793. EDWD. HARPER, AC, to JOSIAH JOBLING, AC, for
Ƚ40, 225 acres N fork Cedar Creek. Lines: THOS. JOPLING's es-
tate - note variation in the spelling - GEO. DAVIS, WM. SHOEMAKER, JNO.
DUNCAN, THOS. LUCAS, dec'd, THOS. MORRIS. Part of land taken up by
HENRY HARPER and surveyed to EDWD. HARPER in 1791. Wit: JAS. JOBLING,
BENJ. CHILDRESS, PLEASANT MARTIN.

Page 317. 21 Oct 1793. JAS. COLEMAN, Alb. Co., to JNO. MATTHEWS HATTER,
AC, for Ƚ50, 139 acres S side Tye. Wit: BARTLETT FITZGERALD,
JAS. COLEMAN, WM. JACOB. (Note: Alb. will of JC shows HATTER was his son
in law. BFD)

Page 318. 19 Oct 1793. JAS. JOBLING, Albemarle, to RICH. FARRAR, of
same, for Ƚ100, 75 acres in Alb. and AC, part of tract pat. to
JAS. HOLBY. Lines: by the road-side; JAS. JOBLING. Wit: HUDSON GARLAND,
SHEROD GRIFFIN JNO. FARRAR, RALPH JOPLING - PHILIP JOBLING's name is
erased in part.

Page 319. 3 Oct 1793. JAS. MORTON, Woodford Co, Ky, and AMBROSE RUCKER,
AC, to ISAAC RUCKER, AC, for Ƚ40, 91 acres N side Paul's Mt.
and Harris Creek. Lines: at the Thourough fare on top of Paul's Mt. Wit:
PHILLIP GOOCH, ANTHONY RUCKER, JESSE WOODROOF, JAS. WILLMORE.

Page 321. 4 Oct 1793. PLEASANT MARTIN & wife REBECCA, AC, to HENRY
ROBERTS, AC, for Ƚ350, 780 acres Rockfish. Lines: JOSIAH JOB-
LING, JNO. MONTGOMERY, WM. LYONS, JAS. WOODS. Wit: JNO. DIGGES, LEWIS
NEVIL, JAS. JOBLING, W. DIGGES.

Page 322. 24 Aug 1793. JNO. PRICE, AC, to HENRY VERNOR(?), Augustia
(sic) Co., (Orig. del. to CHAS. PERROW, atty, 18 Nov 1845)
for Ƚ100, 527 acres N fork Rockfish. Lines: Top of the Blue Ridge, the

282

new road. Wit: JNO. McANALLY, ELIJAH McANALLY, THOS. GREENE, one illegible signature. Memo: If it should include part of PRYOR's survey.

Page 324. 21 Oct 1793. THOS. STOCKTON, AC, to JAS. BROOKS, Alb., for
Ł12-10, 190 acres on Spring Mt. near Rock Rumm. Wit: W. LEE
HARRIS, J. MONTGOMERY, WALTON LEAKE.

Page 325. 21 Sep 1793. JNO. SKELTON - SHELTON in some places - and wife
ELIZ., AC, to WM. BLAIN, Augusta (Orig. del. 7 Jul 1798, to M.
DAWSON per order of BLAIN) for Ł50, 64 acres. Lines: JAS. BURTON, WM.
HARRIS, ROBINSON's grant, Mrs. JOHNSON.

Page 326. 22 Feb 1793. Order to THOS. LANTON & JAS. PATILLO, Charlotte
Co. J.P.'s to quiz ANNE, wife of GEO. JUDE - deed of 30 Nov
1792, to JOSEPH WEAVER - 200 acres. Done, 29 Mar 1793.

Page 327. 3 Oct 1793. JAS. MORTON, Woodford Co. Ky, & AMBR. RUCKER, AC,
to JAS. WILMORE, AC, for Ł30, 83 acres S side Paul's Mt. &
Rutledge. Lines: CREWS, top of Paul's Mt. Wit: P. GOOCH, ANTHONY RUCKER,
JESSE WOODROOF, MOSES & ISAAC RUCKER.

Page 328. 16 Dec 1793. NANCY CALLAWAY, AC, Power of Atty to friend, JNO.
BRECKENRIDGE, Kentucky - under will of late father, RICH. CAL-
LAWAY, late of Ky. Wit: WM. BARRET, CHAS. BECKLEY, W.L. CRAWFORD.

Page 329. Inv. of Est. of JNO. BICKLEY, 13 Dec 1793. Ł325-17-6. CHAS.
BURKS, JNO. EUBANKS.

Page 330. 5 Nov 1793. ISAAC WOOD, Alb., to JAS. BROOKS, Alb., for Ł20,
70 acres N branch and haeadwaters of Rockfish. Lines: ALEX.
PATTEN, THOS. THOMSON. Wit: JNO. BROOKS, OSTON BOLAN, JNO. KNOWS(KNOWLS?)

Page 330. 10 Dec 1793. JNO. KNOLS & wife SARAH, AC, to JNO. DETTON,
Alb., for Ł75-15, 160 acres both sides Patton's branch; N fork
Rockfish. Lines: his own. Wit: JAS. BROOKS, JNO. N. REID, JAS. ANDERSON.

Page 331. 22 Nov 1793. WM. NALLY & wife RACHEL, Alb., to WM. TURNER,
AC, for Ł40, 80 acres branches of Dutch. Lines: HENRY MARTIN
JR, Marrow Bone Mt., NALLY; JNO. MATTHEWS. Wit: JNO. JOBLING, THOS.
MATTHEWS, JNO. SANDERS.

Page 332. 19 May 1793. WM. HIGGINBOTHAM, Elbert Co, Ga., exr. of BENJ.
HIGGINBOTHAM, to JOS. HIGGINBOTHAM, AC, - Memo: This deed
ought to have been recorded among the deeds at Dec. Ct., 1803 - for Ł12,
258 acres. Lines: BENJ. HIGGINBOTHAM, pat. to him, 19 Feb 1781. Wit:
DANL. WHITE, JNO. CLEMONS, BENJ. HIGGINBOTHAM. Final proof, 19 Dec 1803,
by JNO. CLEMENTS(sic). Previously proved 16 Dec 1793 by WHITE & BH.

Page 333. Inv. of JOSHUA HUDSON - called HUNDSON at beginning and HUDSON
in summary - (my wife's ancestor. BFD) - for Ł52-3. JER.
FRANKLIN, NATHL. MANTIPLY, SHEROD BUGG. 26 Sep 1793. (Note my error in
comment above. This man is not my wife's ancestor, but this is Jr. who
died before his father, Sr. See my "H" Wills for data on family. BFD)

Page 334. 16 Dec 1793. BENJ. HARRIS & wife MARY, Alb., to JOSIAH CHEA-
THAM, AC, (Sent to JC 20 Mar 1800 by M. DAWSON per order) for
Ł40, 110 acres Hiccory Creek. Lines: his own.

Page 335. 22 Nov 1793. JNO. LACKEY & wife ANN; RACHEL AYRES, & EVE
LACKEY, AC, to SAML. LACKEY, AC, (Orig. del. to SL 15 May 1795)
for Ł208, 208 acres branch Rutledge. Lines: JOS. HIGGINBOTHAM, WM. CHAP-
PELL, BENJ. STONE, JNO. HIGGINBOTHAM; part of grant of MOSES HIGGINBOTHAM
and by him to WM. MORRISON and by W.M. devised to EVE LACKEY. Wit: JAS.
BROOKS, JOS. HIGGINBOTHAM, JNO. CLARK, TERZAH DAVIS.

Page 336. 16 Dec 1793. JAS. COTTRELL, AC, to ALEX. MARR, AC, for Ł16-8-
15, hogs, furniture, etc. Wit: BARTLETT CASH, SAML. GOOLSBY.

Page 337. 16 Dec 1793. GEO. DAVIS & wife NANCY, AC, to NATHL. HILL, AC,
for Ł40, 88 acres N branch Piney. Lines: CHAS. ROSE, NICHL.

CABELL; part of land devised to GEO. DAVIS by will of PHILLIP DAVIS dec'd.

Page 338. 16 Dec 1793. Inv. of est. of JOS. LIVELY. Ł240-14. LUCAS
POWELL, JAS. STEVENS, WILL LOVING.

Page 339. 16 Jan 1794. WM. CABELL, AC, to LANDON CABELL, AC, for love -
1658 acres both sides Dutch Creek & Rucker's Run. (Orig. del.
12 Nov 1795 to LC) 1180 acres part of tract late that of JNO. HARMER,
British subject and sold by escheat laws. Lines: The Dutch, pat. line.
180 acres on N side and joins first tract and conveyed by deed of indenture to WC from ALLEN BLAIR & JNO. MURRY GRIFFIN and wives, 6 Sep 1790.
297 acres on S side and joins the 1180 - 100 of it by deed from JAS.
GREGORY, 27 Apr 1784. 197 acres by pat. to WC as assignee of JNO. GREG-
ORY 2 Dec 1785.

Page 340. 18 Jan 1794. GABL. PENN to daughter NANCY PENN - love and 5
sh., (Orig. del. to CH(?) E. PENN 3 Oct 1796) - slaves named.
Wit: JAS. CALLAWAY, RO. HOLLOWAY, OWEN HASKINS, GEO. PENN.

Page 341. 18 Jan 1794. GABL. PENN for love of son, EDMOND PENN & 5 sh.,
slaves named. Wit: as above plus JAS. LOCKHART.

Page 341. 18 Jan 1794. GABL. PENN, AC, Power of Atty. to friend, JNO.
BRECKINRIDGE, Ky, to receive pat. lands. Wit: same as p.340.

Page 341. 18 Jan 1794. WM. PENN, late of AC, by will of 13 Aug 1776,
and probated 7 Jul 1777, stated that real and personal est. be
sold by exrs. - GABL. PENN & GEO. PENN, exrs. - WM. instituted claim for
land in western country as Lt. in State Va. Continental line - land warrant issued in Registrar's office, 26 Dec 1785; No. 4055 for 2666 2/3 in
favor of exrs. Power of Atty. to JNO. BRECKENRIDGE, Ky, to receive land
and sell. Signed by exrs. as named. Wit: same as page 340.

Page 342. 14 Jan 1794. CHAS. CHRISTIAN & wife SARAH, AC, to HENRY IS-
BELL, THOS. DILLARD ISBELL, & ZACH. ISBELL, Goochland, for Ł60,
204 acres S branch Buffalo. Lines: JNO. WEST, dec'd, Parks road, HARRY
STRUTTON, CHAS. CHRISTIAN. Wit: JAS. CHRISTIAN, GODFREY TOLER, HENRY
CHRISTIAN.

Page 344. 22 Jul 1793. DUDLEY CALLOWAY, AC, to WM. WHITTEN, Bedford Co,
WW is his bondsman to THOS. LUMPKIN, exr. of STANLEY GOWER -
horses, cattle, etc. - Deed of Trust. Wit: THOS. LUMPKIN, DRURY HOLLARD
(AND?) JNO. STRATTON. Margin: "Not done".

Page 344. 19 Oct 1793. WM. CAMPBELL & wife SARAH, St. Ann's Parish, to
WM. EVENS, same Par., blank sum - (Orig. del. to WE, 11 Sep
1797 to EVANS) 140 acres and 10 acres adj., part of survey, S br. Piney.

Page 346. 20 Jan 1794. PATRICK ROSE, AC, Power of Atty to JNO. BOYD,
Richmond merchant, to sell my share of Jas. River Co. - 1
share. Margin: Not done.

Page 346. 3 Oct 1793. JOEL FRANKLIN, AC, to MICHL. COLTER, Augusta,
for Ł350, 402 acres (Orig. del. to MICHL. COALTER 29 Jan 1796)
Lines: JNO. WIATT, WM. MAYO, Rutledge Creek, JAS. LIVELY, WM. MOOR, ABNER
PADGETT, old pat. line, WM. CHAPPELL, JOS. HIGGINBOTHAM. Wit: JAS. FRANK-
LIN, DAVID S. GARLAND, RO. WALKER, REUBEN PENDLETON, THOS. APLING, JAS.
CALLAWAY, LINDSEY COLEMAN.

Page 347. 20 Jan 1794. HENRY CAMDEN & wife LUCY, to DRURY TUCKER for
Ł50, 26½ acres S branch Buffalo. Lines: his own, HENRY CAMDEN.

Page 348. 20 Jan 1794. JNO. ROSE, AC, Power of Atty. to JNO. BOYD,
Richmond merchant, to sell my 1 share in Jas. River Co. Wit:
DILLD. DONALD, SAML. COLEMAN, RO. H. ROSE. Margin: Not done.

Page 349. 20 Jan 1794. HENRY CAMDEN & wife LUCY, to BURCHER WHITEHEAD
for Ł350, 338 acres S branch Buffalo. Lines: JNO. PENN, Spring
Branch, DRURY TUCKER, WM. CAMDEN.

Page 350. 14 Sep 1793. ELIJAH MORAN & wife ELIZ., AC, to ABRAHAM WARREN, AC, for Ł12, 100 acres branch Stovall. Wit: JAS. KINGSOLVING, CHAS. BOWLES, WM. LUCCH (LUSSH?)

Page 352. AA by RICH. POWELL, admr. of ANTHONY STREET - from 9 Aug 1789- Cash found in the trunk at Mrs. STREET's deas(sic) - Ł24-2-10½ JAS. CARY for coffin, Apr 1790 - 8-9; cash allowed me for services by legatees; JESSE DAWSON for coffin - 1793 item - 10-3. Page 353, Order of Court we made division of estate to SAML., THOS. STREET; to ELIZ. SMITH; to FRANKEY HARRILL; to ANTHONY COX - one of the grandchildren. Other grandchildren: WM. COX, FRANKEY CRAWLEY, ELIZ. COX - all legatees. Returned 20 Jan 1794 by THOS. MOORE, PHILIP BURTON, GEO. McDANIEL, RICH. HARRISON, DAVID TINSLEY.

Page 354. 25 Jan 1794. GABL. PENN & wife SARAH, AC, to WM. CAMDEN, AC, for Ł300, 4 tracts and adj. Tobacco Row Mt. 1) 263 acres by deed from JNO. BARNS to GP 13 Nov 1778. 2) 137 acres by deed from BENJ. WRIGHT, 3 May 1774. 3) 32 acres by pat. 20 Jul 1780. 4) 200 acres by deed from NICHL. CABELL, 6 May 1782. Total: 532 acres. Wit: JAS. PENN, RO. HOLLOWAY, OWEN HASKINS, NANCY PENN, JAS. BALLINGER, CHAS. ELLIS JR, JAS. CALLAWAY.

Page 355. 17 Feb 1794. JNO. BOUSH, AC, to CHAS. WATTS, AC, for Ł105, 110 acres N side Fenely Mt. and N branch Rucker's Run - 82 acres of it conveyed to JB by HENRY KEY 1 Nov 1773, and residue is part of tract conveyed to JB by HENRY KEY on same date. Lines: ABRAHAM WARWICK, WM. CABELL.

Page 356. 17 Feb 1794. JNO. BOUSH, AC, & Parish, to WIATT BOUSH, of same, for Ł50, 100 acres, part of 370 acres pat. to HUGH WILLOUGHBY 7 Aug 1761, at Williamsburg. S. branch Rockfish. Lines: WM. ALFORD, JAS. MATTHEWS.

Page 357. 6 Sep 1793. WM. CAMDEN, AC, to DAVID DUGGINS, (Orig. del. to WM. CAMDEN per order) for Ł50, 140 acres near Huff. Lines: JNO. COLEMAN, top of the mt., BENJ. NOEL, JAS. BIAS, old cove about half way up mt., TYREE HADING.

Page 358. 15 Jul 1793. CORNL. CRASS (CRESS?) and wife ELIZ, AC, to JACOB WHEELER, AC, blank sum, 137½ acres Rockfish. Lines: SAML. WOODS, dec'd. Wit: RO. DINWIDDIE, JNO. DINWIDDIE, JNO. STAPLES. Margin: Lay for further proof.

Page 359. 23 Oct 1793. WM. HOUCHIN to BENJ. WRIGHT, AC, for Ł100, no acres set forth - N side Piney.Wit: JNO. MASSIE, MOSES WRIGHT, BENJ. CAMDEN, JESSE WRIGHT.

Page 359. 29 Nov 1793. PLEDGE PALMER & wife SARAH, AC, to RO. ROBERTSON, AC, for Ł30, 113 acres. Wit: GEO. McDANIEL, JNO. REYNOLDS, HENRY ROBINSON, JAMES LASHELL, JNO. HARRIS, THOS. JOHNSON.

Page 360. 15 Feb 1794. JNO. McCABE, AC, to LANDON CARTER, AC, for Ł25, 100 acres Jack Branch of Pedlar. Wit: JNO. BROWN, ABRAHAM & JESSE CARTER.

Page 361. 17 Feb 1794. BENNETT NALLY, AC, Deed of Trust to RICH. FARRAR, Alb. land, negroes, and stock; bond due to WM. C. NICHOLAS and RF is my bondsman. Orig. del. 4 May 1800 to M. DAWSON.

Page 361. 11 Jan 1794. CHRISTOPHER COY, AC, to JESSE CARTER for Ł6, horse, bed, etc. Wit: NELSON CRAWFORD, DANL. WHITE.

Page 362. 22 Oct 1792. Order to AC J.P.'s to quiz MOLLY, wife of NATHL. CLARK - 12 May 1787, deed to THOS. GOODWIN, Hanover, 360 acres. Lines: THOS. MORRISON, ZACH. CLARK, THOS. ADAMS, SAML. REID. Done 1 Nov 1792 by HUDSON MARTIN & NATHAN CRAWFORD.

Page 363. 12 Jul 1792. Order to AC J.P.'s to quiz SARAH HURT, wife of JNO., 7 Jan 1793 deed to BENJ. TALIAFERRO - 180 acres. Done, 23 Aug 1793, by NICHL. CABELL & SAML. MEREDITH.

Page 363. 22 Apr 1794. PHILIP THURMOND & wife JUDITH, AC, to ISAAC
         WRIGHT, AC, for Ⱡ3000, 3 tracts on Horsley. 1) 422 acres.
Lines: CHAS. TALIAFERRO, WIDOW CARTER. 2) 104 acres adj. - both sides
Horsley. 3) 70 acres adj. both tracts. Lines: JOB CARTER, LUNSFORD LOMAX.

Page 365. 9 Jan 1794. Agreement between THOS. GOODRICH & wife CHATHER-
         INE (sic) AC, to EDMOND GOODRICH, AC, (Orig. del. 3 Jan 1796
to EG) EDMOND is to take full possession of THOMAS' land, manage, pay
debts, and maintain THOS. & wife - 3 slaves named as consideration. Wit:
WM. WARE, JOHN EUBANK, JNO. WARE.

Page 366. 22 Apr 1794. ISAAC WRIGHT & wife SUSANNA, AC, to PHILLIP
         THURMOND, AC, (Orig. del. to JNO. CRAWFORD 9 Mar 1798, per
verbal order) for Ⱡ600, 3 tracts N side Tobacco Row & Horsley. 1) 121 &
5/8 acres. 2) 121 5/8 acres adj.; Rockey Branch. 3) 121 5/8 adj.

Page 367. 8 Mar 1794. JNO. HOPKINS, Goochland, to THOS. HOPKINS, AC,
         (Orig. del. to JNO. LOVING, per JAS. HOPKINS's order) Love of
JNO. for son THOS. & Ⱡ40, Davis Creek & Rockfish; old survey of 285 acres.
Lines: WM. WRIGHT. Also 164 acres adj. pat. to JNO. HOPKINS, assignee of
THOS. MONTGOMERY, assignee of LUKE BINION, 1 Jun 1782. Lines: THOS. MONT-
GOMERY. 449 acres. Wit: EDWARD MARTIN, THOS. POOR(?), JNO. HOPKINS JR,
DAVID CLARKSON, RICH. C. POLLARD, THOS. POWELL.

Page 374. 14 Feb 1794. DANL. GAINES, Wilks Co, Ga. and his trustees,
         HUGH ROSE, GABL. PENN, & JAS. FRANKLIN, AC, & exr. of CHAS.
IRVING, Alb., also trustee to JOS. CREWS, AC, for Ⱡ50 and 1 sh, 52 acres
Crooked Run. Lines: JOSEPH CREWS, JOS. MAYO, now in possession of JC.
Wit: JNO. HILL JR, JAMES. WRIGHT, NIMROD LONG, DAVID S. GARLAND, WIATT
WOODROOF. First three as to GAINES.

Page 376. 12 May 1794. NICHL. PAMPLIN, AC, to JNO. DABNEY, Campbell
         Co., N. POWES, THOS. HUMPHREYS, Lynchburg Merchant. - filed
suit in AC Court and obtained judgment - Deed of Trust - 5 sh. 150 acres
Elk Run tract NP bought of JAS. PAMPLIN. Lines: SAML. ALLEN, Chickahominy
Branch, GEO. HILTON, WM. HORSLEY, DANL. PERROW - except 2 acres whereon
mill stands. Wit: POWHATAN BOLING, THOS. HIGGINBOTHAM, PLEASANT M. MILLER,
SAML. J. HARRISON, CORNL. POWELL, WIATT POWELL, WM. MEREDITH. Orig. del.
to WM. BROWN, merchant, 13 Aug 1794.

Page 378. 16 Jun 1794. THOS. LLEWELLYN LOCKMERE WALL, Camp Creek, AC,
         to wife SALLY, for love - 1 black mare bought of late Capt.
FRANCIS THORP, New london, Bedford Co, saddle, cow bought of CHAS. ROSE,
Esq., AC, and other items.

Page 379. 6 Dec 1793. JNO. McALEXANDER & wife NANCY, AC, to CLEVER C.
         HARRILL, AC, for Ⱡ50, 307 3/4 acres Nelson Co, Ky; Green River.
Lines: ALEX. McALEXANDER, WM. MONTGOMERY. Pat. 27 Oct 1788, No. 16427.
Wit: HUDSON MARTIN, JAS. PHILLIPS, JAS. McALEXANDER.

Page 380. 16 Jun 1794. GEO. GALASPIE & wife MARY, AC, to PATRICK ROSE,
         AC, for 5 sh., Little Piney on N side, no acreage set forth.
Lines: PATRICK ROSE.

Page 381. 16 Jun 1794. WM. CAMDEN, AC, to JNO. CAMDEN SR, (Orig. del.
         13 Feb 1802, to WM. CAMDEN per order) for Ⱡ50, 170 acres top
of the Blue Ridge.

Page 382. 16 Jun 1794. ALEX. DUGGINS, AC, to BENJ. GOODE, AC, (Sent to
         BG per order filed, 11 Nov 1802) for Ⱡ10, 30 acres, part of
tract formerly that of HENRY CHILDRESS on top of Blue Ridge and granted
at Richmond to ALEX. DUGGINS, 24 Jul 1787. Wit; J.W. CAMPBELL, BURCHER
WHITEHEAD, WM. CAMDEN.

Page 383. 16 Jun 1794. ALEX. DUGGINS, AC, to JNO. CAMDEN, (Margin
         either faded or erased - Orig. del. 13(?) Feb 1802, to WM.
DUNCAN(?)) for Ⱡ30, 270 acres. Pat. to AD at Richmond 24 Jul 1787 - both
sides Pedlar. Wit: as above.

Page 384. 16 Jun 1794. CHAS. McCABE, AC, to THOS. MITCHELL, Rockbridge

286

Co., for Ł40, 100 acres H branches of Puppy Creek. Lines: WM. WARE, CHAS.
TALIAFERRO, ridge that lies between the plantation where SOL. CARTER formerly lived and one whereon WM. CARTER now lives; top of the mt., ridge
between Horsley & Puppy.

Page 385. 16 Jun 1794. JAS. LITTRELL, AC & Parish, acting atty for
           ABNER WITT of Knox Co. and territory South of Ohio River - to
JOS. ROBERTS, AC, & parish, for Ł70, N branch Davis. 1) 99 acres formerly
that of JNO. KEY. Lines: his own. 2) Formerly that of JNO. CRAIGHEAD -
35 acres. Lines: his own. Wit: BARTLETT EADES, JAS. TURNER.

Page 386. 11 Apr 1794. REUBEN THORNTON, AC, to WILSON CAREY NICHOLAS,
           Alb., for Ł187-10, 320 acres N side and joining Buffalo. Lines:
HIGGINBOTHAM road, STEPHEN WATTS, SMYTH TANDY. Part of a tract. Wit: RO.
RIVES, JAS. LOVING, DAVID HIGGINBOTHAM.

Page 387. 19 Apr 1794. RACHEL AYRES, AC, to JOS. MONTGOMERY, AC, for
           Ł12, 32 acres S fork Rockfish. Lines: WM. DUVAL, JAS. WOODS.
Wit: THOS. STEWART, JNO. LACKEY, JNO. RYAN.

Page 388. 16 Jun 1794. JNO. MATTHEWS & wife MARY, AC, to BENJ. PAYNE,
           AC, for Ł30, 100 acres S side Cove Creek. Lines: PLEASANT
DAWSON, JOS. MATTHEWS MURRELL, JAS. TURNER SR(?).

Page 389. 26 Mar 1794. HENRY CHRISTIAN, AC, to WM. NOWEL, JR, Campbell
           Co. & Lynchburg - 5 sh, Deed of Trust to secure JNO. & WM.
CHRISTIAN on bond of 24 Jul 1788 to firm of McCREDIE & McMILLAN - 363
acres. Lines: CHARLES CHRISTIAN on E, JOS. HIGGINBOTHAM on W, THOS. ED-
WARDS on N, S by SACKVILLE KING - where HENRY CHRISTIAN now lives. Wit:
JNO. LONDON, WM. HAM, JNO. BULLOCK, WM. LONDON.

Page 391. 27 Nov 1793. Order to WM. HARRIS & JAS. WOODS, AC J.P.'s, to
           quiz REBECCA, wife of PLEASANT MARTIN - deed of 4 Oct 1793, to
HENRY ROBERTS - 780 acres. Done, 27 Mar 1794.

Page 392. 2 May 1794. Order to quiz JUDITH THURMOND, wife of PHILIP, as
           to deed of 12 Oct 1791, to ELIAS WILLS - 121 acres. Done 17
May 1794 by AC J.P.'s: NELSON CRAWFORD & JOSIAH ELLIS. Orig. del. 19 Apr
1802, to EW.

Page 393. 28 Jun 1794. SAML. SPENCER SR, Buckingham Co, to JOS. MAYS,
           SR, AC, for Ł150, 500 acres S side Berry's Mt. Lines: THOS.
LEWIS. No wit. signed, but named in summary as RO. RIVES, JAS. MURPHY,
JNO. NAPPIER.

Page 394. 21 Jul 1794. THOS. LANDRUM, AC, to WM. BANKS, Power of Atty -
           BANKS of Patrick Co. to sell land in Montgomery Co. on W fork
of Little River - 665 acres. Wit: HARMON CRUTZ, SAML. DOTTON, THOS. LAN-
DRUM JR, WM. & ANDERSON MOSS. Orig. del. to BURTON LANDRUM 30 Sep 1794.

Page 394. 28 Apr 1794. THOS. BARRETT & wife ELIZ, AC, to LARKIN SAN-
           DIDGE, AC, for Ł90, 250 acres branches S fork Buffalo and on
Long Mt. Lines: CARNEBY VEAL. Orig. del. to LS 16 Aug 1794.

Page 396. 28 Apr 1794. THOS. BARRETT (BARROTT) and wife ELIZ., AC, to
           REUBIN TINSLEY, AC, for Ł35, 200 acres Bank of Pedlar. Wit:
BENJ. HIGGINBOTHAM, LARKIN SANDIDGE, DANL. COLEMAN, WM. BARROT. Orig.
del. to LARKIN SANDIDGE, 16 Aug 1794.

Page 397. 28 Apr 1794. THOS. BARRETT & wife, as above, to BENJ. SAN-
           DIDGE, AC, for Ł269-5, 294 acres S fork Buffalo - and N side -
"another" - Lines: ISAAC MAYFIELD. Wit: BENJ. HIGGINBOTHAM, DANL. COLEMAN,
LARKIN SANDIDGE, REUBIN TINSLEY.

Page 398. 30 (20?) Mar 1793. GEO. HIGHT, AC, to JNO. ROSE for Ł10-11,
           and Ł1800 Richmond inspected tobacco due by me to ROSE - Deed
of Trust - beds, etc. Wit: DANL. McDANIEL, WM. JACOBS.

Page 399. 11 Jun 1794. VIRGINIA (VIRJUN) TAYLOR & PHILIP THURMOND, AC,
           to MICHL. STONEHOCKER, AC, for Ł100, 170 acres Stovall Creek.

Lines: V. TAYLOR, old fence and plantation. Wit: JNO. TURNER, JNO. KNIGHT, ORSON KNIGHT.

Page 400. 14 Feb 1794. JNO. FLOYED, Ga, Power of Atty to PHILIP THUR-
MOND, AC - DANL. BURFETT(BURFORD) of Va. by will of 1787 bequeathed to VA. TAYLOR 250 acres in AC on headwaters of Stoval - for
life or until she leaves; remainder to me. JF of Wilks Co, Ga. - PT to
dispose of my interest upon removal or death of VA. TAYLOR. Acknowledged
before BENJ. CATCHING, Clk. of Superior Ct., W. STITH JR, one of the
judges. Rec. in AC, 21 Jul 1794. (Writing is poor indeed here. BFD)

Page 401. 7 Dec 1793. MARTIN MILLER, Halifax, to CHAS. STATHAM, AC, for
£15, 200 acres both sides Dutch Creek. Lines: WM. CABELL SR,
THOS. NASH(?) STONE, THOS. JOPLIN. Orig. sent to CS 19 Nov 1799, per
order. Wit: DANL. WILSON, THOS. NASH, ARCHIBALD DOUGLASS.

Page 402. 21 Jun 1794. JESSE MARTIN & wife ELIZ, AC, to ALLEN LAVENDER,
AC, for £50, 59 acres S side Findley Mt. Lines: RICH. PRICHARD,
JACOB EADES - tract of 10 acres and part of 60 acres lately held by PETER
CARTWRIGHT. Lines: JESSE MARTIN, old road, WM. CABELL's purchase of PETER
CARTWRIGHT, JNO. BALL, WM. ALFORD. Tract of 8½ acres S side and joins a
N branch of Joe's Creek. Lines: JAMES MATTHEWS, JESSE MARTIN, and is part
of tract of WM. ALFORD which he bought of HENRY KEY.

Page 404. 20 Apr 1794. DAVID CRAWFORD, Gent. and late Shff. of AC, to
EDMOND WINSTON, Campbell Co, - MILES BURFORD in 1784 was seized of 200 acres and taxes for two years were in arrears. 4 Sep 1785,
CRAWFORD advertised by law, and EW bought the 160 acres surveyed and laid
off. Lines: N bank of Fluvanna, EDMD. WINSTON, MILES BURFORD - survey of
9 Mar 1791, by JAS. HIGGINBOTHAM, AC, surveyor. Wit: RO. HOLLOWAY, WIATT
SMITH, JAS. CALLAWAY, REUBEN CRAWFORD. Enclosed to EW, 14 Mar 1795.

Page 405. 8 Mar 1794. WM. BIBB, AC, to JNO. ALFORD & JNO. WRYHT (sic)
AC, for £216, 180 acres bought by WM. BIBB, dec'd. of LUNSFORD
LOMAX and part of 587½ acres. Lines: TANDY JOHNSON, Naked Creek, WM. TEAS,
GEO. BLAINE, WM. BIBB, dec'd. Wit: THOS. BIBB, WM. MATTHEWS, JOS. LIVELY,
ROWLAND EDMUNDS, JAS. BIBB JR.

Page 407. - Jan 1794. JNO. DRUMMOND & wife MARY, City of Williamsbourgh
(sic) & HENLEY DRUMMOND, AC, to CHAS. TYLER, Charles City, for
£1000, 2000 acres - taken up and surveyed for Col. WM. CABELL, THOS. DOS-
WELL, & JNO. DRUMMOND, the Elder, James City. Partition and conveyed to
JNO. & HENLEY DRUMMOND in 1768. Lines: ABRAM SMITH on S, JOS. STRICKLAND
on N, THOS. GOODWIN on E, JNO. TATE on W. Wit: HENRY SOUTHALL, CRAWLEY
MAYNARD, BENJ. MAYNARD. Chas. City Court, July, 1794. OTWAY BYRD, Presiding Magistrate, by WM. ROYALL. Rec. AC, 21 Jul 1794.

Page 409. 15 Sep 1794. JNO. B. TRENT, AC, Power of Atty to LAWRENCE
WOODWARD to convey to RO. CLARK JR 640 acres in Madison Co,
Ky. on Tate Creek. Part of FLANDERS CALLOWAY's presumption and assigned
to TRENT.

Page 409. 18 Apr 1794. GEO. BURKS & wife JEAN, Buckingham, to WM. BURKS,
AC, (Orig. del. to MICHL. WEST, 20 Oct 1800, per written order)
for £130, 1) 169 acres pat. to RO. DAVIS JR. 3 Mar 1760. Lines: MARVEL
STONE, SAML. BURKS JR, ARTHUR TULEY, MICAJAH CLARK. 2) 20 acres adj.
Lines: JOSIAH ELLIS, DAVID BURKS. 3) 100 acres adj. conveyed by STEPHEN
GOOLSBY to MATT. WILSON 3 Jul 1773. Wit: WM. CABELL JR, JAS. STEVENS JR,
JNO. STAPLES, HEZ. HARGROVE.

Page 410. 22 Apr 1794. WM. BURKS, AC, to NICHL. WEST, AC, (Orig. del.
to NW, 20 Oct 1800) for £75 --- Maple Creek. Wit: WILLIS
WILLS, RICH. TINSLEY, GEO. BURKS, JNO. JOHNSON.

Page 412. 15 Sep 1794. JNO. BOUSH & wife MARY, AC, to EDMOND TRAVELION
& MARTIN BREEDLOVE, Alb., for £80, 100 acres branches Ruckers
Run. Lines: JNO. BOUSH, ABRAHAM WARWICK, CHAS. WATTS.

Page 413. 15 Sep 1794. JNO. BOUSH & wife MARY, AC, to WM. BREEDLOVE,
Cumberland Co., for £120, 158 acres N side Peavine Mt. Part

288

of tract of HENRY KEY. Lines: Top of the Mt., branch of Rucker's Run, HENRY KEY.

Page 414. 15 Sep 1794. JNO. BOUSH & wife MARY, AC, to RICH. BREEDLOVE, Culpeper, for Ł80, 180 acres branches S fork Rockfish. Lines: JNO. BALL, WM. KEY, Glade rode(sic), WM. CABELL, JAS. NEVIL, THOS. KEY.

Page 415. 15 Sep 1794. JNO. BOUSH & wife MARY, AC, to RICH. BREEDLOVE, Culpeper, for Ł50, 100 acres branches S fork Rockfish; part of tract formerly that of HENRY KEY. Lines: WM. ALFORD.

Page 416. 15 Sep 1794. JNO. BOUSH, AC, about to move to Ky, Power of Atty to WM. WARWICK & WM. CABELL JR.

Page 416. 15 Sep 1794. WM. CHAPPELL & wife ANN, to PETER CASHWELL, AC, for Ł110, 253 acres S branches Rugledge. Lines: JOS. HIGGIN-BOTHAM, JR, JOS. WILCHER, CARTER BRAXTON's old pat. line, MICHL. COLTER.

Page 418. 15 Sep 1794. JNO. BROWN JR, & wife FRANCES, AC, to RICE KEY, AC, for Ł12, 182 acres both sides Inchanted Creek; branch of Pedlar. Lines: WM. PRYOR, DANL. BURFORD. Pat. at Williamsburg to JB. Orig. del. to JNO. KEY, 21 Dec 1795.

Page 419. 15 Sep 1794. JNO. BROWN JR & wife FRANCES, AC, to THOS. GOOD-RICH, AC, for Ł100, 200 acres Horsley Creek. Lines: JNO. POW-ELL, ISAAC WRIGHT. (Del. to JNO. EUBANK per order, 2 Oct 1798.) Wit: WM. WARE, CHAS. BROWN, JNO. WARE.

Page 420. 16 Jun 1794. JNO. BROWN as above to ABRAHAM CARTER, AC, for Ł150, N fork Horsley. 1) 94 acres. Lines: tract formerly that of JNO. PEYTON, former tract of PHILIP PEYTON. 2) 59 acres, part of tract of NELSON CRAWFORD. Lines: his own, NELSON CRAWFORD. (Del. to AC 7 Mar 1796) Wit: JNO. CRAWFORD, CHAS. BROWN, JAS. BROWN, ELLIOTT BROWN, EDWD. CARTER.

Page 421. 21 Apr 1794. WM. WITT & wife MILDRED, AC, to SAML. MERRAN, AC, for Ł25, 100 acres Davis Creek. Lines: BARTHOLOMEW MERRAN, RO. GRANT. Part of tract of WW. Wit: HUDSON MARTIN, JAS. VIGUS, WM. WOOD. Orig. del. to JNO. SHELTON, 18 Jun 1795.

Page 422. 15 Sep 1794. HENRY SHELTON & wife MARY, AC, to NATHAN HALL, AC, for Ł40, 93 acres N branch Raven & Buffalo. Part of NICHL. CABELL tract. Lines: JAS. MARTIN, GILBERT BOWMAN, NICHL. CABELL, RICH. ALCOCK, WM. CABELL. Orig. del. to NATHL. HALL, 15 Dec 1803.

Page 423. 3 Jan 1793. Rec'd. of GEO. WORTHAM by JNO. GRIFFIN JR, Ł20-18-6½. Bill of Sale to THOMPSON & TEAS. Wit: GEO. GILLES-PIE, JNO. BROWN, JNO. THOMPSON for T & T.

Page 423. 30 Sep 1794. JNO. H. GOODWIN, AC, to WILLIAM WILLIAMS, AC, for Ł5, ½ acre in Scuffle Town; laid off for JONATHAN DEAKIN; 1st lot laid off in said town. Lines: Lynch road, PHIL JOHNSON, ROYEL(?) & KING. Wit: JNO. BURFORD JR, JNO. HARRIS, JAS. LASHWELL, AMB. BURFORD. Orig. del. to WW, 1799. (Note: This is now Madison Heights just across from Lynchburg on James River. BFD)

Page 425. 15 Sep 1793. JAS. HARRISON & wife BOLLY, Buckingham Co, to RICH. BURKS, AC, for Ł160, 263 acres Harris Creek. Lines: E bank of Harris, JNO. AMBLER, WM. TINSLEY, crossing cree, RICH. SHELTON, JNO. TINSLEY. Orig. del. to RB, 6 Feb 1810.

Page 426. 15 Sep 1794. WM. ABNEY & wife MILDRED, AC, to WM. WOOD, AC, for Ł30, 111 acres Short's Creek. Lines: DAVID WITT, ELIZ. TULEY, LITTLEBERRY WITT. Wit: HUDSON MARTIN, JAS. VIGUS, WM. WITT.

Page 427. 16 Aug 1794. JNO. HOGG, AC, to JNO. BURFORD JR, AC, for Ł80, 392 acres Sside Maple Creek. Pat. 12 Jul 1780. Lines: JNO. BURKS, WM. STEPHENSON. Wit: HARDEN HAYNES, ARCHIBALD BURFORD, BENJ. NOELL, AMB. BURFORD.

Page 428. 20 Nov 1793. DAVID DAVIS, & wife MARY, AC, to DAVID PARROCK,
AC, for Ł70, 156 acres N branches Piney. Lines: CHAS. ROSE,
DAVIS' old pat. Part of 2 tracts of DD. Wit: JNO. PARROCK, JNO. LANCES-
TER, WM. LILLEY, WM. THOMPSON, GEO. DAVIS.

Page 430. 15 Sep 1794. JNO. STINNETT & wife ANN, AC, to JER. WHITTEN,
AC, for Ł101-5, 200 acres Thomas Mill Creek. Lines: ROD. Mc-
CULLOCH, CHAS. DAVIS, JNO. SLEDD. Wit: CHAS. DAVIS, HARDEN HAYNES, JNO.
BURFORD JR, FRANCES VEAL, LARKIN BYAS.

Page 431. 23 Mar 1794. LUCY JOHNSON, Exrx. of RO. JOHNSON, dec'd, Caro-
line, to LARKIN BYAS, AC, (del. to LB 31 Jan 1801) for Ł45,
325 acres, pat. 27 Oct 1766, S side & joining Pedlar. Lines: SAML. GUEST,
S bank Pedlar, S bank. Cornfield branches, JNO. DUNCAN, N fork Cedar,
JOEL WATKINS, JOSIAH ELLIS. Wit: HENRY BROOKS, FRANCIS VEAL, JOS. VEAL,
WM. VEAL.

Page 432. 23 Mar 1794. LUCY JOHNSON, as above, to FRANCIS VEAL, AC, for
Ł50, 294 acres his heirs etc. Pat. 9 Apr 1771 S branch Otter
and N branch Fluvanna, Tarpin (sic) Creek. Wit: LARKIN BYAS, JOS. VEAL,
HENRY BROOKS, WM. VEAL.

Page 434. 23 Mar 1794. LUCY JOHN JOHNSON, as above, to WM. VEAL, AC,
for Ł40, 404 acres Pat. 10 May 1771 N side and adj. Fluvanna
and Otter Creek. Lines: CORNL. THOMAS, Tarpin Creek, Rattle Snake Branch,
Cedar Branch. Wit: as above.

Page 435. 13 Sep 1794. JAS. & GEO. CARPENTER, AC, to JOS. ROBERTS, AC,
(X through "Sent to ROBERTS, 24 Aug 1801) for blank sum, 250
acres. Lines: WM. BARNETT, HENRY SMITH, JOS. ROBERTS. Wit: JNO. E. FITZ-
PATRICK, LANDON BRENT, ALEX. ROBERTS, WM. BARNETT, SAML. LACKEY.

Page 436. 22 Mar 1794. JAS. MANN & wife JANE, to RAYHLEY PENN for Ł50,
400 acres surveyed 22 Nov 1787, Mill and Porrage Creeks. Lines:
JAS. DILLARD, JAS. CHRISTIAN, RO. JOHN, dec'd. Wit: JAS. DILLARD, DANL.
MAYO, STEPHEN WATTS, JAS. DILLARD JR.

Page 438. 13 Sep 1794. EDWD. HARPER to WILLIAM WILLIAMS for Ł20, 12
acres. Lines: WILLIAMS, on the path, ROBINSON. Wit: JNO. BUR-
FORD, JR, JNO. HARRIS, JAS. LASHELL.

Page 439. 24 Feb 1794. ELIZ. DAVIS, exrx., CHAS., ISAM, & JAS. DAVIS;
JNO. BURKS who married ELIZ. DAVIS; JNO. F.P.LEWIS who married
NANCY DAVIS; STEPHEN TERRY who married SALLY DAVIS; JNO. BAGBEY who mar-
ried MILDRED DAVIS; NATHL. & THEODORICK DAVIS, AC, to JNO. BURKS, AC, for
Ł300, 418 acres - we fell heirs by death of our brother, ROBT. DAVIS -
Back Creek of Pedlar. Wit: R. ELLIS, JOSIAH ELLIS, J.P. HEWLINGS, DAVID
BURK SR & JR, WM. SHOEMAKER, LEROY POPE. Note: THEODORICK appears to be
THEODORIC in one place.

Page 440. 29 Aug 1794. EDWD. HARPER & wife FRANCES, AC, to JOSIAH ELLIS,
AC, for Ł30, 365 acres N side and joining Dancing Creek. Lines:
JOSIAH JOPLING, EZEK. SHUMAKER, LARKIN BYAS, DRURY BOWMAN. Wit: J.P.
HEWLINGS, JESSE CARTER, RICH. ELLIS, WM. HAYNES, OBEDIAH MARTIN.

Page 442. 9 Aug 1794. Order to AC J.P.'s WM. CABELL & DANL. WHITE, to
quiz ELIZ. BARRETT, wife of THOS. as to deed of 28 Apr 1794,
to LARKIN SANDIDGE. Done, 22 Aug 1794. Page 443 Same, 9 Apr 1794, as to
294 acres involving same parties. Done: same date. Page 444, 9 Sep 1794,
as to deed by ELIZ. & THOS. to REUBIN TINSLEY - 200 acres. Done 22 Aug
1794.

Page 445. 13 Sep 1794. WM. WITT & wife MILDRED, AC, to JOS. ROBERTS,
AC, for Ł150, 500 acres N branch Davis (Orig. del. to JNO.
ROBERTS, 29 Sep 1794) Lines: RO. GRANT, JOS. SHELTON, JAS. McALEXANDER,
JOS. ROBERTS. Wit: JNO. N. REID, JNO. BONES, ALEX. McALEXANDER, JAS. H.
PONTON.

Page 446. 15 Sep 1794, ANTHONY RUCKER, Tob. Insp., Amherst WH. Bondsman:
BENJ. RUCKER. (Note: ANTHONY RUCKER invented the river barge

and one is referred to data by my good friend, AL PERCY on him in his works on Amherst history. He mentions his patent in his will, but a fire destroyed the original data. BFD)

Page 446.   Same date, GEO. McDANIEL, and same Warehouse. Bondsman: JNO. McDANIEL.

Page 447.   18 Oct 1794. JAS. WILSMORE & wife NANCY, AC, to JNO.CREWS, AC, for Ŀ35, 83 acres branches Rutledge Creek and Paul's Mt. Lines: Top of Paul's Mt., GIDEON CREWS. Wit: JNO. McDANIEL, WM. CASHWILL, WM. MOORE, JNO. MOORE, GIDEON CREWS. Orig. del. to GIDEON CREWS 8 Jan 1796.

Page 448.   17 Mar 1794. JNO. McANALLY & wife RUTH, AC, to ISAAC SCOTT, AC, for Ŀ65, 100 acres Side of the Blue Ridge in Rockfish Gap. Lines: DAVID KINCAID, Thornton's Branch. Wit: JAS. PENDLETON, WM. SKELTON (SHELTON), JNO. KRYSER.

Page 450.   20 Oct 1794. ANN DAVIS, AC, to her children:son, PHILIP - mare, etc. daughter, FRENKEY PENCE DAVIS - mare, etc.

Page 450.   20 Oct 1794. MOSES HALL & wife MOLLY, AC, to CHRISTOPHER COY, for Ŀ35, 100 acres branch Horsley & S branches Buffalo.

Page 451.   6 May 1794. WM. LEACH, AC, to WM. CAMDEN, AC, (Orig. del. to JABEZ CAMDEN, 14 Aug 1805) for Ŀ30, 148 acres. Lines: WM. CAMDEN, AMBR. RUCKER. LEACH bought of GEO. DOUGLAS. Wit: JNO. MASSIE, HENRY CAMDEN, JNO. CAMDEN.

Page 452.   4 Oct 1794. TANDY JOHNSON & wife SALLY, AC, to JAS. WILLS, AC, for Ŀ210, 210 acres branches Naked Creek and N branches Tye, part of tract of WM. BIBB, dec'd. Lines: WM. BIBB, dec'd, JNO. ALFORD. Wit: WM. WARWICK, JAS. THOMPSON, JNO. THOMPSON, WM. POWELL.(Orig. del. to JAS. WILLS, 10 Oct 1806.) Page 453, order to WM. WARWICK & WM. LOVING, AC J.P.'s, to quiz SALLY. Done same day as deed.

Page 455.   10 Dec 1793. Order to REUBEN NORVELL & THOS. MOORE, AC J.P.s to quiz MARTHA CREWS, wife of JOS. CREWS JR as to deed to THOMAS HUMPHREYS, Campbell Co, 24 Aug 1793. Done 13 Sep 1794.   83 acres.

Page 456.   16 Oct 1794. JAS. SAVAGE & wife MARY, AC, to SAML. ANDERSON, Alb. Co, for Ŀ100, 213 acres N branches Buffalo. Lines: JNO. PHILLIPS on N, now sold to ANDERSON & WM. PHILLIPS on W, RICH. ALCOCK & JAS. ROWSEY on S, SMYTH TANDY on E.   213 acres belong to J. SAVAGE.

Page 457.   10 Oct 1794. HUDSON MARTIN & wife ELIZ, AC, to JOS. ROBERTS & ALEX. McALEXANDER & ALEX. ROBERTS, AC, for Ŀ80, 4 acres Davis Creek. Lines: WM. WRIGHT, JAS. WRIGHT, Great Road. Wit: WM. MARTIN, JNO. BONES, SAML. MERIAN.

Page 458.   24 Sep 1794. JAS. TURNER & wife REBECCAH, AC, to STEPHEN TURNER, AC, for Ŀ150, 270 acres adj. Rockfish on both sides & Cove Creek on 1 side and Jermon Creek on other side of said river. Lines: JNO. MATTHEWS on S, JOS. MATTHEWS on E, JNO. MATTHEWS - N & W. Wit: JNO. WILKINSON, LEONARD PHILLIPS, JNO. TURNER, JAS. TURNER JR, JNO. LONDON.

Page 459.   29 Sep 1794. JNO. PHILLIPS & wife SARAH, AC, to SAML. ANDERSON, Alb., for Ŀ160, 359 acres N brnaches Buffalo. Lines: WM. CABELL JR, WM. PHILLIPS, JAS. SAVAGE, SMYTH TANDY, WM. LAYNE. Wit: JER. & WM. PHILLIPS, MARTIN DAWSON.

Page 460.   30 Sep 1794. Order to SAML. MEREDITH, THOS. MOORE, & JOS. BURRUS, AC J.P.'s, to quiz SARAH PHILLIPS as to above deed, 28 Apr 1794, and someone has underlined and put 29 Sep 1794, on margin. Done on the same day by MEREDITH & BURRUS.

Page 461.   11 Oct 1794. Order to SAML. MEREDITH, CHESLEY KINNEY, & REUBEN NORVEL, AC J.P.'s, to quiz MOURNING STEWART, wife of JNO., as to 1788 deed to WM. PHILLIPS - 50 acres. Done by SM & CK, 11

Oct 1794.

Page 462. 13 Sep 1794. LAWRENCE LONG states that he rec'd. of EDWD.
CARTER, dec'd, in lifetime land warrants for 30,000 acres and
gave recpt. in Alb., 10 Mar 1792 - to dispose of and receive ½ as expenses. Wit: PETER DAVIE. 14,130 acres pat. to me; remainder located, but
not pat. EDWD. CARTER in will devised all right, title, etc. in land to
CHAS., EDWD., WM. CHAMPE; ROBT., GEO., WHITAKER, & HILL CARTER, his
younger sons, and they have sued me in AC Chancery to have partition. I
am about to remove to Ky - 6sh. paid by CARTERS - Power of Atty to
PHILLIP GOOCH to convey for me and I have lodged 6020 acres pat. with
GOOCH. Orig. del. to PG, 12 Apr 1795. Wit: MATT. M. GOOCH, CHAS. ELLIS,
JAS. DILLARD.

Page 464. 18 Mar 1794. WM. & JAS. HAY, Exrs. of GILBERT HAY, dec'd, AC,
Power of Atty to JNO. ROSE, AC, to let land on Indian Creek
599 acres otherwise to sell. Wit: JNO. McDANIEL, JNO. HILL. Orig. del.
to Col. JNO. ROSE, 18 Sep 1795.

Page 464. To Mr. LAURENCE LONG - Sir - I wish you to be very particular
when you get to Kentucky - to locate the warrants you have in
hand - one-half to you - try to get the best land laid off - think you
had better call on PARSON CLAY - he has a brother living in that Country-
Wishing you a safe return. 29 Mar 1782. N.B. Wish you to call. P.S. Have
rec'd. no money as yet from Richmond therefore you must make out as well
as you can. EDWARD CARTER. Handwriting attested by HUDSON MARTIN, 20
Oct 1794.

Page 465. 18 Oct 1794. JAS. WATSON, AC, Power of Atty to ANTHONY DI-
BRELL JR, Buckingham Co. for Ky. land - 1800 acres - has bond
of CHAS. LYNCH SR & JR. to lay off and receive as per agreement with
them. Wit: GEO. DILLARD, JNO. PENN, REUBEN PENDLETON, PHILIP GOOCH.
Orig. del. to AD, 17 Dec 1794.

Page 465. 3 Jan 1794. EDWD. HILL CARTER, AC, to CHAS. CARTER, Culpeper,
for ₺135, 135 acres, part of a tract, N branches Buffalo.
Lines: EDWD. CARTER, CHAS. CARTER, down Mill Creek, the great road. Wit:
HUDSON MARTIN, RO. RIVES, P. GOOCH.

Page 467. 20 Oct 1794. JNO. WATKINS & wife KATHERINE, AC, & Parish, to
JACOB PUCKETT, same parish, for ₺50, 3 tracts by survey - 184
acres S branch of N fork David Creek. Lines: JNO. WADE, his own, middle
fork, Davis creek.

Page 468. 15 Oct 1794. Order to NELSON CRAWFORD & WM. WARE, AC J.P.'s
to quiz PEGGY HARRISON, wife of REUBIN HARRISON - deeds of 15
Jul 1793, to JNO. SALE, SR. Done, 20 Oct 1794.

Page 469. 24 Jun 1794. RANDOLPH BIBB, AC to JNO. ALFORD, AC, for ₺92-8-
4, a negro woman, Genney, and boy, Kiah, Moll, a wench, cows
and calves, furniture etc. Wit: WM. MATTHEWS, JAS. BIBB JR, DAVID WRIGHT,
RO. WRIGHT, TANDY JOHNSON.

Page 470. 18 Sep 1794. SAML. BROWN, AC, - Deed of Trust to FRANKLIN &
BALLINGER - because of particular indulgence in waiting on
part not paid - tract whereon I live - 25 acres, part of tract formerly
owned by ISAAC GIBSON, dec'd, mare, etc. Wit: PEACHY FRANKLIN, CHAS.
ELLIS, MICHL. BAILEY.

Page 471. 8 Oct 1794. SAML. MEREDITH & SHERWOOD MARTIN, AC, to DANL.
TRUEHART, Hanover, & St. Paul Parish, 5 sh. - 177 acres, part
of tract SAML. MEREDITH lived on in Hanover and called Wastins(?). Lines:
JNO. HOWARD, JAS. BOTERYTHE, ABSLUM WILTORE(?), JAS. WOODS, JOS. SHELTON.
(Note: the writing is very poor. BFD)

Page 472. 29 Mar 1790. WM. DAMRON & wife SUSANNAH, to THOS. ANDERSON
for ₺40, 56 acres Harris Creek, W side Lynch road. Lines: NOEL
BLANKENSHIP, MICH. ROWER(?), BENJ. RUCKER, a late survey of DAMRON,
Lynch Road. Wit: CHAS. CHRISTIAN, NOEL BLANKENSHIP, JNO. CARTER, DANL.
MEHONE, THOMAS COLEMAN, JOS. WILSON.

292

Page 473. 21 Jun 1794. HUGH ROSE & wife CAROLINE MATILDA, AC, to GEO.
DILLARD, AC, (Orig. del. to GD, 17 Apr 1796) for Ƚ750, 750
acres S side Tye. Lines: WM. CABELL JR, S bank Tye, Stovall's road. Wit:
RO. HOLLOWAY, JNO. TOOL, SAML. ROSE, JAS. BALLINGER.

Page 475. 1 Mar 1794. LARKIN GATEWOOD, Elbert Co., Ga., to JNO. CHRIS-
TIAN, Buckingham Co, Va., for Ƚ50, 100 acres Hooper's Creek.
Lines: JNO. CHRISTIAN, CHESLEY KINNEY (formerly DUVALL), ISAAC WRIGHT.
Tract was formerly sold to PHILIP PENN and by him sold to JAS. CHRISTIAN
dec'd., descended from JAS. CHRISTIAN to JNO. CHRISTIAN by heirship, but
has never been conveyed by either of the parties before. Wit: WALTER
CHRISTIAN, WM. BRIANT, ABSALOM STINCHCOMB.

Page 476. 2 Dec 1794. JAS. CONNER & wife NANCY, to SHEROD GRIFFIN for
Ƚ95, 103½ acres S side Rockfish. Lines: SHELTON GRIFFIN, JOS.
SHELTON, MATT. HARRIS, JNO. GRIFFIN. Wit: WM. HARRIS JR, LINDSEY GRIFFIN,
IVERSON MEDARIS, JNO. GRIFFIN.

Page 476. 15 Dec 1794. WM. MATTHEWS & wife MARY, AC, to THOS. LANDRUM,
Jr, AC, for Ƚ80, 100 acres brnaches Naked Creek, N branch Tye.
Part of a tract. Lines: SAML. JORDAN CABELL, branch in the road from
Courthouse to ABRAHAM WARWICK, JAS. WILLS. Wit: RICH. ALCOCK, GEO.
WRIGHT, WM. LANDRUM. Orig. del. to TL Jr, Dec, 1795.

Page 477. 13 Dec 1794. MICHL. COALTER, AC, Power of Atty to friend, RO.
STEEL, Fayette Co, Ky, to make unto SAML. MURROW, Bourbon Co.
Ky, deed to 250 acres bought in partnership with COALTER, STEEL, & one
RANKIN and bought by RO. WALLACE & RO. CAMPBELL; known as Brooks Bunition
and Settlement on Stone Creek (Note Probably Stoner - if in Bourbon.BFD)
between COALTER & STEEL. (Note: my father was born in Bourbon and has
lines there and in Nicholas and Mason. I am stymied on his JNO. PRESTON
CAMPBELL of Nicholas. ·He married JANE LEE METCALFE, daughter of Gov.
THOS. "STONEHAMMER" METCALFE, 10th Gov. of Ky, and she was my 3rd. great
grandmother. After her death he married her sister, MARY ANN METCALFE.
I am unable to solve parentage problem of JNO. PRESTON CAMPBELL. A
FRANCIS CAMPBELL named son, JNO., in Nicholas Co, Ky, will, but I have no
proof that this is my JNO. PRESTON CAMPBELL. BFD)

Page 478. 15 Dec 1794. RICH. LITTRELL, AC, to son, JAS. LITTRELL, AC,
Power of Atty to recover my part of estate as heir at law of
JNO. LITTRELL; died in Chatham Co, N.C.

Page 478. 22 Oct 1794. WM. CLOPTON, Hanover, to JNO. RICHERSON, AC,
for blank sum, 547 acres. Lines: GURST, LOMAX, JNO. EUBANK,
JOSIAH ELLIS, bank of the river, to Lynnwood. Wit: JNO. EUBANK, JESSE
RICHERSON, JNO. TURNER, JOS. RICHERSON, WM. CLOPTON JR, ELISHA MEREDITH.

Page 479. 21 Nov 1794. GABL. PENN for love of daughter, SALLY PENN &
$1.00, (del. to EDMOND PENN, 7 Oct 1796, for GP) 4 named
slaves. Wit: GEO. DILLARD, WIATE SMITH, JAS. BALLINGER, JAS. M. BROWN,
JAS. PENN.

Page 480. 21 Nov 1794. GABL. PENN for love of daughter, CATHERINE PENN,
for $1.00, 4 named slaves. Wit: as above plus GEO. PENN.

Page 480. 26 Sep 1794. LARKIN SANDIDGE & wife MARY, AC, to HENRY HART-
LESS, AC, for Ƚ30, 35 acres. Orig. del. to WM. HARTLESS, 7
Sep 1805, as admr. of HENRY.

Page 481. 18 Apr 1794. MATT. HARRIS, Sr, & wife ELIZ., AC, to SKILER
HARRIS & ANDREW HART, for Ƚ30, 109 acres S side Buck Creek Mt.
and Hicory Creek. Lines: WM. MORRISON dec'd, RICH. HARE. Wit: JNO. GRIF-
FIN, LINDSEY GRIFFIN, BENJ. CHILDRESS.

Page 482. 18 Apr 1794. MATT. HARRIS & wife ELIZ, AC, to MATT. HARRIS,
AC, for Ƚ100, 2 tracts, 349 acres S branch Buck Creek of Rockfish. Lines: LEE HARRIS dec'd, formerly ALEX. MONTGOMERY, JNO. ROBERTS -
149 acres. Also another tract. Lines: his own, JNO. ROBERTS. Wit: JNO. &
LINDSEY GRIFFIN, BENJ. CHILDRESS.

293

Page 483. 18 Apr 1794. MATT. HARRIS & wife ELIZ, AC, to WM. HARRIS JR,
          AC, for Ł200, 382 acres branches Rockfish. Lines: JAS. HOPKINS,
ZACH. PHILLIPS, JAS. WOODS (formerly JAS. MONTGOMERY) my own, JAS. CONNER,
JOS. SHELTON, ANDREW WRIGHT, PETER MARTIN. Wit: as above.

Page 484. 10 Nov 1794. SAML. SPENCER, Buckingham Co, to JAS. MAYS, AC,
          for Ł150, 500 acres Tye. Lines: JOS. MAYS, CHAS. YANCEY, JAS.
MAYS, WM. CABELL, WM. ALFORD. Wit: GIDEON CREWS, SAML. EDMONDS, WM. BURKS,
ROWLAND EDMONDS, HENRY MASSIE. Orig. del. 28 Jul 1796 to MOSES MAYS.

Page 485. 2 Aug 1794. PETER JOHNSON, AC, to WM. KENNEY, AC, for Ł11-9-4,
          cow & calf; mare about 5 next spring, 2 beds. Wit: WM. POWELL,
NATHAN BARNETT.

Page 485. 10 Dec 1794. LARKIN SANDIDGE & wife MARY, AC, to JACOB PHIL-
          LIPS, AC, for Ł40, 54 acres S fork Buffalo. Lines: JAS. HIG-
GINBOTHAM, his own, just over the branch, ISAAC MAYFIELD, AARON HIGGIN-
BOTHAM. Pat. to grantor.

Page 486. 5 Aug 1794. Order to AC J.P.'s ZACH. TALIAFERRO & JNO. HORS-
          LEY, to quiz BETHEMIAH HYLTON, wife of GEO., 13 Jun 1794, deed
to WM. CAMDEN, AC, 113½ acres. Done, 8 Nov 1794.

Page 487. 18 Jan 1795. REUBEN PENDLETON, AC, to CHRISTOPHER FLETCHER,
          AC, for Ł110, 127 acres Rutledge Creek. Part of tract of RICH.
JONES. Lines: Lynch Road, WIATT POWELL, JOS. CREWS, S branch N fork Rut-
ledge, confluence with N fork of Rutledge, mouth of the Bigg (sic) Hill
Spring Branch. Surveyed 14 Sep 1790.

Page 488. 5 Apr 1794. JNO. THOMAS, AC, to GALT & GARLAND, 5 sh, Deed of
          Trust - stock & furniture. Wit: SAML. MEGHEE, CHRISTIAN MUMMER.

Page 489. 19 Jan 1795. DANL. WHITE & wife SUSANNAH, AC, to JNO. SARGANT,
          Louisa, for Ł150, 400 acres Buffalo. Pat. to AARON TRUEHART,
20 Sep 1759. Orig. del.

Page 490. 1 Sep 1794. BENJ. MARTIN, AC, to JAS. EDMONDS, AC, for Ł30-
          14-1, cattle, furniture, stock. Deed of Trust. Wit: JNO.
CONNERS, WM. EDMONDS.

Page 491. 17 Oct 1794. ISAAC WRIGHT & wife SUSANNA, AC, to ABRAHAM CAR-
          TER, AC, for Ł100, 124 acres Horsley Creek. Lines: PHILIP PEY-
TON, NELSON CRAWFORD. Wit: WM. HALL, PHILIP SMITH, PHILIP LOCKHART, ZACH.
DAWSON, JNO. GOODRICH. Orig. del. to grantee, 7 Mar 1796.

Page 492. AA 24 Nov 1794. JNO. STEWART, exr. of DANL. BURFORD - to JAS.
          BURFORD, MARY GOODWIN, JOS. GOODWIN, JNO. BURFORD, Jr., DANL.
BURFORD SR, ELIZ. GOODWIN. JAS. CREWS signed as legatee. Wit: PHILIP
THURMOND, THOS. ANDERSON.

Page 493. 23 Aug 1794. JOS. HOUSEWRIGHT, AC, to JNO. SPITFATHAM - bed,
          trunk, etc. Orig. del. to JS - WM. DUNCAN, 1796.

Page 494. 19 Jan 1795. RANDAL BIBB, AC, to JNO. ALFORD, AC, for Ł40,
          35 acres by late survey, both sides Naked Creek. Part of tract
of WM. BIBB, dec'd. Lines: his own, ROLAND EDMONDS, JNO. THOMPSON. Wit:
WM. MATTHEWS, MARTIN BIBB JR, JNO. WRIGHT.

Page 495. 19 Jan 1795. JOS. MONTGOMERY & wife JANE, AC & Par. to JAS.
          WOODS of same, for Ł200, 155 acres Lynch Creek, part of tract
of SAML. WOODS, dec'd, and by him devised to his son, WM. WOODS, dec'd,
and lot drawn by JANE WOODS, wife of JOS. MONTGOMERY. Lines: lot of BAR-
BARA WOODS, lot of ELIZ. WOODS. Wit: JAS. BROOKS, RICH. PERKINS, JNO.
PEMBERTON.

Page 496. 20 Jan 1794. GEO. MARTIN & wife BARBARA, Alb., to JAS. WOODS,
          AC, (Orig. del. to JAS. WOODS, 12 Feb 1802) for Ł250, portion
allotted BARBARA, as legatee of SAML. WOODS on part devised to WM. WOODS,
dec'd; as also SARAH WOODS, widow of SAML. WOODS, dec'd. Lynch Creek &
lot of JANE, wife of JOS. MONTGOMERY - about 95 acres known as Mill Tract.

Also Rockfish tract includes meeting House. Lines: THOS. PATANT, HUDSON MARTIN, JNO. MURREL, est. of JAS. DINWIDDIE, dec'd, JNO. MORRISON, THOS. MORRISON, lot drawn by JAS. WOODS, legatee of SAML. WOODS of lands devised to WM. & SARAH WOODS, dec'd. Wit: JAS. BROODS as to Mrs. MARTIN only; RICH. PERKINS -ditto; JNO. PEMBERTON.

Page 497.   3 Dec 1794.   JAS. MONTGOMERY from JNO. MORAN & JNO. BARNETT, all of AC, for Ł130, 166 acres Hatt Creek. Lines: RICH. DOPSON. Wit: JNO. SHIELDS, SAML. FITZPATRICK, OSBON COFFEY.

Page 498.   28 Jul 1794.   MARTIN BIBB JR, AC, to JNO. ALFORD, AC, for Ł60, negro boy, Sammy, about 13; bed, cow, etc. Wit: WM. MATTHEWS, RANDOLPH BIBB,, JNO. WRIGHT.

Page 498.   5 Aug 1793.   Order to AC J.P.'s: HUGH ROSE & wife CAROLINE MATILDA, 15 Jul 1793, to WM. MOSS. Done 20 May 1793, by JOS. BURRUS & JAS. WOODS.

Page 499.   15 Feb 1794.   JNO. MERRITT, AC, to son, THOS., AC, Power of Atty as to dispute over slave, Bob, about 20, taken fraudently from JNO. by one JNO. WALKER from 1 Mar 1791, until now. Wit: JAS. LASHWELL, JNO. HANSARD, WM. BROWN, PHILLIP JOHNSON, PLEDGE PARMER.

Page 500.   16 Feb 1795.   NICHL. CABELL & wife HANNAH, AC, to son WM., AC, for love & support & 5 sh, (Orig. sent 17 Jul 1822, to WM. H. CABELL) 2 tracts which NC bought of WM. RAY. 1) both sides Gilbert Ck. Lines: WM. MAYS, now N.C.'s; 343 acres. 2) Branches of Gilbert Creek. Lines: his own, crossing 2 branches. 80 acres. Someone has written: "Is this a second instrument?" Rec. 16 Feb 1795.

Page 501.   20 Jan 1795.   WM. MEREDITH & wife SALLY, Campbell Co. to STEPHEN WATTS, AC, (Orig. del. to SW, 24 Feb 1795) for Ł150, 400 acres Tye. Lines: STEPHEN WATTS, WM. SPENCER, main road, head of small branch, S branch Tye, new road dividing the mt. to rolling road on top of the mt. Wit: REUBEN THORNTON, DRURY BELL(?), HENRY & BETSY CHRISTIAN, CURDELLAH WATTS.

Page 502.   16 Feb 1795.   NICHL. CABELL & wife HANNAH, AC, to WM. HARE & wife ELIZ, for 5 sh, 693 acres S branch Tye and S side; S fork Castle Creek. Lines: JNO. ROSE, JAS. DICKIE, BENJ. CAMDEN et al.

Page 503.   28 Jun 1794.   JNO. M. GRIFFIN & RO. WRIGHT, AC, to WM. WEDDERBOURN, AC, for Ł26-9, hogs, beds, carpenter's tools, gun etc. Deed of Trust; if not repaid to be advertised at Amherst C.H., 28 Aug next. Wit: JAS. LOVING, BENJ. POWELL. Gun delivered.

Page 504.   16 Feb 1795.   JAS. LASHELL, AC, to PETTIS THACKER, AC, for Ł30, 15 acres. Lines: JNO. HANSARD, Lynch road, MORFUT(?), JNO. WARD.

Page 504.   21 Sep 1794.   REUBEN THORNTON, AC, to HUGH ROSE & WM. WEDDEBOURN, AC, - named slaves - 5 sh. Deed of Trust; debt due FRENCH STRAWTHER, Culpeper. Wit: JNO. HIGGINBOTHAM, JR, WM. TEASE.

Page 505.   15 Feb 1795.   NEH. ROSELL & wife ANNA, AC, to CHAS. JOHNSON, Campbell, for Ł95, 50 acres where NR lately lived. Lines: lower edge BURFORD's old field by side of a branch that has its source in the said old field; east side Bolling's Creek. (Note: This ROZELL name is spelled variously in deeds, but interests me. My wife descends from REUBEN STIVERS who reputedly married SARAH ROZELL in Albany, N.Y. area. He enlisted from Orange in Va. and I wonder if the Orange areas are confused. I can get no proof that EDWD. STIVERS who married BETSY ALDRIDGE in Madison Co, Ky, was son of REUBEN. EDWD. later married BETSY HAPPY, byt my wife's line is by SIDNEY STIVERS who was only child of first marriage. BFD)

Page 506.   3 Jan 1795.   THOS. LLEWELLYNE LACKMERE WALL & wife SALLY, AC, to GEO. DILLARD, AC, (Orig. del. to GD 17 Apr 1796) for Ł60, 50 acres S branches Tye and Stovall's road; part of tract of HUGH ROSE, dec'd. Lines: STOVALL's old road; Col. WM. CABELL JR; crossing Camp

Creek, a road, STOVALL's new road since discontinued by Ct. order. Wit:
WM. PENN, JOS. BURRUS, WIATTE SMITH, JONES REID. Page 507, order to AC
J.P.'s to quiz SALLY, 3 Jan 1795. Done, 16 Feb 1795, by WM. WARE & JOS.
BURRUS.

Page 508.   16 Feb 1795.   JNO. BARNETT, AC, freedom to Tobias, a negro man,
            for Ł30. Orig. del. to TOBIAS, 8 Sep 1795.

Page 508.   16 Feb 1795.   WM. WARWICK & WM. CABELL JR, attys. for JNO.
            BOUSH, AC, to ELISHA ESTES for Ł273, 455 acres branches Ruck-
ers Run. Lines: ABRAHAM WARWICK, his old line, WM. CABELL, CUTHBERT WEBB,
CARROL EADES.

Page 509.   8 Jul 1794.   HENDRICK ARNOLD, Laurence (sic) Co, S.C., to THOS.
            POWELL, AC, for Ł102-10, 288 acres both sides Stone House
Creek, part of a tract of HA & formerly deeded to THOS. POWELL & not ful-
ly proven in AC. Lines: CHAS. CARTER, JNO. MARR, STEPHEN CASH, JNO. CASH.
Wit: JNO. TALIAFERRO, DAVID S. GARLAND, PEACHY FRANKLIN. Memo: THOS.
POWELL rel. claim to 557 acres not fully proven.

Page 511.   20 Jan 1795.   JNO. STEWART, AC, Power of Atty. to friend,
            DAVID S. GARLAND, AC, to recover for me of WM. RICHEY & THOS.
LEWIS by bond to me on Botetourt suit and to receive from Col. JNO. CA-
BELL, Buckingham, for a debt on contract. Wit: ZACH. DAWSON, HENRY DAWSON,
JNO. PHILLIPS, PHILLIP GOOCH. Orig. del. to DSG 9 Jul 1803.

Page 512.   16 Dec 1795.   JNO. AMBLER, James City, to ISAAC TINSLEY, AC,
            (Sent to IT 2 Mar 1812) for Ł12, 12 acres. Lines: TINSLEY, &
fronting present dwelling - Major RICH. HARRISON. Wit: WILL CABELL JR,
N. CABELL.

Page 513.   21 Jul 1794.   DRURY BOWMAN & wife SARAH, AC, to JANE DAVIS for
            Ł50, 250 acres S side and joining Dancing Creek. Lines: JOS.
CABELL, RO. PEYTON, S bank. Wit: ZACH, WM. & JNO. TALIAFERRO.

Page 514.   16 Feb 1795.   WM. BUSTER & wife MARY, to GEO. CABELL for Ł60,
            127 acres known as MOFFET's Old Field. Lines: Major WOODS, WM.
CLARKE - BUSTER & wife entitled to it by decree of AC Court. Wit: PHILLIP
JOHNSON, SAML. MEREDITH, RO. HOLLOWAY.

Page 515.   20 Dec 1794.   WALTER CHRISTIAN, AC, to ISAIAH ATTKERSON, AC,
            for Ł35, 71 acres Rockey Creek (Orig. del. 12 Sep 1816 to IA)
Lines: grantee; JNO. BOLLIN; grantor; near a bridge. Wit: CHAS., HENRY,
& JNO. M. CHRISTIAN.

Page 516.   18 Oct 1794.   JOS. MILSTEAD & wife REBEKEAKEY, AC, to NELSON
            CRAWFORD, AC, for Ł30, 63 acres N fork Horsley; part of a
tract. Wit: JOS. McKEE, ABRAHAM CARTER, STEPHEN SCOBY. Orig. del. to
NC, 18 Sep 1798.

Page 517.   9 Apr 1795.   HENRY TRENT, AC, to GEO. GOODWIN, AC, for 20 sh,
            111 acres. Lines: DAVIS on the river Hill, MICAJAH GOODWIN.
Wit: JNO. B. TRENT, RICH. POWELL, DUDLEY CALLAWAY, THOS. MITCHELL, MICA-
JAH GOODWIN.

Page 517.   18 Apr 1794.   JAS. JOBLING, Alb., to HUDSON MARTIN, AC, for
            Ł30, 391 acres S fork Rockfish. Lines: JAS. MATTHEWS, Beaver
Creek, JOSIAH JOBLING. Wit: RALPH & JAS. JOBLING, WM. MARTIN. Orig. del.
to CHAS. STATHAM, 23 May 1797, per order.

Page 519.   20 Apr 1795.   NELSON CRAWFORD & wife LUCY, AC, to JOS. McKEE,
            Loudoun Co, for Ł12, 6 acres Horsley. Part of tract. Lines:
grantor. Orig. del. to JM, 2 May 1795.

Page 520.   1 Jun 1782 (sic).   RICH. DAVIS, AC, to LARKIN DAVIS, AC, for
            Ł100, 232 acres N branches N fork Horsley; part of tract.
Lines: WM. DAVIS, grantor. Wit: RICH. TALIAFERRO, PETER CARTER, WM. ED-
WARDS. Final proof by RT, 20 Apr 1795.

Page 521.   1 Jun 1782.   RICH. DAVIS SR, AC, to RICH. DAVIS JR, AC, for

Ь100, 200 acres N branches N fork Horsley. Part of tract. Lines: MOSES
DAVIS, RICH. DAVIS. Wit: as above and final proof as above.

Page 522.   1 Jun 1782.   RICH. DAVIS, AC, to MOSES DAVIS, AC, for Ь100,
            200 acres both sides N fork Horsley, part of tract. Lines:
grantor. Wit: as above and proof as above.

Page 523.   9 Mar 1790.   RO. WRIGHT, son & heir of AUSTIN WRIGHT, dec'd,
            & JESSE WRIGHT, AC, to JAS. COCKE, Alb. (Orig. del. to ALEX.
BROWN, 9 Jun 1832) for Ь20, 60 acres both sides Rucker's Run and adj. Gap
of Fenley Mt. Lines: JNO. HARMER, S side of run. Wit: WILL CABELL JR,
JAS. STEPHENS, CHAS. EDMONDS, JNO. STAPLES. Proved 21 Apr 1795.

Page 524.   8 Jan 1795.   AUGUSTINE SHEPHERD to JNO. HAGGARD for Ь130, 200
            acres Taylor Creek. Lines: DUNCAN McLEATH, with the mt. to the
road, ARCHER McDONALD, MATT. HARRIS, JNO. PUGH. Wit: JNO. BENNETT, WM.
McDONALD, GEO. MARTIN.

Page 525.   18 Oct 1794.   JOS. MILSTEAD & wife REBECCA, AC, to JOS. McKee
            for Ь35, 92 acres N fork Horsley. (Orig. del. to JM 2 May 1795)
Wit: NELSON CRAWFORD, ABRAHAM CARTER, STEPHEN SCOBY.

Page 526.   21 Apr 1795.   WM. LAYNE & wife NANCY, AC, to SAML. ANDERSON,
            Alb., for Ь80, 157 acres both sides Raven Creek; branch of
Buffalo. Lines: WM. CABELL at the Rolling Road, NICHL. CABELL's old sur-
sey. Orig. del. to SA 19 Dec 1795.

Page 527.   9 Mar 1791.   JAS. THOMPSON SR, to sons, JNO. THOMPSON & JAS.
            JR, for love, 360 acres S branches Elk Island Creek. Ack. by
grantor 20 Apr 1795.

Page 528.   20 Apr 1795.   PHILIP THURMOND & wife JUDITH, AC, to WM. PAXTON,
            Rockbridge, for Ь80, 90 acres Pedlar, branch of James. Lines:
Top of the Blue Ridge, his own. Wit: MOSES RUCKER JR(?), WM. THURMOND,
JNO. McCABE, DANL. WHITE, JNO. HIGGINBOTHAM, JAS. McCAMPBELL, P. MARTIN.

Page 529.   1 Jun 1782.   RICH. DAVIS, AC, to WM. DAVIS, AC, for Ь100, 200
            acres N branches N fork Horsley. Lines: Grantor, RICH. DAVIS
JR, MOSES DAVIS. Wit: RICH. TALIAFERRO, PETER CARTER, WM. EDWARDS. Final
proof by TALIAFERRO, 20 Apr 1795.

Page 530.   25 Mar 1795.   Order to NELSON CRAWFORD & DANL. WHITE, AC J.P.s
            to quiz SUSANNA CLARKSON, wife of JNO., as to deed to CHAS.
WATTS, Oct 15, 1792; 3 tracts. 926 acres. Done, 20 Apr 1795.

Page 531.   22 Apr 1795.   JNO. JOHNSON, Tob. Insp., Swan's WH. Bdm: JAS.
            WILLS & JAS. STEPHENS, JR.

Page 531.   21 Sep 1795.   Order to Buckingham J.P.'s CLOUGH SHELTON & CHAS
            YANCEY, to quiz MARY SPENCER, wife of SAML. - 28 Jun 1794,
deed to JOS. MAYS SR, 500 acres. Orig. del. to RO. MAYS. Done 3 Feb 1795.

Page 532.   25 Jun 1795.   SAML. MUREAN (MERRAN - his mark) and wife TABBY,
            AC, to JOS. ROBERTS, AC, for Ь50, 100 acres Davis. Lines:
BARTHOLOMEW MERRAN, RO. GRANT, grantee. Wit: HENRY DAWSON, EDMOND BUR-
NETT, JNO. SHELTON, WM. KNIGHT.

Page 533.   6 Apr 1795.   WM. WHITTEN & wife SARAH, Bedford Co, to JER.
            WHITTEN, AC, for Ь70, 136 acres N side Otter. Lines: JNO. HOG,
his own. Orig. del. to WM. DAVIS per order 28 Jul 1796.

Page 534.   AB 21 Jul 1795.   JAS. HENLY, admr. of SAML. DINWIDDIE. Bdm:
            JOS. MONTGOMERY.

Page 535.   6 Apr 1784 (written above as 1795) JER. WHITTEN, AC, to PETER
            WHITTINGHILL, AC, for Ь70, 182 acres. Lines: JOHNSON, SLED,
the division line. Orig. del. to PW 24 Sep 1796.

Page 536.   16 Apr 1795.   HENRY MARTIN SR, AC, to WM. ALLEN AC, for Ь15,
            50 acres Nassau or Dutch. Lines: late HUGH WILLOUGHBY, ENOCH

NASH. Wit: SPARKS MARTIN, JNO. MOSBY, RICH. STATHAM, JOSHUA WILLOUGHBY, JAS. MARTIN.

Page 538. 19 Jan 1795. JNO. SLAUGHTER, Alb., for regard and "effection" for FRANCES DAWSON, daughter of RO. D. DAWSON, AC, negress, Aggey, & increase. Wit: PLEASANT DAWSON, JAS. LEE, JNO. FRANKLIN.

Page 538. 25 Jun 1795. WM. MARTIN, AC, to WM. HARRIS, AC, for Ŀ10, 100 acres, part of tract surveyed for W.M. on N branch Davis. Lines: WM. HARRIS, J.S.C. FOWLER, SAML. MURRIAN; joins HARRIS' land whereon he lives. Wit: THOLY MERRIAN, CHAS. STATHAM, JNO. SHELTON.

Page 539. 22 Nov 1795. WM. HARRIS DIGGS, AC, to WM. LYON, AC, for Ŀ20, 89 acres. Lines: WM. LYON. Wit: PLEASANT & MARTIN DAWSON, MATT HARRIS.

Page 541. 14 Jun 1795. GEORGE HIGHT, AC, to ABRAHAM SMITH & JNO. SMITH, son of ABRAHAM, Deed of Trust - branch Tye; Colestony (?) Run; part of tract bought by GH from WM. COFFEY; also 1 double geered(sic)mill built on the land for his use. Wit: CAMEL GOODE, JESSE WRIGHT, JER. PHILLIPS.

Page 541. 12 Mar 1795. JAS. MATTHEWS, Stokes Co, N.C., to HUGH & JAS. McCABE of "Co. & State of Va." for Ŀ115, 300 acres both sides Pedlar. Lines: N side Pedlar, crossing it. Wit: WM. MATTHEWS, BENJ. POWELL, JNO. WRIGHT, JNO. ALFORD, JAS. HOLLINGSWORTH, RANDOLPH BIBB.

Page 543. 16 Jan 1795. LEONARD & GEO. CLARK, AC, to CHAS. CHRISTIAN, AC, for Ŀ60, 93 acres Buffalo. Lines: CHRISTIAN, ISBELL, near BRAXTON ridge, JNO. CHRISTIAN, a small branch. Part of tract of JOS. WILCHER, dec'd. & willed by him to son, CHAS. WILCHER; subject to widow's life interest - BARBARY WILCHER - sold with this encumbrance and sold to CLARKS by CHAS.; still holds. Wit: JOS. DAVENPORT, ISAIAH ATKERSON, WM. CHRISTIAN, DANL. & GEO. SCRADER. Memo: CHRISTIAN takes title of CLARKS as they did of WILCHER.

Page 544. 20 Jul 1795. JNO. CHRISTIAN & wife JUDITH, AC, to CHAS. CHRISTIAN, AC, for Ŀ20, 300 acres surveyed for both of them, 3 May 1780, and pat. to them, 10 Apr 1781. Branches of Creek. Lines: GEO. HYLTON, WM. HORSLEY dec'd, ELIZ. EVANS, JNO. VIA, dec'd, JNO. SWANSON (formerly REUBEN TYRE), JNO. OLDS. Wit: JACOB G. PEARCE, HENRY STONEHAM, JAS. TURNER. Del. to WALTER CHRISTIAN, Jr, 15 Dec 1798.

Page 545. 12 May 1795. CHAS. CHRISTIAN & wife SARAH; NOTLEY WARREN MADDOX & wife FANNY; JNO. CHRISTIAN & wife JUDITH to JACOB GAROON PEARCE, all of AC, for Ŀ220, 423 acres S side Buffalo (Orig. del. to JP 11 May 1796) Lines: STOVALL's old road, JACOB PEARCE, WILCHER's branch, WM. DILLARD, MIGGINSON's road, below OWNSBY's Cabbins. Wit: JACOB PEIRCE, CHAS. CHRISTIAN, CHAS. DAVENPORT.

Page 546. 3 Jul 1795. RICH. COLEMAN POLLARD, Alb., from WM. FITZPATRICK & wife REBECCA, AC, Ŀ150, 420 acres Head of Dutch Creek and branches; SW side of the horseshoe or Rocky Mt., where grantor now lives. 3 tracts adj. 1) 170 acres conveyed to WF from his father, THOS. late of Alb. 2) 170 acres conveyed to WF by his brother, JNO. FITZPATRICK - 1 & 2 pat. to THOS. FITZPATRICK at Williamsburg 7 Jul 1763, rec. in Secretary's Office and then called a Colony. 50 acres of 1 & 2 excepted for WF sold to JAS. WOODS & is part of POLLARD's own tract - conveyed to him by his father-in-law, JAS. HOPKINS and adjs. 3) 130 acres conveyed to WF by deed from JNO. STAPLES, 1793, and part of tract sold by JS to HENRY MARTIN & adjs. Wit: JNO. M. GRIFFIN, CHAS. MARTIN, JAS. HOPKINS.

Page 549. 21 Jul 1795. CHAS. ROSE about 22 Jun 1790 conveyed to CHAS. IRVING, PATRICK ROSE, WM. S. CRAWFORD, & EDMOND FONTAIN or survivors in trust all of his estate. CRAWFORD & PATRICK ROSE are survivors & trustees to CHAS. WATTS - 606 acres for Ŀ454-10. SALLY, wife of CHAS ROSE, has not rel. dower, but joins - does not sign - N side Tye; part of tract. Lines: LUCAS POWELL, JNO. THOMPSON, small branch to confluence with Tye; JAS. DILLARD, JAS. MAYS. Wit: JAS. PENN, RO. HOLLOWAY, GEO. DILLARD.

Page 551. 13 Jul 1794. JOS. CABELL & wife MARY, Buckingham Co, to WM.
BURKS, AC, for Ⱡ50, 320 acres branches Maple & Cedar Creeks of
Pedlar. Pat. 20 Aug 1792. Lines: BURFORD's Roaling road(sic), his own,
RO. DAVIS dec'd, JOSIAH JOBLING, JNO. GOODRIDGE, JAS. NOWLING. Wit: CHAS.
YANCEY, JOS. CABELL JR, W.H. CABELL, GIDEON CREWS, RO. RIVES.

Page 552. 13 Mar 1795. JAS. HOPLINS, AC, to RICH. COLEMAN POLLARD &
wife ELIZ. BOUSH, Alb., 5 sh., 600 acres SW side Horse Shoe
Mt. & head of Dutch Creek. 3 adj. tracts. 1) to JH from JOSIAS WOOD &
wife RHODA, Feb, 1777 - 455 acres. 2) 70 acres to JH from JNO. WOOD, 2
deeds, some years ago. 3) 76 acres pat. to JH from Comm. 13 May 1785.
Wit: HENRY MARTIN SR, JAS. MARTIN, THOS. FITZPATRICK, JAS. JOPLING.(Note:
See my "H" wills for will of JAS. HOPKINS. It is one of the most interesting documents in AC will books. POLLARD was his son-in-law and JH had
"less than no use" for him. He baits POLLARD's son to change his name to
HOPKINS and the boy did so. BFD)

Page 553. 29 Jun 1795. CHAS. CHRISTIAN & wife SARAH, AC, to JACOB
PEARCE, AC, for Ⱡ87-10, 125 acres Buffalo. Lines: STOVALL's
old road, Wilcher's Branch, JACOB GARRON PEARCE; part of tract. Wit:
BYRD HENDRICK, JAS. CHRISTIAN, HENRY CHRISTIAN. Orig. del. to grantee
11 (15) May 1796.

Page 554. 10 Jul 1795. NOTLEY W. MADDOX & wife FANNY, acknowledged deed
to --- also to JNO. CHRISTIAN & wife JUDITH, also CHAS. CHRIS-
TIAN.

Page 555. 20 Jul 1795. JNO. WRIGHT & wife SUSANNAH, AC, to WM. LEE
HARRIS, AC, for Ⱡ140, 140 acres S branch Rucker's Run; part
of tract of WM. BIBB, dec'd. Lines: WM. LOVING, THOS. BIBB, RO. WRIGHT,
WM. BIBB dec'd, LOMAX's old line. Orig. del. to WH, Jan, 1797.

Page 556. 24 Sep 1792. JNO. KESTERSON & wife REBECCA, AC, to OSBORN
COFFEY, AC, for Ⱡ30, 230 acres Dutch Creek. Lines: ENOCH NASH,
his own, ABRAHAM WARWICK. Wit: JAS. MONTGOMERY, JNO. JOHNSON, GREENBERRY
LANNUM.

Page 557. 20 Jul 1795. JAS. BIBB JR, AC, to THOS. HAWKINS, AC, for Ⱡ200,
200 acres branches of Ruckers Run; N branch Tye. Part of tract
of WM. BIBB, dec'd. Lines: TANDY JOHNSON, WM. BIBB, dec'd.

Page 558. 26 Mar 1795. REUBEN THORNTON & wife MILDRED, AC, to JNO. LOV-
ING, Jr, AC, for Ⱡ368, 800 acres Tye & Buffalo. Lines: mouth
of Buffalo; road at the old muster field Ford, Spring along a valley to
Higginbotham's road; STEPHEN WALL, crossing Raven Creek, road leading
from WM. SPENCER's to where RT formerly lived; road leading to mouth of
Buffalo until it gets to top of the Mt., new ford at Gulph on Tye, chopt
line. Order, page 559, to quiz MILDRED, same date. Done, 8 Apr 1795, by
NICHL. CABELL & WM. WARWICK when they assembled "at the House of REUBEN
THORNTON in the Town of Warminster".

Page 559. 24 Feb 1795. WM. MEREDITH & wife SALLY, Campbell Co; SAML.
MEREDITH & wife JANE, AC, to REUBEN THORNTON, AC, for Ⱡ390,
700 acres fork of Tye and Buffalo. Lines: Mouth of Raven Creek, STEPHEN
WATT's old line, Rolling Road leading to mouth of Buffalo and with it to
top of the Mt.; new line marked by JNO. LOVING, S side Tye. Wit: NICHL.
CABELL, W.S. CRAWFORD, P. GOOCH, CHAS. ELLIS, STEPHEN WATTS, JAS. FRANK-
LIN as to Col. MEREDITH.

Page 560. 24 Feb 1795. Order to Campbell Co. J.P.'s SACKVILLE KING &
THOS. HUMPHREYS to quiz SALLY MEREDITH as to deed above. Done,
28 Feb 1795. Page 561, Another order on same date to same J.P.'s to quiz
SALLY, wife of WM. MEREDITH, as to deed, 20 Jan 1795, to STEPHEN WATTS.
Page 562, order to AC J.P.'s, 24 Apr 1794, to quiz MILDRED THORNTON, wife
of REUBEN as to 12 Oct 1793 deed to JOS. STAPLES, AC - 588 acres. Done,
8 Apr 1795, by NICHL. CABELL & WM. WARWICK.

Page 563. 25 Jun 1795. WM. MARTIN, AC, to THOLEY MERRIAN, AC, for Ⱡ20,
119 acres David Creek. Pat. to W.M. 27 Nov 1794. Wit: HENRY
DAWSON WM. DAWSON, EDMOND BARNETT or BURNETT(?), SAML. MERRIAN.

Page 564. 18 Apr 1795. Order to Elbert Co, Ga. J.P.'s JNO. ROGERS, SAML.
NELSON, BARNABAS PACE, & THOMAS SCOTT to quiz MARY WARE, wife
of JNO., 8 Jan 1793 deed to JNO. CALRKSON, Va. 400 acres. Done by ROGERS
& NELSON 20 May 1795. Orig. del. to JC 7 Dec 1798.

Page 565. 19 Nov 1793. WM. WALTON, AC, to JOS. ROBERTS, AC, for Ŀ140,
3 tracts N branch Rucker's Run & Ragged Mt. 1) 42 acres pat.
to JNO. LOVING JR 5 Jun 1765. Lines: Col. LOMAX, his own, top of a mt.,
JNO. LOVING JR. conveyed to JNO. TUGGLE. 2) 40 3/4 acres granted to him
by deed 5 Oct 1767, from LUNSFORD LOMAX Jr. 3) 72 acres pat. to JNO. TUG-
TLE 1 May 1775. Lines: his own, JNO. MONTGOMERY, JNO. LOVING JR, ABRAHAM
SEAY, top of the mt. Wit: WM. CHAMBERLAIN, BENJ. HENDERSON, EDDY FORTUNE,
THOS. FORTUNE. Receipt by WM. WALTON of TILMAN WALTON, 19 Nov 1793, of
Ŀ140. Orig. del. to JAS. SEAY JR.

Page 567. 21 Nov 1794. JAS. TRUSLER(AR) & wife SUSANNAH, AC, to WM. FOX,
AC, for Ŀ24, 40 acres Head of Indian Branch. Lines: JNO. HEN-
DERSON, SAML. FOX, WM. WILSON. Wit: JNO. MARTIN, WM. CHURCH, CHAS. STA-
PLES, JAS. HUNDLEY. Orig. del. 20 Sep 1796 to WF.

Page 568. 18 Feb 1795. CHAS. TYLER, AC, to JNO. CAMPBELL, AC, for Ŀ12,
24 acres N side Indian Creek, branch of Pina River. Lines:
Said TILER(sic), said CAMPBELL. Wit: JAS. FULCHER, JNO. PHILIPS, J---(?)
REID, WM. LANGHORN. Orig. del. to JC 12 Dec 1798.

Page 569. 19 Apr 1795. GEO. GILLESPIE & wife MARY, AC, to THOS. WILLS,
AC, for Ŀ87, 220 acres surveyed 28 May 1788, S side Shoe Ck,
branch of N fork Piney. Lines: S fork Shoe Creek. Orig. del. to TW, 5
Jun 1797.

Page 570. 6 Apr 1795. WM. WHITTON & wife SARAH, Bedford Co, to JER.
WHITTEN, AC, for Ŀ120, 380 acres branches Thomas Mill Creek &
waters of Otter Creek. Lines: JAS. KITCHEN, JNO. HOG, RO. JOHNSON, HUGH
MORRIS.

Page 572. 20 Jul 1795. WM. HALL & wife MARY, AC, to PULLIAM SANDIDGE,
AC, for Ŀ92, 254 acres branches Buffalo on South Mt. Lines:
ISAAC MAYFIELD.

Page 573. 30 Sep 1794. HUGH ROSE & wife CAROLINE MATILDA, AC, to RO.
HENRY ROSE, their eldest son, for love and 5 sh, 1000 acres
Harris Creek and where JAS. BOWLING now lives; formerly that of HENRY
ROSE. Wit: SAML. IRVINE, RO. AUSTIN, THOS. WORTHAM.

Page 574. 13 Sep 1794. Order to AC J.P.'s WM. HARRIS & JOS. SHELTON, to
quiz MILDRED WITT, wife of WM. - deed of same date to JOS.
ROBERTS - 500 acres. Done 8 Oct 1794.

Page 575. 1 Feb 1795. JACOB KINNEY & wife ANN, Augusta, to RO. DOUTHAT,
Augusta, for Ŀ100, 80 acres. Lines: a branch, JAS. CHRISTIAN,
DAVID PATTERSON. Also 180 acres. Lines: JAS. CHRISTIAN, HENRY BELL,
LARKIN GATEWOOD. JK bought it 2 Nov 1790, of IGNATIOUS RAINS & wife ANN.
Wit: WM. CHAMBERS, D.S. UPSHAW, JNO. BOWYAR, JNO. (?) ALLEN. Margin
blurred. Orig. sent to JNO. CONNER(?) by J. DARTER(?) present owner.

Page 576. 21 Sep 1795. WM. SPENCER AC, Power of Atty to friend, JAS.
ROBERTS, GRanville Co, N.C., to receive title from JNO. MAR-
SHALL of same N.C. county, which WS bought of J.M. Del.to BELDWIN BEAN
by verbal order from WS.

Page 576. 21 Sep 1795. WM. & JNO. LOVING, exrs. of WM. LOVING, dec'd,
AC, to JOS. BARNETT, Madison Co, Ky (Orig. del to JNO. LOVING
Jr. 7 Oct 1795) JB to survey certain lands by location of WM. LOVING,
dec'd. If not done by a Mr. Sullivan and pat. - formerly employed, but no
contracts. JB is to get 1/3 for trouble and pay 1/3 of expenses. Wit:
WM. HARRIS, JOS. SHELTON.

Page 577. 21 Sep 1795. OSBORN COFFEY & wife MARY, AC, to THOS. NASH
(del. to JNO. MARTIN, per order of NASH, 21 Jul 1798) for
Ŀ37-10, 230 acres pat. 7 Apr 1784. Dutch Ck. Lines: ENOCH NASH, HENRY

MARTIN.

Page 579. 16 Sep. 1795. JNO. MAYS & wife FRANKEY, AC, to PETER CASH, AC, for Ł100, 150 acres Stonehouse Creek. Lines: CHAS. TUCKER on N, MAYS on W, JOS. BOND on S, STEPHEN CASH on E. Wit: BENJ. TALIAFERRO, WM. STATON, JAS. MAYS.

Page 579. 29 Apr 1795. GEO. WITT & wife ELIZ, AC, to CHRISTIAN BENNER - indexed BANNER - for Ł225, 200 acres S branch Rockfish. Lines: JOS. STRICKLINE, JNO. WITT, ELISHA WITT, MORRIS HUGHES. Wit: JNO. WITT, MOSES HUGHES, HENRY BENNER.

Page 581. 21 Jun 1795. JNO. WITT & wife ELIZ, AC, to MOSES HUGHES, AC, for Ł500, 220 acres S fork Rockfish. Lines: JOS. WEVER, JOS. STRICKLAND, GEO. WITT, ELISHA WITT, MOSES HUGHES, RICH. ADAMS. Wit: JOS. WEAVER, JNO. HUGHES, JAS. HUGHES, MOSES HUGHES, WM. EDMONDS.

Page 581. 15 Jun 1795. PHILIP BURTON, AC, to GEO. McDANIEL, AC, for Ł300, 300 acres Harris Creek. Formerly that of grantee and by deed to grantor. Wit: RICH. HARRISON, AMBR. RUCKER, GEO. HARRISON.

Page 582. 12 Sep 1795. WM. STATON & wife MARY, AC, to JAS. MAYS, AC, for Ł110, 155 acres N branch Buffalo. (Orig. del. to BENJ. MAYS 28 Nov 1798) Lines: STEPHEN CASH, BENJ. TALIAFERRO, JNO. MAYS, PETER CASH.

Page 583. 21 Sep 1795. JAS. MURPHY, son & heir of SAML. MURPHY dec'd, AC, to JOSIAH WOOD, AC, for Ł145, 162 acres Naked Creek. Lines: BIBB. Wit: JNO. WRIGHT, JNO. SNEAD, SAML. WOOD (JAS. WOOD erased and SAML. written below in one place and over in another). Orig. del. to JNO. HIGGINBOTHAM by written order, 24 Apr 1797.

Page 584. 21 Sep 1795. CHAS. WATTS & wife ELIZ, AC, to JNO. THOMPSON, AC, (Orig. del. per order filed to JAS. WOODS, 12 Sep 1798) for Ł285-12, land on branches of Naked Creek, N branch Tye. Part of tract of CHAS. ROSE now in possession of CHAS. WATTS, formerly that of GEO. GILLESPIE & exchanged to CHAS. ROSE. Lines: Road from CH to ford at JNO. DILLARD's small Island, JAS. DILLARD, JAS. MAYS, JNO. THOMPSON. Part of 606 acres conveyed by CHAS. & PATRICK ROSE, WM. SID CRAWFORD, trustees for CHAS. ROSE, 1795. Wit: GEO. DILLARD, WM. TEAS.

Page 586. 5 Mar 1795. BALLINGER WADE, Franklin Co, to MARTIN PARKS, AC, for Ł47, 94 acres Clarks Creek. Lines: NICHL. DAVIES, his own. Wit: JAS. WAUGH, JNO. HILL JR, ELLIOT BROWN. Orig. del. to MARTIN PARKS 4 Aug 1796.

Page 587. 18 Mar 1795. WM. WEDDEBOURN, AC, to GEO. DILLARD, AC, for Ł267-5-7, penal note, this day, Deed of Trust - 5 sh. 164 acres both sides Piney. Lines: Pat. from Gov. of Va. to WW, 16 Jun 1789, also 506 acres. Lines: HENRY MARTIN, LANDON CABELL, ashivill tract, WM. PURVIS, WM. BLAIR, WM. JOHNSON, ALLEN BLAIR, HUGH WILLOUGHBY, JOSHUA WILLOUGHBY. Tract on Indian Creek; by entry. Lines: JONES JOY; two tracts on Tye and all that he has there. 1) 335 acres. 2) 384 acres. Also named slaves - to satisfy ALEX. BRYDIE & Co. for 12 months. Wit: JNO. HIGGINBOTHAM JR, EZEK. HILL, CHAS. MARTIN, CHAS. TALIAFERRO JR.

Page 588. 19 Sep 1795. THOS. BECKNELL & wife ELIZ; JNO. BECKNELL & wife ANN, AC, to JOS. SMITH, AC, for Ł50, 200 acres both sides Dutch. Lines: Near the old apple orchard, JOS. SMITH, a fence, near Trible fall Creek, JAS. TURNER, JNO. MATTHEWS, THOS. BECKNELL, Spring Branch. Wit: DANL. DUNNCAN, LEONARD PHILLIPS, JNO. MATTHEWS.

Page 589. 21 Sep 1795. JESSE HARRIS, AC, Power of Atty to WM. LEE HARRIS, AC, to recover sum from JNO. SHELTON, AC,.

Page 590. 2 Jul 1794. HENDRICK ARNOLD, Laurens Co, SC, to BENJ. POWELL, AC, for Ł102-10, 292 acres both sides Stone House Creek. Lines: AARON HIGGINBOTHAM, HOWARD CASH, CHAS. CARTER, upper lot, JNO. CASH, MOSES MARTIN. Wit: SEYMOUR POWELL, HENRY BIBB, RANDOLPH BIBB.

Page 591. 21 Sep 1795. JOHNSON BEAN & wife HANNAH, AC, to JACOB PEARCE,
AC, (blank sum) 200 acres N side Buffalo. Lines: DILLARD's
road, JESSE KENNEDY, JNO. CHRISTIAN, EVANS' Spring Branch. Orig. del. to
JP, 11 May 1796.

Page 592. 30 Apr 1794. ISAAC DARNEILL to WM. TEASE, WM. WEDDEBOURN,
LEWIS NEVIL & SEYMOUR POWELL - 5 sh. Slave, Lewis, boy, Alex,
carriage and 3 horses. MATT. HARRIS, AC, has instituted suit vs. me in
County Court for ₺105. Deed of Trust. Wit: WM. H. DIGGS. (I am told
that DARNEILL was an early rector in AC. BFD)

Page 593. 3 Jan 1793. JNO. LOCKHARD, AC, to PHILIP LOCKHARD, for ₺8,
one mare & cow. Wit: ANDERSON MOSS, JNO. BLAN(sic). Final
proof by JNO. BLAND 21 Sep 1795.

Page 594. 3 Sep 1795. ELIZ. DAVIS, widow of JNO. DAVIS dec'd, AC; DAVID
DAVIS & wife FRANCES - DAVID, son of JNO. - FRANCES signed,
but no JNO. save here - to EBINEZER HAYCOCK, AC, 5 sh. All of ELIZABETH's
rights under will of PHILIP DAVIS and DAVID also does the same - where
ELIZ. now lives - 100 acres. Lines: PHILIP DAVIS' survey. Admitted to
record, 1 Oct 1787(sic). FRANCES, wife of DAVID, rel. dower. Orig. del.
to grantee, 14 Feb 1798.

Page 594. 18 May 1795. Order to AC J.P.'s SAML. MEREDITH & JOS. BURRUS
to quiz NANCY, wife of JNO. LACKEY - 22 Nov 1793 deed by JNO.
& wife; RACHEL AYRES, & EVE LACKEY to SAML. (LEMUEL?) LACKEY. Done, 21
Sep 1795.

Page 595. 21 Sep 1795. PETER CLARKSON - Power of Atty to HIRAM McGINNIS,
AC, to receive all sums from estate of JNO. CLARKSON, Alb. Co,
and from any persons in AC for mares with JNO. CLARKSON' stud horse,
Matchless. Wit: WILL LOVING, DAVID CLARKSON.

Page 596. 18 Sep 1795. THOS. NASH, AC, to GREENBERRY LANHAM, AC, for
₺5, 30 acres S side Marrowbone Mt. & Dutch Creek. Part of pat.
to TN 2 Dec 1785 - E end divided by new line in presence of WM. MARTIN
between themselves. Lines: NASH, WALTER KING.

Page 597. 21 Sep 1795. BENJ. POWELL & wife JANE, AC, to JNO. THOMPSON,
AC, for ₺131-8, 292 acres both sides Stone House Creek. Part
of tract of HENDRICK ARNOLD. Lines: AARON HIGGINBOTHAM, HOWARD CASH,
dec'd, CHAS. CARTER, his own lines, MOSES MARTIN. Granted by deed to BP
from HENDRICK ARNOLD, 2 Jul 1794. Orig. del. to NAHTL. OFFUTT, agt. for
JT, 19 Oct 1801.

Page 598. 10 Jun 1795. GIDEON VIA, Buckingham Co, to DANL. PERROW, AC,
for ₺80, 72½ acres both sides N fork of Fishing Creek. Grant-
or's one fourth part of 290 acres granted to JNO. VIA by pat., 1 Sep
1780; includes plantation whereon - at lower end - grantor formerly lived. Wit: JNO. HORSLEY, N. POWELL, WM. CHURCK, RO. B. HILL(HARE?). CHURK
not plain.

Page 599. 7 May 1795. THOS. RICKETS & wife JANE, AC, to CALEB SHINAULT,
AC, (To THOS. A EDWARDS, present owner, 4 Jan 1850) for ₺20,
49 acres. Lines: Begins at Oposom Island road. Wit: JOS. BURRUS, ZACH.
DAWSON, JNO. McDANIEL, DUDLEY CALLAWAY.

Page 600. 19 Oct 1795. JAS. TURNER, AC, Power of Atty to my loving &
trusty friend, JNO. TURNER, AC, - sums due me in Ky. & to sell
or transfer any property there. Orig. del. to JNO. TURNER.

Page 601. 20 Oct 1795. JAS. TURNER, JR, AC, admr. of STEPHEN TURNER,
dec'd, AC, Power of Atty to my true friend, JNO. TURNER, AC,
to sell Ky. land of STEPHEN TURNER.

Page 602. 16 Oct 1795. Order to AC J.P.'s SAML. MEREDITH & JOS. BURRUS,
to quiz FRANCES PENDLETON, wife of REUBEN - 18 Jan 1795, deed
to CHRISTOPHER FLETCHER - 177 acres. Done 16 Oct 1795. Orig. del. to
CF, 10 Nov 1796.

Page 603. 12 Oct 1795. CHAS. SNELSON, AC, Power of Atty. to trusty
        friend, DANL. BATES, Pitsylvania Co., to recover all monies
due me from treasury of United States due to my dec'd sons, JNO. & CHAS,
for themselves during the late War in the Southern division.

Page 603. 19 Oct 1795. SAML. FRANKLIN & wife RACHEL, AC, to JNO. DUNCAN
        (Orig. del. to SF 9 Dec 1795) for Ⱡ120, 156 acres branches
Beaver Creek. Part of 2000 acres pat. to JOS. & RICH. BALLINGER. Lines:
GEO. SEATON; also 10 acres adj. - part of larger tract which was RICH.
OGLESBY's. Lines: FRANKLIN, WM. OGLESBY. Memo: Graveyard on tract excep-
ted as to FRANKLIN's heirs.

Page 604. 19 Oct 1795. JAS. PENDLETON & wife SARAH, AC, to PETER FRENG-
        ER SR, Augusta, for Ⱡ200. 290 acres Rockfish. Lines: JAS.
BROOKS (formerly GEO. CAMPBELL), JNO. CRISON(?blurred), formerly JNO. Mc-
ANALLY, JAS. ANDERSON, formerly WM. KILE. Orig. del. to JNO. COOPER per
verbal order, 9 Mar 1798.

Page 605. 24 Jun 1795. ISAAC SCOTT & wife NANCY, AC, to JNO. SMITH, AC,
        (Orig. del. to JAS. BROOKS 11 Aug 1800) for Ⱡ70, 100 acres.
Lines: DAVID KINCAID, Thornton's Branch. Wit: JAS. ANDERSON, FO GAIN
KRITZER(CRITZER to one side); JAS. PENDLETON, SAML. McCULACK (McCULLOCH).

Page 606. 14 Apr 1795. NEH. ROZEL, AC, to ARCHIBALD REYNOLDS, Campbell
        Co., for Ⱡ15, 1/2 acre N side Lynch road and near Madison
Twon. Lines: JAS. LATHELL, JNO. HENRY GOODWIN. Wit: GEO. McDANIEL, ANTHO-
NY RUCKER, WM. TINSLEY, JNO. CLAYTON, HENRY ROBINSON, BENJ. GUFFEY, JAS.
LASHWELL (probably LATHELL above).

Page 606. 27 May 1795. NICHL. CABELL & wife HANNAH, AC, to SUSANNA WIL-
        COX, daughter of L(?) WILCOX dec'd, for Ⱡ45, land on N side of
Tye; opposite an Ivy Island; Cedar cliffs of Tye. Wit: GIDEON CREWS, JNO.
JOHNSON, W.B. HARE, WILLIS WILLS, WM. H. CABELL. Orig. del to POWHATAN
BOLLING 23 Nov 1795, to be del. to SW, admrx. of DOC(?) WILCOX, dec'd.

Page 607. 19 Oct 1795. CHAS. WATTS & wife BETSY, AC, to WM. SID CRAW-
        FORD, AC, for Ⱡ500, 300 acres, 390; 236 acres - 926 acres in
all (hard to read) (Orig. del. to WSC) bought by CW of JNO. CLARKSON &
BENJ. HIGGINBOTHAM, 24 Apr 1795(?) both sides of Buffalo & branches of
Franklin Creek on Davis Mt. Lines: ZACH. TALIAFERRO, formerly SAML. HIG-
GINBOTHAM's; JACOB SMITH.

Page 608. 19 Oct 1795. JNO. JACOBS, AC, Power of Atty to JOS. BARNETT,
        Madison Co, Ky, to survey and clear all lands located or en-
tered for me. Wit: DAVID JACOBS, JAS. MONTGOMERY. Ack. by JJ, 19 Oct 1795,
and del. to DAVID JACOBS same date.

Page 609. 26 Jul 1794. RICH. BALLINGER & wife ELIZ, to WM. HALL, AC,
        for Ⱡ30, 250 acres. Lines: DAVID MOORE, Nukleston Run, JAS.
FEAGANS. Pat. to ANGUS McDONALD at Richmond, 20 Jul 1784. Also adj.
tract pat. at Williamsburg, to DAVID MOORE, 15 Jan 1773. Orig. del. to
WH, 30 Oct 1797. Wit: JNO. McCABE, RICH. OGLESBY, LINDSEY MAYS.

Page 610. 29 Aug 1795. Mercer(?) Co, Ky. J.P.'s: RO. MOSBY & BENJ. PER-
        KINS have quizzed ELIZ. BALLINGER & MARTHA McDANIEL apart from
husbands. THOS. ALLEN, Clk of Co, 4 Sep 1795. Not clear writing for
county.

Page 611. 19 Oct 1795. JAS. PENN - Power of Atty. to WM. SID CRAWFORD
        to sign for him as security for my sister, ELIZ. CALLAWAY,
admrx. of JAS. CALLAWAY, dec'd. Wit: REUBEN CRAWFORD, JNO. LOVING JR.

Page 611. 19 Oct 1795. DANL. MAHONE, AC, to WM. BURFORD, AC, for Ⱡ10,
        17 acres adj. grantee's land. Line: The road.

Page 612. 19 Oct 1795. JAS. WATSON, AC, Power of Atty. to ANTHONY DI-
        BRELL JR, Buckingham Co., & CHAS. DIBRELL, Madison Co, Ky, -
true intent of a bond to CHAS. LYNCH SR, & JR, 23 Apr 1794 - to act in
KY. to choose for me 800 acres mentioned in the bond. Wit: GEO. DILLARD,
WIATT SMITH, DAVID S. GARLAND.

Page 613.　3 Jun 1795.　WILSON CARY NICHOLAS & wife MARGARET, Alb., to
　　　　　　JAS. SEAY, AC, (Orig. del. to JS 25 Jan 1796) for ₤105, 210
acres N side Buffalo and joining. Lines: SMYTH TANDY, JOS. STAPLES; part
of a tract. Wit: RO. RIVES, JNO. SNEAD, REUBEN SNEAD, JNO. STAPLES.

Page 614.　30 Mar 1795.　WM. LAYNE to his daughter. MILLY LAYNE - love
　　　　　　and 6 sh, 1 girl, Patience. Wit: JAS. FRANKLIN, REUBEN CRAW-
FORD.

Page 615.　19 Oct 1795.　THOS. BRAGG, AC, to JAS. LASHELLS, AC, for ₤5,
　　　　　　1/2 acre S side Lynch. Orig. del. to C. DABNEY 22 Aug 1827.

Page 616.　19 Oct 1795.　THOS. BRAGG to JAS. LASHELLS as above for ₤20,
　　　　　　6 acres N side Lynch Road. Orig. del. as above.

Page 617.　19 Oct 1795.　JNO. BARNETT, AC, Power of Atty to JOS. BARNETT,
Madison Co, Ky, to receive sums after sale of my Ky. land.

Page 617.　18 Oct 1795.　CARREL EADES & wife BARBARY, AC, to ELISHA ES-
　　　　　　TES, AC, for ₤15, 40 acres Rucker's Run. Lines of grantor &
grantee. (The script here is very small and very poor, too.)

Page 618.　12 Oct 1795.　JOS. LANNUM & wife MARY, AC, to JNO. SANDERS,
　　　　　　AC, for ₤30, 98 acres. Wit: DAVID DUNCKEN, WM. BAILEY, JNO.
MATTHEWS.

Page 619.　1 Aug 1795.　JOS. MAGANN, JR, AC, to PLEASANT MAGANN, AC, for
　　　　　　₤100, 66 acres. Orig. del. to MOSES HALL per order, 1800.

Page 619.　19 Oct 1795.　JNO. STRUTTON & wife MARY, AC, to JNO. HINES JR,
　　　　　　AC, for ₤80, 150 acres. Lines: SMYTH TANDY, WM. SPENCER,
Raccoon Creek, NATHAN HALL, Rolling road, SAML. ANDERSON. Orig. del.
to J. JONES(?), 10 Oct 1803.

Page 620.　27 Aug 1795.　JOS. SMITH, AC, formerly of Cumberland, now
　　　　　　Powhatan, and wife PATIENCE, to WM. FLEMING, Chesterfield -
consideration: 1 slave girl, Betty - at ₤100, 140 acres in Chesterfield,
S side Michaux's Branch and N side Buckingham road. Lines: SAML. LANDRUM,
JNO. GODSEY, CHAS. AMONT, FRANCIS HANCOCK (formerly ANTHONY LOUILLEIN).
Bought by FLEMING of RO. MOSLEY and devised to JOS. SMITH by will of
FRANCES WALKER, dec'd, 29 Dec 1767, in Chesterfield. Tract where FRANCES
WALKER lived. (I wonder if FLEMING was connected with BEVERLY FLEMING
who was on bond of FRANCIS DRINKARD who married MARTHA FLEMING in Prince
Edward. They named one son BEVERLY DRINKARD. A daughter of FRANCIS &
wife, MARTHA, married HOLCOMB D. BAILEY and they were my ancestors. BFD)

Page 622.　28 Aug 1795.　JAS. McLAIN & wife SALLY, AC, to WM. MOORE, AC,
　　　　　　for ₤50, 137½ acres. Lines: JONATHAN BRIDGWATER, THOS. FITZ-
PATRICK, HENRY McLAIN, WM. FITZPATRICK - formerly that of HENRY McLAIN,
dec'd. Wit: SAML., JONATHAN, & HANNAH BRIDGWATER.

Page 622.　19 Oct 1795.　JNO. MARTIN, AC, to EDMOND COFFEY, JNO. BARNETT,
　　　　　　& DAVID CLARKSON, AC, Deed of Trust on replevin bond ₤14 -
many articles - Wit: EDMD. COFFEY JR, WM. COFFEY.

Page 623.　9 Sep 1795.　JAS. BIBB JR, AC, to JNO. ALFORD, AC, for ₤65,
　　　　　　slave, Caesar, about 22. Wit: JOHNSON PHILLIPS, CHAS. VIGUS,
WM. W. RAY, JACOB MILLER.

Page 624.　18 Oct 1795.　CARREL EADES & wife BARBERY, AC, to ELISHA ESTES,
　　　　　　AC, for ₤15, 40 acres Rucker's Run. Lines: grantee, grantor.

Page 625.　12 Oct 1795.　JOS. LANNUM & wife NANCEY, AC, to JNO. SANDERS -
　　　　　　(not indexed as SANDERS or LANDERS) for ₤30, - land contiguous
- blank space & no signatures.

Page 625.　22 Jul 1795.　REUBEN THORNTON & wife MILDRED, AC, to WM. B.
　　　　　　HARE & wife ELIZ, all of AC, for ₤352-10, 2½ lots in Warmin-
ster - 14 and 16 opposite RO. RIVES' store. Wit: N. CABELL, GIDEON CREWS,
WILLIS WILLS, WM. H. CABELL. Orig. del. 2 Mar --- to WM. H. CABELL.

304

(NICHL. CABELL had great dreams of his river twon, but it went the way of all flesh. May wife and I drove up to the site and there is only a store there now. BFD)

Page 627. 19 Oct 1795. ISAAC BURNETT & wife MARY; RICH. PERKINS & wife ELIZ., AC, to JAS. WOODS, AC, for Ł55, 50 acres S side Rockfish. Lines: RICH. PERKINS, WM. FITZPATRICK, CLOUGH SHELTON, ISAAC BURNETT and where he now lives - RICH. PERKINS' part. MARY signs, but nothing on ELIZ.

Page 628. 18 Jan 1794. ARCHELAUS MITCHELL SR, & wife HANNAH, AC, to THOMAS MOORE, AC, for Ł140, 198 acres Harris Creek. Lines: THOS. POWELL dec'd, RICHARD SHELTON, JOS. MAGANN - bought of JER. TAYLOR, whereon my son, JNO. MITCHELL, lives. Wit: DAVID WOODROOF JR, JNO. MITCHELL, JNO. MEGANN & final proof by him, 19 Oct 1795.

Page 629. 19 Oct 1795. JNO. LITTRELL & wife ANONIA (ANIA), AC, to HENRY BUNNER, AC, (Orig. sent to HB, 10 Feb 1813, per order filed) for Ł50, 150 acres N side Stoney Creek; branch of Rockfish. Lines: RICH. LEE, MOSES HUGHES on E, line of marked trees made by JNO. & GEO. WITT - known as CAMDEN's Entry.

Page 630. 4 May 1795. JESSE KENNEDY, AC, to HENRY CAMDEN, AC, for Ł20, 80 acres N side Buffalo. Lines: Col. EDWD. CARTER dec'd, Mill Creek, CHAS. PARKS' old corner, Col. BRAXTON - now in possession of LINDSEY COLEMAN - PARKS' place - alias PHILLIP PENN, JAS. WILLIAMSON. JK bought it of MATTHEW TUCKER in 1776. Lately occupied by ELISHA DENNIS. Wit: JAS. CALLAWAY, WIATT SMITH, HENRY STONEHAM, CHAS. BURRUS JR, RO. HOLLOWAY.

Page 631. 19 Oct 1795. JOS. ROBERTS & wife SARAH, AC, to JNO. SEAY, AC, for Ł30, adjoining tracts. (Orig. del. to JS 2 Sep 1813) N side Rucker's Run on the Ragged Mt. 1) 42 acres pat. to JNO. LOVING JR, 5 Jun 1765. Lines: Col. LOMAX; that tract conveyed by the said JNO. LOVING JR. to JNO. TUGGLE. 2) 40 3/4 acres "granted to him by deed, 5 Oct 1767, from LUNSFORD LOMAX. 3) 72 acres pat. to JNO. TUGGLE 1 May 1775. Lines: his own, JNO. MONTGOMERY, JNO. LOVING JR, ABRAHAM SEAY JR, top of a mt.

Page 633. 5 Dec 1795. HENRY BELL, AC, to POWHATAN BOLLING, Campbell Co, for Ł46-4, 330 acres N side and adj. Fluvanna and branches of Bolling & Fall Creek. Lines: ROBT. BOLLING dec'd, Bone Camp, MICAJAH TERRELL; near Bolling or Oppossum Island road. Wit: REUBEN COBBS, JAS. LONDON, JAS. CURLE, KITTIE B. HUGHES, THOS. WILSON, WM. L.(?) WATTS. Orig. del. 4 Mar 1806 to POWHATAN BOLLING's exr., LINEAS BOLLING.

Page 634. 9 Dec 1795. ADAM WHITESIDES, State of North Caroline - freedom to slave, Ben, for Ł60 paid by Ben. Wit: DAVID S. GARLAND, REUBEN PENDLETON.

Page 634. 13 Dec 1795. WM. TURNER, AC, to JNO. JINKINS, AC, for Ł20, 31 acres. Lines: STEPHEN HAM. Wit: JAS. LONDON, JAS. TURNER JR, HENRY TURNER.

Page 635. 21 Dec 1795. JOS. CHILDRESS SR, to REUBIN, JESSE, JOS. CHILDRESS JR, SAML. COLEMAN & wife JUDITH, JAS. COLEMAN & wife NANCY, BENJ. SANDIDGE & wife ELIZ, MAJOR CHILDRESS, & SHADRACK CHILDRESS, Ł500, and for my natural love toweards them - no acreage - on the great Kankawa(sic) - at point of a small island and a hill above the river on a "drean". Wit: WM. PETER, JESSE COLEMAN, THOS. COLEMAN, JESSE PETER, JOS. GARNER. Orig. to SAML. COLEMAN, 4 Sep 1796. (Note: Marriages for most of these are of record here, but NANCY, wife of JAMES COLEMAN, is called ANN in bond.

Page 637. 13 Dec 1795. WM. TURNER, AC, to JNO. JINKINGS, AC, for Ł20, 32 acres. Lines: STEPHEN HAM, JENKINS' own line. Wit: JAS. LONDON, JAS. TURNER JR, HENRY TURNER.

Page 638. 10 Dec 1795. JNO. MAHON & wife AGNES, AC, to POWHATAN BOLLING, Campbell Co., for Ł30, 265 acres where grantor lives - Stoval and Pompey's Creeks. Lines: GEO. STOVALL dec'd (Jr?). Wit: HENRY TURNER, J.W.(?) CURLE, WM. KING, BENJ. SIMMONS. Orig. del. 4 Mar 1806 to exr. of P. BOLLING: LINEAS BOLLING.

Page 639. 30 Dec 1795. ELIZ. STOVALL, exrx, & HENRY TURNER, exr. of GEO. STOVALL dec'd, to SACKVILLE KING, Campbell Co, for Ł50, 44 acres both sides Stovall Creek. Lines: WM. GALT, STEPHEN HAM - where Stovall's mill formerly stood. Wit: WM. LONDON, JAS. LONDON, JAS. TURNER Jr.

Page 640. 26 Oct 1795. HANNAH DAVIS; DAVID & WM. DAVIS, exrs. of PHIL-LIP DAVIS, dec'd, AC, to WM. LILLIE (Orig. del. to WL 6 Apr 1803) PHILLIP by will of 2 Mar 1787, and rec. in AC, 1 Oct 1787, ordered Castle Creek land to be sold - 84 acres to be sold for purposes mentioned in will; for Ł40, N branch Piney and head branches Castle Creek. Lines: HENRY KEY, WM. CABELL. Pat. to PD, 1 Aug 1772. WM. does not sign. Wit: DAVID PARROCK WM. THOMSON, JNO. LANCASTER, EBINEAZOR HAYCOCK.

Page 642. 23 Nov 1795. MARTIN BIBB & wife MARY, AC, to JNO. THOMPSON, AC, (Orig. del. to JT, 19 Apr 1802) for Ł100, 100 acres Naked Creek; part of a tract held by MB as legatee of WM. BIBB dec'd. Lines: JAS. WILLS(?), JNO. ALFORD, JAS. BIBB. Wit: GEO. DILLARD, WIATT SMITH, BENJ. POWELL.

Page 643. 21 Dec 1790. RO. HENRY ROSE, AC, to SAML. TURNER, AC, for Ł140, 140 acres S side Tye and both sides Camp Creek. Part of former tract of Col. HUGH ROSE, AC, dec'd. Lines: DILLARD's road; THOS. L.L. WALLS, STEPHEN TURNER. Ack. in Court, Dec, 1795.

Page 644. 21 Dec 1795. JOS. CHILDRESS SR, to same grantees as shown on page 635, for Ł100 and natural love and affection - 500 acres in AC. Lines: WM. PETER, JNO. COLEMAN, WM. CAMDEN, AMBR. RUCKER - also 350 acres in AC. Lines: JNO. HARVIE, MOSES SWENEY, JNO. COLEMAN; also 8 named slaves; stock, tools, furniture. Orig. del. to SAML. COLEMAN, 4 Apr 1796. Wit: WM. PETER, JESSE COLEMAN, THOS. COLEMAN, JESSE PETER, JOS. GARNER.

Page 646. 4 Dec 1795. RO. HENRY ROSE, AC, to DANL. BURFORD SR, AC, for Ł200, 193 acres both sides Harris Creek. Lines: SHELTON's road, HUGH ROSE dec'd, an old field. Orig. del. to E. WILLS, admr., 11 Jan 1811.

Page 647. 18 Dec 1795. WM. TUCKER, AC, to daughter, FRANCES TUCKER, for Ł5, slave girl. Wit: ISAAC TINSLEY, RICH. PENDLETON, RICH. & BENNETT TINSLEY.

Page 647. 28 Apr 1795. MICHL. COALTER & FRANCES JOHNSON, both of AC, by virtue of marriage contract - to any heirs begotten by me or her heirs by any future marriage - if none, then to her brothers and sis-ters - Ł200 to FRANCES; also power given to him to dispose of 170 acres belonging to her in AC. Wit: JNO. MERRITT.

Page 648. 9 Dec 1795. Order to AC J.P.'s SAML. MEREDITH & WM. WARE to quiz RACHEL, wife of SAML. FRANKLIN - 19 Oct 1795, deed to JNO. DUNCAN - 156 acres. Done, 25 Dec 1795. Note: This stencil was cut on 25 Dec 1964 by BAILEY FULTON DAVIS [in original edition].

Page 649. WM. CRAWFORD, Prot. Epis. minister, 19 Oct 1795. Bdm. NATHAN CRAWFORD & HUDSON MARTIN.

Page 649. 25 Aug 1795. LEROY ROBERTSON, Caroline Co, and at present in the Legion of the U.S.A. in territory of NW of Ohio - Power of Atty. to JAMES HANSBROUGH, formerly of AC and late a soldier in this same Legion, and now of this place, to take possession of land in Caroline devised to me by my father, WM. ROBERTSON, dec'd., and all negroes. Head Quarters Green Ville, N.W. 27 Feb 1795. Wit: THOS. STRATTON, DAVID THOMSON, JR, CHAS. CREWS, CHRISTOPHER MILLER. Ack. before CAMPBELL SMITH, "Ind. Mar & Adv. Genl." Proved in AC, 15 Feb 1796, by STRATTON & CREWS.

Page 651. 9 Feb 1796. DANL, JNO, THOS, JAS. & RALPH JOPLING, legatees of RALPH JOPLING, dec'd, AC, to CHAS. STATHAM, AC, for Ł15, 100

acres S branches Dutch Creek. Lines: THOS. JOPLING, JAS. MATTHEWS. Wit:
THOS. & WM. JOPLING, MARSHALL BOWMAN, GEO. MARTIN. Orig. del. to CS,
17 Nov 1799.

Page 653. 15 Feb 1796. SAML. MEREDITH, AC, to DAVID S. GARLAND for Ł500,
            355 acres Higginbotham Mill Creek and Armon(?) Creek. Part of
a tract. Lines: WM. CABELL, Spencer's road, WM. S. CRAWFORD, MOSES HIG-
HINBOTHAM dec'd, GABL. PENN, the Race Path. (Orig. del. to DSG, 2 Apr
1803.) Wit: JOEL FRANKLIN, RO. H. ROSE, JNO. ROSE JR, GEO. & WM. PENN.
(I have not attempted to trace the title to the property in the village
of Clifford where GARLAND built his pretentious brick home, but I am inclined to believe that this is the estate. My wife has been in the house
and says that it is one of the most fascinating homes in AC. They once
held races at Clifford - then New Glasgow - and this was the center of
activity in the county. The Village of Amherst was then known as The Oaks
and did not steal the lime light until it was selected as site of the new
Courthouse needed after Nelson was formed in 1808. I might state that
this beautiful GARLAND home has been extensively worked over by Mr. and
Mrs. WEBB BABCOCK. She is the daughter of State Senator MOSES of Appomattox who recently died. The GARLAND place has been place on the market
because they are removing to Appomattox.

Page 655. 15 Feb 1796. EDWD. CARTER & wife MARY; RANDOLPH CARTER, AC,
            to JOEL FRANKLIN, AC, for Ł1000, 842 acres. Lines: Big Maple
Run, Piney River, the Main Road. Wit: DAVID S. GARLAND, JAS. M. BROWN,
JAS. BALLINGER.

Page 656. 20 Jun 1795. GIDEON LEE, AC, to CALEB TATE & Co, Lynchburg,
            for Ł0-5, household goods etc., carpenter's and joiner's tools,
plantation utensils standing in a certain AC tenement. Wit: WIATT POWELL,
FREDERICK CABELL, THOS. HUMPHREYS.

Page 657. 28 Aug 1795. ELISHA CARTER, AC, to JAS. KELLY, AC, for Ł37-10,
            59½ acres Horsley. Part of SOLOMON CARTER tract - dec'd. Wit:
WM. WARE, AMBR. RUCKER JR, EDWD. CARTER, JNO. WARE, CHAS. TALIAFERRO JR.

Page 658. 25 Sep 1794. MORRIS HAMNER & wife MARY; AMBROSE RUCKER & wife
            ELIZ., JESSE CARTER & wife FRANCES, & NANCY LUCAS, AC, to GEO.
MORRIS, AC, for Ł50, 265 acres N branch Cedar Creek. Lines: JOEL FRANKLIN.
Wit: PETER CARTER, MICAJAH CAMDEN, THOS. COLEMAN, EDWD. CARTER, ABRAHAM
CARTER, JAS. CARTER, KIT(?) COY. Proved 15 Feb 1796 by PETER, EDWD. &
ABRAHAM CARTER.

Page 659. 25 Sep 1790. MORRIS HAMNER etc. as above, to ELIZ. COLEMAN,
            AC, (Orig. del. to EC, 18 Feb 1802) for Ł30, 50 acres both
sides Harris. Lines: JNO. COLEMAN dec'd, DANL. BURFORD, AMBR. RUCKER,
ELIZ. COLEMAN. Wit: as above & proof as above.

Page 660. 25 Sep 1795. Same grantors as above to AMBR. RUCKER & wife
            ELIZ., AC, for Ł50, 37 acres Harris Creek branches. Lines:
DANL. BURFORD JR, THOS. REID. Wit: as above & proof as above.

Page 661. 25 Nov 1790. Margin: Error ought not to be recorded. RICHARD
            LITTRELL & wife SARAH, AC, to HENRY BENNER, AC, for Ł8, 33
acres S fork Rockfish. Lines: NICHL. RANDAN(?), JNO. LITTRELL. Wit: JOS.
WEAVER, MOSES HUGHES, MOSES HUGHES JR.

Page 661. 13 Nov 1795. JESSE MARTIN, Oglethorpe Co, Ga., to JNO. WAR-
            WICK, AC, for Ł6, 204 acres branches S fork Rockfish and Ruck-
er's Run. Lines: JESSE MARTIN, THOS. TRAIL, RICH. MURRY, WM. CHAMBERLAIN,
JNO. RICHARD, MILLY KEY. Wit: WM. WARWICK, DANL. WHITE, DANL. WARWICK,
ALLEN BLAIR.

Page 663. 27 Oct 1795. BARTHOLOMEW MORRAN(M), AC, to JOS. ROBERTS, AC,
            for Ł75, 163 acres. Lines: LITTLEBERRY WITT, WM. HARRIS, RO.
GRANT; grantee. Wit: ALEX. ROBERTS, THOS. CHILDRESS, JNO. SHELTON.

Page 663. 10 Feb 1796. JNO. MATTHEWS & wife MARY, to PLEASANT MARTIN
            for Ł30, 150 acres N side Cove Creek. Lines: JAS. TURNER,
BENJ. PAINE, WM. PIERCE dec'd, top of the Pine Mt.

Page 665.   13 Aug 1795.   GEO. DILLARD, AC, to ISRAEL DAVIS, AC, for Ł53, negress, Rachel. Wit: JOS. BURRUS, JNO. DAVIS.

Page 665.   29 Aug 1795.   WM. EVANS, AC, to GEO. DILLARD AC, (Orig. del. to GD 17 Jul 1797) EVANS owed ALEX. BRYDIE & Co. - Deed of Trust to secure debts - 529 acres where EVANS lives. Headwaters of Piney; winch, Peggy. Wit: WIATT SMITH, LEML. or SAML. HILL. This seems to have been written by two scribes.

Page 666.   15 Aug 1795.   ISAAC RUCKER, AC, to ANTHONY RUCKER, AC, for Ł4, 14 acres Harris Creek. Lines: Capt. BENJ. RUCKER. Wit: RICHARD ELIZ., & PATSY RUCKER.

Page 667.   26 Dec 1795.   JNO. MARTIN, Alb., to JAS, JENNY, MARY, WM., ELIZ., & ALEX. ANGUS, children of WM. ANGUS & wife ELIZ., 5 sh. and my love for them - negress, Beck, and children, Hannah & Lucy. Wit: WM. DEAN, DAVID & JOS. MARTIN.

Page 668.   24 Dec 1795.   RO. CASH LIVELY, AC, to THOS. NEVIL, AC, for Ł85, wagon, horses, etc. Wit: WILL LOVING & LUCY TILLER.

Page 669.   18 Sep 1795.   ZACH. TALIAFERRO & wife SALLY, to BENJ. TALIA-FERRO - (Orig. del. to ZT 6 May 1799) for 6 sh, 4 acres on S of Buffalo. Lines: small spring, Clift of Rocks, ZACH. TALIAFERRO, S branch of Buffalo.

Page 669.   18 Sep 1795.   ZACH. TALIAFERRO JR. from CHAS. TALIAFERRO for 6 sh, 4 acres - same description except name of BEN. instead of ZACH. in lines. Wit: ANTHONY PERLER(?), CHAS. DAVIS, JAS. TALIAFERRO.

Page 670.   15 Aug 1795.   ISAAC RUCKER, AC, to ANTHONY RUCKER, AC, for Ł104, 104 acres Harris Creek. Lines: TINSLEY. Wit: RICH, ELIZ. & PATSY RUCKER.

Page 671.   23 Oct 1795.   JNO. H. GOODWIN, AC, to JNO. DABNEY, Campbell Co. - WM. BAGBY by a judgment vs. him in Louisa, 12 Nov 1795, was indebted to WM. O. COLLIS, exr. of JNO. BAGBY dec'd., for Ł125 from 25 Dec 1788 - WM. BAGBY, 27 Nov 1792, to secure debt executed Deed of Trust to COLLIS on a Pittsylvania tract on Staunton River - 267 acres. JNO. H. GOODWIN has bought the land of WM. BRACTHET(?) and has disposed of it. Desirous to secure under Deed of Trust so as to pay COLLIS - 5 sh. paid by JNO. DABNEY - Deed of Trust - land in AC next to Town of Madison - both sides main road - 120 acres & where JHG lives. 2 tracts. 1) bought by JG of THOS. WRIGHT and 2) from JNO. HANSARD, the elder. Lines: The Tanyard, LASHELL's lot. If not paid, to be sold at the dwelling house thereon. Inclosed(sic) to JNO. DABNEY, 22 May 1796. Wit: WIATT POWELL, JOEL FRANKLIN, WALTER IRVINE, DAVID HUNTER.

Page 674.   15 Feb 1796.   ROYAL CHILDRESS, AC, to THOS. CHILDRESS, AC, for Ł125, 140 acres Rockfish. Lines: JOSIAH JOPLING, MATT. HARRIS, BENJ. CHILDRESS. Wit: BEN JOHNSON, SAML. CHILDRESS, ISAIA ATTKISSON.

Page 675.   15 Feb 1796.   JAS. FRAZER & wife MARGARET, AC, to JAS. CLARK, AC, for Ł25, 100 acres. Wit: Z. DAWSON, JOS. BALLINGER, WM. STINNETT. Sent to JC by JNO. WARE, 18 Apr 1801.

Page 676.   15 Feb 1796.   PETER JOHNSON & wife ANN, AC, to MATT. HARRIS, AC, for Ł41-16, 44 acres formerly property of JOS. LIVELY. Lines: RO. WRIGHT's old line, WM. GRIFFIN,JOS. & JNO. LIVELY. Wit: HENRY HOLLOWAY, THOS. POWELL, JAS. MURPHY.

Page 677.   15 Feb 1796.   JAS. FRAZER & wife MARGARET, AC, to JAS. CLARK (CLACK?), AC, (Orig. sent to JAS. CLARKE by JNO. WARE, 18 Apr 1801) for Ł30, 166 acres. Lines: JNO. FLINT, DAVID McCLAIN, Blue Ridge - and 100 acres bought by WM. CLARK of FREDERICK HUFFMAN. Wit: ZACH. DAWSON, WM. STINNETT, VOLENTINE COX.

Page 678.   13 Feb 1796.   JAS. SEAY & wife JENNY, AC, to JOS. SEAY, AC, for Ł52-1, 105 acres N side Buffalo. Lines: JNO. LOVING, SMYTH TANDY, JOS. STAPLES, a branch, WILSON CARY NICHOLAS. Bought by JS of

308

NICHOLAS.

Page 679. 28 Nov 1795. PARMENUS BRYANT, AC, to WILLIS WILLS, Deed of
Trust, Ł170, 5 slaves named - to secure debt to ALEX. BRYDIE &
Co. Wit: JAS. P. PARRISH & JAS. LOVING.

Page 681. 15 Feb 1796. SAML. HIGGINBOTHAM & JAS. BROOKS, AC, to HAWES
COLEMAN, AC, for Ł35, 190 acres Spring Hill Mt. near Rock
rimon; a branch of Rockfish. Also 80 acres on S side Springhill Mt. on
N side Spence Creek. Lines: JOS. HIGGINBOTHAM MORRISON (formerly).

Page 682. 15 Feb 1796. Deed of Trust by JOEL FRANKLIN, AC, to EDWD.
CARTER, 5 sh. - several bonds due at dates from 1796 to 1801 -
total of Ł1000. Maple Run, branch of Piney. Land lately sold by CARTER to
FRANKLIN and part of tract held by EC under will of his dec'd. father,
EDWD. CARTER.

Page 683. 23 Dec 1795. Order to AC J.P.'s to quiz NANCY THOMAS, wife
of JESSE - deed to JNO. MILTON, 21 Oct 1793, 207 acres. Done
by JNO. DIGGS & JOS. SHELTON, 15 Feb 1796.

Page 684. -- 1795, rec. 15 Feb 1796. JNO. SHIELDS, SR, AC, to BENJ.
PACE, AC, for Ł37-10, 125 acres "being the land WM. McMULLIN"-
Taylor Creek. Lines: WM. HARRIS, JNO. McCLURE, RO. PAGE, AUGUSTINE SHEP-
HERD. Wit: AUGUSTINE SHEPHERD JR, ALEX. McCLURE, JNO. HAGGARD.

Page 684. 28 Dec 1795. WM. MATTHEWS & wife MARY, to JAS. MURPHY, for
Ł74-13, Deed of Trust - debt due RO. RIVES & Co. by MATTHEWS -
5 sh. 100 acres Naked Creek, N branch Tye - residue of 200 acres which
MARY, wife of WM., is entitled to as one of co-heirs of WM. BIBB, dec'd.
Lines: JAS. WILLS, JNO. WRIGHT, SAML. CABELL - only land that they now
hold; one slave girl, Moll. Wit: WM. CAMDEN, JNO. DUNCAN, WM. H. CABELL,
HENRY HOLLOWAY, PARMENUS BRYANT.

Page 686. 7 Jan 1796. THOS. STONE, Fairfield Co, S.C., to WM. BAILEY,
AC, for Ł50, 200 acres Dutch Creek. Lines: SNIDER, his own
Lain(sic), RALPH JOBLING, to Statonis (STATON's?), THOS. NASH. Wit: JNO.
WATTS, MICAJAH PICKETT, CHRISTOPHER BOWLES. Orig. del. to JNO. MATTHEWS
per order, 25 Aug 1796. Certified that MICAJAH PUKETT (PICKETT in sum-
mary) was witness, by CHAS. PUKETT, Fairfield Co, S.C. J.P. - D. EVANS,
C.F.C.

Page 687. JAS. WOODS, Coroner, 22 Mar 1796 - by appt. of JAS. WOOD, Lt.
Gov. 8 Sep 1795. Bdm.: JOS. SHELTON, JAS. BROOKS.

Page 687. 16 Apr 1796. GEO. DILLARD & wife ELIZ, AC, to ALEX. BRYDIE &
Co, for Ł60, 50 acres. Lines: STOVALL's old road, Col. WM.
CABELL JR, crossing Camp Creek, STOVALL's new road. ALEX. BRYDIE for
McCLURE, BRYDIE & Co.

Page 688. 16 Apr 1796. Same grantors and grantee as above - for Ł750,
750 acres S side Tye. Lines: WM. CABELL JR; S branch Tye,
STOVALL's road.

Page 690. 30 Sep 1795. JOSEPH McKEE & wife SIDNEY, Loudoun Co., to JNO.
PANCOAST, same county, for Ł6, 6 acres Horsley Creek. Part of
tract of NELSON CRAWFORD. Lines: CRAWFORD. Wit: JACOB MYERS, JNO. GREGG,
JOHN LITTLEJOHN. Grantors appeared in Loudoun Court, 12 Oct 1795, and
ack. deed. CHAS. BURRUS(?), clk.

Page 691. 30 Sep 1795. JOS. McKEE & wife SIDNEY, Loudoun, to same grantee as above, for Ł30, 91 acres Horsley Creek. Lines: Down the
branch. Wit: same as above.

Page 692. 18 Sep 1795. JNO. RYAN, AC, to RICH. LEE, AC, mare and other
stock; furniture, etc. Ł25. Wit: RICH. HARRISON, JAS. PETTIT,
ISAAC TINSLEY. Orig. sent to R. LEE by his son, Jan 1799.

Page 693. 28 Mar 1796. BENJ. PLUNKETT, AC, to PHILLIP JOHNSON, AC, for
Ł100, 170 acres by pat. surveyed for SAML. BAUGHAN, dec'd; S

fork Stovall. Lines: HENRY TURPIN, JNO. GOFF, FRY; GEO. STOVALL, JONATHAN
JOHNSON. Wit: HENRY ROBINSON, JAS. LASHELL, WM. GUTTRY, JNO. GARDNER,
THOS. BRAGG, NATHL. GUTTRY, JNO. MERRITT.

Page 694.   -- 1796; rec. 18 Apr 1796. NATHL. GUTTRY & wife NANCY, AC, to
             JAS. LONDON, AC, for Ŀ30, 118 acres by pat. 4 Jul 1759. Bought
of NG of RO. JOHNS, dec'd, estate - both sides Porrage. Lines: JOSHUA FRY,
S side Porrage, a branch. Wit: JAS. LONDON JR, TERISHA TURNER.

Page 695.   18 Apr 1796 - erased, but rec. on that date. Same parties as
             above. Ŀ30 - scratched - 92 acres, pat. 28 Sep 1758. Bought as
above - N br. Porrage. Lines: his own, Wit: as above.

Page 696.   18 Apr 1796. Same grantors & grantee as above. Pat. 14 Jul.1769
             Ŀ10, 30 acres bought as above. S side Porrage. Wit: as above.

Page 696.   2 pages so numbered. 18 Apr 1796. JNO. BURFORD, signed JR, AC,
             to JNO. MAIS for Ŀ100, 267 acres. Lines: on the road, Elbow.

Page 698.   9 Apr 1795. HENRY TRENT, AC, to DUDLEY CALLAWAY, AC, 20 sh, 11 acres
             Lines: DAVIS. Wit: RICH. POWELL, JNO. B. TRENT, GEO. GOODWIN, THOS.
MITCHELL.

Page 699.   30 Jul 1795. LITTLEBERRY WITT & wife JENNY (JANE) AC, to JOS.
             ROBERTS, AC, for Ŀ28, 50 acres, part of a tract. Cove of a mt.
on N fork of Davis Ck. Lines: Said WITT, WM. HARRIS, JOS. ROBERTS. Signed
JANE WITT. Wit: JNO. BALLARD, JESSE OGLESBY, WM. THORP.

Page 700.   17 Apr 1795. NEH. ROZEL, AC, to THOS. BRAGG & JAS. LASHELL, AC,
             for Ŀ10, 1/2 acre S side Lynch road. Wit: GEO. McDANIEL, JNO.
ROBINSON SR, WM. DICKS, WM. HURT, DUDLEY CALLAWAY, MICAJAH GOODWIN, JESSE
WOODROOF.

Page 701.   17 Apr 1795. Same grantor & grantees as above - Ŀ45, 6 acres
             N side Lynch road near Madison Town. Lines: JNO. WARD. Wit:
as above.

Page 702.   18 Apr 1796. JARRED HOTCHKISS & wife ---, AC, to RUSH HUDSON,
             AC, for Ŀ100, 130 acres bought of grantee by grantor 17 Jun
1793.

Page 703.   26 Mar 1796. JNO. WILSFORD & wife ELIZ, AC, to WM. EVANS, AC,
             for Ŀ14, 33 acres N side Indian Creek. Property of JNO. PHIL-
LIPS & conveyed to CHAS. TYLER and by CT to grantor. Lines: JNO. CAMPBELL
on N branch of Indian Creek. Wit: WM. ANGUS, JOSIAH MARTIN, WM. ARRINGTON.

Page 704.   18 Apr 1796. THOS. BRAGG 7 wife LUCY, AC, to THOS. RUCKER, AC,
             for Ŀ315, 350 acres Stovall Creek. Lines: BENJ. RUCKER. Wit:
JNO. WINGFIELD, ELIZABETH SNELSON, CHAS. CHRISTIAN.

Page 705.   21 Mar 1796. JAS. CREWS SR, AC, to GEO. DILLARD, AC, Deed of
             Trust. JC owes HART BROWN & Co, Lynchburg, Campbell Co, Ŀ49-10.
(Orig. del. 14 Aug 1796, to WM. (?) BROWN, merchant, Lynchburg. 5 sh.
from GD; tract whereon JC lives - 72 acres. Lines: JOS. DAWSON, WM.
HUGHES, JAS. LEE, JNO. BURFORD SR, HARRISON HUGHES. All that grantor
owns and part of tract of GEO. CARRINGTON, bought by grantor of GC. Also
slave, Buster, about 40; bed, stock. Wit: SAML. READ, JNO. BROWN, JAS.
STUART, WALTER IRVINE, JAS. LEE.

Page 707.   6 Aug 1794. MILES BURFORD, Warren Co, N.C., to DANL. BURFORD,
             Caswell Co, N.C., for Ŀ100, 290 acres N side Fluvanna and
joining it. Lines: Line formerly JOS. ANTHONY's and now the Hon. EDMOND
WINSTON's. Part of tract pat. to Camp. DANL. BURFORD, late of AC, dec'd,
and conveyed to MILES BURFORD - 377 acres - by taking about 70 or 80
acres lying within lines formerly ANTHONY's and now WINSTON's tract.
(Orig. del. to EDMOND WINSTON, Nov 1800) Wit: ISAAC MARSHALL, DANL. FAINE
QURONT(?), WM. FANINE QURVEL(?), ZACH. SHEARIN, WYATE HAWKINS JR. The
two men called FAINE in summary. Certified Warren Co, N.C. Feb. session,
1796. M. DUKE JACKSON, Co. Clk. WILL JOHNSON, J.P.

Page 708. Two so numbered - 22 Mar 1796. JOS. MAYO SR, Powhatan to
THOS. BRAGG, AC, for Ⱡ225, 331 acres Middle fork Stovall.
Lines: RUCKER, RO. JOHNS, BENJ. RUCKER. Wit: JOS. BURRUS, JOS. DILLARD,
JAS. DILLARD, GEO. DILLARD.

End of Deed Book G

AMHERST COUNTY, VIRGINIA DEED BOOK H

DEDICATION

This deed book work is dedicated to FRANCES DUNN BOWMAN, wife of J.J. BOWMAN, Lynchburg, Virginia. She is a fellow Kentuckian and she and her husband have been friends of the DAVIS family for many years. She is active in DAR, Baptist church work, and civic affairs of Lynchburg.

FOREWORD

I have now abstracted deed books of Amherst County, Virginia, from 1761 as shown in deed books A through H. Deed book I is in process of being prepared. There is no deed book J since they avoided confusion resulting from I and J. We are seeing more and more evidence of the southern and western migrations in these deed books as former residents of Amherst dispose of Amherst lands and interests in estates. We also see Revolutionary soldiers disposing of land warrants in Kentucky and other states.

BAILEY FULTON DAVIS
1965

Page 1.   20 Jun 1796. HENRY LANDON DAVIES, Bedford Co, to JESSE WOOD-
             ROOF, AC, (Orig. del. 15 Oct 1805 to JW; comm. annexed) for
L202, 202 acres John's creek. Part of tract. Lines: THOS. POWELL dec'd,
DUDLEY CALLAWAY, ARCHELAUS MITCHELL. Wit: MICAJAH CAMDEN, JAS. WOODROOF,
REUBEN PENDLETON.

Page 2.   1 Jun 1796. HENRY LANDON DAVIES & wife LUCY, Bedford, to REU-
             BEN PENDLETON, AC, (Orig. del. 5 Aug 1805 to WM. G. PENDLETON,
son to REUBEN) for L450, 500 acres. Lines: JESSE WOODROOF, THOS. POWELL,
dec'd, JNO. B. TRENT, crossing Rockey Creek, ARCHELAUS MITCHELL, Mitchell's road. Wit: MICAJAH CAMDEN, JESSE WOODROOF, JAS. WOODROOF.

Page 3.   20 Jun 1796. GEO. McDANIEL SR, AC, to GEO. McDANIEL JR, AC,
             for L200, 194 acres. Lines: RICH. POWELL.

Page 4.   4 Jan 1796. EDWD. TREVILIAN & wife SUSANNAH, & MARTIN BREED-
             LOVE and wife ELIZ., AC, to RICHMOND STATHAM, AC, for L85, 100
acres N branch Rucker's Run; part of tract to grantors from JNO. BOUSH,
1794. Wit: WM. BREEDLOVE, CHARLES WATTS, WM. WARWICK. Receipt of same
date. Orig. del. to RS, 5 Jun 1798.

Page 5.   18 Jun 1796. JAS. ANDERSON & wife ELIZ, AC, to JAS. FLACK,
             Augusta, for L241-6-3, 214 acres; part of 429 acres headwaters
Rockfish. Lines: FREDERICK WARE, THOS. BRUMHALL, PETER FRANKER(?), JNO.
SMITH; and dividing line agreed upon by parties. Wit: JNO. KNOWLS, FRED-
ERICK WEIR (this name is often spelled WARE or WEIR) CHAS. McCUE, RO.
HENDREN.

Page 6.   25 Nov 1795. DAVID McCUE & wife MARGARET, Greenbryer Co, to
             CHAS. McCUE, AC, for L50, 35½ acres Headwaters Rockfish. Lines:
HENRY VARNER, JAMES ANDERSON, JAS. BROOKS, MARY McCUE. Wit: JAS. ANDERSON,
JAS. BISHOP, JNO. KNOWLS. Orig. del. 5 May 1800, to M. DAWSON.

Page 7.   18 Jun 1796. JNO. BURGER & wife SUSANNAH, Alb., to RO. HEN-
             DREN, AC, (Orig. del. to RH. 30 Apr 179--) for L113, 119 ac-
res Headwaters Beaver Creek branches. Wit: JNO. KNOWLS, JAS. ANDERSON,
CHAS. McCUE, FREDERICK WARE.

Page 8.   11 Dec 1795. JNO. THOMPSON & wife MARY, AC, to JOS. THOMPSON,
             AC, for L100, 63 acres Headwaters Rockfish. Wit: JAS. ANDER-
SON, JNO. THOMPSON, JNO. TODER(?), FREDERICK WEIR, WM. SHELTON.

Page 9.   18 Jun 1796. JNO. KNOWLS & wife SARAH, AC, to JAS. FLACK,
             Augusta (examined, del. to J. BROOKS, atty.) for L167-10, 110
acres Pattens Branch; headwaters of Rockfish. Lines: JAS. BROOKS, JNO.
DETTOR, CHAS. ROADS, JAS. BISHOP. Wit: JAS. ANDERSON, CHAS. McCUE,
FREDERICK WEIR.

Page 10.   8 Apr 1796.   JNO. CARTWRIGHT, AC, to GEO. DILLARD, AC, Deed
           of Trust to secure ALEX. BRYDIE & Co. - beds, stock, etc.
Wit: WIATT SMITH, JOS. DILLARD.

Page 11.   4 Mar 1796.   TILMAN WALTON, AC, to BARTLETT EADES, AC, for 6sh,
           327 acres top and both sides of the Mt. dividing Dutch & Davis
Creeks. Lines: RICH. POLLARD, ARCHER HAMLET dec'd, JNO. LOVING, RO.
WRIGHT, JNO. MILLION(?). Wit: WM. WRIGHT, JAS. McALEXANDER, WM. McDONALD.
Orig. del. 23 Sep 1796 to BE.

Page 12.   15 Apr 1796.   CHAS. CARTER, Culpeper, to LEONARD HENLEY, AC,
           for Ŀ61-10, 41 acres S side and joining Buffalo. Lines: DRURY
TUCKER, grantee. Part of a tract. Wit: DANL. TUCKER, P. GOOCH, WM. BACON,
EDWD. CARTER.

Page 13.   29 Feb 1796.   THOS. EADES, AC, to TILMAN WALTON, AC, for 5 sh,
           377 acres top of the mt. dividing Dutch & Davis Creeks. Lines:
RICH. POLLARD, ARCHER HAMLET, dec'd, JNO. LOVING, RO. WRIGHT, JNO. MILTON
(appears to be MILLION in previous deed) - 3 plats and 1 deed (plats not
herein). Wit: MARY MILTON, BARTLETT EADES, JNO. MILTON.

Page 14.   10 Mar 1796.   HENRY LANDON DAVIES, Bedford Co, to SALLY HARRI-
           SON - lease, 7 yrs. from 20 Nov last - Ŀ10 per year - to plant
100 peach & 100 apple trees. Wit: JOSIAH HARRISON, SAML. B. DAVIES, NATHL.
C. DAVIES, JAS. WOODROOF, MARTIN PARKS.

Page 15.   29 Oct 1795.   ELIZ. BARRETT(OTT), AC, to DAVIS BULLOCK, Louisa,
           (Orig. del. to SAML. OVERTON JR, 8 Dec 1796) for Ŀ914-9-9 debt
deed of trust - 5 sh. 100 acres N side road from Buffalo to Irish Creek;
known as Mitchell's Cove; also 23 negroes named. Wit: CHAS. TALIAFERRO
JR, WM. BARRETT, LARKIN SANDIDGE, RO. HOLLOWAY, WM. BAILEY.

Page 17.   31 Aug 1793.   JACOB GIBSON & wife JANE, Buckingham Co, to
           SAML. BROWN, AC, for Ŀ25, 75 acres S branches Higginbotham
Mill Creek; also 150 acres, late property of ISAAC GIBSON dec'd. Lines:
GABL. PENN, to Lot 1, to lot 4, SMYTH TANDY. Wit: JAS. BALLINGER, WM.
PAMPLIN, DAVID S. GARLAND, PEACHY FRANKLIN.

Page 18.   7 Oct 1794.   Order to AC J.P.'s to quiz JANE, wife of JACOB
           GIBSON. They are styled as being of Buckingham, but done by
AC J.P.'s, SAML. MEREDITH & CHESLEY KINNEY.

Page 19.   11 Nov 1795.   GEO. HIGHT & wife LUCY, AC, to THOS. MASSIE,
           Frederick Co. (Orig. del. to DANL. McDONALD, 21 Sep 1797) for
Ŀ120, 25 acres Stony Creek, branch of Tye; water grist mill. Lines: HIGHT,
S fork Stoney; part of 2 tracts pat. to JAS. BROWN, 16 Feb 1771; sold to
JNO. HIGHT and by him sold to WM. COFFEE, and by WC to grantor 3 Mar 1792.

Page 20.   9 Jun 1796.   JAS. DINWIDDIE, dec'd, AC, owned 300 acres on
           Rockfish. Lines: RO. DINWIDDIE dec'd, JNO. MORRISON dec'd, JAS.
WOODS. He devised it for life to ANN DINWIDDIE and at her death to sons
of his brother, ROBT: JNO, WM.., & RO. JR. RO. JR. bought interest of
his brothers and now sells his interest to HUDSON MARTIN, AC, for Ŀ320;
1/2 acre reserved for cemetery. Examined, 22 Aug 1805, and sent to MARTIN.

Page 21.   25 Nov 1795.   JNO. MATTHEWS & wife MARY, to JAS. TURNER, heir
           of STEPHEN TURNER, dec'd. for Ŀ10, 50 acres Rockfish. Lines:
JAS. TURNER; former lines of MILES BAILEY, end of Perry Mt. Orig. del.
13 Nov 1798 to JNO. WATKINS for TURNER on order.

Page 21.   4 Apr 1796.   JAS. WATSON & wife PATTY, AC, to PHILLIP GOOCH,
           AC, for Ŀ500, 400 acres where JW lives and bought of JAS.
GATEWOOD, S side Buffalo, crossing Tribulation Creek. Wit: REUBEN CRAW-
FORD, HENRY CAMDEN, WM. CAMDEN, WM. MOSS, WM. LONDON. Orig. del. to PG
31 Oct 1799.

Page 23.   18 Jun 1796.   JNO. BARNETT, AC, to JAS. MONTGOMERY for Ŀ20,
           41 acres Hatt Creek. Orig. del. to JM 15 Oct 1798.

Page 24.   18 Jun 1796.   JNO. BARNETT, AC, to ARCHIBALD C. FREAM, Augusta,

for L50, 24 acres S branches Hatt & Raccoon of Tye. Lines: Col. WM. RAN-
DOLPH, JNO. ROSE.

Page 24.   14 Nov 1795.   JNO. BREEDEN & wife SUSANNAH, to JOS. MONTGOMERY
for L55, head of Stonry; branch of S fork Rockfish. Lines:
Bermudian Creek. Wit: NATHAN CRAWFORD, RO. DINWIDDIE, RICH. ADAMS, HENRY
SMITH.

Page 25.   21 Mar 1790.   JNO. MITCHELL, AC, to GEO. DILLARD, AC, for 5 sh,
Deed of trust - negroes; furniture, stock. Wit: JESSE MAYS,
WM. TYREE.

Page 26.   4 Jun 1796.   JNO. DILLARD & wife SARAH, AC, to RO. HOLLOWAY,
AC, for L154, 110 acres, part of where JD lives. Lines: grant-
or, JAS. WALTERS, S side bank Long Branch, JAS. DILLARD, JESSE MAYS, JAS.
WALTERS(WATERS?). Orig. del. to RH, 29 Jul 1797. Wit: WIATT SMITH, HENRY
HOLLOWAY, CHAS. BURRUS JR.

Page 27.   4 Jan 1796.   RICH. TANKERSLEY, AC, to GEO. DILLARD, 5 sh, Deed
of trust - slaves and stock. Wit: PEACHY FRANKLIN, WIATT SMITH.
Page 28 - same date and same parties - another deed of trust - slaves and
stock. Wit: as above.

Page 29.   13 May 1796.   JNO. ROSE & wife CATH, AC, to THOS. MASSIE,
Frederick Co, (Orig. del. to Col. JNO. ROSE by D.W. McDANIEL;
another - del. to DMCD, 21 Sep 1797.) 40 sh. per acre for part of grant
to RO. ROSE, Clerk, and 20 shillings per acre for grant to JNO. ROSE -
Tye - 3111 acres. Lines: order line of RO. ROSE, clk, Castle Creek, old
field, ZACH. TALIAFERRO - formerly JAS. CHURCHILL, N branch Tye. Part of
tract devised to JNO. by father RO. ROSE, and pat. to RO. 30 Aug 1749.
Also tract on Priest Run and branches - 741 acres - 150 acres of it
granted to JNO. ROSE by pat. 3 Mar 1761; 400 acres pat. to JNO, 10 Jul
1767; 191 acres pat. to LEONARD TARRANT, 10 Sep 1767, and by deed to JNO.
ROSE, 5 Nov 1774. Lines: RO. ROSE's order line, JNO. ROSE. Wit: DANL.
McDONALD, JNO. N. ROSE, MATT. HIGHT, EDEN W. ROOTES(?), GEO. HIGHT.

Page 31.   18 Jul 1796.   WM. MATTHEWS & wife MARY, AC, to JNO. JACOBS JR
(?), AC, (del. to JJ 25 Jun 1796(sic), for L150, 100 acres on
branch of Naked Creek and N branch Tye. One half of 200 acres devised to
MARY MATTHEWS by WM. BIBB, dec'd. Lines: WM. BIBB.

Page 32.   1 Jul 1796.   JNO. BALL, AC, to ELISHA PETERS, AC, for L30, 112
acres S branches of S fork Rockfish. Lines: WM. CABELL, WM.
LOVEDAY, waggon road, HENRY KEYS, Glade road. ELIZ. BALL, wife of JNO,
signed.

Page 33.   22 Mar 1796.   JOS. MAYO & wife MARTHA, Powhatan Co, to GEO.
DILLARD, AC, for L130, 260 acres. Lines: Lynch road, Crooked
Run, JAS. MANEES, DANL. GAINES, JNO. STEWART. Wit: JOS. BURRUS, JAS.
FRANKLIN, JAS. DILLARD, WIATT SMITH. Orig. del. to GD, 12 Sep 1804.

Page 34.   16 Jul 1796.   CARROL EADES & wife BARBARY, AC, to DANL. McCoy,
AC, for L40, 132 acres Naked Creek and head of branches of S
fork of Rockfish.

Page 35.   18 Jul 1796.   SAML. EDMONDS & wife ALICE (ELISA), AC, to MINON
WRIGHT, AC, for L50, 3 3/4 acres N side Tye. Part of tract.

Page 36.   29 Apr 1796.   Order to AC J.P.'s, to quiz MARY, wife of JNO.
MATTHEWS as to deed to PLEASANT MARTIN - 150 acres. Done 13
May 1796 by JNO. DIGGS & JOS. SHELTON.

Page 37.   16 Jul 1796.   WM. CABELL, AC, to son, LANDON CABELL, AC, (Orig.
del. 22 Sep 1801, to LC) for love, lot in Town of New Markett,
AC, No. 5 on town plat; next to RO. RIVES store. Only brick or stone
house to be built thereon. Wit: WM. CABELL JR, WM. H. CABELL, RO. RIVES,
N. CABELL.

Page 38.   16 Jul 1796.   WM. CABELL, AC, to sons, SAML. JORDAN, WM. JR,
& HECTOR CABELL, for love, 1½ acres adj. New Markett. Lines:

stake on S side Main Street and Lot 5 of LANDON CABELL. Wit: as in previous deed, but LANDON in place of WM. JR.

Page 38.   16 Jul 1796.   WM. CABELL to NICHL. CABELL for Ł100, Island in
            Fluvanna lately bought of MOSES RAY; uppermost and largest of
Swift Islands. Wit: LANDON, WM. JR, WM. & W.H. CABELL.

Page 40.   13 Feb 1796.   JNO. BURNETT (BARNETT?), AC, to MARY BURNETT,
            AC, for Ł0-13, bed, stock etc. Wit: JAS. VIGUS, THOS. FORTUNE.

Page 40.   18 Jul 1796.   JNO. EDMONDS, AC, to JAS. COCKE, Alb., & THOS.
            BROWN, AC, for Ł25, 25 acres S side Rucker's Run; part of
tract. Lines: EDMOND's mt. line. Wit: JAS. MURPHY, HENRY HOLLOWAY,
AUGUSTINE WRIGHT.

Page 41.   18 Jul 1796.   JAS. EDMONDS & wife MARY, AC, to BENJ. MARTIN,
            AC, for Ł80, 195 acres both sides Rucker's Run. Part of tract
of JNO. EDMONDS. Lines: CHAS. EDMONDS, JAS. COCKE, HARMER's old line,
JNO. BETHEL, RO. C. HARRISON. Wit: JAS. MURPHY, THOS. BIBB, CHAS. MAYSE.

Page 43.   15 Apr 1796.   CHAS. CARTER & wife BETTY, Culpeper, to DANL.
            TUCKER, AC, for Ł174, 116 acres S side Buffalo; part of tract.
Lines of grantor and grantee. Wit: WM. BROWN, WALTER LEAKE, H. HOLLOWAY.
Orig. del. to DT, Aug, 1802.

Page 44.   18 Jul 1796.   JAS. BROOKS, Alb., to JOS. MONTGOMERY, AC, for
            Ł11, 327 acres taken up by JOS. HIGGINBOTHAM MORRISON. Lines:
HAWES COLEMAN, THOS. GOODWIN, JOS. MONTGOMERY, NATHAN CRAWFORD.

Page 45.   18 Jul 1796.   MATT. HARRIS SR, AC, to GEO. BLAINE SR, Alb. -
            HARRIS was granted 150 acres on Cub in 3 pats. Lines: JNO.
THURMOND, PERRIN FARRAR, JNO. MORRISON, MICHL. MORRISON, GUTTRY THURMOND,
top of the mt. Orig. del. to MARTIN DAWSON, 8 Feb 1798. ELIZ, wife of
HARRIS.

Page 46.   12 Sep 1796.   THOS. ANDERSON & wife ELIZ, AC, to RO. ROBINSON,
            AC, for Ł60, 26 acres both sides Lynch road. Lines: RO. CAMP-
BELL, BENJ. RUCKER, GARLAND, JNO. KNIGHT, ABLE BLANKENSHIP. Orig. del.
to ROBERTSON (sic) 1 Sep 1801. Wit: JAS. LASHELL, PHILIP JOHNSON, REUBEN
TAYLOR, MICHL. COALTER, HENRY BROWN.

Page 47.   15 Aug 1796.   JNO. H. GOODWIN, AC, to JAS. LASHELL, AC, for
            Ł12, 1/2 acre N side Lynch road. Lines: LASHELL's lots. Orig.
del. to C. DABNEY 29 Apr 1827. Wit: THOS. JOHNSON, JNO. MERRITT, RO.
ROBINSON, MICHL. COALTER.

Page 48.   3 Aug 1796.   MICHL. COALTER & wife FRANCES, AC, to HENRY
            BOUREN, AC, for Ł400, 402 acres. Lines: JNO. WIATT, WM. MAYO,
crossing Rutledge, JAS. LIVELY, WM. MOON, ABNER PADGETT, old pat. line,
WM. CHAPPLE, JOS. HIGGINBOTHAM. Orig. del. BOURNE(sic) 13 Mar 1803.
Wit: RO. ROBINSON, THOS. ANDERSON, REUBEN TAYLOR.

Page 49.   9 Aug 1796.   GEO. McDANIEL JR, & wife POLLY, AC, to GIDEON
            CREWS, AC, for Ł375, 250 acres Rutledge & Tribulation Creeks.
Bought by GM of WIATT POWELL. Lines: EDWD. WATSON, WIATT POWELL, grantee,
JAS. PENDLETON, an old road, JOS. BURRUS. Orig. del. to GC, 30 Dec 1796.
Wit: THOS. MOORE, ANTHONY RUCKER, JNO. HANSARD, JOS. CREWS, JR.

Page 50.   7 Jul 1796.   JOS. SHIPS to his son, ELIJAH SHIPS, AC, 40 acres
            Harris Creek. Lines: DANL. BURFORD SR, JNO. BURFORD JR (or
SR?). Wit: WM. BURFORD, JAS. MARKHAM, AB(?) CAMPBELL.

Page 51.   15 Feb 1796.   JNO. TOOL to JNO. HORSLEY - deed of trust - debt
            due RO. RIVES & Co. 5 sh. 100 acres Alb. tract - Taylor's
Creek. Lines: ROBIN PAGE, WM. SMITH, BENNETT HENDERSON. Orig. del. to
SAML. PERKINS, 23 Oct 1797.

Page 51.   12 Sep 1796.   DRURY TUCKER, AC, to DANL. TUCKER, AC, for Ł100,
            150 acres S side Mobley's Mt., Buffalo. Part of tract bought
by DRURY of JAS. MOBLEY. Lines: Thoroughfair Branch, DANL. TUCKER,

LEONARD HENDLEY. Wit: GIDEON CREWS, WM. WORTHAM, JAS. WOODROOF.

Page 52.   16 Sep 1796. ARCHELAUS MITCHELL, AC, to THOS. MITCHELL for
            $1.00, a slave, Caleb, about 10 years old. Wit: ARCHELAUS
MITCHELL JR, MICAJAH GOODWIN, JNO. B. TRENT.

Page 53.   24 Jun 1796. ARCHELAUS MITCHELL, AC, to BOWLIN MITCHELL, AC,
            for Ƚ5, 95 acres John's Creek. Lines: mouth of said creek,
JNO. B. TRENT, HENRY LONDON, THOS. MITCHELL, MICAJAH GOODWIN. Wit: THOS.
MITCHELL, JNO. GILES, JNO. B. TRENT.

Page 54.   15 Jul 1796. ARCHELAUS MITCHELL to son, BOWLIN MITCHELL, for
            love, slave, Pompey, about 9, furniture, also slave, Vicey,
to daughter of ARCHELAUS, STILLY MITCHELL, and furniture. Wit: JNO. B.
TRENT, THOS. MITCHELL, DUDLEY CALLAWAY, ARCHELAUS MITCHELL JR.

Page 54.   16 Sep 1796. ARCHELAUS MITCHELL to JNO. B. TRENT for $1.00,
            a slave, Will, about 13 or 14. Wit: ARCHELAUS MITCHELL JR,
THOS. MITCHELL, BOLIN MITCHELL.

Page 55.   23 May 1796. ANDREW SMITH to JAS. WILLS for Ƚ25, horse and
            cows. Wit: JAS. THOMPSON, ELIAS WILLS.

Page 55.   19 Sep 1796. JNO. F.P. LEWIS & wife NANCY, AC, to DAVID
            BURKS for Ƚ250, 200 acres Pedlar. Lines: grantee, JAS. DAVIS,
grist mill on land, one acre included on opposite or E side of river.
Orig. del. 21 Nov 1807 to DB.

Page 56.   13 Sep 1796. JNO. CHILDRESS, AC, to JOS. McADAMS, AC, for Ƚ25,
            100 acres N side Pedlar. Lines: ANTHL. HENDERSON. Acknowledged
by PRISCILLA, wife of JC, 15 Sep 1800. Sent to JM, 26 Nov 1801.

Page 57.   14 Sep 1796. SAML. MEREDITH & wife JANE, AC, to LINDSEY
            COLEMAN, AC, for Ƚ250, 101 3/4 acres both sides Buffalo. Lines:
grantee, above the mill and crossing river, Crooked Run, grantor. Del.
to SM. 26 Sep 1796.

Page 58.   14 Sep 1796. LINDSEY COLEMAN & wife LUCY, AC, to SAML. MERE-
            DITH, AC, for Ƚ5, 3 3/4 acres. Lines: grantor, MEREDITH's
Buffalo Spring Branch. Orig. del. to LC, 26 Sep 1796.

Page 59.   16 Jul 1796. JNO. CHILDRESS, AC, to WIATT STARK, Rockbridge,
            for Ƚ50, 125 acres S side Pedlar. Lines: HENRY CHILDRESS, top
of the Blue Ridge. Orig. del. to GEO. HOWARD ---.

Page 59.   10 Aug 1796. JNO. HARRIS & wife ELIZ, AC, to BOOTH WOODSON,
            Goochland, for Ƚ40, Goochland tract of 125 acres. Lines:
STEPEHN & JOS. WOODSON, WM. SANDERS(?), CHAS. ATKISSON. Sold by JH to
BOOTH WOODSON, dec'd. Sent by mail to BW, 26 Jun 1825.

Page 60.   17 Sep 1796. JNO. SWANSON, AC, to "my natural son, DAVID
            SWANSON", AC, for love - blank acres - Maple Run of Piney;
Turkey Mt. Lines: NATHL. MANTIPLY, LINDSEY COLEMAN, JOSHUA HUDSON, EDWD.
CARTER. Wit: REUBEN CRAWFORD, WIATT SMITH.

Page 60.   16 Aug 1796. SUSANNA PERRY, AC, to son, WM. PERRY, Fluvanna -
            love and $1.00, 3 negroes during my lifetime. Wit: JOS.
WEAVER, LEWIS BALL.

Page 61.   19 Sep 1796. ANNA FISHER, AC, to JNO. MOORE, my friend, of
            Georgia. Power of Atty. to receive my property in Ga. when
due me.

Page 62.   20 Jul 1796. Order to AC J.P.'s to quiz MARY, wife of WM.
            MATTHEWS, deed to JNO. JACOBS, 18 Jul 1796, 100 acres. Done,
30 Jul, by WM. WARWICK & WM. LOVING.

Page 63.   13 Sep 1796. JNO. CHILDRESS, AC, to WM. MITCHELL, AC, for
            Ƚ50, 200 acres N side Pedlar. Lines: grantor, HENRY CHILDRESS,
WIATT STARK. PRISCILLA, wife of JC, ack. deed, 15 Sep 1800. Orig. del.

316

to WM 26 Nov 1801.

Page 63.   20 Sep 1796.   JNO. CHILDRESS, AC, to JNO. HENDERSON, AC, for
Ł200, 90 acres both sides Pedlar. Lines: NATHL. HENDERSON,
crossing river. Orig. del. to JH personally, 16 May 1800.

Page 64.   13 Aug 1796.   ZACH. TALIAFERRO, AC, to son RICH. TALIAFERRO
377 acres N side Tye. Lines: MOSES HUGHES, THOS. STEWART,
Col. JNO. ROSE. Wit: NATHL. OFFUTT, HENDLEY DRUMMOND, BURKENHEAD
TALIAFERRO.

Page 65.   19 Sep 1796.   BENJ. MAYS & wife SUSANNAH, AC, to EATON CARPEN-
TER, AC, for Ł35, 85 acres W side Thrasher's Creek. Wit: RO.
HAMBLETON, JAS. CARPENTER, CORNL. SALE. Margin: 2 Oct 1848, orig. sent
to E.P. TUCKER, exr. of E. CARTER (sic).

Page 66.   21 Nov 1794.   WM. WILSON & wife SARAH, AC, to WM. FOX, AC, for
Ł36, 60 acres Meriwether's Branch, S side dividing ridge be-
tween branch and Ponder branch. Lines: RO. JOHNSON, SAML. FOX, JAS.
TRUSLER, JNO. HENDERSON. Wit: JNO. MARTIN, WM. CHURCH, JAS. HENDLEY.

Page 67.   19 Sep 1796.   YOUNG LANDRUM & wife PATSEY; ARCHILLES WRIGHT &
wife NANCY, AC, to JOS. LOVING, AC, for Ł325, 2 tracts of 500
and 185 acres on N branches Tye; N side Berry's Mt.   500 acres lines:
WM. LAFORD, AUGUSTINE SMITH, RO. RIVES, GEO. STONHAM, MINOS WRIGHT, ACHI-
LLES WRIGHT - ref. to deeds of JOS. BOUSH to WM. HOLLINGSWRITH and WH to
YOUNG LANDRUM.   185 acres part of ACHILLES WRIGHT tract. Lines: WM. AL-
FORD, JOS. MAYS, top of Berry's Mt., JOS. MAYS - formerly SAML. SPENCER.
Orig. del. to YOUNG LANDRUM 29 Nov 1796; del. to JOS. LOVING, 26 Jun 1798.

Page 68.   19 Sep 1796.   SAML. EDMONDS & wife ALCEE, AC, to ROLAND ED-
MONDS, AC, for 6 sh, 242 acres both sides Naked Creek N branch
Tye; part of tract of JAS. & SAML. EDMONDS. Lines: grantors, JNO. THOMP-
SON, mouth of Wold Branch. Orig. sent to W.H. DIGGS, 2 May 1807 per
order.

Page 69.   19 Sep 1796.   WM. HENDERSON & wife JENNY, AC & parish, to
ZACH. FORTUNE, AC & Par., for Ł40, land both sides of Main
branch of Rucker's Run in course of a mt.

Page 70.   20 Jul 1796.   WM. EVANS, AC, to ROLAND JONES, Campbell Co, for
Ł39, 266 acres Stovall and Juniper creeks. Lines: TURNER
CHRISTIAN, Ivory Hill side, STEPHEN HAM, JOS. CREWS, BENJ. COFLAND.

Page 71.   2 Jul 1796.   JOS. SHIPS, AC, to PLEASANT DAWSON, AC, for Ł100,
97 acres branches Harris Creek. Lines: ELIJAH SHIPS, S side
Taylor's branch, RUCKER.

Page 72.   18 Jul 1796.   JOS. LIVELY & wife SALLY; JNO. LIVELY & wife
CLARISSA; RO. CASH LIVELY & wife ELIZ, AC, to MATT. HARRIS JR,
AC, for Ł75, part of tract of JOS. LIVELY dec'd - laid off to grantors as
legatees.   44 acres "Three 132 acres" - references to numbers: 5 etc.
Lines: HEZ. LIVELY, MARK LIVELY, RO. CASH LIVELY, PETER JOHNSON, WM.
BIBB dec'd, JNO. & JOS. LIVELY.

Page 74.   22 Aug 1795.   WM. HAYNES & wife SARAH, AC, to GEO. HOWARD for
Ł40, 138 acres by survey of 30 Dec 1790. Branches of Pedlar.
Lines: JAS. MARTIN, top of the mt. Wit: WM. PARKS, ABRAHAM CARTER,
AMBR. EUBANK.

Page 75.   1 Sep 1796.   JNO. DABNEY, Lynchburg and Campbell Co. to MICHL.
COALTER & PHILIP JOHNSON, AC. JNO. H. GOODWIN, 23 Oct 1795,
executed Deed of Trust to DABNEY - 120 acres adj. town of Madison and
both sides Main road - where JG lives. 2 tracts bought by JG of JNO.
HANSARD the elder and Thos. wright. Lines: Tanyard lot, LASHELL's lot
and porch. Debt due exr. of JNO. BAGBY, but not paid. Grantees bought it
at public sale for Ł120. Wit: JNO. BROWN, JNO. G.(?) POWELL, RO. JOHNSON.

Page 77.   24 Mar 1796.   DANL. BURFORD, Caswell Co, NC, to EDMOND WINSTON,
Campbell Co, Va. for $200 (note that many deeds still use the

old pound system) Lines: N side Fluvanna, grantor (formerly JOS. ANTHONY) conveyed to MILES BURFORD by DANL. BURFORD dec'd, AC. Conveyed for 290 acres and adjustment in ANTHONY land; 160 acres conveyed by DAVID CRAW-FORD, late Shff, by claim of DANL. from MILES BURFORD. Wit: JNO. P. POW-ELL, PATRICK ROSE JR, EDMD. WINSTON JR. Orig. del. to DAVID S. GARLAND 16 Sep 1798.

Page 79.   13 Aug 1796.   JNO. KNIGHT, AC, to DAVID S. GARLAND, AC, for
            L49-9-9, 129 acres Harris Creek. Lines: PETER RUCKER, ALEX.
McCAUL, MAGANN, bottom near the road, ISAAC RUCKER. Bought by JK of WM.
GARLAND dec'd, and JOS. MEGANN. Penal bond by decree to GARLAND's credi-
tors, Aug, 1794. Deed of Trust; KNIGHT is blacksmith. Wit: JAS. GARLAND,
THOS. POWELL, MOSES MARTIN.

Page 81.   16 Oct 1796.   DAVID CRAWFORD, AC, Power of Atty to friend,
            NELSON CRAWFORD, AC, to sell Ky. lands for him. Wit: W.S.
CRAWFORD, JAS. MURPHY.

Page 82.   13 Oct 1796.   JAS. ANDERSON & wife ELIZ, AC, to JACOB ARISMAN,
            AC, for L530, 200 acres Headwaters of Rockfish. Orig. sent to
JA, 5 Oct 1837.

Page 83.   10 Aug 1796.   THOS. GOODRICH, AC, to granddaughter, CATH.
            BROWN, AC, love and 5 sh, slave Anthony; mare, Dutch oven, for
lifetime of wife and me. Wit: WM. WARE, HENRY BROWN, JAS. BROWN.

Page 84.   31 May 1796.   SEYMOUR POWELL, AC, to JNO. THOMPSON, AC, Deed
            of Trust - slave girl, Betty, about 9 or 10. Debt of L47-8-3.

Page 85.   30 Dec 1794.   THOS. L.L. WALL & wife SALLY, AC, to WM. BRAGG,
            AC, consideration, 1 horse, at L8; 76 acres MEGANN's Ordinary.
Lines: JNO. WIATT GILBERT, dec'd, Lynch road. Wit: JAS. BALLINGER, CHAS.
BURRUS, JAS. FRANKLIN, GEO. DILLARD. Order to quiz SALLY WALL, done by
SAML. MEREDITH & JOS. BURRUS, and rec. 19 Oct 1796.

Page 86.   7 Oct 1796.   SAML. LACKEY & wife ----, to PHILLIP GOOCH, AC,
            for L208, 208 acres Rutledge Creek. Lines: JOS. HIGGINBOTHAM,
BENAMMI STONE, JNO. HIGGINBOTHAM. Orig. del. to MATT. M. GOOCH, 31 Oct
1796.   .

Page 87.   12 Mar 1796.   JNO. PUGH, AC, to JNO. STRATTON, AC, 4 sh. Deed
            of Trust as bondsman to GALT & GARLAND - beds, etc. Wit: DAVID
S. GARLAND, WM. STRATTON.

Page 88.   21 Mar 1796.   WM. MATTHEWS, AC, to MARY HOLLINGSWORTH, AC,
            Deed of Trust - cows, etc. Wit: RANDOLPH BIBB, WM. MORROW,
MARY WRIGHT.

Page 88.   1 Jun 1796.   BENJ. POWELL, AC, to GALT & GARLAND - Deed of
            Trust - slaves, beds etc. Wit: JESSE MAY, THOS. BIBB(?),
GEO. BURKS.

Page 89.   3 Jul 1796.   BENJ. POWELL, AC, to THOMPSON & TEAS - Deed of
            Trust - slaves & beds. Wit: SEYMOUR POWELL, WM. POWELL. Orig.
del. to JT 2 Jan 1796 (JNO. THOMPSON)

Page 89.   ---- 1793.   JAS. FERGUSON & wife MARY, Alb., to FRANCIS HODGE,
            AC, for L40, 183 acres Headwaters Rockfish. Line of JNO. PRICE.
Rec. 19 Oct 1796. Wit: ARCHIBALD CAMPBELL, FREDERICK WEIR, JAS. ANDERSON.
Orig. del. to FH, 11 Sep 1802.

Page 91.   21 Jun 1794.   HUGH ROSE & wife CAROLINE MATILDA, AC, to GEO.
            DILLARD, AC, for L750, 750 acres S side Tye and joining.
Lines: WM. CABELL JR, Stovall's road. Wit: RO. HOLLOWAY, JNO. TOOL, SAML.
ROSE, BALLINGER. Page 92, order to quiz CAROLINE MATILDA. Done & rec.,
17 Oct 1796, by JOS. BURRUS & WM. CABELL JR.

Page 93.   21 Sep 1796.   ABRAHAM STEEL, AC, to LINDSEY COLEMAN, AC, all
            interest in estate of father, AUGUSTINE STEEL. Wit: GIDEON
CREWS, PEACHY FRANKLIN, JAS. BALLINGER, HOWARD CASH.

318

Page 93.   12 Apr 1796.   MOSES HALL, AC, to ZACH. TALIAFERRO for Ł48-19-1,
            cows, furniture etc. Wit: WM. CARTER, JASPER FRANKLIN, HOWARD
CASH.

Page 94.   1 Oct 1796.   JAS. BROOKS & wife ELIZ., Albemarle, to JAS.
            NOLIN, AC, for Ł100, 130 acres N fork Rockfish. Lines: grantor,
the road, CHAS. RODES, Shingle Hollow, BENJ. PANNELL, JOS. SMITH. Wit:
MARTIN DAWSON, AUGUSTINE SHEPHERD, WM. FOX, WM. EWERS. Orig. del. to
BROOKS, 19 Oct 1797.

Page 95.   13 Oct 1796.   JNO. BAUGHAN, son & heir of SAML. BAUGHAN dec'd,
            who was son & heir of MICHL. BAUGHAN dec'd, to PHILIP JOHNSON,
158 acres headwaters Boling Creek. In possession of MICHL. BAUGHAN dec'd.
and fell to SAML. BAUGHAN, dec'd, sole heir of MICHL, and sold by SB to
JONATHAN JOHNSON dec'd, and through heirship to PHILIP JOHNSON. Lines:
JOHNSON, COALTER, THOS. MOFFITT's heirs. Wit: JNO. HILL JR, CALEB WATTS,
JNO. MURRILL, NICHL. DAVIES, MARTIN PARKS, GEO. McDANIEL.

Page 96.   2 Sep 1796.   CHAS. CARTER, Culpeper, to LEONARD HENLEY, AC,
            for Ł30, no acreage - S side Buffalo and subject to lease of
JNO. BROCKMAN. Lines: grantee, RICH. OGLESBY, the river. All that CC
holds on this side of river. Wit: RICH. OGLESBY, HENRY CAMDEN, WM. BACON.

Page 97.   14 Sep 1796.   WM. CABELL to RO. RIVES & Co., all of AC, for
            Ł60, 2 lots of 1/2 acre each in New Markett, No. 6 & 10 on
plat - not herein. Wit: W.H. CABELL, LANDON CABELL, WILL CABELL JR. Orig
del. to JAS. MURPHY 19 Oct 1809.

Page 98.   17 Aug 1792.   CHAS. LYNCH, heir of CHAS. LYNCH, dec'd.; SAML.
            MITCHELL & wife ANN (late LYNCH and daughter and joint heir of
CHRISTOPHER LYNCH) to JNO. LYNCH - Campbell Co. residents - 160 acres on
Harris Creek.   CHAS. left land to son, CHRISTOPHER, but error in will
made him only life tenant. It is necessary for CHAS. to join in this deed.
Lines: Jas. River and the mouth of Harris. Wit: GIDEON LEA, JNO. MILLS,
CALEB TATE, THOS. THORPH, MICAJAH GOODWIN, DANL. TUCKER, CHAS. ELLIS,
JOS. MEGANN.

Page 99.   10 Nov 1795.   JAS. MAYS, AC, & parish, to MARGARET WELCH of
            same, for Ł60, 200 acres N side Tye river. Lines: SAML. BURKS.
Wit: WM. WARWICK, CHAS. LAYNE, WM. LAIN, waterman.

Page 101.   16 Oct 1796.   Order to quiz SALLY ROSE, wife of CHAS. ROSE as
            to deed to CHAS. WATTS 21 Jul 1795; del. to CW, 28 Mar 1807.
606 acres by ROSE and trustees, W.S. CRAWFORD & PATRICK ROSE.

Page 102.   Order of 14 Jul 1796, to AC J.P.'s to quiz CATH, wife of JNO.
            ROSE as to 13 May 1796 deed to THOS. MASSIE - 2 tracts of 3852
acres. Done 17 Oct 1796, by NATHAN CRAWFORD & HUDSON MARTIN.

Page 103.   17 Oct 1796.   ZACH. FORTUNE & wife ELIZ, AC, to MAJOR KING, AC,
            for Ł54, 100 acres - scratched - Head branches S fork Rucker's
Run. Line of NICHL. CABELL.

Page 104.   15 Oct 1796.   SACKVILLE KING & wife ANN, Campbell Co, to POW-
            HATAN BOLLING, Lynchburg, for Ł45-10, 44 acres Stovall Creek
and including STOVALL's old mill and seat. Surveyed by JAS. HIGGINBOTHAM
4 Apr 1794. Lines: KING, GEO. STOVALL JR, dec'd, (now WM. GALT's), STE-
PHEN HAM, N side of creek. Wit: THOS. MOORE, WM. TURNER, A. STUART, PHIL.
JOHNSON. Orig. del. to LINEAS BOLLING, exr. of P. BOLLING, 4 Mar 1806.

Page 105.   18 Oct 1796.   RO. GRANT & wife MARY, AC, to ALEX. McALEXANDER,
            AC, for Ł60-10, 119 acres N fork Davis Creek. Lines: JOS.
ROBERTS, WM. BLAINE, ELIZ. JOHNSON, JOSEPH SHELTON. Del. 8 Aug 1801 to AM.

Page 106.   2 Mar 1796.   FLEMING WATKINS, Buckingham Co, to LEWIS NEVIL,
            AC, for Ł20, slave & horse. Wit: CORNL. THOMAS, WM. LEE HARRIS.

Page 107.   6 Oct 1796.   JACOB TYREE SR, to WM. PHILLIPS, AC, for Ł20, 100
            acres S dies Buffalo. Lines: grantee & river. Wit: H.A. GAR-
LAND, JACOB TYREE JR, GABL. PAGE, BARNETT OWEN, P. GOOCH.

Page 108.   4 Aug 1796.   CHAS. CHRISTIAN & wife SARAH, AC, to JNO. CREWS,
AC, for Ŀ173, 270 acres both sides Porrage. Lines: ELIJAH DE-
HART, crossing creek. Wit: GIDEON CREWS, WM. CASHWELL, WM. PENDLETON,
JNO. MAHONE.

Page 109.   -- Oct 1796.   GEO. HYLTON & wife BETHEMIA (BARTHEMIA), AC, to
RICH. WOOD, AC, for Ŀ50, 50 acres both sides N branch Fishing
Creek. Lines: grantor (formerly JNO. JOSLINS's), JAS. PAMPLIN (formerly
WM. CABELL's).

Page 110.   26 Sep 1796.   Order to AC J.P.'s to quiz JANE, wife of SAML.
MEREDITH - 14 Sep 1796 deed of MEREDITHs to LINDSEY COLEMAN -
101 acres. Done & rec. 17 Oct 1796, by JOS. BURRUS & WM. CABELL JR.

Page 111.   Rec. 17 Oct 1796, AC J.P.'s quizzed LUCY COLEMAN, wife of
LINDSEY COLEMAN, as to deed to SAML. MEREDITH, 14 Sep 1796 -
3 1/4 acres. Same J.P.'s as above.

Page 111.   16 Apr 1796.   ARCHELAUS MITCHELL SR, to ARCHELAUS MITCHELL JR.
for 5 sh, 100 acres. Lines: MICAJAH GOODWIN, John's Creek to
mouth. Wit: RICH. POWELL, BOLLING MITCHELL, JOSIAH HARRIS.

Page 112.   14 May 1796.   DANL. MOSBY & wife SARAH, AC, to JNO. MOSBY, AC,
their son, for certain services - 300 acres, lower tract
bought by DM of DAVID MONTGOMERY JR. Lines: W side Marrowbone, E side of
Spur of Rocky Mt., grantee. Wit: JNO. E. FITZPATRICK, CHAS. STATHAM,
JNO. CLARKE, PLEASANT DAWSON.

Page 112.   24 Sep 1796.   RO. CAMPBELL, AC, to PHILIP JOHNSON & MICHL.
COALTER, AC, for Ŀ50, 15 acres. Lines: JNO. FLOYD BURFORD. Wit:
JOS. BURRUS, RICH. BURKS, WM. PERRIGAN(?), CONY(?) WHITEHEAD, JNO. REY-
NOLDS, OBEDIAH REYNOLDS, JNO. MERRITT.

Page 114.   20 Nov 1796.   JNO. GARDNER, AC farmer, sets forth that he drew
draft on his father, JNO. GARDNER, Great Britain, after father
wrote letter permitting it to "my brother, EPHRAIM GARDNER", tanner, City
of Glasgow. Ŀ100 drawn after copy of letter sent of 1 Mar 1796, payable
to SAML. IRVINE & Co. Relinquishes all future rights against estate of
father in Great Britain. Wit: ALEX. STEWART, SAML. IRVINE, WILSON DAVEN-
PORT.

Page 115.   12 Sep 1796.   WM. CABELL & wife MARGARETT, AC, to JAS. POWELL
COCKE, Albemarle Co, (Orig. del. to ALEX. BROWN, 9 Jun 1832)
for Ŀ55, 30 acres. Lines: grantor, JNO. BETHEL, N bank Rucker's Run. Wit:
LANDON, JUDITH S., ELIZ, WM. JR, & WM. H. CABELL.

Page 116.   15 Oct 1796.   JAS. WATSON & wife PATTY, AC, to EZEK. GILBERT
& wife, ANN RUKINGS GILBERT, AC, for Ŀ80, 80 acres where grantees live. Lines: JAMES FRANKLYN, GEO. COLEMAN dec'd. At deaths of grantees, to their children and heirs on equal division. Wit: P. GOOCH,
RICH. F. BERNARD, HENRY R. SNEED.

Page 118.   3 Nov 1796, rec.   Consent of DORCAS LACKEY, wife of SAML., as
to 17 Oct 1796, deed to PHILIP GOOCH. Done by WM. HARRIS &
JAS. WOODS, AC J.P.'s.

Page 119.   16 Dec 1796.   GEO. McDANIEL to MATT. MYLER, AC, for Ŀ9, 3½
acres, part of tract recently bought by grantor of THOS. GIL-
LINGWATERS. Lines: THOS. JOHNSON, Bolling Creek, King's road. Wit: GIDEON
LEA, THOS. JOHNSON, ANTHONY RUCKER.

Page 119.   17 Nov 1796.   PAUL WOOD, AC, & FRANCES WOOD, Bedford Co, to
SUSANNA GILLILAND, AC, for Ŀ47-15, 57 acres Porrage Creek.
Lines: THOS. WILCOX. Wit: JNO. McDANIEL, WM. BURFORD, JNO. HANSARD, JAS.
MARR, SILAS WOOD, WM. KNIGHT, ANTHONY RUCKER.

Page 121.   15 Nov 1796.   SAML. LACKEY & wife DORCAS, AC, to JOS. ROBERTS,
AC, for Ŀ400, 216 acres Corbin Creek, branch of Rockfish.
Lines: LITTLEBERRY WITT dec'd, ROBT. HARDY, WM. BARNETT, grantee. Wit:
JAS. WOODS, WM. WRIGHT, ALEX. ROBERTS, WM. MOORE.

Page 122.   19 Dec 1796.   NICHL. CROSS (CRESS) & wife ELIZ, AC, to DANL.
          BURFORD SR, AC, for Ł130, 222 acres Stovall & Harris creeks in
3 surveys. Lines: DANL. BURFORD JR, Bolling Creek, MICHL. STONEHOCKER,
PHILIP JOHNSON & MICHL. COALTER, RO. CAMPBELL. Orig. del. to E. WILLS'
exr., 11 Jan 1811.

Page 123.   14 May 1796.   SAML. COLEMAN, AC, to THOS. COLEMAN, AC, Deed of
          Trust to secure debt to McCLURE BRYDIE & Co. 5 sh. 140 acres
Head of Huff. Lines: JNO. COLEMAN dec'd, WM. CAMDEN; also tobacco and
wheat. One batch of tobacco due from THOS. STEWART. Wit: WM. TUCKER,
RO. GRISSOM, H. SMITH.

Page 124.   23 Nov 1796.   GARRET LANDS, AC, to WM. THURMOND, AC, for Ł50,
          beds, etc, wroking Iron tools at blacksmith shop and in Lynch-
burg. Wit: CHAS. TUCKER, JNO. McCABE, CHAS. HAYS.

Page 125.   9 May 1796.   Order to AC J.P.'s, SAML. MEREDITH & JOS. BURRUS,
          to quiz LUCY, wife of THOS. BRAGG - 8 Apr 1796, deed to THOS.
RUCKER - 350 acres. Done & rec. 19 Dec 1796.

Page 126.   21 Nov 1796.   WM. GRIFFIN & wife RUTH; ZACH. PETERS & wife
          KEZIAH, AC, to WM. LOVING, AC, (Orig. del. to WL, 26 Jun 1798)
for Ł60, S branches Rucker's Run - 2 adj. tracts. Lines: grantee, where
he lives; part of tract of JOSEPH LIVELY, dec'd, upon equal division
to RUTH & KEZIAH by JOS. LIVELY as his legatees by settlement - 44 acres
each. (Note discrepancy in acres) Page 127, order to quiz wives done and
rec. 23 Nov 1796. Wit: JOS. LOVING, JAS. HANSBROUGH, JNO. BRYANT, JNO.
STAPLES.

Page 128.   26 Oct 1796.   MOSES PENN, AC, to GALT & GARLAND - 5 sh., 3
          slaves. Wit: WIATT SMITH, WM. EDMONDS.

Page 128.   15 Nov 1796.   SAML. LACKEY & wife DORCAS, AC, to JOS. ROBERTS,
          AC, for Ł400, 216 acres Corbin Creek; branch of Rockfish.
Lines: LITTLEBERRY WITT, dec'd, RO. HARDY, WM. BARNETT, grantee. Wit:
JAS. WOODS, WM. WRIGHT, ALEX. ROBERTS, WM. MOORE.

Page 130.   24 Oct 1796.   WM. LAINE, AC, to McCLURE BRYDIE & Co, Ł171-14
          debt - 3 slaves. Wit: GIDEON CREWS, JNO. STRATTON, MICAJAH
GOODWIN.

Page 130.   16 Dec 1796.   JOS. HIGGINBOTHAM JR, AC, to WM. CLARK, AC,
          (orig. del. 28 Apr 1817, to B. TALIAFERRO) for Ł100, 100 acres
S and middle forks Pedlar. Part of tract.

Page 131.   Order of 29 Nov 1796 to AC J.P.'s WM. WARWICK & WM. WARE, to
          quiz PATTY LANDRUM, wife of YOUNG LANDRUM, and NANCY WRIGHT,
wife of ACHILLES WRIGHT, as to deed to JOS. LOVING - 685 acres. Rec. 2
Dec 1796.

Page 132.   15 Sep 1796.   PHILIP SMITH, AC, to JNO. CLARKSON, AC, for Ł225,
          200 acres on Franklin Creek. Part of tract. Wit: JNO. TALIA-
FERRO, RODERICK TALIAFERRO, JAS. TALIAFERRO.

Page 133.   3 Dec 1796.   CHARLEY DAWSON, admr. of JNO. DAWSON, lease for
          9 yrs. of land whereon I live with mansion house - to WM.
TURNER - from above date. Ł15 per year. Wit: THOS. MORE, NELSON C.
DAWSON, JAMES LEE.

Page 134.   19 Dec 1796.   SAML. BROWN & wife MARY, AC, to JAS. SAVAGE, AC,
          for Ł105, 75 acres Buffalo. Bought by SB of JACOB GIBSON.
Lines: GABL. PENN to lot 1; lot 4, SMYTH TANDY. Wit: JAS. FRANKLIN, JNO.
LAMONT, JOS. DILLARD.

Page 135.   16 Dec 1796.   BENJ. PLUNKETT & wife FRANCES, Campbell Co., to
          MADDISON HILL, AC, (Examined and del. to STEPHEN ROBINSON) for
Ł88, 177 acres S branches Stovall Creek. Lines: BENJ. RUCKER, THOS. JOHNS,
S bank Wolf Branch, THOS. RICKETTS. Wit: JNO. WINGFIELD, CHAS. WINGFIELD,
STEPHEN ROBINSON.

Page 136.   14 Dec 1796.   SPRICE(SPRUCE?) PENDLETON, Buckingham Co, to
            MICAJAH PENDLETON, Buckingham Co, for Ƚ50, 200 acres both
sides Elk Island Creek. Wit: JNO. HORSLEY, JNO. HARRIS JR, JOS. HORSLEY,
WARREN TALIAFERRO.

Page 137.   26 Nov 1796.   CHAS. SNELSON, AC, to JNO. WINGFIELD, AC, Deed
            of trust on an appeal bond to Superior Court - del. 13 Oct
1797, to JW - slave, beds, etc. Wit: WILSON DAVENPORT, CHAS. H. WINGFIELD.

Page 139.   17 Aug 1796.   JNO. HO. GOODWIN, Pittsylvania Co, to MICHL.
            COALTER & PHILLIP JOHNSON, AC, (Del. to JNO. WIATT JR, 24 Jan
1794) for Ƚ60, 340 acres branches Bolling Creek. Lines: JONATHAN JOHNSON's
pat. line, 20 Jul 1780, bequeathed by WM. JOHNSON dec'd, to sisters, MARY
now GOODWIN and wife of JNO. H., and FRANCES JOHNSON - lower tract to
MARY. Wit: WM. MUSE, JAS. LASHELL, RO. ROBINSON, GIDEON LEA, JNO. MERRITT.

Page 140.   19 Aug 1794.   DANL. BURFORD SR, & JNO. STEWART, AC, to PHILIP
            THURMOND, AC, for Ƚ100, 54 acres. Lines: VA. TAYLOR, RO. CAMP-
BELL. Wit: JNO. MERRITT, GEO. McDANIEL, STEPHEN ROBINSON.

Page 141.   30 Nov 1796.   JACOB PETTYJOHN & wife ELIZ, AC, to WM. PETTY-
            JOHN, AC, for Ƚ280, 280 acres Harris Creek. Wit: PHILIP JOHN-
SON, STEPHEN ROBINSON, R. NERVELL.

Page 142.   19 Nov 1796.   WM. LAINE, waterman, AC, to children, GEO. &
            SARAH LAINE, for love and 5 sh, slave, Hannah, horse, bed,
cattle, hogs, table etc. Wit: JNO. LOVING, JOS. STAPLES.

Page 143.   19 Dec 1796.   GEO. HIGHT & wife LOVY, AC, to THOS. MASSIE,
            Frederick Co, for Ƚ74-8, 200 acres Stony Run; branch of Tye.
Lines: SAML. POE, GEO. HIGHT, S fork Stony. (Del. to DANL. McDANIEL, 21
Sep 1794) JOS. ALLEN (now HIGHT), SAML. POE (now HIGHT's). Pat. 16 Feb
1771, to JAS. BROWN and conveyed to GH by WM. COFFEY, Jun 1792, and adj.
tracts. One pat. next as of first and same conveyance. Wit: DANL. McDON-
ALD, NATHL. OFFUTT, WILSON PENN, JNO. ROSE.

Page 145.   10 Aug 1796.   JAS. MATTHEWS, Stokes Co, NC, Power of Atty. to
            Capt. WM. TEAS, AC, bills of sale in my possession of property
bought of WM. MATTHEWS of AC. Wit: TANDY MATTHEWS.

Page 146.   25 Mar 1796.   WM. MATTHEWS, AC, to JAS. MATTHEWS, Stokes Co.
            NC, for Ƚ200, slave, Doll, about 16 or 17; horse, etc. Wit:
JNO. BARNES, JNO. COOLEY, WM. TEAS, TANDY MATTHEWS.

Page 146.   21 Nov 1796.   JOS. MAYS JR, & wife JANE, AC, to HENRY STONEHAM,
            AC, for Ƚ100, 199 acres Elk Branch of Tye. Lines: GEO. STONE-
HAM. Wit: JNO. JACOBS, EZEK. HILL, JAS. MURPHY. Page 148, order to AC
J.P.'s to quiz JANE. Done and rec. 2 Dec 1796 by WM. WARWICK, WM. LOVING.

Page 149.   16 Jan 1797.   ZACH. TALIAFERRO & wife JUDTIH, AC, to THOS.
            MASSIE, Frederick Co, for Ƚ393, noted that ZT bought it of
SAML. MARKSBERRY and one part pat. to ZT. 262 acres S side and adj. Tye.
Lines: grantee, JOS. BURGER. Wit: NATHL. OFFUTT, BURKENHEAD TALIAFERRO,
HENDLEY DRUMMOND, WM. HORSLEY, WARREN TALIAFERRO.

Page 150.   16 Jan 1797.   DANL. McDONALD, RICH. & CHAS. TALIAFERRO, attys.
            for devisees of JNO. B. TALIAFERRO, dec'd, to THOS. MASSIE,
Frederick Co, for Ƚ40, 190 acres. (Del. to DMc, 21 Sep 1797.) Branches of
Priest Run, branch of Tye. Line of JNO. ROSE.

Page 151.   5 Nov 1796.   WILSON PENN, AC, & THOMPSON WATKINS, Wilks Co, Va.
            (sic) Power of Atty. to DANL. McDONALD, CHAS. & RICH. TALIA-
FERRO, AC, to sell AC land of JNO. BL TALIAFERRO, dec'd. Wit: GEO. PENN,
JAS. HARRISON.

Page 152.   16 Jan 1797.   LINDSEY COLEMAN, AC, son to RO. COLEMAN, dec'd,
            entitled to share of estate of my dec'd brother, REUBEN COLE-
MAN, of Ga., (Del. to JNO. COLEMAN, 26 Jan 1797) Power of Atty to friend,
JNO. WALLER, S.C., to receive my share. THOS. MOORE & WM. WARWICK certi-
fied that JNO. PENN & BENJ. CHILDRESS, testified under oath that JAS.,

322

CLAYTON, CALEB, LINDSEY, GEO., REUBEN, JOSEPH, SARAH, & MARY COLEMAN were children of ROBT. & ELIZ. COLEMAN, dec'd. 16 Jan 1797.

Page 153. 20 Oct 1796. JOS. H. MORRISON, Elbert Co, Ga., to NATHAN CRAW-
          FORD, AC, (del. to WM. CRAWFORD 19 Nov 1840) for Ł35, 200 ac-
res branches of Rockfish. Lines: his own, DAVID CRAWFORD, JNO. ROBINSON.
Wit: JNO. HIGGINBOTHAM, JR, WM. CRAWFORD JR.

Page 154. 20 Feb 1797. RANDOLPH BIBB, AC, to JNO. PHILLIPS, AC, for
          Ł262-16, 146 acres both sides N branch of Tye. Part of tract
of WM. BIBB, dec'd. Lines: JOHN THOMPSON, WM. BIBB, JNO. ALFORD, Naked
Creek. Wit: WM. LONDON, JNO. CHRISTIAN.

Page 155. 5 Dec 1796. WIATT POWELL, Lynchburg, Campbell Co., to WM.
          NOVILL of same place - Deed of Trust - POWELL owes PHILIP
PAINE & RO. WALKER is bdm. Mtg. on 513 acres on Rutledge - whole of sev-
eral tracts bought by POWELL of JACOB COLEY, JNO. STEWART, GEO. GILBERT
& DAVID JONES. Wit: A. STEWART, C. POWELL, WILSON DAVENPORT.

Page 157. 3 Apr 1789. SAML. RICHESON, Fluvanna, to PHILIP BAILEY, AC,
          for Ł150, 150 acres Rockfish. Part of tract of JNO. WILLIAMSON.
Lines: JONATHAN BRIDGWATER, THOS. FITZPATRICK, HENRY McCLAIN, JNO. WILL-
IAMSON. Wit: JNO. WILLIAMSON, THOS. WILLIAMSON, HENRY SMITH. Final proof
20 Feb 1797, by SMITH.

Page 158. JAS. BUNT - Deed of Trust to JNO. ROSE on land below. Wit:
          KENDALL BUNT, LANDON BRENT.

Page 159. 20 Oct 1796. RICH. DOBSON, Buckingham Co, to JAS. BUNT, AC,
          for Ł820-15, 469 acres Hatt Creek; part of tract conveyed by
THOS. RANDOLPH to PETERFIELD TRENT & by PT to JNO. DOBSON and by JD to
son, RICH. DOBSON. Lines: JNO. SHIELDS, narrow ridge. Wit: as in deed
above, plus RO. MORRISON, RO. DINWIDDIE.

Page 161. 6 Feb 1796. JAS. OWEN & wife BETSY, Bedford Co, to SAML.
          MEREDITH, AC, (Orig. del. to SM 23 Sep 1798) for Ł80, 95 acres
Rocky Run Branch; S branch Buffalo. Part of 2 tracts of JNO. STUART &
JOS. WILCHER. Lines: grantee, CHAS. CHRISTIAN. By deed to OWEN. Signed
BETTY ANN OWEN. Wit: WM. ARMISTEAD, SHEROD BUGG, CHAS. BOWLES, RUSH
HUDSON, WM. CRUTCHER, M. CAMDEN.

Page 162. 15 Feb 1797. ALEX. BRYDIE & wife NANCY - BRYDIE trustee for
          JAS. R. MILLER, PATRICK HART, WM. McCLURE & self - also agt.,
Merchants and partners of firm of McCLURE BRYDIE & Co. (Orig. del. to
W.S. CRAWFORD) firm in Richmond - to WM. S. CRAWFORD, AC, for Ł1000, two
tracts on Tye - 750 acres lately bought by GEO. DILLARD of HUGH ROSE,
dec'd. and by DILLARD sold to firm. Lines: WM. CABELL JR, S branch Tye,
Stovall's road. 50 acres also bought by DILLARD and late property of
THOS. L.L. WALL and transferred to firm and bought by WALL of HUGH ROSE,
dec'd. Camp Creek. Wit: GIDEON CREWS, PEACHY FRANKLIN, LINDSEY COLEMAN.

Page 163. 20 Feb 1796. ALLEN BLAIR & wife MARY, AC, to CHAS. THOMPSON,
          Louisa Co, for Ł180, 179 acres branches Rucker's Run. Lines:
BAINES; JAS. STEVENS. Part of tract of THOS. LOMAX. Signed MARY ANN BLAIR.

Page 164. 20 Feb 1797. WM. KEY & wife ELIZ, AC, to ELISHA PETERS, AC,
          for Ł70, 140 acres S branches Rockfish. Part of WM. ALFORD
tract. Lines: THOS. KEY, JESSE MARTIN, N branches Joe's Creek, JAS.
MATTHEWS, JNO. BUSH. Wit: JAS. LANDRUM, WM. WRIGHT, JNO. ALFORD.

Page 165. 18 Oct 1796. RICH. DOBSON, Buckingham Co, to JNO. SHIELDS,
          AC, for Ł495, 396 acres Hatt Creek, originally granted to WM.
RANDOLPH & devised to his son, THOS. MANN RANDOLPH; transferred to PETER-
FIELD TRENT and by PT transferred to JNO. DOBSON and by him to RICH.
DOBSON. Lines: 3rd lott. Wit: WM. CRAWFORD JR, RO. MORRISON, JAS. BRENT,
JNO. SHIELDS JR.

Page 167. 20 Feb 1797. THOS. JOPLING & wife SALLY, AC, to GEO. VAUGHAN,
          Culpeper, for Ł220, 492 acres H Branches of S fork Rockfish &
branches of Dutch Creek. 2 tracts , 1 of 400 acres and other of 92 acres

in one survey.

Page 168. 11 Feb 1797. THOS. CHILDRESS & wife ELIZ, AC, to BENJ. CHILD-
ERS (sic), AC, for Ł300, 150 acres. Lines: JOSIAH JOPLING,
MATT. HARRIS, WM. L. HARRIS, BENJ. CHILDRESS, to Rockfish river. Wit:
WM. LEE HARRIS, JNO. GRIFFIN, JOS. SHELTON.

Page 169. 22 Sep 1796. Order to Henry Co. J.P.'s HENRY LYNE & JNO.
DILLARD, to quiz SALLY, wife of BALLINGER WADE, as to 5 Mar
1795 deed to MARTIN PARKS - 94 acres. Done, 5 Nov 1796.

Page 170. 21 Jan 1796. Rec'd. of GEO. HIGHT an order on Major THOS.
MASSIE for Ł52-18-10. Signed by WM. COFFEY. Wit: DANL. McDON-
ALD, WM. JACOBS. Orig. del. to GH, 13 Apr 1797.

Page 170. 8 Apr 1797. JNO. ROSE, Roseisle, AC, & wife CAROLINE, to JNO.
ROSE of Westmoreland (del. to SANDY ROSE, 22 Apr 1797)- RO.
ROSE, late of Westmoreland, died in 1793 without issue and single;left
two brothers and two sisters: KATH. md. JNO. ROSE, AC, (CAROLINE above);
MOLLY, widow of THOS. HODGE, dec'd, late of Westmoreland who died Dec,
1775; and ALEX. ROSE (other brother is not named). ROBT. served as sur-
geon in Army of U.S. Estate insufficient to pay debts. JNO. ROSE (probably the other brother) is admr. and JNO. of AC and wife relinquish all
rights in estate-two military warrants and any plats or surveys. Wit:
JNO. THOMPSON JR, JAS. THOMPSON, PLEASANT THOMPSON JR.

Page 172. 17 Feb 1797. WM. LEE HARRIS & wife ELIZ, AC, to WM. H. DIGGS,
AC, (del. to JOS. LOVING, 2 May 1807) for Ł175, 190 acres S
branches Rucker's Run, part of tract of WM. BIBB, dec'd. Lines: WM. LOV-
ING, JNO. LOVING, THOS. BIBB, RO. WRIGHT, MATT. HARRIS, LOMAX's old line.
Wit: WM. PATTERSON, JNO. HIGGINBOTHAM, RO. RIVES.

Page 173. 22 Dec 1796. MOSES PENN, AC, to GEO. PENN (del. 7 Sep 1799)
Deed of Trust securing GEO. PENN for Ł150 - my land portion
bequeathed to me by my father, GEO. PENN, dec'd, in his will, whereon he
lived - all my interest. Wit: REUBIN CRAWFORD, THOS. PENN, JAS. STRATTON
JR.

Page 173. 17 Apr 1797. DANL. TUCKER, gen. of WM., ROBT H., REUBEN, &
LINDSEY COLEMAN, children & orphs. of GEO. COLEMAN, dec'd,
Power of Atty. to friends, NATHL. PERRY, Ga., & JNO. WALLER, S.C.,
children's interest in Georgia in estate of REUBEN COLEMAN dec'd.

Page 174. 15 Apr 1797. NICHL. PRYOR, AC, to WM. PRYOR, AC, (del. to NP
17 Jun 1800) for Ł60, 100 acres Lovelady Creek; branch of
Pedlar. Part of tract.

Page 175. 21 Oct 1796. JNO. McDANIEL, AC, to JNO. WILSON, AC, for Ł25,
244 acres. Lines: ANGUST McDANIEL, S branch Brown Mt. Creek,
NEILL CAMPBELL. Wit: WM. BARRETT, JOS. DILLARD, WM. CAMDEN.

Page 176. 10 Apr 1797. SAML. MEREDITH & wife JANE, AC, to RICH. WILSON,
AC, for Ł262-10, 527 acres. Lines: GILBERT'S tract, 95 acres
bought of JAS. OWEN; JOS. WILCHER, CHAS. CHRISTIAN. 432 acre tract. Wit:
WM. ARMISTEAD, WM. HUGHES, DAVID S. GARLAND.

Page 177. 20 Mar 1797. RO. C. HARRISON & iwfe ANN, Cumberland Co., to
JOSEPH HOLLINGSWORTH, AC, for Ł82, 265 acres, part of tract
conveyed by JOS. CABELL, Buckingham, to ANN HARRISON. Lines: WM. CRISP,
Spencer's road, WM. LOVING dec'd, Bobb's Creek.

Page 178. 20 Mar 1797. RO. C. HARRISON & wife ANN, Cumberland, to CHAS.
EDMONDS, AC, for Ł46-13-4, 140 acres, part of tract as above.
Lines: grantor, N branch Bobb's Creek, BENJ. MARTIN, S bank Rucker's Run.

Page 179. 5 Oct 1796. JOS. LIVELY JR, AC, to NATHL. WADE, AC, for Ł40,
225 acres Rockfish. Lines: JNO. SNYDER, CORNL. THOMAS Dec'd.
SALLY, wife of JOS. LIVELY. Wit: PATRICK TYLER, BENJ. HAMMETT, CHAS.
HAMMETT. Page 180, 29 Dec 1796, certified in Spartingbourgh(sic), S.C.,
that GEO. LAMPKIN, Acting J.P., took oath of BENJ. HAMMETT that he saw

324

JOS. & SALLY LIVELY sign the deed. JNO. LANCASTER certified as to LAMPKIN.

Page 181.   Rec. 17 Apr 1797.   LANDON CARTER & wife MARY, AC, to WM. HOW-
            ARD, AC, for Ŀ25, 78 acres Horsley Creek. Lines: JAS. GOODRICH,
WM. WARE.

Page 182.   14 Jun 1797.   EDWD. WATSON, AC, to daughter, ANN LACKEY &
            children - slaves in trust of my son, WM. WATSON, now loaned
to JNO. LACKEY by me; horse, beds. At ANN's death to her heirs. Wit: JNO.
PENDLETON, THOS. STEWART.

Page 182.   9 Apr 1797.   ABRAHAM WARWICK, AC, to WM. WARWICK, AC, for 5sh,
            436 acres branches Rucker's Run. Lines: JNO. BETHEL, road
crossing Middow or Middle(?) branch on road from Fendlay's Gap to Amherst
Courthouse (CH was then at what is now Colleen in Nelson County) Orig.
sent to JNO. M. OTEY, adm., 3 Oct 1833.

Page 183.   17 Jun 1797.   JAS. H. WEST & wife SUSANNAH, Alb, to DENNITT
            WITT, AC, for Ŀ80, 200 acres Headwaters Rockfish. Lines: Top
of a mt. in WEST's line, WITT.

(I should point out that page numbers are poorly done in this deed book,
but I am putting down pages as numbered. Some of them have no numbers at
all, but I am putting deeds in sequence as they appear.BFD)

Page 184.   19 Jun 1797.   JAS. H. WEST & wife SUSANNAH, Alb., to JESSE
            OGLESBY, AC, (del. to JO, 6 Apr 1805) for Ŀ40, 76 acres S
branches of S fork of Rockfish. Lines: THOMAS WEST, JAS. HURD, ANDREW
REID, JAS. WEST.

Page 185.   30 Nov 1796 (scratched) BENJ. LIVELY, AC, to MARK LIVELY, AC,
            for 40, 44 acres branches Rucker's Run. Lines: WM. LOVING.
Part of tract of JOS. LIVELY dec'd. Lot 1 fell to BENJ. Wit: WILL LOVING,
RICH. WAUGH, GEO. MARTIN. Rec. on 19 Jun 1797.

Page 186.   4 Mar 1797.   THOS. LAINE, AC, to daughter, SALLY LAINE, for
            love, "I am weak, old, and infirm, and Sarah has supported for
years her mother and me." 6 sh. for mare, cattle, furniture etc. Wit:
FRANCES SMITH, HOWARD BALLEW.

Page 187.   21 Oct 1796.   CHAS. LYNCH, Campbell Co, to JAS. WARD, of same,
            (Orig. del. to JW 7 Nov 1815) for 5 sh, 500 acres Jas. river
tract sold to WARD by CHRISTOPHER LYNCH, dec'd. CHAS. is heir and wishes
to fill contract - Ŀ50 pat. to LARCH(?) LYNCH. Lines: JNO. LYNCH (formerly THACKER) PETTUS THACKER, JNO. WARD (formerly THOS. POWELL) TENNISON,
JNO. WARD (formerly THOS. WRIGHT. Wit: JNO. LYNCH, HENRY WARD, WM. MOORE.

Page 188.   8 Mar 1797.   WIATT POWELL & wife MARY, Lynchburg, to GIDEON
            RUCKER, AC, (del. to WP 9 Nov 1797) for Ŀ175, 175 acres Rut-
ledge. Lines: CHRISTOPHER FLETCHER, Lynch road, grantee, Still House
Branch, N fork Rutledge, Mill Pond, GEO. COLEMAN, dec'd, EDWD. WATSON,
Watson's road, Spring Corner. Wit: WM. EDMONDS, WM. KING, JNO. F. POWELL.

Page 189.   23 Sep 1796.   Order to AC J.P.'s ot quiz FRANCES, wife of
            MICHL. COALTER - 3 Aug 1796 deed to HENRY BROWN - 402 acres.
(Del. to HB, 13 Mar 1803.) Done by JOS. BURRUS & REUBEN NORVELL and rec.
19 Jun 1797.

Page 191.   27 Oct 1796.   CLARY HIGGINBOTHAM, AC, to MARY ANN ARNOLD, AC,
            for 3 pence per year, 200 acres where AARON HIGGINBOTHAM SR,
died and was buried. Wit: ELIJAH BROCKMAN, AARON FRANKLIN, REUBEN FRANK-
LIN. (This deed reminds me of a question propounded to me by Mrs. SWEENY
just a short time before her fatal illness. She was in the record room
working across from me and asked me if I knew where AARON HIGGINBOTHAM
was buried. I replied in the negative and she said, "Someone wants to
know, but I am not revealing it. I know exactly where he is buried." I
assume that she had traced down the title on the land, but I have never
attempted to do so. The Amherst chapter of DAR's has benn considering
the project of marking graves, but I know of no work to date on the
problem. I fear that it will ba a hard task, for family graveyards in the

county have been plowed up in many instances. The use of fieldstones, also, makes identification difficult except for approximate sites. I know this to be true from investigation of the sites of graves of JOSHUA HUDSON & GEO. GILLESPIE, two of my wife's ancestors, who were too old to fight, but rendered assistance as shown in Impressed Claims (see my work on these records). The HUDSON plot is still known because a few modern graves have been marked, but the old ones are merely fieldstones. GILLESPIE's site has been destroyed. BFD)

Page 191. 16 Dec 1796. WM. FOX & wife ELIZ, AC, to CHAS. RODES, AC, for Ł50, 40 acres Head of Indian Branch. Lines: JNO. HENDERSON, SAML. FOX, WM. WILSON. Fianl proof 19 Jun 1797. Wit: JNO. MURRELL JR, WM. WILSON, THOS. MARTIN, CHAS. RODES JR.

Page 192. 6 Oct 1796. WM. WILSON & wife SARAH, AC, to CHAS. RODES, AC, for Ł33, 60 acres Headwaters Rockfish. Lines: RO. JOHNSON, WM. FOX, SAML. FOX, JNO. HENDERSON. Wit: as above.

Page 193. 19 Jun 1797. SALLY BURRUS declined provisions of will of her dec'd. husband, CHAS. BURRUS, AC; claims dower. Wit: W.S. CRAWFORD & JNO. CAMM.

Page 193. 9 Jun 1797. WM. HOWARD, AC, to GALT & GARLAND, 4 sh, Deed of Trust, 78 acres Horsley. Lines: JAS. GOODRICH, WM. WARE. Wit: SAML. MEREDITH, JAMES GARLAND, WM. EDMONDS (JR?)

Page 195. 19 Apr 1797. JAS. NEVIL, AC, to JAS. LOVING, Deed of Trust, 5 sh, slave, Hatt, a boy; debt due McCLURE & BRYDIE. Wit: WILLIS WILLS, CLO. SHELTON.

Page 195. 15 Mar 1797. JNO. JOHNSON, AC, to JAS. LOVING for Ł10, 4 slaves, Rachel, Phillis, Ben, and Buck; beds, etc. Deed of Trust for debt due McCLURE & BRYDIE. Wit: as above plus EDMD. READ.

Page 195. 26 Jan 1797. SAML. IRVINE, gdn. of SAML. ROSE, to PHILIP BAILEY, 4 yr. lease, land to ward from Col. HUGH ROSE, dec'd. To repair & fence - known as The Orchard; plant peach trees for brandy - 40 ft. apart. Corn 1st year, wheat 2nd year, wheat 3rd yr. to prevent wasting. Ł100. Wit: WILSON DAVENPORT, DAVID S. GARLAND.

Page 198. 3 Dec 1796. WM. GRIFFIN & wife RUTH, AC, for Ł30, 44 acres S branch Rucker's Run. Part of tract of JOS. LIVELY, dec'd; share of MARY LIVELY under equal division; ref. to deed by MARY to GRIFFIN. Wit: WM. TEAS, EDMD. BURNETT, HENRY SMITH.

Page 199. 17 Apr 1797. WM., GEO., THOS. PENN & DAVID S. GARLAND, exrs. of GEO. PENN, dec'd, AC, to WM. WARWICK, AC,(sent to JNO. M. OTEY, admr. 2 Oct 1833) ref. to will - Ł600, 400 acres N side and joining Burralo. Lines of SAML. MEREDITH & GABL. PENN. Wit: W.S. CRAWFORD, LANDON CABELL, NELSON ANDERSON.

Page 200. 17 Jun 1797. THOS. GOODRICH & ISAAC WRIGHT to WM. WARE, AC, for Ł500, - scratched - 300 acres. Lines: ISAAC WRIGHT, Horsley creek, CALEB RALLS, crossing creek that leads to main road, H. LAINE land. bought of WM. DAVIS; included is Mill seat. Wit: HENRY BROWN, ABRAM CARTER, HENRY LAINE, LANDON CARTER.

Page 201. 30 May 1797. HENRY LANDON DAVIES & wife LUCY WHITING, Bedford, to NICHL. CALYTON DAVIES, AC, for 5 sh, 2951 acres surveyed by SAML. BOYLE DAVIES. Lines: mouth of Crab Creek; branch above Pedlar, near Rolling road, ASHCRAFT ROACH, ARCHELAUS GILLIAM, JNO. BURKS; LEWIS; JAS. DAVIS, Maple Creek, Clark Creek, crossing Pedlar, Major JOSIAH ELLIS, CALEB WATTS, Pedlar road, Indian granve, Green Pond Branch. (Orig. del. to RO. CRAWFORD, 28 Aug 1797. Wit: DANL. WARWICK, JAS. BAILEY, JNO. GRIGSBY.

Page 204. 23 Feb 1796. SAML. MEREDITH, AC, to JOS. WILCHER, AC, for 5 sh, 102 acres, part of tract. Rockey River branches. Lines: BRAXTON's old line, NOTLEY MADDOX, JOS. HIGGINBOTHAM. Wit: DAVIS S. GARLAND, JAS. GARLAND, JAS. P. GARLAND.

326

Page 205. 19 Jun 1797. CHAS. ROSE & wife SALLY; WM. S. CRAWFORD; PAT-
RICK ROSE - surviving trustees, AC, to WM. MOSS, AC, for Ŀ246,
328 acres S side and joining Piney River. Part of tract. Lines: Rockey
Branch, PATRICK ROSE, WM. MOSS. Wit: JOS. BURRUS, GEO. PENN, SAML. MERE-
DITH. Order to quiz SALLY and rec. on same day by BURRUS & MEREDITH who
were also witnesses.

Page 207. 2 Jun 1797. HENRY LANDON DAVIES & wife LUCY WHITING, Bedford,
to CHAS. CLAY, Bedford, (Sent to CC, 17 Mar 1800) for Ŀ144-15,
59 acres N side Fluvanna and both sides Otter Creek. Surveyed by SAML.
BOYLE DAVIES. Lines: N branch Fluvanna, across the little river, Rawley's
Island (alias Big Island), sunken ground. Wit: OSBORN LOCKETT, THOS.
MOORE, SAML. B. DAVIES, SANL. WARWICK, JO. GRIGSBY, JAS. BAILEY.

Page 209. 4 Dec 1796. Order to Bedford J.P.'s WM. HARRIS & SIMON MILLER
to quiz SARAH, wife of WM. WHITTEN, 6 Apr 1795 deed to JER.
WHITTEN - 385 acres. Rec. p.211 another order for 136 acres. Done 19 Dec
1796.

Page 210. 17 Jun 1797. THOS. & EDMOND GOODRICH, AC, to WM. WARE, AC,
for Ŀ200, 162 3/4 acres Headwaters Horsley. Wit: ABRAHAM CAR-
TER, LANDON CARTER, HENRY BROWN, HENRY LAINE.

Page 212. 15 Jul 1797. JNO. BALL & wife ELIZ., to ALBIN GORDING for
Ŀ125, 100 acres Joe's Creek. Lines: Warminster road; WM.
CABELL, NELSON ANDERSON.

Page 213. 30 Jun 1797. WM. McMULLEN of Ky, to JNO. SHIELDS SR, AC, for
Ŀ37-10, 125 acres. Lines: THOS. ROBERTSON, JNO. McCLURE, MAJOR
HARRIS, Capt. AUGUSTINE SHEPHERD. MARTHA, wife of McMULLEN. Wit: RO.
SHIELDS, JNO. SMITH, MARGARET SMITH.

Page 213. 8 Jul 1797. WM. WARWICK & wife SARAH, AC, to JNO. WARWICK, AC,
Parish of Amherst, for Ŀ1000, 436 acres Rucker's Run. Part of
former tract of ABRAHAM WARWICK. Lines: the road, WM. CABELL, JNO. BETHEL.

Page 215. 17 Jul 1797. MARK LIVELY & wife MARY, AC, to WM. LOVING, AC,
(Orig. del. to WL, 26 Jun 1798) for Ŀ100, 100 acres N branches
Bobb's Creek. Lines: grantee. Part of tract of JOS. LIVELY dec'd.

Page 216. 22 Dec 1796. MOSES PENN, AC, to WILSON PENN, AC, for Ŀ50,
furniture, horse, saddle etc. Wit: REUBEN CRAWFORD, GEO. PENN.

Page 216. 15 Jul 1797. EDWD. CAMPBELL, AC, to GALT & GARLAND, 5 sh,
Deed of Trust - bond of JAS. & EDWD. CAMPBELL assigned to
SAML. MEREDITH & DAVID S. GARLAND - stock - 1 black cow bought of Dr.
EZEK. GILBERT. Wit: EDWD. GARLAND, JAS. EDMUNDS, JR, WM. KNIGHT.

Page 218. 5 Oct 1792. RO. DAVIS, Power of Atty for LANDON DAVIS, Dist.
of Ky, Lincoln Co, to BENJ. KELLY, AC, for Ŀ15, 25 acres, part
of tract of RO. DAVIS and now that of DAVID JARRELL - Wilderness Run -
laid off for JNO. FLOYD by RO. DAVIS and by FLOYD willed to LANDON DAVIS.
Lines: JNO. GILLIAM, DAVID JARRELL, RODERICK McCULLOCH, DAVID ROSS, BENJ.
GOODE. Wit: RODERICK McCULLOCH, DAVID JARRELL, THOS. ALLEN,JNO. F.P. LEWIS.

Page 219. 6 Jan 1797. EDWD WARE & wife SALLY, Georgia, to HENRY HART-
LESS, (Orig. del. 7 Sep 1805, to WM. HARTLESS, admr. of H.
HARTLESS) for Ŀ150, 330 acres Horsley Creek. Lines: SOLOMON CARTER, WM.
CABELL, JNO. TALIAFERRO. Wit: WM. WARE, LANDON CARTER, T.N. EUBANK, LAR-
KIN BIAS, JER. DUN, WM. THURMOND, JNO. McCABE, PHILIP THURMOND JR.

Page 220. 17 Jul 1797. JOS. STAPLES & wife MOLLY, AC, to ALLEN BLAIR,
AC, for Ŀ141, 235 acres N branches Buffalo. Part of tract.
Lines: JAS. SEAY, SMYTH TANDY, GABRIEL PENN.

Page 221. 21 May 1797. Order to Cumberland Co, J.P.'s JOS. & MAYO
CARRINGTON to quiz ANN, wife of RO. C. HARRISON - 20 Mar 1797
deed to CHAS. EDMONDS - 140 acres. Done, 14 Jul 1797.

Page 222. --- 1797. RO. CARTER HARRISON & wife ANNE, Cumberland Co, to

WM. LOVING, AC, (Orig. del. to WL, 26 Jun 1798) for ₤300, 400 acres S branches Rucker's Run and adjoins WM. LOVING. Lines: grantee, grantor, GEO. LOVING, RO. RIVES. Part of tract conveyed to ANNE by JOS. CABELL, Buckingham Co, 4 Jan 1791. Order to quiz ANNE to same J.P.'s as above.

Page 224. 17 Jul 1797. RICH. OGLESBY & wife NANCY, AC, to JNO. DUNCAN, AC, for ₤270, 279 acres. Lines: CARTER; LEONARD HENLEY, RICH. OGLESBY, AARON HIGGINBOTHAM, dec'd, JACOB SMITH, HENRY FRANKLIN dec'd.

Page 226. --- 1797. ROBT. ROBINSON, Charlotte Co., to BENJ. WILSON, AC, for ₤80, 101 acres Falls Creek. Line of SAML. BAILEY. Wit: AMBROSE RUCKER, GEO. McDANIEL, WM. GUTTRY SR & JR.

Page 228. 14 Sep 1797. ELIJAH SHIP, AC, to JNO. BURFORD JR, AC,-no sum- 29 3/4 acres. Lines: DANL. BURFORD, then a path.

Page 229. 18 Sep 1797. RICH. TALIAFERRO, exr. of ZACH. TALIAFERRO dec'd, AC, to JNO. JACOBS, AC, (3 Aug 1836, del. to WM. MASSIE, present owner) for ₤267, 267 acres both sides Tye. Lines: THOS. MASSEY, JOS. BURGER, DAVID CLARKSON, WM. COFFEE, MOSES HUGHES.

Page 230. 7 Apr 1797. BENJ. RUCKER & wife ELIZ, AC, to DANL. BURFORD, JR, AC, for ₤229-2-6, 305½ acres S side Stovall Creek. Lines: Possum Island road. Wit: RICH. RUCKER, JNO. WINGFIELD, THOS. RUCKER.

Page 232. 30 Mar 1797. HENRY VARNER, Augusta, to JACOB ARISMAN, AC, for ₤21, 100 acres head branch N fork Rockfish. Lines: JAS. FLACK. MARY, wife of VARNER signed. Wit: FREDERICK WEIR, SAML. McCULLOCH.

Page 233. 15 Aug 1797. WM. CHAMBERLAIN & wife MARY, to DANL. McCOY, all of AC, for ₤24, 60 acres Naked Creek of Rucker's Run. Lines: HENRY KEY, RICH. RICHARDS. Signed MARY ANN. Wit: AUGUSTINE WOODY, JNO. GREGORY, WM. BREEDLOVE.

Page 235. 18 Sep 1797. DAVID VIA & wife ELIZ, AC, to THOS. SPRADLIN,AC, for ₤12, 72½ acres N fork Fishing Creek, part of 290 acres that JNO. VIA left by will to sons GIDEON, DANL, JNO. & WM. VIA. Lines: WM. VIA, WM. LAIN. Wit: JNO. HORSLEY, CHAS. TALIAFERRO, SAML. ARRINGTON.

Page 236. 18 Sep 1797. WM. EVANS & wife JOYSE, AC, to JAS. BRANSFORD, Buckingham, (del. to JB 12 Jul 1799) for ₤250, 186 acres S branch Piney. Line of HENRY ROSE.

Page 237. 18 Sep 1797. WM. GUTTRY SR, AC, to WM. GUTTRY JR, AC, for ₤66, 100 acres on Stovall Creek. Bought from LEONARD GOFF. Lines: JNO. MERRITT, ABRAHAM WARNER, BOWLING CLACK, MICAJAH CLARK, HENRY ROBINSON, MICHL. COALTER.

Page 239. 28 Oct 1796. Order to AC J.P.'s REUBEN NORVELL & THOS. MOORE to quiz DOROTHEA, wife of JOS. SHIPS - 7 Jul 1796, deed to ELIJAH SHIPS - 40 acres. Done, 24 Jul 1797.

Page 240. 18 Sep 1797. WM. ANGUS, AC, power of atty. to friend DANL. McDONALD of AC, to sell, survey etc. all Kentucky lands to which I am entitled - land warrant.

Page 241. 18 Sep 1797. ARTHUR ROBINSON & wife MILLEY, AC, to WM. CLASBY of AC, (del. to WC, 26 Apr 1803) for ₤200, 200 acres N side Tye, and side of Berry's Mt.

Page 242. 9 Aug 1797. STEPHEN ROBINSON & wife JUDY, to JNO. BONDS, all of AC, consideration of one mare - 51 acres Stovall Creek and granted to grantor. Lines: THOS. PUCKETT(?), BENJ. COUGHLAN dec'd, JOS. MAYS. Wit: WM. MUSE, ANTHONY RUCKER, DAVID TINSLEY, GEO. McDANIEL, RICH. POWELL, WM. BROWN, JNO. KNIGHT, JNO. MERRITT.

Page 243. 18 Sep 1797. JNO. WEST & wife SARAH, AC, to JNO. ROBERTSON, AC, for ₤31, (del. to W.H. CABELL, by post - Warminster, Jul, 1799) 107 acres Branches of Mayo Creek. Lines: PETER LEGRAND, WM. CABELL, NICHL. CABELL, NICHL. WEST and where WEST lives.

328

Page 245.   18 Sep 1797.   JNO. HENDERSON, AC, to MICH. McMULLERN, Augusta,
             (del. to A. McMULLEN, 29 Sep 1812) for Ł160, 140 acres both
sides Meriwether Creek. Lines: DANL. LATTERMAN. ELIZ., wife of HENDERSON
signed.

Page 247.   7 Nov 1796.   PAUL WOOD, AC, WM. KNIGHT, AC, FRANCIS WOOD, Bed-
             ford, to JAS. MARR, AC, for Ł225, 200 acres Porrage Creek,
formerly that of JNO. WOOD dec'd. Lines: JNO. KNIGHT, WILCOX's fence.
Wit: JNO. HANSARD, WM. BROWN, WM. BURFORD, T. HIGGINBOTHAM, JNO. McDANIEL,
ANTHONY RUCKER, SILAS WOOD.   The name appears as FRANCES WOOD, Bedford,
in deed, but at end it has this: "FRANCIS WOOD - his mark".

Page 248.   16 Oct 1797.   JOSIAH WOOD & wife PATIENCE, HEZIKIAH HARTGROVE
             & wife SUSANNA, AC, to CONYERS WHITE, Alb., for Ł34105, 162
acres Naked Creek branches and joining BIBB.

Page 249.   26 Sep 1797.   DUDLEY CALLAWAY & wife PATSEY, AC, to JESSE
             WOODROOF, AC, for Ł117, 117 acres John's creek. Wit: THOS.
MOORE, JOSIAH HARRISON, NICHL. C. DAVIES, JAS. LEE, NELSON C. DAWSON.

Page 251.   16 Oct 1797.   GEO. PENN & THOS. PENN, exrs. of GEO. PENN, AC,
             Power of Atty to WM. PENN to recover and receive any lands on
surveyor's books in Kentucky, or any other state, due our father, GEO.
PENN.

Page 252.   15 Apr 1797.   REUBEN, JESSE, JOS. JR, CHILDRESS; SAML. COLEMAN
             & wife JUDITH; JAS. COLEMAN & wife NANCY, BENJ. SANDIDGE &
wife ELIZ., MAJOR & SHADRICK CHILDRESS to JOS. CHILDRESS SR, for Ł1000,
land and slaves - 500 acres. Lines: WM. PETERS, JNO. COLEMAN, WM. CAMDEN,
AMBROSE RUCKER. Also 350 acres. Lines: JOHN HARRIS, MOSES SWINNEY, JNO.
COLEMAN, 7 named slaves, stock. Wit: WM. WARE, AMBROSE RUCKER JR, THOS.
COLEMAN, JESSE CLEMENTS, JOS. WILSON, TAUS. COLEMAN, JOS. GARNER, DANL.
COLEMAN, WM. PETER, ANDREW STATON.

Page 253.   15 Apr 1797.   Same grantors and grantee as previous deed -
             Ł500, land on Kanawaha, no adj. owners. Same witnesses.

Page 255.   15 Jun 1797.   DAVID & JESSE WOODROOF, AC, to JAS. WILMORE, AC,
             for Ł100, 123 acres. Wit: JNO. McDANIEL, THOS. WOODROOF, RICH.
BURKS, WM. STEVENS, SAML. HOLT, JNO. HILL.

Page 256.   12 Apr 1797.   ZACH. TALIAFERRO, AC, to son CHAS. TALIAFERRO,
             for love, no acreage mentioned - N and S forks of Tye. Wit:
NATHL. OFFUTT, JAS. SOUTHWORTH, BIRKENHEAD TALIAFERRO, WM. HORSLEY.

Page 257.   16 Oct 1797.   JOS. MAYS & wife SALLY, AC, to RO. MAYS, AC, for
             Ł275, 275 acres N branches Tye and S side Berry's Mt., sur-
veyed for JOS. MAYS SR. Lines: CHAS. MAYS, old pat. line, THOS. LAYNE,
WM. LAYNE. Wit: CHAS., MOSES, & LEWIS MAYS.

Page 258.   16 Oct 1797.   Same parties as above - Ł275, 275 acres - same
             description. Lines: JAS. MAYS, WM. LAYNE. Wit: same.

Page 260.   14 Oct 1797.   JNO. MERRITT, AC, to DANL. NORCUTT, AC, for Ł12,
"10 or 12 acres". Lines: NORCUTT on S, DANL. BURFORD on W., DANL. MEHONE
on N, MICAJAH CLARK on E. Wit: PHIL JOHNSON, HARRISON HUGHES, WM. HUGHES
JR, ZACH. DAWSON, JNO. TURNER, NELSON C. DAWSON, HENRY ROBINSON, MILLNER
COX.

Page 261.   16 Oct 1797.   JNO. SNIDER & wife ANN, AC, to WM. BAILEY (sent
             to WB 17 Nov 1799) for Ł125, 200 acres Dutch Creek. Lines:
JNO. MATTHEWS, WM. BAILEY, RALPH JOPLING dec'd.

Page 262.   7 Sep 1797.   AMBROSE EUBANK & wife FRANKEY, AC, & Parish, to
             JOHN RICHESON, of same, (Orig. del. to JR, 15 Dec 1797) for
Ł150, 104 acres Horsley branches. Lines: JOSIAH ELLIS, RODERICK McCULLOCH,
EDMD. GOODRICH. Wit: JNO., CORNL., & SAML. SALE.

Page 263.   23 Sep 1797.   JNO. MATTHEWS & wife MARY, AC, to WM. BOWMAN,
             AC, for Ł75, 120 acres. Lines: ALEX. ROBERTS, PLEASANT MARTIN,

JAS. TURNER, down Rockfish to the mouth of Rock Branch; DUNNAKIN. Wit:
RO. RIVES, JNO. HILL, JNO. JOHNSON, JAS. P. PARISH.

Page 264.   16 Oct 1797.   FRANCIS WEST, AC, and wife PEGGY to JNO. PHIL-
           LIPS, AC, for Ⱡ36-10, 107 acres. Lines: Col. NICHL. CABELL,
WM. WEST, LEWIS NEVIL, BRANSFORD WEST.

Page 265.   4 May 1797.   THOS. MATTHEWS & wife ALEY, AC, to JNO. MATTHEWS,
           AC, (del. to JNO., 20 Dec 1799) for Ⱡ100, 210 acres Dutch
Creek.   74 acres of it willed to THOS. by his father, THOS. dec'd. Lines:
WM. TURNER, DANL. DUNNIAN(?), JNO. MATTHEWS, JOS. LANHAM SR. Wit: WM.
BAILEY, WM. ALLEN, JOSHUA WILLOUGHBY, WM. BALL.

Page 267.   16 Oct 1797.   JAS. TINSLEY, Bedford Co, to GEO. McDANIEL JR,
           AC, for Ⱡ70, 53 acres. Wit: JNO. LONDON, AMBROSE & ANTHONY
RUCKER, MOSES TINSLEY.

Page 268.   7 Oct 1795.   JNO. PHILIPS, with power of atty. from ELIZ.
           EVANS, AC, to SAML. ARRINGTON, AC, (15 Nov 1809, del. to SA)
for Ⱡ45, 99 acres S branches Owen Creek and next to JNO. JOSLING. Wit:
GEO. HILTON, HENLEY DRUMMOND, LEWIS TINDALL.

Page 269.   Same parties and date as previous deed. Ⱡ45, 140 acres Branch-
           es of Owen Creek. Wit: same.

Page 271.   12 Oct 1797.   THOS. LAINE & wife MARY, AC, to GEO. LOVING, AC,
           (del. 21 Dec 1812, to J. MURPHY) for Ⱡ200, no acreage mention-
ed, N branches ye Tye River, part of 2 tracts. Lines: JAS. GATEWOOD, RO.
MAYS, THOS. LAINE, N bank Tye, WM. LAINE, Cedar Creek. Wit: CHAS. EVANS,
MINOS WRIGHT.

Page 272.   1 Oct 1796.   JOS. C. MIGGINSON & wife SALLY, Buckingham Co.,
           to SHADRICK CARTER, AC, (del. to SC, 1804) for Ⱡ250, 150 acres
both sides Little Owens Creek. Part of tract and next to WM. HORSLEY,
dec'd. Wit: BENJ. WATKINS, BENJ. JOHNSON, SAML. ARRINGTON, CHAS. LAVENDER.

Page 274.   16 Oct 1797.   WM. DAVIS, AC, to WM. PRYOR, AC, for Ⱡ65, 102
           acres Horsley. Wit: WM. WARE, ISAAC WRIGHT, HENRY BROWN,
L.M. MUNDY.

Page 275.   16 Oct 1797.   WM. DAVIS, AC, to WM. WARE, AC, for Ⱡ100, 106
           acres Horsley. Lines of grantee. (Del. to WW, 10 Apr 1798.)
Wit: HENRY BROWNE, ISAAC WRIGHT, WM. PRYOR, L.M. MUNDY.

Page 276.   14 Oct 1797.   ISAAC WRIGHT, AC, to WM. PRYOR, AC, for Ⱡ40, 60
           acres Horsley. Part of tract and next to WM. DAVIS. SUSANNAH,
wife of ISAAC WRIGHT.

Page 277.   14 Oct 1797.   ISAAC WRIGHT, AC, to NELSON CRAWFORD, AC, (orig.
           del. to NC 18 Sep 1798) for Ⱡ50, 18 acres Horsley.

Page 277.   16 Oct 1797.   Receipt of WM. WARE from WM. DAVIS, on Deed of
           Trust. Wit: BENJ. & ZACH. TALIAFERRO.

Page 278.   16 Oct 1797.   RICH. OGLESBY & wife NANCY; JNO. CASH & wife
           SALLY; JOEL CASH & wife BETSY, to JAS. SHIELDS, Junior, no
sum - 146 acres Stonehouse Creek. Part of tract of BENJ. CASH, dec'd.
Lines: JAS. MAYS, RO. MAYS, AARON HIGGINBOTHAM JR.

Page 279.   16 Dec 1795.   CHAS. TYLER, AC, to JNO. WILSFORD, AC, for Ⱡ8,
           36 acres N side Indian Creek, property of THOS. DICKERSON &
conveyed to JNO. PHILIPS and then to CHAS. TYLER. Lines: JNO. CAMPBELL,
WM. EVANS, Wit: JAS. MARTIN, JAS. WILSFORD, JNO. ARRINGTON, JACOB PHIL-
LIPS, WM. HOOKER, WM. MARTIN.

Page 280.   2 Dec 1796.   JOS. H. MORRISON & wife MARY, AC, & WM. DEPP and
           wife ELIZ, of Kentucky, to GEO. HILTON, AC, for Ⱡ50, 165 acres
Elk Island Creek. Wit: LEWIS TINDALL, JESSE JOPLING, SPOTSWOOD GARLAND,
SAML. FERGUSON.

Page 282.   17 Oct 1797.   JNO. ARRINGTON, AC, to JNO. KIDD, Buckingham Co.
            (del. to JK, 13 Oct 1801) for Ł50, 115 acres both sides Little
Indian Creek. Lines: JNO. PARSON, JNO. WILSFORD, lines in old plantation
made by WILSFORD & ARRINGTON. SUSANNAH, wife of ARRINGTON.

Page 283.   1 Dec 1795.   GREENBERRY LANNUM & wife CATHERINE, AC, to WM.
            BAILEY, AC, for Ł30, 30 acres Dutch Creek. Lines: grantee -
known as SNIDER's tract; TOS. NASH, JNO. SANDERS, WM. NALLY.   Wit: THOS.
MATTHEWS, WM. TURNER, MARY MATTHEWS, JOHN MATTHEWS.

Page 284.   -- Oct 1797.   DAVID PHILLIPS & wife MARY to NATHAN HARRIS
            (Orig. del. to BENJ. MOSBY, 29 Nov 1797) for Ł300, 217 acres.
Lines: Capt. MATT. HARRIS SR, JAS. TURNER SR, PLEASANT DAWSON, JOS.
ROBERTS, JNO. MATTHEWS.

Page 285.   19 Nov 1795.   WM. NALLY & wife RACHEL, Albemarle, to WM. BAI-
            LEY, AC, for Ł30, 80 acres Dutch Creek. Lines: HENRY MARTIN JR,
known as SNIDER's tract, OSBURN COFFEE, WM. TURNER, JNO. SANDERS. Wit:
JOS. SMITH, JOS. MATTHEWS, THOMAS MATTHEWS, JNO. MATTHEWS.

Page 286.   19 Apr 1797.   GEO. BLAIN, AC, to BALDWIN BLAINE, AC, for Ł75,
            stock - seems to be BAINE and not BLAIN for grantee - Wit:
RO. WRIGHT, JNO. FLOOD, JNO. HANGER, JOEL DAVIS, JNO. M. GRIFFIN.

Page 287.   27 Jan 1797.   JNO. BOLLING & wife SARAH; CHAS. CHRISTIAN & wife
            SARAH, AC, to BARNET OWEN for Ł100, 156 acres S side Buffalo.
Lines: Braxton Ridge, JAMES CHRISTIAN, CHAS. CHRISTIAN, RAWLEY PENN,
CHAS. HIGGINBOTHAM. Wit: WALTER CHRISTIAN, HENRY CHRISTIAN, JOS. DAVEN-
PORT, JNO. CHRISTIAN B, JNO. M. JOHNSON, JACOB PIERCE.

Page 288.   16 Oct 1797.   BARNET OWEN & wife RACHEL; WALTER CHRISTIAN &
            wife MARTHA, to CHAS. CHRISTIAN, AC, for Ł100, 180 acres Rocky
Run. Lines: JOEL CAMPBELL, JOSEPH WILCHER, RICH. WILSON, WALTER CHRISTIAN,
ISAIAH ATTKISSON, WILLIAMS' old field, AMBROSE RUCKER. Wit: JNO. TURNER,
JNO. LONDON, JNO. DEHART.

Page 289.   16 Oct 1797.   JAS. LANDRUM & wife MARY, AC, to JOS. WHITE,
            Orange Co, for Ł350, 232 acres, part of tract of AUSTIN SMITH
on Tye. Lines: WM. BIBB dec'd, AMBROSE CAMPBELL, SAML. EDMONDS, HEZEKIAH
HARTGROVE.

Page 290.   16 Oct 1797.   DANL. DUNCAN & wife ELIZ, AC, to PLEASANT DAWSON,
            SC, for Ł65, 224 acres, 2 adj. tracts, S side Marrowbone Mt.
Lines: JNO. MATTHEWS, WM. BOWMAN, JNO. SANDERS, MATT. PHILLIPS dec'd.
Wit: FRANCIS WEST, NICHL. WEST, PEGGY WEST.

Page 291.   21 Nov 1795.   RICH. C. POLLARD, Annadale, AC, to father-in-law
            JAMES HOPKINS, slave for 1 year at Ł1-4 and to be returned.
All are here present save Judy. Wit: THOS. PHILLIPS, SCOTT SCRUGGS.
(Note: later in this book is interesting document wherein HOPKINS names
various of slaves to be worked for so many years by daughter and husband,
POLLARD, and then to be freed. I have referred to my work on H wills
wherein POLLARD is denounced by HOPKINS and bait is used to get POLLARD's
son to change his name. I have seen order book data showing that he took
the bait. BFD)

Page 291.   5 Dec 1797.   WM. CABELL JR, & wife ANNE, AC, by deed of 20 Jul
            1795, conveyed to BYRD HENDRICK 2000 acres (1000 each) held by
SAML. W. VENABLE and BH as tenants in common, on Chaplain Fork of Salt
River in Mercer and one tract on Rowland's fork of same in Nelson. Ł300
for contract and Ł41 paid herein to cancel. Wit: WM. H. CABELL, HENRY
READ, ELVIRA CABELL.

Page 292.   20 Nov 1797.   LANDON CABELL & wife JUDITH SCOTT, to JNO MARR,
            Orange, (orig. sent to JM per D.S. GARLAND, 25 Jul 1810) no
sum set forth - 212 acres on both sides Naked Creek; S branch Piney. Part
of 1872 acres (a corrected figure) of Col. HUGH ROSE dec'd., AC, and divided to legatees by AC court decree - lot #9. Lines: LOT #1, 8 (to
PAULINA ROSE), PATRICK ROSE, WM. MOSS, CHARLES ROSE. Wit: BENJ. JORDAN,
RO. H. ROSE, H.M. ROSE, JNO. PHILLIPS.

Page 293. 16 Apr 1798. JONATHAN WILSON, AC, to THOS. GRISSOM, AC, (del.
to TG 20 Jun 1800) for Ⱡ400, 400 acres S branches Harris Creek.
Lines: WM. COLEMAN, J. AMBLER, D. BURFORD, ELIZ. COLEMAN, WM. PETERS,
THOS. COLEMAN, MILLICENT COLEMAN.

Page 295. 13 Apr 1798. JOS. CHILDRESS SR. & wife MARY to WM. PETER SR,
(del. to WP 28 Apr 1798) for Ⱡ200, 526 acres branches of Harris
between Bear & Cedar Mts. Lines of both. Wit: JOS. WILSON, ANDREW STATON,
AMBR. RUCKER JR, RO. & THOS. GRISSOM, JONATHAN WILSON.

Page 296. 13 Dec 1797. RICH. PERKINS & wife ELIZ; JACOB PUCKETT & wife
MARY, AC, to JNO. NETHERLAND & JAS. WOODS, exrs. of JOS. LIGON
(formerly of Powhatan) for benefit of heirs agreeable to his will - RICH.
& JACOB sold to him in his lifetime for Ⱡ310 the tract where PERKINS
lives on S side of Rockfish. Lines: JAS. WOODS, THOS. MORRISON, WM. FITZ-
PATRICK. Wit: JNO. LOBBAN JR, THOS. EWERS, JAS. McCLAIN, THOS. MORRISON.
Sent to M. DAWSON, for JAS. WOODS.

Page 297. 10 Dec 1797. GEO. DILLARD to JNO. CREWS - JAS. CREWS SR, AC,
did on 21 Mar 1796, execute deed of trust to HART BROWN & Co,
Lynchburg, on 72 acres. Lines: JOS. DAWSON, WM. HUGHES, JAS. LEE, JNO.
BURFORD, HARRISON HUGHES and where he lives. Part of tract which he
bought of GEO. CARRINGTON; also a number of slaves and stock. Default in
payment and duly sold by GEO. DILLARD, 1 Jun 1797, to JNO. CREWS, for
Ⱡ60. Wit: JNO. PENN, ZACH. TUCKER, LITTLEBERRY TUCKER. Feb. Court, 1800,
to JNO. CREWS.

Page 299. 2 Feb 1798. TIMOTHY SCRUGS, AC, to JAS. MURPHY, AC, for Ⱡ47-
9-10, deed of trust. Slave, Violet, stock etc. Debt due RO.
RIVES & Co. Wit: PARMENAS BRYANT, JAS. HANSBROUGH, WM. BRYANT, MARBELL
CAMDEN. Orig. del. to JM 12 Aug 1799.

Page 300. 18 Dec 1797. JNO. CREWS, AC, to WM. MOON, AC, for Ⱡ36, 83
acres. Lines: DAVID WOODROOF, JAS. WILLMORE, ISAAC RUCKER,
JOS. CREWS.

Page 301. 14 Oct 1797. JNO. CREWS, AC, to HARRISON HUGHES, AC, for Ⱡ30,
30 acres Fawn Creek. Lines: PLEASANT DAWSON, grantor, grantee,
JNO. BURFORD. Wit: JESSE WOODROOF, JAS. LEE.

Page 302. 1 Feb 1798. MARTIN DAWSON & wife ELIZ; JESSE DAWSON, their
son, AC, to DANL. BURFORD SR. (Orig. del. to E. WILLS, admr.,
11 Jan 1811) for Ⱡ125, 92 acres on Harris, where JESSE DAWSON lives.
Lines: HARRIS Creek, at mouth of Miller Creek, old line between MARTIN
DAWSON & JNO. WATERS, HENRY GOSNEY, VAL. COX, Miller's Branch, PHILIP
BURFORD, grantee. Wit: NELSON C. DAWSON, ZACH. DAWSON, WM. BURFORD.

Page 303. 2 Oct 1797. JNO. MATTHEWS & wife JANE, AC, to WM. SANDIDGE,
AC, (Orig. sent to WS, 25 Feb 1822) for Ⱡ100, 200 acres Mole
Creek. Lines: JNO. TALIAFERRO, JNO. SALES, RO. CASH, JACOB SMITH, PHILIP
SMITH. Wit: JACOB PHILIPS, THOS. N. EUBANK, DANL. WARWICK, BENJ. SANDIDGE.

Page 304. 29 Sep 1797. DAVID SWANSON, AC, to REUBEN HARRISON (Orig. del.
to RH, 8 May 1799) consideration of 1 mare and saddle - 53
acres S branches Maple Creek of Piney. Conveyed by JNO. SWANSON to son,
DAVID. Lines: NATHL. MANTIPLY, LINDSEY COLEMAN, JOSHUA HUDSON, EDWD. CAR-
TER. Wit: JNO. CAMM, SPOTSWOOD GARLAND, JOS. DILLARD, PEACHY FRANKLIN.

Page 305. -- 1798. JNO. CREWS, AC, to JAS. LEE, AC, for Ⱡ32-10, 32½
acres Fawn Creek. Lines: JOS. DAWSON, a path.

Page 306. 15 Dec 1797. RICH. PERKINS & wife ELIZ, AC, to THOS. MORRISON,
AC, (Orig. sent to TM 14 Feb 1822) for Ⱡ30, 46 acres S side
Rockfish. Lines: THOS. EWERS, JAS. WOODS, grantor and grantee. Wit: JAS.
WOODS, JAS. McCLAIN, THOS. EWERS.

Page 307. 23 Sep 1797. WM. BAILEY, AC, to WM. B. HARE, AC, for 5 sh, a
slave, Fanny. Deed of Trust for debt due WILLIS WILLS for Ⱡ90.
Wit: JAS. P. PARRISH, JAS. LOVING, JAS. HANSBROUGH.

332

Page 307.   10 Oct 1797.   GEO. BLANE, Albemarle, to SKILER HARRIS, of same,
            for L269, 229 acres adj. Hycory Creek. Lines: JNO. COLE, JNO.
PUGH, EPHRAIM BLAINE, RICH. HARE. Wit: SAML. MURRELL, JNO. CHOWNING,
PERRIN FARRAR, JNO. WILKINSON, WM. LEE HARRIS, GEO. BLAINE JR.

Page 308.   9 Nov 1797.   Order to AC J.P.'s, JOS. BURRUS & REUBEN NORVELL
            to quiz SALLY, wife of WIATT POWELL - 8 Mar 1797, deed to
GIDEON RUCKER, 175 acres. Done and rec. 16 Apr 1798.

Page 309.   6 Apr 1795.   HENRY TRENT, AC, to JNO. BLAKE TRENT, AC, for 20
            sh., 400 acres N side Fluvanna and joining it. Lines: mouth
of John's Creek, RICH. TILLER, crossing Cedar Branch. Final proof, 18 Apr
1798, by GEO. GOODWIN. Wit: THOS. MOORE, GEO. GOODWIN, RICH. POWELL, THOS.
MITCHELL.

Page 310.   13 Apr 1795.   HENRY TRENT, AC, to THOS. MITCHELL, AC, for 20
            sh, 111 acres. Lines: John's Creek. Wit: DUDLEY CALLAWAY,
JNO. B. TRENT, GEO. GOODWIN, MICAJAH GOODWIN.

Page 314.   (no page 312 in book; as stated, pages are garbled. 13 Apr
            1795, ARCHELAUS MITCHELL SR, AC, to son, THOS. MITCHELL, for
love and 5 sh, no acreage mentioned - E side Creek. Lines: John's Creek,
GOODWIN, ARCHELAUS MITCHELL's plantation. Wit: as in 310.

Page 315.   27 Feb 1798.   THOS. MITCHELL, & wife EADY, AC, to JESSE WOOD-
            ROOF, AC, for L48-10, 48½ acres on John's Creek. Wit: DUDLEY
CALLAWAY, BOLLING MITCHELL, WM. M. TRENT, REUBIN PENDLETON, JNO. B. TRENT.

Page 316.   24 Sep 1793.   Order to Fluvanna J.P.'s JOS. HADEN & ALLEN
            BAINERD(?) to quiz NANCY, wife of SAML. RICHARDSON - 3 Apr
1789 deed to PHILIP BAILEY, 150 acres. Done, 20 Nov 1797.

Page 317-   16 Apr 1797.   WM. MARTIN & wife PATSY, AC, to HUDSON MARTIN,
            AC, (sent to HM 17 Jan 1804) for L15, 30 acres S fork Rockfish.
Lines: the road adj. THOS. ANDERSON, ABSALOM COX, JNO. JOPLING, JNO. DAM-
RON. GEO. VAUGHAN, grantee. Wit: ABSALOM COX, JNO. JOPLING, JNO. DAMRON.

Page 319.   28 Dec 1797.   BYRD D. HENDRICK, AC, to JAS. MURPHY, AC, for
            L87-15-7, Deed of Trust to RO. RIVES & Co. 5 sh. slaves and
increase. Wit: HENRY HOLLOWAY, RICH. MAYS, WM. BRYANT, HENRY RIVES, HENRY
READ.

Page 320.   14 Apr 1798.   WM. MARTIN & wife PATSY, AC, to GREENBERRY LAN-
            HAM, AC, (del. to JNO. MATTHEWS per order of GL, 21 Jul 1798)
for L22 and L1000 tobacco, 230 acres S branches Rockfish. Lines: CUTHBERT
WEBB, HUDSON MARTIN, NORMOND THOMAS. Wit: HUDSON MARTIN, JNO. JOPLING,
ABSALOM COX.

Page 322.   20 Feb 1798.   Order to AC J.P.'s N. CABELL & JOS. SHELTON and
            WM. LOVING to quiz PATSEY, wife of JAS. JOPLING - deed to
HUDSON MARTIN 18 Apr 1795 for 391 acres. Done 8 Mar 1798 by CABELL &
SHELTON.

Page 323.   14 Feb 1798.   MARTHA HORSLEY, exrx. of WM. HORSLEY, and his
            admrs. JNO. HORSLEY & RODERICK McCULLOCH, AC, to HENLEY DRUM-
MOND, AC, for L113-16, 270 acres. Will directed sale of land lying back
from Rockfish tract. Branches Owens' CreeK. Surveyed by ROD. McCULLOCH
JR. Lines: GEO. HILTON. Wit: SAML. ARRINGTON, JESSE JOPLING, WARREN
TALIAFERRO, JAS. PAMPLIN, WM. HORSLEY.

Page 324.   29 Jan 1798.   JNO. THURMOND & wife SALLY, AC, to GEO. BLAINE,
            Albemarle, for L250, 125 acres Cub Creek, branch of Hickory.
Lines: grantor, GUTRIDGE THURMOND, MORRISON. Wit: SAML. MURRELL, SAML.
ANDERSON.

Page 325.   18 Nov 1796.   ZACH. TALIAFERRO, AC, to DAVID CLARKSON, AC,
            (noted on margin: This deed is not recorded in rotation being
omitted through mistake) for L100, half paid and rest due 1 Jun next and
bond given - Mill is on tract. 76 acres by 2 pats. 1 for 62 and 1 for 14
acres. Lines: N side of the river opposite small Island, crossing Tye;

ELIAS SMITH. 2nd tract: JAS. BROWN and S side Tye. Wit: NATHL. OFFUTT,
RICH. TALIAFERRO, WM. HORSLEY, WARREN TALIAFERRO.

Page 326. 17 Jun 1798. JAS. BROOKS, Albemarle, to DELMUS JOHNSON, AC,
(Orig. del. 16 Nov 1799 to DJ) for Ł45, 65 acres S side Rodes
Creek. Lines: SAML. FOX, CHAS. RODES. ELIZ, wife of JB, signed.

Page 327. 17 Jun 1798. JAS. BROOKS & wife ELIZ, Albemarle, to PETER
BRANNER, AC, for Ł9, 70 acres N branches Rockfish; granted to
WM. WOOD dec'd., and conveyed by him to son, ISAAC WOOD, and then to
BROOKS. Lines: ALEX. PATTON dec'd, THOS. THOMPSON.

Page 328. 24 Jan 1797. Order to AC J.P.'s AMBR. RUCKER & JOS. BURRUS,
to quiz MARY, wife of JNO. H. GOODWIN, for 17 Aug 1796 deed
to MICHL. COALTER & PHILIP JOHNSON. Done, 18 Jun 1798.

Page 329. 12 May 1798. JOS. WILCHER, AC, to ANDREW MONROE (MUNROE), AC,
for Ł300, 231 acres branches Rockey Run. Lines: JOS. HIGGIN-
BOTHAM, PETER CASHWELL, CHARLES CHRISTIAN, RICH. WILSON, SAML. HUCKSTEP.
Wit: CHAS. CHRISTIAN, JACOB PIERCE, RICH. WILSON.

Page 330. 29 Nov 1797. Order to AC J.P.'s JOS. SHELTON & WM. HARRIS to
quiz MARY, wife of DAVID PHILIPS, deed of Oct, 1797, to NATHAN
HARRIS, 217 acres. Done, 18 Jun 1798.

Page 331. 28 Apr 1798. Order to AC J.P.'s DAVID CRAWFORD & WM. WARE to
quiz MARY, wife of JOS. CHILDRESS, 13 Apr 1798 deed to WM.
PETER. Done 18 Jun 1798. 526 acres.

Page 332. 7 Mar 1797. Order to AC J.P.'s SAML. MEREDITH & JOS. BURRUS
to quiz NANCY, wife of ALEX. BRYDIE, deed of 15 Feb 1797, to
W.S. CRAWFORD. Done 18 Jun 1798. 800 acres.

Page 333. 18 Nov 1797. Order to AC J.P.'s SAML. MEREDITH & THOS. MOORE
to quiz ELIZ, wife of JARED HOTCHKISS - 18 Apr 1796 deed to
RUSH HUDSON. Done 18 Nov 1797. 130 acres.

Page 334. 30 Apr 1798. Order to Buckingham J.P.'s DAVID PATTESON JR &
ANTHONY DIBRELL JR, to quiz JOYCE - deed of SMYTH TANDY &
wife JOYCE to JNO. McHENRY & Co. Done, 18 Jun 1798. 470 acres.

Page 335. 30 Apr 1798. Order to AC J.P.'s SAML. MEREDITH & WM. WARWICK
to quiz PATTY, wife of JAS. WATSON, 1 Jan 1787 deed to JNO.
STEWART - 700 acres. Done 18 Jun 1798.

Page 336. 15 Nov 1797. GEO. CARTER, Albemarle, to JOEL FRANKLIN, AC,
for Ł150, Tract bought of EDWD. CARTER and claimed by GEO. as
devisee of EDWD. CARTER, dec'd. GEO. has sued by next friend, PATRICK
ROSE in Chancery - vs. EDWD. CARTER & FRANKLIN - sells whole tract to
FRANKLIN. Lines: Where the old church stood; Piney River; MORSE. Tract
intended by EDWD, dec'd, for son, EDWD. from above where old church
stood to main road. Wit: CHAS. WINGFIELD JR, MARY WINGFIELD, P. MARTIN,
JNO. CAMM, WM. S. CRAWFORD.

Page 337. 15 May 1798. CHAS. A. LEWIS, AC, to JAS. MURPHY, AC, Deed of
Trust (del. to JM 12 Aug 1799) debt due RO. RIVES & Co. 6 sh.
Slave, Thos., and Alsey. Wit: JAS. HANSBROUGH, HENRY HOLLOWAY, MARBELL
CAMDEN.

Page 338. 15 Jun 1798. DAVID CRAWFORD, AC, Power of Atty to friend,
NATHAN CRAWFORD, Ky, to sell any land that I shall give orders
for. Wit: NELSON & REUBEN CRAWFORD, ELIAS WILLS. 22 Aug 1798, sent to
DAVID CRAWFORD by his son.

Page 339. Rec. 18 Jun 1798. JNO. ALFORD & wife ELIZ, AC, to CONYERS
WHITE, Alb.,(WHITE is called SR) for Ł950, 372 acres both
sides Naked Creek of Tye. Part of tract of WM. BIBB, dec'd. Lines: JOS.
WHITE, New Market road, ROWLAND EDMUNDS, JNO. THOMPSON, JNO. PHILLIPS,
WM. TEAS, CONYERS WHITE JR. Wit: EZEKIEL GILBERT, CONYERS WHITE JR,
JNO. PHILLIPS, JNO. M. GRIFFIN, ZACH. WHITE.

Page 340. 19 Feb 1798. RICHMOND STATHAM, AC, to THOS. STATHAM, AC, for
Ь120, 100 acres. Lines: ABRAHAM WARWICK, ELISHA ESTIS, WM.
CABELL SR. survey, CHAS. WATTS. Wit: CHAS. STATHAM, WM. FURBUSH, SPARKS
MARTIN.

Page 341. 20 Sep 1794. JNO. BROWN JR, AC, to STEPHEN RUSSELL, AC, for
Ь100, 140 acres both sides Pedlar. Granted to JACOB BROWN, the
Elder, by pat. 15 Jul 1760. Wit: NELSON CRAWFORD, JNO. MATTHEWS, JNO.
CRAWFORD, PHILIP SMITH JR. Final proof, 18 Jun 1798, by JNO. CRAWFORD.

Page 342. 14 Nov 1797. EZEK. GILBERT, AC, to GALT & GARLAND, Deed of
Trust - 5 sh. mare, horse, colt from my mare by Elers(?). 4
Nov 1800, sent to D.S. GARLAND by EG. Wit: MICAJAH CAMDEN, JAS. GARLAND.

Page 343. 22 Feb 1798. JOS. BURK, AC, Deed of Trust to GALT & GARLAND,
5 sh. beds, etc. large Bible, long list, my sadler tools.
Wit: J.P. GARLAND, JAS. GARLAND, WM. EDMUNDS JR.

Page 343. 18 Dec 1797. JNO. S. DAWSON & wife JANE, to JNO. DAWSON, AC,
for Ь80, (Orig. del. to M. DAWSON, 12 Sep 1799) 80 acres N
side Hicory, part of tract left to JNO. S. by will of JNO. SORRELL, dec'd,
AC. Lines: ZACH. ROBERTS, grantor, on a ridge near Rock Spring, JNO.
DAWSON. Wit: MARTIN DAWSON, JNO. LYON, JNO. BAILEY JR.

Page 345. 18 Jan 1798. JNO. DAWSON & wife SALLY, AC, to JNO. S. DAWSON,
AC, (orig. del. as above) for Ь40, 40 acres Cove Creek. Bought
by JNO. of BENJ. MOORE, dec'd. Lines: JNO. & JNO. S. DAWSON, Spring
Branch of JNO. SORRELL's widow. Wit: as above.

Page 346. 3 May 1797. JAS. GATEWOOD to ALEX. STUART (Orig. del. to B.
JORDAN 20 Feb 1800) HENDERSON McCAUL & CO, Apr. last, Dist.
Court at New London abtained judgment vs. GATEWOOD, admr. of DUDLEY GATE-
WOOD, dec'd. Deed of Trust, 5 sh. 200 acres on Tye. Lines: ARTHUR ROBIN-
SON. Bought by JAS. of THOS. WILTSHIRE, and corn on plantation where JG
lives.

Page 348. 1 Nov 1797. SHEROD MARTIN, AC, to JAS. GAHANS, AC, for Ь38,
140 acres N fork Rockfish. Lines: JNO. SMITH, Capt. AZARIAH
MARTIN, MARTIN's Mt. Wit: HUDSON MARTIN, JNO. MURRELL JR, JNO. MURRELL,
minor, JESSEY MURRELL.

Page 349. 21 Oct 1797. RO. CAMPBELL, AC, to REUBEN RUCKER, AC, for Ь130,
147 acres on Stovall's Creek and Lynch Road. Wit: JNO. WATKINS,
BENJ. SIMMONS, ISAAC RUCKER, RICH.RUCKER.

Page 350. Rec. 18 Jun 1798. NORBORNE THOMAS & wife JUDITH, AC, to WM.
DIXON, AC, (Orig. del. to SAML. DIXON, 22 Dec 1806) for Ь10,
64 acres and joins where DIXON lives. Part of a tract on Bryant's Branch.

Page 351. 15 Aug 1794. JNO. PHILLIPS & wife AVEY; JNO. THOMPSON & wife
REBECCA; WM. TEAS, AC, to WM. EVANS, AC, for Ь10, 97 acres
both sides Indian Creek. Wit: BENJ. POWELL, SEYMOUR POWELL, WM. LOCKHART,
JNO. BROWN. Final proof, 18 Jun 1798, by grantors.

Page 357. 13 Oct 1797. CHAS. DAVIS, AC, Power of Atty. to STEPHEN TEAS,
Kanawha, and JNO. TEAS, Campbell Co, to obtain pat. for me in
Kanawha - preemption warrant for 1000 acres on Horse Shoe Bottom of Cole
River - one side of big falls and to cross below the falls. Wit: RODERICK
McCULLOCH JR. & ARCHL. MITCHELL. Orig. del. to M. ELMORE, per order of
TEAS, 21 Aug 1798.

Page 353. 4 May 1798. SAML. COLEMAN's receipt to JOS. CHILDRESS SR, 350
and Ь50, in full of my claims vs. JOS. as legatee of JOS.
CHILDRESS' estate. Bond given me by JC for his one eighth interest and
mislaid. Wit: ZACH. TALIAFERRO, AMBR. RUCKER JR, ALBISON MORRIS, JOS.
CHILDRESS JR, REUBEN CHILDRESS.

Page 354. 16 Apr 1798. GEO. CARTER & EDWD. CARTER to GEO. CAMPBELL for
Ь300, 611 acres S side Piney; part of their tract. Lines: S
bank Piney at WM. MOSS corner; where main road crosses river. Wit:

RO. RIVES, CHAS. CHRISTIAN, P. GOOCH. Orig. del. to Mrs. CAMPBELL, admx, 23 Nov 1801.

Page 355. 15 Jun 1798. ZACH. TALIAFERRO & wife SALLY, AC, to JNO. TAL-
IAFERRO, AC, for Ƚ175, 364 acres both sides Puppie Creek; that
tract of CHAS. TALIAFERRO, dec'd, which fell to AT by will. Lines: JNO.
CLARKSON.

Page 356. 23 Dec 1797. PRESLEY RAINS, AC, to GALT & GARLAND, 5 sh, Deed
of Trust - a horse. Wit: ALEX. MARR, JAS. P. GARLAND, WILL
EDMUNDS JR.

Page 357. 21 Jan 1796. Order to Orange Co., N.C. J.P.'s. OBADIAH MARTIN
& wife BETTY, 1 Dec 1783 deed to JNO. MARTIN, 200 acres. To
quiz BETTY. Done 1 Dec 1783 by JNO. SLOSS & HARDY HURDLE(?) or HENDLE.

Page 358. 21 Jun 1798. JACOB TYREE, AC, to JOS. WILCHER, AC, for 5 sh.
& love, a slave Sue, for his wife SARAH, who is my daughter.
Wit: FRANCIS BUNT, NICODEMUS VERMILLION.

Page 358. 20 Jun 1798. NATHAN CRAWFORD, AC, to NELSON CRAWFORD, AC, for
Ƚ100, 134 acres N side and branches Rockfish. Lines: JOS. H.
MORRISON, NATHAN CRAWFORD. Wit: JAS. SHIELDS.

Page 359. 20 Jun 1798. NATHAN CRAWFORD, AC, to WM. CRAWFORD, AC, for
Ƚ300, 1200 acres on branches of Rockfish. Lines: WM. MORRISON,
THOS. MORRISON JR, DAVID CRAWFORD, JNO. ROBINSON. Wit: JAS. SHIELDS,
NELSON CRAWFORD.

Page 360. 31 Jan 1798. WM. TILLER, AC, to son, WM. TILLER, and my daughter LUCY TILLER, AC, for love and $1.00, slave, Jno. for son,
and slave, Judah, for daughter. Wit: P. MARTIN, JNO. THOMPSON, RALPH
MARTIN.

Page 361. 20 Mar 1798. THOS. MOOR, AC, to PLEASANT MARTIN for Ƚ50,
slave boy and horse (got from JNO. ALFORD) Orig. del. to PM
1 Apr 1802. Wit: GEO. MARTIN JR, AUGUSTIN SMITH.

Page 362. 13 Apr 1798. Receipt by WM. TALIAFERRO, to ZACH. TALIAFERRO
for money legacy left to WT by dec'd. father, CHAS. TALIAFERRO,
and reference to will. Wit: JNO. TALIAFERRO, JOS. LOVING, WILL LOVING.

Page 362. 17 May 1798. Receipt by RODERICK TALIAFERRO to CHAS. TALIA-
FERRO for Ƚ50, sum left to RT by fahter's will and ref. to it,
as of 30 Jul 1791. Wit: JAS. & ZACH. TALIAFERRO.

Page 362. 17 May 1798. Receipt of WM. TALIAFERRO to CHAS. TALIAFERRO
for a sum left me in my father's will of 30 Jul 1791. Wit:
as above.

Page 363. 7 Sep 1798. WM. WARE, as gdn. of JAS. TALIAFERRO, to BENJ.
TALIAFERRO, sum left ward by father in will of July 1791.

Page 363. 17 Aug 1798. WM. HANSBROUGH, Culpeper, Power of Atty. to
PETER HANSBROUGH to survey tract on Rockcastle creek in Madi-
son or Lincoln counties in Ky. and to lease or sell. Wit: HEN. HOLLOWAY,
J. MURPHY, RO. HOLLOWAY.

Page 364. 28 Oct 1796. Order to AC J.P.'s REUBEN NORVELL & THOS. MOORE,
to quiz DOROTHEA, wife of JOS. SHIPS, 2 Jul 1796 deed to
PLEASANT DAWSON. 97 acres. Done, 24 Jul 1797.

Page 365. 9 Aug 1798. JAS. FLACK & wife MARY, Augusta, to JACOB REUDE-
SIL, AC, for Ƚ200, 110 acres Patton's Branch of Rockfish.
Lines: JAS. BROOKS, JNO. DETTRO, CHAS. RODES, JAS. BISHOP. Sent to JR,
28 Apr 1826. Wit: DANL. COLEMAN, JACOB ARISMAN, JNO. CRITZER, and 3 ille-
geble signatures.

Page 366. 14 Feb 1798. JNO. CAMDEN, AC, to BENJ. GOODE, AC, for Ƚ75 -
no acreage - N of S branches Pedlar. Lines: Top of the Blue

Ridge. Wit: MICAJAH CAMDEN.

Page 367.   28 Jun 1798.   JNO. CAMDEN, AC, to JER. WHITTEN, AC, for Ŀ30,
100 acres Pigg Creek. Lines: JNO. BIAS, MORRIS, JNO. HOG.

Page 368.   26 Mar 1798.   JAS. YELTON & wife MARY, AC, to ENOCH CARPENTER,
AC, for Ŀ50, 100 acres. Lines: JNO. T. WILSFORD, AARON HIGGIN-
BOTHAM dec'd, Thrasher Creek, BENJ. CARPENTER. Wit: JNO. T. WILSFORD,
EATON CARPENTER, JNO. YELTON. Orig. del. to EC, 12 Apr 1799.

Page 369.   31 Jun 1798.   WM. MOON, AC, to THOS. EDWARDS, AC, for Ŀ80,
100 acres Porrage. Lines: ABNER PADGET. Orig. del. 28 Jan 1804
to TE. Signed MOHN. Wit: ABNER & EDMON PADGETT.

Page 370.   12 Sep 1798.   JNO. DUNCAN & wife SALLY, AC, to FLEMING DUNCAN,
AC, for Ŀ1, 265 acres branches Cornfield Branch. Lines: his
own, JNO. BRYAN.

Page 372.   12 Sep 1798.   JNO. DUNCAN & wife SALLY, AC, to WM. DUNCAN, AC,
for Ŀ1, 250 acres S branches Buffalo. Lines: LEONARD HENLEY;
CARTER; RICH. OGLESBY, AARON HIGGINBOTHAM dec'd., JACOB SMITH, schoolhouse.

Page 373.   6 Apr 1798.   JNO. HEIZER (HEIGER?) & wife ELIZ., Alb., to
CHAS. McCUE, AC, (orig. del. 3 May 1799 to RICH. MITCHELL per
order of CM) for Ŀ105, 105 acres near the Blue Ridge; W side of road
from Staunton to RICH. WOODS. Lines: KINCADE's old line, N side Piney
Mt., E side of road and down the Great Road, Headwaters N fork Rockfish.
Wit: JOS. SHELTON, AUGUSTINE SHEPHERD, WM. WARE.

Page 374.   28 Apr 1798.   ARCHIBALD RHEA & wife JANE, AC, to ANDERSON MOR-
GAN, AC, for $85.00, 2 tracts. 1) 30 acres on Blue Ridge and
headwaters of N fork Tye. Lines: DAVID TILFORD, DOWEL & DRUMMOND, TIL-
FORD's Mill, crossing creek. By TILFORD to RHEA, 19 Sep 1789. 2) Head of
Pond Run; N branch of N fork Tye; 270 acres. Lines: grantor, top of Blue
Ridge. Granted to RHEA as the assignee of DAVID TILFORD by pat., 27 Sep
1791. Wit: THOS. JONES, JESSE JONES, BENJ. H. MORGAN.

Page 376.   24 Feb 1798.   JAS. BISHOP & wife ELIZ, AC, to JACOB NEISE,
Albemarle, 5 sh. 150 acres, part of 400 acres surveyed on
Patton's Branch. Lines: JNO. NOWL. Wit: DANL.(?) OAFTMAN, ZEBOUN ORIZBAN,
JACOB CLOUDMAN(?). (Note: There are many signatures which are literally
impossible to read and seem to be an attempt on clerk's part to imitate
them. I am wondering if these are settlers in what is traditionally known
as Nassau or Dutch tract. I find many German or Dutch sounding names so
this only mystifies me. BFD)

Page 377.   9 Aug 1798.   JAS. FLACK & wife MARY, Augusta, to JACOB COFFMAN
SR, Rockingham Co, for Ŀ420, 280 acres Headwaters Rockfish -
whole tract bought by JF of JAS. ANDERSON. Lines: SMITH, JACOB ARISMAN.
Wit: JACOB CLOUDMAN(?), GORHAM PERRY JR(?) - practically illegible sig.

Page 378.   14 Jun 1798.   JNO. CRISER & wife SUSANNAH, AC, to SAML. Mc-
CULLOCH, AC, for Ŀ50, 49 acres. Lines: McKANELLY; SMITH; CHAS.
DELLAR(DETTOR?). Wit: as above.

Page 379.   16 Jul 1798.   Order to AC J.P.'s to quiz ELIZ. HARRIS, wife of
MATT. as to 150 acres conveyed to GEO. BLAINE SR, 18 Jul 1796.
Sent to M. DAWSON per order 20 Mar 1800. Done by JNO. DIGGES & WM.
HARRIS, 12 Sep 1798.

Page 380.   18 Jun 1798.   Order to same J.P.'s to quiz SALLY THURMOND,
wife of JNO. as to 29 Jan 1798 deed to GEO. BLAINE - 125 acres
Margin as above and don, 15 (16) Aug 1798.

Page 381.   17 Sep 1795.   JESSE CARTER, Ky, to JAS. KELLEY, AC, for Ŀ40,
63½ acres on Horsley. Proved by JAS. CARTER, 15 Feb 1796, and
by WARE & LAWLESS, 17 Sep 1798. Wit: WM. WARE, WM. LAWLESS, JAS. CARTER,
SAML. BROWN.

Page 382.   17 Feb 1798.   BENJ. RUCKER, AC, to BARTLETT EADES, AC, for

Ŀ250, 332 acres Stovall Creek. Lines: the road. Wit: ANTHONY & THOS. RUCKER.

Page 383. 15 Mar 1796. WM. MATTHEWS, Albemarle, to SAML. HENSLEY for
Ŀ60, 80 acres, part in AC and part in Albemarle; greater part in AC; both sides Ivy Creek. Lines: JNO. FARRAR, ISHAM BAILEY, SAML. IRV-ING, JNO. WILKINSON. Wit: JAS. BETHEL, JARROTT SUDDARTH, SUSANNAH HENSLEY, SILVEY HENSLEY, SUCKEY HENSLEY. Final proof by SILVEY, 17 Sep 1798.

Page 384. -- 1798. GEO. McDANIEL SR, to GEO. McDANIEL JR, for Ŀ115,
106 acres Harris Creek. Lines: HARRISON; SHELTON; RICH. POWELL. Wit: ZACH. DAWSON, ANTHONY RUCKER, AMBROSE RUCKER, minor, REUBIN PENDLETON.

Page 386. 24 Oct 1796. JOS. HIGGINBOTHAM SR, to ZACH. TALIAFERRO (Orig.
del. to ZT 29 Sep 1798) for Ŀ75, 177 acres N side Buffalo. Part of 300 acres. Lines: N bank of Buffalo, grantor, JOS. DODD, grantee. Final proof, 17 Sep 1798, by BENJ. HIGGINBOTHAM. Wit: JOS. HIGGINBOTHAM JR, BENJ. HIGGINBOTHAM, JNO. TALIAFERRO.

Page 387. 14 Jun 1798. JNO. CRISER & wife SUSANNAH, AC, to CHAS. KELLAR,
AC, (orig. del. to MARTIN, 12 Apr 1827) for Ŀ50, 49 acres. Lines: McANALLY's old line, dividing line of KELLAR & McCULLOCH, JAS. BROOKS, a path, a "holler". Wit: JACOB RUDASILL and two illegible ones. CRISER's signature and mark of wife and his is illegible, too.

Page 389. 17 Sep 1798. JAS. KELLY & wife ELIZ, AC, to JNO. SMITH, AC,
for Ŀ120, 219 acres Horsley. Lines: RICH. LAWLESS, WM. WARE, THOS. MITCHELL, PETER CARTER, top of Job's Mt., grantor.

Page 389. 17 Sep 1798. MARTIN KEY & wife ANN, AC, to LINDSEY BURKS, AC,
for Ŀ100,-no acres- S side and joining Brown's Creek, branch of Pedlar.

Page 391. 18 Sep 1797. WM. HAYNES & wife SARAH, AC, to son, HARDEN
HAYNES, AC, (Orig. sent to EDITH HAYNES, admrx. of HH, 7 Feb 1807) for Ŀ125, 150 acres N side Tobacco Row Mt., Horsley Creek. Lines: PHILIP THURMOND on NE, EDMOND GOODRICH on SW, JNO. EUBANKS & CALEB RALLS on NW & N. Wit: JNO. WARE, CHARLES HAYNES, THOS. GOODRICH, THOS. GOOD-RICH JR, THOS. SLEDD, JNO. EUBANKS.

Page 392. 28 Oct 1796. Order to AC J.P.'s to quiz MILLEY - JAS. CREWS &
wife MILLEY, 4 Sep 1784, deed to JOS. DAWSON. Rec. 17 Sep 1798 by THOS. MOORE & REUBIN NOWELL (NORVELL).

Page 393. 27 Nov 1792. CHAS. LAVENDER to JNO. TYLER & JNO. ALEX. JOHNS
for Ŀ40, 100 acres Buffalo Ridge. SALLY, wife of CL, signed. Lines: NATHAN WINGFIELD, JNO. PHILLIPS, EDLOE. Wit: JAS. FRANKLIN, W. SPENCER, GEO. DILLARD, ELIJAH MORAN. Final proof, 21 Jan 1793, by SPENCER & DILLARD. Then another note that JAS. FRANKLIN proved it on 18 Jun 1798, rec. 15 Oct 1798.

Page 394. 3 Jun 1798. AMBROSE TOMLINSON & wife MARY, AC, to PULLIAM
SANDIDGE, AC, for Ŀ100, 2 tracts. 1) 62 acres both sides N fork Buffalo. Lines: ISAAC MAYFIELD, JNO. HIGGINBOTHAM. 2) 25 acres adj. and between N and S forks Buffalo. Part of 200 acres pat. to MAYFIELD 20 Jul 1768. Lines: MAYFIELD's old line.

Page 396. 17 Sep 1798. NICHL. JONES & wife AMMERALE, AC, to PETER HARK-
LESS, AC, (Orig. del. to H. CAMDEN, per ord., 25 Jun 1803) for Ŀ50,-no acres- S branches Pedlar and S side Blue Ridge. Lines: Top of the Blue Ridge.

Page 398. 31 May 1798. BARTLETT EADES & wife ANN, AC, to JNO. MELTON,
AC, for Ŀ100, 127 acres (Orig. del. to JM, exr. of JNO. MILTON, 24 Sep 1840 - note variation in spelling) S branches Davis. Lines: gran-tor, descent of the mt. by a branch near RICH. POLLARD's line, across top of the mt. above JOS. LOVING. Wit: M.C. NAPIER, RO. WRIGHT, JNO. WRIGHT.

Page 398. 28 Aug 1798. CAROLINE MATILDA ROSE for Ŀ12-1-8 rel. suit vs.
DAVID TINSLEY for dower in 145 acres bought from my late

husband, HUGH ROSE, dec'd. Wit: JNO. WIATT, HUGH ROSE, AMBR. RUCKER, MARTIN DAWSON JR, NICHL. WEST.

Page 398.   28 Aug 1798.   CAROLINE as above rel. suit vs. JOSHUA TINSLEY for 159 acres as above bought. Wit: same.

Page 398.   2 Aug 1798.   CAROLINE as above dismisses suit vs. JNO., ISAAC, DAVID, & JOSHUA TINSLEY for Ł1-18-4 - 23 acres. Wit: as above.

Page 399.   28 Aug 1798.   CAROLINE as above dismisses suit vs. PHILIP BURFORD - 52 acres bought as above. Wit: same as above.

Page 400.   20 Jun 1798.   PLEASANT DAWSON & wife SALLY, Albemarle, to MARTIN DAWSON (del. to MD, 22 Aug 1798) for Ł200, 3 tracts. 1) Pat. to THOS. MATTHEWS 1 Aug 1772 - 64 acres. Lines: JOSIAS WOOD. 2) Pat. to PLEASANT DAWSON 16 Mar 1789 - 100 acres. Lines: JAS. & TERISHA TURNER, ZACH. ROBERTS, bank of N side Rockfish. 3) Pat. to DANL. DUNCAN, 23 Aug 1797, 161 acres S side Marrowbone Mt. Lines: his own, MATT. PHILLIPS, JNO. SANDERS, JNO. MATTHEWS.

Page 401.   6 Jun 1798.   JAS. NOLEN (signed NOLAN) & wife ELIZ, Rockingham Co, to DANL. KERY, AC, (orig. del. to HARLOW per ord, 2 Mar 1799) for Ł150, 130 acres N fork Rockfish. Lines: JAS. BROOKS, on the road, CHAS. RODES, branch known as the Shingle Hollow, BENJ. PANNELL, JOS. SMITH. Wit: JAS. BROOKS, SOLOMON CARY, P. LEMOINE, WM. CARY.

Page 403.   13 Oct 1798.   THOS. BIBBS, AC, to JAS. JOHNSON, Augusta Co, (orig. sent to JJ by JNO. B. SPRICE(?) 22 Aug 1838) for Ł8, no acres - N branch Rodes; survey of 36 acres mentioned later. Lines: Side of the mt.

Page 403.   3 Oct 1798.   WALTER CHRISTIAN & wife PATTY, AC, to ISAIAH ATTKISSON, AC, (one marginal note, scratched and illegible, but another, Orig. del. on 12 Sep 1816, to IA) for Ł22, 23 acres Rocky Run Branches. Lines: grantor, grantee, CHAS. CHRISTIAN. Wit: CHAS, SARAH, & WALTER CHRISTIAN JR.

Page 404.   12 Oct 1798.   MARTIN DAWSON SR, & ZACH DAWSON, AC, to NELSON C. DAWSON, AC, for Ł300, 162 acres Harris Creek. Lines: MARTIN DAWSON, Capt. R. SHELTON, THOS. POWELL dec'd, HENRY L. DAVIES, JNO. DAWSON dec'd. Wit: PLEASANT DAWSON, REUBEN PENDLETON, JESSE WOODROOF, JNO. SHELTON.

Page 405.   13 Sep 1798.   MACE FREELAND & wife ELIZ, Buckingham Co, to STEPEHN WATTS, AC, (Orig. del. to SW 2 Dec 1798) for Ł325, 195 acres both sides Buffalo, fork of Tye. Wit: JNO. HORSLEY, MICAJAH PENDLETON, NICHL. PAMPLIN, WM. JORDAN, JAS. PAMPLIN.

Page 407.   Order of 1 Aug 1796 to J.P.'s of Stokes Co. N.C., GEO. HANSER & CHRISTIAN LASH - deed of GEO. FITZGERALD & wife MARGARET & THOMPSON & TEAS to WM. EVANS - 103 acres 14 Feb 1791. Done, 8 Aug 1796, when MARGARET rel. dower rights. RO. WILLIAMS, CC of Court of Stokes Co. Rec. AC 15 Oct 1798.

Page 408.   15 Oct 1798.   JNO. MAYS & wife FRANKEY, AC, to THOS. WANCE, Rockbrigde, for Ł100, 267 acres Pedlar. Lines: on the path, the road. Wit: ANDREW HAMBLETON, JAS. WILLS JR, JNO. COONEY.

Page 409.   19 May 1798.   JOS. CHILDRESS & wife MARY, AC, to SAML. COLEMAN (Orig. del. to SC, 18 Sep 1799; someone has made date with pencil of 1798) for Ł500, 350 acres Harris Creek. Survey of 13 Nov 1793. Lines: JNO. HARVEY dec'd. Wit: WM. PETER, ANDREW STATON, JNO. PETER, RICH. TANKERSLEY, POLEY COLEMAN.

Page 411.   20 Jun 1798.   THOS. DICKERSON & wife SUKEY, AC, to WARNER GOODWIN, AC, (orig. del. to WG, 7 Dec 1798) for Ł200, 2 tracts N side and joining Buffalo. 1) 185 acres bought by TD of JOS. HIGGINBOTHAM. Lines: ZACH. TALIAFERRO, JOS. DODD, N bank of Buffalo. 2) 28 acres entry of STEWART BALLOW and assigned to ZACH. TALIAFERRO and by him to TD. Wit: DANL. WARWICK, JOS. DILLARD, RICH. DAVIS.

Page 412. 8 Dec 1796. NICHL. & JAS. PAMPLIN, AC, to WILL JORDAN, AC,
          (orig. del. to WJ 8 Nov 1798) for Ł200, 151 acres both sides
Elk Island Creek. Lines: JAS. PAMPLIN, Mill Creek. Wit: CHAS. & GABL.
PENN, EDWD. B. PAGE. Memo: reserve of 2 acres within above tract for JAS.
PAMPLIN & his mill.

Page 414. 15 Oct 1798. LAURENCE CAMPBELL, AC, to JNO. SWANSON, AC, for
          Ł9, 6 acres head of Higginbotham's Mill Creek. Lines: road
from Cabellsburg to New market, WM. CABELL. Part of a tract.

Page 415. 29 Nov 1797. NATHAN HARRIS & wife SARAH, AC, to MATTHEW
          HARRIS JR, for Ł400, 208 acres. Lines: JNO. ROBERTS, MATT.
HARRIS, Still House Branch, JNO. HARRIS, EDWD. HARRIS. Wit: JNO. HARRIS,
HENRY ROBERTS, EDWD. THOMPSON TOMS. Final proof by ROBERTS, 15 Oct 1798.

Page 416. 15 Nov 1798. DANL. McDONALD, RICH. & CHAS. TALIAFERRO, exrs.
          of JNO. B. TALIAFERRO, AC, to NELSON MUNROE, AC, for Ł45, 196
acres S branches Tye. Lines: JOS. BURGER, THOS. MASSIE.

Page 417. 13 Feb 1798. ALEX. McCAUL, Glasgow Merchant, by atty.-in-
          fact, JAS. LYLE, Chesterfield Co, to GEO. McDANIEL, AC, for Ł5,
108 acres Stoval Creek and head of Buck Branch. Pat. to AMc 15 Aug 1764.
Wit: BENJ. JORDAN, JNO. M. ROSE, PATRICK ROSE JR, JNO. LAMONT.

Page 418. 15 Oct 1798. WM. CRISP & wife LUCY, AC, to JNO. ALFORD, AC,
          for Ł640, 640 acres by survey of 21 Mar 1780. S branches
Ruckers Run, part of tract of JNO. HARMER, British subject, and WALTER
KING, same, and sold by DAVID SHEPHERD, Escheator, to WC under two
Assembly acts of 1779. Lines: WM. ALFORD.

Page 419. -- Apr 1798. GEO. HILTON, AC, to WILLSON PENN, AC, - lease of
          land formerly occupied by THOS. SPRADLING near Oles's Mill and
next to GILES DAVIDSON. From 1 Jan 1798, for five years. Annual rent of
25 sh. Wit: JOS. DILLARD, SAML. FRANKLIN, HENLEY DRUMMOND.

Page 421. 15 Oct 1798. JNO. ALEX. JOHNS and wife ONEY; JNO. TYLER &
          wife ELIZ., AC, to PETER PEARCE (orig. del. to PP 29 Sep 1800
by T. TRIPLETT) for Ł100, 100 acres N side Buffalo on Glade road Branches.
92 acres of it surveyed for JOS. WHITTLE and sold to CHAS. WINGFIELD and
pat. in his name, 7 Jan 1780. 8 acres part of land belonging at present
to NATHAN WINGFIELD. Wit: CHAS. CHRISTIAN, JNO. THOMPSON, THOS. JOHNS.

Page 422. 9 Dec 1793. ABSALOM STINCHCOMB, "Albert Co, Ga." to WM. LAYNE,
   .   AC, (orig. del. to SAML. P. LAIN per order, 8 May 1810) for
Ł20, 72½ acres both sides Elk Island, N fork; part of tract of JNO. VIA.
Lines of VIA. Wit: HENRY ARRINGTON, THOS. JOHNS, RICH. GATEWOOD. Final
Proof 15 Oct 1798, and noted that GATEWOOD has died.

Page 424. 15 Oct 1798. RO. HENRY ROSE to SPENCER NORVELL, Alb. (orig.
          del. 18 Aug 1851, to C. McIVER, the present owner) for Ł600,
505 acres Harris Creek. Lines: SHELTON's road, BENJ. RUCKER, DANL.
BURFORD, Rucker's Branch.

Page 425. 24 Sep 1798. JAS. HOPKINS, AC, - deplores miserable condition
          of slaves who are fellow mortals - freedom to Squire to whom
I have given surname of Jackson, and his wife Sarah, after 4 Nov next.
They are about 44 and in good health and able to earn plentiful mainten-
ance; will furnish clothing and will no longer be responsible for them.
Court is to examine them for approval. Wit: JAS. HOPKINS, minro, BENJ.
NORVELL. Rec. 15 Oct 1798.

Page 426. -- 1798. PLEASANT DAWSON & wife SALLY, Alb., to JAS. TURNER,
          AC, for Ł40, 73 acres, (orig. del. to MARTIN DAWSON, 22 Aug
1798) S side and joining Rockfish. Lines: grantee, NATHAN HARRIS, JOS.
ROBERTS. Wit: JNO. CLARKE, JOS. H. IRVIN.

Page 427. 17 Dec 1798. ALLEN BLAIR & wife MARY ANN, AC, to LANDON
          CABELL, AC, (orig. del. 22 Sep 1801 to LC) bond of 22 Feb 1790
to JOSHUA WILLOUGHBY, AC, 150 acres and assigned to THOS. BICKNALL, who
has died intestate; TB's heirs have assigned to LEWIS McQUEEN and he has

assigned to CABELL - now convey to CABELL - Nassau Creek, branch of Rockfish. Lines: grantee, SNIDER, now WM. PURVIS, HARMER & KING (now CABELLs)
JNO. GRIFFIN (now CABELL's) and bought 16 Mar 1789. Granted to BLAIR as
assignee of GRIFFIN's.

Page 429.   22 Sep 1798.   Order of AC J.P.'s to quiz JANE, wife of SAML.
            MEREDITH, as to deed of 23 Feb 1796 to JOS. WILCHER, 102 acres.
Done by WM. WARWICK & DAVID S. GARLAND, 17 Dec 1798.

Page 430.   15 Nov 1798.   JNO. WATKINS & wife CATHERINE, to JNO. KESTERSON
            for Ł80, 90 acres (orig. del. 2 Sep 1799 to JD) on N branch
Davis. Lines: JAS. McALEXANDER dec'd, LEE HARRIS dec'd, ALEX. McALEXANDER.

Page 431.   25 Aug 1798.   Order to AC J.P.'s to quiz MARY, wife of PATRICK
            ROSE - 30 Sep 1776, to CHAS. IRVING, 2 tracts; one known as
Grey's Point - 394 acres and tract bought of THOS. HIGGINBOTHAM by Rev.
ROBT. ROSE - 200 acres, and joining 1st tract. Done by SAML. MEREDITH &
DAVID S. GARLAND, 15 Dec 1798.

Page 432.   10 May 1798.   THOS. D. ISBELL, Greenville Co, N.C. to HENRY
            ISBELL, Fluvanna Co, for Ł25, 57 acres Buffalo - has been in
partnership between THOS. D, HENRY, & ZACH. ISBELL. Lines: CHAS. CHRIS-
TIAN WEST. Wit: JOS. BAINARD, JNO. BAINARD JR, JAS. SMITH, BARTLETT
HUMPHREY, JOS. SOUTHERLAND.

Page 434.   21 Jun 1798.   CAROLINE MATILDA ROSE to BENJ. JORDAN for $1.00,
            rel. dower in 800 acres sold by late Col. HUGH ROSE to CHAS.
IRVING and granted to him by deed of 7 May 1775. Rel. to IRVING's heirs.
Wit: BENJ. JORDAN, WALTER IRVINE, P. GOOCH.

Page 434.   4 Dec 1798.   Agreement between SUSANNA JOPLING, widow of
            JOSIAH JOPLING, and his exrs, JAS. & WM. JOPLING - Ł200, rel.
of all claims vs. estate. Wit: WM. LEE HARRIS, WM. H. DIGGES, GEO. ENNIS.

Page 435.   19 Jan 1798.   JAS. PAMPLIN, AC, to JAS. PAMPLIN JR, AC, (orig.
            del. to JP 27 Nov 1801) for Ł50, 100 acres Elk Island Creek.
Lines: GEO. HILTON, near Chicihominy Branch. Wit: WILSON PENN, THOS.
SPRADLIN, WM. JORDAN.

Page 436.   13 Nov 1798.   NATHL. HENDERSON, AC, to OBEDIAH HENDERSON, AC,
            for Ł60, 140 acres, part of a tract; 30 acres sold off of it;
110 acres conveyed. S side and joining Pedlar. Lines: dividing ridge
leading to Piney Gap. SALLY, wife of NH signed. Wit: JNO. CHILDRESS SR,
& JR, JNO. HENDERSON, NANNY TULEY.

Page 438.   17 Jan 1799.   CHAS. CHRISTIAN to ROBT. PEARCE, both of AC,
            (orig. del. 6 Aug 1799 to JACOB PEARCE) for Ł200, 204 acres
where JACOB PEARCE lives - headwaters Rockey Run. Lines: FRANCIS BURCH
THOS. POWELL's heirs, ANDERSON MONROE. Wit: JAS. HIGGINBOTHAM, WALTER
CHRISTIAN, JOHN CHRISTIAN, B.

Page 439.   7 Jan 1799.   CHAS. CHRISTIAN, AC, to JAS. FLOYD, AC, (orig.
            del. to JF 9 Jun 1800) for Ł126, 50 acres. Lines: E bank
Rockey Run or creek; JNO. CHRISTIAN, mill pond, JF has privilege of
raising water in pond; WM. DILLARD, JACOB G. PEARCE, bank of Buffalo,
Mill Creek mouth; Part of 2 tracts bought of THOS. PENN and included mill
and one tract bought of JNO. CHRISTAIN.

Page 441.   19 Jan 1799.   DANL. PERROW & wife ANNE, AC, to THOS. SPRADLING,
            AC, for Ł30, 72½ acres both sides N fork Fishing Creek; part
of tract left by JNO. VIA to his 4 sons: GIDEON, DAVID, JNO. & WM. VIA.
Wit: WILSON PENN, WM. JORDAN, JAS. PAMPLIN.

Page 442.   24 Nov 1798.   JOS. CREWS SR, AC, to JOS. CREWS JR, AC, for
            $1.00, 250 acres on Rutledge and Tribulation; bought by late
GIDEON CREWS from GEO. McDANIEL JR. Lines: EDWD. WATSON, top of the hill,
WIATT POWELL, late GIDEON CREWS, JAS. PENDLETON, the old road, JOS.
BURRUS. (Orig. del. to THOS. CREWS 31 Jan 1829) Wit: PROSSER POWELL,
JNO. CREWS, DAVID TINSLEY, JNO. PENDLETON, NELSON C. CRAWFORD. (I have
pointed out before that we are dealing with the Sweet Briar campus

whenever we encounter CREWS data mentioning the Rutledge Creek area. It
is known that the beautiful Sweet Briar House occupied by the president
was built by a CRESS, but we still lack definite data on the various
steps in the title. BFD)

Page 445. 11 Jan 1799. REUBEN, WM. & SARAH GATEWOOD, AC, to JACOB
            PEARCE, AC, (orig. del. 18 Jul 1799 to JP) for ₺137, 137 acres
S side Buffalo. Tract bequeathed by WM. GATEWOOD JR, dec'd, to his wife
SARAH, for life and then to her sons, REUBEN & WM. LInes: JACOB GAROON
PEARCE, CHAS. CHRISTIAN, JAS. CHRISTIAN. Wit: JNO. CHRISTIAN B., JAS.
GARLAND, JOS. LAYNE, THOS. APPLING.

Page 446. 11 May 1796. Order to AC J.P.'s. CHAS. CHRISTIAN & wife SARAH,
            NOTLEY MADDOX & wife FANNY, JNO. CHRISTIAN & wife JUDITH, 12
May 1795, to JACOB GAROON PEARCE - 423 acres. Order to quiz SARAH CHRIS-
TIAN. Done 21 Jan 1799, by WM. WARWICK, GEO. DILLARD, & DAVID S. GARLAND.
Page 448, order to quiz SARAH as to 195 acres to same grantee; deed of
29 Jun 1795. Done on same date by same J.P.'s. Page 449, 16 Jun 1797,
order to quiz SARAH as to deed of 4 Aug 1796, to JNO. CREWS. Done by
same J.P's on same date.

Page 450. 15 Oct 1798. THEODORICK WEBB & wife CHRISTY, CUTHBERT WEBB &
            wife MILLY, ADRIAN WEBB & wife LUCY, JNO. WEBB, JAS. WEBB,
ADAM HILLAM & wife CANEY, THOS. HILLAM & wife MARY, ISHAM JARRELL & wife
LUCY, JNO. HARTER & wife SALLY, JACOB WEBB & wife BETTY, Franklin Co, and
WM. TULLEY & wife HANNAH, Alb., to JAS. WOOD, AC, for ₺100, 533 acres in
3 tracts. 1) Granted before Revolution to WM. BRUISE and pat. at Williamsburg 25 Sep 1762, branches S fork Rockfish. Lines: HENRY KEYS. 2) Pat.
to THEODORICK WEBB at same place, 27 Aug 1776. 1 has 150 acres, 2 has
154 acres. 3) Pat. to CUTHBERT WEBB at same place, 5 Jul 1774, 229 acres.
Wit: MOSES GREEN, THOS. THOMPSON, JNO. VANTERSPOLE(?). Monday, 5 Nov
1798, at Franklin Co. and proved "by 1 witness" as to LUCY JARRELL.
Rec. AC, 21 Jan 1799.

Page 454. 27 Dec 1796. NATHL. HARLOE & wife FANNEY, AC, to CHRISTIAN
            SHELLY, Shanandoah(sic) Co., (Orig. sent to HUDSON MARTIN 31
Oct 1799) for ₺300, 289 acres. Lines: SAML. WOODS, SHEROD MARTIN. Wit:
JACOB GOOP(?), RICH. RICHARDSON, WM. HARLOW, PETER FABER. Final proof,
21 Jan 1799, by WH.

Page 456. 14 Sep 1798. NATHL. HENDERSON & wife SARAH, AC, to OBADIAH
            MARTIN, AC, for ₺50, 140 acres Pedlar; to NH by deed. Lines:
Leading ridge from Piney Gap to Pedlar; Irish Creek branches; 1/4 of
tract containing 30 acres - ambiguous in language. Wit: JNO. CHILDRESS   ✗
SR, NANCY(?) TULEY, JNO. CHILDRESS JR.

Page 457. 19 Nov 1798. RICH. TALIAFERRO, AC, to JNO. JACOBS SR, AC, for
            ₺654, 327 acres Tye and joining grantee. Lines: MOSES HUGHES,
THOS. STUART, JNO. ROSE, THOS. MASSEY. Wit: WM. JACOBS, JNO. JACOBS, JNO.
CONEY, DAVID JACOBS, W.S. CRAWFORD.

Page 458. 15 Nov 1798. JAS. BRADY, Knox Co, Tenn., to JNO. HUGHES, AC,
            for ₺200, 173 acres. Lines: crossing branch of Elk Creek.
Signed BRELEN (mark). Wit: JOS. WIATT, MOSES HUGHES. Final proof, 21 Jan
1799, by JESSE OGLESBY.

Page 459. 5 Sep 1793. AARON DEHART, AC, to ELIJAH DEHART, AC, for ₺5,
            30 acres Porrage Creek. Lines: H. CHRISTIAN, H. WOOD, SAC.
KING, AARON DEHART. Wit: CHAS. CHRISTIAN, WM. LONDON, JAS. DEHART. Final
proof, 21 Jan 1799, by CC.

Page 461. 8 Oct 1798. RAWLEY PINN & wife SARAH, AC, to JAS. LONDON, AC,
            for ₺5, 25 acres Porrage Branches and S of Buffalo Ridge.
Lines: grantee, LARKIN LONDON. Wit: R. NOWELL (NORVELL?), PHIL. JOHNSON,
JNO. TURNER, HENRY TURNER. Final proof, 21 Jan 1799, by JNO. TURNER.

Page 462. 20 Nov 1798. RO. HOLLOWAY & wife SARAH, AC, to JONATHAN
            BOLLING, Alb., for ₺205, 110 acres bought by RH of JNO. DILL-
ARD. Lines: JNO. DILLARD, JAS. WATERS, S side bank of Long Branch, JAS.
DILLARD, JESSE MAYS. Wit: JAS. DILLARD, H.M. GARLAND, RICH. WILSON,

342

HENRY STONEHAM.

Page 463.   6 Oct 1798.   CHAS. EVANS, AC, to JAS. MURPHY, AC, Deed of
Trust - $1.00. Stock, bull bought of THOS. ROBERTSON. Wit:
WADDY THOMPSON, THOS. GREGORY, JNO. HAWKINS, MARBELL CAMDEN.

Page 465.   26 Dec 1798.   NATHL. DAVIS, AC, to JOSIAH ELLIS, SR, AC, for
Ł324, 324 acres W side Tobacco Row Mt., N branches Pedlar.
Bequeathed to ND by NATHL. DAVIS, dec'd, and rec. in AC. Lines: RODERICK
McCULLOCH, his own, CHAS. ELLIS' orphans. Wit: JAS. BALLINGER, RICH. S.
ELLIS, JOSIAH ELLIS JR, JNO. ELLIS, CHAS. & JAS. DAVIS, THOS. WILLS.

Page 467.   29 Oct 1798.   JNO. SHIELDS & JAS. MONTGOMERY by mutual consent
bought 396 acres on Hatt of RICH. DOPSON. MONTGOMERY to have
140 acres (later it is put at 147 acres) and SHIELDS conveys for 5 sh,
147 acres. Wit: JNO. N. REID, JAS. BROOKS, JAS. SHIELDS.

Page 469.   10 May 1798.   SPICEY, JNO., BENJ., JAS. & MACE PENDLETON;
JOHN HARRIS, JNO. CABELL, & MACE FREELAND, Buckingham Co, to
MICAJAH PENDLETON, Buckingham Co, for Ł200, 175 acres both sides Buffalo.
Wit: NATHL. OFFUTT, JAS. PATTERSON, SAML. PERKINS.

Page 471.   23 Nov 1798.   Order to AC J.P.'s to quiz SALLY, wife of PLEA-
SANT DAWSON, as to 1798 deed to JAS. TURNER for 73 acres.
Done, 29 Dec 1798, by JNO. & WM. H. DIGGES.

Page 472.   23 Nov 1798.   Order to same J.P.'s to quiz SALLY as above as
to 20 Jun 1798 deed to MARTIN DAWSON, 3 tracts of 325 acres.
Done as above.

Page 474.   1 Feb 1799.   RO. C. HARRISON & wife ANNE, Cumberland Co, to
RO. RIVES, AC, (orig. del. to RR, 2 Mar 1799) for Ł1100, 1290
acres both sides Rucker's Run. Lines: grantee, WM. LOVING, Bob's Creek.
Lots 8, 10 & 11, and small part of two other lots adj. 10; between CHAS.
EDMONDS & JOS. HOLLINGSWORTH. Survey of Mar, 1780, for Commonwealth and
formerly that of JNO. HARMER, Great Britain. (Note: There are many deeds
involving this land of HARMER and KING who were British subjects and
their lands were sold so see my earlier abstracts.)Wit: JESSE & JNO.
HIGGINBOTHAM, WM. B. HARE, SAML. WOOD, JAS. LOVING, WILLIS WILLS, F.
CABELL, CLO. SHELTON.

Page 476.   8 Nov 1798.   Order to AC JP's.   NICHL. PAMPLIN & JAS. PAMPLIN
and wife, RACHEL (of JAS.), 8 Dec 1796, to WM. JORDAN - 150
acres. Orig. sent to CHAS. CHRISTIAN. Done by JAS. DILLARD & JNO. CHRIS-
TIAN, 16 Dec 1798.

Page 477.   11 Feb 1798.   JOSHUA WILLOUGHBY & wife ELIZ, AC, to SPARKS
MARTIN, AC, for Ł10, 30½ acres Dutch Creek. Lines: HENRY
MARTIN, dec'd.

Page 479.   14 Jan 1799.   JNO. CLARKSON & wife SUKEY, AC, to JNO. YOUNG,
Caroline Co, for Ł700 - given for following land and 400 acres
in separate deeds - 30 on Tob. Row Mt. Lines: CHAS. TALIAFERRO, tract of
400 acres. On page 480 is deed for 400 acres at Ł700 on Puppies Creek.
Lines: CHAS. TALIAFERRO, dec'd., JNO. WATKINS, top of the mt., WM. CABELL.

Page 481.   17 Dec 1798.   ALEX. HUMPHREY & wife MARY, Augusta, to JACOB
KINNEY, same Co., for Ł300, 200 acres bought from WM. BIBB &
GEO. GILLESPIE as attys. for JNO. RYAN, and to CHESLY KINNEY and by him
to HUMPHERY - last two deeds are of rec. in Charlottesville Dist. Court.

Page 482.   18 Dec 1798.   JACOB KINNEY & wife ANN, Augusta, to DAVID
CLARKSON, AC, for Ł300, 200 acres and ref. to deed above.

Page 484.   Order of 22 Jun 1792 to Lincoln Co, (Ky).   GEO. LEE, & wife
ELIZ, TO RICH. HARRISON, 2 Dec 1782 - 303 acres. Order to quiz
ELIZ., done on 17 Nov 1796, by JNO. BLANE & DANL. W. McCORMICK. Rec. AC
18 Feb 1799. Orig. del. Dec, 1802, to RH.

Page 485.   12 Dec 1798.   SAML. IRVINE & wife NANCY (formerly ROSE),

Lynchburg & Campbell Co, to WM. SPENCER, for $1,000, 240 acres Tye and
Piney branches. Part of 1872 acres divided lately to heirs of HUGH ROSE
and this is lot of the grantors. Lines: WM. CABELL JR, GEO. DILLARD. Lots
2 and 3; subject to life estate in codicil to THOS. WORTHAM & wife. Wit:
WILSON DAVENPORT, JNO. N. ROSE, F. CABELL, WM. DAVIS, WALTER IRVINE,
PATRICK ROSE, GEORGE NICHOLAS.

Page 486. 8 Dec 1797. STEPHEN TURNER, AC, to SAML. TURNER, his son,
          STEPHEN for love and support of SAML, 400 acres Tye; conveyed
to STEPHEN by JNO. WARE & wife ELIZ, 6 Apr 1789. Lines: Col. HUGH ROSE,
dec'd., Col. WM. CABELL JR, SHELTON, WM. SPENCER, JOS. DILLARD dec'd.
Wit: RO. RIVES, JAS. MURPHY, WILLIS WILLS, CLO. SHELTON.

Page 488. 25 Jan 1799. JNO. KESTERSON, AC, to JOS. SHELTON, AC, Deed
          of Trust - debt due WM. TURNER, AC, - $1.00 - 90 acres N fork
Davis Creek. Lines: LEE HARRIS dec'd, JAS. McALEXANDER dec'd, ALEX. Mc-
ALEXANDER, JAS. THARP. Wit: EDWD. THO. TOMS, WM. LEE HARRIS, JERIAH KIDD.

Page 491. 19 Feb 1799. JNO. PENN, AC, gets release from GEO. DILLARD on
          Deed of Trust - 11 Jan 1803, del. to JP - DILLARD as agt. of
McCLURE BRYDIE & Co., ref. to Deed of Trust of WM. EVANS, AC, 29 Aug 1795,
and wife JOICE, and assigned to JNO. PENN. Five adj. tracts on Indian
Creek. 1) 97 acres. 2) 33 acres and adj. JNO. CAMPBELL on N bank. 3)
EVANS' line, crossing creek - 103 acres. 4) 63 3/4 acres adj. CHAS. TYLER.
5) 119 acres adj. EVANS, JNO. CAMPBELL, WM. LAHORN. Wit: PEACHY FRANKLIN,
CLO. SHELTON, ARCHELAUS MAYS.

Page 494. -- Feb 1799. JAS. BROOKS, Alb., to THOS. GOODWIN, AC, (orig.
          del. to TG, 15 Mar 1802) for Ł5, 120 acres Shoemaker Creek;
branch of Rockfish. Lines: THOS. MORRISON, THOMAS ADAMS. Wit: JO. H.
MORRISON.

Page 497. -- Oct 1798. ELIZ. BRAXTON, to RICH. WILSON by SAML. MEREDITH
          - rel. dower in samll tract sold by MEREDITH to WILSON - part
of tract bought by MEREDITH from Hon. CARTER BRAXTON. Orig. del. 3 Feb
1802 to ROBT. WILSON. Wit: WM. GALT, JNO. ALLEN, DANL. WARWICK, RO.
HOLLOWAY, DAVID S. GARLAND.

Page 497. 9 Feb 1799. JNO. DAWSON & wife SALLY, AC, to MARTIN DAWSON
          (Orig. sent to MD per letter) for Ł200, 139 acres Rockfish.
Part of pat. of JNO. BARRS JR (BURRUS?) 20 Sep 1758, and by JB conveyed
to JNO. DAWSON. Lines: S side Rockey Branch, JNO. DAWSON's old line,
TERISHA TURNER. Another tract to JNO. DAWSON, 9 Sep 1796; 100 acres.
Lines: grantor, PLEASANT DAWSON, top of a mt. Wit: P. GOOCH, NANCY DAW-
SON, POLLY BECKNAL, JNO. S. DAWSON, BENNETT NALLY, RICH. HARRISON.

Page 500. 14 Nov 1795. WM. MATTHEWS, Alb., to JARRATT SUDDARTH, Alb.,
          for Ł50, 87 acres Ivy Creek and 1770 survey. Wit: MEREDITH
LANDERS, JESSE THOMAS, SAML. HENSLEY. Final proof, 18 Feb 1799, by
MATTHEWS.

Page 501. 21 Aug 1798. PHILIP RYAN, AC, to BENJ. JORDAN, Buckingham -
          4 Nov 1799, to GEO. KIPPEN debt is owed - Ł130-9-5. Deed of
Trust - 5 sh. 200 acres. Lines: JNO. ROSE, DAVID CLARKSON. Bought by
RYAN of GEO. GILLESPIE, atty. in fact for JNO. RYAN, heir of JNO. RYAN
dec'd. Part of 400 acres granted to GILLESPIE and WM. BIBB SR. as attys
for JNO. RYAN dec'd., 25 Aug 1789. pat. Wit: ANDREW MORGAN, JESSE
CLARKSON, NATHL. OFFUTT, HUGH CAMPBELL.

Page 503. 18 Feb 1799. JOS. TILFORD, & wife NANCY, AC, to GEO. LAVENDER,
          AC, for Ł300, 150 acres Coffey or Raccoon Creek. Lines: STE-
PHEN JOHNSON, Col. HENRY.

Page 504. 15 Apr 1799. GEO. NICHOLAS & wife NANCY, Buckingham Co, to
          LINDSEY COLEMAN, AC, (orig. del. to LC, 16 Apr 1799) for Ł329,
329 acres S branches Buffalo. Lines: Harvie's old road, JOHN NICHOLAS
dec'd.

Page 505. -- Apr 1799. JAS. McALEXANDER, AC, Power of Atty to DAVID Mc-
          ALEXANDER, AC, (Orig. del. to DM 4 May 1799) to receive Ky.

344

lands to which I am entitled and to sell. Wit: LANDON CABELL, JOS. ROBERTS, JAS. WRIGHT.

Page 506. 15 Apr 1799. JAS. THORP, AC, Power of Atty. to son, WM. THORP, AC, (Orig. del. to WT, 4 May 1799) to receive all Ky lands assigned by Commonwealth of Va. for 3 years of service. Wit: LANDON BRENT, JOS. ROBERTS, SAML. BRIDGWATER, HENRY DAWSON. (is it too much to imagine the sight of the two - McALEXANDER & THORP - as they probably came into the old courthouse at Colleen in present Nelson Co. to pick up the powers granted to them in Kentucky? It is noted that they picked them up on same day and it is logical to assume that they made the trip together. BFD)

Page 506. 25 Feb 1799. Order to AC J.P.'s, JNO. WARWICK & WM. LOVING or WM. B. HARE, to quiz JUDITH - Deed of LANDON CABELL & wife JUDITH SCOTT, to JNO. MARR, 20 Nov 1797, 212 acres. Done by LOVING & HARE 8 Apr 1799.

Page 508. 5 Apr 1799. GEO. McDANIEL, AC, to HENRY ROBINSON, AC, (orig. del. to HR 24 Jan 1801) for Ł80, 180 acres Stovell Creek and Buck Branch. Lines: DANL. NORCUTT, MICHL. COALTER, WM. GUTTRY, DANL. MEHONE. Wit: RICH. POWELL, P. BURTON, GEO. McDANIEL JR.

Page 510. 15 Apr 1799. CALEB RALLS & wife SUKEY to DANL. WARWICK for Ł1200, 500 acres both sides Horsley. Part of tract. Lines: Pedlar road, grantor. Orig. del. to CR, 25 Apr 1799.

Page 511. 2 Mar 1799. CHAS. LAVENDER, AC, to JAS. MURPHY, AC, Deed of Trust - debt due RO. RIVES & Co. - $1.00 - stock. Orig. del. to JM 12 Aug 1799. Wit: HEN. HOLLOWAY, SAML. HANSBROUGH, JNO. CRISP, WM. STAPLES.

Page 512. 26 Jan 1799. THOS. HOPKINS, Sullivan Co, Tenn, to JAS. McALEXANDER, AC, for Ł300, 449 acres composed of 2 tracts adj. 1) The old survey of 285 acres. Lines: WM. WRIGHT, BINION's entry, old pat. line. 2) 164 acres adj., granted JNO. HOPKINS, assignee of THOS. MONTGOMERY, who was assignee of LUKE BINION - date of 1 Jun 1782. Wit: MICAJAH BURNETT, HENRY DAWSON, DAVID McALEXANDER. Later tract adj. THOS. MONTGOMERY.

Page 514. 15 May 1798. SMYTH TANDY & wife JOYCE, to JAS. MURRAY BROWN for Ł20, 1/2 acre in town of Cabellsburg. Lines: N side of lot sold by ST to WM. GALT for IRVING GALT & Co. and on S by Col. WM. CABELL. Wit: P. GOOCH, WM. CAMDEN, DANL. TUCKER.

Page 516. 18 Mar 1799. SAML. ANDERSON, Alb., to THOS TRIPLETT, AC, (Orig. del. to TT, 29 Sep 1800) for Ł150, 157 acres both sides Raven Creek, N branch Buffalo. Lines: WM. CABELL at the Rolling Road; old survey of NICHL. CABELL. Bought from WM. LAYNE, 21 Apr 1795. Wit: CHAS. CHRISTIAN, ABSALOM HOWL, JNO. CHRISTIAN B., JNO. ALLCOCK.

Page 517. 15 Apr 1799. PHILIP DAVIS & wife SARAH, AC, to JNO. THOMPSON, AC, for Ł16, 189 acres Piney near the little Mts.; part of 378 acre pat. 9 Aug 1794, to PD, assignee of PHILIP BUSH. Wit: WM. B. HARE, ALEX. ROSE, MICAJAH CAMDEN.

Page 519. 15 Apr 1799. JNO. ALFORD to THOS. ALFORD, both of AC, for Ł50, 50 acres Tye and Ruckers Run. Part of tract lately bought by JNO. of WM. CRISP. Lines: AUSTIN SMITH, THOS. BIBB, grantor, WM. ALFORD.

Page 519. 15 Jun 1793. ELIJAH STONE, AC, to heirs of PERRIN FARRAR, AC, for Ł125, 190 acres. Lines: ABRAHAM STRANGE, WM. MORRISON, grantor. Final proof on 15 Apr 1799, by STONE. Wit: JAS. MONTGOMERY, BENJ. PAYNE, SAML. PAKINS, DANL. MARTIN.

Page 521. 21 Aug 1798. GEO. GILLESPIE, AC, atty in fact for JNO. RYAN, heir of JNO. RYAN, dec'd, to PHILIP RYAN, AC, for Ł250, 200 acres. Lines: JNO. ROSE, DAVID CLARKSON; part of 400 acres granted to WM. BIBB SR, and GILLESPIE as attys. for JNO. RYAN, heir of JNO. RYAN dec'd, 25 Aug 1789. Balance of unsold tract. Orig. del. to RYAN, 18 Jun 1803 - grantee. Wit: BENJ. JORDAN, ANDREW MORGAN, JESSE CLARKSON, NATHL. OFFUTT.

Page 522.   -- Feb 1799.   JNO. & WM. ALFORD, AC, to AUSTIN SMITH, AC, for
Ŀ32, 32 acres Tye & Rucker's Run. 20 acres of it part of tract
lately bought by JNO. ALFORD from WM. CRISP - 12 acres of it is where WM.
ALFORD lives. Lines: THOS. ALFORD, THOS. BIBB, grantee, JOS. LOVING, WM.
ALFORD.

Page 523.   9 Mar 1799.   JNO. SWANSON, AC, to JAS. M. BROWN, AC, for Ŀ10,
3 acres, part off of tract whreon BROWN has erected a dwelling
house and improved tract. Wit: JNO. CAMM, JAS. DILLARD, SPOTSWOOD GARLAND.
Martin seems to be some figures and Tough and Co.

Page 525.   27 Oct 1798.   ELIZ. BECKNAL, JNO, MARY, NANCY, & SALLY BECKNAL;
JNO. MATTHEWS & wife MARY ANN, AC, to SAML. SCOTT SCRUGGS, AC,
for Ŀ120, 236 acres trible fall creek, branch of Rockfish. Lines: JOS.
SMITH, RALPH JOPLING dec'd, WM. DIXON. Wit: WM. BAILEY, THOS. NASH, WM.
MATTHEWS as to WM. LEE HARRIS.

Page 527.   11 Mar 1799.   MINOS WRIGHT, AC, to JAS. MURPHY, AC, Deed of
Trust for debt due RO. RIVES & Co. (Orig. del. to DANL. HIGGIN-
BOTHAM, 14 Jul 1800) $1.00 - 136 acres N side Tye. Lines: SAML. EDMUNDS,
SR, GEO. STONEHAM, JOS. LOVING. Part of 390 acres. Wit: HEN. HOLLOWAY,
DANL. HIGGINBOTHAM, JAS. HANSBROUGH, PERMENAS BRYANT.

Page 528.   14 Apr 1788.   ELIZ. PATTERSON, AC, to THOMPSON & TEAS, Deed of
Trust - tobacco, stock etc. Wit: DAVID S. GARLAND, ALEX. PAT-
TERSON. Final proof, 15 Apr 1799.

Page 530.   16 Mar 1799.   JNO. HAGER, AC, to GEO. SHRADER, AC, Deed of
Trust - long list of items - debt due from GEO. & DANL. SHRA-
DER - also to JAS. MURPHY for RO. RIVES & Co., exrs. of WM. CABELL dec'd.
Memo: fire shovel and shot gun delivered. Wit: JAS. BALLINGER, HENRY
GILBERT.   (Note: HAGER seekers should consult Johnson's History of Ky.,
3rd Vol. for 2 sketches on later members of the family and PERRIN et al-
8th edition on eastern Ky. (There are 2 8ths, one on Jefferson, too).
Some years ago an army captain stationed in Germany and some distance
from my capt. son, JNO. FULTON DAVIS, who was in another section of Ger-
many, wrote here about a marriage of JNO. HAGER to a SCHRAEDER. The
marriage is not of record, but I recalled the Ky. data. I had gone to
Georgetown College in my native Kentucky with EUGENE HAGER from eastern
Ky. I have not heard about him in many years - and so I looked up the
sketches referred to above. They show that JNO. HAGER went into eastern
Ky. and that he married a woman named SCHRAEDER here. One sketch shows
HAGER as a Revolutionary soldier but another states that he fought with
British. I feel sure that he was one of the Hessians stationed at Albemarle Barracks and that he, like so many, switched sides after his cap-
ture. I would assume the same for the Shrader family, but it is stated in
one sketch that his wife (HAGER's) was born in Virginia and the date
given is pre-Revolution. BFD)

Page 531.   6 Jan 1799.   RUSH HUDSON & wife LUCY, AC, to JAS. FRANKLIN, AC,
for Ŀ10, 10 acres. Lines: WM. CABELL, grantee. Wit: W.S.
CRAWFORD, JNO. CAMM, S. GARLAND.

Page 532.   15 Apr 1799.   BENJ. RUCKER & wife ELIZ, AC, to ELIAS WILLS,
(Orig. del. to EW 17 Sep 1799) for Ŀ545, 414 acres Stoval Cr.
Lines: THOS. RUCKER, the road.

Page 533.   14 Mar 1799.   HUGH ROSE, AC, to WM. SPENCER for Ŀ56-10, 28 1/4
acres Tye. Lines: WM. SID CRAWFORD, lot #4, dower line, lot #
2. Wit: NATHAN HALL, PHILIP SOWELL, SAML. TURNER, JNO. SPENCER.

Page 535.   22 Mar 1799.   GEO. McDANIEL JR, Bedford Co, to PHILIP BURTON,
AC, for Ŀ700, 353 acres. Lines: HENRY LANDON DAVIES, RICH.
POWELL, RICH. SHELTON, GEO. McDANIEL SR. Wit: DAVID TINSLEY, JNO. TINSLEY,
JAS. HARRISON, JAS. TINSLEY, RICH. POWELL, GEO. McDANIEL.

Page 537.   3 Mar 1798.   THOS. HAWKINS & wife ELIZ, AC, to JAS. MURPHY, AC,
Deed of Trust - debt due RO. RIVES & Co. (Orig. del. to JM 12
Aug 1799) 6 sh. - 200 acres Headwaters Boh's Creek. Lines: MATT. HARRIS
JR, MARTIN BIBB, JNO. THOMPSON, CONYERS WHITE - formerly that of JAS. BIBB

to which he was entitled as a co-heir of WM. BIBB, dec'd.; also slaves.
Final proof 15 Apr 1799 by THOS. BROWN. Wit: JNO. SPENCER, THOS. BROWN,
HENRY HOLLOWAY, JNO. CRISP.

Page 538.   15 Apr 1799.   WM. ALFORD, AC, to WM. KEEY,AC, for Ł80, 81 ac-
            res Tye. Lines: JOS. LOVING, grantor, grantee, WM. HOLLINGS-
WORTH.

Page 540.   24 Feb 1797.   JOS. HARLAN & wife TABITHA, Albemarle, to BENJ.
            JORDAN, Buckingham, for Ł100, 1/2 acre lot Warminster. S side
Main Street - No. 6 by town plat now occupied by CLOUGH SHELTON. Wit:
WM. H. CABELL, WM. B. HARE, CLO. SHELTON, JAS. STEWART, JNO. HIGGINBOTHAM.

Page 541.   4 Jun 1799.   WM. LAVENDER to GALT & GARLAND - Deed of Trust -
            2 sh. slave, mare, furniture. Wit: SPOTSWOOD GARLAND, JNO.
ELLIS, WILL EDMUNDS, JR.

Page 541.   11 Apr 1799.   EDMUND DAVIS, AC, to GALT & GARLAND, Deed of
            Trust - furniture, pots, oven and other items. Wit: WILL
EDMUNDS, JR, DANL. McDONALD.

Page 542.   27 May 1799.   WARNER GOODWIN, AC, to HENRY BALLINGER, AC, (del.
            30 Aug 1800, to JNO. S. MIGGINSON per written order from HB)
for Ł120, 2 tracts N side of Buffalo and adj.   1) 185 acres bought by WG
of THOS. DICKERSON. Lines: ZACH. TALIAFERRO, JOS. DODD, old pat. line.
2) 28 acres - entry made by STEWART BALLOW & assigned to ZACH. TALIAFERRO
JR, and by him to THOS. DICKERSON & by TD to GOODWIN. Wit: JABEZ CAMDEN,
WM. CAMDEN, MICAJAH CAMDEN, WILL CAMDEN JR.

Page 544.   15 Apr 1799.   THOS. RUCKER & wife SALLY, AC, to ELIAS WILLS,
            AC, for Ł455, 350 acres Stovall Creek. Lines: BENJ. RUCKER &
CLACK.

Page 545.   17 Jun 1799.   JER. WHITTEN, AC, to ANTHONY NICELY, AC, for
            Ł100, Peg's (Pig's?) Creek. Lines: JNO. BIAS, JON. HOGG, NICHL.
JONES. Orig. del. 19 Aug 1816.

Page 546.   21 May 1799.   JESSE HARRIS, AC, to WM. LEE HARRIS, Deed of
            Trust - debt due ANDREW HART - all interest in estate of JNO.
HARRIS, dec'd. of Green Mt. - Davis Creek land. Wit: JNO. LOVING, JNO.
HARRIS, JNO. CAMM, S. GARLAND.

Page 547.   17 Jun 1799.   JESSE KANADY & wife SUSANNAH, AC, to JOS. ALL-
            COCK, AC, for Ł50, 200 acres next to where JK lives. Lines:
RICH. ALLCOCK, WM. GATEWOOD, dec'd, JAS. FREELAND, GABL. PENN dec'd.,
JAS. ROWSEY.

Page 548.   17 Jun 1799.   JOS. ALLCOCK & wife STILLY, AC, to THOS. NEVIL,
            AC, (Orig. del. to TN 22 Mar 1806) for Ł100, 92 acres N bran-
ches Buffalo. Lines: RICH. ALLCOCK, crooked fall branch, spring that
widow PAGE now makes use of, GABL. PENN dec'd, JAS. ROWSEY. Part of tract.

Page 549.   5 Nov 1798.   JAS. HOPKINS, at present of Annadale, AC, (orig.
            del. to RICH. P. POLLARD, 31 Jan 1805) to daughter, ELIZ.
BOUSH POLLARD, my only surviving child - now at Mt. Liberty with husband
and children - for her support and to alleviate miserable condition of
fellow mortals whose Supreme Creator has put in my hands - Touiamond -
born Apr, 1763; for 7 years; Junin, bought June 1770, for 12 years, Caty,
bought March 1780, and about 8 then; Catey, bought March 1780 and about 8
then, for 12 years, Minor(female) born Feb. 1779, for 17 years; Phillis,
born Jan 1781, for 19 years; Moses, born Jul7, 1784, for 22 years; Tom,
born May of 1786, for 28 years; Emma, born Oct 1788, for 26 years; mulatto, Orange, born to my negro woman, Betsy, May 1791, for 30 years. They
were hired last year to my son-in-law, RICH. C. POLLARD - to be delivered
to me or exrs. at end of specified terms and to be set free. $10.00 to
each male and $15.00 to each female, increase to serve - males for 35
years and females for 30 years. Each one to be certified to court. If my
daughter dies, then to her children. No child to be taken from mother
until weaned or at age of two. POLLARD and wife agreed to terms in a memo.
Wit: GEO. MARTIN, JNO. FORTUNE, JAS. HOPKINS, minor. (I have made

comments on this man before, but cite his will in my H will work. I consider the document to be one of the most interesting in AC. BFD)

Page 556. 1 Jun 1799. BENJ. JORDAN, Buckingham, to JAS. LOVING, AC, Ŀ50, 1/2 acre in Warminster - S side Main Street - lot #6, lately bought by JOS. HARLAN & wife TABITHA. Wit: JOS. SHELTON, WM. B. HARE, WM. H. CABELL, JAS. P. COCKE JR.

Page 557. 5 Jan 1795. Legatees of ELLIOT ROBARDS (they signed as ROBERTS) receipt to exrs. and rel. all claims vs. cattle & hogs in possession of HENRY & ELIZ. ROBARDS - reserving equal parts to all other portions of the estate. Signed by JNO. & HENRY ROBERTS, CONYERS WHITE, JAS. THOMAS, WM. BURKS, WM. HARRIS JR. Wit: JOS. SHELTON, GIDEON CREWS.

Page 558. 8 Dec 1798. ELIZ. & HENRY ROBARDS under powers given us by the heirs of ELLIOTT ROBERTS and love for MATTHEW ROBERTS, son of ELLIOTT, the stock mentioned in previous deed, but reserved for our own lives. Wit: JNO., JOS., ROBT. S., & GEO. FARRAR.

Page 558. 7 Dec 1798. Order to Hanover J.P.'s JNO. THOMPSON & JNO. BULLOCK to quiz SUKEY, wife of THOS. DICKINSON for 20 Jun 1798 deed to WARNER GOODWIN - 2 tracts - 213 acres. Done & rec. AC 17 Jun 1799.

Page 559. 25 Oct 1798. HENRY HUGHES & wife MARTHA, AC, to JNO. WATKINS, AC, for Ŀ36, 50 acres Davis Creek. Lines: LEE HARRIS, DANL. DEVAL, ALEX. McALEXANDER. Part of 150 acres by new chopt line. Page 560, order to quiz MARTHA and done by WM. HARRIS & JAS. MONTGOMERY. Rec. 17 Jun 1799. Wit: to deed: JACOB PUCKETT, JAS. MONTGOMERY, JNO. N. REID, WM. HARRIS, HENRY SMITH.

Page 562. 17 Jun 1799. JNO. WATKINS & wife KATEY, AC, to JNO. ABNEY, AC, (Orig. del. to M. KING per order of JA, 15 Jun 1804) for Ŀ37, 50 acres N fork Davis. Lines: LEE HARRIS dec'd, ALEX. McALEXANDER, JAS. THORP.

Page 563. 13 Dec 1798. MADDISON HILL, AC, to WM. DAMERON, AC, - POLLY, wife of HILL - for $200, 177 acres S branches Stovall. Lines: BENJ. RUCKER, THOS. JOHNS, his own, S branch Wolf Branch, THOS. RUCKER. Wit: ALEX. STUART, REUBIN NORVILL, MOSES TINSLEY, DAVID WOODROOF, DRURY BELL, JESSE WOODROOF.

Page 564. 17 Jun 1799. ALLEN BLAIR & wife MARY ANN; LEWIS McQUEEN & wife POLLY, AC, to JNO., ELIZ, MARY, ANNE, SARAH, & SOOKEY BICKNALL for Ŀ80, 142 acres, granted to AB, assignee of JOSHUA WILLOUGHBY, 17 Sep 1792; branches Rucker's Run. Lines: WM. CRISP, THOS. HAWKINS. Orig. del. to JNO. BICKNALL, 5 Jan 1802. MARY ANN rel. dower, but nothing said about McQUEEN's wife.

Page 565. 4 Mar 1799. Order to Cumberland J.P.'s NATHL. & CODDINGTON CARRINGTON & WM. POWELL - to quiz ANNE, wife of RO. C. HARRISON, deed of 1 Feb 1799, to RO. RIVES - 1290 acres. Rec. AC, 17 Jun 1799. Del. to RR, 1 Mar 1802.

Page 566. 16 Apr 1799. Order to Buckingham J.P.'s WM. CANNON & WM. R. BARNARD, to quiz NANCY, wife of GEO. NICHOLAS - 15 Apr 1799, deed to LINDSEY COLEMAN - 329 acres. Rec. AC, 17 Jun 1799.

Page 567. 1 Dec 1798. Order to AC J.P.'s JOSIAS JONES & JOS. C. MEGGINSON, to quiz ELIZ., wife of MACE FREELAND, deed of 13 Sep 1798 to STEPHEN WATTS - 195 acres. Rec. AC, 17 Jun 1799.

Page 569. 18 Jun 1799. CLAUDIUS BUSTER & wife ANNE, (formerly MOFFETT) and co-heir of THOS. MOFFETT, dec'd, Albemarle, to MILINOR COX, AC, for Ŀ150, 128½ acres. Lines: MICHL. COALTER, HENRY ROBERTSON, GEO. CABELL. ANNE's division of her father's estate.

Page 569. 1 Jun 1799. WM. P. LEWIS & wife ELIZ, Buckingham Co, to NATHL. HARLOW, AC, (sent to NH by R.S. ELLIS, Esq., 25 Apr 1800) for Ŀ70-10, 188 acres on top of Blue Ridge and Rhodes Creek. Conveyed by Col.

348

JOS. CABELL, dec'd, to his daughter, ELIZ. LEWIS. Wit: ANNE BERNARD, MARY
CABELL, JAS. D. CASKE JR.(?)

Page 571.   18 Jul 1799. JAS. BRANSFORD & wife SILEY, AC, to WM. EVNAS,
AC, for Ł250, 186 acres S branches Piney. Line of HENRY ROSE.

Page 572.   15 Jul 1799. HUGH McCABE & wife ELIZ., AC, to WM. HALL (orig.
del. to WH on 27 Oct 1800) for blank sum, 300 acres by pat.,
20 Jul 1768. Lines: N side Pedlar, S side Pedlar.

Page 573.   31 May 1799. NICHL. CABELL & wife HANNAH, AC, to WM. H.
CABELL (Orig. del. to WHC, 8 Nov 1800) for love of their son,
and 5 sh, 800 acres on Fluvanna. Lines: mouth of small branch off upper
part of Swift Islands, SAML. J. CABELL, WM. H. CABELL, former lines of
FRANCIS WEST, dec'd. Also 288 acres surveyed on 17 Nov 1780, on S branches Thomas Mill Creek and S branches Mayo Creek and granted to NC by pat,
16 Sep 1790. Wit: RO. RIVES, JAS. LOVING, WILLIS WILLS, WM. B. HARE.

Page 575.   31 May 1799. NICHL. CABELL & wife HANNAH, AC, to their son,
GEO. CABELL (orig. del. to W.H. CABELL 8 Nov 1800) for love
and 5 sh, 940 acres on Fluvanna. Lines: next to tract sold on same date
to WM. H. CABELL; former tract of FRANCIS WEST dec'd. Lines: STEPHEN
TURNER, Swan Creek, below landing of old ferry commonly called JOS.
CABELL's ferry. Wit: same as above deed.

Page 576.   26 Jun 1799. GALT & GARLAND under AC Court decree vs. EZEK.
GILBERT sold at public auction, 1 Sep 1798, for 5 sh. to
EZEK. GILBERT, in trust - medical books, stock etc., for maintenance of
his children: WIATT ROSKINS GILBERT, ELVIRA GILBERT, PATSY C. GILBERT,
WILLMOUTH GILBERT, ANN GILBERT, EZEK. GILBERT, WM. BLUNT GILBERT, FANNY
WIATT GILBERT, & MARTHA GILBERT. Wit: RALPH MARTIN, JNO. HILL.

Page 577.   23 Feb 1799. Trustees of Warminster, RO. RIVES, DAVID TYNDALL,
WM. B. HARE, CHAS. YANCEY, JNO. JOHNSON, JNO. TURNER, & WM.
CABELL to JOSEPH HARLAN, Albemarle - 5 sh. and Ł17-10-15 paid to NICHL.
CABELL - 2 lots of 1/2 acre each, S side Main Street - Nos. 6 & 8. No.6
is now occupied by CLOUGH SHELTON and 8 by JESSE HARLAN. Wit: CLO. SHEL-
TON, ZACH. NEVIL, JNO. HIGGINBOTHAM, WM. H. CABELL.

Page 578.   14 Jun 1799. Trustees of Warminster (some changes in names)
CHAS. YANCEY, SAML. SPENCER, DAVID TYNDALL, JNO. TURNER, RO.
RIVES, SAML. J. CABELL, WM. B. HARE to WILLIS WILLS, Warminster, 5 sh.
and Ł16-10 and Ł25 paid to NICHL. CABELL - three lots of 1/2 acre each.
N side Main street and Nos. 7,9 and 11. Occupied by WILLIS WILLS and
WILLIS WILLS and Co. Wit: BENJ. JORDAN, JAS. LOVING, JNO. HIGGINBOTHAM,
NELSON ANDERSON.

Page 579.   13 Jul 1799. JAS. LONDON, AC, to JNO. LONDON, AC, for love of
JAS. for his son, JNO. 240 acres both sides Porrage Creek.
Lines: JOSHUA FRY, survey of 92 acres of RO. JOHNS. Wit: LARKIN LONDON,
DRURY CHRISTIAN, WM. JOYNER, CHAS. CHRISTIAN.

Page 580.   22 Feb 1799. WM. LONG & wife ELIZ, AC, to PEACHY FRANKLIN,
AC, for Ł30, 1/2 acre lot S of the store and lots of JAS.
FRANKLIN & WM. CABELL - near town of Cabellsburg on road leading to
Lynchburg. Wit: WIATT POWELL, S. GARLAND, JAS. M. BROWN.

Page 581.   11 Jul 1799. THOS. RICKETTS, AC, to WM. DAMRON, AC, for Ł150,
300 acres, the graveyard of 4 poles square is excepted - Wolf
Branch - Opossum Island road and MATT. RICKETTS adjoin. Wit: WM. STEVENS,
NICK HARRISON, JNO. WINGFIELD, GEO. McDANIEL.

Page 583.   3 --- 1799. EBINEZER HAYCOCK & wife JANE, AC, to JAS. THOMP-
SON, AC, for Ł100, 100 acres, formerly occupied by ELIZ. DAVIS
and pat. to PHILLIP DAVIS (JR or SR?) and lines of his survey.

Page 584.   1 Dec 1797. ABRAHAM WARREN, AC, to JNO. MERRIT, AC, for Ł90,
100 acres Stovall Creek. MERRIT is called Jr. in deed. Wit:
WM. GUTTRY, THOS. MERRIT, MATT. MYLER, JNO. BURFORD JR, JNO. & CHAS.
WINGFIELD.

Page 586. 12 Jan 1799. RO. YOUNG, City of Alexandria, to BERTAND EWELL,
            Pr. Wm., $5.00 -(30 Aug 1799, forwarded by post to BE)- 2000
acres, part of 4000 acres taken up and surveyed by Col. WM. CABELL for
THOS. DOSWELL and JOHN DRUMMOND, the elder, James City, and partitioned
by DOSWELL to JNO. & HENLEY DRUMMOND, 1768; by DRUMMONDs to Hon. JNO.
TYLER, dec'd, in 1794; by JT to JNO. FOSTER, 11 Jun 1796; by FOSTER to
YOUNG, 12 Jan 1799. Lines: ABRAM SMITH on S, JOS. STRICKLAND on N, THOS.
GOODWIN on E, JNO. TATE on W. Wit: WALTER JONES JR, CHAS. ALEXANDER JR,
GEO. YOUNG, JNO. ABERT. Produced from Fairfax to AC.

Page 587. 14 Jun 1799. This name is difficult and could be CHAS. PULEY,
            PALEY, or PERLEY, and wife SARAH, Henrico and City of Richmond
to DANL. NORCUTT, AC, for Ł150, 73 acres Lynch road. Lines of HIGGINBO-
THAM. Seems to be PERLEY in summary from Richmond, 14 Jun 1799. Rec.
AC, 16 Sep 1799.

Page 589. 13 Sep 1799. WM. WARWICK, AC, to JNO. BETHEL, AC, for Ł50, 50
            acres branches Rucker's Run. Part of tract formerly that of
ABRAHAM WARWICK. Lines: grantee, RO. C. HARRISON.

Page 589. 16 Sep 1799. JNO. KESTERSON & wife REBECCA, AC, to MAJOR
            KING, AC, (del. to MK, 14 Jan 1800) for Ł80, 90 acres Head
waters Davis Creek. Lines: JAS. ALEXANDER, LEE HARRIS dec'd, JAS. THORP,
ALEX. McALEXANDER (Note: ALEX. is probably McALEX., but so recorded)

Page 590. 12 Sep 1799. JNO. BAILEY & wife FRANKEY, AC, to PETER LYON,
            AC, for $5.50, 25 acres Cove Creek branch of Rockfish. Part of
70 acres pat. to JB 8 Sep 1787. Lines: grantor, JNO. S. DAWSON, GEO.
BLAIN JR.

Page 591. 12 Sep 1799. JAS. SORRELL, AC, to HENRY HARTLESS, AC, (del.
            to WM. HARTLESS, admr. of HH, Sept, 1805) for Ł25, 83 acres
Head branches Pedlar and on the Blue Ridge. LInes: JNO. JARVIS, top of
Blue Ridge, HENRY HARTLESS. Pat. to JS on 26 May 1794. MARY, wife of JS
signed. Wit: BENJ. HIGGINBOTHAM, JAMES MARTIN, WALTER FRASHER, JACOB
PHILLIPS.

Page 592. 7 Sep 1799. GEO. GOODWIN, AC, to AMBROSE RUCKER JR, AC, (del.
            to AR Jr. 29 Mar 1805) for Ł115, 11 acres near DAVIES' lower
ferry. Lines: HENRY L. DAVIES, MICAJAH GOODWIN, THOS. MITCHELL, JESSE
WOODROOF. Wit: THOS. MOORE, JESSE WOODROOF, JOSIAH ELLIS JR, GEO. Mc-
DANIEL JR.

Page 594. 16 Sep 1799. DAVID S. GARLAND, AC, to JNO. McDANIEL, AC, (del.
            to JM 8 May 1807) for Ł95, 122 acres Harris Creek. Lines: JNO.
KNIGHT, ABEL BLANKENSHIP, ISAAC RUCKER, MAGANN's old ordinary tract. Same
tract sold by WM. GARLAND to JNO. KNIGHT and by JK to DAVID S. GARLAND.

Page 595. 14 Sep 1799. ARCHIBALD REYNOLDS, Campbell Co., to JAS. LASH-
            ELL, AC, (del. to O. DABNEY, 22 Aug 1827) for Ł10, 1/2 acre
N side Lynch road near Madison Town. Lines: grantee, Lynch road. Wit:
WILSON DAVENPORT, GEO. McDANIELL, ANTHONY RUCKER, JOS. KENNERLEY.

Page 596. 28 Aug 1799. JNO. CHRISTIAN & wife MARY, AC, to MICAJAH PEN-
            DLETON, AC, (orig. del. to MP by WILSON PENN, 15 Oct 1799) for
Ł287-5, 191½ acres. Lines: Capt. JNO. CHRISTIAN, near a spring. Wit: WM.
HORSLEY, GILES DAVIDSON, R. HORSELY, WM. CREWS.

Page 598. 28 Dec 1798. BENJ. RUCKER & wife ELIZ, AC, to DANL. BURFORD,
            AC, for Ł60, 100 acres S fork Stovall Creek. DANL. is called
Jr. in document. Wit: JNO. READ, THOS. RUCKER, WIATT READ.

Page 599. 16 Sep 1799. BENJ. RUCKER & wife ELIZ, AC, to JESSE BECK, AC,
            for Ł333-10, 221 acres Main fork Stovall; lower part of tract
surveyed for GEO. STOVALL dec'd. Lines: Path from forks of creek to ELIAS
WILLS, a fence.

Page 600. 18 Mar 1799. BALLENGER WADE & wife SALLEY, Henry Co., to JAS.
            MAYS, son of ROBT. MAYS, (orig. del. to JM 7 Oct 1799) for
Ł30, 170 acres Stonehouse Creek, formerly granted to PEARCE WADE, father

of BALLENGER WADE, by pat. of 20 Sep 1768. Lines: JNO. FREELAND. Wit:
W.S. CRAWFORD, JAS. DILLARD, JAS. CARPNER (prob. CARPENTER).

Page 602.   20 Jul 1799.   LARKIN SANDIDGE & wife MARY, AC, to PETER WATER-
        FIELD, AC, for Ł300, 250 acres S fork Buffalo on Long Mt. ex-
cept 35 acres deeded to HENRY HARTLESS. Lines: CARNABY VEAL. Wit: HENRY
BALLINGER, WALKER ATKINSON, HUGH CAMPBELL. Del. to PW 20 Oct 1811.

Page 603.   7 Sep 1799.   LARKIN SANDIDGE & wife MARY, AC, to PETER WATER-
        FIELD, AC, (orig. del. as above) for Ł100, 300 acres branches
S fork Buffalo; pat. to LS at Richmond 25 Aug 1796. Lines: his own, JOS.
HIGGINBOTHAM SR, WM. CARTER, dec'd, JAS. HENSON, BENJ. SANDIDGE, HENRY
HARCULAS (HARTLESS probably).

Page 605.   12 Sep 1799.   LARKIN SANDIDGE & wife MARY, to PETER CARTER, AC,
        for Ł60, 42 acres both sides Piney Mt. between Horsley & Buffalo.

Page 606.   16 Sep 1799.   JNO. EUBANK & wife PEGGY, AC, to PETER SULMAN,
        AC, (orig. del. to PS, 30 Aug 1806) for Ł450, 300 acres both
sides Wilderness Creek and Laurence Creek. Part of a tract surveyed and
plat (not herein) by JOS. BARNETT.

Page 607.   13 Aug 1799.   POWHATAN BOLLING, Buckingham Co, to WM. ISBELL,
        late of Cumberland Co. - lease - Bolling's Creek low ground on
Fluvanna - upper part. Lines: MICAJAH TERRELL, 10 ft. above high water,
THOS. WIATT, grantor's old pat. line, now fallen - 80 acres, may clear
river hills for dwelling - have fishery, not to waste timber. 10 years at
$120 per year. To cultivate and interesting to see rotation of crops
suggested - 1/2 in tobacco and 1/2 in small grains; hemp may be grown,
but takes care to emphasize small grain items. Wit: JOS. BURRUS, REUBEN
NORVELL, PHIL JOHNSON.

Page 609.   13 Aug 1799.   POWHATAN BOLLING, Buckingham, to WM. & HENRY
        ROBINSON, AC, lease - Wills Creek low ground -lower half.
Lines: bank of Fluvanna, CHRISTOPHER ISBELL. 95 acres. Liberty to clear
low ground and river hills facing river for healthy place in hills for
their families to dwell - $142.50 per year for same period as previous
lease - 10 years. We have the same stipulations as to rotation of crops
herein. Wit: as above.

Page 610.   13 Sep 1799.   WM. NORVELL & WM. EDENFIELD to WM. PETTYJOHN,
        Campbell Co. Ct., Nov 1797, ordered WARRINGTON & KEENE vs.
MICKLE - to appoint WM. BROWN and two grantors named to sell 214 acres on
Harris Creek and PETTYJOHN bought for blank sum, June, 1798. Lines: mouth
of Polecat. Wit: JESSE WOODROOF, JNO. LACKEY, W. ROBINSON, HENRY ROBINSON,
THOS. STEWART.

Page 612.   11 Mar 1799.   CRAVEN PEYTON to JOS. CABELL - Ł275 - 3 slaves.
        Wit: WM. B. HARE & JNO. JOHNSON.   14 Oct 1799, del. to JC
and receipt wits. were RO. RIVES & JESSE HIGGINBOTHAM.

Page 613.   2 Sep 1799.   JNO. LOVING & ELISHA ESTIS, Overseers of Poor of
        Amherst Parish, to HIRAM McGINNIS, AC, order of June, 1799, to
bind out BARNETT CASH, a poor boy whose parents are not adjudged able to
bring him up - 18 years of age- To serve McGINNIS until 21 and to learn
the sadler's trade - he is to deport himself well and McGINNIS is to
furnish drink, clothing, and board, also washing, and teach him reading,
writing and arithmetic to rule of three. He is to pay CASH the sum of
$12.00 at expiration of service.

Page 614.   15 Jul 1799.   Same overseers of the Poor as above to McGINNIS,
        acting under Act of Assembly relating to Bastard children -
they bound out JAS. MURPHY, whose parents are unable to bring him up -
14 years old and to serve until 21 as above to learn sadler's art. He is
not to absent himself from master, to play no games, and isn't to
contract matrimony.

Page 615.   16 Sep 1799.   JNO. BARNETT & wife REBECCA, AC, to RICE BROWN,
        AC, (del. 3 Jan 1800 to RB) for Ł50, 98 acres Hat Creek & Tye.
Lines: JAS. BROWN, RICH. DOBSON, DAVID DUNAHOE, STEPHEN JOHNSON.

Page 616. 16 Sep 1799. JNO. BARNETT & wife REBECCA, AC, to JAS. MONT-
GOMERY, AC, (del. to JM 21 Jun 1800) for $4500, 400 acres Hat
Creek. Devised by Rev. ROBT ROSE to RO. BARNETT & by RB to JNO. BARNETT.
Lines: JNO. ROSE, RICH. DOBSON, CHAS. JONES.

Page 618. 16 Sep 1799. MARY ANN JONES, AC, to CHAS. JONES, AC, for $500,
156 acres Tye. Lines: THOS. JONES, RICH. DOBSON, JNO. BARNETT,
JNO. ROSE, DAVID CLARKSON.

Page 618. 16 Sep 1799. MARY ANN JONES, AC, to THOS. JONES, AC, (del. to
TJ, 7 Nov 1806) for $1000, 244 acres. Lines: CHAS. JONES,
DAVID CLARKSON, THOMAS MASSIE, RICH. DOBSON.

Page 620. 17 Sep 1799. JAS. SAVAGE & wife MARY, AC, to RO. HOLLOWAY, AC,
for Ŀ170, 75 acres where JS lives. Lines: GABL. PENN dec'd.,
lot #1 & #4; land formerly that of SMYTH TANDY, but now that of grantee.
Bought by JS of SAML. BROWN and part of tract of ---- GIBSON, dec'd. Wit:
HENRY CAMDEN, WM. ARMISTEAD, JOSIAH ELLIS JR.

Page 621. 4 Nov 1798. THOS. DILLON & wife ELIZ, Lynchburg, to WM. SPEN-
CER & STEPHEN WATTS, AC, for Ŀ60, 400 acres N branches Buffalo.
Lines: SAML. MEREDITH, JNO. ROWSEY, JNO. PHILLIPS, WM. LAINE, JNO.
STRATTON, WM. SPENCER, STEPHEN WATTS. Wit: JAS. DILLARD, WM. & HENRY
TURNER, STINSON BRYANT, JAS. CHRISTIAN JR.

Page 623. 15 Apr 1799. JNO. JACOBS & wife LUCY, AC, to THOS. HARVIE,
AC, for Ŀ100, 139 acres pat. 20 Nov 1795 - balance of 2
tracts surveyed by DAVID DAVIS on N branches Piney. Lines: CHAS. ROSE,
DAVID PARROCK, WM. BOND(?), BENJ. KILBENN. Wit: PARMENAS BRYANT, HENRY
HARPER.

Page 624. 16 Sep 1799. WM. HOLLINGSWORTH & wife JAMIMA, AC, to ZACHA-
RIAS PHILLIPS JR, AC, (del. to ZP 13 Dec 1801) for Ŀ165, 93
acres S branches Rucker's Run. Part of tract of WM. ALFORD. Lines: WM.
CRISP, WM. ALFORD.

Page 625. 25 Apr 1799. Order of AC J.P.'s DAVID & NELSON CARWFORD -
CALEB RALLS & wife SUKEY, 15 Apr 1799, to DANL. WARWICK -
500 acres - to quiz SUKEY. Rec. 16 Sep 1799. Del. to T.N. EUBANK, 3
Jan 1800.

Page 629. 21 Oct 1797. Order to AC J.P.'s - not named - to quiz SUSAN-
NAH HARGROVE, wife of HEZEKIAH - deed of 16 Oct 1797, to
CONYERS WHITE for 192 acres by JOSIAH WOOD & wife PATIENCE, and HEZ.
HARGROVE & wife. Rec. 16 Sep 1799. (Perhaps the clerk was eager to
finish this book and skipped names of the J.P.'s.)

End of Deed Book H

352

Page 1.   4 Oct 1799. BENAMIMI STONE & wife ELIZ., to WM. LONG, for 6sh,
2 acres both sides Rutledge. 1) 1 acres surveyed 99 Aug 1794
on N side and joining Rutledge. Part of tract of GEO. COLEMAN dec'd, and
condemned by jury for STONE to erect water grist mill - order of Court
Sept., 1793. 2) Surveyed 24 Aug 1799 for both parties and part of tract
of Stone - granary theron and 2 pairs of stones and machinery. Wit:
PEACHY FRANKLIN, JOS. BURRUS, S. GARLAND. Original delivered to WL 7 May
1821.

Page 2.   20 Oct 1799. JOS. WEAVER & wife SUSANA, AC, to MOSES HUGHES,
AC, for $1200, 200 acres; part of 400 acres pat. to GEO.
HEDD(?) 15 Feb 1748. Lines: ANDREW REID, formerly JNO. CHISWELL, NATHL.
BARNETT, formerly WM. MAYO, JAS. HEARD. Wit: JAS. HUGHES, WM. COFFEY,
JNO. HUGHES.

Page 3.   27 Sep 1799. DUNCAN McLAUGHLAN & Co., Fluvanna, to RO. PAGE,
Albemarle, for Ł200, 169½ acres. Co. bought it of MARBEL
STONE - Taylor Creek. Lines: grantee, AUGUSTINE SHEPHERD dec'd. Wit:
MARTIN DAWSON, RICH. S. ELLIS, MOSES MORRIS, ZACH. TALIAFERRO, DAVID S.
GARLAND.

Page 3.   21 Oct 1799. CHAS. REYNOLDS, AC, to JAS. LEE, AC, for Ł10, 9
acres Harris Creek. Lines: grantor. Wit: ARCHELAUS REYNOLDS,
WM. HUGHES, JR, THOS. MERRITT.

Page 4.   21 Oct 1799. JAS. LEE, AC, to CHAS. REYNOLDS, AC, for Ł400,
mill seat; formerly called Wade's old mill, with ½ acres lot
laid off for mill and mill house.

Page 5.   21 Oct 1799. JAS. LEE, AC, to CHAS. REYNOLDS, AC, for Ł20, 15
acres + Harris Creek, near the ford road and bank of mill pond.

Page 6.   30 Sep 1799. JOS. THOMPSON & wife MARGARET, AC, to MICHL.
BROCKMAN, Albemarle, for Ł140, 63 acres. Lines: Grantor, FRED-
ERICK WARE. Wit: WM. WHITE, JNO. PIPER, JAS. HAYS.

Page 7.   21 Oct 1799. BEN SANDIDGE, AC, to WM. MITCHEL, AC, (Orig. del.
to WM 29 Oct 1802) for Ł60, 66 acres on Blue Ridge and branches of Pedlar.

Page 8.   21 Oct 1799. JAS. MAYS & wife CREASY, to HENSLEY CARPENTER,
AC, for Ł45, 170 acres Stonehouse Creek; tract granted to
PIERCE WADE, father of BALLINGER WADE, by pat., 20 Sep 1768. Lines: JNO.
FREEMAN.

Page 8.   8 May 1799. JESSE WRIGHT SR, AC, to JAS. MURPHY, AC, Deed of
Trust to secure debt to RO. RIVES & Co. - $1.00 - debt of
Ł67-16-5. A very long list of personal property - no land mentioned. Wit:
HEN. HOLLOWAY, DANL. HIGGINBOTHAM, WM. MORRIS, WM. BRYANT.

Page 10.   29 Jul 1799. CHAS. YANCEY, Buckingham, to ZACH. WHITE, AC,
(Orig. del. per S. GARLAND to ZW 23 May 1816) for Ł187-10, 250
acres between Tye & Rucker's Run and near Cocke and Brown's Mill. Lines:
DAVID PROFIT, JAS. MAYS. Part of pat. of SAML. SPENCER SR, dec'd. Wit:
RICH. POWELL, GEO. MARTIN, RO. RIVES, CONYERS WHITE, JAS. HANSBROUGH.

Page 10.   21 Apr 1799. STEPHEN CASH, AC, to SAML. FRANKLIN, AC, for Ł5,
1½ acre Stonehouse Creek. Lines: THOS. POWELL, Franklin's Mill
Pond. Wit: BARTLETT, JNO. & WM. CASH.

Page 11.   25 Aug 1799. WM. VEAL & wife ELIZ, AC, to HUGH McCABE, AC,
for Ł40, 404 acres N side Fluvanna (early name for James River)
& Otter Creek. Lines: CORNL. THOMAS, Tarrapin Creek, Rattlesnake Branch.
Wit: WM. BURKS, JNO. FLOOD, ANTHONY LAVENDER, JOS. MILSTEAD, CHAS.
FLOOD, KENSY RALLS, DAVID BURKS JR.

Page 12.   21 Oct 1799. JNO. PHILLIPS & wife RHODAY, AC, to FRANCIS

WEST, for Ƚ36-10, 107 acres Swan Creek. Lines: Col. NICHL. CABELL, WM. WEST, BRANSFORD WEST, NOURBORN THOMAS.

Page 13.   25 Sep 1799.   PETER WHITINGHILL & wife CATH., AC, to SAML. NICELY, AC, for Ƚ80, 200 acres Thomas Mill Creek. Lines: RO. JOHNSON, JNO. SLEDD. Wit: THOS. WAUGH, THOS. WANTZ, DAVID THOMAS, ROD. McCULLOCH.

Page 14.   31 Jul 1799.   WM. BACON & wife NANNY, AC, to ZACH. TALIAFERRO, (Orig. del. to ZT 26 Apr 1800) for Ƚ45, 110 acres N side Buffalo. Lines: DILLARD's road, JESSE KENNEDY, JOHNSON BEAN, BENJ. EVANS, Evans' spring branch. Wit: WM. EDMUNDS JR, ANDREW MORGAN, WM. JACOBS, SAML. MEREDITH.

Page 15.   21 Oct 1799.   CHAS. CHRISTIAN & wife SARAH, AC, to JNO. PADGET, AC, for Ƚ50, 307 acres Porrige Creek. Lines: CHRISTIAN, POWELL dec'd., JNO. CREWS, THOS. EDWARDS. Wit: RICH. WILSON, EPHRAIM PADGET, SAML. L. CHRISTIAN.

Page 16.   21 Oct 1799.   JNO. PADGET, AC, to REUBEN PADGET, AC, for Ƚ15, 60 acres Porage Creek. Lines: grantor, grantee. Wit: CHAS. CHRISTIAN, RICH. WILSON, JAS. CHRISTIAN.

Page 17.   21 Oct 1799.   Same parties for Ƚ15, 60 acres Porrage. Lines: THOS. EDWARDS. Wit: CHAS. CHRISTIAN, RICH. WILSON, SAML. L. CHRISTIAN.

Page 19.   15 Oct 1799.   CHAS. HIGGINBOTHAM, AC, to his brother, JOS. HIGGINBOTHAM, AC, Ƚ100, interest in slaves from estate of father, MOSES HIGGINBOTHAM, in my mother's possession. Wit: DAVID S. GARLAND, WIATT SMITH, WM. HIGGINBOTHAM, HENLEY DRUMMOND, JAS. SAVAGE.

Page 19.   21 Oct 1799.   SARAH ENIX renounces will of husband, DAVID ENIX, and claims dower. Wit: NATHL. WADE, JAS. TRAIL, MESHACK ENIX.

Page 20.   11 Mar 1799.   JNO. LACKEY & wife ANN, AC, and AMBROSE RUCKER SR, AC, to JAS. BALLINGER, AC, for Ƚ10, 42 acres Harris Creek. Lines: WM. PETER (formerly JOS. CHILDRESS) and designated by WM. PETER, ELIZ. & SAML. COLEMAN, THOS. COLEMAN. Wit: JOS. WILSON, WILL PENN, WIATT POWELL, JAS. CHRISTIAN, GEO. DILLARD, REUBEN GATEWOOD.

Page 20.   15 Oct 1799.   JAS. HENLEY & wife ALEY, AC, to RO. DINWIDDIE, AC, (Orig. del. to H. HARRIS 16 Jun 1812) for Ƚ150, 298 acres branches Rockfish at foot of Blue Mts. Lines: HUDSON MARTIN. Wit: THOS. & JAS. MORRISON, JNO. MURRILL JR, THOS. KILLAND.

Page 21.   24 Jul 1799.   JNO. MASSIE, AC, to JAS. MURPHY, AC, (orig. del. to JM 14 Jun 1800) Deed of Trust on debt to RO. RIVES & Co. $1.00 - 100 acres. Lines: JNO. CAMPBELL, JESSE WRIGHT, JR, GEO. CAMPBELL, Crawley Creek, branch of Piney. Ref. to deed: JNO. HOUCHIN to JNO. MASSIE. Wit: PLEASANT MARTIN, BEN CAMDEN, LEWIS MAYS, DANL. THOMAS.

Page 23.   1 Jun 1799.   THOS. TILMAN, AC, to JAS. MURPHY, AC, Deed of Trust. $1.00. Debt to JNO. BALL - a slave. Wit: PARMENAS BRYANT, JAS. HANSBROUGH, ALEX. MARR. Sent to DANL. HIGGINBOTHAM per MURPHY's order - no date.

Page 24.   25 Nov 1799.   WILSON C. NICHOLAS, Albemarle, to STEPHEN WATTS, (Orig. del. to SW 1 Dec 1803) for 5 sh, 110 acres S side and joining Buffalo. Part of a tract. Lines: HIGGINBOTHAM's orad, JOHN LEA, JAS. LEA. Wit: JNO. SNEAD, BURGHER GRIFFIN, WALTER EDDS, STEPHEN MARTIN.

Page 25.   16 Dec 1799.   ABEL BLANKENSHIP & wife FANNY, AC, to WM. GARRETT, Goochland, (orig. del. to REUBEN NORVELL 29 May 1806) for Ƚ70, 100 acres Stovall Creek. Also 10 acres - CREW's entry and joining 100 acres on Lynchburg road. Wit: JNO. COONEY, JNO. ROBERTSON JR, THADDEUS MILES.

Page 26.   5 Dec 1799.   CHAS. ROSE & wife SARAH, AC, to ALEX. MARR, AC, (Orig. del. 19 Jul 1800 to AM) for Ƚ5, 300 acres, part of tract known as Claypool Wit: JNO. MARR, JOS. AMOS, RICH. RUCKER.

Page 27.   21 Oct 1799.   JOSHUA HUDSON, AC, to RUSH HUDSON, AC, for 5 sh,
            27 acres S end of Turkey Mt. Lines: Top of the mt., grantor,
LINDSEY COLEMAN, WM. CABELL, his own, chestnut stump at the old church.
Part of a tract. Wit: GEO., REUBEN, & RUSH HUDSON.

Page 28.   12 Dec 1799.   RICH. WILSON & wife ANNY, to ANDREW MUNROE for
            Ь31, 31 acres. Lines: Grantee. Wit: GEO. DILLARD, MATT.
TUCKER, RICH. DAVENPORT.

Page 29.   24 Oct 1799.   JNO. CABELL & wife ELIZ., Buckingham, to HECTOR
            CABELL, AC, (Orig. del. to HC 17 Feb 1800) for Ь1200, 390 ac.
N side Fluvanna and upper side of Tye - 200 acres of it conveyed to JNO.
by his father, WM. CABELL, and wife MARGARET, 30 Apr 1763; 190 acres pat.
to JNO. 20 Jul 1765. Wit: LANDON CABELL, WM. H. CABELL, WILL CABELL,
JAS. MURPHY, PARMENAS BRYANT.

Page 31.   2 Dec 1799.   NOTLEY W. MADDOX & wife FANNY, to WM. MOORE, all
            of AC, for Ь300 and Ь8000 tobacco - where MADDOX lives and
bought from exrs. of JOS. DILLARD, dec'd., 14 Feb 1793. Lines: GEO.
GILLESPIE on the river; Col. PETER ROSE, JNO. PARSON - except 2 acres
laid off to GEO. GILLESPIE opposite his mill seat on the river. 593 acres
Little Piney & N. branches Indian Creek. Wit: GEO. DILLARD as to MADDOX;
WM. PENN, JAS. FULCHER, WALKER SAUNDERS. Page 33, order to AC J.P.'s to
quiz FANNY MADDOX, 5 Dec 1799. Done and rec. 16 Dec 1799, by SAML. MERE-
DITH & GEO. DILLARD.

Page 34.   1 Nov 1799.   JNO. CHRISTIAN & wife MARY, AC, to MICAJAH PEN-
            DLETON, AC, for Ь552-15, 368½ acres Elk Island Creek. Wit: JNO.
CHRISTIAN, JAS. DILLARD, HENLEY DRUMMOND, WILSON PENN, RO. HORSLEY. Page
35, Order to AC J.P.'s JNO. CHRISTIAN & JAS. DILLARD, to quiz MARY. Rec.
16 Dec 1799.

Page 36.   13 Jan 1800.   WM. TURNER, Albemarle, to JNO. WATKINS, AC, for
            Ь80, (Orig. sent to JW 1815) 80 acres Duck Creek. Lines: JNO.
MATTHEWS, WM. BAILEY, JNO. SANDERS. Wit: the three adjoining owners just
named.

Page 37.   8 Dec 1797.   DAVID DAVIS, AC, to DANL. ALLEN, Rockbridge Co.,
            for Ь8, 31 acres N branch Piney; part of a tract. Lines: DAVID
PARROCK, DAVID DAVIS' late pat. line. Wit: JNO. JACOBS JR, WILL & PETER
JACOBS, ALEX. ROBERTS, WILL CABELL JR, W.S. CRAWFORD, JAS. DILLARD,
NOTLEY W. MADDOX.

Page 38.   18 Jan 1800.   JNO. THOMPSON & wife REBECCA, AC, to WM. TEAS,
            AA (Orig. del. to CHAS. PERROW 2 Feb 1827) for Ь172-12, 2
tracts in one survey on Naked Creek. 1) 198 acres bought in partnership
by THOMPSON & TEAS from WM. OGLESBY. 2) 122 acres bought by THOMPSON
from CHAS. IRVING by virtue of Deed of Trust from GEO. BLAINE & wife
RACHEL, and THOMPSON & TEAS, Merchants. Lines: WM. CABELL, GEORGE BLAINE,
JNO. WRIGHT, WM. BIBB, dec'd, JNO. THOMPSON. Wit: JNO. LOVING, NATHL.
OFFUTT.

Page 39.   12 Aug 1799.   JNO. COFFMAN & wife BARBARA, Rockingham Co, to
            ANDERSON COFFMAN for Ь164-18-8, 93½ acres N branches Rockfish.
Lines: FREDERICK WARE, JNO. COFFMAN, JACOB ARISMAN. Part of tract bought
by grantor from JAS. FLACK - 280 acres and rec. in AC. Wit: JNO. BARNETT,
DAVID CAULDWELL, SAML. COFFMAN, DANL. COFFMAN and illegible signature.

Page 41.   12 Aug 1799.   JNO. COFFMAN & wife as above to JNO. COFFMAN,
            AC, for Ь10, 93½ acres and head of N branches Rockfish. Lines:
FREDERICK WEIR, JNO. SMITH, DANL. CAUFFMAN. Wit: as above. The illegible
signature may be ARMUND LAUFFMAN or COFFMAN.

Page 42.   12 Aug 1799.   JNO. COFFMAN (CAUFFMAN) & wife BARBARA, Rocking-
            ham, to DANL. CAUFFMAN, AC, for Ь10, 93½ acres described as
previous deed, but line of JAS. BRUMHALL added. Wit: as above.

Page 43.   18 Apr 1799.   JOS. SMITH & wife MARY, AC, & JOSIAH SMITH,

their son, to PETER LEMOINE, AC, for $2.00, 250 acres N branches Rockfish.
Formerly that of WM. & JOS. CABELL and conveyed to JOS. SMITH, 1 Jan 1790.
Lines: JOHN SHIELDS JR, JNO. SHIELDS, SHEROD MARTIN. Wit: DILMUS JOHNSON,
SOLOMON CAREY, JOS. MARTIN.

Page 46.   20 Jan 1800.   HUDSON MARTIN & wife ELIZ, AC, to NATHL. ANDER-
SON, atty. in fact for JNO. TATE, THOS. HANSTON, & THOS.
ASTON JR, assignees of HENRY MARTIN & Co., for Ь392-14, 391 acres S fork
Rockfish. Lines: JAS. MATTHEWS, Beaver Creek, JOSIAH JOPLING. Orig. del.
to NA 20 May 1805.

Page 47.   18 Jan 1800.   CHRISTOPHER FLETCHER & wife PHEBY, AC, to WM.
ALLIVER, Orange Co., for Ь200, 127 acres (del. to WA 25 Feb
1804) Lines: Lunch road, GIDEON RUCKER, JOS. CREWS, S branch of N fork
Rutledge, big hill spring branch, WIATT POWELL.

Page 48.   2 Mar 1799.   Order to Rockingham J.P.'s to quiz ELIZ. NOLAN,
wife of JAS., as to deed 6 Jun 1793, to DANL. CAREY - 130 acres. Done by
JNO. WEAN(R?), B. FAWCETT & rec. 20 Jan 1800.

Page 49.   15 Feb 1800.   JAS. BROWN, AC, to SAML. COLEMAN, Albemarle, for
Ь65, 50 acres in 2 tracts, Tye and both sides Ivy Branch. 1)
Surveyed 3 May 1757. 2) Surveyed 13 Feb 1786. Lines: grantor, S side Ivy
Branch, GEO. HAYS.

Page 50.   16 Feb 1800.   RICH. FARRAR, Albemarle, to son JNO. FARRAR,
for love and 1 sh., 250 acres N side Rockfish and in Albemarle
and AC. Lines: JAS. JOPLING, small place known as Stucker's Place; place
known as Towsen low ground. Wit: MOSES PHILLIPS, GEO. FARRAR, BENJ. WATTS,
GEO. WHARTON, JESSE JOPLING.

Page 52.   17 Nov 1798.   RHODA DINWIDDIE, alias BENNETT, and husband, JNO.
BENNETT, AC, to JAS. HUNLEY, AC, for Ь30, 180 acres and 118
acres adj. Rockfish - all rights - property of SAML. DINWIDDIE and at
death to 4 daughters: RHODA, SARAH (now READY), HANNAH & JANE DINWIDDIE;
second tract pat. by father to his 4 daughters. Lines: RO. DINWIDDIE,
JAS. DINWIDDIE, JNO. MURRELL, HUDSON MARTIN. Wit: JAS. BROOKS, RO.
DINWIDDIE, JNO. DAVIS, THOS. KILLAND.

Page 53.   1 May 1799.   HANNAH DINWIDDIE, AC, to JAS. HUNLEY, AC, for Ь30,
180 acres on Rockfish; description and data as above. Wit:
JAS. BROOKS, HENRY BENNER, DAVID McALEXANDER, WM. THORP.

Page 54.   11 Nov 1799.   RANDOLPH DEPRIEST & wife MARIANAH, Richmond Va.,
to ZACH. FORTUNE, AC, & JNO. LEE, AC, (Orig. del. to JL 26
May 1800) for Ь275, 252 acres in Parish of Amherst - devised to grantor
by his fahter, Dec'd, WM. DEPRIEST, and rec. in Henrico. Wit: N. VAN-
STAVERN, RO. RIVES, W.S. CRAWFORD.

Page 55.   1 May 1799.   SARAH DINWIDDIE (now READY) and husband, WM.
READY, AC, to JAS. HUNDLEY, AC, (note spelling differs from
other deeds to him above) for Ь30, description as in other deeds involving Dinwiddie heirs - see p.53. Wit: as on page 53.

Page 56.   16 Aug 1799.   JNO. SAVAGE, AC, to JESSE HIGGINBOTHAM, AC, Deed
of Trust on debt to RO. RIVES & Co., 5 sh. 6 slaves and stock.
Wit: WILLIS WILLS, JAS. LOVING, JNO. HARRIS, JNO. HIGGINBOTHAM, EDWD.
HARRIS.

Page 58.   21 Sep 1799.   JAS. HENRY WEST & wife SUSANNAH, AC, to ISHAM
READY, AC, (orig. del. to JNO. SHIELDS, 27 Jun 1800 per order
of IR) for Ь178-10, 120 acres Hatt & Tye. Part of pat. of THOS. WEST in
1761 and by TW devised to JAMES HENRY WEST. Wit: JAS. WOODS, ALEX. Mc-
ALEXANDER, WM. WRIGHT, JNS. M GOMERY, JNO. SHIELDS.

Page 59.   4 Mar 1800.   CHAS. ROSE & wife SARAH, AC, to JAS. & HENRY
WOODS, AC, for Ь1060, 587 acres both sides Maple Creek and
Carter's Mill Creek. Part of tract. Lines: JOEL FRANKLIN, CHAS. CARTER,
PAT. ROSE. Wit: JAS. M. BROWN, JNO. CAMM, JNO. M. ROSE.

Page 60.   25 Nov 1799.   AMBROSE MORAN, AC, to GALT & GARLAND, AC,-DAVID
            & JAS. GARLAND - for 10 sh., Deed of Trust - negroes, furni-
ture, stock. Wit: JAS. P. GARLAND, RALPH MARTIN.

Page 61.   17 Mar 1800.   Order to Bedford J.P.'s WM. HARRIS & WM. BURTON,
            to quiz LUCY WHITING DAVIES, wife of HENRY L. DAVIES - 2 Jun
1797, deed to CHAS. CLAY - 59 acres. Done 29 Mar 1800 & rec. AC 21 Apr
1800.

Page 62.   7 Feb 1800.   HENRY LANDON DAVIES & wife LUCY, Bedford Co, to
            ARTHUR LANDON DAVIES, AC, for $5.00, (Orig. del. to JAS. GAR-
LAND 21 Jul 1800, per verbal order of AD) 294 acres N side Fluvanna and
Salt Creek, late survey by SAML. BOYLE DAVIES. Lines: McDONALD's Spring,
Green pond branch where Rolling Road crosses it; Pedlar road; around the
Indian grave on the top of Tobacco Row. Mt., PHILIP BURTON, THOS. MOORE,
POWELL, Bethel Road - also tobacco WH at Bethel or DAVIES' lower ferry;
scales etc. for receiving and inspecting tobacco. Also, ferry on N side
of Fluvanna and boat kept there now. Wit: VERNON METCALF, JAS. HARRISON,
SAML. B. DAVIES.

Page 66.   10 Dec 1799.   JAS. WATSON JR, AC, to WALKER SAUNDERS for 5 sh,
            Deed of Trust on debt due GEO. DILLARD. 7 slaves. Wit: JAS.
BALLINGER, SEATON M. PENN.

Page 67.   21 Apr 1800.   LANDON DAVIES, AC, to JAS. HARRISON, AC, lease -
            172 3/4 acres around the dwelling house and tobacco WH -
field above Salt Creek lately occupied by JER. TAYLOR; ferry & boat. 2¼
acres reserved for a storehouse - N bank Fluvanna, near mouth of the
little double creek; the spring, old road, land laid off for a town - 5
years at ₤50 per year. To plant 100 peach trees, 100 apple trees, good
late fruit; to fence. Memo: DAVIES & family to be ferry free and DAVIES
is to furnish a new boat in 1802.

Page 69.   4 Nov 1799.   FRANCIS VEAL, AC, to WM. PEYTON, AC, (Orig. del.
            to C. PEYTON 21 Mar 1851) for ₤56, 294 acres N branches Otter
and N branches Fluvanna. Lines: Terripan Creek. Wit: N. VANSTAVERN, JNO.
PEYTON, BENJ. HOWARD.

Page 70.   20 Jan 1800.   JAS. BROWN, AC, to WM. HAMILTON, AC, for ₤50,
            80 acres Hatt Creek survey of 7 Dec 1771. Lines: THOS. LILLEY.
Wit: JAS. MONTGOMERY, JNO. HUGHES, JNO. WITT, WM. JACOBS, DANL. McDONALD.

Page 71.   15 Nov 1799.   WM. ALCOCK, AC, to WALKER SAUNDERS (Orig. del.
            2 Oct 1800 to GEO. DILLARD) Deed of Trust on debt to GEO.
DILLARD - beds, stock etc. Wit: RO. HOLLOWAY, WM. COLEMAN.

Page 72.   18 Mar 1800.   JNO. HILL SR, AC, to DAVID & JAS. GARLAND, AC,
            Deed of Trust - 5 sh. Slaves, stock etc. Wit: WIATT SMITH,
BARTLETT CASH.

Page 73.   20 Jan 1800.   JNO. HANSBROUGH, Hampshire Co., to WM. HANS-
            BROUGH, Culpeper Co., for ₤50, 1/4 of tract devised to JNO. by
his father, WM. 100 acres. Rec. AC 21 Apr 1800. JNO. JAMESON, Culpeper
Clerk.

Page 74.   5 Feb 1800.   WM. EDMUNDS & wife SALLY, AC, to JOS. STRICKLIN,
            AC, for ₤125, 89 acres head of Cub Creek. Lines: Thoroughfare
corner, MOSES HUGHES, JNO. JACOBS, his own.

Page 76.   9 Nov 1799.   JNO. ROBERTSON & wife SARAH, to WM. H. CABELL
            (Orig. del. to WHC 23 Jul 1800) for $94.25, 107 acres branches
Mayo Creek. Lines: grantee, formerly LE GRAND; formerly WM. CABELL, formerly NICHL. CABELL and NICHL. WEST. Bought by grantor from JNO. WEST
who got it from his father. Wit: JNO. HIGGINBOTHAM, THOS. BIBB, JESSE
HIGGINBOTHAM, RO. RIVES, WILLIS WILLS, JAS. P. COCKE JR.

Page 77.   28 Aug 1799.   DANL. WARWICK, AC, to CALEB RALLS, AC, -(15 May
            1804, filed in Chancery suit RALLS vs. WARWICK) ₤1200, Deed of
Trust debt due RALLS - forks of Horsley, 500 acres, part of tract bought
from RALLS. Wit: JNO. PETER, CALEB RALLS JR, NELSON CRAWFORD, NANCY RALLS,

T.N. EUBANK.

Page 78. 4 Nov 1799. JNO. CHRISTIAN & wife MARY, AC, to JNO. CHRISTIAN,
son to DRURY CHRISTIAN, AC, for Ⱡ700, 132 acres N side and
joining Fluvanna; part of tract of RO. CHRISTIAN's orphans & DRURY CHRIS-
TIAN's orphans. Lines: both of orphans' tracts; the Great Branch. Wit:
DRURY CHRISTIAN, JNO. CHRISTIAN, GILES DAVIDSON, JNO. CHRISTIAN JR,
MICAJAH PENDLETON.

Page 79. 4 Nov 1799. Same parties - Ⱡ700, 400 acres. Lines: RO. CHRIS-
TIAN, RO. CHRISTIAN's orphans, Great Branch. Wit: as above.

Page 81. 29 Mar 1800. MARY BOUSH, wife of JNO. BOUSH, dec'd, Clarke
Co. Ky., to ELISHA ESTIS, AC, 5 sh. - dower in 450 acres.
J.P.'s of Clarke Co.: JNO. BAKER, R. HICKMAN. DAVID BULLOCK, clerk.
Note: All Kentuckians know that this is Clark and not Clarke County. I
was born at county seat of Winchester. BFD)

Page 82. 29 Mar 1800. WM. WALTON BUSH & MARY BUSH, admrs. of JNO. BUSH
dec'd, AARON SHARP & wife ANNA (late BUSH), RO. RICHARDS, gdn.
of JONATHAN(BUSH), WM. BUSH, gdn. of BETSY, POLLY, THOS., TILMAN, NELSON
(one or two names?) LANDON, MERIER & LUCY BUSH, heirs of JNO. BUSH, Clark
Co. Ky. Power of Atty. to WYATT BUSH, Clark Co. Ky. as to AC business.
J.P.'s as above. Rec. in AC 21 Apr 1800.

Page 83. 29 Mar 1800. MARY BUSH, relict of JNO. BUSH, Clarke Co, Ky.,
to CHAS. WATTS, AC, 5 sh., dower in 110 acres. J.P.s as above.

Page 85. 29 Aug 1799. LALINDER DEHART, THOS. TENNISON & wife MARY,
JAS. DEHART & wife CATH., SUSANNAH DEHART, MARY DEHART, wife
of ELIJAH DEHART, Patrick Co., to MATT. STANTON, AC, for Ⱡ92, 90 acres.
Lines: JNO. NICHOLAS, SACKVILLE KING, Porrage Creek, CHAS. CHRISTIAN,
JNO. CREWS. Wit: JAS. TURNER, JAS. LEWIS, RO. ROWAN.

Page 86. 24 Dec 1799. BARTLETT EADES & wife ANN, AC, to JNO. MELTON,
AC, (Orig. del. to BE 24 Jun 1801) for Ⱡ125, 200 acres Head-
waters Dutch creek. Lines: ALEX. MOSS, grantor. Wit: RO. WRIGHT, JNO. S.
MONTGOMERY, JON. WRIGHT.

Page 87. 6 Aug 1799. Order to AC J.P.'s to quiz SARAH, wife of CHAS.
CHRISTIAN, as to deed of 17 Jan 1799, to RO. PEARCE - 204 ac.
Done 4 Mar 1800 by GEO. DILLARD & DAVID S. GARLAND.

Page 88. 14 Jun 1800. JAS. PAMPLIN, AC, to WM. PAMPLIN, AC, (Orig. del.
to WP, 27 Nov 1801) for Ⱡ96, 96 acres Elk Island Creek-balance
of tract where I live - mansion house and plantation. Lines: RICH. WOODS,
WM. JORDAN, GEO. HILTON, JAS. PAMPLIN JR. Wit: ROBT. PAMPLIN, HENLEY
DRUMMOND, WM. WOOD.

Page 89. 16 May 1800. JAMES PENN, exr. of GABL. PENN, to JNO. WARWICK
for Ⱡ678, 357 acres N side Buffalo. Lines: FRANCIS LEE dec'd.,
WM. WARWICK.

Page 90. 27 Apr 1800. JOS. MILSTEAD & wife REBECKAH, AC, to JNO. DEVA-
ZER, AC, for Ⱡ85, 96 acres Buffalo and Horsley. Part of tract.
Lines: JOS. HIGGINBOTHAM, Childress Gap, WM. SCHOFIELD dec'd. Wit: WALLER
SANDIDGE, JOS. MILSTEAD, minor, JNO. C. DAVAS.(Note: See my D marriages,
1801-1854, for DEVASHER family data in Ky. BFD)

Page 91. 16 Jun 1800. JNO. ROBERTS SR, AC, to JNO. KEE (Orig. del. to
NELSON CRAWFORD per verbal order, 24 Apr 1801) for Ⱡ45, 117
acres Pedlar. Part of 2 tracts. Lines: grantor.

Page 93. 17 May 1800. JACOB SMITH, AC, to BENJ. TALIAFERRO, AC, for
Ⱡ118, 59 acres both sides Puppies Creek. Part of tract. Lines:
grantor, Pedlar road. Wit: JOS. C. HIGGINBOTHAM, JNO. TALIAFERRO, BENJ.
HIGGINBOTHAM.

Page 94. 16 Jun 1800. JOS. CABELL HIGGINBOTHAM, AC, to SHADRICK CARTER,
AC, for Ⱡ10-10, 18 acres branches Owen Creek. Lines: Little

358

Owens Creek, BENJ. JOHNSON, GEO. HILTON, grantee. Pat. 24 Dec 1799.

Page 95.   21 Oct 1799.   PAUL GRAYHAM, Hanover Co., to RICH. SHELTON, AC,
           for Ŀ120, 164 acres Harris Creek. Lines: Schoolhouse Branch,
BURKS. Wit: JOSHUA SHELTON, HENRY GOSNEY, VOLENTINE COX.

Page 96.   13 May 1799.   JAS. CHAPMAN & wife PHEBE, AC, to JESSE HAYNES,
           for Ŀ150, 100 acres Horsley (Orig. del. to WM. HAYNES, 21 Sep
1820) also 14 acres adjoining - bought of a part of larger tract of SAML.
SHACKELFORD. Wit: KENSY RALLS, JNO. EUBANK, JNO. FLOOD, JNO. WARE JR.,
HENRY BROWN.   Page 97, undated order to AC J.P.'s to quiz PHEBE; done 16
Sep 1799.   DAVID & NELSON CRAWFORD.

Page 98.   13 Jun 1800.   CALEB WATTS, AC, to WM. TINSLEY, heir to WM.
           TINSLEY, dec'd, AC, for Ŀ100, 100 acres. (orig. del. to JNO.
WARE per order 2 Aug 1803) Lines: ROD. McCULLOCH, NICHL. DAVIES, JOSIAH
ELLIS.

Page 99.   26 Nov 1799.   GEO. WORTHAM, AC, to NOTLEY W. MADDOX, a negress,
           Moll. Deed of Trust on debt due GARLANDS. Wit: JOEL FRANKLIN.

Page 99.   29 Nov 1799.   SUSANNAH MARTIN, AC, to JNO. MONROE, Orange Co.
           (Orig. del. to JM. 15 Dec 1810) for Ŀ100, 100 acres Stovall.
Lines: JNO. KNITE, JOS. HIGGINBOTHAM, JNO. TURNER, old field opposite the
house. Wit: GEO. DILLARD, JOSIAH ELLIS, JACOB PERCE. (Note: ELLIS is JR.)

Page 100. 17 Apr 1800.   ABRAHAM WARWICK & wife AMY, AC, to WM. BATES,
           late of Albemarle and now of AC, for Ŀ736, 368 acres Meadow
Creek, both sides, branch of Rockfish. Part of 2 tracts. Lines: Dutch
creek road; survey made formerly for RO. JOHNSON, dec'd.; grantor, JNO.
WARWICK, road to Findley Gap. Wit: WM. H. CABELL, WM. RYAN, ZACH. TALIA-
FERRO, JNO. WARWICK.

Page 102. 28 Apr 1800.   CHAS. PATTESON, AC, to JAS. MURPHY, AC, Deed of
           Trust on debt due RO. RIVES & Co. $1.00 - slaves & children.
(Orig. del. to JM 18 Jun 1801) Wit: JAS. HANSBROUGH, PARMENAS BRYANT,
HENRY RIVES, JNO. GRIFFIN.

Page 103. 15 Feb 1800.   NICHL. CLAYTON DAVIES, AC, to JNO. WILLIS CLAY-
           TON - lease - 114 acres for 6 years. 4 hands to be worked,
exclusive of negro woman in possession of his mother, MARY CLATON, named
June and boy, Frank. Ŀ5 per year for every plow boy, excepted if under
14, to plant trees and fence, to be peaceable in the neighborhood. (Note:
MARY CLAYTON and not CLATON.BFD). Wit: JAS. GARLAND, THOS. WOODROOF,
SAML. B. DAVIES, RICH. BURKS, JOSIAH ELLIS JR.

Page 105. No date save 1800. CORNL. THOMAS & wife ELIZ., AC, to BRANS-
           FORD WEST, AC, (Orig. del. to BW 1 Aug 1800) for Ŀ69-5, Whole
of tract of 3201 acres allotted to grantor in will of his father, CORNL.
THOMAS, N side Glade road. Lines: THOS. JOPLING, NORBOURN THOMAS, and the
division line between CORNL. & NORBOURN THOMAS of their father's land;
Rockfish, JNO. SNYDER, NATHL. WADE.

Page 107. 12 May 1800.   JNO. MATTHEWS & wife MARY, AC, to DUNMORE DAMRON,
           for Ŀ100, 100 acres N side Anne Laugh Creek. Lines: Branch,
mill seat, WM. BOWMAN, MARTIN DAWSON, DIETSON. Wit: NEALLY, WILEY, &
LEWIS CAMPBELL.

Page 108. 7 Jun 1800.   WM. FURBUSH, AC, to JAS. STEVENS, AC, for Ŀ260,
           199½ acres both sides of N & S branches of Rucker's Run. Lines:
RO. RIVES, JNO. BIBB, dec'd, JNO. STAPLES, dec'd, WM. LOVING dec'd, JAS.
STEVENS, GEO. LOVING. Wit: LANDON CABELL, JNO. CLARKE, CHAS. STATHAM,
RICHMOND STATHAM.

Page 109. 16 Jun 1800.   JNO. McCUE, SR, AC, on 3 Dec 1789, gave DAVID &
           MARY McCUE 71 acres on branch of Rockfish and near Blue Mts.
DAVID conveyed his right to CHAS. McCUE and partition has not been made.
RO. HENDREN married MARY McCUE. CHAS. paid them Ŀ40 for their rights in
the 71 acres. Wit: THOS. PANNELL, JOSIAH SMITH, RO. DINWIDDIE.

Page 111.   18 Sep 1798.   AUGUSTINE SMITH, AC, to JOSIAH SMITH, AC, 5 sh.,
            Deed of Trust for debt to IRVING GALT & Co., 200 acres Rock-
fish. Lines: S side Rockfish, CHISWELL's old line. Wit: PL. MARTIN, JNO.
MASSIE.

Page 112.   20 May 1800.   JNO. STRATTON SR, AC, to DAVID & JAS. GARLAND
            (Orig. del. to DG 10 Sep 1807) Deed of Trust - wagon & gear;
stock etc. Wit: JNO. LOVING, JOSIAH ELLIS JR.

Page 113.   4 Dec 1799.   ZACH. TALIAFERRO, AC, to JNO. CHRISTIAN JR, AC,
            for Ł80, 110 acres N side Buffalo. Lines: DILLARD's road,
JESSE KENNEDY, JACOB PEARCE, EVANS' Spring Branch. Sold by BENJ. EVANS,
dec'd, to SAML. MEGGINSON and by SM sold to AMBORSE GATEWOOD. TALIAFERRO
bought it from GATEWOOD. Wit: CHAS. CHRISTIAN, WALTER CHRISTIAN, WM. C.
CHRISTIAN, WM. CHRISTIAN, CHAS. H. CHRISTIAN.

Page 114.   20 Jun 1799.   Order to Albemarle J.P.'s to quiz ELIZ. HEIGER,
            wife of JNO. 6 Apr 1798, deed to CHAS. McCUE. Done 6 Sep 1799
by SAML. BLACK & CHAS. YANCEY.

Page 115.   22 Jan 1800.   ARCHELAUS MITCHELL & wife SPICEY, & HANNAH MIT-
            CHELL, AC, to JNO. GILES, Bedford Co., for Ł200, 100 acres
Fluvanna & Johns Creek. Lines: MIC. GOODWIN, where AM lives and whole of
tract given to him by his father, ARCHELAUS MITCHELL, dec'd.   (Orig. del.
to JG 12 Sep 1804) Wit: DUDLEY GALLAWAY, OB. H. TRENT, THOS. MITCHELL,
BOLLING MITCHELL, JOSIAS HAWKINS.

Page 116.   7 Jun 1800.   JACOB SMITH to ZACH. TALIAFERRO for Ł125, 101 ac.
            Franklin Creek and N side Buffalo. Lines: his own, WM. CRAW -
FORD, ZACH. TALIAFERRO. Wit: THOS. N. EUBANK, RICH. SMITH, WM. CLARKSON,
JAS. TALIAFERRO. Del. to ZT 3 Mar 1801.

Page 117.   7 Jun 1800.   JACOB SMITH, AC, to JNO. CLARKSON, AC, for Ł375,
            299 acres Franklin Creek. Lines: ZACH. TALIAFERRO, WM. S.
CRAWFORD, crossing the creek, JNO. SALE, PHILIP SMITH, his own. Wit:
same as previous deed.

Page 118.   18 Aug 1800.   JNO. LOVING, AC, owns 1000 acres in Jefferson
            Co. Ky., on Sinking Creek, branch of Green and pat. to me
about 20 Aug 1786. Power of Atty. to his son, JAS. to lease, sell or
exchange.

Page 118.   14 Mar 1800.   THOS. MITCHELL & wife EADY, AC, to AMBROSE
            RUCKER, AC, and son to REUBEN RUCKER, dec'd, for Ł161, 115
acres John Creek. Lines: grantee, MICAJAH GOODWIN, ARCHELAUS MITCHELL
dec'd, REUBEN PENDLETON, JESSE WOODROOF. Wit: THOS. MOORE, THOS. WOODROOF,
JESSE WOODROOF, GEO. McDANIEL SR.   Sent to AR per order 23 Sep 1800.

Page 120.   30 Dec 1799.   JNO. ROBERTSON, AC, to JNO. HOWARD, AC, Deed of
            Trust - long list - trundle bed, carpenter's tools, etc. Wit:
WM. HOWARD JR, JACOB WARRIMER(?), JNO. SCRUGG.

Page 120.   28 Mar 1800.   JACOB PIERCE & wife ELIZ., to JOS. LANE for Ł120,
            200 acres N side Buffalo. Lines: DILLARD's road, JESSE KENNEDY,
JNO. CHRISTIAN, EVANS' Spring Branch. Wit: CHAS. & JNO. CHRISTIAN, JACOB
G. PIERCE, JAS. HATTER.

Page 121.   15 Jul 1800.   MINOS WRIGHT, AC, to JAS. MURPHY, AC, Deed of
            Trust - debt due BROWN RIVES & Co., $1.00, 136 acres N side
Tye. Lines: SAML. EDMONDS SR, GEO. STONEHAM, JOS. LOVING; part of tract
of 390 acres. Wit: PARMENAS BRYANT, JAS. HANSBROUGH, HENRY RIVES, JOS.
WHITE.

Page 123.   28 Apr 1800.   JESSE WRIGHT SR, AC, to JAS. MURPHY, AC, Deed of
            Trust, debt to same firm as above, $1.00 - horse, formerly
that of PARMENAS BRYANT; mare exchanged with LEWIS McQUEEN; many other
items. Wit: as above.

Page 124.   7 Jun 1798.   CHRISTIAN BENNER & wife MARY, Cumberland Township,
            York Co., Penn., to HENRY BENNER, AC, for Ł362, 200 acres.

Lines: JAS. HERD, WM. HERD, HUGH WILLOUGHBY, his corner. Wit: ISRAEL IR-
VIN, DAVID ENIX, WM. EDMONDS, MOSES HUGHES, S. GARLAND. Grantors appeared
in Penn., 2 Jun 1798; SAML. ENIX, one of judges of said County. Rec. AC,
17 Dec 1798. Proved by MOSES HUGHES & EDMUNDS. Dower report to AC 21 Jul
1800.

Page 126.   25 Oct 1799.   Order to AC J.P.'s to quiz ELIZ. STONE, wife of
            BENAMIMI STONE, 4 Oct 1799 deed to WM. LONG - 2 acres on Rut-
ledge. Done by JOS. BURRUS & GEO. DILLARD, 8 Nov 1799. Orig. del. to WL
7 May 1821.

Page 127.   16 Jun 1800.   EZEK. GILBERT, AC, to MATT. WATSON for Ł5, 80
            acres, conveyed to GILBERT by JAS. WATSON, 15 Oct 1796 - life
estate. Lines: JAS. FRANKLIN, GEO. COLEMAN dec'd. Wit: RO. CHRISTIAN,
JNO. MAJOR.

Page 128.   21 Jul 1800.   WM. WARE, AC, to HENRY LANE, AC, (Orig. del. to
            HL 15 May 1801) LANE has exonerated WARE from money due be-
tween LANE & THOS. GOODRICH - WARE was bondsman. Deed of Trust was made
to WARE and WARE conveys to LANE. 298 acres Horsley. Bought by LANE of
ISAAC WRIGHT, except 2 acres for mill and seat. Lines: Road ford of
Horsley; RALLS, LANE's tract bought of WM. DAVIS, JAMES GOODRICH, ABRAM
CARTER.

Page 129.   7 Feb 1800.   RICH. BREEDLOVE & wife MILDRED, to NELSON ANDER-
            SON for $300, 180 acres branches S fork Rockfish. Lines: JNO.
BALL, WM. KEY, Glade road, WM. CABELL, JAS. NEVIL, THOS. KEYS. Wit: ZACH.
NEVIL, ELISHA PETERS, ZACH. PETERS, CAREL EADS.

Page 130.   21 Jul 1800.   JOS. CREWS, AC, to daughter, POLLY CREWS, for
            love and 5 sh., 5 slaves, part of estate of GIDEON CREWS,
dec'd. Wit: JOSIAH ELLIS JR, JNO. ELLIS, THOS. CREWS.

Page 131.   30 Jan 1800.   JAS. H. WEST, AC, to JAS. BROOKS, Albemarle, for
            10 sh., 200 acres headwaters N fork Rockfish, where WEST lives.
Lines: CHAS. KAYLOR, SAML. McCULLOCH. Slaves etc., Deed of Trust - BROOKS
is exr. of THOS. WEST dec'd. Wit: THOS. STOCKTON, BENJ. LOW, WM. RINE,
WM. HILL, SAML. MOSES, AUSTIN BOWLER.

Page 131.   13 Mar 1800.   JAS. FITZ GARRELD, AC, to DAVID & JAS. GARLAND
            and GALT & GARLAND - Deed of Trust - mare, etc. Wit: LINDSEY
COLEMAN, WIATT SMITH. Orig. del. to W. EDMUNDS, 3 Nov 1801.

Page 132.   20 Jun 1800.   JAS. MONTGOMERY, AC, to JNO. SHIELDS, AC, for
            $1575, 362 acres Hat Creek. Lines: RICH. DOBSON, LEE HARRIS
dec'd, JAS. BRENT, grantee.

Page 133.   21 Jul 1800.   JNO. WARWICK, AC, to ABRAM WARWICK, AC, for
            Ł1036, 436 acres N side Rucker's Run. Lines: JNO. BETHEL,
road from Findley's Gap to Amherst Courthouse, W. CABELL.

Page 134.   27 Jun 1800.   Order to AC J.P.'s to quiz SUSANNAH WEST, wife
            of JAS. H. WEST - 21 Sep 1799, deed to ISHAM READY - 120 acres.
Done by HUDSON MARTIN & JAS. WOODS, 21 Jul 1800. Orig. del. to RO.
SHIELDS per written order, 27 Dec 1802.

Page 135.   22 Jul 1800.   Exrs. of SAML. WOODS - GABL. PENN, FRANS. MERI-
            WETHER, JAS. BROOKS & JAS. WOODS to HUDSON MARTIN for Ł7-10,
60 acres Rockfish branches. Part of pat. for 146 acres of 13 Jun 1787.
Lines: SHEROD MARTIN, HUDSON MARTIN, JACOB WHEELER, GIDEON MARTIN. Orig.
sent to HM, memo June Court, 1805, 11 Jul 1805.

Page 136.   20 Mar 1800.   JNO. LACKEY, AC, to JAS. BROOKS, for 20 sh., one
            half of 137 acres both sides Franklin Creek. Lines: AARON
HIGGINBOTHAM JR, dec'd., BALLINGER WADE, JNO. MARTIN. Tract located by
JNO. & AMBROSE RUCKER. Wit: JNO. LOVING, RICH. S. ELLIS, PLEAS. MARTIN.

Page 136.   10 Mar 1800.   MATT GLENN, Gloucester, to JESSE CLARKSON, AC,
            for Ł101-5, slave and her son. Wit: CHRISTOPHER GARLAND, ALMON
DURNSTON, JAS. CLARKSON.

Page 137. 20 Jul 1786. GEO. BLAINE, AC, to NATHL. OFFUTT, AC, & SAML.
OFFUTT, Montgomery Co, Md., Deed of Trust - 5 sh. 202½ acres
between fork of road and courthouse. Lines: KING's former line. Wit:
PETER GARLAND, CHRIS. BOLLING, RANDOLPH BIBB, JNO. PHILLIPS. Final proof
15 Sep 1800, by PHILLIPS. Orig. del. to NO 9 Jan 1804. Tract formerly
part of 7881 acres of LUNSFORD LOMAX, dec'd.

Page 138. 3 Jun 1800. JAS. WILLIAMSON & wife NANCY, to JNO. MORTON for
Ŀ140, 123½ acres. Lines: DAVID WOODROOF, ISAAC RUCKER. Wit:
GEO. DILLARD, ALEX. PENN, ISAAC RUCKER, POLLY STONE, RICH. WILSON, WM.
McDANIEL. Orig. del. to JM 21 Nov 1800.

Page 139. 15 Sep 1800. JNO. MASSIE, AC, to DAVID & JAS. GARLAND, 5 sh.,
Deed of Trust, mare, saddle, etc. Wit: WILL EDMUNDS, JR., JOS.
HOUSEWRIGHT, BENJ. CAMDEN. Orig. del. to DAVID S. GARLAND, 2 Nov 1801.

Page 140. 29 Aug 1800. JOS. C. MIGGINSON & wife SARAH, Buckingham, to
WM. CAMDEN & JAS. FRANKLIN, AC, for $455, 91 acres N side
Fluvanna and Mobley Creek, surveyed for JM 28 Apr 1798. Lines: Little
Mobley Creek, WM. CAMDEN, WARREN TALIAFERRO. Wit: WM. ARMISTEAD, ARCH.
ROBERTSON JR., WM. COLEMAN, BENJ. TALIAFERRO, HENRY BALLINGER. Orig. del.
to WC 5 Aug 1801.

Page 141. 15 Sep 1800. PETER WATERFIELD & wife MILLY, AC, to BENJ.
SANDIDGE, AC, for Ŀ5, 3 acres S side S fork Buffalo and joins
HENRY HARTLESS. Orig. del. to BS 15 May 1804.

Page 142. 12 May 1800. JOS. LANNUM & wife NANCEY, Green Co., Tenn., to
WM. DIXON, AC, for Ŀ67-10, 130 acres Dutch Creek. Lines: JNO.
MATTHEWS, JNO. JOPLING, SAML. SCOT SCRUGGS. Wit: WM. BAILEY, ELIZ. HAYS,
JAS. HAYS, J.P. of Green Co., & DANL. KARNIEL. Rec. AC, 15 Sep 1800.
KARNIEL was clerk of county.

Page 143. 15 Sep 1800. CALEB WATTS, AC, to MARTIN PARKS, AC, Ŀ100, 100a.

Page 144. 15 Sep 1800. JESSE WOODROOF, & wife JUDITH, AC, to JAS. TINS-
LEY, AC, for Ŀ119, 85 acres Johns Creek. Lines: ARTHUR L.
DAVIES, AMBR. RUCKER (son to REUBEN).

Page 145. 15 Sep 1800. THOS. GRAHAM & wife ELIZ., AC, to ARCHILUS MIT-
CHELL, for Ŀ46, 400 acres S branches Cashaw Creek. Lines:
JOHNSTON's Branch. Tract of 400 acres formerly surveyed for RO. JOHNSTON
and transferred to TG. Orig. del. to AM, 31 Oct 1801.

Page 145. 16 Aug 1800. JAS. M. BROWN & wife RHODA, AC, to WM. LONG,
AC, for Ŀ18-15-8, one half acre S of the store and lots of
JAS. FRANKLIN and property of WM. CABELL - near Cabellsburg on road to
Lynchburg. Wit: P. GOOCH, JSO. DILLARD, PEACHY FRANKLIN.

Page 146. 18 Aug 1800. BENJ. FORTUNE, AC, to CHAS. BLOUNT & JAS. STE-
VENS, AC, for Ŀ15, Deed of Trust - 5 sh. Stock, glasses,
joyner's tools. Wit: JNO. CLARKE, WM. VAUGHAN. Orig. del. to JS 18 Apr
1801.

Page 147. 20 Oct 1800. HENRY STONEHAM & wife JANE, AC, to WM. H. DIGGES,
AC, for Ŀ260, 199 acres, branch of Tye; known as Elk Island
Branch. Lines: GEO. STONEHAM, EDMUNDS. Wit: JNO. ELLIS, RO. RIVES, WILLIS
WILLS. Orig. del. to Capt. JNO. CLARKE, 8 Dec 1800.

Page 148. 15 Oct 1800. JACOB WOOD & wife BARTHENA, to BENJ. PHILLIPS
for Ŀ185, all interest in estate of WM. PHILLIPS, dec'd; real
and personal.

Page 148. 15 Oct 1800. PHILIP GOOCH & wife FRANCES, to BENJ. PHILLIPS
for Ŀ185, all interest in estate of WM. PHILLIPS dec'd, real
and personal.

Page 149. 8 Jul 1800. JNO. COFFMAN & wife MARY, Shannandoah Co., to
JACOB MASENCOPE, Dorphin (sic - really Dauphin - also note
spelling of Shenandoah) Co., Penn., for Ŀ135, 93 1/3 acres. Lines: DANL.

362

COFFMAN, FREDERICK WARE. Wit: GEO. HATTER and illegible names, JACOB etc.

Page 150. 28 May 1800. DANL. COFFMAN & wife ELIZ., AC, to JACOB MACEN-
          COPE, Daulphin Co., Penn., 93 1/3 acres Rockfish. Lines: FRED-
ERICK WARE, PETER FRANKE, JNO. COFMAN, BRUMHALL. Wit: JNO. DOTTOR and
illegible signatures.

Page 151. 18 Oct 1800. PETER BRENNER to NATHL. LANDCRAFT, Albemarle,
          for Ł60, 71 acres Headwaters Rockfish. Lines: JNO. McCUE,
RICH. MITCHELL. Wit: JNO. DETTRO, GEO. H. H---?, JACOB CHRISMAN(?). Orig.
del. 7 Feb 1802, to NL.

Page 151. 13 Sep 1800. SAML. McCULLOCH & wife ELIZ., AC, to RICH. MIT-
          CHELL, AC, for Ł40, 49 acres Rockfish branches. Former tract
of JNO. CHISWELL and by him conveyed to JNO. McANALLY and by JM to JNO.
CRIZER and by JC to CHAS. KELLER and by CK to grantor. Lines: KELLER,
McCULLOCH, JAS. BROOKS. Wit: GEO. HATTER, JACOB CHRISMAN(?).

Page 152. 20 Oct 1800. JNO. CASH & wife SALLY, AC, to JNO. BALL, AC,
          for Ł200-4-8, 146 acres Stone house branch. Lines: JNO. THOMP-
SON, THOS. POWELL, STEPHEN CASH dec'd., JAS. MAYS, JOEL CASH. Wit: PHILIP
THURMOND JR.

Page 153. 21 Jun 1800. REUBEN NORVELL & wife POLLY, AC, to FRANCIS
          BURCH, AC, for 5 sh, 100 acres surveyed for RN for 669½ acres
and includes tract sold this day by CHAS. CHRISTIAN & wife SARAH, to
BURCH. Wit: JAS. DILLARD, JNO. & JAS. CHRISTIAN.

Page 154. 15 Oct 1800. JNO.M. THOMPSON & wife REBECCA E., AC, to JAS.
          EDMONDS SR, AC, for Ł43-10, 29 acres Naked Creek branches,
branch of Tye. Part of tract. Lines: grantee, JAS. MAYS, Stillhouse Br.,
his own. Wit: NATHL. OFFUTT, REUBEN WOODY, RO. MAYS.

Page 155. 15 Oct 1800. JAS. EDMONDS SR, & wife MARY, to JNO. M. THOMP-
          SON, AC, for Ł37, 25 acres both sides Naked Creek, branch of
Tye. Part of tract. Lines: ROLAND EDMONDS, grantee, Stillhouse Branch.
Wit: as above. Orig. del. to JT 11 Jun 1805.

Page 156. 15 Sep 1800. BETSY LONG, formerly CALLAWAY, and widow of JAS.
          CALLAWAY, dec'd, and WILL LONG to WM. BROWN, Lynchburg, for
6 sh.,- left me by my late husband, 854 acres, conveyed to late husband
by AUSTIN, JNO., & DERBARTUS SHEPHERD, 5 Jul 1784 - 1 tract of 554 acres
and ref. to Deed Bk. F, page 551. 108 acres conveyed to late husband by
JER. TAYLOR, 4 Aug 1788, ref. to Deed Bk. F, p.259. 192 acres conveyed
to late husband by JAS. LIVELY, 1 Apr 1791, ref. to Deed Bk. F, p.633.
Also any other patents or locations in late husband's name. Wit: JAS.
FRANKLIN, THOS. LUMPKIN, THOS. CREWS, P. GOOCH.

Page 157. 22 Sep 1800. WM. BROWN, Lynchburg, to WM. LONG, AC, for 6 sh,
          all interest in 3 tracts in AC sold to me by WM. LONG and wife
BETSY, 15 Sep 1800. 854 acres and ref. to deed to me. Wit: ARCHELAUS
MAYS, JAS. WOOD, JNO. CAMM, S. GARLAND. Orig. del. to WL 18 Nov 1818.

Page 158. 19 Sep 1800. GEO. DILLARD & wife BETSY, AC, to JAS. FRANKLIN,
          AC, for 6 sh, 2 acres conveyed to GD, 2 Sep 1800, by BENAMIMI
STONE. Wit: W.S. CRAWFORD, WIATT POWELL, WILL EDMUNDS JR. Orig. del. to
JF 25 Sep 1801.

Page 159. 6 Apr 1800. JOS. MATTHEWS & wife LYDIA, AC, to JNO. SHEPHERD,
          AC, for Ł100, 85 acres both sides Kerby Creek. Lines: JAS.
TURNER, JNO. MATTHEWS, HENRY ROBERTS, JOS. SMITH. Wit: JOS. SMITH, ELIZ.
& POLLY MURRILL.

Page 159. 17 Jun 1799. AMBROSE GATEWOOD & wife MARGARET, AC, to JAS.
          SHASTEAD, AC, for Ł50, 100 acres Otter Creek. Lines: JER.
WHITTEN, WM. DAVIS. Wit: BENJ. SHACKLEFORD, THOS. JENKINS, ROLAND BIAS.
Final proof, 20 Oct 1800, by TJ. Orig. del. to JS on 18 Aug 1812.

Page 160. 12 Sep 1800. THOS. WAME & wife MARY ANN, to HUGH McCABE -
          Margin notes "crotvhets in deed for it was torn and unintell-

igible in places" for Ł40, 267 acres, where TW lives. Wit: HENRY BROWN,
---RUCKER, --- BURKS, ---- BALLINGER. Sent to HM by WM. DAVIS 31 Jul 1801.

Page 161.   18 Mar 1800.   RAWLEY PINN & wife SARAH, AC, to GEO. & WM.
            CLARKE, AC, for Ł100, - no acres - Mill Creek branches &
Porrige. Lines: E side Buffalo Ridge.

Page 162.   4 Oct 1800.   WM. BOWMAN & wife SARY, AC, to REUBIN T. MITCHELL,
            Albemarle, for Ł110, 127 acres both sides Rockfish. Lines: JAS.
TURNER, ELEXANDER ROBERTS, MARTIN DAWSON, JOHN MATTHEWS, DUNMORE DAMRON.
Wit: JNO. JOHNSON, BENJ. CHILDS, JNO. HIGGINBOTHAM JR, DAVID CRAWFORD JR,
WM. MURRILL. Orig. del. to R.T. MITCHELL, 4 Nov 1805.

Page 163.   14 Oct 1800.   JNO. MITCHELL, AC, to SAML. HILL, AC, for 5 sh,
            Deed of Trust - furniture, stock etc. Wit: WM. EDMUNDS JR,
JNO. N. ROSE, RICH. S. ELLIS.

Page 163.   29 Aug 1800.   EDWD. WATSON, AC, to PHILIP GOOCH, for Ł98 - for
            buying negroes for Mrs. ELIZ. WATSON, wife of JAS. WATSON,
Deed of Trust on negroes for Mrs. Watson's life time, but not subject to
husband's debts - to him at her death. Wit: GEO. DILLARD, SEATON M. PENN.
Orig. del. to EW, 24 Nov 1824.

Page 164.   20 Oct 1800.   ASHCRAFT ROACH & wife ELIZ., AC, to HENRY ROACH,
            AC, for Ł200, 200 acres branches Wilderness Swamp. Pat. to
ISHAM DAVIS 16 Aug 1756. Lines: JNO. DAVIS and now in line of grantor.

Page 165.   1 Sep 1800.   NELSON ANDERSON & wife AGNES, to ELISHA PETERS
            for Ł12-12, 25 acres S fork Rockfish. Lines: grantee, estate
of ALLEN LAVENDER, glade road, grantor.

Page 165.   29 Aug 1800.   ALEX. BLAIN & wife AILEY, AC, to WM. H. CABELL,
            AC, for Ł120, 2 tracts. 1) 140 acres S side of a mt. and join-
ing line formerly that of JNO. HARMER & pat. to THOS. ALFORD, 25 Sep 1762,
and conveyed by MICAJAH BECKNAL to grantor. 2) 160 acres Ruckers Run
branches and joins first tract. Pat. to MICAJAH BECKNAL, devisee of WM.
BECKNAL, 23 Feb 1793, and by MC conveyed to grantor. Wit: JNO. HIGGIN-
BOTHAM JR, HENRY RIVES, WM. B. HARE, LANDON CABELL. Orig. sent to WHC,
17 Jul 1822.

Page 167.   17 Apr 1800.   WM. BATES & wife ROSANNA, AC, to LANDON CABELL,
            AC, Deed of Trust - debt due ABRAHAM WARWICK - 5 sh. - 368
acres both sides Meadow Creek, branch of Rucker Run. Bought by WB from
W. WARWICK & wife AMY. Lines: Survey of RO. JOHNSTON, dec'd., JNO. WAR-
WICK, ABRAHAM WARWICK, a fence, road to Findley's Gap, Dutch Fork Road.
Wit: WM. H. CABELL, WM. RYAN, JNO. WARWICK.

Page 169.   2 Oct 1800.   WARREN TALIAFERRO, AC, to WM. CAMDEN, and JAS.
            FRANKLIN, AC, for Ł90, 2 tracts Mobley Creek near James River.
1) 92 acres surveyed by WM. MIGGINSON 29 Mar 1771; granted to tenants in
common, HUGH ROSE & DANL. GAINES, by pat., 10 Mar 1781. Lines: GEO.
HILTON, N branch Mobley, RO. FREELAND. 2) 38 acres surveyed 6 Apr 1774,
on S side and joining Mobley Creek. Lines: JAS. FREELAND on N bank, WM.
MIGGINSON. Sent to WC, 6 May 1811.

Page 170.   18 Oct 1800.   WARREN TALIAFERRO, AC, to JOS. LYLE, AC, for Ł80,
            140 acres survey 26 Apr 1798, branches of Fluvanna and joining
Mobley Creek. Lines: JOS. C. MIGGINSON, JAS. FREELAND, WM. HORSLEY dec'd,
steep hill side.

Page 171.   26 Aug 1800.   RANDOLPH BIBB, AC, to JNO. ALFORD, AC, for Ł40,
            mare, cow & calf, steer. Wit: WM. MATTHEWS, MARTIN BIBB.

Page 172.   23 Sep 1800.   Order to AC J.P.'s PHILIP JOHNSON & THOS. MOORE,
            to quiz EADY, wife of THOS. MITCHELL, as to deed to AMBR.
RUCKER, 14 Mar 1800 - 115 acres. Rec. 15 Dec 1800.

Page 172.   13 Dec 1800.   JACOB SMITH gives slaves and stock to each of
            his following children: 6 sh. - PHILIP SMITH, MARY SMITH,
JAMES SMITH, CLARY SMITH, WIATT SMITH, & RICHARD SMITH. Wit: HIRAM

364

McGINNIS, WM. WARE.

Page 173. -- Nov 1800. SOLOMON CARTER - his portion of his father's
         estate - Ь75-0-0 - NELSON CRAWFORD, CHAS. TALIAFERRO. Rec.
15 Dec 1800. This item has a huge X through it in same ink to erase from
record. Usually they put on the margin "Not done", but I see no such
notation here.

Page 173. 10 Dec 1800. MAJOR KING & wife SEALY, to SAML. PUCKET for Ь70,
         100 acres head branch S fork Rucker's Run. Lines: NICHL. CA-
BELL. (Note: SEALY was daughter of JNO. PUCKET - see Amherst marriages
prior to 1801 - MAJOR KING left a will in Estill county, Ky. - see
Scott's Papers, and wife was still living when he wrote it. BFD)

Page 174. 8 Sep 1800. JAS. LUCAS, AC, to WALKER & GARLAND, Albemarle,
         for $1.00, Deed of Trust to JAS. WLAKER - beds, stock etc.
Wit: SAML. SHELTON, WM. BROWN.

Page 175. 2 Sep 1800. BENAMIMI STONE & wife BETSY, AC, to GEO. DILLARD,
         AC, (Orig. del. to JAS. FRANKLIN, 25 Sep 1801) for 6 sh, 2
acres both sides Rutledge. 1) 1 acre surveyed 11 Aug 1794 on N side and
joining Rutledge - part of estate of GEO. COLEMAN dec'd, and condemned by
jury for STONE to erect grist mill in Sept, 1793. 2) 1 acre surveyed 24
Aug 1799, for WM. LONG & STONE and part of STONE's land. Surveyed under
Court order on date above - granary & mill; 2 pairs of stones; complete
machinery; built on bed or channel of Rutledge. Wit: RO. WALKER, WILL
LONG, JACOB WOOD, WALKER SAUNDERS.

Page 177. 30 Oct 1800. AMBROSE BABER & wife AILEY, Albemarle, to JAS.
         FOWLER, Albemarle, for Ь200, 240 acres S side Tye - bought by
grantor of WM. BALL. Lines: Tye, Dr. WILCOX, dec'd. Part of 350 acres
pat. to SAML. BURKS, 25 Jun 1747. Wit: HENRY HOLLOWAY, WM. H. CABELL,
JNO. JOHNSON, JAS. P. PARISH, WILLIS WILLS.

Page 178. 10 Dec 1800. STEPHEN WATTS & DRURY BELL, exrs. of HENRY BELL,
         dec'd, & RICH. PHELPS to PHILIP GOOCH -(Orig. del. to PG, 26
Nov 1802) under will - Ь80, 400 acres Limekiln Creek branches. Lines:
JNO. HIGGINBOTHAM, SAML. BELL, JNO. SWANSON, ALEX. QUARRIER. Pat. to
HENRY BELL, 15 Oct 1789. Wit: WILL LOVING, THOS. WOODROOF, NORVELL SPEN-
CER, GEO. VAUGHAN. PHELPS does not sign.

Page 179. 15 Dec 1800. AMBROSE RUCKER, son of REUBEN RUCKER dec'd, &
         wife BETSY, AC, to GEO. McDANIEL, AC, for Ь200, 322 acres on
head of N fork Pedlar. Lines: JAS. SMITH. Wit: WM. TYREE, JAS. TYREE JR,
ELIJAH STATON.

Page 180. 26 Nov 1799. SAML. FRANKLIN, AC, to DAVID & JAS. GARLAND,
         Deed of Trust - slaves, stock, beds, too many items to mention.
Wit: THOS. POWELL, WILSON PENN, JOEL FRANKLIN.

Page 180. 2 Jun 1800. JNO. HARVIE, Henrico, to PHILIP GOOCH, AC, for
         Ь100, paid by GOOCH to RICH. HARVIE for use and benefit of
JNO. HARVIE - all interest in mine tract - Buffalo and W of Buffalo Ridge,
400 acres and devised by JNO. HARVIE, dec'd to his four sons RICHARD, JNO.
DANL. & WM. Wit: P. ROSE JR, JNO. CAMM, WM. F. BRAXTON, BENJ. PHILLIPS,
H.M. GARLAND.

Page 181. 22 Sep 1800. JNO. BOWLING, AC, to DAVID & JAS. GARLAND, Deed
         of Trust - 5 sh. stock, furniture etc. Wit: WM. EDMUNDS JR,
JAS. FRANKLIN JR, EDMD. T. COLEMAN.

Page 182. 17 Oct 1800. JNO. CARR, AC, to JAS. & DAVID GARLAND, Deed of
         Trust - 3 tracts where I live - 54 acres on S fork Tye; stock.
Wit: as above, but JER. & not JAS. FRANKLIN JR.

Page 183. 2 Dec 1800. NATHL. HILL, AC, to son, WM. HILL JR, AC, Power
         of Atty. to manage my estate in Va. Wit: JAS. P. CAMDEN,
THOS. BIBB. Orig. del. to WH, Jr 11 Nov 1801.

Page 183. 17 Feb 1800. Order to Buckingham J.P.'s, JOSIAS JONES &

ANTHONY DIBRELL, to quiz ELIZ., wife of JNO. CABELL - deed to HECTOR CABELL, 390 acres. Rec. 19 Jan 1801, as to her dower assent. Del. to RO. RIVES, 5 Mar 1805.

Page 184. 20 Jan 1801. DANL. CONNER & wife ELIZ., PARMENAS BRYANT & wife PEGGY, JNO. BRYANT & wife ELIZ., SYLVANUS BRYANT, WM. BRYANT, RICH. H. BRYANT & wife JUDY, DAVID P. BRYANT, all of AC, to REUBEN HUGHES, Fluvanna Co. (Orig. del. to DAVID S. GARLAND 22 Feb 1802) it is recited that JNO. BRYANT, late of Fluvanna, and now dec'd, did by will devise to wife ELIZ. (now wife of DANL. CONNER) for her lifetime and then to his sons, PARMENAS, JNO., SYLVANUS, WM., RICH. H., & DAVID P. BRYANT. All of record in Fluvanna - HUGHES paid Ь80 for 168 acres in Fluvanna. Lines: RO. QUARLES, JAS. QUARLES, CALEB STONE. Wit: WM. H. CABELL, CHAS. BLOUNT, R. NORVELL - except to CONNER & wife. (Note: Just why this Fluvanna deed shows here is a mystery, but I know that PARMENAS lived here; so did the others according to the deed. BFD)

Page 185. 1 Jan 1801. WM. LANE, wagoner, AC, to MIDDLETON LANE, for Ь97-8-5, slave named Geo. Wit: WM. STRATTON, JNO. STRATTON. Orig. del. to SAML. P. LAINE 13 Aug 1808.

Page 186. Order of 23 Jul 1800, to AC J.P.'s WM. B. HARE & NICHL. CABELL as to deed of 9 Nov 1799 - to quiz SARAH ROBERTSON, wife of JNO. - 107 acres to WM. H. CABELL. Done 5 Nov 1800, and rec. 19 Jan 1801.

Page 187. 8 Dec 1800. Order to AC J.P.'s WILL LOVING & JOS. LOVING, to quiz JANE, wife of HENRY STONEHAM, as to deed of 20 Oct 1800, to WM. H. DIGGES, 199 acres. Rec. after quiz: 19 Jan 1800.

Page 187. 17 Jan 1801. ISAAC WRIGHT & wife SUSANNAH, AC, to PHILIP GOOCH, AC, for $900, 300 acres both sides Limekiln Creek. Lines: PHILIP PENN. Bought by IW from LARKIN GATEWOOD. Wit: W.S. CRAWFORD. Orig. del. to PG 25 Apr 1802.

Page 188. 1 Jan 1792(sic). REUBIN HARRISON, AC, to RO. HAMBLETON, AC, (Orig. del. to RH 2 Apr 1801) Lease for 14 years - lot #1 on Main road; CARTER's old back line, Stonehouse Creek. Ь600 tobacco per year - Warminster inspection. Wit: JNO. BROCKMAN, LEWIS DAVIS, AARON FRANKLIN, JOEL DAVIS. Proved by BROCKMAN & DAVIS 18 Jun 1792; proved by JOEL DAVIS 19 Jan 1801.

Page 189. 21 Jul 1800. NELSON CRAWFORD & wife LUCY, AC, to WM. H. CA-BELL, AC, for Ь64, 4350 acres both sides Pedlar (Orig. sent to WHC, 17 Jul 1822) Pat. to NELSON CRAWFORD & NICHL. CABELL about 29 Sep 1797, except 600 acres sold by them to SAML. DEAN - does not warrant 300 acres near MARTIN KEYS on Piney Mt. and now LINDSEY BURKS'. Wit: JACOB KINNEY, JAS. WOODS, RO. GARLAND, WADDY THOMPSON.

Page 190. 8 Jan 1801. WM. LANE, AC, to REUBEN & WM. GATEWOOD, AC, slave and child. Wit: JOS. LAYNE, RANSOM GATEWOOD, THOS. APPLING.

Page 190. 10 Oct 1774. GEO. III, by the grace of GOD, etc, to JNO. QUARLES, WM. AYLETT, & JNO. ROANE, Gent. Justices - CARTER BRAXTON, esq., and wife ELIZ., deed of 6 Oct 1774, to HENRY GILBERT - 2113 acres in AC - signed by EDMD. WILCOX. Done 29 Oct 1774, as to ELIZ. and dower rights, by QUARLES & AYLETT. Rec. in AC 17 Feb 1801, but no reference as to reason for delay.

Page 191. 13 Dec 1800. JOS. MILSTEAD & wife REBECCA, AC, to JNO. DEVA-ZER, AC, (Orig. del. to JD 31 Jan 1803) for Ь72, 117 acres Long Branch of Buffalo and Horsley; part of tract. Wit: PETER WATERFIELD, ABEL WOOD, ISHAM D. WASSER(?).

Page 192. 3 Oct 1800. HENRY LANE SR, AC, to HENRY LANE, JR, AC, (Orig. del. to HL JR, 21 Apr 1806) for $1.00, 80 acres. Lines: JNO. WARE, ABRAHAM CARTER. Wit: DANL. WARWICK, OBEDIAH MARTIN, PETER MARTIN.

Page 192. 30 Dec 1800. NOTLEY SMOOT & ABRAHAM STRATTON, AC, to JAS. & DAVID GARLAND - Deed of Trust - stock & furniture. Wit: WILL EDMUNDS JR, EDMD. T. COLEMAN, EZEK. HILL. Orig. del. to DAVID S.

GARLAND 22 Feb 1802.

Page 193.   26 May 1800.   Order to Henrico J.P.'s JOS. SEDDAN & WM. MAYS
            JR, to quiz MARINAH, wife of RANDOLPH DEPRIEST - deed of 11
Nov 1799, to ZACH. FORTUNE & JNO. LEE - 252 acres. Done 23 Jan 1801.
Rec. AC, 17 Feb 1801.

Page 194.   1 Nov 1800.   AMBROSE MORAN, AC, to DAVID & JAS. GARLAND, Deed
            of Trust - stock. Wit: WM. EDMUNDS JR, WM. BADER, THOS. LAN-
DRUM. Orig. del. to DAVID S. GARLAND 22 Feb 1802.

Page 194.   15 Dec 1800.   JAS. MAYS & wife ISABELLA, to JAS. DILLARD, for
            blank sum, 100 acres N branches Tye. Lines: JAS. EDMONDS, JNO.
THOMPSON, JAS. DILLARD, JONATHAN BOLLING, JESSE & MOSES MAYS. Part of 200
acres.

Page 195.   16 Feb 1801.   JAS. DILLARD & wife SUSANNAH, AC, to JAS. MAYS,
            AC, for L100, 90 acres. Lines: grantee, N bank Tye, JNO.
DILLARD, JAS. WALTERS.   Part of tract on N side & joining Tye. The
receipt is signed JAS. MAYS SR.

Page 196.   14 Aug 1800.   JNO. CARTWRIGHT, AC, to DAVID & JAS. GARLAND,
            Deed of Trust - stock. Wit: THOS. LANDRUM, JAS. P. GARLAND,
WIATT SMITH.   Orig. del. to DAVID GARLAND, 22 Feb 1802.

Page 196.   1 Oct 1800.   GEO. DILLARD & wife ELIZ., AC, to JACOB PIERCE,
            Jr, AC, for L257, 257 acres. Lines: BENJ. RUCKER, RICH. WILSON,
Gaines' road, CHAS. CHRISTIAN, WALTER CHRISTIAN.   Orig. del. to JP, 3
Dec 1801.

Page 197.   6 May 1800.   WALTER CHRISTIAN & wife MARTHA, AC, to CHAS.
            CHRISTIAN, AC, (Orig. del. to CC by his son, 23 Sep 1801) for
L100, 74 acres Rockey Creek, part of where grantor lives and sold by JAS.
LONDON, dec'd, to CHAS. CHRISTIAN, dec'd. and given by CHAS. CHRISTIAN
by will to his son, WALTER CHRISTIAN. Lines: ISBEL, MIGGINSON road,
PARKS' road, BENJ. RUCKER, GAINES' road, WALTER CHRISTIAN's old line,
JOSIAH ATKINSON, AMBROSE RUCKER, STOVALL's old road. Memo: small tract
on BENJ. RUCKER's line and between PARKS' road, formerly sold to WALTER
CHRISTIAN by CHAS. CHRISTIAN and never conveyed by deed. Wit: JOS. DAVEN-
PORT, JAS. & SAML. L. CHRISTIAN.

Page 198.   20 Sep 1800.   JAS. COLEMAN, AC, to WALKER SAUNDERS, 5 sh,
            Deed of Trust - stock, debt due GEO. DILLARD. Wit: OBEDIAH
TANKERSLEY, DAVID HUNTER.   Orig. del. to GEO. DILLARD per order of WS,
24 May 1802.

Page 199.   15 Dec 1800.   JOS. WHITE & wife COTNEY, AC, to CONYERS WHITE
            SR, AC, for L68-12-6, 30½ acres Naked Creek; branches of Tye.
Lines: CONYERS WHITE JR, JOS. WHITE, POWLIN EDMONDS.

Page 199.   17 Jan 1801.   JNO. SHIELDS SR, AC, to ISHAM READY, AC, for
            L150, 50 acres Hatt and Cubb Creeks. Survey of 29 Oct 1798.
Lines: survey made for THOS. WEST dec'd, for 29 acres. Delivered to RO.
SHIELDS 27 Dec 1802.

Page 200.   5 Aug 1800.   HUDSON M. GARLAND, AC, to JNO. CAMM, AC, Deed of
            Trust - $1.00 - debt due WM. LONG, AC, - slave. Wit: WM.
KNIGHT, WM. DAWSON.   Orig. del. to JC 12 Aug 1801.

Page 200.   30 Oct 1800.   JNO. HARDIN & wife PHEBY, AC, to JNO. HIGGIN-
            BOTHAM, AC, Deed of Trust - debt due RO. RIVES & Co. - 5 sh.
300 acres, devised by GROVES HARDIN dec'd, to EDWD. HARDIN and by him
sold to JNO. HARDIN. Also slaves. Wit: WM. H. CABELL, WM. B. HARE,
WILLIS WILLS, JESSE HIGGINBOTHAM.   Orig. del. to JAS. MURPHY 8 Jan 1805.

Page 201.   2 Oct 1800.   LANDON DAVIES & wife LUCY WHITING, Lynchburg, to
            NICHL. DAVIES, AC, & THOS. W. COCKE, Lynchburg, for L1200, 403
acres N side Fluvanna; late survey by SAML. B. DAVIES. Lines: McDONALDS
Spring, mouth of Crab, Green Pond branch where the rolling road crosses;
big double creek; also the Warehouses at Bethel on DAVIES' lower ferry;

as well as ferry boat on N side of river. Wit: JAS. WARE, PROSSER POWELL, EZEK. HILL. Page 203, order to Campbell Co. J.P.'s THOMAS HUMPHREYS & SAML. SCOTT to quiz LUCY, 17 Apr 1801; rec. AC, 20 Apr 1801.

Page 203.   20 Apr 1801.   SAML. PUCKETT & wife POLLEY, AC, to ZACH. KING, AC, for $50, 45 acres Hatt & headwaters of Rucker's Run. Lines: JNO. CAMPBELL, waggoner, JAS. WILLS.

Page 204.   17 Jan 1801.   CHAS. LAVENER, AC, to JAS. MURPHY, Deed of Trust debt due BROWN RIVES & Co. - $1.00 - stock and furniture. Wit: DANL. HIGGINBOTHAM, SAML. EDMUNDS JR, JAS. GREGORY, HENRY REED.

Page 205.   4 Apr 1801.   CHAS. CHRISTIAN & wife SARAH, AC, to CHRISTOPHER FLETCHER, AC, (Orig. del. to CF 25 Jun 1801) for Ⱡ192-10-0, 154 acres Rocker Creek. Lines: RO. PEARCE, THOMAS POWELL dec'd, REUBEN PADGETT, EPHRAIM PADGETT, PETER CASHWELL, ANDREW MONROE. Wit: JNO. NICHOLS, WM. C. CHRISTIAN, ANDREW MONROE, JNO. BURCH.

Page 206.   19 May 1801.   JOSIAH ELLIS, AC, Power of Atty to son, JOSIAH ELLIS JR, (Orig. del. to JE Jr, 3 Jun 1801) to act as to Ky. lands or Tenn. or Ga. - to sell. Wit: D.W. CRAWFORD, SAML. J. CABELL, SAML. IRVING, AMBROSE LEE.

Page 206.   20 Apr 1801.   JAS. MURPHY, AC, to RO. RIVES, & Co. - JNO. MASSIE owned the company and made Deed of Trust about 24 Jul 1799, to MURPHY - 100 acres. Lines: JNO. CAMPBELL, JESSE WRIGHT, GEO. CAMPBELL, Crawley Creek, branch of Piney. Sold 8 Jun 1800, at Amherst Courthouse to RO. RIVES & Co. for Ⱡ39. Sent to MURPHY 9 Jun 1802.

Page 207.   30 Mar 1801.   DAVID S. GARLAND & wife JANE, AC, to HENRY HARPER, AC, (Orig. sent to D. PARROCK, 21 Feb 1852) for Ⱡ200, 84 acres Tye - granted to ELIAS SMITH JR by pat. 26 Sep 1764. Lines: bank of Cub Creek. Also 60 acres surveyed 20 Apr 1761. Lines: S side Tye, opposite mouth of Cub, SMITH. Also 200 acres pat. to GARLAND on 24 Jan 1800. Lines: his own, DAVID CLARKSON, JOS. BURGER, S bank Cripple Creek.

Page 208.   25 Sep 1800.   WM. BOWMAN, AC, to GEO. S. HARE, AC, Deed of Trust - debt due WILLIS WILLS - 5 sh. 2 slaves, Jesse & Hannah. Wit: JAS. P. PARISH, LAURENCE H. WILLS, WM. B. HARE.

Page 209.   19 Sep 1800.   JNO. HILL JR, AC, to PLEASANT MARTIN, AC, bay horse about 5 and raised by JNO. HILL SR. Ⱡ36. Wit: JOS. BURRUS, GEO. MARTIN. Orig. del. to PM, 13 Oct 1801. Proved by BURRUS, 17 Feb 1801.

Page 209.   15 Dec 1798.   JAS. KELLY, AC, to WM. LAWLESS, AC, for Ⱡ25, 68 acres. Lines: JNO. SMITH, Mrs. CARTER, EDWD. CARTER, ISAAC RIGHT, WM. PRYOR, RICH. LAWLESS. Wit: WM. CARTER, RICH. LAWLESS, SOLOMON CARTER, EDWD. CARTER JR. Sent to WL 9 Apr 1803. Final proof by WM. CARTER 20 Apr 1801.

Page 210.   20 Apr 1801.   NICHL. PRYOR & wife MARY, AC, to DAVID PRYOR, AC, for Ⱡ15, 73 acres Lovelady Creek and part of a tract. Orig. sent to PRYOR 19 Mar 1803.

Page 210.   20 Apr 1801.   NICHL. PRYOR & wife MARY, to MARTIN BIBB for Ⱡ230, 230 acres both sides Lovelady Creek and S side Pedlar. Part of a tract.

Page 211.   20 Apr 1801.   HENRY BENNER & wife ELIZ., AC, to WM. EDMONDS, AC, for $1020, 200 acres.

Page 211.   18 Apr 1801.   WM. SPENCER & STEPHEN WATTS, AC, to THOS. CURRY, AC, for Ⱡ65, 121 acres Buffalo - part of tract. Lines: ALLEN BLAIR, ARCHER ROWSEY, HIGGINBOTHAM's road, SAML. ANDERSON. Wit: JNO. LOVING, HENRY RAINS, THOS. TRIPLETT, DAVID HUNTER, JAS. MAYS.

Page 212.   3 Apr 1801.   WM. MARTIN & wife PATSEY, AC, to REUBEN T. MITCHELL, AC, (Orig. sent to W.M. 4 Nov 1805) for Ⱡ20, 20 acres Rockfish. Lines: mouth of Rocky Branch, grantee, WM. MURRELL, CORNL.

GILLUM, common high water mark. Part of tract bought by MARTIN from JNO. MATTHEWS. Wit: WM. MURRELL, JNO. MATTHEWS, MARY MATTHEWS.

Page 213.   4 Nov 1800.   HIRAM ALLEN AC, to JAS. & DAVID GARLAND, Deed of Trust - Ŀ50, stock, plates, etc. Wit: WM. EDMUNDS, ANDERSON MOSS, WM. KNIGHT.

Page 214.   20 Apr 1801.   SAML. MEREDITH & wife JANE, AC, to WM. ARMISTEAD, AC, for $1000, 3 1/4 acres. Lines: stake in race path in DAVID S. GARLAND's line; near head of race path on side of the ridge between HIGGINBOTHAM's Mill Creek and CIMON's(?) Creek; part of tract. Wit: WM. EDMUNDS, WM. KNIGHT, DAVID S. GARLAND.

Page 215.   20 Apr 1801.   JNO. WARE JR, to WILLIAM WARWICK, Deed of Trust. 6 sh, debt due DANL. WARWICK. 100 acres where I live; slave, stock, etc. Wit: CHAS. L. BARRETT, JOHN HAYSLIP, JNO. BARKER.

Page 216.   18 Apr 1801.   JNO. MATTHEWS & wife MARY ANN, AC, to JOS. MATTHEWS, AC, for Ŀ50, 100 acres both sides Kirby Creek. Lines: CORNL. MURRELL, BENJ. PAYNE, JAS. TURNER, BENJ. LANHAM, JNO. MORE, BENDICT LANHAM. Wit: WM. MURRELL, JNO. WATKINS, PLEASANT BAILEY.

Page 217.   15 Jun 1801.   RICH. C. POLLARD, AC, to JAS. HOPKINS, AC, Deed of Trust - Ŀ150, five slaves and "cutt knife". Debt due exors. of HENRY MARTIN dec'd.

Page 219.   18 Apr 1801.   JNO. MURRILL JR, & wife ANNE, AC, to NATHL. HARLOW, AC, for Ŀ600, 575 acres Rockfish at foot and on side of Blue Ridge. All of grantor's AC land. Lines: JAS. WOODY, HUDSON MARTIN, JAS. FLACK, ANNE DINWIDDIE. Wit: WM. HARLOW, JNO. ROBERTSON, NATHL. HARLOW JR, BENJ. CHILDRESS, JER. HAYS, EDWD. PAGE, WM. BARNETT JR.

Page 220.   29 Dec 1800.   JNO. McDANIEL, Wilson Co, Tenn., to SARAH GEORGE, AC, for Ŀ85, 121 acres Harris Creek. Lines: Lynch road. Wit: THOS. WILCOX, WM. GARRETT, MATTH. WATSON, JAS. HILL JR, JNO. McBRYDE, JAS. HILL, WM. KNIGHT.

Page 221.   10 Dec 1800.   SUSANNAH MARTIN, AC, to DANL. DAY, AC, for Ŀ100, 214 acres Stovall & Porrage. Lines: JNO. TURNER, JOS. NICHOLAS, TAYLOR, BENJ. RUCKER, JNO. KNIGHT, JNO. MONROE, an old field. Wit: ABEL & NOEL BLANKENSHIP, JNO. DEHART.

Page 222.   8 Nov 1800.   ELIZ. TOOLEY, widow of CHAS. TOOLEY, late of AC, to JNO. TOOLEY, for Ŀ25 - son and heir of CHAS. - dower in 100 acres. Lines: MATT. HARRIS, CLOUGH SHELTON dec'd, WM. WOOD, DAVID WITT. Wit: JOS. ROBERTS, JNO. HARRIS, MATT. HARRIS JR.

Page 223.   30 Sep 1800.   JNO. HAGGARD to SARAH SHEPHERD, AC, for Ŀ450, 292 acres S branches Taylor Creek. Lines: top of the mt., RO. PAGE, road by ARCHIBALD McDONALD. Wit: HUDSON MARTIN, AUGUSTINE SHEPHERD, THOS. PATTON, JAS. CLACK(CLARK).

Page 224.   15 Jun 1801.   JAS. FRANKLIN, AC, to ELVIRIA, PATSY C., WILMOUTH ANN, FANNY WIATT, & MATILDA GILBERT, children of EZEK. GILBERT (daughters) AC - Oznabirg tick, feathers, tables, pots, flax wheel - sold to FRANLKIN on court execution - HENRY MASSIE, assignee of FRANKLIN vs. EZEK. GILBERT - deed of gift. Wit: P. MARTIN, WM. COLEMAN, S. GARLAND.

Page 225.   21 Mar 1801.   GEO. MARTIN, AC, to RICH. POWELL, AC, Deed of Trust - debt due WM. BROWN & Co. - 5 sh. - 2 slaves, Will & Polly; mare, colt, etc. Orig. del. to RO. IRVING for RP, 8 Sep 1804. Wit: HEN. HOLLOWAY, JAS. VIGUS, JAS. P. PARISH.

Page 226.   11 Oct 1800.   JNO. RUCKER & wife NANCY, MOSES RUCKER & wife ELIZ., REUBEN RUCKER & wife ELIZ., JAS. TINSLEY & wife SUSANNA, ARCHELAUS REYNOLDS & wife ELIZ., to RICH. RUCKER, AC, for Ŀ66, 97 acres. Lines: REUBEN RUCKER. Wit: PHILIP THURMOND JR, ORSON KNIGHT, JAS. HILL JR, LEWIS CAMPBELL, JAS. HILL SR. Orig. del. to RR, 16 Oct 1802.

Page 226.   11 Oct 1800.   RICH. RUCKER & wife MARGARET, and others above
            (save REUBEN) to REUBEN RUCKER, AC, for Ł100, 100 acres.
Lines: my line. Wit: JNO. RUCKER, JAS. LIVELY, and other wits. above
(save REUBEN). Orig. del. to RR, 16 Oct 1802.

Page 227.   29 Dec 1800.   JNO. McDANIEL, Wilson Co. Tenn., atty. for HUGH
            GILLILAND, to THOS. WILCOX, AC, for Ł40, 100 acres Porrage
Creek. Lines: THOS. WILCOX. Wit: WM. GARRETT, WM. KNIGHT, MATT. WATSON,
JAS. HILL, JNO. McBRIDE. (GILLILAND is called HEIGHT GILLILAND in deed.)

Page 228.   14 Nov 1800.   THOMAS WANCE, AC, to JNO. BARKER, AC, for 6 sh,
            Deed of Trust - debt due EDWD. SAUNDERSON - black colt -
THOMAS MORRIS is named as grantee and then BARKER. Wit: JAS. & THOS.POPE.

Page 228.   8 Jun 1801.   WM. LILLEY, AC, to ISAAC WRIGHT, AC, for Ł200,
            65 acres both sides Horsley. Lines: CALEB RALLS.

Page 229.   15 May 1801.   Order to AC J.P.'s DAVID CRAWFORD, CHAS. TALIA-
            FERRO, & THOS. MORRE, to quiz PATTY WARE, wife of WM. WARE -
deed of 21 Jul 1800, to HENRY LANE - 298 acres. Done by CRAWFORD & TALIA-
FERRO; rec. 15 Jun 1801. Orig. del. to HL 15 May 1806.

Page 229.   15 May 1801.   AC J.P.'s JOS. BURRUS & PHILIP JOHNSON to quiz
            MARY POWELL, wife of OBEDIAH POWELL - deed of 25 Sep 1797, to
HENRY LANE. Done by BURRUS & JOHNSON; rec. 15 Jun 1801.   50 acres. Margin
as above.

Page 230.   17 Mar 1801.   PLEASANT MARTIN, AC, to JNO. HIGGINBOTHAM, AC,
            Deed of Trust - debt due BROWN RIVES & Co., 5 sh., slaves(8).
Wit: WM. H. CABELL, RICH. CLARKE, N. VANSTAVERN, W. BATES. Original sent
to R. RIVES by D. WARWICK, 26 Feb 1804.

Page 231.   15 Jun 1801.   JNO. SMITH & wife SALLY, ELIJAH BROCKMAN & wife
            FRANCES, AC, to THOS. POWELL, AC, for Ł42-10, 2 tracts. 1)
2 1/4 acres sold by JNO. SMITH. 2) 33 acres sold by BROCKMAN. Both on
Stonehouse and Carter's Mill Creeks. 2 1/4 acre lines: grantor, CARTER,
a spring. 33 acres lines: JNO. SMITH, CARTER, main road, a spring. Parts
of tracts of grantors.

Page 231.   13 Jun 1801.   SHEROD MARTIN & wife MARY, AC, to NATHL. HARLOW,
            AC, for Ł9, 67 acres (Orig. sent to NH 9 Jan 1804) Lines: CHAS.
SMITH, grantee, RICH. RICHARDSON, JAS. WOODS. Wit: BENJ. CHILDRESS, EDWD.
PAGE, W. BARNETT JR, NATHL. HARLOW JR.

Page 232.   13 Jan 1801.   CHAS. CHRISTIAN & wife SARAH, AC, to JINKINS
            OXLEY, AC, for Ł141, 141 acres. Lines: ANDREW MONROE, Capt.
WILSON, grantor, ISAIAH ATTKISON, branch of Rocky Run, JOEL CAMPBELL,
FRAS. BURKS, RO. PEARCE. Wit: CHAS. H. CHRISTIAN, JOSEPH DAVENPORT, JAS.
DILLARD. Receipt by HENRY CHRISTIAN & WALTER CHRISTIAN.

Page 233.   16 Feb 1801.   JAS. CHRISTIAN & wife MARY, AC, -MARY is a lega-
            tee of ROBT. CHRISTIAN - to DRURY CHRISTIAN, WM. HANSARD, &
JOS. KENNERLEY, AC, for Ł100, all rights in estate of ROBT. CHRISTIAN
dec'd.   RO. CHRISTIAN, son of the dec'd. ROBT, came to lawful age -
tract where DRURY CHRISTIAN lives of 624 acres to be sold under will and
balance of lands, including his plantation, where RO. lived at death;
widow, MARY, now lives thereon for life and at her death to be sold and
then equal division to legatees. Set forth that it has not been sold.
Wit: CHAS., CHAS. H., WM. C., & SAML. L. CHRISTIAN.

Page 233.   30 Dec 1800.   MICAJAH PENDLETON & wife POLLY, AC, to DANL.
            PERROW, AC, for Ł100, 82 acres on Fluvanna and Elk Island
Creeks. Lines: WM. JORDAN (formerly RO. HORSLEY) dec'd, grantee, JNO.
CHRISTIAN. Wit: WM. HORSLEY, SAML. H. ALLEN, RO. WINGFIELD, GURERANT
PERROW.

Page 234.   4 Apr 1800.   HENRY LANE to JNO. CRAWFORD - Deed of Trust to
            secure MARY(?) RICHESON, admrx. of JNO. RICHESON - Ł209 -
6 slaves. Wit: ZACH. TALIAFERRO, WM. TALIAFERRO, JAS. FRANKLIN JR.

370

Page 235.   1 Dec 1800.   WM. MARTIN & wife PATSEY, AC, to HENRY SMITH, AC,
(Orig. del. to HS 3 Aug 1807) for ₤100, 60 acres S fork Rock-
fish. Lines: JOSIAH JOPLING dec'd., GEO. VAUGHAN, HUDSON MARTIN. Wit:
SAML. SCRUGGS, PHIELD SMITH, THOS. MATTHEWS, WM. MURRELL.

Page 236.   19 May 1801.   WADDY THOMPSON, AC, grants freedom to slave,
Robt. - recently bought from SAML. HILL, AC,. Wit: JNO.
JACOBS JR, NELSON CRAWFORD.

Page 236.   17 Jul 1801.   JAS. LOVING, AC, to JNO. JOHNSON, AC, for ₤80,
equal moiety in one half of Warminster lot - No. 4 on S side
Main Street; bought by LOVING from BENJ. JORDAN, June, 1799.

Page 237.   23 Mar 1801.   WM. HAMBLETON, AC, to DAVID S. & JAS. GARLAND,
AC, Deed of Trust - 10 sh. Horse bought of GARLAND, cow
bought of JAS. BROWN, beds, etc. Wit: WM. EDMUNDS JR, EDMD. T. COLEMAN,
JAS. FRANKLIN JR.

Page 237.   20 Jul 1801.   WM. BURKS & wife NANCY, AC, to NICHL. WEST, AC,
(Orig. del. 17 Nov 1801 to NW) for ₤141-5, 137 acres. Lines:
Maple Creek branches; CHAS. BURKS, grantee, JNO. BURKS.

Page 238.   17 Jun 1801.   LINDSEY COLEMAN, AC, to PETER ROSE, SR, & DAVID
S. GARLAND, AC, for ₤655, Deed of Trust - debt due EDWD. SCOTT
& ELIZ. NICHOLAS, Buckingham Co., for 2 tracts in AC and conveyed by EDWD
SCOTT & wife MARTHA, & ELIZ. NICHOLAS, 8 Jun 1801 - 5 sh. and the 2
tracts on Buffalo Ridge and river. Reference to 2 plats, but not herein,
and surveyed by JAS. HIGGINBOTHAM. 970 acres. Wit: JNO. CAMM, JAS. WOODS,
JAS. M. BROWN.

Page 239.   20 Jun 1801.   ANNA PERROW, AC, renounces will of late husband,
DANL. PERROW, and claims dower. Wit: MICAJAH PENDLETON, RO.
WINGFIELD, JOSIAH WINGFIELD.

Page 240.   29 Nov 1800.   RO. HOLLOWAY & CHAS. B. PENN, AC, to SAML.
BURKS, AC, for ₤160, 80 acres. Lines: SAML. BURKS, tract of
about 90 acres allotted to POLLY PENN, infant of JOS. PENN, dec'd. 80
acres is lot of CHAS. B. PENN from JOS. PENN dec'd. CHAS. B. is now an
infant under 21 and will execute deed at majority. Wit: JNO. CRAWFORD,
THOS. WOODROOF, PHIL JOHNSON. Final proof 20 Jul 1801, by JNO. CRAWFORD.

Page 240.   14 May 1801.   JOS. SHIPS, AC, to PLEASANT DAWSON, AC, for
₤150, 110 acres Harris Creek. Lines: JNO. BURFORD. Wit: VERNON
METCALFE, ISHAM ROYALTY, WM. NEIGHBORS. Orig. del. to PD 16 Apr 1801.

Page 241.   15 Jul 1801.   BENAMMI STONE, AC, to SPOTSWOOD GARLAND, AC,
for love of my daughter, POLLY wife of GARLAND - 15 slaves;
stock, horses named, furniture. Wit: ANTHONY FRANKLIN, JAS. WOOD, ARCHE-
LAUS MAYS. (Note: STONE lived in what is known as Hunting Tower and it
is now owned by MADISON SETTLE who is a member of Amherst Baptist Church.
He tells me that some GARLANDS are buried in the old cemetery on the
place, but I have never visited it to see which ones are therein. BFD)

Page 242.   24 Jun 1801.   BENJ. JOHNSON & wife MARTHA, BENJ. WATKINS &
wife MARY, AC, to GEO. HYLTON, AC, - blank sum - 50 acres
surveyed 30 Jan 1800, for WATKINS - Owens Creek and part of JOHNSON
tract. Lines: MIGGINSON road. Wit: JAS. L. TURNER, HENLEY DRUMMON, LEROY
PAMPLIN, SHADRICK CARTER, JOS. DAVENPORT. Order to AC J.P.'s to quiz
wives and rec. 20 Jul 1801. J.P.s: JNO. HORSLEY & JNO. CHRISTIAN.

Page 243.   20 Jul 1801.   PHILIP SMITH, AC, to WM. TALIAFERRO, AC, (Orig.
del. to WT 21 Jul 1803) for ₤390, 300 acres Franklin & Moll's
Creek, branches of Buffalo. Lines: JNO. CLARKSON. Wit: JNO. EUBANK JR,
HIRAM McGINNIS, THOS. N. EUBANK, JNO. TALIAFERRO.

Page 244.   4 Jul 1801.   JESSE WOODROOF, AC, to JAS. WARE, AC, for ₤46-4,
33 acres John's Creek. Part of where JW lives. Lines: MITCH-
ELL's road. Wit: JNO. E. HARRISON, ISAAC TINSLEY, JAS. HARRISON, AMBROSE
RUCKER JR.

Page 244. 8 Feb 1801. AMBROSE RUCKER & wife BETSY, AC, to JAS. WARE, AC,
for Ŀ18-4, 13 acres, part of where RUCKER dwells. Lines: MICA-
JAH GOODWIN, grantor, grantee, BOWLING MITCHELL, REUBEN PENDLETON.

Page 245. 8 Jun 1801. JOS. LAYNE & wife PATSEY, AC, to DAVID & JAS.
GARLAND for Ŀ164, 200 acres N side Buffalo. Lines: DILLARD's
road, JESSE KENNEDY, JNO. CHRISTAIN, EVANS' spring. Wit: WM. EDMUNDS JR,
JNO. COLEMAN, EZEK. HILL, JAS. POWELL. Orig. del. to WM. EDMUNDS 13 Jan
1802.

Page 245. 23 Jan 1801. THOS. JOHNS, AC, to DAN. HIGGINBOTHAM, AC, Deed
of Trust - debt due BROWN RIVES & Co. of New Market - $1.00
- furniture, stock, etc. To advertise in Lynchburg and Richmond papers,
if defaulted. Wit: JAS. MURPHY, RICH. CLARKE. Orig. del. to JAS. MURPHY
15 Jul 1802.

Page 246. 6 Jun 1801. CHAS. THOMPSON, AC, to JAS. MURPHY, AC, Deed of
Trust for debt to same firm as above, del. to MURPHY 4 Mar
1805 - 5 sh. 179 3/4 acres on S fork Rucker's Run. THOMPSON bought it of
ALLEN BLAIR; stock, etc. Wit: JAS. HANSBROUGH, DANL. HIGGINBOTHAM, PAR-
MENAS BRYANT, JNO. EUBANK SR.

Page 247. 28 Jul 1800. MARTIN BIBB, AC, to JAS. MURPHY, AC, (Orig. del.
15 Jul 1802 to JM) Deed of Trust for debt to same firm as p.
245 - $1.00 - 100 acres, part of tract. BIBB was entitled to it as heir
of WM. BIBB dec'd. and where he lives. Lines: CONYERS WHITE, JOS. WHITE,
WM. H. DIGGES, THOS. HAWKINS, JNO. THOMPSON JR. Wit: PARMENAS BRYANT,
JAS. HANSBROUGH, W. CLARKE, DANL. HIGGINBOTHAM.

Page 249. 20 Jun 1801. JNO. ALFORD, AC, to DANL. HIGGINBOTHAM, AC - JAS.
MURPHY is bondsman for ALFORD to WM. CRISP - suit pending in
Dist. Court at Charlottesville for appeal from AC st. and debt to BROWN
RIVES & Co. - Deed of Trust - 5 sh. 576 acres Rucker's Run. Lines: THOS.
ALFORD, JAS. BIBB SR, CHAS. EDMUNDS, JOS. HOLLINGSWORTH, JNO. LOVING,
THOS. BIBB. It is set forth that ALFORD bought tract from CRISP; also
6 slaves, stock, furniture, etc. Wit: RICH. CLARKE, DAVID TRAIL, JAS.
HANSBROUGH.

Page 251. 21 Apr 1801. BENJ. WHITESIDES "for.love and affection for
negro woman, Betty, and her child Polly" -my slaves and bought
from REUBEN PENDLETON - their freedom. Wit: DAVID S. GARLAND, EDMD. T.
COLEMAN.

Page 251. 8 Jun 1801. EDWD. SCOTT & wife MARTHA (late NICHOLAS) and
ELIZ. NICHOLAS, his wife (sic), Buckingham Co. to LINDSEY
COLEMAN, AC, (Orig. del. 23 Jun 1801 to SCOTT) 2 tracts of 970 acres on
Buffalo Ridge and river - 2 separate surveys and plats (not herein) by
JAS. HIGGINBOTHAM. 1) 400 acres S branches Buffalo and N side Buffalo
Ridge. 2) 570 acres N side Buffalo. Lines: JNO. HARVIE dec'd., old pat.
line, MIGGINSON's road. Wit: RO. NICHOLAS, WALTER IRVINE, OGLESBY SCRUGGS.

Page 252. 20 Jul 1800. JNO. THOMPSON & wife JUDITH; JAS. THOMPSON &
wife ELIZ., AC, to PHILIP GOOCH & BENJ. PHILLIPS, AC, for $720,
360 acres S branches Elk Island Creek. Lines: former line of Col. JNO.
CHRISTIAN, SAML. BELL, JNO. HIGGINBOTHAM. Pat. to WM. EVANS, 15 Jun 1773.
Two margins: 1. Orig. del. 26 Nov 1802 to P. GOOCH. 2) 29 Aug 1806 to
WM. B. GOOCH.

Page 252. 20 Jul 1801. MICAJAH PENDLETON & wife MARY C., AC, to GILES
DAVIDSON, AC, for Ŀ300, 195 acres S fork of Elk Island Creek.
Lines: GEO. PENN, JNO. THOMPSON, JNO. CHRISTIAN's old line, S branch of
Creek, grantor, JNO. HIGGINBOTHAM. Del. to GEO. PENN, 6 Jun 1806.

Page 253. 20 Jul 1801. MICAJAH PENDLETON & wife MARY C., AC, to GEO.
PENN for Ŀ300, 195 acres and located as above. Del. as above.

Page 254. 20 Jul 1801. MICAJAH PENDLETON & wife MARY C., AC, to WM.
JORDAN, AC, for Ŀ100, blank acres Elk Island Creek. Lines:
DANL. PERROW dec'd, grantor, RICH. WOOD, grantee.

Page 254. 1 Jun 1798. EZEK. GILBERT & wife ANNE ROOKINS GILBERT, to JAS. FRANKLIN for Ł15, part of execution of HENRY MASSIE, assigned, vs. GILBERT - mare. Wit: JAS. WATSON JR, BETSY WATSON. Proved 20 Jul 1801 by EG.

Page 255. 26 May 1801. SAML. BURKS, Buckingham Co., to JAS. MURPHY, AC, and New Market, Deed of Trust - debt due BROWN RIVES & Co.-5 sh. - male slave bought of JOS. C. MIGGINSON. (Del. to JM 15 Jul 1802) Wit: JNO. HORSLEY, JOS. C. MIGGINSON, SAML. PERKINS, JOSIAH WINGFIELD, CHAS. TALIAFERRO.

Page 255. 20 Jul 1801. CHRISTOPHER FLETCHER, AC, to JNO. CASHWELL, AC, for Ł82-10, 66 acres Rocky Run branches. Lines: REUBEN PADGETT, near a spring, EPHRAIM PADGETT, PETER CASHWELL, ANDREW MONROE. Part of a tract.

Page 256. 18 Jul 1801. JNO. KNIGHT, AC, to SUSANNAH GILLILAND, AC, for Ł60, 50 acres. Lines: grantee on E, JAS. LIVELY on N, W by grantor, S by THOS. WILCOX. Wit: WM. EDWARDS, THOS. EDWARDS, REUBEN PADGETT.

Page 256. 18 May 1801. CHAS. CHRISTIAN, AC, to HENRY CHRISTIAN, AC, (orig. del. to THOS. EDWARDS 5 Jan 1802) for respect and 1 sh. and 6 pence, 237 acres Porrage Creek. 270 acres sold to JNO. CREWS by HENRY CHRISTIAN and for his sole benefit deeded to CREWS by CHAS. CHRISTIAN. Lines: JNO. CREWS, THOS. EDWARDS, CHAS. H. CHRISTIAN, HENRY CHRISTIAN, MATT. STANTON, SACKVILLE KING, JNO. TURNER, JOS. HIGGINBOTHAM. Wit: WM. EDWARDS, THOS. EDWARDS, REUBEN PADGETT.

Page 257. 5 Jun 1801. HENRY CHRISTIAN, AC, to THOS. EDWARDS, AC, for Ł200, 138 acres Porrage Creek. Lines: E by JNO. CREWS, N by grantee, W by JOS. HIGGINBOTHAM, S by JANK(?) NICHOLS & MATT. STANTON. Wit: WM. EDWARDS, CHRISTOPHER FLETCHER, REUBEN PADGETT. Orig. del. to TE, Oct, 1801.

Page 258. 15 Jul 1801. HENRY CHRISTIAN, AC, to CHRISTOPHER FLETCHER, AC, Ł30 paid by AARON DEHART dec'd - 56 acres Porrage. Sold by HC to AARON DEHART and by his heirs to MATT. STANTON and by STANTON to FLETCHER. Lines: E by CHAS. H. CHRISTIAN, N by JNO. CREWS, W by JNO. NICHOLS, S by DEHART's old line. Wit: THOS. EDWARDS, REUBEN PADGETT, WM. EDWARDS.

Page 259. 10 May 1800. CHAS. CARTER & wife BETTY, to JNO. SMITH (Orig. del. 1 Oct 1801 to JS.) for Ł500, 459 acres. Lines: Bank of Carter's Mill Creek, grantor, old pat. line, THOS. POWELL, ELIJAH BROCKMAN, main road. Wit: ELIJAH BROCKMAN, LUDWELL BACON, LEWIS DAVIS, WM. BACON.

Page 259. 9 Apr 1801. GEO. CLARKE & wife LOUISA ANN, AC, to JNO. BURKS, AC, (Orig. del. 3 Nov 1815 to JB) for Ł33, 104 acres Christian Mill :Creek. Lines: JNO. & CHAS. CHRISTIAN, JAS. DILLARD. Wit: CHAS. CHRISTIAN, RO. ALLEN, CHAS CHRISTIAN (two named as noted).

Page 260. 10 May 1800. CHAS. CARTER & wife BETTY, AC, to ELIJAH BROCKMAN, AC, for Ł500, 286 acres. Lines: 194 acres, S bank Stonehouse creek on main road in grantor's line, N bank Buffalo, tract of 92 acres, main road, Carter's Mill Creek, Stonehouse Creek - seemingly lines of the 286 acres. Wit: JNO. SMITH, JOEL FRANKLIN, REUBIN HARRISON, LEWIS DAVIS. Orig. del. to EB 1 Oct 1801.

Page 260. 14 Jul 1801. NATHAN CRAWFORD, AC, Atty. in fact for PETER CRAWFORD, Columbia Co, Ga., to WM. BARNETT, AC, for Ł30, --- At Bottom is written "Mistake" and deed is incomplete.

Page 261. 16 Feb 1801. Order to AC J.P.'s to quiz SARAH, wife of CHAS. ROSE, as to 5 Dec 1799 deed of 300 acres to ALEX. MARR. Done and rec. 20 Jul 1801 by JOS. BURRUS & PHIL JOHNSON.

Page 261. 15 Jun 1801. ALEX. OFFUTT, Montgomery Co, Maryland, Power of Atty. to PHILIP GOOCH to transact AC business. Wit: BENJ.

BROWN. Memo: ISAAC MILLER is to act as atty., but no fee if suit is lost.

Page 262.   21 Nov 1800.   Order to AC J.P.'s AMBR. RUCKER & GEO. DILLARD
to quiz NANCY, wife of JAS. WILLMORE, as to 3 Jun 1800 deed to
JNO. MORTON.   Rec. 21 Sep 1801.

Page 262.   20 Sep 1801.   PETTIS THACKER, AC, to JONATHAN DAKIN, AC, for
Ŀ30, 15 acres W side Lynch road. Lines: JNO. WARD, JNO. HANS-
FORD. Wit: WM. TURNER, SAML. HILL, ABNER PADGETT, JNO. HANSARD. (Note:
Clerks had hard time with HANSARD & HANSFORD.)

Page 263.   21 Sep 1801.   JNO. MILLER, Campbell Co, to JNO. HANSARD, AC,
(Orig. del. 8 Oct 1834 to PETER HANSARD) for Ŀ100, 110 acres,
part of JOS. FROST's land - from him to MILLER & JOHNSON, from MILLER to
RIDGWAY, from RIDGWAY to SAML. IRVING, Lynchburg merchant, from IRVING
to RO. JINNINGS, from JINNINGS to JNO. HANSARD - in FROST's pat. Lines:
the spring, WARD, ALLEY, CLARK. Wit: WM. TURNER, SAML. HILL, ABNER
PADGETT, JONATHAN DAKIN.

Page 263.   29 Aug 1801.   THOS. STEWART, AC, to JAS. & DAVID S. GARLAND,
Deed of Trust - 5 sh. as bondsmen to NATHAN CRAWFORD, AC shff.
Slave, Bob, 16 years old. Wit: THOS. WOODROOF, WM. EDMONDS JR.

Page 264.   30 May 1801.   PETER WATERFIELD, AC, to JOS. CHILDRESS, AC, for
Ŀ11000 tobacco - WATERFIELD & HUGH CAMPBELL are bound to LAR-
KIN SANDIDGE - Deed of Trust - 5 sh.   500 acres, sold by SANDIDGE to
WATERFIELD. Lines: N by HENRY HARTLESS, E by BENJ. SANDIDGE, S by JOS.
HIGGINBOTHAM, stock. Wit: TABITHA BALLINGER, BARTLETT CLENENTS, JAS.
BARRET(?), JNO. SMITH, BENJ. SANDIDGE.

Page 265.   18 Jul 1801.   JAS. FRANKLIN & wife NANCY, AC, to WM. CAMDEN,
AC, (Orig. sent to WC 14 Apr 1802) for $1400, 3 tracts.   1)
N side and joining Fluvanna and Mobley Creek - 1 acre. Lines: Mouth of
Mobely, Little Mobley, grantee, WARREN TALIAFERRO. Bought by CAMDEN and
FRANKLIN from JOS. C. MIGGINSON 29 Aug 1800.   Other 2 tracts on Mobley
near James River. 1) 92 acres. Lines: GEO. HILTON, RO. FREELAND. 2) 38
acres S and joining Mobley. Lines: JAS. FREELAND dec'd., WM. MIGGINSON.
Boufht by both from WARREN TALIAFERRO 2 Oct 1800, with storehouse, ware-
house, and tavern. Wit: MICAJAH CAMDEN, WILL CASHWELL, FREDK. PRICE,
WILL CAMDEN JR.

Page 266.   1 May 1800.   JNO. HUGHES & wife SARAH C., AC, to RICH. LEE, AC,
for Ŀ35, 2 tracts. 1) 94 acres branches S fork Rockfish.
Lines: JNO. DODD, the falling Rock. 2) 95 acres S branches of Stoney of
Rockfish. Wit: WM. EDMUNDS, MOSES HUGHES, MOSES HUGHES JR.

Page 267.   27 Feb 1801.   WM. MOON, AC, to JAS. LIVELY, AC, for Ŀ60, 44
acres Porrige Creek. Lines: grantee on N and W., SUSANNAH
GILLILAND on S, THOS. EDWARDS on E. Wit: JNO. COONEY, JAS. HILL SR, WM.
GREGORY, WM. JONES, BENJ. RUCKER.

Page 267.   21 Sep 1801.   BENJ. GOODE & wife ELIZ, to LEONARD ROWSEY for
Ŀ52, 170 acres on Pedlar.

Page 268.   21 Sep 1801.   CHAS. ROSE & wife SALLY, AC, to PATRICK ROSE JR,
son of CHAS., for $1.00, 240 acres Allin's Creek, branch of
Piney. Lines: old order line of the late Rev. RO. ROSE, Claypool tract
of CHAS. ROSE, CHAS. IRVING, dec'd. Wit: W.S. CRAWFORD, SAML. GARDINER,
ALEX. B. ROSE.

Page 269.   21 Sep 1801.   WM. & JNO. LOVING, exrs. of WM. LOVING dec'd.,
AC, to JNO. SEAY, AC, for Ŀ45, 154 acres - under will of WM.
LOVING. Lines: JAS. THOMPSON & TILMAN WALTON - to be paid to JOS. LOVING.
Surveyed 13 Dec 1795, and pat. 5 Sep 1788 - Rucker's Run. Lines: THOS.
HAWKINS (now JAS. WILLS), JAS. STEVENS, top of a mt. near a flat rock.

Page 269.   21 Sep 1801.   JAS. WATSON SR, AC, to daughter. FANNY N. WATSON,
AC, for love and 5 sh, slave and her child.

Page 270.   21 Sep 1801.   JAS. WATSON, AC, to CHAS. DIBRELL, Wayne Co, Ky.

Power of Atty. to take bond executed to me by CHAS. LYNCH SR & JR, 23 Apr 1794, and to choose some 1800 acres mentioned in a new bond. Orig. del. 29 Oct 1801 to JW.

Page 270.   15 Aug 1801.   LUKE PANNELL & wife MARY, AC, to HUGH PAUL, Augusta, for Ƚ60, 170 acres Cribben Creek(?), S side Blue Ridge. Lines: JNO. McANALLY, JNO. PANNELL. Wit: JAS. BROOKS, THOS. STOCKTON, KILLIS BABER, RO. BROOKS. Orig. del. to HP Nov 1801.

Page 271.   11 Mar 1801.   JOSIAH SMITH, AC, to HUDSON MARTIN (Orig. del. Apr 1803 to WM. WOODS) & WM. WOODS, Bedford, Deed of Trust - debt due WOODS - $1.00 - 100 acres on S side Rockfish and tract on N side bequeathed to me by my father. Wit: JAS. BROOKS, WILLIS BABER, RICH. MITCHELL, ROBT. BROOKS.

Page 272.   14 Sep 1801.   MARGARET HENDERSON, acting exrx. of GEO. CAMPBELL, dec'd, AC, to JAS. BROOKS, AC, - MARGARET was formerly CAMPBELL - Ƚ31 under will - 2 tracts N fork Rockfish - part of tract. 1) 62 acres. Lines: SHEROD MARTIN, JNO. HENDERSON dec'd., grantee. 2) 130 acres. Lines: JNO. HENDERSON dec'd. Wit: THOS. STOCKTON, RO. BROOKS, WM. RICE, WILLIS BABER. Orig. del. 12 Mar 1806 to JB.

Page 273.   15 Jun 1801.   WM. SANDIDGE & wife TAMSEY, AC, to SAML. PAXTON SR, AC, for Ƚ50, 144 acres S fork Pedlar and joining ADAM REID.

Page 273.   21 Sep 1801.   JNO. CARTWRIGHT, AC, to MOSES WRIGHT, AC, for Ƚ200, 71 acres S branches of N fork Piney on spur of Bald Fyyer(sic) Mt.

Page 274.   20 Oct 1800.   JNO. ROSE, AC, atty. in fact for WM. & JAS. HAY, exrs. of GILBERT HAY, dec'd, power of 18 Mar 1794 and rec. in AC 20 Oct 1794 - to HENRY ROSE, Fairfax, Ƚ250, 476 acres Piney. Lines: HENRY ROSE, tract formerly of JNO. HARRIS. Wit: ALEX. ROSE, S.M. ROSE, CHAS ROSE JR. Orig. del. to D. McDONALD 3 Mar 1804.

Page 274.   13 Mar 1801.   BENJ. LANHAM, AC, to JOS. MATTHEWS, AC, for Ƚ40 100 acres Kirby Creek. Lines: JOS. SMITH, JNO. MATTHEWS, JNO. MOORE. Wit: WM. MURRILL, JNO. & MARY MATTHEWS. Orig. sent to JM 24 Aug 1811.

Page 275.   21 Sep 1801.   RICE KEY & wife SARAH, AC, to THOS. TUCKER, AC, for Ƚ15, 182 acres. Lines: WM. PRYOR, Inchanted Creek, DANL. BURFORD. Wit: PHILIP SMITH, BARTLETT CASH, JOEL CASH. Orig. del. 21 Feb 1831, to THOS. TUCKER, one of the heirs of THOS. TUCKER.

Page 275.   18 Sep 1801.   ELIJAH BROCKMAN & wife FRANCES, AC, to WM. SANDIDGE, AC, for Ƚ126, 78 acres Stonehouse Creek branches. Lines: Main rode(sic), THOS. POWELL, grantor, CHAS. CARTER. Wit: THOS. POWELL, JNO. BALLARD, WIATT F. CAMDEN, WM. MANTIPLY. Orig. del. to WS 13 Oct 1803.

Page 276.   21 Sep 1801.   WM. HALL & wife MARY, AC, to JNO. KEY, AC, for Ƚ100, 100 acres S branches Horsley on Bankston's Mt., part of 900 acres pat. to WH. Lines: MOSES HALL, JER. DEAN, NELSON CRAWFORD. Orig. del. 26 Nov 1801 to JK.

Page 277.   22 Jan 1801.   ANN JOHNSON, MICHL. COALTER, FRANCES COALTER, JNO. H. GOODWIN, MARY GOODWIN, WM. BUSTER, MARY BUSTER, CLAUDIUS & ANN BUSTER, to PHILIP JOHNSON, AC, 142 acres Fawls Creek; no sum. Wit: LEWIS DAWSON, JAS. LEE, JNO. YOST, JNO. BURFORD JR, JACOB STRATTON, SPOTSWOOD GARLAND, THOS. LANDRUM, WM. MOSS.

Page 278.   24 Jan 1801.   PHILIP JOHNSON joins same grantors as in deed just given, p.277, to WM. ROBINSON, AC, for Ƚ50, 145 acres branches Falls Creek. Wit: as above.

Page 279.   19 Sep 1801.   JAS. SHIELDS & wife ELIZ., AC, to NANCY HIGGINBOTHAM, for Ƚ170, 146 acres Stonehouse Creek; part of tract. Lines: JAS. MAYS, RO. MAYS, AARON HIGGINBOTHAM, JR, dec'd. Wit: JNO. BALLARD, SAML. GOOLSBY, WIATT CAMDEN.

Page 280. 21 Sep 1801. JNO. KEY & wife BELINDA to JNO. BURKS for ₺80, 117 acres Pedlar. Part of two tracts of JNO. ROBERTS. Orig. del. to JB 2 Jul 1831.

Page 281. 16 Oct 1801. SKILER HARRIS & wife FRANCES, Albemarle, to JNO. ROBERTS, AC, for ₺500, 200 acres; also 29 acres Hicory Creek and adj. first tract. Orig. del. 17 Apr 1805 to JR.

Page 281. 21 Sep 1801. JAS. WATSON, SR, AC, to daughter, KITTY WATSON, AC, for love and 5 sh., slaves.

Page 282. 15 Oct 1801. DANL. CAREY & wife SUSANNAH, AC, to JAS. BROOKS, AC, for ₺212, 144 acres Rockfish. Lines: S bank Rockfish, JOS. SMITH dec'd, grantee, the road, CHAS. ROADS, BENJ. PANNELL. Wit: RO. BROOKS, WM. RICE, ANN CAREY, H. PAUL, LUKE PANNELL. Orig. sent to JB, 28 Nov 1801.

Page 283. 2 Oct 1801. ELIZ. COLEMAN, widow of JNO. COLEMAN; SAML. COLE- MAN & wife JUDITH; RICH. HARDWICK & wife NANCY; JAS. COLEMAN & MARY COLEMAN to THOS. COLEMAN for ₺50, 237 acres Harris Creek. Wit: AMBR. RUCKER JR, WM. PETERS, JNO. PETER, JOS. CHILDRESS, TINSLEY RUCKER. Orig. del. 5 Apr 1802 to TC.

Page 284. 19 Oct 1801. CHAS. WATTS & wife ELIZ., AC, to RICH. BREEDLOVE AC, for ₺125, 110 acres. Lines: THOS. STATHAM and where he lives; small tract of 130 acres granted to LANDON CABELL 9 Dec 1800 - WM. CABELL in right of wife ELIZ., and devised to her by WM. CABELL, dec'd; ABRAHAM WARWICK. Part of tract of JNO. BUSH conveyed to CW.

Page 285. 15 Oct 1801. JOEL CASH & wife ELIZ., AC, to BEVERLY WILLIAM- SON, AC, for ₺204-8, 146 acres Stonehouse Creek. Lines: RO. CASH dec'd, MOSES MARTIN, JNO. THOMPSON, JAS. MAYS, NANCY HIGGINBOTHAM, AARON HIGGINBOTHAM JR, dec'd. Orig. del. 16 Oct 1802 to BW.

Page 286. 15 May 1801. DAVID PATTERSON SR, Buckingham, to DAVID R. PATTERSON, Buckingham, for ₺500, Fishpond tract on James river; larger Sycamore Islands are excepted - part of tract willed by Col. ALLEN HOWARD to son, JNO. HOWARD and by him sold to THOS. ANDERSON dec'd. and by ANDERSON to DAVID PATTERSON SR. Lines: JNO. HOWARD's indenture to THOS. ANDERSON and rec. in AC 8 May 1780. Wit: JAS. P. PARRISH, LANDON CABELL, RICH. POWELL, JAS. VIGUS. Orig. del. to SAML. P. CHRISTIAN 22 Sep 1828.

Page 288. 21 Aug 1801. TERISHA TURNER, AC, to JNO. TURNER, AC, for $10, 10 acres Rockfish. Lines: grantor, WM. TEASE, JAS. TURNER. Wit: JNO. DAWSON, WM. LANKFORD, BENJ. PAYNE, NATHAN LANKFORD.

Page 288. 15 Oct 1801. JAS. MAYS & wife LUCRESY, AC, to BEVERLY WILLIAM- SON, AC, for ₺200, 155 acres N branches Buffalo. Lines: STE- PHEN CASH, dec'd.

Page 289. 18 Oct 1800. ADAM SIGLER, AC, & wife SUSANNAH, to JNO. HOGG, AC, for ₺100, 100 acres Otter Creek. Lines: Big branch of Otter, to the mouth, WM. DAVIS. Wit: JAS. POPE, JAS. WRIGHT, JAS. SHASTED, DAVID THOMAS. Orig. del. 13 Jun 1807 to BENJ. NOELL.

Page 290. 1 Nov 1800. STEPHEN RUSSELL & wife REBECAH, AC, to MOSES HALL, AC, for ₺60, 140 acres S side Pedlar and N side Pedlar. Wit: EDWD. TAYLOR, JOS. MARTIN, SAML. DEAN. Orig. del. 9 Feb 1805 to HALL.

Page 291. 19 Sep 1801. AMBROSE GATEWOOD & wife MARGARET, AC, to WM. DAVIS for ₺100, 200 acres Otter Creek branches; pat. 19 Dec 1799. Lines: JAS. SHASTED, JNO. HOGG, RO. NICHOLS, HENRY L. DAVIES. Wit: THOS. MORE, JAS. POPE, SAML. NICELY.

Page 292. 8 Oct 1799. SAML. ARRINGTON & wife MARY, AC, to BENJ. JOHNSON, AC, for ₺104, 69 acres S branches Owen Creek; part of HENLEY DRUMMOND tract. Lines: GEO. HILTON (formerly JNO. JOSLING), HENLEY DRUM- MOND. Wit: LEROY PAMPLIN, BEN WATKINS, RO. PAMPLIN, ISHAM JOHNSON. Final proof by SA 19 Oct 1801. Orig. del. to BJ 23 Dec 1802.

376

Page 293. 28 Sep 1801. ISAAC RUCKER, AC, to WM. McDANIEL, AC, for
          $2330.33, 318 acres. Lines: DAVID WOODROOF, JNO. MORTON, EDMD.
WINSTON, JNO. AMBLER, AMBORSE RUCKER. Wit: JNO. McDANIEL, HENRY WOODS,
JAS. PENDLETON, PEACHY FRANKLIN, JOS. BALLINGER.

Page 293. 19 Oct 1801. LANDON CABELL & wife JUDITH, AC, to LUCINDA &
          EMILY ROSE who are sisters of JUDITH CABELL, for love and $1.00
200 acres, part of tract known as Geddes - belonged to Col. HUGH ROSE
and allotted to PAULINA ROSE. Ł8 on commissioner's report. Lines: No. of
lots and PATRICK ROSE. (Note: Geddes still stands and is an interesting
old house. It belongs to the CLAIBORNE sisters of Clifford and they have
graciously shown my wife and me through the old place. BFD)

Page 295. 19 Oct 1801. THOS. GRAYHAM & wife ELIZ. to HENRY CAMDEN for
          Ł250, 250 acres on Three forks of Pedlar. Orig. del. 4 Nov
1811, to HENRY CAMDEN.

Page 296. 21 Mar 1801. GREENBERY LANHAM & wife CATY, AC, to GEO. MARTIN
          & wife MILDRED, AC, for Ł80, 230 acres S branches Rockfish.
Lines: CUTHBERT WEBB, THOS. JOPLING dec'd. Wit: HUDSON MARTIN, REUBIN
MARTIN, WM. BAILEY.

Page 297. 19 Oct 1801. WM. DAVIS & wife FRANCES, AC, to ISAAC TINSLEY,
          AC, for Ł200, 200 acres Otter Creek. Pat 19 Dec 1791. Lines:
JAS. SHASTED, JNO. HOGG, RO. NICHOLAS, HENRY L. DAVIES. Orig. del. 16
Aug 1802 to IT.

Page 297. 24 Sep 1801. JAS. SHIELDS & wife ELIZ., AC, to WM. SANDIDGE,
          AC, for Ł189-16-4, 146 acres Stonehouse branches. Lines: fork
of the road, HENDRICK ARNOLD, old field, CHAS. CARTER. Orig. del. 13
Oct 1803 to WS.

Page 298. 19 Oct 1801. JNO. COLE & wife REBECAH, AC, to JNO. ROBERTS,
          AC, for Ł250, 200 acres Hicory; branch of Rockfish. Lines:
JNO. PUGH SR, SKILER HARRIS, JNO. MORRIS, JOSIAH CHEATHAM.

Page 299. 15 Oct 1801. WM. HALL & wife MOLLEY, AC, to JNO. MASE, AC,
          (Orig. del. to JNO. MAYS, 28 Sep 1820) for Ł100, 100 acres
Pedlar. Lines: ISAAC WRIGHT, NICHL. PRYOR, JAS. MATTHEWS. The writing
on this page is very dim. It looks as if WM. HALL also adjoins.

Page 300. 20 Oct 1801. WM. HALL & wife MARY, AC, to FRANCIS TAYLOR, AC,
          (orig. del. to FT 13 Feb 1804) for Ł50, blank acres. Lines:
Ridge path to RICE KEY & JNO. ROBERTS, S bank Pedlar, STEPEHN RUSSELL.

Page 300. 20 Oct 1801. WM. HALL & wife MARY, AC, to EDWD. TAYLOR, AC,
          for Ł100, 100 acres not far from Pedlar and lines of JNO.
SANDIDGE and JERRY DEAN.

Page 301. 19 Oct 1801. Tobias, a free negro, AC, to JAS. MONTGOMERY,
          AC, for Ł15, 47 acres, bearing date of 15 May 1793, N branch
Hatt Creek. Lines: grantee, JNO. BROWN.

Page 302. 19 Oct 1801. WM. CLARKE & GEO. CLARKE - also signed by ANN &
          LOUISA CLARKE - AC, to MADISON HILL, AC, for Ł31-10, 104 acres
Christian Mill Creek. Lines: RO. ALLEN, JAS. DILLARD, JNO. BURCH, REUBEN
NORVELL. Wit: CHAS. CHRISTIAN, WALTER CHRISTIAN JR, CHAS. CHRISTIAN (two
of them).

Page 303. 15 Oct 1801. JAS. BROOKS & JAS. WOODS, AC, exrs. of SAML.
          WOODS, dec'd, to CHAS MASSIE JR, Albemarle, no amount - 82
acres Rockfish; near top of a mt., STINSON's entry.

Page 303. 10 Oct 1801. JACOB KING, AC, to JAS. WILLS JR, AC, for Ł7-17,
          cow and calf; sheep. Wit: JNO. WILLS & JNO. TOLL.

Page 304. 19 Oct 1801. THOS. GRAYHAM & wife ELIZ., AC, to HENRY CAMDEN,
          AC, for Ł90, 46 acres surveyed 15 Nov 1770, N branches Pedlar.
Orig. del. 14 Nov 1811 to HC.

Page 305.   20 Oct 1801.   WM. HALL & wife MARY, AC, to RICH. HATTEN, AC,
            for Ł60, 54 acres by survey of 23 Oct 1799, S branches Horsley.
Lines: WM. CABELL's old line, PHILIP PAYTON, RICH. ELLIS' old line, WM.
PETER's old line.   Orig. del. 13 Oct 1803 to RH.

Page 305.   20 Oct 1801.   WM. HALL & wife MARY, AC, to JNO. HARDEN, AC,
            for Ł100, 150 acres. Lines: BURKS' ridge path, STEPHEN RUSSELL,
JACOB BROWN.   Orig. del. 6 Sep 1808, to MARTIN BIBB per order of JH.

Page 306.   6 Jun 1801.   PHILIP RYAN to JOS. SHELTON & WM. H. DIGGS to
            secure JNO. ALFORD - Deed of Trust - $1.00.   200 acres where
PR lives. Lines: Col. JNO. ROSE, DAVID CLARKSON, LUCY DANGERFIELD. Wit:
CARY BIBB, WM. LEE HARRIS, WADDY THOMPSON. Orig. del. to WM. H. DIGGS,
1 Dec 1801.

Page 307.   9 Jun 1800.   Order to AC J.P.'s JNO. CHRISTIAN & REUBEN NOR-
            VELL, to quiz SARAH CHRISTIAN, wife of CHAS. for 7 Jan 1799
deed to JAS. FLOYD - 58 acres. Rec. 20 Oct 1801. Orig. del. 31 Dec 1801
to FLOYD.

Page 308.   17 Aug 1801.   BENJ. FORTUNE, AC, CHAS. BLUNT, 2nd part; JAS.
            STEVENS JR, 3rd. part, AC - Deed of Trust to secure STEVENS.
5 sh. Stock, carpenter's tools. Wit: JNO. CLARK, WM. KEES, JNO. JACOBS
JR. Orig. del. 3 Mar 1801 to BLUNT.

Page 309.   23 Sep 1801.   Order to AC J.P.'s JAS. DILLARD & JNO. CHRISTAIN
            to quiz MARTHA, wife of WALTER CHRISTIAN, for deed of 6 May
1800 to CHAS. CHRISTIAN - 74 acres. Done and rec. 19 Oct 1801.

Page 310.   23 Aug 1799.   ALEX. McALEXANDER to JAS., WM., & JNO. McALEX-
            ANDER - JAS. McALEXANDER dec'd, had bond of JNO. WARD, Bedford
Co., to JAS. McALEXANDER SR, AC, for 2000 acres in Pittsylvania Co. and
conveyed to sons, WM. & JNO.   JAS. devised to son, JAS., 28 acres in AC
on Davis Creek. Said JAS. died in Jan of 1798, intestate and left 4 sons;
JAS., WM., JNO., & ALEX. McALEXANDER.   JAS. had 6 tracts of 585 acres in
AC on Davis Creek.   JAS., one of heirs, not satisfied with 70 acres as
full part of father's land and brought 70 acres into hog pot and ALEX,
one of the sons, paid JAS. Ł150 for his right in 585 acres. JAS. has
right to one fourth and sells to ALEX. for Ł50 his rights. WM. & JOHN,
heirs, concur that they have rec'd. their parts and for 5 sh. relinquish
to ALEX. all interests.   Wit: MICAJAH BURNETT, WM. McDONALD, M.C. NAPIER.
Memo: WM. McALEXANDER for Ł60 sells all interest in father's estate to
ALEX. McALEXANDER. Wit: as above. Orig. del. to ALEX. McALEXANDER 18 Jul
1804.

Page 311.   10 Oct 1800.   JNO. SMITH & wife BARBARA, AC, to HUGH PAUL,
            Augusta, for Ł100, 100 acres. Lines: DAVID KINCADE, Thornton
Branch.   Acknowledged in Augusta 27 Oct 1800. Rec. AC 20 Oct 1801.

Page 312.   22 Mar 1801.   EDMUND WINSTON, Campbell Co., to son, GEO. DAB-
            NEY WINSTON, for support of son - where EW hitherto resided
and bought of JOSEF ANTHONY from his heir, CHRISTOPHER ANTHONY - 160
acres - and conveyed from DAVID CRAWFORD.   Also 300 acres by deed from
DANL. BURFORD and joins. Wit: JAS. STEWART, ARCH ROBERTSON, HENRY P.
CALLAWAY, WM. DAVENPORT, HENRY RIVERS or RIVES, BENJ. WINSTON. Orig.
sent to Lynchburg by S. GARLAND, 26 Dec 1803.

Page 312.   24 Jun 1801.   Order to AC J.P.'s to quiz ANN, wife of BARTLETT
            EADES for 24 Dec 1799 deed to JNO. MILTON; 200 acres. Rec. 19
Oct 1801.

Page 313.   22 Oct 1799.   HENRY VARNER, Tenn., to HUGH PAUL, Augusta, for
            Ł50, 477 acres Priest Mt. near Rockfish Gap. Lines: FRANCIS
HODGE, JACOB ARISMAN. Pat. to JNO. PRICE(?) 13 Aug 1788, for 577 acres-
100 acres excepted and sold to JACOB ARISMAN. Wit: CLAUDIUS BUSTER, WM.
WHITE, JNO. SILVERS(?). Orig. del. to PENN, 18 Nov 1845 - seems to be
C. PENN.

Page 314.   21 Dec 1801.   NELSON CRAWFORD & wife LUCY, to NICHL. CABELL
            & wife HANNAH of first part - This is marked through with
huge X - incomplete.

378

Page 314.	4 Jun 1801.	GEO. MARTIN (signed GEO. G.) to JAS. MARTIN for
Ł8-5, 11 acres. Lines: JOSHUA WILLOUGHBY, grantor and grantee;
agreeable to their father's will. Wit: RICH. C. POLLARD, SPARKS MARTIN,
ELIZ. H. GREEN.

Page 315.	8 Dec 1801.	JNO. WARWICK, AC, to ELISHA PETERS, for Ł45, 204
acres branches S fork Rockfish & Rucker's Run. Lines: JESSE
MARTIN, THOS. TRAIL, RICH. MURRAY, WM. CHAMBERLAINE, JNO. RICHARDS, MILLY
KEY. Bought from JESSE MARTIN by WARWICK. Wit: WM. EDMUNDS JR, WALKER
SAUNDERS, JNO. CAMM.

Page 315.	25 Jun 1801.	GEO. STONEHAM, AC, to WM. H. DIGGS & ELIJAH MAYS,
AC, Deed of Trust (Orig. del. 22 Sep 1818 to WHD) debt due
MARY STONEHAM - $1.00 - 150 acres where STONEHAM lives. Lines: WM. DIGGS,
JOSEPH LOVING, MENLENOUS WRIGHT, SAML. EDMUNDS, MOSES MAYS, AMBR. CAMP-
BELL,. Wit: JAS. KIDD, SAML. DICKINSON, WM. HAWKINS.

Page 316.	10 Dec 1801.	WM. WRIGHT, AC, to ESTHER WRIGHT - love and $1.,
slave, Ned. Wit: JAS. H. BURTON, JAS. WRIGHT.

Page 317.	17 Sep 1801.	PHILIP GOOCH, agt. for ELIZ. BRAXTON, widow of
CARTER BRAXTON, to RO. HOLLOWAY, for blank sum, 470 acres -
her dower part - Buffalo - whole tract bought by HOLLOWAY from SMYTH
TANDY. Wit: D.S. GARLAND, WM. EDMUNDS JR, EDMD. COLEMAN.

Page 317.	21 Dec 1801.	ZACH. PHILLIPS & wife ELIZ., AC, to JAS. BIBB,
AC, for Ł165, 245 acres; several tracts and adjoining. 1) 95
acres to PHILIPS from WM. HOLLINGSWORTH & wife JEMIMA, 16 Sep 1797 -
Rucker's Run. Lines: WM. CRISP, WM. ALFORD. 2) Surveyed for HOLLINGS-
WORTH and bought by PHILIPS. Lines: Both sides of ----Mt., 152 acres in
tract - WM. CRISP, CHAS. EDMUNDS, SAML. SPENCER's old line, WM. HOLLINGS-
WORTH, grantor.

Page 318.	22 Apr 1801.	JAS. LOVING JR & wife NANCY, AC, to WM. VAUGHAN,
AC, for Ł50, - also wife of WM. VAUGHAN, ELIZABETH - 100 acres
for natural lives - Rucker's Run and both sides of road from Amherst
Courthouse to Loving's Gap and extends from road to path from CHAS.
PURVIS' line to JAS. STEVENS. Wit: JNO. THOMPSON, JNO. CAMM, THOS. WOOD-
ROOF, JAS. MONTGOMERY, JAS. MURPHY. (Note: Courthouse was at what is
now Coleen or Colleen in Nelson. Loving's Gap was to be site of present
Nelson courthouse at what is now Lovingston. BFD)

Page 319.	26 Nov 1801.	Order to AC J.P.'s to quiz MARY, wife of WM.
HALL, as to deed to JNO. KEY - 100 acres - 21 Sep 1801. Done
by WM. WARE & CHAS. TALIAFERRO. Rec. 12 Dec 1801. Orig. sent to JK, 1802.

Page 319.	10 Dec 1801.	JAS. MATTHEWS, Stokes Co, N.C., to JOS. HOLL-
INGSWORTH, AC, Power of Atty. to HOLLINGSWORTH to sell 100
acres in AC in possession of WILLIAM MATTHEWS, AC, also negress, Doll,
furniture. Wit: WM. HOLLINGSWORTH, THOM T. AMSANS(?), ISAAC DALTON J.P.
& RO. WILLIAMS, Clerk of Stokes Co, N.C.

Page 320.	17 Dec 1801.	Order to AC J.P.'s, JOSIAH ELLIS & DAVID CRAW-
FORD, to quiz NANCY, wife of WM. BURKS, as to deed to NICHL.
WEST, 20 Jul 1801. Rec. 21 Dec 1801.

Page 321.	5 Jan 1802.	Order to GEO. DILLARD & REUBEN NORVELL, AC J.P.'s
to quiz SARAH, wife of CHAS. CHRISTIAN - 18 May 1801 deed to
HENRY CHRISTIAN. Rec. 18 Jan 1802.

Page 322.	10 Oct 1801.	Order to AC J.P.'s JAS. & GEO. DILLARD, to quiz
MARTHA, wife of HENRY CHRISTIAN, for deed of 5 Jun 1801, to
THOS. EDWARDS - 138 acres. Rec. 18 Jan 1802. Orig. sent to EDWARDS, 28
Jan 1804.

Page 322.	15 Dec 1801.	HENRY TURNER & wife RACHEL, AC, to JAS. LONDON
for $100, 50 acres N side Porrage. Lines: grantor, grantee.
Wit: JNO. LONDON, WM. TURNER, ALLEN WADE.

Page 323.	26 Nov 1801.	Order to AC J.P.'s DAVID CRAWFORD & WM. WARE to quiz wives of SAML. COLEMAN & RICH. HARDWICK - JUDITH & NANCY - deed of 2 Oct 1801 to THOS. COLEMAN - 237 acres. Done 18 Jan 1802; sent to THOS. COLEMAN 11 Feb 1802.

Page 324.   -- Jan 1802.   DAVID CLARKSON, AC, to PETER CLARKSON, Albemarle, for Ł385, 285 acres in Fluvanna on Byrd's Creek. Lines: JOS. TATE, EDMD. TILLY, BENJ. JOHNSON. Wit: JNO. JACOBS, WM. COFFEY, JAS. CLARKSON, LANDON BRENT. Margin: Certified to County Court of Fluvanna and huge X is through the deed.

Page 325.   15 Dec 1801.   JAS. LONDON & wife MARY to HENRY TURNER for $100, 50 acres S side Porrage. Lines: grantee. Part of former tract of RO. JOHNS. Wit: JNO. LONDON, WM. TURNER, ALLEN WADE. Orig. del. to JESSE MUNDY 15 Dec 1828.

Page 325.   16 Oct 1801.   Order to AC J.P.'s to quiz DOLLEY, wife of JOS. SHIPS, as to deed of 14 May 1801, to PLEASANT DAWSON. Done, 7 Nov 1801, by PHILIP JOHNSON & THOS. MOORE.

Page 326.   26 Nov 1801.   Order to AC J.P.'s SAML. MEREDITH & DAVID S. GARLAND, to quiz NANCY, wife of WM. TUCKER, as to deed of 5 Apr 1790 to RO. MAYS. Rec. 18 Jan 1802.

Page 327.   19 Dec 1801.   SAML. MITCHELL & wife NANCY, Campbell Co., to WM. SCOTT, for Ł250, 32½ acres Hardwick's Island in James and about 3 miles above Lynchburg. Wit: W.B. BANKS, SAML. IRVINE, SAML. ROSE, THOS. M. COCKER, WILSON DAVENPORT, CALEB TATE. To WM. B. BANKS, 10 Feb 1802.

Page 328.   22 Oct 1801.   GEO. HILTON, AC, to JESSE ALLEN, AC, for Ł400, 195 acres Elk Island Creek where WILSON PENN lives - in addition, an exchange of two tracts of ALLEN's and "for superiority" of the soil. Wit: HENLEY DRUMMOND, ROBT. VIA, CHAS. A. LEWIS, JNO. SCRUGGS, LEWIS TINDALL, JESSE JOPLING.

Page 329.   23 Dec 1801.   JAS. JOPLING & wife MARTHA; EDMD. POWELL & wife LUCY; PLEASANT MARTIN & wife REBECCA; HANNAH ALLEN, ANN CHILDRESS, & JNO. GRIFFIN to EDWD. & HOLMAN JOPLING - $10.00 - 1813½ acres in Kanawha County on right hand fork of 13 Mile Creek; branch of great Kanawaha. Lines: HENRY BANKS. Pat. to THOS. JOPLING. Wit: WM. LEE HARRIS, BENJ. CHILDRESS, RICH. C. POLLARD, JESSE JOPLING, WM. DIXON.

Page 330.   22 Oct 1801.   JESSE ALLEN & wife NANCY, AC, to GEO. HILTON, AC, 350 acres both sides Rich Branch. Lines: WM. HORSLEY's orphans. Consideration - tract where WILSON PENN lives of 195 acres. Wit: JNO. SCRUGGS, HENLEY DRUMMOND, RO. VIA, CHAS. A LEWIS.

Page 231.   29 Oct 1801.   CHAS. PATTESON, AC, to JAS. MURPHY, New Market, AC, Deed of Trust - debt due BROWN RIVES & Co. 5 sh. 3 slaves. Orig. del. to JM 15 Jul 1802. Wit: DANL. HIGGINBOTHAM, C.L. BARRETT, WM. EDMUNDS JR.

Page 332.   18 Jan 1802.   MINOS WRIGHT & wife ELIZ. L.(S), AC, to JORDAN WRIGHT for Ł200, 138½ acres. Lines: JOS. LOVING, SAML. EDMUNDS, GEO. STONEHAM. On Tye River. Also Apple Orchard tract reserved out of tract and sold to SAML. EDMUNDS - 150 acres, 22 Nov 1793. Deed bears date of 1802 and 1793 date seems to refer to sale to EDMUNDS. Orig. del. to HCAS. M. BURKS, 21 Feb 1819.

Page 333.   9 Dec 1799.   RICH. WILSON & wife ANNY(?), AC, to GEO. DILLARD, AC, for Ł200, 257 acres. Lines: BENJ. RUCKER, grantor, Gaines' road, CHAS. CHRISTIAN, WALTER CHRISTIAN. Wit: RO. HOLLOWAY, JAS. WATSON JR, MOSES PHILIPS.

Page 334.   13 Jul 1801.   Order to AC J.P.'s JNO. DIGGS & HUDSON MARTIN to quiz ANN, wife of JNO. MURRELL, as to deed of 18 Apr 1801 to NATHL. HARLOW - 575 acres. Rec. 18 Jan 1802.

Page 334.   18 Nov 1801.   Order to AC J.P.'s HUDSON MARTIN & JAS. WOODS to quiz KEZIAH, wife of WM. HAMILTON, as to deed of 16 Nov 1801

to JAS. MONTGOMERY & JNO. CLARKE. 80 acres. Done 18 Jan 1802. Orig. del.
to MONTGOMERY 10 Nov 1803.

Page 335. 10 Jan 1801. JARROT SUDDITH & wife SALLEY, Albemarle, to MATT.
           ROBERTS, AC, for Ŀ40, 87 acres Tye (Fry?) Creek. Lines: grant-
ee, JOS. SMITH, SAML. HENSLEY. Wit: SAML. IRVINE JR, PLEASANT BAILEY,
JNO. HARRIS JR, SAML. HENSLEY.

Page 336. 10 Jan 1801. SAML. HENSLEY & wife LEBBY Albemarle, to MATT.
           ROBERTS, AC, for Ŀ25, 40 acres Ivory Creek. Lines: grantee,
Long Mt., grantor, WM. MATTHEWS. Wit: as above.

Page 337. 12 Feb 1802. MARTHA HORSLEY, exrx. of WM. HORSLEY, & JNO.
           HORSLEY & RODERICK McCULLOCH, exrs. of WM. HORSLEY dec'd., AC,
to MICAJAH PENDLETON, AC, for Ŀ123-15, 275 acres Pat. 20 Jul 1780. Lines:
RO. HORSLEY, CHAS. PERROW, DRURY CHRISTIAN, JNO. FREELAND dec'd., S bank
Elk Island Creek, GEO. HILTON. Wit: JESSE ALLEN, JAS. PAMPLIN, WARREN
TALIAFERRO, WM. HORSLEY, SAML. HORSELY.

Page 338. 4 Jan 1802. HENRY LANDON DAVIES, Bedford Co., to GEO. GILLES-
           PIE JR, for Ŀ100, 387 acres Cedar Creek, branch of Pedlar.
Lines: THOS. MORRIS, JOSHIAH JOBLING, JNO. GOODRICH. Wit: WM. THURMOND,
GEO. GILLESPIE SR, JESSE CLARK JONES, PHILIP LOCKHARD. Orig. del. to GG,
19 May 1804.

Page 338. 13 Feb 1802. JAS. BROOKS & wife ELIZ., AC, to HENRY McCLAIN,
           AC, for Ŀ209015, 142½ acres N fork Rockfish. Sold to BROOKS
by DANL. CAREY - except 1½ acres adjoining river for Mill seat. Lines:
JOSIAH SMITH, grantor, the road, CHAS. RODES, BENJ. PANNELL. Orig. del.
to HMc. 2 Apr 1805.

Page 339. 15 Jan 1802. CHRISTIAN SHERLEY(SHENLEY?), Augusta, to CHAS.
           SMITH, AC, for Ŀ400, 289 acres Rockfish. Lines: SAML. WOODS,
dec'd. Wit: JAS. LOBBEN, RUBEN HARLOW, JNO. McCLURE, FREDERICK SHAFER,
NANCY SMITH, BETSY SMITH, WM. SMITH. Orig. del. to JNO. WATERS May 1802.

Page 340. 10 Nov 1801. Order to AC J.P.'s HUDSON MARTIN & JAS. WOODS,
           to quiz JANE, wife of WM. BARNETT, as to deed of 13 Nov 1801
to MICHL. WOODS, 15 Feb 1802. Margin: "The deed ought to have been recorded here, but was omitted. It may be seen in this book, p.637."

Page 341. 15 Feb 1802. GEO. MENG, late of Culpeper, Power of Atty. to
           NATHAN BARNETT, late of AC, but now of Kentucky - to sell
Franklin Co. tract about 12 miles from Frankfort - 499 acres surveyed.
Part of 1000 acres sold to me by GEO. MENG & NIMROD LONG and pat. to
ISAAC HITE. Lines: COFFMAN's Settlement, Bailey's Run. RO. REEVES, AC,
to receive money. Original sent to RO. REEVES.

Page 342. 4 Sep 1801. RO. ROBINSON, AC, to JNO. McBRIDE, AC, for Ŀ60,
           76 acres both sides Lynch road. Lines: RO. CAMPBELL, BENJ.
RUCKER, GARLAND, JNO. KNIGHT, ABEL BLANKENSHIP. Wit: PL. DAWSON, PATRICK
HIGGINS, WM. WILLMORE. Wife joined, but is not named. Orig. del. to
JM 14 Jun 1813.

Page 343. 20 Jul 1801. JOS. C. HIGGINBOTHAM, AC, to HUDSON M. GARLAND
           for Ŀ300, 87 acres Owens Creek. Lines: JNO. CABELL, THOS.
STAPLES.

Page 344. 27 Nov 1801. JNO. KIDD & wife SELIA, AC, to ISAAC SCOTT, AC,
           for Ŀ57-10, 115 acres Little Indian Creek. Lines: JNO. PARSON,
N fork of Creek, JNO. WILSFORD, JNO. ARRINGTON. Wit: THOS. WOODROOF,
GEO. DILLARD, JNO. TYLER.

Page 345. 10 Jan 1802. JARROT SUDDITH & wife SALLEY, Albemarle, to MATT.
           ROBERTS, AC, for Ŀ40, 87 acres Ivy Creek. Lines: JOS. SMITH,
grantee, SAML. HENSLEY. Wit: SAML. IRVING JR, PL. BAILEY, JNO. HARRIS JR,
SAML. HENSLEY.

Page 345. 3 Dec 1801. WM. BATES, AC, to WM. LOVING & JAS. MURPHY, AC.
           BATES has this day by indenture rented tavern at Amherst

Courthouse from SAML. J. CABELL and cleared land on N side of road for 5 years. Yearly rent fo Ŀ160. Deed of Trust - 5 sh. 5 negroes and stock. Wit: EDMUND BURNETT, JAS. GREGORY, GEO. W. VARNUM, RICH. MURRAY, FRANCIS WEST, PETER MARTIN. Orig. del. to RO. RIVES, 30 Dec 1803.

Page 346. 10 Jan 1802. SAML. HENSLEY & wife SEBBY (LEBBY) Albemarle, to
MATT. ROBERTS, AC, for Ŀ25, 40 acres Ivory Creek. Lines: grantee, up the Long Mt., grantor, WM. MATTHEWS. Wit: Same as SUDDITH deed
on p. 345.

Page 347. 5 Feb 1802. TANDY DEMPSEY, AC, to JAS. WILLS, for Ŀ20, cows
and other items. Wit: JNO. WILLS, WM. HENDERSON.

Page 348. 15 Feb 1802. JOS. HOLLINGSWORTH, AC, to ELISHA PETERS, AC,
for Ŀ50, 130 acres S fork Rockfish. Lines: CORNL. NEVIL, DOLLY
KEY, RICH. BREEDLOVE. Wit: D. WARWICK, BENJ. CHILDRESS, LANDON CABEL.

Page 349. 15 Feb 1802. WM. BATES & wife ROSANNAH, AC, to JAS. WILLS SR,
AC, for Ŀ536, 368 acres bought of ABRAHAM WARWICK on both
sides Meador Creek, branch of Rucker's Run. Lines: Dutch Creek, former
survey of ROBT. JOHNSON dec'd., ABRAHAM WARWICK, road to Findley's Gap,
Dutch Creek road. Wit: JNO. & DANL. WARWICK, EDMD. BURNETT. Orig. del.
1 Oct 1802 to JW by JNO. WARWICK.

Page 350. 19 Apr 1802. PATRICK ROSE & wife MARY, AC, to JNO. NICHL.
ROSE, AC, - love for their son and $1.00, 500 acres, part of
tract wher they live. Lines: S side of road from courthouse to New
Glasgow, Piney river, little below a mill, CARTER. Wit: JOHN CHAMPE
CARTER, GEO. NICHOLAS. Orig. del. to JR, 2 May 1805.

Page 351. 15 Dec 1801. ROBT. TUCKER to DANL. TUCKER - ROBT. is entitled
to certain lands under will of dec'd. father, DRURY TUCKER -
Ŀ30 for all rights in them. Wit: JAS. BALLINGER, L BERRY TUCKER, REUBEN
COLEMAN, ZACH. TUCKER, PL. TUCKER.

Page 351. 19 Apr 1802. CATH. ROSE declines to admr. estate of dec'd.
husband, JNO. ROSE. Wit: JESSE CLARKSON, CHAS. ROSE JR.

Page 351. 15 Apr 1802. HENRY ROBERTSON (ROBINSON) & wife FANNY, AC, to
LUKE RAY, Bedford Co., for Ŀ400, 133 acres. Lines: MICHL.
COALTER, CLARK, DANL. NORCUTT.

Page 352. 5 Mar 1802. RO. RIVES & wife PEGGY, AC, to GEO. MENG, late of
Culpeper, but now of AC, for $1000, 2 acres adjoining town of
Warminster. Lines: Lot 36, S side Main Street. Wit: JNO. HIGGINBOTHAM,
JR, RICH. POWELL, JAS. P. PARISH.

Page 353. 20 Dec 1798. HECTOR CABELL & wife PAULINA; SAML. JORDAN
CABELL; WM. & LANDON CABELL, AC, to RO. RIVES, AC, (Orig. sent
to LANDON CABELL 23 Feb 1807 per letter filed) for Ŀ1613, 1130 acres on
branches of Joe's Creek. Part of HECTOR's tract. Lines: old church road,
WM. HANSBROUGH dec'd., Rolling road, Richard's road, RICH. MURROW, Warminster road, ELISHA PETERS, ALLEN LAVENDER, old glade road. Also 390
acres on N side Fluvanna and upper side of Tye - conveyed to HECTOR CA-
BELL by JNO. CABELL & wife ELIZ., Buckingham Co., 25 Oct 1799. Wit: WM.
H. CABELL, RICH. MURRAY, BENJ. JORDAN.

Page 355. 19 May 1802. PATRICK ROSE, WM. CABELL, exrs. of Col. HUGH
ROSE, late of AC, & CAROLINE M. ROSE, widow of HUGH ROSE,
Power of Atty. to SAML. ROSE, Lynchburg, as to Henry County tract of
1968 acres - part of 5250 acres granted JACK POWER and SAML. JORDAN by
pat. 20 Jul 1768. Devised to be sold by HUGH ROSE & to make deed to Capt.
JNO. SALMONS, Henry Co., for 25 acres; to collect sum due from Col.
HENRY LYNE. Wit: THO. WOODROOF, WILSON DAVENPORT, JNO. LOVING, WM. ROSE,
GUSTAVUS A. ROSE. Orig. sent to GUSTAVUS A. ROSE 25 May 1802.

Page 356. 1 Jan 1802. BENJ. RUCKER, AC, to SPOTSWOOD GARLAND, AC, for
Ŀ423, 470 acres S branches Rutledge - part of 1113 acres for-
merly that of HENRY GILBERT. Lines: BENJ. MILES, Parks' road, pat. line,
Migginson road, HENRY GILBERT. Wit: JNO. McDANIEL, THOS. WOODROOF, CHAS.

CHRISTIAN, JOS. DAVENPORT, B. STONE. Orig. del. 29 Oct 1804 to SG.

Page 357.   26 Feb 1802.   JAS. GOODWIN & wife ISAMMA, AC, to GEO. M. TINS-
LEY for Ł262, 131 acres. Lines: path on DAVIS' line; small
branch, WM. GOODWIN, LEE, Spring Branch. Wit: GEO. TINSLEY, THOS. CLE-
MENTS, BANISTER TINSLEY, WM. BROWN as to GOODWIN. Orig. del. to GMT 20
Mar 1815.

Page 357.   4 Mar 1802.   CHAS. CHRISTIAN & wife SARAH, AC, to RO. PEARCE,
AC, for Ł27-15, 18 acres branches Rockey Run. Lines: JINKINS
OXLEY, grantee, ANDREW MUNROE. Wit; RICH. WILSON, REUBEN L. HOMAN, CHAS.
H. CHRISTIAN. Orig. del. to RP 16 Jan 1806.

Page 358.   20 Mar 1802.   CHAS. CHRISTIAN & wife SARAH, AC, to ELIZ. HOMAN,
AC, for Ł51, 40 acres Rockey Creek. Lines: JOSIAH ATTKISON,
JINKINS OXLEY, JOEL CAMPBELL. Wit: JNO. GRIFFIN JR., JINKINS OXLEY,
WALTER CHRISTIAN JR, BENJ. PHILLIPS.

Page 359.   17 Apr 1802.   CHAS. CHRISTIAN & wife SARAH, AC, to WM. JORDAN,
AC, for Ł250, 250 acres. Lines: GEO. HILTON, HENLEY DRUMMOND,
SAML. ARRINGTON, THOS. SPRADLIN. Wit: JAS. CHRISTIAN, HENRY CHRISTIAN,
WALTER CHRISTIAN JR, SAML. L. CHRISTIAN, BENJ. PHILLIPS.

Page 360.   1 Jan 1802.   JNO. LONDON, AC, to JAS. LONDON JR, AC, for Ł250,
240 acres both sides Porrage. Lines: JAS. LONDON SR, RAWLEY
PINN, JAS. DILLARD, WM. ANDERSON ENGLAND. Wit: HENRY ROBINSON, THOS.
MERRITT, TERISHA TURNER, REUBEN NORVELL, RICHARD & WM. TURNER.

Page 361.   14 Apr 1802.   JNO. BURFORD SR, AC, to AMBROSE BURFORD, AC, for
Ł100, 84 acres where JB, Sr, lives. Lines: HARRISON HUGHES,
PL. DAWSON, the Path, DANL. BURFORD SR., JOS. DAWSON. Wit: PL. DAWSON,
HARRISON HUGHES, PHIL BURFORD.

Page 362.   18 Apr 1802.   HARRISON HUGHES, AC, to PLEASANT DAWSON, AC, for
Ł8, 8 acres. Lines: PL. DAWSON, grantor, AMBR. BURFORD.

Page 362.   1 Jan 1802.   WM. MOORE & wife BETSY, AC, to SAML. BRIDGWATER,
AC, for Ł55, 63 acres. Lines: JONATHAN BRIDGWATER, THOS. FITZ-
PATRICK, JONATHAN REID's entry, McCLAIN's Mt., WM. MOORE, JAS. W. McCLAIN.

Page 363.   20 Nov 1801.   HENRY TURNER & wife RACHEL, AC, to SACKVILLE
KING, for 5 sh, 6 acres Porrige and N side. Lines: ford at
KING's mill; grantee. Wit: REUBEN NORVELL, WM. TURNER, JAS. LONDON, WM.
PETTYJOHN, JAS. DAVIS.

Page 363.   13 Nov 1801.   WM. TURNER, AC, to JNO. & CHAS. MUNDY, Fauquier
Co., for $1.00, 70 acres S branches Porridge. Lines: SACKVILLE
KING, HENRY TURNER, JNO. TURNER. Wit: WM. PETTYJOHN, HENRY TURNER, JAS.
DAVIS, R. NORVELL.

Page 364.   6 Mar 1802.   JNO. TURNER & wife MILLEY, AC, to RICH. JONES,
AC, for Ł800, 622 1/3 acres Porrage. Lines: JOS. HIGGINBOTHAM,
JNO. NICHOLAS, CHAS. MUNDY, WM. TURNER, JOS. NICHOLAS, DANL. DAY, JNO.
MONROE. Wit: REUBEN NORVELL, JESSE BECK, JNO. McDANIEL, WM. JONES. Orig.
del. to RJ, 24 Sep 1804.

Page 364.   20 Nov 1801.   SACKVILLE KING & wife ANNA, Campbell Co. to
HENRY TURNER, AC, for 5 sh., 6 acres N side Porrige. Lines:
grantor - part of tract bought by KING of RALPH LAMASTER. Wit: same as
p. 363 HENRY TURNER to KING.

Page 365.   15 Mar 1802.   JNO. HENDERSON to RICE KEY for Ł21, 90 acres
Pedlar - bought by JH from JNO. CHILDRESS and contains HENDER-
SON's old mill seat and apple orchard; reference to deed of 1796 - CHILD-
RESS to HENDERSON. Wit: WALTER LEAKE, WM. LEE HARRIS, JAS. L. TURNER.

Page 365.   21 May 1802.   CHAS. ROSE, the elder, AC, to DAVID S. GARLAND,
AC, for Ł1854-10, 1074 acres Tye and Piney; Claypool tract.
Lines: JNO. ROSE, ALEX. MARR; also 378 acres adjoining. Part of ROSE
Common divided by court decree of AC. Lines: JNO. ROSE, PATRICK & HUGH

ROSE. Also 109 acres adjoining Rose Common. Lines: CHAS. IRVING, dec'd,
CHAS. ROSE. Wit: JAS. M. BROWN, HUDSON M. GARLAND, EDMD. T. COLEMAN,
PATRICK ROSE JR.

Page 366. 19 Apr 1802. JACOB PHILLIPS & wife SARAH, AC, to PULLIAM
         SANDIDGE, AC, for Ł50, 39 acres N side of S fork Buffalo.
Lines: JOS. HIGGINBOTHAM, JR., grantee.

Page 367. 15 Sep 1798. JACOB PHILLIPS & wife SARAH, AC, to PULLIAM SAN-
         DIDGE, AC, for Ł100-10, 228 acres head of S branch of S fork
Buffalo and head branch Horsley. Lines: SOL CARTER, JNO. SANDIDGE, WM.
CARTER dec'd., AARON HIGGINBOTHAM. Wit: JNO. SANDIDGE, JOSHUA SANDIDGE,
JACOB PHILLIPS JR. Ack. by grantor, 21 Jun 1802.

Page 368. 26 Jun 1801. Order to AC J.P.'s REUBEN NORVELL & GEO. DILLARD
         to quiz SARAH, wife of CHAS. CHRISTIAN, as to deed of 4 Apr
1801, to CHRISTOPHER FLETCHER. 154 acres. Rec. 21 Jun 1802.

Page 369. 2 Dec 1801. MATT. TUCKER to DANL. TUCKER - consideration,
         horse named High Flyer - MATT sells all interest in estate -
certain lands - of his late father, DRURY TUCKER;ref. to will. Wit: JNO.
CAMM, JAS. BALLINGER, ZACH. TUCKER, L BERRY TUCKER, PL. TUCKER.

Page 369. 20 Oct 1801. WM. HOWARD & wife AMY, AC, to WM. WARE, AC, for
         Ł100, 143 acres on Puppy Creek and where HOWARD lives. Wit:
WM. CARTER, ABRAHAM SMITH, JOS. DUNKIN. Orig. del. to WH, 30 Jul 1802.

Page 370. 21 Jun 1802. JAS. LONDON JR, AC, to RO. ALLEN, AC, for Ł90,
         90 acres, part of survey of 92 acres formerly that of RO.
JOHNS, dec'd., pat. 28 Sep 1758, N branches Porage. Lines: grantee. Orig.
del. to RA, 17 May 1806.

Page 370. 21 Jun 1802. JACOB PHILLIPS & wife SARAH, to HENRY BALLINGER
         for Ł60, 140 acres S branches of N fork Buffalo; side of Cold
Mt. (Note: Cold Mt. is an old landmark of AC and on clear days may be
seen from traffic circle as one looks to west and Blue Ridge. Amherst
countians speak of Cold Mt. cabbage and it is quite delicious. BFD)

Page 371. 28 Mar 1802. JAS. GATEWOOD, Jessamine County, Kentucky, to
         JOS. NICHOLS, AC, for Ł60, my fishery rights on James River -
from WM. SCOTT, Caroline, 1784. 1150 acres on both sides of James River
and lying in AC, Bedford, and Campbell counties. One half conveyed. THOS.
BODLEY, Lexington District, County clerk, 28 Mar 1802; JAS. G. HUNTER,
Presiding judge. Rec. AC 21 Jun 1802.

Page 372. 25 Mar 1802. PHILIP THURMOND & wife JUDITH, AC, to WM. THUR-
         MOND, AC, for Ł400, 125 acres N side Tobacco Row Mt.; part of
where grantor lives. Lines: PARSON CRAWFORD near the road on a ridge; WM.
THURMOND, Punchboal(sic) Field, small spring, the path, Meador Br., ELIAS
WILLS, DAVID CRAWFORD. Wit: THOS. N. EUBANK, P. GOOCH, HARDEN HAYNES,
PHILIP THURMOND JR., PHILIP LOCKARD, JNO. WATKINS, NELSON CRAWFORD. Orig.
del. to PT, trustee, 5 Feb 1812.

Page 373. 20 Apr 1802. ACHILLES BALLINGER, Garrard Co., Ky, and RICH.
         BALLINGER, Knox Co., Ky, to JAS. BALLINGER, AC, - JOS. BALLIN-
GER, father of the parties hereto, lately departed this life and made
will - bequeathed in fee simple estate in 3 AC tracts to all three parties - Ky. heirs to sell to JAS. BALLINGER, AC, for Ł60 their interest in
the 3 tracts. Wit: SAML. MEREDITH, ANDREW MORGAN, JOEL FRANKLIN, NELSON
CRAWFORD, HUDSON M. GARLAND, DAVID S. GARLAND. Rec. AC 21 Jun 1802.

Page 374. 1 Oct 1801. Order to Culpeper J.P's. CHAS. CARTER & wife
         BETTY, to ELIJAH BROCKMAN, 10 May 1800 - 286 acres. BETTY rel.
dower - SAML. SLAUGHTER & BIRDD HAYWOOD, J.P.'s. Rec. AC 21 Jun 1802.
Same page - order to same men as to deed by CARTER & wife BETTY, to JNO.
SMITH: done and rec. on same date - BURDD(?) HAYWOOD. Orig. del. to
SMITH 12 Nov 1809.

Page 375. 15 Feb 1802. HUDSON M. GARLAND, AC, to JAS. MURPHY, AC, Deed
         of Trust - debt to RIVES & Co., 5 sh. Slaves & furniture.

Wit: JNO. HAWKINS, DANL. HIGGINBOTHAM, JNO. W. CAMDEN. Orig. del. to JM
26 Apr 1802.

Page 376. 27 Aug 1801. JAS. GATEWOOD & wife FRANCES, Fayette Co, Ky.,
           to JAS. R. PENN, Bedford Co, Va., for Ł140, 200 acres S side
Berry's Mt. Lines: ARTHUR ROBINSON, WM. TYREE, SAML. SPENCER, THOS. LANE
(marked by LAYNE & THOS. WILSHER), top of Berry Mt. Part of 385 acres
pat. 20 Jul 1780 to THOS. LANE and by him conveyed to THOS. WILSHER, 2
Jan 1785. Wit: WM. TODD, THOS. BODLEY, Clk of Ct., BUCKNER THRUSTON,
judge of Dist. Orig. del. 7 Sep 1811 to PENN.

Page 377. 21 Jun 1802. JAS. R. PENN & wife POLLY Bedford Co., to WM.
           CLASBY, AC, for Ł400, 200 acres S side Berry's Mt. Lines as
in previous deed. Orig. del. to WC, 29 May 1804.

Page 377. 16 Jun 1802. MOSES WRIGHT & wife ELIZ., AC, to JNO. CAMPBELL,
           AC, for Ł100, 52 acres S side and joining Crawley Creek, br.
of Piney. Lines: grantee, JESSE WRIGHT, GEO. GILLESPIE. Whole of tract.

Page 378. 26 May 1801 MARTIN DAWSON, AC, to HENRY GOSNEY, AC, for Ł30,
           13+ acres Harris Creek. Lines: grantor, VALENTINE COX, grantee,
near DAWSON's dwelling, RICH. SHELTON. Wit: NELSON C. SAWSON, JOSIAH
ELLIS JR., THOS. WOODROOF, REUBIN PENDLETON, DUDLEY CALLAWAY, RICH.
HARRISON, JNO. BOLLING, JNO. SHELTON.

Page 379. 8 Apr 1802. SAML. MEREDITH & wife JANE, AC, to WILLIAM WAR-
           WICK, Campbell Co., for Ł400, 400 acres both sides Bolling's
Creek, branch of James. Wit: DAVID S. GARLAND, WM. ARMISTEAD, JNO. CAMM,
THOS. WOODROOF. Orig. sent to JNO. M. OTEY, admr., 3 Oct 1833.

Page 379. 24 Dec 1798. JACOB PHILLIPS & wife SARAH, AC, to BENJ. SAN-
           DIDGE, AC, for Ł60, 54 acres branches S bork Buffalo. Lines:
JAS. HIGGINBOTHAM,grantor, grantee. Wit: WM. TOMLINSON, WALLER SANDIDGE,
PULLIAM SANDIDGE. Final proof, 21 Jun 1802 by grantor & wife. Orig. sent
to BS 15 May 1804.

Page 380. 6 May 1802. THOS. HAWKINS & wife ELIZ., AC, to JAS. MURPHY,
           AC, Deed of Trust to BROWN RIVES & Co., 5 sh. 200 acres head
branches Bob's Creek. Lines: MATT. HARRIS JR, MARTIN BIBB, JNO. THOMPSON,
CONYERS WHITE JR. Former tract of JAS. BIBB as co-heir of WM. BIBB
dec'd. Also 6 slaves. Wit: DANL. HIGGINBOTHAM, D.W. CRAWFORD, WM. TEAS,
NATHL. OFFUTT, JAS. HANSBROUGH.

Page 381. 21 Jun 1802. BROWN RIVES & Co. give receipt to Capt. PL.
           MARTIN and Col. WM. WARE for $500 on MARTIN's Deed of Trust.
Wit: BENJ. BROWN.

Page 381. 9 Feb 1802. NATHAN CRAWFORD, AC, to JNO. JACOBS, AC, several
           slaves "for a valuable consideration", also woman's saddle,
etc. Wit: PETER C. JACOBS, EDMUND COFFEY. Deed of gift.

Page 382. 9 Nov 1801. ANDREW MORELAND, AC, to JOEL PONTON, AC, for Ł18,
           stock. Wit: THOS. FORTUNE SR., THOS. E. FORTUNE.

Page 382. 21 Jun 1802. RO. & HENRY HOLLOWAY & CHAS. WATTS to SAML.
           BURKS - ROBT. HOLLOWAY & CHAS. B. PENN, infant of JOS. PENN,
dec'd, have conveyed to SAML. BURKS, 29 Nov 1801, tract adj. where BURKS
lives - part of CHAS. B. PENN from father, JOS. PENN, dec'd. This is
bond to protect BURKS. Wit: JNO. CAMM, WM. WARE, WM. LEE HARRIS, THOS.
WOODROOF.

Page 383. 21 Jun 1802. HENRY ROBERTS SR, AC, to MATT. ROBERTS, AC, 5 sh.
           - love of HENRY for nephew, MATT. ROBERTS - 108 acres N side
Rockfish; Eagles Nest Branch - also negress devised to MATT. by ELLIOTT
ROBERTS dec'd. and held for life by HENRY ROBERTS. Wit: WM. H. CABELL,
RICH. BURKS, LANDON BRENT. Orig. del. 8 Nov 1805, to ZACH. ROBERTS,
admr. of MATT. ROBERTS by MAJOR PERKINS.

Page 383. 17 Jun 1802. WM. WARWICK, Lynchburg, to JNO. CAMM, AC, for
           Ł800, 400 acres N side & joining Buffalo. Ref. to deed in AC

of 17 Apr 1797, from GEO. PENN's exrs. Wit: D.S. GARLAND, JNO. WARWICK, WILSON DAVENPORT. Orig. del. to JC, 1 Oct 1802.

Page 384. 17 May 1802. SAML. BELL & wife ---- to PHILIP GOOCH, AC, for
$192, 192 acres Elk Run Branches. Lines: LARKIN GATEWOOD, HENRY BELL, JAS. THOMPSON, JNO. HIGGINBOTHAM. Wit: S. GARLAND, RO. GARLAND, N. VANSTAVERN, JAS. BROOKS.

Page 385. 2 Feb 1802. WM. BATES, AC, to JAS. MURPHY, AC, Deed of Trust.
Debt to JNO. WARWICK. 5 sh. Stock, tobacco, etc. Wit: D.W. CRAWFORD, DANL. HIGGINBOTHAM, JAS. HANSBROUGH. Orig. del. to JNO. CAMM, 20 Jun 1803.

Page 385. 28 May 1802. LINDSEY WRIGHT & JESSE WRIGHT, JR, AC, to DANL.
HIGGINBOTHAM - Deed of Trust - debt due BROWN RIVES & Co. Stock, etc. Wit: JAS. MURPHY, CHAS. L. BRENT, JAS. HANSBROUGH, D. TRAIL. Orig. del. to JAS. MURPHY 22 May 1804.

Page 386. 21 Jun 1802. MOSES MAYS & wife LUCY, AC, to RO. MAYS, AC, for
Ł500, 192 acres Tye branches; part of tract of JOS. MAYS Sr, dec'd.

Page 387. 21 Jun 1802. RO. MAYS & wife ELIZ., AC, and parish, to MOSES
MAYS of same, for Ł500, 275 acres N branch Tye and S side Berry's Mt. Part of tract of JOS. MAYS Sr, dec'd. Lines: CHAS. MAYS, THOS. LANE, WM. LANE.

Page 388. 21 Jun 1802. DAVID S. GARLAND & wife JANE, AC, to JNO.
SHIELDS, AC, for $30, 50 acres Hat. Lines: THOS. WEST dec'd.

Page 389. 21 May 1802. RO. H. ROSE, Orange, & wife FRANCES, to WM. B.
BANKS, Lynchburg, LANDON CABELL, security for ROSE in Charlottesville District Court, Apr, 1801, and in AC by CHAS. CROUGHTON, assignee of RO. KING, Tenn. - injunction in Richmond by ROSE - MARTIN DAWSON, agt. for BROWN RIVES & Co. at their Milton store - injunction bond to exrs. of JAS. SHORT - Deed of Trust to secure CABELL - 505 acres. Lines: SPENCER NORVELL, DANL. BURFORD SR, JR, BENJ. RUCKER. Part of tract conveyed to ROSE in 1794 by father, Col. HUGH ROSE dec'd, AC; also 8 slaves. Wit: NELSON CRAWFORD JR, JACOB KINNEY, W.L. CRAWFORD.

Page 391. 26 Oct 1801. WM. LONG & wife ELIZ, Richmond, to JAS. FRANKLIN,
AC, for Ł100, 192 acres both sides S fork Huff Creek. Lines: BENJ. HIGGINBOTHAM, PATRICK NEWLAND, JNO. COLEMAN - also 13 acres adjoining. Lines: WM. CAMDEN, MOSES PENN. Wit: JNO. CAMM, JOEL FRANKLIN, S. GARLAND.

Page 392. 28 Oct. 1802. WM. LONG & wife BETSY, Richmond, to JACOB WOODS,
for $300, 260 acres and 180 acres Lime Kiln Creek. Lines: JAS. CHRISTIAN, DAVID PATTESON. Wit: JNO. CAMM, JNO. COLEMAN, SALLEY PENN, DANL. TUCKER.

Page 393. 22 Jun 1802. WARNER GOODWIN & wife ESTHER, AC, to RO. WALKER,
AC, for Ł69, 23 acres S branches Huff at Mill pond in JNO. PENN's line; part of tract. Orig. del. to RW 2 Jun 1823. (This is very fancy script.)

Page 393. 22 Jun 1802. RO. HOLLOWAY & wife SALLEY, AC, to WARNER GOOD-
WIN, AC, for Ł160, 158 acres Huff. Lines: School House Spring, Parks' road. Orig. del. 23 Jan 1807 to WG.

Page 394. 19 Jul 1802. JAS. CLARK & wife ANNE, AC, to HENRY HARTLESS,
AC, for Ł30, 166 acres. Lines: JNO. FLINT, DAVID McCLURE, the Blue Ridge, line of 100 acres bought by WM. CLARKE from FREDERICK HUFFMAN.

Page 395. 19 Jul 1802. JAS. CLARK & wife ANN, AC, to HENRY HARTLESS,
AC, for $100, 100 acres.

Page 395. 2 Dec 1801. HENRY ROSE, Fairfax, to NICHL. C. DAVIS, AC,
slave, Ł105. Wit: WM. MOSS & W.S. CRAWFORD.

Page 396. 9 Feb 1802. AC ct. execution of 9 Jun 1795 ANN CRAWFORD vs.
RACHEL AYERS & bdm., EVE LACKEY - RACHEL, slave, supposed pro-
perty of both - slave sold by shff. and GEO. DILLARD bought her for Ł35.
JOS. H. MORRISON still clamins interest in her and $8.30 paid to him by
DILLARD. Wit: JNO. CAMM, ABRAM CARTER Orig. del. 14 Mar 1804 to NELSON
CRAWFORD.

Page 396. 21 Jun 1802. JNO. JACOBS & wife LUCY, AC, to PARMENAS BRYANT,
AC, for Ł250, 100 acres branches Naked Creek and N branch Tye.
1 moiety of 200 acres devised to WM. MATTHEWS wife by WM. BIBB, dec'd.
WM. MATTHEWS' wife is not named. Lines: WM. BIBB.

Page 397. -- Dec 1801, rec. 19 Jul 1802. BENJ. CHILDRESS & wife ANN, AC,
to JOS. SHELTON, AC, (Orig. del. 21 Nov 1803 to JS) for Ł1000,
295 acres. Lines: JNO. GRIFFIN, grantee, WM. LEE HARRIS, MATT. HARRIS JR,
--- JOPLING dec'd, Rockfish.

Page 397. 19 Sep 1795. CHRISTOPHER COY & wife ELIZ., AC, to ABRAHAM
CARTER, AC, for Ł40, 100 acres Glady branch. Wit: GARRETT
LANDS, LANDON CARTER, THOS. ADCOCK, JAS. McCABE. Final proof by ACCOCK,
19 Jul 1802.

Page 398. 25 Sep 1801. Order to AC J.P.'s SAML. MEREDITH & DAVID S.
GARLAND, to quiz BETSY, wife of BENAMIMI STONE as to deed of
2 Sep 1800, to GEO. DILLARD. Rec. 19 Jul 1802.

Page 399. 21 Jun 1802. JNO. SHIELDS, AC, to ISHAM READY, AC, for Ł50,
29 acres survey mentioned as line. Hat & Cub creeks, branches
of Tye. Lines: THOS. WEST, dec'd. Wit; LANDON BRENT, JAS. MT GOMERY, NEL-
SON CRAWFORD JR, RO. SHIELDS. Orig. del. to RO. SHIELDS 27 Dec 1802.
(Note: The name of ISHAM READY appears in ALLEN's list of settlers in
Green County, Ky. BFD)

Page 399. 23 Jun 1802. Order to Buckingham J.P.'s, PETER GUERRANT &
DANL. GUERRANT, to quiz MARTHA, wife of EDWD. SCOTT, as to
deed of 8 Jun 1801, to LINDSEY COLEMAN. Rec. 19 Jul 1802.

Page 400. 11 Oct 1800. JNO. RUCKER & wife NANCY; MOSES RUCKER & wife
ELIZ.; REUBEN RUCKER & wife ELIZ.; RICH. RUCKER & wife MAR-
GARET; JAS. TINSLEY & wife SUSANNAH; ARCHILLES REYNOLDS & wife ELIZ., to
PHILLIP THURMOND JR, AC, for Ł60, 92 acres. Lines: JNO. McDANIEL, EDMD.
WINSTON, top of the mt.(Paul's). 22 Sep 1802, orig. sent to PT by PHILIP
LOCKART.

Page 401. 18 Sep 1802. RICH. LAWLESS & wife ELIZ. (ELIRABETH), AC, to
WM. PRYOR, AC, for Ł100, 100 acres branches Horsley. Lines:
ISAAC WRIGHT, Lomarde, WM. LAWLESS, WM. WARE. Wit: RICH. SMITH, WM.
CARTER, JNO. PRYOR, WM. WARE. Orig. del. 12 Feb 1805 to WP.

Page 402. 21 Oct 1801. WM. WARE & wife PATSEY, AC, to WM. HOWARD, AC,
for Ł100, 143 acres Puppy Creek - blank sum. Orig. del. 1801
to WARE from HOWARD & wife AMEY. Wit: WM. CARTER, ABRAH SMITH, JOS.
DUNKIN.

Page 402. 17 May 1802. RO. RIVES & wife PEGGY, AC, to WM. LOVING, AC,
for Ł85, 85 acres S side and joining Rucker's Run; part of
tract. Lines: JAS. STEVENS, grantor, grantee. Wit: LANDON CABELL, NELSON
ANDERSON, JNO. CAMM, W.S. CRAWFORD.

Page 403. 3 May 1802. WM. LOVING & wife SARAH, AC, to RO. RIVES, AC,
for Ł102, 34 acres - joins grantee and most contigious to his
dwelling house. Part of tract bought by LOVING of RO. C. HARRISON. Lines:
grantee. Wit: as in previous deed.

Page 404. 31 Jul 1802. JNO. ALFORD & wife ELIZ., AC, to TERISHA TURNER,
AC, (Orig. del. 15 Nov 1841, to --- DILLARD, atty. for TURNER)
for $3000, 575 acres, part of 640 acres surveyed 21 Mar 1780, S branches
Rucker's Run. Part of JNO. HARMER tract and WALTER KING, British Subjects,
and sold by DAVID SHEPHERD, Escheator, to WM. CRISP. Lines: WM. ALFORD-
645 acres and 70 acres taken off - 50 acres for THOS. ALFORD and where he
lives - 20 acres for AUGUSTINE SMITH adj. THOS. ALFORD, THOS. BIBB, WM.

ALFORD & JOS. LOVING. Wit: RO. RIVES, JAS. MURPHY, JAS. SEAY, RANDOLPH
BIBB.

Page 405.   17 Sep 1802.   MARGARET SHIELDS, relinquished administration of
            dec'd. husband, JNO. SHIELDS - "burthen too great" and asked
that son, ROBT. SHIELDS, be appointed. Wit: JAS. & JOS. MONTGOMERY.

Page 406.   15 Sep 1802.   THOS. WILLS to JNO. & THOS. N. EUBANK, AC, (Orig.
            de. 2 May 1814 to J.S. ELLIS, per order of TNE) for $500, 220
acres surveyed 28 May 1788, S fork of Shoe Creek, branch of N fork Piney.
Wit: RICH. S. ELLIS, A.B. WARWICK, WM. BURKS, JNO. BROWN, JNO. MAGAN.

Page 407.   16 Sep 1802.   RO. JENNINGS, AC, to secure ISAAC RUCKER & JNO.
            HANSFORD, bdm. on debt to SAML. IRVINE, Lynchburg - to AMNR.
RUCKER - 3 slaves. Wit: PHIL JOHNSON, HENRY HOLLOWAY, WIATT SMITH.

Page 408.   19 Oct 1801.   ELIZ. ENGLAND, widow of WM. ENGLAND; ELISHA
            ENGLAND; JANE & ANNE ENGLAND (WILLAIM's children), AC, to WM.
ENGLAND, AC, for Ⱡ6, all interest in land pat. to WM. ANDERSON ENGLAND,
14 Oct 1789, 174 acres.   Signed by ELIZ., ELISHA, GUINEA ENGLAND; ANNA
ENGLAND, JOSIAH MARTIN.   Orig. del. to WE 18 Feb 1802. Wit: DABNEY HILL,
JNO. FULCHER, EDWD. BOWLING.

Page 408.   13 Feb 1802.   ELIJAH MORAN & wife MARY, AC, to JAS. HATTER,
            AC, for Ⱡ15-5, 66 acres S side Tye. Lines: JNO. M. HATTER; pat.
5 Dec 1795. To JESSE HATTER, 20 Sep 1821 admr. of JAS. HATTER, orig. was
del. (Note: Some man came here to look for MORAN data and told me that
they went "somewhere in Ky." HATTERS in Simpson - from Madison, but do
not know that they are these from AC and Nelson. BFD)

Page 409.   8 May 1802.   PLEASANT TUCKER, entitled to equal share of lands
            of dec'd. father, DRURY TUCKER, with other legatees - $120.
ZACH. TUCKER buys his interest in estate. Wit: P. MARTIN, WM. COLEMAN, J.
LACKEY, RO. ALLEN, RO. H. COLEMAN.

Page 410.   8 Apr 1802.   NANCY LEE, AC, for love of JNO. DILLARD, AC, for
            Ⱡ250, slaves. Ⱡ100-12. Ⱡ18 from JOS. CANDAY; Ⱡ15 from WM.
NIGHT; Ⱡ26 from ZACH. MARTIN; Ⱡ12 from SAML. FRANKLIN; Ⱡ29 from NICHL.
HARRISON - furniture, stock, etc. Wit: JACOB SCOTT, MILDRED SCOTT. Orig.
del. to JD 4 Aug 1803.

Page 410.   30 Aug 1789.   JNO. SPENCER, AC, atty. for EDWD. LYON, Washing-
            ton, N.C., to JOS. NICHOLS, for Ⱡ50, 150 acres Stovall Creek.
Lines: MARTIN BIBB, JNO. MERRITT, BENJ. RUCKER, PETER DAY dec'd. Wit:
ZACH. DAWSON, WM. MAYFIELD, RO. D. DAWSON, THOS. DAY, JNO. WOOD.   Proved
by two DAWSONS, 5 Apr 1790. Proved by DAY, 20 Sep 1802.

Page 411.   20 Sep 1802.   JOS. NICHOLS & wife ANNE, Campbell Co., to JAS.
            DAVIS, AC, for Ⱡ147-15, 197 acres Stovall and Porage Creeks
on both sides Stovall's road. Lines: RICH. JONES On N and NE; DANL. DAY
on NW; grantee on S and JNO. LONDON & MARY DAY on S and SE. Bought by JN
from WM. BAILEY. Orig. del. to DAVIS by JNO. LONDON on order of 6 Jan
1803.

Page 412.   18 Sep 1802.   MARTIN DAWSON, Albemarle, to ZACH. ROBERTS, AC,
            for Ⱡ40, 37 acres Rockfish and Morrison's Mt. Lines: JNO.
DAWSON, grantee. Pat. 25 Sep 1800. Wit: WM. TURNER, JNO. S. DAWSON,
CHAS. CHRISTIAN.

Page 413.   15 Sep 1802.   WM. COFFEY, AC, from PETER RIPPETOE & wife SARAH,
            AC, Ⱡ7400 tobacco, 215 acres E side Cub Creek, branch of Tye.
Lines: WM. HOOKER, MOSES MARTIN, THOS. STURAT, GEO. LAVENDER.

Page 413.   3 Jul 1802.   WM. MARTIN (F) & wife SUSANNAH, AC, to JNO. HUD-
            SON, AC, for Ⱡ25, 108 acres Little Piney. Pat. 20 Jul 1796.
Lines: JNO. HARRIS, NOTLEY MADDOX. Wit: JAS. MARTIN, JACOB MADDOX,
JOSIAH MARTIN.

Page 414.   1 Aug 1801.   WM. EVANS, AC, to JAS. MURPHY, AC, (Orig. del. to
            JM 24 Nov 1802) Deed of Trust - debt to BROWN RIVES & Co.

388

5 sh. 350 acres both sides Little Piney. Lines: WM. MOORE, STEPHEN
TURNER, DAVID CLARKSON, where EVANS lives - also one negress. Wit: DANL.
HIGGINBOTHAM, PARMENAS BRYANT, RICH. CLARKE.

Page 415. 26 Oct 1797. Order to AC J.P.'s, PHILIP JOHNSON & THOS. MOORE
to quiz PATSEY CALLAWAY, wife of DUDLEY, deed of 26 Sep 1797,
to JESSE WOODROOF. 117 acres. Done 24 Jul 1802.

Page 416. 19 Jul 1802. Order to AC J.P.'s to quiz AMY, wife of WM.
HOWARD - deed of 20 Oct 1801, to WM. WARE. Rec. 20 Sep 1802;
JOS. BURRUS & CHAS. TALIAFERRO. Orig. del. to WH, 7 Jun 1803.

Page 417. 18 Oct 1802. JNO. ABNEY & wife PATTY, AC, to MAJOR KING, AC,
for Ł45, 50 acres N branch of N fork Davis Creek. Orig. del.
to MK 15 Jun 1804. (Some of these KINGS went to Estill Co, Ky. BFD)

Page 418. 14 Oct 1802. BENJ. PANNELL & wife MARY, AC, to JAS. FLACK,
Augusta, (Orig. del. to C. PERROW 18 Nov 1845) for $500, 100
acres Rockfish. Conveyed to PANNELL by THOS. PANNELL, 31 Jul 1779. Lines:
ROBERTSON, MARTIN. Wit: JAS. BROOKS, EDMD. PANNELL.

Page 418. 3 Dec 1801. PLEASANT MAGANN, Bedford, to PROSSER POWELL, AC,
(Orig. del. 12 Sep 1804 to PP) for Ł100, 66 acres. Wit: THOS.
CREWS, ANTHONY RUCKER, DAVID TINSLEY, WILSON DAVENPORT, ARCHIBALD
ROBERTSON.

Page 419. 26 Apr 1802. ACHILLES, RICH. & JAS. BALLINGER, legatees under
the will of JOS. BALLINGER - to TABITHA BALLINGER - rel. of
all rights in estate left her by NEIL CAMPBELL - land and negroes; and
also in estate of JOS. BALLINGER - horses, sheep, furniture, etc. Wit:
HUGH CAMPBELL, JOS. CHILDRESS, JAS. FRANKLIN. Orig. del. to JAS. BARRET
9 Nov 1808. (See my C will works. TABITHA was mother of natural child
of NEIL CAMPBELL's and he names her in his will. She later married JOS.
BALLINGER. BFD)

Page 420. 5 Aug 1802. JNO. M. GRIFFIN, AC, to DANL. HIGGINBOTHAM, AC,
Deed of Trust - debt due BROWN RIVES & Co. 5 sh. Stock, furn-
iture, etc. Wit: EZEK. GILBERT, JESSE PROFFITT, JAS. MURPHY, CHAS. L.
BARRETT.

Page 420. 8 Jun 1802. BENJ. SNEAD, AC, to DANL. HIGGINBOTHAM, AC, Deed
of Trust - debt due BROWN RIVES & Co. 5 sh. Beds, stock, etc.
Wit: CHAS. L. BARRET, JAS. MURPHY.

Page 421. 21 May 1802. JOS. ALLEN, AC, to NATHL. HILL, for Ł12, bay
mare, about 13 and 4 ft 5 or 6 inches tall. Wit: WM. HILL JR,
JNO. P. HILL. Orig. del. to WM. HILL JR, 13 Dec 1804.

Page 422. 18 Oct 1802. HUGH CAMPBELL & wife ELIZ, AC, to ANGUS McCLOUT
& JNO. H. CLEMENTS for $644, 161 acres both sides S fork Buff-
alo. Part of 190 acres granted to AARON HIGGINBOTHAM at Williamsburg 30
Aug 1763. Deeded to NEIL CAMPBELL 3 Oct 1768. Lines: BENJ. SANDIDGE, his
own. Orig. del. to AM 9 Aug 1805.

Page 423. 18 Oct 1802. HUGH CAMPBELL & wife ELIZ., AC, to BENJ. SAN-
DIDGE, AC, for $116, 29 acres E side Long Mt. Part of 190
acres pat. to AARON HIGGINBOTHAM as above and deeded to NEIL CAMPBELL 3
Oct 1768. Lines: grantee; his own.

Page 424. 11 Oct 1802. Agreement between parties above - grantors warrant title, but 28 acres here. Discount for all paid within
year at 12½%. Wit: NICHL. VANSTAVERN, MOZA PETER, ANGUSH McCLOUT, JAS.
BARRET. Orig. del. to BD 27 Apr 1805.

Page 424. 16 Oct 1802. HUDSON MARTIN & wife JANE, AC, to NATHL. HARLOW,
AC, for $100, 7 acres plus - 2 adjoining tracts - conveyed by
JNO. MURRELL dec'd., to NH. Lines: grantor, tract adj. tract conveyed on
North - 457 acres. Wit: ELIJAH L. WILLIAMS, PEGGY CLARK, MARY W. MARTIN.

Page 425. 4 Aug 1802. HENRY CAMPBELL, AC, to EM. EDMUNDS, Deed of Trust

debt due JAS. BOLLING - negress. JAS. BAILEY's name at end and not BOLL-
ING's name. Wit: P. GOOCH.

Page 426. 20 Jul 1801. PULLIAM SANDIDGE & wife LUCY, AC, to WALKER AT-
KINSON, AC, for Ь30, 134 acres Luck Mt. Part of 254 acres of
grantor's. Lines: JOS. HIGGINBOTHAM, JNO. SANDIDGE SR, WM. WILMORE. Wit:
JNO. & JOSHUA SANDIDGE. (I have not checked on PULLIAM SANDIDGE, but
recall seeing deeds later from Kentucky. He was son-in-law of JOSHUA
HUDSON who was my wife's ancestor. BFD)

Page 427. 25 Aug 1802. JOS. MILSTEAD, SR, & wife REBECCAH, AC, to DANL.
SHRADER, AC, "for value rec'd" 107 acres. Lines: JNO. DEVAZIER,
grantor, the road. Wit: BENJ. HIGGINBOTHAM, JNO. C. DEVASHER, JOS. MIL-
STEAD JR, JNO. KEY.

Page 428. 15 Feb 1802. WM. PENDLETON & wife MARTHA, AC, to MILLNER COX,
AC, for Ь30, 30 acres. Lines: WM. MUSE, grantee. Wit: HARRISON
HUGHES, REUBEN COX., WM. HUGHES.

Page 429. 18 Oct 1802. WM. HALL, AC, & wife POLLY, to JNO. FRYER HALL
for Ь30, 40 acres N branches Pedlar. Lines: SUSANNA BROWN,
STEPEHN RUSSELL, SAML. DEAN, NELSON CRAWFORD, JNO. McCABE. Granted to
HALL Dec. 1795.

Page 429. 18 Oct 1802. EDWD. TAYLOR & wife NANCY, AC, to THOS. MORRIS,
AC, for Ь100, 100 acres not far from Pedlar River. Lines:
JNO. SANDIDGE, JERRY DEAN. Orig. del. to ET 18 Dec 1815.

Page 430 . 16 Sep 1802. EZRA MORRISON to THOS. COPPEDGE, AC, for Ь100,
no acreage mentioned - Harris & Huff creeks. Lines: JNO. HAR-
VEY. Wit: WM. EDMUNDS JR, THOS. LANDRUM, THOS. ALDRIDGE, RICH. HERNDON,
W.R. MILSTEAD. Orig. del. to TC, 18 Oct 1808.

Page 431. 15 Oct 1802. THOS. POWELL & wife NANCY (mark of ANN), AC, to
BEVERLY WILLIAMSON, AC, for Ь230, 147 acres both sides Stone-
house creek; part of a tract. Lines: JNO. MORE dec'd, STEPHEN CASH, JNO.
CASH, BENJ. POWELL.

Page 431. 15 Oct 1802. HENRY ISBELL, Goochland, and ZACH. ISBELL, AC,
to CHAS. CHRISTIAN, AC, for Ь218, 204 acres S side Buffalo.
Lines: JNO. WEST dec'd., Parks' road, Migginson road, CHAS. CHRISTIAN,
HENRY STRATTON, WEST's road.

Page 432. 18 Sep 1802. STEPHEN WATTS & wife MARTHA, AC, to BENJ. WATTS,
AC, for Ь10, 300 acres Tye. Lines: JNO. LOVING, Rolling road,
WM. SPENCER, Main road., LAVENDER LONDON. Orig. del. to SW 1 Dec 1803.

Page 433. 13 Sep 1802. JAS. McCLAIN & wife SALLY, AC, to WM. FITZPAT-
RICK, AC, for Ь330, 150 acres, where grantor lives. Lines:
SAML. BRIDGWATER, grantee. Wit: JAS. BROOKS, JAS. MONTGOMERY, BENJ.
FORTUNE, JNO. RIVERS.

Page 434. 19 Aug 1802. GEO. McDANIEL SR, AC, to PHILIP BURTON, AC, for
Ь240, 434 acres W side Cold Mt. and N fork of head of Pedlar.
Lines: JAS. SMITH's former line. Wit: JNO. McDANIEL, JAS. GARLAND, AM-
BROSE RUCKER, DAVID TINSLEY, SAML. BURKS, PHILIP BURFORD, ANTHONY
RUCKER. Orig. del. to WM. SHELTON, 4 Oct 1810.

Page 435. 26 Jun 1802. JAS. MURPHY & WM. H. CABELL, exrs. of THOS.
BROWN, late of AC, to JAS. P. COCKE, Albemarle (Orig. del. to
ALEX. BROWN, 9 Jun 1832) Indenture between COCKE & THOS. BROWN, 2 Jun
1800 - co-partnership for 10 years as millers and distillers from 1 Jan
1798 - survivorship clause. Accts. to be made for settlement and tracts
sold. 1) 60 acres Rucker's Run, bought by COCKE of JESSE WRIGHT et al.
2) 70 acres adj. and bought by COCKE of CHAS. EDMUNDS before grant for
same; part of 130 acres, pat. to COCKE as assignee of EDMUNDS. 3) 30
acres on Rucker's Run whereon is mill and distillery and where business
is managed. Bought by COCKE of WM. CABELL dec'd. 4) Near Tye Warehouse
and bought by COCKE & THOS. BROWN from HECTOR CABELL. 5) 24 acres S side
Rucker's Run and pat. to THOS. BROWN. 6) 25 acres S side Rucker's Run

and bought by partners from JNO. EDMUNDS. 7) 2 acres on Rucker's Run and bought by them from JAS. EDMUNDS. Also 3 slaves, horses, utensils etc. Three fourths to COCKE and one fourth to BROWN. THOS. BROWN died 1 Dec 1800, testate, and named exrs. who have qualified and act under will. Ł569-5-7. Wit: WILLIS WILLS, JNO. JOHNSON, JNO. HIGGINBOTHAM JR, ELISHA ESTIS, JESSE HIGGINBOTHAM. (Note: JESSE HIGGINBOTHAM later went to Tenn. and then came back here and opened Higginbotham Academy on Main Street in Village of Amherst - see my H will works. BFD)

Page 438. 1 Oct 1802. Order to AC J.P.'s WM. H. DIGGES & WILL CABELL to quiz ROSANNA, wife of WM. BATES as to deed of 15 Feb 1802 to JAS. WILLS SR. - 368 acres. Rec. 18 Oct 1802.

Page 438. 17 Feb 1802. Order to Campbell Co. J.P.'s SAML. SCOTT & THOS. W. COCKE to quiz NANCY, wife of SAML. MITCHELL, as to deed of 19 Dec 1801 to WM. SCOTT. 32½ acres. Done and re. AC 18 Oct 1802. Orig. del. to WM. B. BANKS, 22 Feb 1803(?).

Page 440. 24 Feb 1795. Order to Campbell Co. J.P.'s SACKVILLE KING & THOS. HUMPHREYS, to quiz SALLY, wife of WILLIAM MEREDITH, as to deed of 20 Jan 1795 to STEPHEN WATTS - 400 acres. Done 28 Feb 1795, and returned 18 Oct 1802. Orig. del. to SW, 3 May 1809.

Page 441. 10 Nov 1795. PETER WATERFIELD, AC, to JNO. CAMDEN SR, AC, for Ł30, 184 acres on Roberts' Creek; S branch of Pedlar. Lines: WM. PRYOR. Wit: WM. HIGGINBOTHAM, WM. HARTLESS, THOS. ALLEN, THOS. GRIF-FITH, JOS. HIGGINBOTHAM JR, JAS. SMITH. Proved by JOS. HIGGINBOTHAM & JAS. SMITH 18 Apr 1796, and final proof by WM. HIGGINBOTHAM 20 Dec 1802.

Page 441. 13 Dec 1802. GEO. HYLTON to WM. EVANS - receipt in full on judgment in AC court obtained in 1792. EVANS as security of RICH. GATEWOOD on bond rec. in Georgia. Wit: SAML. ARRINGTON, ADAMSON BERRY.

Page 442. 18 Oct 1802. GEO. VAUGHAN & wife SUSANNA (signed SUCKEY), AC, to JAMES TURNER, JR, AC, (Orig. del. to BF, 8 Jan 1803) for Ł114-15, 170 acres N branches S fork Rockfish. Lines: HENRY SMITH, grantor, THOS. ANDERSON dec'd, JNO. JOPLING, CHAS. STATHAM. Part of tract divided by Warminster road. Wit: JAS. MT GOMERY (MONTGOMERY and often so signed), JAS. LOVING JR, JNO. LOVING. Memo as to delivery by VAL. BALL and others as above (wits.).

Page 443. 22 Nov 1802. JAS. ROWSEY & wife BETSY, AC, to ALLEN BLAIR, AC, for $250, 50 acres grantor bought from JNO. ROWSEY and 10 acres bought from GEO. PHILLIPS and adj. Lines: ARCHIBALD ROWSEY, JNO. ANDERSON, THOS. NEVIL, RICH. ALCOCK, STEPHEN WATTS. Wit: JNO. LOVING, WM. L. WATTS, JNO. PUGH.

Page 444. 6 Dec 1802. RO. L. ROSE & wife JANE L., Stafford Co., to JNO. CAMDEN, AC, for 5 sh, 260 acres. Lines: mouth of Little Piney. Wit: JAS. CAMDEN, P. ROSE JR, PATRICK ROSE, JNO. N. ROSE. Orig. del. to JC 17 May 1803.

Page 445. 7 Dec 1802. JNO. CAMDEN & wife ONEY, AC, to RO. L. ROSE, Stafford, 5 sh., 260 acres. Lines: mouth of Little Piney. Wit: as above deed.

Page 446. 20 Dec 1802. ELIJAH BROCKMAN & wife FRANCES, AC, to HENRY CAMDEN, AC, (Orig. del. to HC, 23 May 1810) for Ł200, 194 ac. Stonehouse Creek and Buffalo. Lines: The main road from TALIAFERRO's store to Amherst Courthouse; CARTER's, now WM. SANDIDGE.

Page 446. 6 Oct 1802. THOS. MASSIE & wife SALLY, Frederick Co, to JNO. JACOBS JR, AC, for Ł892-10, 350 acres, part of tract. N. side and joining Tye. Lines: STEPHEN JOHNSON. Wit: DANL. McDONALD, WM. HILL JR, EDWD. H. CARTER.

Page 447. 20 Dec 1802. HILL CARTER, AC, to JNO. HENDERSON, Albemarle (Orig. del. to JH, 2 May 1803) Kentucky land (not described) devised to HILL CARTER by his father, EDWD. CARTER.

Page 448.   14 Nov 1802.   JAS. PENN, exr. of GABL. PENN, Campbell Co., to
STEPHEN WATTS, AC, for Ƚ80, 146 acres surveyed 27 May 1791 -
both sides Freeland Creek, N branch of Buffalo. Lines: JAS. FREELAND,
dec'c., JESSE KENNIDY (Now THOS. NEVIL), REUBIN THORNTON(now JOS. STAPLES)
ALLEN BLAIR, SMYTH TANDY (now ARTHUR ROWSEY), JAS. ROWSEY. Wit: WM. CAM-
DEN, RO. COLEMAN, LINDSEY COLEMAN, HEN. HOLLOWAY.

Page 449.   2 Nov 1802.   MARTIN BIBB & wife MARY, AC, to JNO. THOMPSON, AC,
for Ƚ250, 100 acres branches of Naked Creek, N branch Tye.
Balance of survey of 200 acres laid off to BIBB out of estate of WM. BIBB.
100 acres of which THOMPSON has bought before of MARTIN BIBB. Lines:
Grantee, where 100 acres was devised, CONYERS WHITE, THOS. HAWKINS. Wit:
WM. BATES, THOS. E. FORTUNE, RO. RIVES.   Page 450, order to AC J.P.'s on
5 Nov 1802, to quiz MARY BIBB. Done and rec. 27 Nov 1802 by WILL LOVING
& WM. H. DIGGS. Also another order for 100 acres bought on 3 Nov 1795 -
same J.P.'s. Rec. 20 Dec 1802. Both del. to THOMPSON 13 Jul 1803.

Page 451.   17 Nov 1802.   JOS. MAYO SR, & wife MARTHA, Powhatan Co., to
GEO. DILLARD, AC, (Orig. del. to GD. 12 Sep 1804) for $1.00,
175 acres Crooked Run. Lines: JOS. HIGGINBOTHAM, JNO. WYATT, JOS. CREWS.
Proved in Powhatan, J(?) POINDEXTER, Clk., 17 Nov 1802. Rec. AC 17 Jan
1803.

Page 452.   23 Oct 1802.   JOS. HIGGINBOTHAM JR, to BENJ. SANDIDGE, AC, for
Ƚ100, 340 acres both sides Middle Fork Pedlar. Lines: WM.
HIGGINBOTHAM, GEO. McDANIEL. Wit: HENRY BALLINGER, WM. TOMBLINSON, AMBR?)
TOMBLINSON. Orig. del. to BS 15 May 1804.

Page 453.   7 Jan 1803.   JNO. LONDON, AC, to JAS. DAVIS, AC, (Orig. del.
31 Aug 1831, to JD) for $96, 48 acres Porage Creek. Lines: JNO. JINKINS,
WM. TURNER, grantee, RICH. JONES, PETER DAY dec'd. Wit: JAS. L. LAMKIN,
JNO. MONDAY, JAS. LONDON.

Page 454.   11 Oct 1802.   JNO. GRAVILY, Pendleton Dist. SC, Power of Atty.
to WM. LINCH, same dist., to receive from JOEL FRANLIN & HENRY
BALLINGER, exrs. of JOS. BALLINGER, my legacy left him by me. Wit: CHAS.
LAY & A. LADD SR. 13 Oct 1802, JNO. BAYLIS EARLE, Clk. of Dist. Cert.
by JNO. COCKRAN, Acting J.P. Receipt by WM. LYNCH, atty. in fact for
JNO. GRAVILY, S.C., to JOEL FRANKLIN, AC, legacy of PEGGY HENSLEY GRAVILY
to be paid by ACHILLES, RICH., & JAS. BALLINGER, sons of JOS. BALLINGER -
PEGGY, formerly BALLINGER and now GRAVILY. Ƚ60 paid to LYNCH, 29 Dec
1802. W.S. CRAWFORD, wit. (See my B will work for BALLINGER data. BFD)

Page 455.   15 Jan 1803.   JNO. CAMPBELL & wife FANNY, AC, to JNO. PENN, AC,
for Ƚ158-8, 144 acres. Lines: HENRY ROSE, Indian Creek. Orig.
del. to JNO. PENN JR, 15 Aug 1808.

Page 456.   -- Jan 1803.   JNO. THOMPSON & wife REBECCA, AC, to BEVERLY
WILLIAMSON, AC, for Ƚ325, 292 acres both sides Stonehouse
Creek, part of tract of HENDRICK ARNOLD. Lines: AARON HIGGINBOTHAM, HOW-
ARD CASH, dec'd., MOSES MARTIN. Granted to JT by BENJ. POWELL by deed
1 Sep 1795.

Page 457.   9 Jun 1802.   DANL. BURFORD, AC, to SAML. ROSE, Lynchburg - del.
to SAML. IRVINE, 15 Oct 1804) for Ƚ347-3-4, Deed of Trust for
debt due SAML. IRVINE - $1.00, 500 acres. Lines: BENJ. RUCKER, RO. H.
ROSE, BOLLING CLARK, DANL. BURFORD SR, ARCHIBALD BURFORD, BEUBEN RUCKER
and where grantor lives. Wit: STERLING CLAIBORNE, WILSON DAVENPORT, WM.
L ADAMS.

Page 458.   25 Oct 1802.   HILL CARTER, AC, to WHITTAKER CARTER, Albemarle,
(Orig. del. 24 Mar 1803 to BENJ. BROWN) - EDWD. CARTER, father
of both parties left will in Spotsylvania Co., devised that AC tract be
sold or divided when sons of age or words to that purport - HILL CARTER
is now 21 and partition made. Lines: Old Church road to New Glasgow; N
side to HILL CARTER and S side to WHITTAKER CARTER. $1.00 for rel. by
HILL in WHITTAKER's part. Wit: TUCKER M. WOODSON, PHIL SLAUGHTER, WM.
ARMISTEAD, EDWD. H. CARTER, BENJ. BROWN, JOEL FRANKLIN, WASH. HILL.

Page 459.   25 Oct 1802.   WHITTAKER CARTER rel. rights in tract of HILL

CARTER as derived in deed above. WHITTAKER of Albemarle.

Page 460.   6 Dec 1802.   ALEX. MOORE & wife ELIZ., Stokes Co, N.C. to LUKE
EMELY, AC, (Orig. del. 21 Feb 1814 to LE) for Ł15, 77 acres N
branches Tye or Cub Creek. Lines: WM. GARLAND, dec'd, GEO. MUNROE's old
line, ISAAC DALTON, and JNO. A.WOLF, J.P.'s and also JAS. RIPPETOE, J.P.
Stokes Co. RO. WILLIAMS, Clk. Order on p.461 to Stokes Co. J.P.'s, 2
Feb 1790, for 77 acres. No names of J.P.'s herein. Rec. AC 17 Jan 1803.

Page 462.   5 Oct 1796.   STEWARD BALLOW & wife HANNAH, AC, to JOS. HIGGIN-
BOTHAM, JR, AC, for Ł130, 340 acres surveyed 7 Apr 1775. Both
sides middle fork Pedlar. Lines: WM. HIGGINBOTHAM, GEO. McDANIEL. Wit:
BENJ. SANDIDGE, BENJ. HIGGINBOTHAM, THOS. DICKINSON. Final proof 17 Jan
1803 by BENJ. SANDIDGE. Page 463, Order to AC J.P.'s to quiz HANNAH, 29
Oct 1802. Done by GEO. DILLARD & SAML. MEREDITH. Rec. 17 Jan 180(?).

Page 463.   2 Sep 1802.   Order to AC J.P.'s WM. WARE, JOSIAH ELLIS & CHAS.
TALIAFERRO, to quiz REBECCAH, wife of JOS. MILSTEAD, as to
deed of 15 Oct 1792, to BETSY SCHOFIELD, widow of WM. SCHOFIELD, for benefit of WM.'s grandchildren. 100 acres. Done by WARE & TALIAFERRO 17 Jan
1803.

Page 464.   16 Oct 1802.   Order to AC J.P.'s SAML. MEREDITH & GEO. DILLARD
to quiz wives of JNO., MOSES, & REUBEN RUCKER; JAS. TINSLEY, &
ARCHELAUS REYNOLDS - NANCY, ELIZ., ELIZ., SUSANNAH, & ELIZ., as to deed
of 11 Oct 1800, to RICH. RUCKER - 97 acres. Certified in return that
NANCY & ELIZ. RUCKER rel. dower rights. 17 Jan 1803.

Page 465.   8 Feb 1803.   SAML. EDMUNDS SR, AC, to SAML. EDMUNDS JR, AC,
3 slaves, Chas., Hannah & Reuben. Wit: WM. DICKSON, JOS. LOV-
ING, JNO. DICKSON, JOS. DICKSON. Orig. del. to SE Jr, 31 Jul 1811.

Page 465.   1 Aug 1802.   JAS. MARTIN, AC, to WM. MARTIN, AC, for Ł50, horse.
Wit: JOSEF MARTIN, AUGUSTINE DAVIS.

Page 466.   14 Dec 1802.   THOS. JOPLING, Kanawaha Co., to JAS. STEVENS, Jr,
AC, Power of Atty. to transact business in my absence. Wit:
THOS. JOPLING, THOS. PENN.

Page 466.   27 Jan 1803.   JAS. BALLINGER, AC, to HENRY HARTLESS, AC, for
Ł42-10, 90 acres both sides Swoping camp creek. Lines: JAS.
SMITH, NEAL CAMPBELL. Wit: PETER P. THORNTON, WM. PRYOR, CHAS. CRAWFORD,
JAS. WARE. Orig. del. to HENRY HARTLESS JR, admr. of HH, dec'd, 29 Mar
1805.

Page 467.   8 Jan 1803.   Order to AC J.P.'s JOS. LOVING & LANDON CABELL,
to quiz SUSANNA, wife of GEORGE VAUGHAN, as to deed to JAS.
TURNER JR, 18 Oct 1802. Rec. 20 Jan 1803.

Page 468.   17 Jan 1803.   WM. CABELL & wife ANNE, AC, to DAVID S. GARLAND,
AC, for Ł1500, 431 acres New Glasgow tract. Devised to WC by
WM. CABELL, dec'd., by will. Lines: LAURENCE CAMPBELL, JAS. FRANKLIN,
Church road, JOSHUA HUDSON, RUSH HUDSON, SAML. MEREDITH, Grantee, WM. S.
CRAWFORD. Exception of 10 ft. square where SMYTH TANDY has child buried
and 1 acre where JAS. FRANKLIN has storehouse; also 1/2 acre of PEACHY
FRANKLIN, 6 acres of JNO. SWANSON dec'd. Wit: S. GARLAND, N. VANSTAVERN,
JAS. B. EDWARDS. Orig. del. to DAVID S. GARLAND, 2 Apr 1803.

Page 469.   15 Feb 1803.   CHAS. TALIAFERRO & wife LUCY, AC, to JNO. TALIA-
FERRO, AC, for Ł134, 67 acres adj. grantee. Lines: the old
road near Puppy Creek; CHAS. TALIAFERRO, Wildcat Branch. Part of tract
to CHAS. TALIAFERRO from CHAS. TALIAFERRO & agreeable to will. Orig. del.
to CT, 9 Nov 1805.

Page 470.   28 Dec 1802.   ISHAM READY & wife ELEANOR, Augusta, to MATT.
HARRIS, SR., AC, for Ł200, 50 acres. Lines: old survey of THOS.
WEST of 29 acres. 170 acres in all. THOS. WEST, dec'd. 120 acres adj.
to make total of 170. Wit: HAWES COLEMAN, JNO. DIGGS JR, HENRY L. HARRIS,
RO. SHIELDS, BENJ. HARRIS.

Page 471. 21 Feb 1803. JAS. BALLINGER, AC, to TABITHA BALLINGER & NICHL. VANSTAVERN, AC, for Ł40, 80 acres Brown Mt. Creek. Pat. 3 Mar 1801. Lines: WM. HARTLESS, PHILIP SMITH.

Page 473. 17 Feb 1803. JAS. LEWIS, CORNELIUS NEVIL, ROWLAND EDMUNDS & Wife ELIZ., CHAS. A. LEWIS & wife SALLY, WM. O. MURRAY & wife LUCY, CLOUGH SHELTON & wife MARY, SAML. EDMUNDS & wife ESTHER, AC, to ZACH. NEVIL, AC, for Ł213-7-6, 142½ acres. Lines: S fork Rockfish, JAS. NEVIL, ZACH. NEVIL, CORNL. NEVIL, PETER LEGRAND, Dutch Creek road. There is doubt whether brothers and sisters of JAS. NEVIL, in case he dies without issue, would not be entitled to tract by virtue of their father's will; they rel. all rights. Wit: HARDIN P. LEWIS, JNO. B. WEST, JNO. STAPLES.

Page 474. 16 Jan 1803. DAVID S. GARLAND, AC, to JNO. SAVAGE JR, AC, for Ł17-14, lot in New Glasgow - S side New Street, No. 9 on plat (not herein) - 35 yds. in front and 70 yds. in back from street. Wit: JAS. C. HIGGINBOTHAM, EDMD. T. COLEMAN, W. HIGGINBOTHAM.

Page 475. 17 Feb 1803. JNO. SAVAGE, JR, AC, to DAVID S. GARLAND, AC, for Ł6-10-7½, and note for Ł17-14 for lot above; also horse named - bought of MORGAN, beds, etc. Wit: as above.

Page 475. 17 Sep 1802. JNO. LONDON, AC, to DAVID S. GARLAND, AC, for Ł21, 70 acres Porrage Creek; N branches of Fluvanna. Lines: JAS. DILLARD, JOS. MAYO, SACKVILLE KING, LONDON, GARLAND. Wit: JOS. BURRUS, EDMD. T. COLEMAN, JOS. DILLARD, SAML. MEREDITH. Orig. del. to DG by WM. G. PENDLETON, 3 Jan 1804.

Page 476. 10 Feb 1803. DAVID S. GARLAND, AC, to SUSANNAH, WM., CHAS., THOS., JNO., BETSY, JESSIE, & POLLY MASSIE, AC, for 5 sh. and love, friendship, and principles of justice, 5 acres S waters Piney. Pat. 24 Mar 1802. Lines: JESSE WRIGHT, JNO. CAMDEN, GEO. CAMPBELL, JNO. MASSIE.

Page 477. 4 Apr 1801. JNO. CAMDEN SR, AC, to HENRY CAMDEN, AC, for Ł115, 220 acres S side Pegg's Creek. Lines: WM. MORRIS, ANTHONY NICE-LY, THOS. VANCE, road crossing Stoney branch, JER. WHITTEN, SAML. NICELY, Widow MORRIS, JNO. SLEDD. Wit: MICAJAH CAMDEN, WM. CAMDEN JR, JABEZ CAMDEN.

Page 478. 19 Sep 1802. CALEB RALLS & wife SUCKEY, AC, JNO. EUBANK & wife PEGGY, AC, to HARDIN HAYNES, AC, for $100, 26 acres surveyed 8 Mar 1798, branches Horsley. Lines: grantor & grantee, JOB CARTER, CHAS. CRAWFORD, PHILIP THURMOND. Wit: THOS. N. EUBANK, WM. BURKS, A.B. WARWICK. Orig. del. to CR 17 Dec 1803.

Page 479. 10 Jul 1803. CHAS. H. CHRISTIAN & wife JANEY, HENRY CHRISTIAN & wife MARY, AC, to CHAS. CHRISTIAN, AC, for Ł55, 372 acres Porrage. Lines: order line of CHRISTIAN & BROWN in Glade near Jumping Branch; POWELL; JNO. CREWS; DATCHESS(?), HENRY TURNER. Wit: DRURY CHRISTIAN, WM. C. CHRISTIAN, WALTER CHRISTIAN JR, SAML. L. CHRISTIAN, CHAS. CHRISTIAN JR.

Page 480. 21 Feb 1803. BURCHER WHITEHEAD & wife NANCY, AC, to HENRY CAMDEN, AC, for Ł500, 152 acres - 2 tracts - both sides Hoof (sic Huff?) Creek. Lines: NOEL JOHNSON, JNO. HIGGINBOTHAM, BENJ. NOEL, JNO. WHITEHEAD, dec'd. 100 acres adj. Lines: JABEZ CAMDEN, WM. CAMDEN SR. JNO. WHITEHEAD died seized of it - except 150 acres sold by commrs. for debt to ALEX. SPIERS JNO. BOWMAN & CO. Wit: JAS. WARE, JAS. GARLAND, DAVID GARLAND. Page 481, order to quiz NANCY, 20 Jul 1801. Ret. by SAML. MEREDITH & DAVID GARLAND, 21 Feb 1803. So written.

Page 482. 22 Dec 1802. Order to AC J.P.'s (sic, but these are not AC J.P.'s) SAML. SCOTT & THOS. W. COCKE - to quiz ANNE, wife of JOS. NICHOLS, as to deed of 20 Sep 1802, to JAS. DAVIS; 197 acres. "Ret. to AC,"2 Feb 1803.

Page 483. 9 Jan 1803. JAS. NEVIL, LEWIS NEVIL, ROLAND EDMUNDS & wife ELIZ., CHAS. A. LEWIS & wife SALLEY, WM. MURRAY & wife LUCY, CLOUGH SHELTON & wife MARY, ZACH. NEVIL, CORNELIUS NEVIL, SAML. EDMUNDS &

394

wife ESTHER, to NELSON ANDERSON for Ł280, 260 acres branches S fork Rockfish. Lines: WM. CABELL, JAS. NEVIL. Wit: JAS. HANSBROUGH, JNO. CRISP,
SAML. DIKSON, DANL. HIGGINBOTHAM, ELISHA PETERS.

Page 485. 21 Sep 1802. DAVID ROSS, surviving partner of merchantile
house of DAVID ROSS & CO, to JAS. FRANKLIN, survivor of trustees - authorized to sell estate of DANL. GAINES. ROSS of -- County, and
FRANKLIN of AC - to JOS. MAYS, Powhatan Co. - Chancery decree of Richmond
2 Mar 1801 - $1.00 - 175 acres Crooked Run. Lines: JOS. HIGGINBOTHAM, JNO.
WYATT, JOS. CREWS - in possession of GEO. DILLARD. Wit: JNO. F. PRICE,
MICAJAH DAVIS, WM. BOOKER, WM. B. JAMES, P. MARTIN, L. BERRY TUCKER, WM.
COLEMAN, JAS. BALLINGER, JNO. FOSTER (as Mayor of Richmond). Cert. by
him as to ROSS. 30 Sep 1802. Rec. AC 21 Feb 1803.

Page 487. 14th day of 5th month, 1790. MICAJAH TERRELL, Gilford Co, NC,
to JNO. LYNCH & ACHILLES DOUGLAS, Campbell Co. (Orig. sent to
LYNCH 19 Jul 1819) for Ł50, 476 acres both sides of Boling Creek. Lines:
HENRY HAYS(?), BOLING, Fluvanna bank, BURFORD. Wit: JOS. ANTHONY, WM. &
ANNE TERRELL. Memo: 25½ acres and enclosing fork of Boling Creek and ½
acres adj. BOLLING excepted. Proved by both TERRELLS 21 Jul 1800 and by
ANTHONY 21 Mar 1803.

Page 488. 9 Oct 1802. DAVID DAVENPORT, Cumberland, to GLOVER DAVENPORT,
now of Powhatan (Orig. sent to GD, 18 Apr 1804) for 5 sh,
DAVID for love of his son, GLOVER, 100 acres out of my 300 acres in AC.
Wit: ALLEN BOWLES, JNO. & WM. HAMBLETON.

Page 489. 15 Apr 1803. WM. MOON, AC, to WM. HILL, AC, for Ł50, 100
acres. Lines: THOS. WILCOX, LIVELY. Wit: WM. WILLIAMS, JNO.
MOON.

Page 490. 10 Mar 1803. JNO. WIATT & wife MINA, AC, to JNO. ADAMS, Rich-
mond, for Ł333, 1/4 of Buckingham tract on James & S--? Rivers.
Pat. to SAML. JORDAN - 4449 acres - grantors claim as JORDAN's heirs. Wit:
GEO. CABELL JR, WILL NORVELL, ANN NORVELL, THOS. WOODROOF, S. WIATT, JAS.
WOODROOF.

Page 491. 11 Apr 1803. SAML. MOSES & wife MARIA , AC, to THOS. JOPLING,
AC, Deed of Trust - debt due JNO. W. KINNEY, admr. de bonis
non of CHAS. FLOYD, dec'd. - execution in hands of shff. - 5 sh. 134
acres on top of Blue Ridge; N fork Rockfish. The whole tract. Lines:
PAULEY, COOPER, SHROPSHIRE et al. Stock, beds, etc. Wit: JAS. BROOKS,
JESSE JOPLING, RO. BROOKS.

Page 492. 29 Jan 1803. EZEKIEL HILL, AC, to REUBEN PENDLETON, AC, Deed
of Trust - debt due THOS. MOORE -(1 Jul 1803, del. to TM) -
$1.00. Slave, Jacob and horse. Wit: THOS., JESSE, & JAS. WOODROOF.

Page 493. 25 Sep 1802. JAS. CLARKE, Town of Staunton, Va., to JACOB
KINNEY of same, (Orig. del. 3 Jan 1805 to RICE MORRIS for J.
STEWART) Deed of Trust - debt due JANE STEWART, Staunton - $1.00 - 300
acres in AC; pat. 17 Jun 1800. Lines: CHAS. BRIDGWATER, JAS. FLACK,
HUDSON MARTIN, SAML. WOODS, MICHL. McMULLAN, Meriwether's Branch. Wit:
RICE MORRIS, JOS. DICKEY, JNO. STEELE. Proved by wits., Tuesday, 1 Mar,
1803. Rec. AC 17 May 1803.

Page 495. 20 Feb 1803. DANL. NORCUTT & wife RACHEL, AC, to WM. MUSE,
AC, for Ł150 - no acres mentioned. Lines: grantee. Orig. sent
to WM. by post, 4 Jul 1803.

Page 496. 7 Jun 1802. SACKVILLE KING & REUBEN NORVELL to JNO. & CHAS.
MUNDY, for Ł1130, Porrige Creek, 801 acres. Lines: RICH. JONES,
JNO. NICHOLS, CHRISTOPHER FLETCHER, ELIAS DEHART's old survey, CHAS.
CHRISTIAN, HENRY TURNER, WM. TURNER. Wit: WM. TURNER, WM. PETTYJOHN,
THOS. WILSON (his mark). Orig. del. to CM 2 Jun 1803.

Page 497. 25 Oct 1802. JESSE MILLS, Green Co., Ky, sued in Charlottesville vs. admrs. of JOSHUA HUDSON, dec'd, and they have sued
in AC; my bdm. in ANDERSON MOSS. Power of Atty. to MOSS to act. Wit:
RO. GARLAND, JACOB KINNEY, THOS. L. McCLELLAND.

Page 498.   14 Apr 1802.   Order to AC J.P.'s JOS. BURRUS & GEO. DILLARD to quiz NANCY FRANKLIN, wife of JAS. as to deed of 18 Jul 1801, to WM. CAMDEN - 3 tracts of 91, 92, and 38 acres. Rec. 20 Jun 1803.

Page 498.   20 Jun 1803.   SAML. ANDERSON, AC, to JNO. ANDERSON, AC, for Ь100, 213 acres which SA bought of JAS. SANDIDGE, AC, Lines: PHILLIPS' last survey, CHAS. STEWART, JAS. ROWSEY, SMITH TANDY.

Page 499.   14 Dec 1802.   JNO. KEY & wife BELINDA, AC, to THOS. MORRIS, AC for Ь100, 100 acres S branches Horsley on Bankston's Mt.; part of 300 acres given WM. HALL by pat. Lines: MOSES HALL, JER. DEAN, NELSON CRAWFORD, JNO. BROWN. Wit: DANL. WARWICK, ABRAM CARTER, THOS. N. EUBANK, HENRY BROWN, THOS. O'NEILL, JNO. RICHESON, JNO. FLOOD.

Page 500.   20 Jun 1803.   RICH. WILSON & wife ANNA, AC, to BENJ. MILES, AC, for Ь31, 62 acres Rutledge Creek. Lines: GAINES' road, SAML. HUCKSTEP, JACOB PEARCE, SPOTSWOOD GARLAND, grantee. Wit: CHAS. CHRISTIAN, SARAH CHRISTIAN, WM. C. CHRISTIAN.

Page 501.   3 Jun 1803.   GEO. MARTIN, AC, to JOSHUA WILLOUGHBY, AC, for Ь20, 20 acres both sides Dutch Creek and part of where MARTIN lives. Lines: RICH. C. POLLARD, JAS. MARTIN, GEO. MARTIN, just above small island. Wit: LANDON CABELL, SPARKS MARTIN, BENJ. MOSBY.

Page 502.   22 Mar 1803.   HENRY WOODS, JAS. WOODS & wife ELIZ., AC, to WM. GALT, Richmond, for Ь1467, 587 acres. Lines: JOEL FRANKLIN, Maple Run, CHAS. CARTER, CARTER's Mill Creek, PATRICK ROSE. WM. ANGUS now lives on tract. Wit: JOEL FRANKLIN, WM. ARMISTEAD, JAS. P. GARLAND. Orig. sent to JOEL FRANKLIN, 10 Aug 1803.

Page 503.   20 Jun 1803.   SALLY ROSE, widow of CHAS. ROSE, late of AC, dec'd, to HENRY & JAS. WOODS for Ь1056, all her interest in 587 acres both sides Maple Run and conveyed to grantees by late husband, 4 Mar 1800. Wit: PATRICK ROSE JR, JNO. JORDAN, CHAS. BLOUNT.

Page 504.   20 Jun 1803.   SALLY ROSE, as above, to ELIZA SCOTT (now WOODS) and ALEX. ROSS for Ь100, 587 acres Indian Creek and Piney. Conveyed to grantees by late husband 4 Mar 1800. Wit: as above.

Page 505.   3 May 1803.   DANL. WARWICK & wife SALLY to GILBERT & KERBY for Ь1900, 500 acres both sides Horsley. Lines: Pedlar road, CALEB RALLS. Wit: JNO. EUBANK JR, WM. S. PRYOR, THOS. N. EUBANK, JESSE HAYNES. Orig. del. to DW, 2 Oct 1803.

Page 506.   17 Aug 1802.   NOAH BLANKENSHIP, Lincoln Co. Ky, Power of Atty. to JNO. WARREN, same county in Ky, to act in AC business. Wit: JNO. DAVIS, MICHL. HEDRICK, and J.P.'s of Lincoln: WM. OUSLEY & WM. PEARL. THOS. MONTGOMERY, Depty. clk. of Lincoln.   Rec. AC, 20 Jun 1803.

Page 507.   29 Jan 1803.   WM. LONG & wife BETSY, Richmond, Va., to JAS. FRANKLIN, AC, for Ь200, 2 acres. Conveyed by BENAMIMI STONE, 4 Oct 1799, to LONG and dated 21 Oct 1799. Wit: S. GARLAND, PL. MARTIN, RO. WINGFIELD, W.L. CRAWFORD, THOS. CREWS.

Page 508.   3 May 1803.   JESSE HAYNES & wife MILLEY to GILBERT & KERBY for Ь10, 9 acres plus. Lines: Wincanton Road, JNO. RICHERSON dec'd. Wit: THOS. N. EUBANK, WM. S. PRYOR, JNO. EUBANK JR, D. WARWICK. Part of tract. Orig. del. to THOS. N. EUBANK, 14 Jun 1808.

Page 509.   11 Apr 1803.   RICH. BALLINGER & wife ELIZ., Garrard Co, Ky, to HENRY CAMDEN, AC, for Ь100, 99 acres S branches S fork Pedlar. Lines: his own. Wit: JNO. HARRISON, SAML. RENSHAW. BENJ. LETCHER, clk. of court. JNO. HARRISON, Pres. justice as to LETCHER. ELIZ. rel. dower, 18 Apr 1803. Rec. AC, 20 Jun 1803.

Page 510.   11 Arp 1803.   RICH. BALLINGER & wife as above, to HENRY CAMDEN, AC, for Ь100, 250 acres. Lines: DAVID MOORE, Nicholson Run, JAS. FRAZIER.   Cert. as above.

Page 511.   1 Mar 1803.   MICAJAH CLARK, AC, to DANL. NORCUTT, AC, for Ь10,

396

9 acres W side Lynch road and joins RAY. Wit: THOS. MERRIT, THOS. WRAY, WM. CLARK.

Page 512.   11 Apr 1803.   ANJUS McDANIEL & wife MARTHA, Garrard Co, Ky, to
            HENRY CAMDEN, AC, for Ł30(?), 110 acres head branches Pedlar
and Richeson Creek. Lines: DAVID MOORE, JAS. FRAZIER, NICHOLSON Run, WM.
TAYLOR. Pat. to grantor. Cert. as for RICH. BALLINGER above p.509f.

Page 513.   12 Nov 1802.   JNO. CLARKE, AC, to JAS. MONTGOMERY, AC, for Ł40,
            100 acres Hatt Creek. Conveyed to both parties by WM. HAMBLE-
TON & wife KEZIAH in 1801. To be paid later. Wit: WM. CLARKE, WM. SHIELDS,
PEGGY CLARK. Orig. del. to JM 8 Oct 1803.

Page 515.   14 Aug 1779.   PATRICK LOWRY & wife RACHEL, Rockbridge, to JAS.
            BAILEY, Rockbridge, for Ł300, 200 acres N side and joining N
fork Pedlar and on side of Long Mt. Pat. to JAS. SMITH, 10 Jul 1766, and
by him conveyed to LOWRY 7 Sep 1767. Lines: JOS. HIGGINBOTHAM. Wit: DAVID
TAYLOR, MARY TAYLOR, DAVID EDMONDS JR, JNO. WELCH, JNO. LUSK. Proved by
WELCH & JNO. --erased-- LUSK, 6 Mar 1780, and by EDMUNDS, 20 Jun 1803.

Page 516.   15 Apr 1803.   JAS. BAILEY & wife ANNEY, Rockbridge, to DAVID
            BAILEY, AC, for $1000, tract above and so described. Wit: JNO.
WHITTON, HIRAM BYERS, SALLY & PATSEY BAILEY, WM. BAILEY, DAVID EDMUNDS.
(Were these folks kin to DAVID BAILEY who shows in Charlotte in 1769?
His son, HOLCOMB D. BAILEY, married MARTHA DRINKARD in Pr. Edwd. and HDB
finally settled at Holt's Summit in Calloway Co, Mo., and was my great-
great grandfather.   HDB had son, WM.HENRY BAILEY, my great-grandfather,
who married MARTHA JOHNSON in Montgomery Co, Tenn, and they came to Graves Co. Ky. There was some relationship between ROGER COCKE BAILEY and
PETER COCKE BAILEY to DAVID of CHARLOTTE, but what was it? BFD)

Page 517.   2 Jun 1802.   W. HIGGINBOTHAM Power of Atty to JNO. WARE & JNO.
            TALIAFERRO to act as to will of JNO. SANDIDGE. Wit: WM. TALIA-
FERRO, BENJ. HIGGINBOTHAM, CHAS. TALIAFERRO.

Page 518.   20 Jun 1803.   THOS. LUMPKIN & wife ANN, Bedford, to JABEZ CAM-
            DEN, AC, - no acres - (Orig. sent to LUMPKIN 16 Sep 1803) It
is set forth that JNO. WHITEHEAD, AC, owed SPIERS BOWMAN & Co. at Amherst
store and Deed of Trust on land and a slave of rec. in AC. Sold by Ct.
decree by commrs, DAVID S. GARLAND & GEO. DILLARD & RO. WALKER. LUMPKIN
bought tract for Ł150.

Page 519.   6 Jan 1803.   WM. TUCKER & wife NANCY, AC, to DANL. TUCKER, AC,
            interest in estate of DRURY TUCKER - Ł30-5-3. Wit: JAS.
BALLINGER, BURCHER WHITEHEAD, ISHAM JOHNSON, LINDSEY COLEMAN JR.

Page 519.   25 Feb 1803.   See page 473 (Deed Book I) for long list of
            grantors - NEVILS et al - to CHAS. YOUNG, Buckingham, for
Ł250-18, 324 acres S fork Rockfish. Part of land inherited by JAS. NEVIL
from father, JAS. Lines: PETER LEGRAND, the fork of road, WM. CABELL,
NELSON ANDERSON, Dutch Creek. Wit: as in previous deed. Margin: "Should
have been recorded at June Court, 1804, but by mistake was not. Orig.
del. to WM. H. DIGGS, 20 Aug 1804.

Page 521.   20 Feb 1803.   HENRY ROBINSON, AC, to MICAJAH CLARK, for Ł500,
            88 acres Lynch road. Lines: DANL. NORCUTT, WM. GUTHRIE, BOLL-
ING CLARKE, MEHONE. Wit: THOS. MERRITT, JOS. BURRUS, WM. TURNER, JESSE
BECK, DANL. NORCUTT.

Page 522.   11 Nov 1802.   GEO. DILLARD, AC, to DAVID S. GARLAND & JNO.
            CAMM, AC, Deed of Trust. DILLARD & BURRUS partners - debt due
RO. GORDON & Co., Richmond; WM. GALT, Richmond, WM. McKINSIE & Co.,
Richmond - DILLARD does so to protect BURRUS - $1.00 - 435 acres where
DILLARD lives and bought from WM. MAYO. Wit: S. GARLAND, RO. WALKER,
GIDEON RUCKER.

Page 524.   20 Jun 1803.   LANDON CABELL & wife JUDITH, AC, to HECTOR CA-
            BELL, AC, for Ł50, fishery in Fluvanna River; devised to LC by
WM. CABELL. Orig. del. to LC, 18 Jun 1803.

Page 525. 18 Jun 1803. Same NEVIL group - see I-473 - to JAS. MURPHY,
AC, (Orig. del. to him 22 Jul 1803) Deed of Trust to RO. RIVES
& Co. on 319 acres devised to LEWIS NEVIL by father, JAS. NEVIL. Heirs
have moved somewhat: WM. MURRAY & wife LUCY, Buckinhgam, CLOUGH SHELTON &
wife MOLLY, of South Carolina. It is set forth that ELIZ., SALLY, ESTHER,
LUCY, & NELLY (MOLLY?) are daughters of JAS. NEVIL, dec'd. Debt of Ł550
Deed of Trust for 5 sh. Wit: JESSE JOPLING, WM. HANSARD, EDWIN H. WARE,
WM. F. CARTER, RO. MOORE, JNO. JOHNSON, JAS. VIGUS JR.

Page 528. 10 Feb 1803. RICH. C. POLLARD, AC, to ELIAS HAMLETT, AC, for
Ł150, 414 acres headwaters Dutch Creek. Lines: GEORGE MARTIN,
the road. Orig. del. to RP, 4 Aug 1803.

Page 529. 10 Feb 1803. RICH. C. POLLARD, AC, to JNO. WRIGHT, AC, for
Ł70, 164 acres Dutch Creek. Margin as to del. as above.

Page 531. 10 Feb 1803. RICH. C. POLLARD, AC, to JNO. MELTON,AC, for Ł60,
119 acres Dutch Creek. Lines: slong a road. Wit: GEO. W. VAR-
NUM, HENRY REED, DANL. CAMRON. Margin as above.

Page 533. 9 Nov 1802. CHAS. LEWIS & wife SALLY, AC, - SALLY is daughter
of JAMES NEVIL, late of AC - to ZACH. NEVIL - SALLY at death
of mother, MARY NEVIL, will be entitled to her share - mother has life
estate - also by deaths of any brothers and sisters. LEWIS executes·Deed
of Trust for wife and children - now or future - apart from him. When
child or children reach 21 or get married. Wit: HENLY DRUMMOND, CORNL.
NEVIL, POLLY HENDRICKS, SHARLOTT HENDRICKS, JESSE HENDRICKS.

Page 534. 15 Mar 1803. CHAS. TALIAFERRO, AC, to JNO. CAMPBELL, AC, for
Ł50, 2 tracts. 1) 78 acres S side and joining N fork Tye.
Lines: EDMD. COFFEY. 2) 98 acres surveyed 1 Feb 1797 - N side of N fork
Tye. Lines: Pannell's Branch. Wit: WM. JACOBS, DANL. JACOBS, EDMD. COFFEY,
D. McDONALD. Orig. del. to JC, 23 Jan 1807.

Page 536. 14 Apr 1803. JNO. B. TRENT & wife PATSEY, Rockbridge, to JAS.
WILLS, AC, for Ł900, 400 acres N side Fluvanna and joining.
Pat. to RICH. BURK, 16 Aug 1756. Lines: mouth of John's Creek, Burks'
Creek, Cedar Branch. Wit: NELSON ANDERSON, SAML. SPENCER, LAURENCE WILLS,
DAVID W. CRAWFORD. Orig. del. to JW 14 Oct 1803.

Page 537. 10(20?) Jun 1803. JAS. MARTIN & wife REBECCA, AC, to JAS.
WILLS, AC, (Orig. del. to JW 10 Oct 1806) 209½ acres exchanged
out of 368 acres. Lines: ABRAHAM WARWICK, HECTOR CABELL. Conveyed to JM
by JAS. WILLS & wife MILLEY - 10 sh. both sides Dutch Creek. Lines:
SPARKS MARTIN, JOSHUA WILLOUGHBY, GEO. MARTIN, RICH. C. POLLARD.

Page 538. 20 Jun 1803. JAS. WILLS, AC, to JAS. MARTIN, AC, exchange of
209½ acres on Dutch; lines as above - 10 sh. 368 acres. Formerly that of ABRAHAM WARWICK and bought of WM. BATES by WILLS.

Page 539. 17 Jan 1803. JNO. HAWKINS, AC, to WM. C. JOHNSON, AC, (Orig.
del. to WJ 24 Nov 1803) Deed of Trust - horse, beds, stock.
Wit: WILSON DAVENPORT, WILL LOVING.

Page 539. 5 Oct 1801. EDWD. CARTER & wife LUCY, Albemarle, to CHAS.
CARTER, Culpeper, for Ł1200. Lines: JOEL FRANKLIN on E, JNO.
SMITH on W, CHAS. ROSE on N, main road, HILL & WHITTAKER CARTER on S.
Includes grant of 160 acres conveyed heretofore by EDWD. CARTER to CHAS.
CARTER. Lines: CARTER's Mill Run, Maple Run, JOEL FRANKLIN. Surveyed by
JAS. HIGGINBOTHAM for CHAS. CARTER, 26 Apr 1800. Wit: WM. W. HENNING, C.
JOUITT, THOS. C. FLETCHER. Order to quiz LUCY, p.540f, 7 Apr 1802. Done
in Albemarle by G. CARR & W. WARDLAW. Rec. AC 20 Jun 1803.

Page 542. 17 Dec 1802. CHAS. CARTER & wife BETTY, Culpeper, to LINDSEY
COLEMAN, AC, (Orig. del. 16 Mar 1805 to LC) for $7630, 763
acres Buffalo. Lines: S side road not far from CARTER's Old Mill on Mill
Creek; JNO. SMITH, HUGH CAMPBELL, EDWD. CARTER (formerly WHITTAKER CARTER)
Proved in Culpeper, 20 Dec 1802. Page 543, order to J.P.'s of Culpeper to
quiz BETTY. Done 8 Jan 1803 by RO. SLAUGHTER & WILL BROADDUS. Rec. AC
20 Jun 1803.

Page 543. 23 Feb 1803. WM. ANGUS, AC, to JAS. ANGUS - blank sum - to
          secure his son and for love; on a bond. $1.00 - 3 slaves; 2
mulattos who are children of one of the 3; stock, pine chest, walnut
chest, carpenter & joiner tools.

Page 545. 4 Apr 1803. Order to AC J.P.'s NELSON CRAWFORD & CHAS. TALIA-
          FERRO, to quiz REBECCA, wife of JOS. MILSTEAD, as to deed of
25 Aug 1802 to DANL. SHRADER - 107 acres. Rec. 15 Jun 1803.

Page 546. 20 Jun 1803. SAML. DAY, AC, to DANL. & SOLOMON DAY, AC, for
          Ƚ80, 250 acres; part of tract bought by PETER DAY and JNO.
CRITTENDEN. Lines: JAS. DAVIS, JOS. NICHOLS on N; N branches Stovall Ck.
on W., JESSE BECK & BARTLETT EADES on E. Wit: HENRY SMITH, WILEY CAMP-
BELL, ELIJAH MORAN. Orig. del. to SD, 6 Oct 1819.

Page 546. 20 Jun 1803. ABRAM CARTER & wife MARYAN, AC, to EDWD TAYLOR,
          for Ƚ40, 100 acres Horsley and S branches Buffalo. Orig. del.
to AC, 20 Jan 1812.

Page 547. 17 Apr 1803. WM. SPENCER & STEPHEN WATTS, AC, to ARCHEY ROW-
          SEY, for Ƚ60, 122 acres. Lines: SAML. ANDERSON, ALLEN BLAIR,
STEPHEN WATTS. Wit: ARCHELAUS MAYS, JNO. ANDERSON, GEO. ENNIX. Orig. del.
to AR, 9 Jan 1804.

Page 549. 19 Jun 1802. THOS. WAUGH & wife FRANCES, Bedford, to JAS.
          WAUGH, AC, for Ƚ100, 100 acres on James River - one half of
tract lately occupied by THOS. WAUGH. Wit: HENRY BROWN, DAVID BAILEY, WM.
PRYOR, RICH. ELLIS, THOS. WILLS, JNO. ELLIS.

Page 550. 19 Jun 1802. Same parties - Ƚ200 paid by JAS. WAUGH for 280
          acres on James. Lines: NICHL. DAVIES, NATHL. DAVIS, opposite
upper end of NICHL. DAVIES' island. Wit: as above. Surveyed 11 May 1774.

Page 551. 26 Apr 1803. JNO. CLARK, AC, to DAVID & JAS. GARLAND, (Orig.
          del. to DG 22 Jul 1833)-75 interest in Hat Creek tract bought
by JC & JAS. MONTGOMERY of WM. HAMBLETON - to sell and apply on debt -
Deed of Trust - also farm gear etc. Wit: A. MORGAN, EDMD. T. COLEMAN,
RO. COLEMAN, THOS. ALDRIDGE.

Page 552. 18 Dec 1801. WM. H. CABELL, AC, to WM., JOS., & LANDON CABELL,
          AC (Orig. del. to WHC, 28 Oct 1803) for love of the three
children of his much beloved wife ELIZ., who hath lately departed this
life and only issue of their two bodies and for their support - 10 sh.
All slaves which WHC got by marriage to ELIZ.; also any other slaves due
at death of MARGARET CABELL, mother of ELIZ. - very long list of slaves
(7 in one family alone) to be divided when NICHL. CABELL is 21 and to
deliver to LOUISA CABELL her share at 21 or marriage; also to ABRAHAM
CABELL when 21. Sons are trustees, if WM. dies. Slaves may be sold, if
money needed. WM. H. is to hold and hire until time of delivery to each
child - if NICHL. or ABRAHAM die before 21, same as to LOUISA; to husbands or wives or children, if any. ABRAHAM is to deliver to the 3 a
tract of 800 acres devised to ELIZ. CABELL by her father, WM. CABELL.
Wit: RO. RIVES, NELSON ANDERSON, JESSE HIGGINBOTHAM, JNO. HIGGINBOTHAM
JR., FLEMING TURNER. Ack. by WHC, 20 Jun 1803.

Page 560. 19 Mar 1803. JNO. PHILLIPS, Overseer of AC, to WM. ARMISTEAD,
          AC, Deed of Trust. Debt due DAVID & JAS. GARLAND - $1.00 beds,
etc. Wit: EDMD. COLEMAN, JAS. WOODS. Orig. del. to DAVID S. GARLAND by
H. HIGGINBOTHAM 21 Jun 1805.

Page 561. 10 Mar 1803. JOS. DAVENPORT, AC, to JNO. CAMM, AC, Deed of
          Trust - debt due to GARLANDS above - $1.00 - slaves. Wit:
EDMD. TO. COLEMAN, WM. G. PENDLETON, WM. CAMDEN. Orig. del. to JAS.
GARLAND 9 Jun 1805.

Page 563. 15 Jun 1803. SAML. EDMUNDS, Sr, AC, to SAML. EDMUNDS, Jr, AC,
          for love and 5 sh, 150 acres, part of tract where MINOS
WRIGHT lives on Tye and both sides Great Branch. Lines: YOUNG LANDRUM
(now JOS. LOVING). Wit: JNO. DICKSON, JOS. DICKIE, JOS. LOVING, WM. DICK-
SON. Orig. del. to SE Jr, 31 Jul 1811.

Page 364. 12 Jan 1803. JNO. COLEM AC, to THOS. LUMPKIN, NATHAN REID, & BENJ. MOORE, Bedford & JOS. SHELTON, AC, Deed of Trust. Debt due WILLS, Warminster mct. and WILLIS WILLS & WM. HARRIS - HARRIS on bond in Court of AC to ELIJAH STONE - $1.00. 6 slaves. Wit: WM. HARRIS, WM. DOUGLAS, WM. KIDD.

Page 365. 18 Jun 1803. JAS. H. BURTON, AC, to JOS. SHELTON, WM. WRIGHT & ALEX. McALEXANDER, AC, trustees for erecting houses - for worship by any society. Lines: JOS. SHELTON, toward the Mt. Wit: WM. HARRIS, HENRY DAWSON, MATT. HARRIS, JNO. MELTON.

Page 566. 22 Jun 1803. NICHL. FORTUNE, AC, to ANDREW HART, Albemarle, Deed of Trust- judgment secured by HART vs. FORTUNE - $1.00 - household items; debt due from JAS. WILLS & Mrs. ELIZ. LOVING. Wit: JAS. STEVENS JR, THOS. PENN. Orig. del. to JAS. WILLS, 26 Oct 1811.

Page 567. 2 Mar 1803. JOHN S.(T) WILSFORD & wife ELIZ., AC, to HENRY & JAS. WOODS, AC, for L60, 226 acres - old pat. surveyed. Lines: S branch Little Indian Creek. Also 20 acres adj. on Little Thresher. Lines: JAS. YELTON. Wit: JNO. CAMM, THOS. WOODROOF, WM. EVANS. Orig. del. to HW 5 Jul 1806.

Page 569. 3 Jun 1803. CHAS. CHRISTIAN & wife LUCY, AC, to CHRISTOPHER FLETCHER, AC, for L15, 11 acres Porrage. Lines: JNO. CREWS, himself. Wit: WALTER CHRISTIAN JR, JAS. & SAML. CHRISTIAN.

Page 569. 18 Jul 1803. CHRISTOPHER FLETCHER & wife PHEABE, AC, to MATT. STANTON, AC, for L91, 91 acres Rockey Creek. Lines: JNO. PAD- GETT, JNO. CASHWELL, ANDREW MONROE, RO. PEARCE and where STANTON lives. Wit: CHAS. CHRISTIAN.

Page 570. 18 Jul 1803. MATT. STANTON & wife NANCY, AC, to CHRISTOPHER FLETCHER, AC, for L91, 39 acres Porrige. Lines: JNO. MONDAY, AARON DEHART's old line, CHAS. CHRISTIAN, grantee, HENRY CHRISTIAN's old line. Bought by STANTON of legatees of AARON DEHART, dec'd. Wit: CHAS. CHRISTIAN.

Page 571. 11 Dec 1802. WM. GILES, AC, to THOS. NASH, AC, for L9, bay mare. Wit: HUDSON MARTIN, WM. H. MOSBY.

Page 572. 4 Jul 1803. THOS. MERRITT JR, AC, to PHILIP JOHNSON, AC, and ARCHIBALD ROBERTSON, Campbell Co, Deed of Trust - (Orig. del. to A. MAYS 1 Sep 1804) Debt due to WM. BROWN & Co., Lynchburg store - $1.00 - slave BOB, about 30, stock, etc. Wit: ARCHELAUS MAYS, NATHL. OFFUTT, WM. IRVINE.

Page 573. 13 Mar 1802. Order to AC J.P.'s to quiz MARTHA, wife of HENRY CHRISTIAN, as to deed of 15 Jul 1801, to CHRISTOPHER FLETCHER - 56 acres. Rec. 18 Jul 1803. REUBEN NORVELL & GEO. DILLARD, JP's.

Page 574. 26 May 1803. RICH. C. POLLARD, AC, to RICH. POWELL, AC, for L446-7 and 5 sh, 309 acres head branches Dutch Creek. Deed of Trust . Lines: JAS. MARTIN, JNO. MELTON, estate of Dr. JAS. HOPKINS. Residue of a tract. Wit: WM. H. CABELL, HEN HOLLOWAY, ELISHA MEREDITH.

Page 575. 24 Jun 1803. PETER MARTIN, AC, to ARCHIBALD ROBERTSON, Camp- bell Co., GEO. DILLARD, PHILIP JOHNSON, and SPOTSWOOD GARLAND, AC, Deed of Trust - debt due WM. BROWN & Co. at Albemarle store.(Orig. del. to ARCHELAUS MAYS, 17 Apr 1804) 7 slaves. Wit: ARCHELAUS MAYS, JNO. L. McGEHEE, NATHL. OFFUTT.

Page 576. 19 Oct 1802. JOS. SHELTON & WM. H. DIGGS, AC, to JNO. ALFORD, AC, - PHILIP RYAN owed JNO. ALFORD and about 6 Jun 1801, made Deed of Trust to grantors above on 200 acres and where RYAN then lived. Lines: Col. JNO. ROSE, DAVID CLARKSON, LEROY DAINGERFIELD. Sold Monday, 1 Mar at ACH - opposite tavern door (then occupied by REUBEN BATES) - JNO. ALFORD bought tract for $261.00.

Page 578. 20 Jun 1803. THOS. LANDRUM & wife DOROTHY, AC, to WM. HOLLAN- SWORTH, AC, for L220, 100 acres Naked Creek, N branch Tye. Part of tract of WM. MATTHEWS. Lines: SAML. J. CABELL, branch in road from CH to ABRAHAM WARWICK, JAS. WITT. Orig. del. to SPOTSWOOD GARLAND, 16 Jan 1815.

Page 579.   15 Jan 1803.   JAS. LUCAS, AC, to WM. WALKER, Albemarle, Deed of Trust - $1.00. Stock. Wit: JAS. WALKER, DABNEY BRYANT, SAML. LUCAS.

Page 580.   12 Mar 1803.   Order to Campbell Co. J.P.'s THOS. HUMPHREY & SAML. SCOTT, to quiz MARY, wife of JNO. H. GOODWIN, as to deed of & Aug 1796, to MICHL. COALTER & PHILIP JOHNSON - 170 acres. Rec. 22 Mar 1803.

Page 581.   1 Dec 1801.   JOB CARTER & wife JUDITH, Lancaster Co., to NICHL. VANSTAVERN, AC, for L2000, 220 acres N side and joining Fluvanna; both sides of Cawshaw Creek. Lines: Rockrow Creek. Proved in Lancaster 22 Feb 1803, JAS. TOWLES, Clk.

Page 581.   15 Aug 1800.   Order to --- Co. J.P.'s to quiz CATH., wife of PETER WHITINGHILL, as to deed of 25 Sep 1799, to SAML. NICELY. 200 acres. County in Kentucky is not set forth, but J.P.'s were JNO. T. COAGIN & JESSE HALL. No date is given. Rec. AC, 19 Sep 1803. (I knew a Miss WHITTINGHILL at Cadiz, Ky, when I was pastor. She was a home demonstration agent and attended our church. She was from Falls of Rough. BFD)

Page 582.   17 Sep 1803.   ISABELL HARTLESS - my husband departed this life on 9 July last, intestate. I am in low state of health and unable to admr. Requested that my husband's four sons be appointed: HENRY, JAS., WM. & RICH. HARTLESS. Wit: BENJ. HIGGINBOTHAM, WM. SLEDD, JOS. MILSTEAD, NICHL. VANSTAVERN.(This does not show in will book items, but the sons show as qualifying. BFD)

Page 583.   24 Aug 1803.   WM. S. CRAWFORD, AC, to RO. S. ROSE, Stafford Co. Deed of Trust - 1004 acres Indian Creek. Lines: WM. GALT, HENRY & JAS. WOODS who bought it of PATRICK & JNO. ROSE, JR, WC got by conveyance from RO. S. ROSE on equal date. Wit: JO. CAMM, S. GARLAND, JOEL FRANKLIN.

Page 584.   4 Mar 1803.   RO. HARDY & wife MARY, AC, to DAVID WITT, AC, for L880, 2 tracts. 1) where RH lives - 140 acres. Lines: grantee, JONATHAN BRIDGWATER, WM. SMALL, JOS. ROBERTS. 2) 80 acres. Lines: WM. SMALL, THOS. FITZPATRICK, MICHL. WOODS. Wit: WM. SMALL, WM. WOOD, BURGESS WITT.

Page 585.   25 Jul 1803.   JNO. MORRIS & wife MARY, AC, to ZACH. MORRIS, AC, for L30, 50 acres Hickory Creek of Rockfish. Part of tract pat. to JM 1798. Lines: JNO. FARRAR, Chimney Hill Ridge. Wit: THOS. PUGH, JNO. PUGH, PETER H. MORRIS. Orig. del. to ZM 27 Feb 1813.

Page 586.   18 Sep 1803.   JOICE PARROCK, AC, sister of WM. HARPER, late of Wilks Co, Ga., and at present a widow and femme sole, Power of Atty. to my brother, HENRY HARPER, AC, to receive my share of WILLIAM's estate. Wit: DANL. McDONALD. Orig. del. to HH, 24 Sep 1803.

Page 586.   16 Aug 1803.   JAS. PENN, exr. of GABL. PENN, Campbell Co, to HENRY HOLLOWAY, - under will - $2000, 385 acres N side and joining Buffalo. Lines: WM. PHILLIPS, WM. CABELL JR, Higginbotham Mill Creek, JACOB GIBSON, SMYTH TANDY, N bank Buffalo at mouth of Higginbotham Mill Creek. Wit: EDMD. PENN, JOS. C. HIGGINBOTHAM, JNO. PIGG.

Page 588.   10 Sep 1803.   NICHL. VANSTAVERN & wife CATEY, AC, to TABITHA BALLINGER, AC, for L22, 80 acres both sides Brown Mt. Creek. Pat. to JOS. BALLINGER at Richmond, 3 Mar 1801 - with all mills etc. Conveyed by JAS. BALLINGER to TABITHA BALLINGER and VANSTAVERN. Wit: ELIZ. CAMPBELL, PHILY WATERFIELD, WM. WILLSON, JOS. CHILDRESS. (Was this ELIZ. CAMPBELL the natural daughter of NEIL CAMPBELL & TABITHA BALLOWE who is named in CAMPBELL's will? BFD)

Page 589.   15 Sep 1803.   JOS. NICHOLS & wife ANNA, Campbell, to JAS. DAVIS, AC, for L186, 186 acres both sides N fork Stovall.

Lines: grantee, DANL. DAY, REUBEN NORVELL, ELIAS WILLS, BARTLETT EADES.
Wit: SAML. IRVINE, MADISON J. HILL, CHAS. YELTON, THOS. W. COCKE.

Page 590. 18 Aug 1803. JNO. LAIN, AC, to JNO. HIGGINBOTHAM, AC, Deed of
           Trust - debt due to BROWN MURPHY & Co. - 5 sh. Stock & furni-
ture; poplar boat marked on each side "JOHN LAIN" Bible etc. Wit: CHAS.
L. BARRET, JAS. HANSBROUGH, SAML. BLAIR(?).

Page 591. 15 Aug 1803. HENRY REED, AC, to DANL. HIGGINBOTHAM, AC, for
           Ł34, Deed of Trust - debt due BROWN RIVES & Co. 5 sh. House-
hold goods. Wit: CHAS. L. BARRETT, JAS. GREGORY, JNO. EDMONDS SR,

Page 593. 11 Apr 1803. MICHL. STONEHAWKER & wife ANNE, AC, to JAS.
           BOLLING, AC, for $612. Lines: near the old graveyard. Wit:
REUBEN NORVELL, WM. KNIGHT, WM. BURFORD, JNO. BOLLING. Orig. del. to JB
3 Nov 1803.

Page 593. 7 Mar 1803. DAVID TRAILE, New Market, AC, to JNO. HIGGINBO-
           THAM, AC, Deed of Trust - 5 sh. debt due BROWN MURPHY & Co.
Negress and 2 children - one a yellow boy about 1. Wit: D.W. CRAWFORD,
THOS. BIBB SR, JAS. HANSBROUGH, CHAS. L. BARRETT, RO. KENNEDY. Orig. del.
to SAML. TURNER per order of JAS. MURPHY, 12 Jun 1805.

Page 595. 12 Aug 1803. JOS. AMOS, AC, to JNO. CAMM, AC, Deed of Trust
           Debt due GARLANDS - $1.00. 2 Negro girls, Hannah & Mary. Wit:
THOS. ALDRIDGE, WALKER SAUNDERS, JAS. P. GARLAND. Orig. del. to DAVID
GARLAND by WM. G. PENDLETON, 3 Jan 1804.

Page 596. 18 Jul 1803. PLEASANT MARTIN, AC, to SPOTSWOOD, GARLAND, AC,
           Deed of Trust - debt due GARLANDS - $1.00 - beds, slaves etc.
Wit: JAS. B. EDWARDS, JAS. P. GARLAND, WM. G. PENDLETON.

Page 597. 13 Sep 1803. SHEROD BUGG, AC, to JNO. CAMM, AC., Deed of
           Trust. Debt due GARLANDS - $1.00. Slaves, stock, furniture.
Wit: WM. G. PENDLETON, J.B. GARLAND.

Page 598. 2 Jul 1803. WM. HARRIS, AC, to DANL. HIGGINBOTHAM, AC, Deed
           of Trust - debt due RIVES MURPHY & Co. - 5 sh. 260 acres where
HARRIS lives. Lines: WM. BLAINE, JNO. ROBERTS(?) dec'd, JNO. HARRIS
(Green Mt.); stock. Wit: BALDWIN BAIN, WM. TEAS, WM. B. HARE, NELSON
ANDERSON. Orig. del. to J. MURPHY, 8 Jan 1806.

Page 599. 30 Oct 1800. JNO. HALL, AC, to WM. WARWICK, AC, Deed of Trust
           debt due DANL. WARWICK. 6 sh. 3 adj. tracts and where JH
lives. 432 acres, stock, etc. Wit: CHAS. L. BARRET, JNO. HAYSLIP, JNO.
B. BURK(?), JNO. BARKE. Final proof of BARRET, 19 Sep 1803.

Page 601. 18 Sep 1803. MOSES MARTIN, AC, & wife ELIZ., to DAN. McDONALD,
           AC, for Ł370, 185 acres Cub Creek. Part of tract. Lines: JNO.
JACOBS, old grant line, PETER RIPPETOE, road through Dock Gap.

Page 602. 20 Apr 1803. JAS. TURNER & wife REBECCAH, AC, to JOS. SMITH,
           AC, - this day exchanged 15 acres on S side Rockfish. Lines:
TURNER, near Dutch Creek, THOS. JOPLING's old line. Part of 20 acres sur-
veyed for MILES RAILY 1 Aug 1772, by pat. Wit: JAS. TURNER JR, ALEX.
ROBERTS, WM. MARTIN.

Page 603. 26 Sep 1802. JNO. WILSON, Wane(sic) Co. Ky, (really Wayne) to
           WM. WILSON, AC, for Ł100, 244 acres Pedlar. Lines: ANGUS McDON-
ALD, S branch Brown Creek Mt. Creek, NEIL CAMPBELL. Wit: JOS. HIGGINBO-
THAM JR, JAS. SMITH, WM. HIGGINBOTHAM, WALTER FRAZIER.

Page 605. 9 Jul 1803. PHILIP DAVIS, AC, to JAS. P. GARLAND, AC, Deed of
           Trust - $1.00 - 175 acres head branches Davis Creek. Lines:
JNO. THOMPSON, JAS. THOMPSON, WM. B. HARE, stock. Wit: WM. HILL JR, JESSE
JOPLING, WM. RYAN.

Page 606. 4 Apr 1803. WM. CLARK, AC, to DANL. McDONALD - Deed of Trust-
           debt to GARLANDS - 5 sh. tobacco on plantation where WC lives;
corn, rye, gun, stock, books, etc. Wit: LANDON CABELL, WM. LEE HARRIS,

JESSE JOPLING.

Page 607.   17 Sep 1803.   TOBIAS, a free black man, Power of Atty. to
                DANL. McDONALD to settle all accts. for me. Ack. by TOBIAS
in open court, 19 Sep 1803.

Page 608.   24 Aug 1803.   RO. S. ROSE & wife JANE L, Stafford, to WM. S.
                CRAWFORD, AC, for Ł2484, 1004 acres Indian Creek. Lines: WM.
GALT; late that of HENRY & JAS. WOODS, who bought of JNO. & PAT. ROSE JR.
Part of tract obtained by RR from father, PATRICK ROSE, AC, & originally
that of Rev. RO. ROSE, dec'd., and given by him to his son, HENRY ROSE,
dec'd. Wit: JNO. CAMM, S. GARLAND, JOEL FRANKLIN. Orig. del. to WC,Nov--.

Page 609.   24 Aug 1803.   SAML. ROSE, AC, seized of part of 1872 acres
                devised by my father, HUGH ROSE and to me by Chancery commrs.
of AC #5 - 200 acres to LANDON CABELL - Power of Atty. to lease or sell.
Wit: S. GARLAND, THOS. O'NEILL, SEATON M. PENN, JAS. B. EDWARDS, DANL.
TUCKER. Orig. del. to CABELL by G.A. ROSE, 21 Sep 1803.

Page 610.   29 Jul 1803.   JOS. SMITH & wife PATIENCE, AC, to WM. H. MURPHY,
                AC, for Ł240, 240 acres both sides Rockfish & Dutch. Lines:
BENDICK LANHAM, JNO. SHEPHERD, JAS. TURNER, SAML. S. SCRUGGS. Wit: HUDSON
MARTIN, HENRY EMMERSON, RICH. C. POLLARD.

Page 611.   29 Jul 1803.   JOS. SMITH & wife PATIENCE, AC, to JAS. TURNER,
                AC, for Ł15, 14 acres Dutch. Lines: WM. MARTIN, WM. MOSBY,
JAS. TURNER, HENRY EMMERSON. Part of tract. Wit: as above.

Page 611.   18 May 1803.   LEWIS McWAINE, AC, to DANL. HIGGINBOTHAM, AC,
                Deed of Trust. 5 sh. debt to BROWN RIVES & Co, suit March
Ct. last. Stock. Wit: ALEX. B. ROSE, WADDY THOMPSON, SEYMOUR POWELL,
MARK LIVELY. Orig. del. to J. MURPHY, 12 Apr 1808.

Page 613.   19 Sep 1803.   DANL. ALLEN & wife MILLY, Rockbridge Co, to WM.
                CAMPBELL, AC, 5 sh. 36¾ acres N branches Piney. Lines: DAVID
PARROCK dec'd, GEO. HIGHT. The deed reads WM. CAMPBELL & wife SALLY,
but her name is scratched. Wit: JAS. CAMPBELL, JAS. RANSEY(?). WM. RAMSEY.

Page 614.   15 Sep 1803.   DANL. McDONALD, AC, to JAS. DURHAM, AC, for Ł25,
                65 acres S side and joining N fork Tye. Lines: THOS. DURHAM,
ZACH. TALIAFERRO.

Page 615.   12 Aug 1803.   SAML. MOSES, AC, to JNO. FITZPATRICK, AC, Deed
                of Trust - $1.00. stock, gun etc. Wit: JNO. BARNETT, JAS.
WOODS, WM. FITZPATRICK.

Page 616.   29 Jul 1803.   JOS. SMITH & wife PATIENCE, AC, to WM. MARTIN,
                AC, for Ł10, 15 acres Dutch Creek. Lines: grantee, TURNER's
fence, MOSEBY (part of same tract) SAML. S. SCRUGGS. Wit: HUDSON MARTIN,
HENRY EMMERSON, RICH. C. POLLARD.

Page 617.   17 Oct 1803.   JAS. TURNER, AC, to BENJ. DAWSON, Kentucky,
                Power of Atty. to receive any accts. due TURNER in Ky., debts
or lands. Orig. del. to JT, 5 Nov 1803.

Page 618.   22 Nov 1803.   THOS. HAWKINS, & wife ELIZ., to JOHN LOVING JR
                for Ł450, 200 acres head branches Rucker's Run. Lines: JNO.
THOMPSON, WM. H. DIGGES, MATT. HARRIS. Wit: JNO. THOMPSON, JAS. WILLS,
JAS. POWELL, NATHL. OFFUTT.

Page 619.   28 Apr 1803.   JACOB PHILLIPS, AC, to THOS. N. EUBANK, Deed of
                Trust - debt due DANL. WARWICK - 5 sh. 142 acres S fork Buf-
falo and where I live; also 4 tracts on N fork Buffalo - 499 acres. Wit:
JNO. BURKS, WM. PRYOR, HENRY BROWN, JNO. EUBANK JR, BENJ. TALIAFERRO,
CHAS. TALIAFERRO JR, JNO. TALIAFERRO. Orig. del. to CHAS. TALIAFERRO JR,
12 Apr 1804.

Page 620.   26 Jun 1802.   ELIAS WILLS SR, Fluvanna, to WM. THURMOND, AC,
                "Should have been recorded with those of Oct. Ct., 1802, but
thro mistake was not" (Short spelling is thus shown not to be a new thing

- note thro. BFD) for Ł250, 3 tracts Horsley branches. 1)BURFORD's entry,
38 acres adj. PHILIP THURMOND. 2) adjoins - 121 acres. Lines: DAVID CRAW-
FORD on E, by No.3 on S, PHILIP THURMOND on W; formerly known as BENJ.
WALLISES' place and now that of WM. THURMOND. 3) 84 acres adj. Lines:
DAVID CRAWFORD, WM. THURMOND, PHILIP THURMOND. Note: 2nd is ambiguous
and reads "now in possession of WM. THURMOND". Wit: I. WILLS, JNO. TOM-
KINS, LITTLEBERRY WEAVER, JNO. SNEAD. JNO. TIMBERLAKE, Fluvanna Clk.
Rec. AC 18 Oct 1802.

Page 621. 16 May 1803. JNO. MARTIN, dec'd, late of AC - intestate -
owned 360 acres on Meriwether's branch, of Tye. Lines: Col.
JNO. COLES, SHEROD MARTIN, AZARIAH MARTIN, CHAS. BRIDGWATER, STEPHEN
MARTIN, dec'd, GIDEON MARTIN. Widow, SARAH, as since married JNO. DIN-
WIDDIE - life dower sold by JNO. DINWIDDIE & wife SARAH, to OBEDIAH MAR-
TIN (heir of JNO. MARTIN) Ł200 - all interest in tract. Wit: HUDSON MAR-
TIN, HUDSON MARTIN JR, NATHL. HARLOW JR. Page 622, order to quiz SARAH,
20 May 1803. Done by NATHAN CRAWFORD & HUDSON MARTIN. Rec. Oct 17 1803.

Page 622. 21 Mar 1803. WM. FITZPATRICK & wife REBECCA, AC, to THOS.
FITZPATRICK, son of JNO - AC - Ł29-5, 9 and 3/4 acres Rockfish.
Lines: grantor, grantee, THOS. WARE.

Page 623. 14 Oct 1803. STEPHEN WATTS & wife MARTHA, AC, to LAVENDER
LONDON, AC, for Ł48, 80 acres Tye. Lines: ALEX. CHISNALL,
JNO. LOVING.

Page 624. 17 Oct 1803. HENRY PEYTON & wife ELIZ., AC, to JESSE BLAND,
AC, for Ł50, 87 acres Puppie Creek. Lines: CHAS. TALIAFERRO,
WM. CLEMENTS. Part of tract bequeathed to ELIZ. PEYTON by will of THOS.
POWELL, 18 Mar 1783. Orig. del. to CHAS. TALIAFERRO 10 Jun 1808.

Page 624. 1 Oct 1803. HENRY PEYTON & wife ELIZ, AC, to ASHCRAFT ROACH,
AC, for Ł60, 100 acres N side and joining Fluvanna. Lines:
below mouth of Hooker's Branch, grantee.

Page 625. 17 Oct 1803. WM. LEE, AC, to JAS. LEE, AC, for Ł186, 124 ac.
Lines: JOS. DAWSON, GEO. McDANIEL TINSLEY, JAMES' separate
tract.

Page 625. 17 Oct 1803. WM. LEE, AC, to RICH. WHITEHEAD, AC, for Ł316,
105½ acres. Lines: on the river. Orig. sent to RW; no date.

Page 626. 8 Oct 1803. WM. HANSFORD, AC, to JOSIAH ALLEY, AC, for Ł10,
small tract of 15 poles. Wit: RALPH MITCHELL, JAS. JONES, JNO.
MERRITT, HENRY TENNISON, WM. ISBELL.

Page 626. 4 Oct 1803. JNO. HARDING & wife PHEBE, AC, to WM. BALL, AC,
for Ł300, 300 acres both sides S fork Rockfish. Lines: Cold
Branch, WM. JOHNSON, JESSE JOPLING, WM. BALL, DAVID ENOX, dec'd, JNO.
SNIDER, EDWD. HARDING, RALPH JOPLING, CORNL. THOMAS. Deeded to JNO. HARD-
ING by his brother, EDWD. HARDING. Wit: JNO. HIGGINBOTHAM, JR, JESSE
FIDLER, SAML. & JAS. HANSBROUGH. Orig. del. to JAS. P. GARLAND, 1817.

Page 627. 27 Jul 1803. LUCY ROBINSON, AC, to HENRY TENNISON, AC, for
Ł45, 38 acres. Wit: ISAIAH ALLEY, SIMON ROBINSON, RALPH MIT-
CHELL, JOS. ROBINSON, JAS. JONES.

Page 628. 19 Sep 1803. WM. CAMPBELL & wife SARAH, AC, to JNO. PAINTER,
AC, for 5 sh, 36 acres N branch Piney. Lines: DAVID PARROCK,
dec'd, GEO. HIGHT.

Page 628. 18 May 1803. Order to Stafford Co. J.P.'s THOS. MOUNTJOY &
JNO. PRIMM; also JNO. NICHOLAS, to quiz JANE L. ROSE, wife of
RO. S. ROSE, as to deed of 6 Dec 1802, to JNO. CAMDEN - 260 acres. Done,
10 Aug 1803; Rec. AC 17 Oct 1803.

Page 629. 28 Nov 1801. Order to AC J.P.'s NATHAN CRAWFORD & HUDSON
MARTIN to quiz SUSANNA CAREY, wife of DANL., as to deed to
JAS. BROOKS, 15 Oct 1801. 144 acres. Ret. 2 Jul 1803.

404

Page 630.   29 Arp 1803.   HUGH PAUL, Augusta, to JACOB KINNEY, Staunton,
             Deed of Trust to secure debt to ALEX. WASSON, Rockingham- in
favor of GEO. WILLS, assignee of WASSON in Staunton Dist. Court - $1.00.
2 tracts. 1) 230 acres whereon JNO. LANGFORD lives. 2) 200 acres whereon
JNO. VINES lives and sold to PAUL by JAS. BROOKS. Wit: CHAS. PAGE, WM.
BRECKENRIDGE, JNO. COALTEN, JOHN McARTHUR.

Page 631.   16 Sep 1803.   Order to Bedford J.P.'s ISAAC & JAS. OTEY, to
             quiz ANN, wife of THOS. LUMPKIN, as to deed of 20 Jun 1803, to
JABEZ CAMDEN.   Rec. AC 17 Oct 1803.

Page 632.   15 Oct 1802.   DAVID S. GARLAND & wife JANE, AC, to THOS. AL-
             DRIDGE, AC, for $150, 2 acres and 3 poles. Part of tract.
Lines: WM. CABELL.

Page 633.   10 Aug 1803.   Order to AC J.P.'s JOEL FRANKLIN & JNO. WARWICK
             to quiz ELIZ., wife of JAS. WOODS, as to deed by husband and
HENRY WOODS to WM. GALT, 22 Mar 1803 - 587 acres. Done and rec. 17 Oct
1803. Orig. del. to WG, 4 May 1812.

Page 633.   18 Sep 1798.   AUGUSTINE SMITH, AC, to IRVING GALT & Co., Deed
             of Trust. 5 sh. 200 acres Rockfish. Lines: CHISWELL's old line.
Wit: PL. MARTIN, RALPH MARTIN, HENRY BIBB, JNO. MASSIE. Final proof, 18
Oct 1803, by DAVID S. GARLAND who swore that he saw MASSIE & RALPH
MARTIN sign; both now dead. Orig. del. to JNO. CAMM 28 Jun 1811.

Page 634.   15 Oct 1803.   HUGH McCABE & wife ELIZ, AC, to RICH. TINSLEY,
             AC, for Ł100, 206 acres Otter Creek. Lines: Terrapin Creek,
Rattle Snake Branch, N bank Fluvanna, mouth of Cedar Branch, CORNL.
THOMAS, WALCHE's Spring.

Page 634.   16 Sep 1803.   JNO. CARTWRIGHT, AC, to ABRAM CARTER, AC, Deed
             of Trust to secure WM. EVANS & THOS. ALDRIDGE - $1.00. Beds,
furniture, utensils etc. Wit: JAS. P. GARLAND, WM. G. PENDLETON, WM.
ENGLAND, CHAS. BOWLES. Orig. del. to WE, 16 Nov 1805.

Page 635.   9 Aug 1802.   Order to Culpeper J.P.'s RO. SLAUGHTER & WM.
             BROADDUS, to quiz BETTY, wife of CHAS. CARTER, as to deed of
15 Apr 1796, to DANL. TUCKER. 115 acres. Rec. AC, 19 Oct 1803.

Page 636.   14 Aug 1800.   HENRY LANDON DAVIES, Bedford, to THOS. MOORE, AC,
             for Ł143, 159 acres. Lines: Both of them; DAVIES lower ferry
road; RICH. POWELL, JOS. MAGANN. Wit: THOS. WOODROOF, JAS. GARLAND,
LEWIS DAWSON, REUBEN PENDLETON, JESSE WOODROOF. Final proof by JESSE
WOODROOF 18 Jan 1802.

Page 637.   13 Nov 1801.   WM. BARNETT & wife JANE, AC, to MICHL. WOODS,
             Albemarle, for Ł1250, 470 acres Rockfish. Wit: JOS. MONTGOM-
ERY, SAML. REID, RO. DINWIDDIE, SAML. BRIDGWATER. Final proof 15 Feb
1802, by REID, DINWIDDIE & BRIDGWATER.

End of Deed Book I

405

AMHERST COUNTY, VIRGINIA DEED BOOK K

DEDICATION

It is only fitting that this particular deed book should be dedicated to
my college fraternity, KAPPA ALPHA (Southern Order). Alpha chapter was
organized at Washington and Lee University, 21 Dec 1865. The charter
members were JAMES WARD WOOD, WILLIAM NELSON SCOTT, STANHOPE McCLELLAND
SCOTT, and WILLIAM ARCHIBALD WALSH. National headquarters at Lexington,
Virginia, were dedicated in our centennial year, 1965. I was initiated
into Beta Delta chapter at Georgetown College in my native Kentucky,
April 17, 1926. I later affiliated with Kappa chapter, Mercer University,
Macon, Georgia, where I received my degree in 1929. I attended Washington and Lee law school for one year before going into the ministry, and
attended chapter meetings of Alpha and ate at the house a good bit of the
time.

My brother, BERNARD BYRD DAVIS, was initiated at Kappa and transferred to
Alpha. He is now a Commissioner on Court of Appeals in Kentucky. My
brother-in-law, CLARENCE MILLER one-time Assistant Secretary of Agriculture, Shelbyville, Kentucky, was initiated by the Theta chapter at University of Kentucky. My oldest son, Capt. JOHN FULTON DAVIS, Regular Army,
was also initiated at Theta.

My third son, THURMAN BLANTON DAVIS, was initiated into Sigma Nu at the
University of Kentucky. The three fraternities, Kappa Alpha, Sigma Nu,
and Alpha Tau Omega were all founded in Lexington, at Washington and Lee,
or Virginia Military Institute.

                                        BAILEY FULTON DAVIS
                                        1966

Note: Deed Book K follows Deed Book I, as there is no Deed Book J.

Page 1.   15 Jul 1803. Order to AC J.P.'s WILL LOVING & WM. B. HARE, to
           quiz JUDITH CABELL, wife of LANDON CABELL, as to deed of 20
Jun 1803, to HECTOR CABELL - fishery - Woods' Island. Done and recorded
19 Dec 1803.

Page 1.   4 Jan 1802. Order to same J.P.'s as above to quiz JUDITH, as
           above, deed of 19 Oct 1802, to LUCINDA & EMILY ROSE - 200
acres, part of a tract. Done and recorded as above.

Page 2.   28 Oct 1803. Order to Buckingham County J.P.'s DAVID PATTESON
           & A. DIBRELL, to quiz SALLY WARWICK, wife of DANL. WARWICK, as
to deed of 3 May 1803, to GILBERT KIRBY - 500 acres. Done 14 Dec 1803;
rec. in AC. Margin: Del. to THOS. N. EUBANK, 17 (?) Aug 1807.

Page 2.   19 Dec 1803. NATHL. WADE & wife MARY, AC, to JNO. FARIS for
           Ŀ180, 225 acres on Rockfish. Lines: JNO. SNIDER.

Page 3.   5 Dec 1803. BENJ. WATTS & wife FANNY, AC, to FRANCIS SLAUGH-
           TER, Culpeper Co, for Ŀ550, 300 acres on Tye River. Lines:
JNO. LOVING, rolling road, main road, LAVENDER LONDON. Orig. del. to FS
12 Oct 1811. Wit: JNO. LOVING, STEPHEN WATTS, BETSY CHRISTAIN, PATSY LAIN.

Page 4.   14 May 1802. Order to Augusta J.P.'s JAS. COCKRAN & JNO. FACK-
           LER, to quiz FANNY, wife of CHRISTIAN SHIRLEY, as to deed of
15 Jan 1802 to CHAS. SMITH; 289 acres. Rec. in AC 19 Dec 1803.

Page 5.   5 Dec 1803. GEO. HYLTON, AC , to JNO. HAGER, AC, for Ŀ110,
           110 acres S side Buffalo Ridge. Lines: JAS. PETER, S fork
Owens' Creek. Wit: SAML. ARRINGTON, RO. VIA, JORDAN ARRINGTON, JNO. HAGER
JR. Orig. del. to JH, 27 May 1805.

Page 5.   19 Jul 1803.   CORNL. MURRIL, AC, for love of Methodist Church,
             to JNO. SHEPHERD, WM. BREEDLOVE, & BENJ. PAYNE. Lines: PAYNE,
the road. Part of tract where CM lives. Wit: THOS. MURRILL, WM. PAYNE,
REUBEN MITCHELL. Orig. del. to J.G. PAMPLIN(?), 16 Jan 1856. (Note:
Those who have studied previous deed books will realize that these delivery items are noted on the margins of the deeds and may bear much later
dates. BFD)

Page 6.   9 Dec 1803.   ALEX. CHISNAL, AC, to LAVENDER LONDON for love
             and $1.00 - all of my estate except slave, Gilbert, whom I
intend to liberate; mare, small mulatto girl slave, Patto(Rittlo?); bed,
furniture. Then he conveys to ONEY LAIN and heirs - remaining property
of 150 acres. Lines: WM. SPENCER, STEPHEN WATTS, ACHILLES WRIGHT.   He
then conveys slaves to ONEY LAIN. LAVENDER LONDON is to support CHISNAL
for rest of life. Wit: SAML. EDMUNDS SR & JR, THOS. ALFORD, SILVANUS
BRIENT JR.

Page 7.   1 Nov 1803.   THOS. DAVIS, Lincoln Co, Ky, Power of Atty. from
             JEAN DAVIS, widow of same county, to HOLEMAN JOPLING, AC, for
Ь100, 250 acres S side and joining Dancing Creek. Pat. 20 Jun 1780. Lines:
JOS. CABELL, RO. PAYTON. Wit: JAS., BENNETT, & THOS. JOPLING.

Page 8.   21 Nov 1803.   MARY GILLESPIE to children of late husband,
             GEORGE, Ь300 for her interest in his estate. Wit: PHILLIP
GOOCH, WM. & JAS. WARE. (We have dealt with this family of GILLESPIE
before. I have pointed out that GEO. was ancestor of my wife, MILDRED
MILLER DAVIS, and she descends from WM. GILLESPIE, son of GEO., who married a daughter of JOSHUA HUDSON's here in 1777. WM. & wife went to our
native Kentucky. The children of GEORGE GILLESPIE are all by his unknown
wife, MARY----, who was living here in 1775 when she and GEO. sold land
which is of record in Albemarle. I feel sure that she was a MOORE, but
can't establish it. This second MARY - in this item - was MARY FARIS and
she married GEO. GILLESPIE in Louisa - see Dr. MALCOLM HARRIS' Louisa
data. She was a widow and two of her gilrs married in AC to sons of
GEO. GILLESPIE. BFD)

Page 8.   8 Oct 1803.   PHILIP GOOCH, AC, to DAVID S. GARLAND, AC, Deed
             of Trust - GOOCH has sold WM. WARE a slave, James, and title
is vested in children of GOOCH: LUCY F. & WM. B. GOOCH. GOOCH puts lien
upon 400 acres on W side of Buffalo - "The Folly". Lines: LINDSEY COLE-
MAN, JNO. CHRISTIAN, WM. DILLARD. "When children are of age, they will
make title." (We have mentioned "The Folly" before - quite a place for
gambling, racing, and fighting. It was located just east of the present
Wayside Park on U.S. highway 60 to the east of Amherst on Richmond road.)
Wit: WALKER SAUNDERS, HUDSON M. GARLAND, WALTER LEAKE.

Page 8.   6 Oct 1803.   WM. WARE, NELSON CRAWFORD, & JOS. HIGGINBOTHAM
             JR, exrs. of JACOB SMITH, and his children JAS., WIATT, RICH.,
MARY, & CLARY SMITH to WM. SANDIDGE, AC, for Ь1250, 570 acres both sides
Buffalo. Lines: AARON HIGGINBOTHAM dec'd, JNO. DUNCAN, EDMD. POWELL, old
line, survey made for JACOB SMITH, dec'd, mouth of a lane, BENJ. TALIA-
FERRO, the main road, JNO. CLARKSON, WM. TALIAFERRO, WM. SANDIDGE, RO.
CASH, dec'd, Throasher's Creek. It was where JACOB SMITH lived at time
of death and got from his brother, JAS. SMITH, RICH. & EDMD. POWELL -
save what he gave the widow of WM. SMITH & WILLIAM's children - WM. is
deceased - and what he sold to BENJ. TALIAFERRO. The will directed sale
and prodeeds to go the five children above named. Wit: JNO. SMITH, PHILIP
SMITH JR, WM. TALIAFERRO, JACOB PHILLIPS JR. Memo: half acre reserved
for a cemetery. Orig. del. to "WM. SANDIDGE's son, 28 Feb 1822."

Page 10.   13 Nov 1803.   WM. G. ALLEN, AC, to DANL. HIGGINBOTHAM, AC,
             Deed of Trust - to secure debt due RIVES MURPHY & Co. and
WILLIS WILLS - 5 sh. Three slaves. Wit: NORVELL SPENCER, SAML. HANS-
BROUGH, TERISHA TURNER, WM. F. CARTER. Orig. del. to WILLIS WILLS, "exr.
of JAMES", 8 Jul 1806.

Page 11.   22 Nov 1803.   PATRICK ROSE JR & wife JANE, to WM. B. HARE for
             $1500, 244 acres - Allen's Creek, branch of Piney. Lines: CHAS.
IRVING dec'd; claimed by JABEZ DAVIS, ALEX. MARR. Grantor got it from
his dec'd. father, CHAS. ROSE, by AC deed. Also 15 acres bought from

JABEZ DAVIS. Wit: WM. LEE HARRIS, RO. GARLAND, S. GARLAND, JNO. CAMM, JAS. B. EDWARDS. Orig. del. to WBH, 4 Jul 1804.

Page 11.   19 Nov 1803.   Order to AC J.P.'s JAS. WOODS & JAS. MONTGOMERY
            to quiz ELIZ., wife of JAS. SHIELDS, as to deed of 24 Sep
1801, to WM. SANDIDGE. Rec. 19 Dec 1803. Orig. del. or sent to WS, 3
Feb 1823.

Page 12.   20 Sep 1803.   Order to Stafford Co. J.P.'s, JNO. NICHOLAS &
            E. MASON, to quiz JANE L., wife of RO. S. ROSE, as to deed of
24 Aug 1803, to WM. S. CRAWFORD - 1004 acres. Rec. in AC 19 Dec 1803.
Orig. del. to WSC, 15 Aug 1805.

Page 13.   17 Oct 1803.   BETSY GANDY does not intend to admr. estate of
            ELIAS GANDY. Wit: JNO. DIXON, WM. SETTLES, WM. EDMUNDS.

Page 13.   2 Jul 1803.   Order to Campbell Co. J.P.'s JAS. MILLER & DANL.
            B. PERROW, to quiz ANN, wife of SACKVILLE KING; POLLY, wife of
REUBEN NORVELL, as to deed of 7 Jun 1802, to JNO. & CHAS. MUNDY - 801
acres. Done: 7 Jul 1803; rec. AC 16 Jan 1804.

Page 14.   14 Jan 1804.   JONATHAN BRIDGWATER, AC, to NATHL. BRIDGWATER
            for $2000, 300 acres on Rockfish. Lines: THOS. FITZPATRICK,
WM. SMALL, grantor, DAVID WITT, estate of CLOUGH SHELTON, SAML. BRIDGWAT-
ER. Wit: JAS., CLAYTON, & JOS. MONTGOMERY, WM. DOUGLASS, HOLEMAN JOPLING,
WM. LEE HARRIS.

Page 14.   2 Jun 1803.   PHILIP LOCKHARD to THOS. N. EUBANK - Deed of
            Trust to secure debt due WM. GALT, assignee of DANL. WARWICK,
$1.00 - a mare - 9 last spring. Wit: HENRY BROWN, JNO. DUNCAN, JNO. FLOOD.

Page 15.   1 Dec 1803.   FRANCIS SLAUGHTER, Culpeper Co, to BENJ. WATTS,
            AC, Deed of Trust - tract between Tye and Buffalo. Lines: WM.
SPENCER, STEPHEN WATTS, JNO. LOVING, LAVENDER LONDON. 4 years to pay.
Wit: STEPHEN WATTS, BETSY CHRISTIAN, PATSY LAINE. Orig. del. to BW,
1 Jan 1808.

Page 16.   22 Oct 1803.   BENJ. JOHNSON JR, & wife NANCY, AC, to LEROY
            PAMPLIN, AC, for Ł104, 69 acres S branches Owen Creek; part of
HENLEY DRUMMOND tract. Lines: GEO. HYLTON & formerly that of JNO. LOFTON
(LAWSON?). Wit: WM. PAMPLIN, SAML. FRANKLIN, JAS. & JNO. PAMPLIN.

Page 16.   22 Dec 1802.   Order to AC J.P.'s JNO. HORSLEY & JNO. CHRISTIAN,
            to quiz MARY, wife of SAML. ARRINGTON, as to deed of 8 Oct
1799, to BENJ. JOHNSON - 69 acres. Rec. 17 Sep 1803.

Page 17.   10 Jan 1804.   THOS. GRISSOM SR, AC, in trust to RICH. HARDWICK,
            JESSE CLEMENTS, & RO. GRISSOM, by subscription of 25 Jun 1803,
Ł50, one fourth of an acre on N side of Harris - for gospel preaching.
Wit: RANDOLPH CASH, TINSLEY RUCKER, THOS. GRISSOM JR, FRANCIS CLEMMENS.

Page 18.   10 Aug 1803.   GEO. HYLTON, AC, to RO. HORSLEY, AC, for Ł58,
            58 acres Elk Island creek. Part of 217 acres. Lines: JAS. PAM-
PLIN, WM. HORSLEY. Wit: SAML. FRANKLIN, LEROY PAMPLIN, RO. VIA.

Page 18.   20 Sep 1803.   RO. HORSLEY, AC, to JAS. PAMPLIN, AC, for Ł64,
            58 acres Elk Island. Part of 270 acres. Lines: JAS. PAMPLIN,
WM. HORSLEY. Wit: MICAJAH PENDLETON, MARY C. PENDLETON, JUDITH HORSLEY.

Page 19.   28 Oct 1803.   HENRY CAMPBELL, AC, to WM. H. CABELL & DAVID S.
            GARLAND, Deed of Trust - debt due WM. B. HARE. 5 sh. 476 acres
Castlr Creek; bought from HARE on same date. Part of tract of NICHL. CA-
BELL, dec'd, and where HARE now has a plantation. Wit: N. SPENCER, H.M.
GARLAND, PHIL JOHNSON, D. WARWICK.

Page 21.   14 Jan 1804.   ARCHIBALD ROWSEY & wife ELIZ., AC, to ALLEN
            BLAIR, AC, for Ł200, 122 acres Buffalo branches. Lines: SAML.
ANDERSON, grantee, STEPHEN WATTS - to BLAIR's tract bought of JAS. ROWSEY.

Page 22.   16 Jan 1804.   MOSES HALL & wife MARY, AC, to CHARLES BROOKS for Ł10, 25 acres Horsley Creek. Lines: EDWD. WARE.

Page 22.   16 Jan 1804.   WM. HIGGINBOTHAM & wife CATH. L., AC, to JNO.
PATTERSON, Rockbridge Co, for Ł15, 70 acres branches S and
middle fork Pedlar. Lines: THOS. STATON, JOS. HIGGINBOTHAM JR, top of the
mt., JOS. HIGGINBOTHAM SR. Pat. to grantor, 12 May 1783. Wit: JNO.
FRASER, WALTER FRASER, SAML. McCLAIN. Orig. del. to JP, 1808.

Page 23.   4 Nov 1803.   JESSE PROFFITT, AC, to DANL. HIGGINBOTHAM, AC,
Deed of Trust, debt due JNO. & ROWLAND PROFFITT, admrs. of
DAVID PROFFITT, dec'd.   5 sh.   180 acres S waters Rucker's Run. Lines:
JNO. EDMUNDS, SR, HECTOR CABELL, TERISHA TURNER, stock, furniture etc.
Wit: SAML. BLAIR, JAS. HANSBROUGH, JOS. LOVING, DAVID P. BRYANT. Orig.
del. to JH, 2 Jan 1805.

Page 24.   6 Jan 1804.   JOS. WHITE, AC, to JNO. HIGGINBOTHAM, JR, AC,for
Ł275-5-9, Deed of Trust; debt due BROWN MURPHY & CO. 5 sh.
232 acres Naked Creek. Lines: CONYERS WHITE SR, dec'd, ROWLAND EDMUNDS,
AMBROSE CAMPBELL SR, ELIJAH MAYS, WM. H. DIGGES, CONYERS WHITE JR, dec'd.
Where JW lives; slave and ages also. Wit: WAML. BLAIR, JOS. LOVING, JAS.
HANSBROUGH, WM. A HOWARD. Orig. del. to J. MURPHY 21 Jan 1805.

Page 25.   31 Oct 1803.   WM. LAINE SR, AC, to DANL. HIGGINBOTHAM, AC,
Deed of Trust - debt due JNO. & ROWLAND PROFFITT, admrs. of
DAVID PROFFITT. 5 sh.   4 slaves. Wit: DAVID P. BRYANT, SAML. BLAIR, WM.
SHANER. Orig. del. to DH, 12 Jan 1805.

Page 26.   25 Nov 1803.   ABRAHAM CARTER & wife MARY, AC, to DAVID BURKS
JR, for $100 and --- 203 acres N side Banks' Mt. and joining
Pedlar. Lines: THOMAS MANICE(?), JER. DEAN, JNO. SANDIDGE, WM. CARTER
dec'd, BENJ. HIGGINBOTHAM, PETER CARTER, JNO. BROWN. Wit: THOS. SALE,
MANNICE(?) ROBERTS, PETER CARTER. Orig. del. to DB, 26 Sep 1825.

Page 27.   29 Dec 1803.   DAVID & JAS. GARLAND, AC, to ZACH., GEO., &
HARRY ANN MITCHELL or survivors - stock and furniture now at
JNO. MITCHELL's - to the three children in trust and their mother, BETSY
MITCHELL, for support. Wit: DEMUND HOLEMAN.

Page 27.   14 Nov 1803.   AUSTIN SMITH & wife NANCY, to BYRD SKINNER for
Ł200, 138 acres N branches Tye. Lines: WM. ALFORD, THOS. AL-
FORD, THOS. BIBB, ELIJAH MAYS, WM. H. DIGGES, JOS. LOVING. Wit: WM. H.
DIGGES, JOS. LOVING, JNO. ALFORD, THOS. ALFORD.

Page 28.   29 Oct 1803.   RO. & MARGARET WRIGHT, wife, AC, to JNO. MELTON,
AC, for Ł91-2-6, 15 acres. Wit: JNO. OWENS, JAS. GENTRY, JAS.
WRIGHT, LEVY OWENS. Orig. del. to JNO. MELTON, exr. of JNO. MELTON, 24
Sep 1840.

Page 29.   23 Nov 1803.   GEO. MENG, AC, to DANL. HIGGINBOTHAM, AC, Deed
of Trust on debt to RIVES MURPHY & Co.   5 sh.   Houses and lots
in Warminster and where MENG lives - bought of RO. RIVES; slaves. WILLIS
WHITE, RO. MOSELY JR, & Dr. DAVID PATTESON to be umpires in dispute with
RO. RIVES. Wit: WM. LEE HARRIS, D.W. CRAWFORD, WM. H. CABELL, WALTER
LEAKE, WM. L. CRAWFORD. Orig. del. 16 Jul 1804 to JAS. MURPHY.

Page 30.   30 Dec 1803.   SUSANNA GILLILAND, AC, to JAS. MARR, AC, for Ł85,
75 acres both sides S fork Porrige Creek. Lines: THOS. WILCOX,
grantee. Wit: JNO. MONROE, ISAAC SCOTT, WM. KNIGHT, MADISON HILL. Orig.
del. to JM, 3 Nov 1817.

Page 31.   30 Dec 1803.   WM. HILL & wife NANCY, AC, to SUSANNA GILLILAND,
AC, for Ł85, 100 acres. Lines: THOS. WILCOX, LIVELY. Wit: WM.
KNIGHT, JNO. MONROE, ISAAC SCOTT, JAS. MARR.

Page 32.   23 Oct 1802.   JOS. HIGGINBOTHAM SR, AC, to BENJ. HIGGINBOTHAM,
AC, for Ł300, 235 acres S branches Buffalo. Lines: JOS. HIG-
GINBOTHAM, JOS. HIGGINBOTHAM JR, Spring road. Wit: HENRY BALLINGER, BENJ.
SANDIDGE, JACOB PHILLIPS, SR. Final proof by PHILLIPS, 16 Jan 1804.

Page 33.   23 Oct 1802.   JOS. HIGGINBOTHAM SR, AC, to JOS. HIGGINBOTHAM

JR, AC, for 5 sh, 117 acres S side and joining Buffalo. Lines: grantor; part of 300 acres of grantor. Wit. and proof as deed above.

Page 34.   23 Oct 1802. JOS. HIGGINBOTHAM SR, AC, to SUSANNA HIGGINBO-
THAM, AC, for 5 sh, 258 acres Horsley Creek. Lines: WM. CARTER, dec'd. Wit. and proof as above.

Page 35.   27 Apr 1803. JONATHAN BRIDGWATER, WM. FITZPATRICK & wife REBECCA, AC, to SAML. BRIDGWATER, AC, for 555 (no pounds or dollars given) 216 acres Rockfish. Laid off from larger tract of WM's; 100 acres a part of where JONATHAN lives and laid off for SAML. Lines: CLOUGH SHELTON's estate, WM. FITZPATRICK, SAML. BRIDGWATER, JONATHAN BRIDGWATER. Wit: JAMES GENTRY, MATT. WHITE, WM. DOUGLAS. Orig. del. to JOS. BURRUS, 6 May 1806.

Page 36.   31 Oct 1803. JNO. & ROWLAND PROFFITT, admrs. of DAVID PROF-
FITT, dec'd, AC, to JESSE PROFFITT, AC, for Ŀ188, 180 acres. Lines: JNO. EDMUNDS, HECTOR CABELL, a spring branch, TERISHA TURNER. Wit: SAML. BLAIR, ZACH. WHITE, DANL. HIGGINBOTHAM, WM. LAIN SR.

Page 37.   16 Jan 1804. JOS. BURRUS, AC, to WM. PENN JR, AC, for Ŀ500, 342 acres both sides S fork Huff Creek. Lines: BRAXTON's patent; JAS. LIVELY, crossing the road. Ack. by BURRUS, 16 Jan 1804.

Page 38.   7 Jan 1804. JAS. BERRY & wife JANE, Augusta Co, to JOS. STRICKLAND, AC, for Ŀ85, 160 acres, tract of estate of JAS. SHIELDS, dec'd, and claimed by BERRY & wife by descent by JANE by AC decree. Wit: WM. B. JACOBS, SAML. REID, MONTGOMERY(sic), HAWES COLEMAN, DAVID JACOBS, JAS. WOODS. Orig. del. to RO. SHIELDS, 16 Dec 1804.

Page 39.   28 Jul 1803. CHAS. & WALTER CHRISTIAN, AC, to JACOB PEARCE, AC, for Ŀ140, 6 acres Rockey Creek. Lines: ISAIAH ATKINSON, JINKINS OXLEY, RICH. WILSON, grantee, WALTER CHRISTIAN. Signed also by SARAH, wife of CHAS. CHRISTIAN, and MARTHA, wife of WALTER CHRISTIAN. Wit: JNO. CHRISTIAN(B), HENRY CHRISTIAN, WM. S.(L) CHRISTIAN. Orig. del. to JP, 11 Nov 1805. (Note: I have previously noted that (B) with JNO. CHRISTIAN signified that he was the one who lived on Buffalo. BFD)

Page 39.   20 Feb 1804. PHILIP SMITH, AC, to JNO. WARE, AC, for $50, 164 acres on Pedlar. Lines: grantee, JOS. BALLINGER, THOS. BARRETT, N bank Brown Mt. Creek.

Page 40.   18 Feb 1804. JOS. ROBERTS & wife SALLY, AC, to his son, JNO. ROBERTS, AC, for love and 5 sh, 400 acres Davis Creek. Lines: WM. HARRIS, WM. BLAIN, JOS. SHELTON, ALEX. McALEXANDER, grantor. Wit: JOS. ROBERTS, ANN ROBERTS, THOS. FITZPATRICK, WM. THORP. Orig. del. to ALEX. ROBERTS, 3 Mar 1806.

Page 41.   26 Jan 1804. JOS. ROBERTS & wife SALLY, as above, to son, ALEX. ROBERTS, AC, for love and 5 sh, 326 acres Rockfish. Lines: JAS. TURNER SR, NATHAN HARRIS, JNO. MATTHEWS, REUBEN T. MITCHELL. Wit: JOS. C. ROBERTS, WM. KIDD, WM. THORP, ANN ROBERTS. Del. as above.

Page 42.   4 Aug 1803. HANNAH & NANCY DUNNON, AC, to THOS. V. GOODRICH, AC. NANCY, with her mother's approval, apprentices herself until 18 to GOODRICH - which will be 1 Sep 1813, to learn art of spinning, weaving, and housework (done about house - by a woman). Her clothing and food will be furnished by GOODRICH and at end of time he is to pay her Ŀ3-10 and "one strong sute(sic) of cloathes(sic) suitable for an apprentice. He will "learn her to read, in case such a thing can be, in his own family - knowing that her colour will exclude her from going to school". Wit: BENJ. TALIAFERRO, THOS. GOODRICH, JUBAL WARYS(?), JOS. HOUSEWRIGHT.

Page 43.   13 Feb 1804. ZACH. FORTUNE & wife ELIZ., AC, to JNO. FORTUNE, AC, for Ŀ50, 70 acres both sides main branch Rucker's Run in mt. cove. Part of tract deeded from LAURENCE SUDATH to WM. HENDERSON. Lines: crossing the branch to line on the other mt. Orig. sent to JF Feb 1823.

Page 44.   16 Feb 1804. NORBORNE THOMAS & wife JUDITH, AC, to JAS.

TURNER, AC, for Ł25, 100 acres; part of tract whereon NT and wife live. Lines: grantor, CORNL. THOMAS, grantee. Wit: JOS. C. HIGGINBOTHAM, TERISHA TURNER, FRANCIS WEST. Orig. del. to L.N. LYON (LIGON?) 7 Aug 1829.

Page 45.   20 Feb 1804. JNO. LONDON, AC, to RO. ALLEN, AC, for $500, 140 acres S branches Porrage. Lines: DAVID S. GARLAND, PLEASANT STORY, JAS. DILLARD, ALEX. JEWELL, SACKVILLE KING. Orig. del. to RA, 4 Nov 1804.

Page 45.   20 Feb 1804. RO. ALLEN & wife ELIZ., AC, to JNO. LONDON, AC, for $1000, 322 acres Porage Creek. Lines: JAS. LONDON JR, JAS. DILLARD, MADISON HILL, WIATT SMITH, JAS. LONDON. ELIZ. rel. dower, 19 Sep 1808.

Page 46.   26 Aug 1803. P. MARTIN to JAS. W. JOPLING for Ł60, negress, Edy. Wit: JNO. CAMM, HENRY WOODS, GEO. MARTIN.

Page 46.   10 Jan 1804. JNO. WIATT & wife WILLHAMINA, AC, to HENRY BROWN, AC, for $1.00, S branches Rutledge. Lines: JNO. McDANIEL, JAS. LIVELY, MIGGINSON's road. Wit: JNO. McDANIEL, DAVID WOODROOF SR. & JR, WILL WOODROOF. Orig. del. to HB, 16 Aug 1804.

Page 47.   15 Feb 1804. GEO. HYLTON, AC, to BENJ. WATKINS, AC, for Ł57, 50 acres Owens' Creek. Part of BENJ. JOHNSON's tract. Lines: MIGGINSON. Wit: SAML. FRANKLIN, JAS. PETERS, SAML. ARRINGTON, SETH MACOMBER.

Page 48.   15 Feb 1804. BENJ. WATKINS & wife MARY, AC, to JAS. CUNNINGHAM, AC, for Ł57, 50 acres Owens' Creek. Part of tract of BENJ. JOHNSON. Lines: MIGGINSON. Wit: as above. Orig. del. 22 Aug 1807, to JC.

Page 49.   16 Oct 1803. JESSE HOUCHINS, AC, to WM. CAMPBELL, AC, for Ł31-10-1, Deed of Trust on debt due JAS. & DAVID GARLAND. Corn, tobacco, etc. Wit: JOS., DANL., & CAMPBELL GOODE.

Page 49.   4 Aug 1803. Order to AC J.P.'s to quiz ELIZ. B., wife of RICH. C. POLLARD, as to deed of 10 Feb 1803, to ELIAS HAMLETT. 414 acres. Done, 13 Feb 1804, and rec. 20 Feb 1804. JOS. SHELTON & WM. H. DIGGES, J.P.'s.

Page 50.   2 Aug 1803. Order to same J.P.'s to quiz ELIZ. POLLARD, as above, as to deed of 10 Feb 1803, to JNO. WRIGHT - 164 acres. Done as above.

Page 50.   2 Aug 1803. Order to same J.P.'s to quiz ELIZ. POLLARD, as above, as to deed to JNO. MELTON, Feb. -- 1803. Done as above.

Page 51.   17 Dec 1803. CHAS. CARTER & wife BETTY, Culpeper, to JAS. FRANKLIN, AC, for $9000, 1006 acres. Lines: JNO. SMITH, HUGH CAMPBELL, EDWD. CARTER (formerly WHITAKER CARTER), JOLE FRANKLIN, Maple Run, Main Co. road. Certificate from Culpeper, 20 Feb 1804, rec--p.520 order of 8 Jan 1803, to Culpeper J.P.'s to quiz BETTY. Done, 20 May 1803, by RO. SLAUGHTER & WILL BROADUS. Orig. del. 24 Aug 1832 to HENRY L.DAVIES.

Page 53.   6 Aug 1803. JNO. CREWS & wife CHRISTIANA, AC, to JAS. LEE, AC, for Ł30, 34½ acres. Lines: Fawn Creek. Wit: NELSON C. DAWSON, WM. LEE, PLEASANT DAWSON, THOS. POWELL, WM. PETTYJOHN.

Page 54.   17 Sep 1804. PLEASANT TUCKER, AC, Power of Atty. to RO. H. COLEMAN, AC, LITTLEBERRY & ZACH. TUCKER, LIncoln Co, Ky. Any claims or interests "by discent" or purchase in Kentucky.

Page 54.   17 Sep 1804. RICH. HARRISON, AC, Power of Atty by RH of AC to RO. H. COLEMAN, AC, and WM. WOODFORK, Woodford Co, Ky, to act as to any Ky. lands.

Page 55.   28 Jul 1803. LITTLEBERRY TUCKER, AC, to RICH. HARRISON, AC, for Ł105, 2 negro boys: Davy and Jno. Wit: ISOM JOHNSON, MATT. TUCKER, and proved by them, 20 Feb 1804. Orig. del. to RH, 12 Oct 1804.

Page 56.   13 Oct 1804.   GEO. MENG & wife MARY, AC, to JAS. MURPHY, AC,
            for Ł420, 2 acres Warminster; where RO. RIVES formerly lived
and sold by him to MENG - save a carriage house. Wit: HEN. HOLLOWAY, JAS.
TURNER, CHAS. IRVING, RO. MOORE, LANDON CABELL, SAML. WINFREY, SAML.
WOOD. Orig. del. to JM, 24 Oct 1804.

Page 56.   31 May 1802.   SAML. BELL, AC, to DRURY LEE & JAS. DILLARD, AC,
            and ARCHIBALD ROBERTSON, Lynchburg - Deed of Trust to secure
debt to WM. BROWN & Co., Lynchburg - $1.00. 2 women slaves; Sis, about
25, and Sarah, about 13 years old. 2 boys, Wiatt, about 7 or 8, and Bur-
well, about 5 or 6. Wit: WM. JOHNSON, GEO. POWELL, JOSIAH LEAKE, EDMUND
READ, ALEX. SHARP. (Note: Slavery, thank the good Lord, has long since
dsaappeared, but the Amherst reliance upon Lynchburg in a commercial way
is still very much in style. Amherst Courthouse is merely a village and
all residents call it The Village. There are grocery, drug, and hardware
outlets here and one clothing store, but those seeking a wide choice in
goods always go to "Town". Lynchburg, or "Town" is sixteen miles south
of us and just across the James River. We also rely upon them for hospital facilities and they operate three fine institutions: Virginia Baptist,
General, and Memorial. BFD)

Page 57.   1 Jan 1804.   THOS. MITCHELL, AC, to STERLING CLAIBORNE, Lynch-
            burg, Deed of Trust to secure debt to SAML. IRVINE. $1.00.
woman slave, girl slave. Wit: JAS. BENAGH, BENJ. A WINSTON, JAS. ADAMS,
WILSON DAVENPORT, WM. BULLOCK. Orig. del. to SC, 29 Dec 1804.

Page 59.   28 Jul 1803.   ZACH. TUCKER, AC, to RICH. HARRISON, AC, for Ł60,
            slave girl, Patty. Wit: ISHAM JOHNSON & MATT. TUCKER.

Page 59.   21 Jul 1803.   EDWD. CARTER certifies that compromise has been
            made with LARKIN SANDIDGE as to property in CARTER's possess-
ion by virtue of CORNL. VAUGHAN's will; made safe to CARTER by bill of
sale of SANDIDGE; CARTER relinquishes all claims vs. VAUGHAN estate. Wit:
CHAS. TALIAFERRO, NELSON CRAWFORD, ABRAM CARTER. Orig. del. to WM. SAN-
DIDGE, 22 Jun 1805.

Page 59.   1 Aug 1803.   LITTLEBERRY TUCKER, AC, to RICH. HARRISON, AC,
            slave, Jesse, secured to me by will of my father, DRURY TUCKER.
Wit: NATHL. OFFUTT, JNO. WARE, RO. COLEMAN.

Page 60.   1 Feb 1804.   JNO. PHILLIPS & wife FRANKEY, AC, to JNO. ALFORD,
            AC, for Ł275, 146 acres both sides N branch Tye. Part of tract
of WM. BIBB, and now that of CONYERS WHITE SR, dec'd. et al. Lines: JNO.
THOMPSON, WM. TEAS, WM. BIBB, Naked Creek, CONYERS WHITE SR, dec'd. Wit:
JAS. KIDD, ISAAC WHITE, LEWIS WHITE.

Page 61.   27 Jul 1803.   ZACH. TUCKER, AC, to RICH. HARRISON, AC, for
            Ł66-13, two undivided lots in lands of DRURY TUCKER, dec'd,
AC - Buffalo - as legatee of DRURY TUCKER; also lot bought from PLEASANT
TUCKER. Wit: ISHAM JOHNSON, MATT. TUCKER, LITTLEBERRY TUCKER, ISAAC
TUCKER.

Page 61.   11 Feb 1804.   WM. WEST, Clark Co, Ky., to FRANCIS WEST, AC,
            for Ł25, 107 acres S branches Swan Creek. Lines: NICHL. CABELL
on S; W by FRANCIS WEST, N by NORBORN THOMAS, E by STEVEN TURNER. Wit:
WM. BEMIS, BRANSORD or BRANSFORD WEST, NANCY WEST. Ack. in AC by WW,
20 Feb 1804. Orig. del. 3 Oct 1817, "p son" (sic).

Page 62.   18 Feb 1804.   RO. MAYS & wife SUSANNAH, AC, to HENSLEY CARPEN-
            TER, AC, for $1.00 and love for HC and wife, RHODA - Stone-
house Creek. 12 acres. Lines: grantor, HIGGINBOTHAM, grantee. Wit: JNO.
TALIAFERRO, JNO. EUBANK JR, DABNEY HILL, THOS. N. GOODRICH.

Page 63.   18 Feb 1804.   HENSLEY CARPENTER & wife RHODA, AC, to RO. MAYS,
            AC, for $1.00, 110 acres N branches Stonehouse Creek. Lines:
Near the spring, down the branch; grantee. Wit: as in previous deed.

Page 63.   12 Nov 1801.   WM. HALL & wife MARY, AC, to HENRY BROWN, AC,
            for Ł200, 200 acres both sides Pedlar. Lines: ABRAHAM CARTER.
Part of 300 acres. Wit: DANL. WARWICK, JNO. BARKER, THOS. N. EUBANK,

A.B. WARWICK, NELSON CRAWFORD, ABRAM CARTER. Final proof, 20 Feb 1804, by DANL. WARWICK.

Page 64. 12 Nov 1803. JNO. WRIGHT & wife SUSANNAH, AC, to PARMENAS BRYANT, AC, for Ь260, 87 acres Naked Creek, branch of Tye. Lines: CONYERS WHITE SR, dec'd, WM. TEAS, JNO. THOMPSON, grantee, Col. SAML. J. CABELL. Wit: EDMD. BURNETT, JAS. MONTGOMERY, WM. H. DIGGES, PEACHY FRANKLIN, JAS. GREGORY. Orig. del. to PB, 30 Jan 1805.

Page 66. 21 Feb 1804. HENRY LANE & wife FRANCES, AC, to WM. WARE, AC, for Ь100, 100 acres Horsley Creek. Lines: JESSE & JNO. RICHE- SON, THOS. GOODRICH, JESSE HAYNES, CALEB RALLS. Orig. del. to WW, 12 Jul 1806.

Page 66. 17 Dec 1803. Order to AC J.P.'s: CALEB RALLS & wife SUCKEY, and JNO. EUBANK & wife PEGGY, deed of 19 Sep 1802, to HARDEN HAYNES; 26 acres. Done by JOSIAH ELLIS & NELSON CRAWFORD, 20 Feb 1804.

Page 67. 9 Jan 1804. RO. HARDY & wife MARY, AC, to MICHL. WOODS, AC, for $100, 21½ acres Rockfish. Part of 84 acres transferred from ALEX. REID to HARDY. Lines: JOS. MONTGOMERY, top of the mt. Wit: WM. SMALL, THOS. JOPLING, DAVID WITT, JNO. TULER. Orig. del. to H.T. HARRIS, 16 Jun 1812.

Page 68. 16 Nov 1803. SARAH, JNO. & JOS. JARVIS, heirs of JNO. JARVIS, dec'd, AC, to JNO. DEFRIES, Rockbridge - $186 in property; horse $100.80; cart, harness, gun - balance due before they start to Ky. 99 acres and all estate rights. S branches Pedlar and where they live. Wit: JNO. PAXTON, JNO. FRASER, WALTER FRASER, THOS. PAXTON, AND. ALEXANDER.

Page 69. 14 Jan 1804. RICH. WILSON & wife ANNA, AC, to SAML. HUCKSTEP, AC, for Ь44-2, 31½ acres Rockey Creek. Lines: grantor, grantee, Gaines' road, ANDREW MONROE. Part of where WILSON lives. Wit: CHAS. CHRISTIAN, CHAS. H. CHRISTIAN, BETSY WITEN.

Page 70. 3 Jan 1803. JNO. WITT, AC, to MOSES HUGHES, AC, for Ь15, 10 or 12 acres; part of a tract; head of Rockfish. Lines: WM. EDMUNDS, mouth of dry branch. Wit: JNO. & SALLY HUGHES, ELIJAH GANIL.

Page 71. 18 Jun 1804. THOS. N. EUBANK to JACOB PHILLIPS - all title vested in EUBANK by Deed of Trust - PHILLIPS to DANL. WARWICK - 142 acres - now satisfied. Wit: JNO. TALIAFERRO.

Page 71. 9 Jan 1804. RO. HARDY & wife MARY, AC, to JOS. MONTGOMERY, AC, for Ь40, 61½ acres, part of tract from ALEX. REID to HARDY by transfer of 84 acres. On Rockfish. Lines: grantee, top of the mt. Wit: WM. SMALL, THOS. JOPLING, DAVID WITT, JNO. TULEY.

Page 72. 5 Nov 1803. HENRY DAWSON & wife MARY, AC, to THOS. PRATT, AC, for Ь30, 47 acres Corbin's creek, branch of Rockfish. Lines: JAS. BARNETT (now MICHL. WOODS), WM. BARNETT (now MICHL. WOODS). Wit: MICHL. WOODS, WM. SMALL, THOS. PRATT JR.

Page 72. 13 Jun 1804. JACOB PHILLIPS & wife SARAH, AC, to BENJ. SAN- DIDGE, AC, for Ь100, 148 acres both sides Buffalo. Lines: old line of PULLIAM SANDIDGE on river bank; on the mt., mouth of a branch. Wit: JNO. TALIAFERRO, CHAS. L. BARRETT, JNO. SPITFATHOM. Orig. del. to BS, 29 Mar 1813.

Page 73. 12 May 1804. JAS. EDMUNDS, JR, AC, for love of his four in- fant children: LEJES L., LAVENDER L., MARYANN G., & JANE EDMUNDS - 6 sh. - for use of children - to WM. EDMUNDS - slaves named; beds, kitchen utensils - WM. to use for education of the children and equal distribution when of age. Wit: JNO. N. ROSE, SEATON M. PENN, TERENCE COONEY.

Page 75. 16 Apr 1804. CHAS. CHRISTIAN, AC, to CHAS. HUNT CHRISTIAN for Ь150, 125 acres Buffalo. Lines: WALTER CHRISTIAN, SPOTSWOOD GARLAND, heirs of A. BRYDIE, dec'd, dividing line from grantor whereon he lives. Wit: WALTER CHRISTIAN JR, PETER P. THORNTON, JNO. PENN. Orig.

sent to CHAS. HUNT CHRISTIAN by R. HUCKSTEP, 28 Apr 1808.

Page 75. 13 Sep 1804. JNO. McCLURE & wife ELIZ., to WM. SMITH for Ⱡ980,
          no acres Rockfish. Lines: Col. CHISWELL. Wit: LYDIA, POLLY &
JNO. WALTERS, JAS. & JNO. McCLURE. Orig. sent to SMITH 18 Dec 1804.

Page 76. 8 Mar 1802. JORDAN WRIGHT, AC, to JAS. MURPHY, AC, Deed of
          Trust; debt due BROWN RIVES & Co. $1.00, 138¼ acres N side
Tye. Lines: JOSPEH LOVING, SAML. EDMUNDS, GEO. STONEHAM. Wit: DANL. HIG-
GINBOTHAM, DAVID P. BRYANT, JAS. HANSBROUGH, CHAS. L. BARRETT. Orig.
del. to DANL. HIGGINBOTHAM, 3 Jan 1805.

Page 77. 23 Apr 1804. CHAS. CHRISTIAN & wife SARAH, AC, to JACOB G.
          PEARCE, AC, for Ⱡ91-10, no acres; Buffalo. Lines: STOVELL's
old road, grantee, MIGGINSON's Ferry road, JNO. TYLER, AMBROSE RUCKER,
grantor, new road; part of a tract. Wit: DAVID S. GARLAND, SAML. HUCKSTEP,
ANDERSON MOSS, ISAAC RUCKER. Orig. del. 25 Mar 1805, to JP.

Page 78. 27 Feb 1804. WM. EVANS, AC, to WM. JORDAN, AC, Deed of Trust.
          debt to WM. PAMPLIN. $1.00. 2 mares - black and grey. Wit:
HUDSON M. GARLAND, RO. COLEMAN, NORVELL SPENCER.

Page 79. 15 Jun 1804. MATT. STANTON & wife NANCY, AC, to JNO. CASHWELL,
          for Ⱡ160, 88 acres Rockey Run branches. Lines: RO. PEARCE,
THOS. POWELL, REUBEN PADGETT, grantee, ANDREW MONROE. Wit: JNO. LONDON,
SAML. HUCKSTEP, JOS. HIGGINBOTHAM. Orig. del. to JC, 22 Feb 1807.

Page 80. 28 Feb 1804. EDWD. THOMPSON TOMS, AC, to JOS. SHELTON for
          Ⱡ150, 4 negroes; Milly, Eliza, Geo., & Nancey; 2 cows and
calves. Wit: HARRISON GRIFFIN, WM. H. SHELTON.

Page 80. 15 Jun 1804. WM. MOORE & wife BETSY, AC, to THOS. FITZPATRICK,
          son of JNO., for Ⱡ70, 75 acres Rockfish. Lines: SAML. BRIDG-
WATER near top of the mt., WM. FITZPATRICK, THOS. WARE. Wit: DAVID S.
GARLAND.

Page 81. 17 Nov 1803. NATHAN CRAWFORD, AC, to WM. CRAWFORD, AC, for
          $1000, 211 acres Rockfish. Lines: N by grnator, W by grantee,
S by JAS. WOODS, E by RO. DINWIDDIE. Wit: NELSON ANDERSON, NELSON CRAW-
FORD JR, D.W. CRAWFORD.

Page 81. 14 Oct 1803. Order to blank J.P.'s to quiz PATSY, wife of
          JNO. B. TRENT, as to deed of 14 Apr 1803, to JAS. WILLS; 400
acres. Done by AC J.P.'s JNO. CHRISTIAN & THOS. MOORE; rec. 18 Jun 1804.

Page 82. 20 Feb 1804. PETER JOHNSON, AC, to JNO. FITZPATRICK, Deed of
          Trust, $1.00 - stock, furniture, etc. Wit: WM. FITZPATRICK,
SCHUYLER BARNETT, ALEX. FITZPATRICK, THOS. FITZPATRICK JR.

Page 83. 14 Apr 1804. HENRY BROWN & wife NANCY, AC, to JNO. MAYS, SR,
          AC, for $1000, 200 acres both sides Pedlar. Lines: ABRAM CAR-
TER. Part of 300 acres formerly that of WM. HALL. Wit: THOS. N. EUBANK,
JNO. EUBANK JR, ABRAM CARTER, HUGH McCABE, JOSIAH ELLIS JR, ROBINSON
RALLS, RICH. L. ELLIS.

Page 83. 9 Dec 1803. JNO. MATTHEWS & wife JANE, Barren Co, Ky, to
          PETER P. THORNTON, AC, for Ⱡ150, 220 acres Dancing & Pedlar -
surveyed 11 Mar 1767. Lines: SAML. GEST, WM. SHOEMAKER. Wit: JNO. FLOOD,
REUBEN CRAWFORD, WM. S(L) PRYOR, GEO. GILLESPIE, JNO. EUBANK, LINZA
BURKS, HENRY BROWN. Orig. del. to THOS. S. McCLELLAND 24 Oct 1806.

Page 84. 9 Oct 1803. JESSE WEST, Madison Co, Ky. - WEST gives Power of
          Atty. to THOS. HOOTON or HORTON, same Co., to settle accts.
with WEST's brother, BRANSFORD WEST - they have been partners. Wit: JNO.
HOCKADAY. Produced 9 Dec 1803, before WM. IRVINE, Clk. of Madison Co,
Ky. JNO. KINCAID certified as J.P. as to IRVINE.

Page 85. 11 Feb 1804. JAS. TURNER JR, & wife LUCY, AC, to CONRAD
          MOIRER, AC, for Ⱡ40, 25 acres Rockfish branch. Lines: grantor,
GEO. VAUGHAN, CHAS. STATHAM. Wit: HUDSON MARTIN, ABSALOM COX, LEONARD
MOYER.

Page 86.   27 Feb 1804.   DANL. TYLER & wife SARAH, Bedford Co., to JAS.
            KIDD, AC, no amount given, 128 acres Little Indian Creek.
Proved in Bedford and rec. in AC, 18 Jun 1804. Orig. del. to JK 7 Jan 1808.

Page 87.   2 Jan 1804.   DAVID S. GARLAND, AC, to JOS. ARBUCKLE, AC, for
            $52, "lott" in New Glasgow; No. 8. N side of new street;
starting at an alley. Wit: EDMD. TO. COLEMAN, WM. HALL, JAS. HALL.

Page 87.   15 Jun 1804.   JNO. LONDON, AC, to STEPHEN HAM, AC, for 5 sh,
            53½ acres Stovall Creek. Lines: grantee, POWHATAN BOWLING,
grantor. Orig. del. to JESSE BECK, exr. of HAM, 19 Jan 1824.

Page 88.   11 Feb 1804.   MICAJAH GOODWIN & wife ELIZ., AC, to PROSSER
            POWELL, AC, for £240, no acres given, adj. N side Fluvanna and
where MG lives. Lines: JOS. GOODWIN. Wit: THOS. MOORE, RICH. HARRISON,
NICHL. C. DAVIES, NELSON CRAWFORD, JNO. SHELTON, JAS. WARE.

Page 89.   18 Jun 1804.   PHILIP GOOCH & wife FRANCES, AC, to JOS. HIGGIN-
            BOTHAM,   son of MOSES HIGGINBOTHAM, for $410, 41 acres Rut-
ledge creek branches. Lines: JOSEPH HIGGINBOTHAM SR, PETER CASHWELL dec'd,
JOS. HIGGINBOTHAM JR, JNO. HIGGINBOTHAM. Part of a tract. Sent to
grantee, 8 Jun 1805.

Page 89.   14 Mar 1804.   JNO. LONDON, AC, to DANL. NORCUTT, AC, for $40,
            109 acres Stovall Creek. Lines: WM. GARRETT, MICHL. COALTER,
JAS. BOLLING, ELIAS WILLS, REUBEN NORVELL, JNO. KNIGHT. Wit: WILL LEE,
JER. COATS, CHAS. CHRISTIAN.

Page 90.   2 Jan 1804.   ZACH. NEVIL, AC, to JNO. LUCAS SR, AC, for 5 sh,
            Deed of Trust for debt due LEWIS NEVIL - small bay horse,
commonly called The Stud; formerly that of LEWIS NEVIL. Wit: RICH. BRIANT,
CHAS. STINNETT.

Page 91.   26 May 1804.   JNO. LONDON, AC, to DAVID S. GARLAND, AC, for
            £15, 76½ acres N branches Stovall. Lines: grantee, SACKVILLE
KING, STEPHEN HAM, POWHATAN BOWLING dec'd, WM. GALT. Wit: WM. G. PENDLE-
TON, JAS. GARLAND, EDMD. T. COLEMAN. Orig. del. to DSD 20 Jul 1805.

Page 92.   26 May 1804.   JNO. LONDON & DAVID S. GARLAND, AC, to KEZIAH
            COFFLAND, AC, for 5 sh, relinquishment of rights in land
"pretended" to be surveyed by KEZIAH's father, BENJ. COFLIN (note two
spellings) - 200 acres on Porrage. Lines: JOS. NICHOLS, JAS. DILLARD,
CHRISTIAN's orphans.

Page 92.   19 Jun 1804.   SEATON M. PENN, AC, to NICHL. HARRISON, AC, for
            £200, 110 acres Harris Creek. Lines: JNO. AMBLER. Part of
tract of JOS. PENN dec'd.

Page 93.   19 Mar 1804.   HOALMAN JOPLING & wife SARAH, AC, to WM. JOPLING
            of AC, for £100, 100 acres Cedar & Dancing creeks. Surveyed
16 Apr 1791. Lines: JOSIAH JOPLING, DRURY BOWMAN, JOS. CABELL. Wit: HENRY
DAWSON, EDWD. PAGE, JESSE JOPLING. Orig. del. 8 Dec 1829, to HJ. "RD
rec. Deed Book T:330". Produced AC, 22 Mar 1831; SARAH rel. dower rights.

Page 94.   8 May 1804.   BENJ. PHILLIPS, AC, to PHILIP GOOCH, AC, for
            $720, 360 acres on Elk Run - S side Buffalo Ridge. Lines:
GILES DAVIDSON, GEO. PENN, PHILIP GOOCH, JNO. HIGGINBOTHAM. Tract con-
veyed by JAS. & JNO. THOMPSON to both parties. On 9 Nov 1805, del. to
WM. GOOCH, one of exrs. of P. GOOCH. Wit: E. GILBERT, WILL CAMDEN JR,
GEO. RULEY. (Note: I can see Buffalo Ridge from the window which is
close to my typewriter. BFD)

Page 94.   23 Jan 1804.   Order to AC J.P.'s: SAML. BELL & wife SALLY,
            17 May 1802, deed to PHILIP GOOCH, 192 acres. Rec. 18 Jun 1804
by JAS. DILLARD & JNO. CHRISTIAN, J.P.'s.

Page 95.   8 May 1800.   JAS. J. FORREST & wife CATH., Botetourt Co., to
            RO. McCHESNEY, Rockbridge Co., for £100, 93 acres Head bran-
ches N fork Tye. Lines: JAS. TILFORD, top of the blue ridge. Wit: DAVID
BAILEY, EZEK. WRAY, JNO. PAGE. Proved in Botetourt, H. BOWYER, Clk. Rec.

AC, 20 Jun 1804. Orig. del. to RMc 21 Nov 1877(? hard to read).

Page 96. 9 Nov 1803. Order to AC J.P.'s: CHAS. TALIAFERRO & wife LUCY,
deed of 15 Apr 1803, to JNO. TALIAFERRO - 67 acres. Rec. 2 Feb
1804; NELSON CRAWFORD & WM. LOVING.

Page 97. 21 Jul 1803. Order to AC J.P.'s as to LEWIS NEVIL, JAS. NEVIL,
ZACH NEVIL & wife NANCY, CORNL. NEVIL, ROWLAND EDMUNDS & wife
ELIS., CHAS. LEWIS & wife SALLY, SAML. EDMUNDS & wife ESTHER, WM. MURRAY
& wife LUCY, CLOUGH SHELTON & wife MOLLY - 18 Jun 1803, to RIVES MURPHY
& Co. - 319 acres - to quiz NANCY, ELIZ., SALLY & ESTHER. Done, 3 Aug
1803. WM. LOVING & WM. H. DIGGES.

Page 98. 21 Jul 1803. Order to Buckingham J.P.'s, PRICE PERKINS &
LINEAS BOLLING, same parties as order above - NEVILS et al -
to quiz LUCY, wife of WM. MURRAY. Rec. AC 20 Jun 1804.

Page 98. 9 Jun 1804. JNO. PUGH SR, & wife ANNE, AC, to JNO. PUGH JR,
AC, for $100, 100 acres Taylor's Creek whereon Jr. lives.
Lines: JAS. WOODS. Wit: JNO. MORRIS, ELIJAH PUGH, ZACH. MORRIS.

Page 99. 17 Setp 1799, order to AC J.P.'s, JOS. BURRUS & THOS. MOORE,
as to deed by THOS. RUCKER & wife SALLY, 15 Apr 1799, to ELIAS
WILLS - 350 acres. Done 27 Sep 1799, but not rec. until 16 Jul 1804.

Page 100. 16 Jul 1804. HANNAH CAMRON, widow of DUNCAN CAMRON dec'd, to
JNO. CAMPBELL, AC, for Ł10, no acres given - her dower in
Piney River tract. Lines: GEO. GILLESPIE, dec'd, grantee, MOSES WRIGHT.

Page 101. 16 Jul 1804. WM. CAMDEN SR, AC, to his son, MARBELL CAMDEN,
Alb. Co., for love and $1.00, 113½ acres. Lines: N bank Flu-
vanna, WM. MIGGINSON dec'd, GEO. HYLTON, JAS. FREELAND, dec'd, Little
Mozley Creek mouth, including CAMDEN's Warehouse.

Page 102. 16 Jul 1804. WM. CAMDEN SR, AC, to son HENRY CAMDEN, AC, for
love and $1.00, 414 acres Bever Creek, part of tract formerly
that of GABL. PENN, dec'd. Lines: CHAS. BURRUS, JNO. DUNCAN, JNO. YOUNG
on top of the mt., high peak of the mt., WM. CAMDEN JR, JABEZ CAMDEN, at
the dug road. Margin: (very dim) Orig. del. to HC, 6(?) Nov 1811.

Page 103. 19 Nov 1803. JAS. WILSFORD, AC, to CLIFTON GARLAND, Alb. Co,
Deed of Trust - $1.00 - debt to DENNETT WITT; horse, mare,
furniture etc. Wit: OZBORNE HENLEY, JAS. WALKER, HOLMAN SNEAD. Orig. del.
to RO. GARLAND, 22 Mar 1805.

Page 104. 29 Mar 1804. JNO. LUCAS, AC, to DANL. HIGGINBOTHAM, AC, Deed
of Trust - debt due BROWN RIVES & Co., 5 sh, stock and furniture etc. Wit: JAMES MURPHY, JNO. HIGGINBOTHAM JR.

Page 105. 16 Feb 1804. Order to AC J.P.'s WM. H. DIGGES & WM. LOVING -
THOS. HAWKINS & wife ELIZ, 22 Nov 1803, to JNO. LOVING JR, 200
acres. Done 18 May 1804.

Page 106. 18 Apr 1804. JORDAN WRIGHT, AC, for love of parents (not named). Land - no acres set forth. My wife to live thereon, if
she chooses. Wit: ELIJAH MAYS, JNO. EDMUNDS JR, PETER CAMPBELL. (Note:
JORDAN WRIGHT seemingly was ill when he deeded this land. My will notes
show that in Will Book 4:151 his inventory was taken on 26 Jun 1804, by
JOS. LOVING, SAML. EDMUNDS JR, ACHILLES WRIGHT, SAML. EDMUNDS SR - total
of Ł540-12-0. On page 383 of same book, LEVINA WRIGHT qualified to admr.
his estate, 14 Jun 1804. Bdm: CHAS. BURKS. I find no marriage for JORDAN
WRIGHT in AC and no estate data on ACHILLES WRIGHT.

Page 106. 11 Dec 1803. WM. PARKS, AC, to ARCHIBALD ROBERTSON, THOS.
CREWS, & ARCHELAUS MAYS, Campbell Co., Deed of Trust - debt
due WM. BROWN & Co. - $1.00 - 2 negroes: Charlotte, about 24, and child
Hannah, about 18 months old. Wit: GEO. POWELL, THOS. MOORMAN, JNO. MUR-
RALL, REUBEN PENDLETON. Final proof by PENDLETON, 16 Jul 1804. Orig. del.
to A. MAYS, one of the trustees, 21 Aug 1805.

Page 108.   16 Jul 1804.   WM. TYREE, AC, to JACOB PIERCE, AC, for Ŀ16, 18
acres N side of Buffalo. Lines: JESSE KENNEDY dec'd, Tyree's
spring branch. Orig. del. to JP, 11 Nov 1805.

Page 108.   13 Dec 1803.   MICAJAH GOODWIN, AC, to THOS. MOORE & PHILIP
JOHNSON, AC, & ARCHIBALD ROBERTSON, Campbell Co, Deed of
Trust - debt due WM. BROWN & Co. - $1.00 - 2 negro watermen: Peter &
Dick. Wit: ARCHELAUS MAYS, THOS. MOORMAN, GEO. POWELL. (Note: Watermen
were used on the James to get tobacco down to Richmond on boats. BFD)

Page 109.   4 Feb 1804.   REUBIN T. MITCHELL & wife MILDRED, AC, to DUNMORE
DAMERON, AC, for Ŀ4-10-6, 6 acres and part of where RM lives -
Marrowbone Mt. Lines: dividing line of both and made in presence of THOS.
MURRELL & WM. MARTIN. Both of them were wits. along with ALEX. ROBERTS
& JAS. TURNER JR.

Page 111.   2 Jun 1804.   ELIJAH STATON, AC, to JNO. STAPLES, AC, Deed of
Trust - debt due ELISHA PETERS - 5 sh. 17 acres. Lines: ELI-
SHA ESTIS, ELISHA PETERS. Wit: JNO. HIGGINBOTHAM, JAS. GREGORY, JAS.
MURPHY, JNO. TURNER JR.

Page 112.   16 Jan 1804.   JOS. WHITE, AC, to his 3 children SALLY, JNO.
D. & ELIZ. DAWSON WHITE, by wife PRISCILLA (N DAWSON) negroes
given to his dec'd wife - also stock and furniture - to be delivered at
majority or marriage. Wit: PLEASANT DAWSON, JNO. L. DAWSON.

Page 112.   17 Sep 1804.   ANGUSH McCLOUD, AC, to AMBROSE TOMLINSON, AC,
for Ŀ90, 3 tracts N fork Buffalo. 1) 100 acres pat. to AM, 7
Sep 1796. Lines: AARON HIGGINBOTHAM, Mitchell's Cove Creek, JOS. HIGGIN-
BOTHAM, JER. TUNGET, AMBROSE TOMLIN (Note TOMLIN and SON are both used in
data here) 2) 19 acres N fork Buffaloe, pat. to AM, 27 Sep 1796. Lines:
N bank of N fork of Buffaloe. 3) 73 acres on N side of Buffalo; N fork.

Page 114.   28 May 1804.   BOLLING MITCHELL, AC, to JAS. WARE, AC, for
Ŀ124-12, 89 acres James River and Johns' creek. Lines: old
field, JAS. WARE (formerly HENRY L. DAVIES), JNO. GILES, JAS. WILLS,
grantee. Wit: ANTHONY RUCKER, REUBEN PENDLETON, DAVID TINSLEY.

Page 115.   14 Jul 1804.   REUBEN PENDLETON & wife FRANCES, AC, to JAS.
WARE, AC, for Ŀ5, 62 acres on Big Branch; part of where RP
lives. Lines: MITCHELL's road, JNO. B. TRENT, grantor, MITCHELL's old
field.

Page 116.   15 Sep 1804.   JNO. CHILDRESS SR, & wife PRISCILLA, AC, to
JOHN CHILDRESS JR, for Ŀ60, both sides Pedlar. Part of 2
tracts pat. to Sr. 1) 20 Jul 1780. 2) 24 Jul 1787. Lines of 1) are HENRY
CHILDRESS & MOSES SWEENY. To hold 280 acres. Del. to Sr. 12 May 1806.

Page 116.   17 Sep 1804.   JER. DEAN & wife ELIZ, AC, to RO. HAMILTON, AC,
for Ŀ60, 100 acres on Horsley. Del. to RH, 10 Feb 1805.

Page 117.   5 Mar 1804.   NICHL. C. DAVIES & wife ELIZ., AC, to ALLERSON
MORRIS, AC, for Ŀ64, 100 acres NW side Pedlar and surveyed by
SAML. B. DAVIES. Lines: JARRETT GILLUM. Wit: THOS. MORRIS, JOS. MAGANN,
JNO. BROWN. Del. to AM, 24 Dec 1826.

Page 118.   31 Aug 1804.   JAS. FULCHER, AC, to RO. L.(T) ROSE, Stafford
Co., for Ŀ228-12, 114 acres. Lines: JAS. WOODS, big Piney
bank, mouth of Little Piney. Wit: HILL CARTER, RO. H. & JNO. M. ROSE.

Page 119.   22 Mar 1804.   DRURY HUDGINS, AC, to WM. HUDGEN, AC, beds and
stock. Wit: FLEMING CARTER, SARAH CARTER, GEO. CURRY, WM.
CAMDEN, WM. CUNNINGHAM.

Page 120.   6 Sep 1804.   BENJ. COLEMAN & wife SALLY, AC, to JNO. WARE, AC,
for $150, 104 acres both sides Irish Creek, S branches of Ped-
lar. Lines: grantee, THOS. TUCKER. Wit: JAS. MARTIN, SR, VIRGIL COLEMAN,
N. VANSTAVERN.

Page 120.   10 Aug 1799.   JAS. WEBSTER, Baltimore Md, to NATHAN LUFBOROUGH,

Lancaster, Pa, for $1.00, 5682 acres Buff. & Owens' Creeks - N side of &
joining Fluvanna River and S side & joining Tye. Pat. signed by JAS. WOOD,
Lt. Governor in Richmond, 24 Apr 1794, to WEBSTER. Wit: WASHINGTON LEE,
JNO. DONONAN(?). Proved in Baltimore by JW, JAS. CALHOUN, mayor. Rec.
in AC 17 Sep 1804. Orig. del. to NL, 14 Nov 1806.

Page 122.   22 Feb 1804.   NICHL. PRYOR, AC, to THOS. N. EUBANK, AC, Deed
of Trust - debt due DANL. WARWICK - $1.00 - 103 acres on Ped-
lar and where PRYOR lives. Lines: SAML. GUEST, MARTIN BIBB. Wit: HENRY
BROWN, ELLIS WRIGHT, JNO. ROBERTSON, JAS. POPE. Orig. del. to TE, 24
Sep 1805.

Page 123.   25 Aug 1804.   JAS. P. COCKE & wife LUCY, Alb. Co., to SHELTON
CROSTHWAIT, AC, for ₤4000, 260 acres Rucker's Run. Bought by
JC of Col. WM. CABELL, dec'd - with mills, distillery, shops, and houses;
also slaves - Jas., a cooper by trade, MOSES, also 3/4 interest in Cyrus;
wagons, etc. - lately in occupation by both men. Wit: JAS. MURPHY, PAR-
MENAS BRYANT, WM. H. CABELL, ELISHA MEREDITH, D.W. CRAWFORD, AB. SEAY.
Orig. sent to JC, 17 Oct 1806.

Page 124.   7 May 1804.   BEVERLY PADGETT, AC, to JNO. CAMM, AC, Deed of
Trust - debt due to DAVID & JAS. GARLAND - $1.00 - slaves,
Milley & Polly; stock. Wit: THOS. ALDRIDGE, WILL G. PENDLETON, CHAS. W.
CHRISTIAN. Orig. del. to JAS. GARLAND, 12 Mar 1807.

Page 125.   17 Sep 1804.   NATHAN CRAWFORD, HUDSON MARTIN, & MATT. HARRIS,
AC, to THOS. H. PROSSER, Henrico - grantors appointed commiss-
ioners by AC court in THOS. H. PROSSER, exr. of THOS. PROSSER, vs. SAML.
BRIDGWATER, guardian of SALLY, PATSY, POLLY WOODSON, BETSY, REBECCA PAR-
SONS, NATHL. & JUDITH CLARKE, children and heirs of NATH. CLARKE, dec'd.
5 sh. - 517 acres. Bought by NATHL. CLRAKE from THOS. GOODWIN & rec.in AC.

Page 126.   21 Aug 1804.   JNO. BETHEL, & wife MARY, AC, to JNO. BETHEL JR,
for love & ₤50, 346 acres on Rucker's Run and N side Findley's
Mt. in 2 surveys. 1) 296 acres. Lines: ABRAHAM WARWICK, RO. RIVES, his
mill tract, CHAS. EDMUNDS, JNO. BALL, WM. CABELL, now HECTOR CABELL. 2)
50 acres adj., surveyed for ABRAHAM WARWICK and sold by him to JNO. BETH-
EL. Wit: WM. FOSTER, FRANCIS SMITH. Orig. del. to JB, 25 Sep 1830.

Page 127.   17 Sep 1804.   WM. JORDAN, AC, to MICAJAH PENDLETON, AC, for
₤100, 6 acres both sides Elk Creek. Lines: grantee, a steep
hill. Wit: WM. JOS., & RO. HORSLEY.

Page 128.   16 Jul 1804.   BURCHER WHITEHEAD, AC, to HUDSON M. GARLAND, AC,
Deed of Trust - debt due JAS. & DAVID GARLAND - $1.00 - negress
Fan, and her three children: Jinney, Lilly & Edmd.; also horses and all
of my tract on S side of road and joining JNO. PENN JR. Wit: ANDERSON
MOSS, WM. HALL, WM. G. PENDLETON.

Page 129.   2 Jan 1804.   DAVID S. GARLAND, AC, to WM. HALL, AC, for $56,
lot 18 in New Glasgow between old and new streets; beginning
at alley-front of 56 yards and 51 yards deep; adjoins the old garden;
alley between 17 & 18. Wit: JOS. ARBUCKLE, JAS. HALL, EDMD. T. COLEMAN.
(Note: I think that in previous works that I have pointed out that the
town of New Glasgow is now known as Clifford.

Page 130.   6 Aug 1804.   THOS. NEVIL, AC, to HUDSON M. GARLAND, AC, Deed
of Trust - debt to JAS. & DAVID S. GARLAND - $1.00 - tract
where NEVIL lives - 92 acres. Lines: JOSEPH ALCOCK, RICH. ALCOCK, STEPHEN
WATTS, ALLEN BLAIR. Bought of JAS. & WM. ALCOCK; also mare (?) years old
last spring and raised by JNO. STAPLES. Wit: WILL CAMDEN JR, CHAS. W.
CHRISTIAN, WM. G. PENDLETON.

Page 131.   13 Apr 1804.   DANL. McCOY & wife NANCY, AC, to ELIJAH STATON,
AC, for ₤27, 17 acres. Lines: ELISHA ESTIS, ELISAH PETERS,
grantee. Wit: JNO. WOOD, JAMES McCOY, NELSON ANDERSON, SAML. HANSBROUGH,
ISHAM STATON.

Page 132.   8 Sep 1804.   JOSIAH CHEATHAM, AC, to JNO. HIGGINBOTHAM, AC,
Deed of Trust - 5 sh. 110 acres Hicory Creek. Lines: BENJ.

HARRIS, JNO. ROBERTS, SAML. PERKINS, JOHN FARRAR; also 5 slaves. Wit:
JNO. VIGUS JR, RO. MOORE, SAML. HANSBROUGH, NELSON ANDERSON. Orig. del.
to J. MURPHY, 8 Jan 1806.

Page 133. 31 Aug 1804. JNO. MATTHEWS to ELEX. ROBERTS, AC, for Ŀ86-5,
275 acres Marrowbone Mt. and joins ROBERTS. Deed of Trust,
5 sh. Stock, beds, etc. Wit: ROBT. RIVES, F. McHENRY.

Page 133. 17 Sep 1804. JNO. MATTHEWS & wife MARY, AC, to ALEX. ROBERTS,
AC, for Ŀ82-10, 275 acres N side Marrowbone Mt. Lines: REUBIN
MITCHELL, NATHAN HARRIS, grantee, PHILLIPS, dec'd, MARTIN DAWSON. Wit:
WM. MATTHEWS, ELIZ. SNEAD, ANN MATTHEWS.

Page 134. 24 Jul 1804. JAS. McALEXANDER & wife PATIENCE, AC, to NATHAN
BARNETT, AC, for Ŀ480, 435 acres Davis Creek. Lines: JAS.
WHITE, WM. WHITE, red house let, WM. WRIGHT, ALEX. FORBUS, old pat. line,
top of the mt., MARTIN KEY - now in hands of JNO. C.(?) FITZPATRICK; JAS.
WRIGHT. Wit: MATT. HARRIS, MICAJAH BURNETT, SALLY BURNETT.

Page 135. 20 Jan 1804. HUGH CAMPBELL & wife ELIZ, AC, to PHILLIP
SLAUGHTER, Culpeper, for Ŀ2772-18, 949 acres. Lines: JNO.
SMITH, JAS. FRANKLIN, EDWD. CARTER - formerly WHITTAKER CARTER. Bought by
HC of CHAS. CARTER and wife BETTY, 16 Dec 1802. Lines: main road, not far
from CARTER's old mill on Mill Creek, LINDSEY COLEMAN. Deed of Trust.
Wit: JAS. FRANKLIN JR, CHAS. L. BARNETT, JNO. SMITH, REUBEN HARRISON.
Orig. del. to PS, 13 May 1805.

Page 138. 27 Jul 1804. DAVID GEORGE, AC, to JAS. BULLOCK, Lynchburg,
Deed of Trust - debt due THOS. WIATT, Lynchburg - $1.00 - beds,
etc. Wit: JNO. LYNCH, B.W. MOSELEY.

Page 139. 1 Nov 1802. ISAAC TUCKER & wife ELIZ., AC, to DRURY TUCKER's
son, DANL. TUCKER, AC, interest of ISAAC under will of DRURY
TUCKER to 1/11th of tracts in AC, Ŀ30. Wit: L BERRY TUCKER, NELSON CRAW-
FORD, RO. H. COLEMAN, REUBEN COLEMAN, WM. TUCKER. Proved by WT 15 Oct
1804.

Page 139. 16 Jul 1804. HENRY HOLLOWAY, exr. of RO. HOLLOWAY, AC, to
EDMD. PENN, AC, for $290, 29 acres Buff. Part of a tract.
Lines: FRANCIS LEE, dec'd, RO. HOLLOWAY. Wit: WM. HALL, W. SAUNDERS,
ALEX. PENN, NATHL. OFFUTT, JAS. WOODS. Orig. del. to EP, 16 Dec 1814.

Page 140. 16 Jul 1804. EDMD. PENN, AC, to HENRY HOLLOWAY, AC, for $100,
11 3/4 acres N side Buff. Lines: old line of RO. HOLLOWAY,
old line of JACOB GIBSON. Part of a tract. Wit: as above.

Page 141. 12 May 1804. WM. HENDERSON, AC, to JNO. FORTUNE, AC, for lifetime support of WH - mare, furniture, etc. Wit: MARTIN DAWSON,
THOS. C. FORTUNE.

Page 142. 14 Sep 1804. CHAS. MASSIE SR, to WM. SMITH, - MASSIE to pay
part of purchase price - Rockfish tract. Lines: Main ridge
above a big rock; the stack rock; side of the Mt. Wit: JAS. WALTERS, JNO.
WALTERS, LYDIA WALTERS, POLLY WALTERS, JNO. McCLURE, JAS. McCLURE.

Page 142. 15 Oct 1804. JAS. MURPHY, AC, to NICHL. CABELL for Ŀ420, Warminster lot, adjoining town - 2 acres. Sold to JM by GEO. MENG,
except carriage house. Wit: HEN. HOLLOWAY, RO. MOORE, JAS. FARRAR, CHAS.
IRVING. Orig. del. to NC, 12 Feb 1805.

Page 143. 11 Oct 1804. STEPHEN WATTS & wife MARTHA, AC, to ALLEN BLAIR,
AC, for $100, 20 acres. Lines: JOS. SEAY, grantee, grantor,
THOS. CURRY.

Page 144. 10 Jan 1804. JNO. WIATT & wife WILHELMENIA, AC, to DAVID
WOODROOF JR, AC, for $1.00, no acres mentioned - S branches
Rutledge. Lines: The Church Road. Wit: JNO. McDANIEL, WIATT MOON, WM.
WOODROOF, DAVID WOODROOF SR. Orig. del. to DW Jr, 26 Sep 1805.

Page 145. 10 Jan 1804. JNO. WIATT & wife WILHELMENIA, AC, to JNO.

McDANIEL, AC, for $1.00, no acres mentioned, S branches Rutledge. Lines: JAS. LIVELY, bank of creek, THOS. CREWS. Wit: same as above save for JNO. McDANIEL.

Page 146.   10 Jan 1804. JNO. WIATT & wife WILHELMENIA, AC, to DAVID WOOD-
ROOF SR, for $1.00, no acres, S branches Rutledge. Lines: THOS. CREWS, Grantee, DAVID WOODROOF JR, JNO. McDANIEL. Wit: JNO. McDANIEL, DAVID WOODROOF JR, WILL WOODROOF, GEORGE CABELL JR, WIATT MOON.

Page 146.   15 Oct 1804. THOS. POWELL, AC, to WM. SALE, AC, for Ł354-10,
2 tracts. 1) 142 acres. 2) 35¼ acres both on Carter's Mill Creek and Stonehouse Creek. Lines of 142 acres: CHAS. CARTER's old line, JNO. MORE dec'd, --- WILLIAMSON, BENJ. POWELL. Line of 35¼ acres: JNO. SMITH, CARTER, main road.

Page 148.   3 May 1804. WM. SANDIDGE & wife TAMSEY, AC, to MOSES MARTIN
for Ł500, 224 acres branches Stonehouse. Lines: grantee, the old field, main road, ELIJAH BROCKMAN, AARON HIGGINBOTHAM, dec'd. Wit: NELSON CRAWFORD, CHAS. TALIAFERRO, WALKER ATKINSON. Page 149, order to quiz TAMSEY, 1 May 1804(sic). Done by CHAS. TALIAFERRO & NELSON CRAWFORD 15 Oct 1804. Orig. del. to MM, 30 Oct 1805.

Page 150.   10 Mar 1804. NICHL. PRYOR, AC, to LEROY BROWN, AC, for Ł26-16,
82 acres Head of Irish Creek. Lines: side of Blue ridge on E side; WM. PAXTON; top of Blue Ridge. Wit: GODFREY TOLER, JOSIAH ELLIS, JNO. C. PRYOR, CHAS. HAYNES, JNO. ELLIS, S(L) ELLIS, SOLOMON CARTER, AN-DERSON EVANS, THOS. N. EUBANK, GEORGE M. BROWNE.

Page 150.   10 Oct 1804. WIATT POWELL & wife SALLY, AC, to RO. WALKER, AC,
for $2000, 260 acres and where grantor lives. Wit: JNO. CAMM, RICH. POWELL, JAS. M. BROWN. Orig. del. to RW, 23 Sep 1818.

Page 151.   11 Oct 1804. RO. WALKER, AC, to WIATT POWELL & wife SALLY, AC,
for Ł50, for natural lives - tract above, but can't transfer without consent of RW. Wit: as above.

Page 152.   4 Oct 1804. GIDEON MARTIN SR, AC, to son WM. MARTIN, for love,
interest of dec'd son, ANDERSON, single and without will - 5 sh. GIDEON's interest in his dec'd son's estate. Wit: HUDSON MARTIN JR, NATHL. HARLOW.

Page 153.   6 Oct 1804. JAS. WOODS & wife SARAH, AC, to THOS. PUGH, AC,
for Ł378, 168 acres N side Rockfish. Lines: HENRY ROBERTS, WM. LYON. Part of tract. Wit: JNO. & ELIJAH PUGH, ZACH. MORRIS. Orig. del. to TP, 20 Mar 1807.

Page 154.   13 Oct 1804. JACOB WOOD, & wife BARTHENY, AC, to HENRY HOLLO-
WAY, AC, for Ł400, 258 acres branches Limekiln Creek. Lines: DRURY BELL, DRURY CHRISTIAN, est. of JNO. CHRISTIAN dec'd, PHILLIP GOOCH, JAS. CHRISTIAN, dec'd, HENRY BELL, exc'd. To HENRY HOLLOWAY, 8 Jun 1805, by P. GOOCH - delivered.

Page 155.   15 Oct 1804. PHILIP GOOCH & wife FRANCES, AC, to JACOB WOOD,
AC, for Ł487-10, 162½ acres. Lines: JNO. HIGGINBOTHAM, GIDEON RUCKER, JOS. HIGGINBOTHAM SR & JR. Orig. sent to JW, 8 Jun 1805.

Page 156.   28 May 1804. JNO. C. PRYOR, AC, to THOS. N. EUBANK, AC, Deed
of Trust - 6 sh.; debt due JNO. & RICH. ELLIS and assigned to WM. THURMOND - very long list of articles. Wit: JNO. DAVIS, G. LANE, LINZA BURKS, JOS. DUNCAN, GODFREY TOLER, JNO. FLOOD, JNO. EUBANK. Orig. sent to Major JNO. ELLIS 5 Oct 1808.

Page 158.   9 Feb 1801. JOS. DAWSON, AC, to LEWIS DAWSON, AC, for Ł282,
Harris Creek. Lines: grantor, Whitten's Spring branch, the path. Wit: NELSON C. DAWSON, JAS. LEE, GEO. SULLIVAN, PLEASANT DAWSON.

Page 159.   -- Aug 1804. RO. H. ROSE & wife FRANCES, Orange Co, to SPOTS-
WOOD GARLAND & wife LUCINDA (formerly ROSE) and EMILY ROSE - love and $1.00 - all of their interest 1/10th - in 200 acres. Part of GEDDES tract of Col. HUGH ROSE- lot of PAULINA ROSE, now dec'd. by AC

420

commrs - Lot 2. Lines: old field, lot 1, 6, 7; PATRICK ROSE. Wit: THOS. WOODROOF, JAS. B. EDWARDS, WILL CAMDEN JR.

Page 160. 15 Oct 1804. PHILIP THURMOND, Amelia Co, to EDMD. WINSTON, AC, for ₤45, 91 acres N side Paul's Mt., Harris Creek. Lines: JNO. McDANIEL, THOS. CREWS, WM. MOON, JNO. MORTON, grantee. Orig. del. to EW, 15 Apr 1835. (Note: I can see Paul's Mt. from my kitchen window. BFD)

Page 161. 19 Jul 1803. HENRY HOLLOWAY, exr. of RO. HOLLOWAY, dec'd, & SALLY HOLLOWAY, widow of RO., to DAVID S. GARLAND - 5 sh. and ₤382-10 paid to RO. in lifetime - 170 acres S side Buff., part of tract. Lines: Mill lot, JAS. WATSON JR, JAS. FRANKLIN, BENJ. PHILLIPS. Wit: WM. BRYANT, JAS. WARREN, JNO. SWANSON. 16 Oct 1807, del. to DSG.

Page 162. 19 Jul 1803. HENRY HOLLOWAY as above and SALLY HOLLOWAY as above for 5 sh. and ₤105 paid in lifetime of RO. HOLLOWAY - water grist mill and joins both parties - 4½ acres. Lines: S bank Buff., FRANCIS LEE, dec'd. Wit: as above. (grantee - DAVID S. GARLAND)

Page 163. 15 Oct 1804. HENRY HOLLOWAY, as exr. of RO. HOLLOWAY, to DAVID S. GARLAND for ₤300, 1/2 water grist mill on Buff. Lines: as above.

Page 164. 13 Oct 1804. DAVID S. GARLAND, AC, to WM. ARMISTEAD, AC, for $100, no acres mentioned - both sides Otter Creek. Lines: DAVID BURKS, S bank Otter, crossing creek, HENRY L. DAVIES.

Page 164. 13 Oct 1804. PETER JOINER & wife MILLEY, Campbell Co, to FREDERICK FULTZ, AC, for $1809, 201 acres both sides Rockey Run. Lines: JNO. TYLER, AMBROSE RUCKER, NATHAN WINGFIELD, Stovall's road, BENJ. WARREN, his spring, WM. DILLARD.

Page 165. 21 Oct 1804. HENRY CAMDEN, AC, to EDMD. HUDSON, for ₤70, 88 acres N side Buff.; Lines: Col. EDWD. CARTER, dec'd, Mill Creek, Col. BRAXTON - now LINDSEY COLEMAN; CHAS. PARKS' old corner - alias PHILIP PENN; JAS. WILLIAMSON. Bought by HC of ELISHA DENNIS. Orig. del. to EH, 1 Feb 1808.

Page 166. 15 Oct 1804. JNO. COWPER, late of AC, 2 Apr 1790, conveyed to NATHAN CRAWFORD & WM. HARRIS - Deed of Trust - to secure NATHL. ANDERSON & HUDSON MARTIN, attys. for HENRY MARTIN - 196 acres - top of Blue Mts - sold to SOLOMON & DANL. CAREY - 5 sh. paid by them. Tract conveyed to JNO. COWPER by DAVID McANNALLY & JNO. PANNELL. Lines: LUKE PANNELL (formerly).

Page 167. 15 Oct 1804. PETER JOINER & wife MILLEY, AC, to JNO. TYLER, AC, for ₤47 paid by TYLER - 47 acres Rockey Creek. Lines: JACOB G. PEARCE, AMBROSE RUCKER, WM. DILLARD. Wit: CHAS. CHRISTIAN, SAML. COLEMAN, JNO. ELLIS.

Page 168. 27 Sep 1802. Order to DAVID HOLLOWAY & WM. McKIM, J.P.'s of Richmond City, Va. - WM. LONG & wife BETSY, 28 Oct 1801, to JACOB WOOD - 2 tracts, 180 & 80 acres. Done, 21 Nov 1803.

Page 169. 17 Jul 1804. CHAS. CHRISTIAN & wife SARAH, AC, to ISAIAH ATKINSON, AC, for ₤12, 8 acres Rockey Creek. Lines: grantee, ELIZ. HOMAN, JOEL CAMPBELL, RUCKER, grantor. Wit: CHAS., HENRY CHRISTIAN, & WALTER CHRISTIAN JR.

Page 170. 20 Arp 1804. PLEASANT MARTIN, AC, to JAS. MURPHY, Warminster, Deed of Trust, debt due JNO. HIGGINBOTHAM JR. 5 sh. Boy slave, Squire. Wit: WM. F. CARTER, RO. MOORE, JAS. P. PARRISH.

Page 171. 17 Dec 1804. JNO. LONDON, AC, to WM. GARRETT, AC, for $11.30, 120 acres Stovall Creek. Lines: DANL. NORCUTT, JNO. KNIGHT, JNO. McBRIDE, JNO. BOLLING.

Page 171. 16 Jul 1804. JOS. HENSON & wife JEMIMY, AC, to ELISHA EVANS, Buckingham Co, for ₤25, 300 acres both sides Lovelady Creek. Lines: grantor, CABELL. Wit: JOHAN(?) S. WADE(?), JNO. DAVIS, WM. SANDIDGE.

Page 172.   27 Oct 1804.   WM. CARTER & wife CATY, Washington Co, Ky, to
             THOS. N. EUBANK, AC, for $500, 105 acres Puppies' Creek. Lines:
HENRY HARTLESS, dec'd, HENRY HEW(?), JNO. TALIAFERRO. Part of 2 tracts
bequeathed to WC by father, SOLOMON CARTER, AC,. Wit: JNO. FLOOD, EDMD.
GOODRICH, JNO. EUBANK, THOMAS MORRIS, JNO. EUBANK JR, ABRAM CARTER, G.
LANE, BENJ. SALE. (Note: if one does not know Kentucky counties, Washington County was formed in 1792 from Nelson County. I spent over 8 years
as pastor of Baptist Church at Springfield - county seat. I have many
records which I copied during my stay there. Here one sees the marriage
data on parents of ABRAHAM LINCOLN and Lincoln Homestead Park is out in
the county. Their records are in excellent condition. BFD)

Page 173.   28 Nov 1804.   PARMENAS BRYANT, AC, & wife PEGGY; RANDOLPH CASH
             & wife SALLY; WM. C. JOHNSON & wife ELIZ., AC, to THOS. & JNO.
BIBB, AC, for Ŀ157-7, to be paid by BIBBS to their brother, WM. BIBB, and
to be equally divided between THOS. & JNO. (sic) - all int. in tract on
Rucker's Run - 394 acres - whereof JNO. BIBB, dec'd, died in possession.
Wit: LANDON CABELL, JAS. MONTGOMERY, JNO. BETHEL.

Page 174.   17 Dec 1804.   THOS. N. EUBANK, AC, to CHAS. OVERSTREET, Alb.,
             for $400, 105 acres Puppy Creek. Lines: HENRY HARTLESS dec'd,
HENRY HEWS, JNO. TALIAFERRO; part of tract bought by TE of WM. CARTER,
Washington Co, Ky. Orig. del. to CO, 28 Sep 1805.

Page 175.   3 Nov 1804.   THOS. JONES, AC, to JESSE JONES, AC, for $1.00
             and love - slave, Frances. Wit: SHELTON JONES. Orig. del. to
JJ, 5 May 1807.

Page 176.   13 Oct 1804.   JNO. LONDON, AC, to THOS. GILLENWATERS, AC, for
             Ŀ66, 120 acres N branches Porrage. Lines: MADDISON HILL, WIATT
SMITH, grantor, JAS. DILLARD. Wit: JNO. CHRISTIAN.

Page 177.   20 Aug 1796.   JOS. DAWSON, AC, to son, PLEASANT DAWSON, AC,
             for love & Ŀ5, 37 acres. Wit: ZACH. DAWSON, N.C. DAWSON, JESSE
WOODROOF. Final proof by NELSON C. DAWSON, 17 Dec 1804.

Page 178.   20 Aug 1796.   JOS. DAWSON, AC, to son, PLEASANT DAWSON, AC,
             for love and Ŀ5, 100 acres. Lines: Harris Creek, JAS. CREWS,
JNO. BURFORD. Wit: as above and proof as above.

Page 179.   13 Apr 1804.   THOS. MOORE & wife SALLY, AC, to DAVID TINSLEY,
             AC, for $2560, 320 acres on James below town of Bethel-Rasp-
berry Neck. Lines: JESSE WOODROOF, ARTHUR L. DAVIES. Wit: NELSON C. DAW-
SON, ANTHONY G. TINSLEY, JAS. WARE, REUBEN PENDLETON. Orig. sent to TM,
25 Oct 1805.

Page 180.   21 Jun 1804.   REUBEN NORVELL & wife POLLY, AC, to BENJ. RUCKER,
             AC, for Ŀ38-17, 47 acres Stovall Creek, 2 tracts. 1) 47 acres
Lines: JAS. DAVIS, BARTLETT EADES, DANL. DAY. 2) 17 3/4 acres. Lines:
Rucker's road. Wit: RICH. WOOD, GIDEON RUCKER, NELSON C. DAWSON.

Page 181.   17 Dec 1804.   CHAS. CHRISTIAN & wife SARAH, AC, to JACOB
             PEARCE, AC, for Ŀ321, 160½ acres Buff. and where CC lives.
Lines: MIGGINSON's Ferry road, grantee, Stovall's old road, WM. COWLES
CHRISTIAN, CHAS. HUNT CHRISTIAN, WALTER CHRISTIAN, ISAIAH ATKINSON, AMBR.
RUCKER. Wit: RICH. WILSON, JACOB G. PEARCE, JAS. CHRISTIAN. Orig. sent
to CHRISTIAN - no date.

Page 182.   24 Oct 1804.   Order to AC J.P.'s - 13 Oct 1804, GEO. MENG &
             wife MARY, to JAS. MURPHY - 2 acres Warminster. Done, 17 Dec
1804, by LANDON CABELL & WM. B. HARE.

Page 183.   1 Sep 1804.   RICE BROWN & wife NANCY, AC, to JAS. MONTGOMERY,
             AC, for $200, 98 acres Hatt Creek. Lines: grantee, THOS. JONES,
ARCHIBALD FRAME, STEPHEN JOHNSON. Wit: JNO. TOOL, THOS. HAYS, WM. BROOKS,
CLAYTON MONTGOMERY, RO. SHIELDS, ALEX. SALE, MATT. HIGHT, JAS. FITZGERALD,
WM. FITZGERALD.

Page 185.   21 Jan 1805.   LANDON CABELL, AC, to NORVELL SPENCER, AC, (del.
             to NS, 7 May 1807) - SAML. ROSE, late of Va., but now of Ky. -

Power of Atty, 24 Aug 1803, to CABELL - for L300, 200 acres, part of 1872 acres of Col. HUGH ROSE, late of AC - SAML. derived title as devisee of HUGH ROSE - lot #5. Lines: WM. CABELL, #4 - now WM. SPENCER's, #2, #1; Tract bought by N. SPENCER from S. GARLAND & wife. Wit: DAVID S. GARLAND, WILL LOVING, JOEL FRANKLIN.

Page 187. 15 Jan 1805. GEO. HYLTON, AC, to RICH. WOOD, AC, for L144, 96
            acres; part of tract on Elk Island Creek. Lines: CHAS. CHRIS-
TIAN, JESSE ALLEN, WM. JORDAN. Wit: VALENTINE HYLTON, WM. PAMPLIN, WM.
WOOD, CALEB WOOD.

Page 188. 21 Jul 1804. JNO. WRIGHT, AC, to JNO. HIGGINBOTHAM, AC, Deed
            of Trust - debt to BROWN MURPHY & Co., for 5 sh; slaves. Wit:
JAS. HANSBROUGH, JOS. LOVING, WM. A. HOWARD. Orig. del. to SAML. BLAIN
3 Oct 1805.

Page 189. 19 Nov 1804. WM. SMITH, AC, to JAS. MURPHY, AC, Deed of Trust
            Debt to BROWN PERKINS & Co, Bent Creek, for 5 sh. Stock, etc.
Wit: STEPHEN WATTS, J.P. GARLAND, WM. PETTYJOHN, JAS. LEE.

Page 190. 1 Jan 1805. SPOTSWOOD GARLAND & wife LUCINDA, AC, to NORVELL
            SPENCER, AC, for L750, 180 acres Naked Creek, S branch Piney.
Part of 1872 acres of Col. HUGH ROSE & share of grantors - lot #6 to
LUCINDA GARLAND. Lines: WM. CABELL, lots #5, 1, 8. - 200 acres. Lines:
PATRICK ROSE, Lots #1, 6, 7; old field - PAULINA ROSE's share, too, by
AC decree. Their interest in 3/10th or 60 acres. Wit: LANDON CABELL,
LEROY ROBINSON, W. SPENCER, JAS. SPENCER.

Page 192. 24 Sep 1804. Order to Sumner Co. Tenn. J.P.'s THOS. BLACKMORE
            & JONA HANNUM - JNO. TURNER & wife MILLEY, 6 Mar 1802, deed to
RICH. JONES - 622 1/3 acres. Done, 18 Feb 1805.

Page 193. 11 Feb 1805. LAWRENCE CAMPBELL & wife HENRIETTA, AC, to JAS.
            M. BROWN, AC, for L212, 53 acres Higginbotham Mill Creek and
part of where LC lives. Lines: School House Spring, WM. S. CRAWFORD,
grantee, DAVID S. GARLAND, Courthouse road, the old road. Wit: WM. BATES,
WM. KINNIDY, JNO. CAMM.

Page 194. 16 Apr 1804. LAWRENCE CAMPBELL & wife HENRIETTA to JAS. M.
            BROWN, as above, for L60, 10½ acres on Higginbotham Mill
Creek. Lines: as above. Wit: WM. BATES, BENJ. TALIAFERRO, ALEX. PENN.

Page 195. 16 Feb 1805. SAML. S. SCRUGGS & wife JANEY, AC, to WM. MARTIN,
            AC, no amount mentioned, 15 acres S branches Dutch Creek and
Becknal's Spring Branch. Lines: grantee, WM. DIXON, WM. H. MOSBY.

Page 196. 18 Feb 1805. SAML. S. SCRUGGS & wife JANEY, AC, to WM. SMITH,
            AC, for L70, 70 acres S branches Rockfish. Lines: JOS. SMITH,
trible fall branch, WM. H. MOSBY.

Page 197. 16 Jan 1805. Order to AC J.P.'s, THOS. MOORE & PHILIP JOHNSON.
            Deed of MICAJAH GOODWIN & wife ELIZ., 11 Feb 1804, to PROSSER
POWELL. Done, 14 Feb 1805.

Page 198. 2 Nov 1804. JAS. L. TURNER, AC, to HUDSON M. & SPOTSWOOD GAR-
            LAND, AC, Deed of Trust - debt due JAS. & DAVID GARLAND. 6 sh.
Beds and slaves in hands of TERISHA TURNER. Wit: WILL G. PENDLETON, EDMD.
T. COLEMAN, RO. COLEMAN. Orig. del. to DAVID S. GARLAND, 7 Oct 1805.

Page 199. 5 Jan 1805. JNO. CREWS, AC, to LEWIS DAWSON, AC, for $100, 24
            acres Fawn Creek. Lines: JOS. DAWSON, JAS. LEE, AMBR. BURFORD,
PLEASANT DAWSON, JNO. CREWS. Wit: WILL CAMDEN JR, PLEASANT DAWSON, NELSON
C. DAWSON, BENJ. WATTS, BURL SNEAD.

Page 200. 17 Nov 1804. FRANCES TUCKER, widow of DRURY TUCKER, dec'd, AC,
            to Major RICH. HARRISON of Harris Creek - she is advanced in
years and wishes to pay debts and be supported - for $1.00 - all lands,
slaves, etc. Wit: W.S. CRAWFORD, WM. HARRISON, THOS. MOORE, JNO. SHELTON,
JAS. HARRISON, GEO. CARY. Orig. del. to NICHL. HARRISON, 22 Jun 1805.

Page 201. 22 Oct 1804. WM. HORSLEY, AC, to GEO. HYLTON, AC, for Ł224,
112 acres out of estate of WM. HORSLEY, dec'd. N side James.
Lines: ALLEN on river, GEO. HYLTON. Wit: LEROY PAMPLIN, JAS. P. GARLAND,
JAS. PAMPLIN, MARY B. DRUMMOND, RACHEL FRANKLIN. Orig. del. to CHAS.L.
CHRISTIAN 10 May 1813.

Page 202. -- Jul 1804. REUBEN RUCKER & wife BETSY, to JNO. BOLLING for
5 sh, no acres mentioned - Stovall Creek. Lines: DANL. BURFORD,
SR, near Lynch road, MICHL. COALTER. Wit: JNO. McDANIEL, MATT. LIVELY,
JAS. BOLING.

Page 203. 15 Jan 1805. ALEX. REID, dec'd, AC, by will directed that
lands be sold; duly advertised on 1st of this month and sold
at public sale to JAS. HUGHES. Exrs. convey: JAS. WOODS, SAML. REID, &
HUDSON MARTIN for Ł45, Rockfish - part of pat. to AR, 283 acres, 10 Sep
1767 - 140 acres sold. Lines: JAS. WOODS. Wit: HUDSON MARTIN JR, RO.
SHIELDS, NATHAN BARNETT, RICH. LEIGH.

Page 204. 16 Jul 1804. DAVID S. GARLAND, AC, to WM. KNIGHT, AC, for Ł24,
lot #5 in New Glasgow - E side of new street. Lines: alley,
No. 4. Wit: JAS. GARLAND, WM. G. PENDLETON, H.M. GARLAND. Orig. del. to
WK, 10 Apr 1817.

Page 204. 20 Nov 1804. BENJ. HARRIS & wife MARY, Alb., to JNO. BETHEL,
AC, for Ł1032-10, 347 + acres Eastern waters Rockfish; Taylor's
Creek. Lines: WM. SMITH, THOS. ROBERTSON, WM. HARRIS JR, JNO. McLURE. Wit:
THOS. MORRISON, NICHL. CAKSON (CALSON?), JNO. DIGGES, MARY W. HARRIS.
Orig. del. to JNO. W. HARRIS, per order, 9 Apr 1806.

Page 206. 16 Feb 1805. JNO. ANDERSON & wife POLLY, AC, to MOSES PHIL-
LIPS, AC, for Ł75, 50 acres Aaron's Branch; N branch Buff.
Part of tract. Lines: RICH. ALCOCK, SAML. ANDERSON, PHILLIPS' old line.
Orig. del. to MP, 27 May 1805.

Page 207. 7 Feb 1805. SAML. HANSBROUGH, AC, to JAS. HANSBROUGH, AC, for
Ł75-12, one-fourth of a tract which my father, WM. HANSBROUGH,
devised to me by will - or my interest therein. Wit: NELSON ANDERSON,
EDWIN H. WAIDE.

Page 208. 30 Oct 1804. LUCY HUDSON, AC, to DAVID & JAS. GARLAND, AC,
for Ł55 - she is widow of RO. HUDSON and daughter of GEO.
GILLESPIE, dec'd - all of her interest in tract on S side Piney - where
GG lived at death. Wit: EDMD. T. COLEMAN, WM. KNIGHT, THOMPSON NOELL,
BENNETT HUDSON.

Page 208. 18 Feb 1805. JACOB WOOD & wife BARTHEMIA, AC, to WIATT SMITH,
for Ł487-10, 162½ acres Rutledge Creek. Lines: JNO. HIGGINBO-
THAM, GIDEON RUCKER, JOS. HIGGINBOTHAM, Sr. & Jr. Bought of PHILIP GOOCH
by JW and commonly called LACKEY's Tract.

Page 209. 14 Sep 1803. JACOB WOOD to WIATT SMITH for Ł45, all interest
in estate of SALLY H. & NANCY PHILLIPS - due me at decease of
their mother by my marriage. Ł100 bond, if wife, BARTHENY, fails to relinquish dower. Wit: GEO. MARTIN.

Page 210. 17 Oct 1804. JAS. FLOYD, AC, to JACOB WOOD, AC, for $2000, 58
acres. Lines: E side Rockey Creek, JNO. CHRISTIAN, mill pond,
CHISNELL's old stamping mill, WM. DILLARD, JACOB G. PEARCE, Buffaloe,
mouth of Mill Creek. Wit: WIATT SMITH, JAC TYREE, MOSES PHILLIPS, WM.
TYREE.

Page 211. 29 Oct 1802. THOS. WATT, AC, & wife JANCY, to WM. WALLER
HENING, Alb., for Ł10, 1/2 acre lot in Charlottesville - No.
20. Bought by TW of SAML. WOODS. Wit: D.W. CRAWFORD, CARY BIBB, JNO.
THOMPSON.

Page 212. 18 Aug 1804. Order to AC J.P.'s WM. LOVING & WM. H. DIGGES.
Deed of JAS. NEVIL, LEWIS NEVIL, ZACH. NEVIL, CORNL. NEVIL,
ROWLAND EDMUNDS & wife ELIZ., WM. O. MURRAY & wife LUCY, CHAS. A. LEWIS
& wife SALLY, CLOUGH SHELTON & wife MARY, SAML. EDMUNDS & wife ESTHER,

to CHAS. YANCEY, 25 Feb 1803 - 324 acres. To quiz ELIZ., LUCY, SALLY,
MARY, & ESTHER apart from husbands: ROWLAND, WM. O., CHAS. A., CLOUGH &
SAML. Done as to wives of ROWLAND EDMUNDS, WM. O. MURRAY, CHAS. A. LEWIS,
& SAML. EDMUNDS, 12 Feb 1805.

Page 213. 13 Nov 1804. JNO. CHILDRESS & wife MARGAREY, Knox Co, Tenn.,
to JESSE BLAND, AC, for $250, 100 acres. Lines: CHAS. TALIA-
FERRO. Bequeathed to JC by THOS. POWELL, dec'd, by will of 18 Mar 1783,
& rec. in AC. Wit: JAS. WHITE, J.P. & JOSIAH NICHOL(?) J.P. Orig. del.
to JB, 2 Jun 1808. CHAS. McCLUNG, Clk, JAS. WHITE, Pres. J.P.

Page 214. 31 Jan 1805. FRANCIS TAYLOR & wife NANCY, AC, to JNO. F. HALL,
AC, for Ł50, 40 acres. Lines: Ridge path, RICE KEY, JNO.
ROBERTS, STEPHEN RUSSELL.

Page 215. 16 Feb 1805. DANL. NORCUTT, AC, to JAS. BOLLING, AC, for Ł130,
129 acres headwaters Stovall. Orig. del. to JB, 19 Aug 1805.

Page 215. 7 Jul 1804. RO. DINWIDDIE, AC, to NATHAN CRAWFORD, AC, Deed
of Trust - $1.00. RD has conveyed to HUDSON MARTIN & JAS.
WOODS - 200 acres where RD lives. Lines: CRAWFORD, WM. CRAWFORD, JAS.
MORRISON, ANN DINWIDDIE. Wit: JESSE JOPLING, WM. CRAWFORD, NELSON CRAW-
FORD, JR. Sent to H. MARTIN 11 Jul 1805.

Page 217. 4 Jul 1804. Order to DAVID PATTISON & A. DIBRELL, Buckingham
J.P.'s. Deed of PATRICK ROSE JR, & wife JANE, 22 Nov 1803, to
WM. B. HARE - 244 acres. Done 13 Feb 1805.

Page 218. 18 Feb 1805. CHAS. CHRISTIAN & wife SARAH, AC, to RO. ALLEN,
AC, for Ł200, 135 acres where CC lives. Lines: Stovall's old
road, JAS. CHRISTIAN, JACOB PEARCE, CHAS. H. CHRISTIAN, ALEX. BRYDIE,
dec'd, top of Braxton's ridge, West's old road. Orig. del. to RA, 30 Dec
1805. Memo: agreement by CC & RO. ALLEN - CC reserved to self, ISAAC
RUCKER, & JAS. FLOYD - present managers of "an house, now a bldg." on
Stovall's old road. It is to be free for Presbyterian or Methodist Society and all others willing to associate and commune with the same - one
half acre - at forks of Wests' and Stovall's old road and includes meeting house and 20 Sq. ft. for burying ground. Wit: WILL CAMDEN JR, JOS.
ALLCOCK, JAS. CHRISTIAN.

Page 220. 17 Dec 1804. GEO. CABELL & wife SARAH, Lynchburg, to WM. COX,
AC, for $400, known as Moffitt's old field. Lines: MAJOR WARD,
WM. CLARKE. Conveyed by WM. BURTON & wife MARY, by AC decree - 127½ acres.
Wit: RO. RIVES, THOS. S. McCLELLAND, F. McHENRY, LANDON CABELL, WM.
KENNIDY.

Page 221. 7 Apr 1804. JNO. ROBERTS, AC, to CHAS. P. TALIAFERRO, AC, for
Ł38, 145 acres S waters Pedlar. Lines: grantor, JNO. BURKS,
JESSE PRYOR. Wit: BENJ. TALIAFERRO, JNO. TALIAFERRO, JNO. SPITFATHOM,
JOS. HOUSEWRIGHT. Orig. del. 11 Mar 1806 to JNO. TALIAFERRO.

Page 222. 14 Dec 1802. Order to WM. LOVING & WM. H. DIGGES, AC J.P.'s,
Deed of WM. ALFORD & wife LETTY, 18 Nov 1792, to ELIJAH MAYS.
103 acres. Done 12 Feb 1805.

Page 223. 18 Feb 1805. JAS. TURNER & wife LUCY, AC, to HENRY SMITH, AC,
for Ł200, 145 acres N branches S. fork Rockfish. Lines: GEO.
VAUGHAN, grantee, THOS. ANDERSON dec'd, JNO. JOPLING, CHAS. STATHAM, CON-
NARD MOYER. Orig. del. to J. TURNER JR, 8 May 1806.

Page 224. 25 Mar 1805. Order to AC J.P.'s, DAVID S. GARLAND & JOS. BUR-
RUS. Deed of SPOTSWOOD GARLAND & wife LUCINDA, 1 Jan 1805, to
NORVELL SPENCER - 240 acres. Done, 26 Mar 1805.

Page 225. 13 Oct 1804. WM. TUCKER, Bedford Co, to AMBROSE RUCKER, Jr,
AC, Deed of Trust - WM. owes DRURY TUCKER"s committee - 2 neg-
ro girls. Wit: SPOTSWOOD GARLAND, JAS. B. EDWARDS, LINDSEY COLEMAN JR,
TERENCE COSNEY, LEWIS DAWSON, PLEASANT MARTIN.

Page 226. 17 Jun 1805. ABRAHAM SMITH, AC, to son ELIAS SMITH, Claiborn

Co, Tenn, Power of Atty - to act as to my land in Buncum Co, N.C. Bought
of NATHAN DEAVER & rec. in N.C. To AS, 2 Jul 1805; county seal annexed.
(Note: How I would like to see one of the old county seals of Amherst
County. No one knows what became of the official seal and we have no
copies of it. I was asked to serve as Director of Amherst's celebration
of her 200th birthday and also to help prepare a new seal. The committee
did so, but I should like to see the original and we could then use it.)

Page 227. 23 Sep 1802. JAS. CREWS & wife ELIZ., AC, to WM. ADAMS, Lynch-
           burg, for Ŀ120, 50 acres where JC lives. Lines: E side Bolling
Creek. Wit: SAML. ROSE, VERNON METCALFE, THOS. W. COCKE, J.P., REUBEN
CRAWFORD, WILSON DAVENPORT. Orig. del. to WA, 24 Jul 1805.

Page 228. 1 Jan 1805. DANL. BURFORD, Jr, AC, to STERLING CLAIBORNE,
           Campbell Co, Deed of Trust - debt due SAML. IRVINE, FOR $1.00,
500 acres. Lines: BENJ. RUCKER, RO. H. ROSE, BOLLING CLARKE, DANL. BUR-
FORD SR, ARCHIBALD BURFORD, REUBEN RUCKER & where DB, Jr, lives. Wit:
ANTHONY RUCKER, DAVID TINSLEY, JNO. CREWS, THOS. WOODROOF, ARCHILAUS
REYNOLDS, HARSON(?) HUGHES.

Page 229. 4 Mar 1805. RICH. TANKERSLEY, AC, to WM. PENN, Deed of Trust
           for 6 sh. debt due JNO. PENN SR - 2 negroes. Wit: JOS. & GEO.
DAVENPORT, GEO. DILLARD.

Page 230. 23 Feb 1805. THOS. MITCHELL, AC, to STERLING CLAIBORNE,
           Lynchburg, Deed of Trust; debt to SAML. IRVINE; 2 negroes.
Wit: GEO. DILLARD, WILSON DAVENPORT, JAS. BENAGH.

Page 231. 17 Dec 1804. RO. ALLEN & wife ELIZ, AC, to WM. TOLLE, AC, for
           Ŀ110, 140 acres S branches Porage. Lines: DAVID GARLAND,
PLEASANT STORY, JAS. DILLARD, ALEX. JEWELL, SACKVILLE KING. Wit: THOS.
COPPEDGE, P. MARTIN, WM. PENN JR, WM. COLEMAN. Orig. del. to WT, 1 Aug
1806.

Page 231. 10 Apr 1805. JNO. MUNDY, AD, to CHAS. MUNDY, AC, for Ŀ560,
           all interest in 801 acres on both sides Porage and bought by
both from SACKVILLE KING & REUBEN NORVELL. Wit: WM. TURNER, REUBEN NOR-
VELL, JNO. LONDON, HENRY TURNER.

Page 232. 1 Dec 1804. SACKVILLE KING & wife ANN, Campbell Co, to DAVID
           S. GARLAND for Ŀ324, 360 acres N branches Fluvanna. Lines:
JOS. MAYS, dec'd, WM. GALT, near Stovall's ferry, grantee. Wit: REUBEN
NORVELL, THOS. S. McCLELLAND, JNO. LONDON, WM. TURNER. Orig. del. 17
Feb 1806, to DG.

Page 232. 27 Mar 1805. Order to AC J.P.'s to quiz NANCY BROWN, wife of
           HENRY BROWN, deed of 14 Apr 1804 to JNO. MAYS SR. 200 acres.
Done 28 Mar 1805 by WM. WARE & DAVID S. GARLAND.

Page 232. (2 pages so numbered) 9 Apr 1805. Order to AC J.P.'s:
           LAWRENCE CAMPBELL & wife HENRIETTA, 11 Feb 1805, to JAS. M.
BROWN, deed of 53 acres. Done by SAML. MEREDITH & DAVID S. GARLAND, 17
Jun 1805.

Page 233. 9 Apr 1805. Same order and parties - 10½ acres sold to JAS.
           M. BROWN. Same return.

Page 234. 22 Nov 1804. JAS. CLARKE JR, Manchester in Chesterfield, to
           JNO. MONDAY, AC, for Ŀ1142-8, 544 acres Duck bill; branch of
Bolling Creek. Surveyed by Capt. REUBEN NORVELL. Lines: Capt. PHILLIP
JOHNSON, JNO. MILLER, JNO. HANSFORD, PLEDGE PALMER, JNO. WARD. Tract
pat. to CHAS. CLARKE, 14 Feb 1761. Wit: REUBEN NORVELL, JNO. LONDON, WM.
TURNER, JAS. L. LAMKIN, RO. SHIELDS. Orig. del. to JAS. L. LAMKIN, 16 Dec
1833, by JNO. M. WILLIAMS.

Page 235. 2 May 1805. WM. WOODS & wife RUTH, Rockingham Co, to JOS.
           TOMS, AC, for Ŀ403, 96 acres N fork Rockfish. Part of tract of
JOS. SMITH, dec'd. Lines: HENRY McCLAIN, AUGUSTINE SMITH; tract devised
by JOS. SMITH to his three daughters, SARAH, JUDY & MARY; JAS. BROOKS.
Wit: JAS. BROOKS for WM. WOODS only, RO. BROOKS - same; AZARIAH MARTIN,

426

HENRY McCLAIN.

Page 235. 17 Jun 1805. NATHL. ANDERSON, atty. in fact for JNO. TOLLE &
THOS. ASTON, surviving partners or assignees of HENRY MARTIN &
Co. to LUNSFORD LOVING for Ł230-10, 391 acres S fork Rockfish. Lines:
JAMES MATTHEWS, Beaver Creek, JOSIAH JOPLING.

Page 236. 13 Oct 1804. PATRICK ROSE & wife MARY, AC, to THOS. LANDRUM,
AC, for Ł416, 208 acres both sides Naked Creek; part of tract
and where ANDREW MORGAN lives. Lines: ANDERSON MOSS, HUGH ROSE dec'd, JAS.
FRANKLIN, RO. ROSE dec'd. Wit: DAVID S. GARLAND, THOS. POWELL, ANN POWELL.
Page 237, order to AC J.P.'s to quiz MARY ROSE, 27 Oct 1804. Done 15 Mar
1805, by SAML. MEREDITH & DAVID S. GARLAND.

Page 237. 31 Mar 1795. JAS. PAMPLIN, AC, to RO. ROGERS, Buckingham Co,
for Ł200, 2 acres grist mill on Fishing Creek. The 2 acres
excepted in deed by JAMES PAMPLIN to NICHL. PAMPLIN. Wit: JNO. PATTISON,
CHAS. FITCH, THOMAS NORTH, JAS. PHELPS. Final proof by FITCH, 17 Jun 1805.

Page 238. 1 Mar 1805. JOS. AMOS, AC, to LINDSEY COLEMAN, AC, Deed of
Trust; debt to WM. EDMUNDS. 6 sh. Negro woman and child. Wit:
SHAROD BUGG, TERENCE COONEY, JNO. SPITFATHOM. Orig. del. to EDMUNDS, 9
Nov 1805.

Page 239. 2 May 1805. JOS. TOMS, AC, & wife MAPSEY, to WM. WOODS, Rock-
ingham Co., Deed of Trust; debt to WW. $1.00 paid by JAS.
BROOKS - 96 acres N fork Rockfish; part of tract of JOS. SMITH dec'd and
sold this day by WM. WOODS to JOS. TOMS. Lines: see 235, WM. WOODS's deed.
Wit: RO. BROOKS, WM. SMITH, ANNE BROOKS, JAS. MONTGOMERY, NELSON ANDERSON,
JOS. SHELTON, HUDSON MARTIN.

Page 240. 17 Jun 1805. PATRICK ROSE & wife MARY, AC, to JNO. NICHOLAS
ROSE, AC, for Ł250, 105 acres and part of where PR lives.
Lines: S side Main road, N side of road, Landrum's branch, WM. MOSS.

Page 240. 6 Mar 1805. THOS. WOODROOF, AC, from GEO. SHRADER, AC, Deed
of Trust; debts due JAS. L. TURNER & DAVID & JAS. GARLAND. For
$1.00 all interest in tract where HENRY ARRINGTON lives & mill - 10 acres.
Bought from GEO. HYLTON. Wit: JAS. S. LAINE, HUDSON M. GARLAND, WM. G.
PENDLETON.

Page 241. 28 May 1805. ALEX. F. ROSE to WM. GALT, Richmond, for Ł639-4,
290 acres. Lines: JOEL FRANKLIN, grantee, WM. S. CRAWFORD,
JAS. WOODS. Wit: W.R.(?) MILSTEAD, JAS. WOODS, D.S. GARLAND, JAS. GARLAND.
Orig. del. to WG, 4 May 1812.

Page 242. 17 Jun 1805. DAVID RODES, AC, to CHAS. YANCEY, Alb., for
$1000, slaves etc. Wit: JOEL YANCEY, DILMUS JOHNSON of Alb.

Page 242. 15 Jun 1805. RO. ROGERS, Buckingham, to WM. PAMPLIN, AC, for
Ł100, grist mill and 2 acres. Fishing Creek. Orig. del. to WP
10 Dec 1807.

Page 243. 7 Jun 1805. HAWES COLEMAN, LEWIS NICHOLAS, ZACH. ROBERTS,
commrs., to LINDSEY BURKS, AC, Nov. Court, 1801 decree: BENJ.
HARRIS, HAWES COLEMAN, JAS. WOODS, RO. FARRAR, LEWIS NICHOLAS & ZACH
ROBERTS - or any 3 - to sell 2 tracts of est. of THOS. JOPLING - not
mentioned in his will. Sold to L BURKS at CH, 15 Feb 1802, for Ł97-10;
228 acres Dancing creek. Lines: WM. BURKS, WM. JOPLING, WM. SHOEMAKER.
Wit: JOS. SHELTON, WM. LEE HARRIS, JNO. FARRAR, Sr, RICH. C. POLLARD,
JNO. W. HARRIS, WM. DOUGLAS.

Page 244. 15 Jun 1804. WM. WARE & wife PATTY, AC, to WM. PRYOR, AC, for
Ł8, 18 acres on Horsley creek. Lines: CHAS. CRAWFORD, DAVID
CRAWFORD, main road. Wit: JNO. CRAWFORD, ABRAM CARTER, JOS. DODD, JNO.
DAVIS, MOSES MARTIN, WM. EVANS. Orig. del. to WP, 18 Jun 1810.

Page 244. 15 Jun 1805. WM. WARE & wife PATTY as above to WM. PRYOR as
above for Ł75, 48¼ acres N fork Horsley & S fork. Lines: main
road, JNO. CRAWFORD, grantee. Wit: as above, but margin has del. to JNO.

PRYOR, 17 Aug 1841.

Page 245. 6 Nov 1804. WM. B. HARE & WM. H. CABELL bound to NATHL. HILL
          for $10,000 HARE has conveyed to HILL 664 acres Castle Creek
& believed HANNAH H. & SARAH E., infants of WM. HARE, are entitled to
undivided moiety when 21. Bond to protect HILL until they mature. Wit:
THOS. HARVIE, NATHL. HILL JR, WM. HILL JR. Ack. by grantor 17 Jun 1805.

Page 246. 6 Nov 1804. WM. B. HARE to NATHL. HILL, both of AC, for Ŀ4460
          tobacco, 664 acres Castle Creek. Part of tract formerly owned
by NCIHL. CABELL dec'd. Lines: DAVID S. GARLAND, the thoroughfare, Castle
Creek.

Page 247. 13 Apr 1805. ADAMSON BERRY, AC, to JAS. WARE, AC, Deed of
          Trust - debt due DAVID & JAS. GARLAND, for $1.00, beds, etc.
Wit: ALEX. MARR, WM. KNIGHT, S. GARLAND.

Page 248. 15 Jun 1805. WM. PRYOR certifies that WM. WARE & wife PATTY
          have conveyed 48½ acres on Horsley. WARE may raise his mill
dam as high as ISAAC WRIGHT had at present place & pointed out by NELSON
& JNO. CRAWFORD, HENRY LANE, JNO. EUBANK, EDWD. CARTER & ISAAC WRIGHT. If
any higher, to pay damages. Wit: JNO. CRAWFORD & WM. EVANS.

Page 248. 15 Aug 1805. WM. PRYOR, AC, to WM. WARE, AC, for Ŀ60, 42 ac-
          res Horsley. Lines: grantee, WM. LAWLESS. Wit: JNO. CRAWFORD,
ABRAM CARTER, MOSES MARTIN, JOS. DODD, JNO. DAVIS, WM. EVANS.

Page 249. 17 Feb 1804. ISAAC WRIGHT & wife SUSANNAH, AC, to WM. WARE
          for Ŀ100, 50 acres in fork of both sides N fork Horsley. Lines:
WM. PRYOR, JNO. CRAWFORD. Wit: REUBEN CRAWFORD, HENRY BROWN, NELSON CRAW-
FORD, JNO. FLOOD, EDWD. CARTER, JNO. BARKER.

Page 249. 1 Jun 1805. JNO. HAGER & wife MARY, AC, to GEO. HYLTON, AC,
          for Ŀ110, 110 acres S side Buff. Ridge. Lines: JAS. PETER,
S fork Oweney's Creek. Wit: VALENTINE HYLTON, JORDAN ARRINGTON, JNO.
HAGER JR.

Page 250. 17 Jun 1805. JAS. EDMONDS & wife MARY, AC, to JAS. FLOYD, JNO.
          ALCOCK, GEO. WRIGHT, JNO. ALFORD & JAS. BIBB JR, trustees, for
$100, 1 acre West Naked Creek and including New Kingswood Meeting House -
Meth. Epis. Church - including use of spring west of the house; for
Conference use.

Page 251. 5 Sep 1791. JACOB PHILLIPS & wife SARAH, AC, to WM. SANDIDGE
          AC, for Ŀ20, no acres mentioned, N branches S fork Pedlar.
Lines: ADAM REID. Wit: PULLIAM SANDIDGE, LARKIN SANDIDGE, AMS. TOMLINSON.
Final proof, 17 Jun 1805, by LARKIN SANDIDGE.

Page 252. 17 Jun 1805. ABRAM CARTER & wife MARY, AC, to THOS. GOODRICH,
          AC, for Ŀ157, 157 acres N side Pedlar. Lines: grantor, grantee,
near Lovelady Mt., SAM GEST. Orig. del. to TG, 7 Sep 1807.

Page 253. 18 Feb 1805. GEO. MARTIN & wife MILDRED, AC, to THOS. CHILD-
          RESS, AC, for Ŀ200, 230 acres surveyed 26 May 1795 S branches
S fork Rockfish. Lines: CUTHBERT WEBB, THOS. JOPLING dec'd. Wit: HUDSON
MARTIN, PETER MARTIN, GEO. VAUGHAN.

Page 254. 4 Mar 1805. THOS. BIBB Sr., AC, to WM. H. DIGGES, AC, for
          Ŀ550, 190 acres S branches Rucker's Run-part of tract of WM.
BIBB dec'd. Lines: THOS. ALFORD, TERISHA TURNER, JNO. LOVING, grantee,
ELIJAH MAYS, BURDETT SKINNER. Wit: WILL LOVING, CARY BIBB, RO. RIVES.
Orig. del. to JOS. LOVING, 2 May 1807.

Page 254. 20 Apr 1805. JAS. GILES, JUDIA GILES, NELSON MONROE for
          SUSANNA GILES, WM. COFFEE for ELIZ. GILES, REUBEN COFFEY for
NANCY GILES, AC, Power of Atty. to friend, WM. GILES - to sell our joint
interest in tract in Fluvanna on Cunningham Creek; part of tract bequeathed to us as joint heirs of GEO. ROD, dec'd, Fluvanna. Wit: DANL. Mc-
DONALD, EDMD. COFFEY, ISABEL MONROE, NANCY R. MONROE.

Page 255.   17 Jun 1805.   ALEX. REID, AC, by will directed exrs. to sell
            AC lands - Ŀ1610-10 pd. to SAML. REID, JAS. WOODS, & HUDSON
MARTIN by THOS. GOODWIN - 287 acres Headwaters S Rockfish. Tract where
SAML. REID died as owner & resident. Wit: PLEASANT MARTIN, JNO. JOPLING,
JNO. THOMPSON, HAWES COLEMAN. Orig. del. to TG, 26 Nov 1805.

Page 256.   20 Nov 1804.   THOS. GOODWIN, AC, to WM. H. CABELL, WM. CRAW-
            FORD, NELSON CRAWFORD, HUDSON MARTIN JR, - 2nd part - & HAWES
COLEMAN, 3rd part to secure COLEMAN on 14 bonds to exrs. of SAML. REID
Deed of Trust. $1.00, 460 acres where TG lives. Wit: P. MARTIN, JAS.
JOPLING, JNO. THOMPSON, EDMOND BURNETT.

Page 257.   20 Nov 1804.   THOS. GOODWIN, AC, Deed of Trust to same men as
            previous deed above, for $1.00, 287 + acres. Headwaters Rock-
fish - South and whereon SAML. REID lived. Wit: as previous deed.

Page 258.   18 Jun 1805.   HUDSON MARTIN frees slave, Danl.

Page 258.   4 Jun 1805.   THOS. PHILLIPS & wife SARAH, AC, to JNO. BARNETT,
            AC, for Ŀ60, 182 where TP lives. Lines: JNO. HATTER, JNO.
MASTERS, D.S. GARLAND; known as Waller Hall. Wit: BARTLETT GARRNELD(?),
ALLEN DAVIS, JAS. DEMASTERS, WM. COFFEY, JOS. HORSLEY, JNO. CARKEON,
JESSE JONES.

Page 259.   21 Mar 1805.   JNO. OWENS, AC, to JNO. THOMPSON, Overseer, Deed
            of Trust to secure GEO: LOVING & HENRY SMITH as bondsmen to
EDWD. LEWIS - 6 sh. - slave. Wit: NICHL. VANSTAVERN, WALTER LEAKE, AUGUS-
TINE SHEPHERD.   Orig. del. to GEORGE LOVING, 3 Jun 1806.

Page 260.   23 Nov 1804.   PATRICK ROSE & wife MARY, AC, to JNO. THOMPSON,
            AC, - about 30 Sep 1776, PATRICK ROSE & wife sold to CHAS.
IRVING a tract known as Grey's Point - 834 acres and adj. tract at upper
end - bought of THOS. HIGGINBOTHAM by Rev. RO. ROSE - 200 acres. No dispute as to 200 acres, but the description was vague; should have been 240
acres and pat. to THOS. HIGGINBOTHAM 12 Jul 1750 and described as 140
acres - N side N branch Piney.   JNO. M. ROSE & wife MARTHA, late IRVING,
exrx. of CHAS. IRVING and widow, and WM. HUGHES, acting under will have
sold to JNO. THOMPSON on 17th of this month.   5 sh. to rectify description. Wit: WM. H. CABELL, MARK LIVELY, JNO. CAMM, THOS. POWELL.

Page 261.   13 Jul 1805.   EDWD. CARTER & wife LUCY, AC, to NATHL. MANTIPLY,
            AC, for Ŀ1620, 647½ acres Maple Run. Lines: PATRICK ROSE, old
church road. Wit: DANL. HIGGINBOTHAM, HENRY CAMDEN, JAS. M. BROWN, JAS.
GARLAND, JAS. WOODS.   Orig. del. to NM, 10 Jun 1808.

Page 262.   11 Jul 1805.   JNO. HIGGINBOTHAM SR, & wife RACHEL, AC, to WM.
            CAMDEN, Sr., AC, for Ŀ24,000 tobacco. 3 tracts. 1) 172 acres
S branch N fork Huff of Buff.; pat. to JH, 10 Mar 1756. Lines: JAS. STIN-
NETT.   2) 200 acres pat. to JH, 3 Mar 1760; E side Tobacco Row. Lines:
JAS. STINNETT, his own, JAS. HIGGINBOTHAM. 3) 53 acres pat. to JH. 15 Jul
1793, branches of Huff. Lines: grantor, BENJ. HIGGINBOTHAM.   425 acres.
Wit: SAML. MEREDITH, DAVID S. GARLAND, PETER P. THORNTON, GEO. W. HIGGIN-
BOTHAM, ISAAC RUCKER.   Page 263, order to quiz RACHEL on same date; done
12 Jul 1805 by MEREDITH & DAVID GARLAND.

Page 264.   13 Jul 1805.   JNO. CARR, AC, to HUDSON M. GARLAND, AC, Deed of
            Trust for debt to DAVID & JAS. GARLAND, for $1.00, 54 acres N
side of S branch Tye. Lines: WM. & EDMUND COFFEE and which CARR located
by treasury warrant; also 98 acres on S side S branch Tye. Lines: McCLAIN
& JNO. M. HATTER & bought of RO. HORSLEY; also stock. Wit: J.P. GARLAND,
RO WALKER, MICAJAH CAMDEN.   Orig. del. to JNO. EUBAN, 25 Sep 1807.

Page 265.   15 Mar 1805.   JAS. HANSBROUGH, AC, to SAML. HANSBROUGH, AC,
            Deed of Trust, debt to BROWN MURPHY & Co., 5 sh.   2/5 of tract
to which JAS. is entitled by will of WM. HANSBROUGH, and where JAS. lives,
head branches Joe's Creek. Wit: WILL A. HOWARD, REUBEN HIGGINBOTHAM, WM.
EDMUNDS.   Orig. del. to JAS. MURPHY, 16 Sep 1805.

Page 266.   28 Jan 1805.   DAVID & SOLOMON HICKS & DAVID HICKS JR, of first
            part, to WM. LEE HARRIS & JAS. WOODS, 2nd part - Deed of Trust.

Debt due in suit of JNO. FITZPATRICK, for $1.00, full set of blacksmith
tools. Wit: JNO. W. HARRIS, LOVEY FITZPATRICK, WM. FITZPATRICK.

Page 267. 13 Apr 1805. LITTLEBERRY & PLEASANT TUCKER, Lincoln Co, Ky,
by deed in writing to DANL. TUCKER, all interest in estate of
our dec'd. father, DRURY TUCKER, and held by our mother, FRANCES, for
life. Ł82-11-6. Wit: JOS. BURRUS, WM. L. CHRISTIAN, RO. H. COLEMAN,
BUCHER & JNO. WHITEHEAD. Also another deed on same page from same
grantors to same grantee - all estate - for Ł174-15-8, due us at death of
FRANCES TUCKER from DRURY TUCKER - 2/11ths - to be divided to 11 children
at her death. Wit: WM. COLEMAN, RO. H. COLEMAN, JNO. MEHONE, ISAAC RUCKER,
JOS. BURRUS, JNO. & BURCHER WHITEHEAD. Receipt by grantors on same date.

Page 268. 17 Nov 1804. JNO. M. ROSE & wife MILIA, late wife of CHAS.
IRVING, Buckingham, and WM. HUGHES, Alb., to JNO. THOMPSON -
CHAS. IRVING by will of about 25 Apr 1792, directed exrs. to sell Piney
River tract in AC - 2200 acres. MILLIE proved will in Alb. and NICHL.
CABELL, now dec'd, AC, WM. HUGHES, & JNO. JORDAN, bdm. for her. ROSE &
wife failed to give counter security and JNO. THOMPSON has bought 480
acres at Ł1462. Wit: WM. H. CABELL, JAS. P. PARISH, JAS. VIGUS JR, JNO.
B. WEST.

Page 270. 9 Jul 1805. JAS. BROOKS & wife ELIZ., AC, to NATHL. HARLOW,
AC, for Ł250, 62 acres in AC & Alb. on Lynch Creek whereon is
grist mill. Part of 70 acres sold by JACOB GOOD to JB and NH in partnership. Lines: grantee, RICH. RICHARDSON. Orig. del. to NH Jr, 4 Oct 1805.

Page 271. 17 Nov 1804. JNO. M. ROSE & wife MILIA, widow of CHAS. IRVING,
Buckingham - see p.268 for details - to THOS. PENN, AC, 733
acres for Ł1466. Lines: JNO. CARTER. Wit: as on p.268. Orig. del. to WM.
B. HARE, 15 Sep 1806.

Page 272. 17 Nov 1804. Release of all claims by JNO. M. ROSE & wife
MILLIA for Ł500 to WM. B. HARE, JNO. THOMPSON, & THOS. PENN,
AC, 2200 acres on Piney. Wit: as on p.268.

Page 273. 13 Jul 1805. HENRY BALLINGER & wife MARY, AC, to PULLIAM SAN-
DIDGE, AC, for Ł227, 2 adj. tracts N side and joining Buffl.
1) 185 acres bought by HB of WARNER GOODWIN. Lines: ZACH. TALIAFERRO, JOS.
DODD. 2) 28 acres - entry of STEWART BALOE & assigned to ZACHARIAH TALIA-
FERRO JR, and by him to THOMAS DICKERSON & by him to WARNER GOODWIN and
by him to HB. Wit: JOHN DAVIS, JAS. SANDIDGE, JNO. CARTER. Orig. del. to
HB, 22 Aug 1806.

Page 274. 17 May 1805. HECTOR CABELL, AC, to LANDON CABELL, AC, Deed of
Trust, debt to JAS. MURPHY & Co., 5 sh, 4 slaves & children
named. Wit: WILL CABELL, SAML. BLAIR, RICH. MURROW. Orig. del. to JAS.
MURPHY, 12 May 1808.

Page 275. 13 Jul 1805. HECTOR CABELL, AC, 1st part; JNO. CABELL, Buckingham, 2nd part; & PAULINA CABELL, wife of HECTOR, 3rd part.
HECTOR for love of wife & children - 10 sh. paid by JC, 390 acres N side
Fluvanna and upper side Tye. 200 acres of it to JNO. CABELL from his
father, WM., and wife MARGARET, 30 Apr 1763. 190 acres - other part - pat.
to JNO. CABELL, 26 Jul 1765. Lines: grantor, grantee. 2nd tract conveyed
by JNO. CABELL & wife ELIZ., to HECTOR CABELL, 25 Oct 1799. Wit: REUBEN
BATES, JNO. BETHEL, JOS. HARGROVE, WILLIS H. WILLS, RICH. MURRAY.

Page 277. 18 Jun 1805. SYLVANUS BRYANT, AC, to JNO. HIGGINBOTHAM, Warminster, AC, Deed of Trust - debt to JAS. MURPHY; $1.00; slave
woman and 2 children; man slave & stock. Wit: NORVELL SPENCER, SAML.
BLAIR, ISAAC WHITE. 2 margins: 8 Jan 1806, del.to MURPHY; 11 Jul 1806,
del. to RICH. CLARKE.

Page 278. 17 Nov 1804. JNO. M. ROSE & wife MILLIA (see p.268) to WM. B.
HARE, AC, for Ł1911-7, 889 acres. Lines: Piney River road.
Wit: WM. H. CABELL, JAS. P. PARISH, JAS. VIGUS JR, JNO. B. WEST. Orig.
del. to WH, 16 Sep 1806.

Page 279. 17 Jun 1805. GEO. GILBERT to REUBEN RUCKER for Ł308-5, 102 acres Harris Creek. Lines: Grantor, RICH. RUCKER, grantee, Mrs. GEORGE, JNO. KNIGHT. Wit: RICH. GARRETT, ARCHELAUS COX, JONATHAN R. DAWSON, WM. GARRETT, HENRY GILBERT.

Page 280. 21 Feb 1805. AGNES CLARKSON, exrx. of JNO. CLARKSON, late of Burbon (sic) Co. Ky, Power of Atty to friend, HENRY BALLINGER, AC, as to business in Va. THOS. HUGHES & SAML. WILLIAMS, J.P.'s of Bourbon, WM. GARRARD, Clk. Orig. del. to HB, 8 Apr 1806.

Page 280. 15 Jul 1805. WM. & WALLER SANDIDGE, AC, exrs. of JNO. SANDIDGE, AC, to GODFREY TOLER, AC, for Ŀ600, 603 acres both sides Horsley. Lines: Said SANDIDGE, JNO. DAVASHAR, JOS. HIGGINBOTHAM, WALKER ATKERSON, PULLIAM SANDIDGE, WM. CARTER, dec'd, DAVID BURKS, MORRIS, NELSON CRAWFORD, JOS. MILSTEAD, ELIZ. SCOFIELD.

Page 282. 26 May 1804. AMBROSE CAMPBELL, Piney River, AC, to DAVID & JAMES GARLAND, Ŀ55 for CAMPBELL & wife in est. of GEO. GILLESPIE tract. CAMPBELL married NANCY GILLESPIE, daughter of GEO. GILLESPIE, the elder, who died intestate and left NANCY & 11 other children. Left Piney river tract "of considerable value" and free of widow's claims. Wit: WM. G. PENDLETON, JER. FRANKLIN, JOS. SWANSON.

Page 282. 21 Jul 1804. LEROY ROBINSON, AC, to JNO. HIGGINBOTHAM, Warminster, Deed of Trust - debt due BROWN MURPHY & Co., 5 sh. 62 acres Cedar Creek. Lines: GEO. LOVING, MOSES MAYS, WM. CLASBY, where "ROBERTSON" lives, slave, stock. Wit: JAS. HANSBROUGH, JOS. LOVING, BURDETT SKINNER, JNO. WRIGHT.

Page 283. 23 Feb 1805. HENRY LANDON DAVIES & wife LUCY, Bedford, to THOS. MOORE, AC, for Ŀ528, 320 acres Raspberry Neck. Lines: Fluvanna River, JESSE WOODROOF, ARTHUR L. DAVIES. Wit: RO. TURNER, JESSE WOODROOF, GEO. DILLARD, WM. TURNER, R. NORVELL, ARCHELAUS CROWS.

Page 284. 14 Aug 1800. HENRY LANDON DAVIES & wife LUCY, Bedford Co, to LEWIS DAWSON, AC, for Ŀ152-15, 152 3/4 acres. Lines: REUBIN PADGET or PONTERS(? - hard to read) JNO. TRENT, JAS. GOODWIN, REUBIN PENDLETON, est. of THOS. POWELL. Wit: THOS. MOORE, THOS. WOODROOF, JAS. GARLAND, REUBEN PENDLETON, JESSE WOODROOF.

Page 285. 31 Oct 1804. JAS. PETERS, AC, to JNO. HIGGINBOTHAM, AC, Deed of Trust; debt due BROWN MURPHY & Co.; 5 sh. bay mare called Jolly Toper, beds etc. Wit: SAML. BLAIN, THOS. BIBB, RO. KENNEDY.

Page 286. 16 Mar 1805. JESSE A. PROFFITT, AC, to DANL. HIGGINBOTHAM, AC, Deed of Trust; debt to JAS. MURPHY & Co.; 5 sh; cows, beds, etc. Wit: WM. S. HOWARD, REUBIN HIGGINBOTHAM, JNO. PROFFITT, AUSTIN WRIGHT.

Page 287. 28 Nov 1804. THOS. MERRITT, AC, to PHILIP JOHNSON & JAS. WOODROOF, AC, Deed of Trust - bondsman, DANL. NORCUTT, sued by THOS. WIATT & CABELL - $1.00. Furniture, stock etc. - some stock in hands of DANL. BURFORD. Wit: LEROY CAMDEN, WALKER SAUNDERS, DAVID ----.

Page 288. 28 Apr 1802. HECTOR CABELL & wife PAULINA, AC, 1st; RO. RIVES, 2nd, WM. & LANDON CABELL, 3rd. RIVES has bought of HECTOR CABELL at Ŀ1200, 1130 acres Joe's Creek. Part of tract. Lines: old church road, ALLEN LAVINDER, RICH. MURROW, Prichard's road, Warminster road. Deed of 1799 or 1800, SAML. JORDAN CABELL, WM. & LANDON CABELL, parties thereto relinquished int. in will of WM. CABELL, late of AC. HECTOR had only life estate. WM. & LANDON CABELL to RO. RIVES 300 acres S & joining Tye. Conveyed to HECTOR CABELL by JNO. CABELL & wife ELIZ., Buckingham Co., 21 Oct 1799. HECTOR is to occupy. Wit: ABRAM MARTIN, HUDSON MARTIN, JNO. HORSLEY, CHAS. WATTS. Rec. 1 Apr 1805 with wits: WM. A. HOWARD, DANL. HIGGINBOTHAM, AUSTIN WRIGHT, WILLIS WILLS.

Page 293. 28 Mar 1805. HARRISON HUGHES, AC, to AMBROSE BURFORD, AC, for Ŀ50, 11 acres where HH lives. Lines: PLEASANT DAWSON, grantee. Wit: JAS. MITCHELL, REUBEN CREWS.

Page 293. 17 Dec 1802. CHAS. CARTER & wife BETSY, Culpeper, to HUGH

CAMPBELL, AC, for $900, 949 acres. Lines: JNO. SMITH, JAS. FRANKLIN, EDWD.
CARTER (formerly that of WHITTAKER CARTER) CARTER's old mill, LINDSEY
COLEMAN. Page 294, order to Culpeper J.P.'s, 8 Jan 1803. Done, 20 May
1803, by RO. SLAUGHTER & WM. BROADUS.

Page 295. 22 Jul 1805. JNO. ANDERSON, AC, to LINDSEY COLEMAN, AC, Deed
of Trust; debt due WM. EDMUNDS; 6 sh; slave. Wit: PEYTON KEITH,
JNO. SPITFATHOM, TERRENCE COONEY.

Page 296. 9 Sep 1805. RICH. C. POLLARD, AC, to THOS. GLASS, for £54,
no acres mentioned; Dutch. Lines: ELIAS HAMLET, SPARKS MARTIN,
grantor. Wit: W.B. SHAMROCK(?), RO. SHIRLEY, JNO. MALLON, MARY MALLON
(or MELLON.) 14 Jan 1806, del. to TG.

Page 296. 16 Sep 1805. SAML. REID & wife LUTE, AC, to JAS. HUGHES, AC,
for £120, 136 acres N branches Stoney Run of Rockfish. Pat.
to ALEX. REID, dec'd, 3 Aug 1771. Lines: his own, WM. MURRELL's orphans.

Page 297. 16 Sep 1805. SAML. REID & wife LUTE, AC, to HAWES COLEMAN,
AC, for £1500, 25 acres by pat., S branches Rockfish. Lines:
THOS. PRATT, JOS. MONTGOMERY.

Page 297. 17 May 1805. RO. HAMBLETON, AC, to MAURICE MORRIS, AC, for
£40, 100 acres on Horsley. Wit: WALLER SANDIDGE, ISHAM WADGER,
JOS. MAGANN.

Page 298. 18 Jul 1805. HECTOR CABELL, SAML. J., WM. & LANDON CABELL,
AC, to THOS. MASSIE, AC, for 10 sh, 1/2 acre Nside and joining
Tye. Lines: opposite Warehouse at New Market; supposed st. line. Wit:
JAS. M. BROWN, RICH. MURRAY, JAS. MURPHY.

Page 299. 30 Jan 1805. Order to AC J.P.'s WM. LOVING & THOS. MOORE -
deed of JNO. WRIGHT & wife SUSANNA, to PARMENAS BRYANT, 12
Nov. 1803. Done 19 Aug 1805.

Page 300. 6 Sep 1805. Heirs Of JER. WHITTEN, dec'd, AC, WM. NOWELL &
wife LUCINDA, RO. NUCKLES & wife FRANCES, JAS. FRANKLIN &
wife NANCY, JAS. BIAS & wife ELIZ., TABITHA WHITTEN, Mercer Co. Ky, and
her guardian, WM. WHITTEN, to BENJ. NOWELL, "same Co. & state" for $83.33,
50 acres Thomas Mill Creek; survey of 11 Oct 1802. Lines: SAML. NICELY.
Part of tract. Wit: THOS. N. EUBANK, THOS. GOODRICH, CHAS. DAVIS, BENJ.
SHACKLEFORD.

Page 300. 6 Sep 1805. RODERICK McCULLOCH, AC, to BENJ. SHACKLEFORD, AC,
for £200, 200 acres by pat. Lines: crossing the road. Wit:
MICAJAH CAMDEN, THOS. N. EUBANK, THOS. GOODRICH. Orig. del. to BS 5 Oct
1808.

Page 301. 16 Sep 1805. WM. CAMDEN & wife SYBELL, AC, to JABEZ CAMDEN,
AC, for £150, 130 acres. Lines: AMBROSE PATEN, JNO. WHEELER,
GEO. BRAXTON, Gent.

Page 302. 16 Sep 1805. WM. CAMDEN, AC, to JABEZ CAMDEN, AC, for $1.00
and love of WM. for son JABEZ, 5 adj. tracts on headwaters of
Huff Creek. 1) 138 acres by deed to WC from JOS. CHILDRESS, 6 Jul 1778.
2) 138 acres by deed from JNO. CHILDRESS, Alb., to WC, 6 Jul 1778. 3)
74 acres pat. to WC at Richmond 16 Jul 1780. 4) -- acres pat. to WC at
Richmond, 4 Nov 1783. 5) 148 acres to WC by deed from WM. LEACH, 6 May
1794.

Page 303. 16 Sep 1805. HENRY CAMDEN & wife LUCY, AC, to JABEZ CAMDEN,
For £291, 194 acres Huff branches; part of tract. Lines: CAM-
DEN's road, grantee, WM. CAMDEN, grantor. Signed by WM. CAMDEN, but ack.
by HENRY CAMDEN, 16 Sep 1805.

Page 303. 29 Aug 1805. WM. TALIAFERRO & wife NANCY W., AC, to JAS.
TALIAFERRO, Richmond, for £200, 154 acres Franklin & Molls
Creeks, branch of Buff. Lines: JNO. CLARKSON, WM. SANDIDGE. Wit: ANSELM
CLARKSON, BENJ. TALIAFERRO, WM. SANDIDGE, CHAS. L. CHRISTIAN.

Page 303. 16 Sep 1805. HENRY CAMDEN & wife LUCY, AC, to MICAJAH CAMDEN, AC, for Ł60, 48 acres Huff branches; part of tract. Lines: JABEZ CAMDEN, WM. CAMDEN, grantor. Orig. del. to MC, 31 Dec 1812.

Page 304. 15 Apr 1805. WM. CAMDEN, AC, to MICAJAH CAMDEN, AC, for love of WM. for son, MICAJAH, & 5 sh., WM. relinquishes all claims on land - 425 acres on branches of Huff. Lines: JAS. STINNETT, JAS. HIGGINBOTHAM. Wit: THOS. N. EUBANK, EDMD. T. COLEMAN, WM. HARRIS.

Page 305. 17 Jun 1804. RICH. LAWLESS & wife ELIZABETH, WM. LAWLESS & wife SUSANNA, AC, to WM. WARE, AC, for Ł115, 107 acres. Lines: grantee, JNO. SMITH, WM. LAWLESS, Shop Branch, R. LAWLESS, JNO. SMITH's Still House at the road, LOMAX, top of the Mt. Wit: PETER P. THORNTON, WALKER SANDIDGE, WM. THURMOND, HOLEMAN JOPLING, JNO. EUBANK JR, JNO. WARE. Orig. del. to WW, 12 Jul 1806.

Page 306. 28 Aug 1805. THOS. FITZPATRICK JR, & wife ELIZ.; CHAS. TOOLEY & wife MARY, AC, to WM. WITT JR, for $100, 202 acres. Lines: DAVID WITT, JOS. ROBERTS, WM. WOOD. Tract of LITTLEBERRY WITT,& ELIZ. & MARY are two of his children. LW is dec'd - all interest of ELIZ. & MARY. Wit: WM. LEE HARRIS.

Page 307. 10 Jul 1805. ISAAC WRIGHT SR, & wife SUSANNA, AC, to EDWD. CARTER, AC, for Ł164, 82 acres Horsley Creek. Lines: ABRAM CARTER, along the road, WM. PRYOR, WM. LAWLESS, grantee. Wit: ABRAM CARTER, RICH. ELLIS, HENRY BROWN, JNO. ELLIS, WM. PRYOR. Orig. del. 24 Jun 1806 to NELSON CRAWFORD.

Page 307. 9 Sep 1805. JOS. C. HIGGINBOTHAM, AC, to FREDERICK CABELL, AC, for Ł130, 304 acres surveyed 7 Sep 1798 N side and joining Fluvanna River. Lines: JAS. CABELL, THOS. STAPLES, GEO. HYLTON, WM. HORSLEY dec'd. Wit: SAML. BLAIR, DAVID P. BRYANT, JNO. CABELL. Orig. del. 27 Feb 1807 to JH.

Page 308. 2 Sep 1805. GARRET SANDS, AC, to THOS. N. EUBANK, AC, for 6 sh, Deed of Trust; debt due HENRY BROWN on execution of WM. THURMOND who has enjoined High Court of Chancery, Richmond - bay horse.

Page 309. 16 Sep 1805. ZACH. ROBERTS & wife SALLY, AC, to MARTIN DAWSON, Alb. & Town of Millon, for Ł40, no acres mentioned, Rockfish. Lines: both parties, top of Morrison's Mt.

Page 309. 8 Apr 1805. JAS. McALEXANDER & wife PATIENCE; MICAJAH BURNETT & wife SALLY, AC, to HENRY DAWSON & JNO. C.(E) FITZPATRICK, AC - BURNETT is styled McCAMDEN in deed, but signed BURNETT - for Ł100, 10 acres; 2 small tracts adjoining - Red House lot of 4 acres adjoins. Lines: WM. WRIGHT, JAS. WRIGHT, HOPKINS, NATHAN BARNETT. Wit: NATHAN BARNETT, WM. WATKINS, WM. BUTTERSWORTH, WM. BLAIN, JNO. WRIGHT, JNO. MELTON.

Page 311. 16 Sep 1805. JAS. McALEXANDER & wife PATIENCE; ALEX. McALEXANDER & wife PATSEY, AC, to JNO. McALEXANDER, AC, for $2000, 267 acres S branches Davis Creek. Lines: ALEX. McALEXANDER, JACOB PUCKETT, FORTUNE.

Page 312. 3 Sep 1804. DENNIS MANN, AC, to CHAS. LEWIS, AC, Deed of Trust; debt due WM. LEWIS; $1.00; furniture etc. Wit: CORNL. NEVIL, WM. W. RAY, Final proof by DM, 16 Sep 1805.

Page 313. 21 Sep 1805. JNO., BENJ., & JAS. LIVELY, AC, to MARK LIVELY for Ł70 to each - tract left them by father in will - all land of grantors - S side Rockfish. Lines: DAVID ENNICK. Wit: GEO. FARRAR, PLEASANT BAILEY, JNO. FARRAR JR.

Page 313. 16 Aug 1805. PETTIS THACKER & wife MARY, AC, to DANL. BURFORD SR, AC, for Ł500, 339 acres both sides Stovall Creek. Lines: JESSE BECK, STEPHEN HAM, LINEAS BOLLING, J.B. COFFLAND, WM. DAWSON dec'd. Wit: WM. BURFORD, JNO. L(?) BURFORD, CHAS. MAYS. Orig. del. to E. WILLS, admr., 11 Jan 1814(?).

Page 314. 16 Aug 1804. Order to Lynchburg J.P.'s THOS. WIATT & WM.

433

WARWICK; deed of JNO. WIATT & wife WILHELMENIA, 10 Jan 1804, to HENRY
BROWN, S branches Rockfish. Done, 27 Sep 1805, rec. 21 Oct 1805.

Page 315. 10 Aug 1805. ARCHIBALD BURFORD, AC, to PHILIP BURFORD, AC,
          Deed of Trust; debt due JNO. BURFORD SR, $1.00; beds etc.
Wit: THOS. McCLELLAND, REUBEN CREWS, AMBR. BURFORD, W. & JNO. L. BURFORD.
Orig. del. to PB, 14 Aug 1806.

Page 316. 31 Jul 1805. JNO. ANDERSON & wife MARY, AC, to JNO. ALCOCK,
          LEWIS DAWSON, GEO. WRIGHT, & JNO. ENNIS, trustees, for Ŀ4-10,
1 acre for Meth. Epis. Church in America; use of spring to west. Wit:
THOS. LANDRUM, THOS. TRIPLET, WM. TILLER JR.

Page 317. 17 Aug 1805. JNO. MOORE (signed MOON), AC, to MARTIN DAWSON,
          Alb. & town of Milton, for Ŀ450, 323+ acres Cove Creek. Lines:
PETER LYON, SAML. ANDERSON, TERISHA TURNER, JNO. DAWSON dec'd. Wit: JNO.
S. DAWSON, REUBIN T. MITCHELL, JOS. SMITH, TERISHA TURNER, JAS. P. GAR-
LAND. Orig. del. to MD, 30 Mar 1807.

Page 317. 25 May 1805. DAVID S. GARLAND, AC, to PEYTON KEITH, AC, for
          Ŀ20, lot in town of New Glasgow; "plate" of town (not herein)
#6. E of Main Street & begins at an alley. Orig. del. 25 Jan 1806 to PK.

Page 318. 21 Oct 1805. JNO. JOPLING & wife ELIZ., AC, to FIELD SMITH,
          AC, for Ŀ50, 100 acres Treble Fall Creek. Lines: JOS. SMITH,
SAML. S. SCRUGGS, RALPH JOPLING's old line.

Page 318. 21 Oct 1805. HUDSON M. GARLAND, agt. of ELIZ. BRAXTON, widow
          of CARTER BRAXTON, to BENJ. MILES for $100, all dower claims
to 190 acres. Wit: WM. EVANS. Orig. del. 12 Oct 1807 to J. CAMM.

Page 319. 2 Apr 1805. DAVID BAILEY, Rockbridge, to THOS. N. EUBANK, AC,
          Deed of Trust - 6 sh; debt due ABRAM CARTER, JNO. RICHARDSON,
& LINZA BURKS, bondsmen for LUSK & BAILEY on injunction bond to JAS. GOLD
for benefit of MEEKER(?) DUNMAN. 200 acres headwaters of Pedlar. Lines:
WM. HIGGINBOTHAM. Wit: JAS. CARPENTER, JNO. WAUGH, HENRY BRYANT, HENRY
BROWN. Orig. del. to TE, 9 Apr 1806.

Page 319. 12 Sep 1798. JOS. CREWS JR. & wife MARTHA, to WM. PENDLETON
          for Ŀ100, 49 acres. Lines: WM. GOODWIN dec'd., grantor. Wit:
THOS. MOORE, JESSE WOODROOF, WM. PETTYJOHN, RICH. WHITEHEAD, REUBEN PEN-
DLETON. Final proof, 21 Oct 1805, by MOORE. Orig. del. to WP, 15 May
1807.

Page 320. 8 Jul 1805. WIATT SMITH, AC, to JAS. FLOYED (sic), AC, for
          6 sh., Deed of Trust; debt due FLOYD. 162½ acres Porrage.
Lines: JNO. HIGGINBOTHAM, GIDEON RUCKER, JOS. HIGGINBOTHAM SR, & JR. Wit:
JAS. BALLINGER, JACOB SCOTT, RICH. WILSON, JAS. PAGE, JAS. CHRISTIAN.

Page 321. 15 Feb 1805. HENRY L. DAVIES, Bedford, to NATHL. J. MANSON,
          AC, for 6 sh, 746 acres by survey for NICHL. C. DAVIES. Lines:
NICHL. C. DAVIES, N side Fluvanna, Rocking Branch, grantor, HENRY ROACH,
ASHCRAFT ROACH, RODERICK McCULLOCH. Wit: NELSON C. DAWSON, JESSE WOOD-
ROOF, THOS. MOORE, ARCHELAUS CREWS.

Page 322. 25 Jul 1805. BENJ. PHILLIPS, AC, to JAS. FRANKLIN, AC, for
          Ŀ21-5, 8½ acres Rutledge Creek; part of tract. Lines: grantee.
Wit: PLEASANT MARTIN, SAML. WOOD, WM. COLEMAN, WM. PENN JR, RO. COLEMAN.

Page 322. 7 Sep 1805. DAVID TRYALL, AC, to JAS. PARKER GARLAND, AC,
          Deed of Trust to secure JAS. STEPHENS, JR. on bond to JAS. &
DAVID GARLAND. $1.00 - house and lot in Warminster. Wit: JNO. HIGGINBO-
THAM, CHAS. EDMUNDS, JAS. MURPHY. Orig. del. 20 Mar 1811 to SPOTSWOOD
GARLAND, Gent., for STEVENS(sic) exr.

Page 323. 3 Jun 1805. JAS. MONTGOMERY & wife RACHEL; THANKFUL SHIELDS &
          PEGGY SHIELDS, AC, to RO. SHIELDS, AC, for Ŀ400, 247 acres
both sides Hat Creek; tract of JNO. SHIELDS dec'd., and fell to JAS. MONT-
GOMERY who married RACHEL SHIELDS - RO. SHIELDS, THANKFUL & PEGGY SHIELDS
by commrs: NATHAN CRAWFORD, JAS. WOODS, & HAWES COLEMAN, in chancery suit

to divide. Lines: JAS. MONTGOMERY, JAS. SHIELDS, LEE HARRIS dec'd., MAR-
GARET SHIELDS' part as widow of JNO. SHIELDS, WM. SHIELDS' part, ALEX.
SHIELDS, NATHAN SHIELDS, & REBECCA SHIELDS. Wit: LANDON BRENT, JAS.
BARNET, WM. SHIELDS, GEO. & ALEX. SHIELDS.

Page 324. 4 Sep 1805. BENJ. PHILLIPS, AC, to JACOB WOOD, AC, Deed of
         Trust to secure all debts; $1.00; all AC land. Wit: THOS.
WOODROOF, JAC TYREE, MOSES PHILLIPS, WM. DAVENPORT, WM. TYREE.

Page 324. 31 Jul 1805. AMBROSE CAMPBELL, AC, to THOS. ALDRIDGE, AC,
         Deed of Trust; debt due JAS. & DAVID GARLAND: $1.00; Negress,
furniture, etc. Wit: JOHNSON PHILLIPS, JAS. & WM. CAMPBELL.

Page 325. 21 Oct 1805. AMBROSE RUCKER, son of REUBEN RUCKER, dec'd, &
         wife BETSY, AC, to ANTHONY RUCKER, AC, for Ł511-4, 213 acres
both sides John's Creek. Lines: JAS. TINSLEY, DAVID TINSLEY, PROSSER
POWELL, JAS. WARE. Wit: DAVID TINSLEY, EZEK. HILL, JNO. MAGANN. Orig.
de. to AMBR. RUCKER per order of ANTHONY RUCKER, 9 May 1806.

Page 326. 21 Nov 1805. NICHL. WEST, AC, & wife ELIZ, to BRANSFORD WEST,
         AC, for Ł16, 107 acres; deeded to NW by father, FRANCIS WEST.
Lines: WM. CABELL, JNO. WEST - now WM. H. CABELL's; NEVIL's or entry by
PETER LEGRON; JESSE WEST's tract from his father, FRANCIS WEST; Mayo Ck.

Page 326. 21 Oct 1805. CHAS. DAVENPORT, AC, to JOS. DAVENPORT, AC, 2nd
         part; & ISAAC RUCKER. Deed of Trust to secure JOS. $1.00
paid by ISAAC RUCKER - slaves.

Page 327. 15 Oct 1805. CHAS. CHRISTIAN SR, & RO. ALLEN, AC, to JAS.
         FLOYED, ISAAC RUCKER & SAML. MEREDITH, trustees - 10 sh; 1
acre. Lines: EAST's old road - to congregations which may meet there of
M.E. & Presbyterian churches of USA. Wit: WALTER CHRISTIAN, JACOB PIERCE,
THOS. EDMONDS. Orig. del. 15 Oct 1809 to IR.

Page 328. 12 Mar 1805. WM. CAMDEN, AC, to his son, MARBEL CAMDEN, AC,
         for love & 6 sh, 91 acres N side and joining Fluvanna & Mobley
Creek. Lines: grantor. Bought by WC & JAS. FRANKLIN from JOS. C. MIGGIN-
SON & JF has conveyed his part to WC. Mention of 92 acres. Lines: GEO.
HYLTON, RO. FREELAND. Also 38 acres S side & joining Mobley Creek.
Bought by WC and FRANKLIN of WARREN TALIAFERRO, 2 Oct 1800, & by FRANKLIN
to WC; store, Warehouse, tavern. Wit: HUDSON M. GARLAND, WM. ARMISTEAD,
HENRY CAMDEN, DAVID S. GARLAND.

Page 329. 30 Sep 1805. CHAS. HAYNES, AC, to THOS. N. EUBANK, AC, Deed
         of Trust; 6 sh; debt to JNO. EUBANK JR, & JESSE HAYNES - bdm.
for CHAS. HAYNES & MARY RICHESON, gdn. for PATSEY RICHESON - stock, furniture, etc. Wit: PETER P. THORNTON, ELLIS M. EUBANK, JNO. EUBANK JR.

Page 330. 17 Apr 1802. HENRY CHRISTIAN, AC, to JNO. NICHOLS, AC, for
         Ł20, 38 acres. Lines: THOS. EDWARDS, CHRISTOPHER FLETCHER,
JOS. HIGGINBOTHAM, RICH. JONES. Wit: JAS. CHRISTIAN, REUBIN NORVELL,
DRURY BELL.

Page 330. 26(?) Nov 1804. GEO., ALEX., LEWIS GILLESPIE for self and
         for SHERODMORE GILLESPIE; JAS. BOWLING & wife LETTICE, CHAS.
JONES & wife BETSY, HOWARD CASH & wife SALLY, JESSE WRIGHT & wife DICEY -
all heirs of GEO. GILLESPIE, dec'd., AC, to DAVID S. GARLAND, AC, for
Ł66-13-4, 403 acres on Piney - they own 1/12th each. Wit: JOEL FRANKLIN,
JAS. CAMDEN, MOSES & BENJ. WRIGHT. Memo: reserved - not over 1/4 acre for
family graveyard where GEO. GILLESPIE is buried. (Note: I've commented
on this graveyard before. I had long search, but finally located it. It
is on farm of TAYLOR WRIGHT, dec'd., near Piney River Baptist parsonage.
There is no sign of graveyard now for it was plowed up by a later buyer.
There is another deed from the Kentucky heirs of GEO. GILLESPIE and they
are heirs of son, WM. GILLESPIE, who married here in 1777, ANN or NANCY
HUDSON, daughter of JOSHUA HUDSON. WM. & wife went to Madison Co, Ky,
and daughter, MARY, married HENDERSON THURMAN and my wife, MILDRED MILLER
DAVIS, is descendant of THURMAN and wife. BFD)

Page 331. 13 Sep 1805. WM. CABELL & wife ANNE, AC, to THOS. S.

McCLELAND (McLELAND) & wife MARGARET, Campbell Co, for good will and affection and 5 sh, 216 acres both sides Higginbotham Mill Creek; part of tract. Lines: JAMES HIGGINBOTHAM, HENRY HOLLOWAY, ISAAC GIBSON's legatees, EDMD. PENN.

Page 332.   20 Aug 1805. WM. TEAS, AC, to JNO. HIGGINBOTHAM, AC, Deed of Trust; debt to JAS. MURPHY; 5 sh; 320 acres Naked Creek. Lines: WM. CABELL, GEO. BLAIN, JNO. WRIGHT, WM. BIBB dec'd, JNO. THOMPSON. Wit: THOS. L. McCLELAND, NATHL. OFFUTT, WM. MOSS. Orig. del. to JM 10 Feb 1807.

Page 333.   24 Jul 1805. Order to Campbell Co. J.P.'s THOS. HUMPHREYS, THOS. W. COCKE, & SAML. SCOTT, for deed of JAS. CREWS & wife ELIZ., 23 Sep 1802, to WM. ADAMS - 50 acres. Done by COCKE & HUMPHREYS, 23 Oct 1805.

Page 333.   31 May 1805. WM. THURMOND, AC, to ELIAS WILLS, PHILIP THUR- MOND SR & JR, & WM. JAS. THURMOND, AC, for $1.00 and love for wife LUCY THURMOND & children - Deed of Trust for their benefits - tract where I live; between 400 and 500 acres next to PHILIP THURMOND dec'd; DAVID CRAWFORD, & CHARLES CRAWFORD; also 13 negroes named and stock. Also rights in estate of my father and that of ELIAS WILLS Sr. Wit: P. GOOCH, REUBEN CRAWFORD, PHILIP LOCKARD. Margin: 20 May 1811, WM. THURMOND rel- inquished tr.   and proved by E. WILLS. Comm. to settle accts. of WT: THOS. N. EUBANK, JAS. WARE, PETER P. THORNTON, MARTIN PARKS, WM. JOPLING. (Note: WM. THURMOND was sentenced to two years in pen for murder at a later date. In will book 5:70, 20 May 1811, this is set forth and a comm. had to be appointed to take care of his business. JOHN TUCKER made bond; ELIAS WILLS was security. BFD)

Page 334.   14 Dec 1805. JNO. WARE & wife ELIZ., AC, to NICHL. VANSTAVERN, AC, for $100, 55 acres both sides Irish Creek. Lines: grantor.

Page 335.   13 Dec 1805. ELISHA PETERS to DANL. LEEBRICK for Ł420, 200 acres S waters Rockfish; part of tract. Lines: AGGEY LAVENDER, RO. RIVES, NELSON ANDERSON, old glade road, DOLLY KEY, RICH. BREEDLOVE. Orig. del. to WM. D. LIGON - no date.

Page 336.   16 Dec 1805. DANL. LEEBRICK, AC, to NELSON ANDERSON, AC, Deed of Trust - owes ELISHA PETERS. $1.00; mtg. on 200 acres bought of ELISHA PETERS.

Page 337.   6 Dec 1805. NICHL. HARRISON & wife NANCY, AC, to WM. EDMUNDS, AC, for Ł300, 110 acres Harris Creek and where NH lives. Lines: JNO. AMBLER. Wit: DAVID & WILL WOODROOF, JAS. EDMONDS. Orig. del. May, 1806, by direction of WE.

Page 337.   4 Oct 1779. NATHL. & MILES BURFORD, AC, to JNO. HANSARD, AC, for Ł18, 70 acres Boling Creek. Lines: THOS. WRIGHT, JNO. LYNCH. Wit: JAS. SYMONS, JNO. FRANKLIN, ---- BURFORD JR, WM. BROWN, JNO. HENRY GOODWIN. Proof by SYMONS & WM. BROWN, 4 Oct 1779, and by a "third wit.", 16 Dec 1805. Margin: "Blanks because deed was torn". Orig. del. to PETER HANSARD, 8 Oct 1834.

Page 338.   7 Oct 1805. WM. GATEWOOD & wife MILLY; REUBEN GATEWOOD & wife ELIZ.; SAML. WRIGHT & wife NANCY; WM. LAYN & wife JUDITH, AC, to WM. EDMUNDS, AC, for Ł146, 146 acres Buff.; where WM. GATEWOOD lives. Lines: Cedar Branch, JNO. CHRISTIAN, JNO. COLEMAN, WM. S. CRAWFORD, LIND- SEY COLEMAN, REUBEN GATEWOOD, Watermilion (sic) branch on bank of Buff. Wit: THOS. ROWSEY, WM. FOSTER, WM. SAVAGE, TERENCE COONEY, SEATON M. PENN, S. GARLAND. Page 339, order to AC J.P.'s to quiz the wives; same date and done same date: JOS. BURRUS & JNO. WARWICK.

Page 340.   28 Nov 1805. DAVID S. GARLAND & wife JANE, AC, to WM. S. CRAWFORD, JOS. BURRUS, JNO. CAMM, JOEL FRANKLIN, SAML. MERE- DITH, RO. WALKER, WM. H. CABELL, HUDSON M. GARLAND, JAS. M. BROWN, CHAS. CRAWFORD, WM. CABELL, & EDMD. PENN, trustees of New Glasgow Academy, for $100, 4 acres in New Glasgow on which Academy, lately erected, now stands. Lines: near the brick kiln. Wit: WM. ARMISTEAD, DANL. HIGGINBOTHAM, THOS. WOODROOF. Order to quiz JANE, 16 Dec 1805; done on same date by SAML. MEREDITH & JOS. BURRUS. (Note: I have mentioned home of DAVID S. GARLAND before. It is located in village of Clifford and was recently bought from WEBB BABCOCK by LYNN K. BRUGH, III, who is from Maryland. BRUGH has become an associate in a local law firm. It is thought that the Academy stood on site of the present Clifford school. It was in the old Academy that ELIAJH FLETCHER once taught. His letters have recently been published by Mill MARTHA VON BRIESEN, Publicity Director of Sweet Briar College.)

Page 341. 14 Dec 1805. ELIZ. PARSONS, widow of JNO. PARSONS, dec'd, and his children: JOHN PARSONS, JNO. ENGLAND & wife MARY (N PARSONS); GEO. LAWHORN & wife NANCY (N PARSONS); ELIZ. & MARGARET PARSONS to CHARLES TUCKER. JOHN died owning 100 acres on Indian Creek; part of 400 acres pat. to JNO. HARRIS, 10 Sep 1755, and 100 acres conveyed to JNO. PARSONS, 6 Mar 1769. Lines: HENRY ROSE. JNO. died after execution of deed - Ł140. Wit: BARTLETT CASH, BENJ. & WM. ROGERS.

Page 342.. 16 Dec 1805. WM. HIGGINBOTHAM & wife CATH, AC, to FIELDING HOLLIDAY for Ł750, 3 tracts: 1) 300 acres pat. to WH, 10 Jul 1766. 2) 154 acres both sides N fork Pedlar & pat. to WH, 20 Jul 1780. 3) 57 acres branches N fork Pedlar. Lines: his own, DAVID BAILEY. Orig. del. to FH, 21 Sep 1818.

Page 344. 2 Dec 1805. Same parties - HOLIDAY puts mtg. on tract to HIGGINBOTHAM. Wit: HENRY BALLINGER, ANDREW HAMBLETON, JNO. TALIAFERRO.

Page 344. 8 Apr 1805. RO. S. ROSE & wife JANE, N.Y. state, to JNO. FULCHER, AC, for $1500, 206 acres. Lines: N by Little Piney and mill lot; MOOR, CRAWFORD, JAS. FULCHER. Orig. del. to CHAS. H. CHRISTIAN 22 Jun 1819. Memo: RO. S. ROSE & wife, village of Geneva, N.Y., came before TIMOTHY HORNER, 1st judge of common pleas of said court; Cert. by THOS. TILLOTSON, Sect. of N.Y. - Ontario Co., N.Y. Albany, 19 Apr 1805, MORGAN LEWIS, Gov. of N.Y., Gen. & Commander in Charge of all the militia & Admiral of the Navy of the same. Rec. AC, 16 Dec 1805.

Page 345. 19 Aug 1805. HUGH CAMPBELL & wife ELIZ., AC, to RO. RIVES, Greensville Co, Va., for Ł2586, 862 acres. Lines: LINDSEY COLEMAN, JNO. SMITH, JAS. FRANKLIN, EDWD. CARTER. Is tract conveyed by CHAS. CARTER & wife BETTY, to HC, 17 Dec 1802 - CC of Culpeper - above CARTER's old mill. Wit: JOEL FRANKLIN, CHAS. WINGFIELD, BEV. WILLIAMSON, LUDAH WILLIAMSON. Order to AC J.P.'s to quiz., ELIZ., 20 Aug 1805; done on next day by JOEL FRANKLIN & JAS. MONTGOMERY.

Page 347. 19 Aug 1805. RO. RIVES & wife, Greensville, Va., to PHILIP SLAUGHTER, Culpeper, for Ł2546-5, Lines as above. 862 acres. Main co. road. Wit: as above. Orig. del. to PS, 22 Aug 1814.

Page 348. 4 Apr 1805. JNO. ROBERTS to CHAS. P. TALIAFERRO for Ł17, 31 acres S waters Pedlar. Lines: grantee. Orig. del. to JNO. TALIAFERRO, 11 Mar 1806.

Page 349. 1 Aug 1805. P. GOOCH to MOSES PHILLIPS - negro girl & included in trust with increase for benefit of my wife, FRANCES - consideration - her part in her sister's estate which I have disposed of. Wit: JNO. PHILLIPS, HUDSON M. GARLAND.

Page 349. 16 Dec 1805. MOSES MAYS & wife LUCY, AC, to THOS. HAWKINS for Ł215, 223 acres S side Berry's Mt. Lines: CHAS. MAYS, old pat. line on S side mt., LEROY ROBERSON, Cedar Creek, GEO. LOVING, WM. LAYNE. Part of tract - 52 acres sold to LEROY ROBERSON. Orig. del. 20 Dec 1830 to SPENCER(?) FALCONDER who married one of the heirs.

Page 350. 16 Dec 1805. RICH. WILSON & wife ANNE, AC, to THOS. CLASBEY for Ł177-12, 101½ acres, part of where RW lives. Lines: GAINES' road; SAML. HUCKSTEP, JACOB PEARCE, Rockey Creek.

Page 350. 18 Nov 1803. Order to Alb. J.P.'s, CLIFTON GARLAND & JNO. STAPLES - BENJ. CHILDRESS & wife ANN, Dec -- 1801, to JOS. SHELTON. 295 acres. Done 1 Nov 1805. Rec. AC 20 Jan 1806.

Page 351. 6 Dec 1805. JAS. FRANKLIN & wife NANCY, AC, to HUDSON M.

GARLAND, AC, for $1000, 1 acre adj. Cabellsburg or New Glasgow. Lines:
Lumber house occupied by WM. EDMUNDS; main road, PEACHY FRANKLIN's lot,
burying ground. Wit: JAS. P. GARLAND, JNO. W. HARRIS, THOS. WOODROOF, S.
GARLAND, JAS. B. EDWARDS.

Page 352. 25 Oct 1805. WIATT SMITH & wife POLLY, AC, to BENJ. PHILLIPS,
           AC, for £215, all their interest in estate of WM. PHILLIPS -
real and personal - which POLLY may have. Wit: WM. G. PENDLETON, CHAS. W.
CHRISTIAN, GUSTAVUS A. ROSE. Order on same date to quiz POLLY; done on
same date by SAML. MEREDITH & DAVID S. GARLAND.

Page 353. 29 Apr 1796. WM. GOODWIN, AC, to JOS. CREWS, AC, for £50, 49
           acres, part of tract. Lines: both. Wit: WM. PETTYJOHN and del.
to him, 15 Feb 1806; CARY WHITEHEAD, JNO. MERRITT.

Page 354. 25 Nov 1805. THOS. ALDRIDGE & wife CATH, AC, to WM. HIGGIN-
           BOTHAM, AC, & JOS. SWANSON, AC, - firm of SWANSON & HIGGINBO-
THAM - for £26-5, one half of lot - 3/4 acre in New Glasgow - #1; E side
Main Street. Lines: N by Church lot, DAVID S. GARLAND. Wit: DANL. HIGGIN-
BOTHAM, JOS. DILLARD, WILKINS WATSON, DAVID SWANSON. Order to quiz CATH,
9 Dec 1805. Done by SAML. MEREDITH & GEO. DILLARD, 8 Jan 1806.

Page 355. 20 Feb 1804. WALTER CHRISTIAN, JR, AC, to PHILIP GOOCH, AC,
           for $104, 26 acres Glade Creek. Lines: grantee, LINDSEY COLE-
MAN, JNO. COLEMAN, RO. MEANS. Wit: LUCY GOOCH, CHAS. CHRISTIAN, WM. LANE.
Orig. del. to WM. B. GOOCH, one of the exrs. of P. GOOCH, 7 Jun 1806.

Page 356. 20 Jan 1806. HENRY EMMERSON JR, AC, to LANDON CABELL, AC,
           Deed of Trust - to secure JNO. MOSBY on bond to JNO. S. DAWSON,
exr. of JNO. DAWSON, AC, for 10 sh, 150 acres S side Rockfish. Lines:
JAS. TURNER, SR (now JT, JR); Dr. WM. MARTIN, WM. DIXON SR, DUNMORE DAM-
ERON, REUBIN T. MITCHELL. Also 3 slaves & horse. Orig. sent to LC, 21
Apr 1807.

Page 357. 9 Dec 1805. NORBORNE THOMAS, & wife JUDITH, AC, to JNO. &
           SAML. DIXON, AC, for £166, no acres mentioned. Lines: S fork
Rockfish, grantor, WM. DIXON SR, BRYANT's branch. Wit: LANDON CABELL, WM.
& JOS. DIXON. Orig. del. to SD, 22 Dec 1806.

Page 358. 2 Jan 1806. JOS. HORSLEY, AC, to GEO. HILTON, AC, for £150,
           114 acres, part of tract on Rich Branch & willed to him by
father, WM. HORSLEY dec'd; Lot #5. Wit: LEWIS TINDALL, VAL. HYLTON, SAML.
ARRINGTON. Orig. del. to CHAS. L. CHRISTIAN, 10 May 1813.

Page 358. 2 Jan 1806. SAML. HORSLEY, AC, to GEO. HYLTON, AC, for £150,
           110 acres; derived as above - Lot #6. Wit: as above, plus JOS.
HORSLEY. Margin as above.

Page 359. 16 Sep 1805. THOS. GOUGE, Harrison Co, Ky., to friend, JACOB
           POWERS, same Co., to receive from SHELTON CROSTHWAIT, AC,
legacy of my wife, ANN BOURN GOUGE (alias CROSTHWAIT). Harrison J.P.'s:
ISAAC MILLER, GARVIN MORRISON. WM. MOORE, Clerk. Rec. AC, 20 Jan 1806.

Page 360. 2 Jan 1806. JACOB WOOD, AC, to SEATON M. PENN, AC, - BENJ.
           PHILLIPS, AC, 4 Sep 1805, executed Deed of Trust to JACOB WOOD,
all lands on both sides Buff. WOODS advertised on --- and SEATON M. PENN
was buyer at £456; 152 acres. Lines: JAS. FRANKLIN, DAVID S. GARLAND, N.
bank. Rutledge, CHAS. HIGGINBOTHAM, PHILLIPS, BENJ. PHILLIPS. Tract
bought of RO. HOLLOWAY. Wit: DANL. HIGGINBOTHAM, THOS. ALDRIDGE, WM.
EDMUNDS, NICHL. HARRISON.

Page 361. 20 Jan 1806. JNO. FARRAR SR. (so signed) & wife MARY, AC, to
           SAML. PERKINS, AC, for £24, 136 acres N side Hickory Creek.
Lines: SCILER HARRIS, JNO. MORRIS, JOSIAH CHEATHAM, grantee. Wit: JNO. W.
HARRIS, JNO. DIGGS, WM. H. SHELTON. Orig. del. 27 Mar 1855, to S.H.
LOVING, for Dr. D(?) WATSON, the supposed owner of the land.

Page 362. 26 Nov 1805. RUSH HUDSON SR, to JAS. FLOYD, both of AC, for
           $600, 150 acres N branches Buff.; part of tract. Lines: DAVID
S. GARLAND, SAML. MEREDITH, LINDSEY COLEMAN, grantor, old church road.

438

Wit: S. GARLAND, DANL. HIGGINBOTHAM, W.G. PENDLETON. Orig. del. 3 Jun
1806, to JF.

Page 362. 1 Jan 1806. RO. ALLEN & wife ELIZ., AC, to WM. C. CHRISTIAN,
AC, for Ł200, 134 acres. Lines: Stovall's old road, JAS.
CHRISTIAN, JACOB PEARCE, CHAS. H. CHRISTIAN, ALEX. BRYDIE, dec'd, top of
Braxton's ridge, West's old road. Wit: RICH. WILSON, GEO. DILLARD, THOS.
WOODROOF.

Page 363. 31 Oct 1805. RANDOLPH LIVELY, Kanawhay Co. to MARK LIVELY,
AC, for Ł20, tract devised to RL by his father and all on
which RL claims; S side of Buff. Lines: DAVID ENICKS. Wit: FLEMING COBBS,
JNO. CASEY, LEWIS THOMAS, ISAM BAGLEY.

Page 364. 11 Jan 1806. SHELTON CROSTHWAIT & JAS. MURPHY, AC, to ROWLAND
PROFFITT - Nov. Court, 1805, Chancery: JNO., RANDOLPH, JESSE,
ROWLAND, ELIZ. & NANCY PROFFITT, children of DAVID PROFFITT, dec'd, &
DUNCAN CAMERON & wife MOLLY (late PROFFITT & daughter of DAVID PROFFITT)
& DAVID & AUSTIN PROFFITT, infants of AUSTIN PROFFITT, dec'd. (son of
DAVID PROFFITT) by JNO. PROFFITT, gdn. vs. WM. JOSLIN & wife SALLY, JOS.
WILCHER & wife SUSANNA, & DAVID PROFFITT (SALLY, SUSANNA & DAVIE are
children of DAVID PROFFITT dec'd) decreed that commrs. above & ABRAHAM B.
WARWICK sell land. Sold 4 Jan 1806, to ROWLAND PROFFITT - Ł160, 180 acres
S waters Rucker's Run & on Berry's Mt. Lines: JNO. EDMONDS, HECTOR CABELL,
Spring Branch, TERRISHA TURNER. Wit: BENJ. JOHNSON, JNO. CREWS, JNO.
BARTLEY, MARBELL EASTHAM.

Page 365. 17 Jun 1805. JAS. CHRISTIAN, AC ,to STEPHEN WATTS & JAS. MUR-
PHY, AC, love for wife and family - Deed of Trust; $1.00; all
estate and at death of JAS. to divide. 1) To wife, CURDILLAH, for life,
and then to children. Wit: WM. H. CABELL, PARMENAS BRYANT, THOS. BIBB JR,
JNO. WRIGHT. Orig. del. to JM, 28 Jan 1807.

Page 365. 2 Nov 1805. JNO. JOHNSON & wife NANCY, AC, to NICHL. CABELL,
AC, for Ł80, 1/2 acre lot in Warminster; Main St. and opposite
store of WM. BROWN & Co. Wit: EDWD. H. CARTER, HEN. HOLLOWAY, RICH.
POWELL.

Page 366. 10 Dec 1805. JNO. SAVAGE JR, AC, to ANDERSON MOSS, AC, for
Ł145, horses, furniture, etc. Wit: JAS. B. EDWARDS, WM. SAVAGE.

Page 366. 15 Jul 1805. JAS. MONTGOMERY, AC, to JNO. N. ROSE, AC, Deed
of Trust - to protect CHAS. JONES, bdm. - 8 Dec 1803, bond to
JAS. FULCHER, assignee of CHAS. JONES & JAS. MURPHY, acting for est. of
GEO. GILLESPIE, dec'd, 3 slaves. Wit: HUDSON M. GARLAND, THOS. ALDRIDGE,
MATT. HIGHT.

Page 367. 20 Jan 1806. JNO. SAUNDERS, AC, to SHELTON CROSTHWAIT, & RICH.
CLARKE, AC, Deed of Trust; debt due RIVES MURPHY & Co. and
JAS. MURPHY & Co.; 6 sh; 98 acres surveyed, 18 Nov 1772 - Dutch Creek
between 2 tops of Marrow Bone Mt.; 105 3/4 later used. Lines: WM. BAILEY,
THOS. NASH, JNO. MOSELY, DANL. MOSELY; also horse bought of WM. BAILEY,
etc. Orig. del. to JM. 19 Sep 1808.

Page 368. 18 Sep 1805. RO. JOHNSTON, late of St. Margaret's Parish,
Caroline, dec'd, owned AC land and died about 10 Feb 1780, &
left widow, LUCY, and 2 children: RO. & LUCY. LUCY has married RICH.
PEATROSS and RO. died intestate and without issue. Title now vested in
widow LUCY, and RICH. PEATROSS & wife - all of same Caroline Parish.
Power of Atty. to THOS. GUY, same Co. & parish, to sell AC tract. Wit:
WM. & GEO. GUY, HENRY PEATROSS. Cert. by Caroline J.P.'s: FRANCIS CORBIN
& THOS. BURKE. Wit: WILL NELSON. Rec. in AC, 18 Mar 1806.

Page 369. 11 Feb 1805. WM. EVANS, AC, to JNO. HIGGINBOTHAM JR, AC, Deed
of Trust, debt to BROWN MURPHY & Co., 5 sh.; 2 surveys both
sides little Piney - 350 acres. Lines: WM. MOORE, STEPHEN TURNER, DAVID
CLARKSON and where WE lives. Also slave, Peg, and issue. Wit: WM. EDMUNDS,
ISAAC WHITE, WILL F. CARTER, AUSTIN WRIGHT, REUBEN HIGGINBOTHAM.

Page 370. 1 Feb 1806. ARCHIBALD BURFORD & wife ELIZ., AC, to WM.

BURFORD, AC, for Ŀ140, 49¼ acres Lynch road & Harris Creek. Bought by AB
from DANL. MEHONE. Lines: DANL. BURFORD. Wit: HARRISON HUGHES, BENJ.
PALMORE, JNO. L. BURFORD.

Page 371. 10 Feb 1806. RO. HENDREN, AC, to JNO. THOMPSON, AC, for $1.00,
8½ acres headwaters Rockfish near Alb. line. Lines: JNO.
THOMPSON's entry of 11 acres; BROCK.

Page 371. 10 Feb 1806. JNO. THOMPSON, AC, to RO. HENDREN AC, for $1.00,
8½ acres head branches of a N fork Rockfish near Alb. line.
Lines: Widdow(sic) WALLACE. Sent to RH by JNO. HENDREN, 7 May 1822.

Page 372. 13 Feb 1798. ALEX. McCAUL, Glasgow mct., by atty-in-fact,
JAS. LYLE, Chesterfield Co., to JNO. KNIGHT, AC, for Ŀ5, 400
acres branches Porrage. Pat. to AM 15 Aug 1764. Wit: BENJ. JORDAN, JNO.
M. ROSE, PATRICK ROSE JR, JNO. LAMONT. Proved, 15 Oct 1798, by ROSES.
17 Feb 1806, JAS. MURPHY swore as to signature of BENJ. JORDAN, now dec'd.

Page 373. 16 Sep 1805. JNO. MITCHELL, Madison Co, Ky, to WALLER SAN-
DIDGE, AC, for Ŀ150, 2 slaves. Wit: JNO. SANDIDGE, STEPHEN
CARTER & proved by them in AC, 17 Feb 1806.

Page 373. 29 Oct 1805. JOS. HOLLONSWORTH & wife MARY, Stokes Co, NC,
to WM. HOLLONSWORTH, AC, for $1000, 265 acres bought by JOS.
of RO. HARRISON & part of a tract. Lines: WM. CRISP, Spencer's road, WM.
LOVING, HARRISON, Bobb's Creek. Wit: CAREY BIBB, JNO. ALFORD, WM. ALFORD.
8 May, 1806, del. to WH.

Page 374. 17 Feb 1806. WM. BLANE & wife FANNY, AC, to ZACH. FORTUNE,
AC, for Ŀ220, 120 acres N fork Davis. Lines: JAS. H. BURTON,
JOS. SHELTON, ALEX. McALEXANDER, JNO. ROBERTS, WM. HARRIS.

Page 374. 19 Dec 1791. Ord. to Alb. J.P.'s, SAML. MURRELL & TANDY KEY.
WM. IRVINE & wife ELIZ., 30 Sep 1785, to THOS. WILLIAMSON -
245 acres branches of Rockfish near Blue Mts. Done 22 Dec 1791. Rec. AC,
17 Feb 1806.

Page 375. 19 Dec 1791. Ord. to AC J.P.'s NATHAN CRAWFORD & HUDSON MAR-
TIN - THOS. WILLIAMSON & wife JUDITH, 7 Feb 1791, to ALEX.
HENDERSON - 245 acres as above. Done 24 Dec 1791, rec. AC, 17 Feb 1806.

Page 375. 15 Dec 1797. Order to AC J.P.'s AMBROSE EUBANK & wife FRANKEY,
17 Sep 1797, to JNO. RICHESON - 104 acres. Done 22 Dec 1797,
by DAVID CRAWFORD & JOSIAH ELLIS. Rec. AC, 17 Feb 1806.

Page 376. 31 Oct 1799. Order to AC J.P.'s: NATHL. HARLOW & wife FANNY,
27 Dec 1796, to CHRISTIAN SHELLY - 289 acres. Done, no date,
by HUDSON MARTIN & JAS. WOODS. Rec. AC, 17 Feb 1806.

Page 377. 12 Mar 1792. Order to Bedford J.P.s: NATHAN REED & wife
SOPHIA, 22 Dec 1787, to JNO. & THOS. FITZPATRICK - 400 acres
Rockfish. Done, 18 Jul 1792, by WM. HARRIS & JAS. CALLAWAY. Rec. AC, 17
Feb 1806.(Note: It must have been a snowy day and clerk decided to "catch
up" on all of these over-due items. BFD)

Page 377. 19 Dec 1805. JINKINS OXLEY & wife HESTER, AC, to RO. PIERCE,
AC, for Ŀ222-10, 141 acres Rockey Creek. Lines: grantee, AND-
REW MONROE, RICH. WILSON, JACOB PIERCE, ISAIAH ATTKINSON, ELIZ. HOMAN,
JOEL CAMPBELL, WM. KINGSCALE. Bought from CHAS. CHRISTIAN, AC. Wit: CHAS.
& SARAH CHRISTIAN, WM. DAVENPORT. Order to quiz HESTER, 16 Jan 1806.
Done by REUBEN NORVELL & GEO. DILLARD next day.

Page 378. 31 Oct 1791. Order to AC J.P.'s: ELIZ., wife of SAML. MIG-
GINSON, 23 Sep 1791, to THOS. APLING - 300 acres Buff. Done,
5 Nov 1791, by JAS. DILLARD & REUBEN THORNTON. Rec. AC, 17 Feb 1806.
Orig. sent to TA, 18 Aug 1809.

Page 379. 22 Jul 1805. JNO. SERGEANT & wife FRANKEY, Louisa Co, to JNO.
POINDEXTER, Louisa Co, for $200, 400 acres Buff. Granted by
pat., 20 Sep 1759, to AARON TRUEHART. 6 Jun 1815, del. to Mr. POINDEXTER.

Louisa Clerk, JNO. POINDEXTER JR, 9 Dec 1805 (sic).

Page 380. 18 Jun 1805. JACOB WOOD & wife BARTHENY, to HENRY HOLLOWAY,
            13 Oct 1804 - order to quiz - 258 acres. Done by JNO. CHRIS-
TIAN & JAS. DILLARD, 21 Apr 1806.

Page 380. 12 Mar 1806. JAS. EDMUNDS SR, frees slave, GILBERT, "supposed
            to be about 40". Wit: THOS. WOODROOF.

Page 381. 5 Sep 1805. WIATT SMITH, AC, to WM. ARMISTEAD, AC, Deed of
            Trust; debt to JAS. FLOYD; 10 sh; slave. Wit: P. MARTIN, S.
GARLAND, WM. SAUNDERS. "Scratched, 6 Jun 1815, to Mr. POINDEXTER".

Page 382. 4 Jan 1806. GEO. GILBERT, AC, to NICHL. HARRISON, AC, for
            Ƚ460, 200 acres Migan's Ordinary - road from Lynchburg to New
Glasgow. Lines: SUSAN GILILAND, JAS. LIVLIE, JAS. HILL, REUBEN RUCKER.
Sent to NH, 17 Jul 1807, by THOS. WOODROOF.

Page 382. 19 Mar 1806. WM. WATTS, AC, to BARTLETT THOMPSON, AC, for
            Ƚ5-8-11, Deed of Trust; debt to THOMPSON & NOELL; $1.00; beds
etc. Wit: STERLING CLAIBORNE, WM. L. SLAUGHTER, W. SAUNDERS.

Page 383. 21 Apr 1806. HENRY LAIN JR, & wife SUSANNAH, AC, to ABRAM
            CARTER, AC, for Ƚ4, 2½ acres Horsley Creek. Part of tract sold
to JESSE RICHERSON. Lines: RICHERSON, mill dam.

Page 384. 17 Sep 1805. JAS. BIAS, AC, from JAS. FRANKLIN & wife NANCY,
            AC, for Ƚ80, 105 acres N branches James, surveyed by CARS(sic)
CHRISTIAN JR; taken from larger tract of heirs of JERRY WHITTEN, dec'd.
Lines: TABITHY WHITTEN, BENJ. NOEL, SLEDD. Wit: THOS. N. EUBANK, RICH.
S. ELLIS, ABRAM CARTER, MOSES RUCKER, CHAS. DAVIS. Order to quiz NANCY,
19 Sep 1805; done, by WM. WARE & CHAS. TALIAFERRO, 21 Sep 1805.

Page 385. 11 Nov 1805. RICH. HARRISON & wife SUSANNA, AC, to AMBROSE
            RUCKER, son of REUBEN RUCKER, dec'd, AC, for $2298, 287 acres
S side Miller Creek. Lines: RICH. SHELTON, GEO. McDANIEL, JNO. AMBLER,
ISAAC TINSLEY, PHILIP BURTON, dec'd. Wit: NELSON C. DAWSON, JAS. WARE,
PROSSER POWELL, LEROY CAMDEN, THOS. POWELL, NICHL. HARRISON. Orig. sent
to AR, 1 May 1806.

Page 386. 20 Feb 1806. Order to AC J.P.'s: BENJ. SANDIDGE & wife ELIZ.
            ---1799, to WM. MITCHELL - 66 acres. Done by WM. WARE & CHAS.
TALIAFERRO, 21 Apr 1806.

Page 387. 10 Oct 1805. Order to Bedford J.P.'s: HENRY LANDON DAVIES &
            wife, LUCY WHITING, 7 Feb 1800, to ARTHUR LANDON DAVIES - 2948
acres; also on same page HENRY & wife to NICHL. C. DAVIES - 2951 acres;
30 May 1797. Done on 18 Feb 1806 by ANDREW DONALD & WM. BURTON.

Page 388. 11 Dec 1805. THOS. GUY, agt. for heirs of RO. JOHNSTON, Caro-
            line Co, to LARKIN BYAS, AC, for $1.00, 325 acres Pedlar. Wit:
THOS. N. EUBANK, JNO. EUBANK JR, MOSES RUCKER, GODFREY TOLER, REUBEN
CRAWFORD.

Page 389. 18 Dec 1804. Order to Beaver Co, Pa. J.P.'s. JNO. McCUE &
            wife ELIZ., 13 Sep 1804, to WM. SMITH. Done, 19 Oct 1805, by
DAVID POTTER & MARTIN HOLMAN.

Page 389. 24 Nov 1801. GEO. RIVELEY, RO. WATKINS, & DUNCAN McLAUGHLIN
            to JOS. KENNERLEY for Ƚ507, tan yard & grounds; Town of Mad-
dison, AC; formerly that occupied by SACKVILLE KING & Co., & bought by
grantors. Wit: SAML. IRVINE, CALEB TATE, WM. SHELTON. Final proof by
SHELTON, 21 Apr 1806. (Note: Maddison(sic) is now Madison Heights and one
also finds it called Scuffletown in some deeds. It is an unincorporated
Sanitary District in AC and the area is teeming with people. It overlooks
James river and Lynchburg on the other side of the James.

Page 390. 3 Nov 1805. HENRY LAINE & wife FRANCES, AC, to JESSE RICHESON,
            AC, for Ƚ213, 230 acres S side Horsley. Lines: Harris branch,
THOS. GOODRICH. Wit: NELSON CRAWFORD, WM. WARE, JNO. ELLIS, MICAJAH

CAMDEN. Orig. del. to JR, 19 May 1807.

Page 391. 21 Apr 1806. HENRY LAIN JR, & wife SUSANNA, AC, & HENRY LAIN
           SR, & wife FRANCES, AC, to JESSE RICHESON, AC, for Ł110, 73¼
acres Horsely. Orig. del. to JR, 29 May 1807.

Page 391. 21 Apr 1806. THOS. GUY, agt. for heirs of RO. JOHNSTON, Caro-
           line, to THOS. N. EUBANK, AC, - heirs: LUCY JOHNSTON, wife &
relict of ROBT., PETROSS & wife LUCY, late JOHNSTON, and only surviving
heir, for $200, 197 acres pat. 8 May 1771, to RO. JOHNSTON. Lines: EDWD.
SANDERSON, Pegg's Creek, THOS. MORRIS, ALLISON MORRIS, JNO. SLEDD, DAVID
DAVENPORT.

Page 392. 21 Apr 1806. WM. LEE HARRIS & wife POLLY, AC, to JON TOOLEY,
           AC, for Ł10, 12 acres. Lines: WM. WOOD, CLOUGH SHELTON, top
of a mt.

Page 393. 21 Apr 1806. JNO. CAMDEN SR, AC, to JAS. MARTIN, son of PETER,
           AC, for Ł90, 270 acres; pat. to ALEX. DUGGINS in Richmond, 24
Jul 1787 - both sides Pedlar. Lines: NEILL CAMPBELL's est., JNO. CHILD-
RESS, MOSES SWINEY. Orig. del. to JM, 13 May 1808.

Page 393. 22 Apr 1806. GEO. STONEHAM, AC, - $1.00 paid by slaves:
           Lettia, Will, Ben, Cath., Susan, Tabitha, Sampson, Rachel, &
Jno. and named children of Cath. - freedom at end of 5 years for most of
them, but Jno. after 15 years and Robinson & Lettia after 25 years. To
have privileges of free negroes and mulattoes. To Mr.(?) LOVING, atty.
for Lettia, 11 Aug 1807, delivered. (Note: In next deed book is item
showing STONEHAM's heirs and they divide the salves, but refer to this
document to cast doubt upon the division. BFD)

Page 394. 11 Dec 1805. THOS. GUY, agt. for heirs of ROBT. JOHNSTON,
           Caroline, to THOS. N. EUBANK, AC, for $100, 74 acres Horsley
Creek. Lines: CHAS. CRAWFORD, WM. WARE. Part of 125 acres entry by RJ and
known as Johnston's Gun Mt. Entry. Mtg. to ALEX. GORDON, factor for
SPEARS BOWMAN & CO. alluded to. Wit: REUBEN CRAWFORD, JNO. EUBANK JR,
MOSES RUCKER, WM. PRYOR, HENRY BROWN.

Page 394. 31 Dec 1803. GEO. HUDSON, AC, to RUSH HUDSON, AC, for Ł75,
           80 acres Naked Creek. Part of tract. Lines: grantee, JAS.
FRANKLIN, old Church road, a bridge, REUBEN HUDSON, uop of Turkey Mt.
Wit: JAS. GARLAND, EMDM(?) HOLEMAN, CHARLES BURRUS.

Page 395. 16 Sep 1805. SAML. REID & wife LUTE, AC, to HAWES COLEMAN,
           AC, for Ł1500, 139 acres S fork Rockfish. Lines: grantee,
THOS. GOODWIN. Wit: JAS. MONTGOMERY, MICHL. WOODS, MOSES HUGHES, BENJ.
HUGHES. Page 396, order to quiz LUTE, 5 Oct 1805; done 8 Oct 1805 by
NATHAN CRAWFORD & JAS. WOODS.

Page 397. 6 May 1806. Order to AC J.Ps: JOS. BURRUS & wife SOPHIA, 16
           Feb 1804, to WM. PENN JR, 342 acres - done by SAML. MEREDITH
& DAVID S. GARLAND, 16 May 1806.

Page 397. 17 Feb 1806. Order to AC J.Ps: SACKVILLE KING & wife ANNA,
           1 Dec 1804, to DAVID S. GARLAND - 360 acres. This is so
written, but was done by Campbell Co. J.P.'s SAML. SCOTT & JAS. MILLER,
25 Mar 1806.

Page 398. 6 Jan 1806. Order to Henry Co. J.P.'s: GEO. MARTIN & wife
           MILDRED, -- Oct 1805, to THOS. CHILDRESS - 230 acres. Done by
BALLINGER WADE & JNO. DILLARD, 15 Jan 1806.

Page 398. 9 May 1806. Order to AC J.P.'s: AMBROSE RUCKER & wife BETSY,
           -- Oct 1805, to ANTHONY RUCKER - 230 acres. Done, 10 May 1806
by JOS. BURRUS & REUBEN NORVELL.

Page 399. 21 Apr 1806. Order to AC J.P.'s: HENRY LANE & wife FRANCES,
           3 Oct 1800, to HENRY LANE JR. Done by WM. WARE & NELSON
CRAWFORD, 26 Apr 1806.

442

Page 400. 5 May 1806. ARTHUR L. DAVIES & wife ELIZ. W., Gloucester co.
to EDWD. TINSLEY, Bedford, for Ŀ555-15, 370½ acres fork of
Bethel & Pedlar roads; surveyed by REUBEN NORVELL. Wit: NATHL. J. MANSON,
NICHL. C. DAVIES, RO. TINSLEY, NICHL. WEST, ANTHONY G. TINSLEY. Page
401, order to Gloucester J.P.'s as to above deed; done, 5 May 1806, by
MORGAN (TOMKIES?) & JOS. (CLUVARIES?).

Page 401. 4 Jan 1806. DANL. BURFORD JR, AC, to EDWD. WATSON, AC, for
Ŀ160, 100 acres where GEO. KNIGHT lives and bought by DB of
JNO. HARDWICK. Wit: ALEX. WATSON, JAS. LAYNE, WILKINS WATSON. Orig. del.
to HAMM, 9 Aug 1807.

Page 402. 3 Jan 1806. FREDERICK FULTS, AC, to RO. WALKER, GEO. DILLARD,
& THOMAS CREWS, AC, Deed of Trust; debt to WM. BROWN & Co.,
Lynchburg, & JAS. FRANKLIN Co. of Amherst - suit in Dist. Ct., Charlotts-
ville; $1.00; 201 acres where FF lives & conveyed to him by PETER JOINER.
Lines: AMBROSE RUCKER, REUBEN PADGETT, WM. DILLARD, JNO. TYLER - also
slaves. C. ACHILLES MAYS for WM. BROWN. Wit: JAS. BALLINGER, WIATT POWELL,
FREDERICK PRICE, EDWD. WATSON.

Page 404. 17 Mar 1806. CHAS. CHRISTIAN SR, AC, to BENJ. SANDIDGE, AC,
for Ŀ10, 50 acres S branches S fork Buff. Lines: JACOB PHIL-
LIPS, WILMORE; PULLIAM SANDIDGE. Wit: JOS. CHILDRESS, ANSELM CLARKSON,
SAML. CASH, DAVID S. GARLAND, FERDINAND LEIGH, JNO. CHRISTIAN(B).

Page 404. 17 Feb 1806. JAS. WARE & wife NANCY G., AC, to JOS. HAWKINS,
AC, for Ŀ32, 16 acres James River and John's Creek; part of
where JW lives. Lines: JAS. WILLS, grantor, N Bank Johns' Creek. Wit:
JNO. MAGANN, MICAJAH GOODWIN, JESSE WOODROOF, NICHL. HARRISON, EDWD.
TINSLEY, BENJ. RUCKER JR.

Page 405. 22 Feb 1806. JNO. MARTIN, AC, to JAS. & DAVID S. GARLAND, AC,
Deed of Trust; debt due them - suit in AC - 5 sh. Mare in
hands of SHEROD BUGG; many other items. Wit: BARTLETT THOMPSON, SHEROD
BUGG, JNO. SAVAGE JR, GEO. RULEY. Orig. del. to JG, 13 Jan 1809.

Page 406. 11 Mar 1806. GEO. PHILLIPS, AC, to JNO. EUBANK Jr, AC, Deed
of Trust - debt to J & D. GARLAND & DANL. HIGGINBOTHAM JR; 6
sh.; stock, furniture, etc. 50 acres on Elk Creek. Lines: FRANCES CAMP-
BELL. Pat. to JNO. PHILLIPS, 8 May 1805. Wit: CHAS. W. CHRISTIAN,
BARTLETT THOMPSON, RICH. HERNDON. Orig. del. to JAS. GARLAND, 10 Aug
1807.

Page 407. 14 May 1806. PULLIAM SANDIDGE & REUBEN HUDSON, exrs. of
JOSHUA HUDSON, AC, to GEO. HUDSON, AC, - under will authorized
to sell land; Ŀ550, 161 acres; part of tract; Naked Creek branches.
Lines: PATRICK ROSE, REUBEN HUDSON, top of Turkey Mt., RUSH HUDSON, old
church road, JNO. WIATT's old survey. Wit: JNO. CAMM, ANDERSON MOSS, RUSH
HUDSON, WM. EDMUNDS. Orig. del. to RO. RIVES, 13 Jun 1844.

Page 408. 10 Mar 1806. JAS. HALL, AC, to JNO. EUBANK JR, AC, Deed of
Trust; debt due J. & D. GARLAND - 6 sh. Lot #17 in New Glas-
gow. Wit: J.P. GARLAND, CHAS. W. CHRISTIAN, MICAJAH CAMDEN. Also owes
DANL. HIGGINBOTHAM & Co. To JG, 23 Mar 1807.

Page 409. 30 May 1806. JNO. WILLS, AC, HUDSON M. GARLAND, GASPER POTTER,
Rockbridge - Deed of Trust - debt due POTTOR - $1.00; where
JW lives - Lot #-- in New Glasgow. Wit: S. GARLAND, WM. SAVAGE, JAS. B.
EDWARDS, ARTHUR B. DAVIES. Orig. del. to HMG, 10 Jun 1807.

Page 410. 17 Dec 1805. WIATT R. GILBERT, AC, to MATT. WATSON, AC, for
Ŀ18, all int. in 80 acres conveyed by deed from JAS. WATSON,
dec'd, late of AC, to EZEK. & ANN RUKINGS GILBERT, his wife, 15 Oct 1796.
Wit: S. GARLAND, JAS. HALL, WM. HALL.

Page 411. 19 Nov 1805. Agreement between CHAS. ADAMS, & wife MARY,
Charlotte Co, Va., & JNO. S. DAWSON, AC, all int. in est. of
JNO. DAWSON, dec'd - except dower of SALLY, widow of JNO. - Ŀ200. Wit:
WALTER LEAKE, BEN DAWSON, CHAS. LANKFORD, FLEMING FARRAR, NELSON DAWSON.
Orig. del. to JSD, 27 Feb 1809.

Page 411. 19 Feb 1805. CHAS. ADAMS & wife, as above, to JNO. S. DAWSON, AC, for L60, 1 undivided int. of 1/8th. Hickory Creek. 512 acres. Lines: TERISHA TURNER, dec'd, JNO. MOORE, JNO. S. DAWSON. Tract of JNO. DAWSON, dec'd - MARY ADAMS, late DAWSON, is distributee of JNO. DAWSON. Orig. sent to JSD, 1809. Wit: same as previous deed.

Page 412. 10 Dec 1805. ABNER FORD & wife ELIZ., AC, to NANCY DAWSON, AC, for L60, all int. in est. of JNO. DAWSON, dec'd - 1/8th. Widow's third first taken out. Wit: WM. BERLEY, TERISHA TURNER, CHAS. LANKFORD, JNO. MOSBY.

Page 412. 19 Nov 1805. BENJ. DAWSON & wife MOLLY, Lincoln Co, Ky, to JNO. S. DAWSON, AC, for L60, 512 acres Hickory Creek - 1/8th as above in JNO. DAWSON's land - minus widow's part. Wit: THOS. PUGH, NELSON DAWSON, CHAS. LANKFORD. Orig. del. to JD, 27 Feb 1809.

Page 413. 21 May 1806. WM. G. ARMS to BARTLETT THOMPSON - several slaves and mare - no amt. Wit: STERLING CLAIBORNE, JNO. P. COBBS, JAS. GARLAND.

Page 414. 2 Dec 1805. THOS. GUY, agt. for heirs of RO. JOHNSTON, Caroline Co., heirs are LUCY, widow of RO. JOHNSTON, RICH. W. PEATROSS & wife LUCY, formerly JOHNSTON, and only surviving child of RO.; Caroline, to HUGH McCABE, AC, for $200, 404 acres Otter Creek; pat. 20 Nov 1784. Lines: CORNL. THOMAS, Tarapin Creek, Rattlesnake Branch, N bank Fluvanna; Cedar branch - also amt. includes costs also vs. VEAL in AC Court. Wit: THOS. N. EUBANK, MOSES RUCKER, HENRY BROWN, ABRAM CARTER, BENJ. NOEL, JNO. FLOOD, REUBEN CRAWFORD.

Page 415. 11 Jun 1806. REUBEN TINSLEY & wife PHANNEY, AC, to PETER MARTIN, AC, for L70, 150 acres Pedlar, N side.

Page 415. 1 May 1806. Order to Patrick Co. J.P.'s: RICH HARRISON & wife SUSANNAH, 11 Nov 1805, to AMBROSE RUCKER - 287 acres. Done 29 May 1806, by D. BANKS (WM. in order) & GEO. PENN.

Page 416. 20 Feb 1806. ELIZ. COFLIN, AC, to DAVID S. GARLAND & JNO. LONDON, AC, for 6 sh. and $200 per year - her life estate in tracts bequeathed to her by her dec'd husband, BENJ. COFLIN, on Porage - where she lives. Wit: Major J.B. COFLIN, THOS. GILLENWATERS, HENRY TURNER, WM. BRYANT, JAS. LONDON JR, RO. GRANT, PLEASANT STORY, MARTIN LONDON. Orig. del. to DG, 12 Aug 1806.

Page 417. 20 Feb 1806. KEZIAH SMITH, AC, to DAVID S. GARLAND & JNO. LONDON, AC, for 6 sh. & $10 per year, all int. in tract above and bequeathed to her by dec'd father, BENJ. COFLIN. Wit: as above.

Page 418. 10 Jun 1806. JNO. LONDON, AC, to RO. GRANT, AC, for L160, 210 acres N branches Porrage. JL bought it from RO. ALLEN. Lines: JAS. DILLARD, THOS. GILLENWATERS, LARKIN LONDON, JAS. LONDON SR, & JR.

Page 418. 20 Jan 1806. BROWN RIVES & Co, AC, to SUSANNA MASSIE, AC, for L91-19-3, 100 acres Crawley Creek; branch of Piney. Lines: JNO. CAMPBELL, JESSE WRIGHT JR, GEO. CAMPBELL. Tract sold by decree to pay debt - JNO. MASSIS's tract. Wit: STEPHEN WATTS, WM. SANDIDGE, THOS. JONES, LEWIS DAVIS, BEV. WILLIAMSON, JNO. ANDERSON, EDMD. MASSIE.

Page 419. 15 Feb 1806. WM. MITCHELL & wife JANE, Botetourt, to JNO. ROBINSON, Rockbridge, for L150, 2 tracts. 1) granted to THOS. GOLDSBY 16 Feb 1771 - 66 acres on blue ridge & Pedlar. 2) 200 acres; part of 400 acres pat. to JNO. CHILDRESS SR, 25 Jul 1780. Lines: HENRY CHILDERS, Shady Mt. Creek. Wit: JULIAN(?) WASS or WAAS, WALLER SANDIDGE, JNO. DEVASHER, JOS. MILSTRED. Orig. del. to WM, 5 Apr 1808, per order.

Page 420. 16 Jun 1806. THOS. NEVIL & wife ELIZ., AC, to JOS. ALCOCK, AC, for L100, 92 acres N branches Buff. Lines: RICH. ALCOCK, Crooked Fall branch-head of; the Spring used by grantor, GABL. PENN dec'd, ALLEN BLAIR. Part of tract. Wit: JAS. STEVENS JR, JESSE FIDLER, JESSE CLARKSON.

Page 421. 16 Jun 1806. REUBEN TINSLEY & wife FANNY, AC, to WM. GRISSOM,
AC, for Ł60, 125 acres both sides Pedlar. Lines: PETER MARTIN,
HENRY CAMDEN, JAS. MARTIN, JNO. CRAWFORD, WM. GALT. Signed: PHANUABE
TINSLEY.

Page 421. 16 Jun 1806. WM. PENN, AC, to RO. WALKER, AC, for Ł129-15,
86+ acres to WALKER. Lines: the main road up the mt., VERNON
MEDCALF, WM. CAMDEN, JAS. HIGGINBOTHAM, grantee. Part of tract sold to
WP by Major JOS. BURRUS. Wit: RO. COLEMAN, WM. & JAS. HALL. Orig. del.
to PETER WALKER, 9 May 1811.

Page 422. 16 Jun 1806. JNO. BETHEL & wife JEAN, AC, to BENJ. HARRIS,
Alb., for Ł783, 347+acres. Taylor Creek. Lines: WM. SMITH,
THOS. ROBERTSON, WM. HARRIS JR, JNO. McCLURE. Deed of Trust; debt due
HARRIS.

Page 423. 30 Nov 1805. JNO. WRIGHT, AC, to JNO. HIGGINBOTHAM, AC, Deed
of Trust; debt to JAS. MURPHY & Co, 5 sh; slave, Pat, and her
four children and a man slave, Edwd. Wit: SHELTON CROSTHWAIT, CORNL.
NEVIL, NATHL. OFFUTT, JNO. DAWSON, JNO. CREWS. Orig. del. to RICH. CLARK
21 Jul 1806.

Page 424. 8 May 1806. DANL. TILMAN, AC, to CORNL. THOMAS, AC, for Ł16 -
10, Deed of Trust - debts to NORBORN THOMAS. $1.00. stock.
Wit: JNO. HIGGINBOTHAM, JAS. MURPHY, ELISHA PETERS, JAS. TURNER, WM. L.
BELL.

Page 425. 22 Feb 1806. WM. MEGUFFIN, AC, to JNO. THOMPSON, overseer,
Deed of Trust - debt to GEO. W. VARNUM; $1.00; horse bought of
JACOB SWISHER of Augusta; 1 bought of JNO. STEWART, 1 bought of PENN, 1
bought of JNO. YORKSHIRE of Augusta; 1 bought of CHAS. THOMPSON SR, 1
bought of GEO. W. VARNUM; beds, etc. Wit: THOS. E. FORTUNE, WM. GOWING,
HENRY MASSIE. Orig. del. to BARTLETT THOMPSON, 16 Feb 1807.

Page 427. 18 Nov 1805. SAML. J. CABELL & wife SARAH, AC, to JNO. THOMP-
SON, AC, for Ł50, 1 lot in town of Cabellsville; No. 35 on
plat - 1600 sq. yds. Wit: RO. NIMMO, WM. NIMMO, SETH WARD, DAVID DAWSON.
Orig. del. to JAS. MURPHY, 22 Jul 1806.

Page 427. 23 Aug 1805. JAS. MONTGOMERY, AC, to RO. MOORE, AC, Deed of
Trust - debt to RIVES MURPHY & CO, 5 sh; 7 slaves. Wit: NATHAN
BURNETT, JNO. ALFORD, EBEN HICKOK, J. FREELAND, JESSE PROFFITT, RO.CLARKE.

Page 428. 5 Aug 1805. Order to Bedford J.P.s. HENRY L. DAVIES & wife
LUCY, 1 Jun 1796, to REUBEN PENDLETON - 500 acres. Done by
WM. BURTON & ANDREW DONALD, 1 Feb 1806. Page 429, order to same men, 15
Oct 1805, as to DAVIES & wife LUCY, to JESSE WOODROOF; 202 acres. Done
18 Feb 1806.

Page 430. 7 May 1805. Order to AC J.P.'s. WM. CABELL & wife ANNE, 17
Jan 1803, to DAVID S. GARLAND - 31 acres. Done, 16 Jun 1806,
by SAML. J. & LANDON CABELL. Orig. del. to DG, 18 Oct 1806.

Page 430. 21 Jun 1806. SAML. J. CABELL, AC, to JAS. TAYLOR of Ky, to
superintend land business in Ohio - entries and to convey etc.
Wit: WM. S. CABELL, SAML. J. CABELL JR, LANDON & WM. CABELL. Orig. del.
to SJC, 24 Jul.

Page 431. 4 Jul 1806. Order to AC J.P.'s. JACOB WOOD & wife BETHENY,
14 Sep 1803, to WIATT SMITH, all int. of JW & wife in est. of
SALLY H. & NANCY PHILLIPS, dec'd. Done 15 Jul 1806, by DAVID S. GARLAND
& GEO. DILLARD.

Page 432. Order to same J.P.'s, 14 Jul 1806. JACOB WOOD & wife BARTHENY,
18 Feb 1805, to WIATT SMITH - 162½ acres. Done, 15 Jul 1806.

Page 433. 8 Jun 1805. Order to AC J.P.'s. PHILLIP GOOCH & wife FRANCES,
-- Oct 1804, to JACOB WOOD - 162 acres. Done by REUBEN NORVELL
& GEO. DILLARD, 10 Jun 1805.

Page 433.   14 Jan 1806.   Order to AC J.P.'s.   RICH. C. POLLARD & wife
ELIZ. B., 9 Sep 1805, to THOS. GLASS; Done 27 May 1806, by
JOS. SHELTON & WM. H. DIGGES.

Page 434.   10 Jul 1806.   WM. WARE & wife PATTY, AC, to JNO. CRAWFORD, AC,
for ₤75, 51 acres Horsley. Lines: CALEB RALLS, JESSE RICHESON.
Orig. del. to JC, 20 Mar 1810.

Page 435.   25 Nov 1805.   Dispute between WM. WARE, AC, & THOS. GUY, agt.
for heirs of ROBT. JOHNSTON, Caroline, by Power of Atty, HENRY
GRIFFEY enters 50 acres under Tobacco Row Mt. and joins CRAWFORD & LOMAX;
13 Apr 1762, and entry by co. curveyor, 6 May 1791, and transferred to
THOS. ALLEN and surveyed by him, 28 May 1791; and by him the said Works
transferred to WM. WARE & pat. by him (Gov. HENRY LEE) 6 Aug 1793.   WARE
derives claim as above. GUY claims by entry & survey of 200 acres, 7 Sep
1764, and 125 acres out of the survey of 200 acres was surveyed and pat.
issued, 17 Jul 1780; being a prior date to WARE's.   Agreed that 50 acres
is part of the 125 acres claimed by GUY - to be settled by DAVID S. GAR-
LAND, JAS. HIGGINBOTHAM, & W.S. CRAWFORD. They decided that 50 acres
belongs to WARE.

Page 436.   28 Oct 1805.   BALDWIN BAIN, AC, Power of Atty to JAS. BROOKS,
AC. Wit: THOS. STOCKHAM, KILLIS BABER, WM. CANORE(?).

Page 436.   21 Jul 1806.   BENJ. RUCKER, AC, to BENAMIMI STONE, AC, for ₤16,
16 acres Crooked Run; branch of Rutledge. Lines: grantor, JNO.
HIGGINBOTHAM, JOS. HIGGINBOTHAM. Wit: ANTHONY RUCKER, DAVID TINSLEY, JNO.
McDANIEL.

Page 437.   28 Jun 1806.   JOS. WHITE & wife COURTNEY, AC,. to WM. H. DIGGES,
AC, for ₤26-10, 18 or 20 acres Tye. Part of tract sold to JW
by JAS. LANDRUM. Lines: S side road from JNO. THOMPSON, merchant, to
SHELTON CROSTHWAIT's mill; ELIJAH MAYS, houses now occupied by TEMPERANCE
FLOED, grantee, HENRY STONEHAM, AMBROSE CAMPBELL, ROLAND EDMONDS, mouth
of lane between WHITE & EDMONDS.   Orig. del. to WHD, 2 May 1807.

Page 437.   3 Jun 1805.   JNO. SMITH, AC, & wife KESIAH, late COFLAND, &
ELIZ. COFLAND, AC, to JESSE SPINNER, AC, for ₤200, 250 acres.
Lines: Capt. JAS. DILLARD, RICH. PETERS - whole of lands bequeathed to
KESIAH SMITH, late COFLAND, by her dec'd. father. JAS. COFLAND also
signed. Wit: JAS. CHRISTIAN, CHAS. CHRISTIAN, JAS. WADE. Orig. del. to
JS, 27 Jul 1806.

Page 439.   19 Jul 1806.   CHAS. DAVIS & wife SUSANNAH, AC, to WM. NOEL, AC,
for ₤30, 74 acres N branches Otter Creek; laid off by NICHL.
C. DAVIES by agreement. Lines: grantor, NICHL. C. DAVIES, DAVID NOWLIN,
JER WHITTON, JNO. STINNETT.   Orig. del. to BENJ. NOEL, 13 Jun 1807.

Page 439.   9 Jul 1806.   HENRY L. DAVIES & wife LUCY WHITING, Bedford, to
CHAS. DAVIS, AC, for ₤30, 83 acres N branches Otter. Lines:
NICHL. C. DAVIES, grantee, DAVID NOWLAND, JER. WHITTEN, JNO. STINNETT.
Wit: NATHL. J. MANSON, JOSIAH LEAKE, ANTHONY RUCKER, DAVID TINSLEY.
Orig. del. to JOSIAH ELLIS, 21 Apr 1807.

Page 440.   14 May 1806.   SAML. S. SCRUGGS & wife JANEY, AC, to WM. SMITH,
AC, for ₤30, 26 acres S branches Rockfish & Dutch. Lines: WM.
DIXON, grantee, WM. H. MOSBEY. Wit: WM. MARTIN, WM. H. MOSEBY, NATHAN
HARRIS.   Orig. del. to WS, 13 Jan 1807.

Page 441.   18 May 1806.   WM. CAMDEN & wife LUCY, AC, to JAS. MARKHAM, AC,
for ₤60, 140 acres Huff. Lines: JNO. COLEMAN, top of the mt.,
BENJ. NOEL, JAS. BYAS, SLAIDING. Wit: DANL. HIGGINBOTHAM, PEYTON KEITH,
JAS. GARLAND.   Orig. del. to JM, 5 Jan 1807.

Page 442.   21 Jul 1806.   REBEKAH MILSTEAD & JOS. MILSTEAD, AC, Deed of
Trust; debts due TALIAFERRO & LOVING; CHAS. P. & PETER TALIA-
FERRO; 6 sh. to BENJ. HIGGINBOTHAM.   310 acres. Lines: BETTY SCOFIELD,
JNO. DEVASHER, JNO. C. DEVASHER, DANL. SWADER, GODFREY TOLER - where we
live; also 7 slaves; stock etc.   3 Jul 1807, orig. del. to CHAS. P.
TALIAFERRO.   BENJ. HIGGINBOTHAM is to pay "over plush" to REBEKAH

445

MILSTEAD: POWHATAN, NEWMAN, MULLICE & MARTIN PRICE MULLICE - sons of
FRANCES MILSTEAD. Wit: JAS. LOVING JR, STEPHEN CARTER, JNO. WASER(?).

Page 443. 10 Feb 1806. EZEK. GILBERT & wife ANN ROOKING, MATT. WATSON,
          & ELVIRA GILBERT, AC, to JNO. PENN JR, AC, Deed of Trust;
$1.00; debt due NANCY SHIELDS - 80 acres - conveyed by JAS. WATSON, late
of AC, to EZEK. GILBERT & wife for life and then to their children, 15
Oct 1796. MATT. WATSON conveyed int. of WIATT R. GILBERT (conveyed to MW
by WG), Dec -- 1805. ELVIRA conveys int. due at death of EZEK. & wife,
as one of the children. Wit: LINDSEY COLEMAN, WM. COLEMAN, WM. LEE.

Page 445. 21 Jul 1806. JOSIAH CHEATHAM, AC, to RICH. CLARK & SHELTON
          CROSTHWAIT, AC, Deed of Trust; debt due JAS. MURPHY & Co.;
6 sh; 110 acres Hickory Creek. Lines: BENJ. HARRIS, JNO. ROBERTS, SAML.
PERKINS, JNO. FARRAR, 5 slaves, stock. Wit: MOSES PHILLIPS, ELIJAH
STATON, JNO. STEWART. Orig. del. to JAS. MURPHY, 10 Feb 1807.

Page 446. 17 Mar 1806. NATHL. HARLOW JR, & wife JANE, AC, to DAVID
          SHIELDS, AC, - JANE was formely SHIELDS - $400 Hatt creek;
tract is share of JANE from est. of JNO. SHIELDS, dec'd. Lines: JAS.
SHIELDS lot; GEO. SHILEDS' lot. Wit: GEO. W. HIGGINBOTHAM, JAS. & GEO.
SHIELDS. Orig. del. to JAS. SHIELDS, 6 Oct 1807.

Page 447. 21 Jul 1806. JAS. SHIELDS, AC, & wife ELIZ., to GEO. SHIELDS,
          AC, for $400, Hatt creek - JAMES' share of tract of JNO. SHI-
ELDS, dec'd. Lines: MARGARET SHIELDS, GEO. SHIELDS near N & S forks Hatt;
DAVID SHIELDS, WM. ALEX., REBEKAH, & NATHAN SHIELDS.

Page 448. 6 May 1806. HANNAH ALLEN, AC, to daughter, BETHEMIAH ALLEN,
          AC, for love and 5 sh, negro, Sam. Wit: JAS. FRANKLIN JR,
LEWIS TINDALL, JOS. BRYANT.

Page 448. 21 Jul 1806. JAS. FLOYD, AC, from WIATT SMITH, AC, Ŀ64 in
          full on Deed of Trust on slave, Squire, WM. ARMISTEAD, trustee.
Wit: J.B. EDWARDS, H.M. GARLAND.

Page 449. 30 Jan 1806. JNO. KNIGHT, AC, to WM. KNIGHT, AC, for Ŀ700,
          347 acres N headbranches Stovall. Lines: JAS. MORRIS, JAS.
PETTIT, WM. GARRETT, JNO. MUNROE, JAS. MARR. Wit: RICH. BURKS, JNO. COX,
JAS. PETTIT, NICHL. HARRISON, ABSALOM RUCKER.

Page 450. 21 Jun 1806. THOS. ALFRED, AC, to JOS. KENADY, AC, for Ŀ100,
          one-third of Buff. tract which JESSE KENNEDY owned at death
& dower of my wife, SUSANNAH, formerly KENNEDY, on order of AC court;
also slaves - for life of my wife, whose former husband was JESSE KENNEDY.
Wit: ALEX. PENN, JOS. DILLARD, JAMES GARLAND, WM. GRISSOM.

Page 450. 4 Jul 1806. BARKSDALE SNIDER & wife SARAH, Lynchburg, to
          PHILIP JOHNSON, AC, for Ŀ40, SARAH's dower as widow of PLEDGE
PALMER; sold by AC ct. decree & PHILIP JOHNSON bought it. Wit: JOSIAH
LEAKE, THOS. WOODROOF, ED. PENN, GEO. DILLARD. Orig. del. to PJ, 17 Sep
1806.

Page 451. 13 Jan 1806. JNO. KNIGHT, AC, to JAS. PETIT, AC, for Ŀ385-14,
          203 acres Head branches Porrage & Stovall. Lines: SUSANNA
GILILAND, WM. GARRET, WM. KNIGHT, JAS. MARR. Wit: ABSALOM RUCKER, JNO.
COX, WM. KNIGHT, RICH. BURKS, NICHL. HARRISON. Orig. del. to JP, 1 Dec
1817.

Page 452. 15 Mar 1806. AMBROSE RUCKER, SR, AC, to his son, ISAAC RUCKER,
          AC, for love, 400 acres both sides Rockey Run. Lines: JOEL
CAMPBELL, NATHAN WINGFIELD, FREDERICK FULTZ, JACOB PEARCE, ISAIAH ATKIN-
SON. Wit: REUBEN RUCKER, BENJ. RUCKER, JNO. RYON.

Page 453. 20 Jan 1806. WM. DILLARD, AC, to BENJ. WARREN, AC, no amount,
          9 acres both sides Adams' branch of Rocky River creek. Lines;
PHILIP GOOCH, dec'd, grantee, grantor. Wit: WM. B. GOOCH, ABSALOM HOWL,
WILEY CAMPBELL, WALTER CHRISTIAN, JNO. CHRISTIAN (B). Orig. del. to
CHAS. CHRISTIAN SR, 8 Aug 1806.

Page 454. 11 (14?) Mar, 1806. BENJ. WARREN, AC, to WALTER CHRISTIAN,
            AC, L is the middle initial of CHRISTIAN - for Ł50, where BW
lives - both sides Adams' Branch. Lines: REUBEN PADGETT, FREDERICK FULTZ,
WM. DILLARD, PHILLIP GOOCH, dec'd, glade road. Wit: as above, minus
WALTER CHRISTIAN. Orig. del. to CHAS.CHRISTIAN 8 Aug 1806.

Page 455. 5 Mar 1806. HENRY FOGES, AC, to JNO. LOVING, AC, Deed of
            Trust - SHELTON CRESTHWAIT, security, to exrs. of CHRISTOPHER
SMITH, Louisa, 6 sh; slaves. Wit: JNO. DAWSON, JNO. WILLCOCK(?), MILDRED
THOMPSON. Orig. del. to JL, 9 May 1807.

Page 456. 30 Nov 1804. NICHL. PRYOR & wife MARY, AC, to CALEB RALLS,
            AC, for Ł47-10, 104 acres Pedlar. Lines: MARTIN BIBB, THOS.
LUCAS, dec'd, SAML. GEST, HENRY BROWN, JNO. MAYS. Wit: JNO. ELLIS, THOS.
N. EUBANK, DANL. WARWICK, BENJ. SALE, JNO. WARE. Orig. del. to CR, --
Sept 1806.

Page 457. 8 Feb 1806. WM. JONES, AC, to WILSON DAVENPORT, Campbell Co,
            Deed of Trust; debt to SAML. IRVINE; $1.00; negress & 2 child-
ren, male slaves, beds, stock, etc. Wit: JAS. BENAGH, THOS. C. CLAYTON,
BENJ. A. WINSTON, JOSIAH LEAKE. 30 Jan 1807, del. to SAML. IRVINE, by
mail.

Page 458. 22 May 1806. THOS. CREWS, AC, to VERNON METCALFE, AC, for
            Ł712-10, 237½ acres Rutledge & Tribulation. Lines: EDWD. WAT-
SON, WIATT POWELL, grantor, JAMES PENDLETON, the road, grantee. Orig.
del. to HOLLOWAY's exrs, 25 Feb 1812.

Page 459. 29 Nov 1805. WM. CHASE, AC, to DANL. HIGGINBOTAHM, AC, Deed
            of Trust; debt to JAS. & DAVID GARLAND: $1.00; stock, furni-
ture, etc. Wit: WM. G. PENDLETON, HUDSON M. GARLAND, ANDERSON MOSS.

Page 460. 3 Sep 1803. JNO. FARRAR, AC, to DANL. HIGGINBOTHAM, AC, Deed
            of Trust; debt to RIVES MURPHY & Co., 5 sh; 136 acres Hickory
Creek; taken up and surveyed by JF. Lines: RICH. HARE, SAML. PERKINS,
JNO. ROBERTS, JOSIAH CHEATHAM, woman slave & child, blacksmith tools,
sorrel mare with one eye - supposed to be 5 last spring and her colt
which was got by Cor Ira and was "folded" the last spring. Wit: WM. F.
CARTER, JAS. VIGUS JR, WM. BAILEY, JAS. P. PARISH, RO. MOORE. Orig. del.
30 Sep 1806, to JAS. MURPHY by letter.

Page 461. 1 Jul 1806. WM. H. DIGGES & SHELTON CROSTHWAIT, Overseers of
            the Poor, Amherst Parish, to JNO. HAWKINS, AC, - have put
MOSES SMITH, free negro boy, 3 yrs. old, as apprentice to HAWKINS, until
21, by Act of Assembly - carpenter's trade. Next page - same men -
REUBIN SMITH, free negro boy, 8 yrs. old, bound out on same date to
HAWKINS.

Page 463. 15 Sep 1806. PETER SOULMON & wife CHRISTINA, AC, to JNO.
            GILLIAM, AC, for Ł650, no acres - both sides Wilderness &
Lawrence Creeks. Part of a divided tract. 16 Sep 1806, to JG, by WM.
DUNCAN.

Page 464. 21 Oct 1803. RICH. FARRAR, Alb., to DANL. HIGGINBOTHAM, AC,
            Deed of Trust; debt to RIVES MURPHY & Co, 5 sh; slaves &
supposed ages. Wit: RO. MOORE, WM. F. CARTER, SAML. HANSBROUGH, SAML.
TURNER. Orig. del. to JAS. MURPHY, 30 Sep 1806.

Page 465. 18 Aug 1806. SHELTON CROSTHWAIT came before DAVID S. GARLAND,
            J.P., and swore that on night of 23 July last, Mr. ISAAC
THOMPSON had considerable part of his right ear bit off by one JNO. WIL-
COX as this affiant believes. They had been working in the tanyard to-
gether some little time and in the previous evening to THOMPSON's mis-
fortune they had some angry words as this affiant was informed and after
THOMPSON had gone to bed, as this affiant informed, WILCOX dashed sudden-
ly on him, THOMPSON, and bit off his ear as it appears at present. WIL-
COX went off suddenly without power of civil authority to interpose.
Both in my imploy(sic) & I well know the Ear of THOMPSON must be mangled
in the manner it is by WILCOX or some person in night aforesaid.

Page 466. 6 Aug 1806. JAS. FULCHER, AC, to THOS. PENN, AC, - PENN may
build dam across Piney adj. FULCHER's lands for water grist
mill on JF's lands on opposite side of river; may join my banks, but not
to damage lands. Wit: JAS. GENTRY, JAS. STEVENS, JR.

Page 466. 15 Sep 1806. JOS. & BENJ. HIGGINBOTHAM, exrs. of JOS. HIGGIN-
BOTHAM, AC, to CHRISTOPHER HOILMAN, Rockbridge, for $52.50,
110 acres surveyed 15 Apr 1775; S branches Pedlar. Lines: HUGHS, McDANIEL,
WM. TAYLOR, JOS. KING, JAS. FRASHER, ANGUS McDANIEL. Wit: WALLER SANDIDGE,
STEPHEN CARTER, JAS. SMITH. Orig. del. to CH, 14 Aug 1807, by JOS.
HIGGINBOTHAM.

Page 467. 8 May 1806. WM. C. CHRISTIAN, AC, to ISAAC RUCKER, AC, Deed
of Trust to secure ANDREW MONROE & WM. GALT & Co., no amt.,
slaves. Wit: RICH. WILSON & JER. WILSON. Orig. del. to MONROE 23 Apr 1807.

Page 468. 13 Sep 1806. WM.HANSARD & wife MARTHA, AC, to JNO. MILLER,
Lynchburg, for Ь150, 73 acres. Wit: ELIAS WILLS, PHIL JOHNSON,
THOS. B. MEHONE, ANTHONY RUCKER. Orig. sent to JM, 9 Oct 1806.

Page 468. 15 Sep 1806. JNO. CAMDEN, THOS. PENN & JESSE WRIGHT, AC, to
JOHN CAMPBELL, Piney River - Nov. 1805, conditional decree in
favor of JNO. BROWN, surviving partner of ALEX. SPEARS & JNO. BROWN & Co,
agt. HENRIETTA CAMRON, widow of DUNCAN CAMRON; DANL. HUNTER & wife PEGGY;
DUNCAN & ANDREW CAMRON, EDWD. CAMPBELL & wife FRANCES, MARY CAMRON; THOS.
CASH & wife JANE, ALLEN CAMRON, DINAH CAMRON, DANL. CAMRON, & RO. CAMRON,
legatees of DUNCAN CAMRON and above grantors authorized to sell to JNO.
CAMPBELL who was highest bidder - 377 acres Piney at Ь72-11.

Page 469. 30 Sep 1806. WM. CLASBEY & wife MOLLY, AC, to THOS. CLASBEY,
AC, for Ь200, 100 acres N branches Tye. Lines: GEO. LOVING,
ACHILLES WRIGHT, MOSES MAYS. Part of tract.

Page 470. 21 Oct 1805. Order to AC J.P.'s. JAS. BROOKS & wife ELIZ.,
9 Jul 1805, to NATHL. HARLOW - 62 acres in AC and Alb. Done,
22 (12?) Apr 1806, by NATHAN CRAWFORD & HUDSON MARTIN.

Page 470. 4 Aug 1806. ELIZ. HOMAN, AC, to RO. PEARCE, AC, for Ь82, 40
acres Rockey Creek. Lines: ISAIAH ATKINSON, JINKINS OXLEY,
JOEL CAMPBELL. Wit: RICH., ANNA, & ELIZ. WILSON. Orig. del. to RP, 27
Jan 1808.

Page 471. 15 Mar 1806. FRANCIS BURCH & wife PENELOPE, Campbell Co, to
WM. CLINKSCALES, AC, for Ь662, 331 acres Rocky Run. Lines: RO.
PEARCE, JOEL CAMPBELL, Stovall's old road, REUBIN NORVELL. Wit: REUBEN
NORVELL, TERISHA TURNER, ARCHILEAUS REYNOLDS, REUBEN PENDLETON, ANDREW
MONROE, RO. PEARCE. Order to Campbell J.P.'s to quiz PENELOPE, 28 Mar
1806; done, 12 Apr 1806, by JAS. STEWART & RODERICK TALIAFERRO.

Page 473. 1 May 1806. Order to Bedford J.P.'s. JOS. NICHOLS & wife
ANNA, 15 Sep 1806, to JAS. DAVIS - 186 acres. Done by JNO.
WATTS & WM. BURTON, 22 Jul 1806. Orig. del. to JD, 31 Aug 1831.

Page 474. 1 Aug 1806. WM. GARRETT & wife ANNE, AC, to EDWD. WATSON, AC,
for Ь259-10, 2 tracts with total of 173 acres. 1) Where WG
lives - 118½ acres. Lines: JNO. BOLLING, MICHL. COALTER, JAS. BOLLING,
WM. KNIGHT, JNO. McBRIDE, Lynch road. 2) 54½ acres, part of tract bought
by WG of sundry legatees of SARAH GEORGE, dec'd; both sides Lynch road.
Lines: REUBEN RUCKER, LODOWICK GEORGE, JAS. PETIT. Wit: BARTLETT EADES,
RICH. GARRETT, SAML. HILL, JNO. LACKEY, ALEX. WATSON. Orig. del. to EW,
7 Oct 1806.

Page 475. 30 Sep 1806. JAS. FRANKLIN, acting for EDMD. BOLES & wife
TABITHA, to RO. NUCKLES, AC, for Ь58, part of tract of JER.
WHITTEN, dec'd. Lines: CHAS. DAVIES, BENJ. SHACKELFORD, JNO. SLEDD. 90
acres by division at WHITTEN's death to daughter, TABITHA.

Page 475. 15 Mar 1806. SAML. COLEMAN & wife JUDITH, AC, to THOS. COLE-
MAN & wife NANCY, AC, for Ь214-10, 2 tracts Harris Creek, S
side Bare(sic) Mt. Lines: JNO. AMBLER, MOSES SWEENY, JNO. COLEMAN - 390

acres - JNO. AMBLER's was formerly JNO. HARVEY, dec'd. - JNO. COLEMAN is
later termed "dec'd.", JOS. CHILDRESS.

Page 476. 30 Sep 1806. Heirs of JER. WHITTEN: JAS. BIAS & wife BETSY,
          JAMES FRANKLIN & wife NANCY, WM. NOEL & wife LUCY, EDMD. BOLES
& wife TABITHA, to RO. NICKLES, AC, for Ł20, 136 acres N side Otter.
Lines: JER. WHITTEN, JNO. HOG. Wit: RO. TINSLEY, PETER SULIMAN, JNO.
GILLIAM. Orig. del. to RN, 5 Oct 1809.

Page 477. 19 Aug 1805. PHILIP SLAUGHTER, Culpeper Co, relinquished all
          title in mtg. from HUGH CAMPBELL to RO. RIVES & me. New bonds
made. Wit: CHAS. WINGFIELD, JOEL FRANKLIN, BEV. WILLIAMSON, JUDAH WILL-
IAMSON.

Page 478. 21 Jul 1806. WM. BOWMAN, AC, to LANDON CABELL, Deed of Trust
          for benefit of BOWMAN's children: RALPH, JNO.,GILBERT, SHEROD,
WM. BOWMAN, ELIZ. FOWLES, MARY WILKINSON, AILSE BABER, LUCY WILKINSON,
SARAH BURKS, NANCY BOWMAN, SUSANNA & REBEKAH BOWMAN - $1.00; tract where-
on WB lives. Lines: TERISHA TURNER, WM. JOHNSON, CORNL. THOMAS. 360 acres.
Also Alb. tract of 400 acres. Lines: WILLIAM HOWARD, JNO. CRANK, CHAS.
IRVING's est. Also Buckingham tract of 100 acres. Lines: JAS. WILKINSON,
JAS. PATESON. Also 20 slaves named; furniture. WB is to live on land
and manage. AC tract to SHEROD & GILBERT BOWMAN, his sons - divided by
Joblares Branch. Alb. tract to SHEROD - Canoe branch, that tract on
Rockfish to JNO. & RALPH BOWMAN. Buckingham Tract to WM., son of WM.
Furniture to be divided to all heirs named above, but REBECAH is not
named. Wit: JAS. JOHNSON, SAML. HARDIE, VAL. BALL.

Page 479. 17 Apr 1806. RO. HAMBLETON, AC, to THOS. N. EUBANK,, AC, Deed
          of Trust, debt to JNO. & RICH. S. ELLIS, AC, $1.00; stock,
furniture, etc. Wit: OBA. TURPIN, DANL. DUMIFIN(VIN?), REUBEN CRAWFORD,
JNO. GILLIAM, JAS. FRANKLIN, RO. KNUCKLES, PETER SULMON. Orig. del. to
TE, 20 Jan 1808.

Page 480. 28 Jul 1806. EDMD. BOLES & wife TABITHA, Mercer Co, Ky, Power
          of Atty. to JAS. FRANKLIN, AC, - to convey to RO. KNUCKLES, AC,
90 acres. Lines: CHAS. DAVIES on N, JNO. SLED on N. Bequeathed to TABI-
THA by father, JER. WHITTEN. Wit: RO. B. WAFER, J. WOODS, JNO. HAGGIN,
ARBD. BILBO, J.P.s: THOS. ALLEN, Clk. THOS. FREEMAN, Pres. Justice. Rec.
AC 15 Sep 1806.

Page 481. 12 Jul 1803. Agreement between REUBEN CRAWFORD, AC, & JNO.
          WOODS & RO. WARNER LEWIS, Alb., for Ł500, 500 acres in Ky. by
will of father, DAVID CRAWFORD, dec'd. Wit: THOS. MOORE, P. MARTIN, SAML.
SHIELD. Final proof 20 Oct 1806, by MOORE. Orig. del. to WM. S. CRAWFORD,
1 Nov 1806.

Page 482. 15 Sep 1806. JONATHAN BOLLING, AC, & wife SUSANNA, to JNO.
          DILLARD, AC, for Ł300, 110 acres, part of where JD lives.
Lines: grantee, JAS. WALTERS, S side Long Branch, JESSE MAYS, JAS. DILL-
ARD. Wit: WM. B. HARE, HENRY F. CARTER.

Page 483. 26 Aug 1806. WM. TYREE, AC, to SEATON M. PENN, AC, for Ł675,
          Deed of Trust - debt to NANCY SHIELDS. 2 tracts. 1) 175 acres
bequeathed to WT by father, dec'd. Lines: S by JACOB TYREE, dec'd, Saw
Pitt Branch; where I live. 2) 100 acres. Lines: JESSE KENNEDY, dec'd,
JAS. HIGGINBOTHAM, Buff., where I formerly lived on Buffl. Wit: RICH.
WILSON, JNO. LOWGAN, CHAS. HIGGINBOTHAM, WM. CHASE.

Page 484. 15 Sep 1806. LUNSFORD LOVING & wife PEGGY N., AC, to HENRY
          SMITH, AC, for $435, 175½ acres Dutch Creek. Lines: DAVID S.
GARLAND, NORBORNE THOMAS, grantee, the road. Wit: JAS. TURNER JR, JNO.
HAWKINS, HEZ. HARGROVE. 3 Aug 1807, del. to HS.

Page 485. 22 Sep 1806. MORRIS HAMNER & wife MARY, AMBROSE RUCKER & wife
          ELIZ., JESSE CARTER & wife FRANCES, SAML. HAMNER & wife NANCY,
to ELIZ. COLEMAN, for Ł30, 37 acres both sides Harris. Lines: JNO. COLE-
MAN, dec'd, Col. AMBROSE RUCKER, grantee, DANL. BURFORD, THOS. GRISSOM
SR. Wit: BERRY COLEMAN, BLANSFORD HICKS, JAS. COLEMAN, TINSLEY RUCKER,
SAML. COLEMAN. Memo: This deed is for same land & sum of 25 Sep 1790, and

wit: PETER, ABRAM, EDWD. CARTER. Signed: ELIZ. COLEMAN.

Page 486.   20 Oct 1806.   WM. CLASBEY & wife POLLY, AC, to DABNEY BRYANT,
            AC, for Ƚ200, 100 acres N side and joining Tye. Part of tract.
Lines: GEO. LOVING, grantor.

Page 486.   16 Dec 1805.   REUBEN NORVELL & wife POLLY, AC, to THOS. JEWELL,
            AC, for Ƚ100, 100 acres Porrage. Lines: HENRY TURNER, ENGLAND,
ALEX. JEWELL.   Orig. del. to TJ, 6 Dec 1806.

Page 487.   7 Oct 1806.   Order to AC J.P.'s.   WM. GARRETT (GRAVETT) & wife
            ANN, 1 Aug 1806, to EDWD. WATSON - 173 acres. Done, 15 Oct
1806, by REUBEN NORVELL & GEO. DILLARD.

Page 488.   20 Oct 1806.   WM. WILSON, Rockbridge, to ARCHIBALD ROWSEY, AC,
            for Ƚ170, 269 acres Brown Mt. Creek. Lines: HUGH CAMPBELL,
HENRY CAMDEN, WM. GALT, WM. TOMLINSON.   Orig. del. to AR, 14 Nov 1806.

Page 489.   21 Oct 1806.   ARCHIBALD ROWSEY & wife ELIZ., AC, to HENRY
            BALLINGER & RICH. HERCULES, AC, Deed of Trust; debt to WM.
WILSON, Rockbridge; 6 sh.; Brown Mt. Creek and Pedlar. Lines: HENRY BALL-
INGER, WM. TOMBELIN(sic), WM. HALL, HUGH CAMPBELL, HENRY CAMDEN. Wit:
BARTLETT, ANDREW & BURSILLER CHILDRESS & JAS. ROWSEY.

Page 490.   1 Oct 1806.   GEO. BLAIN JR, AC, to GUTRIDGE THURMOND, AC, for
            Ƚ175, 275 acres Hickory Creek; branch of Rockfish. Lines:
grantee, JNO. BAILEY, JNO. S. DAWSON, JNO. MORRISON - 125 acres of it
deeded to him by JNO. THURMOND; 150 acres of it devised to him by his
father, GEO. BLAIN SR, 150 acres pat. to MATT. HARRIS and by him conveyed
to GB, SR.   Wit: THOS. & JNO. THURMOND, TERISHA BAILEY.

Page 491.   24 Jun 1806.   Order to AC J.P.s.   ISAAC WRIGHT & wife SUSANNA,
            10 Jul 1805, to EDWD. CARTER - 82 acres. Done, 26 Jul 1806,
by JOSIAH ELLIS & NELSON CRAWFORD.

Page 491.   15 Aug 1806.   COONROD MOYER, AC, to WM. MURRELL, AC, for Ƚ7,
            25 acres Dutch. Lines: Fork of the rd., GEO. VAUGHAN, HENRY
SMITH, CHAS. STATHAM. Wit: HUDSON MARTIN, THOS. CHILDERS(?), JNO. W.GREEN.

Page 492.   13 Sep 1806.   DILMUS JOHNSON & wife NANCY, AC, to JAS. JOHNSON,
            Augusta, for Ƚ45, 65 acres S side Rodes Creek. Lines: SAML.
FOX, CHAS. RODES. Wit: CHAS. MARTIN, WM. MARTIN, THOS. TILMAN.

Page 493.   20 Oct 1806.   JAS. MAYS & wife ISABEL, AC, to son, ARCHELAUS
            MAYS, AC, for $1.00 and love, 250 acres Tye. Lines: ZACH.
WHITE, HECTOR CABELL, JAS. MAYS, JR, JAS. BIBB SR.   Orig. del. to AM,
28 Jun 1807.

Page 493.   20 Oct 1806.   JAS. MAYS, AC, & wife ISABEL, to son, JAS. MAYS
            JR, for $1.00 and love, 250 acres Tye. Lines: ARCHELAUS MAYS,
JAS. Sr., WM. ALFORD.

Page 494.   20 Oct 1806.   MAJOR KING & wife COLE, AC, to ALEX. McALEXANDER,
            AC, for $300, 2 tracts N fork Davis Creek. Lines: grantee,
SAML. FORD, JAS. THORPE, LEE HARRIS dec'd.   90 acres - 50 acres part of
a survey of 150 acres; other part belongs to grantee. Lines: LEE HARRIS
dec'd, JAS. THORP, grantee.

Page 495.   15 Sep 1806.   Order to Buckingham J.P.'s.   JNO. M. ROSE & wife
            MILLIA, late widow of CHAS. IRVING, dec'd, and WM. HUGHES &
WM. B. HARE, 889 acres. Done by CHAS. YANCEY & ANTHONY DIBRELL, 1 Oct
1806.   19 Nov 1818, del. to HILL CARTER.   Deed of 17 Nov 1804, p.496,
same order - ROSE & wife MILLIA, to JNO. THOMPSON, 15 Apr 1807, done as
above. Page 496, same order. ROSE & wife to THOS. PENN - 733 acres. Done
as above. Del. to TP, 29 Sep 1819. Page 497, same order to check as to
ROSE & wife to WM. B. HARE; JNO. THOMPSON, & THOS. PENN, 2200 acres, 27
Nov 1818, to HILL CARTER.

Page 498.   20 Oct 1806.   JNO. CLARKSON, AC, to his son, ANSELM CLARKSON
            for $1.00 and love, 250 acres surveyed 30 Sep 1806. Lines:

Franklin Creek, part of 2 tracts of grantor, ZACH. TALIAFERRO, WM. SAN-
DIDGE, WM. TALIAFERRO. Orig. del. 7 Sep 1810, to A.C. Wit: HUGH CAMP-
BELL, DAVID CLARKSON, DUDLEY SANDIDGE.

Page 499. 7 Oct 1806. JNO. INNIS & wife RACHEL, AC, to PRESLEY SAUNDERS
JR, Loudoun Co., for $750, 150 acres. Lines: SMITH TANDY at
Rolling road - at present SPENCER's, WM. SPENCER, Raven Creek, NATHAN
HALL, WM. CABELL, SAML. ANDERSON - now THOS. TRIPLETT. Wit: STEPHEN
WATTS, THOS. TRIPLETT, THOS. CURRY.

Page 500. 29 Nov 1805. DAVID S. GARLAND, AC, to JAS. M. BROWN, AC, for
Ŀ97-10, 13 acres, part of tract. N Buff. Lines: grantor, JNO.
SWANSON's original tract, WM. S. CRAWFORD, near the schoolhouse. Wit:
W.G. PENDLETON, JAS. GARLAND, DAVID SWANSON.

Page 500. 20 Oct 1806. WM. BARNETT, Ky, to THOS. PRATT JR, AC, for
blank sum, 13 acres Corbey's Creek.

Page 501. 10 Oct 1806. MOSES WRIGHT, AC, to BENJ. WRIGHT, AC, for 5 sh,
71 acres S branches Big Piney. MW bought it from JNO. CART-
WRIGHT.

Page 502. 11 Jan 1806. JACOB WOOD, AC, 1st; JAS. FISHER & JNO. L. LE-
SUERUER, Richmond, 2nd; DAVID S. GARLAND, AC, 3rd. Deed of
Trust; debt to 2nd parties; firm FISHER & LESUERUER - 5 sh. paid by 3rd
party - 62½ acres where JW lives - Buff. and bought of JAS. FLOYD; water
grist mill, saw mill and distillery. Wit: TEMPLE GWATHMEY, GEO. TURNER,
B. McCRACKEN.

Page 503. 28 Jun 1806. DAVID S. GARLAND, AC, by Deed of Trust advertised tr., 28 Jun 1806, and FISHER & LESEUER bought JACOB
WOOD tr. Ŀ220-6.

Page 503. -- Oct 1806. THOS. PRATT SR, & wife ELIZ, AC, to THOS. PRATT,
Jr, AC, blank sum, 197 acres S branches S fork Rockfish; by
2 pats. & joining - 150 acres pat. to Sr. and other to HENRY DAWSON &
conveyed to Sr - 47 acres. Lines: MICHL. WOODS, DAVID WITT, JOS. MONT-
GOMERY, HENRY SMITH. Orig. del. to Jr, 6 Dec 1809.

Page 504. 10 Oct 1806. SAML. PUCKETT & wife POLLY; ZACH. KING & wife
CREASY, AC, to JAS. WILLS JR, AC, for Ŀ100, 100 acres head
branches S fork Rucker's Run. Lines: NICHL. CABELL.

Page 504. -- Oct 1806. JABEZ DAVIS & wife CHRISTIAN, to WIATT CAMDEN,
AC, for Ŀ180, 180 acres N branches Piney in 2 surveys. 1) Pat.
27 Dec 1799, for 84 acres. Lines: JNO. THOMPSON, WM. DAVIS, grantor, CHAS.
IRVING, dec'd. 2) Surveyed 20 Aug 1795; 100 acres. Lines: WM. DAVIS, WM.
B. HARE. Tracts adjoin.

Page 505. 2 Jul 1806. CHAS. MAYS, AC, to JNO. LOVING, AC, Deed of Trust
Debt to WM. SPENCER; 6 sh.; 275 acres S side Berry's Mt.,
slaves. Wit: WM. BATES, LAVENDER LONDON, NORVELL SPENCER. Orig. del. to
JL, 28 Nov 1806.

Page 506. 15 Oct 1806. ARCH RHEA & wife JEAN, Rockbridge, to JABEZ
DAVIS, AC, for Ŀ180, 2 tracts. 1) 130 acres surveyed 21 Dec
1785 on Blue Ridge, head branches Tye and N fork. Lines: JAS. TILFORD,
DOSWELL & DRUMMOND; near a mill. 2) 100 acres surveyed for ARCH RHEA
SR, dec'd, 28 Feb 1795 - head branches Tye. Orig. del. to JD, 8 Mar 1813.

Page 507. 18 Oct 1806. JNO. MARTIN SR, & wife MARY, AC, to ABRAM MARTIN,
AC, for Ŀ20, 20 acres, part of 150 acres where JM lives. N
and joining AM.

Page 507. 20 Oct 1806. JAS. WILLS SR & wife MILDRED, AC, to ANN PHIL-
LIPS, AC, for Ŀ209-10, 209½ acres both sides Dutch. Lines:
SPARKS MARTIN, JOSHUA WILLOUGHBY, GEO. MARTIN, RICH. C. POLLARD.

Page 508. 20 Oct 1806. WM. MARTIN SR, & wife SUSANNA, AC, to JNO. MAR-
TIN SR, AC, for Ŀ61-10, 250 acres both sides Franklin Creek.

452

Lines: JACOB SMITH, crossing creek.

Page 508.   23 Dec 1805.   JNO. H. GOODWIN & wife MARY, Pittsylvania, to
            PHILLIP JOHNSON, AC, for Ł100, E side Colings Creek, tract
which JG got as legatee of JAS. COALTER, dec'd - one fourth part of 170
acres. Wit: JNO. BURFORD JR, JAS. L. LAMKIN, JOS. BRADSHAW, BENJ. RUCKER,
JR, JOS. KENNERLY, WM. ISBELL,JR, JNO. MERRITT, SR.   Final proof by
BRADSHAW, 20 Oct 1806.

Page 509.   17 Sep 1806.   Order to Lynchburg Corp. Ct. J.P.'s.   BARKSDALE
            SNIDER & wife SARAH, 4 Jul 1806, to PHILLIP JOHNSON - SARAH's
life est.- except her dower - sold by AC Ct. decree. JNO. LYNCH in order,
but signed JOS. LYNCH & JAS. STEWART, 15 Oct 1806.

Page 510.   24 Sep 1806.   WM. CAMDEN, AC, to ESTHER GOODWIN, AC, for 6 sh.
            and love for her as his daughter & her children, (a slave?)
(apart from ?) WARNER GOODWIN, her husband.

Page 510.   22 Aug 1806.   NICHL. FORTUNE, AC, to BARTLETT THOMPSON, AC,
            Deed of Trust; debt due WM. G. ARMS; $1.00; bay horse. Wit:
STERLING CLAIBORNE, JNO. W. HARRIS, J.P. GARLAND.   Orig. del. to BT, 16
May 1807.

Page 511.   9 Oct 1804.   EPHRAIM BLAIN, Halifax Co, to JNO. ROBERTS, AC,
            for Ł30, 64 acres Buck Creek Mt. Lines: HENRY ROBERTS, RICH.
HARE, his own.   Wit: ABRAHAM MARTIN, MATT. HARRIS JR, WM. H. BLAYDES.
Final proof, by A. MARTIN, 21 Oct 1806.

Page 512.   9 Dec 1806.   SPOTSWOOD GARLAND, AC, & wife LUCINDA, to JAS.
            PARKER GARLAND, AC, for 10 sh, 187 acres N branches Rutledge
surveyed by CHAS. L. CHRISTIAN, asst. Co. surveyor. Part of tract bought
by SG of BENJ. RUCKER. Lines: Parks' road, BENJ. MILES, JACOB PEARCE JR,
N end of tract.   Wit: CHAS. PERROW, JAS. B. EDWARDS.   Orig. del. to JG,
6 Feb 1807.

Page 513.   19 Nov 1806.   SALLY PHILLIPS, widow of THOS. PHILLIPS, AC, to
            JNO. BARNETT, AC, for $1.00, int. in tract late husband sold
in lifetime - to JB.   182 acres Tye. Lines: JNO. MASTERS, DAVID R. CLARK-
SON, JR. WINSTON RYAN, JESSE CLARKSON.

Page 513.   17 Oct 1806.   CORNL. NEVIL & wife AILSEY, & MARY NEVIL, AC, to
            JAS. MURPHY, AC, for Ł496-10, 165½ acres S fork Rockfish. Part
of tract under will of JAS. NEVIL - N side & joining S fork Rockfish.
Lines: NORBORN THOMAS, ZACH. NEVIL.   Wit: SAML. JONES, SAML. HANSBROUGH,
JONES GILL, LEWIS NEVIL, JERE YAGER, DUNCAN CAMRON, REUBEN B. PATTERSON,
JNO. CREWS.   Orig. del. to JM, 10 Feb 1807.

Page 514.   19 Jan 1807.   JNO. EDMUNDS & wife SALLY, AC, to SHELTON CROS-
            THWAIT, AC, for Ł400, 500 acres bought by JE from JNO. JOPLING.
Lines: S side RUCKER's Run, BERRY's Mt. Sent to SC by JNO. CREWS, 29 Jan
1807.

Page 515.   27 Oct 1806.   EDWD. HARRIS SR, AC, from THOS. JOPLING, late of
            AC, for Ł240, 77¾ acres Buck Creek. Lines: JNO. HARRIS, JNO.
DIGGES, grantee. Wit: NATHAN BARNETT, WM. SHELTON, WM. LEE HARRIS.

Page 515.   14 Nov 1806.   PLEASANT MARTIN & wife BETSY, AC, to JNO. TURNER,
            AC, for Ł125, 150 acres Cove Creek; branch of Rockfish. Lines:
WM. LEIGH, REUBEN T. MITCHELL, JAS. TURNER, BENJ. PAIN. Wit: NELSON AN-
DERSON, JAS. TURNER JR, TERISHA TURNER, LANDON B. BRENT.

Page 516.   3 Jan 1807.   JOS. WHITE & wife COATNEY, AC, to NATHL. POWELL,
            WM. MOSS, & JNO. LOVING, AC, for $1.00, 200 acres; Deed of
Trust. Lines: WM. H. DIGGES, ROWLAND EDMUNDS, ISAAC WHITE, slaves. For
benefit of JOSEPH's children: SALLY, JNO. & BETSY (by a former wife) JAS.
& LORENZO by present wife, COATNEY; stock, beds.   JOS. to oversee, but
not to sell; for support of family; at his death, to deliver slaves to
children and tract to present wife and 2 children. Wit: LEWIS POWELL JR,
WM. HARTGROVE, ELIJAH MAYS.   Orig. del. to JW, by order, 12 Aug 1808, of
JNO. LOVING.

Page 517.   26 Nov 1806.   JOSIAH ELLIS, WM. S. CRAWFORD, WM. LAWLESS &
               wife SARAH, JOSIAH TANKERSLEY & wife MILLEY, JNO. CARTER &
wife JEMIMAH, AC, CHAS. CARTER & wife DINAH, PETER CARTER & wife ANNEY,
JESSE CARTER & wife FRANCES, EDWD. CARTER & wife NANCY, SOLOMON CARTER &
wife NANCY of Ky. (ELLIS & CRAWFORD as exrs.) - children of PETER CARTER
dec'd, AC, to HENRY BALLINGER, AC, for Ŀ427, 425½ acres Horsley. Lines:
JNO. SMITH, RICH. HARTLESS, JOSEPH MILSTEAD, EDWD. TAYLOR. Wit: PETER
P. THORNTON, HENRY BROWN, WALLER SANDIDGE, WM. SANDIDGE, THOS. N. EUBANK,
BENJ. HIGGINBOTHAM, ABRAM CARTER, RICH. S. ELLIS.

Page 518.   26 Nov 1806.   Same grantors as previous deed to NELSON CRAW-
               FORD, AC, for Ŀ260, 371½ acres Horsley. Lines: grantee, EDWD.
CARTER, DANL. SHRADER, JOHN SMITH. Wit: as above.

Page 519.   29 May 1804.   Order to Bedford J.P.'s.   JAS. R. PENN & wife
               POLLY, 21 Jun 1802, to WM. CLASBY, 200 acres. Done by WM. BUR-
TON & BALDO(A) McDANIEL, 11 Dec 1806. Rec. AC, 19 Jan 1807. Orig. del.
to WC, 25 Mar 1812.

Page 520.   16 Feb 1807.   JNO. RICHESON & wife NANCY, AC, to JESSE RICHE-
               SON, AC, for Ŀ75, 99 acres Brown's & Enchanted Creek. Orig.
del. May 1812 to JESSE RICHESON.

Page 521.   6 Jun 1806.   Order to AC J.P.'s.   MICAJAH PENDLETON & wife
               MARY C., 1801 to GILES DAVIDSON; 195 acres. Done by JNO.
HORSLEY & JAS. DILLARD, 13 Feb 1806. Same page and grantors to GEO. PENN,
195 acres. Done, 14 Feb 1807.

Page 522.   5 Sep 1806.   CHAS. HOYLE, Lynchburg, to WM. PETERS MARTIN,
               Campbell Co, Deed of Trust; debt to STEPHEN ROBINSON, AC, for
Ŀ330, 159 acres where BENJ. WATTS lives. CH bought of GEO. McDANIEL on
date of these presents; slaves. Wit: GEO. McDANIEL, SAML. IRVINE, A.
ROBERTSON, BURL SNEAD, HENRY ROBINSON, S. WIATT, BENJ. WATTS, JNO. W.
ROBINSON.

Page 523.   11 Jul 1806.   WIATT SMITH, AC, to DANL. HIGGINBOTHAM, AC, Deed
               of Trust; debt to JAS. & DAVID GARLAND; $1.00; 2 slaves. Wit:
JNO. EUBANK JR, D. McDONALD, C.W. CHRISTIAN, VERNON METCALFE.

Page 524.   5 Feb 1807.   JUDITH TUCKER, admrx. of DANL. (DRURY in deed)
               TUCKER, dec'd, AC, from GEO. RUCKER & wife MARTHA, Bedford Co,
for Ŀ40, all interest in estate - 1/11th - tract where DRURY TUCKER lived
and devised by will to GEO. RUCKER. Wit: LINDSEY COLEMAN JR, WM. COLEMAN,
JONATHAN RUCKER.

Page 524.   14 Sep 1805.   BENJ. PHILLIPS & WM. WOODROOF, AC, from MOSES
               PHILLIPS, AC, for Ŀ120, 62 acres. Lines: JACOB TYREE, grantee,
JAS. HIGGINBOTHAM. Wit: HENRY HOLLOWAY, JACOB TYREE, WM. GRISSOM. Final
proof, 16 Feb 1807, by JACOB TYREE.

Page 526.   20 Nov 1806.   BENJ. COLEMAN to BENJ. TALIAFERRO for Ŀ6, 80
               acres Blue Ridge and branches Shady Mt. Creek. Lines: JNO.
CHILDRESS, top of Blue Ridge. Wit: CHAS. P. TALIAFERRO, PETER TALIAFERRO,
WALLER SANDIDGE, JACK CARTER.

Page 526.   13 Aug 1806.   CHAS. CHRISTIAN, the Elder, AC, to JACOB PEARCE,
               AC, for Ŀ25, 15 acres Buff. Lines: JOSHUA FRIES' old line,
grantee, Wilcher's Branch, GATEWOOD's old line, near Braxton's Ridge,
BARNETT OWENS, survey lately made for JNO. CHRISTIAN. Wit: JAS. CHRISTIAN,
JACOB SCOTT, CORNL. PEARCE, JNO. SMUTE.

Page 527.   8 Nov 1806.   MARGARET HENDERSON, acting exrx. of GEO. CAMPBELL
               dec'd, & also of JNO. HENDERSON, dec'd, AC, to CLAYTON C.
MONTGOMERY, late of Ky., for Ŀ540, 178¾ acres branches N fork Rockfish.
Part of tract of GEO. CAMPBELL. Lines: JOS. MARTIN, JAS. BROOKS, JNO.
SHIELDS, ALEX. SHIELDS. Wit: JOS. MONTGOMERY, THOS. CHURCH, CHAS. BROOKS,
THOS. STOCKTON, JOS. MARTIN.

Page 528.   28 Nov 1806.   LEROY PAMPLIN & wife MARTHA, AC, to MARY BOUT-
               WELL DRUMMOND, AC, for Ŀ100, 69 acres S branches Owen Creek;

part of tract formerly of WM. HORSLEY, dec'd. Lines: GEO. HYLTON (former-
ly JNO. JOSLING), WM. HORSLEY, dec'd. (now HENLEY DRUMMOND, dec'd.) Wit:
FRED CABELL, VAL. HYLTON, ZACH. DRUMMOND. Orig. del. to L. DRUMMOND, 10
Nov 1812.

Page 529. 17 Dec 1806. RO. ROSE & wife MARY SEYMOUR ROSE, Fauquier Co,
to ANDREW MORGAN, AC, for $3333.30, 333 1/3 acres both sides
Hatt Creek. Lines: JAMES MONTGOMERY, CHAS. JONES, JAS. CLARKSON. Wit:
ALEX. PENN, BENJ. H. MORGAN, HILL & WM. F. CARTER. Orig. del. to AM, 23
Feb 1807.

Page 529. 16 Feb 1807. JAS. HIGGINBOTHAM, AC, to BENJ. SANDIDGE, AC,
for Ł687-10, 275 acres N branches S fork Buff. Lines: JOS.
HIGGINBOTHAM, survey made for LEONARD BALOW, grantee, grantor, GEO. W.
HIGGINBOTHAM. Wit: JOS. DILLARD, ABSALOM HIGGINBOTHAM, GEO. WASH. HIGGIN-
BOTHAM. Orig. del. to J. DILLARD, 24 Apr 1807.

Page 530. 29 Jan 1807. ELISHA ESTES, AC, to JAS. MURPHY & JNO. HIGGIN-
BOTHAM, Warminster, AC, Deed of Trust; debt to ELISHA PETERS;
6 sh.; 573 acres Rucker's Run. Lines: ABRAM WARWICK, WM. BREEDLOVE, JAS.
WOODS, ELIJAH STATON, DANL. McCOY. Wit: RICH. POWELL, JERE YAGER, ELIJAH
STATON, CHAS. CHRISTIAN, JAMES VIGUS JR. Orig. del. to JM 11 Jan 1807.

Page 531. 16 Feb 1807. JNO. RICHESON & wife NANCY, to JESSE RICHESON,
AC, for $500, 254 acres Brown's Creek; branch of Pedlar. Orig.
del. to JESSE RICHESON, May, 1812.

Page 532. 30 Oct 1806. JNO. ALFORD & wife ELIZ., to RICH. PHILLIPS, for
Ł350, 150 acres both sides N branch Tye; part of tract of WM.
BIBB, dec'd. - now estate of CONYERS WHITE SR, dec'd. Lines: JNO. THOMP-
SON, WM. TEAS, WM. BIBB, Naked Creek, CONYERS WHITE SR, dec'd. Wit: JNO.
LOVING, THOS. BIBB, LEWIS WHITE, TANDY CAMPBELL, NELSON WRIGHT. Order to
AC J.P.'s to quiz ELIZ.; done, 13 Nov 1806, by WM. H. DIGGES & JOS. LOV-
ING. Orig. sent to RP, by ASA VARNUM, 27 May 1807.

Page 533. 22 Nov 1806. PRESLEY SANDERS & wife MARY, Loudoun Co., to
DANL. TRIPLETT, Loudoun, for $850, 150 acres. Lines: SMITH
TANDY at rolling road; WM. SPENCER, NATHAN HALL, WM. CABELL JR, SAML.
ANDERSON, Raven Creek. Wit: OBADIAH CLIFFORD, RO. HAMILTON, WM. AUSTIN.
Signed SAUNDERS. Orig. del. to DT, 17 Sep 1808.

Page 534. 16 Feb 1807. JNO. RICHESON & wife MARY, AC, to JESSE RICHESON,
AC, for Ł75, 148 acres both sides Brown's Creek; S branch
Pedlar. Orig. del. to JESSE RICHESON, May, 1812.

Page 534. 14 Feb 1807. CALEB WILCHER, AC, to MARTIN PARKS, AC, for Ł50,
60 acres. Lines: ARTHUR L. DAVIES, top of Tobacco Row Mt. Wit:
RO. H. COLEMAN, GIDEON GOODRICH, ABRAM CARTER, JAS. WAUGH.

Page 535. 16 Nov 1806. JESSE CLARKSON, AC, to JAS. GARLAND, AC, Deed of
Trust; debt to DAVID S. GARLAND - 6 sh. JESSE is bdm. for WM.
SPENCER, AC, - 5 slaves and children. Wit: HUDSON M. GARLAND, JNO. EUBANK
JR, DANL. HIGGINBOTHAM, CHAS. W. CHRISTIAN. Orig. del. to DANL. HIGGIN-
BOTHAM, 23 Feb 1809.

Page 536. 27 Dec 1806. WM. TOLLE & wife DINAH, AC, to RO. ALLEN - WM.
TOLLE for Ł130 sells to RO. ALLEN 140 acres S branches Porrage.
Lines: DAVID S. GARLAND, PLEASANT STORY, JAS. DILLARD, ALEX. JEWELL,
SACKVILLE KING. Tract sold by ALLEN to WM. TOLLE, 17 Dec 1804. Wit: WM.
EDMUNDS, MICAJAH CAMDEN, ALLEN BUGG. Orig. del. to RA, 30 Jan 1808.

Page 537. 22 Dec 1806. Order to AC J.P.'s. NORBORNE THOMAS & wife
JUDITH, 1798, to WM. DIXON - 64 acres. Done, 24 Dec 1806, by
WM. CABELL & JOS. LOVING.

Page 538. 22 Dec 1806. Order to AC J.P.'s. NORBORNE THOMAS & wife
JUDITH, to JNO. & SAML. DIXON, 7 Dec 1805. Done as above by
same J.P.'s.

Page 538. 14 Feb 1807. PETER CARTER & wife BETSY, AC, to JNO. TAYLOR,

AC, for ₤26, 42 acres both sides Piney Mt. - between Buff. & Horsley.
Wit: JNO. FLOOD, JNO. BROWN JR, ABRAM CARTER. Orig. del. to NICHL.
VANSTAVERN, 26 Mar 1808.

Page 539.   22 Dec 1806.   THOS. W. COCKE & wife SALLY, Lynchburg, to NEL-
        SON CRAWFORD, AC, for ₤600, Bethel tract on N side James River;
403 acres surveyed by SAML. B. DAVIES in 1800. Lines: Crab Creek, McDaniel's Spring, Green Pond Branch; Big Double Creek. Tract bought by NICHL.
C. DAVIES & THOS. W. COCKE from ARTHUR L. DAVIES, 2 Oct 1800; rec. 28 Apr
1801 - one half tract; Ware houses in Bethel, 1/2 ferry boat on N side
James; reserved 1/2 acre lots in Bethel by Act of Assembly for N.C.
DAVIES & COCKE. Orig. del. to NC, 21 Aug 1809.

Page 541.   29 Jan 1807.   Order to AC J.P.s.   JNO. EDMUNDS & wife SALLY,
        19 Jan 1807, to SHELTON CROSTHWAIT, 500 acres. Done by JOS.
LOVING & WM. H. DIGGES, 5 Feb 1807. Orig. del. to SC by mail, 9 Mar 1807.

Page 541.   12 Mar 1806.   JNO. LUCAS, AC, to JNO. EUBANK, AC, Deed of
        Trust; debt to DANL. HIGGINBOTHAM & Co, 6 sh; stock. Wit: CHAS.
W. CHRISTIAN, BARTLETT THOMPSON. Orig. del. to JAS. GARLAND 2 Oct 1807.

Page 542.   12 Nov 1805.   JNO. THOMAS, AC, to SPOTSWOOD GARLAND, AC, Deed
        of Trust; debt to JAS. & DAVID GARLAND; $1.00; stock, furni-
ture, etc. Wit: WM. G. PENDLETON, DANL. HIGGINBOTHAM, ABRAM STRATTON.
Orig. del. to JAS. GARLAND, 21 May 1808.

Page 543.   25 Jul 1806.   SAML. HILL, Henry Co., to REUBEN NORVELL & STERL-
        ING CLAIBORNE, AC, & JOSIAH LEAKE, Lynchburg; Deed of Trust;
debt to WM. CABELL & PATRICK ROSE, exrs. of HUGH ROSE & SPENCER NORVELL,
bdm.; $1.00; slaves. Wit: URIAH BOBBITT, SPENCER D. NORVELL, HUGH NORVELL.
Orig. del. to SC, 7 Mar 1807.

Page 544.   16 Oct 1806.   JNO. ANDERSON & wife POLLY, AC, to THOS. ALD-
        RIDGE, AC, for $810, 162 acres; sold by SAML. ANDERSON to JNO.
ANDERSON 20 Jun 1803; except 50 acres sold to MOSES PHILLIPS 16 Feb 1805.
Also 1 acre sold in tract to JNO. ALCOCK, LEWIS DAWSON, GEO. WRIGHT, JNO.
ENNIS for erecting meeting house - leaving 162 acres. Wit: RO. NIMMO,
CHAS. WATTS, JNO. PENN JR. Page 545, order to AC J.P.'s to quiz POLLY,
18 Oct 1806; done by JNO. BURRUS & GEO. DILLARD, 18 Oct 1806.

Page 545.   24 Dec 1806.   MATT. WATSON, AC, to RO. COLEMAN, AC, Deed of
        Trust to secure JNO. PENN JR, bdm. on judgment by WM. LONG;
also debt to JAS. & DAVID GARLAND vs. MW as exr. of JAS. WATSON dec'd;
$1.00; 225 acres whereon MW lives. Also slaves. Wit: JAS. GARLAND, DANL.
HIGGINBOTHAM, HUDSON M. GARLAND.

Page 546.   10 Feb 1807.   NANCY N. TALIAFERRO, widow of WM. TALIAFERRO
        dec'd, to CHAS. & BENJ. TALIAFERRO, exrs. of WM. TALIAFERRO,
for ₤120, all claims to them and JAS. TALIAFERRO. Tract bought by WM.
TALIAFERRO of PHILLIP SMITH - 300 acres, but 150 of it conveyed by WT to
JAS. TALIAFERRO, 29 Aug 1805. Wit: JNO. FLOED, WM. HOWARD, MARY EUBANK,
THOS. N. EUBANK.

Page 547.   1 Aug 1806.   WM. GARRETT & wife ANNE; JAS. CHEATHAM & wife
        FRANCES; DAVID GEORGE & wife SALLY; DANL. TAYLOR & wife JANE,
to ELIZ., POLLY, & LODOWICK GEORGE, for $1.00, 45½ acres near Lynch Road
on Harris Creek. Lines: REUBEN RUCKER, WM. GARRETT, REUBEN RUCKER's road.
Wit: BARTLETT EADES, RICH. GARRETT, SAML. HILL.

Page 547.   2 Feb 1807.   FREDERICK FULTZ, AC, to THOMAS ALDRIDGE, AC, Deed
        of Trust; debt to DAVID HANGER, AC, $1.00; stock etc. Wit:
HUDSON M. GARLAND, S. GARLAND, REUBEN PADGETT.

Page 548.   19 Mar 1803.   RICH. FARRAR, Alb., to RO. L.(S) FARRAR, AC, for
        love & $1.00, all my AC land S side Rockfish. Lines: THOS.
FARRAR. Wit: JESSE JOPLING, GEO. FARRAR, JNO. FARRAR SR.

Page 548.   16 Apr 1807.   THOS. STEWART & wife TIRZAH, Bedford, to WM.
        PENN, JR, AC, for 5 sh.; 56 acres by survey, 18 Jun 1795;
branches Rutledge & Huff; granted to TS as assignee of heirs at law of

456

JNO. DAVIS dec'd. by pat., 10 Jul 1795. Lines: JAS. CALLAWAY dec'd., JNO.
LACKEY, JOS. BURRUS, GEO. McDANIEL, JAS. PENDLETON. Wit: JNO. EUBANK JR,
JAS. B. EDWARDS, BARTLETT THOMPSON, JNO. P. COBBS. Orig. del. to Col.
JOS. BURRUS, 25 Apr 1807.

Page 549. 11 Dec 1806. JNO. SHELTON, AC, to RO. FRANKLIN & JAS. VIGUS,
          Warminster, Deed of Trust; debt to JAS. MURPHY & Co.; $1.00;
slaves. Wit: REUBEN B. PATTERSON, SAML. JONES, SAML. HANSBROUGH, CHAS.
CHRISTIAN. Orig. del. to JAS. MURPHY, 11 Jan 1807.

Page 550. 12 Apr 1807. RO. HORSLEY, AC, to GEO. HYLTON, AC, for Ł168,
          112 acres, part of Rich Branch tract. Wit: VAL. HYLTON, WM.
LEWIS, ZACH. DRUMMOND. Orig. del. to CHAS. L. CHRISTIAN, 10 May 1813.

Page 551. 22 Sep 1806. LEWIS BRYANT to THOS. N. EUBANK, Deed of Trust;
          debt to JNO. & RICH. ELLIS - $1.00; 100 acres Tarripin Creek,
branch of Fluvanna. Lines: MOSES RUCKER, RICH. TINSLEY, BERRY BRYANT, one
batteau, stock, furniture. Wit: DAVID CLEMENTS, DANL. DONAVIN, CHAS.
ELLIS, PETER P. THORNTON, ABRAM CARTER, WM. PRYOR SR, HENRY & JAS. BROWN.
Orig. del. to TE, 20 Jan 1808.

Page 552. 15 Sep 1806. JNO. AUGUSTINE HARRIS, Lynchburg, to WM. WILL-
          IAMS, AC, for Ł60, 70 acres; branch of Bowling's Creek. Lines:
TERREL, HARPER, grantee. Wit: RO. TURNER, JNO. WILLIAMS, JAS. LONDON,
JAS. BUCK, BENJ. WATTS.

Page 552. 13 Feb 1807. EDWD. SANDERSON & wife MOLLY, Tenn., to THOS.
          MORRIS, AC, for Ł400, 310 acres both sides Maple Creek, branch
of Pedlar. Lines: ARTHUR TOOLEY. Wit: RICH. S. ELLIS, JNO. ELLIS, THOS.
M. POPE, GEO. MORRIS, JNO. BARKER, LINZA BURKS. Orig. del. to TM, 15
Oct 1807.

Page 553. 17 Apr 1807. JNO. HOGG of Va. to JNO. MORRIS, AC, for Ł7, no
          acres mentioned, Cedar & Maple Creeks. Lines: grantee, Burks'
road, GEO. GLASBY. Wit: LINZA BURKS, JNO. BARKER, GEO. MORRIS, MAURICE
MORRIS, GEO. MORRIS (2 named).

Page 554. 7 Oct 1806. MARYANN CARTER, entitled by will of dec'd husband,
          PETER CARTER, to life estate in lands & slaves; disposed to
move to Ky. Power to sell her int. to exrs. of PETER CARTER: JOSIAH ELLIS,
W.S. CRAWFORD. Wit: ABRAM CARTER, EDWD. CARTER, NELSON CRAWFORD, RICH.
LAWLESS.

Page 554. 8 Oct 1806. JOS. TANKERSLEY, WM. LAWLESS, JNO. CARTER direct
          that Ł500 be set aside for MARYANN CARTER who wishes to move
to Ky. - for support. Also joined by CHAS., JESSE, EDWD., SOLOMON CARTER.
Wit: JNO. ELLIS, ABRAM CARTER, CHAS. DAVIS, GEO. ROACH, MAURICE BROWN,
ELIZ. EPPERSON, JNO. McDANIEL, SALLY NORCUTT. Memo: signatures of CHAS.,
JESSE, EDWD & SOLOMON executed in Ky., doubt may arise as to legality.
CHAS. CARTER produced Power of Atty signed in Ky. and acting for others
in Ky. Rec. AC, 20 Apr 1807. Wit: NELSON CRAWFORD, HENRY BROWN, BENJ.
TALIAFERRO as to AC wits. MAURICE BROWN et al wits. in Ky.

Page 555. 30 Oct 1806. JESSE, EDWD., & SOLOMON CARTER, Lincoln Co, Ky.
          Power of Atty to brother CHAS. CARTER, Lincoln Co, Ky, to act
in our behalf as to est. of our father, PETER CARTER, and to give our
mother, MARY ANN CARTER, any part for her support. THOS. MONTGOMERY, Clk.
of Lincoln; JOEL ADKERSON & VAL. PEYTON, J.P.'s of Lincoln - (ADKINSON
or ADKERSON).

Page 556. 18 Oct 1806. THOS. MOORE, REUBEN PENDLETON, JOHN ELLIS, NEL-
          SON CRAWFORD, LEWIS DAWSON, & JAS. WARE, trustees of town of
Bethel to MOSES RUCKER, AC, for $66.25, 3½ acres lots in Bethel - #10, 11
& 16 by plat (not with deed); Act of Assembley on lands of NICHL. C.
DAVIES & THOS. W. COCKE, 31 Dec 1801. Wit: ABRAM CARTER, JESSE WOODROOF,
WM. WATTS, HENRY BROWN, WM. G. HEYWOOD, WM. CLAYTON. Orig. del. to THOS.
N. EUBANK, 1 Jul 1807.

Page 556. 18 Oct 1806. Same trustees of Bethel to MOORMAN JOHNSON,
          Lynchburg, for $70, 4 lots of 1/2 acre each; #21, 22, 23.

Wit: as in previous deed.

Page 558.   18 Oct 1806.   Same trustees of Bethel to CHAS. JOHNSON, Lynchburg, for $45, 1 lot of 1/2 acre - #17. Wit: as above.

Page 559.   18 Oct 1806.   Same trustees of Bethel to JNO. RUCKER, AC, for
$50, Lot #8, 1/2 acre. Wit: as above.(Note: Bethel had same
fate as that of Warminster. Lynchburg was to grow, but Bethel was on the
Amherst side of the James and did not share her neighbor's growth. She is
now no more, but I know about where it was located. BFD)

Page 560.   30 Oct 1806.   THOS. JOPLING, Bedford, to JNO. HARRIS, AC, for
Ŀ600, 210 acres Buck Creek. Lines: JNO. DIGGS, BENNETT JOPLING,
HENRY ROBERTS, grantor. Wit: JNO. W. HARRIS, ASA VARNUM, BENJ. RUCKER, JR,
WM. LEE HARRIS.

Page 561.   22 Nov 1806.   JNO. CAMPBELL, son of GEO., & wife POLLY, AC, to
JACOB PUCKETT JR, for Ŀ25, Hatt Creek owned by JNO. CAMPBELL,
waggoner, at death. Lot #4 fell to JNO. & POLLY as heirs of JNO. - commissioners act. Wit; WINTON RYAN, WM. BATES, CHAS. JONES, BENJ. H.MORGAN.

Page 562.   26 Feb 1807.   Order to AC J.P.'s. SPOTSWOOD GARLAND & wife
LUCINDA, 9 Dec 1806, to JAS. PARKER GARLAND - 187 acres. Done,
26 Feb 1807, by JOS. BURRUS & JOS. SHELTON.

Page 562.   27 Feb 1807.   Order to AC J.P.'s.   JOS. C. HIGGINBOTHAM & wife
LUCY, on 9 Sep, 1805, to FREDERICK CABELL - 304 acres. Done by
JOS. BURRUS & DAVID S. GARLAND, 2 Mar 1807.

Page 563.   Receipt, AC Court, Nov, 1796. HENDERSON McCALL & Co. vs.
PHILIP BAILEY & CHAS. BOWLS, bdm. Rec'd in full, 19 Dec 1796,
by BENJ. JORDAN for Co. Wit: PLEASANT MARTIN - Ŀ9-5-4 with int. from 14
Aug 1795. W.S. CRAWFORD, Clk. Proved by MARTIN, 20 May 1807.

Page 563.   4 Mar 1806.   WM. LANHORN, AC, to DAVID & JAS. GARLAND & JNO.
EUBANK, JR, AC, Deed of Trust; debt to GARLANDS; 5 sh. paid by
EUBANK. 140 acres Thrasher's Creek; pat. to WL; stock. Wit: CHAS. BURRUS,
CHAS. W. CHRISTIAN, JAS. L. TURNER, GEO. RULEY. Orig. del. to JG, 11 Aug
1807.

Page 564.   21 Mar 1807.   Order to AC J.P.'s.   JAS. WOODS & wife SARAH, 6
Oct 1804, to THOS. PUGH - 168 acres. Done 4 Apr 1807, by
NATHAN CRAWFORD & HUDSON MARTIN.

Page 565.   25 Apr 1807.   Order to Bedford J.P.'s.   THOS. STEWART & wife
TIRZAH, to WM. PENN - 56 acres. Done by SAML. HANCOCK & WM.
DICKERSON, 8 May 1807.

Page 565.   15 Feb 1806.   Order to AC J.P.s.   WM. GOODWIN & wife FRANCES,
29 Apr 1796, to JOS. CREWS - 49 acres. Done by THOS. MOORE &
PHILIP JOHNSON,21 May 1807.

Page 566.   15 May 1807.   Order to Bedford J.P.'s.   JOS. CREWS, JR, & wife
MARTHA, 12 Sep 1798, to WM. PENDLETON - 49 acres. Done by WM.
BURTON & BALDA McDANIEL, 21 May 1807. CHAS. CLAY also named in ord. as JP.

Page 567.   4 Mar 1801.   CHAS. ROSE & wife SALLY, AC, to ELIZA SCOTT &
ALEX. ROSE - son and daughter of ROSE - love and 5 sh; 587 acres; one half remainder - other half sold to HENRY & JAS. WOODS for benefit of J.M. & PATRICK ROSE, JR. Commonly called Rose Mount on Piney &
Indian Creeks. Wit: D.S. GARLAND, JAS. WOODS, J.M. ROSE. Proved by WOODS,
22 May 1807; others on 15 Jun 1801.

Page 567.   13 Jun 1807.   THOS. S. McCLELLAND & wife MARGARET, Lynchburg,
to WM. ARMISTEAD, AC, for Ŀ824, 216 acres surveyed 19 Jun 1805;
plat annexed (not so) both sides Higginbotham's Mill Creek. Part of tract
of WM. CABELL. Lines: JAS. HIGGINBOTHAM, HENRY HOLLOWAY, ISAAC GIBSON's
legatees, GABL. PENN, dec'd. Sent by mail to TMc, 19 Jun 1807.

Page 568.   15 Jun 1807.   JNO. McDANIEL & wife LUCY, AC, to JAS. LIVELY,

458

AC, for Ł24, 8 acres Rutledge Creek. Wit: LINDSEY McDANIEL, BETSY McDAN-
IEL, PEGGY McDANIEL, HENRY & JESSE BROWN.

Page 569.   17 Nov 1806. WM. MAYS, AC, to ALEX. SALE, for Ł36, colt. Wit:
            BARTLETT CASH, WM. SALE.

Page 569.   8 Jan 1807. REUBEN, NATHAN, MARY, ZACH. TYREE, ELIZ. LEGGINS
            (formerly TYREE), children of WM. TYREE, dec'd, AC, to LEWIS
TINDALL, AC, for Ł180, 180 acres N side Tye. Lines: GEO. LOVING, WM.
GLASBY, LEWIS TINDALL. All of pat. of WM. TYREE. Wit: WM. ENOX, VALENTINE
BALL, JESSE FIDLER, JNO. SCRUGGS, TIM. SCRUGGS, PATTERSON SCRUGGS, JAS.
NEVIL.

Page 570.   2 Jun 1807. JAS. FLOYD & wife ELEANOR, AC, to REUBEN HUDSON,
            AC, for Ł280, 150 acres N branches Buffaloe; part of tract
formerly that of RUSH HUDSON. Lines: DAVID S. GARLAND, SAML. MEREDITH,
LINDSEY COLEMAN, RUSH HUDSON, old Church road. Wit: S. GARLAND, JACOB
MYERS, JAS. B. EDWARDS, N.C. HORSLEY.

Page 571.   30 May 1807. Order to AC J.P.'s. JAS. WARE & wife NANCY, 17
            Feb 1806, to JOS. HAWKINS, 16 acres. Done, 6 Jun 1807, by THOS.
MOORE & PHILIP JOHNSON.

Page 572.   25 Nov 1806. GEO. HYLTON, AC, to NATHAN LUFBROUGH, Georgetown,
            D.C.; HYLTON has right to certain iron ore mines & LUFBROUGH
has eligible seat for furnace N of Owen's Creek about 4 miles eastwardly
from the mines. $1.00 - NL may search for and take away all iron ore on
HYLTON's lands. Lines: Widow DRUMMOND, JAS. PAMPLIN, WM. PAMPLIN, RICH.
WOODS, WM. JORDAN. Tract bought by GH from PHILIP PENN - 1 ton per year
to GH. Wit: JNO. SCRUGGS, CHAS. O. PATTERSON, VAL. HYLTON.

Page 573.   15 Jun 1807. JNO. CHILDRESS JR, & wife SARAH, AC, to ARCHI-
            BALD ROWSEY, AC, for Ł135, 2 tracts both sides Pedlar - 290
acres. 1) 380 acres, part of 2 tracts pat. to JNO. CHILDRESS SR, 20 Jul
1780 & 24 Jul 1787. Lines: HENRY CHILDRESS, MOSES SWEENY. 2) 10 acres
surveyed for JNO. CHILDRESS SR. Orig. del. to AR, 26 Sep 1807.

Page 574.   26 Mar 1807. WM. DAVENPORT, AC, to RO. & THOS. WINGFIELD, AC,
            for love of DAVENPORT's children: NANCY H., MAHALA, SALLY,
ACHILLES, & WILLIS DAVENPORT by his wife, ELIZ., who has lately departed
this life - only issues. 10 sh. All int. of his late wife, ELIZ., in
estate of her father, NATHAN WINGFIELD, dec'd. - at her death of ANN
WINGFIELD, mother of ELIZ. - will rec. in AC. For benefit of children
until 21 or married. Wit: S. GARLAND, CHAS. DAVENPORT, THOS. WOODROOF,
JAS. B. EDWARDS.

Page 575.   26 May 1807. REUBEN GATEWOOD, AC, to FRANCIS HALL, AC, for
            Ł33, 33 acres, part of tract of WM. GATEWOOD, dec'd. Lines:
COLEMAN. Wit: RO. WINGFIELD, NATHAN HALL, CHAS. L. CHRISTIAN, WM. WILCHER.

Page 576.   15 Jun 1807. WIATT SMITH & wife POLLY, AC, to JOS. HIGGINBO-
            THAM, JR, AC, for Ł487-10, 162½ acres Rutledge Creek. Lines:
JNO. HIGGINBOTHAM SR, grantee, SUSANNA HIGGINBOTHAM, GIDEON RUCKER. Tract
bought by WS of JACOB WOOD and he bought it from PHILLIP GOOCH. Orig.
del. to WS, 10 Jul 1807.

Page 576.   15 Jun 1807. JOS. HIGGINBOTHAM & wife RACHEL, AC, to AMBROSE
            TOMLINSON, AC, for Ł300, 385 acres both sides N fork Buff.
Lines: JAS. HIGGINBOTHAM, JNO. HIGGINBOTHAM JR.

Page 577.   18 May 1807. JNO. BARNETT, AC, to BEZEBELL BROWN, Alb., for
            Ł100, Deed of Trust; Bought by JB of THOS. PHILLIPS - N side
and joining Tye. Pat. to TP on 20 Jul 1780; also 2 lots laid off to WM.
& JNO. CAMPBELL out of a larger tract of their late father, JNO. CAMPBELL,
waggoner - Hatt Creek. 80 acres bought by JNO. CAMPBELL of WM. CAMPBELL;
1st tract of PHILLIPS - 182 acres. Wit: BENJ. BROWN, JAS. B. EDWARDS,
JNO. LOVING, RO. GARLAND. Orig. del. to BB, 23 May 1810.

Page 578.   Order to AC J.P.'s, 12 Feb 1805. RICH. LAWLESS & wife ELIZ.,
            18 Sep 1802, to WM. PRYOR - 100 acres. Done by CHAS. TALIAFERRO

& NELSON CRAWFORD, 15 Jun 1807.

Page 579. 15 May 1807. WM. PRYOR to NANCY ATKINS, AC, for Ŀ3 - marriage
intended between them. Wit: NELSON CRAWFORD, WM. HOWARD,
HENRY BROWN.

Page 579. 27 Dec 1806. WM. EDMUNDS & wife POLLY ANN, AC, to WM L. &
CHAS. L. CHRISTIAN, AC, for Ŀ230, 146 acres S side Buff.
Lines: REUBEN GATEWOOD, LINDSEY COLEMAN, JNO. CHRISTIAN, JNO. COLEMAN,
WM. S. CRAWFORD, mouth of watermilion branch. Wit: WM. B. GOOCH, JNO.
CHRISTIAN(B), JNO. CHRISTIAN JR., WALTER L. CHRISTIAN.

Page 580. 2 Feb 1807. ANNE PHILLIPS, AC, to JAS. MARTIN, AC, Deed of
Trust; debt due JAS. WILLS SR, $1.00; 209½ acres both sides
Dutch. Lines: SPARKS MARTIN, JOSHUA WILLOUGHBY, GEO. MARTIN, RICH. C.
POLLARD. Wit: SPARKS MARTIN, ELIJAH L. CHRISTIAN, JNO. W. GREEN.

Page 581. 19 Nov 1805. RICH. ADAMS & wife SUSANNA, Charlotte Co, to
JNO. S. DAWSON, AC, for Ŀ60, 1/8th of tract on Hickory of 512
acres. Lines: TERISHA TURNER, JNO. MOORE, grantee. Tract whereon JNO.
DAWSON died possessed thereof. ADAMS & wife are distributees of JNO.
DAWSON. Wit: CHAS. LANKFORD, JNO. MOORE, LINDSEY GRIFFIN, BEN. DAWSON.
Orig. del. to RO. GARLAND, 21 Aug 1809.

Page 582. 6 Jan 1807. SAML. CASH, BARNETT CASH, LUKE RAY, & RICH.
SLAUGHTER on behalf of wives: LUKE RAY for wife PAMELA CASH,
daughter of RO. CASH, dec'd, RICH. SLAUGHTER for wife FRANCES CASH, dau.
of said RO. CASH - they have rec'd. of WM. SANDIDGE & wife TAMSEY, exrx.
of RO. CASH. SAML. CASH has rec'd. full quota of land & 3 slaves from
my father's estate (RO. CASH est.) - and all my interest in est. of AARON
HIGGINBOTHAM; same as to BARNETT CASH; RAY & SLAUGHTER. Wit: WIATT
SMITH, JOS. HIGGINBOTHAM, CORNL. SALE, RICH. SMITH.

Page 583. 17 May 1806. JAS. GAHAGINS & wife SALLY, Franklin Co, Va.,
to AZARIAH MARTIN, AC, for Ŀ174, 151½ acres. Lines: grantee,
SHEROD MARTIN. Wit: RICH. C. POLLARD, NATHAN BARNETT, WM. DOUGLAS, NATHL.
HARLOW JR. Page 584, order to quiz SALLY, 17 Nov 1806. AC J.P's. Done
by WM. H. DIGGES & GEO. DILLARD on same date. Final proof by BARNETT,
15 Jun 1807.

Page 585. 7 Apr 1807. Memo of compromise between LENNIS (LINEAS) BOWLING,
devisee of POWHATAN BOWLING, dec'd, Buckingham, & JNO. LONDON,
AC, - 2 caveats pending in Dist. Court at Charlottesville - LB is cavea-
tor & claiming under POWHATAN BOWLING, and LONDON is cavetee - entered
to prevent examination of grants to LONDON on 2 surveys on 2 plats returned to him by Register's Office. 1 for 200 acres and 2 for 1496
acres in AC - tedious and expensive to both & to terminate, have agreed.
BOWLING agrees to dismiss both caveats at next term and each to pay
costs & relinquish claims to 200 acres. Lines: JOS. MAYS, DAMERON's
heirs, WM. ROBINSON - surveyed by LONDON. PHILIP JOHNSON & BOWLING will
pay $160. LONDON will obtain grant for residue and to convey to BOWLING.
If they die, heirs are to carry out agreement. Wit: THOS. S. McCLELLAND,
THOS. LANDRUM, CHAS. MUNDAY, STERLING CLAIBORNE.

Page 586. 17 Jan 1807. RICH. HERNDON, AC, to JNO. EUBANK JR, AC, Deed
of Trust; debt to JAS. & DAVID GARLAND, SARAH ROSE, & DANL.
HIGGINBOTHAM. $1.00; stock, etc. Wit: BARTLETT THOMPSON, RO. PAMPLIN,
JNO. PAMPLIN. Orig. del. to JAS. GARLAND, 10 Oct 1807.

Page 587. 18 May 1807. ANDREW MORGAN & wife MARY, AC, to GEO. WILLIAMS,
AC, for $3333.30, 333 acres both sides Hatt Creek. Lines: JAS.
MONTGOMERY, CHAS. JONES, JAS. CLARKSON, HENRY ROSE. Wit: THOS. MASSIE,
DANL. HIGGINBOTHAM, WM. G. PENDLETON, WM. KNIGHT, S. CROSTHWAIT, P.C.
JACOBS, THOS. JONES, JAS. MONTGOMERY, DAVID JACOBS. May 19, 1809, rec'd
of GEO. WILLIAMS from THOS. MASSIE - & GEO. WILLIAMS's bonds: THOS. MAS-
SIE & RO. ROSE, bdm. Wit: ELIJAH MORAN. Orig. del. to GW, 5 Dec 1812.

Page 588. 15 Jun 1807. JNO. THOMPSON & wife JUDITH, JAS. WILLS SR, &
wife MILDRED, AC, to HAWES COLEMAN, AC, for Ŀ1000, 2 tracts
Naked Creek which grantors bought of MARTIN BIBB & TANDY JOHNSON. 1) 200

460

acres. Lines: JAS. BIBB, JNO. LOVING, TANDY JOHNSON, JAS. WILLS SR, WM.
BIBB, dec'd - now estates of CONYERS WHITE, SR & JR, dec'd, JOS. WHITE,
WM. H. DIGGES. 2) 210 acres which JAS. WILLS SR, bought of TANDY JOHNSON.
Lines: WM. BIBB, dec'd., JNO. LOVING, WM. LOVING, WM. HOLLINSWORTH, PAR-
MENAS BRYANT, est. of CONYERS WHITE Sr., JNO. THOMPSON - 410 acres.

Page 590. 8 Apr 1807. WM. TEAS & wife SARAH, AC, to PARMENAS BRYANT,AC,
              for ₺48, 32 acres, part of a tract; Naked Creek; 1 mile SE of
Courthouse. Lines: SAML. J. CABELL, both parties. Wit: GEO. W. VARNUM,
B. SNEAD. Orig. del. to CHAS. PERROW, 20 Feb 1827.

Page 591. 28 Nov 1806 - in 4 parts - RO. ROSE, Fauquier - 1st. HENRY
              ROSE, Alexandria, Fairfax Co.; 2nd. ALEX. BROOKE ROSE, Rose
Isle, AC, for self and late Dr. CHAS. ROSE, AC, 3rd. WM. H. FITZHUGH,
atty. for THOS. FITZHUGH & wife ANN, Stafford Co. 4th. children of late
Col. JOHN ROSE, Rose Isle, AC. Partition of 5 equal parts. 1) RO. ROSE
tract. Lines: S of dwelling of JESSE CLARKSON, JNO. CAMPBELL, dec'd, JAS.
MONTGOMERY - 1000 acres - lot #1. 2) HENRY ROSE. Lines: S of house of
JESSE CLARKSON, JNO. CAMPBELL, dec'd - 1170 acres. Lot 2. 3) ALEX.
BROOKE ROSE as heir of late Dr. CHAS. ROSE. Lines: Bank of Hatt., lots
2 and 3, Tye, THOS. MASSIE - 2530acres, lots 4 and 5. THOS. FITZHUGH &
wife ANN, E side Hatt - 1005 acres. Lot 3, RO. ROSE - 74 acres - lot 4.
ALEX. BROOKE ROSE - 74 acres Lot 3 and 148 acres; lots 1 and 2 - THOS.
FITZHUGH & wife ANN - 74 acres; lot 5. Wit: MERIWETHER FORTUNE, CHAS.
MOORE, EDWD. H. CARTER, JESSE CLARKSON. (Note: a bit confusing in spots,
but abstracted as given. BFD)

Page 594. 19 Nov 1806. JNO. ROSE, AC, died owning 6075 acres and his
              children are entitled to tracts. 1) RO. ROSE - one fifth. 2)
HENRY ROSE - one fifth. 3) ALEX. B. ROSE - one fifth and one fifth under
will of his dec'd. brother, CHAS. ROSE. 4) THOS. FITZHUGH - one fifth in
right of wife, ANN, daughter of JNO. ROSE, dec'd. Commissioners: EDWD.
CARTER, HILL CARTER, ANDREW MORGAN, NATHL. MANTIPLY, JOS. BURRUS, JNO.
THOMPSON (overseer), WM. DIGGS, & JAS. STEVENS. 1) Where JNO. ROSE's
house stands - 5705 acres. 2) The Commons - 370 acres. ALEX. B. to have
the house in lieu of dower of CATH., wife of JNO. ROSE, dec'd. CATH. to
get 200 acres from each part. Wit: JOHN C. CARTER, JAS. MONTGOMERY, JAS.
LANDRUM.

Page 596. 11 Nov 1806. THOS. FITZHUGH, Stafford Co, Power of Atty. to
              son, WM. FITZHUGH, to act in division of est. of JNO. ROSE,
dec'd, AC - wife is legatee. Wit: JAS. SUTHARD, WM. SUTHARD, ALLEN SU-
THARD.

Page 596. 17 Jul 1807. WM. RIPPETOE, AC, to JNO. EUBANK JR, AC, Deed of
              Trust; debt to JAS. & DAVID GARLAND & DANL. HIGGINBOTHAM. 6 sh.
Stock, beds, etc. Wit: THOMPSON NOEL, WM. ARMSTEAD, STERLING CLAIBORNE,
WM. HALL, CHAS. A. JACOBS. Orig. del. to DH, 15 Mar 1808.

Page 597. 17 Jul 1807. JAS. RIPPETOE, AC, to JNO. EUBANK JR, AC, Deed
              of trust; debts due as above; 6 sh; stock,furniture, tools etc.
Wit: as above. Margin as above.

Page 599. 7 Jul 1807. DAVID S. GARLAND, AC, to WM. MOSS, AC, for $191,
              Lot 23 W side Main Street in New Glasgow. (Later appears to be
No. 2) Wit: JNO. EUBANK JR, DANL. HIGGINBOTHAM, S. GARLAND.

Page 599. 8 Dec 1806. JAS. LONDON SR, to his son, JAS. LONDON JR, for
              love, 200 acres Porrage Creek. Part of where Sr. lives. Lines:
RO. GRANT, LARKIN LONDON, REUBEN NORVELL, JNO. LONDON, glade road. Wit:
REUBEN NORVELL, HENRY TURNER, JNO. LONDON. Final proof by NORVELL, 20 Jul
1807. Orig. del. to JL (no Sr. or Jr) 1 Nov 1813.

Page 600. 19 Mar 1807. NATHAN SHEPARDSON, AC, to DANL. McDONALD & JNO.
              MASTERS, AC, Deed of Trust; debt to JAS. MURPHY & Co., $1.00;
slave, Nelly, about 15, and future increase. Wit: EDMD. COFFEY, WM. FOR-
BUS JR, PEBEY & REUBEN COFFEY. Orig. del. to DM 26 Mar 1808.

Page 601. 4 Dec 1806. WM. LONG, Richmond, to DAVID S. GARLAND, AC, for
              $1500, 500 acres. Lines: RO. MEANS, JNO. SWANDSON, Lime Kiln

Creek, JNO. CHRISTIAN, CHRISTIAN Mill Creek, JNO. A. JONES. Orig. del.
to DG, 17 Oct 1807.

Page 602.   4 Aug 1806.   JAS. THOMPSON JR, AC, to RICH. CLARKE, AC, Deed
of Trust; debt to JAS. MURPHY & Co.; $1.00; 2 slaves. Wit:
JOS. LOVING, JAS. STEVANS, JR, RODERICK . TALIAFERRO, JNO. STEVENS, W.F.
CARTER, DRURY BELL, JAS. VIGUS JR, JNO. HIGGINBOTHAM. Orig. del. to JM,
19 Sep 1808.

Page 603.   4 Aug 1806.   DAVID OWENS, AC, to RICH. CLARKE, AC, Deed of
Trust; debt to JAS. MURPHY & CO, $1.00; 339 acres where DO
lives and bought of WALTER FORD. Wit: as above. Margin: as above.

Page 604.   13 Apr 1807.   JOS. HENSON & wife JEMIMAH, AC, to CHAS. P.
TALIAFERRO, AC, for $410, 3 tracts Lovelady Creek. 1) 300 ac-
res.   2) 60 acres. Lines: NICHL. PRYOR, HEZEKIAH SHOEMAKER, JNO. ROBERTS.
3) 50 acres. Lines: JNO. KEY, NELSON CRAWFORD, his own. Wit: PETER TALIA-
FERRO, JAS. BROWN, WM. CLEMENTS.

Page 605.   2 Jul 1807.   CHAS. YANCEY, Buckingham Co., & WM. CABELL - 2 of
the commissioners in decree of High Court Chancery, Richmond,
17 Sep 1806 - suit between JAS. GOVEN & GEO. WEIR & WILLIS WILLS & wife
ELIZ., vs. JNO. CABELL, Buckingham. Ŀ211-1 paid by JNO. CABELL for 3 lots
of 1/2 acre each in Warminster; property of WILLIS WILLS - Main St. #'s
7, 9, 11. Lines: WM. BROWN & Co., NICHL. CABELL, W.F. CABELL, ANN &
CLEMELINA CABELL.

Page 607.   20 Jul 1807.   RIVES & MURPHY Co, Warminster, to JAS. MURPHY,
AC, for Ŀ550, 319 acres devised by JAS. NEVIL to LEWIS NEVIL.

Page 608.   12 Jun 1807.   JNO. ROBERTS, AC, to MURRY HENSON,AC, for Ŀ70,
100 acres both sides Sinking Creek; where JR lives. Lines:
JNO. F. HALL, WM. H. CABELL, JNO. BROWN. Wit: ABRAM CARTER, JOS. HENSON,
JEMIMA HENSON.   Orig. del. to MH, 19 Apr 1824.

Page 609.   17 Jul 1807.   PRESLEY RAINES, AC, to WM. F. CARTER & SHELTON
CROSTHWAIT, AC, Deed of Trust, debt to JAS. MURPHY & Co.,
BROWN & Co. $1.00; sotck etc.

Page 610.   21 Nov 1806.   JESSE FORTUNE & wife BETSY, Iredal Co., N.C.,
& ZACH. FORTUNE & wife BETSY, AC, to JNO. GRIFFIN, AC, for
Ŀ180, 250 acres Headwaters Dutch Creek; bequeathed by THOS. FORTUNE to
his son, JESSE. Lines: JNO. FORTUNE, DAVID OWENS, JNO. McALEXANDER, JACOB
PUCKETT, EDDY FORTUNE. Wit: A. McALEXANDER, THOS. E. FORTUNE JR, WM. LOV-
ING. Page 611, Iredell Co. N.C. J.P.s, 1 Nov 1806(sic)- BETSY FORTUNE
appeared as to deed - Davis Creek of Rockfish. GEO. ROBINSON & WILL
YOUNG, ABNER SHARPE, Clk.

Page 611.   3 Feb 1807.   JNO. MATTHEWS, AC, to JNO. HIGGINBOTHAM & RO.
FRANKLIN, Warminster, Deed of Trust; debt to JAS. MURPHY & Co.
5 sh.; stock. Wit: WM. HOWARD, JAS. P. PARISH, JERE YAGER. Orig. del.
to JM, 19 Sep 1808.

Page 612.   17 Jun 1806.   BEVERLY WILLIAMSON & wife LIZA, AC, to JUDAH &
EDMD. WILLIAMSON, AC, for Ŀ216-13-4, 200 acres. Lines: EDMD.
WILLIAMSON, Ball's Spring Branch, MOSES MARTIN. Wit: EDMD. LANIER, RO.
RIVES, ALEX. SALE, MOSES MARTIN. Also joins JUDAH WILLIAMSON on Stone-
house Creek.   Orig. del. to JW, 2 Oct 1807.

Page 613.   19 Jun 1807.   Order to Campbell J.P.'s.   THOS. McCLELLAND &
wife MARGARET McCLELLAND, 13 Jun 1807, to WM. ARMISTEAD - 216
acres. Done 29 Jul 1807, by THOS. HUMPHREYS & THOS. W. COCKE. Orig.
del. to WA, 6 Jun 1818.

Page 614.   1 Dec 1806.   JAS. CAMPBELL, BARTHOLOMEW WHITEHEAD & wife NANCY
(late CAMPBELL), CATH. CAMPBELL, JNO. CAMPBELL JR, WM. CAMP-
BELL JR, POLLY CAMPBELL, SAML. CAMPBELL, & CORNL. CAMPBELL, children &
heirs of GEO. CAMPBELL, dec'd, to GEO. CAMPBELL for $1.00 and considera-
tion of Ŀ106 paid by GEO. CAMPBELL to GEO. CAMPBELL dec'd - GEO. died
intestate and deed was never made in lifetime. Part of survey of 611

acres. Lines: Main road, Piney river - 100 acres. Wit: JNO., WIATT CAMP-
BELL & BENJ. WRIGHT. Orig. del. to GC, 17 Nov 1807.

Page 615.   1 Dec 1806.   JNO. CAMPBELL JR, AC, to GEO. CAMPBELL, AC, for
            Ł50, all int. in est. of GEO. CAMPBELL dec'd, as one of his
children. Wit: as above. Orig. del. to GC, 12 Dec 1808.

Page 616.   15 Apr 1807. Order to Lynchburg J.P.'s.   JNO. WIATT & wife
            WILHELMENIA 14 Apr 1790, to JOS. CREWS. Done by M. LAMBERTH &
RODERICK TALIAFERRO, 21 Sep 1807.   Page 617, 21 Apr 1807: Order to Bedford J.P.'s.   HENRY L. DAVIES & wife LUCY, to CHAS. DAVIS, 9 Jul 1806.
83 acres.   WM. BURTON & BALDA McDONALD 19 Sep 1807, J.P.s.

Page 618.   5 Aug 1807.   Order to AC J.P.'s.   WM. CABELL & wife ANNE, 13
            Sep 1805, to THOS. S. McCLELLAND, 216 acres. SAML. J. & LANDON
CABELL, 29 Aug 1807   Also MARGARET McCLELLAN was a grantee as wife of
THOS. S.

Page 618.   21 Sep 1807.   JOS. BURRUS & wife SOPHIA, AC, to WM. PENN, AC,
            for Ł1200, 2 tracts Buff. 1) Bought by JB of PHILIP BURTON,
25 Apr 1786 - 400 acres. Lines: MATT. TUCKER, N bank Buff. 2) S side
Buff. & bought of WM. BURTON, 1 Jul 1786 - 76 acres. Part of 400 acres
of WM. BURTON. Lines: P. BURTON.

Page 619.   22 Aug 1807.   Order to AC J.P.'s.   BENJ. WATKINS & wife MARY,
            15 Feb 1804, to JAS. CUNNINGHAM - 50 acres. Done by JNO.
HORSLEY & JNO. CHRISTIAN, 16 Sep 1807.

Page 620.   22 Jan 1807.   JOS. HAWKINS, AC, to JESSE WOODROOF, AC, for
            Ł180, Deed of Trust; debt to WOODROOF - tract bought by HAW-
KINS of JAS. WARE. Wit: REUBEN PENDLETON, JNO. MEHONE, H. GUTHRIE,
GIDEON POWELL.

Page 621.   21 Jan 1807.   JAS. WARE & wife NANCY, AC, to JOS. HAWKINS, AC,
            for Ł180, 62 acres and part of where WARE lives. Lines: JAS.
WILLS, grantor, PROSSER POWELL, John's Creek. Wit: JESSE WOODROOF,
REUBEN PENDLETON, JNO. MEHONE, ANTHONY RUCKER.

Page 622.   8 Jun 1807.   JNO. JACOBS & wife SALLY, AC, to their sons:
            DAVID & PETER C. JACOBS, AC, for love and $1.00, 13 acres N
side and joining Tye. Lines: JNO. HUGHES. Wit: JAS. MONTGOMERY, JESSE
BURGHER, JOS. BURGHER, WM. COFFEY SR.

Page 623.   20 Sep 1807.   CHAS. BURRUS & wife ELIZ., AC, to JABEZ CAMDEN,
            AC, for Ł450, 232½ acres. Orig. del. to JC, 10 Oct 1807.

Page 623.   20 Sep 1807.   CHAS. BURRUS & wife ELIZ, AC, to LEONARD HENLEY,
            AC, for Ł1250, 523 acres. Lines: JNO. DUNCAN, dec'd; on the
mt. Orig. del. to LH, 10 Oct 1807.

Page 624.   27 Aug 1807.   HUDSON M. GARLAND to JAS. & SPOTSWOOD GARLAND.
            Deed of Trust; $1.00 paid by JAS. GARLAND. 1 acre adj. New
Glasgow and where HG lives and bought of Major JAS. FRANKLIN. SPOTSWOOD
GARLAND has become surety at suit of WM. CABELL, assignee of JAS. & DAVID
GARLAND.

Page 625.   28 Feb 1807.   JAS. PAMPLIN, AC, & wife MARY, to JAS. CUNNING-
            HAM, AC, for Ł50, 33 acres James River. Lines: GEO. HYLTON,
W.S. GARLAND, JAS. HARRIS, JAS. B. EDWARDS. Order to quiz MARY; done by
JNO. HORSLEY & JNO. CHRISTIAN, 16 Sep 1807.

Page 626.   8 Sep 1807.   NATHAN WILLIAMSON, AC, to JNO. LONDON, Campbell
            Co., Deed of Trust; debt to THOS. HIGGINBOTHAM & Co., & HIG-
GINBOTHAM, BROWN & Co., beds, stock, etc. Wit: REUBEN MITCHELL, GEO.
TOWNS. Orig. del. to Mr. HIGGINBOTHAM, 17 Jul 1810.

Page 627.   23 Mar 1807.   RO. WALKER, GEO. DILLARD, & THOS. CREWS, AC, to
            WM. BROWN & Co. - FREDERICK FULTZ, 3 Jan 1806, to grantors as
trustees - 201 acres & where FF lived at time. Bought by FF of PETER
JOINER. Ł210 paid at sale by grantee. Lines: JNO. TAYLOR, AMBROSE RUCKER,

NATHAN WINGFIELD, Stovall's road, REUBEN PADGETT, BENJ. WARREN's spring.
Orig. del. to JNO. CAMM, for grantee, 9 Apr 1808.

Page 628.   29 Aug 1807.   REUBEN GATEWOOD & wife ELIZ., AC, to WM. B.
          GOOCH, AC, for Ł50, 68 acres. Lines: STEPHEN WATTS, MIC. PEN-
DLETON, RO. COLEMAN, EDMD. WILCOX dec'd, WM. GATEWOOD, dec'd, LINDSEY
COLEMAN. Wit: THOS. BEDDOW, FRANCES & ELIZ. GOOCH. BEDDOW later appears
to be Jr. Orig. del. to WG, 27 Mar 1810(?).

Page 629.   20 Jul 1807.   JAS. THOMAS & wife ELIZ. (late ROBERTS), Kanawha,
          to HENRY ROBERTS, AC, for $250, 1500 acres, part of tract of
ELIOT ROBERTS, dec'd. and by him del. to son, MATT. ROBERTS, and all that
MR owned at death. Both sides Rockfish. Lines: RICH. FARRAR dec'd, ISHAM
BAILEY, SAML. HENLEY, JOS. SMITH, MARK LIVELY, JNO. MOORE. Wit: MATT.
HARRIS JR, JNO. ROBERTS, LINDSEY GRIFFIN.

End of Deed Book K

Following are lists of Surveys, Tax Lists, Voters Lists, etc. found in
Deed Book F. The names have been alphabetized here; consequently, these
names will not be found in the index.

Page 65. Survey list: A list of all surveys of land in Amherst County
during the preceding twelve monts, 6 Jul 1786. WM. CABELL, JR, AC Surveyor. a = acres.

JNO. BAILEY   70 acres
WM. BARNETT   130 a
JNO. BETHEL   296 a.
JAS. BOWLER   16 a.
EDWD. BOWMAN   160 a.
RICH. BROOKS   250 a.
NICHL. CABELL   700 a.
DAVID CLARK   54 a.
EDMD. COFFEY   208 a.
CORNL. CROSS   137½ a.
DANL. GOODE   80 a.
JNO. GRIFFIN   150 a.
LEE HARRIS   320 a.
GEO. HILTON   240 3/4 a.
JOS. LANNUM   70 a.
BETHEL LIVELY   300 a.

WM. LOVING   154 a.
JNO. MATTHEWS   275 a.
WM. MATTHEWS   345 a.
JAS. McALEXANDER   73 a.
DAVID MONTGOMERY 95 & 45 a.
JOS. HIGGINBOTHAM MORRISON 120 a.
LEONARD & MATTHEW PHILLIPS   73 a.
JNO. SHIELDS   120 a.
JOS. SMITH   300 a.
WM. SPENCER   36 a.
DAVID TILFORD   126 a.
JAS. TILFORD   130 a.
FRANCIS TURNER   280 a.
JOEL WALKER   400 a.
WM. WALTON   400 & 290 a.
ACHILLES WRIGHT   370 a.

Page 82. List indents received for the following peoples taxes for 2/3
1785. JNO. CRAWFORD, Deputy Shff.; DAVID CRAWFORD, Shff.

HENDRICK ARNOLD   3-8-8
THOS. BARRETT   7-8-0
EDWD & CHAS. CARTER 45-18-0

PETER CARTER   4-9-6
CHAS. ROSE   14-13-2½

Page 83. Court of AC held on 4 Sep 1786 - JNO. CRAWFORD, Deputy Shff.
for DAVID CRAWFORD, Shff. - returned this list of Indents collected for
2/3 of taxes. WM. LOVING, Clerk.

JOS. BALLENGER   4-16-0
CHAS. BURKS   1-3-2
JNO. BURKS   1-12-9
DAVID BURKS   2-5-7
WM. BURTON   1-16-8
EDWD. CARTER   0-14-10
WM CARTER   1-4-6
ELIZ. COLEMAN   1-18-0
MILLY COLEMAN   2-4-3
JOS. DAVENPORT   1-18-6
JNO. EUBANK   1-3-11¼
HENRY FRANKLIN   0-19-9
REUBIN HARRISON   0-15-1¼
WM. HAYNES   0-15-3/4
AARON HIGGINBOTHAM   1-0-0 3/4
WM. HIGGINBOTHAM   0-19-4
THOS. HILLEY   0-6-4
JOSHUA HUTSON   2-9-2
RO. HUDSON   0-12-7
JNO. MARR, SR.   1-9-4
JNO. MARR, JR.   0-6-0
JAS. MARTIN   0-13-8

BENJ. MAYS   0-5-2
RO. MAYS   0-11-8
WM. MAYS   0-4-2
RODERICK McCULLOCH   7-7-9½
ARCHEY MITCHELL   4-0-7½
RICH. OGLESBY   2-11-10
WM. OGLESBY   1-6-10
WIATT POWELL   2-13-2
BENJ. ROGERS   0-8-2 3/4
BENJ. RUCKER   9-4-3
JNO. SALE   4-19-9 3/4
WM. SANDADGE   1-5-2½
JACOB SMITH   7-0-1
BENJ. STATON   0-4-0
WM. STINNETT   0-10-0
MATT. TUCKER   3-16-0
WM. VEAL   0-10-10
EDWD. WARE   0-13-1 (Jr)
CALEB WATTS   1-6-11
JNO. WHITEHEAD   3-9-9¼
JNO. WOOD   0-10-2
JNO. WOODROOF   1-2-6

Note: The collector often combined reports. On this page these names are
found with others as follows: (Page 88)

WM. ALFORD-THOS. HAWKINS
JNO. CASH - MOSES CAMPBELL
WM. HANSBROUGH estate with JNO.
LOVING

JNO. INNIS - THOS. HAWKINS
JNO. JOSLING - GEO. HILTON
DAVID PATTERSON with MOSES CAMPBELL

Page 88.   2 Oct 1786.   2/3 of taxes reported by NELSON CRAWFORD, Depty.
Shff. for DAVID CRAWFORD, Shff.

THOS. BALLOW - see JNO. BIBB
JNO. BETHEL 0-6-0
JNO. BIBB & THOS. BALLOW 2-2-0
WM. BIBB 4-4-0
JAS. EVANS BURNET 0-5-0
JNO. BUSH 2-10-0
NICHL. CABELL 22-19-0
SAML. J. CABELL 7-12-8
WM. CABELL Sr. 42-3-4
WM. CABELL JR. 7-1-8
MOSES CAMPBELL, JNO. CASH &
   DAVID PATTERSON 12-18-0
WM. CRISP 1-10-0
JNO. EDMOND estate 0-18-0
GROVES HARDING estate 1-16-0
THOS. HAWKINS, JNO. INNIS &
   WM. ALFORD 3-12-0

GEO. HILTON & JNO. JOSLING 6-0-0
JAS. HOPKINS 4-16-0
JNO. & RO. HORSLEY 6-15-0
WM. HORSLEY 6-12-0
WM. HOWARD 14-0-0
JNO. LOVING & WM. HANSBROUGH estate
                          5-2-0
WM. LOVING 6-0-0
JAS. NEVIL's eatate 9-15-0
CHAS. ROSE 8-0-0
SAML. SHELTON 2-2-0
MENNIS WRIGHT 0-12-0
JNO. WARREN 0-7-0½
JOHN WEST's estate 2-14-4
JNO. WINKFIELD 2-6-0½

Page 88.   Court of 2 Oct 1786.   JOS. BURRUSS, Depty. Shff. for DAVID
CRAWFORD, Shff. 1785 tax.

RICH. ALLCOCK 0-17-11
JOHNSON BAIN 1-4-11
SAML. BELL 0-19-6
RO. BOWLING estate 26-6-10½
WM. CABELL Jr. 3-8-7
JOEL CAMPBELL 0-14-0
CHAS. CHRISTIAN 1-12-7
ELIJAH CHRISTIAN 1-11-6
HENRY CHRISTIAN 3-7-6½
JNO. CHRISTIAN 0-17-6
JNO. CHRISTIAN (B) 1-10-11
(Note: In previous work I have
noted this (B). It was for one
living on Buffalo. BFD)
JNO. CHRISTIAN (H?) 2-4-0
MICAJAH CLARK 0-15-6
JAS. DILLARD 4-13-11
WM. DILLARD 0-18-5
JNO. EDLOW 0-17-6
RICH. GATEWOOD 1-10-11

HENRY GILBERT's estate 2-17-0½
EDWD. HARPER 0-19-2½
SNELLING JOHNSON 1-6-2
WM. LAYNE (W) 2-8-2 (waggoner)
ABRAHAM LEMASTER 0-9-11
JNO. LEMASTER 0-6-0
RALPH LEMASTER 0-9-2
DANL. MAYO 0-16-0
JAS. PATTERSON 6-1-8
GABL. PENN 14-9-4½
PHILLIP PENN 0-16-2
DANL. PERROW 1-12-7½
JNO. PHILLIPS 1-13-7
WM. PHILLIPS 0-19-8
HUGH ROSE 12-14-3
JNO. ROWSEY 0-12-0
WM.SCOTT 0-7-3
JNO. STRATTON 0-16-5
JNO. UPSHAW 0-8-7
JOEL WALKER

Page 89.   Court of 2 Oct 1786.   JNO. CRAWFORD, DS for DAVID CRAWFORD,
Shff. List of indents to pay in the Treasure(sic) 2/3 of the following
persons tax agreeable to Act of Assembly.

ANN BANKS 1-4-2
LINN BANKS 1-0-5
RUBIN BANKS 0-12-2
JAS. BOWLING 1-4-0
CHAS. BURRUS 6-5-2
JAS. CALLAWAY 5-15-1
WM. CAMDEN 0-16-6
DUNCAN CAMRUN 0-7-0
JNO. CLARKSON 4-4-4
ELIZ. DAVIS 4-19-10½
JNO. DAWSON 0-15-0
RO. DAWSON 0-18-0
GEO. DOUGLAS 1-5-1
EDWD. GARLAND 0-17-0
PERRON GILES 1-3-1
ARCHEBELL GILLUM 0-14-8
JNO. GILLUM 1-3-6
JNO. GOODRICH 0-19-5½
THOS. GOODRICH 2-4-3
BATTLE HARRISON est. 1-15-10
DANL. HARVIE 4-7-4 (?)

CALEB HIGGINBOTHAM 1-10-0
DANL. HUNTER 0-6-0
THOS. LUCAS 4-14-5
GEO. McDANIEL 1-3-0
SAML. MEREDITH 12-19-6
JAS. MORTON 1-11-0
JAS. NOWLING 0-14-6
JNO. PARKS 1-4-0
GEO. PENN 4-12-0
JNO. PENN 8-0-0½
JOS. PENN 3-10-0
MOSES PENN 1-17-5¼
AMBROSE RUCKER 8-11-7
ISAACK RUCKER 3-11-3
EDWD. SANDERSON 0-18-9
JNO. SANDIDGE 1-15-3
PULLUM SANDIDGE 0-9-3
PHILIP SMITH 0-12-4
JNO. STINNETT 0-9-0
PHILIP THURMOND 6-0-8
JNO. TINSLEY 2-13-1

WM. TINSLEY   1-18-10
JAS. TOOLEY   1-0-0
HENRY TRENT   3-18-8
EDWD. WARE, SR.   5-4-1
JAS. WARE   0-18-7
WM. WARE   3-0-3½

EDWD. WATSON   3-11-10
JAS. WATSON   4-12-3
THOS. WAUGH   2-16-1
EDMD. WINSTON   2-18-8
DANL. WOODROOF   3-9-9

Page 89.   The following indents for the different persons tax for 1785 and not exceeding 2/3 of tax. NATHAN CRAWFORD, D.S. for DAVID CRAWFORD, Shff. WM. LOVING, Clerk.

GEO. BLAINE   1-3-0
JAS. BROOKS   3-0-10
NATHAN CRAWFORD   40-2-0
JNO. DAWSON   9-12-0
ALEX. REID   2-8-0

JNO. ROSE   37-4-0
PATRICK ROSE   16-10-0
JAS. STEVENS   6-0-0
JAS. WOODS   3-5-9

Page 91.   List of indents 2/3 taxes for 1785.   Returned 9 Aug 1786, by JNO. CRAWFORD, D.S. for DAVID CRAWFORD, Shff.

JNO. BURFORD SR.   1-10-10¼
WM. BURFORD   0-15-8
JOS. CHILDRESS   2-13-6½
JAS. CREWS   0-18-8
HENRY & NICHL. DAVIS   11-8-0
JOS. & MARTIN DAWSON   6-10-4
THOS. GRISON 0-9-4½
MARTHA, RICH. & WM. HARVIE 13-6-9
JNO. HOGG   0-12-10½
WM. HUGHES   2-16-4½
WM. LEE's estate 3-10-2¼
JAS. LIVELY   16-3-3/4
WM. MAYS   -18-0

GEO. McDANIEL SR.   3-16-3½
MARY PARKS   0-14-9 3/4
ELIZ. PENDLETON   0-17-4
RICH. PENDLETON   0-10-4
CHAS. REYNOLDS   1-13-1
ELINOR RUCKER   2-11-11
JAS. SIMMONS   0-17-0
JNO. SLEAD   0-13-0
CHAS. TALIAFERRO   6-16-3
DANL. TUCKER 0-8-10
DRURY TUCKER   3-17-10½
JAS. WARE   0-9-9

Page 92.   List of taxes received in Indents for 1785.   Six figures in some columns.   JOS. BURRUS, D.S.   Returned 9 Aug 1786.   DAVID CRAWFORD, Shff.

RICH. BAINE 19-10½-13-3
WM. BROWN CHRISTIAN 1-16-1½-1-4-1
LAURENCE CAMPBELL 2-3-11½-1-9-3½
PETER CASHWELL 10-10½-0-7-3
WM. CASHWELL 4-2-8
DRURY CHRISTIAN 6-4-11½-4-3-3½
JNO. CHRISTIAN 6-0-6-4-0-4
RO. CHRISTIAN 6-15-9½-4-10-6
RO. CHRISTIAN's son (not named)
    7-0-4-8
GEO. COLEMAN 7-2-8-3/4-4-15-1½
JNO. CRITTENDON 1-2-7-15-0½
JOS. FRANKLIN 4-6-2-17-4
JAS. GRESTHAM 4-4-6½-2-16-4
WM. GUTTRY 1---13-4
JAS. HIGGINBOTHAM 7-19-6½-5-6-4
JNO. HIGGINBOTHAM 7-6-7½-4-17-9

MARY JOHNSON 3-6-3-2-2
EVE LACKEY 18-7½-12-5
FRANCIS LEE 2-14-8-1-16-5
JAS. LONDON 1-13-1¼-1-2-0½
JOS. MAYHO   21--14--
HENRY McDANIEL 2-8-2-1-12-5
JER. McDANIEL -7--4-8
PLEDGE PALMER -9-3½-6-2
GEO. PHILLIPS 1-2-5--14-11
HUGH ROSE 18-0-5-12-0-3
JNO. STEWART 3-3-10½-2-2-7
JAS. STOVALL -19-8¾--13-1
HENRY TURNER 4-4-5½-2-16-1 3/4
JNO. TURNER   2-6-8-1-11-8
THOS. WILCOX -12-6--8-4

Page 111.   List of Indents 2/3 of taxes for 1785.   Returned 1 Jan 1787 by JNO. CRAWFORD, D.S., for DAVID CRAWFORD, Late Shff.

BENJ. ARNOLD 1-0-6
WM. CAMDEN   1-9-9
WM. CHAPPLE 2-2-0
ARCHELAUS COX 2-13-6
DAVID CRAWFORD 5-15-9
CHAS. ELLIS 1-9-5
MICAJAH GOODWIN 1-0-3

HENRY HARTLESS 0-16-2
DANL. HARVIE 4-6-6
AARON HIGGINBOTHAM SR. 4-10-16
SAML. HIGGINBOTHAM 3-8-6
RUSH HUTSON 1-10-0
GEO. LEE 2-14-10
THOS. POWELL 3-15-3

CORNL. SALE   1-10-0
JNO. SCOTT   3-7-8
SAML. SCOTT   1-16-0

BENAMMI STONE 1-5-0
SMYTH TANDY 4-7-8
JNO. WIATT 6-8-4

Page 130. Rec'd. the following list in Indents for the different Persons Tax for 1785 not exceeding 2/3 of tax. Returned 5 Feb 1787, by NATHAN CRAWFORD, D.S. for DAVID CRAWFORD, late Shff.

WM. ALLEN 0-7-4
RACHEL AYRES   4-4-0
JAS. BELL 1-4-0
THOS. BELL 2-0-0
WM. BONES 0-5-0
BENJ. CAMDEN 0-6-0
JNO. CAMDEN 0-9-0
JNO. CAMPBELL 0-6-0
BENJ. CARPENTER 0-10-0
BENJ. CHILDRESS est. 1-2-0
BENJ. CLARK 0-7-0
DAVID CLARK 0-12-6
JNO. CLARK 0-6-0
NATHL. CLARK 2-10-0
DAVID CLARKSON 1-8-0
WM. COFFEE 0-17-4
OSBOND COFFEE 0-8-6
JNO. COLE 1-16-0
JNO. COOPER 0-6-0
DAVID DAVIS 0-6-0
JAS. DICKEY 0-16-0
JNO. DIGGES 4-19-0
ANN DINWIDDIE 0-8-0
JOS. DODD 0-6-0
THOS. DOSWELL 1-10-0
JNO. DRUMMON 1-10-0
THOS. FORTUNE 0-6-0
SAML. FOX 0-8-0 (Tax?)
JNO. GILMER 0-16-0
JNO. GRIFFIN 1-1-0

JNO. HALL 0-6-0
RO. HARDY 2-5-0
HENRY HARPER 1-6-0
HEZ. HARTGROVE 0-18-0
JNO. M. HATTER 0-8-0
JNO. HENDERSON 1-4-0
WM. HENDERSON 0-13-0
WM. KILE 0-8-0
WM. KILES 0-16-0
JNO. LANKESTER 0-4-6
WM. LYON 1-8-0
JNO. MARTIN est. 0-11-0
STEVEN MARTIN 0-10-0
JNO. MT GOMERY est. 3-0-0
JOS. MT GOMERY 2-12-0
JNO. MORRIS 0-6-0
BENJ. PANNEL 0-10-0
JNO. POPE 3-10-0
THOS. POWELL 1-16-0
PETER RIPETOE 0-14-0
JOS. ROBERTS 3-4-0
AUGUSTINE SHEPHERD 1-10-0
WM. SMALL 0-10-0
ABRAHAM STRANGE 0-14-0
RICH. TANKERSLEY 0-18-0
RO. THOMPSON 1-2-0
JNO. WILLIAMSON 1-0-0
THOS. WILLIAMSON 0-18-0
GEO. WITT 0-9-0
JAS. WRIGHT 1-7-0

Page 131. List of Indents for 1785; not over 2/3 Returned 8 Nov 1786, by NATHAN CRAWFORD, D.S. for DAVID CRAWFORD.

WM. BARNETT 2-0-4
ANNE CRAWFORD 1-16-0
PHILLIP DAVIS 0-10-6
THOS. EWERS 0-10-0
AZARIAH MARTIN 3-2-0
DAVID McANALLY 0-12-6
JNO. McANALLY 0-8-6
JNO. McCLURE 0-14-0
JNO. MT GOMERY 2-2-0
NICHL. MORAN 2-0-0
THOS. MORRISON SR. 2-12-0
THOS. MORRISON JR. 1-4-0

JNO. PHILLIPS 0-4-0
ALEX. REID 0-16-0
DAVID REID 1-0-0
THOS. ROBINSON 0-12-6
CLOUGH SHELTON 3-6-0
DAVID SHELTON 3-0-0
JNO. SHIELDS 1-4-0
SAMER(LAMER?) SHROPSHIRE 0-12-6
ZACHS. TALIAFERRO 9-6-0
JAS. TILFORD 9-14-6
NICHL. WREN 0-13-0

Page 132. Indents for 1785 not exceeding 2/3 Returned 9 Nov 1786, NELSON CRAWFORD, D.S. for DAVID CRAWFORD, Shff.

SAML. ALLEN 6-6-0
JAS. DILLARD 1-4-0
MILLEY LAVENDER 0-18-0

JAS. PAMPLIN 2-8-0
STEPHEN TURNER 6-18-0
ANDREW WRIGHT 1-4-0

468

Page 134. Rec'd Indents not exceeding 2/3 for 1785. Returned 7 Mar 1787
by NELSON CRAWFORD, D.S. for DAVID CRAWFORD, Shff.

JNO. CABELL 12-0-0
JNO. CARTWRIGHT 0-14-0
JAS. CONNER 0-12-0
WM. DIXON 0-16-0
THOS. FARRAR 0-18-0
JNO. GRIFFIN 0-16-0
EDWD. HARDING 0-18-0
MATT. HARRIS 8-0-0
JNO. LYON, dec'd. 1-18-0
HENRY MARTIN 2-8-0

WM. MATTHEWS 0-8-0
DAVID MONTGOMERY 1-4-0
JAS. MONTGOMERY 0-12-0
RICH. MURROW 0-10-0
SUSANNAH NASH 0-12-0
ROBT. ROBERTSON 0-16-0
WM. TILLER 1-2-0
RO. WRIGHT 1-13-6
WM. WRIGHT 1-18-6

Page 134. The undermentioned is a list of Indents rec'd 1785 - not exceeding 2/3 - Errors excepted. NATHAN CARWFORD, D.S. Returned 6 Mar
1787, by him for DAVID CRAWFORD, late Shff.

WM. DEPRIEST 1-16-0
ABRAHAM SMITH 1-14-0

WM. WALTON 4-10-0

Page 147. 2/3 Indents - year not stated. Returned 8 May 1787 by JNO.
CRAWFORD, D.S. for DAVID CRAWFORD, late Shff.

BENJ. ARNOLD 1-0-3
ANNA BANKS 1-4-1
BENJ. COLEMAN 1-0-6
JNO. DAWSON 0-18-0
WM. GALT 1-16-11
SAML. GEFT(?) 1-10-0
PERRIN GILES 1-2-8
ALEX. GORDIN 0-14-6
RICH. HARRISON 1-10-0
DINAH HAY 0-18-0
PHILIP HOLT 0-10-0
RUSH HUDSON 1-10-0
CHAS. IRVING 2-3-0
DAVID JARRELL 1-15-6

RO. JOHNSON 0-10-0
JNO. JONES 4-8-1
GEO. LEE 2-15-8
WM. PETERS 1-0-9
LEROY POPE 2-2-0
WALTER POWERS ---
DAVID ROSS 2-4-0
GEO. ROUT 0-12-0
PETTIS THACKER 1-6-9
JNO. TENISON 0-11-0
WM. TUCKER 1-3-6
JNO. WARD 1-4-6
ISAAC WRIGHT 4-2-6

Page 220. A list of surveys made in the County of Amherst during the preceding 12 mos. 6 Jul 1787. WILL CABELL JR., Surveyor. a = acres

JNO. BELL 72 a
NICHL. CABELL 165 a
JNO. CAMPDEN 100 a
EDMOND COFFEY 135 a.
MAJOR DOWELL 50 a
THOS. DURHAM 65 a
JNO. ENNIS 52 a
THOS. FORTUNE 100 a
JNO. HATTER 50 a
THOS. HAWKINS 103 a
JNO. HENDERSON 180 & 180 a
JOS. HIGGINBOTHAM JR. 100 a
THOS. JOPLING 400 a
CHAS. KNUCKLES 56 a
WM. LOVING 85 a
JAS. MATTHEWS 204 a

WM. McANALLY 60 a
JOS. MONTGOMERY 69 a
JOS. H. HENDERSON 327, 134, 80 a
JAS. NEVIL 85 a
JNO. POPE 190, 103 a.
JNO. PRICE 340 a.
GEO. PURVIS 50 a
ABRAHAM SMITH 196 a
CHAS. STEWART 140 a
ZACHS. TALIAFERRO 98 a
CORNL. THOMAS, dec'd. 400, 400,
  400, 400, 225, 300 a.
DAVID TILFORD 270 a
JAS. TILFORD 100 a
STEPHEN TURNER 165a
FRANCIS WEST 390 a

Page 237. Indents - 2/3 for 1785. Returned 2 Jun 1788. NELSON CRAWFORD,
D.S. for DAVID CRAWFORD, Shff.

ARCHER HAMBLET 0-9-0
THOS. JOPLING 5-14-0
WM. MEREDITH 4-5-0
BENJ. MOORE 7-12-0

JAS. TURNER 4-0-0
BENNETT NALLEY 0-18-0
CHAS. WATTS 0-7-0
STEPHEN WATTS 2-4-0

Page 261. A list of all surveys of land made in the County of Amherst during the preceding 12 months. 6 Jul 1788. WM. CABELL Jr, Surveyor of AC. Truly recorded, WM. LOVING, Clk.

HENRY BELL   400, 330 a
SAML. BELL   192 a
RO. BOLLING, dec'd.   2 3/4 a
CHAS. BURKS   4 a
DAVID BURKS   36 a
NICHL. CABELL   970 a
WM. CABELL   1000 a
WM.CABELL JR.   1/2 a
GEO. CAMPBELL   163 a.
JOB CARTER 220 a
JOS. CHILDERS   40 a
ELIJAH CHRISTIAN   118 a
NATHL. CLARK   372, 235 a.
JESSE CLEMENTS   123 a
JNO. COLEMAN dec'd.   60 a
GEO. DAVIS   50 a
PLEASANT DAWSON   100 a
JAS. DILLARD   400, 360 a.
SAML. DINWIDDIE, dec'd.   118 a
JNO. DUNCAN   140 a
SAML. EDMOND   8a
WM. ANDERSON ENGLAND   174 a
JNO. EUBANKS   13 a
WM. EVANS   266 a
GEO. FITZJARRALD 400 a
GEO. GALASPIE   200, 164 a
EDWD. GARLAND 28 a
JAS. GOODWIN   12 a
EDWD. HARPER   244 a
MATT. HARRIS   57 a
Capt. WM. HARRIS   320 a

JNO. HENDERSON 90 a
JAS. & JNO. HIGGINBOTHAM   695½, 400, 400 a
JOS. HIGGINBOTHAM   140 a
ABRAHAM LEMASTER   272 a
JAS. LONDON   120 a
JNO. LOVING   85 a
MARTIN KEY   123 a
JNO. MATTHEWS   27 a
JOS. MATTHEWS   85 a
GEO. McDANIEL   20, 92 a
THOS. MOFFIT   80 a
SARAH NEW   108 a
JNO. NICHOLAS   16 a
JNO. PHILLIPS   250 a
THOS. PHILLIPS   172, 14 a
CHAS. REYNOLDS   28 a
JNO. RICHARDSON   148, 125 a
THOS. RICKETS 146, 110 a
ASHCRAFT ROACH 150 a
JNO. ROBERTS   238 a
ZACH. ROBERTS   307 a
JNO. SALE   8 a
JNO. SHASTEEN   280 a
SEYMOUR SHROPSHIRE   140 a
ABRAHAM SMITH 190 a
JNO. SMITH   180 a
DAVID TILFORD   372 a
ISAAC TINSLEY   120 a
JNO. WARE   90, 95 a
THOS. WILLIAMSON 77a

Pages 292-294. Poll of election. Summary at end: Clerk of above Poll has made oath before me a magistrate that he has taken the same justly and impartially this 7 Jan 1789. WILL CABELL, JR. Truly recorded, WM. LOV-ING, Clerk. (One will note that some names appear in more than one list for some elections, so we assume that they had several candidates before them and could vote for two. In some cases we are not told just what the office was in contest. The following voted for WM. CABELL SR. GENL. STEVENS was running against WM. CABELL SR, and page 292 gives him 0 votes) For WM. CABELL, SR:

WM. ALCOCK
JNO. ALFORD
JNO. BAILEY
STEWART BALLOW
WM. BARNETT
RICH. BEAN
MICAJAH BECKNALL
HENRY BELL
WM. BIBB
GEO. BLAIN
ALLEN BLAIR
WM. BONES
WM. BOWMAN
JNO. BOUSH
CHAS. BRIDGWATER
JNO. BROCKMAN
JNO. BROWN SR.
JNO. BROWN
SHEROD BUGG
JNO. BURGY
CHAS. BURKS
DAVID BURKS
JNO. BURKS

NICHL. CABELL
SAML. J. CABELL
WM. CABELL JR.
JAS. CALLAWAY
AMBROSE CAMPBELL
FRANCIS CAMPBELL
GEO. CAMPBELL
JNO. CAMPBELL
LAURENCE CAMPBELL
THOS. CARPENTER
ABRAHAM CARTER
EDWD. CARTER
PETER CARTER
WM. CARTER
BARTLETT CASH
STEVEN CASH
WM. CHAPPLE
ALEX. CHISNALL
ELIJAH CHRISTIAN
DAVID CLARK JR.
DAVID CLARKSON
JNO. CLARKSON
OSBON COFFEY

LINDSEY COLEMAN
DAVID CRAWFORD
NELSON CRAWFORD
WM. SID CRAWFORD
JAS. CREWS
JNO. DAWSON
JOS. DAWSON
ZACHARIAS DAWSON
JAS. DILLARD SR.
JAS. DILLARD
JOS. DILLARD
JOSIAH DODD
GEO. DOUGLAS
JNO. DUNCAN
CARROL EADS
THOS. EADS
JAS. EDMONDS
SAML. EDMONDS
JOSIAH ELLIS
DAVID ENIX
THOS. EVANS
RICH. FARRAR
THOS. FARRAR

GEO. FITZGERALD
THOS. FITZPATRICK
WM. FITZPATRICK
THOS. FORTUNE
SAML. FOX
HENRY FRANKLIN
GEO. GILLESPIE
ISAAC GIPSON
DANL. GOODE
EDMD. GOODRICH
MICAJAH GOODWIN
JNO. GRIGORY
HEZAKIAH HARGROVE
EDWD. HARPER
HENRY HARPER
BENJ. HARRIS
JNO. HARRIS
WM. HARRIS
JAS. HARRISON
HENRY HARTLESS
THOS. HAWKINS
CHAS. HAY
ALEX. HENDERSON
AARON HIGGINBOTHAM
CALEB HIGGINBOTHAM
CHAS. HIGGINBOTHAM
JAS. HIGGINBOTHAM
JNO. HIGGINBOTHAM
JOS. HIGGINBOTHAM
JOS. HIGGINBOTHAM Jr.
MOSES HIGGINBOTHAM
SAML. HIGGINBOTHAM
WM. HIGGINBOTHAM
JAS. HILL
NATHAL. HILL
GEO. HILTON
JAS. HOPKINS
CLEVER HORRILL
JNO. HORSLEY
JOSHUA HUDSON
RUSH HUDSON
HENRY HUGHES
WM. HUGHES
JNO. INNIS
JNO. JACOBS
STEPHEN JOHNSON
TANDY JOHNSON
WM. JOHNSTON
CHAS. JONES
JAS. JOPLING
JOSIAH JOPLING
THOS. JOPLING JR.
JESSE KENNEDY
SAML. LACKEY
CHAS. LAINE
THOS. LAINE
WM. LAINE
THOS. LANDRUM
YOUNG LANDRUM
FRANCES LEE
GEO. LEE
RICH. LEE
BETHELL LIVELY
JAS. LIVELY
JOS. LIVELY
WM. LOVING, SR.

ALEX. McALEXANDER
JAS. McALEXANDER
NOTLEY MADDOX
NATHL. MANTIPLY
JNO. MARR SR.
GIDEON MARTIN
HENRY MARTIN
HUDSON MARTIN
MOSES MARTIN
PETER MARTIN
PLEASANT MARTIN
SHEROD MARTIN
WM. MARTIN
JNO. MASSEY
JAS. MATTHEWS
JNO. MATTHEWS
WM. MATTHEWS
JAS. MAYS
JOS. MAYS SR.
JOS. MAYS
SAML. MEREDITH SR.
SAML. MIGGINSON
JOS. MONTGOMERY
NICHL. MORAN
THOS. MORRISON JR.
JAS. MORTON
CORNL. MURRELL
RICH. MURROW
BENNETT NALLEY
RICH. OGLESBY
WM. OGLESBY
THOS. PATTERN
JAS. PENDLETON
GABL. PENN
GEO. PENN
DANL. PERROW
DAVID PHILLIPS
JNO. PHILLIPS
WM. PHILLIPS
JOELL PONTON
FRANCIS POWELL
LUCAS POWELL
OBEDIAH POWELL
THOS. POWELL
WIATT POWELL
JNO. PRICHATT
DAVID PROFFITT
NICHL. PRYOR
GEO. PURVIS
IGNATIUS RAINS
ALEX. REID
SAML. REID
HENRY ROBERTS
JOS. ROBERTS
ARTHUR ROBERTSON
BENJ. ROGERS
CALEB ROLLS
HUGH ROSE
PATRICK ROSE
JAS. ROWSEY
JNO. ROWSEY
ANTHONY RUCKER
ISAAC RUCKER
CORNL. SALE
JNO. SAILS
JNO. SANDIDGE

LARKIN SANDIDGE
WM. SANDIDGE
EDWD. SAUNDERSON
ABRAHAM SEAY
CLOUGH SHELTON
HENRY SHELTON
JOS. SHELTON
SAML. SHELTON
AUGUSTIN SHEPHERD
JAS. SIMMONS
WM. SMALL
AUSTIN SMITH
HENRY SMITH
JACOB SMITH
JNO. SMITH
PHILIP SMITH
JNO. SNIDER
WM. SPENCER
JNO. STAPLES
CHAS. STEWART
JNO. STEWART
MARBLE STONE
GEO. STONEHAM
JNO. STRUTTON
CHAS. TALIAFERRO
SMYTH TANDY
CHAS. TATE
JNO. THOMPSON   (3)
JAS. TILFORD
ISAAC TINSLEY
JNO. TINSLEY
JOSHUA TINSLEY
CHAS. TUCKER
DANL. TUCKER
DRURY TUCKER
JAS. TURNER
TERISHA TURNER
NATHL. WADE
JOELL WALKER
TILMAN WALTON
WM. WALTON
JAS. WATERS
JNO. WATKINS
EDWD. WATSON
STEPHEN WATTS
BRANSFORD WEST
FRANCIS WEST
FRANCIS WEST JR.
JNO. WEST
ELISHA WILL
JNO. WILLIAMSON
JAS. WILLS
DAVID WITT
GEO. WITT
JNO. WITT
LITTLEBERRY WITT
WM. WITT
JAS. WOODS
ANDREW WRIGHT
ARCHELAUS WRIGHT
BENJ. WRIGHT
JSS. WRIGHT
MENOS WRIGHT
RO. WRIGHT
WM. WRIGHT

Pages 496-497. Poll kept and held in AC for candidates for Congress in
the Albemarle District 2 Feb 1789. "I do hereby certify that the fore-
going poll was kept by me, having first sworn, and that the number of
voters, when I delivered the Polls, stood as follows: for JAMES MONROE,
Esq., 174. for JAMES MADISON Jr., Esq., 92. Signed: JAS. FRANKLIN.
WM. CABELL, Jr. took his oath.

For JAMES MADISON:
JNO. BAILEY
JNO. BARNETT
EPHRAIM BLAINE
JAS. CALLAWAY
PETER CARTER JR.
WM. CARTER
RICH. CHANDLER
WM. CHAPEL
CHAS. CHRISTIAN
JNO. CHRISTIAN
BENJ. CHILDRES
JNO. COLE
LINDSEY COLEMAN
DAVID CRAWFORD
JNO. CRAWFORD
NELSON CRAWFORD
WM. S. CRAWFORD
JOS. CREWS
DAVID DAVIS
WM. DAVIS (2?)
ZACH. DAWSON
JOS. DILLARD
WM. EVANS
JNO. FITZHUGH
HENRY FRANKLIN
JAS. FRANKLIN
JNO. GRIFFIN
RICH. HAIR
BENJ. HARRIS
JNO. HARRIS
WM. HARRIS (2?)
WM. L. HARRIS
REUBIN HARRISON
NATHL. HILL
JOSHUA HUDSON
RUSH HUDSON
HENRY HUGHES
JOSIAH JOPLING
FRANCIS LEE
WM. LOVING
PETER LYON
MOSES MARTIN
PLEASANT MARTIN
RODERICK McCULLOCH
JNO. McDANIEL
SAML. MEREDITH
JOS. MT GOMERY
BENNETT NALLEY
THOS. PARROCK
GABL. PENN
GEO. PENN
JOS. PENN
WIATT POWELL
IGNATIUS RAINS
PETER RIPETOE
HENRY ROBERTS
JNO. ROBERTS
ZACH. ROBERTS
CALEB ROLLS
HUGH ROSE
JNO. ROSE
PATRICK ROSE

AMBROSE RUCKER
ANTHONY RUCKER
BENJ. RUCKER
ISAAC RUCKER
JNO. RUCKER
JOS. SHELTON
AUGUSTIN SHEPHERD
JOS. SMITH
WM. SPENCER
JNO. SWANSON
CHAS. TALIAFERRO
ZACHS. TALIAFERRO
SMYTH TANDY
JOS. TILFORD
JAS. TURNER
EDWD. WARE
JAS. WARE
WM. WARE
JNO. WATKINS
CHAS. WATTS
STEVEN WATTS
JNO. WIATT
JAS. WILLS
DAVID WITT
DAVID WOODROOF
JAS. WOODS
ANDREW WRIGHT
WM. WRIGHT

For JAMES MONROE:

JNO. ALFORD
WM. ALFORD
JNO. BALL
WM. BALL
STEWART BALLOW
WM. BARNETT
MICAJAH BECKNALL
WM. BIBB
GEORGE BLAINE
ALLEN BLAIR
JOS. BOND
WM. BONES
WM. BOWMAN
JNO. BROCKMAN
JAS. BROWN
JNO. BROWN
JNO. BROWN JR.
WM. BURFORD
JOS. BURGEE
CHAS. BURKS
DAVID BURKS
JNO. BURKS
JNO. BUSH
JNO. CABELL
SAML. J. CABELL
WM. CABELL
WM. CABELL JR.
BENJ. CAMDEN
JNO. CAMDEN
WM. CAMDEN
AMBROSE CAMPBELL
GEO. CAMPBELL JR.

JNO. CAMPBELL
LAURENCE CAMPBELL
MOSES CAMPBELL
EDWD.CARTER
JAS. CARY
BARTLETT CASH
JNO. CASH
STEVEN CASH
JNO. CLARKSON
OSBON COFFEY
PHILIP DAVIS
JNO. S. DAWSON
JAS. DILLARD (Tay)
WM. DIXON
JNO. DUNCAN
CARRELL EADS
JAS. EDMONDS
SAML. EDMONDS
THOS. EWERS
RICH. FARRAR
DANL. GOODE
WM. FITZPATRICK
GEO. GALASPIE
EDMD. GOODRICH
JNO. GREGORY
JNO. M. GRIFFIN
EDWD. HARDING
HEZEKIAH HARGROVE
HENRY HARPER
RICH. HARRISON
HENRY HARTLESS
THOMAS HAWKINS
WM. HAYNES
AARON HIGGINBOTHAM
CALEB HIGGINBOTHAM
JAS. HIGGINBOTHAM
JNO. HIGGINBOTHAM
JOS. HIGGINBOTHAM (2?)
MOSES HIGGINBOTHAM
SAML. .HIGGINBOTHAM
WM. HIGGINBOTHAM
CLEVER HORRELL
JNO. HORSLEY
WM. HORSLEY
WM. HOWARD
MOSES HUGHES
JNO. INNIS
JNO. JACOBS
THOS. JOHNS
CHAS. JONES
THOS. JONES
THOS. JOPLING JR.
JESSE KENNEDY
SAML. LACKEY
WM. LAINE (wagr)
YOUNG LANDRUM
WM. LAVENDER
GEO. LEE
RICH. LEE
JAS. LIVELY
JOS. LIVELY
GEO. LOVING
JNO. LOVING

472

For James Monroe Cont.
WM. LYON
JNO. MARR
HENRY MARTIN
PETER MARTIN
JNO. MASSEY
JAS. MATTHEWS
JNO. MATTHEWS
JAS. MAYS
JNO. MAYS
JOS. MAYS SR. & JR.
RO. MAYS
SAML. MEGGINSON
JOS. MILSTEAD
NICHL. MORAN
JOS. H. MORRISON
THOS. MORRISON
RICH. MURREY
JAS. NEVIL
LEWIS NEVIL
RICH. OGLESBY
JAS. PAMPLIN
RICH. PERKINS
DANL. PERROW
JNO. PHILLIPS
WILLIAM PHILLIPS
ZACHS. PHILLIPS

LUCAS POWELL
THOS. POWELL
DAVID PROFFITT
NICHL. PRYOR
JNO. PUGH
JNO. ROBERTS
JOS. ROBERTS
ARTHER ROBINSON
BENJ. ROGERS
JAS. ROWSEY
JNO. SALE
LARKIN SANDIDGE
JNO. SCOTT
ABRAHAM SEAY
CLOUGH SHELTON
SAML. SHELTON
WM. SMALL
ABRAHAM SMITH
JACOB SMITH
PHILIP SMITH
FRANCIS SPENCER
JNO.STAPLES
JNO. STEWART
MARBIL STONE
GEO. STONEHAM
CHAS. TATE
DAVID THOMPSON

JAS. THOMPSON
JNO. THOMPSON
DAVID TINSLEY
AMBROSE TOMPLINSON
DANL. TUCKER
DRURY TUCKER
STEPHEN TURNER
TILMAN WALTON
WM. WALTON
ABRAHAM WARWICK
JAS. WATERS
JNO. WEST
JNO. WILLIAMSON
JOS. WILSHER
JAS. WOOD
BENJ. WRIGHT
ISAAC WRIGHT
JAS. WRIGHT
KILLIS WRIGHT
MINOS WRIGHT
MOSES WRIGHT
RO. WRIGHT

Page 298. 4 Feb 1789. This day PLEASANT MARTIN made oath that the above poll of 66 votes for JAS. MONROE and 51 for JAMES MADISON was taken with Justice and Impartiality. HUGH ROSE. Truly recorded WM. LOVING, Clerk. This summary follows the tabulation now given:

For JAMES MADISON

MARTIN BIBB
NOELL BLANKENSHIP
SHEROD BUGG
THOS. CARPENTER
ABRAHAM CARTER
PETER CARTER
WM. CLARK
JAMES CREWS
CHAS. DAVIS
SAML. DAY
JNO. DEMASTERS
JOSIAH DODD
JOSIAH ELLIS
THOS. GRISSOM
EDWD. HARPER
LEE HARRIS
CHAS. HAY
JAS. HILL
JNO. HOGG
NOTLEY MADDOX
HENRY McCLAIN JR.
DANL. MEHONE
WM. MOON
JAS. MORTON
EZRA MORRISON
JAS. MURPHY (just below is his sworn statement before ZACH. TALIAFERRO)
WM. OGLESBY
ABNER PADGETT
JNO. PARSONS
JAS. PENDLETON
JNO. PENN
MOSES PENN

DAVID PHILLIPS
CHAS. PURLEY
SAML. REID
PETER ROSE Esq.
ISAAC RUCKER Jr.
JNO. RUCKER Jr.
MOSES RUCKER
HENRY SHELTON
JNO. SHIELDS
JAS. SIMMONS
AUGUSTIN STEEL
CHAS. STEWART
BENAMI STONE
JOHN THOMAS
CHAS. TYLER
DAVID VIA
JOELL WALKER
THOS. WARE
EDWD. WATSON
JAS. WATSON
THOS. WILCOX
ELISHA WITT
GEO. WITT
JNO. WTII

For JAMES MONROE:

WM. ALCOCK
THOS. BECKNALL
JOHNSON BEEN
HENRY BELL
JNO. BETHEL
FRANCIS CAMPBELL
GEO. CAMPBELL
PETER CARTWRIGHT
ALEX. CHISNELL

WM. COFFEY
JNO. DAVIS
PLEASANT DAWSON
DAVID DONOHOU
GEO. DOUGLAS
ALEX. DUGGINS
THOS. EADS
DAVID ENIX
AMBROSE EUBANK
JNO. EUBANK
THOS. FORTUNE
ISAAC GIBSON
ARCHER GILLUM
JNO. HATTER
JAS. HARRISON
WM. HUGHES
THOS. JINKINS
STEPHEN JOHNSON
WM. JOHNSON
RALPH JOPLING
THOS. JOPLING SR.
THOS. LAINE
THOS. LANDRUM
BETHELL LIVELY
JAMES LONDON
NATHL. MANTIPLY
JESSE MARTIN
GEO. McDANIEL SR.
SAML. MEREDITH Esq.
THOS. MORRIS
JAS. MURPHY (partially erased, but name is in both columns)
THOS. PATTON
RICH. PENDLETON
JACOB PHILLIPS

For JAMES MONROE cont.
JOELL PONTON
FRANCIS POWELL
WM. PRYOR
THOS. PUGH
JNO. RICHARDSON
ASHCRAFT ROACH
BENJ. SANDIDGE
JNO. SANDIDGE
PULLIAM SANDIDGE
WM. SANDIDGE (Our present clerk is so named and his father served before him. BFD)

EDWD. SAUNDERSON
HEZ. SHOEMAKER
JNO. SLEDD
JNO. SMITH
JNO. SNYDER
WM. STINNETT
ELIJAH STONE
GUTRIDGE THURMOND
JNO. THURMOND
JAS. TILFORD
ISAAC TINSLEY

JOSHUA TINSLEY
WM. TINSLEY
JEREMIAH TUNGET
HENRY TURNER
JNO. TURNER
WM. TURNER
FRANCIS WEST
BURCHER WHITEHEAD
JONATHAN WILSON
JAS. YELTON

Pages 315-320. This is a peculiar table for no date given, but evidently in 1789. It is not stated just what the election was for in any place. Several men seem to have gleaned a few votes and may have been comparable to our modern-day "write'in"candidates. I am giving these first.

WM. CABELL, SR: RICH. CHANDLER, WM. LAINE, DAVID WOODROOF, WM. CABELL, BENJ. RUCKER. (Note that we run into names in more than one candidate's list.)
GEO. GALASPIE - JOS. CREWS
HUGH ROSE - MOSES MARTIN, JAS. LIVELY
AMBROSE RUCKER - POWHATAN BOWLING

NICHOLAS CABELL Supporters:

JNO. ALFORD
JNO. BAILEY
PHILIP BAILEY
JNO. BALL
JOS. BALLENGER
STEWART BALLOW
WM. BARNETT
THOS. BARRETT
MICAJAH BECKNALL
THOS. BECKNALL
HENRY BELL
JNO. BETHEL
WM. BIBB
GEO. BLAINE
NOELL BLANKENSHIP
WM. BOWMAN
CHAS. BRIDGWATER
JONATHAN BRIDGWATER
JNO. BROCKMAN
JNO. BROWN
SHEROD BUGG
JNO. BURFORD
JOS. BURGER
CHAS. BURKS
DAVID BURKS
SAML. BURKS JR.
JOS. BURRUS
JNO. BUSH
WM. CABELL
JAS. CALLAWAY
BENJ. CAMDEN
JNO. CAMDEN
JNO. CAMDEN JR.
WM. CAMDEN
AMBROSE CAMPBELL
GEO. CAMPBELL
GEO. CAMPBELL JR.
JOELL CAMPBELL
JNO. CAMPBELL
JNO. CAMPBELL (wag)
LAURENCE CAMPBELL

EDWD. CARTER
PETER CARTER
WM. CARTER
BARTLETT CASH
STEPHEN CASH
WM. CHAPELL
ALEX. CHISNELL
CHAS. CHRISTIAN
JOHN CHRISTIAN
RO. CHRISTIAN
TURNER CHRISTIAN
DAVID CLARK JR.
NATHL. CLARK
ZACHARUS CLARK
JNO. CLARKSON
WM. COFFEE
JAS. CONNER
VALENTINE COX
JNO. CRAWFORD
NATHAN CRAWFORD
NELSON CRAWFORD
JAS. CREWS
WM. CRISP
CORNL. CROSS
CHAS. DAVIS
DAVID DAVIS
ISAM DAVIS
JABUS DAVIS
WM. DAVIS
JOS. DAWSON
JAS. DILLARD
JOS. DILLARD
WM. DIXON
GEO. DOUGLASS
JNO. DUNCAN
CARRELL EADS
JAS. EDMUNDS
SAML. EDMUNDS
THOS. EDWARDS
JOSIAH ELLIS
DAVID ENIX

WM. FITZPATRICK
HENRY FRANKLIN
JAS. FRANKLIN
JAS. FRASER
GEO. GALASPIE
AMBROSE GATEWOOD
ISAAC GIBSON
ARCHELAUS GILLIAM
DANL. GOODE
EDMOND GOODRICH
JNO. GREGORY
JNO. GRIFFIN
JOHN HALL
WM. HALL
RO. HARDEY
EDWD. HARDING
EDWD. HARPER
HENRY HARPER
JNO. HARRIS
JAS. HARRISON
RICH. HARRISON
HENRY HARTLESS
THOS. HAWKINS
CHAS. HAY
WM. HAYNES
ALEX. HENDERSON
JNO. HENDERSON
CALEB HIGGINBOTHAM
JAS.   "
JNO.   "
JOS.   "   (2)
JOS.   "   Jr.
MOSES   "
SAML.   "
JAS. HILL
CLEVER HORRELL
JNO. HORSLEY
WM. HORSLEY
RUSH HUDSON
WM. HUGHES
JNO. HUTCHERSON

JNO. JACOBS
STEPHEN JOHNSON
WM. JOHNSTON
PETER JOINER
JOSIAH JOPLING
RALPH JOPLING
JESSE KENNEDY
JNO. KNIGHT
SAML. LACKEY
CHAS. LAINE
THOS. LAINE
WM. LAINE
WM. LAINE (W)
WM. LAVENDER
FRANCIS LEE
GEO. LEE
JNO. LEMASTER
BETHEL LIVELY
JAS. LIVELY
JOS. LIVELY
JAS. LONDON
LARKIN LONDON
GEO. LOVING
JNO. LOVING
WM. LOVING
THOS. LUCAS
PETER LYON
WM. LYON
NOTLEY MADDOX
JNO. MARR
GIDEON MARTIN
HENRY MARTIN
JAS. MARTIN
PETER MARTIN
STEPHEN MARTIN
JAS. MATTHEWS
JNO. MATTHEWS
DANL. MAYO
JAS. MAYS
JNO. MAYS
JOS. MAYS
JOS. MAYS JR.
RO. MAYS
ALEX. McALEXANDER
JAS. McALEXANDER JR.
RODERICK McCULLOCH
GEO. McDANIEL
JNO. McDANIEL
JOS. MILSTEAD
NICHL. MORRAN
JOHN MORRIS
JNO. MIRRISON
JOS. HIGGINBOTHAM MORRISON
THOS. MORRISON JR
CORNL. MURRELL
JNO. MURROW
RICH. MURROW
BENNETT NALLEY
JAS. NEVIL
RICH. OGLESBY
WM. OGLESBY
BENJ. PANNELL
THOS. PATTERN
JAS. PENDLETON
GEO. PENN
JAS. PENN
JOS. PENN
PHILIP PENN
RICH. PERKINS
DANL. PERROW

ZACH. PHILLIPS
JOELL PONTON
FRANCIS POWELL
WALTER POWERS
DAVID PROFFETT
JNO. PUGH
THOS. PUGH
GEO. PURVIS
HENRY ROBERTS
JOS. ROBERTS
ARTHUR ROBERTSON
BENJ. ROGERS
JNO. ROWSEY
ANTHONY RUCKER
ISAAC RUCKER
JOHN RUCKER
BENJ. SANDIDGE
JNO. SANDIDGE
PULLIAM SANDIDGE
EDWARD SAUNDERSON
JNO. SCOTT
ABRAHAM SEAY
CLOUGH SHELTON
HENRY SHELTON
WM. SHELTON
WM. SMALL
ABRAHAM SMITH
JACOB SMITH
JNO. SMITH
JOS. SMITH
PHILIP SMITH
JNO. SNYDER
WM. SPENCER
JNO. STAPLES
CHAS. STEWART
BENAMI STONE
ELIJAH STONE
JNO. STRATTON
JNO. SWANSON
CHARLES TALIAFERRO
SMYTH TANDY
CHAS. TATE
JER. TAYLOR
WM. TEAS
JAMES THOMPSON
JNO. THOMPSON
GUTRIDGE THURMOND
DAVID TINSLEY
ISAAC TINSLEY
JOSHUA TINSLEY
THOS. H. TOLBERT
AMBROSE TOMBLIN
DANL, DRURY &
THOS. TUCKER
JAS. TURNER
STEPHEN TURNER
WM. TURNER
JACOB TYREE
NATHL. WADE
JOELL WALKER
WM. WALTON
WM. WARE
ABRAHAM WARWICK
JAS. WATERS
JNO. WATKINS
EDWD. WATSON
STEPHEN WATTS
JOS. WELCH
BRANSFORD WEST
FRANCIS WEST SR.

FRANCIS WEST JR.
JNO. WEST
NICHL. WEST
THOS. WILCOX
JNO. WILLIAMSON
JONATHAN WILSON
JOS. WILTSHIRE
JNO. WITT
JAMES WOOD
JNO. WOODROOF
ANDREW WRIGHT
BENJ. WRIGHT
ISAAC WRIGHT
JAS. WRIGHT
RO. WRIGHT
WM. WRIGHT JR.

For JNO. NICHOLAS

JNO. BARNETT
EPHRAIM BLAINE
POWHATAN BOWLING
JNO. CASH
RICH. CHANDLER
BENJ. CHILDRESS
WALTER CHRISTIAN
JNO. COLE
WM. S. CRAWFORD
JOS. CREWS
ZACHARIAS DAWSON
MATT. HARRIS
WM. HARRIS JR.
NATHL. HILL
CHAS. IRVING
WM. KILE
MOSES MARTIN
PLEASANT MARTIN
JOS. MEGANN
WM. MEREDITH
JOS. MONTGOMERY
JAS. MORTON
THOS. PARROCK
JNO. PENN
MOSES PENN
WIATT POWELL
IGNATIUS RAINS
HUGH ROSE
PATRICK ROSE
AMBROSE RUCKER
BENJ. RUCKER
WM. SCOTT
JOS. SHELTON
JNO. THOMAS
ROBERT WALKER
JNO. WARE
JNO. WIATT
JAS. WILLS
DAVID WOODROOF
JAS. WOODS

Page 317. For
GABRIEL PENN

JOS. BALLENGER
JNO. BARNETT
HENRY BELL
EPHRAIM BLAINE
NOELL BLANKENSHIP
POWHATAN BOWLING
JONATHAN BRIDGWATER

SHEROD BUGG
JNO. BURFORD
JOS. BURRUS
JAS. CALLAWAY
JOELL CAMPBELL
LAURENCE CAMPBELL
PETER CARTER
RICH. CHANDLER
WM. CHAPELL
BENJ. CHILDRESS
CHAS.CHRISTIAN
JNO. CHRISTIAN
ROBERT CHRISTIAN
TURNER CHRISTIAN
WALTER CHRISTIAN
JNO. COLE
VALENTINE COX
JOHN CRAWFORD
NATHAN CRAWFORD
NATHAN CRAWFORD
NELSON CRAWFORD
WM. S. CRAWFORD
JAS.CREWS
JOS. CREWS
CHAS. DAVIS
ISHAM DAVIS
WM. DAVIS
JOS. DAWSON
ZACH. DAWSON
JOSEPH DILLARD
THOS. EDWARDS
JOSIAH ELLIS
HENRY FRANKLIN
JAMES FRANKLIN
AMBROSE GATEWOOD
EDWD. GOODRICH
EDWD. HARPER
MATT. HARRIS
WM. L. HARRIS JR.
JAS. HARRISON
JNO. HARRISON
RICHARD HARRISON
WM. HAYNE
JNO. HIGGINBOTHAM
JOS. HIGGINBOTHAM
SAML. HIGGINBOTHAM
JAS. HILL
NATHL. HILL
RUSH HUDSON
WM. HUGHES
JNO. HUTCHERSON
CHAS. IRVING
JNO. JACOBS
STEPHEN JOHNSON
PETER JOYNER
JESSE KENNEDY
JNO. KNIGHT
WM. LAINE
WM. LAVENDER
FRANCIS LEE
GEO. LEE
JAS. LONDON
LARKIN LONDON
WM. LOVING
THOS. LUCAS
NOTLEY MADDOX
JNO. MARR
PLEASANT MARTIN
DANL. MAYO
JAS. MAYS

JOS. MAYS   SR.
JOS. MAYS   JR.
RO. MAYS
JNO. McDANIEL
RODERICK McCULLOCH
GEO. McDANIEL
JOS. MEGANN
WM. MEREDITH
JOS. MONTGOMERY
JNO. MORRIS
JAS. MORTON
RICH. OGLESBY
WM. OGLESBY
THOS. PARROCK
JAS. PENDLETON
GEO. PENN
JAS. PENN
JNO. PENN
JOS. PENN
MOSES PENN
PHILIP PENN
WIATT POWELL
JNO. PUGH
IGNATIUS RAINS
HUGH ROSE
PATRICK ROSE
JNO. ROWSEY
AMBROSE RUCKER
ANTHONY RUCKER
BENJ. RUCKER
ISAAC RUCKER
JNO. RUCKER
JNO. SANDIDGE
PULLIAM SANDIDGE
EDWD. SAUNDERSON
JNO. SCOTT
WM. SCOTT
HENRY SHELTON
JOS. SHELTON
JACOB SMITH
JNO. SMITH
PHILIP SMITH
WM. SPENCER
BENAMMI STONE
JNO. STRATTON
JNO. SWANSON
CHARLES TALIAFERRO
SMYTH TANDY
JER. TAYLOR
JNO. THOMAS
DAVID TINSLEY
ISAAC TINSLEY
JOSHUA TINSLEY
THOS. H. TOLBERT
JACOB TYREE
THOS. TUCKER
HENRY TURNER
JAS. TURNER
JOELL WALKER
RO. WALKER
JNO. WARE
WM. WARE
JAS. WATERS
EDWD. WATSON
STEPHEN WATTS
JNO. WIATT
THOS. WILCOX
JAS. WILLS
JOS. WILSHER
JONATHAN WILSON

JNO. WITT
DAVID WOODROOF
JNO. WOODROOF
JAS. WOODS
ISAAC WRIGHT

For SAML. J. CABELL

JNO. ALFORD
JNO. BAILEY
PHILIP BAILEY
JNO. BALL
JOS. BALLENGER
STEWART BALLOW
JNO. BARNETT
WM. BARNETT
THOS. BARRETT
MICAJAH BECKNALL
THOS. BECKNALL
HENRY BELL
JNO. BETHEL
WM. BIBB
GEO. BLAINE
NOELL BLANKENSHIP
WM. BOWMAN
CHAS. BRIDGWATER
JONATHAN BRIDGWATER
JOHN BROCKMAN
JNO. BROWN
SHEROD BUGG
JOS. BURGER
CHAS. BURKS
DAVID BURKS
SAML. BURKS JR.
JOS. BURRUS
JNO. BUSH
JAS. CALLAWAY
BENJ. CAMDEN
JNO. CAMDEN SR. & JR.
WM. CAMDEN
AMBROSE CAMPBELL
GEO.CAMPBELL SR. & JR.
JOELL CAMPBELL
JNO. CAMPBELL (W)
JNO. CAMPBELL
LAURENCE CAMPBELL
EDWD. CARTER
PETER CARTER
WM. CARTER
BARTLETT CASH
JNO. CASH
STEPHEN CASH
WM. CHAPPELL
ALEX. CHISNELL
CHAS. CHRISTIAN
JNO. CHRISTIAN
RO. CHRISTIAN
TURNER CHRISTIAN
WALTER CHRISTIAN
DAVID CLARK JR.
NATHL. CLARK
ZACH. CLARK
JNO. CLARKSON
WM. COFFEE
JAS. CONNER
VALENTINE COX
JNO. CRAWFORD
NATHAN CRAWFORD
NELSON CRAWFORD
WM. S. CRAWFORD

JAS. CREWS
WM. CRISP
CORNL. CROSS
CHAS. DAVIS
DAVID DAVIS
ISHAM DAVIS
JABUS DAVIS
WM. DAVIS
JOS. DAWSON
ZACH. DAWSON
JAS. DILLARD
JOS. DILLARD
WM. DIXON
GEO. DOUGLASS
JNO. DUNCAN
CARROLL EADS
JAS. EDMONDS
SAML. EDMONDS
THOS. EDWARDS
JOSIAH ELLIS
DAVID ENIX
WM. FITZPATRICK
HENRY FRANKLIN
JAS. FRANKLIN
JAS. FRASER
GEO. GALASPIE
AMBROSE GATEWOOD
ISAAC GIBSON
ARCHELAUS GILLUM
DANL. GOODE
EDMD. GOODRICH
JNO. GREGORY
JNO. GRIFFIN
JOHN HALL
WM. HALL
EDWD. HARDEN
RO. HARDY
EDWD. HARPER
HENRY HARPER
JNO. HARRIS
WM. L. HARRIS JR.
JAS. HARRISON
JNO. HARRISON
RICH. HARRISON
HENRY HARTLESS
THOS. HAWKINS
CHAS. HAY
ALEX. HENDERSON
JNO. HENDERSON
JAS. HILL
CALEB HIGGINBOTHAM
JAS. HIGGINBOTHAM
JNO. HIGGINBOTHAM
JOS. HIGGINBOTHAM SR & JR
JOS. HIGGINBOTHAM
MOSES HIGGINBOTHAM
SAML. HIGGINBOTHAM
CLEVER HORRELL
JNO. HORSLEY
WM. HORSLEY
RUSH HUDSON
WM. HUGHES
JNO. HUTCHESON
CHAS. IRVING
JNO. JACOBS
WM. JOHNSTON
JOSIAH JOPLING
RALPH JOPLING
JESSE KENNEDY
WM. KILE

JNO. KNIGHT
SAML. LACKY
CHAS. LAINE
THOS. LAINE
WM. LAINE (W)
WM. LAVENDER
FRANCIS LEE
GEO. LEE
JNO. LEMASTER
BETHELL LIVELY
JOS. LIVELY
JAS. LONDON
LARKIN LONDON
GEO. LOVING
JNO. LOVING
THOS. LUCAS
PETER LYON
WM. LYON
NOTLEY MADDOX
JNO. MARR
GIDEON MARTIN
HENRY MARTIN
JAS. MARTIN
PETER MARTIN
SHEROD MARTIN
JAS. MATTHEWS
JNO. MATHEWS
JAS. MAYS
JNO. MAYS
JOS. MAYS
RO. MAYS
ALEX. McALEXANDER
JAS. McALEXANDER JR.
GEO. McDANIEL
JNO. McDANIEL
RODERICK McCULLOCH
JOS. MEGANN
WM. MEREDITH
JOS. MILSTEAD
JOS. MONTGOMERY
NICHL. MORAN
JOS. H. MORRISON
THOS. H. MORRISON JR.
JAS. MORTON
CORNL. MURRELL
JNO. MURROW
RICH. MURROW
BENNETT NALLEY
JAS. NEVIL
RICH. OGLESBY
WM. OGLESBY
BENJ. PANNELL
THOS. PARROCK
THOS. PATTON
JAS. PENDLETON
GEO. PENN
JAS. PENN
JNO. PENN
JOS. PENN
MOSES PENN
PHILIP PENN
RICH. PERKINS
DANL. PERROW
ZACHARIAS PHILLIS(sic)
JOELL PONTON
FRANCIS POWELL
WIATT POWELL
WALTER POWERS
DAVID PROFFITT
JNO. PUGH

THOS. PUGH
GEO. PURVIS
HENRY ROBERTS
JOS. ROBERTS
ARTHER ROBERTSON
BENJ. ROGERS
JNO. ROWSEY
AMBROSE RUCKER
ANTHONY RUCKER
ISAAC RUCKER
JNO. RUCKER
BENJ. SANDIDGE
JNO. SANDIDGE
PULLIAM SANDIDGE
EDWD. SAUNDERSON
JNO. SCOTT
WM. SCOTT
ABRAHAM SEAY
CLOUGH SHELTON
WM. SHELTON
WM. SMALL
ABRAHAM SMITH
JACOB SMITH
JNO. SMITH
JOS. SMITH
PHILIP SMITH
WM. SPENCER
JNO. SNYDER
JNO. STAPLES
CHAS. STEWART
BENEMI STONE
ELIJAH STONE
JNO. STRATTON
THOS. H. TALBERT
CHAS. TALIAFERRO
SMYTH TANDY
CHAS. TATE
JER. TAYLOR
WM. TEAS
JNO. THOMAS
JAMES THOMPSON
JNO. THOMPSON
GUTRIDGE THURMOND
DAVID TINSLEY
ISAAC TINSLEY
JOSHUA TINSLEY
AMBROSE TOMBLIN
DANL. TUCKER
DRURY TUCKER
THOS. TUCKER
HENRY TURNER
JAS. TURNER
STEPHEN TURNER
WM. TURNER
JACOB TYREE
NATHL. WADE
JOELL WALKER
RO. WALKER
WILLIAM WALTON
JNO. WARE
ABRAHAM WARWICK
JNO. WAST (sic)
JAS. WATERS
JNO. WATKINS
STEPHEN WATTS
JOS. WELCH
BRANSFORD WEST
FRANCIS WEST SR & JR
NICHL WEST
JNO. WIATT

THOS. WILCOX
JNO. WILLIAMSON
JOS. WILSHER
JONATHAN WILSON

JAS. WOOD
JNO. WOODROOF
ANDREW WRIGHT
BENJ. WRIGHT

ISAAC WRIGHT
JAS, WRIGHT
RO. WRIGHT
WM. WRIGHT JR.

My guess is that the poll of the above election was for Delegates to the General Assembly and this explains tha appearance of names of voters more than once. There was one more candidate for it seems that several CABELLS were pitted against each other. BFD.

Page 319. For
WILLIAM CABELL JR.

JNO. ALFORD
JNO. BAILEY
PHILIP BAILEY
JNO. BALL
STEWART BALLOW
WM. BARNETT
THOMAS BARRETT
MICAJAH & THOS. BECKNALL
JNO. BETHEL
EPHRAIM BLAINE
GEO. BLAINE
WM. BIBB
WM. BOWMAN
CHAS. BRIDGWATER
JNO. BROCKMAN
JNO. BROWN
JNO. BURFORD
JOS. BURGER
CHAS. BURKS
DAVID BURKS
SAML. BURKS JR.
JNO. BUSH
JNO. CAMBELL (W)(sic)
BENJ. CAMDEN
JNO. CAMDEN JR. & SR.
WM. CAMDEN
AMBROSE CAMPBELL
GEO. CAMPBELL JR. & SR.
JNO. CAMPBELL
EDWD. CARTER
WM. CARTER
BARTLETT CASH
JNO. CASH
STEPHEN CASH
BENJ. CHILDRESS
ALEX. CHISNALL
DAVID CLARK JR
NATHL. CLARK
ZACHARIAS CLARK
JNO. CLARKSON
WM. COFFEE
JNO. COLE
JAS. CONNER
WM. CRISP
CORNL. CROSS
DAVID DAVIS
JABES DAVIS
JAS. DILLARD
WM. DIXON
GEO. DOUGLASS
JNO. DUNCAN
CARROLL EADS
JAS. EDMONDS
SAML. EDMONDS
DAVID ENIX
WM. FITZPATRICK
JAS. FRASER

GEO. GALASPIE
ISAAC GIBSON
ARCHELAUS GILLUM
DANL. GOODE
JNO. GREGORY
JNO. GRIFFIN
JNO. HALL
WM. HALL
EDWD. HARDING
RO. HARDY
HENRY HARPER
JNO. HARRIS
MATT. HARRIS
HENRY HARTLESS
THOS. HAWKINS
CHAS. HAY
WM. HAYNES
ALEX. HENDERSON
JNO. HENDERSON
CALEB HIGGINBOTHAM
JAS. HIGGINBOTHAM
JOS. HIGGINBOTHAM JR
JOS. HIGGINBOTHAM SR.
MOSES HIGGINBOTHAM
NATHL. HILL
CLEVER HORRELL
JNO. HORSLEY
WM. HORSLEY
STEPHEN JOHNSTON
WM. JOHNSTON
JOSIAH JOPLING
RALPH JOPLING
PETER JOYNER
WM. KILE
SAML. LACKEY
CHAS. LAINE
THOS. LAINE
WM. LAINE (W)
JNO. LEMASTER
BETHEL LIVELY
JAS. LIVELY
JOS. LIVELY
GEO. LOVING
JNO. LOVING
WM. LOVING
PETER LYON
WM. LYON
GIDEON MARTIN
HENRY MARTIN
JAS. MARTIN
MOSES MARTIN
PETER MARTIN
PLEASANT MARTIN
SHEROD MARTIN
JAS. MATHEWS
JNO. MATHEWS
DANL. MAYO
JNO. MAYS
JOS. MAYS JR.
CORNL. MURRELL

JNO. MURROW
RICH. MURROW
ALEX. McALEXANDER
JAS. McALEXANDER JR.
JOS. MILSTEAD
NICHL. MORAN
JNO. MORRIS
JOS. H. MORRISON
THOS. MORRISON JR.
BENNETT NALLEY
JAS. NEVIL
BENJ. PANNELL
THOS. PATTERN
RICH. PERKINS
DANL. PERROW
ZACH. PHILLIPS
JOELL PONTON
FRANCIS POWELL
WALTER POWER
DAVID PROFFITT
THOS. PUGH
GEO. PURVIS
IGNATIOUS RAINS
HENRY ROBERTS
JOS. ROBERTS
ARTHER ROBERTSON
BENJ. ROGERS
HUGH ROSE
PATRICK ROSE
BENJAMIN SANDIDGE
ABRAHAM SEAY
CLOUGH SHELTON
HENRY SHELTON
JOS. SHELTON
WM. SHELTON
WM. SMALL
ABRAHAM SMITH
JOS. SMITH
JNO. SNYDER
JNO. STAPLES
CHARLES STEWART
ELIJAH STONE
JNO. SWANSON
CHAS. TATE
WM. TEAS
JAS. THOMPSON
JNO. THOMPSON
GUTRIDGE THURMOND
AMBROSE TOMBLIN
DANL. TUCKER
DRURY TUCKER
STEPHEN TURNER
WM. TURNER
NATHL. WADE
WM. WARE
WM. WALTON
JNO. WATKINS
EDWD. WATSON
ABRAHAM WARWICK
JOS. WELCH

478

JAS. WELLS	JNO. WILLIAMSON	BENJ. WRIGHT
BRANSFORD WEST	JNO. WITT	JAS. WRIGHT
FRANCIS WEST SR. & JR	JAS. WOOD	RO. WRIGHT
JNO. WEST	JAS. WOODS	WM. WRIGHT JR.
NICHL. WEST	ANDREW WRIGHT	

Page 601. A Poll for the Election of Delegates to Represent the County of Amherst in General Assembly taken at the Courthouse of the said County on Monday, April 4, 1791.

SAMUEL MEREDITH supporters:

WM. ABNEY	MICAJAH CLARK	JNO. GRIFFIN
WM. ALFORD	DAVID CLARKSON	THOS. GRIMES
WM. ALLCOCK	JNO. CLARKSON	THOMAS GRISTHAM
JNO. ALLEN	JESSE CLEMENTS	MOSES HALL
SAML. ANDERSON	WM. COFFEE	WM. HALL
JNO. BAILEY	JNO. COLE	ARCHEY HAMLET
PHILIP BAILEY	HAWS COLEMAN	STEPHEN HAM
JNO. BALL	SAML. COLEMAN	ROBT. HARDY
LEWIS BALL	THOS. COLEMAN	RICH. HARE
WM. BALL	VALENTINE COX	NATHL. HARLOW
JOS. BALLINGER	JNO. CRAWFORD	EDWD. HARPER
STEWART BALLOW	NATHAN CRAWFORD	HENRY HARPER
JOHNSON BANE	NELSON CRAWFORD	WM. HARPER
RICH. BANE	GIDEON CREWS	JNO. HARRIS
JNO. BARNETT	JAS. CREWS	LEE HARRIS
WM. BARNETT	JOS. CREWS JR. & SR.	WM. HARRIS (2)
MICAJAH BECKNALL	WM. DAMERON	WM. L. HARRIS
HENRY BELL	PETER DAVIE	JAS. HARRISON
MARTIN BIBB	CHAS. DAVIS	REUBIN HARRISON
EPHRAIM BLAINE	GEO. DAVIS	RICH. HARRISON
GEO. BLAINE	PHILIP DAVIS	HENRY HARTLESS
NOELL BLANKENSHIP	WM. DAVIS	JNO. M. HATTER
POWHATAN BOWLING	JNO. & JOS. DAWSON	THOS. HAWKINS
WM. BONES	MARTIN DAWSON	WM. HENDERSON
DRURY BOWMAN	RO. D. DAWSON	JAS. HENSON
JNO. BRADEN	ZACH. DAWSON	CALEB HIGGINBOTHAM
JONATHAN BRIDGWATER	ELISHA DENNIS	CHAS. HIGGINBOTHAM
JAS. BROWN	DANL. DENNY	JAS. HIGGINBOTHAM
SHEROD BUGG	JNO. DIGGES	JOS. HIGGINBOTHAM & JR
JNO. BURFORD	JAS. DILLARD	SAML. HIGGINBOTHAM
JOS. BURGEE	JNO. DILLARD	JAS. HILL
EDWD. BURNETT	WM. DIXON	NATHL. HILL
WM. BURNETT	JNO. DODD	SAML. HILL
PHILIP BURTON	JOSIAH DODD	JNO. HOGG
CHAS. BURRUS	SAML. EDMONDS	WM. HOLLANDSWORTH
JOS. BURRUS	THOS. EDWARDS	CLEVER HORRELL
JNO. BUSH	JOSIAH ELLIS	WM. HOWARD
JAS. CALLAWAY	AMBROSE EUBANK	SAML. HUCKSTEP
GEO. CAMPBELL	JNO. EUBANK	JOSHUA HUDSON
FRANCIS CAMPBELL	JNO. FARRAR	RUSH HUDSON
JOEL CAMPBELL	RICH. FARRAR	MOSES HUGES
JNO. CAMPBELL	THOS. FITZPATRICK	WM. HUGHES
LAWRENCE CAMPBELL	WM. FORBUSH	JNO. HUTCHERSON
WM. CAMPBELL	JNO. FORTUNE	JNO. INNIS
BENJ. CARPENTER	THOS. FORTUNE	JNO. JACOBS
THOS. CARPENTER	HENRY FRANKLIN	JNO. JOHNSON
ABRAM CARTER	JAS. FRANKLIN	PHILIP JOHNSON
EDWD. CARTER	THOS. GARLAND	THOS. JOHNSON
JESSE CARTER	AMBROSE GATEWOOD	THOS. JONES
WM. CARTER (2)	JACOB GIBSON	JOSIAH JOPLING
BARTLETT CASH	DANL. GOODE	PETER JOYNER
JNO. CASH	EDMD. GOODRICH	JESSE KENNEDY
STEPHEN CASH	JAS. GOODWIN	JNO. KESTERSON
RICH. CHANDLER	JNO. H. GOODWIN	JNO. KNIGHT
BENJ. CHILDRESS	MICAJAH GOODWIN	WM. KNIGHT
CHAS. CHRISTIAN	THOS. GOODWIN	JNO. LACKEY
JNO. CHRISTIAN SR & JR	HENRY GOSNEY	SAML. LACKEY
WALTER CHRISTIAN	RO. GRANT	WM. LAINE (wag)

JAS. LANDRUM
YOUNG LANDRUM
WM. LAVENDER
JAS. LEE
WM. LITTRELL
JAS. LIVELY
JOS. LIVELY
JNO. LOCKARD
PHILIP LOCKARD
JAS. LONDON
WM. LOVING
JNO. LYNCH
PETER LYON
WM. LYON
NOTLEY MADDOX
NATHL. MANTIPLY
JNO. MARR
GIDEON MARTIN
HENRY MARTIN
HUDSON MARTIN
JAS. MARTIN
MOSES MARTIN
PETER MARTIN
PLEASANT MARTIN
SHEROD MARTIN
WM. MAYO
JAS. MAYS (2)
JNO. MAYS
JOS. MAYS
RO. MAYS
GEO. McDANIEL
JNO. McDANIEL
ARCHIBALD McDONALD
HENRY McLANE
JOS. MEGANN
DANL. MEHONE
WM. MEREDITH
JNO. MERRET
SAML. MIGGINSON
BENJ. MILES
JOS. MILSTEAD
JNO. MITCHELL
JOSEPH MONTGOMERY
MORDECAI MOON
WM. MOON
THOS. MORRIS
JAS. MORTON
DANL. MOSBY
JNO. MOSBY
NICHL. MOURNING
JAS. MURPHY
BENNETT NALLEY
THOS. NASH
JAS. NEVIL
LEWIS NEVIL
JOS. NUKOLS
RICH. OGLESBY
BARNETT OWEN
JAS. OWEN
ABNER PADGETT
BEVERLY PADGETT
JAS. PAMPLIN
BENJAMIN PANNELL
JAS. PENDLETON
REUBEN PENDLETON
RICH. PENDLETON
GEO. PENN
JNO. PENN
JOS. PENN
MOSES PENN
WM. PENN

RICH. PERKINS
DANL. PERROW
WM. PETER
GEO. PHILIPS
JNO. PHILIPS
THOS. PHILIPS
WM. PHILIPS
RAWLEY PINN
JOEL PONTON
LUCAS POWELL
RICH. POWELL
THOS. POWELL
WIATT POWELL
NICHL. PRYOR
JACOB PUCKETT
JNO. PUGH
THOS. PUGH
GEO. PURVIS
CALEB RALLS
SAML. REID
CHAS. REYNOLDS
JNO. RICHESON
MATT. RICKETTS
THOS. RICKETTS
PETER RIPPETTO
ASHCRAFT ROACH
JNO. ROBERTS
JOS. ROBERTS
ZACH. ROBERTS
STEPHEN ROBERTSON
BENJ. ROGERS
HUGH ROSE
JNO. ROSE
PATRICK ROSE
NEHEMIAH ROSELL
AMBROSE RUCKER
ANTHONY RUCKER
BENJ. RUCKER
ISAAC RUCKER (2)
ISAAC RUCKER, JR.
JNO. RUCKER
MOSES RUCKER
THOS. RUCKER
CORNL. SALE
JOHN SALE
EDWD. SAUNDERSON
ABRAHAM SEAY
THOS. SHANNON
HENRY SHELTON
JOS. SHELTON
RICH. SHELTON
AUGUSTINE SHEPHERD
JNO. SHIELDS
JAS. SIMMONS
JNO. SLEDD
WM. SMALL
AUGUSTIN SMITH
AUSTIN SMITH
HENRY SMITH
JACOB SMITH
JNO. SMITH (2)
JOS. SMITH
PHILIP SMITH JR.
SAML. SPENCER
THOS. SPENCER
WM. SPENCER
JOHN STAPLES
WM. STINNETT
BENAMI STONE
ELIJAH STONE
JNO. STRATTON

JNO. SWANSON
THOS. TALBERT
CHAS. TALIAFERRO
ZACH. TALIAFERRO
CHAS. TATE
JER. TAYLOR
WM. TEAS
CORNL. THOMAS
NORBON THOMAS
JAS. THOMPSON
JNO. THOMPSON
REUBEN THORNTON
JNO. THURMOND
PHILIP THURMOND
JAS. TILFORD
JOS. TILFORD
DAVID TINSLEY
ISAAC TINSLEY
JNO. TINSLEY
HENRY TRENT
CHAS. TUCKER
HENRY THRNER
JNO. TURNER
TERISHA TURNER
WM. TURNER
JACOB TYREE
NATHL. WADE
JOEL WALKER
RO. WALKER
TILMAN WALTON
WM. WALTON
EDWD. WARE
JAS. WARE
JNO. WARE
WM. WARE
ABRAHAM WARWICK
JAS. WATERS
JNO. WATKINS
EDWARD WATSON
CHAS. WATTS
STEPHEN WATTS
THOS. WAUGH
THOS. WILCOX
JOSHUA WILLOUGHBY
JAS. WILLS
JONATHAN WILLSON
JOS. WILTSHIRE
NATHAN WINGFIELD
DAVID WITT
GEO. WITT
JNO. WITT
LITTLEBERRY WITT
WM. WITT
FRANCIS WOOD
DAVID WOODROOF
JNO. WOODROOF
JAS. WOODS
ANDREW WRIGHT
BENJ. WRIGHT
ISAAC WRIGHT
RO. WRIGHT
WM. WRIGHT
JAS. YELTON

480

Pages 604-607
For SAML. J. CABELL

WM. ABNEY
WM. ALCOCK
JNO. ALFORD
WM. ALFORD
JNO. ALLEN
SAML. ANDERSON
JNO. BAILEY
PHILIP BAILEY
JNO. BALL
LEWIS BALL
WM. BALL
JOS. BALLINGER
STEWART BALLOW
JOHNSON BANE
RICH. BANE
JNO. BARNETT
WM. BARNETT
MICAJAH BECKNAL
JOS. BENGEE
MARTIN BIBB
WM. BIBB
JOHN BIGGS
EPHRAIM BLAIN
GEO. BLAIN
ALLEN BLAIR
WM. BONES
DRURY BOWMAN
WM. BOWMAN
JNO. BRADEN
JONATHAN BRIDGWATER
JAS. BROWN
SHAROD BUGG
JNO. BURFORD
CHAS. BURKS
DAVID BURKS
JNO. BURKS
EDWD. BURNET
WM. BURNET
CHAS. BURRUS
JOS. BURRUS
PHILIP BURTON
JNO. BUSH
NICHL. CABELL
JAS. CALLAWAY
BENJ. CAMDEN
JABEZ CAMDEN
JNO. CAMDEN (2)
WM. CAMDEN
AMBROSE CAMPBELL
FRANCIS CAMPBELL
GEO. CAMPBELL
JOELL CAMPBELL
JNO. CAMPBELL (2)
LAURENCE CAMPBELL
ABRAM CARTER
EDWD CARTER
LANDON CARTER
WM. CARTER (2)
BARTLETT CASH
JNO. CASH
STEPHEN CASH
CHAS. CHRISTIAN
JNO. CHRISTIAN
BENJ. CHILDRESS
ALEX. CHISNELL
DAVID CLARKSON
JNO. CLARKSON
EDMUND COFFEE

WM. COFFEE
JNO. COLE
HAWS COLEMAN
JAS. CONNER
VALENTINE COX
JNO. CRAWFORD
NATHAN CRAWFORD
NELSON CRAWFORD
GIDEON CREWS
JAS. CREWS
JOS. CREWS SR & JR
WM. CRISP
WM. DAMERON
CHAS. DAVIS
GEO. DAVIS
PHILIP DAVIS
WM. DAVIS
JNO. DAWSON (2)
PLEASANT DAWSON
RO. D. DAWSON
ZACH. DAWSON
ELISHA DENNIS
DANL. DENNY
JAS. DILLARD
JAS. DILLARD (T)
JNO. DILLARD
WM. DIXON
JOSIAS DODD
GEO. DOUGLAS
JNO. DUNCAN
DANL. DUNNAKIN
RO. DINWIDDIE
CARRELL EADS
SAMUEL EDMOND
JAS. EDMONDS
THOS. EDWARDS
JOSIAH ELLIS
DAVID ENIX
AMBROSE EUBANK
JNO. EUBANK
THOS. EWERS
RICH. FARRAR
THOS. FITZPATRICK
WM. FITZPATRICK
WM. FORBUSH
JNO. FORTUNE
THOS. FORTUNE
HENRY FRANKLIN
JAS. FRANKLIN
GEO. GALISPIE
THOS. GARLAND
AMBROSE GATEWOOD
JACOB GIBSON
JNO. GILLIAM
DANL. GOODE
EDMD. GOODRICH
JAS. GOODWIN
MICAJAH GOODWIN
THOMAS GOODWIN
HENRY GOSNEY
RO. GRANT
JNO. GRIFFIN
THOS. GRYMES
MOSES HALL
WM. HALL
STEPHEN HAM
ARCHY HAMLET
RO. HARDY
RICH. HARE
NATHL. HARLOW
EDWD. HARPER

HENRY HARPER
WM. HARPER
JNO. HARRIS
WM. HARRIS
WM. L. HARRIS
JAS. HARRISON
REUBIN HARRISON
RICH. HARRISON
HENRY HARTLESS
JNO. M. HATTER
THOMAS HAWKINS
STEPHEN HENDERSON
WM. HENDERSON
LEONARD HENLEY
GEO. HIGHT
AARON HIGGINBOTHAM
CALEB HIGGINBOTHAM
CAHS. HIGGINBOTHAM
JAS. HIGGINBOTHAM
JOS. HIGGINBOTHAM SR.
JOS. HIGGINBOTHAM JR.
SAML. HIGGINBOTHAM
NATHL. HILL
SAML. HILL
JNO. HOGG
WM. HOLLANDSWORTH
CLEVER HORREL
JNO. HORSLEY
WM. HORSLEY
WM. HOWARD
JOSHUA HUDSON
MOSES HUGHES
WM. HUGHES
JNO. HUTCHERSON
JNO. INNIS
JNO. JACOBS
THOS. JOHNS
THOS. JOHNSON
WM. JOHNSON
THOS. JONES
JOSIAH JOPLING
JESSE KENNEDY
JNO. KESTERSON
JNO. KNIGHT
WM. KNIGHT
SAML. LACKEY
CHAS. LAINE
WM. LAINE (Wag.)
JAMES LANDRUM
YOUNG LANDRUM
THOS. LANE
WM. LANE (Watm)
WM. LITTRELL
BETHEL LIVELY
JAS. LIVELY
JOS. LIVELY
JNO. LOCKARD
PHILIP LOCKARD
JAS. LONDON
GEO. LOVING
JNO. LOVING
WM. LOVING
JNO. LYNCH
PETER LYON
WM. LYON
NOTLEY MADDOX
NATHL. MANTIPLY
JNO. MARR
BENJ. MARTIN
GIDEON MARTIN
HENRY MARTIN

JAS. MARTIN
PETER MARTIN
PLEASANT MARTIN
SHEROD MARTIN
JAS. MASTERS
JNO. MASTERS
JNO. MATTHEWS (2)
WM. MAYO
JAS. MAYS (2)
JNO. MAYS
JOS. MAYS
RO. MAYS
ALEX. McALEXANDER
JAS. McALEXANDER
JNO. McALEXANDER
GEO. McDANIEL
JNO. McDANIEL
ARCHIBALD McDONALD
HENRY McLANE
JOSEPH MEGANN
SAML. MIGGINSON
BENJ. MILES
JOS. MILSTEAD
JOS. MONTGOMERY
THOS. MORRIS
THOS. MORRISON
DANL. MOSBY *
(see end of list)
JNO. MOSLEY
NICHL. MOURNING
JAMES MURPHY
RICH. MURRAH
BENNETT NALLEY
THOS. NASH
JAS. NEVIL
JOS. NICHOLS
RICH. OGLESBY
JAMES PAMPLIN
BENJ. PANNEL
THOMAS PATTON
JAS. PENDLETON
JOS. PENN
MOSES PENN
RICH. PERKINS
DANL. PERROW
WM. PETER
GEO. PHILLIPS
THOS. PHILLIPS
WM. PHILLIPS
ZACH. PHILLIPS
RAWLEY PINN
JOEL PONTON
LUCAS POWELL
RICH. POWELL
THOS. POWELL
WIATT POWELL
DAVID PROFFIT
NICHL. PRYOR
JACOB PUCKET
JNO. PUGH
THOS. PUGH
GEO. PURVIS
CALEB RALLS
CHAS. REYNOLDS
JNO. RICHESON
JOS. ROBERTS
JNO. ROBERTS
ZACH. ROBERTS
ARTHUR ROBERTSON
RO. ROBERTSON
BENJ. ROGERS

AMBROSE RUCKER
ANTHONY RUCKER
ISAAC RUCKER SR & JR
JNO. RUCKER
MOSES RUCKER
CORNL. SALE
JNO. SALE
LARKIN SANDIDGE
WM. SANDIDGE
EDWD. SAUNDERSON
ABRAHAM SEAY
THOS. SHANNON
JOS. SHELTON
RICH. SHELTON
AUGUSTIN SHERHERD
JNO. SHIELDS
SAML. SHROSHIRE
JNO. SLED
WM. SMALL
AUGUSTINE SMITH
AUSTIN SMITH
HENRY SMITH
JACOB SMITH
JNO. SMITH (2)
JOS. SMITH (2)
PHILIP SMITH SR & JR
JNO. SNIDER
SAML. SPENCER
THOS. SPENCER
WM. SPENCER
JNO. STAPLES
WM. STINNETT
BENAMI STONE
ELIJAH STONE
GEO. STONEHAM
CHAS. TATE
WM. TEAS
JESSE THOMAS
NORBON THOMAS
JAS. THOMPSON
JNO. THOMPSON (2)
JNO. THURMOND
JAS. TILFORD
JOS. TILFORD
DAVID, TINSLEY
ISAAC TINSLEY
JAS. TINSLEY
JNO. TINSLEY
JOSHUA TINSLEY
WM. TINSLEY
AMBROSE TOMLINSON
HENRY TRENT
DANL. TUCKER
HENRY TURNER
JNO. TURNER
TERISHA TURNER
WM. TURNER
CHAS. TYLER
NATHL. WADE
JOEL WALKER
TILMON WALTON
WM. WALTON
JAS. WARE
JNO. WARE
WM. WARE
ABRAHAM WARWICK
JAS. WATERS
JNO. WATKINS
EDWD. WATSON
CHAS. WATTS
STEPHEN WATTS

THOS. WAUGH
JOS. WELSH
BLANSFORD WEST
FRANCIS WEST
JNO. WEST
NICHL. WEST
BURCHER WHITEHEAD
THOS. WILCOX
JOSHUA WILLOUGHBY
JAS. WILLS (WELLS?)
JONATHAN WILSON
JOS. WILTSHIRE
NATHAN WINKFIELD
DAVID WITT
GEO. WITT
LITTLEBERRY WITT
WM. WITT
JAS. WOODS (2)
ANDREW WRIGHT
BENJ. WRIGHT
ISAAC WRIGHT
JAS. WRIGHT
KILLIS WRIGHT
ROBT. WRIGHT
WM. WRIGHT

Page 609.
For DAVID WOODROOF

JNO. MITCHELL

For JNO. WIATT

REUBEN PENDLETON
CHAS. TALIAFERRO

For HUGH ROSE

POWHATAN BOLLING

For JOS. BURUS

JER. TAYLOR

For POWHATAN BOLLING

HENRY BELL
NOEL BLANKENSHIP
RICH. CHANDLER
WALTER CHRISTIAN
MICAJAH CLARK
JESSE CLEMENTS
SAML. COLEMAN
THOS. COLEMAN
JOS. DAWSON
MARTIN DAWSON
GEO. DOUGLASS
JNO. H. GOODWIN
THOS. GRISTHAM
SAML. HUCKSTEP
PHILIP JOHNSON
JAS. LEE
DANL. MEHONE
JNO. MERRITT
MORDICAI MOON
WM. MOON
JAS. MORTON
BARNET OWEN
JAS. OWEN
ABNER PADGETT
BEVERLY PADGETT

RICH. PENDLETON
WM. PENN
MATT. RICKETTS
THOS. RICKETTS
STEPHEN ROBERTSON
NEHEMIAH ROSIL
BENJ. RUCKER
ISAAC RUCKER
JAS. SIMMONS
CORNL. THOMAS
PHILIP THURMOND
DANL. TUCKER
RO. WALKER
FRANCIES WOOD
JNO. WOODROOF

For WM. CABELL JR

JABEZ CAMDEN
JNO. CAMDEN
BENJ. CARPENTER
WM. LAVENDER
JNO. LOVING
LEWIS NEVIL
GEO. PENN
JNO. PENN
RO. ROBERTSON
PATRICK ROSE
HENRY SHELTON
REUBIN THORNTON
DAVID WOODROOF
JAS. YELTON

For WM. CABELL

JNO. ALFORD
WM. BIBB
JNO. BIGGES
ALLEN BLAIR
WM. BOWMAN
CHAS. BURKS
DAVID BURKS
JNO. BURKS
NICHL. CABELL
BENJ. CAMDEN
JNO. CAMDEN
WM. CAMDEN
AMBROSE CAMPBELL
JNO. CAMPBELL
WM. CAMPBELL
THOS. CARPENTER

JESSE CARTER
ALEX. CHISNELL
JNO. CHRISTIAN
EDMD. COFFEE
JAS. CONNER
WM. CRISP
PETER DAVIE
JNO. DAWSON
PLEASANT DAWSON
JNO. DIGGES
JAS. DILLARD (T)
RO. DINWIDDIE
JNO. DODD
JNO. DUNCAN
DANL. DUNNAKIN
CARROL EADS
JAS. EDMOMDS
DAVID ENOX
THOS. EWERS
JNO. FARRAR
WM. FITZPATRICK
GEO. GALISPIE
JNO. GILLIAM
LEE HARRIS
WM. HARRIS
STEPHEN HENDERSON
LEONARD HENLEY
JAS. HENSON
AARON HIGGINBOTHAM
GEO. HIGHT
JAS. HILL
JNO. HORSLEY
WM. HORSLEY
RUSH HUDSON
JNO. JOHNSON
WM. JOHNSON
PETER JOINER
THOS. JONES
JNO. LACKEY
WM. LAINE(Watm)
THOS. LANE
CHAS. LAYNE
BETHEL LIVELY
GEO. LOVING
BENJ. MARTIN
HUDSON MARTIN
MOSES MARTIN
JAS. MASTERS
JNO. MASTERS
JNO. MATTHEWS (2)
ALEX. McALEXANDER

JAS. McALEXANDER
JNO. McALEXANDER
WM. MEREDITH
THOS. MORRISON
RICHD. MURRAH
THOS. PATTON
JNO. PHILLIPS
ZACH. PHILLIPS
DAVID PROFFITT
SAML. REID
PETER RIPPETTO
ASHCRAFT ROACH
ARTHUR ROBERTSON
HUGH ROSE
JNO. ROSE
LARKIN SANDIDGE
WM. SANDIDGE
SIMEON SHROPSHIRE
JOS. SMITH
PHILIP SMITH
JNO. SNIDER
GEO. STONEHAM
JNO. STRATTON
JNO. SWANSON
THOS. TALBERT
ZACH. TALIAFERRO
JESSE TALIAFERRO
JESSE THOMAS
JNO. THOMPSON
JAS. TINSLEY
JOSHUA TINSLEY
WM. TINSLEY
AMBROSE TOMLINSON
CHAS. TUCKER
CHAS. TYLER
JACOB TYREE
EDWD. WARE
JOS. WELSH
BLANSFORD WEST
FRANCES WEST
JNO. WEST
NICHL. WEST
BURCHER WHITEHEAD
JNO. WITT
JAS. WOODS
JAS. WRIGHT
KILLIS WRIGHT

The researcher will note that a great many new names appear on the last poll lists. This is due to young men who attained voting age or new families slowly making their ways to the western country. It is interesting to comtemplate the enormous changes in leadership over the years. In these long ago days the CABELL family was quite prominent. Others taking places of prominence were the CRAWFORD, ROSE, LOVING, PENN, MEREDITH, KEY & WILCOX families. These are but a few of the leaders. In the next century we find that the TALIAFERRO, THOMPSON, GARLAND, WHITEHEAD, SANDIDGE and other clans were county leaders. Some of the earliest families have completely disappeared from the rolls of Amherst. Others, such as the LOVING family, are to be found in Nelson County in the foreground. This summary is not to be taken as an exhaustive list for any student of Amherst history can easily supply additional names to the list just made. Two of the biggest operators in land in the next century were DAVID S. GARLAND and JNO. THOMPSON JR. GARLAND was known as "King David" because of his many land holdings. His home still stands in Clifford and is a thing of beauty. It is owned by the BABCOCK family.

* A note on the MOSBY surname found in the list of supporters for SAML.
J. CABELL, Deed Book F, pp 604-607: The "Grey Ghost" of the Confederacy
was born in Nelson County - daughter of Amherst - and was descended from
these early Amherst folk of the same name. The "Ghost" had sons who
attended Kenmore University High School which was just a short distance
out of the village of Amherst. The building still stands and is the
property of a descendant of the STRODE family which ran the school.
This owner is Chairman of Dunn and Bradstreet and he has kept the place
in excellent condition. I have copied the original register of the
school which ran from 1870 to 1900. In it are names of students who
came from all over the country and the two MOSBY boys are listed. One
interesting feature of the register is the data showing birthdays of
many students. The names of parents or guardians also appear along with
their addresses. It is a very interesting volume. One of the descendants of one of these MOSBY boys at Kenmore married MARCIA BOWMAN who is
the daughter of Rev. J.J. & FRANCES DUNN BOWMAN of Lynchburg. JOE J.
BOWMAN and wife are fellow Kentuckians and he is pastor of College Hill
Baptist Church. Marcia is also a native of Kentucky and her husband is
at present in the U.S. Army in Alaska. BFD. 1963.

Deed Book G, pages 257-262. A pole (sic) kept for AC for the election
of an additional member to Congress for the District of
Albemarle, Amherst, Fluvanna, and Goochland on Monday, the 18th of March,
1793.

SAML. J. CABELL - candidate and supporters:

WM. ABNEY	DAVID BURKS	DAVID CLARKSON
RICH. ALLCOCK	JNO.(JOS?) H. BURTON	JESSE CLEMONDS
WM. ALLCOCK	or BUNTON	EDMOND COFFEE
JNO. ALFORD	LARKIN BYAS	OSBORN COFFEE
WM. ALFORD	HECTOR CABELL	WM. COFFEE
JNO. ALLEN	NICHL. CABELL	BENJ. COLEMAN
THOS. APLIN	WM. CABELL	JESSE COLEMAN
SAML. ARRINGTON	WM. CABELL JR.	SAML. COLEMAN
JNO. BAILEY	BENJ. CAMDEN	THOS. COLEMAN
SAML. BAILEY	JABUS CAMDEN	JAS. CONNER
STEWART BALEW	JNO. CAMDEN	VOLENTINE COX
JNO. BALL	AMBROSE CAMPBELL	DAVID CRAWFORD
WM. BALL	EDWD. CAMPBELL	JNO. CRAWFORD
ARCHELAUS BALLINGER	FRANCIS CAMPBELL	NELSON CRAWFORD
JOS. BALLINGER	GEO. CAMPBELL	WM. CRISP
JNO. BARNETT	JOEL CAMPBELL	WM. DAMRON
WM. BARNETT	JNO. CAMPBELL	CHAS. DAVIS
JNO. BEAN	LAURENCE CAMPBELL	DAVID DAVIS
JOHNSON BEAN	DUNCAN CAMRON (2)	GEO. DAVIS
MICHJAR BECKNA(sic)	BENJ. CARPENTER	ISHAM DAVIS
HENRY BELL	ABRAHAM CARTER	JABUS DAVIS
SAML. BELL	EDWD CARTER (2)	NICHL. DAVIS (DAVIES)
JNO. BERGER	JESSE CARTER	PHILIP DAVIS
JNO. BETHEL	WM. CARTER (2)	WM. DAVIS (2)
THOS. BIBB	BARTLETT CASH	JNO. DAWSON
WM. BIBB	JAS. CASH	JOS. DAWSON
PETER BIBEE	JNO. CASH	MARTIN DAWSON
GEO. BLAINE	PETER CASH	PLEASANT DAWSON
JNO. BOLING	STEPHEN CASH	ELIJAH DENNIS
WM. BONES	WM. CHAMBERLAIN	JNO. DIGGS
WM. BOWMAN	BENJ. CHILDRESS	WM. DIGGS
JNO. BRADER	ESEX. CHISNEL	JAS. DILLARD (2)
JONATHAN BRIDGWATER	CHAS. CHRISTIAN	JNO. DILLARD
JNO. BOEKINAM(?)	HENRY CHRISTIAN	WM. DILLARD
JAS. BROWN (2)	JAS. CHRISTIAN	RO. DINWIDDY
JNO. BROWN (4)	JNO. CHRISTIAN (2)	JNO. DODD
JNO BURFORD	WALLER CHRISTIAN	JOS. DODD
JNO. BURGER	WM. CLARK	JOSIAH DODD

DANL. DUNAKIN
THOS. EADES
JAS. EDWARDS
THOS. EDWARDS
SAML. EDMONDS
WM. EDMONDS
JNO. ELLIS
LUKE EMBLEY
JAS. ENNIX
JNO. EUBANKS
JNO. FARRAR (2)
RICH. FARRAR
THOS. FARRAR
THOS. FITZPATRICK
WM. FITZPATRICK
EDWD. FORTUNE
JNO. FORTUNE
THOS. FORTUNE
ZACH. FORTUNE
SAML. FOX
GEO. GILLESPIE
DANL. GOODE
EDMOND GOODRICH
JAS. GOODRICH
JNO. GOODRICH
THOS. GOODRICH
MICAJOR GOODWIN
THOS. GOODWIN
RO. GRANT
JNO. GREGORY
JNO. GRIFFIN
THOS. GRIFFIN
MOSES HALL
WM. HALL
ARCHER HAMBELTON
EDWD. HARDEIN
ROBIN HARDY
JOS. HARKIS(?)
WM. HARKLESS
EDWD. HARPER
HENRY HARPER
CLEVER HARRILL
JNO. HARRIS(2)
MATT HARRIS
WM. HARRIS
JAS. HARRISON
RICH. HARRISON
KIAH HARTGROVE
HENRY HARTLESS
JNO. M. HATTER
WM. HAYNES
NATHL. HENDERSON
STEPHEN HENDERSON
JOS. HENSON
LEONARD HENLEY
AARON HIGGINBOTHAM
CHAS. HIGGINBOTHAM
JAS. HIGGINBOTHAM(2)
WM. HIGGINBOTHAM
GEO. HIGHT
JAS. HILL
NATHL. HILL
WM. HOLLANDSWORTH
JNO. HOLLODAY
JNO. HORSLEY
JESSE HOUCHINS
MOSES HOUCHINS
WM. HOWARD
JOSHUA HUDSON
RUSH HUDSON

JNO. HUGHES
MOSES HUGHES
WM. HUGHES
JNO. JACOBS
JNO. JOBLIN
JOSIAH JOBLIN
RALPH JOBLIN
THOS. JOBLIN
ELLICK JOHNS
THOS. JOHNS
PHILLIP JOHNSON
STEPEHN JOHNSON
TANDY JOHNSON
WM. JOHNSON (2)
PETER JOINE(JOINER?)
CHAS. JONES
THOS. JONES
JNO. JORDAN
WM. KEY
JNO. KESTERSON
JNO. KNIGHT
CHAS. LAIN
THOS. LAIN
WM. LAINE
JNO. LANDERS
JAS. LANDRUM
YOUNG LANDRUM
RICH. LEE
JNO. LEMASTER
JNO. F.P. LEWIS
JNO. LITTRELL
BETHEL LIVELY
JAS. LIVELY
JNO. LOBBARD
GEO. LOVING
JNO. LOVING (2)
JNO. LOVING JR.
WM. LYON
NOTLEY MADDOX
JNO. MAN(?)
NATHL. MANTIPLY
ALEX. MARR(?)
JNO. MASSEY
BENJ. MARTIN
GEO. MARTIN
HENRY MARTIN
HUDSON MARTIN
JAS. MARTIN
JNO. MARTIN
PETER MARTIN
PLEASANT MARTIN
WM. MARTIN (2)
JNO. MATTHEWS
ELIJAH MAYS
JAS. MAYS
JOS. MAYS (2)
JOS. MAYS JR.
RO. MAYS
ALEX. McALEXANDER
JAS. McALEXANDER
HUGH McCABE
JNO. McCABE
TEODORICK McCULLOCH
ARCHABEL McDANNOLD
DANL. McDONALD
HENRY McLAINE
SAML. MEREDITH
BENJ. MILES
JOS. MILSTEAD
ARCHELAUS MITCHELL

JOS. MONTGOMERY
WM. MOON
THOS. MOORE
THOS. MOPPIN
NICHL. MORAN
WM. MORE
JNO. MORENING(?)
THOS. MORRIS
THOS. MORRISON
WM. MOSEBEY
JNO. MOSELY
JAS. MURPHY
RICH. MURROW
BENNETT ANLLEY
RICH. OGLESBY
JNO. PEDGET
JAS. PAMPLIN
DANL. PERROW
THOS. PATTON
JAS. PENDLETON
RICH. PENDLETON
RICH. PERKINS
ELIJAH PETERS
HENRY PEYTON
DAVID PHILLIPS
THOS. PHILLIPS
WM. PHILLIPS
BENJAMIN PLUNKET
JOEL PONTON
LUCAS POWELL
THOS. POWELL
DAVID PROFIT
NICHL. PRYOR
WM. PRYOR
JACOB PUCKET
JNO. PUGH
THOS. PUGH
GEO. PURVIS (2)
WM. PURVIS
JAS. RAMSEY
HENRY REID
SAML. REID
JNO. RICHESON
RO. RIEVES
RO. RIGHT (2)
PETER RIPPETOE
ELLEXENDER ROBERTS
HENRY ROBERTS
JNO. ROBERTS (2)
JOS. ROBERTS
ZACH. ROBERTS
ARTHUR ROBERTSON
BENJ. ROGERS
ANTHONY RUCKER
JNO. RUCKER
MOSES RUCKER
JNO. SALES
LARKIN SANDIDGE
WM. SANDIDGE
ABRAM SEAY
JNO. SKELTON(SKELLON)
HENRY SHELTON (2)
JOS. SHELTON
JAS. SHIELDS
JNO. SHIELDS
WM. SMALL
ABRAHAM SMITH
AUGUSTINE SMITH
AUSTIN SMITH
HENRY SMITH

JACOB SMITH
JNO. SMITH (2)
JOS. SMITH
PHILLIP SMITH
JNO. SNEED
JNO. SNYDER
SAML. SPENCER
WM. SPENCER
JNO. STAPLES
JAS. STEVENS
JNO. STINNETT
GEO. STONEHAM
HENRY STONEHAM
JAS. STRICKLAN
CHAS. TATE
WM. TEAS
EDMOND THOMAS
JNO. THOMAS (2) -
(439 by name)
NORBORN THOMAS
JAS. THOMPSON
JNO. THOMPSON (3)
PHILIP THURMOND
WM. THURMOND
JAS. TILFORD
JOS. TILFORD
JAS. TINSLEY
JOSHUA TINSLEY
AMBROSE TOMLIN
CHAS. TUCKER
DANL. TUCKER
THOS. TUCKER
HANRY TURNER
JNO. TURNER
STEPHEN TURNER
TERISHA TURNER
WM. TURNER
JNO. TYLER
CHAS. TYLOR
DANL. TYLOR
NATHL. WADE
THOS. L.L.WALL
TILMAN WALTON
WM. WALTON
RO. WARE
JAS. WATERS
JNO. WATKINS
EDWD. WATSON
CALEB WATTS
CHAS. WATTS
STEPHEN WATTS
THOS. WAUGH
BRANSFORD WEST
FRANCIS WEST
JNO. WEST
NICHL. WEST
JOSEPH WEVER
GEO. WILL (2)
LEWIS WILLIAMS
BEVERLY WILLIAMSON
JOSHUA WILLOBY
JAS. WILLS

JONATHAN WINKFIELD
DAVID WITT
DENNET WITT
ELISHA WITT
JNO. WITT
LITTLEBERRY WITT
WM. WITT (2)
HENRY WOOD
JAS. WOOD
JOSIAH WOOD
SAML. WOOD
WM. WOOD (2)
AKILLES WRIGHT
ANDREW WRIGHT
ISAAC WRIGHT
JAS. WRIGHT (2)
JESSE WRIGHT
JNO. WRIGHT
MENOS WRIGHT
MOSES WRIGHT
WM. WRIGHT

ELIAS LANGHAM rec'd
1 vote-BENJ. JOHNSON

ROBT. JOUETT supporters:

WM. CAMDEN
WM. GILES
THOS. GRIMES
CHESLEY KINNEY
MOSES MARTIN
WM. MORAN
JONATHAN REID
BURCHER WHITEHEAD

FRANCIS T. WALKER
supporters:

JAS. BAILEY
JAS. BALLINGER
JESSE BECK
ALLEN BLAIN
POWHATAN BOLLING
JNO. BOUSH
SAML. BROWN
CHAS. BURRUS
MICAJOR CAMDEN
JESSE CANNADY
JAS. CARPENTER
WM. CHAPPEL
LINDSEY COLEMAN
NATHAN CRAWFORD
WM. S. CRAWFORD
ZACH. DAWSON
HENLEY DRUMMOND
WM. EVENS
JAS. FRANKLIN
JOEL FRANKLIN
SAML. FRANKLIN
THOS. GRISSOM
MATT. HARRIS JR.

JOS. HIGGINBOTHAM
SAML. HUCKSTEP
JNO. HUTCHERSON
JNO. INNIS
WM. LAVENDER
WM. LEACH
WM. LOVING
WM. NEWTON
LEWIS NICHOLAS
ABNER PADGET
REUBEN PENDLETON
GABL. PENN
GEO. PENN
JNO. PENN
RICH. POWELL
WIATT POWELL
HUGH ROSE
JNO. ROSE
PETER ROSE
JAS. ROWSEY
AMBROSE RUCKER & JR.
ISAAC RUCKER
JAS. SAVAGE
PHILIP SMITH
CHAS. STEWART
WM. STINNETT
BENAMMI STONE
JNO. STRATTON
JNO. SWANSON
BENJ. TALIAFERRO
CHAS. TALIAFERRO (2)
JNO. B. TALIAFERRO
DAVID TINSLEY
WM. TINSLEY
RO. WALKER
JAS. WATSON
ABRAHAM WARWICK
WM. WARWICK
DANL. WHITE
THOS. WILCOX
JONATHAN WILSON
JAS. WOODS
JESSE WOODROOF
WIATT WOODROOF
DAVID WOODROOF

JNO. GUREANT or
GUEREANT supporters

ISAIAH ADKISSON
LEWIS BALL
WM. CLARKSON
LEONARD HENLEY
JNO. HERNDON
THOS. JOHNSON
BARTHOLOMEW MURRIAN
BARNET OWEN
CALEB RALLS
JAS. VAUGHAN

Hensley, Cont.
Saml. 337, 343, 380, 381
Sebby 381
Silvey 337
Suckey 337
Susannah 337
Henson, Jas. 350
Jemimah 461
Jemimy 420
Henson, Jno. 8, 23
Jos. 420, 461
Murry 461
Wm. 130
Hercules, Rich. 450
Herd, Abraham 33
Geo. 177
Jas. 145, 235, 272, 360
Jno. 177, 235
Stephen 33
Thos. 184, 244
Wm. 360
Herndon, Owen 110, 125, 132,
141, 156, 233
Rich. 389, 442, 459
Herrill, ___ 220
Herrin, Wm. 61
Herston, Andrew 9
Heubank (Eubank), Jno. 215
Hewlings, J. P. 289
Hews, Henry 421
Heywood, Wm. G. 456
Hibbit (Hibbits), Wm. 64, 187,
191, 206
Hibbits, Jane 187, 206
Hibit, Wm. 55, 107
Hickman, ___ 28, 32, 33, 49,
58, 60
Edwin 4, 6, 11, 21, 27,
29, 57, 92, 159, 186
R. 357
Thos. 66
Wm. 32
Hickok, Eben 444
Hicks, Blansford 449
David 428
Jno. 36, 71
Solomon 428
Wm. 174
Hieman, Edwin 158
Higason, Eliz. 66
Higgenbotham (Sweeny), Lenora
21
Higgenbotham, M.(?) 139, 227
Higginbotham, ___ 47, 73, 75,
108, 113, 160, 162, 166,
206, 207, 243, 286, 349,
367, 368, 411
A. 211
Aaron 2, 21, 36, 73, 82,
83, 92, 99, 111, 115, 124,
128, 129, 131, 133, 144,
152, 156, 157, 167, 168,
173, 176, 183, 189, 211,
212, 213, 221, 232, 266,
267, 271, 278, 300, 327,
336, 383, 388, 391, 406,
416, 419, 459
Aaron, Jr. 360, 374, 375
Aaron, Sr. 324, 329
Absalom 21, 454
Benj. 2, 21, 71, 102, 127,
128, 129, 139, 156, 163,
164, 176, 195, 198, 212,
213, 214, 215, 216, 226,
240, 266, 267, 282, 286,
302, 337, 349, 357, 385,
389, 392, 396, 400, 408,
428, 445, 448, 453
Caleb 163, 164, 168, 174,
192, 195, 213, 214, 216,
222, 236, 245, 248
Cath. 408, 436
Chas. 330, 353, 437, 449

Higginbotham, Clara 111, 157
Clary 73, 221, 324
Danl. 345, 352, 353, 367,
371, 379, 384, 385, 388,
394, 401, 402, 406, 408,
409, 413, 415, 428, 430,
435, 437, 438, 442, 445,
447, 453, 454, 455, 459,
460
David 286
Dolly 213
Eliz. 71, 163, 213
Frances 21, 196, 263
Geo. W. 428, 446, 454
H. 398
Hannah 111
J. 252
Jas. 21, 22, 71, 75, 79,
84, 104, 109, 114, 124,
135, 144, 146, 148, 150,
156, 159, 161, 164, 167,
169, 172, 175, 176, 184,
186, 187, 191, 198, 199,
201, 202, 207, 212, 214,
216, 217, 218, 223, 227,
230, 239, 240, 245, 287,
293, 318, 340, 370, 371,
384, 397, 432, 435, 444,
445, 449, 453, 454, 457,
458
Jas. C. 393, 457
Jane 266., 271
Jeane 266, 267
Jesse 342, 350, 355, 356,
366, 390, 398
Jno. 21, 71, 84, 109, 132,
148, 153, 206, 207, 216,
282, 296, 300, 317, 322,
323, 337, 342, 346, 348,
355, 356, 364, 366, 369,
371, 385, 393, 401, 414,
416, 417, 419, 422, 423,
428, 429, 430, 433, 435,
444, 445, 458, 461
Jno., Jr. 281, 294, 300,
363, 381, 390, 398, 403,
408, 415, 420, 438, 458
Joseph (Jos.) 2, 21, 79, 83,
90, 102, 109, 111, 128,
129, 130, 131, 132, 163,
164, 171, 178, 198, 201,
208, 212, 213, 214, 215,
226, 227, 232, 238, 239,
240, 242, 243, 251, 263,
269, 272, 273, 282, 283,
286, 314, 317, 325, 333,
338, 353, 357, 358, 371,
372, 373, 382, 389, 390,
391, 394, 396, 408, 413,
414, 416, 423, 430, 433,
434, 445, 448, 454, 459
Jos., Jr. 277, 288, 320,
337, 383, 390, 391, 392,
401, 406, 408, 409, 419,
423, 458
Jos., Sr. 337, 350, 408,
409, 419, 423
Jos. C. 357, 380, 400, 410,
432
Jos. Cabell 357
Lucy 457
Mary Ann (Maryan) 164, 192,
236
Moses 2, 21, 22, 71, 73,
79, 99, 113, 136, 137,
146, 182, 189, 207, 213,
227, 230, 232, 251, 252,
257, 269, 282, 306, 353,
414
Nancy 374, 375
Rachel 217, 428, 458
Reuben 428, 430, 438
Rufus Anderson 21

Higginbotham, Samuel (Saml.)
73, 149, 167, 168, 194,
195(2), 203, 207, 209,
217, 220, 228, 236,
246, 263, 266, 267, 271,
272, 302, 308
Susanna 409, 458
T. 252, 328
Thos. 2, 25, 162, 164, 165,
207, 285, 340, 428, 462
W. 393, 396
Wm. 132, 163, 192, 195, 213,
247, 255, 263, 282, 353,
390, 391, 392, 401, 408,
433, 436, 437
Higgins, ___ 57
Eliz. 42
Patrick 380
Hight, Geo. 270, 286, 297,
312, 313, 321, 323, 402,
403
Jno. 143, 268, 270, 312
Jos. 321
Lovy 321
Lucy 312
Mary 268
Matt. 236, 246, 313, 421,
438
Patrick 236, 246, 268
Saml. 236, 321
Hill, Dabney 387, 411
Ezek. 263, 300, 321, 365,
366, 371, 394, 434
Jas. 32, 34, 53, 192, 215,
216, 227, 233, 252, 267,
279, 368, 369, 440
Jas., Jr. 368
Jas., Sr. 368, 373
Jno. 194, 208, 223, 291,
328, 329, 348
Jno., Jr. 285, 300, 318,
367
Jno., Sr. 356, 367
Jno. P. 388
Leml. 307
Maddison 320, 347
Madison 376, 408, 410, 421
Madison J. 401
Nancy 408
Nathl. 148, 260, 268, 282,
364, 388, 427
Polly 347
Ro. B. 301
Saml. 197, 198, 243, 247,
269, 307, 363, 370, 373,
448, 455
Thos. 2
Wash. 391
Wm. 2, 8, 13, 14, 23, 237,
248, 260, 360, 394, 408,
427
Wm., Jr. 278, 364, 388,
390, 401
Hillam, Adam 341
Caney 341
Mary 341
Thos. 341
Hilley, Mary 203
Mary Walker 236
Thos. 194, 203, 223, 236,
255
Hilton, Bethema 97
Geo. 2, 27, 38, 45, 48, 50,
51, 53, 97, 117, 124, 125,
130, 134, 157, 176, 215,
236, 237, 245, 264, 285,
329, 332, 339, 340, 357,
358, 363, 373, 375, 379,
380, 382, 437
Hester 27
Jas. 18, 48, 51, 63
Hines, Caleb 25
Jno., Jr. 303

Hines, Cont.
  Mary 62
  Wm. 62
Hinslee, Samuel 72
Hird, James 73
  Wm. 174
Hitchcock, Mary 209
  Wm. 8, 54, 172, 194, 209
Hite, Isaac 380
  Jno. 126, 131
Hix, Jno. 34, 128, 129, 130,
  264
  William 83, 123, 129, 131,
  138, 144, 155, 167, 172,
  174, 219
Hockaday, Jno. 413
Hodge, Edmd. 133
  Francis 317, 377
  Molly 323
  Thos. 323
  Chas. 273
  Thos. 123, 136, 138
Hodnat, Jno. 43
  Lucy 43
Hodnett, Jno. 4, 5, 25, 35, 39
Hog, Jno. 296, 299, 336, 449
Hogg, Jno. 127, 143, 199, 202,
  209, 281, 288, 346, 375,
  376, 456
Hoggat(t), Anthony 15, 27, 29
Hoggatt, Nathl. 15, 27, 29, 38
Hoilman, Christopher 448
Holby, Jas. 281
Holeman, Demund 408
  Emdm(?) 441
  Jas. 15
Hollady, Any (Amy?) 212
Holland, ___ 66
  Dick 61
  Hezekiah 58
  Jno. 59
  Michl. 7, 8, 14, 27, 34, 56
  Rich. 46, 82, 85
  Sarah 46, 85
Hollandsworth, Wm. 178, 179,
  183, 190, 236, 399
Hollard, Drury 283
Holliday, Fielding 436
  John (Jno.) 221, 236
  Lettes 236
Hollings, Saml. 8
Hollingshead, Saml. 8
Hollingsworth, Jamina 351
  Jas. 297, 323
  Jemima 378
  Jos. 342, 378, 381
  Mary 317
  Wm. 220, 346, 351, 378, 460
Hollingswrith, Wm. 16, 378
Holloday, Agnes 19
  Danl. 9, 19, 21
  Jno. 222, 281
  Lettice 281
Hollonsworth, Jos. 439
  Mary 439
  Wm. 439
Holloway, David 420
  H. 314
  Hen. 335, 344, 345, 352, 368,
  391, 399, 411, 418, 438
  Henry 226, 307, 308, 313,
  314, 332, 333, 346, 364,
  384, 387, 400, 418, 419,
  420, 435, 440, 453, 457
  Ro. 180, 222, 278, 280, 283,
  284, 287, 292, 295, 297,
  304, 312, 313, 317, 335,
  341, 343, 351, 345, 370,
  378, 379, 384, 385, 418,
  420
  Robt. 384
  Salley 385, 420
  Sarah 341

Holman, Cont.
  Martin 440
  Tandy 35, 38
  Wm. 19
Holmes, Geo. 18
Holms, Geo. 2
Holt, Ann 236
  Eliz. 28
  Philip 229, 236, 245
  Robt. (Ro.) 28
  Saml. 328
Homan, Eliz. 382, 420, 439,
  448
  Reuben L. 382
Hood, Jas. 219
Hook, John 215
Hooker, Wm. 222, 236, 253,
  265, 329, 387
Hooper, Martha 17
  Thos. 99
  Wm. 2, 10, 17, 34, 41, 64
Hooton, Thos. 208, 213
Hopkins, ___ 206
  Arthur 2, 15, 19, 20, 28,
  35, 39, 41, 50, 51, 52,
  56, 66
  Jas. 61, 66, 101, 166, 171,
  172, 190, 206, 209, 210,
  219, 281, 285, 293, 297,
  298, 330, 339, 346, 368,
  399
  John (Jno.) 20, 23, 24, 25,
  28, 171, 196, 217, 281,
  285, 344
  Jno., Jr. 285
  Saml. 39, 50, 66
  Thos. 285, 344
  W. 166, 172
Hopper, Eliz. 86
  George 86, 90, 91
  Jane 236
  Thos. 138, 172, 179, 218,
  236
Hopson, Henry 97
  Martha 97
Hord, James 174
Horner, Timothy 436
Horrall, Mary 152, 169
  (Horral), Wm. 98, 104, 131,
  133, 135, 140, 152, 153,
  169, 178, 185
Horrell, Clever 220
  Eliz. 208, 210
  Wm. 208, 210, 259, 264
Horril, ___ 259
Horrill, Howsan 277
  Howsend 277
Horsburgh, Alex. 224
Horsley, Benj. 221
  Eliz..114, 271
  John (Jno.) 77, 114, 122,
  146, 162, 163, 215, 222,
  236, 245, 271, 277, 278,
  293, 301, 314, 320, 327,
  332, 338, 370, 372, 380,
  407, 430, 453, 462
  Jos. 237, 271, 321, 428,
  437
  Judith 159, 271, 407
  Martha 196, 237, 271, 332,
  380
  Mary 77, 271
  N. C. 458
  Nichl. 271
  R. 349
  Ro. 122, 159, 162, 163, 215,
  354, 369, 380, 407, 417,
  428, 456
  Robt. 20, 50, 77, 114, 271
  Roland 20
  Rowland 8, 30
  Saml. 271, 380, 437
  Susanna 30

Horsley (Horseley, Cont.
  Wm. 26, 61, 76, 77, 97,
  98, 99, 101, 105, 106,
  109, 114, 115, 125, 134,
  146, 156, 159, 161, 163,
  164, 174, 176, 178, 182,
  183, 184, 196, 202, 204,
  206, 215, 216, 232, 236,
  237, 245, 248, 256, 258,
  271, 278, 285, 297, 321,
  328, 329, 332, 333, 349,
  363, 369, 379, 380, 407,
  423, 432, 437, 454
  Wm., Jr. 237, 254
  Wm. Jos, 417
Horton, Thos. 413
Hotchkiss, Eliz. 333
  Gerard 276
  Jarred 309, 333
Houchen, ___ 152
Houchin, Jno. 111, 135, 142,
  171, 353
  Wm. 234, 260, 284
Houchings, Wm. 171
Houchins, Edwd. 217
  Jas. 171
  Jesse 410
  Jno. 112, 138
Houchins (Houtchins), Wm.
  112, 126, 177
Housewright, Jos. 293, 361,
  409, 424
Houtchin, Jno. 130
Howard, ___ 22
Howard(s), Allen 2, 14, 20,
  65, 74, 192, 203, 375
  Amey 386
  Amy 383, 388
  Benj. (Ben.) 46, 50, 83,
  101, 112, 119, 123, 151,
  356
  Geo. 316
  Jno. 375
  Jean 158
  Jno. 9, 20, 35, 38, 74,
  91, 119, 122, 151, 192,
  198, 203, 222, 291, 359
  Judith 64, 65
  Mary 192
  Wm. 23, 33, 42, 60, 64,
  158, 164, 193, 198, 246,
  324, 325, 383, 386, 388,
  430, 449, 455, 459, 461
  Wm., Jr. 359
  Wm. A. 408, 422, 428, 430
Howl, Absalom 446
Howland(?), Jno. 5
Howle, Wm. 2
Hoy, Jno. 18, 47
  John Booker 47
Hoyle, Chas. 453
Hubbard, Jno. 2, 42, 44, 48
Hubbard & Co. 262
Hucker, Phillip 37
Huckstep, R. 413
  Saml. 217, 251, 333, 395,
  412, 413, 436
Hudgins, Ambrose 33
  Drury 416
  Wm. 35, 416
Hudnell, Wm. 56
Hudon, Joshua 133
Hudson, ___ 17, 41, 191
  Ann 264, 434
  Bennett 423
  Chas. 11, 27, 28, 46, 54,
  162
  Christopher 46
  Edmd. 420
  Geo. 354, 441, 442
  Guilielmus 8
  Jno. 25, 46, 52, 387